ENCYCLOPEDIA OF
WORLD ARTISTS

Consulting Editor
PROFESSOR WILLIAM VAUGHAN

Grange
BOOKS

Published 2007 by Grange Books
an imprint of Grange Books Ltd
The Grange
Kingsnorth Industrial Estate
Hoo, Near Rochester
Kent ME3 9ND
www.Grangebooks.co.uk

The Brown Reference Group plc
(incorporating Andromeda Oxford Limited)
8 Chapel Place
Rivington Street
London
EC2A 3DQ
www.brownreference.com

ISBN: 978-1-84013-916-7

Printed and bound in Thailand

Consulting Editors

William Vaughan
BIRKBECK COLLEGE, UNIVERSITY OF LONDON

Contributors

Christopher Ackroyd
Michael Bird
Maria Constantino
Michael Ellis
Flavia Heseltine
Michael Howard
Debbie Lewer
Rebecca Lyons
Claire O'Mahony
Mike O'Mahony
Chris Murray
Alive Peebles
Anthea Peppin
Ailsa Turner
Giles Waterfield
Iain Zaczek

Picture Credits

t = top, b = bottom, c = centre, l = left, r = right

Cover: AKG Images: bl, br

AKG Images: 53, 182, 265, 275, 293, 385; DACS 199, 243; **Albbright-Knox Art Gallery, Buffalo, New York:** 55; Bequest of A. Conger Goodyear 231; Gift of Seymour H. Knox 387; **Board of Trustees of The National Museums and Galleries on Merseyside (Walker Art Gallery, Liverpool):** Lucien Freud 157; **Carl van Vechten, Gallery of Fine Arts, Fisk University, Nashville:** 321; **City of Salford Museum and Art Gallery:** 263t, 363b; **Cleveland Museum of Art:** DACS 309; **Collection Kroller-Muller Museum, Otterlo:** DACS 177; **Corbis:** 82; Academy of Natural Sciences of Philadelphia 23; Alexander Burkatowski 114, 283b, 337; Araldo de Luca 43, 404; Araldo de Luca/DACS 87t; Archivo Iconografico, S.A. 31, 129b, 162, 266, 267, 340, 377, 436, 437; Arte and Imagini srl 14, 15, 17, 103, 179, 284, 285, 326, 374; Austrian Archives; Osterreichische Galerie, Vienna 241; Bettmann 45, 250; Bettmann/DACS 443; Burstein Collection 12, 81, 91, 95, 99, 117, 135, 138, 141, 153, 205, 229, 253, 289, 297, 347; Burstein Collection/DACS 67, 118, 121, 371, 391, 415, 435; Burstein Collection/Succession Picasso 329t; Danny Lehman/DACS 325; Edimedia 84; 270, 393; Elio Ciol 73b; Francis G. Mayer 10, 21, 39, 47, 58, 68/69, 98, 113, 115, 129t, 145, 152, 163, 191t, 191b, 201, 207, 221, 238, 247, 249, 261, 277, 295, 345, 349, 355, 361, 379, 381, 389, 408, 428, 429, 430, 441Francis G. Mayer/Succession Picasso; Franz Marc Frei 42; Gianni Dagli Orti 143, 251, 395, 422; Godfrey Clements 13; Historical Picture Archive 9, 46, 353b; Horree Zirkee Produk 6; Kimbel Art Museum 149, 296, 313, 403; Leonard de Silva 83; Massimo Listri 193; Michael Freeman 359; Mimmo Jodice 73t; National Gallery Collection: by kind permission of the Trustees of the National Gallery 7b, 18, 29, 37, 71, 75, 79, 85, 89, 96, 97, 101, 107, 109, 119, 123, 137b, 147, 159, 161, 171, 185t, 185b, 203, 217t, 217b, 219, 259, 281, 299t, 299b, 312, 341, 354, 357, 373, 375, 383, 405, 406, 407, 411, 413, 416, 417, 418, 419, 420, 421, 423, 431; North Carolina Museum of Art 88; North Carolina Museum of Art/Andrew Wyeth 445; Philadelphia Museum of Art 57, 211, 224, 227, 239, 291, 333, 409, 439, Philadelphia Museum of Art/DACS 139, 197; Robert Holmes/DACS 87b; Scala Group S.p.A. 165; Solomon R. Guggenheim Museum 327; State of New York 369; Ted Spiegel 8, 344; State Russian Museum 187, 233; Vanni Archive 7t; **Cortauld Gallery, London:** 271; **Des Moines Art Center:** Michael Tropea, Chicago 25, 223; **Estate of Eva Hess:** Art Institute, Chicago 209; Giraudon: 225, 255, 303, 305; **Kunsthistorisches Museum, Vienna:** 19, 63t, 63b; **Manchester City Art Gallery:** 401; **Metropolitain Museum of Art, George A. Hearn Fund:** Metropolitan Museum of Art 338/339; **Musee Rodin, Paris:** 364, 365; **Museum of Modern Art, New York:** 269; DACS 27, 33; **Nasjonalgalleriet:** J. Lathion/DACS 311; **National Gallery London:** 425; **Nolde-Siftung Seebull:** 319; **Offentliche Kunstammlung Basel:** Martin Buhler/DACS 125; **Phototheque des Collections du Mnam:** Cci/DACS 59, 397; **Printed by permission of the Norman Rockwell Family Trust:** The Norman Rockwell Family Museum at Stockbridge 363; **Private Collection:** 112; **Royal College of Art:** Lucien Freud 156; **Scala Group S.p.A.:** 35, 48/49, 51, 60, 61, 76, 77, 93, 105, 133, 137t, 167, 169, 173t, 173b, 175, 181, 183, 195, 237, 245, 257, 273t, 273b, 279, 283t, 287t, 287b, 327, 331,335l, 335r, 343, 427, 447; DACS 432/433; **Seattle Art Museum:** Susan Dirk 155; **Tate Gallery:** 65, 235, 367; DACS 111, 151, 189, 315, 398/399; David Hockney 215; Estate of Sidney Nolan 317; John Siberman Associates 131; Paula Rego 351; **V&A Museum:** 212, 213, 307; **Witney Museum of American Art:** 127; Claes Oldenburg 323

Brown Reference Group has made every effort to trace copyright holders of the pictures used in this book. Anyone having claims to ownership not identified above is invited to contact Brown Reference Group.

Contents

Introduction *by William Vaughan*

All human societies produce art, even if they do not always call it that. The very earliest communities we know of, living perhaps some 30,000 years ago, decorated the walls of caves with colors and images, and shaped figures made of clay and stone. There is clearly a basic urge in humans to make things not just because they have a practical use, but also because they satisfy by their appearance. The bison that was drawn millennia ago on a cave wall at Altamira in Spain was not just a reminder of the need to get some food. It had a fascination of its own, became an object of desire in itself.

It may be that this kind of object—one made apparently for the appeal of its appearance—originally had a religious purpose. It is certainly true that almost all the ancient religions we know of (and most modern ones too) make use of images in their rituals. Religions deal with the mysterious, the unknowable, the invisible. Images can provide a representation of that which cannot be seen and that exists otherwise only in the imagination. Certainly there is something magical about the power of images to represent, to reproduce the appearance of something else in a lively and convincing manner. We still do not know how it is that a few lines can come together to give us the image of an object or a person. It still remains a mystery, and is still one of the basic reasons why we find images so appealing. There is every sign that this power of representation fascinated the makers and users of images from the start. The person who drew the bison on the cave wall at Altamira did not just make a rough approximate shape of an animal. He or she showed us the exact features of a bison, the hairy hump on its back, the joints and hooves of the legs, the lowering look on the face. All this was done with a naturalism as consummate as that achieved by any trained artist of our own times. The amazing ability of this early painter also tells us that from the start artists were people with high and special skills. The changes that have taken place in the way works of art have been made since then are not due to alterations in ability, but are responses to changes in needs and in perception.

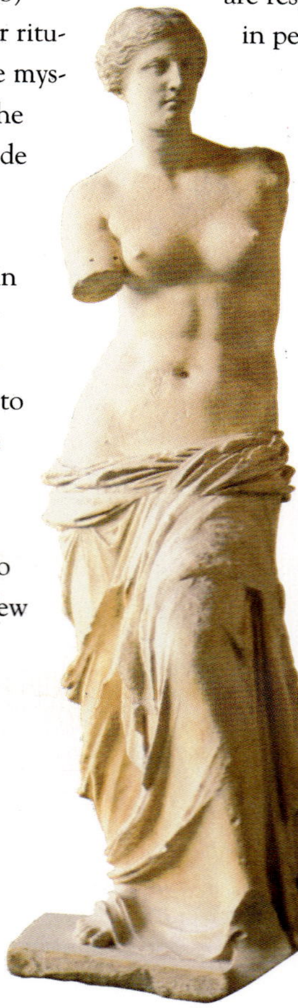

***Venus de Milo** c150–100 BC. Marble. 71 in (180 cm) high. Musée du Louvre, Paris.*

It is these changes that give art a history, or perhaps one should say histories. For each community has its own past, and has developed particular art forms with their own traditions and practices. The paintings, sculptures, and prints focused on in this book come from the art that has developed in Western societies. It is this tradition that the introduction surveys.

The works produced by the ancient civilizations of the Near East, in regions such as Mesopotamia and Egypt, form the first visible links in the chain that leads to modern Western art. In these we can see that art was used principally to bolster religious and secular authority. The great pyramids—such as Gizeh, constructed c3000 BC—commemorated powerful kings and their officials. The pyramids were intended to preserve their bodies as mummies for eternity, but it was also felt important to use the representational powers of painting and sculpture to record their images and their earthly achievements.

Egyptian art, once formulated, remained essentially unchanged for thousands of years. Western art, by contrast, is dynamic and ever changing. Though today such changes take place perhaps too rapidly, in the early days they took place slowly, over centuries; long enough, in fact, for the development of distinct practices. The first of these is the art of ancient Greece, of the seventh to fifth century BC. Western philosophy, science, literature, and democracy all look back to that time as the "classic" moment of their origin, and the spirit of debate, exploration, and enquiry that lay behind such development can also be seen in the visual arts. Originally based on Egyptian models, the statues of ancient Greece seemed gradually to come to life, the simple, stylized images became infused with greater degrees of observed detail and naturalistic movement. It never went beyond a certain point, however. The tendency toward representation was always held in check by a respect for the dignity of harmonious shapes and forms. The "classic" form of such work was achieved in Athens in the fifth century by the sculptor Pheidias and his followers.

The Romans carried on, by and large, with the forms of Greek art. Brilliant engineers, they added the dome and the arch to the relatively simple forms of Greek buildings, using these to

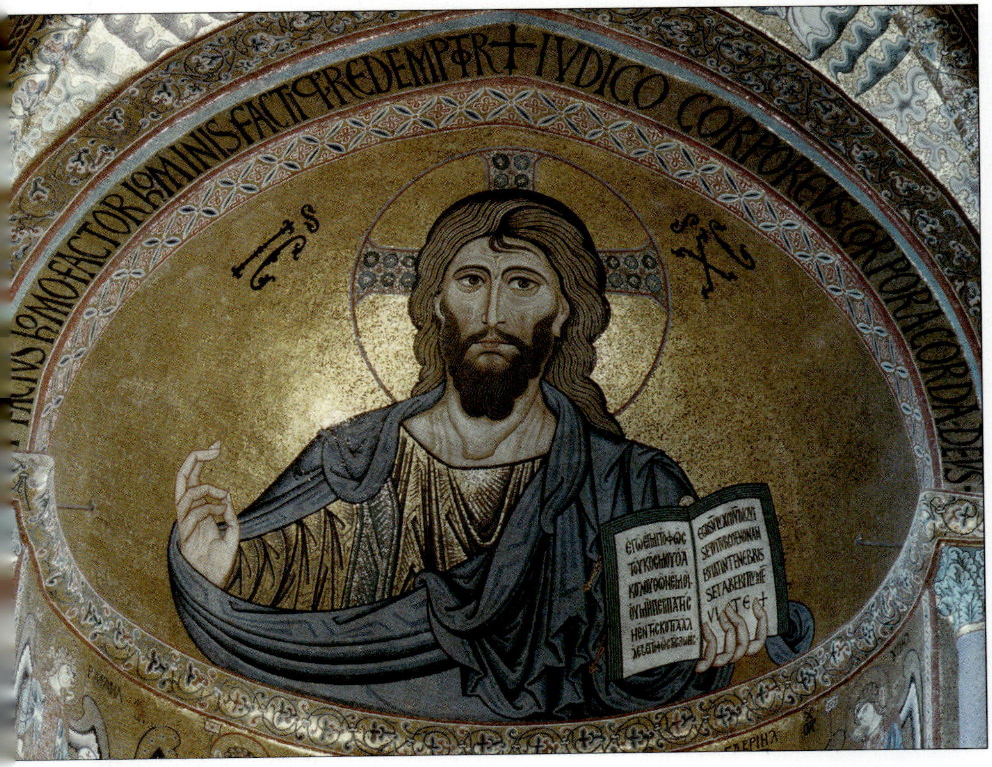

Cristo Pantocrator *1148. Ceiling mosaic. Cefalu Cathedral, Italy.*

produce buildings on a new scale, such as the Colosseum in Rome (completed AD 82). They brought a new degree of realism to painting and sculpture, as can be seen in the landscape frescos preserved on the walls of their villas and the remarkably realistic portrait busts. With the decline of Rome and (some would say) the introduction of Christianity as the official religion, there was a return to less realistic forms of art in which the influence of the East is evident. It was this that led to such splendid achievements as the awe-inspiring mosaics of Byzantium, in which saints and deities are represented, emblazoned in gold and other rich colors.

After the fall of Rome the axis of power in Europe moved more to the north. While the principal artistic interchanges had previously been between East and West, these were now largely replaced by ones between north and south. In the early days at least this was largely evident in the efforts to emulate the achievements of the classical past. When the great ruler Charlemagne came to power around 800—uniting all the Christian lands of western Europe in what came to be known as the Holy Roman Empire—he instigated a revival of classical forms in the art and architecture of his court. Subsequently the Romanesque style that spread throughout Europe showed a continued use of such forms, though invested with a native vigor that gradually asserted its own independence. Even more independence appeared in the sequence of styles that flourished from the 12th to the 16th century, which were later given the generic name of Gothic. Such art expressed a new form of imaginative spirituality. Its great achievements are the soaring cathedrals of the Middle Ages (made possible by the innovation of the pointed arch and the vaulting systems that derived from it), paintings and sculptures of sinuous elegance, rich and luminous stained-glass windows, exquisite illuminated manuscripts. It is an art of extremes, in which daring and delicacy are brought together, and of growing naturalism and individualism, in which Western art seems once again to return to direct observation.

The Gothic period is fundamental to the whole history of modern Western art, yet it was the return to a closer emulation of classical antiquity that began to occur around 1300 that can be said to have established its main direction. Now known as the Renaissance, this movement was a wholesale intellectual and cultural movement that emulated the achievements of the classical world and then developed them in new directions. In the representational arts this can be seen first in a recovery of the full skills of naturalistic depiction. This came earliest in Italy, rich as it was in the remains of ancient Rome. In painting the first step in this direction is attributed to the Florentine Giotto di Bondone, who brought a new humanity into his representations of religious

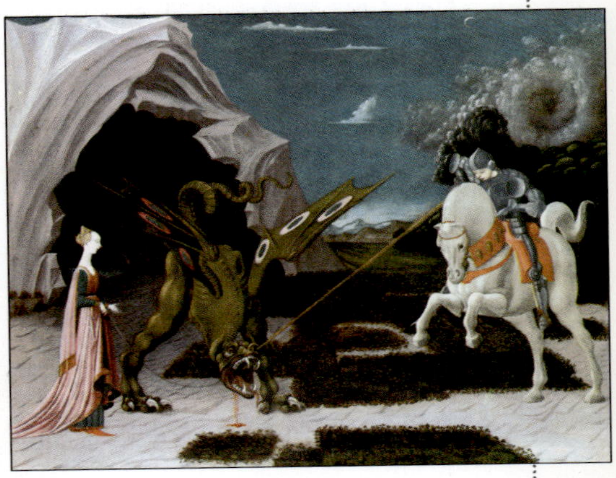

***Saint George and the Dragon* Paolo Uccello** *c1460. Oil on canvas. 22¼ x 29¼ in (56.5 x 74 cm). National Gallery, London.*

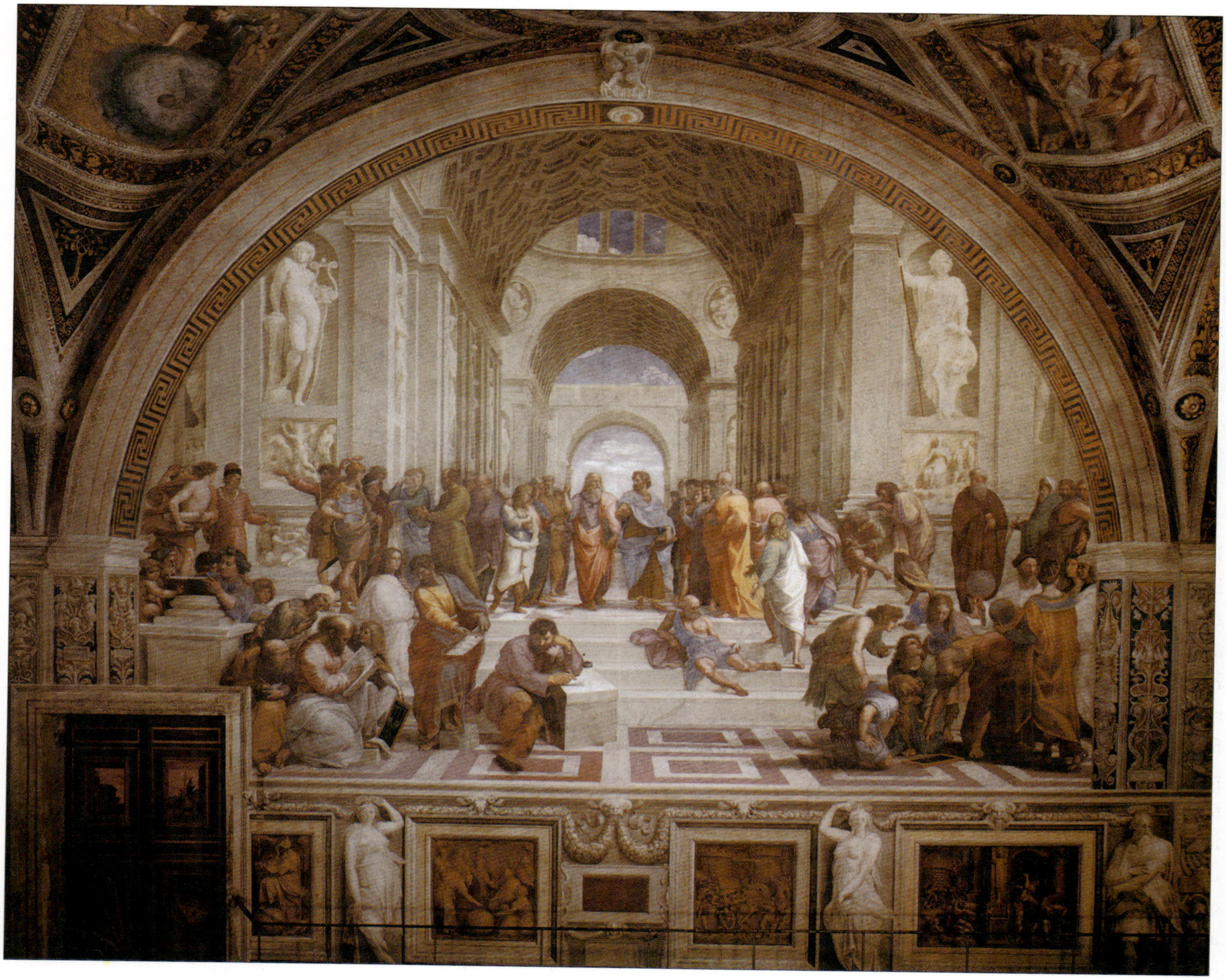

scenes. Later a whole galaxy of artists rivaled each other to recover the skills of perspective and anatomical exactitude—figures such as Masaccio, Paolo Uccello, and Piero della Francesca. Farther north, in Flanders, a more craft-based development of painting was also leading to new heights of realistic representation, particularly in the works of Jan Van Eyck, who showed in an unprecedented way how oil painting could give the illusion of three-dimensionality.

The Renaissance was at the same time a period of classical revival and technical innovation. The dialogue between north and south that it represented remained a dominant feature in Western art up to the 20th century. In the 16th century the movement reached its own form of classical manifestation. This was the art of the High Renaissance, represented most fully in the work of Leonardo da Vinci, Raphael, and Michelangelo Buonarroti. The last two, in particular, exercised a huge influence over subsequent generations through the frescos that they painted for the Pope in Rome, notably Raphael's *Stanze* and Michelangelo's Sistine Ceiling, both in the Vatican. The magnitude of these achievements was felt acutely by contemporaries. One of them, Giorgio Vasari, charted the whole history of artistic development from the time of Giotto in his *Lives of the Artists* (1550). This work set a new standard for documenting and celebrating the achievements of individual artists that has been emulated ever since. Vasari can, in that sense, be called the founder of the history of art.

The achievements of the Italian Renaissance had a massive impact throughout western Europe and beyond.

***School of Athens* Raphael** *c1510–12. Wall fresco. Stanza della Segnatura, Vatican Palace, Rome.*

Many artists were invigorated by this impact. The German artists Albrecht Dürer and Hans Holbein were among them, as was the Flemish artist Pieter Breugel the Elder, who used the newly acquired knowledge to paint the everyday life of the people of his country. In Italy itself there were responses, most notably in Venice, where Titian combined the new sense of form with his own rich sense of color and light.

This process of assimilation and reaction remained the tendency in Western art up to the 19th century. In a succession of styles—mannerism, baroque, rococo—one can see different types of reactions. None of the artists associated with these movements would have challenged the supremacy of a classical norm. Rome remained the Mecca for artists. Usually, though, conditions prevailing in their own countries were more influential on their careers. So in Holland Protestantism and a new commercialism (the birth of the modern capitalist system) seem to have encouraged an art of unprecedented matter-of-factness, while paradoxically preparing the ground for the introspective and spiritual art of Rembrandt. The art of southern Europe took on a grandiosity at this time that seems to have been stimulated by the need to reassert the authority of the Catholic faith in the face of the challenge that had been mounted in the 16th century by the Protestant breakaway from the Church of Rome.

In France the emulation of Italy tended to be closer than elsewhere, stimulated no doubt by a sense of a shared culture with roots in Latin. Many of the key artists in Rome in the 17th century, such as Nicolas Poussin and Claude Lorraine, were French. With the rise to power of Louis XIV at the end of the century, a deliberate policy of wholesale promotion of the visual arts was instigated. It is hardly an exaggeration to say that the dominating position that French art came to achieve in the 18th century, which it maintained with increasing strength up to the middle of the 20th century, was an outcome of this policy. In no other country did artists receive better training or more generous state support. After the French monarchy was swept away in the Revolution of 1789, the policy was continued by subsequent regimes, republican, monarchist, and imperialist alike.

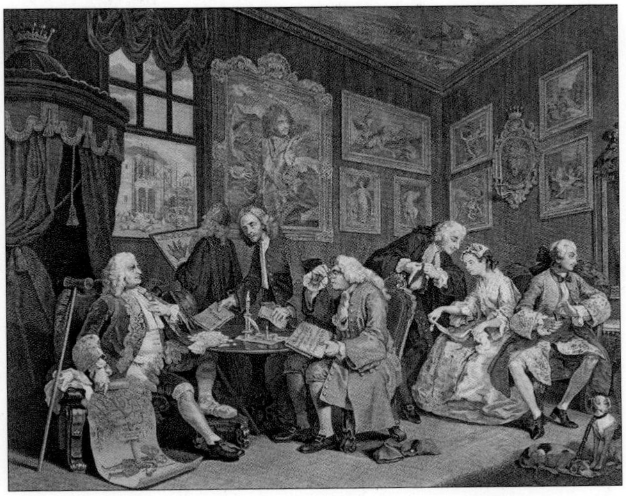

***Marriage à la Mode (1. The Marriage Settlement)* William Hogarth** *c1745. Engraving. 28 x 36 in (71 x 91 cm). National Gallery, London.*

The neoclassical movement of the later 18th century still had its focus in Rome, but the French painter Jacques-Louis David was its principal pictorial exponent. Romanticism, though spread throughout northern and western Europe, had its leading figure in Eugène Delacroix. Frenchman Gustave Courbet became the chief representative of the reactive movement of realism. It was impressionism, though, that confirmed Paris as the undisputed center of the Western art world.

Just as important as this sequence of styles were fundamental changes that were taking place in the way that art was produced and that the art world was organized. Traditionally artists had worked to commission, receiving patronage from powerful institutions such as the Church or the monarchy. The new market economy that had emerged in Holland also encouraged artists to begin to sell their works in the open market. They began to produce works speculatively, rather than waiting to receive commissions. This tendency grew in the 18th century, particularly in Britain, where William Hogarth became the first artist to make his fortune through the sale of prints based on his works.

The history of art in the 19th century is to an extent the history of the struggle between art commissioned and approved of by established authorities and art that exploited opportunities offered by the new bourgeois society. Typically at this time the art world was controlled by academies, learned associations set up and patronized by monarchs or comparable political authorities. Usually the academies controlled the most prestigious exhibitions in the capital city—places where reputations were made or lost. This was certainly the case in Paris, where the Academy's annual Salon became the focal point for all ambitious artists.

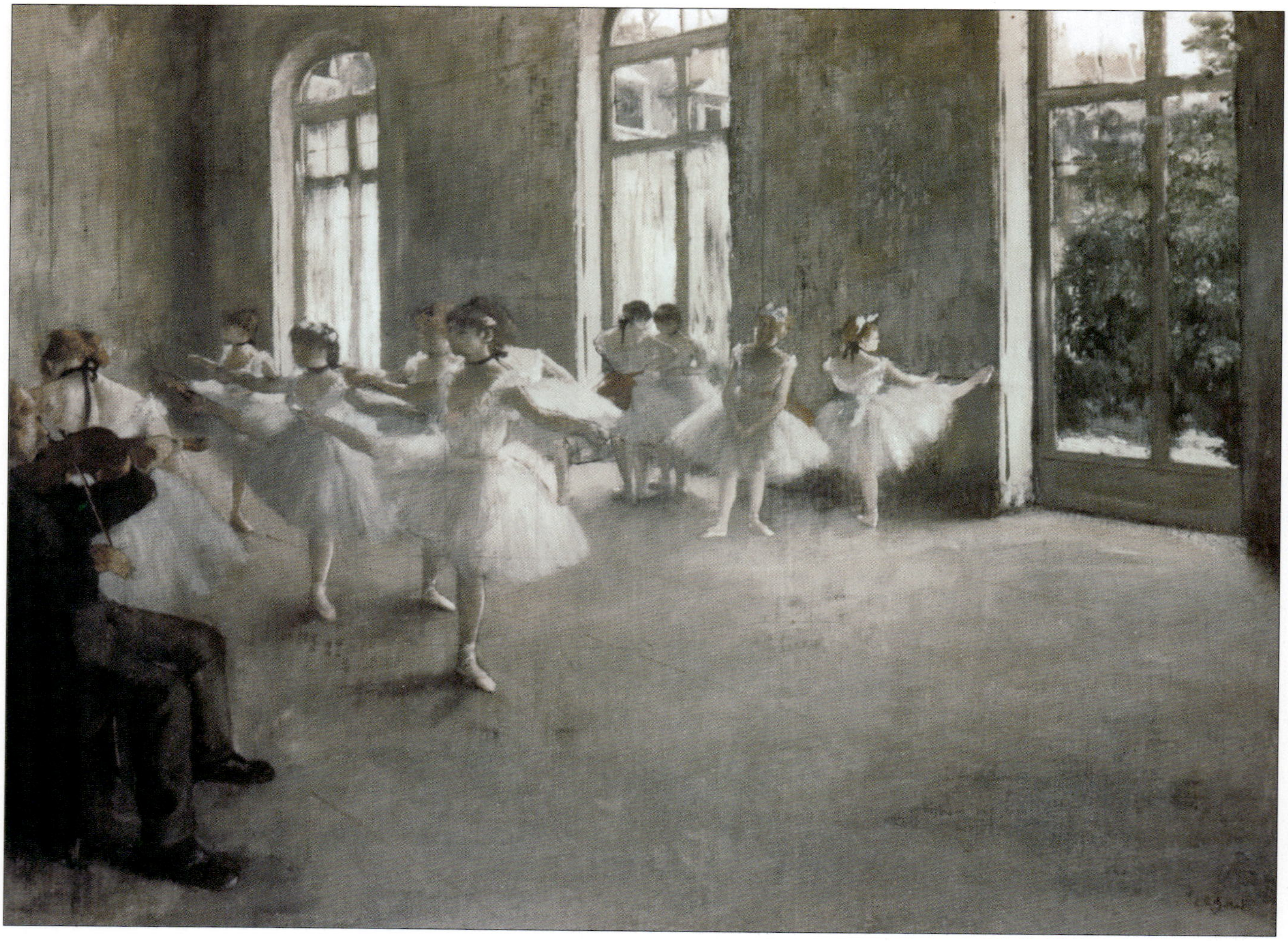

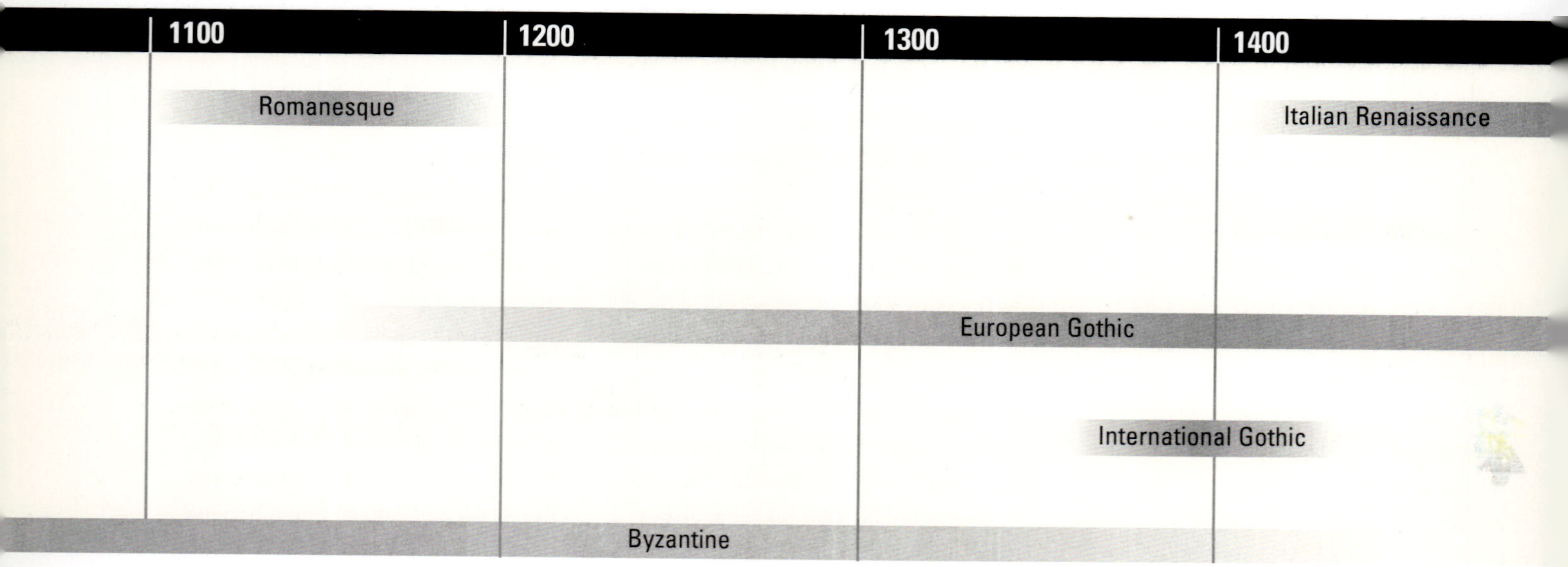
1100
1200
1300
1400
Romanesque
Italian Renaissance
European Gothic
International Gothic
Byzantine

Gradually, however, the power of the commercial market became such that artists were able to turn their backs on the academies and their exhibitions and deal with the public through the alternative venues offered them by art dealers. The impressionists were the first group of artists to benefit fully from this process. After years of having their innovative and fresh form of direct painting rejected by the official Salon in Paris, they put on their own exhibition in 1874. Although not immediately successful, dealers were able to keep the work of the impressionists before the public, gradually gaining them popularity and success.

Once they had established their credentials for artistic discernment, the dealers became increasingly important in the process of validating new artists. They were aided in this by the art critic. The journalist art critic had come into being in the later 18th century. On the whole art critics had found themselves at odds with the largely conservative tastes of the academies that ran the exhibitions. With dealers, however, they were in a different position. The dealer needed the publicity their reviews could offer to help promote the work they were selling. The "critic-dealer" system has dominated the art world ever since.

Whatever the advantages or disadvantages of the critic-dealer system, there is no doubt that it has been a system that has promoted a continuous display of innovation and talent of the highest order. In most Western societies there has been an ongoing tradition of art critical of the status quo. This is the "avant-garde," which has, since the later 19th century, viewed innovative art as being at the cutting edge of social and intellectual developments. In the 20th century the avant-garde has led to a particular kind of story of art, with art seeking to establish its independence, to explore with increasing boldness new forms of perception. This trend is exemplified in the succession of "isms" that chart new moves. Following impressionism there was postimpressionism, which sought to revise impressionism and give it a more powerful base. This is the tendency that can be seen in the work of Vincent Van Gogh and Paul Gauguin, who sought to make art more powerful and expressive. It is a move followed in France by fauvism and in Germany and northern Europe by expressionism. But these movements are themselves less radical than cubism, the great development of Pablo Picasso and Georges Braque in Paris around 1910. Cubism constituted the first effective challenge to the form of realistic representation developed during the Renaissance.

Cubism remained representational, although it explored representation in new ways. But it provided the stimulus for abstract art, the new form of painting that emerged just before World War I (perhaps initially with the work being produced by the Russian artist Wassily Kandinsky in Munich) and grew in importance to become the most prestigious type of art in the 1950s. By this time the center of the art world had

***Dance School* Edgar Degas** *c1873. Oil on canvas. 18 x 24½ in (46 x 62 cm). Fogg Art Museum, Harvard University, Cambridge, MA.*

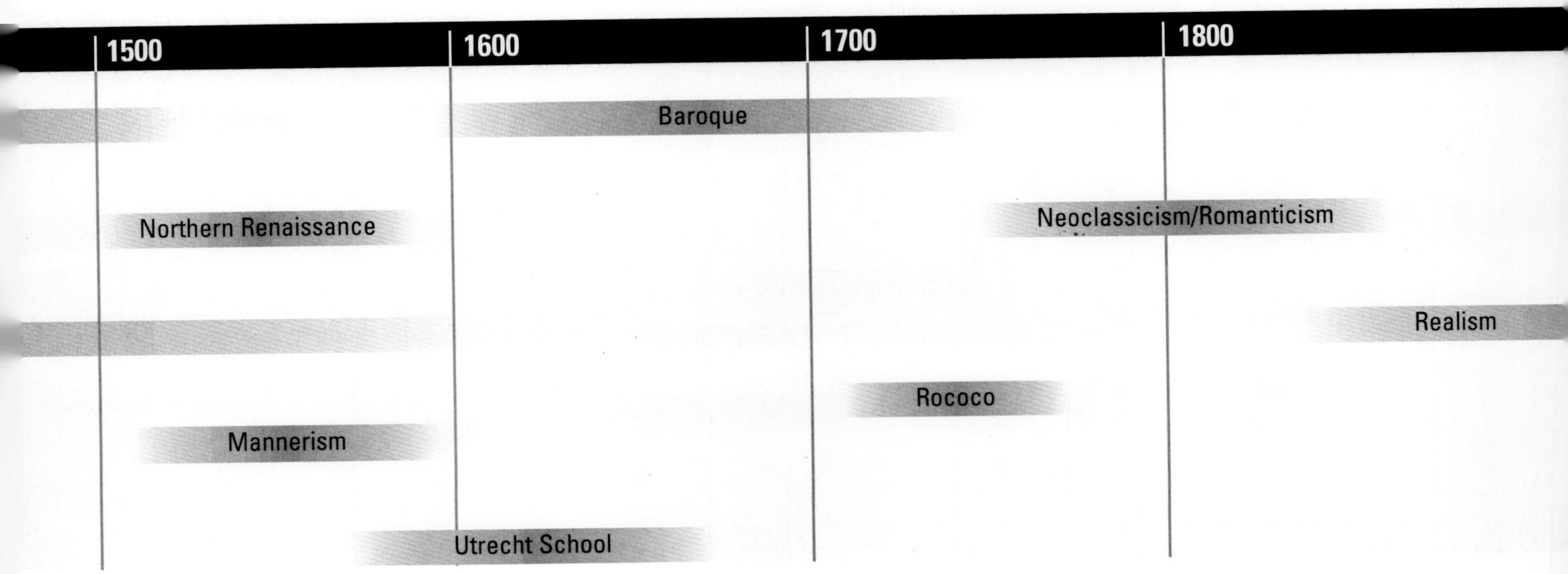

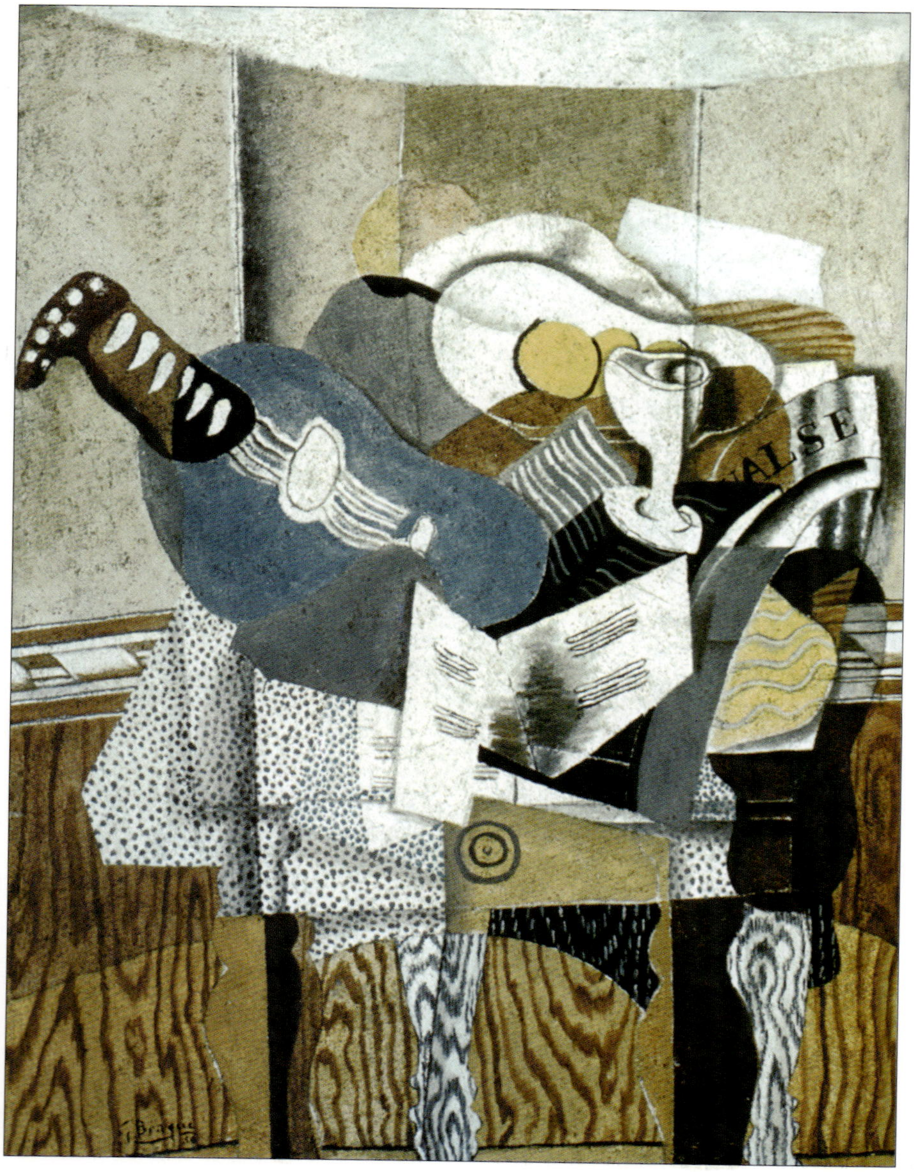

The Blue Mandolin **Georges Braque**
1930. Oil on canvas. 31½ x 24 in (80 x 60.5 cm). Saint Louis Art Museum, Saint Louis, MO.

moved to New York. The ravages of World War II had left Europe both culturally and economically impoverished. It was at this moment that the United States—by now indisputably the wealthiest and most powerful country in the world—became the self-appointed guardian of the Western tradition.

The rise of abstract expressionism in New York at this time was hailed as a sign that the great tradition of modernism that had originated in Paris in the mid-19th century now had its home in the New World. This was, of course, a simplification and exaggeration. In the first place, the history of Western art since the mid-19th century was not a simple development toward increasing abstraction. There were many other art forms that had developed that explored quite different aspects of experience, such as the revolutionary anti-bourgeois movement of dada, or the imaginative

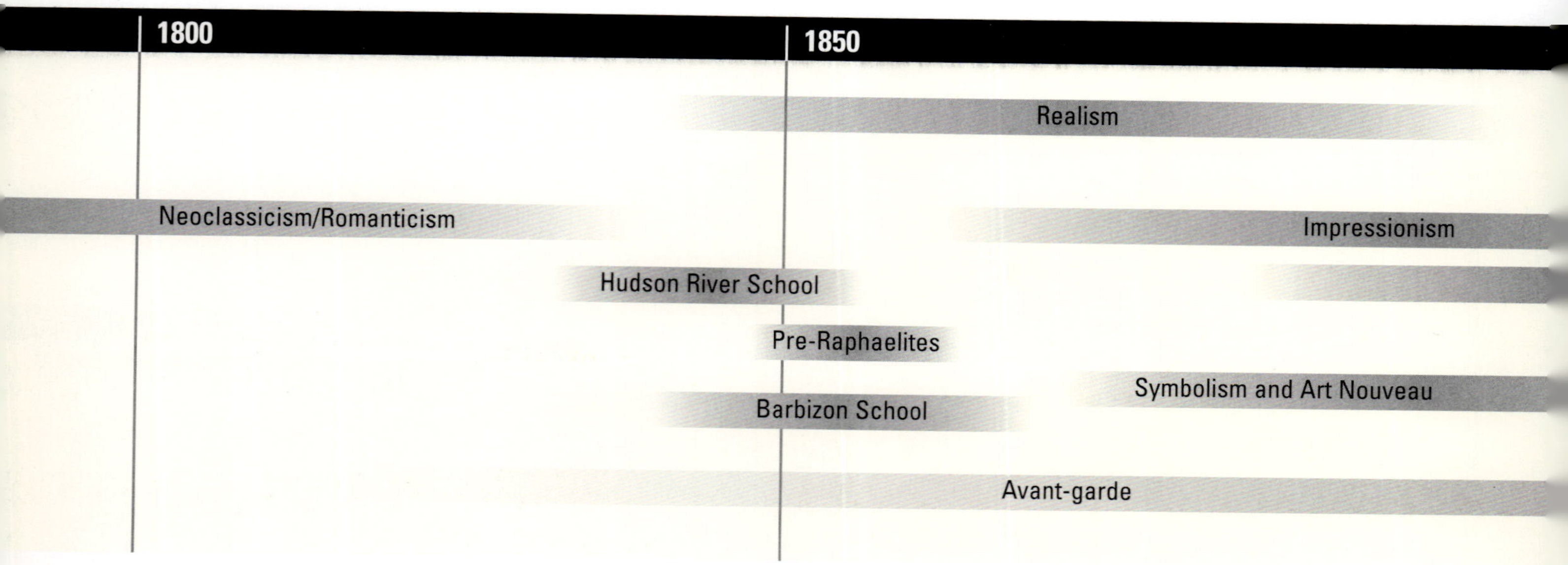

and symbolic art of the surrealists, who used the writings of Freud to aid them in uncovering the rich world of the subconscious. There was as well a vigorous persistence of forms of realist art, which had led to such great achievements as the murals of the Mexican artist Diego Rivera. In the United States itself there had been a highly distinguished tradition of realism that reached from such figures as Winslow Homer and Thomas Eakins in the late 19th century to the regionalists of the 1930s.

In view of this, it is not surprising to see that this story of the triumph of modernism became increasingly challenged in the 1960s, for example through the pop art movement. Such brilliant practitioners as Andy Warhol turned to the despised commercial art of the market place and re-presented it in a form that gave it all the authority of fine art. It was a rebellion appreciated throughout the world and it opened up the way for a whole series of other rejections of an authoritative "high art" practice. Happenings, environmental art, the feminist critique of male empowerment; all this has taken place since then in a seemingly endless succession of new ways of presenting art. This series of critiques of modernism has been brought together under one concept of reaction and denial: postmodernism. We are now, it is claimed, living in a postmodern age, in which the pretensions of abstraction have been overturned and almost any kind of alternative goes. This is claimed as a radical departure. Has everything really changed, though? Not really. The critic-dealer system is still in place, and challenging avant-garde art still gets most publicity. All that has happened is that the art market has grown and become more global than it was before.

Is this the rejection of modernism, or simply another stage in its triumphant progress? We do not know. As with other aspects of our culture and society, we are less certain now than at almost any time in recent history where we are going. But we know we are going somewhere, if only as a continuation of the technological revolution that appears at present to be unstoppable. Ultimately, though, however thoroughly one can explain the circumstances under which a particular work of art is produced, art itself remains mysterious and unexplained. The created image still holds us in its thrall as much as it did those first cavemen who made and then perceived a shape upon a wall.

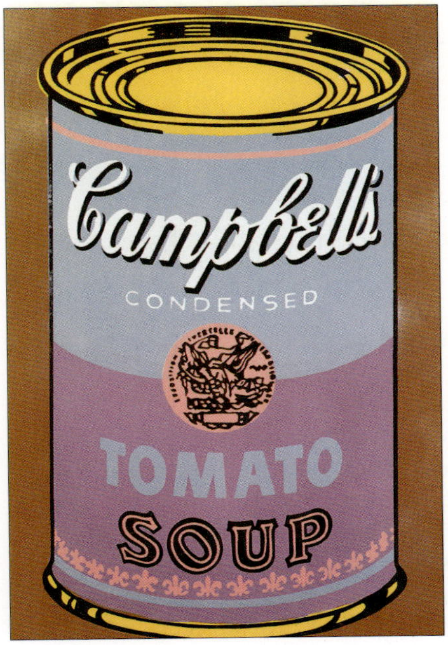

Campbell's Soup **Andy Warhol** *1965. Oil silkscreened on canvas. 36⅛ x 24⅛ in (92 x 61 cm). Museum of Modern Art, New York, NY.*

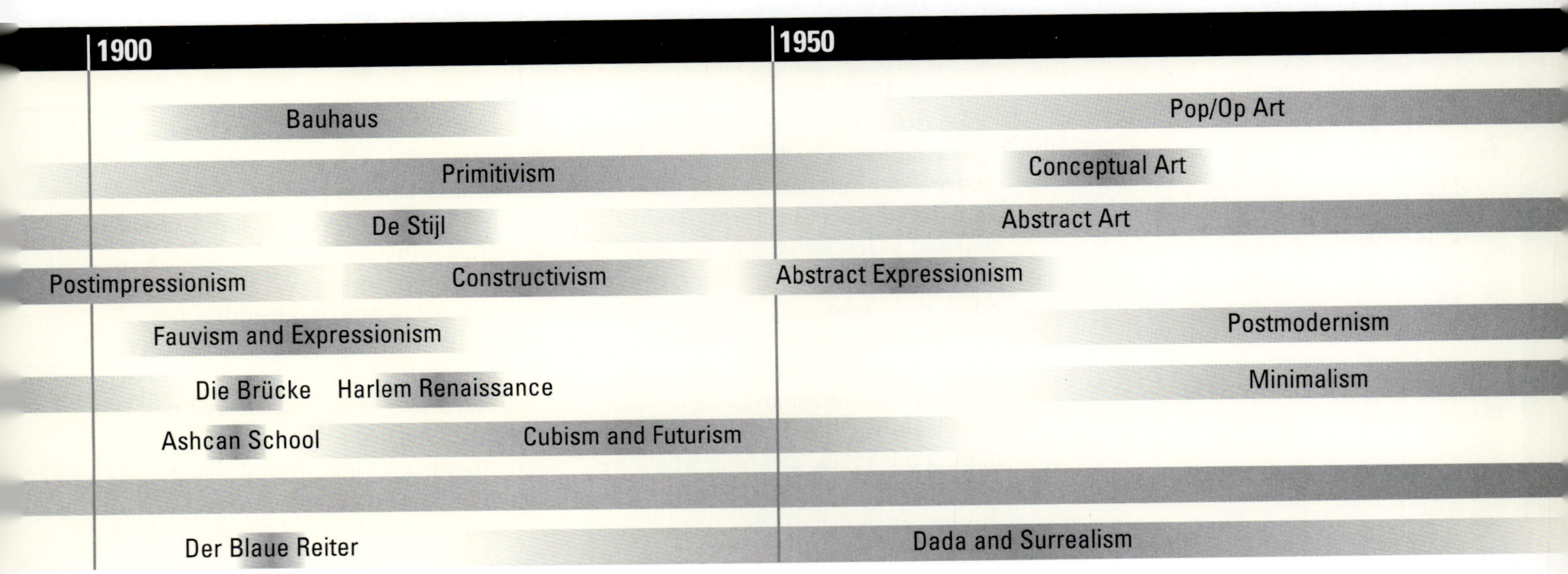

ANDREA DEL SARTO

HISTORICALLY, ANDREA DEL SARTO has been overshadowed by the great artists of the High Renaissance—Leonardo, Michelangelo, and Raphael. But he was one of the most important artists of his day, and his abilities and sensitivities surpassed those of most of his peers.

Life and work

Andrea del Sarto, the son of a tailor, was born in Florence. Apprenticed to a goldsmith at the age of seven, he then studied painting under various masters, notably Piero di Cosimo. In his early twenties, after he had qualified as a master and was able to enter the artists' Guild of Saint Luke, he received his first important commission: a series of frescos illustrating the *Miracles of San Filippo Benizzi* (c1510) in Santissima Annunziata. His artistic development can be gauged from the *grisaille* (monochrome) frescos of scenes from the life of Saint John the Baptist in the Chiostro dello Scalzo, begun c1510 and continued until 1526. Drawing much from the example of Leonardo da Vinci, he explored the possibilities of subtly modulated light to build up mass and detail within a subdued, atmospheric setting.

In 1518 he went to France at the invitation of the French king, François I, at Fontainebleau, and he might have gone on a visit to Rome soon afterward. Apart from these visits, however, he was to spend the whole of his short career in the city of his birth.

While Michelangelo Buonarroti and Raphael are seen as the most important artists in Rome during the 16th century, Andrea del Sarto was, with Fra Bartolommeo, one of the most important painters in Florence. It was a period of profound change in art. The painstaking efforts of 15th-century artists to solve the technical problems associated with the rendering of the human figure reached a point of resolution in the works of Leonardo, Michelangelo, and Raphael. All three artists were resident in Florence between 1501 and 1508; it was in 1508 that Andrea ended his training and established himself as an independent master. Despite his skills as a draftsman and colorist, Andrea's reputation has suffered by comparison with these major representatives of the High Renaissance.

The perception of Andrea as brilliant, but limited, began with the artist and art historian Giorgio Vasari, who trained in Andrea's workshop during the 1520s, and from whom we have learned most of what is known of his life. Although he described Andrea's art as "truly excellent," he said that it lacked the inspiration of an "elevated mind." Vasari's standards were formed primarily by Michelangelo's "nobility" of conception and power of drawing. For him, Andrea thus fell short in terms of "those ornaments of grandeur, richness, and force" with which artists of his and succeeding generations had to contend. Furthermore, Vasari linked this poverty of intellectual elevation with a weakness in the artist's moral character.

A sense of melancholy and contemplation

During Andrea's lifetime the main Italian focus of patronage and artistic innovation shifted to Rome, although Florence and Venice continued to be significant centers of activity. Andrea's mature style combined elements from the schools of each of these cities.

The *Pietà* (or *Deposition*) of 1524 was painted for a monastery at which Andrea stayed in order to avoid the plague epidemic of that year. Although the figure of Christ is based on one painted a few years before by Fra Bartolommeo, Andrea's ability to differentiate between the various psychological states of the surrounding

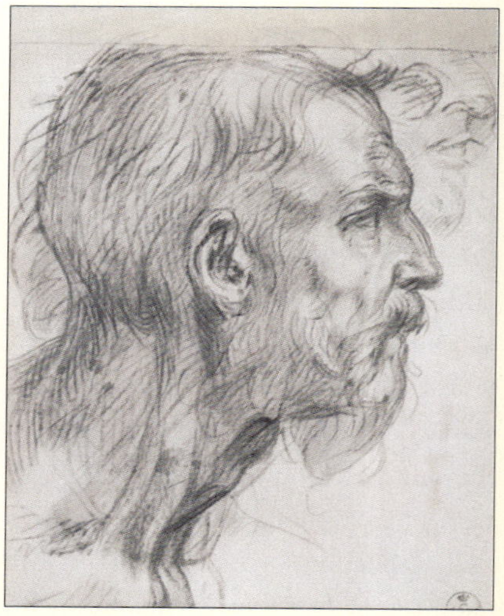

Apostle *c1522–23. Black chalk. $8\frac{1}{2}$ x 7 in (21.5 x 18 cm). Galleria degli Uffizi, Florence.*

Data file

Full name: Andrea del Sarto

Nationality: Italian

Style: High Renaissance

Dates: born 1486 in Florence, died 1531 in Florence

Key works:
- *Miracles of San Filippo Benizzi* c1510
- scenes from the life of Saint John the Baptist c1510–26
- *Birth of the Virgin* 1514
- *Madonna delle Arpie* 1517
- *Apostle* c1522–23
- *Pietà (Deposition)* 1524
- *Madonna del Sacco* 1525
- *Portrait of a Sculptor* c1528

Things to look for:
- a classical sense of balance and order
- an often melancholy mood of stillness
- detailed drawing
- soft, atmospheric coloring
- individualized facial types

Comparisons: Fra Bartolommeo, Leonardo da Vinci, Raphael, Giorgione, Albrecht Dürer, Pontormo

Glossary terms: *grazia, grisaille*

figures surpasses his older Florentine contemporary. This is particularly noticeable in the treatment of hands as being expressive of an emotional condition, and clearly owes much to his study of Leonardo's work (which was concerned with the ways in which the human body conveyed what Leonardo described as "movements of the mind").

The sense of melancholy created by this group of inward-looking people also echoes the effect achieved during this period in works by Giorgione, a Venetian. The subdued atmosphere is emphasized by a masterly handling of the still relatively new (to Italians) medium of oil paint. A softening of the light around the figures not only helps to harmonize them and their coloring into a unified whole, but also underlines the meaning of the picture: each individual's contemplation of the significance of profound tragedy.

The drawing *Apostle* (c1522–23) indicates another influence on Andrea, this time not Italian: the German graphic artist and painter, Albrecht Dürer. Andrea's meticulous attention to detail in the recording of an individual rather than an ideal type was at odds with contemporary tendencies in Italian art.

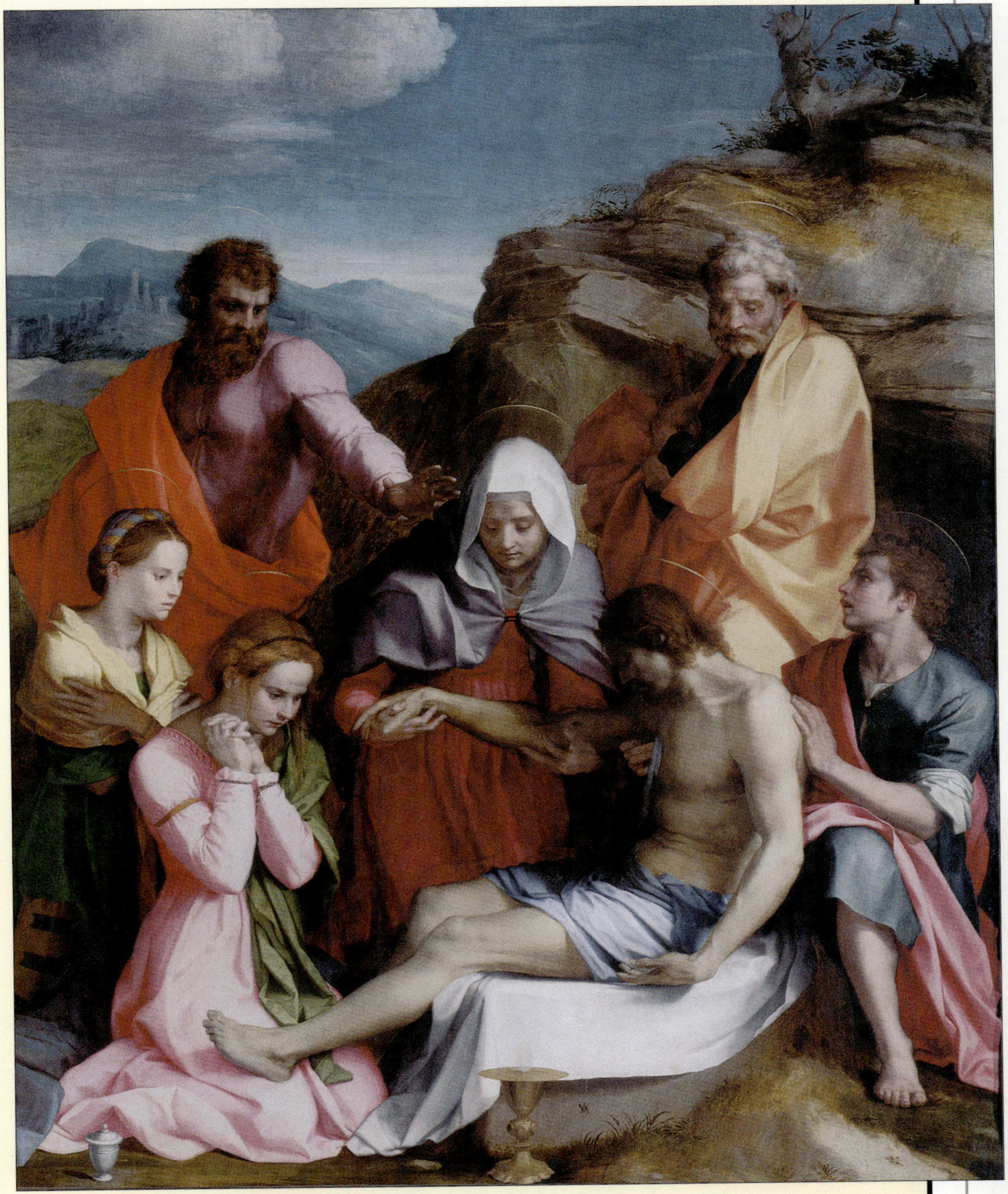

Pietà (Deposition) *1524. Oil on panel. 93¾ x 78 in (238 x 198 cm). Palazzo Pitti, Florence.*

Andrea's self-effacing devotion to his wife, Lucrezia (he was said to have broken his contract in France in order to return to her), was said to have been bound up with his general timidity in art, as in life. Yet such historical judgments can blind us to qualities in Andrea's art with which Vasari was ultimately unsympathetic. Andrea's works typically convey a spirit of gentle melancholy, often in keeping with the meaning of the subject. Their dramatic sense is quietly introspective, quite different from the vigor and strength that Vasari admired. Vasari did, however, credit Andrea with a near-flawless technique and a capacity for *grazia* (a refinement of grace) beyond the abilities of many of his peers.

Some art historians have interpreted Andrea's art as being a less-than-successful synthesis of the 15th-century tradition of naturalistic realism and the new, classicizing manner. Andrea did indeed learn much about balance of composition from his more illustrious contemporaries. However, his limited education would not have given him great access to classical humanist learning.

Until his death from the plague in 1531, Andrea was the master of an artist's workshop. Among his assistants were painters who were soon to become important figures in the evolution of Florentine mannerism—a style that was alien to Andrea's restrained classicism: Pontormo, Rosso Fiorentino, Francesco Salviati, and Vasari himself.

ANGELICO Fra

FRA ANGELICO WAS A DOMINICAN FRIAR. He began his hugely successful artistic career as a book illuminator and ended it as one of the most renowned artists of his time, responsible for huge fresco paintings in both the Vatican and Saint Peter's Basilica in Rome. His most famous work is the fresco decoration of the Dominican priory of San Marco in Florence.

Life and work

Fra Angelico was born Guido di Pietro, and took the name Fra Giovanni when he entered a Dominican priory sometime between 1417 and 1425. (The name by which we now know him, Fra Angelico, was not used until after his death.) Before entering the order, Fra Angelico had been a book illuminator, having trained alongside his brother in Florence. The techniques and characteristics of book illumination (brilliance of color and fine brushwork, for example) remain apparent in his work, even when he concentrated on grander panels, altarpieces, and frescos.

Although it is difficult to discover much about his work during the first years of his career, it is thought that he created three altarpieces for the church of San Domenico in Fiesole. The earliest of his surviving paintings whose date is certain is *The Linaiuoli Tabernacle* (1433–36), a triptych that was commissioned by the Florentine linenworkers' guild and depicted the Virgin and Child with Saints John, Mark, Peter, and John the Baptist.

It is obvious from this point onward that Fra Angelico was fully aware of the developments in Florentine art at the time, including innovations in the representation of "real" space and a more naturalistic approach to figures. However, he often chose to ignore them if he felt that his subject was better suited to a more unrepresentational or symbolic style. The success of the triptych led the great patrons of the time, the Strozzi and Medici families, to commission such works as *The Deposition* (c1436) and the Annalena altarpiece (c1437–40) from him.

By the 1440s Fra Angelico had a large workshop in Florence. Early that decade he began work on the monastery of San Marco, financed by his Medici patrons. He created a magnificent altarpiece, as well as decorating the public and private spaces of the monastery with frescos. An enormous undertaking, it provided a perfect fusion of religion and art that the friars could contemplate in their everyday surroundings.

In 1446 Fra Angelico left San Marco for Rome for about four years. In Rome, the pope immediately assigned him to create frescos in both the Vatican and Saint Peter's Basilica. The cycle of *The Lives of Saints Stephen and*

Data file

Full name: Guido di Pietro or Giovanni da Fiesole (known as Fra Angelico)

Nationality: Italian

Style: late Gothic/early Renaissance

Dates: born c1395–1400 near Viccio, died 1455 in Rome

Key works:
- *The Linaiuoli Tabernacle* 1433–36
- Annalena altarpiece c1437–40
- San Marco frescos 1440–45
- *The Lives of Saints Stephen and Lawrence* 1448–49
- *The Annunciation* c1450

Things to look for:
- work that shows the crossover between the late Gothic style and the new Renaissance ideas about three-dimensional space, naturalistic light, and geometric precision
- a continued interest in the use of symbols in religious works for devotional purposes
- a transition from the tranquility and timelessness of the San Marco frescos to the cycle of *The Lives of Saints Stephen and Lawrence*, which engages more with human activity

Comparisons: Gentile da Fabriano, Masaccio

Glossary terms: *arriccio*, fresco, Gothic, *intonaco*, Renaissance, *sinopia*, triptych

The Annunciation in fresco

Fra Angelico's *The Annunciation* (c1450) was painted in true fresco, a method that required the artist to paint onto wet or fresh plaster (the term "fresco" comes from the Italian for "fresh").

The fresco depicts the moment when the Archangel Gabriel appears to the Virgin Mary to tell her that she is going to bear the Son of God. Gabriel's bowed head denotes salutation, while Mary's lowered head both mirrors his and reveals her humility and willingness to do God's will; her folded hands also suggest acceptance.

This kind of composition became widespread in the representation of annunciations in 15th-century Florence, but it was Fra Angelico who first devised it. Mary is depicted in a confined area; the columns simultaneously delineate her space, represent her separateness from the world, and act as an artistic framing device. As Fra Angelico was depicting a spiritual space, it did not need to conform to any ordinary expectations of reality. Mary is larger than the Archangel and her head and halo reach higher than his; she is also larger than her surroundings if they are compared proportionally. These devices convey her importance.

Fra Angelico also experimented with light within the painting. The light appears to shine from the left-hand side of the work, casting a shadow behind Mary. However, it leaves no shadow behind Gabriel because he is a messenger of God.

Fra Angelico must have worked in conjunction with Michelozzo di Bartolommeo, architect for the Dominican priory of San Marco, in placing the painting to maximize the illusionistic effects of his

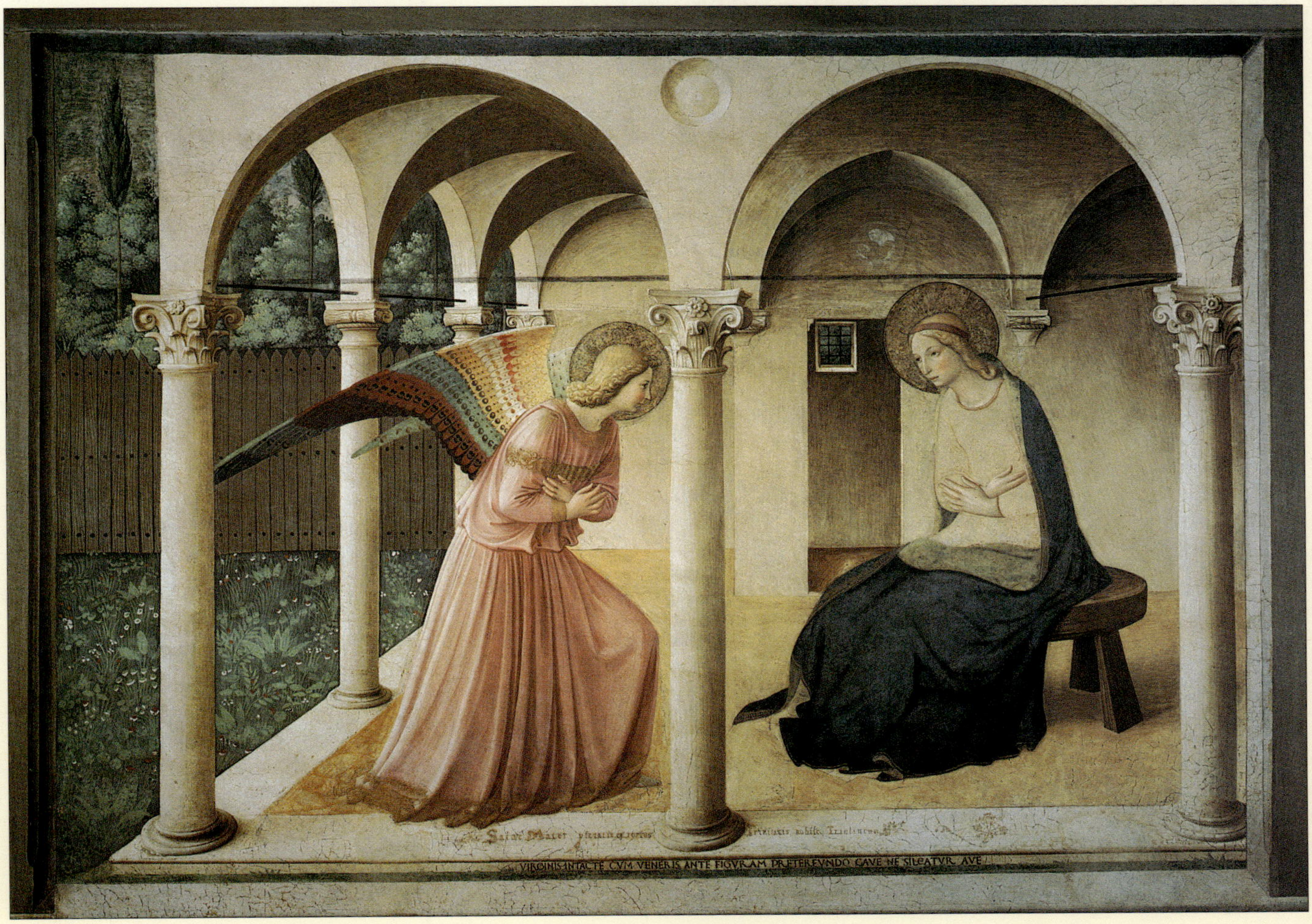

work. *The Annunciation* was placed at the top of a staircase, ensuring that it was the first painting to greet any visiting friars to the private dormitory wing, as well as the first art seen each day by the Dominicans themselves. The center of the staircase is directly opposite the central column portrayed in the work, while the painted-stone edge of *The Annunciation* echoes the stone of the surrounding walls. Viewers would approach from a dark space and be confronted by the scene, which was illuminated by a natural light source falling upon the painting.

The Annunciation *c1450. Fresco. 90½ x 126¼ in (230 x 321 cm). Museum of San Marco, Florence.*

Fresco layers *In the technique of* buon fresco *or true fresco, wet plaster was used. The artist applied a coat of plaster* (arriccio) *over coarse plaster, then drew his design with red-earth pigment, or* sinopia*. Next he covered the area he intended to paint that day with a thin layer of smooth plaster or* intonaco*. He then painted the design on the wet layer using pigment mixed with water.*

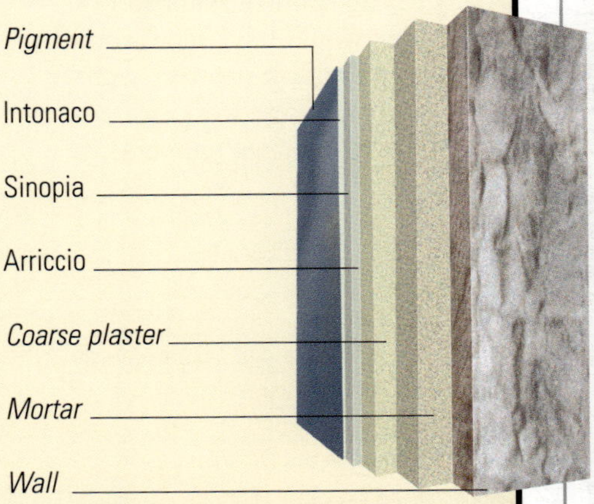

Lawrence (1448–49) are the only surviving frescos from this period. They depict more active scenes than the works in San Marco, and also reveal Fra Angelico's interest in Roman architecture. Both of these features are typical characteristics of the new Renaissance art world, in which real human actions were regarded as being as important as the symbolic gestures of the late Gothic style, and an interest in the classical world was also "reborn."

Fra Angelico returned to Tuscany in 1450 and became the prior of the church and convent of San Domenico in Fiesole. He continued to receive Medici commissions during this two-year period, but in 1452 refused a prestigious commission in Prato, probably because something better had been offered to him in Rome. This was possibly the cloister decoration of San Maria sopra Minerva, where he was buried upon his death in 1455.

ANTONELLO DA MESSINA

ANTONELLO DA MESSINA PLAYED A PART in bringing the oil-painting technique of early Netherlandish painters such as Jan Van Eyck to Italy, and his work reflects Netherlandish treatment of details in its use of light and depiction of objects. In 1475 Antonello visited Venice, where his work greatly influenced Giovanni Bellini.

Life and work

As his name indicates, Antonello da Messina came from Messina, a town in northeast Sicily (the large island off the southern end of the Italian mainland), which was at that time part of the Kingdom of Naples. Sicily is dominated by a live volcano—Mount Etna—and through the centuries has had a history of geological instability. Two large earthquakes, in 1783 and 1908, destroyed 90 percent of the historic town of Messina. As a result many art works (including early paintings by Antonello) and historic buildings have been lost.

It seems that Antonello studied and worked on the mainland in Naples, where, at the court of Alfonso I of Aragon, he would have seen works by early Netherlandish painters such as Jan Van Eyck. These works were in oil paint (rather than egg tempera), a medium that allowed artists to create startling new effects of light, texture, and detail. Antonello used oils in the Netherlandish manner, which was unusual for an Italian painter at this time, but how he learned to do this is not clear (although it has been suggested that he was taught by Van Eyck himself).

In 1457 Antonello returned to Messina, where he remained until 1474. During this time he produced *Salvator Mundi* (1465); the striking *Portrait of a Man* (c1472) probably dates from this period, too.

In 1475 Antonello traveled to Venice, where he so impressed the Venetians that he was offered a state income. During his stay he painted the San Cassiano altarpiece. This was remarkable for the way it depicted the solidity of the figures through the observation of light and perspective.

The design that Antonello used for the altarpiece was also relatively new. Instead of the saints being given separate framed "compartments" of their own within the polyptych, they were incorporated into a single scene so that the Virgin Mary and Jesus seem to be in the same room and almost seem to be having an informal conversation with the saints. This type of composition is often known as a *sacra conversazione* ("holy conversation" in Italian). Only two fragments of this altarpiece survive but, as with other works by Antonello, its combination of northern European and Italian artistic influences had a profound effect on Venetian painters, notably Giovanni Bellini.

By 1476 Antonello had returned to Messina. He died there in 1479.

Data file

Full name: Antonello da Messina

Nationality: Italian

Style: early Renaissance

Dates: born c1430 in Messina, died 1479 in Messina

Key works:
- *Portrait of a Man* c1472
- San Cassiano altarpiece 1475–76
- *Saint Jerome in His Study* 1475–76

Things to look for:
- similarities with 15th-century Netherlandish paintings in use of light and depiction of objects

Comparisons: Jan Van Eyck, Rogier Van der Weyden, Giovanni Bellini, Robert Campin

Glossary terms: egg tempera, polyptych, *sacra conversazione,* saintly attribute

Light, texture, and detail

Although the exact date of this painting is not known, it seems likely that it was done in about 1475–76 when Antonello was in Venice. Saint Jerome, the subject of the painting, lived from about 342 to 420, and is famous for having made the first Latin translation of the Bible from Hebrew. He spent some time living in the desert as a hermit, where it was said that he won the friendship of a lion by removing a thorn from its foot.

Saint Jerome was a popular subject for paintings at this time, being depicted as either a scholar (as Antonello has done here), or out in the wilderness, and he is often shown with his saintly attributes—a lion and his red cardinal's hat. Although the office of cardinal had not been invented in his day, he is often depicted wearing a cardinal's hat and robes—he seems to have been informally "promoted" to the position retrospectively!

Here he sits reading in a kind of cubicle within a Gothic church. He is surrounded by a clutter of everyday objects—pots, boxes, and books—and there are potted plants, a

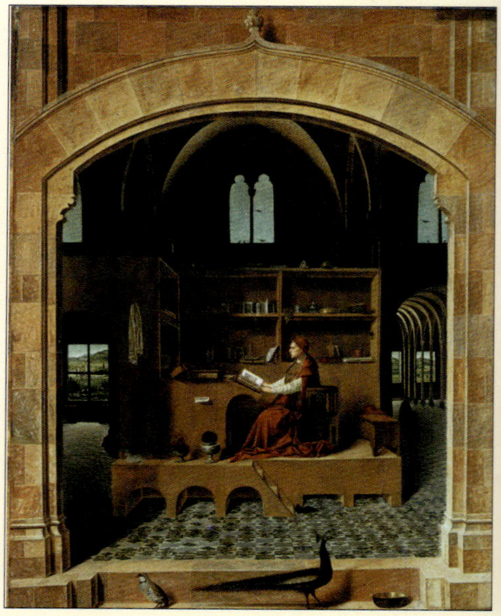

Saint Jerome in His Study *1475–76. Oil on panel. 18 x 14¼ in (46 x 36.5 cm). National Gallery, London.*

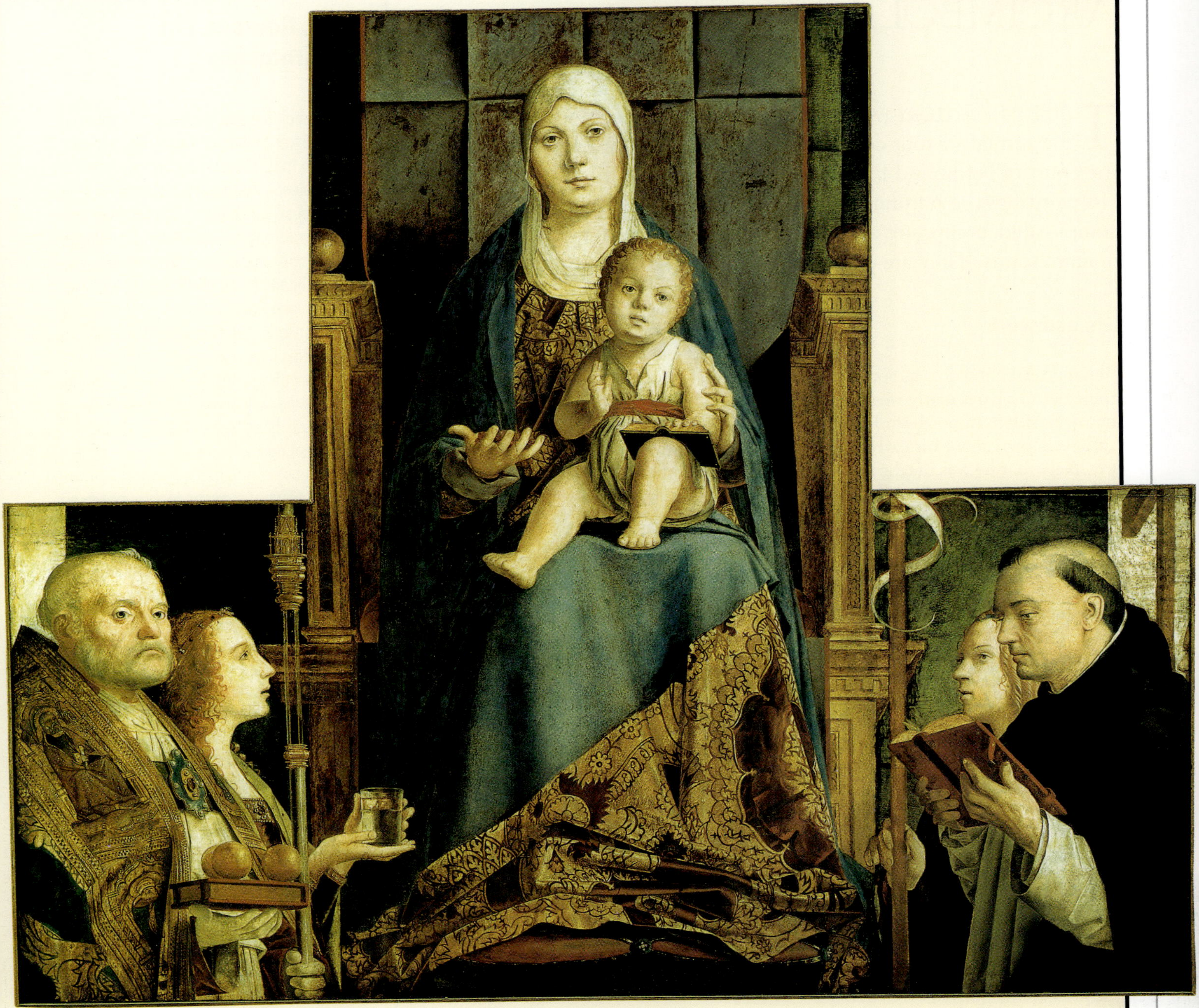

crucifix, his cardinal's hat, and a towel on a hook. A small cat dozes on a ledge while a rather small lion can be seen padding towards him in the shadows of the church on the right-hand side.The birds on the front ledge are almost certainly there to add symbolic meaning—the partridge is a symbol of the Church and of truth, while the peacock is symbolic of immortality.

Saint Jerome in His Study is not at all typical of Italian painting of this time. In its use of detail and light it is reminiscent of the work of the Netherlandish artists Jan Van Eyck and Rogier Van der Weyden. Among the characteristics that makes it comparable with early Netherlandish works are the view through an open doorway, the exquisite detail of the brass dish and the birds in the foreground on the stone step, and the views through the windows at the back of the church, giving us a glimpse of the sun-drenched Italian landscape.

San Cassiano altarpiece *(fragment) 1475–76. Oil on panel. 45 x 52 in (115 x 133 cm). Kunsthistorisches Museum, Vienna.*

ARCIMBOLDO Giuseppe

THE 16TH-CENTURY PAINTER ARCIMBOLDO provided inspiration for the surrealists four centuries later. Born in Italy, he was called to the court of Ferdinand I in Prague and became a favorite court artist. His paintings use natural forms, such as fruit and vegetables, in complicated, composite arrangements to portray other, usually human, forms. They are disturbing as well as entertaining.

Life and work

Giuseppe Arcimboldo was born into a noble but not particularly wealthy family in Milan, in northern Italy. Little is known about his early life, but it is likely that he was taught to paint by his father, an artist. By 1551 he was employed as a painter of decorative schemes for public buildings, including the enormous Milan Cathedral. There he repainted the front of the building and produced a decorative scheme for the main door, as well as designs for the stained-glass windows showing the life of Saint Catherine.

In about 1560 Arcimboldo joined the court of the Holy Roman Empire, the complex of European territories under the rule of the Frankish, or German, king who bore the title of Holy Roman Emperor. The emperor, in theory at least, ruled over a large area of Europe, including territories that are now Germany and Austria. His court moved between various major cities, but was situated mainly in Vienna and Prague.

Arcimboldo received a regular pension, which allowed him to live in comfort. He was sometimes required to execute straightforward portraits for the emperor, but from 1563 he was described as a "painter of heads." Typical of his work at this time was a fantasy painting showing a head made up entirely of fruit. Arcimboldo was commissioned by Emperor Maximilian II to depict many of the members of his court in this style of composite portrait. He continued to work in this manner throughout his life, applying the same technique to whole figures, landscapes, and a variety of objects.

His work was much admired at court, and in the 1570s he came under the patronage of Rudolf II, Maximilian's successor. This highly eccentric ruler, who was passionately interested in science, learning, and the arts, and was one of the most important collectors of all time, lived an increasingly secret life in his palace in Prague and was suspected of being a magician. His interest in the occult may have attracted him to the curious compositions for which Arcimboldo became famous.

As Official Painter, Arcimboldo played an important role in the extravagant and bizarre life of the imperial court. He was responsible for organizing festivities such as balls, processions, and open-air parties, which allowed him to use his imagination to the full. He also advised the emperor on his picture collection and traveled around Europe to make suitable acquisitions, creating a remarkable art collection. A man of many other talents, he also worked as a stage designer, an architect, and as an engineer, and he designed and

Data file

Full name: Guiseppe Arcimboldo
Nationality: Italian
Style: fantasy
Dates: born c1527 in Milan, died 1593 in Milan
Key works:
Seasons series 1563, including *Summer*
Fantasy Figure 1563
Elements series 1566
Seasons series (II) 1573
Things to look for:
- fantasy paintings using fruits, vegetables, and flowers to make up human forms
- a sense of the grotesque and the humorous

Comparisons: Hieronymus Bosch, Salvador Dalí
Glossary terms: fantasy, surrealism

Fruit, flowers, and the grotesque

Arcimboldo made his reputation as a painter of highly imaginative pictures in which fruit, flowers, animals, a variety of other objects, and even people, are meticulously depicted so that together they show another form—a head or a human figure, for example. He often showed fantasy heads made up of apples, lemons, oranges, and flowers.

His style is clearly seen in *Summer* (1563). This was a very popular subject, often part of a series of paintings showing the seasons, which would be shown as landscapes or as human or quasi-human allegorical figures.

Arcimboldo returned a number of times to the subject of summer. In this version he shows summer as a personification: a human figure, probably a woman, is shown reclining on the ground. The body is made up of fruit and vegetables, as well as a basket. All the elements of the figure (head, limbs, and torso) are recognizable, and the painting can be read as a still life with an abundance of fruit. A rapid study of the picture, however, makes it clear that a different subject is also intended.

At one level Arcimboldo's paintings are humorous, if in a rather ironic and grotesque way. But they also raise disturbing questions, for example: What is the nature of apparently solid matter? Is the human body as solid as it appears, or will it decay almost as rapidly as the fruit of which it is composed in Arcimboldo's vision? When we look at an image, do we see what we expect to see, or what is actually there? He creates strange connections between the human and the natural worlds, which not only entertain us but lead us to deeper questioning.

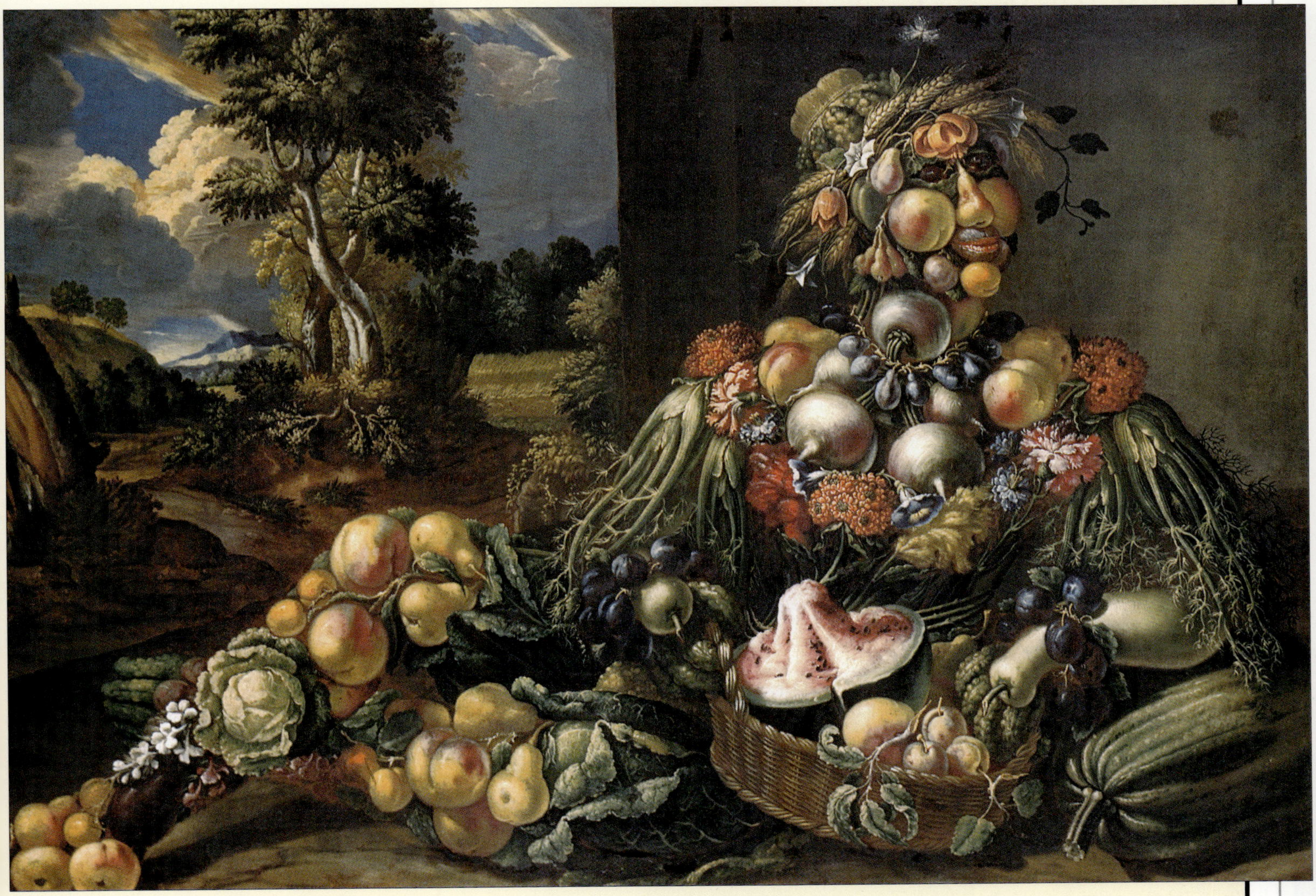

Arcimboldo was not the first artist to have painted works of this sort. Hieronymus Bosch, perhaps the most famous of all fantasy painters, worked in a similar mode during the early 16th century (although most of his works took as their subjects religious themes or allegories about the folly of human beings), and Arcimboldo would have seen the work of the older painter. But he carried this approach further, in a manner that attracted many imitators. His paintings, like those of Bosch, appear strangely modern.

In the 1920s Arcimboldo's style was appreciated anew by the surrealists, who were fascinated by connections between apparently disparate objects and the strange metaphors his work suggested. Today he is regarded as a highly creative artist who worked in the realm of the imagination rather than to official dictates of the court or the Church.

Summer *1563. Oil on canvas. 39 x 55 in (99 x 140 cm). Wadsworth Atheneum, Hartford, CT.*

constructed waterworks. He was also fond of music; he invented a style of musical composition that compared musical notes to color, and his music was performed at court.

By 1587 Arcimboldo had made a large fortune. He returned to Italy, where he died a few years later.

Outside court circles, the sophisticated and slightly sinister quality of his work was not to people's tastes. His work came to be seen as unhealthy, and even decadent, reflecting a strange, inward-looking court culture where playing with appearances and theatrical effects seemed to be given higher priority than moral issues. It is only in the 20th century that an interest in dreams and subconscious meanings has brought his work back into the art history mainstream. His paintings are now much in demand, and many fakes have found their way onto the art market.

AUDUBON John James

THE ARTIST, WRITER, AND ADVENTURER JOHN JAMES AUDUBON is America's greatest and most popular natural-history painter. His ambition to paint every species of bird in the United States was never achieved, but his two great works, *The Birds of America* and *The Viviparous Quadrupeds of North America*, are superb records of the wildlife of a country that, at the time, was still largely unexplored.

Life and work

John James Audubon was born on the Caribbean island of Haiti. He was the son of a French planter and sea-traveling merchant, Jean Audubon, and a French Creole mother. Following his mother's death in 1789, Audubon was taken with a half-sister to live in France with his father and his father's wife, Ann Moynet, who later adopted both children when she realized that she would not bear any of her own.

Audubon's only formal artistic education came when he was 17 years old, and consisted of six months' study in the atelier (artist's studio) of the great French neoclassical painter Jacques-Louis David, who exerted a major influence on French taste from the outbreak of the Revolution in 1789 to the fall of Napoleon in 1815.

Audubon, however, preferred to draw from nature itself. In 1803 he left Paris for Mill Grove, his father's plantation near Philadelphia. Here he was at last able to study at first hand the animals and birds of the region. It was here that Audubon's ambition to draw every single species of North American bird was to develop.

After a brief visit to France in 1806, Audubon returned to the United States, where he married his neighbor and sweetheart Lucy Bakewell, and moved to Kentucky. He formed a business partnership with his brother-in-law, but in 1812 it foundered, leaving them virtually penniless. More upsetting for Audubon, though, was the loss of 200 wildlife drawings that were eaten by rats. It would take him three years to redraw them.

In 1819 Audubon went to work as a taxidermist in Cincinnati before traveling down the Mississippi in 1820. The experience was to prove valuable to him in his later work, as he collected skins and pelts of trapped animals during expeditions, and reconstructed them on a wire framework for drawing. The information on these specimens was augmented by his notebooks, in which he detailed every aspect of an animal's appearance in life.

In 1826 he traveled to England to try to sell subscriptions to his great work, *The Birds of America* (1827–38), and to find an engraver able to translate his paintings and drawings into aquatints. The first 10 plates were

Data file

Full name: John James Audubon

Nationality: American

Style: natural history illustration

Dates: born 1785 in Santo Domingo (now Haiti), died 1851 in New York, NY, United States

Key works:
The Birds of America (four volumes, 1827–38. 435 illustrations of birds reproduced in colored aquatints)

The Viviparous Quadrupeds of North America (three volumes, 1845–48. 156 illustrations of animals by J. J. Audubon and his son, J. W. Audubon, reproduced in colored lithographs)

Things to look for:
- images of birds and animals, often in action
- animals depicted in or against a background of natural habitat
- compositions and poses of animals and birds carefully arranged to demonstrate coloring of plumage or marking of fur
- variable scientific accuracy as some "plain" species are "worked up" (made more elaborate), and some poses are incorrect

Comparisons: George Catlin, Thomas Cole, Frans Snyders, Thomas Bewick, Melchior Hondecoeter, Edwin Henry Landseer

Glossary terms: aquatint, engraving, lithograph, neoclassicism

A collector's prize

Audubon's *The Birds of America* was engraved and published in London by Robert Havell and Son over the period 1827 to 1838. It was produced in a huge "double-elephant" folio size, measuring 26¾ x 40 in (68 x 101.5 cm).

The work was published in parts; each part contained five plates. The original total cost to each subscriber for all four volumes was £187.10s (about $115). This was a significant amount of money in 1827, and many original subscribers defaulted on later parts. Because Audubon refused to sell individual prints, fewer than 200 complete editions were sold. This is one reason why Audubon's work is so rare and so valuable today.

In its original form, *The Birds of America* contained 435 hand-colored engravings after Audubon's original paintings, most of which are in the collection of the New York Historical Society. A further 65 hand-colored lithographs dealing with birds from western North America was added to a smaller book in seven volumes.

In the original book the overall dimensions of the plates were about 29 x 39 in (73.5 x 99 cm) but many of the complete sets were later broken up, and individual prints were cut down in size to fit into frames.

Carolina Parrot (c1827–30) is an interesting example, for it is one of the few bird paintings (which include the *Bald Eagle*, the *Ruffed Grouse* and the *Pileated Woodpecker*) that was painted in its entirety by Audubon. For the most part, the botanical habitats of the creatures were painted by Audubon's assistant, Joseph Mason. There is even one figure of a bird in the book that was painted by Audubon's wife, Lucy.

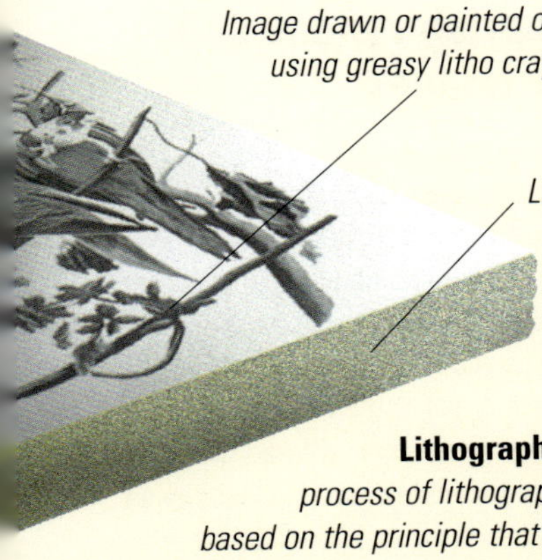

Lithography *The process of lithography is based on the principle that water and grease do not mix. An image is drawn on the stone with a grease-based drawing material, such as a lithographic crayon or ink. The surface of the stone is then chemically treated with a mixture of gum arabic and dilute nitric acid. When the stone is dampened and the printing ink is applied by a roller, the non-image areas repel the ink and retain water, while the image areas accept the ink and repel the water. A print is made when paper is placed on top of the inked stone and the image is transferred to the paper under pressure, using a litho press. Audubon's prints would then be hand-colored, using watercolors.*

Many of the species that Audubon painstakingly recorded in his books are now extinct—another reason why Audubon's work is so prized. The Carolina parrot (*Conuropsis Carolinensis*) was a small green and gold parakeet with scarlet cheeks. Once widespread, it could be found even in New York state, but its last recorded sighting was in 1904.

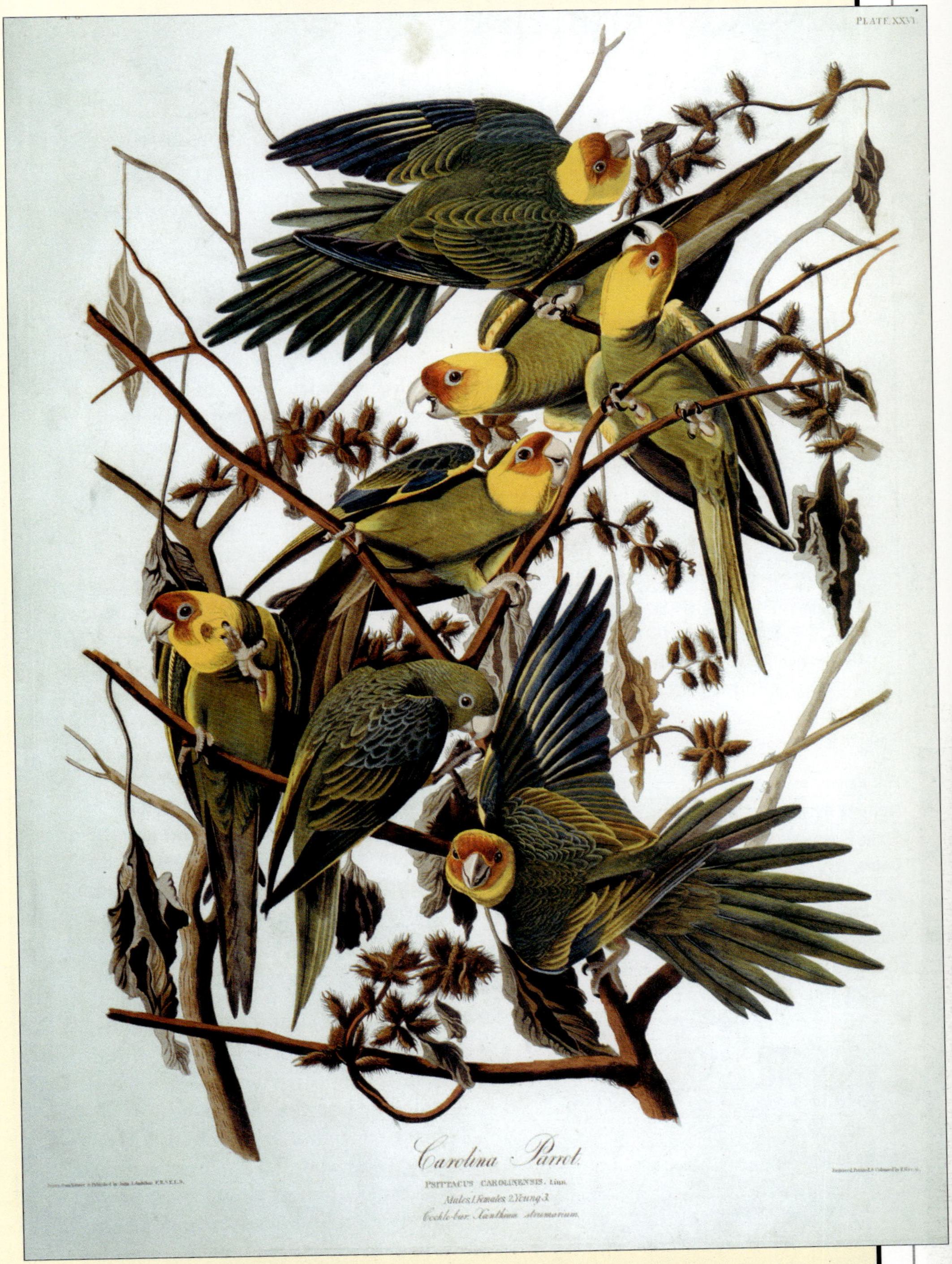

Carolina Parrot *c1827–30. Hand-colored aquatint. 33 x 24 in (84 x 61 cm). The Academy of Natural Science, Philadelphia, PA.*

engraved by Lizars of Edinburgh, the remainder by Havells of London. A trip to France to find buyers for his book met with limited success, and in 1829 Audubon returned to the United States.

By October 1831 he was on an expedition to the southern states. There he met with Reverend John Bachman, who would act as his agent, selling *The Birds* and encouraging him in his next great work, *The Viviparous Quadrupeds of North America* (1845–48)(viviparous quadrupeds means four-legged animals that give birth to live offspring rather than laying eggs). Audubon was assisted by his two sons, John and Victor.

Audubon died in New York in 1851. In 1858, by an Act of Congress, 100 miniature sets of his two major works were presented to governments around the world. His name lives on in the National Audubon Society, dedicated to the conservation of natural resources and wildlife.

BACON Francis

BACON WAS A SELF-TAUGHT ARTIST who sprang to fame in his mid-thirties with his dark and powerful images of contorted and mutilated figures. He lived a life of excess amid the Bohemian artists and marginal figures of London's pubs, clubs, and gambling dens.

Life and work

Francis Bacon suffered greatly from asthma as a child, and his illness resulted in his lack of formal education. He grew up in Dublin, Ireland, and London, England, then left home at the age of 17 in 1927 in order to experience more fully the cultural life of Europe. His first port of call was Berlin, where he stayed for two months and was introduced to the decadent pleasures that were then infusing the German capital (sex, drinking, and gambling were vigorously pursued in Berlin in the 1920s). The French capital, Paris, provided stimulation of a different order. There he visited the galleries and museums that exposed him to the world of art, from the Old Masters of Western painting to the latest works of the modernists, including, most influentially for Bacon, Pablo Picasso and Fernand Léger.

In 1929 Bacon returned to London and set up a studio, where he dabbled in drawings and watercolors, taking the first tentative steps in his new vocation. In order to finance himself during this period he worked as an interior decorator, achieving some success with his furniture designs.

By imitating the great artists of the early 20th century (Léger and Picasso in particular) Bacon learned technique, but his own style took shape initially only by small degrees. *Crucifixion* (1933) reveals the emergence of his own form of visual expression, with its distorted human form and severe style, stripped down to what he regarded to be the essential elements of this theme: a sticklike, crucified body, starkly set against a black background. Despite this promising work, for the next decade Bacon lost almost all of his artistic motivation and nearly abandoned his career as a painter in favor of running an illegal casino.

During World War II Bacon was considered unfit for duty because of his poor health, provoking in him a renewed interest in painting. His *Three Studies for Figures at the Base of a Crucifixion* (1944) not only marked his reemergence as a painter, but also proved his worth as a compelling, forceful artist working in a style that was all his own. This triptych (picture made up of three panels) effectively established the visual vocabulary that Bacon would use for the rest of his career. His compressed figures are stretched in contortions of anguish and leering revelry, more nightmarish creatures of a savage imagination than creatures of the natural world. Each of the three figures is isolated within its own canvas, and each is set within an

Full name: Francis Bacon

Nationality: Irish

Style: figurative/expressionism

Dates: born 1909 in Dublin, died 1992 in Madrid, Spain

Key works:
- *Three Studies for Figures at the Base of a Crucifixion* 1944
- *Head VI* 1949
- *Dog* 1952
- *Three Studies of a Human Head* 1953
- *Study After Velázquez's Portrait of Pope Innocent X* 1953
- *Head Surrounded by Sides of Beef* 1954
- *Triptych May–June* 1973

Things to look for:
- unpainted patches of raw canvas
- semiabstract settings
- dry brushstrokes clinging to the surface of the canvas
- ghostly figures, thinly sketched in oil paint
- deformity of the human physique

Comparisons: Edvard Munch, Pablo Picasso, Willem De Kooning, Vincent Van Gogh, Diego Velázquez, Rembrandt

Glossary terms: expressionism, figurative, Old Masters, triptych

Nightmarish visions and ghostly images

There was an urgency to Bacon's painting that we can see in his treatment of both the main images and the backgrounds of his works. Although he often used acrylic resin or household paint to cover large areas of the canvas rapidly, he did not feel that acrylic offered the same degree of subtlety and malleability as oil paint. When painting figures he would therefore change mediums in order to concentrate his efforts on the most essential elements of his paintings.

When he worked on figures in oil, as in *Study After Velázquez's Portrait of Pope Innocent X* (1953), he would drag the paint across the dry surface of the canvas using his brush, allowing the paint to cling to the ridges of the canvas's woven fabric. Very little repainting over the same area of the picture is evident, and it almost seems as if he feared painting too much. Indeed, his technique resembles sketching with paint, but the effect is very expressive, conveying as it does his sense of urgency, while also presenting an ethereal, ghostly image.

In order to give a rawness to the surface texture he would sometimes throw or rub sand, fibers, or dust from his studio onto the still-wet paint. He would also occasionally flick or squirt paint directly onto the canvas, in an act that demonstrated the work's immediacy. This practice implied that he was gambling with the painting: the gesture could either add a startling element to it or destroy the quality of the image.

Avoiding discussions regarding technique, Bacon preferred the intuitive, the direct, and the raw over labored consideration and development. He wanted to capture a trace of reality—the acts and memories of living.

Bacon based his figures on photographs, usually those that had been reproduced in newspapers and magazines rather than any taken by himself. Even when his imagery was based on great works of the past, such as *Study After Velázquez's Portrait of Pope Innocent X*, he still preferred to work from reproductions. He also used the imagery of the cinema as source material; in several of his pieces he made similar use of an open, apparently screaming, mouth, an image that he took from the 1925 Sergei Eisenstein movie *Battleship Potemkin*.

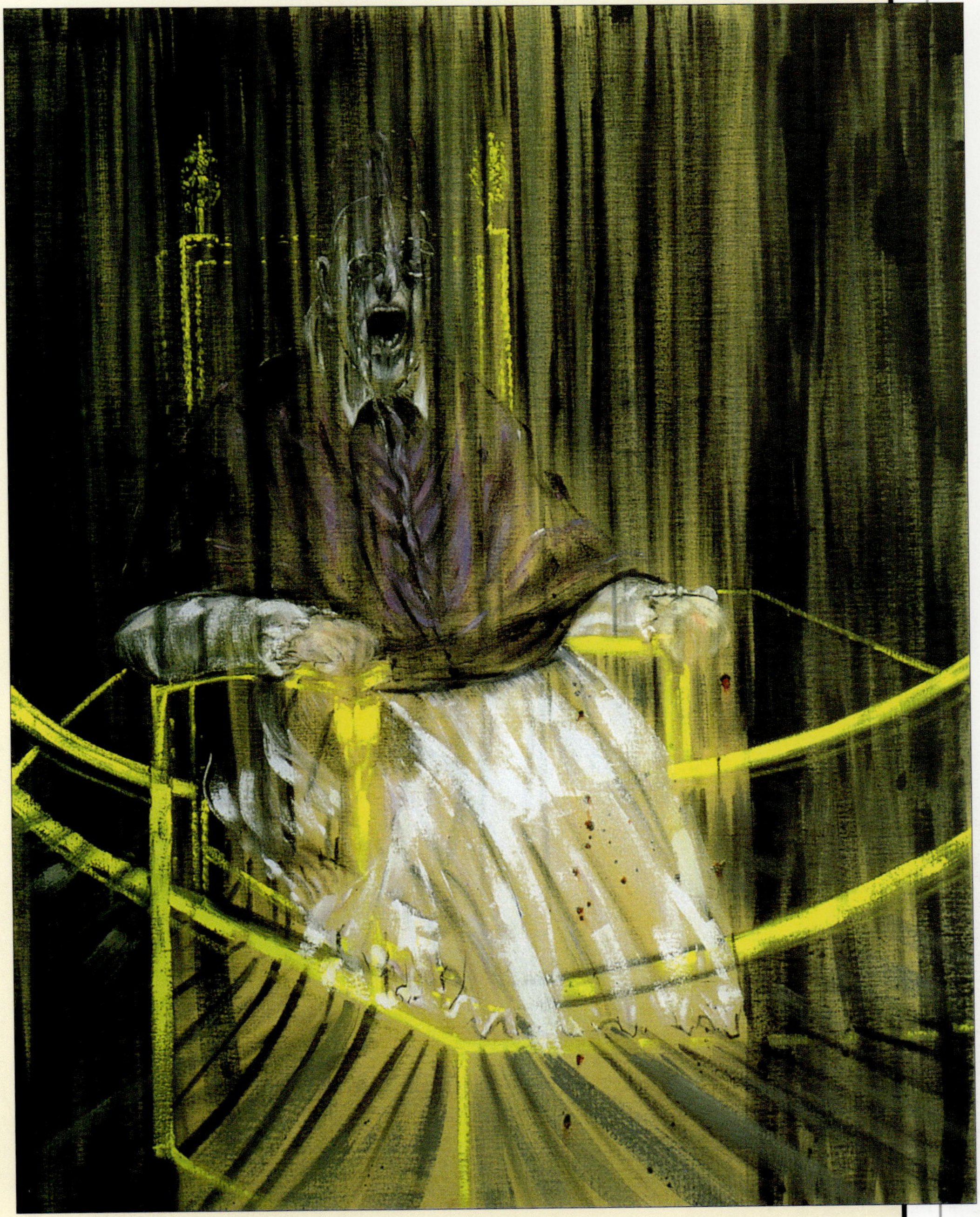

Study After Velázquez's Portrait of Pope Innocent X *1953. Oil on canvas. 60 1/4 x 46 1/2 in (153 x 118 cm). Des Moines Art Center, Des Moines, IA.*

abstract world, which is reduced to a blank, almost empty, space defined by simple lines of geometry. There seems to be no way in which these beings can escape from their predicament to another world; they appear to be stuck within a space that seems both confined and infinite. In their stance and expression these creatures resemble caged animals: furious, pathetic, powerful, and yet impotent.

Bacon's greatest creative period was the 1950s, when he developed his style and range fully, producing some of the most startling images of the 20th century. An image that he used repeatedly was the screaming head of a pope, as seen in such paintings as *Head VI* (1949) and *Head Surrounded by Sides of Beef* (1954). He rapidly became a very successful artist who attracted wide media attention. As his life became a rollercoaster of social excess, his art became increasingly autobiographical. After the 1950s he tended to paint portraits of his close friends and associates, such as the painter Lucian Freud. He also depicted the major psychological and emotional events of his life, of which one of the most startling examples is *Triptych May–June* (1973), which deals with the suicide of his lover during the early 1970s.

BALLA Giacomo

GIACOMO BALLA WAS A KEY MEMBER OF THE FUTURIST GROUP that gathered around the Italian writer Filippo Tommaso Marinetti. Balla, who was fascinated by the scientific and technological developments of his day, sought to capture a sense of the new, and the experience of motion and speed, in his painting.

Life and work

Giacomo Balla, born in 1871 in Turin, was the oldest of the artists associated with the Italian futurist movement. He inherited an interest in science and technology from his father, an amateur photographer, but received little formal artistic training, attending drawing lessons for only a brief period.

Balla left Turin for Rome in 1895, where he became an avid supporter of socialism. After traveling to Paris in 1900, he encountered the work of the French impressionists and divisionists. The divisionists, who included painters such as the neoimpressionist Georges Seurat, were trying to develop the techniques of the impressionist painters in a more scientific way. Their method was to apply small points or patches of unmixed color to their canvases; these were supposed to fuse in the spectator's eye and create a vibrant "optical mixture" when the paintings were viewed from a certain distance. Returning to Rome, Balla began to experiment with this technique, breaking up the surface of his paintings with small, directed brushstrokes.

He was keen to express his socialist sympathies in his work, an ambition that is evident in his first major piece, entitled *The Worker's Day* (1903–04). In 1909 Balla met the poet and theorist Filippo Tommaso Marinetti, the founder of the futurist movement. The futurists were anarchists who rejected the art of the past and advocated new artistic practices that would embrace symbols of modernity and technological progress, such as the automobile, the airplane, and movie theaters. They tried to evoke speed and dynamic motion in their art.

Balla exhibited work at the Venice Biennale for the first time in 1909, and in that year produced his first futurist-inspired painting, *The Street Lamp: Study of Light*. He joined several other artists in signing the *Manifesto of Futurist Painting* in 1910. The group included Umberto Boccioni and Gino Severini, who had begun to frequent Balla's studio from about 1901.

The futurists aimed to represent the dynamic pace of modernity by creating a sense of movement in their paintings and sculptures. Balla turned to several sources of inspiration for this. Cubism was one of them. He was particularly fascinated with cubism's rejection of the traditional single viewpoint in favor of a shifting perspective, whereby an object could be viewed simultaneously from a number of different angles.

Balla was also intrigued by the work of the photographers Etienne-Jules Marey and Anton Giulio Bragaglia, who had both tried to represent movement through the photographic techniques of timed and multiple exposures. In their experiments a moving person or animal would be photographed several times, or over a period of time; the resulting images were presented within a single photograph to give the impression of movement. Balla's response to these experiments is evident in *Dynamism of a Dog on a Leash* (1912), in which the multiplication of the dog's limbs and tail effectively suggests rapid motion.

By the end of 1913 Balla's works were becoming more diagrammatical and geometrical. In his series of works entitled *Abstract Speed* (1912–14) and *Iridescent Compenetrations* (1912–14) the subject becomes increasingly difficult, if not impossible, to identify. Balla was trying to express the experience of movement, instead of presenting a concrete representation of the physical world as viewed in a single moment from a single point of view.

By the start of World War I, in 1914, Balla's politics had shifted to militaristic nationalism. Although too old to serve, he was an enthusiastic supporter of Italy's war effort. During the years after the war he increasingly worked in the fields of theater and costume design. In 1929 he also briefly flirted with the second wave of futurism, which had once again been launched by Marinetti. By the late 1930s, however, Balla had returned to a figurative style, including portraits and urban landscapes, which he maintained until his death in 1958.

Data file

Full name: Giacomo Balla

Nationality: Italian

Style: futurism

Dates: born 1871 in Turin, died 1958 in Rome

Key works:

The Worker's Day 1903–04

The Street Lamp: Study of Light 1909

Dynamism of a Dog on a Leash 1912

The Hand of the Violinist 1912

Abstract Speed: The Car Has Passed 1913

Iridescent Compenetration No. 4 c1913

Things to look for:

- bright colors representing light
- multiple viewpoints simultaneously showing a figure or animal in several positions
- lines of force
- dynamic compositions

Comparisons: Umberto Boccioni, Gino Severini, Carlo Carrà, Luigi Russolo, Giovanni Segantini, Etienne-Jules Marey, Anton Giulio Bragaglia

Glossary terms: cubism, divisionism, futurism, impressionism, neoimpressionism, Venice Biennale

A futurist style

The futurist movement was officially founded in 1909, when Filippo Tommaso Marinetti published his first manifesto in the Parisian newspaper *Le Figaro*. Marinetti's cry for a rejection of the past and a celebration of modernity appealed enormously to Balla, who immediately started work on his first truly futurist painting, *The Street Lamp: Study of Light* (1909).

Balla focused in this painting on an important symbol of the modern, urban world: an electric street lamp of the kind that had just been introduced to Rome. He emphasized the glaring light that emanated from the lamp, giving it an almost material existence. And he contrasted the powerful electric light with the pale glow of the sickle moon that is seen in the top right-hand corner of the painting.

By including the moon in this piece Balla may have been making a reference to an article that had been published by Marinetti entitled "Let's Murder the Moonshine" (1909), in which Marinetti hailed Balla as one of his new futurist friends.

At this point in his career Balla was still heavily influenced by the divisionist techniques that he had encountered in Paris. He built up the image by applying hundreds of V-shaped brushstrokes in reds, yellows, and greens, all radiating from the centrally positioned lamp.

The darker reds and greens gradually diminish, giving way to bright yellows and white around the lamp itself, thereby giving the effect of intense, glaring light. The surrounding dark border, which is similarly represented with short, broken brushstrokes, encloses the light in the shape of a bulb, further emphasizing the power of electric street lighting—at the time a very modern concept.

The Street Lamp: Study of Light set an agenda for Balla, who would strive for the rest of his life to express pictorially the passage of light through space and time.

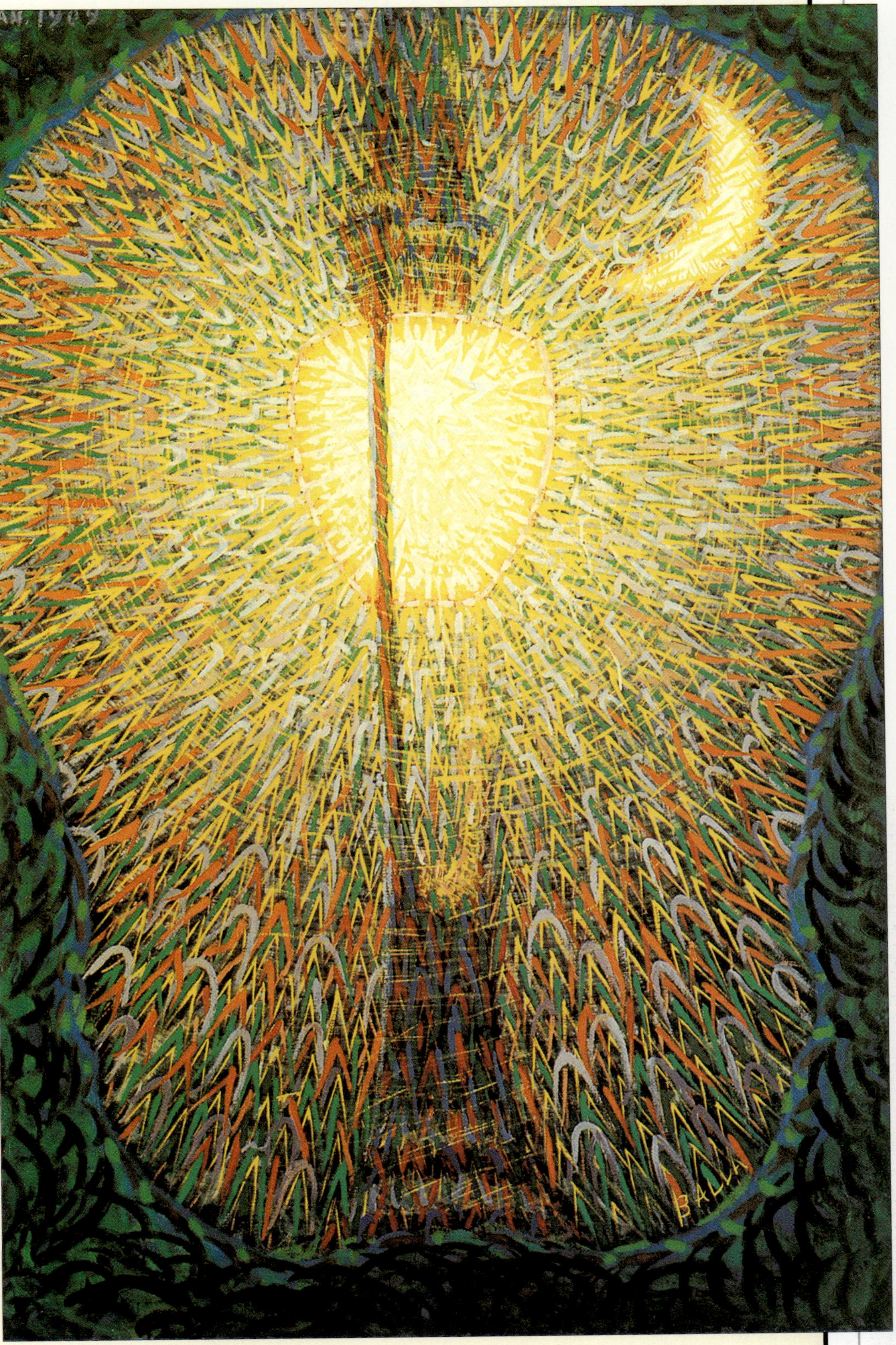

The Street Lamp: Study of Light *1909. Oil on canvas. 69 x 45.5 in (174.5 x 114.5 cm). Museum of Modern Art, New York, NY.*

BARTOLOMMEO Fra

THE HARMONIOUS CALM AND ORDERLINESS of Fra Bartolommeo's mature style suggest little of the political and religious tensions affecting Florence during the decades immediately before and after 1500. Artistically too, this was a period of significant change. Fra Bartolommeo's work reflects a point of transition in Italian art, from the increased realism of the early Renaissance to the monumental classicism of the High Renaissance.

Life and work

Fra Bartolommeo was born Baccio della Porta sometime in the early 1470s. He spent most of his life in Florence, the city of his birth. He trained as an apprentice with Cosimo Rosselli, an artist of moderate ability who nevertheless received important commissions, producing frescos to be used alongside those by Sandro Botticelli and Domenico Ghirlandaio in the Sistine Chapel in the early 1480s. Surviving examples of Fra Bartolommeo's early work, such as *Last Judgment* (1499–1501), painted for the Church of Santa Maria Nuova, depend on the tradition of the early Renaissance. The figures seem separately posed and rather awkwardly related to the composition as a whole.

Fra Bartolommeo's career coincided with a period during which Rome was superseding Florence as the major center of artistic activity and innovation in Italy. He was important as an artist principally because he was able to adapt the formal and psychological complexities of more gifted artists to a style that assimilated them more simply.

In the later 1490s, like a number of other Florentine artists (such as Botticelli), Fra Bartolommeo became aware of the teachings of Fra Girolamo Savonarola, prior of the Convent of San Marco. This charismatic and controversial Dominican priest repeatedly denounced from the pulpit the worldliness and what he saw as corruption of contemporary art. Savonarola urged that art should serve as a visual Bible for the illiterate and should therefore promote an ideal of human and natural beauty in keeping with the divinity of God's creation.

So deeply was Baccio della Porta affected by these ideas that he took holy orders in 1498 and, as a Dominican friar, adopted the name Fra Bartolommeo. He gave up painting for several years and is said to have destroyed all his drawings of the nude. He resumed painting in about 1504 and became head of the monastery workshop. Thereafter he worked entirely on ecclesiastical commissions.

By this time, the artistic scene in Florence was being influenced by the return (in 1501) of Leonardo da Vinci, from Milan, and Michelangelo Buonarroti, from Rome. Fra Bartolommeo responded to the classical principles on which their work was partially based. This change is evident, for example, in his two versions of the *Marriage of Saint Catherine* (1511 and 1512). In contrast to his earlier works, these compositions balance and

Data file

Full name: Baccio della Porta (changed his name to Fra Bartolommeo in 1498)

Nationality: Italian

Style: High Renaissance

Dates: born between 1472 and 1475 in Florence, died 1517 in Florence

Key works:

Last Judgment 1499–1501

Vision of Saint Bernard 1504–07

The Virgin Adoring the Child with Saint Joseph before 1511

Marriage of Saint Catherine 1511 and 1512

Things to look for:

- elements of both early and High Renaissance styles
- Christian subject matter
- nobility of figures but treated with a quiet humanity
- clarity of composition

Comparisons: Domenico Ghirlandaio, Pietro Perugino, Leonardo da Vinci, Raphael, Andrea del Sarto

Glossary terms: cartoon, *grazia*, Renaissance

Highlighting the divine world

In 1514, three years before his death, Fra Bartolommeo visited Rome in order to observe the spectacular recent creations of Michelangelo and Raphael in the Vatican. According to the 16th-century artist and art historian Giorgio Vasari, Fra Bartolommeo was both impressed and discouraged by what he saw. His own art was more modest in scope and in achievement.

The Virgin Adoring the Child with Saint Joseph (before 1511) provides a good example of Fra Bartolommeo's response to the new style of art introduced by Michelangelo and Raphael during the early 1500s. A previously lost cartoon of a similar subject by Leonardo da Vinci had been publicly exhibited in Florence in 1501. This set a standard for the depiction of members of the Holy Family as an intimate group of figures set against an open landscape. Raphael, among others, produced a series of such paintings during the early years of the century, and there are several indications that Fra Bartolommeo was affected by the younger artist's example.

Fra Bartolommeo's exposure to Venetian art is evident both in the details of the landscape and a softened handling of light and color. The figures are arranged formally in a triangular or pyramidal composition, which helps to emphasize the spiritual significance of their interrelationship.

Something of Fra Bartolommeo's own religious background appears to heighten the sense of mystery expressed in simple human terms. Vasari, an important contributor to the critical vocabulary of his time, described one of the qualities of Fra Bartolommeo's paintings as that of *grazia*. The word literally means "grace" in Italian, but Vasari uses it to imply more than grace alone. It conveys rather that there is a sense of ease and refinement in the figures, which elevates them above mere human significance.

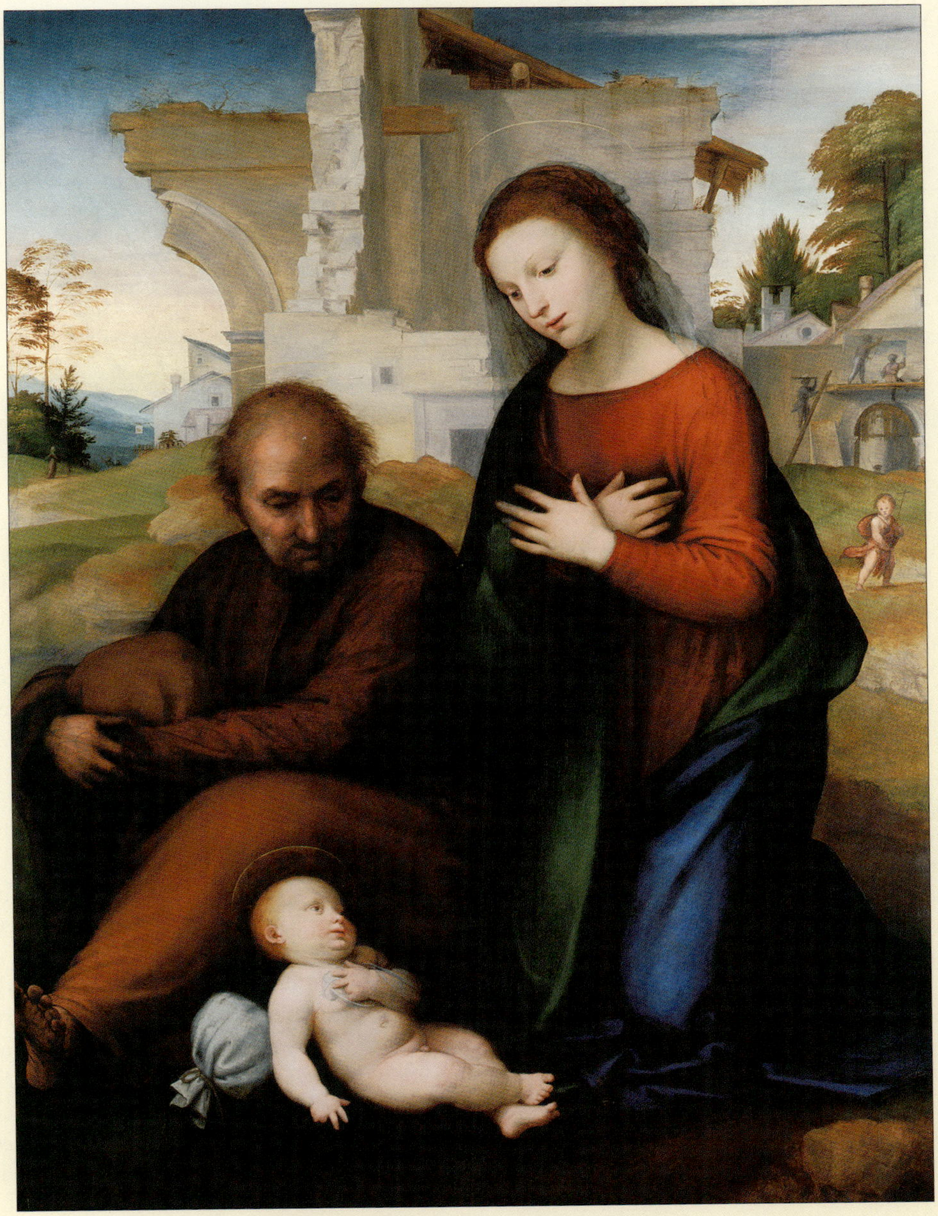

The Virgin Adoring the Child with Saint Joseph *(before 1511). Oil on panel. 54 1/4 x 41 1/4 in (138 x 105 cm). National Gallery, London.*

counterbalance more harmoniously the elements within an overall governing design. The figures are idealized rather than direct portrait studies. Moreover, they are dressed in antique draperies, emphasizing the difference between the ordinary and the divine worlds. They also tend to be arranged in relation to carefully proportioned classical architectural settings, and their poses are more dramatically heroic.

After the departure of Leonardo, Michelangelo, and Raphael from Florence, all in 1508, Fra Bartolommeo was, for a decade or so, the chief representative of the new style in Florence. As such he exercised a formative influence on younger artists such as Andrea del Sarto and Jacopo Pontormo.

The altarpieces he produced for various religious foundations after 1509 represent the maturing of his art. *God the Father with Saints Mary Magdalen and Catherine of Siena* (1509), *The Virgin in Glory with Saints* (1511–12), and *The Annunciation* (1515) indicate a gradual progression away from 15th-century altarpiece schemes inherited from artists such as Pietro Perugino. In addition to the more obviously applied classical characteristics, there is an increasingly subtle manipulation of light and color. Here again, Leonardo is likely to have been a profound influence, but it would seem that Fra Bartolommeo also learned from Giovanni Bellini, whose work he would have seen during a visit to Venice in 1508. After Fra Bartolommeo's death in 1517, his own work went on to influence later Renaissance artists.

BECCAFUMI Domenico

DOMENICO BECCAFUMI WAS A FOUNDER OF THE MANNERIST STYLE of painting in 16th-century Tuscany. His works are notable for their dramatic light effects and bright, iridescent colors with strong contrasts. He himself drew inspiration from the work of Raphael and Michelangelo Buonarroti, but his compositions had a great impact on his contemporaries, and on the painters of the following generation.

Life and work

Little is known about the life or artistic training of Beccafumi, but he is believed to have been born near Siena, in Italy, in about 1486. Giorgio Vasari, in *The Lives of the Great Italian Architects, Painters, and Sculptors* (1550), noted that Beccafumi was the son of a farmer, and was apprenticed to an "obscure artist." It is likely that Beccafumi learned his trade from either Pietro di Domenico or Girolomo di Benvulto, who both had successful workshops in Siena around 1500. It is understood that the artist adopted the name Beccafumi in honor of a Sienese patron who sponsored his studies in Rome and Florence.

Beccafumi's earliest surviving work is an altarpiece, *The Stigmatization of Saint Catherine* (c1514–15), at the Benedictine Convent of Monte Oliveto. At about the same time he completed another altarpiece, *Saint Paul Enthroned* (c1515). The single figure of a saint was a popular altarpiece image during the 13th century, but by the 16th century this type was rare, so it has been suggested that Beccafumi's *Saint Paul* was commissioned as a replacement for a much older, damaged altarpiece.

In 1518, the painter Giovanni Bazzi—known as Il Sodoma—returned to Siena. Older than Beccafumi, Sodoma is thought to have been his master; certainly in his early career Beccafumi was influenced by his work. However, Beccafumi's own style, with its strong Sienese colors mixed with elements drawn from new developments in Florentine and Roman art, itself influenced older artists.

In 1518 Beccafumi worked with Girolomo del Pacchia and Sodoma painting frescos depicting scenes from the life of the Virgin for the Oratory of San Bernadino. Beccafumi completed two frescos: *The Marriage of the Virgin* and *The Death of the Virgin*.

After a visit to Rome in 1519, Beccafumi was strongly influenced by the works of Raphael. On his return to Siena his tendency towards mannerism —displayed in his earlier works with dramatic light effects and figures arranged in fantastic settings—was replaced by a more classical style. Beccafumi was now chiefly occupied with designs for scenes for an inlaid pavement in Siena Cathedral (1519–24), which he would return to throughout the rest of his career.

The mannerist, nonrational tendencies in Beccafumi's art were to re-emerge in the altarpiece of *The Nativity* for San Martino in Siena (1524). This was followed by a commission for an altarpiece of *The Fall of the Rebel Angels* for San Niccolo al Carmine in Siena (c1525). According to Vasari, Beccafumi's first attempt at the altarpiece (now in the Siena Pinacoteca) was abandoned before it was completed. A second version in the Carmine appears to have been painted as a replacement in about 1527–28.

Beccafumi was very much in demand during the mid-1520s. In 1524 he was commissioned to paint frescos for the ceiling of the Palazzo Bindi-Sergardi in Siena. These were based on the life of Scipio, the Roman general who defeated Hannibal. The decorative scheme he devised reflects his knowledge of the classical works painted by artists such as Raphael.

In 1529 Beccafumi was commissioned to paint frescos in the Sala del Concistoro in the Palazzo Pubblico in Siena. Didactic and allegorical, the frescos, finally painted in 1535, showed examples of correct and heroic civic behavior, and were designed to remind the Sienese government of their duty.

The paintings of the last years of Beccafumi's life represent the summit of his style's development. They show his originality in arranging figures, in rendering space, and in his use of light and delicacy of color.

Data file

Full name: Domenico di Giacomo di Pace (known as Domenico Beccafumi)

Nationality: Italian

Style: High Renaissance/mannerism

Dates: born c1486 near Siena, died 1551 in Siena

Key works:
- *The Stigmatization of Saint Catherine* c1514–15
- *Saint Paul Enthroned* c1515
- *Story of Scipio* ceiling frescos for Palazzo Bindi-Sergardi, Siena 1524
- *The Fall of the Rebel Angels* c1525 and c1527–28
- ceiling frescos for the Sala del Concistoro, Palazzo Pubblico, Siena 1535
- *Christ in Limbo* c1535
- *Birth of the Virgin* c1540

Things to look for:
- imaginative interpretations of religious dramas with sinuous figures in architectural settings
- bright, often unbalanced colors, with forms distributed across compositions to create movement and excitement

Comparisons: Francesco Primaticcio, Francesco Parmigianino, Fra Bartolommeo, Raphael, Michelangelo Buonarroti, Agnolo Bronzino, Pontormo, Andrea del Sarto

Glossary terms: allegorical, classical, *contrapposto*, didactic, frescos, mannerism, narrative, Renaissance, triptych, vanishing point

Emerging from the light

Beccafumi's visits to Rome coincided with a period of great artistic activity that culminated in the paintings by Raphael for the Vatican apartments and Michelangelo's paintings for the ceiling of the Sistine Chapel. The treatment of the human figure by these late Italian Renaissance masters was the starting point for the mannerist style that Beccafumi adopted. Mannerist painting is characterized by the use of elongated figures, often in exaggerated, unnatural postures (*contrapposto*). The figures are placed in fantastic settings in which space is deployed for dramatic effect. The effects are further enhanced by inharmonious, often acid colors.

Beccafumi's *Birth of the Virgin* (c1540) is a reworking of a 1342 altarpiece by Pietro Lorenzetti. This altarpiece was in Siena Cathedral during Beccafumi's lifetime. Lorenzetti's altarpiece is a triptych, and he used the wooden frames of each panel as integral architectural features of his painting so that they appear as walls of a room. Beccafumi did not copy Lorenzetti's design. Instead he compresses the three sections of Lorenzetti's altarpiece into a single, imaginative interpretation.

In *Birth of the Virgin* Beccafumi moves the action from the foreground, past the bed in the middle ground, into the back room, where Joachim dozes in front of a fire that casts flickering shadows over him. It is this emphasized recession—the thrusting into depth by way of a narrow channel—that makes this painting significant. The painting is opened up by the position of the door in the background, with its view into the rear room, and by the striking lighting, enhanced by the unusual placement of the vanishing point close to the painting's edge. In the foreground, the characters emerge from shadows into light. Their fingers are elongated and highly expressive. Beyond them, illuminated by a pool of light, Saint Anne reclines on the bed. The edge of the headboard frames the middle ground.

Beccafumi was fascinated by light in all its permutations. In *Birth of the Virgin* he presents a nightlit interior scene. In all his paintings, Beccafumi used light theatrically to heighten the emotional impact, and focus attention on significant figures or actions. He used a wide range of colors, sometimes with strong contrasts, at other times with rich gradations.

Images such as *Birth of the Virgin* would have been understood clearly by a contemporary audience. Beccafumi has included in his picture the familiar objects and people related to the "rituals" of confinement and childbirth: the white sheet, the pillow, the ewer and basin, the attendants, including the wetnurse. Many items were specially made and decorated to celebrate childbirth, and as such would be familiar to women living at the time.

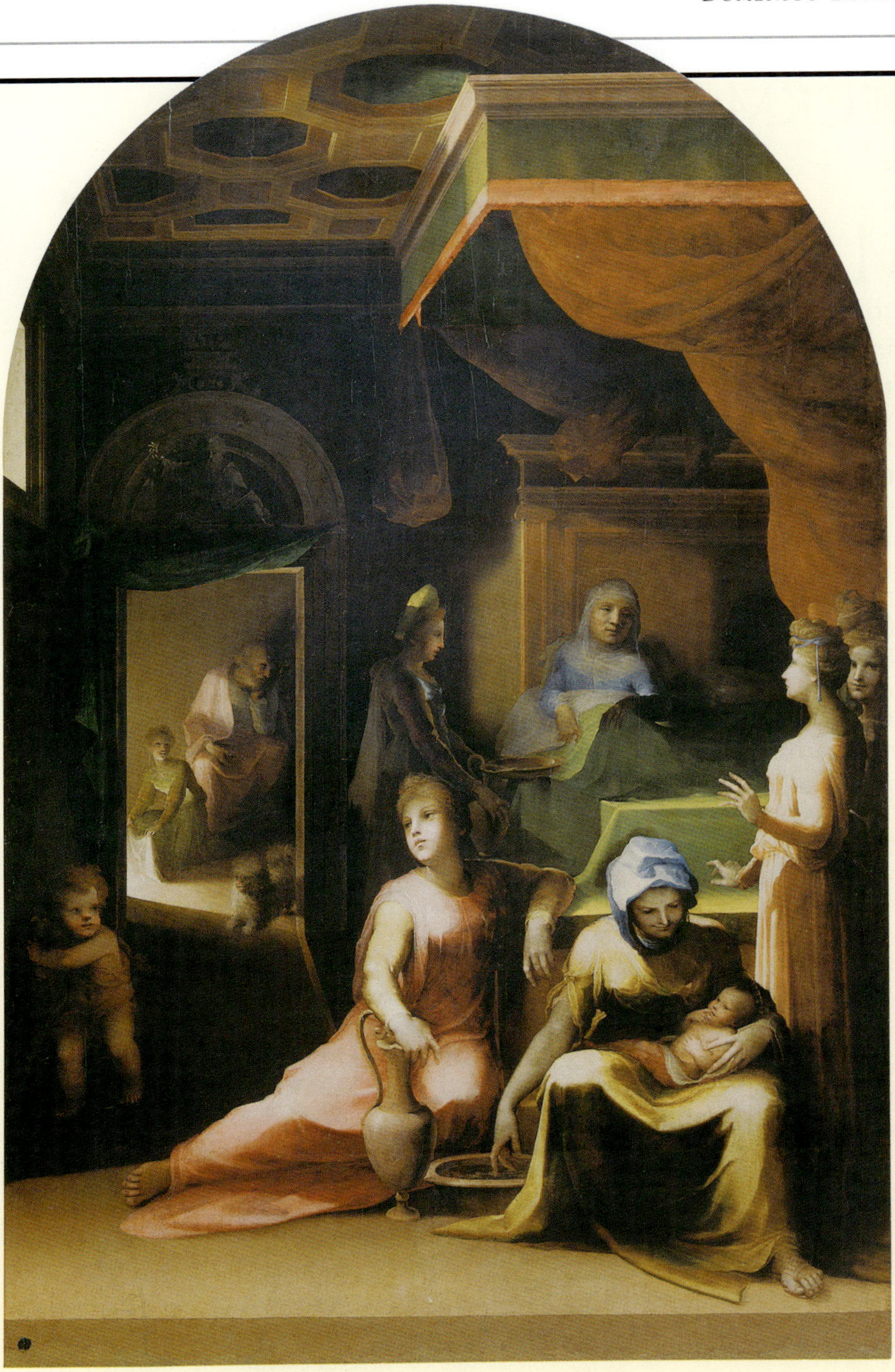

Birth of the Virgin *c1540. Oil on panel. 92 x 57 in (234 x 145 cm). Pinacoteca Nationale, Siena.*

BECKMANN Max

MAX BECKMANN WAS A LEADING GERMAN EXPRESSIONIST whose artistic career reflected the political and cultural turmoil of 20th-century Germany. Following his early success as an avant-garde painter, Beckmann was branded as a "degenerate" artist by Adolf Hitler's National Socialist (Nazi) regime, and had to leave Europe.

Life and work

Max Beckmann was born into a prosperous merchant family in Leipzig in 1884. At the age of just 15 he applied to study at the Dresden Academy of Arts, but after failing the entrance examination, he instead moved to Weimar to pursue his studies. Here he received a traditional artistic education and spent a lot of time sketching from antique plaster casts and life models. He soon developed impressive technical abilities, and also gained a solid knowledge of the art of the past. He was particularly drawn to the works of the great German, Netherlandish, and Flemish masters, including Lucas Cranach, Mathis Grünewald, Pieter Bruegel the Elder, Rembrandt, and Peter Paul Rubens.

After completing his studies, Beckmann traveled to Paris, where he adopted impressionist techniques. Back in Germany he achieved some success exhibiting with the artists of the Berlin Sezession. This was a group of artists who had resigned from academic institutions and societies in order to promote modern works. He was elected a board member of the Sezession while still in his early twenties, but withdrew from it in order to dedicate all his time and energy to painting.

On the outbreak of World War I Beckmann was inducted into the German army as a medical orderly. Traumatized by the experiences of war, however, he had a mental breakdown and was discharged in 1915. It was not until 1917 that he returned to serious painting, producing a number of important works, including *Self-portrait with Red Scarf* (1917).

Beckmann's work took on a more sinister quality during the early postwar years. In such paintings as *The Night* (1918–19), for example, he depicted scenes of violence and torture within confined, claustrophobic spaces. Although these pieces clearly referred to the brutality and violence of the politically divided, postwar Germany, they simultaneously drew upon the work of the 16th-century German painter Grünewald, especially his Isenheim altarpiece, completed in 1515.

Beckmann had acquired an international reputation by the mid-1920s, and his works were exhibited in cities such as Paris, Basel, Zurich, and New York. His paintings also featured prominently in an exhibition mounted in the German city of Mannheim in 1925, which launched a new tendency in modern German painting known as *Neue Sachlichkeit* ("New Objectivity"). This term referred to the increasing tendency by certain artists to move away from expressionism in favor of a highly detailed, figurative style, and Beckmann (along with George Grosz and Otto Dix) became a major figure within the new movement.

Data file

Full name: Max Beckmann

Nationality: German

Style: expressionism/*Neue Sachlichkeit*

Dates: born 1884 in Leipzig, died 1950 in New York, United States

Key works:
- *Self-portrait with Red Scarf* 1917
- *The Night* 1918–19
- *Family Picture* 1920
- *Departure* 1932–33
- *Carnival* 1942–43
- *Blindman's Buff* 1945

Things to look for:
- strong, emphatic forms
- tight, claustrophobic spaces
- theatrical and carnivalesque characters
- large-scale, triptych formats

Comparisons: George Grosz, Otto Dix, Mathis Grünewald, Lucas Cranach, Pieter Bruegel the Elder, Peter Paul Rubens, Hieronymous Bosch

Glossary terms: German expressionism, impressionism, *Neue Sachlichkeit*, realism, Sezession, triptych

Images of a nightmarish world

Beckmann produced nine major triptychs during the last two decades of his life: *Departure* (1932–33) was the first of them. It was begun in 1932, before Hitler came to power, but at a time when the violent and aggressive policies of the Nazi Party were already much in evidence.

In both of the side panels of *Departure*, Beckmann represents a nightmarish world that is reminiscent of the Gothic fantasies of Hieronymus Bosch and Pieter Bruegel the Elder. In the left-hand panel Beckmann depicts a scene of torture, in which the victims have been bound with rope, gagged, and horrifically mutilated. The right-hand panel focuses on degradation and suffering. A woman in a nightgown is being escorted across a dimly lit stage by a blindfolded figure. Inexplicably, a man has been tied upside down to the woman, while another male figure, banging a huge drum, marches in front of the stage in the foreground.

Although the precise meaning of these figures is deliberately obscure, Beckmann seems to be alluding to the brutality and degradation that was being inflicted on society by the Nazis. The drummer, in particular, recalls the noisy street demonstrations that they staged in an attempt to intimidate those who were politically opposed to them.

The central panel portrays a group of heroic figures aboard a boat. The cramped and claustrophobic spaces of the side

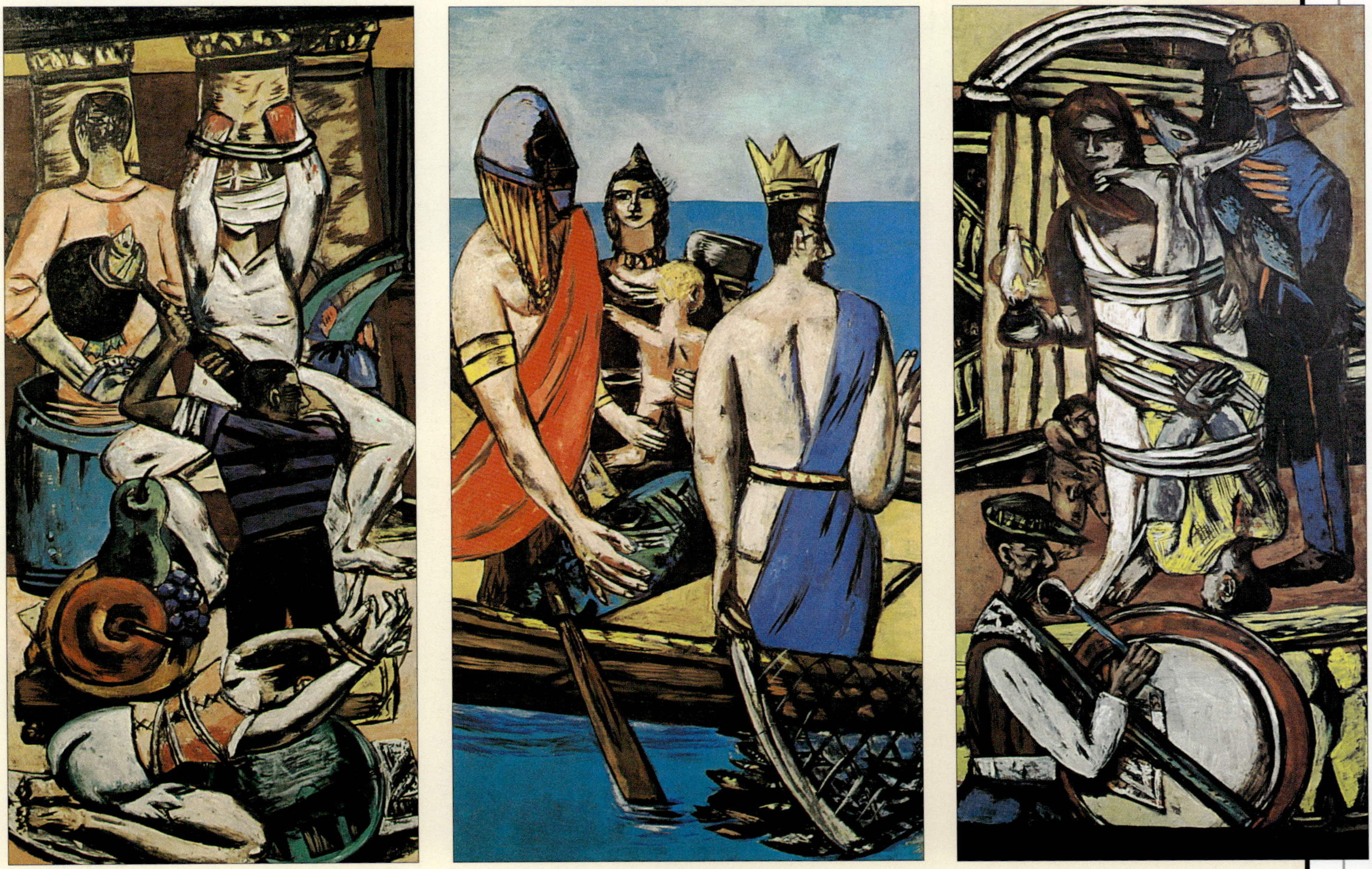

panels have given way to an image of the open sea beneath a bright, expansive sky. This panel represents salvation—and an escape from the horrors of the modern world to a more hopeful future. The crowned, Christlike figure and red-cloaked, mythological character shelter a family of three. The child, carried by its mother, symbolizes freedom as it is transported into a new realm.

Although it was painted several years before he actually left Europe, Beckmann's *Departure* prophesied his own escape from the troubled Germany of the 1930s, and his eventual journey across the ocean to the United States.

Departure *1932–33. Oil on canvas. Center panel 84¾ x 45¼ in (215 x 115 cm), side panels each 84¾ x 39¼ in (215 x 100 cm). Museum of Modern Art, New York, NY.*

Beckmann's reputation soared even higher between 1925 and 1933. He held an important teaching post in Frankfurt am Main, and many of his paintings were purchased and displayed by major German museums (the National Gallery in Berlin had a special room dedicated to his work). His fortunes were to change dramatically, however, when Adolf Hitler came to power in 1933.

During the first few years of their rule, the National Socialists (Nazis) forced dramatic changes onto the German art world, condemning artists who had been associated with such modern movements as expressionism, and removing their works from public collections. They made no exception for Beckmann. In 1937 some of his pieces were included in the notorious "Degenerate Art" exhibition that was staged by the Nazis in order to discredit any type of art that did not promote their regime.

In 1937 Beckmann abandoned his native Germany for Amsterdam, in the Netherlands. He left Europe for good after World War II ended, settling in the United States in 1947. After a couple of years teaching, Beckmann turned his attention toward the production of large-scale, three-panel paintings, or triptychs. These works depict mysterious scenes, peopled with a strange assortment of characters who are frequently dressed in carnival costumes, such as *The Actors* (1942), *Carnival* (1942–43), and *Blindman's Bluff* (1945). These works have often been interpreted as disguised criticisms of Hitler and the Nazis.

BELLINI Gentile

GENTILE BELLINI WAS A HIGHLY ESTEEMED VENETIAN PAINTER who provided the Venetian government and the rulers of the court in Constantinople with lively and detailed visual narratives of important events in his native city. The paintings that survive now offer a fascinating insight into the daily life and appearance of late 15th-century Venice.

Life and work

Gentile Bellini came from an artistic family. His father, Jacopo, had a workshop, and it was here that the young Gentile would have received his training, alongside his brother, Giovanni Bellini. As the elder son, Gentile inherited his father's sketchbooks, and later took over the running of the workshop. Before this he collaborated with his father on many works—mainly altarpieces for churches in Venice and Padua. Some of Gentile's early portrait paintings and religious works show evidence of influence from Padua, particularly that of Andrea Mantegna, who was brother-in-law to Gentile and Giovanni, and was known for producing paintings in a sharp, clear, linear style. However, Gentile soon developed his own distinctive style, and his acute attention to detail became the overriding characteristic of his work.

By 1466 Gentile had taken over a series of paintings of Christ's Passion started by his father in the Scuola Grande of Saint Mark in Venice. He was greatly admired for these works, and his reputation grew, earning him a knighthood from Emperor Frederick III.

In 1474 Gentile was commissioned to redecorate part of the Doge's Palace in Venice. This was a great honor, as the doge was the ruler of Venice. He was asked to paint all the new doges (rather like a court painter would paint all the members of the royal family) and so he is often referred to as the First Painter of Venice. Sadly, all the scenes of the Passion from the Scuola Grande, as well as the paintings for the Doge's Palace, were destroyed by fire, the former in 1485, the latter in 1577. For this reason it is difficult to record the extent of Gentile's production, or to follow in detail the development of his style.

In 1479 Gentile was sent to the court of Sultan Mehmed II in Constantinople, where he stayed for two years, painting members of the court. A portrait of the sultan survives in the National Gallery in London.

On his return to Venice, Gentile resumed his work in the Doge's Palace, also undertaking, in the 1490s, a series of narrative paintings for the School of Saint John the Evangelist. The painting shown above is one of this series of eight, commissioned from several artists (Gentile painted three), depicting scenes from the Legend of the True Cross. This legend asserted that the relic of the cross on which Christ had died had been found in the 4th

Data file

Full name: Gentile Bellini

Nationality: Italian

Style: Venetian 15th century

Dates: born 1429 in Venice, died 1507 in Venice

Key works:
- *Virgin and Child Enthroned* c1475–85
- *Young Man Reading* c1479–81
- *Procession of the Relic of the True Cross in the Piazza San Marco* 1496
- *The Miracle of the True Cross at the Bridge of San Lorenzo* 1500
- *Saint Mark Preaching* (completed by Giovanni Bellini) 1507

Things to look for:
- large narrative paintings depicting views of Venice
- meticulous attention to detail in architecture and costume
- portraits of Venetian dignitaries and Turkish courtiers, painted in a very precise style

Comparisons: Giovanni Bellini, Giovanni Canaletto, Vittore Carpaccio

Glossary terms: orthogonal, perspective, *scuola*

A visual narrative

This painting depicts a very important event in Venice—the feast day of Saint Mark, patron saint of the city. It also shows the procession of the relic of the True Cross (supposedly the cross on which Christ died) through the main city square or piazza. It is carried by the men in white in the foreground of the painting.

Gentile's picture creates a sense of steady movement. Notice how the posts of the canopy over the reliquary (container for sacred relics) lean toward the left-hand side of the painting, and how it has passed over the white line that divides the square, giving a sense of the procession.

Gentile was interested in the perspective of the scene he is depicting. If we follow the diagonal lines from the bottom of the painting, they converge on the main door to Saint Mark's Basilica (see diagram). By choosing to have the lines of perspective (orthogonals) running toward these doors, the artist draws the viewer's eyes to the entrance of the basilica and perhaps even into it, so that the viewer is drawn into the ceremony and can celebrate, like the townspeople depicted in the painting.

The painting now serves as a valuable historical record of the time, and is tremendous in its storytelling. On the left-hand side of the painting, women lean out of the upstairs windows of the buildings, where oriental carpets are also draped. The middle of the piazza shows a cross-section of Venetian society, with lots of anecdotal and incidental detail. The façade of the basilica shows scenes from the story of the relics of Saint Mark coming to Venice, just as the real basilica's mosaics tell the same story. On the right-hand side of the painting the doge is joining the procession.

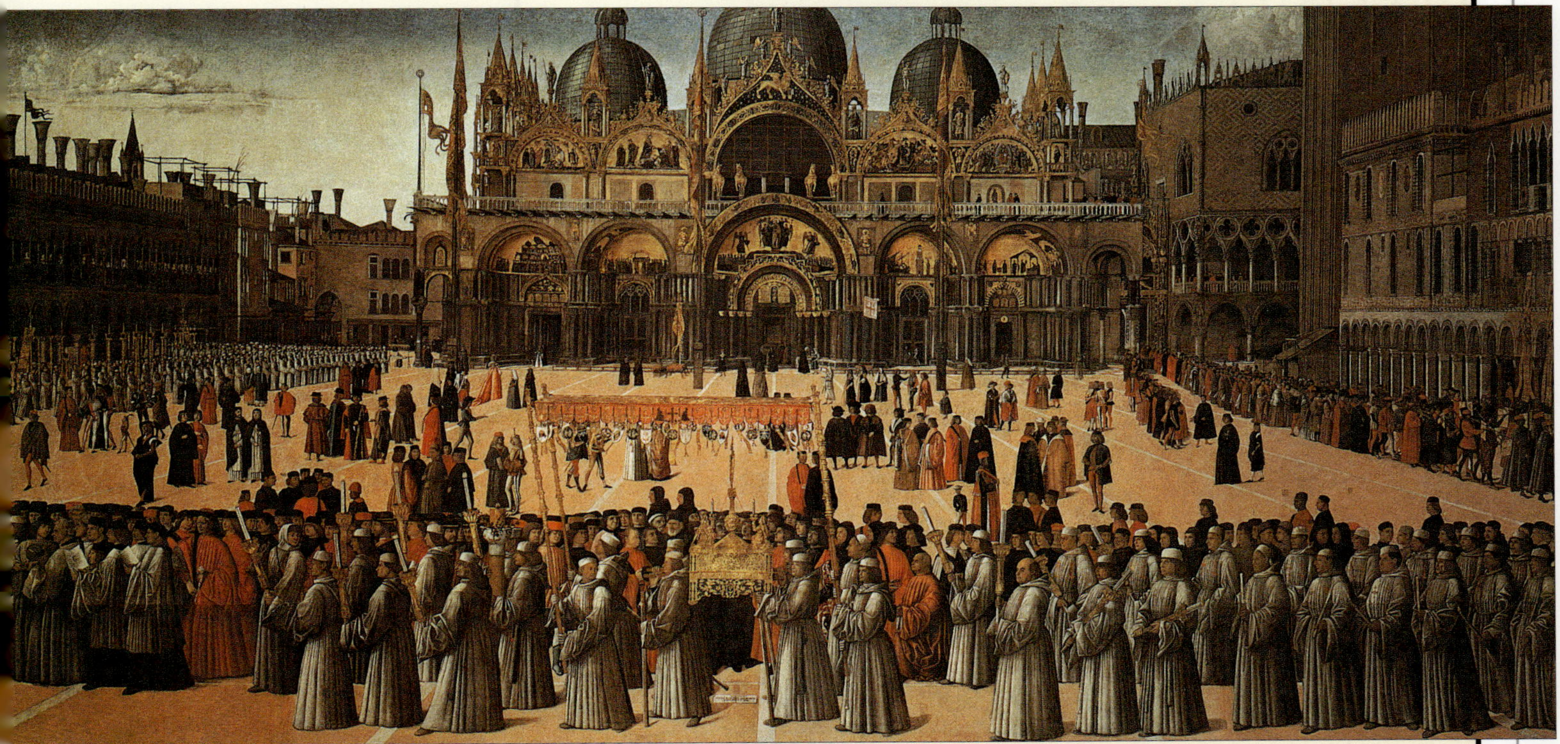

Procession of the Relic of the True Cross in the Piazza San Marco *1496. Tempera on canvas. 144½ x 293 in (367 x 745 cm). Galleria dell'Accademia, Venice.*

The work also contains a story within the main narrative. In the group in the foreground, one man, dressed in red and positioned just behind the reliquary, has dropped to his knees. This is Jacopo de'Salis, a merchant from Brescia, whose son was dying of a fractured skull. He prayed to the true cross for a miracle, and his son was dramatically healed. Gentile commemorates this in his painting, creating a gap in the procession to reveal Jacopo. But Jacopo's intense concentration on the cross also helps to guide the viewer's eye back toward it, as the central focus and reason for the painting.

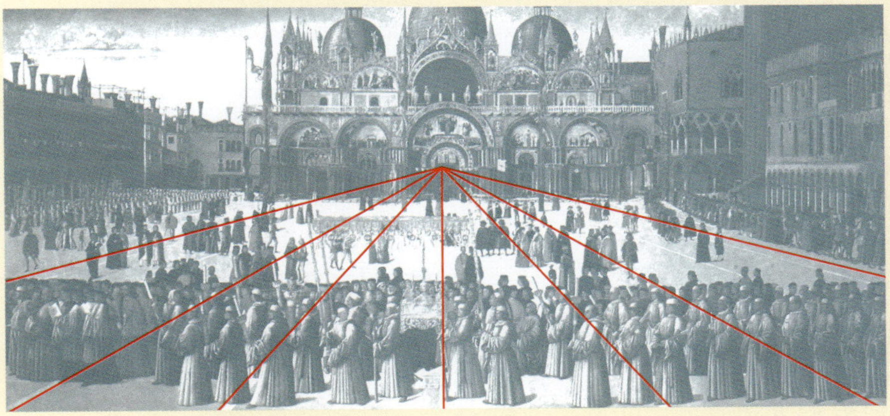

Drawing the viewer in *Gentile used lines of perspective (orthogonals, shown above) to help structure the composition. The white lines on the ground draw the viewer's eyes to the door of Saint Mark's Basilica, and allow us to focus back and forth in the painting. Notice also the off-center position of the canopy and how it contrasts with the orderliness of these orthogonals, thereby attracting the viewer's attention to it.*

century. One of these paintings, *The Miracle of the True Cross at the Bridge of San Lorenzo* (1500) includes portraits of foreign dignitaries among the onlookers. It is rich in detail and humor, showing some of Gentile's careful observation of the different responses of some of the individuals in the crowd. This painting, and *Procession of the Relic of the True Cross* (1496), are his most famous works.

Commissions continued into the 1500s, but when Gentile's health deteriorated, his brother, Giovanni, had to complete the work he had started on *Saint Mark Preaching* (1507). The fact that many of Gentile's major works have not survived means that today he is less well known than Giovanni. However, there are still four portraits of Gentile in existence, including a self-portrait incorporated into his painting of Saint Mark.

Gentile's style of painting has become less popular than that of his brother, but still provides a meticulous record of life in 15th-century Venice.

BELLINI Giovanni

GIOVANNI BELLINI WAS THE MOST TALENTED MEMBER of a distinguished family of painters, which included his father, Jacopo, and brother, Gentile. He succeeded in making Venice a rival to Florence and Rome as a capital of Renaissance art. In the course of his career he drew on a diverse range of influences and incorporated new technical advances into his work.

Life and work

Like his elder brother, Gentile, Giovanni Bellini was trained in the Bellini family workshop, and his earliest known works are collaborations with Jacopo and Gentile. Venetian art at this time was experiencing a change in influences: on the one hand artists remained true to the eastern, Byzantine style, and on the other they began to appreciate the new, experimental Renaissance techniques that concentrated on the study of perspective and human anatomy.

Data file

Full name: Giovanni Bellini

Nationality: Italian

Style: Renaissance

Dates: born c1431–36 in Venice, died 1516 in Venice

Key works:

The Agony in the Garden c1460

Saint Vincent Ferrier polyptych c1464–68

Saint Francis in Ecstasy c1480–85

Portrait of Doge Leonardo Loredan 1501

Madonna of the Meadow 1505

Pietà 1505

San Zaccharia altarpiece 1505

Things to look for:

- religious subjects, painted with intense devotion and seriousness
- gentle, rounded forms in a broad, luminous setting
- interest in nature, both in the details of his backgrounds and in the subtleties of lighting

Comparisons: Antonello da Messina, Giorgione, Piero della Francesca, Andrea Mantegna

Glossary terms: Byzantine, devotional, egg tempera, Pietà, polyptych, Renaissance, vanishing point

Giovanni was also influenced by his brother-in-law, Andrea Mantegna, and the subject of Giovanni's important early work, *The Agony in the Garden* (c1460), closely resembles that of Mantegna's painting of the same name. Giovanni became increasingly concerned with the depiction of real space in paintings. He moved away from the more traditional Byzantine style with its flat and decorative altarpieces divided into a number of sections, and began to paint single scenes with both foreground and background events. Because he retained the intense concentration and visionary style of Byzantine art, his works had great devotional appeal.

In 1475–76 Antonello da Messina visited Venice, and is said to have taught Giovanni the new technique of painting using oil instead of egg tempera. Giovanni became one of the earliest masters of this technique and his art broadened from its earlier, more linear style to a grand, calm, and dignified art with special emphasis on the use of color and light. Students of his, such as Giorgione and Titian, would later take this interest in color and light much further in their works, strengthening the reputation of the Venetian school begun by Giovanni.

Alongside the private devotional images of his early career, Giovanni undertook public works for Venetian confraternities (brotherhoods) and churches. In 1479 when Gentile traveled to Constantinople, he agreed to continue his brother's work in the Doge's Palace. In 1483 he became Painter to the Republic of Venice. He was a highly regarded artist both in his native city and abroad. In the 1490s he was approached by Isabella d'Este of Mantua, who wanted allegorical scenes painted for her study (which he refused to do, preferring a religious subject). In 1501 he painted his most famous

A sense of sorrow and tenderness

Giovanni Bellini's *Madonna of the Meadow* (1505) shows the Virgin Mary with the infant Christ asleep on her lap. The solid, rounded form of the baby takes up the foreground of the painting and stretches right across his mother's lap. Although he is sleeping peacefully here, his mother looks on with an expression of sorrow mingled with tenderness. We are expected to remember the traditional Pietà position—the dead adult Christ lying across his mother's lap after his body has been taken down from the cross—and realize that Giovanni is making reference not just to the beginning of Christ's life but also to the end. The poses in this picture anticipate later events in an innovative way.

Although Giovanni often used horizontal planes to build up his backgrounds, here he also uses triangles to give a sense of depth (see diagram). The Madonna herself forms a triangle, but if we look closely at the edges of the background fields and trace the lines out toward the sides of the painting, we can see how another triangle is formed, enabling us to move into and out of the background.

Unlike early Renaissance or Byzantine representations of the Madonna and Child, there is a warm, rural landscape and real life continuing in the background rather than a flat, decorative surface. Herdsmen tend their cattle outside the city walls, and a bird fights with a snake—perhaps representing the struggle between good forces and bad. High in the tree a vulture (often a symbol of death) looks down.

The atmosphere is not dark and foreboding, however. There is a great sense of calm from this painting, perhaps because of the warm, earthy tones and the gentle golden light. The blue of the Virgin's

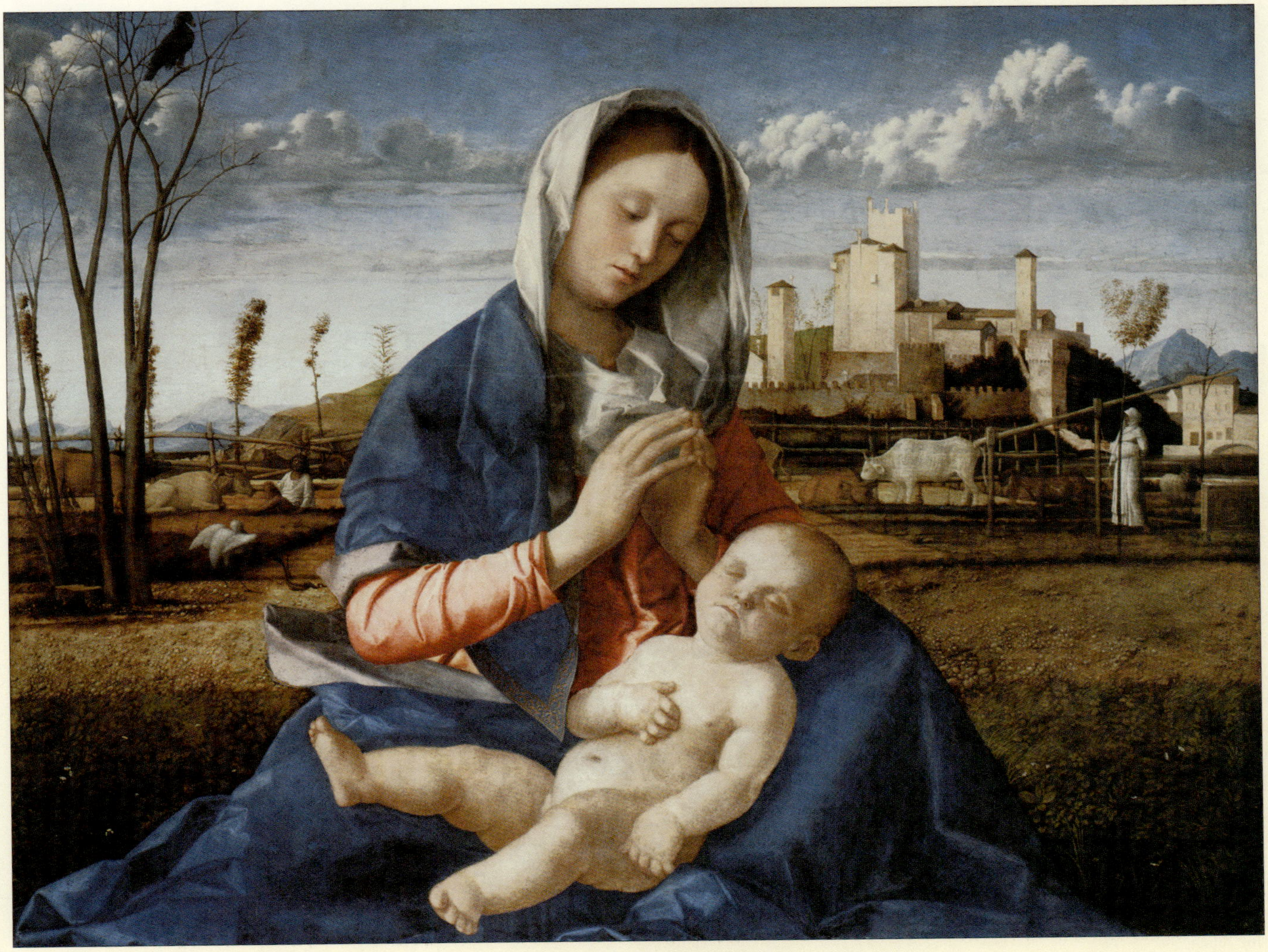

robe also echoes the sky and, though her position is a humble one, sitting on the ground, we are reminded of her later coronation as Queen of Heaven.

The blue of Mary's robes in Renaissance pictures is almost always painted in ultramarine, the most costly pigment of the time, which was made from the semiprecious stone lapis lazuli. Scientific tests have revealed that both oil and egg tempera were used in this picture, although Giovanni was predominantly using oil paint by this stage in his career.

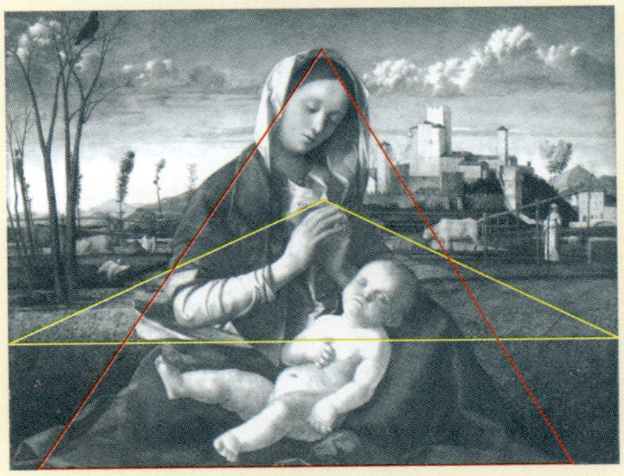

Madonna of the Meadow *1505. Oil and egg tempera on panel, transferred from wood. 26 1/2 x 34 in (67 x 86 cm). National Gallery, London.*

Composition and depth *The two triangles formed (see text) create one "vanishing point," or focus, on the Madonna's head, and one behind her, giving a greater sense of depth.*

portrait of Doge Leonardo Loredan. This masterpiece combines the formality of state portraiture with a sensitive portrayal of the old man's face.

Throughout his long life Giovanni continued to assimilate new ideas and remained extremely inventive in his interpretations of religious subjects. The Madonna and Child was a favored subject that was endlessly reinvented by Giovanni.

During a visit to Venice in 1505–07, the German graphic artist and painter Albrecht Dürer recorded that, although Giovanni Bellini was "very old," he was still "the best painter" in Venice. Giovanni's influence on painting during his lifetime was by far the most dominant and inspirational of any painter in the history of Venice, and it continued long after his death.

BELLOWS George

GEORGE BELLOWS' EXUBERANT PAINTINGS OF CITY LIFE captured the mood of excitement and adventure in New York in the early 20th century. His depiction of everyday subjects and use of a coarse, anti-academic painting style contributed to his reputation as an astute commentator on the values of his time.

Life and work

George Bellows was born in Ohio in 1882. His father was an architect and an influential member of the local methodist church. In high school, Bellows was an outgoing and popular student and an excellent athlete. He played on both the basketball and baseball teams. At home, however, he devoted most of his time to drawing. He loved to copy illustrations from the many newspapers and journals of the time. In 1904, after studying for a time at Ohio State University, the young Bellows decided to pursue a career as an artist, and moved to New York City to study.

Bellows joined the class of Robert Henri at the New York School of Art, and began to focus on themes of modern city life. Henri was a highly influential teacher, who had been inspired by the realism of Gustave Courbet and by Frans Hals and Diego Velázquez. He encouraged his students to reject the classical themes then dominant in the National Academy, in favor of subjects and styles that more accurately reflected modern life.

While studying with Henri, Bellows gained critical success with a painting that represented the excavations of the site for the newly proposed Pennsylvania Railroad Station. At that time there was a great deal of press interest in the project, which was regarded as a spectacular engineering and construction enterprise. Following his success with the *Pennsylvania Excavations* series of paintings (1907–09), Bellows was elected to the National Academy of Design. By 1911 he had held his first one-man exhibition.

Bellows was influenced by the work of French 19th-century artists such as Gustave Courbet, Jean François Millet, and Edouard Manet, as well as the American realist painters Thomas Eakins and John Sloan, and he shared the artists' fascination with modern life subjects. Among his most successful works at this time were his paintings depicting the dark and seedy boxing halls of New York City. Bellows focused on prizefighting, and his pictures suggested the raw, brutal nature of the sport. His *Stag at Sharkey's* (1909), a vividly impressionistic picture of an illegal boxing match, was particularly well received.

This was not the first time everyday life had captured Bellows' imagination. In *Forty-two Kids* (1907), he represented young boys from the poverty-stricken Lower East Side of Manhattan enjoying a swim in the East River. Many critics regarded this focus on the poor as an inappropriate subject for serious art. Bellows was severely criticized in the press for being a political, as well as an artistic, radical.

Data file

Full name: George Wesley Bellows

Nationality: American

Style: realism

Dates: born 1882 in Columbus, OH, died 1925 in New York, NY

Key works:

Forty-two Kids 1907

Pennsylvania Station Excavation (from the *Pennsylvania Excavations* series) 1907–09

Beach at Coney Island 1908–10

Stag at Sharkey's 1909

Cliff Dwellers 1913

Dempsey and Firpo c1924

Things to look for:

- urban scenes and modern life subjects
- bold, loose painting
- low or distant viewpoints

Comparisons: Robert Henri, John Sloan, George Luks, Thomas Eakins, Gustave Courbet, Edouard Manet, Jean-François Millet

Glossary terms: academic, classical, lithograph, realism

The dark world of the boxing halls

Boxing fascinated Bellows throughout his life. He was first inspired by the American painter Thomas Eakins and his images of boxers produced during the 1890s. Like his contemporary, Bellows regarded boxing as an appropriate subject for his art. His works, however, reveal an ambiguous attitude toward the sport. In the first decade of the 20th century boxing was a controversial sport. It was promoted by some as an appropriately "masculine" activity, and even the president at the time, Theodore Roosevelt, was known to be an avid spectator and participant. But boxing was also condemned in many quarters as a sport that brutalized and dehumanized the fighters. Bellows' boxing paintings do not link him to either side of the debate.

In his early works on the boxing theme, such as *Stag at Sharkey's* (1909), Bellows deliberately used dark, thickly applied paint and coarse brushstrokes to convey the seedy atmosphere of the boxing halls. His fighters were anonymous, and, significantly, Bellows placed just as much emphasis on the spectators, who appear to revel in the violent scene before them. By adopting a low viewpoint, Bellows placed us, as viewers of the painting, down among the crowd. It is difficult to determine, however, whether we should be horrified or thrilled by the spectacle that is shown.

By the 1920s, Bellows had forged a considerable reputation as a painter of boxing scenes. He was even commissioned by the *New York Evening Journal* to produce a painting of a major fight.

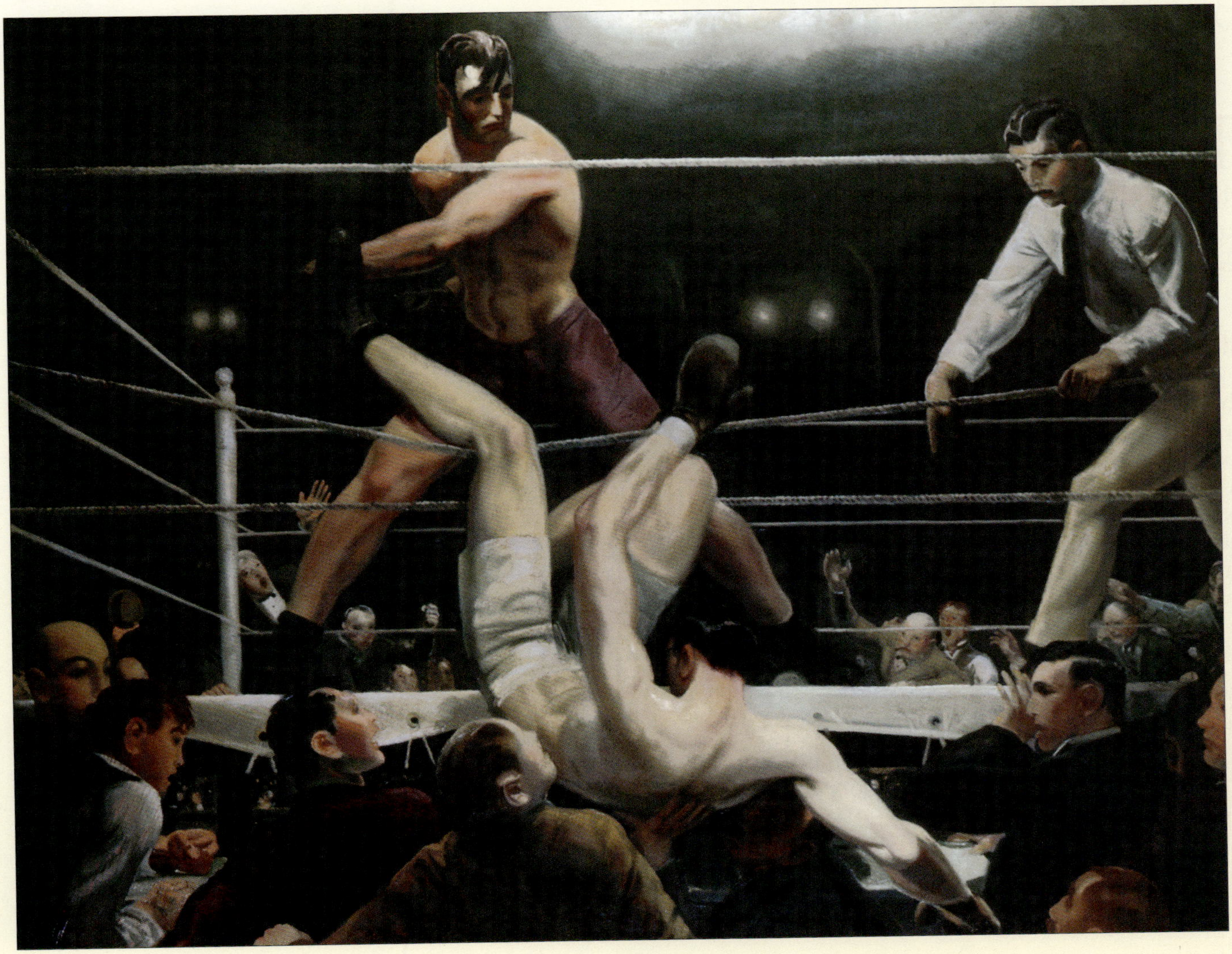

The fight between Jack Dempsey and Luis Firpo was staged in September 1923. In this work, Bellows again used a low viewpoint to give the impression of actually being in the boxing hall. He also chose a specifically brutal moment—when Dempsey knocked Firpo out of the ring and into the laps of the spectators.

Notably, Bellows used a more highly finished style for this work, presenting both competitors and spectators in a harshly glaring spotlight. Yet, despite this shift in artistic style, Bellows still managed to reveal the two sides of boxing: excitement at the spectacle of the sport and horror at its violence.

Dempsey and Firpo *c1924. Oil on canvas. 63¼ x 51 in (159 x 130 cm). Museum of Modern Art, New York, NY.*

Bellows' work captured the spirit of excitement and adventure in New York. His bold freshness and the strength of his subject matter placed him among the leaders of American realism.

In 1913 he joined the ranks of the left-wing journal *The Masses*, and published a number of illustrations. Prominent among these was a drawing entitled *Why Don't They Go to the Country for a Vacation?*, which Bellows soon reworked into a major canvas, *Cliff Dwellers* (1913). Here Bellows focused once again on the crowded city slums, emphasizing the squalor and claustrophobia of New York.

In 1913 a New York exhibition, known as the Armory Show, revealed to American audiences for the first time the breadth of modern art activity in Europe. Bellows was one of the people who helped to organize the exhibition, and he was deeply affected by what he saw. From this point, he increasingly rejected his early emphasis on coarse handling in favor of a smoother finish and symmetrical forms.

Bellows' attention to formal balance is apparent in *Dempsey and Firpo* (c1924). He produced this work both in oil and lithograph; it is one of the best-known lithographs by Bellows produced between 1916 and his early death in 1925.

BENTON Thomas Hart

THOMAS HART BENTON WAS A REGIONALIST PAINTER, who celebrated the countryside and ways of life of his native state of Missouri. One of the most famous of the American mural painters, his colorful, large-scale visual narratives were also observations on contemporary social and political issues.

Life and work

Thomas Hart Benton was born in Neosha, Missouri, when it was still a frontier town. In 1896, following his father's election to Congress, he began spending much of the year with his parents in Washington D.C. In his early teens, he received some formal art training, but in 1906 entered the Western Military Academy. In 1907 he finally persuaded his parents to let him study at the Art Institute of Chicago. From 1908 to 1911 he studied in Paris.

In Paris Benton met Stanton Macdonald-Wright, who would later develop synchronism, a form of painting in which the faceted planes of cubism were combined with brilliant prismatic colors. Macdonald-Wright introduced Benton to the works of Paul Cézanne, and later, under Macdonald-Wright's influence, Benton would paint a few abstract paintings such as *Bubbles* (1914–17).

On his return to the United States, Benton settled in New York and began painting brightly colored figure works. By 1920, however, he had rejected abstraction. He became interested in mural painting, working in distemper (dry pigments mixed with glue and water) and tempera (dry pigments mixed with egg yolk and water). He also began making sculptural models to set up multiple-figure compositions.

In the 1920s he painted an entire mural program, *The American Historical Epic* (1921–27), consisting of 18 panels depicting the endeavors of ordinary people from colonial times on. The critical success of these murals encouraged him to undertake three further mural cycles in the space of three years. The *America Today* murals (1930), based on sketches made during a trip across the United States in 1928, were for the boardroom of the New School for Social Research in New York City. They were the first major American murals to abandon historical subjects and depict the contemporary scene. Painted in a realistic style, and aimed at a popular audience, they helped prompt the Federal Art Project mural program of the 1930s.

In 1932 Benton completed *The Arts of Life in America* for the library of the Whitney Museum of American Art in New York. These murals showed Americans enjoying leisure activities. Benton went on to design *A Social History of the State of Indiana* (1933), 12 feet high and 250 feet long. He painted

Data file

Full name: Thomas Hart Benton

Nationality: American

Style: regionalism

Dates: born 1889 in Neosha, MO, died 1975 in Kansas City, MO

Key works:

The American Historical Epic 1921–27

America Today 1930

The Arts of Life in America 1932

A Social History of the State of Missouri 1936

The Sowers 1942

The Year of Peril 1942

Things to look for:

- early works showing influence of synchronism
- large-scale depictions of the American Midwest, especially rural and small-town life
- richly colored murals painted in distemper, tempera, polymer paints, and acrylics
- flat, often cartoonish figures
- heavy cross-hatching and dark watercolor washes accentuating industrial atmosphere
- American "types" introduced into images of Greek mythology and the Bible

Comparisons: John Steuart Curry, Charles Burchfield, José Clemente Orozco, Salvador Dalí, Stanton Macdonald-Wright, Vincent Van Gogh, Grant Wood

Glossary terms: abstract art, abstract expressionism, avant-garde, cubism, modernism, mural, naturalism, regionalism, Renaissance, surrealism, synchronism

Depicting the enemy

In the late 1930s Benton concentrated on advertising and editorial commissions. In 1937, for example, *Time* magazine sent him to Hollywood to paint a picture of the motion picture industry. The painting was rejected because he depicted the studios as places of work not unlike coalmines or steel foundries. Later he contributed to a tobacco advertising campaign featuring American artists.

With the American entry into World War II, however, Benton once again turned to art with social and political content. This time the visions were apocalyptic.

For six weeks following the attack on Pearl Harbor, Benton closeted himself in his Kansas City studio, and painted what have been described as the eight bloodiest paintings of his career: *The Year of Peril* series (1942). Originally, he had intended to display the paintings in Kansas City's Union Station, but was persuaded to sell the original paintings to a drugs company, which then published them in a pamphlet. The pamphlet also included captions and an essay by Benton. Copies were distributed worldwide by the Office of War Information. In April 1942 the original paintings were shown at the Associated American Artists gallery in New York and attracted over 70,000 viewers.

Content for the pictures in the series came from both fine art sources and from popular culture. *Starry Night* plays on the title of Vincent Van Gogh's 1889 painting, but features a drowning sailor derived from news photographs. Wartime propaganda cartoons provided stereotyped figures of German, Italian, and Japanese aggressors. *The Sowers* reworks Van Gogh's 1888

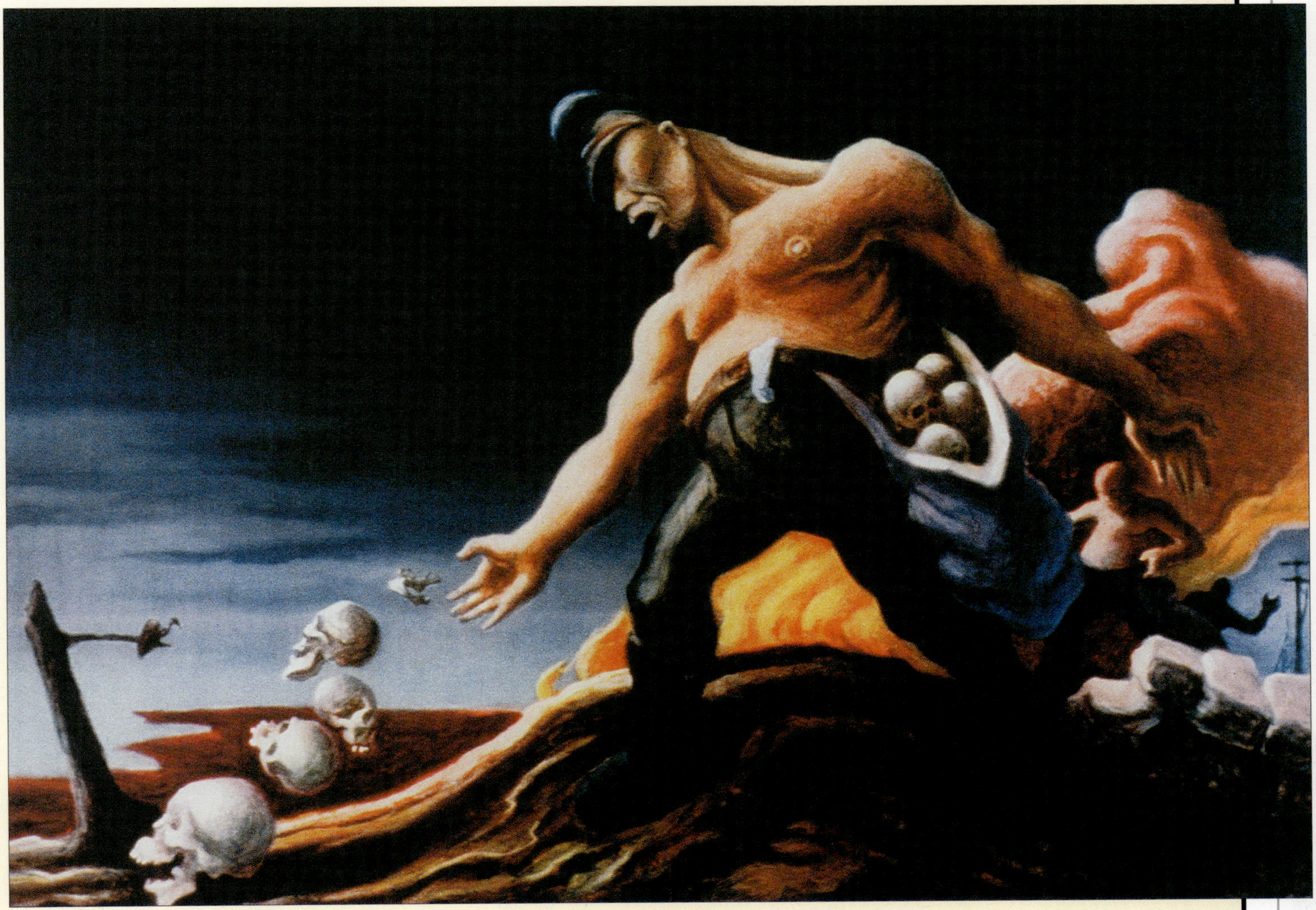

painting of the same name, but Van Gogh's sower is replaced by a personification of the "yellow peril," who scatters—instead of seeds—human skulls across a barren and desolate landscape.

In style, *The Year of Peril* paintings are in marked contrast to Benton's earlier murals. In his easel paintings in the 1930s, he had already begun to turn from regionalism to what is often called "magic realism": objects are depicted with a photographic naturalism, but because they are strangely juxtaposed or because the paintings contain seemingly paradoxical elements, there is an overall sense of unreality. The paintings also paralleled work by the surrealist Salvador Dalí, in particular his paintings *The Persistence of Memory* (1931) and *The Spectre of Sex Appeal* (1934). Benton had seen both of these works in 1941.

The Sowers *1942. Wartime poster of the original painting. National Archive, Washington, D.C.*

it in just six months for the Chicago Century of Progress Exposition.

In December 1924, Benton was featured on the cover of *Time* magazine, which linked him with the regionalists, a group of artists that included Grant Wood, John Steuart Curry, and Charles Burchfield. Benton accepted his role both as a celebrity and as the chief spokesman of a movement that for him "symbolized esthetically what the majority of Americans had in mind—America itself." A few months later, Benton left New York to paint *A Social History of the State of Missouri* (1936) for the Missouri state capitol, and to teach at the Kansas City Art Institute.

He wrote articles on art and was the author of two autobiographies, *An Artist in America* (1937) and *An American in Art* (1966). In the second, he explained his rejection of modern art, saying that it had become "a simple smearing and pouring of material, good for nothing but to release neurotic tensions." His view of contemporary art as "a bowel movement or a vomiting spell," seems aimed at the work of his former pupil, Jackson Pollock.

Benton continued to paint in the same manner long after the regionalist movement had ceased to be a topical artistic force.

BERNINI Gianlorenzo

BERNINI IS CONSIDERED THE GREATEST SCULPTOR of the 17th century. His work as a sculptor and architect, and the positions of power he held, made him a leading figure of the Italian baroque. He is responsible for much of the city of Rome as we see it today.

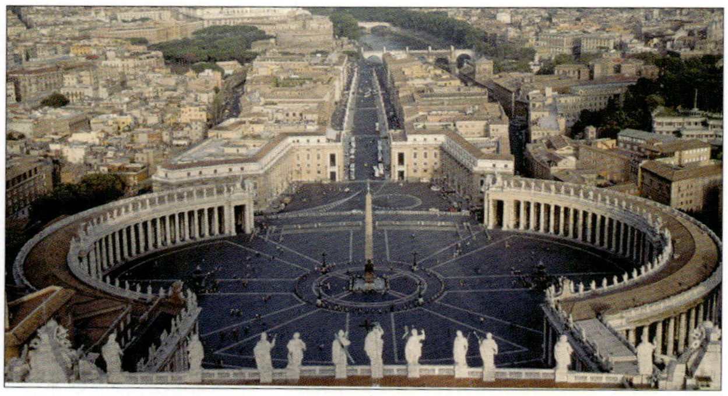

Saint Peter's Square, Rome *1656–67. Saint Peter's Basilica, the focus of the square, was designed by Carlo Maderno, Michelangelo Buonarroti, and Bernini; Bernini designed the semi-circular colonnades around the oval piazza.*

Life and work

Gianlorenzo Bernini was a child prodigy. He was trained by his father, a distinguished sculptor, from the age of eight. By the time he was 10 years old, he had begun to make his own works in a more individual style that showed keen observation of nature and the influence of antique and Renaissance sculpture. It was at this early stage in his life that he met Cardinal Maffeo Barberini, who became his lifelong patron and supporter. Works that the cardinal commissioned later, to decorate his new villa, made Bernini famous throughout Europe, and in 1621 he was knighted by Pope Gregory XV.

In 1623 Cardinal Barberini was elected Pope Urban VIII. This was fortunate for Bernini; he was now a close friend of the most powerful man in Rome and in the Catholic Church. He was given a top position at the papal court in Rome, including being pronounced architect for Saint Peter's Basilica in 1629. He designed several major buildings and made many sculptural works to celebrate the Counter-Reformation, the reform movement in the Roman Catholic Church that was a reaction to the Protestant Reformation.

Bernini's good fortune did not last. In 1644 Urban VIII died, and the next pope, Innocent X, preferred a rival sculptor, Alessandro Algardi. Bernini turned to working mainly on private commissions. The Cornaro Chapel in Santa Maria della Vittoria, Rome, dates from this period (1647–52), and remains one of his greatest triumphs, achieving a fusion of sculpture, painting, and architecture. The baroque style, characterized by its vigor and exuberance, also featured a deliberate blurring of boundaries between the arts—facades were highly sculptural, for example—and many artists at this time were both sculptors and painters.

In 1647 Pope Innocent X was persuaded to view Bernini's work, and was so impressed by his model for the proposed *Fountain of the Four Rivers* in the Piazza Navona that he restored Bernini to favor. This fountain, which still stands in Rome, is the largest and most spectacular designed by Bernini.

Bernini continued to design for Innocent X, and for his successor as pope, Alexander VII, working predominantly in churches, in particular Saint Peter's. From 1656 to 1667 he worked on Saint Peter's Square—a dramatic colonnaded piazza in front of the basilica. Bernini conceived the colonnades surrounding the oval piazza as the arms of the Church embracing its followers.

In 1665 Bernini took a break from working on the piazza and accepted an invitation from the French king Louis XIV to design part of the Louvre in Paris. Although his plans for these were eventually rejected, he also made an imposing marble bust of the king; this became a model for images of power in Europe throughout the century. On his return to Rome, Bernini continued with his sculptural projects for the city and Pope Alexander VII.

Bernini was deeply religious, and as an expression of his beliefs, the last work he carved was a bust of Christ, for himself, in preparation for his death. When he died an engraving of one of his designs of the crucified Christ was placed at the foot of his bed.

Data file

Full name: Gianlorenzo Bernini

Nationality: Italian

Style: baroque

Dates: born 1598 in Naples, died 1680 in Rome

Key works:

- *Apollo and Daphne* 1622–24
- *baldacchino* (canopy) in Saint Peter's 1624–33
- Cornaro Chapel, Santa Maria della Vittoria, including *The Ecstasy of Saint Theresa* 1647–52
- *Fountain of the Four Rivers*, Piazza Navone 1648–51
- Saint Peter's Square (colonnade) 1656–67
- *Cathedra Petri*, Saint Peter's 1657–66
- bust of Louis XIV 1665

Things to look for:

- mythological subjects for early sculptures and fountains
- dramatic combinations of sculpture, painting, and architecture in churches, often with illusionistic devices (ways to trick the spectator's eye)
- baroque style: works of movement, vitality, and vigor designed to encourage celebration of the Catholic faith in the Counter-Reformation period

Comparisons: Michelangelo Merisi da Caravaggio

Glossary terms: antique, baroque, basilica, Renaissance

Movement in stone

This sculpture depicts the god Apollo chasing Daphne, who was transformed at her request, by divine intervention, into a laurel tree to escape him. The piece occupied Bernini and his workshop for three years. When it was completed, Bernini's biographer records that crowds flocked to see it and marvel at the work of the 18-year-old genius.

As his inspiration for the figure of Apollo, Bernini had looked to the most famous Apollo from ancient times, the *Apollo Belvedere*, adapting the pose to suit his more animated figure.

The differing textures and surfaces within the composition show Bernini's skill as a sculptor; without using paint or color, Bernini suggests the different textures and materials that make up his composition. The flesh of his figures is polished and smooth, in contrast to Apollo's cloak, which appears matt and clothlike. Daphne's flowing locks are conveyed by chiseled grooves and then drilled curls at the ends, while Apollo's tousled curly hair is suggested by deep drilling all over the head. Even the laurel leaves have been chiseled to look crinkled. We are expected to wonder at two kinds of transformation: the mythological—Daphne into a tree—and the artistic—marble into human flesh, drapery, tree bark, and leaves.

The way the two figures are positioned is also very cleverly contrived. The statue would have been placed so that on entering the room, only the back of the running Apollo and Daphne's hair, arm, and hand, as it changes into the tree, would have been visible. In order to understand the story completely, the spectator would be obliged to walk around to the front and therefore to examine the group from all angles. The spectator's movement toward the statue mirrors the forward movement of the figures themselves, which is further accentuated by the diagonal running from Apollo's raised leg to Daphne's outstretched arm. The sculptor controls our experience and, as we get closer, different parts of the story are revealed to us in stages. Later in his career, Bernini used this kind of device in many of his religious works for Saint Peter's and the Cornaro Chapel in Santa Maria della Vittoria. It is typical of the baroque style.

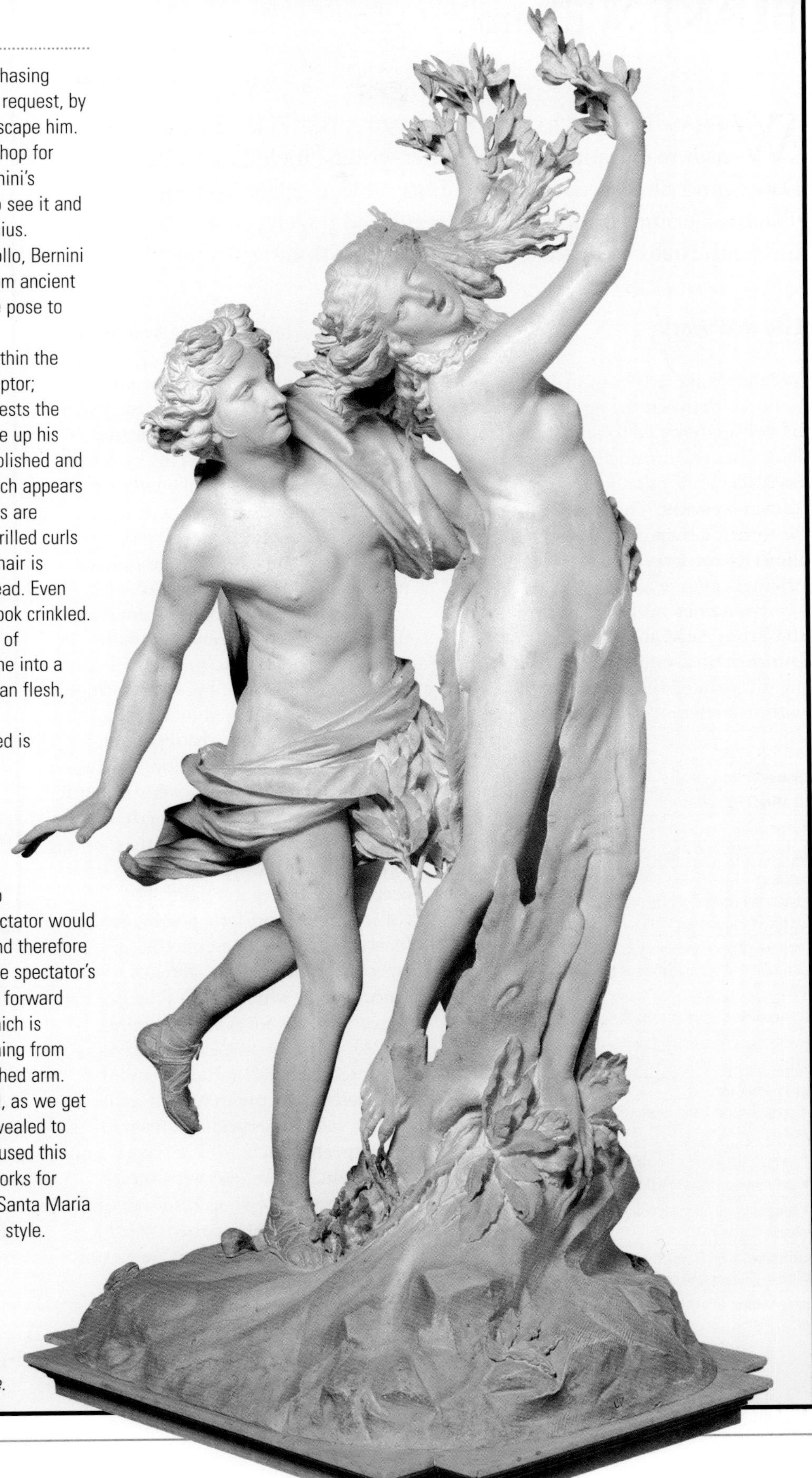

Apollo and Daphne *1622–24. Marble. 95 in (243 cm). Galleria Borghese, Rome.*

BLAKE William

WILLIAM BLAKE WAS AN ARTIST AND A POET. He illustrated his own works and those of earlier writers, including Milton, Dante, and Shakespeare. Many of his subjects appeared to him in visions. During his lifetime he experienced poverty; it was only after his death that he earned widespread recognition for his talent.

Life and work

William Blake was born in 1757 in London. Between the ages of 14 and 21 he was apprenticed to an engraver, James Basire, learning how to make book illustrations and copies of well-known artworks. Throughout his career, he earned a living by producing illustrative engravings, as well as original creative work.

For a brief period he studied art at the Royal Academy, the center of the British artistic establishment. Blake greatly disliked the academy's style, with its preference for grand subjects and classical forms derived from Greek and Roman art. These were the standards demanded by the academy's president from 1723 to 1792, Sir Joshua Reynolds, whom Blake came to see as an enemy of creativity. "This man was hired to depress art," Blake later wrote.

Blake began working as a commercial engraver, developing his own style, which shows the influence of medieval Gothic art combined with highly individual visionary scenes and figures. He also experimented with printing techniques to produce illustrated editions of his own writings, which he often colored by hand.

Blake's art cannot be separated from his writings. Both belong to the heart of the Romantic movement, with their celebration of the strength and purity of human desires, and their rejection of authority figures who try to keep those desires in chains. His collection of short lyric poems, *Songs of Innocence* (1789), presents the sunny aspects of childhood as states of innocence in which God's presence can be seen. In the *Songs of Experience* (1794), this innocence is shown to be corrupted by harsh authority and the materialism of early industrial society.

As well as oustandingly memorable lyrical poems, such as "The Tyger" and "Jerusalem," Blake also wrote much longer works, known as his Prophetic Books. These combine theological, political, and psychological themes in an unfolding drama, peopled by symbolic figures. He illustrated these works, ranging from *The Book of Thel* (1789) to *Jerusalem: The Emanation of the Giant Albion* (1804–20), with hand-colored etchings.

Data file

Full name: William Blake

Nationality: English

Style: Romantic

Dates: born 1757 in London, died 1827 in London

Key works:
- illustrated poems: *Songs of Innocence* 1789 and *Songs of Experience* 1794
- Prophetic Books, including *Milton* 1804 and *Jerusalem: The Emanation of the Giant Albion* 1804–20
- watercolors illustrating the Book of Job 1826
- watercolors illustrating Dante's *Divine Comedy* 1826

Things to look for:
- combined text and illustrations of his own writing
- powerful visionary images
- an interest in the imaginary world
- emphasis on line and contour rather than tonal qualities

Comparisons: John Flaxman, Henry Fuseli, Samuel Palmer, Edward Calvert

Glossary terms: engraving, etching, Gothic, Romantic

Swirling movement

From his early career, Blake was drawn to the art of the Middle Ages, characterized by decorative vegetal forms and intricately folded drapery. This art was known as "Gothic," which in Blake's time meant crude and barbaric, like the Goths who had overrun the Roman Empire.

Blake also admired the dramatic and imaginative power of works by Michelangelo Buonarroti. Another influence was the simple, linear style of his lifelong friend, the artist John Flaxman.

Watercolor and printmaking were Blake's chosen media. He did not work in oil paints, perhaps partly because he associated this medium with what he considered to be the corrupt materialism of artists such as Sir Joshua Reynolds, and with observation from nature—another technique valued by the Royal Academy.

Blake's illustration of Shakespeare's play *A Midsummer Night's Dream* shows the nighttime world of a fairies' dance. The standing figures on the right have flowing lines that echo medieval sculpture. The luminous figures are also typical of Blake, combining weightless swirling movement with a strong, fluid sense of design.

A Midsummer Night's Dream *1785–87. Watercolor with pen and pencil. 18¾ x 26½ in (47.5 x 67 cm). Tate Gallery, London.*

Blake also produced single pictorial prints, including a series of 12 large color prints, showing scenes from the Bible and the works of Milton and Shakespeare, as well as from his own imagination. *Newton* (1795) shows the naked figure of the 17th-century scientist Sir Isaac Newton bending over a mathematical diagram. Newton was seen as a champion of reason, and Blake believed that reason and imagination were opposed.

Blake's art was deeply influenced by his religious views, which were unconventional for his time. He believed in the humanity of Jesus, and rejected the image of God as a stern arbiter. He saw the Church as having

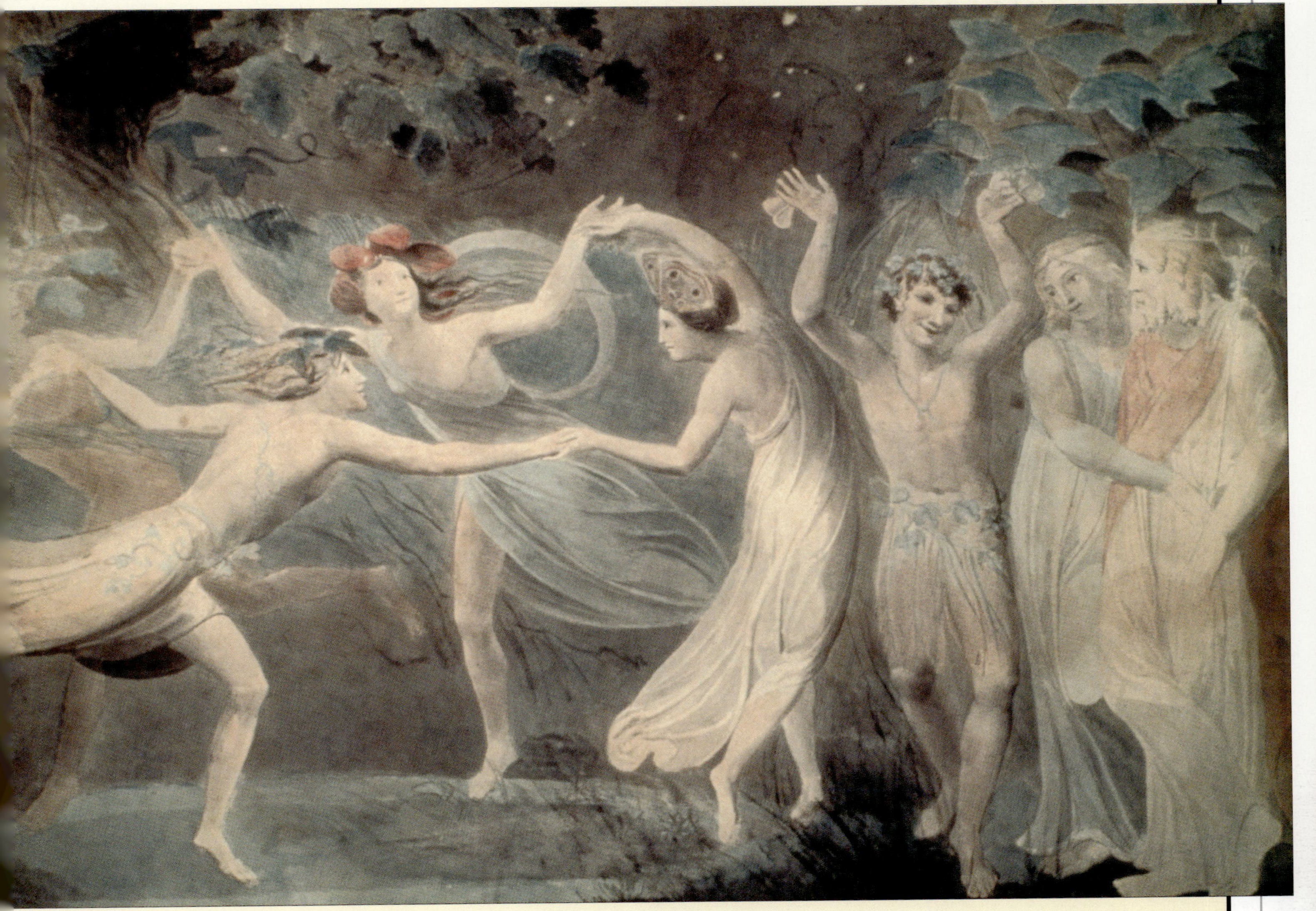

distorted the true Christian qualities of "mercy, pity, peace, and love" in the interests of worldly power. In politics, his sympathies were with the radical movements of the period; he was imaginatively stirred by the French Revolution when it began in 1789.

During the 1790s Blake had some professional success, but toward the end of the decade he found it more difficult to get commissions for work. In 1800, aged 42, he moved to Felpham in Sussex in southern England, to take up a job as general assistant to the poet William Hayley, some of whose poems he illustrated. While at Felpham, he was reportedly overheard one day in 1803 saying such things as "Damn the King!" In the tense atmosphere of the period, when England was at war with revolutionary France, these words were enough to have Blake charged with high treason. It was an alarming experience, but Blake was eventually acquitted.

His unusual views made him an isolated figure, but he found a sympathetic patron in the wealthy young artist John Linnell, who commissioned him to paint 100 watercolors to illustrate Dante's *Divine Comedy*.

Blake moved to London, where he found it difficult to get enough work. At one point he attempted to reach a wider public by staging a year-long exhibition in his own house. The catalog that he produced to accompany it now provides important insights into his work.

Toward the end of his life, Blake did gain a following of younger English artists, including Samuel Palmer and Edward Calvert. Both artists shared his love of medieval, rather than classical, art, and his vision of an innocent, pastoral world, untouched by materialism. Together they formed a group known as the Ancients. It was not until the mid-19th century, however, that the painters of the self-styled Pre-Raphaelite Brotherhood rediscovered Blake's art and brought his work greater appreciation.

BONNARD Pierre

PIERRE BONNARD WAS ONE OF THE LEADING SO-CALLED "INTIMISTE" painters of the 20th century, whose paintings are appreciated for their color and luminosity.

Life and work

As a young man, Bonnard combined his law studies with his love of painting, producing works of great charm and facility in the manner of Jean-Baptiste-Camille Corot. In 1887 he enrolled at the Académie Julian, where he met Maurice Denis, Paul Ranson, and Paul Sérusier. In the same year he began his studies at the Ecole des Beaux-Arts and met Edouard Vuillard, who would become his great friend. In October 1888, Sérusier returned from a visit to Brittany and introduced his friends to Gauguin's ideas and art. They formed themselves into a group called the Nabis (a Hebrew word for prophets).

In 1889 Bonnard failed his law exams, but gained first prize in a poster competition with his design for France-Champagne, which was admired by Henri Toulouse-Lautrec. After a year's military service, Bonnard set up a studio with Vuillard and Denis, and over the next few years he worked in a variety of media. He produced not only oil paintings but also decorative panels, posters, illustrations, and designs for theater sets and costumes, most famously for Alfred Jarry's play *Père Ubu* in 1896.

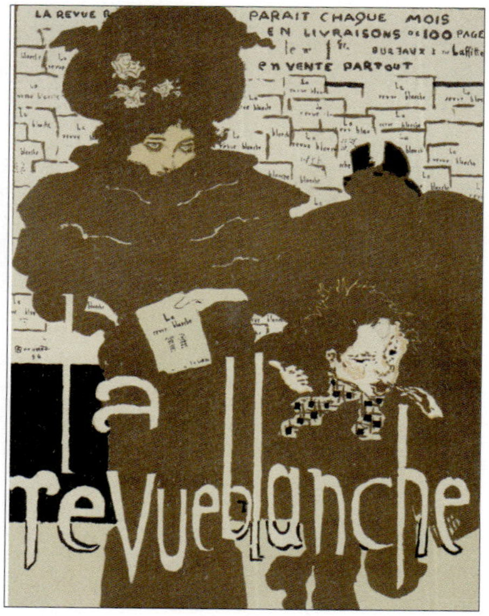

Poster for La Revue Blanche *1894. Lithograph. 31½ x 24½ in (80 x 62 cm). Historical Picture Archive.*

Known as "le Nabi très Japonnard," because of his love for Japanese prints, Bonnard made the public and private life of the city his subject matter. His domestic paintings were seen as examples of "intimisme," a type of impressionist painting that portrayed intimate, domestic interior scenes.

From 1900, the Mediterranean became an important influence, and he began to paint landscapes, some of which were inspired by the 16th-century painter Titian and had mythological themes.

In 1915 Bonnard expressed dissatisfaction with his painting, fearing that he had sacrificed form to experimentation with color, and he decided to introduce a new rigor into his work. In the 1920s he completed a series of ambitious interiors, still lifes, and landscapes of great coloristic and spatial complexity; they were expressive paintings that both celebrated and questioned the nature of perception.

Bonnard lived simply, dividing his time between his two modest homes in Vernon in Normandy—where he lived close to Claude Monet—and, after 1925, at his small residence at Le Cannet, near Cannes. Although he made use of professional models, he generally preferred less formal arrangements, and much of his work features a young woman, Marthe de Méligny (née Maria Boursin). They married in 1925.

Marthe suffered from a troubled mental state, one symptom of which was an obsession with cleanliness. Bonnard's paintings of her in the bath and at her toilette, once perceived as merely celebrations of color and light, are now seen as a complex reaction to his relationship with her. His difficult relationship with Marthe, and the suicide of his first fiancée, were never publicized. During his later life, art increasingly became a solace for a troubled existence.

Bonnard's good friend Vuillard died in 1940, and Marthe died two years later. Bonnard continued to paint, now in an expressionist style; his later works included the eerie painting *The Circus Horse* (1936–46) and a number of self-portraits. He died in 1947, leaving an artistic legacy that reveals a kinship not only with Monet and Renoir, but also with the darker style of expressionist and symbolist artists such as the Norwegian Edvard Munch.

Data file

Full name: Pierre Bonnard

Nationality: French

Style: intimisme

Dates: born 1867 in Fontenay-aux-Roses, died 1947 in Le Cannet

Key works:
- *L'Indolent* 1889
- poster for *La Revue Blanche* 1894
- *The Bathroom* 1908
- *The Window at Le Cannet* 1925
- *Self-portrait (In the Mirror)* 1938
- *The Circus Horse* 1936–46
- *The Almond Tree in Blossom* 1945–47

Things to look for:
- intensity of color and subtle use of light
- innovative composition

Comparisons: Titian, Henri Toulouse-Lautrec, Paul Cézanne, Paul Gauguin, Maurice Denis, Claude Monet, Edouard Vuillard, Henri Matisse, Pierre-Auguste Renoir, Edvard Munch

Glossary terms: expressionism, intimisme, lithography, Nabis, symbolism

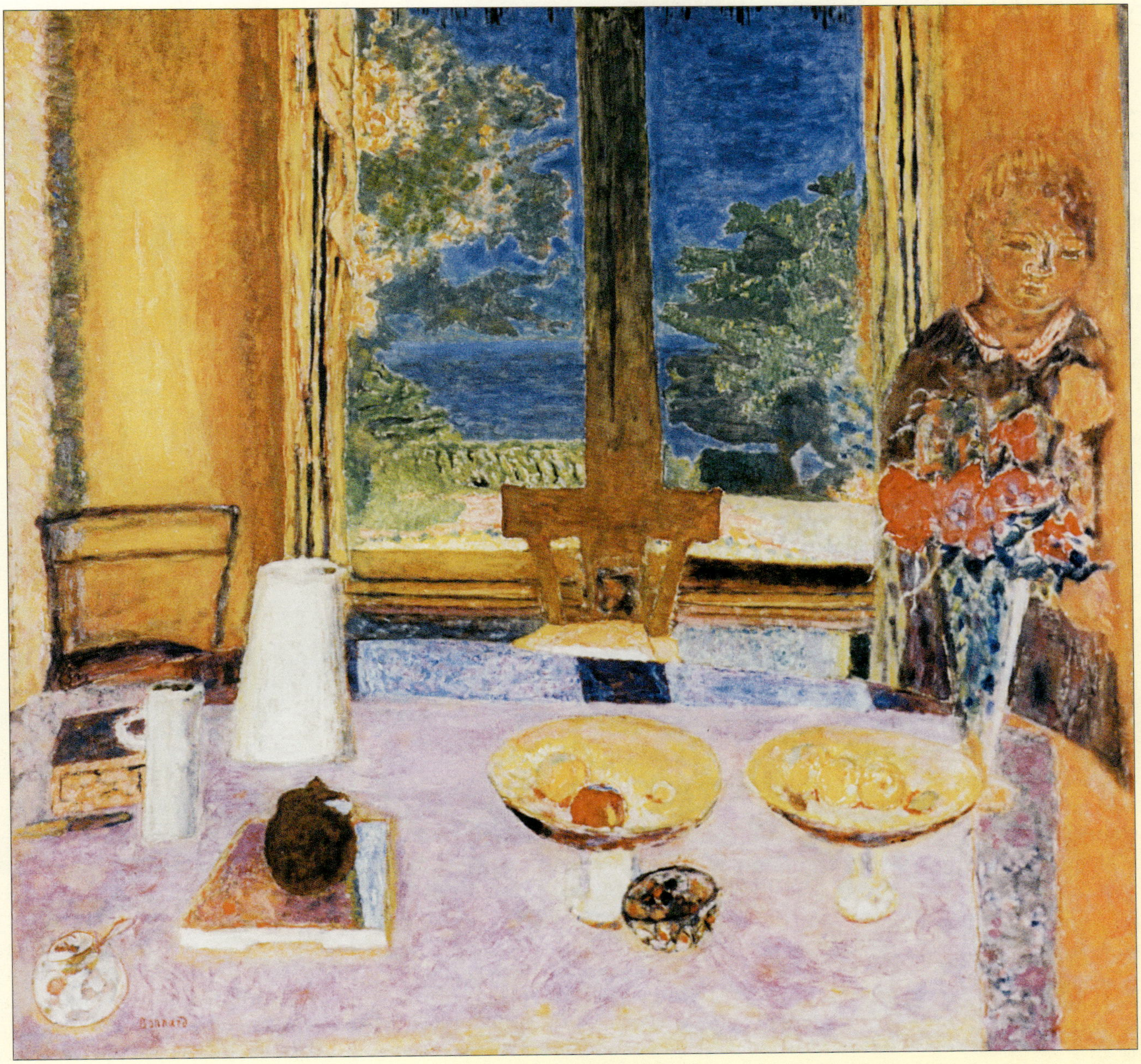

To paint...to dream

Bonnard described the process of painting in the following way: "I have all my subjects to hand, I go and look at them. I take notes. Then I go home. And before I start painting I reflect, I dream."

Bonnard rarely had his subject in front of him as he painted, but tried to capture from memory what his first moment of perception had been, sometimes using tiny pencil sketches to help him remember details. He often painted on canvas pinned to the wall, adding touches of color, revising and overworking with the brush, his thumb, a pencil, or a rag until the desired effect was achieved. This idiosyncratic and lengthy process allowed Bonnard opportunity for constant revision until the finished canvas matched the vision in his mind.

Bonnard's style changed throughout his career. Before 1900 Bonnard's paintings are often somber and atmospheric, and reveal the influence of tapestries, Japanese prints, and the art of 17th-century Dutch artists such as Jan Vermeer.

Dining Room on the Garden *1935. Oil on canvas. 50 x 53 in (127 x 135 cm). Solomon R. Guggenheim Museum, New York, NY.*

After the turn of the century, perhaps influenced by the graphic work he was doing, Bonnard began to put colors onto his canvases in layers, which gave them an extraordinary richness. Bonnard's paintings are celebrations of the splendor of natural light—explorations of the inner spaces of individual perception and the outer spaces of the physical world.

BOSCH Hieronymus

BOSCH WAS BORN IN THE 15TH CENTURY, but his work was unlike any other painter of his age; it is often compared to that of 20th-century surrealist artists. The fantastical imagery and symbolism that he used in his paintings are still not fully understood.

Life and work

Bosch was born in a town called 's-Hertogenbosch in a part of present-day Holland. He seems to have lived most if not all of his life there, too. He is mentioned in public records from 1474, and in 1481 a marriage is recorded between him and an older, wealthy woman. Bosch appears to have sold off much of his wife's property, presumably to finance his painting career, and by 1500 he had become one of the town's richest inhabitants.

Bosch's earliest commissions came through his membership in the Brotherhood of Our Lady, a group of Christians. The work that he produced specifically for the Brotherhood has all been lost now, but certain paintings commissioned for individual members still exist. The Brotherhood was well respected in high circles, and this brought Bosch into contact with courtiers and Dutch nobles. By carrying out work commissioned by such important people, Bosch developed his reputation as an artist. He was regarded as a painter of great technical ability and an awesome imagination.

The nobility seemed particularly drawn to those works of Bosch that were huge in scope and crammed with imagery relating to the devil. Bosch's triptych with the *Last Judgment* (c1504) was a commission for Philip the Handsome, King of Castile, while the triptych *The Garden of Earthly Delights* (c1510) is thought to have been commissioned by Count Hendrik III of Nassau for his castle in Brussels.

However, in addition to such vast religious paintings, Bosch also produced works of a quieter nature. Of these, some were devotional, such as *Christ Crowned with Thorns* (c1490–1500), and *Ecce Homo* (c1475–85). Such works express the dutifulness and endless patience of Christ, particularly *Christ Crowned with Thorns*, in which the tilted head of Christ fixes the viewer with a sad but calm gaze. By contrast, the figures torment him, their expressions leering, and filled with hatred and glee.

A number of paintings attempt to make moral points. Some of these works (such as *Blind Leading the Blind*, undated) unfortunately no longer exist. With these paintings, Bosch allies himself with the wealthier "bourgeois" people and their values, and shows a patronizing attitude toward the lower classes, who are often shown as deformed, and prone to foolish and wicked behavior.

Data file

Full name: Hieronymus Bosch

Nationality: Netherlandish

Style: early Netherlandish

Dates: born c1450 in 's-Hertogenbosch, died 1516 in 's-Hertogenbosch

Key works:
- *Ecco Homo* c1475–85
- *Christ Crowned with Thorns* c1490–1500
- *The Hay Wain* c1500
- *Temptation of Saint Anthony* c1505
- *The Vagabond* c1510
- *The Garden of Earthly Delights* c1510

Things to look for:
- invention of startling imagery
- complex visions of hell

Comparisons: Jan Van Eyck, Rogier Van der Weyden, Pieter Bruegel, Salvador Dali

Glossary terms: devotional, fantastical, imagery, medium, surrealism, symbolism, triptych

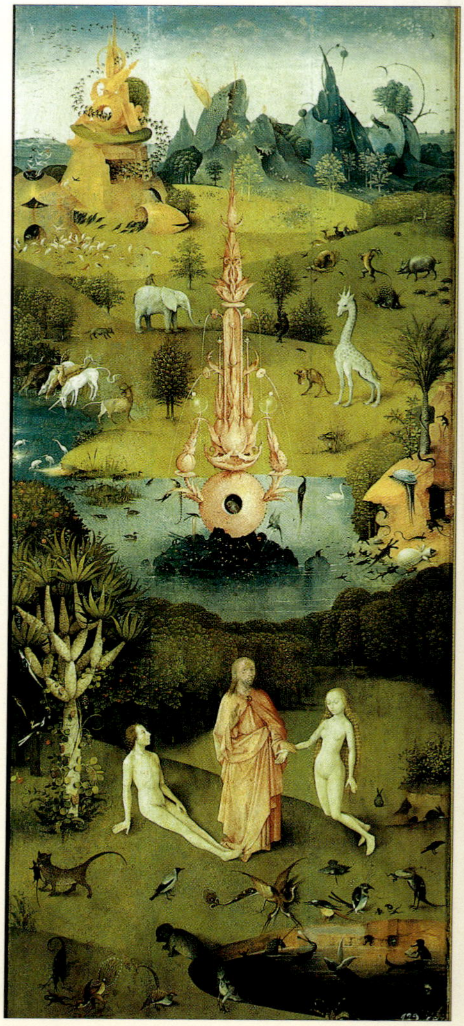

Heaven and hell

Though Bosch used the same medium (oil on panel) as his immediate predecessors, such as Jan Van Eyck and Rogier Van der Weyden, his paintings are unlike anything that they produced. Bosch's style of painting is thinner and sketchier than Van Eyck's or Van der Weyden's, and the colors do not seem as luminous as in the work of these two great painters. But it is for his startling imagery and curious symbolism that Bosch is prized.

The Garden of Earthly Delights (c1510), for example, depicts four views of the world. When the side panels are closed over the central image, the outer panels are revealed. These show a representation of the newly created world (a flat earth within a celestial sphere). When the side

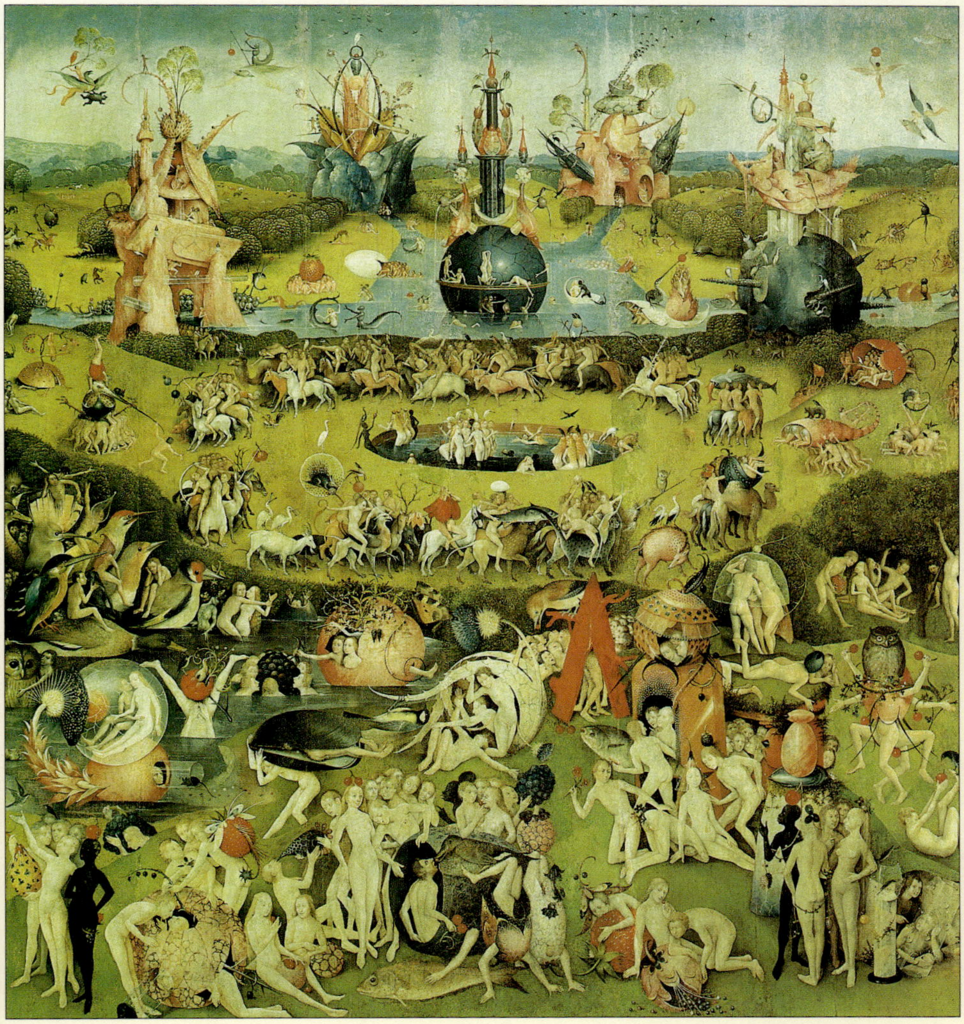

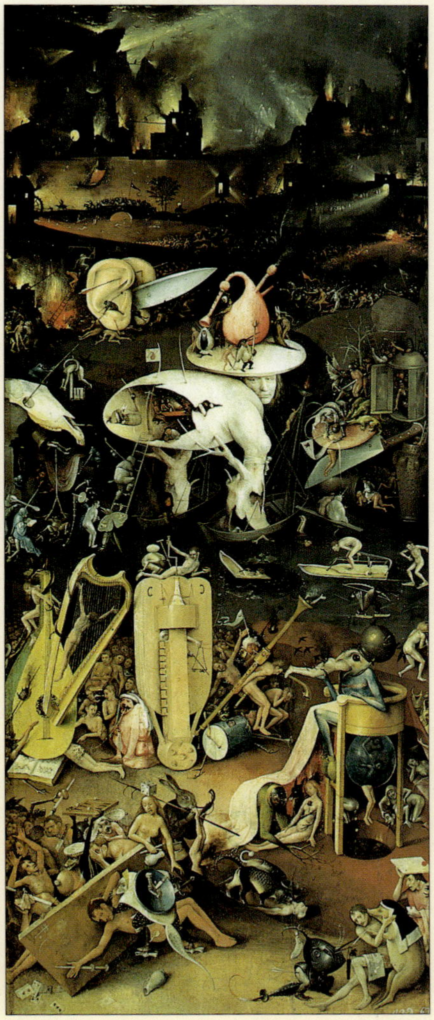

The Garden of Earthly Delights *(triptych) c1510. Oil on panel. 87 x 153 in (220 x 389 cm). Museo del Prado, Madrid.*

panels are opened out (as here), the Garden of Eden (paradise) is revealed on the left; in the foreground God unites Adam and Eve to live in harmony with nature. On the right is a powerful depiction of the torments of hell. The central panel is a little more difficult to interpret. It depicts a more fantastical place than earth, and contains elements of both paradise and hell. The ambiguity of this realm, between the earthly and the supernatural, is part of Bosch's message.

Human folly was a favorite theme for Bosch; here he seems to be warning against the pleasures of the flesh. Demons have encroached upon the central panel, either to encourage the humans into sexual acts or to torment them because of their unrestrained behavior. The right-hand panel is a reminder of where it will all end. Although Bosch is supposed to be offering a warning to the wicked (who seem here to include humanity in general), it is the darker elements of his paintings that draw the attention of the viewer. The images of torture and devastation in the right-hand panel are particularly detailed and vivid.

Sometimes Bosch's message seems quite clear, but it is often difficult to work out the story behind his work. The description above is just one interpretation. Although the elements of hell, sin, and paradise are clearly religious, Bosch's own beliefs may not have been of a conventional Catholic sort. The confused messages in his work may be the result of attempting to please his clients while also subtly expressing his own thoughts on religious matters. He might have included ideas in his work that challenged the traditional views of the Church. For example, in many of his paintings you see the staring eyes of an owl. In the Middle Ages the owl was frequently seen as a symbol of darkness and specifically of the devil. In this painting, the owl is in the foreground, toward the right edge of the central panel, puffed up and propped on top of the naked bodies of two dancing figures. The owl is a still point amid the revelry in which the twisted human forms frolic wildly, and some even change into fish.

We cannot say for sure what Bosch's religious and moral beliefs were, but in the large scenes he painted, everything—even the natural world, which is usually presented as a harmless landscape—seems capable of being corrupted.

BOTTICELLI Sandro

SANDRO BOTTICELLI WAS NOTED FOR THE THOUGHTFUL FORMS and delicate details of his paintings, and invented a new kind of painting using ideas from poems. By the time he died his style was considered old-fashioned, but his idea of perfect beauty inspired painters and historians in the 19th century, who revived his reputation.

Life and work

Sandro Botticelli trained for a short time as a goldsmith but decided to become a painter and joined Fra Filippo Lippi's workshop. Here he received an excellent grounding in the materials and techniques of painting and was strongly influenced by Lippi's style.

His earliest known painting—of fortitude, one of the four cardinal virtues—was made for the Palazzo Signoria, the home of Florence's government. Following the pattern set by Piero Pollaiuolo (the painter of the other virtues), Botticelli had to show fortitude as a beautiful young woman sitting on an ornate throne. He brought her pose to life with a dramatic twist emphasized by the exuberant folds of her theatrical costume.

Botticelli's reputation grew swiftly and he was soon employed on a wide range of projects, including altarpieces, portraits, and, in 1475, decorations for Giuliano de' Medici's joust. He painted several circular pictures with scenes of the Virgin Mary and Angels and the Adoration of the Magi, using the round shape to great effect. The bright colors, patterned clothes, and lively groupings of people echoed the pageants and processions in Florence at the time.

The city had its share of violence. One of Botticelli's more gruesome tasks was painting, in fresco, the members of the Pazzi conspiracy hanged for their part in the attempted rebellion of 1478 against the powerful Medici family. The task was considered an honor and was a further indication of his renown.

In 1481 Botticelli was summoned to Rome by the pope to join Domenico Ghirlandaio, Cosimo Rosselli, and Pietro Perugino in painting frescos on the side walls of the newly built Sistine Chapel. The project included portraits of popes and scenes from the life of Christ and the life of Moses. Botticelli skillfully combined several episodes within each of his three scenes, without losing sight of the overall composition.

Botticelli returned to Florence in 1482 and continued to work for Lorenzo de' Medici and his friends. The painter had already invented a new type of picture for them in about 1478 when he painted *Spring*. Some of these pictures were probably designed as parts of furniture—*Spring* as a backboard for a bench and *Mars and Venus* (c1485) as a headboard for a bed—while others, such as *The Birth of Venus* (c1484), were hung on walls. They were beautiful to look at and enjoyable for the ideas they represented. The gods and goddesses were known from

Data file

Full name: Alessandro di Mariano Filipepi (known as Sandro Botticelli)

Nationality: Italian

Style: Renaissance

Dates: born c1444/45 in Florence, died 1510 in Florence

Key works:
- *Adoration of the Magi* c1470–75
- *Portrait of a Young Man with a Medal* c1470
- *Spring* c1478
- *The Youth of Moses* 1481
- *The Birth of Venus* c1484
- *Mars and Venus* c1485
- *Mystic Nativity* 1500

Things to look for:
- imaginative compositions
- expressive outlines
- Renaissance idea of beauty, especially in depicting angels and goddesses

Comparisons: Fra Filippo Lippi, Domenico Veneziano, Piero della Francesca, Antonio and Piero Pollaiuolo

Glossary terms: fresco, Gothic, Renaissance

Graceful forms and idealized beauty

Botticelli's paintings combined contemporary Renaissance ideas with some characteristics of the Gothic past, such as graceful curving outlines, long elegant bodies, and gold patterned surfaces. He applied perspective and lifelike details as required, but would sometimes vary the size of people in proportion to their surroundings depending on the type of painting in question and its intended location. *Spring* (c1478) belongs to a new type of painting invented by Botticelli for members of the Medici family or people connected with the Medici circle. They would have recognized who the characters were from descriptions in classical mythology. In the center of *Spring* stands Venus, the beautiful goddess of love, with blindfolded Cupid flying just above her. He is taking aim with his bow and arrow at one of the three dancing graces on the left—the one looking toward Mercury, the elegant messenger of the gods, at the extreme left. Flying in on the opposite side of the painting is the wind god, Zephyr, who has just caught up with the fair nymph Chloris. She immediately turns into Flora. Botticelli shows this dramatic transformation: flowers come out of Chloris's mouth and appear on her dress as she merges into Flora and scatters more flowers from her loosely bunched robe.

Inspired by classical authors such as the Greek poet Hesiod and the Roman writer Seneca, the architect and theorist Leon Battista Alberti recommended the three graces as suitable subjects for painters in his book, *Della Pittura* (1436). Botticelli probably based the poses of his figures on such sources, or—as with Venus in *The*

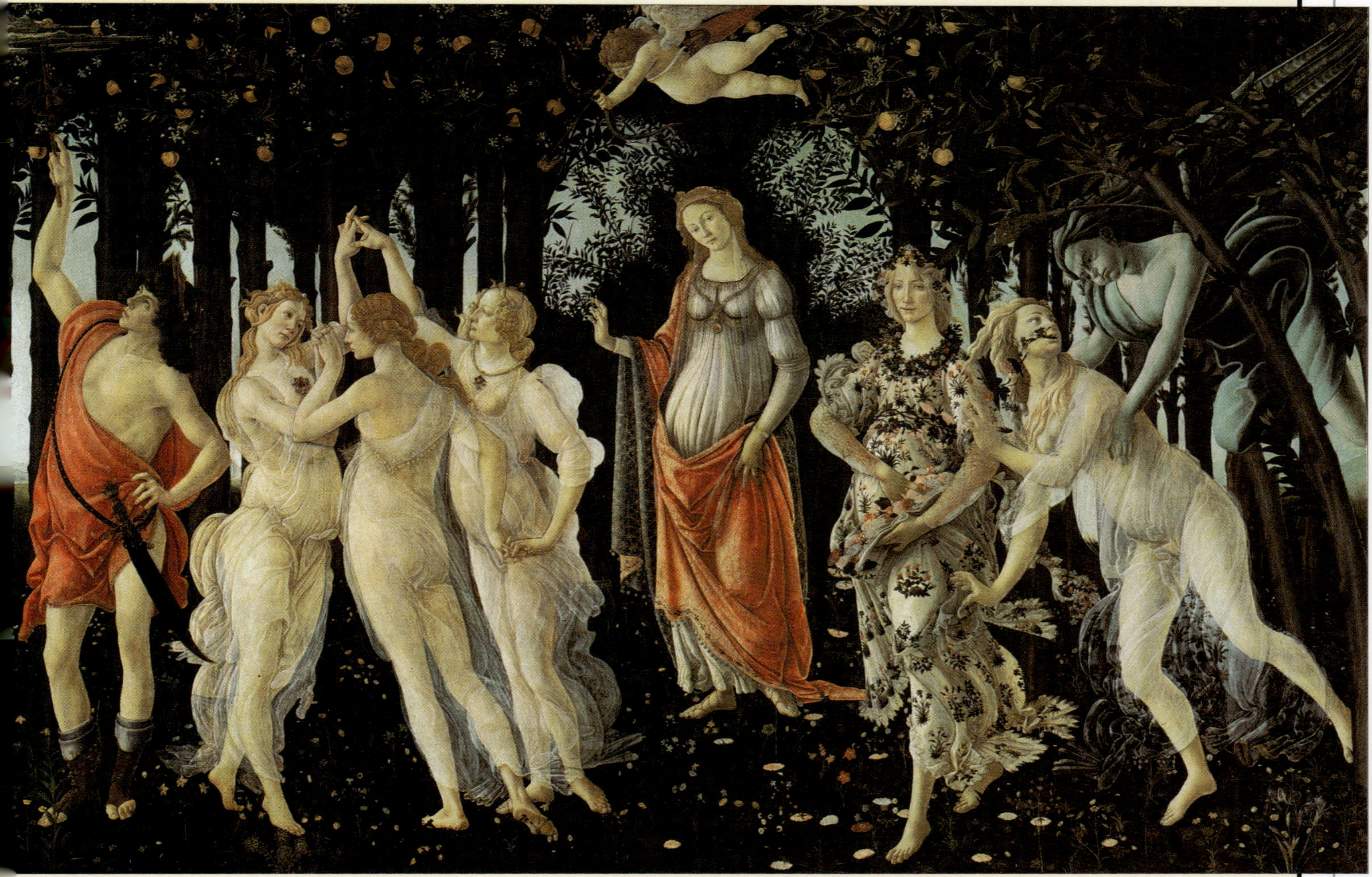

Birth of Venus (c1484)—on well-known classical sculpture. Then he transformed them into his own idea of beautiful goddesses or nymphs. He was more interested in sensuous line than anatomical accuracy, and less interested in naturalistic landscape than a stylized flattened-out pattern, as seen in the orange grove and carpet of flowers. This is in keeping with the tapestry-like effect of *Spring*.

Not all artists approved. Leonardo da Vinci was highly critical of Botticelli's landscapes. Nevertheless, Botticelli's paintings met many of Alberti's recommendations. It is possible that they complemented the prevalent ideas inspired by classical philosophy: Venus, the goddess of love, could represent beauty, and beauty was equal to truth, so looking at a picture of Venus could inspire a love of beauty and therefore of truth. Whatever meaning was intended, Botticelli's paintings could be enjoyed in a variety of ways perfectly in harmony with Renaissance culture.

Spring *c1478. Tempera on panel. 80 1/2 x 124 1/2 in (203 x 314 cm). Uffizi Gallery, Florence.*

classical mythology but their role in Botticelli's paintings was inspired by Renaissance poetry and philosophy, and they had never before been painted on such a grand scale.

After Lorenzo de' Medici's death in 1492, political unrest increased in Florence, and the public preaching of a Dominican friar, Girolamo Savonarola, against Florentine wealth and luxury contributed to a general unease. Botticelli's *Mystic Nativity* (1500) and other late works reflect a change in his style. People appear large or small according to their significance rather than to their location in the painting, colors are darker and deeper, body movements and gestures are more angular, and the mood is one of intense emotion. There is still a strong rhythm, however, in the way people are grouped together and in the detailed drapery of their clothes. Botticelli produced fewer paintings in his later years and concentrated instead on producing illustrations for Dante's epic 14th-century poem, *The Divine Comedy*.

BOUCHER François

FRANÇOIS BOUCHER WAS AN INFLUENTIAL ROCOCO ARTIST in France in the 18th century, who flourished under the patronage of Madame de Pompadour, and later became First Painter to Louis XV. His paintings of allegorical scenes came to embody the carefree spirit, elegance, and excesses of the French court, and the light, decorative, playful character of the rococo style.

Life and work

Boucher's earliest lessons in drawing and painting were probably with his father, Nicolas, who was also a painter. Although his family came from relatively humble origins, the young man's ability was soon noticed by important people in the Paris art world and, as a result, he was able to obtain a better education.

Data file

Full name: François Boucher

Nationality: French

Style: rococo

Dates: born 1703 in Paris, died 1770 in Paris

Key works:

The Triumph of Venus 1740

Diana after the Bath 1742

The Rape of Europa 1747

Reclining Nude 1752

The Rising of the Sun and *The Setting of the Sun* 1753

Madame de Pompadour 1756

Pan and Syrinx 1759

Things to look for:

- imaginary scenes of gods and goddesses or shepherds and shepherdesses in outdoor settings
- designs for tapestries, porcelain, stage sets, and other objects as well as paintings and engravings
- bright colors and a loose, free style of painting, often referred to as "bravura" or "virtuoso" handling
- curves and movement in compositions, in keeping with the rococo style

Comparisons: Pietro Bernini, Jean-Honoré Fragonard, Jean-Antoine Watteau

Glossary terms: Academy, allegorical, baroque, bravura, engravings, neoclassicism, printmaking, Prix de Rome, rococo

In 1723 Boucher won the prestigious Prix de Rome. This was a prize for painting that usually enabled the winner to travel to Rome to study art. However, the trip was awarded instead to one of the French king's favorites. This was an unfortunate start to Boucher's career, because most of the important official commissions went to those artists who had been to school in Rome.

To earn his living, Boucher took a job with an engraver and publisher. He worked from 1723 to 1728, making engravings of his own and other artists' works and producing a series of illustrations for a book. Boucher used the money he saved from this job to go to Italy to study the baroque masters, in particular Gianlorenzo Bernini, and Venetian art. It is easy to see the influences of the flourishes and curving lines of baroque sculptures and the brilliant colors of Venetian paintings in Boucher's own works after this trip. In 1731 he returned to Paris, where he continued printmaking and illustrating. He also worked on a series of large paintings with subjects taken from ancient Greek and Roman legends.

In 1734 Boucher was made a member of the state-run Academy, and obtained his first commission from the royal family—to make four paintings for the palace at Versailles. From this point onward, Boucher became much more successful. Private collectors wanted smaller paintings to decorate walls and cabinets in their homes, tapestry makers used Boucher's designs for their works, and Boucher also produced drawings for porcelain and china factories (most famously at Sèvres). He designed costumes and stage sets for opera and theater, and little pictures for ladies' fans and slippers. An interest in decoration and design was part of the whole movement in art called rococo (from the French *rocaille*, the shell- and rockwork that was used in the design of grottos at the time). The style was characterized by its

The epitome of elegance and refinement

This work, although it is a sketch and much smaller and simpler than a lot of Boucher's more grand decorative paintings, nevertheless embodies many of the distinctive characteristics of his style. Its subject, Madame de Pompadour, who became the mistress of King Louis XV in 1745, supported Boucher until her death in 1764, commissioning portraits of herself, mythological subject paintings, and tapestries.

This oil sketch was almost certainly made as a preparation for a larger portrait, but no such portrait exists today, or is mentioned in past historical records. As the portrait would have been a private commission, there is no reason to assume that it should have been viewed and then recorded by anyone at the time. The fact that it does not survive perhaps links to the French Revolution. Such an image, with its emphasis on aristocratic refinement and the pursuit of pleasure, would have been one that the revolutionaries would have delighted in destroying. This, however, is all conjecture. What is certain is that the bright, playful nature of the sitter and of the rococo spirit are both very much in evidence in the sketch itself.

Madame de Pompadour was a vivacious and witty member of the king's society and, like the king, enjoyed and supported the arts. In this oil sketch she is shown as an accomplished and refined woman of taste, surrounded by books, portfolios, and a globe. The touch of color in Madame de Pompadour's cheeks is picked up by the clutch of roses pinned to her dress. They are echoed in the flowers strewn along the floor. As well as adding color and decoration, the roses serve as a symbol for her fresh youthful bloom and natural beauty. They are also associated with love.

Madame Pompadour's hand lightly touches the keys of a harpsichord, making reference to another of her talents and her love of the arts. Boucher's quick brushstrokes, and the continuous use of curving and curling shapes, enliven the portrait and echo the carefree spirit of rococo painting.

The scene is set within a quintessentially rococo room, with a profusion of decoration that was fashionable at the time. The lines of the furniture do provide some verticals to offset all the swirls of Madame Pompadour's dress, the pile of objects, and the ornate gold mirror frame and candlestick, and perhaps hint at the imminence of the neoclassical style, which would become popular in decoration after the excesses of the rococo.

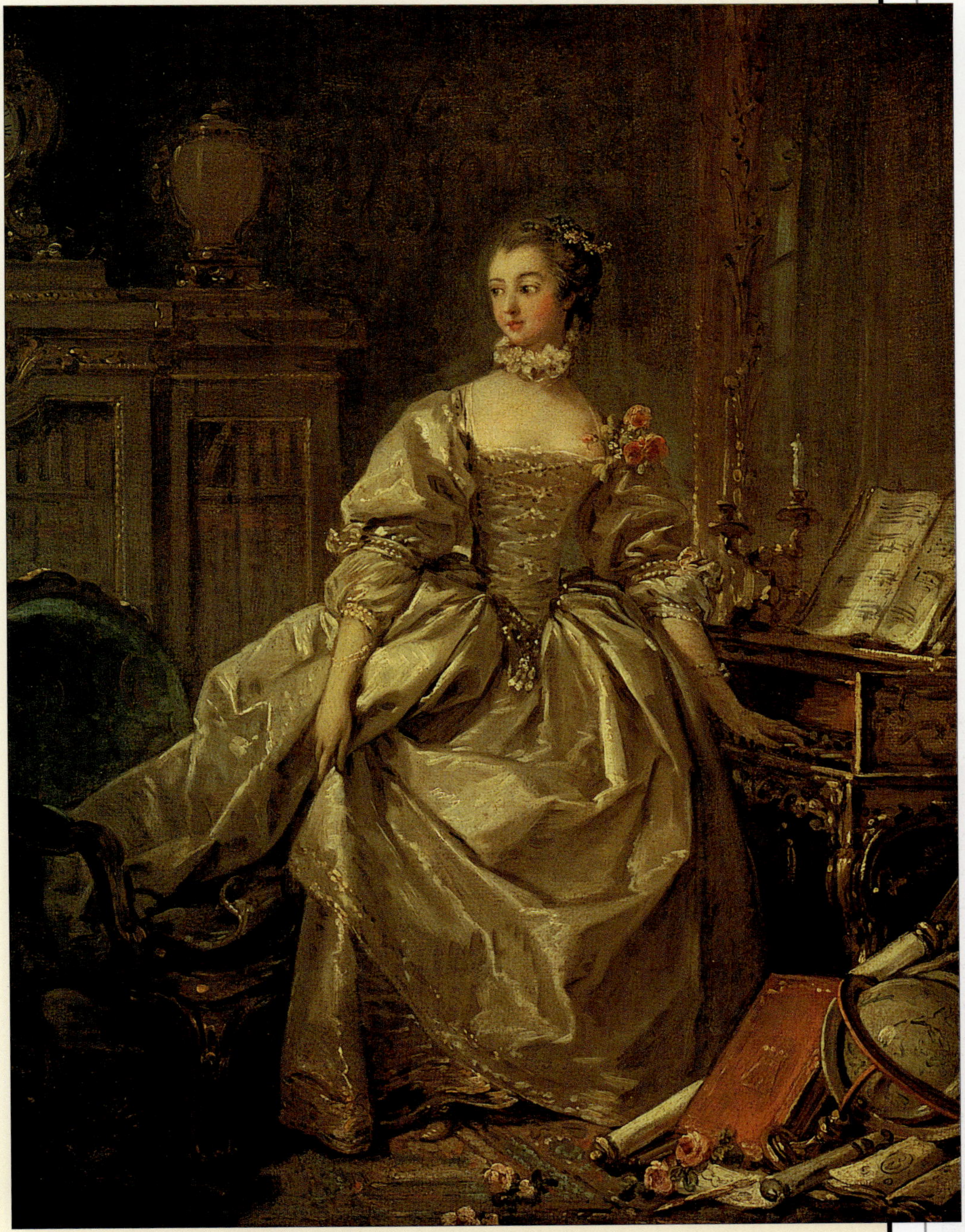

Madame de Pompadour *1756. Oil on canvas. 23 1/2 x 18 in (60 x 45.5 cm). Musée du Louvre, Paris.*

attention to intricate detail, figures in mythological or pastoral scenes (dressed as shepherds and shepherdesses), and a profusion of curling, twisting lines. Boucher was not interested in painting real-life shepherds or nature, and preferred elegant and frivolous subjects that he could invent and imagine.

In the 1740s, Boucher produced some of his most celebrated works, including several commissioned by the Swedish royal family and others by the French king, Louis XV, and his mistress Madame de Pompadour. It was Madame de Pompadour, in particular, who continued to support Boucher. She commissioned portraits of herself, mythological subject paintings, and tapestries, and also took lessons in etching from Boucher until her death in 1764. In 1765 Boucher was appointed the king's First Painter and elected director of the Académie Royale. His art brilliantly captured the spirit of the French court during this period—witty, elegant, superficial, and charming. He had gained the highest honors in the world of fine arts, and continued to produce large, decorative paintings until the end of his life.

BOURGEOIS Louise

ONE OF THE GREAT INDEPENDENT ARTISTS OF THE 20TH CENTURY, Louise Bourgeois began her artistic career as a painter and engraver before she turned to making the highly imaginative, provocative, and individual sculptures for which she is now famous. In the enormous body of work she has created, Bourgeois has consistently challenged accepted definitions of art.

Life and work

Louise Bourgeois was born in Paris in 1911. Her parents owned and ran a gallery dealing primarily in historical tapestries. It was here that Bourgeois first displayed her artistic talents by drawing the missing fragments of tapestries. The drawings were then used as patterns to restore them. After she graduated from the Lycée Fénélon in Paris in 1932, she did not go to art school but enrolled at the Sorbonne to study math. It was only in 1935, at the age of 24, that she decided to pursue a career as an artist.

Although Bourgeois was accepted at the prestigious Ecole des Beaux-Arts, she found the formal academic nature of the program restricting, and left to continue her studies in studios run by leading artists such as the cubist painters Fernand Léger and André Lhote. At this time Bourgeois was still studying painting, but her early interest in math and geometry was soon encouraging her toward three-dimensional work, and she became fascinated by the relationships created by positioning forms in space.

Her shift to working in three dimensions coincided with her move to the United States: in 1938 she met and married the art historian Robert Goldwater and moved to New York. Her earliest sculptures there were tall structures—symbolic representations of her friends and family in which carved wooden segments were arranged on top of each other.

In 1947 she published the suite of engravings *He Disappeared into Complete Silence*. The images of empty rooms found in this series are related to Bourgeois' earlier *Woman-House* paintings in which female forms have houses for heads. Bodies that are fused with buildings or constructions, or appear to emerge out of the material from which they are made, are a recurrent theme in her work, appearing later in the *Lair* series (from 1962) and the *Cell* series (1980s).

During the 1960s Bourgeois divided her time between teaching and sculpting. In 1966 her work was included in the Eccentric Abstraction exhibition organized by the critic Lucy Lippard, which brought her to the attention of a wider public. At this time Bourgeois became involved with the feminist movement, and also began experimenting with a wide range of materials: from plaster, cement, and latex rubber to the materials more

Data file

Full name: Louise Bourgeois

Nationality: American

Style: abstract sculptures based on organic forms

Dates: born 1911 in Paris

Key works:
- *Brother and Sister* 1946–49
- *He Disappeared into Complete Silence* 1947
- *Cumul I* 1969
- *The No March* 1973
- *Articulated Liar* 1983
- *Nature Study: Eyes* 1984
- *Untitled (with Foot)* 1989

Things to look for:
- abstract sculptures and large-scale installations
- references to parts of human bodies
- use of organic forms: nature is an indirect source for images
- works derived from personal experiences and memories
- use of a range of materials from hard (bronze, marble) to soft and semisoft (latex, rubber)

Comparisons: Eva Hesse, Bruce Nauman, Richard Serra, Mel Bochner, Robert Smithson

Glossary terms: abstract, cubism, engraving, etching, surrealism

Personal experiences on public display

In all her sculptures, Bourgeois uses a personal symbolism. She often describes her works as "autobiographical," frequently referring to events in her childhood and adolescence. In particular she recalls the presence in her family household of Sadie, an English tutor who became her father's mistress and lived with the family for some 10 years. Her father's relationship was seen by Bourgeois as an act of betrayal; in her art she expresses her emotions and memories in terms relevant to her own experiences as a woman. Frequently Bourgeois depicts women in fantastic situations: in the *Woman-House* series, women and buildings are merged. At other times, Bourgeois refers to her work as dealing with notions of sexuality and gender.

On the whole, it is "universal themes" that preoccupy Bourgeois: life and death, love, sex, and alienation, and identity. *Untitled (with Hand)* and *Untitled (with Foot)* (both 1989), in which a childlike or doll-like hand or foot emerges from a marble sphere, have the phrases "I Love You" and "Do You Love Me?" carved around the bases. These can be seen to refer to each and all of these themes. But Bourgeois herself identifies the basic human condition as fear. She describes her work as a means of coming to terms with and accepting certain fears.

Bourgeois has mastered numerous sculpting techniques: carving, modeling, assembling, and casting. She has used a range of materials—wood, latex rubber, marble, and bronze—as well as incorporating found objects into her works.

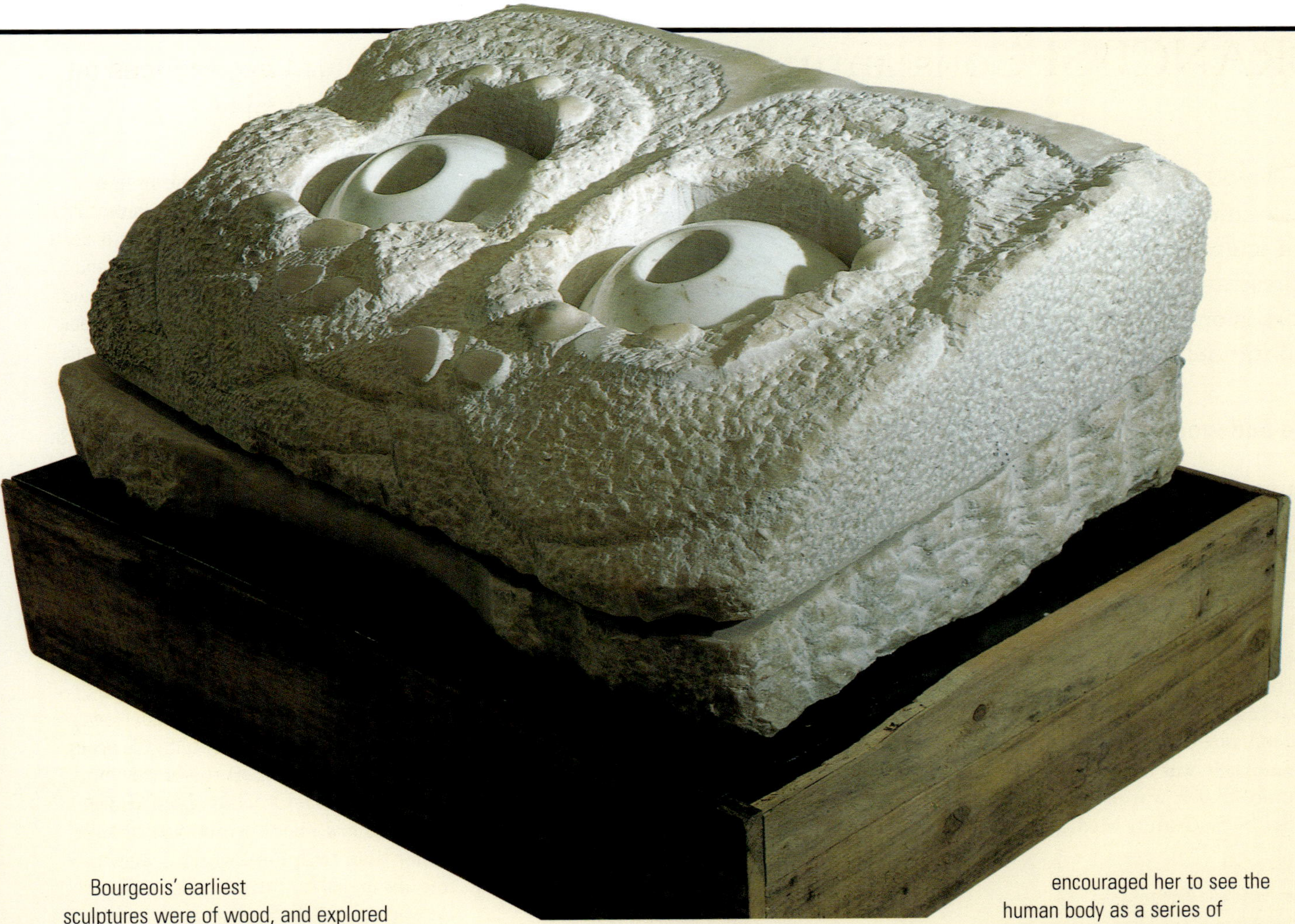

Nature Study: Eyes *1984. Pink and white marble on steel and wood base. 20 x 45½ x 31½ in (51 x 115.5 x 80 cm). Albright-Knox Art Gallery, Buffalo, NY.*

Bourgeois' earliest sculptures were of wood, and explored the way people can be seen to correspond psychologically to the spaces and structures they occupy. *The Blind Leading the Blind* (c1947–49) is an arrangement of black and red wooden posts that can be interpreted as a group of figures as well as a fencelike structure enclosing them.

In the 1960s Bourgeois began working with plaster and moved away from the strong vertical axis toward more horizontal forms. In the 1970s she combined carving in marble with latex-rubber casts of objects taken from life; these would become models for later bronze sculptures.

For Bourgeois, making her sculptures is a way of making "order out of chaos." This sense of ordering is partly derived from her interest in math and geometry, which encouraged her to see the human body as a series of independent parts. It is these parts of the body—hands, feet, arms, ears, and eyes—that are used to create her sculptures. Removed from the context of the whole body, these parts become objects that are subject to the spectator's gaze. *Nature Study: Eyes* (1984) is made up of three parts: the wood and metal base; what seems like a pock-marked pink marble "face," and eyeballs. The eyeballs are not attached to the sockets but just rest inside them; the spectator's look is returned by a blank, expressionless stare.

traditionally used in sculpture, such as bronze, which she used in *Lair* (1964).

In the 1980s, Bourgeois turned to marble—often pink colored. In this material she exploited the potential and qualities of the stone. In her 1989 piece, *Untitled (with Growths)*, highly polished clusters of organic growths appear to sprout out of roughly hewn marble blocks.

In 1991 Bourgeois showed her six-part installation, *Cells*. These are based on her experiences as a woman, and represent different types of pain: physical, emotional, psychological, mental, and intellectual. Six separate spaces were joined by doors (some had windows). These kept the spectator firmly outside each "cell," but able to look in. Inside the cells were a variety of objects: a mattress, perfume bottles, marble carvings of body parts—legs, arms, hands, ears, all seeming to belong to a small child or a doll; a metal stool, and two giant carved wooden spheres.

Today there is a strong interest in Bourgeois' work and she is receiving recognition as one of America's greatest sculptors. She continues to work from her Brooklyn studio.

BRANCUSI Constantin

CONSTANTIN BRANCUSI WAS A HIGHLY SKILLED and influential sculptor who contributed to the revival of direct carving as a sculptural practice in the early 20th century. He rejected the representational styles of traditional sculpture in favor of simple, more geometrical shapes, and produced works of great beauty and tranquility.

Life and work

Constantin Brancusi was born into a peasant family in 1876, in a small village in southern Romania. As a boy he was apprenticed to a carpenter and cabinet maker. This training developed his skills in wood carving and finishing.

At the age of 18, Brancusi entered the Bucharest Academy of Arts, where he developed his sculptural technique. (Indeed, one of the studies he did of the human body was thought to be so accurate that it was used as a teaching model by Bucharest Medical School.)

In 1902 Brancusi left Bucharest for Paris. He took two years to make the trip, spending time in Vienna and Munich on the way.

On his return he enrolled at the Ecole des Beaux-Arts in Paris. Here, his ability to work in many different materials—including wood, stone, and metal—attracted the attention of some of the leading figures in the Paris art world. Not least among these was the famous sculptor Auguste Rodin. Rodin was so impressed by Brancusi's work that he invited the young Romanian to work in his studio as his assistant. Brancusi refused, however, stating famously, "Nothing grows well in the shadow of a big tree."

In 1906 Brancusi left the Ecole des Beaux-Arts and began a career characterized by isolation and an almost monastic simplicity. The following year he produced the first of many works on the theme of the kiss, a subject he would return to throughout his career.

Brancusi's early works reflect the influence of one of the leading Italian sculptors of the 19th century, Medardo Rosso. Rosso's highly original works, frequently modeled in colored wax, concentrated on light and texture, qualities that appealed enormously to Brancusi. Soon, however, Brancusi rejected the traditional practice of modeling, and adopted instead the technique of direct carving. He was influenced by the great number of non-Western works that he had seen in the ethnographical museum in Paris. He was also following in the footsteps of Paul Gauguin and André Derain—painters who had turned to carving.

In 1909 Brancusi met the Italian artist Amedeo Modigliani, who shared his interest in African art. Brancusi persuaded Modigliani to take up sculpture, teaching him to carve.

From 1910 Brancusi's work began to focus more on the natural world. The mythical title of *Maiastra* (1912), meaning magical bird, revealed the artist's fascination with the folklore and peasant culture of his native Romania.

In 1920 Brancusi's work was attracting much popular attention, although this was not all positive. That year, his work *Princess X* (1916), was rejected from a French exhibition, the Salon des Indépendants; it was considered indecent because of a clear resemblance to a phallus. A few years later, in 1926, Brancusi became involved in a dispute with U.S. Customs when he tried to import the bronze *Bird in Space* (1925). Officials claimed the work was raw metal, which was taxable, rather than sculpture, which was duty free. Brancusi had to pay the tax as he wanted to exhibit the work in his one-man show at the Brummer Gallery in New York.

Following these controversies, Brancusi increasingly withdrew from the art world. His studio became the center of his universe, providing a calm and peaceful sanctuary in the midst of the modern world. Here, for over 30 years, Brancusi worked and reworked the same themes, regularly photographing his works in what he perceived to be their ideal setting.

Brancusi's only major public monuments were three works set in a park in Tirgu Jiu, near his birthplace in Romania, which he completed in 1938. Together, *Endless Column*, *The Table of Silence*, and *The Gate of the Kiss* were a memorial to the soldiers who had died in World War I. The works captured the essence of simplicity, contemplation, and the raw materials that were characteristic of Brancusi's work throughout his life.

Data file

Full name: Constantin Brancusi

Nationality: Romanian

Style: primitivism

Dates: born 1876 in Hobitza, died 1957 in Paris, France

Key works:

Sleeping Muse 1908 (one of several versions)

The Kiss c1912 (one of several versions)

Maiastra 1912

Princess X 1916

Golden Bird 1919

Prodigal Son 1925

Bird in Space 1925

Endless Column, The Table of Silence, and *The Gate of the Kiss* 1937–38

Flying Turtle 1943

Things to look for:

- simple forms and materials
- influence of non-Western art forms, including African and Oceanic sculpture
- truth to materials

Comparisons: Auguste Rodin, Medardo Rosso, André Derain, Amedeo Modigliani

Glossary terms: avant-garde, Oceanic art, primitivism

Brancusi's variations on a theme

The Kiss (c1912) is one of a number of versions on this theme that Brancusi produced throughout his lifetime. In 1907, when he produced the first version of the work, Rodin's great marble statue of the same title was only a few years old. However, in contrast to Rodin's highly representational and sensuous treatment of the theme, Brancusi rejected the realistic depiction of the body in favor of simple, geometrical shapes.

Starting with a rough-hewn block of stone, Brancusi carved two upright forms to represent the male and female figures. All details were reduced to an absolute minimum, with simple inscribed lines indicating arms, eyes, and hair. Brancusi made no attempt to disguise the stone from which he carved these figures. Instead he emphasized the rough surface and coarse texture of the material, using this tactile quality as a feature of the work.

By abandoning traditional sculptural styles for a more simple form of representation, Brancusi expressed his awareness of, and fascination with, the art of non-Western cultures. In particular, he would have seen examples of African and Oceanic art displayed in museums throughout Paris. Brancusi's interest in non-Western art was also shared by many turn-of-the-century avant-garde artists, including Paul Gauguin, André Derain, Henri Matisse, and Pablo Picasso.

The theme of the kiss emerged in several different contexts in Brancusi's work. In 1912 a version was used to adorn a gravestone in the Montparnasse cemetery in Paris. The theme also re-emerged in one of Brancusi's last great works, *The Gate of the Kiss* (1937–38), one of three pieces erected in Tirgu Jiu in Romania. Here Brancusi reduced the forms of the two figures even further, until they seem to disappear, leaving little more than two rectangles and two intersecting circles—all that is left of the original work.

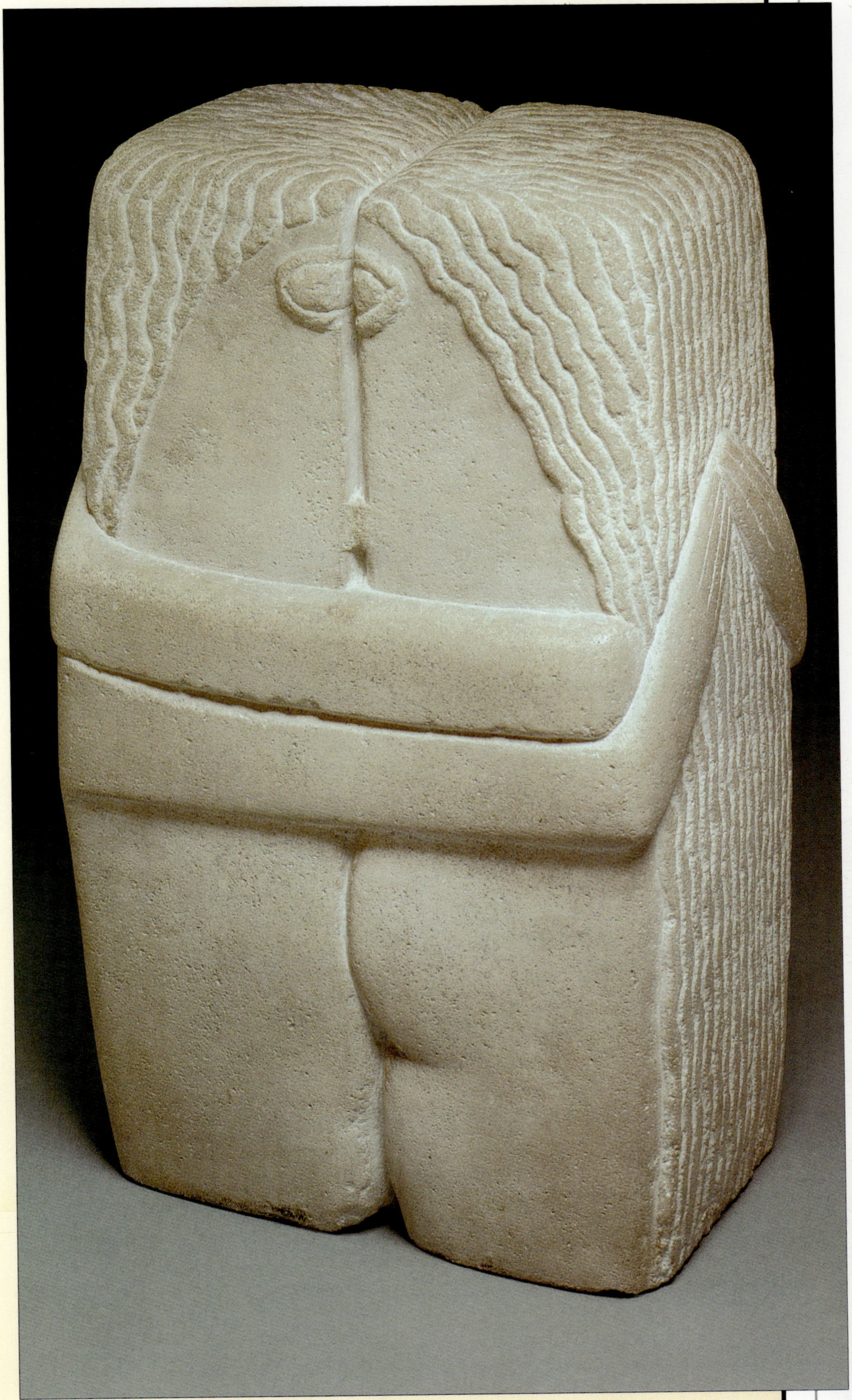

The Kiss *c1912. Stone. 23 in (58.5 cm). Museum of Modern Art, Philadelphia, PA.*

BRAQUE Georges

GEORGES BRAQUE WAS ONE OF THE FOUNDING FATHERS of modern art. Together with Pablo Picasso, he developed cubism, a style that radically altered the way in which artists saw and represented the world around them. Although often overshadowed by the more charismatic Picasso, Braque remains one of the most important and influential artists of the 20th century.

Life and work

Georges Braque was born in 1882 in Argenteuil, a quiet riverside town outside Paris much frequented by impressionist painters. While still a young boy, Braque and his family moved to Le Havre, a seaside town also popular among artists. The Braque family's interests in painting were, however, of a more practical nature. Both Braque's father and grandfather had worked as house painters and, while still a youth, Georges undertook an apprenticeship in the family trade. In Le Havre, however, Braque began to develop an interest in the fine arts, and in his mid-teens he enrolled for evening lessons at the local school of art.

By 1900, Braque had left Le Havre for the bustling artistic community of Montmartre on the northern outskirts of Paris. In the city, he regularly visited the Louvre and the Luxembourg Museum to study the work of the great artists of the distant and more recent past. Like many of his contemporaries, Braque frequently spent the summer months traveling in the south of France, producing paintings for exhibition back in the city at the newly founded Autumn Salon. In 1907 Braque produced a number of canvases representing the small southern fishing port of La Ciotat. In these works, Braque's use of bright colors and forms broken up into divisionist strokes revealed his affinities with the fauvist movement, which was dominated by Henri Matisse and André Derain.

Another of Braque's major interests at this time was the work of Paul Cézanne. Cézanne's reputation had grown dramatically in the first years of the 20th century, culminating in the staging of a major retrospective exhibition in Paris in 1907, one year after Cézanne's death. The following summer, Braque visited the town of L'Estaque near Marseilles, a site frequently visited by Cézanne. Here, he produced a series of landscapes in which he adopted the simplified forms and muted colors typical of Cézanne. When Braque exhibited these works in Paris, one critic referred to the abundant use of cubes. This reference is probably the origin of the term that came to designate one of the most influential art movements of the 20th century: cubism.

During this period, the young art dealer Daniel Henry Kahnweiler exhibited Braque's works. Through Kahnweiler, Braque was introduced to a Spanish painter who was also acquiring a considerable reputation in Parisian artistic circles: the young Pablo Picasso. Between 1909 and 1914 Braque and

Data file

Full name: Georges Braque

Nationality: French

Style: cubism

Dates: born 1882 in Argenteuil, died 1963 in Paris

Key works:
- *The Bay at La Ciotat* 1907
- *Houses at L'Estaque* 1908
- *Still Life on a Table* 1911
- *Still Life on a Table "Gilette"* 1914
- *The Duo* 1937
- *The Studio V* 1945–51

Things to look for:
- use of multiple viewpoints
- inclusion of words and musical signs
- real newsprint and labels attached to the canvas

Comparisons: Pablo Picasso, Paul Cézanne, Raoul Dufy, Henri Matisse

Glossary terms: cubism, divisionism, fauvism, impressionism, *papiers-collés*, Renaissance, Salon

Braque's cubism

Braque's cubist paintings, such as *Still Life on a Table* (1911), abandoned the conventions of representation that had dominated artistic practice since the Renaissance. Instead of depicting a scene as seen from a single viewpoint, he represented objects as if seen simultaneously from several different angles. In this still life, fragments of a café table, a glass, and a violin emerge from a kaleidoscope of forms and shapes, all represented in muted tones of brown and ocher.

Braque's inclusion of signs in his paintings, such as the music notation in *Still Life on a Table*, was also accompanied by the representation of fragments of words, and by illusionistic representations

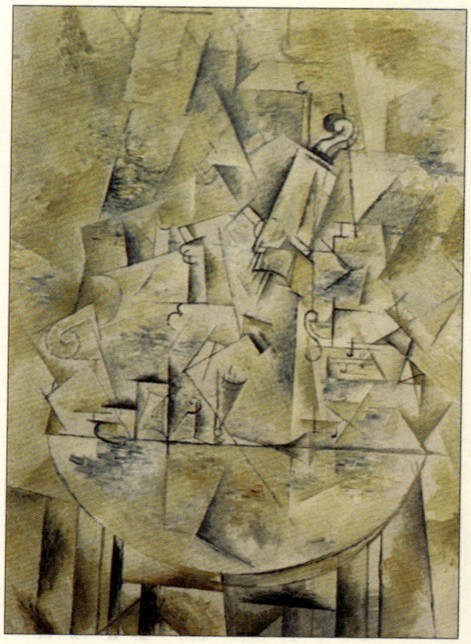

Still Life on a Table *1911. Oil on canvas. 45½ x 32 in (116 x 81 cm). Musée National d'Art Moderne, Paris.*

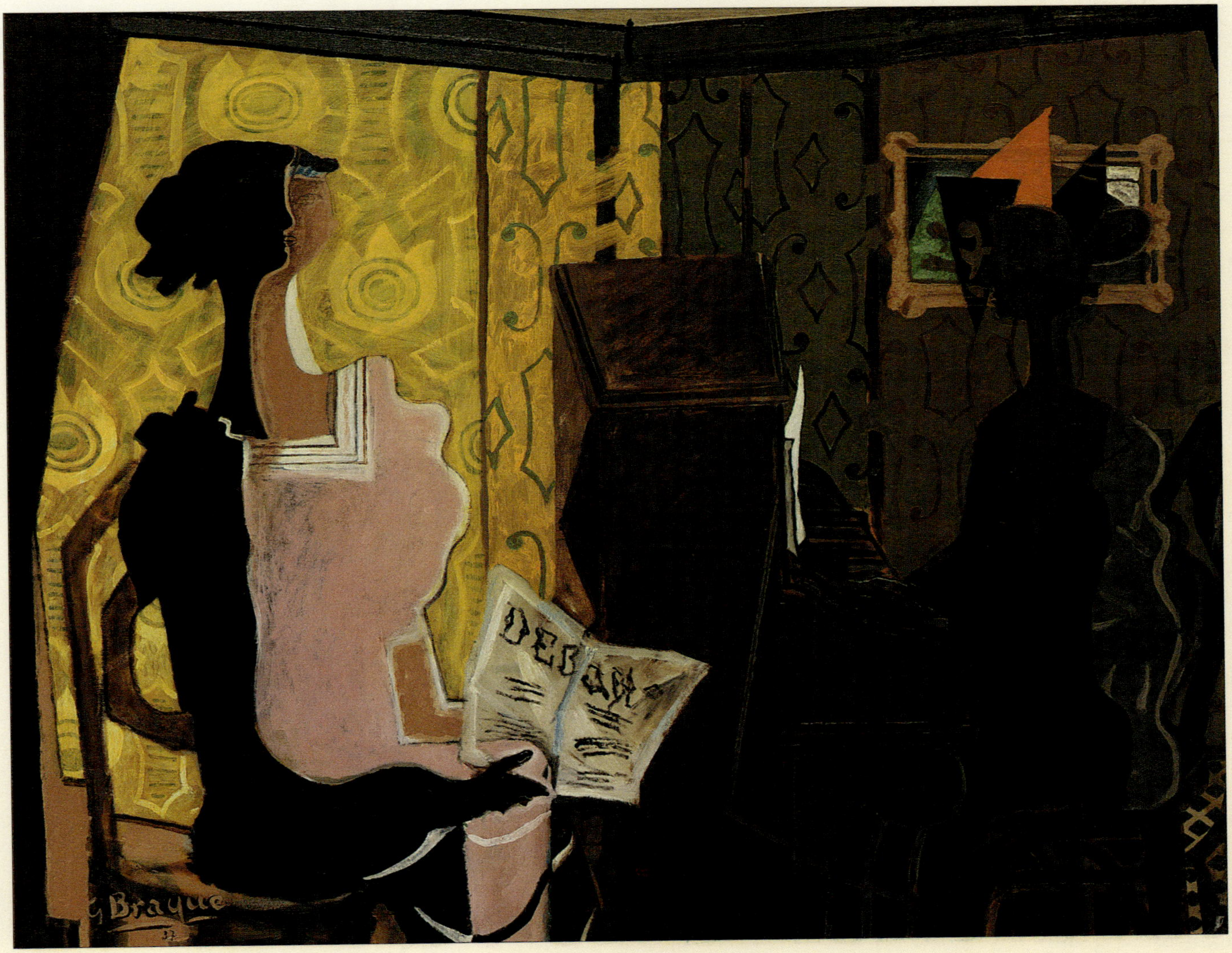

The Duo *1937. Oil on canvas. 51½ x 64 in (131 x 162.5 cm). Musée Nationale d'Art Moderne, Centre Georges Pompidou, Paris.*

of different textured surfaces, such as wood grain and wallpaper. In 1912–14, Braque and Picasso took this idea one stage further when they included actual newspaper cuttings and labels in their works. In these collages, known as *papiers-collés*, Braque and Picasso once again transformed the very nature of art by introducing materials from the world of modern popular culture.

Braque continued to use multiple viewpoints and illusionistic effects. In *The Duo* (1937), for example, he uses light to distinguish between two views of the singer seated on the left of the image. The dark, shadowy form suggests that this figure is seen in profile, while the lit right side shows the singer as seen in frontal view. In the background is imitation wallpaper reminiscent of the wallpaper Braque used in his *papiers-collés*.

Picasso embarked upon a project of intense experimentation, working together constantly and sharing ideas. Their cubist works of this period altered the entire landscape of art history and continue to influence artists to this day.

With the outbreak of World War I, the period of great experimentation came to an end. Braque was sent to fight while Picasso, ineligible for military service, remained in Paris. Within a year, Braque was on his way home again, having suffered a head injury during the conflict. Ultimately discharged as unfit for military service, Braque returned to painting. In the immediate postwar period, Braque increasingly focused on the production of cubist-inspired still-life paintings. In the early 1920s, he also undertook commissions to produce a number of set designs for the then highly popular *Ballet Russe* (Russian ballet) company.

Braque continued to paint throughout the remainder of his long life, focusing predominantly on studio interiors and still lifes. In his last years, however, he introduced images of birds into his canvases, evoking a sense of flight and boundless space.

BRONZINO Agnolo

BRONZINO WAS ONE OF THE LEADING EXPONENTS of the elaborate mannerist style that was fashionable in Italy in the 1500s. His cool, detached approach, courtly elegance, and sophistication earned him success among aristocratic patrons, including the powerful Medici family.

Life and work

The young Bronzino had a special relationship with his teacher, Pontormo, who became his adoptive father and exerted a strong influence on his painting style. Pontormo painted in a style known as mannerism, which was characterized by the use of intense colors and compositions of figures in elaborate poses.

Bronzino began by painting religious subjects for churches in Florence, working closely with Pontormo, and copying his style. However, after spending two years in Pesaro, he returned to Florence, painting smaller altarpieces in a more individual style. Moving away from the more flowing lines of his master, he created works that had a much stiller atmosphere, with carefully posed figures and an enamel-like finish. This made some of his religious paintings seem artificial, full of elegant posturing and empty of feeling. However, when he turned the same detached style to portrait painting, he created a new kind of portrait—aloof and superior—well-suited to many of the haughty aristocrats he was portraying.

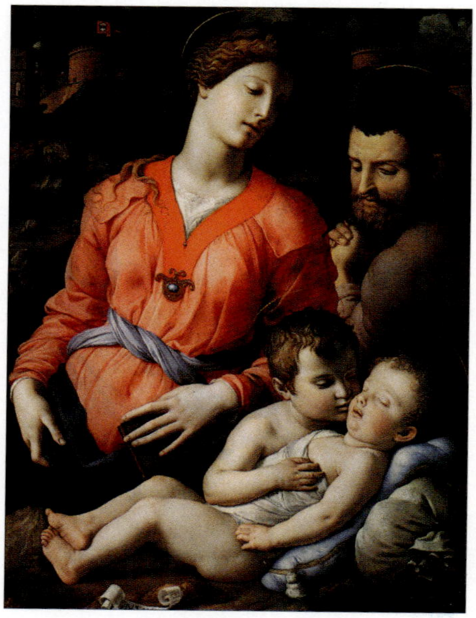

The Holy Family with Saint John *c1540. Oil on panel. 46 x 35 in (117 x 89 cm). Galleria degli Uffizi, Florence.*

It was as a portrait painter that Bronzino became most popular, painting the nobility and the leading poets, musicians, and scholars of his day. He became Court Painter in 1539, and produced several portraits of Duke Cosimo I de' Medici and his family.

Data file

Full name: Agnolo Bronzino (born Agnolo di Cosimo)
Nationality: Italian
Style: mannerism
Dates: born 1503 in Monticelli, died 1572 in Florence
Key works:
- *Portrait of a Young Man* c1538
- *The Holy Family with Saint John* c1540
- *An Allegory with Venus and Cupid* c1544–45
- *Portrait of Cosimo I in Armor* c1545
- *Eleonora of Toledo and Her Son Giovanni* 1545
- *Lamentation* 1545
- *Christ in Limbo* 1552

Things to look for:
- smooth, polished surfaces of paintings
- stylish and sophisticated portraits, often in three-quarter length
- elaborate compositions, painted with great detachment

Comparisons: Pontormo
Glossary terms: allegory, mannerism

Keeping a sense of distance

This portrait of Duke Cosimo I in armor shows us the patron who supported Bronzino. The painting does not commemorate a specific event, rather, Duke Cosimo dressed up to have his portrait painted. He is presented to us in half-length, looking over his shoulder in an alert and slightly suspicious way. He has removed his helmet, and rests his hand in a posed manner on the top of it. This is necessary for us to see his face, of course, but also shows us that although he is not engaged in combat he is always on the lookout, even when at rest.

His watchfulness and stern expression convey to the viewer that Cosimo is a man to be wary of, while the armor tells us of his strength and power. The armor also creates a more detached image for us, a protective layer of hard, metal covering separating the real person from the public scrutiny. Of course, this "layer" is really made of paint, but we are almost convinced otherwise by the artist's skill. The turning of his head suggests that he is aloof, not interested in looking at us, and reinforces the sense of unapproachability. Together with the use of light and shade around the face, the pose also makes the head look more three-dimensional and adds volume to the portrait.

The way Bronzino distances himself from his sitters and stylizes them often means that we appreciate their status rather than their personalities. In this portrait we get a sense of Cosimo as quite a brooding, dangerous character and a military ruler. However, he was also a loyal

Alongside the portraits, Bronzino continued to paint decorative scenes for chapels and tapestries at the Medici court. In c1544–45 he painted the famous *An Allegory with Venus and Cupid*, showing Venus, the mother of Cupid, kissing the winged god, and taking away his arrow as he touches her breast. This is perhaps Bronzino's best-known work, and has been the subject of a great deal of discussion and friend to artists and a patron of the arts.

The hard, shining armor provides a contrast with the other materials and textures of the painting, for example the draped curtain used as a simple backdrop, and the hair and flesh of the man himself. Bronzino conveys his interest in the fabrics and the surfaces with outstanding technical expertise. His extraordinary ability to paint surfaces makes us believe that we are looking at real, shining metal, and that if we get too close to this powerful and watchful Medici leader the protective spikes might just swing round to face us. The metal surface also reflects the light source in the painting, suggesting the outside world where this great ruler is prepared to go and, if need be, to do battle.

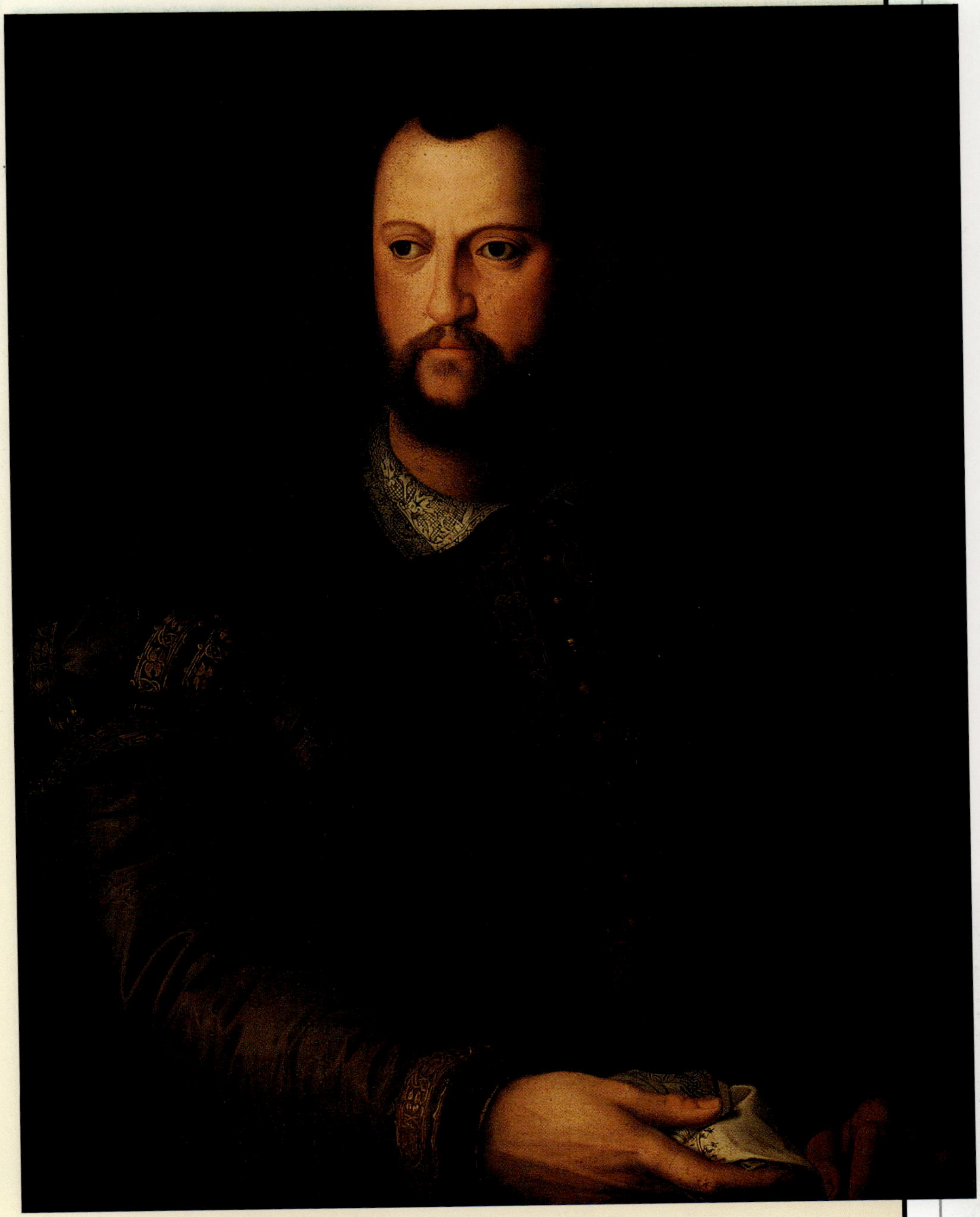

Portrait of Cosimo I in Armor *c1545.*
Tempera on wood. 28 x 22½ in (71 x 57 cm).
Galleria degli Uffizi, Florence.

disagreement about the central figures who form a complex allegory, the meaning of which is not entirely clear to us now. It is painted with the most expensive pigments and has a flawless surface, typical of Bronzino's style. It embodies the intelligence, intrigue, and danger of the Medici court. Rather like a precious jewel, it is an icy, polished, beautiful object for our contemplation. It is typical of mannerist style to fill the painting with lots of figures and objects, giving a sense of claustrophobia that is often characteristic of Bronzino's work. The complicated symbolism and moral tone of the painting would have delighted both Duke Cosimo, who commissioned it, and King Francis I of France, who received it as a gift.

Bronzino's work was seen to be sophisticated and scholarly, and he enjoyed a high reputation for his intellect and his poetry as well as his art. He continued painting religious subjects, portraits, and mythological paintings for the Medici. However, by the end of his life, his style was becoming slightly outdated. Later patrons were transferring their preferences to the new baroque style which showed greater interest in dynamic movement and dramatic, elaborate effects.

BRUEGEL Pieter

PIETER BRUEGEL WON FAME FOR HIS VIVID AND OFTEN HUMOROUS scenes of peasant life. Beneath the surface, however, his paintings often dealt with moral or political issues. He was also a great painter of landscapes.

Life and work

There is very little firm evidence about Bruegel's life, but it seems likely that he was born in Breda, in the Netherlands. At the time the country was still under Spanish rule, although during the artist's lifetime there were increasing moves to free it from foreign control.

The earliest available records show that Bruegel undertook his artistic training in Antwerp. He studied first under Pieter Coecke Van Aelst, a successful artist and publisher of the day. Coecke's teaching had little impact on his style, but Bruegel eventually married his daughter, Mayken, in 1563.

Bruegel qualified as a master painter in 1551 and, in the following year, embarked on a trip to Italy. There he worked for a time in the studio of a miniaturist named Giulio Clovio, before returning home in 1553. The journey was intended to set the seal on Bruegel's artistic education, acquainting him with the latest developments in the Italian Renaissance. However, it was the sight of the Alps on the return journey that proved to have the most influence on his work.

Back in Antwerp, Bruegel took employment with the printer Jerome Cock, who had published a number of engravings based on Bruegel's designs. Apart from a few landscapes, these mainly consisted of pastiches of the grotesque fantasies of his fellow Netherlander Hieronymus Bosch. Bosch's work was currently undergoing a revival in popularity, and Cock was keen to exploit the trend—so keen that he actually tried to pass off some of Bruegel's images as Bosch originals. In fact, some of Bruegel's later paintings—*Dulle Griet (Mad Meg)* (1562), and *The Triumph of Death* (c1562)—did have a pronounced Boschian flavor.

While in Antwerp, Bruegel may have become associated with a religious group known as the "Family of Love." This group advocated tolerance and a strict morality. Because it gave greater weight to individual conscience than to the authority of the Church, membership was secret, so it is impossible to be sure if Bruegel joined. Nevertheless, echoes of the group's ideals can be found in the strong ethical content of many of his pictures, in particular in the larger peasant scenes. Some of his contemporaries regarded these lively compositions as vulgar jollities that pandered to popular taste, but in fact they are eloquent sermons about the dangers of sinfulness.

In 1563 Bruegel settled in Brussels with his wife. One early source cryptically suggests that the move was prompted by the artist's mother-in-law, who wanted to separate Bruegel from a former girlfriend. Whatever the reason, the move presented the painter with new challenges and helped to transform his art. Brussels was a major political

Data file

Full name: Pieter Bruegel
Nationality: Netherlandish
Style: northern Renaissance
Dates: born c1525, possibly in Breda, died 1569 in Brussels (now in Belgium)
Key works:
The Fall of Icarus c1558
Netherlandish Proverbs 1559
Dulle Griet (Mad Meg) 1562
The Triumph of Death c1562
Hunters in the Snow c1565
Peasant Dance c1567
The Parable of the Blind 1568
Things to look for:
- moral messages
- peasant subjects
- sweeping, mountainous landscapes

Comparisons: Hieronymus Bosch, Albrecht Dürer, Peter Paul Rubens
Glossary terms: allegory, Book of Hours, engraving, frieze, miniature, monumental, pastiche, Renaissance

Landscape pioneer

When Bruegel traveled to Italy in the early 1550s, he was captivated by the majestic scenery of the Swiss Alps, and became determined to reproduce it in his paintings. This was not easy because, at the time, landscapes were not regarded as a respectable art form. They were generally only found as background details in subject paintings, or as tiny illustrations for the calendar in a Book of Hours (a type of prayer book that people used at home). Bruegel was one of the first artists to create full-size paintings in which the landscape was the dominant feature.

Hunters in the Snow (c1565), was one of a series of pictures based on the months of the year that Bruegel painted for Niclaes Jonghelinck, a wealthy merchant from Antwerp. It is assumed that originally the complete set was hung together, forming a long frieze (ornamental strip) around the walls of a single room, but only five pictures survive. In essence, Bruegel treated each theme as an enlarged version of a traditional calendar scene. Like the miniaturists, he identifies the month by a relevant agricultural activity (in this case the singeing of a pig on the left-hand side of the picture), as well as by the snow-covered landscape, bare trees, and winter sporting activities.

Hunters in the Snow demonstrates how Bruegel could combine different aspects of his artistic and life experience in order to fuse them into something quite new. The panoramic structure of the landscape is based on his memories of his Alpine trip, patiently refined through scores of careful drawings. Similarly, his work as a printmaker gave him an eye for the tiny,

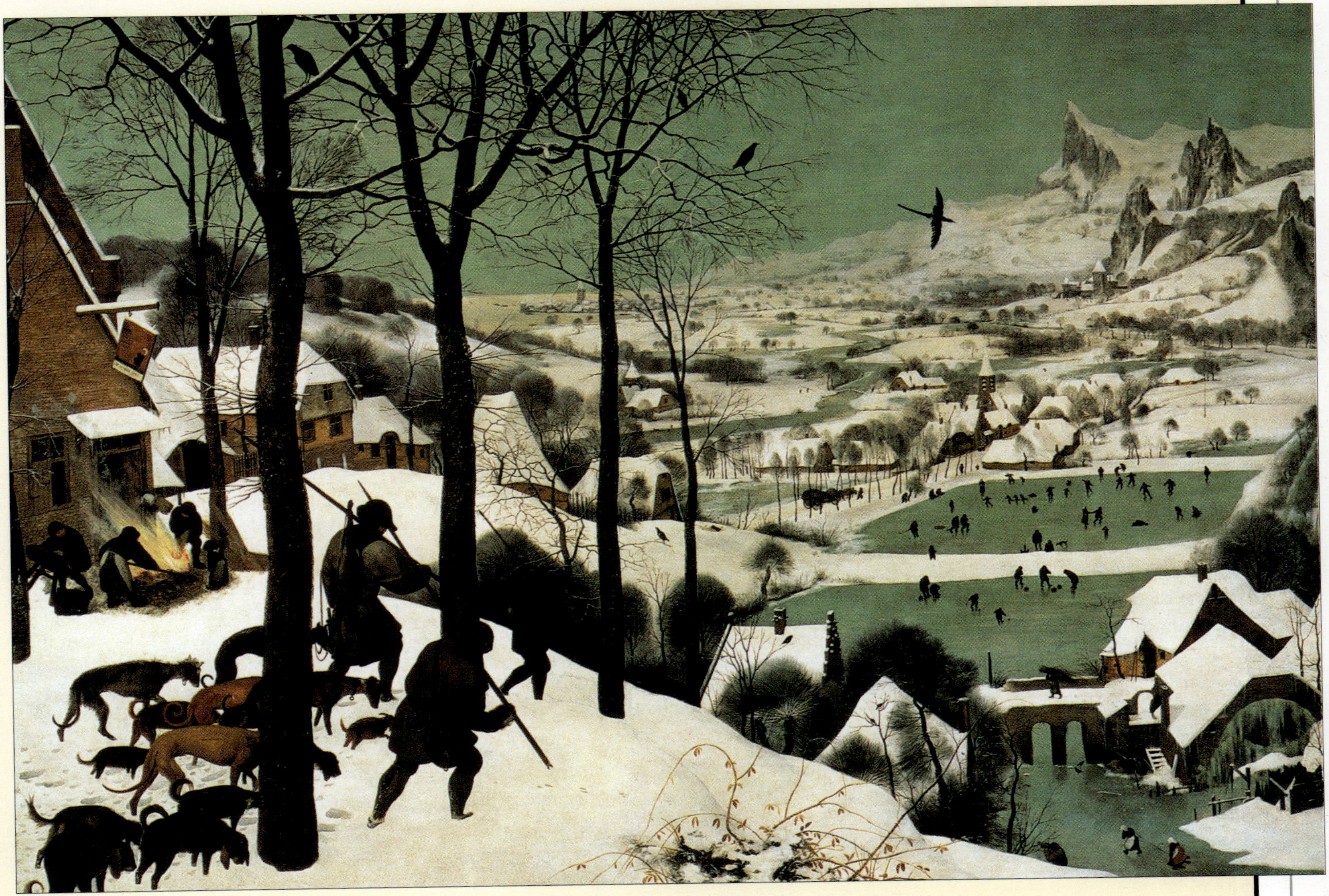

incidental details that delight the observant spectator. For example, there are figures skating, spinning tops, and playing hockey. There is even a group of people trying to extinguish a fire in a distant chimney, left of the church. The combination of these features conjures up an utterly convincing image of a chill winter's day, one that would inspire later Dutch and Flemish artists.

It is clear that Bruegel painted this series very quickly, with an astonishing sureness of touch. He applied the paint very thinly, making sure that the brush was almost dry. In some places the underpainting is still visible, adding to the spontaneity of the scene. Peter Paul Rubens greatly admired this aspect of Bruegel's technique, and employed it in some of his own compositions.

Hunters in the Snow *c1565. Oil on panel. 46 x 64 in (117 x 162 cm). Kunsthistorisches Museum, Vienna.*

center, with a more discerning, aristocratic clientele than Antwerp. As a result, Bruegel modified his style, replacing the slightly cluttered composition of his early paintings, which were packed with scores of tiny figures, with a simpler and more monumental approach.

Growing political tensions cast a shadow over Bruegel's final years. As the Netherlands drifted toward war, his paintings increasingly reflected his pessimistic mood. This culminated in *The Parable of the Blind* (1568), a great but bitter allegory about political folly.

His sons, Pieter and Jan, became artists; the Pieters are now referred to as Bruegel the Elder and the Younger.

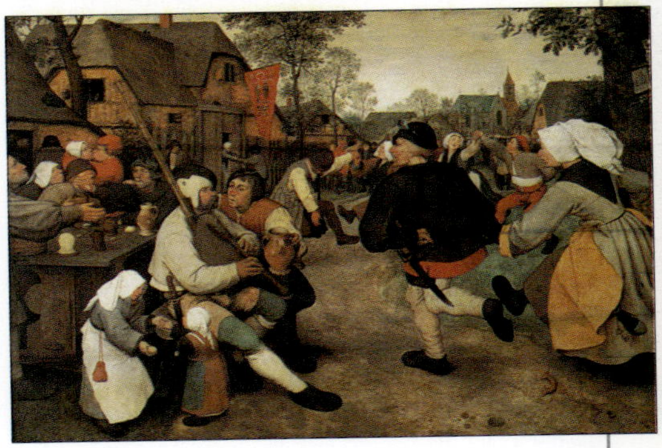

Peasant Dance *c1567. Oil on panel. 45 x 64 1/2 in (114 x 164 cm). Kunsthistorisches Museum, Vienna.*

BURNE-JONES Edward

THE GRACEFUL AND MYSTERIOUS PAINTINGS OF BURNE-JONES conjured up a romantic vision of the past, while his work as a designer helped to inspire a revolution in taste. He became one of the most influential English painters and illustrators of the 19th century.

Life and work

Edward Burne-Jones came from a comfortable, middle-class background, but his childhood was tinged with sadness. His mother died just a few days after he was born, and he was brought up by his father and a maiden aunt named Miss Sampson. His father, also called Edward, was a quiet, distant man, while Miss Sampson was highly religious and fastidious. Both were kind to the boy, but they could not provide the warmth and affection he craved.

Burne-Jones's initial ambition was to enter the Church, but his interest shifted to art during his days at Oxford University. The initial stimulus came from a fellow student, William Morris, who was to become a lifelong friend and collaborator. Morris had a passion for the Middle Ages, which Burne-Jones rapidly came to share. The pair went on holiday together in 1855, making a tour of the Gothic churches in northern France, and it was during this trip that Burne-Jones decided to become a painter.

The medieval interests of the two young students led them to the work of the Pre-Raphaelite Brotherhood. This group of artists also drew much of their inspiration from the Middle Ages, in pursuing their ambition to revive an interest in the painters who had preceded Raphael. So, it was a natural move for Burne-Jones to seek out the leader of the Pre-Raphaelites—Dante Gabriel Rossetti—and persuade him to become his teacher. This was a casual arrangement, which did not involve formal examination or qualifications, but gave Burne-Jones a solid grounding in his chosen profession.

Meanwhile, Burne-Jones remained in close contact with Morris. They both took part in a scheme organized by Rossetti, to provide a series of murals for the debating hall at Oxford University (1857), and Burne-Jones also helped Morris create an elaborate set of decorations for his new home. This inspired Morris into making an important career change. Abandoning his aim of becoming an architect, he founded a firm, Morris, Marshall, Faulkner and Co., which produced fine quality, hand-crafted furnishings. With this new company it was his intention to reverse the increasing trend toward cheap, mass-produced goods, and to restore the high standards of traditional design, manufacture, and finishing that he associated with the workmanship of the Middle Ages.

Burne-Jones played a vital role in Morris's firm. Over the next 30 years, he produced some of his finest work in designs for a huge variety of objects, ranging from stained-glass windows and furniture to tapestries and tiles. His principal achievements in this field include *The Adoration of the Magi* (1887–90), a tapestry that he designed for his old college at Oxford University, and his book illustrations for the Kelmscott Press—another of Morris's projects. In a broader sense, the work produced at Morris's firm proved a major source of inspiration for the Arts and Crafts movement.

At the same time, Burne-Jones forged a unique reputation with his paintings. He continued to work in a Pre-Raphaelite vein, although his style acquired a distinctly Italianate flavor, following his many visits to that country. He was greatly influenced by the works of Italian masters such as Sandro Botticelli and Andrea Mantegna. His style made a strong impression on the illustrator and artist Aubrey Beardsley, as well as on other leading players of the Art Nouveau movement, which was influential at the end of the 19th century. His compositions, along with those of other Pre-Raphaelites, centered largely on medieval subjects, Arthurian legends, and mythology.

Before 1877, Burne-Jones did not exhibit much of his work. When he did, at the Grosvenor Gallery, London, his paintings caused a considerable stir. They achieved even greater acclaim when displayed at the World Fairs held in Paris in 1878 and 1889. At the latter, Burne-Jones was awarded an important prize, the Cross of the Legion of Honor. The reasons for his success in France are quite clear. His mysterious, evocative pictures tallied closely with the experiments of the symbolist painters, and he was rapidly acknowledged as a leading figure in this movement.

Data file

Full name: Edward Coley Burne-Jones

Nationality: English

Style: Pre-Raphaelite

Dates: born 1833 in Birmingham, died 1898 in London

Key works:

- *Le Chant d'Amour* 1868–77
- *Briar Rose* series 1873–90
- *The Annunciation* 1874
- *The Golden Stairs* 1876–80
- *King Cophetua and the Beggar Maid* 1884
- *The Adoration of the Magi* 1887–90
- *Love among the Ruins* 1893

Things to look for:

- linear approach
- elongated figures; mysterious subjects

Comparisons: Sandro Botticelli, Piero della Francesca, Dante Gabriel Rossetti, Andrea Mantegna, William Morris

Glossary terms: Art Nouveau, Arts and Crafts movement, Pre-Raphaelite, symbolism

Grace and mystery

The paintings of Burne-Jones fused elements of the past with hints of the future. His homage to ancient history stemmed mainly from his links with the Pre-Raphaelite Brotherhood. In accordance with their ideals, he drew much of his inspiration from early Italian artists, who were still dismissed as "primitive" by many of the critics of his own time. In particular, his figures closely resemble those of Sandro Botticelli and Piero della Francesca. They have pale skin and idealized faces, and they wear long, flowing robes. They might easily pass for angels. Stylistically, they are conveyed in a very precise, linear manner. For *The Golden Stairs,* (1876–80) the artist produced scores of preparatory drawings of the draperies, the hands, and the feet, to ensure that the details of the painting would look convincing.

Burne-Jones also liked to set his pictures in an ancient world. Sometimes he painted legendary characters from mythology, such as Perseus or Merlin, and sometimes he chose to portray fairytales, as in his version of the Sleeping Beauty story (the *Briar Rose* series, 1873–90). Increasingly, though, he preferred to depict an imaginary past that he described as, "a beautiful romantic dream, of something that never was, never will be...in a land no one can define or remember, only desire." *The Golden Stairs* is typical of this approach. The archaic musical instruments, the garlands, and the strange architecture all suggest the distant past, but there is no firm evidence about the time, the place, or the meaning of the image.

The viewing public found this baffling, and many of them actually wrote to Burne-Jones asking for an explanation. In fact, though, it was the very elusiveness of the subject matter that linked the painter with the symbolist movement. Originally a French literary movement, in the late 19th-century symbolism began to cross over to the visual arts. Followers of this style found it more poetic to conjure up a mood or an emotion rather than simply record the details of a story. They argued that painting should aspire to the condition of music, so that every art lover could interpret a picture in his or her own way. This may well be one of the reasons why so many of Burne-Jones's images contain musicians and musical instruments.

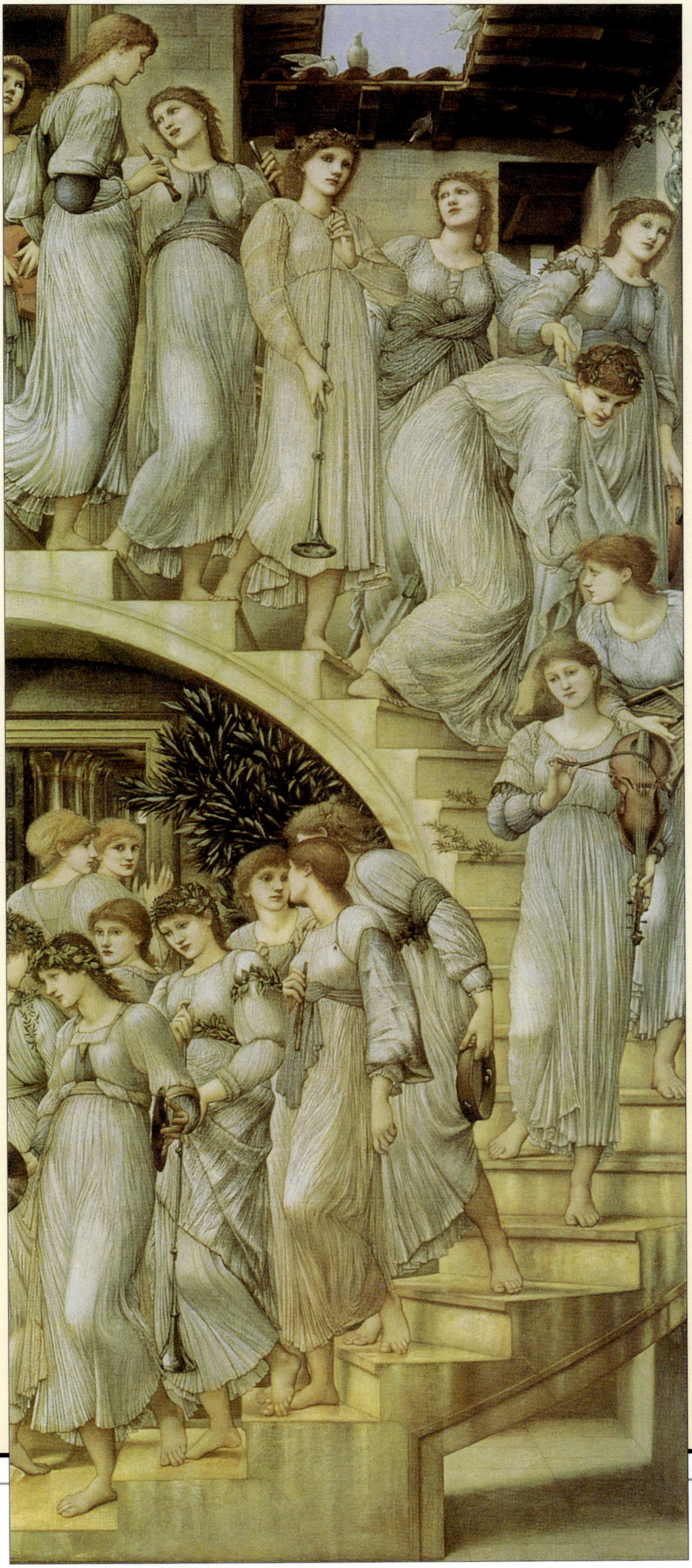

The Golden Stairs *1876–80. Oil on canvas. 109 x 46 in (277 x 117 cm). Tate Gallery, London.*

CALDER Alexander

ALEXANDER CALDER IS BEST KNOWN FOR HIS KINETIC SCULPTURES or mobiles in which abstract, organic forms are delicately balanced or suspended. He created "stabiles," or stationary sculptures, ranging in size from just a few feet to nearly 100 feet tall. His work challenged and altered the definition of sculpture, opening doors for younger artists to explore movement and other effects in their work.

Life and work

Alexander Calder was born in 1898 in Lawnton, now part of Philadelphia. His father, Alexander Stirling Calder, was a noted sculptor, and his mother, Nanette Lederer, was a well-known portrait painter. In 1906 the Calder family moved west to Arizona and then to California; it was hoped the climate there would benefit Calder Senior, who was suffering from a heart condition.

Data file

Full name: Alexander Calder

Nationality: American

Style: abstract sculptures

Dates: born 1898 in Lawnton, PA, died 1976 in New York, NY

Key works:

Aztec Josephine Baker c1929

Lobster Trap and Fish Tail 1939

Constellation 1943

Big Red 1959

Teodelapio 1962

Under the Half Moon 1972

Flamingo 1974

Things to look for:

- mobiles and large-scale static sculptures, or "stabiles"
- use of strong, often primary colors, with red frequently dominant
- abstract, organic shapes
- balanced and counterbalanced forms
- hand-finished appearance rather than slick, mechanized surface finish

Comparisons: Joan Miró, Piet Mondrian, Marcel Duchamp, Naum Gabo, László Moholy-Nagy, Jean Arp

Glossary terms: abstraction, avant-garde, lithography, palette, De Stijl, surrealism

The family returned to the East Coast to New York state in 1910, but moved again to California in 1913 when Calder Senior was appointed acting chief of sculpture for the World's Fair to be held in San Francisco in 1915. In each new home, the young Calder, surrounded by artistic activity, set up his own little workshops where he made toys and gadgets.

In 1919 Calder graduated as a mechanical engineer from Stevens Institute of Technology in New Jersey. A series of apprentice engineering jobs culminated in 1922 when Calder became a fireman on a passenger ship, the *H. F. Alexander*; there he invented a shaped metal baffle to direct cool air into the hot boiler room where he was working during a voyage to Guatemala. While at sea, the experience of seeing the red glow of the sun rising against the silver of the setting moon left him with a lasting sensation of the universe, themes that were to be the main subjects of his work as an artist.

On his return to New York in 1922, Calder began drawing classes at night school, and from 1923 to 1926 he studied at the Art Students' League. During this time he was commissioned by the *National Police Gazette* to sketch the Ringling Brothers and Barnum and Bailey circuses, which marked the beginning of his fascination with the theme. Around the same time Calder also began making his first portraits in wire.

In 1926 Calder left the United States for Paris, where he was to meet many of the leading figures of the European avant garde. Key among his new friends were the Catalan painter once associated with the surrealists, Joan Miró, whose compositions called *Constellations* were to provide Calder with stylistic references; and the Dutch De Stijl painter Piet Mondrian, who encouraged Calder to turn from representation to abstraction and to introduce color—albeit in the limited palette of the three primary colors plus black and white—into his art.

In the early 1930s Calder became fascinated with the problem of motion

Ingenuity and engineering

The word kinetic comes from the Greek *kinesos* (movement); kinetic art means art that involves motion. For centuries artists tried and developed ways of representing movement, but in kinetic art movement is an integral part of the work. Experiments by artists such as Naum Gabo and László Moholy-Nagy made important contributions in the 20th century to the development of kinetic art, and today kinetic art can be grouped as four main types. There are works that move; works that involve movement on the part of the onlooker (such as those by Victor Vasarely); works that involve the use of light and light projections; and works where the spectator can take part in and transform elements of the work. This can range from simply setting a work in motion or stopping it, to actually constructing it!

Whatever form kinetic art takes today, the movement itself can be said to date from Alexander Calder, since it was he who "solved" the problem of motive power by replacing a mechanical device or motor with the simplest, most elegant, and most obvious means: the movement of the air itself.

Calder's work includes three kinds of mobiles: those that stand, like *Indian Feathers* (1969); mobiles that are attached to walls, like *Swizzle Sticks* (1936), and—the most numerous—mobiles that hang from the ceiling like *Red, Black, and Blue* (1968). All Calder's mobiles vary hugely in size from those that can be held in the

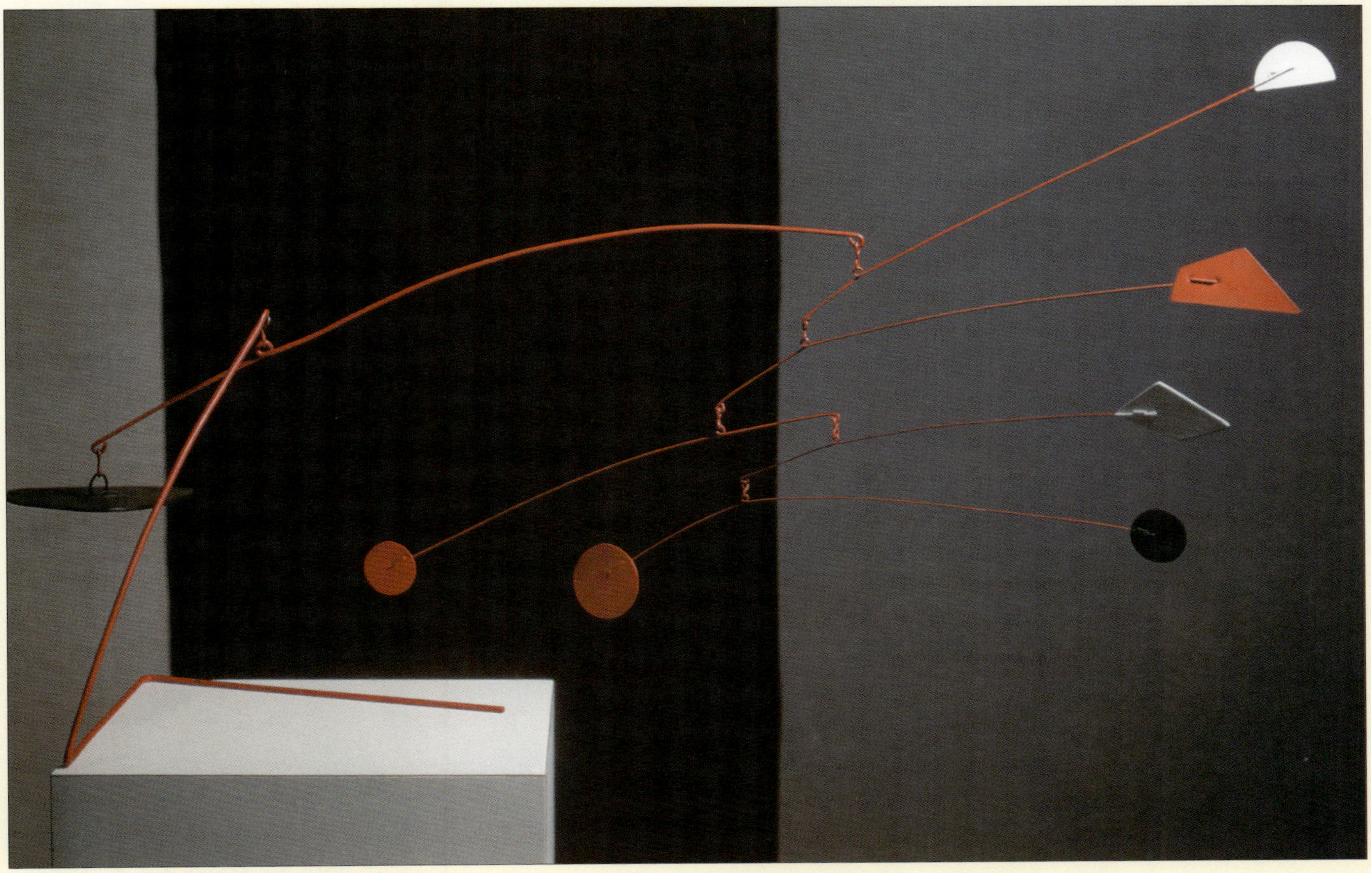

palm of the hand, to works such as *Man* (1967), a stabile (non-moving work) that Calder created for the Expo '67 show in Montreal, which is 94 feet (31 m) high.

The larger the mobile, the slower the movement but, regardless of size, each mobile began life as a scale model made from forms cut from sheet aluminum. The shapes were filed smooth, then arranged on a flat surface with wire between them to establish the overall design. Alterations to shape and size were made to each element, but this time Calder would—with a gadget he invented himself—calculate the center of gravity and the balance of the piece.

With the very large mobiles came engineering problems: Calder had to limit the angles and amount of movement, otherwise the suspended elements would get tangled, or even fly off in high winds. For the large outdoor-sited mobiles, Calder pretested the models in a wind tunnel.

Under the Half Moon *1972. Metal. Pucker Safrai Gallery, Boston, MA.*

in sculpture. In his mobiles of the 1930s, such as *Universe* (1934), different sized spheres painted in primary colors move up and down curved wires at different speeds. Some of Calder's constructions were driven by electric motors, others were "motivated" by hand cranks. Soon Calder was investigating the potential of wind movement to introduce more unpredictable motion.

"Stabiles" was the name invented in 1931 by the sculptor Jean Arp, whom Calder met first in Paris in 1920. Calder seized on the name to describe those works of his that appear to be the complete opposite of his mobiles. The non-moving stabiles frequently convey humorous suggestions of animal shapes: *The Crab* (1962), *Stegosaurus* (1973), and *Flamingo* (1974) retain the organic forms that suggest their animal origins. Almost all the stabiles are painted solid red or black, and although they may weigh several tons, the sense of motion remains: the angles, planes, and curves constantly change as the spectator walks around, through, and under them. The idea of movement was so strong for Calder that in 1973 he began designs for what is possibly the world's biggest mobile—*Flying Colors*—a Braniff International DC-8 passenger jet.

Although primarily considered a sculptor, Calder's work includes paintings and lithographs, book and magazine illustrations, jewelry, toys, and even gadgets that have been described as "whatchama-Calders."

CAMPIN Robert

THE WORK THAT IS NOW ATTRIBUTED TO ROBERT CAMPIN makes him one of the most important and influential figures in early-Netherlandish art. Along with Jan Van Eyck and Rogier Van der Weyden, he guided the direction that art took in northern Europe in the 15th century.

Life and work

Robert Campin is first mentioned as a painter in 1405, when he was working in the town of Tournai. Nothing is known of his place of birth or his artistic training, but it is known that he worked in Tournai for several years until the end of his life. Although he carried out many commissions for the town and for the Church, none of his documented paintings survives intact.

The paintings that are now (and contentiously) thought to be Campin's were, in the past, attributed to several different artists, ranging from Jan Van Eyck to Hans Memling. Campin is also thought to have been the artist formerly called the Master of Flémalle and the Master of Mérode. (The term "Master of…" is used by art historians to label the author of a group of anonymous works in discussing them, and the master is often named after a particular painting or collection.)

The Master of Mérode was so named by an art historian called W. Von Bode in the late 19th century in reference to one particular work: the Mérode altarpiece. The Master of Flémalle received his name at around the same time from another art historian, H. Von Tschudi. "Flémalle" refers to three panel paintings that were (wrongly, as it turned out) thought to have been produced at the Abbey of Flémalle, near the town of Liège in present-day Belgium. These paintings—*The Virgin and Child*, *Saint Veronica*, and *The Trinity* (all undated)—along with the Mérode altarpiece, share similarities of style with the work of two painters of the day, Jacques Daret and Rogier Van der Weyden, though the works are not thought to be by either artist. Later, speculation turned to painters associated with these two painters, and in particular to their teacher, Robert Campin; it has now been assumed that Campin, the Master of Mérode, and the Master of Flémalle are all the same person.

Because of the prosperity of Campin and documentary evidence of his works, we know that he had a large and highly productive workshop. Several apprentices would have worked alongside him, and it is impossible to know how much of the work in any painting would have been undertaken by Campin himself.

Data file

Full name: Robert Campin (also known as Master of Flémalle, Master of Mérode)

Nationality: Netherlandish

Style: early Netherlandish

Dates: active in Tournai 1405–44

Key works:
- *Portrait of a Man* c1420–30
- *Portrait of a Woman* c1420–30
- *The Virgin and Child before a Firescreen* c1425–30
- Mérode altarpiece c1426
- *The Nativity* date unknown

Things to look for:
- clarity throughout the composition from the foreground to details of the world beyond
- orderliness and composure
- varying perspective

Comparisons: Rogier Van der Weyden, Jacques Daret, Jan Van Eyck, Hans Memling, Petrus Christus, Gerard David

Glossary terms: cubism, Netherlandish school, perspective, Renaissance

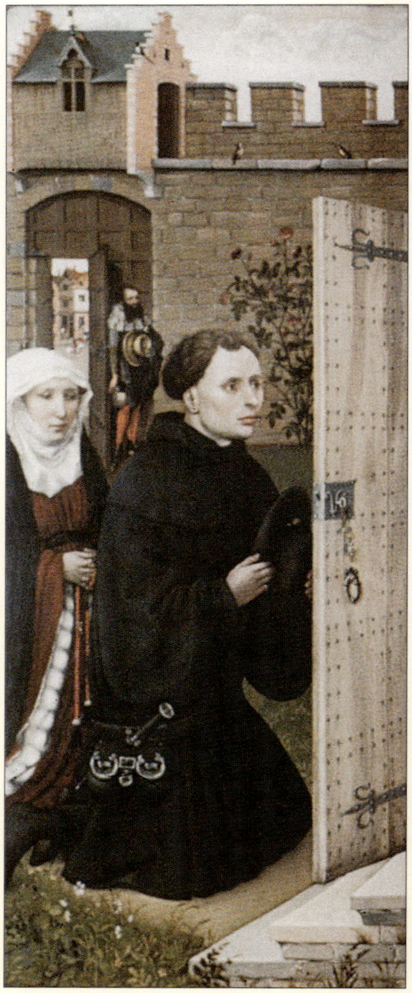

The spiritual and domestic realm

A work such as the Mérode altarpiece (c1426) reflects a particular concern within the Netherlandish school of painting at this time: how to take a biblical theme—in this case the Annunciation—and put it into a domestic setting. Previously, such a painting would have shown an unrealistic world: a mystical landscape, perhaps, or a place abstracted from the natural world. But here the artist has created a very real, homely interior, within which very unreal, or miraculous, events take place. The juxtaposition of the spiritual and domestic worlds would have been striking at the time. It is a device that was also used by Campin in *The Virgin and Child before a Firescreen* (c1425–30) in

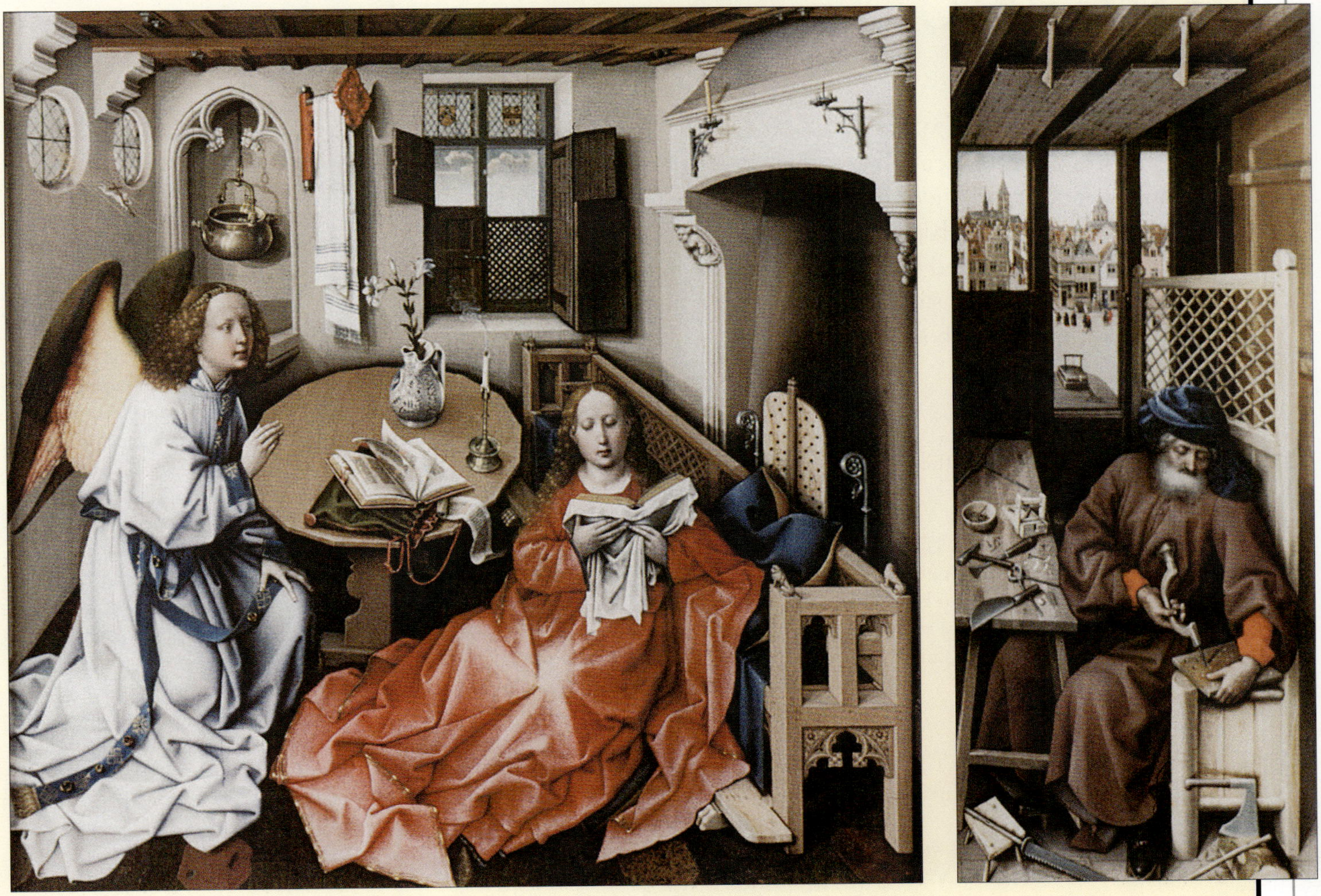

which even the halo behind the Virgin's head is given a domestic equivalent, taking the form of a circular rushwork firescreen.

The central panel of the Mérode altarpiece is its main focus. The Virgin sits reading, at the moment when Archangel Gabriel appears and the Holy Spirit descends toward her on rays of heavenly light, carrying a cross, symbol of Christ's life on earth. The event is, of course, miraculous, but the setting is entirely bound to the everyday world of the 15th-century Netherlands.

The right-hand panel shows Joseph working at his carpentry while the miracle unfolds in another room. As we look through the open window behind him, we see the gabled roofs, church spires, and the open square of a typical Netherlandish town. The image is based on the artist's observation of a local townscape rather than his idea of the Holy Land or spiritual realms.

The left-hand panel shows the donors who presumably paid for the painting, kneeling by a door that appears to open onto the central panel with the Virgin and Archangel. Campin has lavished attention on the different qualities of every surface to achieve a sense of realism. He has used light and dark tones and modulations of color to give the objects a three-dimensional solidity.

Compared to the majority of Western paintings since the Renaissance, however, which we have grown accustomed to seeing as structurally accurate, there is a striking irregularity in the perspective in the Mérode altarpiece. The table in the middle panel and workbench in the right-hand panel appear to slope toward us. We look down upon the tables from above, while at the same time viewing the figures of Mary, Gabriel, and Joseph almost straight on. It is as if the scene has been flattened, or as if the artist is tilting his head in different directions to view the ceiling, the items of furniture, the figures, and the floor.

The Mérode altarpiece *(open) c1426. Oil on panel. Central panel 25 x 24 1/4 in (63.5 x 63 cm). Cloisters, New York, NY.*

During the Renaissance, a stricter form of perspective would be developed, in which works centered on a single viewpoint, and a consistent geometry was used throughout the composition. It was not until cubism and associated movements in the 20th century that art abandoned the compulsive use of the single-point perspective and again worked with multiple viewpoints and a modulating perspective. There is a fascinating affinity, therefore, between what we see in Campin's work and the cubist paintings of Juan Gris, Fernand Léger, Georges Braque, and Pablo Picasso.

CANALETTO

CANALETTO PRODUCED MANY PAINTINGS OF VENICE. His views, conveying the romance of the canals and palaces and depicting important events in the life of the city, were popular with tourists as souvenirs. So many English people bought his paintings that he visited London and painted local landscapes, hoping to make his fortune, but he was not as successful there as he had expected, and he returned to Venice after about 10 years.

Life and work

Canaletto was trained by his father, Bernardo, who was a painter of theatrical scenery. They worked together, visiting Rome around 1720. It was when he returned to his native Venice, however, that Canaletto began to make his name as a painter of views (or *vedute* in Italian) of Venice, and he sold some of these at open-air exhibitions.

His pictures soon attracted attention, and people began to commission him to paint particular views for them. His fame and popularity grew quickly, and he was soon a firm favorite with the many wealthy English aristocrats and businessmen who visited Venice. This was partly due to the support he received from an English merchant named Joseph Smith, who was made British consul in Venice in 1744. Consul Smith bought Canaletto's paintings for himself and he also acted as an agent, arranging many important commissions for him. For example, he arranged that Canaletto should do a series of 24 paintings for the English Duke of Bedford. A steady stream of Englishmen doing the Grand Tour ensured that from the 1730s onward Canaletto had plenty of work. Consul Smith sold his own collection of paintings by Canaletto to the English king, George III, in 1762; the English Royal Collection now contains the finest collection of the artist's works to be found anywhere in the world—50 paintings and 143 drawings.

The outbreak of war in Europe in 1740 meant that fewer tourists came to Venice, and Canaletto decided that his best course of action was to go to England. He arrived in 1746, settled in London and, apart from a couple of short trips home, he stayed for about ten years. In spite of a rumor that it was not the real Canaletto who had come to London, but an impostor, he received a number of important commissions. He produced works showing major London sites and other views of stately homes and important buildings around the country.

By 1755 or 1756 he had returned home to Venice, where he continued to produce views until his death in 1768.

Data file

Full name: Giovanni Antonio Canale (known as Canaletto)

Nationality: Italian

Style: Venetian

Dates: born 1697 in Venice, died 1768 in Venice

Key works:

many views of Venice, including *The Grand Canal: The Stonemason's Yard* c1728, *Venice*, and *The Rialto Bridge from the South* c1729, *A Regatta on the Grand Canal* c1740

works painted while he was in England, including: views of Windsor Castle, Eton College, Whitehall, and Warwick Castle

Things to look for:

- acutely observed scenes
- wide-angle or bird's-eye views
- paintings that evoke the effects of light

Comparisons: Francesco Guardi, Bernardo Bellotto

Glossary terms: camera obscura, Grand Tour, perspective, vanishing point, *vedute*

Grand canal scenes

This view of a regatta on the Grand Canal in Venice is very typical of Canaletto's work. It shows a dramatic long view down the canal—the largest one in Venice. The view carefully uses perspective; the lines of the roofs of the buildings, for example, all converge toward a "vanishing point," which is where the canal turns a corner far in the distance. The picture still has great appeal today because it evokes the feel of Venice; many of the buildings depicted are still standing.

Canaletto sometimes made slight alterations to the views in order to improve the composition of the painting, and some views (such as *The Piazzetta: looking North,* c1727) would have been impossible. However, it was the detailed recreation of Venetian scenes that appealed to tourists, who wanted to take home a reminder of the places they had visited. (Visitors to Venice at this time, centuries before the age of mass tourism, were usually members of the nobility.) Photography as we know it had not been invented, so paintings and drawings were the only means of recording such views.

To achieve his pictures, Canaletto made many drawings, some of which must have been done while he was sitting on a gondola on the canal. It cannot have been easy to make detailed drawings with the everpresent movement of the boat.

Canaletto is also thought to have used a device called a camera obscura, which projected the view onto a piece of paper so that he could trace the outlines of the buildings. The paintings themselves would have been done indoors in his studio; people rarely painted outside in the 18th century.

The Venetians had many special feasts and carnivals, some of them organized in honor of distinguished visitors, throughout the year. The regatta (the word comes from Venetian dialect, meaning a series of boat races) was part of a carnival held between December 26 and the start of Lent, and featured many different types of boat. This view shows a race for one-oared gondolas—the type of boat exclusive to Venice and still used there today.

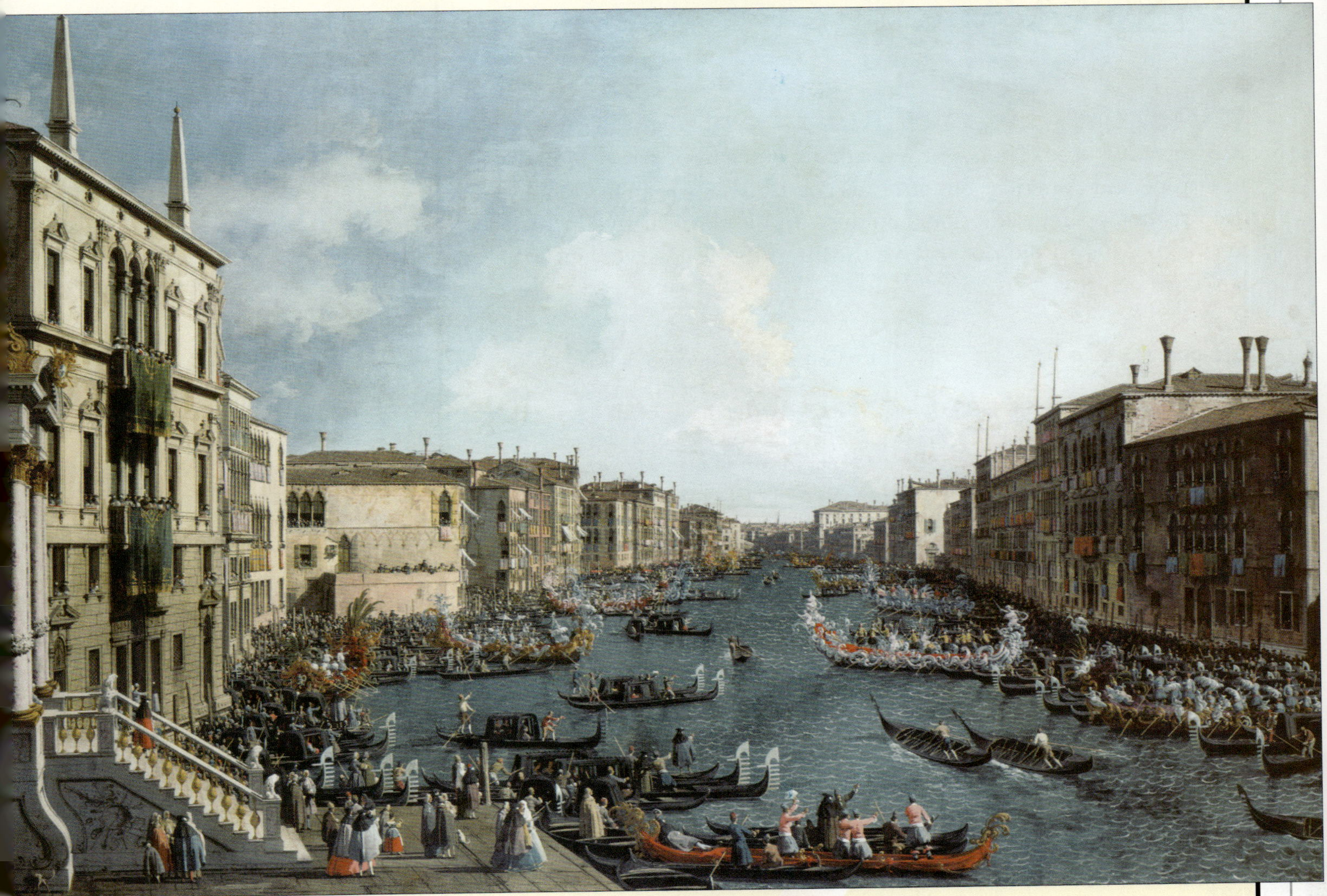

A Regatta on the Grand Canal *c1740. Oil on canvas. 48 x 72 in (122 x 183 cm). National Gallery, London.*

Practically everyone in the painting is watching the race—spectators cheer from every balcony and window, and from all the many different craft along the edges of the Grand Canal. The landing stage on the left (at the front of the picture) was a temporary structure on which one can just see a pavilion (made of painted wood, plaster, and papier-mâché), which was taken down when the regatta was over. It was here that the winners were awarded colored pennants (long flags) as prizes. The picture also shows some people wearing black-and-white masks and cloaks. These were carnival costumes that were not allowed at any other time of year.

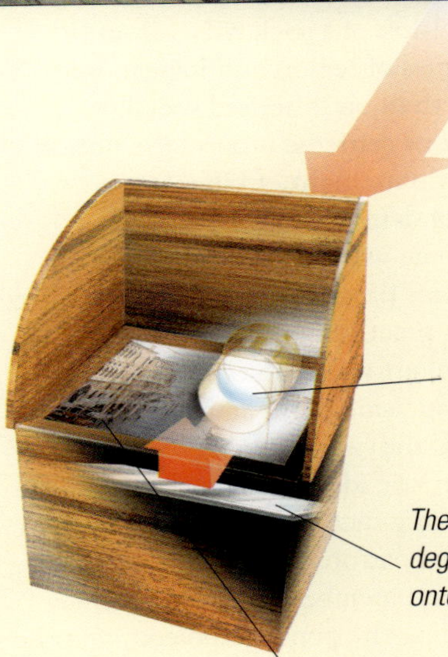

The camera obscura, *which Canaletto is thought to have used, had been in existence from the 16th century and was the forerunner of the modern camera. Photography as we know it today began when ways of fixing the image with chemicals were announced in Paris in 1839. The French painter Paul Delaroche believed that the new process would mean the death of painting.*

CANOVA Antonio

During his lifetime Antonio Canova was the most highly regarded of sculptors, earning commissions from powerful patrons in Europe and America. But after his death there was a reaction against the apparent emotional coldness of his classical style, which meant that his art did not receive the attention it deserved until the late 20th century.

Life and work

Antonio Canova was born in 1757, in the small town of Possagno near the northern edge of the Venetian mainland state. When his father died his mother remarried and left him in the care of his grandfather, a stonecutter and mason. Because he showed indications of having unusual artistic talent, he was apprenticed at the age of 11 to the Venetian sculptor Giuseppe Bernardi, who specialized in decorative sculpture for garden settings. The surviving examples of Canova's work from this period indicate his acceptance of the late baroque and rococo styles that prevailed at the time. His achievements in Venice enabled him to visit Rome in 1779, where he was encouraged by the Venetian ambassador to the Vatican, Girolamo Zulian, who also introduced him to quite different artistic ideas.

A renewed interested in ancient Greek and Roman art and society had blossomed earlier in the century. In addition, archaeological excavations, such as those at Herculaneum and Pompeii, as well as lavish publications featuring engravings of paintings and painted pottery, did much to modify previous perceptions of classical art. To the writers and philosophers of the 18th-century Enlightenment, classical culture offered a historical model for their vision of a society based on the principles of reason and logical order, rather than on inherited social traditions centered around the notion of the divine right of kings to rule without democratic sanction.

Rome was then the international center for progressive theories regarding artistic practice, and this interest in classical art was soon translated into neoclassicism. As an ambitious young artist, Canova was quick to respond to such artistic ideas. His rapid and continuing success meant that he often attracted patrons who were absolute rulers and members of the aristocracy (including the pope, Napoleon, and the Habsburg and Bourbon dynasties). These regimes were at odds with the Enlightenment ideas that underpinned the American and French revolutions;

Full name: Antonio Canova

Nationality: Italian

Style: neoclassicism

Dates: born 1757 in Possagno, died 1822 in Venice

Key works:
- *Daedalus and Icarus* 1779
- *Tomb of Pope Clement XIV* 1783–87
- *The Homeric and Socratic Reliefs* 1787–92
- *Cupid and Pysche* 1787–93
- *Teaching the Ignorant* 1796
- *Perseus* 1797–1801
- *Napoleon* 1809–12
- *The Three Graces* 1815–17

Things to look for:
- idealized forms, but realistic details
- smoothly finished surfaces
- flattened compositions in reliefs and figure groups
- restrained emotional charge

Comparisons: Jacques-Louis David, Gianlorenzo Bernini, Michelangelo Buonarroti, François Boucher, William Blake

Glossary terms: baroque, classical, Enlightenment, neoclassicism

Data file

Art as education and propaganda

In the sculptural relief *Teaching the Ignorant* (1796) Canova moved away from the classical subjects—such as the scenes from Homer or the life of Socrates—that had dominated his work between 1787 and 1792. *Teaching the Ignorant* represents a transition from these classical works, with their emphasis on moral stories, and from the Enlightenment, the 18th-century philosophical movement that stressed the importance of reason and, therefore, education for all.

In terms of style, Canova was also turning away from baroque principles, such as relief sculpture building an illusion of deep pictorial space (a technique borrowed from painting). The narrow flatness within which the figures are arranged, against a plain, abstract ground, reflects the way in which artists at this time often drew from antique painted pottery and classical reliefs. In this piece, Canova has conveyed details of gesture and posture realistically, but each element works within a careful pattern of counterbalancing forms. Neoclassical painters like the French artist Jacques-Louis David were similarly simplifying their compositions in order to dramatize the narrative within their work.

David and Canova were regarded by contemporary critics as being the foremost artists working in the new neoclassical style, and both attracted the attention of Napoleon, the self-styled "Man of Destiny" and conqueror of numerous territories who commissioned artists to propagate his image. In 1802 Canova was invited to Paris to make a larger-than-life-sized statue of Napoleon as Mars (two versions exist: a marble one in London, and another in bronze in Milan).

The conversations that Canova appears to have had with Napoleon raise interesting questions as to how a modern ruler might or ought to be portrayed. Napoleon was soon to present himself as a modern emperor, and, although he was self-made, also encouraged his portrayal as a demigod guided by divine forces. Napoleon's French monarchical

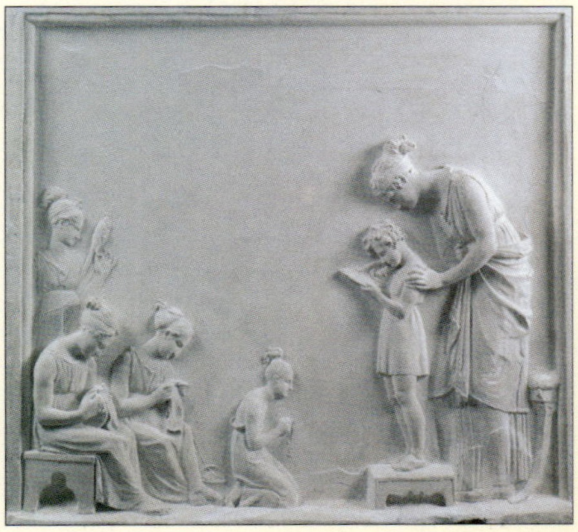

Teaching the Ignorant *1796. Plaster. 46 x 50 in (117 x 127 cm). Museo Correr e Quadreria, Venice.*

predecessors, such as Louis XIV, had worn elaborate robes which were in themselves emblems evocative of divine rulership. For Canova, however, classical sculptural tradition outweighed Napoleon's desire to be represented wearing clothes. The result combines a partially idealized head of Napoleon on the wholly idealized body of a Roman god as conceived by an early 19th-century artist. By the time it was finished in 1812, however, Napoleon's fortunes had waned in the Peninsular War and the Russian campaign; his armies were later defeated at Leipzig (1813). This meant that the statue could never be used for the propaganda purposes for which it was originally intended.

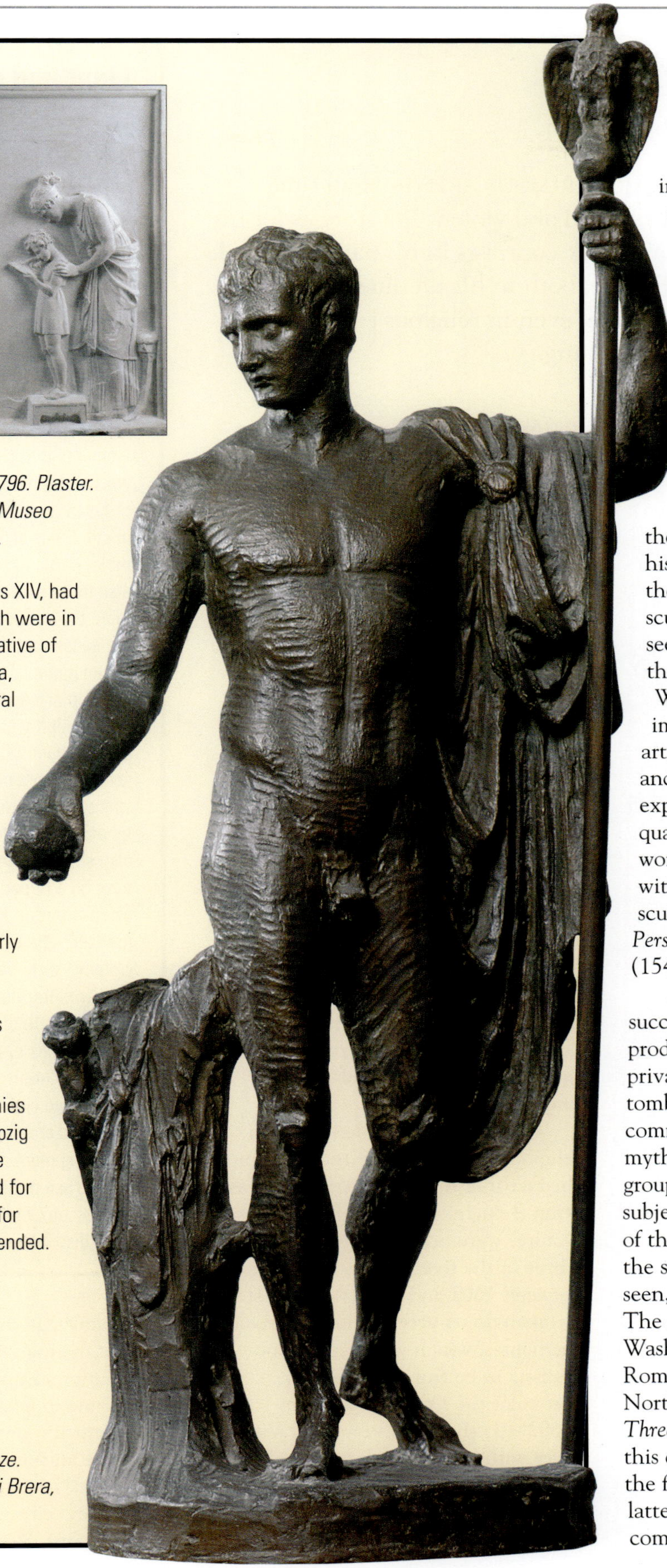

Napoleon *1809–12. Bronze. 128 in (325 cm). Palazzo di Brera, Milan.*

in effect, Canova's art was often used to help bolster their status. That Canova worked for rival European powers during a period of extraordinary political upheaval is a testament to the high value placed upon his powers as an artist.

A major commission, the *Tomb of Pope Clement XIV* (1783–87), received immediate acclaim, while *Perseus* (1797–1801) established him as the leading neoclassical sculptor of his time, drawing comparisons with the greatest of the ancient Greek sculptors. His later work in particular seemed to embody some of the theories of Johann Joachim Winckelmann, one of the most important neoclassical writers on art, who wrote that "noble simplicity and sedate grandeur in gesture and expression" were the ultimate qualities of Greek sculpture. Canova's work was also favorably compared with the famous High Renaissance sculpture by Benvenuto Cellini, *Perseus Holding the Head of Medusa* (1545–54).

As the master of a large and successful *bottega* (workshop), Canova produced a prolific body of public and privately commissioned work: more tombs and civic monuments; commemorative portrait statues; mythological and religious figures and groups; and several series of classical subjects in shallow relief. The character of these sculptures varied according to the situation in which they were to be seen, that is, in public or in private. The now destroyed figure of George Washington wearing the costume of a Roman general, for the state senate of North Carolina (1817–18), and *The Three Graces* (1815–17) are typical of this diversity. The austere seriousness of the former and the sensuousness of the latter are equally representative of the complex historical period.

CARAVAGGIO

CARAVAGGIO IS ONE OF THE MOST FAMOUS ARTISTS of all time, known almost as well for his wild and violent life story as for his art. His dramatic use of light and dark contrasts in his paintings made him well known throughout Europe, both in his lifetime and long after his death. His naturalistic style, even in religious paintings, makes his work all the more compelling.

Life and work

Born in northern Italy, Caravaggio (who was named after his home town) was influenced by different styles of painting, from Titian and other artists of the Venetian school, with their evocative use of color and light, to Leonardo da Vinci, who used *sfumato* (gradations of tone and softened lines) to suggest three-dimensional figures.

Caravaggio traveled to Rome in 1592, and had several patrons in his early years there, the most important being the del Monte family. From 1595 to 1598 Caravaggio painted still lifes and undramatic subjects such as *Young Bacchus* (c1595), but his subject matter was to shift quite dramatically during his career.

It was probably through the influence of the del Montes that Caravaggio received his first public commissions for a church in Rome. Scenes from the life of Saint Matthew (1599–1602) were made for the Contarelli Chapel, followed by *The Crucifixion of Saint Peter* (1601) and *The Conversion of Saint Paul* (1601) for Santa Maria del Popolo, Rome. These works were vital to Caravaggio's career, establishing him as one of the leading religious painters of his time, alongside the more traditionally classical artist Annibale Carracci. They also contained the fundamental elements of his mature style: a strongly contrasting use of light and dark (known as chiaroscuro), realistic figures drawn from models, and dramatic compositions.

Caravaggio continued painting religious works into the 1600s, despite the fact that his naturalistic style was often thought so shocking that the pictures were not actually displayed. Three of the five altarpieces he painted between 1602 and 1605 were rejected or taken down very quickly because of the figures, which were seen as too realistic to be truly religious. In particular the *Death of the Virgin* (1602–03) showed a very plain Virgin Mary with bloated body and swollen feet. This caused a great deal of controversy, because Mary was usually depicted as an idealized woman.

Caravaggio had a quick temper and violent manner, and in May 1606 he killed another man after a quarrel. He fled Rome in fear of the death penalty, and spent the next few years on the run from the authorities.

In 1607 he arrived in Naples, where he continued to paint commissions. He then traveled to

Data file

Full name: Michelangelo Merisi da Caravaggio

Nationality: Italian

Style: chiaroscuro (light-dark)

Dates: born 1571 in Caravaggio, died 1610 in Porto Ercole

Key works:
- scenes from the life of Saint Matthew 1599–1602
- *Supper at Emmaus* 1601
- *The Crucifixion of Saint Peter* 1601
- *The Conversion of Saint Paul* 1601
- *The Beheading of Saint John the Baptist* 1608
- *David with the Head of Goliath* 1610

Things to look for:
- still lifes as early works
- striking use of light contrasted with dark shadows
- religious paintings with theatrical compositions, movement, and drama
- realistic figures, often with tattered clothes and dirty hands and feet

Comparisons: Annibale Carracci, Leonardo da Vinci, Titian

Glossary terms: altarpiece, chiaroscuro, classicism, foreshortening, naturalism, realism, *sfumato*, still life

Light and shadow

Caravaggio's painting *Supper at Emmaus* (1601) depicts a scene inside a roadside inn. The two disciples (the men seated on the left and right of the picture) have just recognized their mysterious companion as the risen Christ, as he stretches his arm out in a gesture of blessing. An innkeeper looks on as the disciples express their amazement with dramatic gestures. The episode is taken from the Bible text, Luke 24: 13–31.

This painting contains many of the elements that characterize Caravaggio's work as he moved from his earlier still lifes to his later religious subjects. His interest in still life is shown by the objects on the table, particularly the bowl of fruit, which also looks as if it might topple from the table top at any moment. This heightens the sense that the artist has captured a frozen moment, just before the disciples jump up and the basket falls.

The elbow of the disciple closest to us, and the hand of the disciple on Christ's left seem to reach out of the picture into our space: these are examples of Caravaggio's theatrical use of foreshortening. We can also see that the elbow is poking out through a ripped sleeve. Caravaggio was often criticized for making his figures too realistic—he often pictured them with torn clothing, dirty fingernails, or dusty feet—as it was felt that this took away from the sacred nature of the subjects.

The faces of the disciples and the innkeeper are rough and unidealized; Caravaggio copied the faces of ordinary people to create his characters, rather than inventing more striking figures.

The use of light and shadow, or chiaroscuro, in this painting is perhaps the most distinctive feature of Caravaggio's

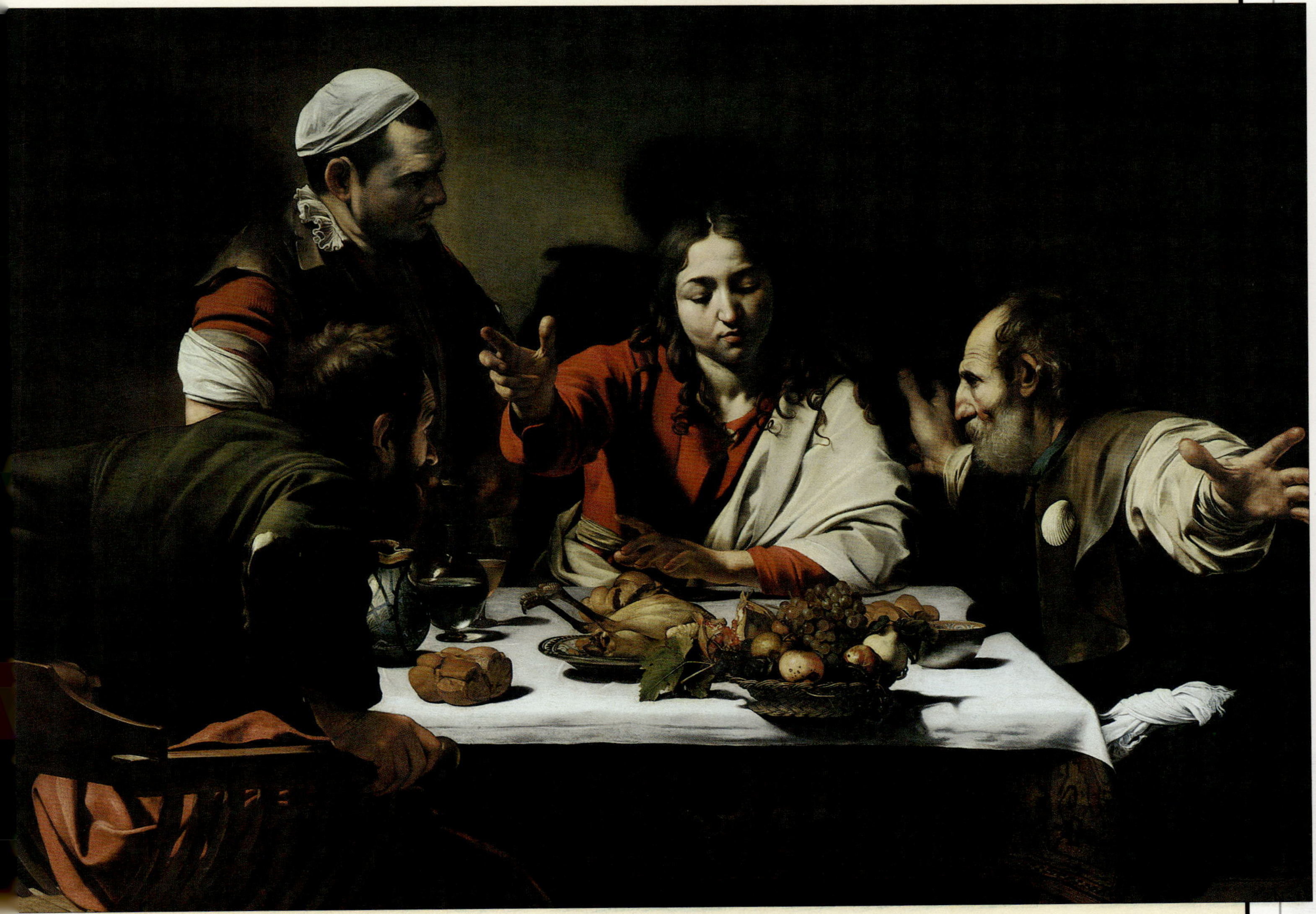

style. His works are often lit from the top left-hand side, as if the light is coming from an outside window. This creates areas of deep shade that make the figures seem more three-dimensional. It also casts a slant of light across the plain background, which makes the composition more interesting. In this painting the light also provides shadows shaped like a halo and an angel's wing behind the seated figure of Christ.

We are persuaded to see the scene as naturalistic, but in reality the innkeeper would block the shaft of light, putting Christ's face in shadow. Caravaggio emphasizes Christ's divine nature by having the light shine directly onto his face.

Supper at Emmaus *1601. Oil on canvas. 55 x 77 in (141 x 196 cm). National Gallery, London.*

Malta, where he was commissioned by the grand master of the knights of Jerusalem to paint *The Beheading of Saint John the Baptist* (1608), a dramatic work in which the brutal death of Saint John contrasts with the motionless onlookers, presenting a vivid and terrifying life-size vision of the realities of martyrdom.

Caravaggio was made a Knight of Saint John, in Malta, but later quarreled with a senior knight and was imprisoned. He escaped and fled first to Sicily and then to Naples. In a tavern there, he got wounded in a fight.

In 1610 a pardon was obtained for him in Rome, and he sailed north with some of his works of this period, including *David with the Head of Goliath* (1610), in which the biblical giant's severed head has Caravaggio's own features. Unfortunately, Caravaggio was mistakenly arrested at Porto Ercole, and the ship sailed on without him. He was soon released, but by then he had fallen ill with a fever. He died in Porto Ercole a few days later.

CARPACCIO Vittore

CARPACCIO LIVED AND WORKED IN VENICE, where he was known particularly for his paintings of the lives of saints—scenes that were full of imaginary stories and detail. Often set in his own time, his paintings tell us much about everyday life in Venice around 1500.

Life and work

Very little is known about Vittore Carpaccio's life. It is thought that he may have traveled to Dalmatia and the Near East as a young man and that he may have been trained by the Venetian artist Gentile Bellini. Whether or not this is true, he was certainly influenced by Gentile's work. It is known that in 1507 he was an assistant to Giovanni Bellini, the most famous member of the Bellini family of painters. Although we do not know the year of Carpaccio's birth, we do know when many of his paintings were made because he often placed a *cartellino* (painted card) on his pictures on which he put the date. These looked like folded paper or card attached to something in the picture.

Carpaccio's most famous works are a series or cycle of paintings now in L'Accademia di Belle Arti (The Academy of Fine Arts) in Venice. These paintings show scenes from the life of Saint Ursula, and were made in the 1490s for La Scuola di San Orsola, in Venice. They are typical of Carpaccio's style, for although Saint Ursula is said to have lived in the 5th century, Carpaccio paints her as if she were living in the late 15th century, showing the detail of his own time.

By about 1451 many people from Dalmatia (a region of eastern Europe that had been ruled by Venice since 1420) had arrived in Venice. These people spoke a Slavonic language, so were known as Slavs. Because so many Dalmatian Slavs had settled in Venice, the Venetian authorities allowed them to build their own *scuola*—La Scuola di San Giorgio degli Schiavone (The School of Saint George of the Slavs). These *scuole* (Italian for "schools"), were not schools in the modern sense at all. They were more like societies—fraternities or brotherhoods—for groups of people with similar professions and interests.

In the first 10 years of the 1500s Carpaccio was hired to paint pictures showing stories of the Dalmatian Slavs' patron saints. These were placed high up, rather like a frieze, around the walls of the main room of the *scuola*. There are nine paintings on canvas, all of which still occupy their original position. Two of them are pictured: *Saint George and the Dragon* and *Saint Jerome Leading the Tame Lion into the Monastery* (1502–07).

In addition to these series of works, Carpaccio also painted some striking individual portraits.

Data file

Full name: Vittore Carpaccio
Nationality: Italian
Style: Renaissance
Dates: active 1490 in Venice, died 1525/26 in Venice
Key works:
- scenes from the life of Saint Ursula 1490s
- scenes from the lives of Saint George and Saint Jerome 1502–07

Things to look for:
- attention to storytelling
- attention to detail
- vibrant colors

Comparisons: Gentile and Giovanni Bellini, Antonello da Messina
Glossary terms: *cartellino*, cycle, patron saint, Renaissance, *scuola*

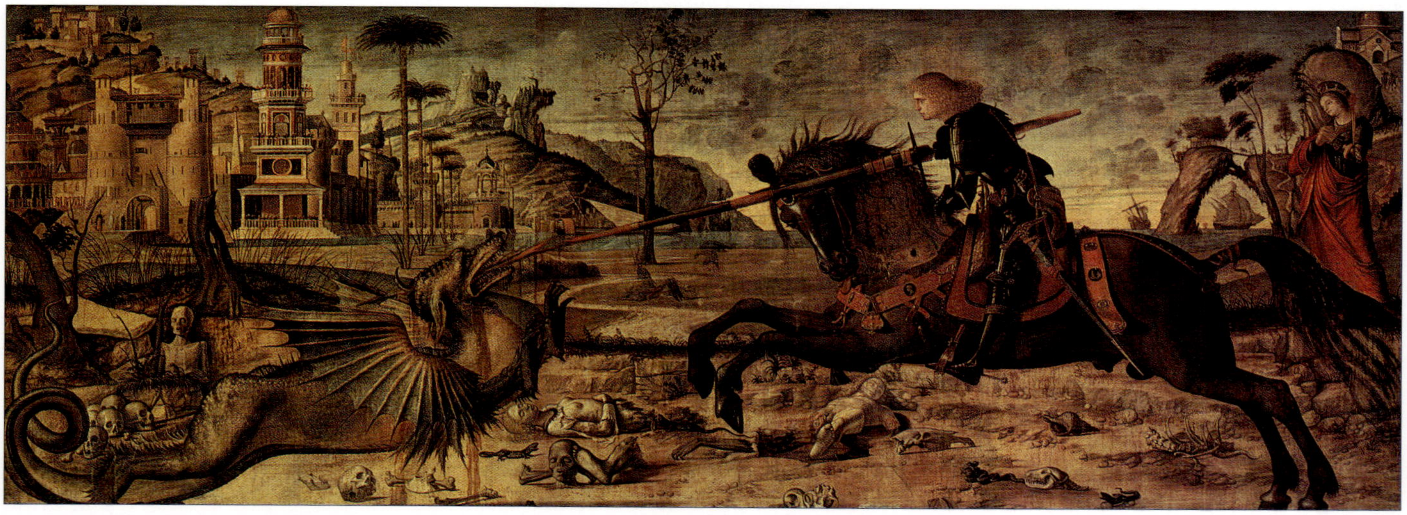

Saint George and the Dragon *1502–07. 55 1/2 x 142 in (141 x 360 cm). La Scuola di San Giorgio degli Schiavoni, Venice.*

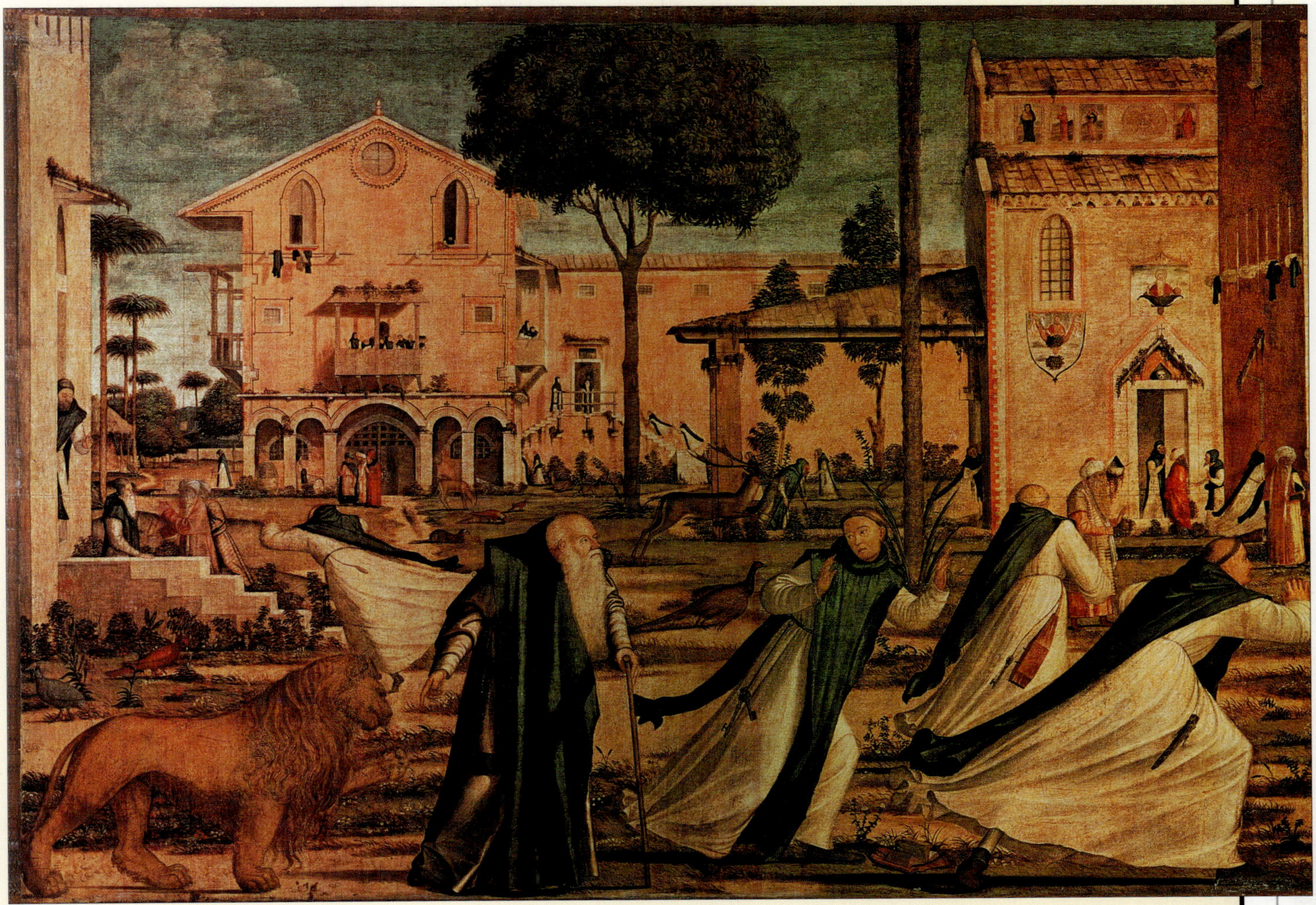

Observation and detail

In spite of the fact that he was influenced by other artists of his day who were more famous than he was, Carpaccio developed a very distinctive style—one that did not change much throughout his working life. Although his painting lacks the realism of some of his contemporaries' work, his style is distinguished by his narrative skill and use of vibrant color.

This painting of *Saint Jerome Leading the Tame Lion into the Monastery* is fairly typical of Carpaccio's style. The story that provides the inspiration for the picture is a delightful one. According to legend, Saint Jerome spent four years on his own in the desert. While he was there he met a lion and removed a thorn that was stuck in its paw. From then on the lion became his devoted friend. When Saint Jerome is shown in a painting he is nearly always accompanied by a lion.

Here Carpaccio has imagined what would have happened if the lion had gone home to the monastery with Saint Jerome. Notice all the details—weeds growing on the ledges, washing hanging out, wall paintings decorating the church. Some of the monks have panicked at the lion's arrival and are running away; others have not yet seen it and are going about their usual business. The deer taking flight in the middle of the picture looks as if it was an afterthought— it appears almost transparent, with the background beneath showing through. This is because oil paint becomes more transparent as it gets older.

Carpaccio enjoyed producing large panoramic paintings featuring many figures. His compositions can seem very busy, with lots of of people (often wearing striking clothes, hats, and jewelry), and all sorts of animals and birds, domestic and exotic. Although this painting is on a slightly smaller scale, it is still full of minutely observed details. Carpaccio tended to paint the world he knew, therefore we find saints who lived long before his time set in the domestic interiors of his own day and dressed in the sorts of clothes that would have been worn at the time. As Venice was a very important port for trade with eastern Europe and the Far East, it is likely that he would have seen many visiting merchants from other lands wearing exotic clothes, such as the long robes and turbans that some people in this painting are wearing.

Saint Jerome Leading the Tame Lion into the Monastery *1502–07. 55 1/2 x 83 in (141 x 211 cm). La Scuola di San Giorgio degli Schiavoni, Venice.*

CARRACCI Annibale

ANNIBALE CARRACCI CREATED BEAUTIFUL AND CHALLENGING paintings and frescos. His natural and observant eye for detail was coupled with a love of classical grandeur and ideal proportions. He, his brother Agostino, and their cousin Ludovico were the leading artists in Bologna, Italy, at the end of the 16th century.

Life and work

Annibale Carracci was born in Bologna in 1560. His cousin, Ludovico, was his first teacher. Early biographers record that Ludovico sent the young man on a trip around Italy to learn about painting in Lombardy and in Venice. Annibale's early style reflects the work of Leonardo da Vinci, as well as the loose, vigorous brushwork of Venetian painters such as Titian and Paolo Veronese, and the acute observation and naturalism of the Lombardy painters (painters in the north of present-day Italy, known for their fresh approach to painting and color).

In 1583, the Carracci, as the brothers Annibale and Agostino and their cousin Ludovico were collectively known, founded a private teaching academy. The academy became known for its rejection of the artificial style of mannerism that was still prevalent in Italy at the time. When Annibale applied his fresh, natural vision and technique to traditional religious subjects instead of to genre (or everyday) scenes, he encountered some criticism, but his ability was such that commissions still came his way.

In 1595 Annibale was called to Rome by a very powerful patron, Cardinal Odoardo Farnese, who wanted Annibale to decorate his study, or *camerino*, and the gallery in the Farnese family palace. It was in decorating the study that Annibale began to refer to the work of the ancient Romans, modeling some of the figures in his frescos on classical statues, while also using the bright, fresh coloring he had learned from northern Italian painters.

The decoration of the ceiling of the gallery, in fresco, was Annibale's great masterpiece. The subjects were all taken from classical mythology and concentrated on the power of love. The commission provided the perfect opportunity for Annibale to show his interest in classical figures and proportions, while also maintaining the naturalism and freshness of his early style. The fusion of these two kinds of painting—the old and the new—in such an exuberant way was seen as revolutionary both then and by future generations of artists. Annibale worked on the Farnese Gallery ceiling for about four years, from 1597 to 1601, while also doing easel-painting commissions for religious works.

In 1601 Annibale was asked to produce *The Assumption of the Virgin* for a church in Rome. The two paintings either side of his central altarpiece were made by his rival, Michelangelo Merisi da Caravaggio, who portrayed his

Data file

Full name: Annibale Carracci

Nationality: Italian

Style: naturalism and classicism

Dates: born 1560 in Bologna, died 1609 in Rome

Key works:

The Butcher's Shop 1582–83

Pietà with Saints Francis and Claire 1585

The Resurrection 1593

Farnese Gallery ceiling 1597–1601

The Assumption of the Virgin 1601

"Domine, Quo Vadis?" 1601–02

The Flight into Egypt c1603–04

Things to look for:

- early natural and vigorous style
- later paintings/frescos focusing on the ideal human forms and classical proportions
- an interest in the landscape backgrounds of his paintings, where he creates an evocative mood

Comparisons: Michelangelo Merisi da Caravaggio, Raphael, Titian, Paolo Veronese

Glossary terms: baroque, classicism, fresco, genre painting, mannerism

Realism, dynamism, and idealism

The early works of Annibale Carracci display an original approach to subject matter and free and natural brushwork, as in the genre painting, *The Butcher's Shop* (1582–83). This was in keeping with the emphasis that the Carracci placed (both in their teaching and in their own work) on direct observation and impressions. By the 1590s, Annibale had adopted a more classical approach, which means that his figures became more idealized than in his previous, more naturalistic works. However, Annibale's style remains a mixture of the realism of the Lombard painters, of the dynamism of the early baroque, and of Raphaelesque perfection.

The painting *"Domine, Quo Vadis?"* (1601–02) was probably commissioned by Pope Clement VIII for his nephew. It shows Christ meeting Peter on the Appian Way, outside Rome. Peter is fleeing Rome to escape persecution. On his way along the road he meets Christ, who has already died and been resurrected. He asks, "Lord, where are you going?" (which is the translation of the Latin title of the painting), and Jesus replies that—since Peter is running away—he, Christ, is going to Rome be tortured in his place. When he learns this, Peter turns back to Rome and dies for his faith. The picture records a moment of great importance, therefore, where life and death, faith and courage are put to the test.

Annibale Carracci's composition narrates the story for us. As Peter shrinks back in surprise and fear, Christ indicates Rome with both his outstretched arm and the direction of his step. The road leads us back into the distance, but the figure of Christ urges us onward. We are included in the momentous decision by the fact that, as viewers, we seem to be traveling down the road away from Rome. The base of the wooden cross also reaches into "our" space, while the top silhouettes itself against the blue sky. Its position echoes the tension between the two directions already set up in the composition.

The figure of Christ embodies past suffering, shown by the nail marks in his feet, the spear wound in his side, and the crown of thorns that he wears. He also reminds us of his resurrection by appearing here to Peter, and the trickle of fresh blood at the side of his face shows his renewed suffering and his willingness to undergo further persecution for his people. Christ's body also shows us the fusion of the ideal human form, modeled on the proportions of classical sculpture, and the naturalism of the muscles and the dynamic pose.

In this painting, Christ is at the same time the divine ideal and the real man. He is real enough to cast shadows on the ground, and for his muscles to show the effort of walking and carrying a heavy load, but his features display the idealized expression of a divine martyr.

The Venetian influence on Annibale's work is apparent in Christ's flowing crimson robe, and in the landscape, where light plays over trees and hills. Venetian painters had been the main influence on Annibale's style for almost a decade; some of his work in this period has also been described as early baroque.

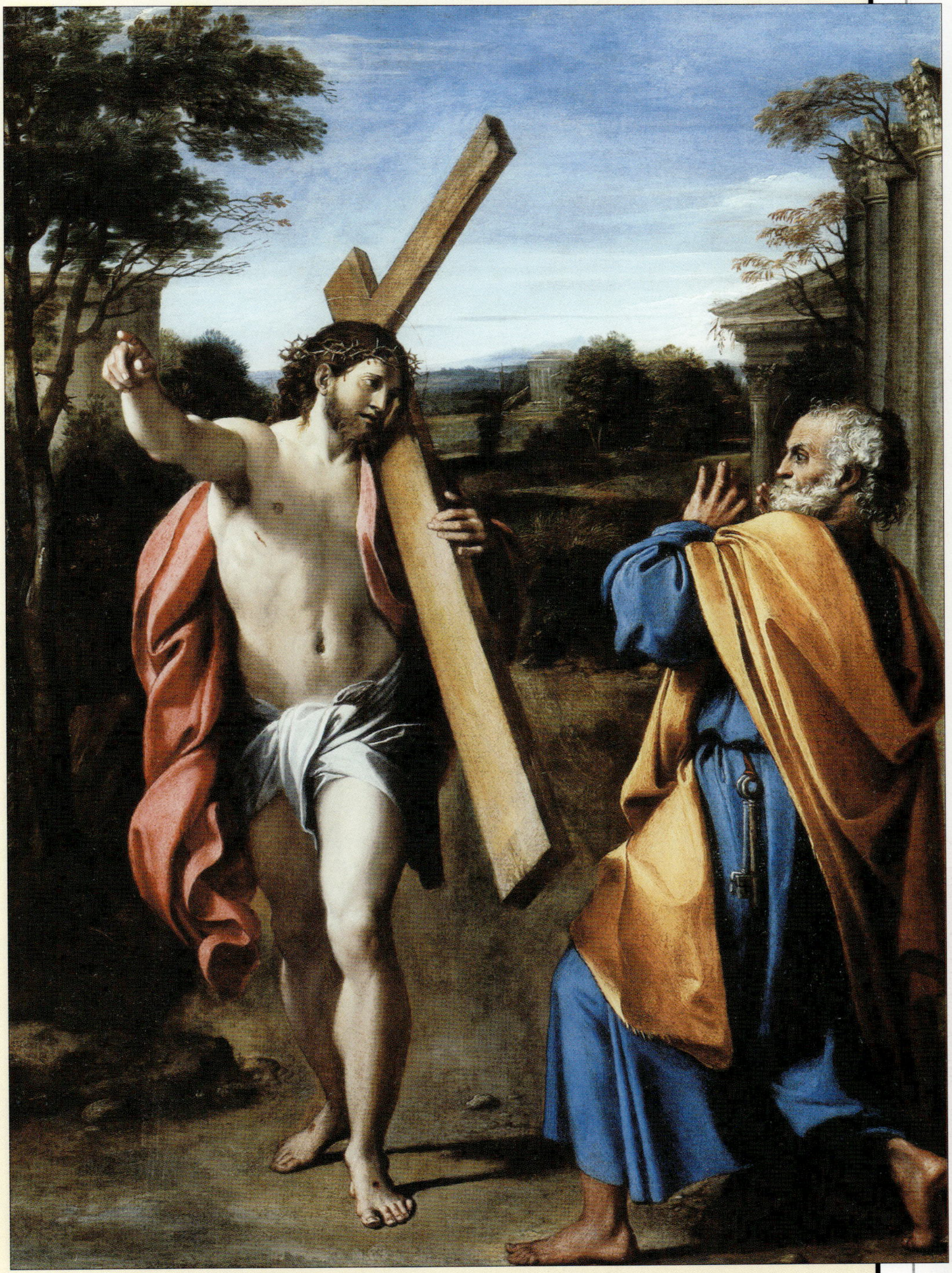

"Domine, Quo Vadis?" *1601–02. Oil on panel. 30½ x 22 in (77.5 x 56 cm). National Gallery, London.*

subjects in a totally unidealized way. Annibale painted in a more traditional style. His blend of the ideal with the true-to-nature style of the Lombard painters is now sometimes called hyper-idealism. He continued to paint in this way, turning more and more to the baroque concept of creating emotional responses in the viewer by depicting figures displaying those emotions.

The Farnese commissions continued, but in 1605 Annibale became offended by the small sums of money offered him, and retired from the cardinal's service. He became increasingly depressed and ill, and completed fewer commissions. He did, however, produce *The Flight into Egypt* (c1603–04) seen now as the perfect example of an ideal landscape, with its harmonies of nature, architecture, and the human figure. He died in Rome in 1609, and was buried in the Pantheon next to the tomb of Raphael.

CASSATT Mary

A PIONEERING AMERICAN PAINTER AND GRAPHIC ARTIST, Mary Cassatt forged her unique reputation far from her native land. She worked mainly in Paris, where she became a leading member of the impressionist circle.

Life and work

Mary Cassatt came from a cultured and prosperous background. Her father was a stockbroker, and while Mary was still a child, the family traveled extensively in Europe. This included a four-year stay in Paris in the 1850s. During this time, Mary learned French and German, and had the opportunity to visit many different galleries. These stimulated her interest in art and, on her return to the United States, she decided to enroll at the Pennsylvania Academy of Fine Arts.

Mary's family had been happy enough to encourage her interest in art, but were horrified when she announced her intention of becoming a professional artist. They had assumed that, like most women of her class, she would settle down to married life. Nevertheless, she was very determined, and in 1866 she returned to Paris to complete her training. There she studied under a minor painter named Charles Chaplin; she made enough progress to have a painting accepted by the Salon (a prestigious but conventional exhibiting body) in 1868.

In 1870, France went to war with Germany, and Cassatt had to leave Europe. She returned two years later, however, touring through Italy, Spain, and Belgium before settling once more in Paris in 1874. The first impressionist exhibition was held in the same year; this was a style of painting that had begun to fascinate Cassatt.

In 1877 Cassatt gained her introduction to the impressionists' circle through Edgar Degas, who admired one of her paintings in a gallery and invited her to join them. Cassatt was delighted. "I accepted with joy," she confided to a friend. "Finally, I would be able to work with absolute independence.... I rejected conventional art. I began to live...."

Cassatt soon became one of the most loyal members of the group, contributing pictures to four of their eight shows from 1879 to 1886. She became particularly close to Degas, forging a friendship that would last until his death in 1917. Under his guidance she developed a more impressionistic technique, adopting unusual viewpoints and cropping the edges of her pictures to give them the informal air of a snapshot.

In common with other impressionist artists, Cassatt wanted to paint scenes of modern Parisian life. She was limited, however, by her sex and her respectable background: it was impossible for her to frequent the bars, dance-halls, and brothels that featured in the work of her male associates.

Data file

Full name: Mary Stevenson Cassatt

Nationality: American

Style: impressionism

Dates: born 1844 in Pittsburgh, PA, died 1926 in Beaufresne, France

Key works:

- *Little Girl in a Blue Armchair* 1878
- *At the Opera* 1879
- *Young Woman Sewing in the Garden* 1884–86
- *Set of Ten* (series of colored engravings, including *In the Omnibus*) 1890–91
- *The Bath* 1891–92
- *The Boating Party* 1894

Things to look for:

- intimate domestic scenes
- influence of Japanese prints
- pictures of children
- images of modern female life

Comparisons: Berthe Morisot, Edgar Degas, Pierre Auguste Renoir

Glossary terms: aquatint, drypoint, impressionism, perspective, Salon

A Japanese vision

Cassatt produced her finest work in the graphic arts, where her prints rank alongside those of Edgar Degas. Here, her chief influence came from Japanese woodblock prints, which created a huge impact in the West in the late 19th century. All the impressionists admired them because they had a freshness that was lacking in Western engravings. They displayed a lively approach to composition, with a greater emphasis on decoration than on accurate perspective, and their colors were bright and pure.

Cassatt had learned about printmaking while studying in Europe, but she did not exhibit any work in this field until 1880, when a version of *At the Opera* (1879) was included in the fifth impressionist show.

Her style was transformed after May 1890, when she witnessed an exhibition of Japanese *ukiyo-e* ("floating world") prints in Paris. Drawing inspiration from these, she produced the so-called *Set of Ten* (1890–91), a series of colored drypoint engravings. Stylistically, the series has a very Japanese flavor. Cassatt concentrated on creating an air of spontaneity, at the expense of laborious detail, and made use of simple, bold color schemes.

The printmaking process was a lengthy one. First, the artist made a preliminary drawing in crayon. She then made a transfer copy of the design onto a softground base (a metal plate covered with wax), adding the fine detail with a sharp needle.

Drypoint engraving is a sensitive medium, as the blackness of the lines on the completed image is determined by the pressure of the artist's hand. Cassatt realized this, but believed that the discipline improved her technical skills. "That is what teaches me to draw," she commented. "In drypoint, you are down to the bare bones, you can't cheat."

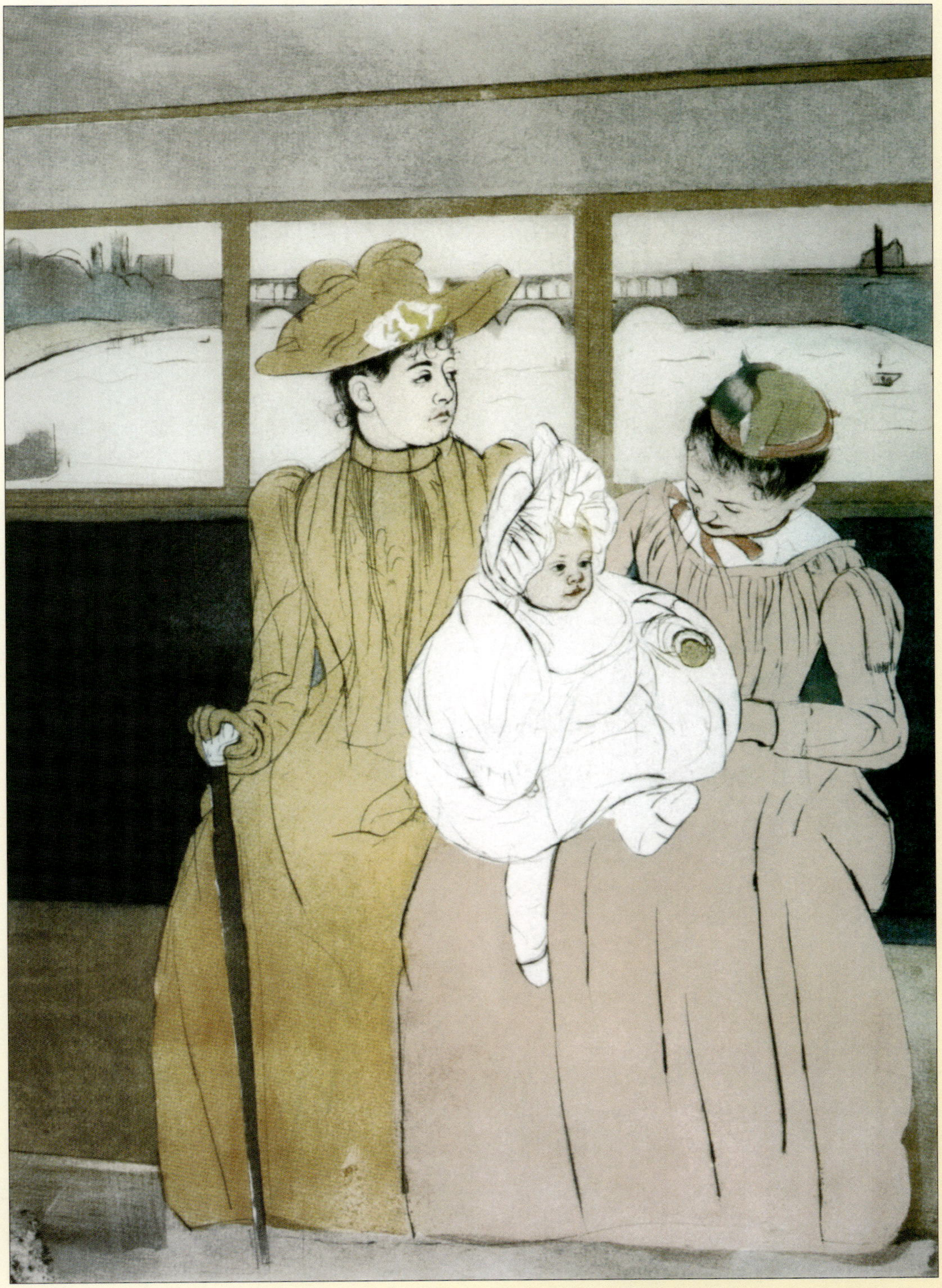

In the Omnibus *(from the* Set of Ten *series) 1890–91. Colored engraving. 14 1/4 x 10 1/2 in (36 x 27 cm). Private collection.*

Undaunted, Cassatt produced vivid portrayals of women of her own class: with their children, visiting the theater, playing music, or traveling on a bus.

Belatedly, Cassatt began to win recognition in her own country. In 1893 she was commissioned to paint a 50-foot mural on the subject of *Modern Women* for the Women's Pavilion at the Chicago World's Fair. While in the United States she also did much to promote the impressionists' cause, persuading her wealthy friends to buy their pictures.

Cassatt's later work was marred by her failing eyesight. She eventually retired to the Château de Beaufresne, in southern France, where she died.

CATLIN George

GEORGE CATLIN WAS AN ARTIST AND ETHNOGRAPHER who devoted his life to portraying Native Americans. His landscapes captured a land that was yet to be fully explored, while his portraits and his paintings of ceremonies and hunting scenes recorded the culture of a people that was in danger of extinction as white settlers advanced westward through America.

Life and work

George Catlin was born on a farm on the banks of the Susquehanna River in Pennsylvania. His mother was from a family of settlers in the Wyoming Valley; at the age of seven she had been captured and held hostage (though later released) during the "Wyoming Massacre" of 1778. George was the fifth of her 14 children.

In 1819 Catlin began practicing law. However, by 1821 he had a reputation as an accomplished amateur portrait painter. In 1823 he moved to Philadelphia to paint and was elected to the Philadelphia Academy of Art. Catlin might have remained a society portraitist had it not been for a delegation of Native American chieftains that arrived that year in Philadelphia en route to Washington D.C. The sight of them in their ceremonial robes rekindled a boyhood interest in that culture (no doubt fed by his mother's stories of Wyoming). He decided to record Native American life.

In 1824 Catlin went to Albany, New York, where, unable to finance an expedition west, he continued to paint portraits. But he made numerous trips to nearby reservations of the Senecas, Oneidas, and Tuscaroras, as well as of the Ottowas and Mohegans.

In 1830, with his wife, Clara, safely settled in Albany, Catlin set off for Saint Louis, the gateway to the West. He was received by General William Clark, who commissioned a portrait. In July Catlin accompanied Clark to Prairie du Chien and Fort Crawford on the upper Missouri River to attend a treaty council with the Ioways, Missouris, Sioux, and Omahas. In the fall, he was in northeast Kansas, painting the Ioway chief Notch-e-ming-a, also known as White Cloud.

Between 1832 and 1837, traveling by foot, on horseback, and by boat, Catlin visited 48 different tribes and painted the portraits of their leaders, as well as documenting everyday village and ceremonial life. During this period he amassed a huge collection of ethnographical artefacts and made copious and detailed notes. His research was published in 1841 in *Letters and Notes on the Manners, Customs, and Conditions of the North American Indians*, and in 1844 in *North*

Data file

Full name: George Catlin

Nationality: American

Style: realism

Dates: born 1796 at Wilkes-Barre, PA, died 1872 in Jersey City, NY

Key works:
- *Self-portrait* 1824
- *General William Clark* 1830
- *La-Doo-Ke-A (The Buffalo Bull, Grand Pawnee Warrior)* 1831
- *Pigeon's Egg Head Going To and Returning From Washington* 1832
- *Letters and Notes on the Manners, Customs, and Conditions of the North American Indians* published 1841
- *North American Indian Portfolio: Hunting Scenes and Amusements of the Rocky Mountains and Prairies of America* published 1844
- *Shooting Flamingos* 1857

Things to look for:
- portraits of Native Americans
- scenes of Native American life and customs
- elements of genre painting and portrait painting combined
- carefully painted details
- clear areas of color
- strong simplified compositions

Comparisons: John James Audubon, Thomas Cole, George Caleb Bingham, James Otto Lewis, Peter Rindisbacher, Samuel Seymour

Glossary terms: ethnography, realism

Ee-cha-zoo-kah-wa-kon: Medicine painter

In March 1832 George Catlin joined the passengers of the *Yellow Stone*, a river boat whose goal was to reach Fort Union, the American Fur Company's farthest outpost, situated some 2000 miles up the Missouri River. Among the passengers was a group of Assiniboine Indians returning from Washington to their lands near Fort Union. Outstanding among the group was Wi-jun-jon or Pigeon's Egg Head, once a warrior of rank.

Catlin documented the man's change in both character and dress in a double portrait, *Pigeon's Egg Head Going To and Returning From Washington* (1832). On one side Wi-jun-jon is dressed in an outfit

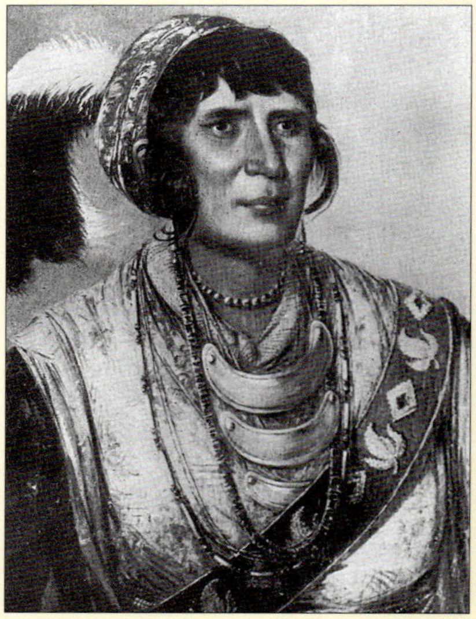

Oseola *c1837. Book illustration for* Letters and Notes on the Manners, Customs, and Conditions of the North American Indians *(published 1841).*

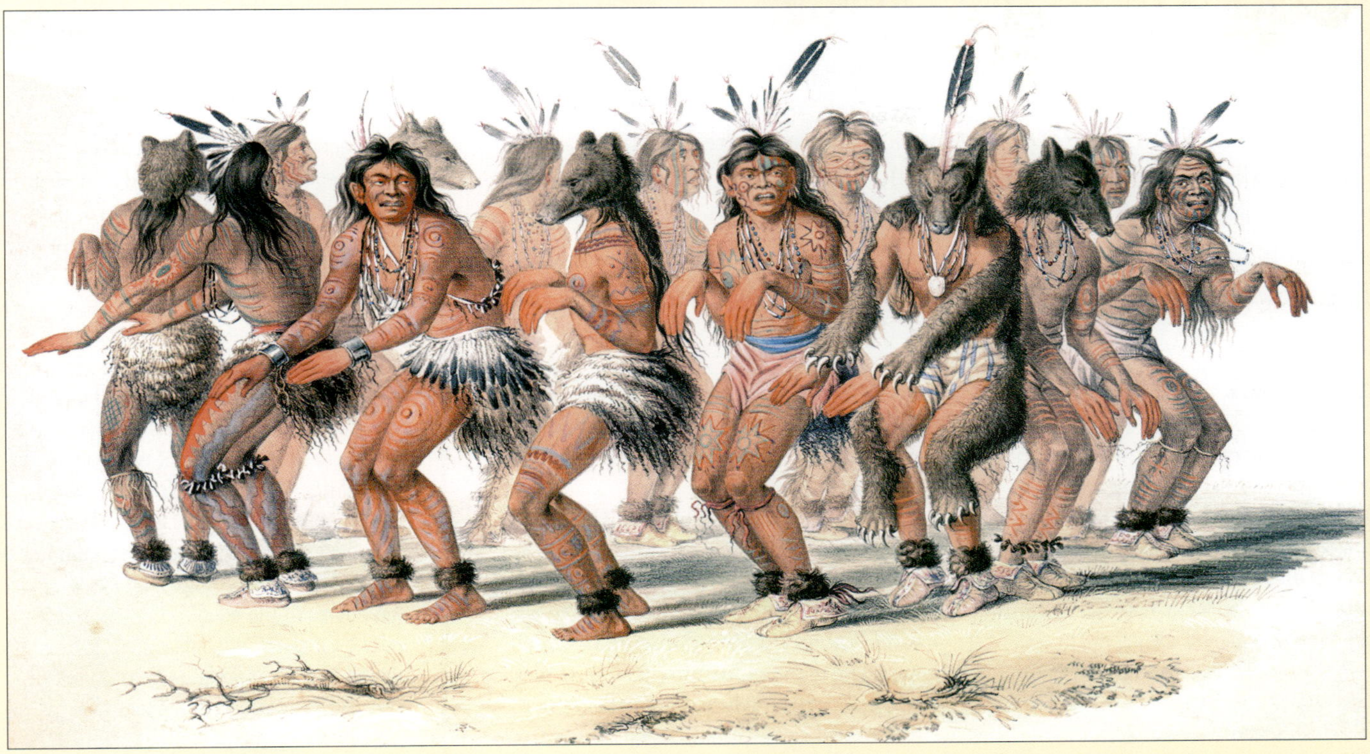

described by Catlin as "richly garnished with the quills of the porcupine…his head decked with the war eagle's plumes." On the other side he is shown in "full dress en militaire," wearing a coat with epaulettes, stiff collar, high-heeled boots, white gloves, and a blue umbrella—and he carries a fan!

As the *Yellow Stone* made its way through wild, untamed lands, Catlin sketched the scenery and made notes about each of the places where the boat docked. When the boat ran aground, he left it to join an expedition crossing 200 miles of plains to Fort Pierre at the mouth of the Teton River (now the Bad River), some 1200 miles north of Saint Louis. This was Sioux country. At Fort Pierre Catlin painted the portraits of native dignitaries and made notes on their customs, in particular, dance ceremonies such as the Bear Dance and the Scalp Dance. The Sioux made him an honorary medicine man, renamed *Ee-cha-zoo-kah-wa-kon*: medicine painter. When the *Yellow Stone* was afloat and pushing upriver once more, Catlin rejoined it, and arrived at Fort Union in June 1832.

Catlin was careful in documenting his work. He enlisted government agents and military officers who had witnessed his painting sessions to verify certificates of authentication. Everywhere he traveled Catlin carried sketchbooks and pieces of canvas that, when painted, could be rolled up in a carrying tube. Most of the canvases were of uniform size—28 x 23 inches (71 x 58.5 cm) making them easier to pack. In the time

Native American Bear Dance *1844. Book illustration for* North American Indian Portfolio: Hunting Scenes and Amusements of the Rocky Mountains and Prairies of America *(published 1844).*

Catlin spent exploring the Upper Missouri, he painted 66 portraits from life, a further 36 scenes of Indian life, 25 landscapes, and at least eight hunting scenes.

Probably his most important ethnographic observations were at the Mandan village near Fort Clark. He recorded in pictures and text the O-Keepa torture ceremony, an initiation rite for young men. First-hand documentation became impossible after this—smallpox arrived in the plains and, by 1838, fewer than 100 Mandan were alive.

American Indian Portfolio: Hunting Scenes and Amusements of the Rocky Mountains and Prairies of America.

In 1837 Catlin began to plan an "Indian Gallery." He wanted to found a national museum, but although his exhibitions attracted huge audiences, Congress refused to provide funds. In 1839 Catlin took his Indian Gallery to England, and exhibited it in London until 1841. Four years later he took the exhibition, which now included some Ioway Indians, to Paris, where they were received by the king, Louis Philippe. Unfortunately many of the Ioways became homesick, and some developed tuberculosis.

In the same year Catlin's wife, Clara, died suddenly of pneumonia. With three children to support, Catlin returned to portrait painting. In 1853, however, he resumed his explorations, traveling from South to North America and across the Bering Sea to Siberia.

In 1870, after an absence of more than 30 years, Catlin returned to New York. He was invited to display his comprehensive pictorial record of Native Americans in the Smithsonian Institution in Washington D.C.

CÉZANNE Paul

FOR MOST OF HIS LIFE, PAUL CÉZANNE was considered by many to be artistically incompetent. However, his style, which became known as postimpressionism, linked developments in late 19th-century art with the beginnings of 20th-century modernism, and had a profound influence on cubist artists such as Pablo Picasso and Georges Braque.

Life and work

Cézanne grew up in Aix-en-Provence in the south of France, the son of a wealthy banker. He wanted to learn to paint, but his father was skeptical about his son's artistic ability, and forced him to study law, a subject for which he had little aptitude.

At school Cézanne had become friends with the future novelist Emile Zola; it was mainly due to his encouragement that Cézanne, in 1861, made the first of his attempts to make his way in Paris. Having failed to gain entrance to the Ecole des Beaux-Arts, he tried to improve his skills at the Académie Suisse, a private studio where he met, among others, the artist Camille Pissarro.

Given Cézanne's nature (he was shy and oversensitive, and prone to outbursts of furious temper), his relationship with Pissarro was remarkable. Pissarro perceived something extraordinary in Cézanne's work at a time when many thought it crude and unresolved. It was Pissarro who encouraged him to turn away from the dark and Romantic subjects that characterized much of his work of the 1860s. Influenced to some extent by Eugène Delacroix, these frequently involved themes of eroticism, violence, and death, as in *The Orgy* (1870).

In 1869 Cézanne met Hortense Fiquet, who became his mistress, and in 1872 they had a son. Terrified of his father's reaction to this relationship, Cézanne kept his family a secret, but he did finally marry Hortense, six months before his father died, in 1886.

In the early 1870s Cézanne began to paint in a quite different style, and he was included in the first of the impressionist exhibitions in 1874. Most critics were hostile to the sketchiness of impressionist methods, but Cézanne was particularly ridiculed for his lack of ability. In 1877 he exhibited with them again, and was met with the same kind of critical disdain.

Cézanne, however, who was largely self-taught, remained doggedly single-minded. Over the years that followed he worked for the most part in isolation in Aix. There he gradually, and with great patience and determination, developed the style for which he eventually became famous.

Cézanne had an extensive knowledge of and respect for artists of the past. The task he set himself was to combine the freshness and truth of the impressionists' response to what was in front of them, with the balance and harmony that could be seen in the work of the Old Masters. In the past this balance had been achieved almost

Data file

Full name: Paul Cézanne

Nationality: French

Style: postimpressionism

Dates: born 1839 in Aix-en-Provence, died 1906 in Aix-en-Provence

Key works:

The Orgy 1870

Landscape: Nature Study c1876

Mountains in Provence c1886

Still Life with Apples and Oranges c1895–1900

The Large Bathers c1895–1906

Mont Sainte-Victoire 1904

Things to look for:

- simplified geometrical forms
- images built up by dabs of color
- careful color harmonies

Comparisons: Georges Braque, Eugène Delacroix, Camille Pissarro, Vincent Van Gogh, Paul Gauguin, Pablo Picasso

Glossary terms: avant-garde, cubism, impressionism, modernism, Old Masters, perspective, postimpressionism, Romanticism, still life

Analyzing the structure of nature

Cézanne's *Still Life with Apples and Oranges* (c1895–1900) and *Mountains in Provence* (c1886) are examples of his paintings in later years. He devoted his career to still lifes and the landscape of Provence, and to portraits of his wife.

Cézanne believed that art should not just be a representation of things seen, but a reflection of the relationship between natural forms and colors. He always wanted to have the subject of a painting in front of him. This might seem odd, given that he appears to distort forms in his pictures (look at the odd angles of the table in the still life, for example, and the abruptness of the edge at the foot of the irregular rocks in the landscape). But he argued that in nature pure lines do not exist. He therefore built up his forms by focusing on small "patches of color."

He was secretive about his working methods, but there is evidence that he

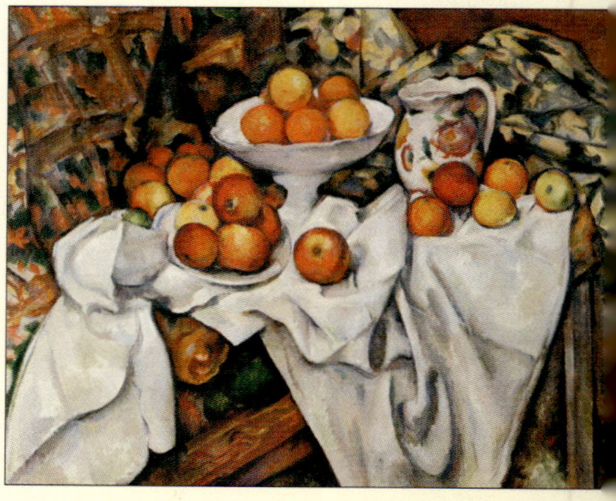

Still Life with Apples and Oranges
c1895–1900. Oil on canvas. 28¾ x 36¼ in (74 x 93 cm). Musée d'Orsay, Paris.

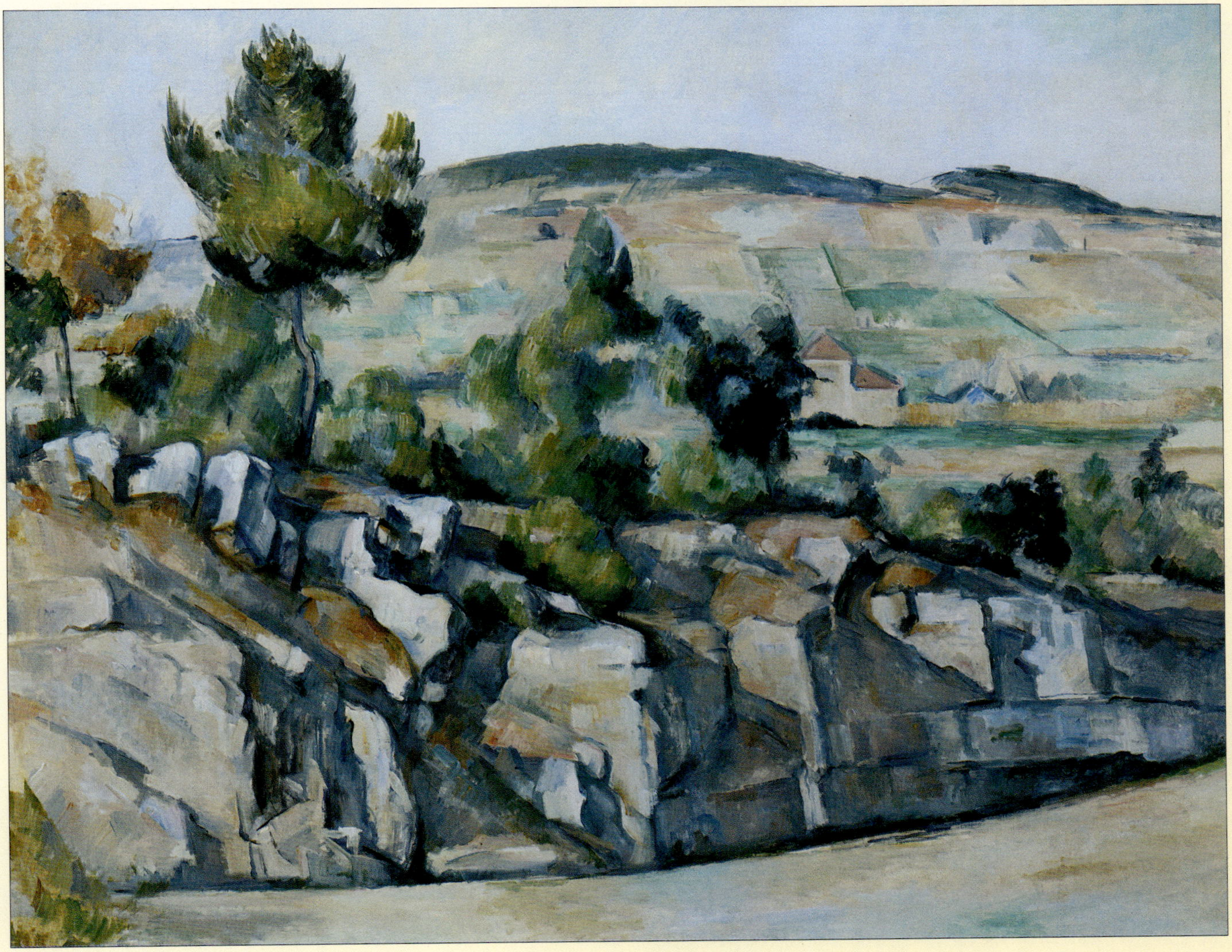

applied layer after layer of subtly selected hues. This meant he had to consider the canvas as a whole, so as not to disturb the harmony of the piece. However, he realized that we do not see every part of a scene at the same time in equal detail; so in *Still Life with Apples and Oranges*, for example, there is a sense that the objects that we are looking at from above are also seen from other points of view.

With Cézanne we are always aware that we are looking at a painting: we see the brushstrokes and the patterns in which they are arranged. Nevertheless, the effect he achieves is a vivid enrichment of the whole, which is like the experience of vision itself.

Mountains in Provence *c1886. Oil on canvas. 25 x 31 1/4 in (63.5 x 79.5 cm). National Gallery, London.*

mathematically, by means of perspective. Cézanne wanted to work directly from nature, studying its structure and recreating the forms he saw by painting them as patches of color. His favorite subjects were still lifes, portraits, and the landscape of Provence, depicted in paintings such as *Mountains in Provence* (c1886) and *Mont Sainte-Victoire* (1904).

During the 1890s an increasing number of younger critics and artists began to value Cézanne's example. His paintings of the later 1870s and 1880s had rarely been exhibited, partly because he was nervous about showing them, and partly because he had inherited his father's estate, so was wealthy enough not to have to depend on the sale of his work. His first one-man exhibition was organized by the dealer Ambroise Vollard in 1895, and after that his reputation grew.

The large retrospective exhibition held in Paris in the year of his death impressed young avant-garde artists such as Pablo Picasso and Georges Braques, and Cézanne's work came to exert a profound effect on the development of modern art.

CHAGALL Marc

MARC CHAGALL'S LONG WORKING LIFE SPANS THE 20TH CENTURY. Brought up in a provincial Russian Jewish community, he became one of the leading international artists of the modern period. His colorful, lyrical works express a very personal vision, but at the same time embrace universal themes of love and of joy in life.

Life and work

Marc Chagall was born Moyshe Shagal in the Belorussian town of Vitebsk in 1887. Situated in the so-called "Pale of Settlement," a western region of the Russian Empire in which Jews were permitted to live, Vitebsk was a thriving provincial town. It had an active cultural life, including an art school, where Shagal studied. His earliest works include portraits of himself and his fiancée, Bella Rosenfeld, and scenes of Jewish community life in Vitebsk.

In 1906, aged 19, he moved to the Russian capital, Saint Petersburg, where his work began to attract attention. In 1910, with financial help from a patron, he traveled to Paris.

Paris inspired Shagal with new ideas and images—he called it "my second Vitebsk." He changed his name to the French-sounding Marc Chagall. The city was the center of the art world at that time, particularly of the artistic avant-garde (the word literally means "vanguard," or "leading division"). These artists set out to find new ways of doing things, breaking with old-established traditions, often producing results that shocked the public.

Chagall lived for a time at La Ruche ("The Beehive"), a circular building crammed with the studios of young artists, and experimented with new styles such as fauvism and cubism. Fauvism involved a striking use of strong color in structuring a picture, a technique pioneered by Henri Matisse; cubism was a way of fragmenting visual forms, which was developed by Pablo Picasso and Georges Braque.

Chagall's paintings—always marked by glowing color and his own very personal imagery—were exhibited in Paris, Germany, and Moscow. When World War I broke out, Chagall returned to live in Russia; he married Bella in July 1915. In 1917 Russia was swept by revolution; the revolutionary government that took control there was keen to use the skills of artists to spread its message, and to help educate the Russian people. Chagall was appointed Commissar for Art for the Vitebsk region.

During his early thirties, he taught at Vitebsk Art School and designed stage sets for the State Yiddish Chamber Theater. He produced a short illustrated autobiography, *My Life* (1931), a whimsical account of his development as an artist. Soon, however, the Russian government became less sympathetic to avant-garde artists such as Chagall, and he moved again to Paris with his wife and young daughter, Ida. To begin with, times were hard, but Chagall was kept busy with new work, including paintings and sets of book illustrations. In 1926 he had his first exhibition in New York; in the following decade his international reputation grew, and he traveled widely in Europe, and to Palestine.

In 1939 World War II began with the German invasion of Poland. The German army struck westward too, reaching Paris in 1940. The Nazis wanted to destroy all Jewish people; they also targeted contemporary artists. It was not safe for Chagall to remain in France, and he took up an invitation to go to New York.

In the United States he exhibited with other European artists in exile, and again designed stage sets. By this time, New York was succeeding Paris as the hub of the art world. After the war, major exhibitions of Chagall's work were held in New York and Chicago, as well as in Paris, London, and other European capitals.

In 1944 Chagall's wife, Bella, died suddenly. Chagall was distraught. In 1948, aged 61, he returned to live in France. He was now regarded as one of the towering figures of the modern movement, rivaled—among living artists—only by Picasso. From this time onward he received a constant stream of prestigious commissions: for stained-glass windows for cathedrals in Metz and Reims, and for public buildings in Jerusalem and New York. He also created a vast painted design for the domed ceiling of the Paris Opéra.

For the last two decades of his life, Chagall lived in the south of France at Saint-Paul-de-Vence, where he died in 1985, aged 97.

Data file

Full name: Marc Chagall

Nationality: Russian

Style: modernism

Dates: born 1887 in Vitebsk, died 1985 in Saint-Paul-de-Vence, France

Key works:
- *To Russia, to Asses and Others* 1911–12
- *The Praying Jew (Rabbi of Vitebsk)* 1914
- *The Birthday* 1915
- set designs for ballet *Aleko* 1942
- *Yellow Crucifixion* 1943
- *Peace* stained-glass window for United Nations Building, New York, NY 1964

Things to look for:
- personal, poetic images
- exuberant color and dreamlike figures
- themes of love and religion

Comparisons: Paul Gauguin, Robert Delaunay, Chaïm Soutine, Pablo Picasso

Glossary terms: abstract, avant-garde, cubism, fauvism, gouache, postimpressionism

The color of love

Many of Chagall's early paintings show scenes of Jewish and Russian life in Vitebsk. He returned to these themes throughout his life. *The Praying Jew (Rabbi of Vitebsk)*, 1914, is one of his best-known works, showing a rabbi in a black-and-white prayer shawl. Even in late works such as *The Event*, painted in 1978 when Chagall was over 90, he used images from his Vitebsk boyhood with freshness and vitality.

A love of life can clearly be felt in Chagall's work. He began by adopting the vibrant colors of postimpressionist artists such as Paul Gauguin and Vincent Van Gogh, together with primitivistic folk art forms—an interest he shared with his Russian contemporaries Mikhail Larionov and Natalia Goncharova. He went on to experiment with many different types of composition and media, ranging from oil paint and gouache (opaque watercolor paint), to stained glass, and printmaking.

In Paris, Chagall was particularly attracted to the color-based cubism of Robert Delaunay. This can be seen in the breaking-up of the forms in *To Russia, to Asses and Others* (1911–12), which at the same time evokes the traditional, folk-tale world of a Russian village. The title of this work was suggested by Chagall's friend, the poet Blaise Cendrars. The "asses" may refer to fellow artists, with whom Chagall had exhibited at the "Ass's Tail" exhibition in Moscow, while the cow suckling a child may refer to folklore, or to ancient Roman or Egyptian images.

Chagall never felt comfortable with art movements based on intellectual theories; his work always expressed a very individual poetic vision. Although he worked for a time with Russian abstract artists, who concentrated solely on geometric forms and color, Chagall nearly always based his compositions on the human figure. Even his portraits seem dreamlike.

His celebrations of his relationship with his wife, Bella, are among his most tender and lyrical paintings. In *The Birthday* (1915), Bella's flowing black dress appears in rich contrast to the red floor and white walls of the room in which Chagall seems to float as he kisses her.

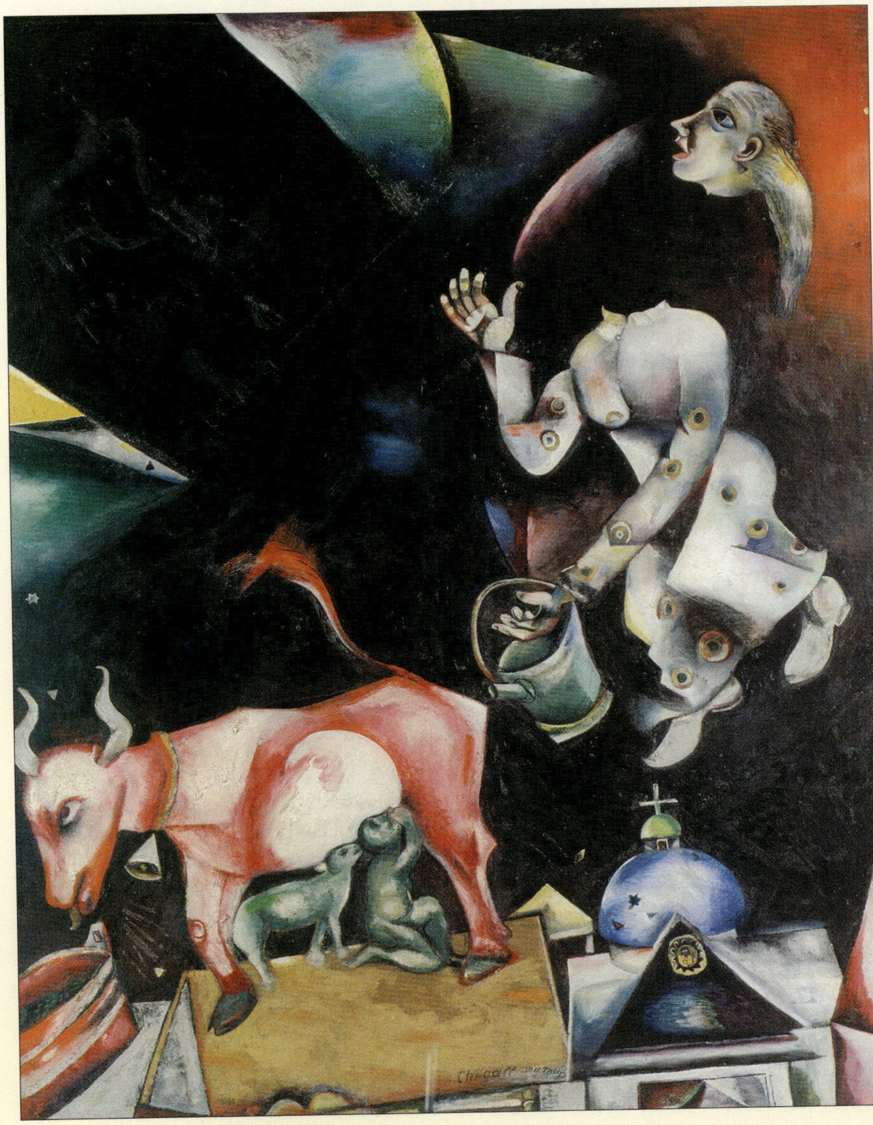

To Russia, to Asses and Others *1911–12. Oil on canvas. 61¾ x 48 in (157 x 122 cm). Musée National d'Art Moderne, Paris.*

From the 1930s onward, his figures became softer and more idealized, with color an even stronger element in the composition of his pictures. Chagall's religious images increasingly tended to be drawn from both Judaism and Christianity, as in the *Yellow Crucifixion* of 1943.

In his later career, Chagall enjoyed working on a monumental scale in different media, as shown by his set designs for the ballet *Aleko* (1942) for the American Ballet Theater, and his stained-glass windows.

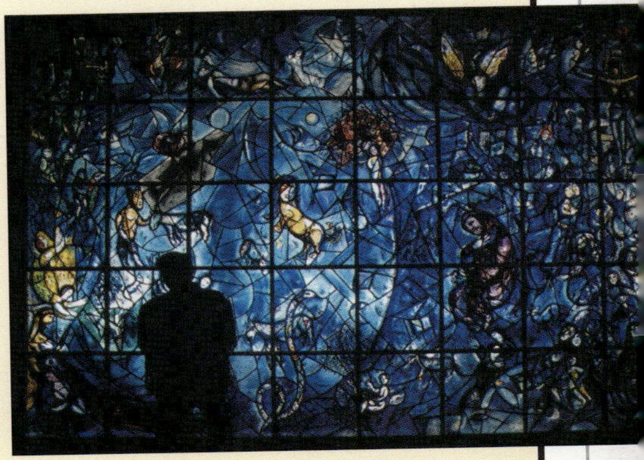

Peace Window *1964. This window at the United Nations Building in New York was one of many stained-glass works that Chagall created for public buildings.*

CHARDIN Jean-Baptiste-Siméon

ALTHOUGH BOTH HIS BACKGROUND AND HIS SUBJECTS were humble, Jean-Baptiste-Siméon Chardin became one of the most influential painters in 18th-century France, raising still lifes and domestic scenes to a new level of importance.

Life and work

Chardin began his career as an artist in a less traditional way than many of his contemporaries, but he did take lessons in which he learned to draw from classical sculpture and from a model. However, his interest in observing nature closely and recording what he saw soon became apparent.

He produced his first still lifes in the 1720s, though it is difficult to know exactly when, since many of them are not dated. He chose simple, everyday objects, enjoying the variety of textures and shapes that even these ordinary items provided. He may also have been attempting to paint different subjects than those of the established still-life painters, such as Jean-Baptiste Oudry, who depicted dead rabbits, partridges, and other game.

In 1728 he became a member of the French Academy, where he was received as a "painter of animals and fruits." This was considered the lowest kind of painting by the Academy, which preferred grand paintings with classical or historical significance. Chardin's output during this period was prolific, however, and several versions of his paintings exist, suggesting there was a good market for his work. He remained dedicated to the Academy, staging its exhibitions for many years, and much later, in 1755, became its treasurer.

Chardin married in 1731, and began to receive commissions from rich patrons. As he became more successful, he decided to paint figures. He did not choose grand and historical subjects, but instead, rather like his simple still-life subjects, depicted ordinary people, usually in domestic roles. These "genre" scenes became very popular with the viewers at the Paris Salon (the exhibition held every year by the Academy), and Chardin soon had a rich international clientele. Less wealthy clients bought engravings of his work. In this way he reached an extremely wide public.

His first wife had died in 1735; in 1744 he married a widow. In the 1750s Chardin returned to painting still-life subjects, both kitchen objects and also game subjects. From 1752 he received a royal pension, and from the 1760s onward he received commissions from the king. He continued to exhibit at the Salon until his death in 1779.

Data file

Full name: Jean-Baptiste-Siméon Chardin

Nationality: French

Style: still-life and genre paintings

Dates: born 1699 in Paris, died 1779 in Paris

Key works:

The Ray-Fish 1728

Still Life with Ray-Fish and Basket of Onions 1731

The House of Cards 1735

The House of Cards 1736–37

The Governess 1739

Bird-Song Organ 1751

Attributes of the Arts and *Attributes of Music* 1764

Self-portrait with Spectacles 1771

Things to look for:

- still-life arrangements using basic kitchen utensils and ordinary foodstuffs
- domestic scenes with children and servants occupied in work and play
- a natural style, based on direct observation

Comparisons: Jean-Baptiste Oudry, Gerard Dou

Glossary terms: Academy, cabinet pictures, classicism, genre painting, Salon, still life

A fresh look at everyday life

The still-life composition of ray-fish and onions was repeated by Chardin at least 10 times, but we do not know why the subject was so popular with him. Indeed, he was a very private man, and we know little of his working methods. In *Still Life with Ray-Fish and Basket of Onions* (1731), the brushwork is particularly smooth and fluid. All the objects are carefully positioned to maximize the varieties of texture and color and the contrast between light and dark.

The dark jug and the copper pot provide two different hard surfaces, and the patches of reflected light suggest roundness and three-dimensionality. They also set up a contrast with the soft feathers of the dead turkey and its scaly feet. The turkey's neck drapes over the shelf, contrasting the hard stone and the soft, broken neck of the bird. The neck also provides some downward motion in the painting, to balance the hanging onions and ray-fish.

The ray-fish, with its scaly grey skin and pink flesh, can be contrasted with the shiny

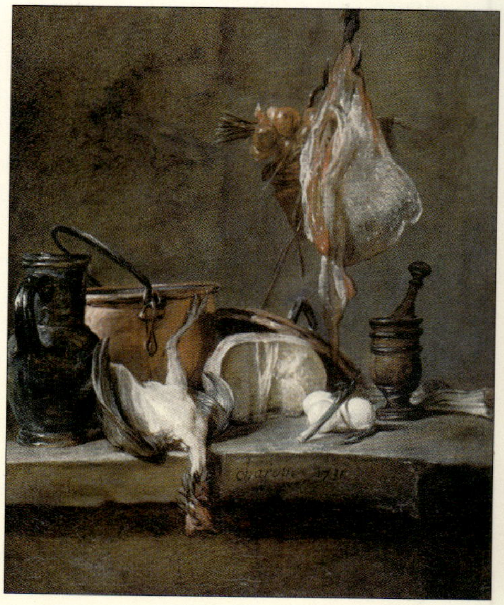

Still Life with Ray-Fish and Basket of Onions *1731. Oil on canvas. 16 x 12½ in (40.5 x 32 cm). North Carolina Museum of Art, Raleigh, NC.*

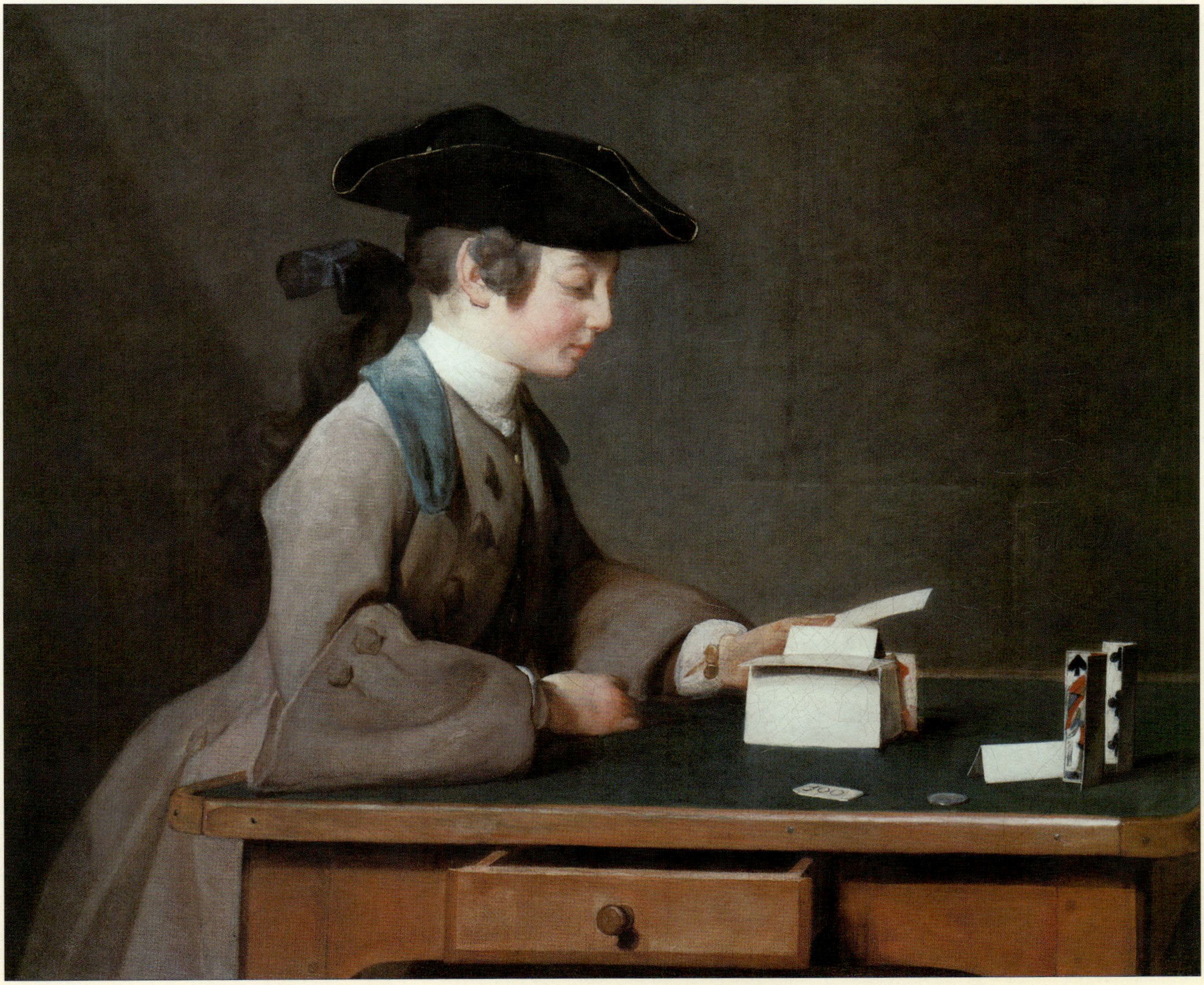

The House of Cards *1736–37. Oil on canvas. 23 1/2 x 28 in (60 x 72 cm). National Gallery, London.*

skin and regular shape of the onions. The cheese, eggs, and white turkey-breast provide brighter notes against the shadows of the pot lid, the darker tones of the mortar and pestle, and the muted background. Every element is chosen to complement and contrast with the others and produce a richness in texture and surface, yet all are everyday kitchen items. Chardin worked hard at arranging objects before he began to paint them, but his skill lay more in observation of objects rather than imaginative composition.

The basic, domestic subjects of Chardin's still lifes and the careful observation of nature carries into his later genre scenes of daily life. In *The House of Cards* (1736–37), we can see from the look of concentration on the boy's face how intently he is absorbed in his game. The table, the cards, and the child's costume are basic and unfussy, but they capture our attention with their geometric balance and simplicity. We focus on the subject just as the boy focuses on his task. Chardin's carefully observed and serious subjects appealed to buyers more than the dramatic history paintings—many people were interested in the small cabinet pictures done at the easel by Dutch and Flemish artists of the 17th century, and Chardin's work seems close to this in subject and size.

His paintings often seemed to contain simple moral messages, reflecting on basic duties and human emotions, the difficulties of love, or the passing of time; these themes appealed to contemporary viewers. *The House of Cards* was a favorite subject for Chardin and other painters at the time. The idea of a house made of cards was interpreted as representing the transience, or shortlived nature, of life and human endeavor: the cards will be easily knocked down, replaced, and knocked down again. Although they were moral pictures, Chardin's paintings of children were never sentimental or patronizing. His natural style, closely following what he saw in front of him, always provides a fresh view of ordinary life.

CHIRICO Giorgio de

GIORGIO DE CHIRICO'S WORK IS FRAUGHT with suggestions of alienation and loss. His paintings have a haunting, enigmatic beauty, in which the familiar and the banal are transformed by their placement in imaginary landscapes into subjects of strange stillness and calm. He was co-founder of the metaphysical painting movement, Pittura Metafisica.

Life and work

De Chirico was born in Greece, the son of a Sicilian railway engineer. He began his studies in Athens, and from 1906 to 1909 studied in Munich, where he discovered the mythological art of Arnold Böcklin and the fantasy-inspired etchings of Max Klinger.

In 1908 he went traveling in Italy, and was entranced by its medieval cities and the paintings of the early and High Renaissance. He later described a key event in his life, a period of "morbid sensitivity" that culminated in 1910 in some sort of mental crisis while he was in front of the church of Santa Croce in Florence. Whatever the specific nature of this event, his work after this date carried its imprint.

In 1911 de Chirico went to Paris, where he stayed until 1915. He produced grand paintings of brooding figures, set in dark, foreboding landscapes (some of which have echoes of the piazzas of Turin and Ferrara), and bizarre groupings of objects. *The Uncertainty of the Poet* (1913), for example, has a classical plaster cast of a female torso, an arcade, bunches of bananas strewn on the ground, and a distant train. His work was shown at the autumn Salon from 1912 to 1914, where it was praised by the avant-garde poet and critic Guillaume Apollinaire.

De Chirico went back to Italy in 1915 and served in the army during World War I. It was while he was in the hospital in Ferrara that he met Carlo Carrà, one of the original members of the futurist movement. Together they formed the movement Pittura Metafisica ("metaphysical painting"), which in many ways anticipated surrealism. De Chirico's brother, Alberto Savino, became the theorist of the group.

After World War I, de Chirico's work lost something of its elemental sense of foreboding, and he became interested in the work of Renaissance painters—especially Titian—as well as baroque artists, and the early 19th-century paintings of Eugène Delacroix.

The foundations of de Chirico's art were his childhood memories and anxieties, informed by his extensive reading, and his ambition to outclass the masters of the past. He claimed to have been influenced by the Greek poet Homer's *Iliad* and *Odyssey*, and the Italian poet Dante's *Divine Comedy* (1309–20)—an allegorical account of the author's journey through hell, purgatory, and paradise. He was also deeply affected by the writings of the 19th-century German philosopher Friedrich Wilhelm Nietzsche. He claimed that Nietzsche's book *Thus*

Data file

Full name: Giorgio de Chirico

Nationality: Italian

Style: metaphysical painting

Dates: born 1888 in Volos, Greece, died 1978 in Rome

Key works:
- *The Silent Statue (Ariadne)* 1913 (one of six pictures featuring the statue of Ariadne)
- *The Uncertainty of the Poet* 1913
- *The Song of Love* 1914
- *Gare Montparnasse (The Melancholy of Departure)* 1914
- *Mannequin Metaphysique* 1915
- *The Disquieting Muses* 1916
- *The Jewish Angel* 1916
- *The Great Metaphysician* 1917
- *The Prodigal Son* 1922

Things to look for:
- elements of the classical world
- strange, dreamlike elements of imaginary cities juxtaposed with ordinary objects
- dark, melancholy images, evoking loss

Comparisons: Arnold Böcklin, Max Klinger, Max Ernst, Yves Tanguy, Salvador Dalí, René Magritte

Glossary terms: baroque, classical, early Renaissance, expressionism, futurism, High Renaissance, metaphysical painting, Neue Sachlichkeit (new objectivity), Old Masters, surrealism

A strange stillness

De Chirico's paintings present simple juxtapositions of everyday objects and strange, haunting settings that resemble stage sets. Classical statues or half-humanized mannequins are seen alongside the most familiar of daily objects, such as gloves, cooking molds, and biscuits familiar from Ferrara shop windows. Memories of de Chirico's childhood are evoked by his repeated allusions to engineering drawings and railways. Open piazzas are populated by statues and decorated by arcades and flags. Strange clouds or puffs of white smoke from distant trains punctuate the sky. The uncanny scenes he creates—half familiar, half alien—conjure up the landscape of a dream.

De Chirico's subdued handling of paint, his idiosyncratic style of drawing, low-toned color, sharp contrasts, and avoidance of all overt painterly effects creates a paradox of security and strangeness. *Gare Montparnasse (The Melancholy of Departure)* (1914) exemplifies this, with its startling shifts from immediate foreground to deep space, its juxtaposition of dark, shadowy recesses and open areas lit by the late-afternoon sun, and the inexplicable presence of a bunch of bananas and what seems to be a bathing hut in the foreground.

Gare Montparnasse (The Melancholy of Departure) *1914. Oil on canvas. 55 x 73 in (140 x 184.5 cm). Museum of Modern Art, New York, NY.*

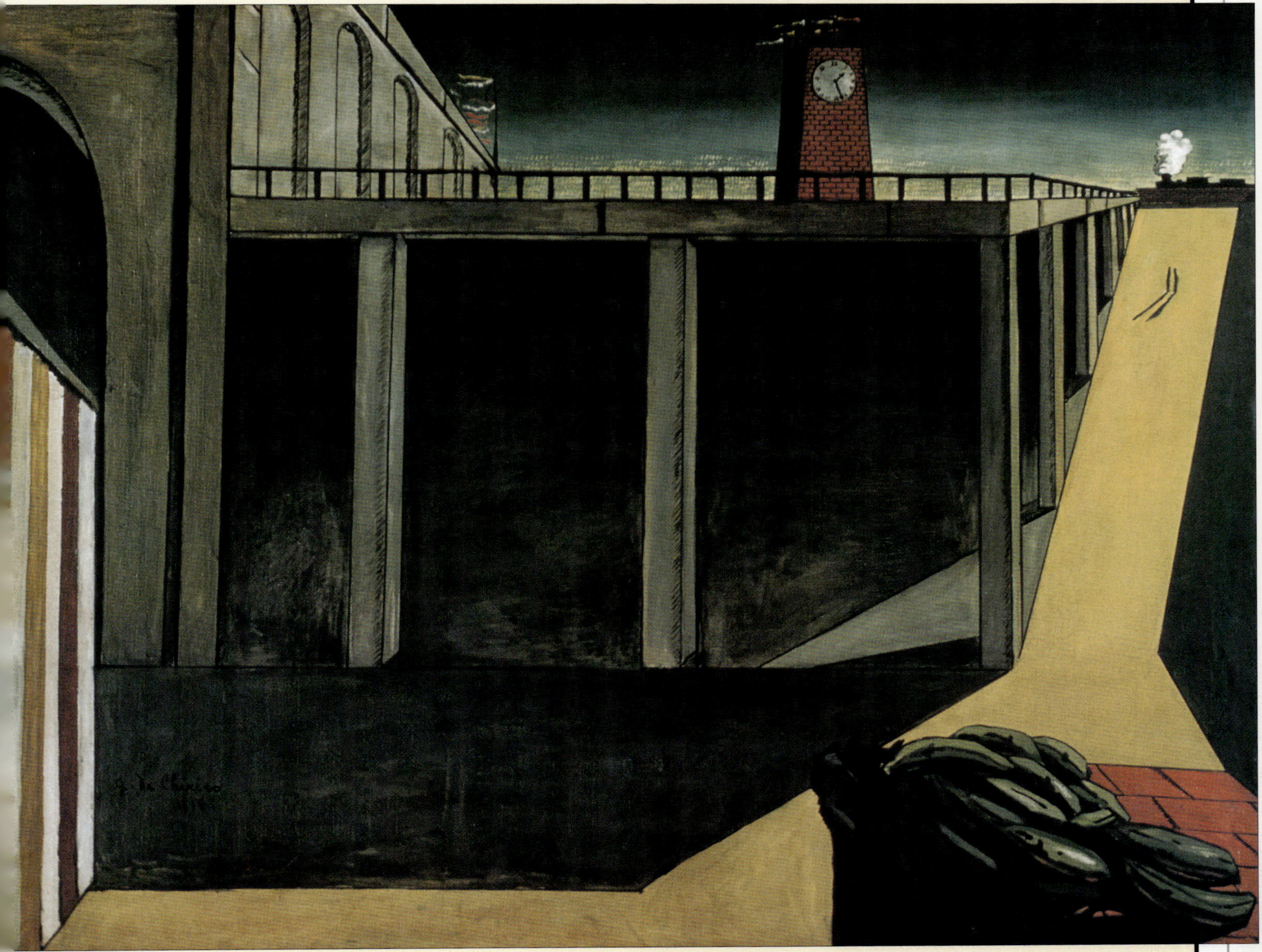

Spake Zarathustra (1883–91) was equally significant in his artistic development as his childhood discovery of Carlo Collodi's *The Adventures of Pinocchio*.

However private the roots of his art, his style has been influential in modern art, if not through his own work then through the paintings of Max Ernst, Salvador Dalí, René Magritte, and other surrealist artists. De Chirico also influenced artists associated with the realist trends of the 1920s, such as George Grosz and Otto Dix, and painters in the German Neue Sachlichkeit ("new objectivity"), a movement formed in 1923 (partly as a reaction against expressionism) which focused on the realistic representation of objects.

During the 1930s de Chirico suddenly rejected his earlier ideas, becoming an implacable opponent of modern styles and embracing a mannered academic style that came close at times to pastiche of the Old Masters. However, his radical change of attitude did not prevent him from continuing to produce replicas and variants of his earlier style, as his 18 later versions of *The Disquieting Muses* (1916) prove. He remained faithful to his classical vision, however, and his later paintings, which often contain bathers or athletes set in dreamlike seascapes, are imbued with a melancholic quality.

In more recent times de Chirico's influence on collective ideas can be seen in film—especially in the use of light and dark, elongated shadows, and evocative settings that may be found in the work of the English director Alfred Hitchcock and the Italian directors Michelangelo Antonioni and Sergio Leone.

CIMABUE

CIMABUE HAS BEEN CREDITED AS ONE OF THE ARTISTS who changed the course of western European painting, but that is almost certainly an exaggeration. He did, however, display great vision and originality, breaking away from the flat and decorative Byzantine style of his day and making his figures and scenes seem three-dimensional and more realistic. He probably influenced Giotto di Bondone, who is sometimes regarded as the founder of modern painting.

Life and work

Cimabue lived around 700 years ago and not much is known about him; few documents survive to tell us about his life and work and he did not sign his pictures. The Italian poet Dante in his epic work *The Divine Comedy* (c1315) referred to this once-esteemed artist as having been superseded by Giotto:

Of painters, Cimabue deemed his name
Unrivalled once; now Giotto is in fashion:
And has eclipsed his predecessor's fame…

The only documented work by Cimabue is not a painting at all but a mosaic picture of St John in the apse of Pisa Cathedral. It is part of a much larger mosaic and is executed very much in the Byzantine style of Cimabue's predecessors.

In the 16th century, Cimabue was mentioned in the very first art history book, *The Lives of the Most Excellent Painters, Sculptors, and Architects*, written by the Italian Giorgio Vasari and first published in 1550 in Florence. Vasari tell us that: "Instead of studying his letters, Cimabue spent all his time covering his paper and his books with pictures showing people, horses, houses, and various other things he dreamt up."

As this book was written more than 200 years after Cimabue's death, we cannot be sure about its accuracy. Certainly, one of the pictures that Vasari attributes to Cimabue—the *Rucellai Madonna* in Florence—has since turned out to be by another artist who was working at around the same time. The painting was probably produced by Duccio di Buoninsegna rather than Cimabue. It was formerly in the church of Santa Maria Novella and is now in the Uffizi Gallery (both in Florence).

Nevertheless, Vasari attributed to Cimabue a group of works that have a distinct style and that can fairly confidently be attributed to the artist. These include a famous crucifix that was in the church of Santa Croce in Florence (which was badly damaged in floods in 1966), some of the numerous frescos in the upper and lower churches of San Francesco in Assisi (parts of which were damaged in an earthquake in 1997), and a huge painting on a wooden panel showing the Madonna and Child (illustrated opposite), originally created for the church of Santa Trinità in Florence and now in the Uffizi Gallery.

The frescos Cimabue produced for the church at Assisi were very important. The church itself is large—in fact, it consists of two churches, one on top of the other—and it seems that no expense was spared in getting the best painters of the day to decorate the church's plastered walls with biblical figures and scenes.

Vasari wrote: "He [Cimabue] was asked to the City of Assisi in Umbria.... [In the upper church] he showed the four evangelists, larger than life-size and so well done that even today one can see how good they are; and from the freshness of the colors used for their flesh one can see what great strides were made through Cimabue's exertions in the art of fresco."

Many other painters were working in Assisi at this time, including the young Giotto, and it is therefore difficult to assess exactly which painter executed which works of art. However, it is almost certain that Cimabue, who was well established by this time, would have had a strong influence on the younger painters who were working alongside him.

The Byzantine and Romanesque styles had dominated art from about 330 to 1200. In these styles, figures and scenes appeared flat, decorative, and unrealistic rather than solid; little attempt was made to create any sense of depth or to create an illusion of three-dimensional reality. However, during the 13th century all this began to change. Cimabue, with his well-proportioned figures softly modeled in light and shade, was a pioneer of this greater realism, which would continue with the influence of Giotto in the next generation and culminate in the Renaissance.

Data file

Full name: Bencivieni (Cenni) di Pepo (known as Cimabue)

Nationality: Italian

Style: late Byzantine/pre-Renaissance

Dates: born c1240 in Florence, died c1302 in Florence

Key works:
- frescos in the Church of San Francesco in Assisi (datable to second half of 13th century)
- *Santa Trinità Madonna* c1260/80
- mosaic of Saint John in Pisa Cathedral c1301

Things to look for:
- large-scale works in mosaic, fresco, and tempera
- Christian subject matter
- more realistic figures than his contemporaries

Comparisons: Pietro Cavallini, Giotto di Bondone, Duccio di Buoninsegna

Glossary terms: apse, Byzantine, fresco, gold leaf, mosaic, Renaissance, Romanesque, tempera

Achieving a sense of solidity

Although this picture of the Madonna enthroned with angels and prophets may look old-fashioned to modern viewers, we must remember that it would have looked remarkably new and modern when it was first painted. The subject, however, is a traditional one—the Virgin and Child seated together on a throne in heaven. For centuries the Virgin Mary had been worshiped throughout the Christian world because she was thought to be devoid of sin.

However, compared with earlier pictures of this subject, Cimabue's Madonna is portrayed in a three-dimensional and hence more realistic way. Her face has highlights and shadows, which make it seem real. Both she and her son engage us with their stare. The angels supporting the throne seem to recede behind the two central figures; the angels at the front are larger than the ones at the back and they overlap each other, which in turn makes the throne seem solid. Framed by the arches below, the four prophets have each been given distinct personalities and characters.

The whole scene would have appeared to be bathed in heavenly light—the folds of the garments and the halos are made of gold leaf, which would have reflected the light from the candles in the dark interior of the church.

The panel originally stood above the high altar of Santa Trinità Church in Florence. Pictures such as this were placed over the altars as a focus for people who had come to worship.

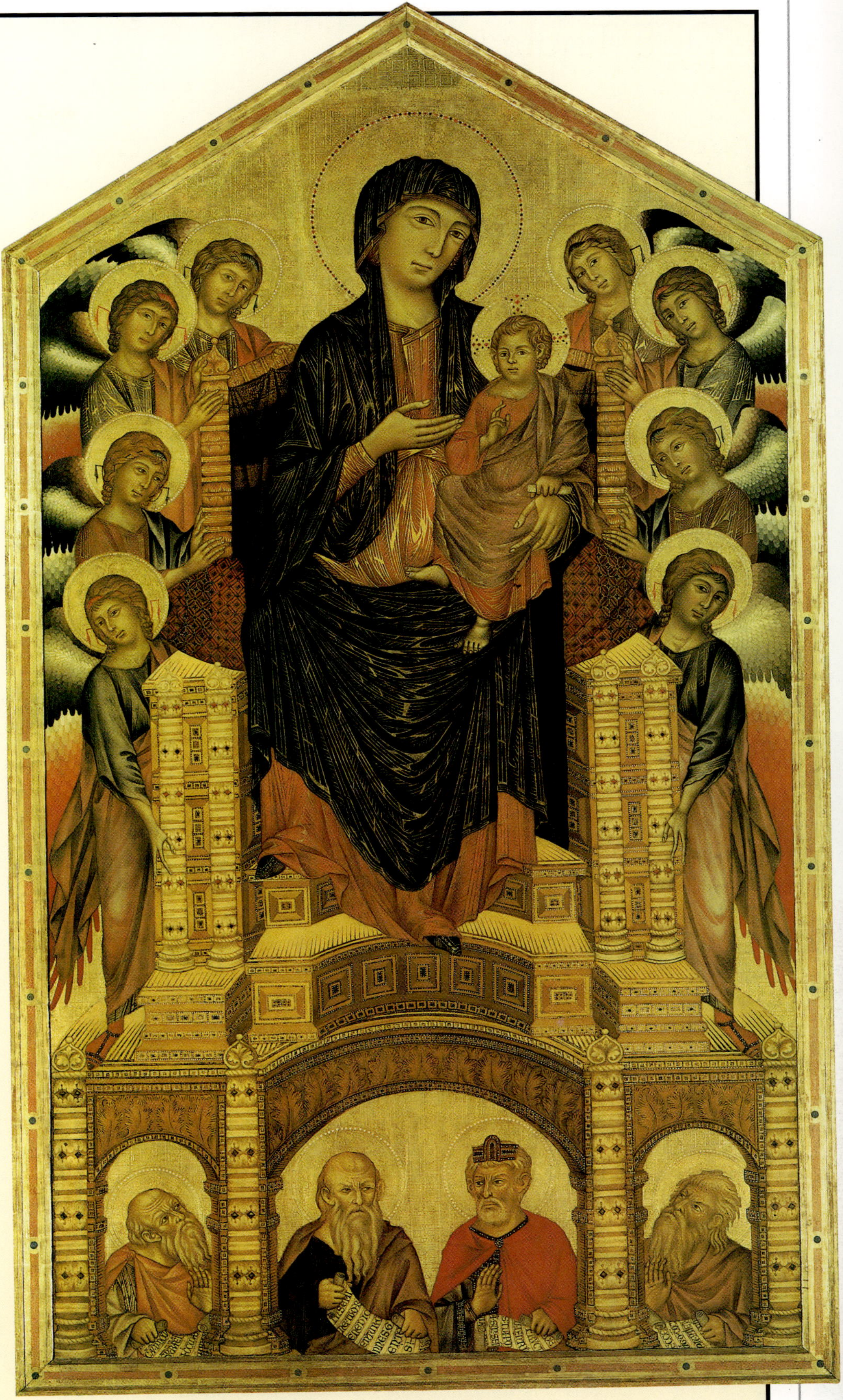

Santa Trinità Madonna *c1260/80. Tempera on panel. 151 1/2 x 87 3/4 in (385 x 223 cm). Galleria degli Uffizi, Florence.*

COLE Thomas

In his paintings of the American landscape, Thomas Cole attempted to capture the sense of wilderness, unlimited space, and awesome power of a land that had yet to be explored and tamed. Cole's belief that "God is in Nature," and that humanity's union with nature was the highest moral state, inspired the first national painting movement in the United States: the Hudson River school.

Life and work

Born in Bolton, northwest England, in 1801, Thomas Cole was 17 when his family left England for the United States, arriving in Philadelphia before setting out for Ohio by wagon. Although he had no formal training in art, to help to support his family Cole traveled from one frontier settlement to another, painting portraits of the inhabitants. Finding himself penniless in Pittsburgh, in 1823 Cole returned to Philadelphia, where he did odd jobs to fund his studies at the Pennsylvania Academy of Fine Arts. After seeing some European landscape paintings in the Academy's collection, Cole decided to concentrate on landscapes, too, guided by his own love of nature.

Although landscape paintings were not highly sought after by American patrons and collectors at the time, when Cole arrived in New York in 1825 there was growing interest in romantic views of nature. The romanticized concept of the American landscape had also been encouraged by writers such as James Fennimore Cooper and Washington Irving, as well as the poet William Cullen Bryant. Cole's close friendship with Bryant led him into a circle of artists and writers who would often work together in publishing illustrated narratives on American scenery. In 1839 they also formed the Apollo Association, which later became the American Art-Union.

In 1825 Cole displayed three paintings of the Catskill Mountains in the window of a framemaker's shop. These caught the eye of the revolutionary war veteran and history painter Colonel John Trumbull. Trumbull bought one of Cole's paintings for $25 and immediately returned with his friends William Dunlap and Asher Brown Durand. Dunlap, who would later become the first chronicler of the arts in the United States, purchased the second painting by Cole, while the artist and engraver Durand bought the third.

In 1826 Cole became one of the founder members of the U.S. Academy of Design and settled in the town of Catskill, New York. From there he traveled to, and sketched, the surrounding countryside, aiming to portray the American landscape in all its grandeur. Three years later, in 1829, he made his first return trip to Europe, visiting England, France, Switzerland, and Italy. In Europe, in addition to the paintings of the English artist J. M. W. Turner, Cole admired the works of Claude Lorraine, Titian, Nicolas Poussin, Salvator Rosa, and Raphael, but he was more pleased to discover that the landscape and scenery of

Data file

Full name: Thomas Cole

Nationality: American

Style: Romanticism/Hudson River school

Dates: born 1801 in Bolton, England, died 1848 in Catskill, NY

Key works:
- *Sunny Morning on the Hudson River* c1827
- *Scene from "The Last of the Mohicans"* 1827
- *The Course of the Empire* (series) 1835–36
- *View from Mount Holyoke, Northampton, Massachusetts, After a Thunderstorm* 1836
- *The Voyage of Life* (series) 1839–42
- *The Architect's Dream* 1840
- *Valley of the Vaucluse* 1841

Things to look for:
- atmospheric, fantastical landscapes
- symbolic content and allegorical references
- dramatic light effects

Comparisons: George Catlin, Claude Lorraine, Nicolas Poussin, George Inness, J. M. W. Turner, Asher Brown Durand, Thomas Doughty, Samuel Morse, Sanford R. Gifford, Salvator Rosa

Glossary terms: engraving, fresco, Gothic Revival, history painting, Hudson River school, realism, Romanticism, sublime

Romantic views

The Hudson River school was the United States' first real landscape-painting movement. All the artists associated with it shared the conviction that the American landscape was more beautiful than that of Europe. Furthermore, because it was still largely untouched by industry, they believed the American landscape was closer to the "original," even "divine form," and should therefore be represented as accurately as possible. Nevertheless, many of the artists, including Cole, combined realism with Romanticism.

Romanticism was marked not only by an interest in nature, but also by a preoccupation with the concept of the sublime. The Romantic view of nature was one that emphasized humanity's union with it. Prominent American writers like Washington Irving, James Fennimore Cooper, and William Cullen Bryant all wrote about the virtues of humanity's "natural state" as the highest state of "moral being." Literary works like Cooper's *The Last of the Mohicans* (1826) introduced these ideas to the public.

Cole's paintings of the late 1820s often drew on either narratives from the Bible or from the latest popular novels. In *Scene from "The Last of the Mohicans"* (1827) Cole has captured the moment of high drama in Cooper's novel when Cora kneels at the feet of Tamenund. But Cole has painted the episode on his own terms, in that the figures and literary action are subordinated to the overwhelming presence of nature.

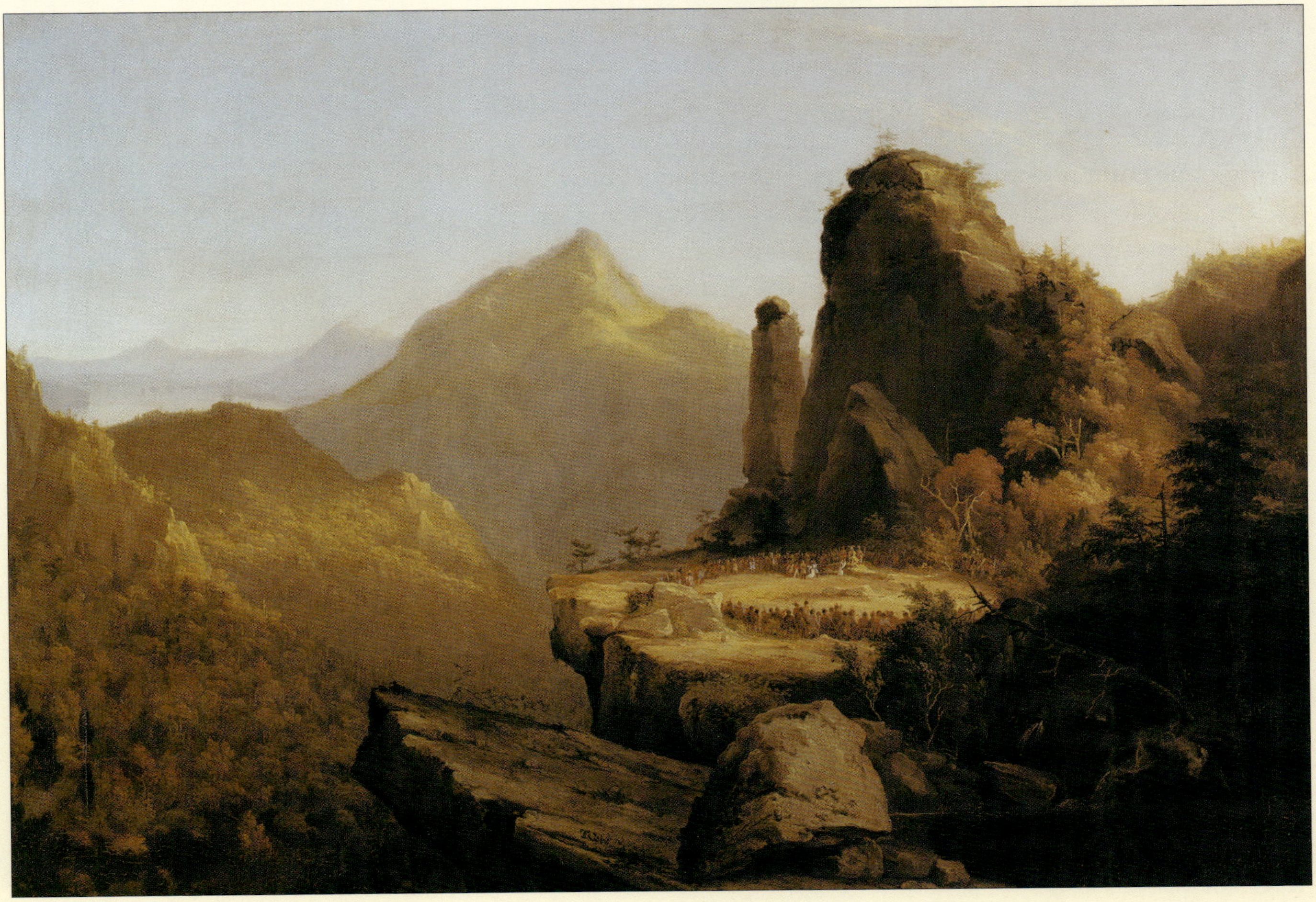

The painting contains many of the aspects of the American natural world that Cole was later to define in his "Essay on American Scenery," which he first delivered as a lecture in 1835. Firstly, the scene includes what Cole believed to be the most distinctive and impressive characteristic of the American landscape: its wildness, represented by its mountains. Secondly, Cole likened the presence of water (in the form of either lakes or waterfalls) to the "eye in the human countenance, its most expressive feature." Then there was the sky: the "source of all scenery." Whether it was the serenity of a summer's sky or the dark tumult of an impending storm, the sky "could speak of many emotions." Finally, the autumnal colors and "every stage of vegetable life and decay" call attention to the passage of time.

Scene from "The Last of the Mohicans"
1827. Oil on canvas. 25 1/4 x 36 in (64 x 91.5 cm). Wadsworth Atheneum, Hartford, CT.

Europe could not, in his opinion, equal those of the United States.

In Italy Cole began what he called a "romantic landscape," with "appropriate savage figures." These became the first canvases of *The Course of the Empire* (1835–36), a series of five paintings showing the progress of humanity from the "savage" state to its ultimate destruction and the desolation of the landscape. In each of the paintings Cole used the central motif of a mountain with which to symbolize nature. It is presented from different angles and in different lights, from dawn to dusk, in order to emphasize the changing states of civilization.

After painting a pair of pictures called *Departure* and *Return* (both 1838), which were based on his memories of the medieval monuments that he had seen in Europe, in 1839 Cole embarked on a new cycle of paintings, called *The Voyage of Life* (completed in 1842). The series consisted of two pairs of paintings: *Childhood* and *Youth*, which were contrasted with *Manhood* and *Old Age*. So popular were these paintings that the American Art-Union issued more than 15,000 engravings of them in one year alone.

A second trip to Europe followed in 1841, where Cole painted a number of landscapes, including *Valley of the Vaucluse* and *An Evening in Arcady* (both 1841). In 1845 he embarked upon a third cycle of paintings, to be called *The Cross and the World*, but he completed only a few preliminary sketches before his untimely death at the age of 47 in 1848.

CONSTABLE John

Constable is considered by many to be the greatest English landscape painter of the 19th century. His works, evoking the subtle effects of light and season, have become part of a romantic image of England itself. His paintings were an instant success when they were shown in Paris, and had a lasting effect on French painting.

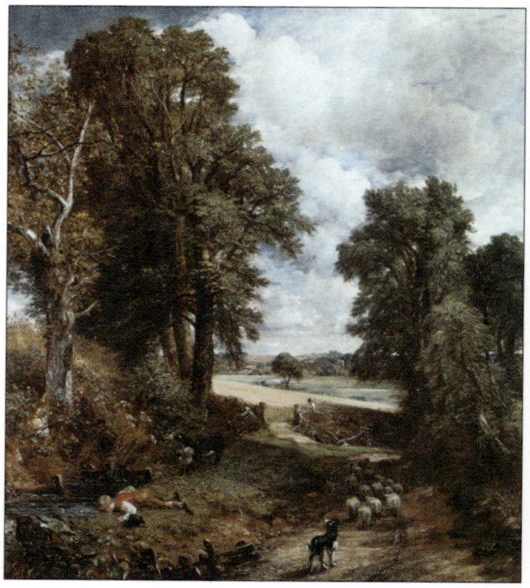

The Cornfield *1826. Oil on canvas. 56 1/4 x 48 in (143 x 122 cm). National Gallery, London.*

Life and work

John Constable's art was intimately connected with the place where he grew up. He was born in East Bergholt (a small, rural town in the county of Suffolk in southeastern England) and was expected to follow the trade of his father, a prosperous grain-mill owner. In 1795, however, he went to London to study art, and in 1799 he enrolled as a student at the Royal Academy.

His near contemporary, J. M. W. Turner (born a year before him), was already an associate member of the Royal Academy, and became a full member three years later, in 1802. Constable passed through these stages of acceptance only gradually: attaining the first honor in 1819 and the second in 1829.

The reasons for this discrepancy are partly due to the artists' different approaches to landscape painting. Early on in his career Turner had mastered the conventions of the picturesque (a way of idealizing nature that depended a good deal on the example of the 17th-century French artist Claude Lorraine). We can gain an insight into how radical Constable's contrasting approach was by understanding how much importance was attached to this historical tradition. Although he learned from Lorraine in terms of composition, as well as from other respected Old Masters of landscape, Constable's guiding principle was the desire to evoke the landscape that he had loved since boyhood by studying it first-hand. Unusually, he worked from sketches drawn from nature.

Both painters were susceptible to the ideas associated with the Romantic movement, especially the notion that painting should not merely be about recording a scene, but should also reflect the emotional response of the artist to it. For Turner, this often meant emphasizing the sublime aspects of nature. By contrast, Constable's emotional engagement was quieter and more private, which is perhaps why his view of nature seems closer to the modern one.

Constable's landscapes have become part of the notion of Englishness. Yet his representation of a tranquil, idyllic countryside was a partial distortion, even during his own lifetime. The new agricultural techniques and machinery that had been introduced to Suffolk and elsewhere had reduced the number of farm laborers needed, which prompted outbreaks of social unrest. There would have been little contemporary demand for paintings of hayrick burnings, however, and such social tensions are not depicted in his paintings.

In 1816, following the death of his father, he was finally able to marry the woman to whom he was devoted. In the years that followed he produced a series of large canvases that eventually gained him success and critical respect, including *The White Horse* (1819), *The Hay Wain* (1821), *A View on the Stour* (1822), and *Landscape (The Leaping Horse)* (1824–25). In 1824, after his work was shown in Paris, he was awarded the gold medal by the Salon.

The death of his wife in 1828 caused a noticeable change of mood in Constable's art. *Hadleigh Castle* (1828), for example, is a somber, desolate, coastal scene spread out beneath a turbulent, cloudy sky. His work of the 1830s (which was not always so gloomy) continued to draw upon his boyhood memories. Indeed, in later life he wrote of the solace that painting brought him by enabling him to forget the present.

Data file

Full name: John Constable

Nationality: English

Style: Romanticism

Dates: born 1776 in East Bergholt, died 1837 in London

Key works:

- *Flatford Mill from the Lock on the Stour* 1811
- *Weymouth Bay* 1816
- *The Hay Wain* 1821
- *The Cornfield* 1826
- *Salisbury Cathedral from the Bishop's Grounds* 1828
- *Hadleigh Castle* 1828

Things to look for:

- attention to the effects of weather and light on the land and sky
- compositions that gradually lead the eye from foreground to distance

Comparisons: Claude Lorraine, Thomas Gainsborough, J. M. W. Turner, Eugène Delacroix, Claude Monet, Alfred Sisley, Gustave Courbet, Camille Corot

Glossary terms: Barbizon school, picturesque, Salon, sublime

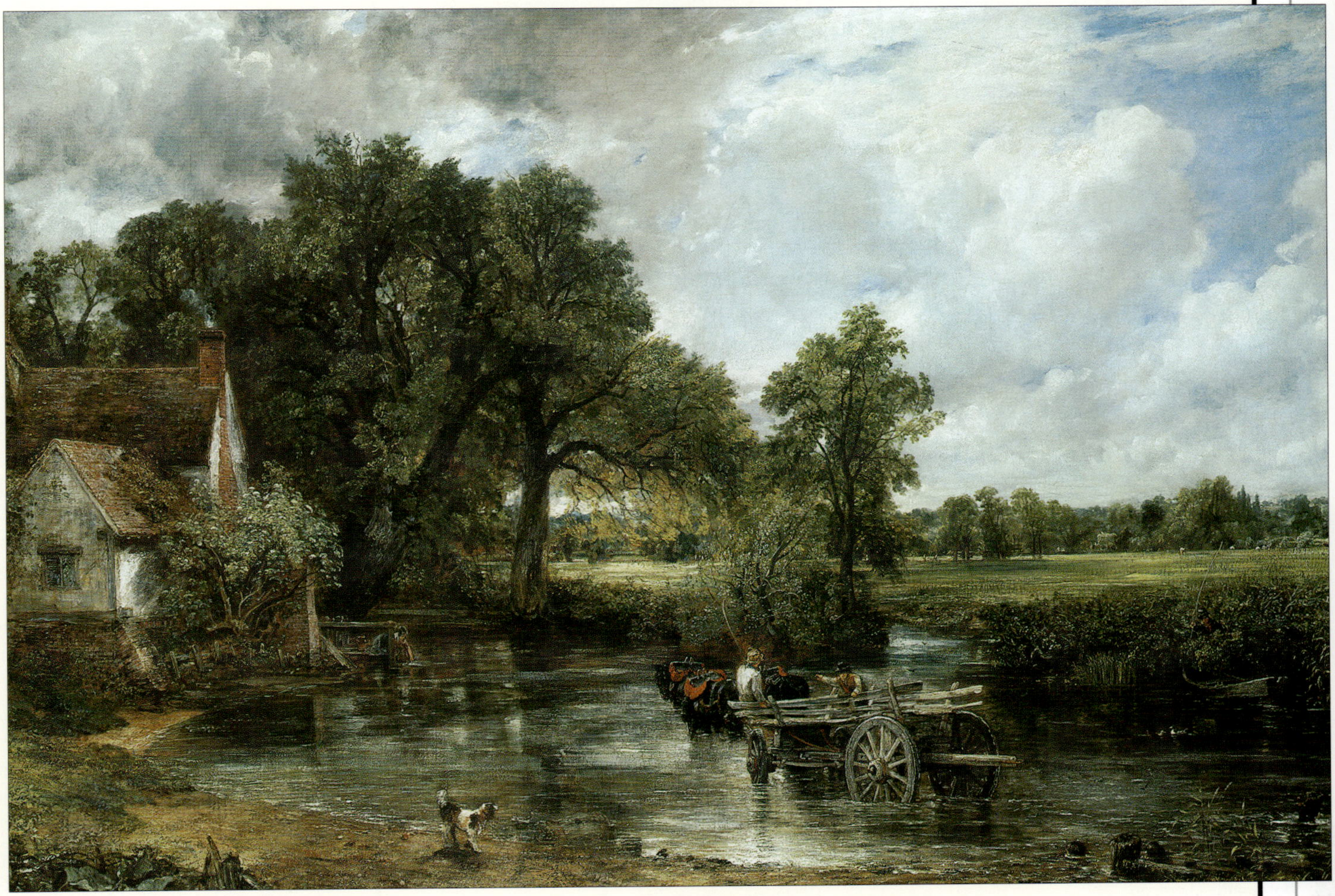

The Hay Wain *1821. Oil on canvas. 51 x 73 in (130.5 x 185.5 cm). National Gallery, London.*

Studies of land, life, and sky

Perhaps no painter before Constable attached such importance to the ways in which the sky could serve as a crucial element in the painted landscape. Indeed, early in his career he adopted the practice of noting down on the backs of his sketches the precise details of the time and weather conditions when he had made them.

It was from the sky, or rather from the peculiar qualities of light that it created, that all else in Constable's paintings evolved. Although trying to ensure that the depiction of the sky in a painting did not become too overwhelming often caused him problems, he was completely dismissive of the common convention that the sky should be a "white sheet thrown behind the objects." His numerous drawn studies of cloud formations, as well as such paintings as *Weymouth Bay* (1816), suggest that he had a scientific interest that was in keeping with the age in which he lived. Yet he also declared that the sky is the "chief organ of sentiment" in a picture. He thus linked the emotion that he wanted to convey to the detailed rendering of the effects of light on leaves and water, surfaces and textures, as if by capturing a particular moment in a particular place he could contain the past.

It was this approach that led to his work being so well received in France. *The Hay Wain* (1821), a depiction of rural life in the Stour valley, was shown at the Paris Salon in 1824, famously causing Eugène Delacroix to add details of contrasting color to the shadows of his *The Massacre at Chios* (1824). Constable, he realized, had carefully juxtaposed tones and hues to enhance his picture's sense of freshness and luminosity.

The Hay Wain is now so well known that it is difficult for us to appreciate how novel this approach was. His use of natural colors that were not obscured by a mist of muted brown glazes earned Constable only moderate recognition in England, where he had few followers. In France, however, it was seen as a breakthrough, and later had a strong influence on the impressionists. More immediately, Constable's gentle scenes of everyday rural life and direct observations of the landscape were emulated by artists of the Barbizon school (named after the small village southwest of Paris), such as Gustave Courbet and Camille Corot, who took their easels into the countryside to paint people at work in the fields.

COPLEY John Singleton

JOHN SINGLETON COPLEY SPENT THE FIRST HALF OF HIS CAREER in America, where he painted portraits of colonial settlers. He was extremely influential in the formation of pre-revolutionary art and culture in Boston at this time. With his move to England in 1774, he developed a different style of painting and took on more ambitious subject matter.

Life and work

John Singleton Copley began painting in his teenage years. His earliest influences were his stepfather, who was an engraver of portraits, and emigrant artists from the British Isles. He also studied prints of English portraits, which he then copied. As a result he initially developed a rather outdated English style, reminiscent of the 17th century. However, modeling many of his early works on black-and-white prints lent them a strong and dramatic character, which, coupled with his love of bold color and straightforward composition, led to the evolution of his own distinctive style. He worked to achieve likenesses in portraits that would please his clientele, while also testing his abilities as an artist.

Although Copley became very successful in America, his desire to set high standards for himself led in 1765 to his first participation in the London art scene, when he sent *Boy with a Squirrel* (1765) to England to see how it would compare with the work of artists there. Upon seeing his work some English artists encouraged him to cross the Atlantic to complete his artistic education. He remained mainly in Boston for another nine years, however, where he continued his profitable business.

During the early 1770s, pre-revolutionary events in Boston caused him concern. He accordingly left Boston, traveling first to England and then to Italy, where he remained for a year, returning to England in 1774. Due to the influence of the Old Masters in Italy, his art took on a different character, with more complex compositions showing several figures rather than one or two. He also decided to try his hand at history painting, as well as portraits. In 1779 he exhibited *Brook Watson and the Shark* (1778), which led to his being elected a member of the Royal Academy. He continued to paint history paintings into the 1780s; *The Death of Major Peirson* (1782–84) is perhaps the best of his dramatic and historical scenes. Copley painted portraits and history paintings for the rest of his career.

Data file

Full name: John Singleton Copley

Nationality: American

Style: portraiture, history painting

Dates: born 1738 in Boston, died 1815 in London

Key works:

Boy with a Squirrel 1765

Portrait of Paul Revere 1768

Portrait of Samuel Adams c1770–72

Mrs John Winthrop 1773

The Copley Family 1776–77

Brook Watson and the Shark 1778

The Death of Major Peirson 1782–84

Things to look for:

- large-scale history paintings of contemporary subjects, often appealing to the patriotic sentiments of his American or English audience
- early work modeled on 17th-century English portraits, giving it a studied, posed, and slightly old-fashioned character
- acute observation and minute attention to detail, particularly in his late American work

Comparisons: Benjamin West, Jean-Baptiste-Siméon Chardin

Glossary terms: history painting, Old Masters

Originality and detail

This portrait, *Boy with a Squirrel* (1765), is a likeness of Copley's half-brother, Henry Pelham. It is a very important work because it was intended as a showpiece to send to London. Copley reveals his awareness of painting for a European market by the way in which he changes his style in this portrait. Where he had previously paid great attention to detail, in this portrait he generalizes Henry's features. The English preferred this gentler, more reflective mood in a portrait to the sharp accuracy of observation associated with Copley's earlier, and more original, "colonial" style. However, the attention to material reality thought to be typical of the "New World" artist is present in the depiction of the squirrel, the solid wood of the tabletop with the glass of water reflected in it, the sheen of the boy's satin collar, and the detailed links of the chain.

The gold chain, although decorative, keeps this pet squirrel captive and domesticated. Squirrels, which were trained to obey their masters, often appear in paintings of children at this time. Indeed, it was believed that the correct way in which to raise children was similar to the taming of squirrels: by means of a gentle

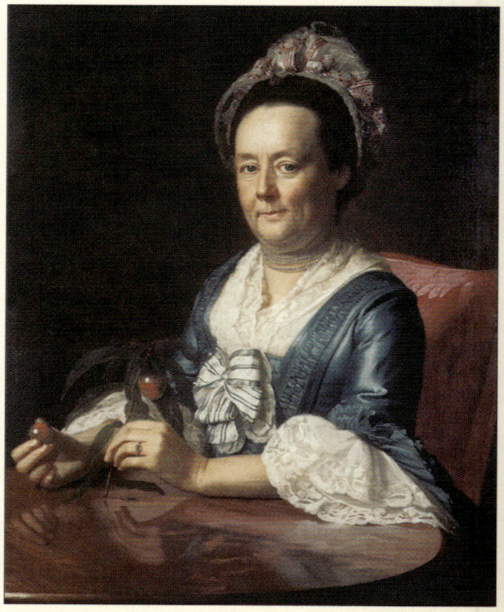

Mrs. John Winthrop *1773. Oil on canvas. 35 1/2 x 28 3/4 in (90 x 73 cm). Metropolitan Museum of Art, New York, NY.*

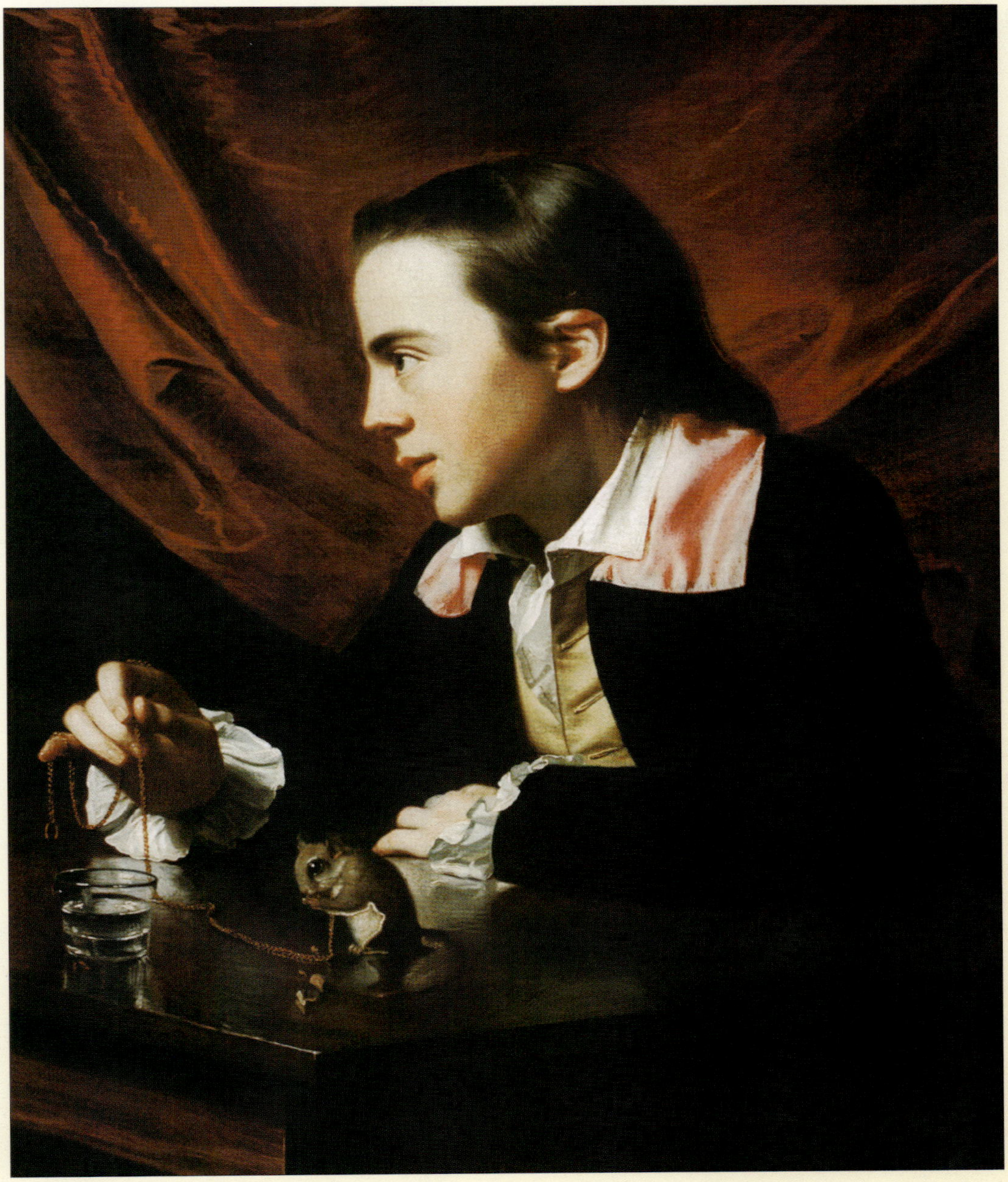

Boy with a Squirrel *1765. Oil on canvas. 30¼ x 25 in (77 x 63.5 cm). Museum of Fine Arts, Boston, MA.*

approach, mixing freedom with restriction. Squirrels cracking open nuts were also regarded as emblems of patience, hard work, and perseverance. These layers of meaning meant that *Boy with a Squirrel* would be compared to the moralizing paintings of Jean-Baptiste-Siméon Chardin.

It becomes easier to see the similarities and differences between *Boy with a Squirrel* and what is traditionally thought of as Copley's American style if we compare this portrait to *Mrs. John Winthrop* (1773). Mrs Winthrop's features are sharp, unidealized, and meticulously observed and recorded. Although he is obviously much younger than her, Henry Pelham's complexion is painted in a softer style. He is shown in profile, which is unusual in Copley's work and echoes the supposed origin of portraiture, when a young lover is said to have traced her beloved's silhouette on a wall in ancient times.

Mrs. Winthrop's head is proportionally larger than the rest of her body, a device common to many of Copley's portraits. However, in the painting of Henry Pelham, he has adjusted the proportions to appear more normal, and therefore more in line with the expectations of his London viewers. Mrs. Winthrop holds nectarines, which shows that she is wealthy because they were then a delicacy in America. The fruit may also refer to the contemporary belief that women were better educated if they learned about gardening.

Despite having been painted with different viewers in mind, these portraits also reveal similarities, both in the use of objects with which to provide a wider meaning, and in the detail of the depicted surroundings.

COROT Camille

COROT WAS A LEADING FRENCH ARTIST WHO SPECIALIZED in landscapes. In his day Corot's work was enormously popular: he enjoyed the dubious distinction of inspiring more forgeries than any other painter. After his death his reputation was eclipsed by the impressionists, but his work is now enjoying renewed popularity.

Life and work

Corot was born into a world of uncertainty, less than a decade after the French Revolution of 1789 had turned society upside down. His parents did their utmost to provide a secure background for him. His father was a successful cloth merchant, while his mother ran a thriving millinery business. It was their money that enabled Corot to forge a career in art.

This vocation was slow to develop. After his schooling in Rouen, Corot obeyed his father's wishes and became apprenticed to a Parisian draper in 1815. He followed this trade for the next seven years—even working for a time in "The Caliph of Baghdad," an exotic fabric shop—before persuading his family that his future lay in art. These early years were not wasted, however, for he learned a lot about color harmonies from his handling of dyed materials. Also, many of the contacts he made in the business world became the first purchasers of his paintings.

Corot's principal teachers were Achille-Etna Michallon and Jean-Victor Bertin. Both specialized in classical landscapes, following in a tradition that had been established by the 17th-century artists Nicolas Poussin and Claude Lorraine. In 1817 Michallon had become the first recipient of the Prix de Rome in the newly-created category of "historical landscape" painting. Corot was hugely influenced by both these painters, and he adopted Michallon's favorite piece of advice—"Look closely at Nature and render it truthfully"—as a guideline for his own art.

Most classical landscapes had a strong Italian flavor, which prompted Corot to make an extended visit to Italy (1825–28), where he began to develop his personal style. After this, traveling became a regular part of the artist's routine. During the summer months he made sketching trips around France or in other parts of Europe, before spending the winter in his Paris studio.

Corot started to make his mark at the Salon in the 1830s. He won his first medal in 1833. Then, in 1846, Corot won the most coveted award of all, the Legion of Honor. By now the artist had extended his repertoire. In addition to his landscapes, he began to paint figure studies of French and Italian peasants in traditional costume. He also introduced a note of lyricism into his landscapes, bathing them in a soft light and giving them a misty, shimmering appearance.

Data file

Full Name: Jean-Baptiste-Camille Corot

Nationality: French

Style: Romanticism

Dates: born 1796 in Paris, died 1875 in Paris

Key works:

The Bridge at Narni 1826–27

Recollection of Mortefontaine 1864

Gust of Wind 1865

The Bridge at Mantes 1868

The Waggon 1874

Things to look for:

- feathery brushwork
- tiny, romanticized figures
- blurred foliage

Comparisons: Claude Lorraine, Nicolas Poussin, John Constable

Glossary terms: academic art, classicism, impressionism, Legion of Honor, Prix de Rome, realism, Salon

A lyrical vision

Corot painted this remarkable little picture in the last year of his life. It encapsulates many of the artistic ideals that he had developed during the course of his career. First and foremost, it betrays a strong debt to the past. Its gentle lyricism is firmly in the tradition of classical landscape painting in France, typified by such artists as Claude Lorraine and Nicolas Poussin. In addition, the subject harks back to John Constable's famous picture of *The Hay Wain* (1821), which had made a huge impression on Corot at the Salon of 1824.

In keeping with normal academic practice, Corot's landscapes are constructed rather than observed. During the summer months, he would make copious sketches in the countryside. Then in the winter he would produce the finished landscapes in his studio, often combining elements from different drawings. Here, as in many of his pictures, he features a single, large tree at the side of the canvas, where it acts as a framing device. The gentle diagonal of the pathway links the foreground with the background, binding the composition together, while the horse, cart, and farm buildings provide the main focal points. The light is warm and tinged with gold. With the exception of his various versions of *Gust of Wind*, nature is always portrayed by the artist as a passive, benevolent force.

Corot's landscape style changed over the years. In the earlier part of his career, buildings and natural objects were often portrayed in a precise, sharply focused manner. From the late 1840s, however, he developed a softer approach, in which his foliage appeared blurred and feathery. Some critics have suggested that Corot acquired this technique after making a close study of Rembrandt's etchings, but it is more probable that the artist was influenced by photography. This art was still very much in its infancy, and moving

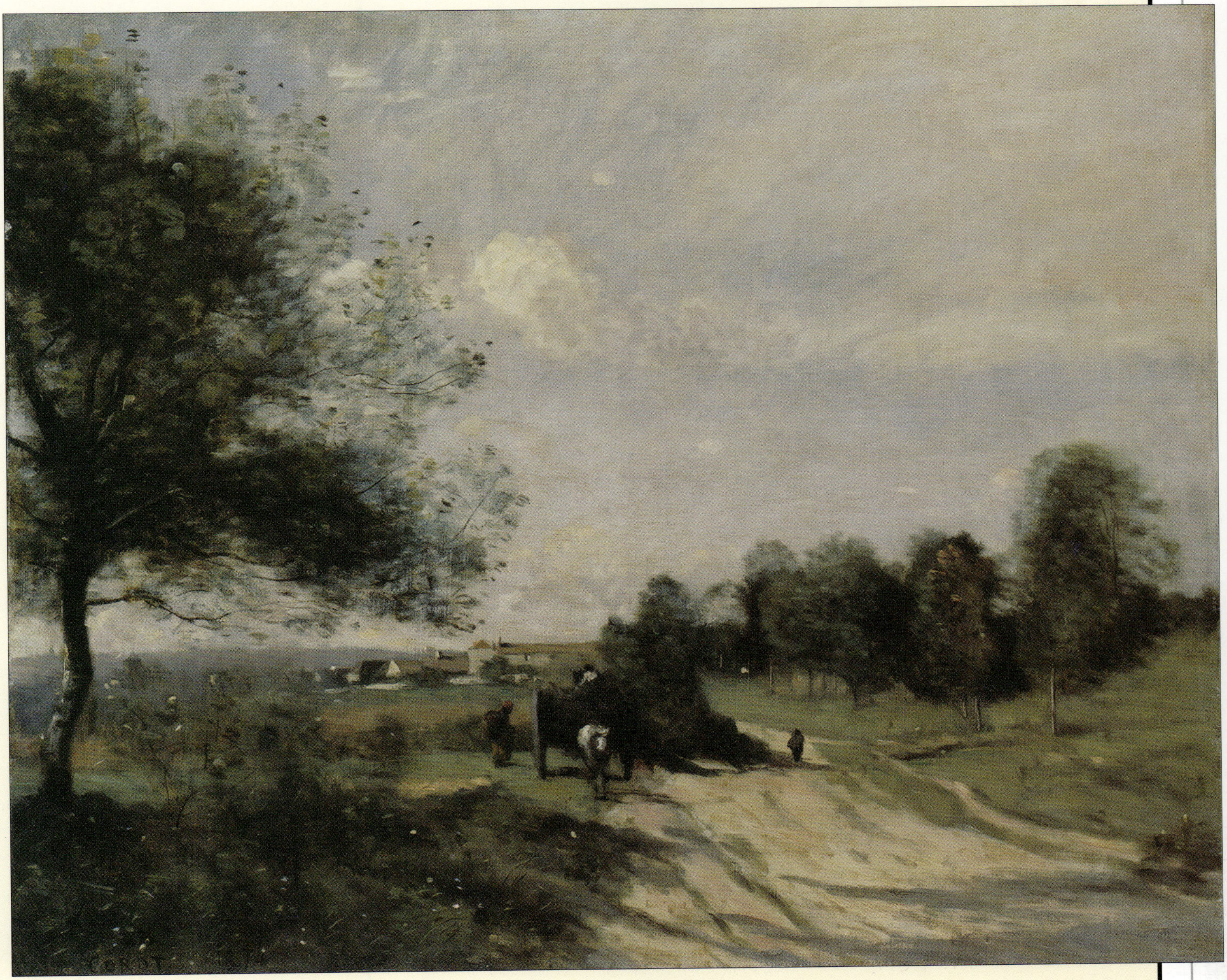

objects—the branches of a tree shaken by the wind, for example—would often appear blurred when caught on film. In addition there was a similar effect known as "halation," which occurred when a strong light made forms appear ill-defined. This was particularly noticeable after the late 1840s, when the use of specially prepared glass plates began to replace calotypes and daguerrotypes (two early photographic processes). Corot is known to have owned about 300 photographs, and it is very likely that he was influenced by them.

Although Corot made greater use of open-air sketches than his predecessors (and these became highly collectable), it was the familiarity of his style that made him such a favorite with art-lovers. Nevertheless, it was a style that would soon be regarded as old-fashioned. *The Waggon* was painted in 1874, the year the first impressionist exhibition was held, which ushered in an entirely different approach to landscape painting.

The Waggon *1874. Oil on canvas. 18½ x 22½ in (47 x 57 cm). National Gallery, London.*

These idyllic scenes were a far cry from the brash experiments in landscape painting that Gustave Courbet and the other realists were undertaking, but they were enormously popular. These landscapes, depicted in muted gray-green tones, triggered many copies. Critics hailed Corot as France's greatest landscape artist, although he never received official patronage, and was dependent on private collectors for money. However, one Parisian store named a color after him—"Corot gray"—an accolade that even his father would have appreciated.

CORREGGIO Antonio

CORREGGIO PAINTED ALTARPIECES, FRESCOS, AND MYTHOLOGICAL works for the Mantuan court. He had a dramatic style that reflected a multitude of artistic influences and was extremely original for his time. Correggio's influence on the development of Italian art was far-reaching.

Life and work

Antonio Allegri took the name Correggio from the small town in Emilia, Italy, where he was born. We do not know a great deal about his life, but the first great influence on the young painter was the painter and engraver Andrea Mantegna, who died in 1506, when Correggio was in his mid-teens. Correggio certainly knew Mantegna's work, and may even have been part of his workshop. Correggio's style shows a softer touch than Mantegna's, however.

Leonardo da Vinci, with his *sfumato* ("shaded") painting style was also a great influence on the younger artist. *Sfumato* was a technique particularly developed by Leonardo da Vinci—the word comes from his idea that tones or colors should blend together smoothly and subtly, without sharp lines. This darker, more rounded way of painting human anatomy is evident in all of Correggio's work. However, he also enjoyed using bright colors, which shows yet another influence—that of the Bolognese painters, such as Lorenzo Costa. Combined, these very different influences helped Correggio develop his own particular style.

He is recorded as working on a commission for an abbey in Mantua in 1514, and by about 1518 he had moved to Parma, the nearest large city. It is also thought, though not proven, that he traveled to Rome at this time, because by 1520 his work, especially his depictions of the human body, showed the influence of Michelangelo Buonarroti and Raphael. Both of these artists had painted great fresco works for the pope's palace, the Vatican, which could have been studied there by Correggio.

Correggio began his time in Parma with a series of frescos for the Benedictine church of Saint John the Evangelist. By 1525 he had completed fresco work in the dome, the main body of the church, the choir vault, and the apse. During this time, Correggio also received his most prestigious commission, when he was asked to decorate Parma Cathedral. He finally completed the magnificent *Assumption*

Data file

Full name: Antonio Allegri (known as Correggio)

Nationality: Italian

Style: High Renaissance

Dates: born c1489 in Correggio, died 1534 in Correggio

Key works:

Virgin of Saint Francis 1514–15

frescos in the church of Saint John the Evangelist 1520–25

Rest on the Flight into Egypt with Saint Francis 1520–21

Venus with Mercury and Cupid ("The School of Love") c1525

Adoration of the Shepherds 1530

Assumption of the Virgin c1530

Loves of Jupiter 1530–33

Things to look for:

- absence of sharp lines and a soft touch
- influence of Leonardo da Vinci, particularly in the use of *sfumato* and in the gentle, smiling faces of females
- an interest in busy, complicated, and multifigure compositions
- interest in the representation of space—three-dimensionality, perspective, and the creating of technically brilliant illusions

Comparisons: Gianlorenzo Bernini, Lorenzo Costa, Leonardo da Vinci, Andrea Mantegna, Michelangelo Buonarroti, Raphael

Glossary terms: fresco, *sfumato*

Solidity and softness

This is Corregio's altarpiece made for the Munari Chapel in the church of Saint Francis in Correggio. The fact that the church is dedicated to Saint Francis explains his presence in the work—he is the kneeling figure on the right-hand side. The depiction of the flight of Mary and Joseph into Egypt (to escape King Herod's persecution) does not seek to be historically accurate; indeed, Saint Francis lived several centuries later than when this event is supposed to have occurred. The setting is also a woodland glade, more in keeping with the Italian countryside than a landscape in the Middle East.

Correggio shows detailed attention to nature, from the little plants in the foreground to the leaves and branches of the receding forest. We have a convincing sense of depth and perspective: this was a skill that Correggio continued to develop throughout his career.

In the same way that Correggio creates a believable environment for his figures, his skill and use of *sfumato* impress upon us a sense of their three-dimensionality, but also give them a softness. Look at the arms and legs of the infant Christ and notice how the dark shadows blend gradually into the brighter flesh, giving us a sense of the chubby limbs of a small child.

The Madonna and Child are positioned according to convention in the center of the painting, but the slope of the Madonna's legs, and the positions of Saint Francis, Jesus, and Joseph add a sense of movement along a rising diagonal from right to left; this dynamic energy and interest in space characterized Correggio's work. Later baroque artists, such as Gianlorenzo Bernini, were influenced by Correggio's style.

Rest on the Flight into Egypt with Saint Francis *1520–21. Oil on canvas. 48 1/2 x 42 in (123.5 x 106.5 cm). Galleria Palatina, Palazzo Pitti, Florence.*

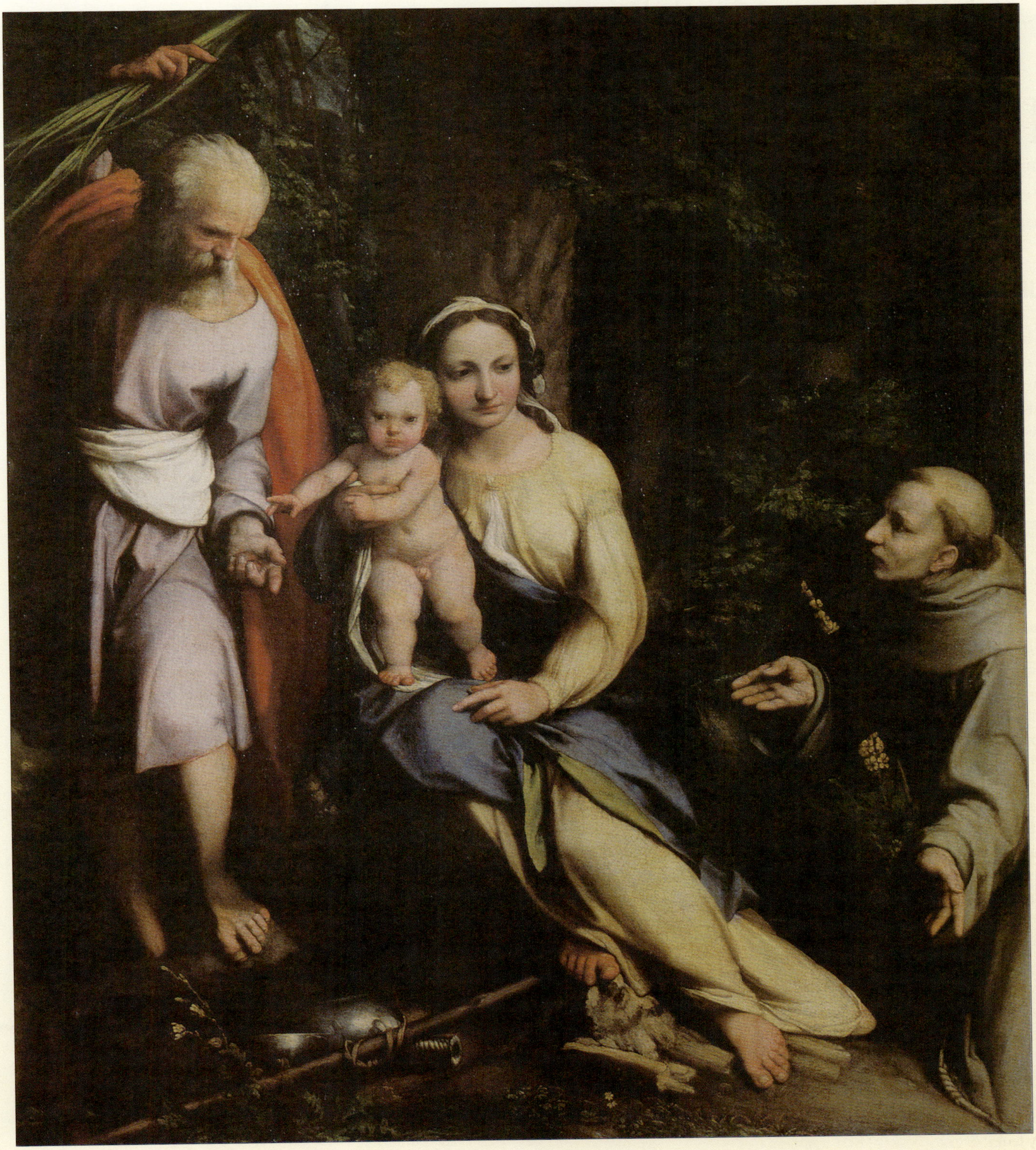

of the Virgin, which adorned the dome, around 1530. The cathedral decorations were his final works in Parma. They were not well liked; one critic called the designs a "stew of frogs' legs."

Correggio had always been interested in painting mythological scenes as well as religious ones, and during the late 1520s and early 1530s he produced many such scenes for prestigious private collectors such as the Gonzaga family at the Mantuan court.

COSSA Francesco del

IN THE 15TH CENTURY FRANCESCO DEL COSSA was a leading artist in Ferrara, which, under the rule of the d'Este family, was a center of humanist activity in Renaissance Italy. It was here, in the Palazzo Schifanoia, that Cossa painted the fresco cycle, *The Months* (1470), for which he is best remembered.

Life and work

The exact dates of Francesco del Cossa's birth and death are uncertain, but it is likely that he was born around 1435 or 1436. He is known to have been the son of a stonemason in Ferrara. Like most artists of the Renaissance, after his primary education had been completed, at around the age of 13, Cossa would have begun an apprenticeship in a *bottega* (workshop), studying under a master such as Angelo Maccagnino da Siena, Court Painter to the d'Este family in Ferrara during the 1450s.

Nothing is known for certain about Cossa's early work, but it seems that he left Ferrara when he was in his late twenties or early thirties; he was in Bologna in 1467. Here he designed a stained-glass window for the church of San Giovanni in Monte, and painted *Madonna and Angels* (1468).

Some time around 1469 Cossa returned to Ferrara, where a major commission awaited him: the decoration of the Hall of the Months in the Palazzo Schifanoia. The Palazzo Schifanoia was one of a number of country villas and summer residences owned by the d'Estes. In addition to this palace there were Belriguardo, Belfiore, and Belvedere. Leonello d'Este had previously commissioned Maccagnino da Siena and his assistant, Cosimo Tura, to create a decorative scheme based on the muses for a *studiolo* (study room) at Belfiore.

When Leonello was succeeded by his brother, Borso d'Este, the renovation of the palaces continued, and in 1466 Borso began work on the Palazzo Schifanoia. Although Tura may have provided some cartoons for the planned scheme, he never worked at Schifanoia. Instead, the commission fell largely to Cossa, who completed the work with the help of his assistant, Ercole d'Antonio de' Roberti, as well as some anonymous painters. Despite their large scale, Cossa completed the *The Months* frescos relatively quickly, in 1470. The most famous images are from the east wall, which depict the months of March, April, and May.

Data file

Full name: Francesco del Cossa
Nationality: Italian
Style: Renaissance
Dates: born c1435/1436 in Ferrara, died c1477 in Bologna
Key works:
Madonna and Angels 1468
The Months 1470
The Annunciation 1470–72
Griffoni altarpiece 1473
The Crucifixion, Saint Lucy, and *Saint Florian* c1473
Mercanti altarpiece 1474
Things to look for:
- illusionistic perspective
- sculptural treatment of drapery
- heads have domed foreheads and short chins
- use of ornamental and "antique" motifs
- repetition of forms
- statuesque figures set against backgrounds of landscapes and architectural forms

Comparisons: Piero della Francesca, Andrea Mantegna, Cosimo Tura, Ercole d'Antonio de' Roberti, Lorenzo Costa, Francesco Squarcione
Glossary terms: cartoon, classical, fresco, humanism, illusionistic perspective, polyptych, *predella,* Renaissance, tempera, triptych

Symbolism and space

The Hall of the Months would have been used as a reception hall by Borso d'Este. This huge room was completely covered in frescos, whose scheme is thought to have been devised by Guarino da Verona, the d'Este family's tutor. Today, little is left of the frescos that adorned the west and south walls. (At one stage the room was used as a granary and the frescos were covered with whitewash. When the whitewash was removed, during the 1950s, only the north and east walls could be rescued and restored.) Only the middle section of *August,* and, on the east wall, *March, April,* and *May,* are believed to be by Cossa.

The overall pattern of the frescos was established by a series of painted pilasters dividing the walls into 12 vertical panels. Each panel was divided horizontally into three sections. Classical deities were depicted in the top section of each panel. In *April,* for example, the chained figure of Mars, the Roman god of war, kneels before the goddess of love, Venus. Each of the gods in the panels is shown riding triumphantly in a chariot across a lush landscape. Venus's chariot is drawn by a pair of stately swans. Lascivious scenes between men and women are depicted either side of the river, with rabbits (symbols of fertility) cavorting beside them.

The sign of the zodiac for the month in question is depicted in the middle section of each panel. In *April* it is Taurus, the bull. The draped figure hovering above the bull and holding a large key symbolizes the "unlocking" of the season of spring. The other astrological figures represent the

Soon after completing the frescos, Cossa left Ferrara in disgust. He had been paid by the square foot for his work, and now complained in a letter to Borso d'Este that he deserved a higher reward for his labors, pointing out that he was being treated on a par with the "worst dauber in Ferrara." Perhaps unsurprisingly, from the late spring of 1470 Cossa (probably

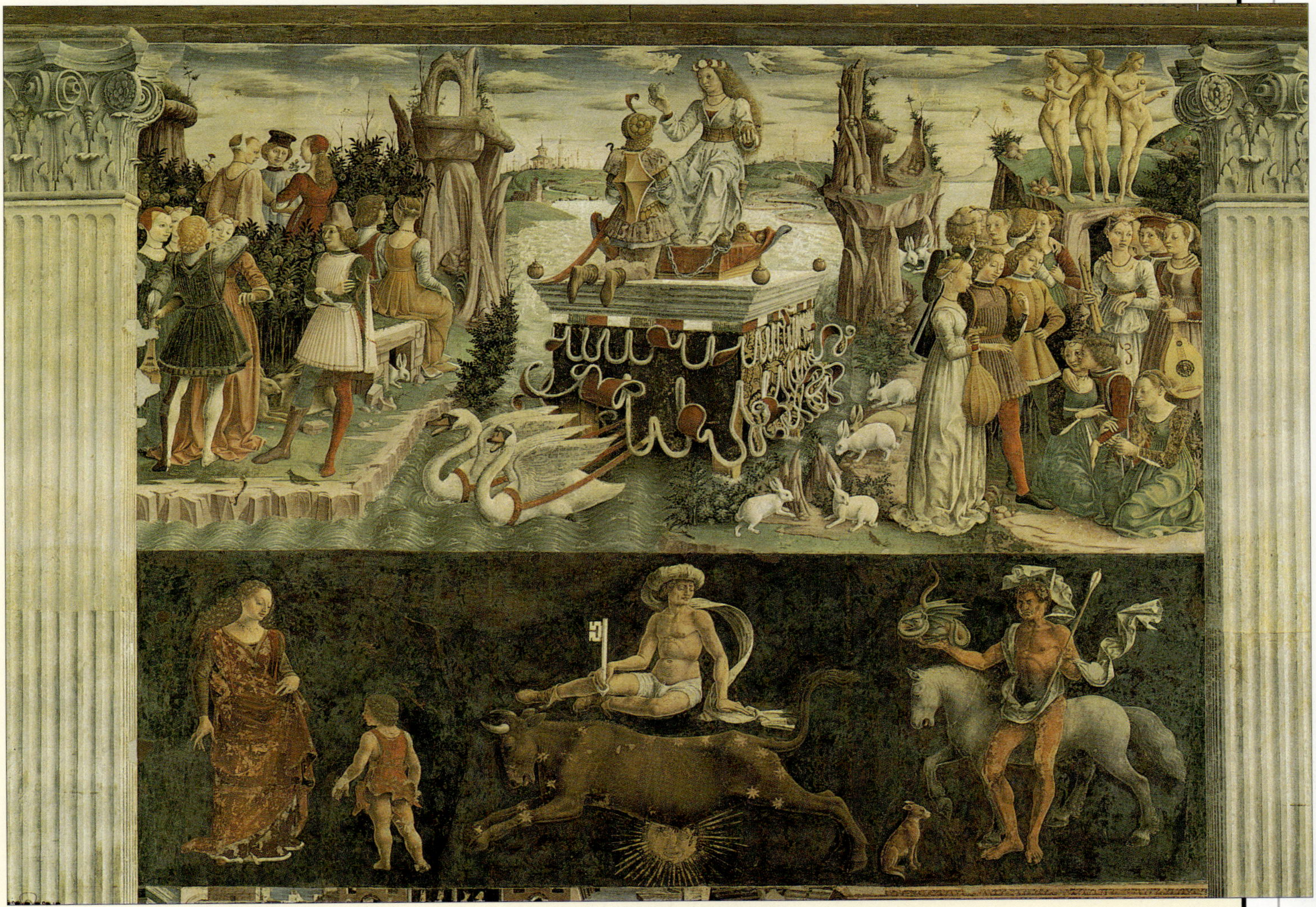

decans (the three divisions of ten degrees that make up each sign of the zodiac).

In the bottom sections of the panels are represented the "labors" of the months, tasks like plowing and harvesting, as well as scenes of feasting. These "labors" are mixed with depictions of the courtly activities of the d'Este family. In a form of visual propaganda designed to impress visitors and celebrate the d'Este family's patronage of art, the smiling figure of Borso d'Este figures in each of the sections, surrounded by courtiers.

Cossa's manipulation of spatial conventions throughout each of the three sections is often remarked upon. In the upper zones (featuring the gods) the space has been compressed, so that the figures appear as if set against a backdrop of scenery or a theater set. In the middle sections the astrological figures seem to "float" in symbolic space, while in the lower sections that deal with earthly life, the space is given a sense of illusionistic perspective.

The Months: April (top and middle sections)
1470. Tempera on plaster. 40 x 80 ft (12 x 24 m). Palazzo Schifanoia, Ferrara.

accompanied by his assistant, de' Roberti) was once again in Bologna. *The Annunciation* (1470–72), with its *predella* painting, *The Nativity*, dates from this period. In 1473 Cossa completed the main portions of the triptych for the Griffoni Chapel in San Petronio, Bologna. This consisted of a central panel depicting Saint Vincent Ferrer, with Saint Peter and Saint John the Baptist either side. The Griffoni altarpiece (1473) is now believed to have been a much larger polyptych. Because they all have gold grounds and a perspective that indicates that they were designed to be seen from below, it is thought that three further panels by Cossa, *The Crucifixion*, *Saint Lucy*, and *Saint Florian* (c1473), were meant to have been placed above the triptych.

The Mercanti altarpiece (1474), showing the Madonna enthroned between saints Petronius and John the Evangelist, was painted for the altar of the Fora dei Mercanti (the Guild of Merchants' lodge, or headquarters) in Bologna, and was commissioned by Alberto de' Cattanei. Cossa died around 1477, three years after finishing the Mercanti altarpiece.

COURBET Gustave

A CONTROVERSIAL ARTISTIC FIGURE with outspoken political views, Gustave Courbet was the leader of the 19th-century realist movement. The realists took aspects of modern life as their inspiration, rather than classical subjects. Their work formed a bridge between the Romantics and the impressionists.

Life and work

Gustave Courbet was born and raised in Ornans, a small town in eastern France, not far from the Swiss border. His family came from prosperous farming stock and had lived in the area for generations. As a result, Gustave grew up with a fierce loyalty to his native region, which was to feature prominently in his painting.

As a schoolchild, Courbet was bright but rebellious, a foretaste of his future career. He developed an early interest in art and, after training under a succession of minor painters, he settled in Paris in 1839. He intended to make his mark by exhibiting at the Salon, an important annual art show, which provided a valuable showcase for ambitious painters. Between 1841 and 1847, he sent in a variety of different subjects—portraits, landscapes, hunting scenes, religious pictures—but none of them created much of an impact.

Despite this, Courbet was building up a reputation among a radical group of writers, artists, and critics, who used to meet at a bar close to his studio. Jokingly, they dubbed it the "Temple of Realism," because it was here that they worked out the details of this new artistic movement. In essence they wanted to sweep away the mythological and historical paintings that were so popular at the Salon, and replace them with pictures that dealt with the realities of modern life. As Courbet himself put it, "painting is a concrete art and must be applied to real and existing things."

The breakthrough came at the 1849 Salon, when Courbet was awarded a gold medal for one of his paintings, *After Dinner at Ornans* (1848–49). He hoped to repeat this success when he submitted another scene of local life, the enormous *Burial at Ornans* (1849–50). This time, however, his work was greeted with derision and outrage. The critics mocked it, because they thought that the ungainly figures of the Ornans townsfolk were intended as a joke. The authorities, on the other hand, were more worried about its possible political overtones. It was a sensitive time. In 1848 King Louis-Philippe had been forced to abdicate the throne, and many people feared that a second French revolution was about to break out. In such a climate, any controversial painting of the peasantry caused concern.

This was to be the first of many clashes between Courbet and the authorities. The most significant of these occurred in 1855, when the organizers of the Paris World's Fair invited him to produce a painting for

Data file

Full name: Jean Désiré Gustave Courbet

Nationality: French

Style: realism

Dates: born 1819 in Ornans, died 1877 in La Tour de Peilz, Switzerland

Key works:
- *After Dinner at Ornans* 1848–49
- *Burial at Ornans* 1849–50
- *Stonebreakers* 1850
- *Bonjour Monsieur Courbet* 1854
- *The Painter's Studio* 1855
- *The Winnowers* 1855
- *Young Ladies by the Banks of the Seine* 1856–57
- *The Kill* 1867

Things to look for:
- unsentimental view of the countryside
- unidealized figures and images of work
- thickly applied paint

Comparisons: Jean-François Millet, Edouard Manet, Pieter Bruegel the Elder

Glossary terms: classical, realism, Salon

A realistic approach

In mid-19th-century France, paintings were expected to conform to a strict moral and educational code. Artists were meant to tackle uplifting subjects, preferably from ancient history or mythology, and their figures were supposed to be noble and idealized.

Courbet's pictures challenged these preconceptions in several ways. He chose themes that both the public and the critics found trivial—usually scenes of peasant life or labor. Courbet also painted them on a huge scale, which implied that the subjects themselves had great significance.

His human figures also caused an outcry. Art-lovers were accustomed to seeing pictures with beautiful or heroic figures, often based on classical statues. Courbet adopted a more prosaic approach. He painted people as he saw them, with all their physical blemishes, and rejected the idealization of his subjects. However, many of his contemporaries did not believe Courbet was trying to be realistic; they were convinced he was actively seeking out ugliness and squalor in an attempt to shock people.

This particular painting aroused controversy because of its immoral overtones. The scene shows two young women relaxing by the river Seine, in just the sort of public place where respectable Parisians strolled with their families. They have decided to lie down on the grass—itself a breach of decorum—and one of them has taken off her dress, to use it as a pillow. For Courbet's public, this was unacceptable behavior, and it raised all sorts of questions about the women's motives. Were they prostitutes plying their trade? Was this the reason why the nearest girl was gazing dreamily at the

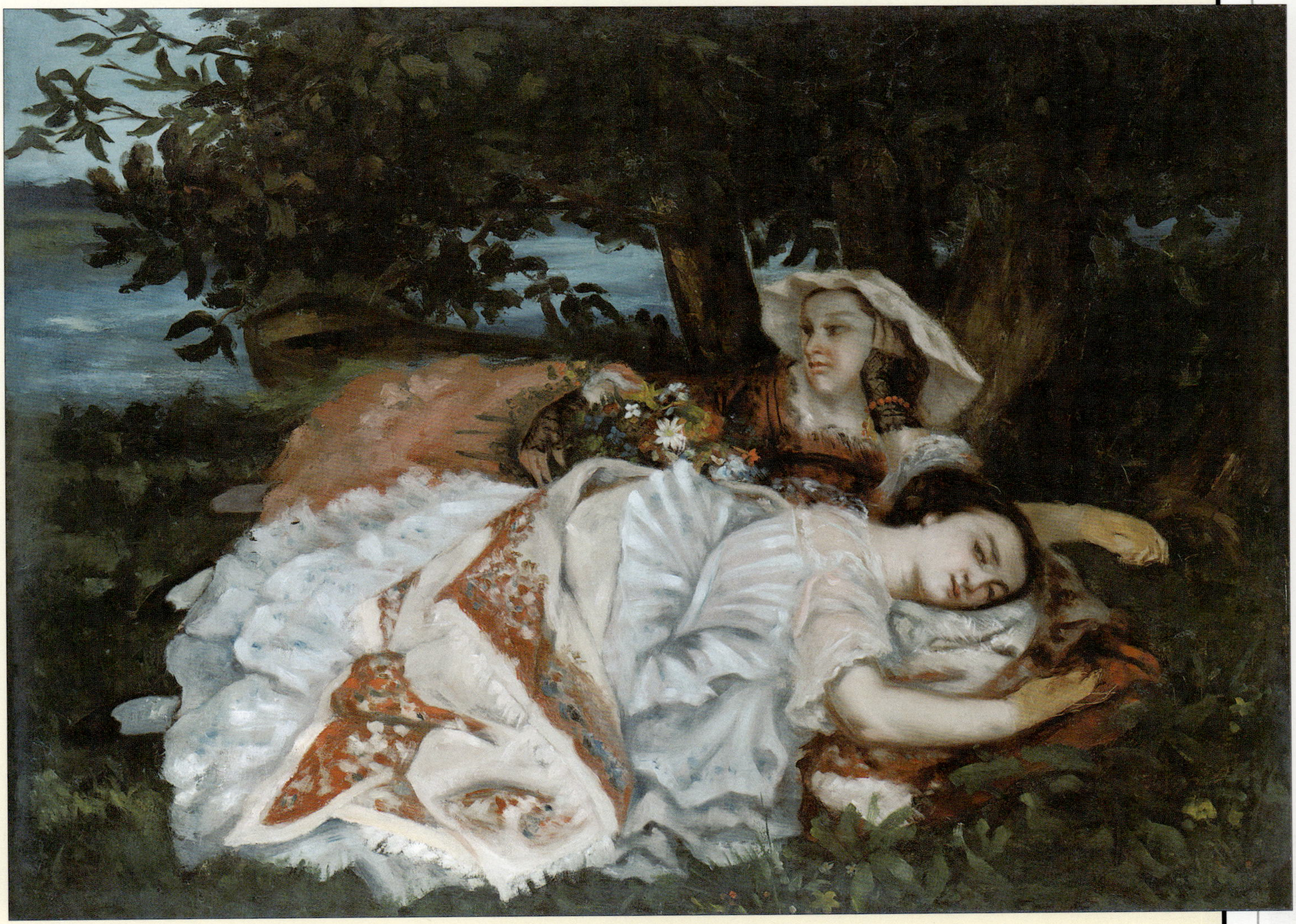

spectator? Was the viewer of the painting being placed in the position of a prospective client? Such was the air of suspicion inspired by Courbet's work that many critics looked for hidden meanings and symbolism that the artist had probably never intended. Here, for example, some critics suggested that the plucked blooms were symbols of the women's lost virginity.

Courbet would certainly have been aware that this picture would upset many people, but he probably had little interest in the moral implications of the scene. Instead, it is more likely that he was attracted by the idea of portraying a slice of contemporary life, however unseemly it might appear. In this respect, he can be seen as a precursor of the impressionists.

Young Ladies by the Banks of the Seine *1856–57. Oil on canvas. 38 x 51 in (96.5 x 130 cm). National Gallery, London.*

their show, provided that they could see a sketch of it in advance. Courbet refused indignantly, believing that this was meant as a form of censorship. Instead, he staged a rival exhibition of his own work, which he advertised under the banner of "realism." The show was a comparative failure, but it set an important precedent for the independent exhibitions organized by the next generation of artists, most notably the impressionists.

Courbet's antagonistic attitude eventually landed him in serious trouble during the days of the Paris Commune after the deposition of Napoleon III (1870–71). Courbet took part in this violent uprising, and served as a councillor in the shortlived revolutionary government. Once order was restored, however, he was fined and imprisoned by the new administration. In 1873 he chose to go into voluntary exile in Switzerland, settling in La Tour de Peilz. He never returned to France, and died four years later.

CRIVELLI Carlo

LIKE OTHER EARLY RENAISSANCE ARTISTS, CARLO CRIVELLI explored perspective and proportion in his paintings. But his work has a less natural appearance than that of his contemporaries. Crivelli celebrated the devices in art that heighten and intensify an image, through vivid color, the clarity of the foreground and background detail, and the illusion of space.

Life and work

Carlo Crivelli is the most famous member of a family of painters who flourished in the mid- to late 15th century in Italy. He signed himself a Venetian, and so it is probable that he was born in Venice. It is also fair to assume that he learned his craft from his father, Jacopo. He would also have joined an artist's workshop to develop his style and technique.

The first factual document relating to Crivelli reveals two pieces of information: that he served a six-month prison sentence for the crime of adultery in 1457; and that his profession was independent painter. Painting at this time was being elevated to a position of primacy, and artists used pictures to show off their skills. Attention to detail was already a feature of Gothic art, but now perspective and proportion were being explored, and art was becoming more challenging for its audience.

In about 1460 Crivelli moved from Venice across the Adriatic Sea to the town of Zara (then part of the Venetian republic and now within Croatia). About that time Crivelli produced *Virgin and Child* (c1460), which shows an almost devotional attention to clarity and detail.

By 1470 he had moved again, to Fermo in central Italy. In Fermo he worked on several altarpieces for local churches, which gained him a good reputation in the region. Here, throughout the 1470s, Crivelli developed his distinctive style through commissions from the Catholic Church and from private patrons.

In the 1480s Crivelli moved to Ascoli Piceno, the largest and most prosperous town in this region; presumably he wanted to take on more lucrative commissions. There he produced his most famous work, *The Annunciation with Saint Emidius* (1486), which was painted in celebration of the town's newly won independence. The independence was short-lived, however; in 1490 the town came under the control of the kingdom of Naples. It is likely that Crivelli had a political hand in this takeover, for, in the same year, he was knighted by the future King of Naples. From then until his death, five years later, Crivelli proudly used his new title when signing his name.

Data file

Full name: Carlo Crivelli

Nationality: Italian

Style: Renaissance

Dates: born 1435 in Venice, died 1495 in Naples

Key works:

Virgin and Child c1460

The Annunciation with Saint Emidius 1486

The Madonna of the Swallow c1490–92

The Virgin and Child with Saints Francis and Sebastian 1491

Things to look for:

- paintings of religious subjects
- intense coloration from use of gesso and paint
- dramatic use of geometry and linear perspective
- dense patterning

Comparisons: Andrea Mantegna, Giovanni Bellini, Cosimo Tura, Sandro Botticelli

Glossary terms: altarpiece, gesso, perspective, polyptych

Delighting in detail and perspective

Crivelli's *The Annunciation with Saint Emidius* is a powerful depiction of its biblical subject matter—the announcement by the Archangel Gabriel to the Virgin Mary that she would bear the Son of God. The most striking feature of the painting, however, is its elaborate detail and its strong sense of linear perspective. Crivelli used the work to show off his mastery of "foreshortening" (drawing objects so that they appear to recede into the distance), which gives a sense of three-dimensional space on the surface of the painting. The orthogonal lines, which converge and meet at the "vanishing point," also help to guide the eye over the painting toward significant elements of the story; directly above the vanishing point is the ray from the heavens, which penetrates the wall of the palace and on which the dove of the Holy Spirit descends to the Virgin Mary.

The painting shows Crivelli's clear delineation of form—a style more akin to drawing than painting—and his attention to, and delight in, detail throughout the composition. For example, a carpet blows in the breeze and is anchored by a flowerpot.

At the front of the picture are an apple and gourd, both of which have shadows to enhance their realism, and appear as if part of a still-life painting. The apple is a symbol of mankind's fall from paradise and the gourd is a symbol of the Resurrection of Christ.

Crivelli painted this work at Ascoli Piceno in 1486. Four years previously the town had been granted self-government by Pope Innocent VIII. The people of Ascoli celebrated this declaration annually in a procession on the day (March 25) when the independence was granted, which coincided with the day observed by the church to commemorate the Annunciation. Though more reserved and stately in tone than celebratory, this painting combines its main subject with reference to the town's new status. On the bridge (above the vanishing point), a town dignitary receives a message, sent by carrier pigeon, stating that the pope has awarded Ascoli self-

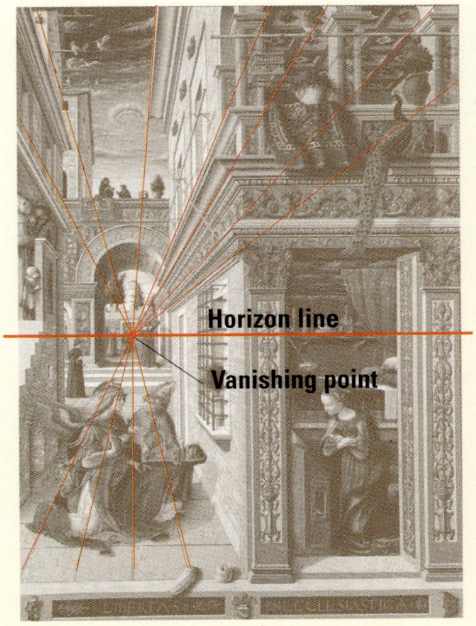

Linear perspective *The lines of perspective ("orthogonals") on the tiles on the floor and on the building are directed toward a single point on an imaginary horizon line. The orthogonals converge on the "vanishing point," and this gives a strong sense of distance between the foreground and background. The height of the figures throughout the painting is determined with reference to these converging lines; architectural elements, such as the window grid, also enhance the effect. The orthogonals (and elements such as the man's bright red cap), help to guide the eye toward significant elements of the story—in this case a ray of light from the heavens.*

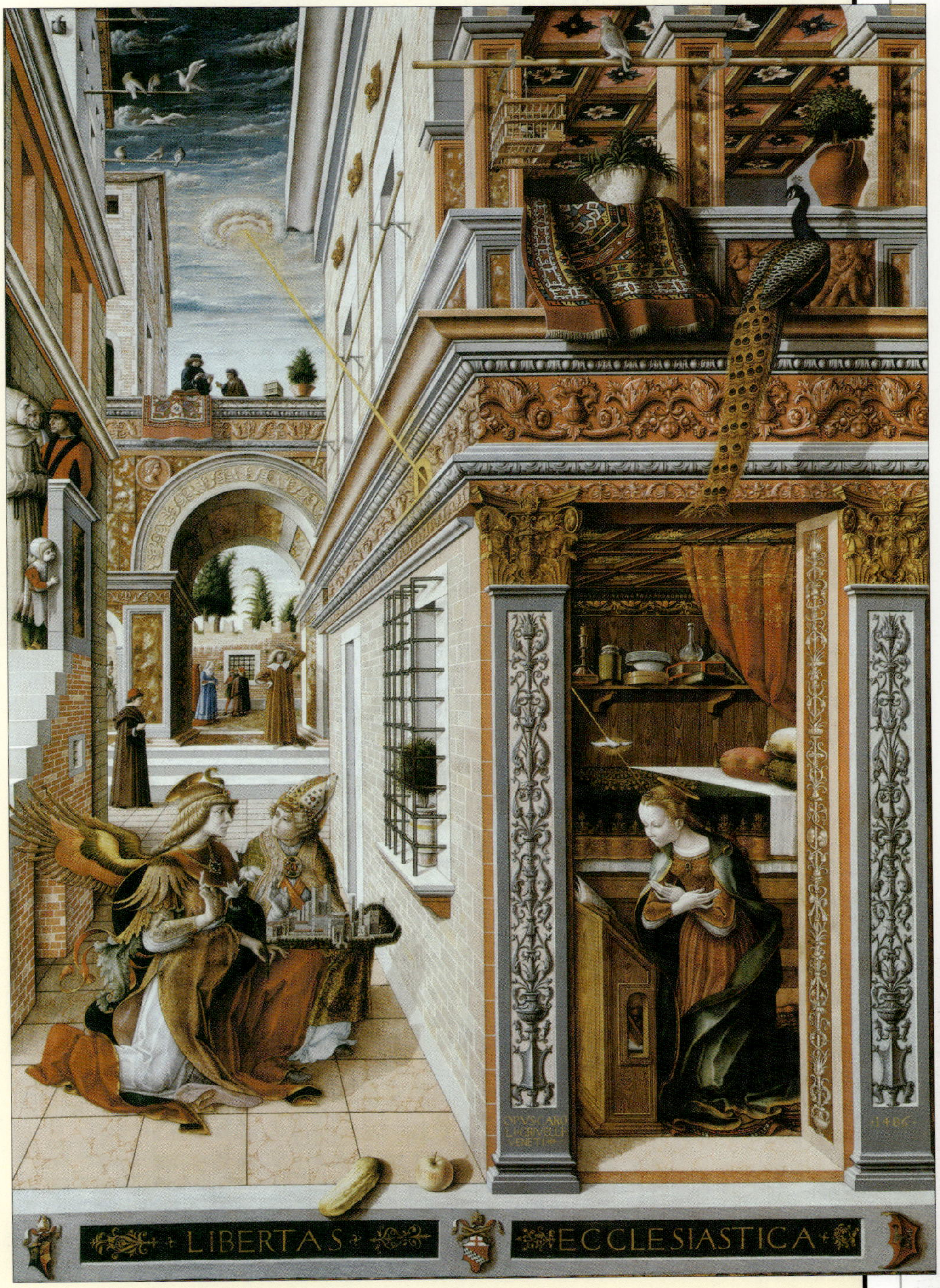

The Annunciation with Saint Emidius
1486. Oil on canvas, wood. 81½ x 58 in (207 x 147 cm). National Gallery, London.

government. Saint Emidius, the patron saint of the town, kneels next to the Archangel Gabriel, a model of the town of Ascoli in his hands. Further reference to the town includes the Latin inscription along the base of the panel, which reads *Libertas Ecclesiastica* (Freedom under the Church)—a phrase that referred to the town's new status.

Many of Crivelli's surviving works are panels from polyptychs that would once have formed a church altarpiece. Most of these panels have been separated over the centuries since Crivelli completed them, and they are often presented in museums as individual works. (This is the case with three side panels from the *Virgin and Child*, which are now in the National Gallery in London). Such panels from altarpieces frequently have flat but highly patterned backgrounds. Crivelli often used gold leaf or gold color mixed with gesso to create a textured, decorative surround to the main characters. In contrast, *The Annunciation* is a complex, detailed, and fully developed scene.

DALÍ Salvador

SALVADOR DALÍ IS ONE OF THE WORLD'S MOST POPULAR ARTISTS, whose mysterious, dreamlike, and scrupulously detailed paintings are immediately recognizable. His name has become synonymous with surrealism, even though most of his most famous paintings were produced after his expulsion from the movement in 1935.

Life and work

The son of a well-respected notary, Salvador Dalí was born in Figueras in Catalonia, a province of Spain known for the richness of its culture and the independent attitudes of its people. A child prodigy, he rapidly absorbed a variety of avant-garde styles. By the age of 17, he was already recognized by Catalan critics as a major talent. He was admitted to the San Fernando Academy in Madrid, where he embarked on a four-year course of study, but he became involved in a student fracas and was expelled.

From then on he dedicated his life to exploring his dreams and obsessions and cultivating an eccentric persona.

Full name: Salvador Felipe Jacinto Dalí
Nationality: Spanish (Catalan)
Style: surrealism
Dates: born 1904 in Figueras, died 1989 in Barcelona
Key works:
The Accommodation of Desire 1926
The Persistence of Memory 1931
Birth of Liquid Desire 1932
The Metamorphosis of Narcissus 1937
Dream Caused by the Flight of a Bee around a Pomegranate One Second before Waking Up 1944
Christ of Saint John of the Cross 1951
Things to look for:
- flamboyant but meticulous technique
- dreamlike, hallucinatory imagery
- incongruous juxtaposition of images
- metamorphic subjects

Comparisons: Joan Miró, André Masson, Max Ernst, René Magritte
Glossary terms: naïve, surrealism

Data file

His anarchic ambitions were fuelled by his close friend, the poet Frederico Garcia Lorca. His early paintings were also influenced by the English Pre-Raphaelites, the naïve style of the French painter Douanier Rousseau, and his fellow Spaniards Joan Miró and Pablo Picasso (whom he visited in Paris in 1926). He was also influenced by the detailed, historical paintings of the French 19th-century artist Ernest Meissonnier, who, along with Jan Vermeer and Jean-François Millet, became a focus of interest.

Dalí became one of the surrealists, a group with a fascination for the bizarre and irrational. The group, which included poets, painters such as Yves Tanguy, and the film director Luis Buñuel, attempted to marry dreams and reality, to create an "absolute reality," or "surreality." In 1927 Dalí began to produce works that reflected this quest. André Breton, the leader of the surrealists, later commented, "The coming of Dalí marks perhaps for the first time that the windows of the mind have been thrown wide open."

In 1928 Dalí collaborated with Luis Buñuel, making a shocking film, *Le Chien Andalou* (1929), with its famous opening featuring the slicing of an eye. Its narrative follows the delirious logic of a dream, Dalí's own obsession with decay, and his interests in subconscious urges, violence, and sexuality. With Buñuel he also made the film *L'Age d'Or* (1930); he later made a dream sequence for Alfred Hitchcock's film *Spellbound* (1945).

The great psychoanalyst Sigmund Freud, whose theories of the subconscious and submerged impulses were revolutionizing many fields of art and culture, was a strong influence for Dalí. The artist invented the pseudo-scientific term "paranoic-critical method" to refer to his conscious (or "critical") manipulation of reality.

Dalí's paintings, often depicting dreamlike landscapes, reveal a world of illusion and fantasy, in which objects set in strange juxtapositions melt and metamorphose into each other. His work includes such bizarre, hallucinatory images as the human figure made up of open drawers, and oversize watches melting (*The Persistence of Memory*, 1931).

In 1929 Dalí fell in love with Gala, then the wife of surrealist poet Paul Eluard; Gala became become his life-long companion and inspiration.

Stunned by his paintings and intrigued by his outrageous behavior, the surrealists initially embraced Dalí as one of their own, but by the mid-1930s his support of General Francisco Franco caused unease, and, despite his renown, Breton expelled him from the group.

In 1942 Dalí and Gala emigrated to the United States. By a combination of masterly promotion, skill, and the sheer force of his personality, Dalí became immensely wealthy. He published his autobiography, *The Secret Life of Salvador Dalí*, in 1942, and his first novel, *Hidden Faces*, in 1944.

Many of his later works (such as *Christ of Saint John of the Cross*, 1951) display a fascination with the Old Masters, Christian imagery, and the processes of perception. He also produced paintings of Gala and experimented with several other media, such as jewelry and theater sets.

By the time Dalí returned to Spain in 1955, André Breton had re-christened him Avida Dollars (Dollar Greedy), an unkind anagram of his name. In old age he became a recluse. Eccentric and subversive to the end, Dalí died one of the most famous and controversial artists of the 20th century.

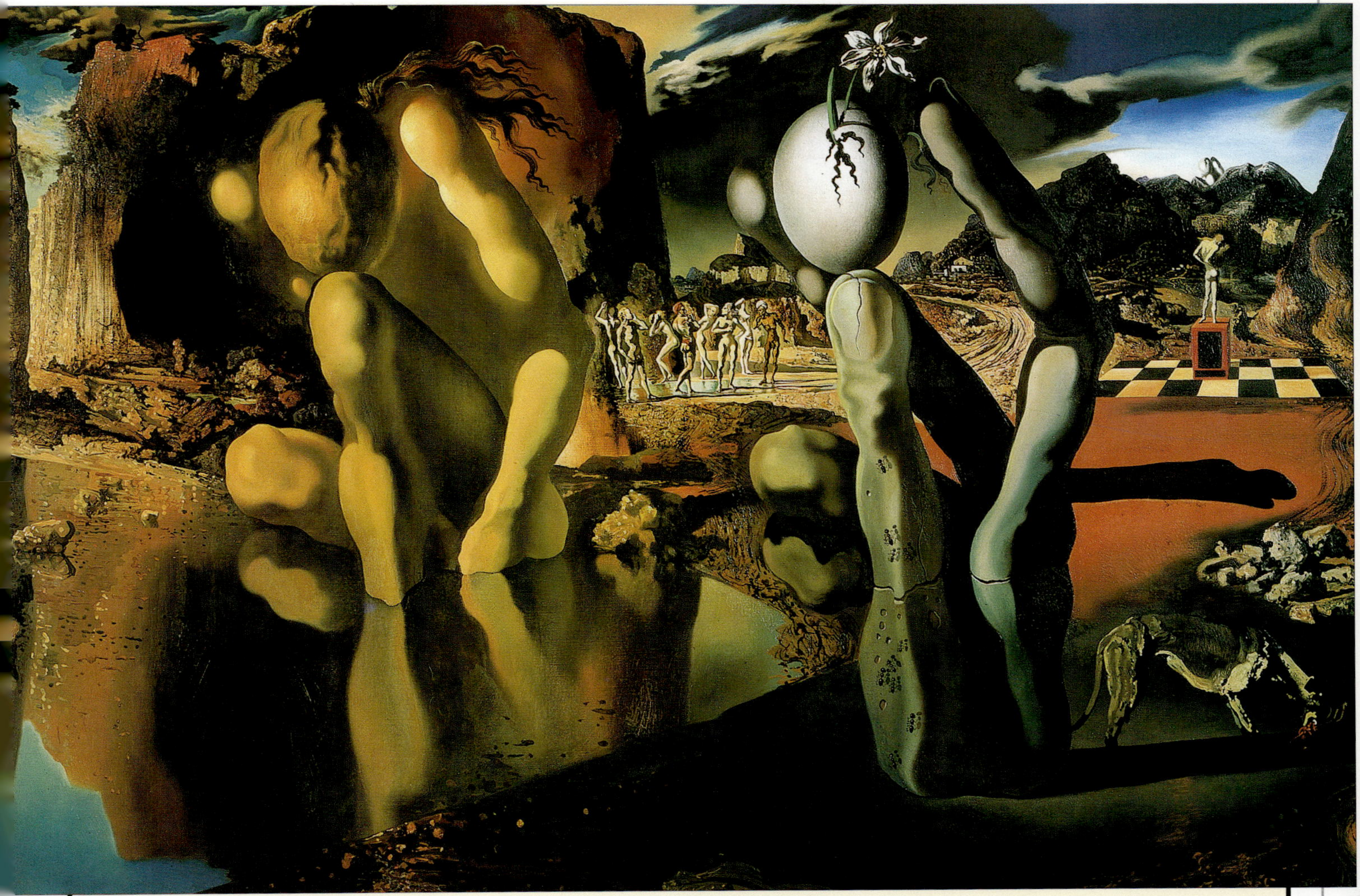

Dream sequences

The dreamlike quality of Dalí's paintings and the themes explored in them reflect the influence of Sigmund Freud, whose writing brought to public awareness the concept of subconscious desires and the symbolic importance of dreams themselves.

Like the other surrealists, Dalí was fascinated by the unconscious. *The Metamorphosis of Narcissus* was painted after his break with surrealism, but reflects this fascination, and explores the theme (also classically Freudian) of self-love.

The painting was inspired by an overheard conversation about a villager obsessed by his own reflection, who some local fishermen called a "bulb head" (a Spanish nickname for someone who is self-obsessed). Narcissus was the tragic figure of Greek mythology who fell hopelessly in love with his own image reflected in a pool, and was then transformed into a flower.

In the painting, Narcissus appears (on the left) as the figure of a boy kneeling down in a pool or lake. Bathed in sun, the figure resembles, or perhaps is, a rock reflected in the still waters. On the shore (on the right), the figure is echoed by a giant hand, the ants running up the thumb suggesting age or decay. The knee of the first figure corresponds to a finger on the hand in the second figure, and the head or "bulb" is now an egg from which bursts a narcissus flower, a symbol of rebirth.

The landscape of the painting belongs to an imaginary world. The intense coloration, sudden juxtapositions of scale, and ambiguous fantasy images describe a dreamscape in which time, space, and meaning are outside the control of the conscious mind.

The Metamorphosis of Narcissus *1937. 20 x 30¾ in (51 x 78 cm). Oil on canvas. Tate Gallery, London.*

DAUMIER Honoré

HONORÉ DAUMIER WAS ONE OF THE GREAT DRAFTSMEN and printmakers of the 19th century. Today he is considered an innovative sculptor and painter, although his sculptural works were only studies to help him define the figures in his satirical lithographs, and his paintings were little known until after his death.

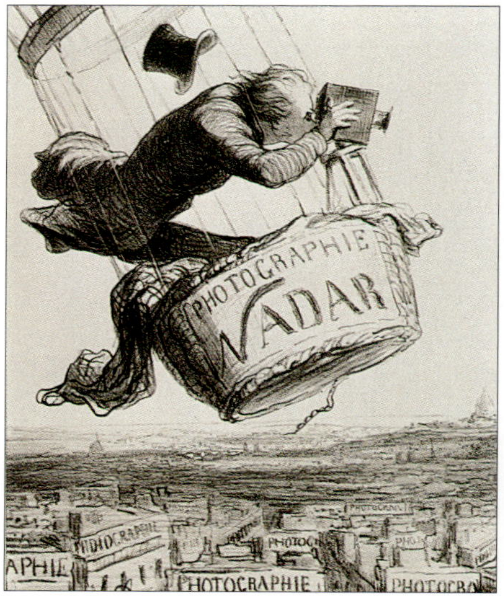

Nadar Elevating Photography to the Level of Art *(above) c1862. Lithograph. 10¾ x 8¾ in (27 x 22 cm). Private collection.*

Crispin and Scapin *(right) 1858–60. Oil on canvas. 23¾ x 32¾ in (60.5 x 82 cm). Musée d'Orsay, Paris.*

Life and work

The son of a glazier in Marseilles, Daumier lived his early life in near poverty. His father moved to Paris to try to establish a reputation as a poet and playwright, and the family eventually followed. The young Daumier entered the studio of the academic artist Alexandre Lenoir, but left as soon as he could to attend the Académie Julian, whose bohemian reputation attracted him. His talent for draftsmanship was consolidated by his visits to the Louvre, where he copied drawings by the Old Masters.

Working as a lithographer in 1830, he came to the attention of the radical journalist Charles Philipon, editor of *La Caricature*, a left-wing weekly journal. During the troubled days that followed the July revolution, Daumier's political caricatures caused offense to the king, Louis Philippe, and in 1832 Daumier was arrested, fined, and imprisoned for six months.

The 1835 censorship laws forced Daumier to avoid direct political comment and concentrate on the manners and customs of Parisian life. In 1845 he moved to Ile St Louis, and a year later married Marie-Alexandrine Dassy (Didine). These were his happiest years. He was friendly with Eugène Delacroix and Camille Corot, and admired by the great poet and critic Charles Baudelaire, who considered Daumier one of the greatest draftsmen of the century.

Daumier welcomed the socialist government that came to power after the revolution of 1848, but hopes for reform were shattered when Louis-Napoleon Bonaparte declared himself emperor in 1852. In this period Daumier created a number of paintings and reliefs that obliquely refer to Louis-Napoleon's oppressive regime: images of outcasts, exodus, clowns, and *saltimbanques* (wandering theatrical performers). Although deeply poignant in effect and ambitious in scale, these works were never critically very successful.

Ever a radical, Daumier was vocal in the call for artistic reforms that characterized the period. He used his prints to satirize the status quo, but with the suppression of press freedom, he once again had to avoid direct political comments and focus on less controversial subject matter. In the mid-1830s he began a series about an imaginary charlatan and trickster he named Robert Macaire; following the success of this he created the bedraggled agent provocateur Ratapoil ("the skinned rat") in the 1850s. A little later Daumier also mimicked the self-satisfied bourgeoisie with his character M. Joseph Prud'homme. He also produced many drawings and paintings of Cervantes' fictional character Don Quixote, a tragi-comic figure with whom Daumier clearly identified.

Increasingly plagued by problems with his sight, Daumier produced his last lithograph in 1872. An exhibition of his prints, paintings, drawings, and sculptures was held in 1878, but was not financially successful. Nevertheless, he was hailed by his friend Etienne Carjat as "the Michelangelo of the people." Reduced to near poverty, he was supported by his friends, and died in 1879 at the home that had been bought for him by the painter Jean-Baptiste-Camille Corot at Valmondais on the outskirts of Paris.

Data file

Full name: Honoré-Victorin Daumier

Nationality: French

Style: realism and caricature

Dates: born 1808 in Marseille, died 1879 in Paris

Key works:
- *Rue Transonain, April 15, 1834* 1834
- *La République* 1848
- *Ratapoil* 1850
- *Crispin and Scapin* 1858–60
- *Nadar Elevating Photography to the Level of Art* c1862
- *A Literary Discussion on the Second Gallery* 1864
- *Don Quixote and Sancho Panza* c1870

Things to look for:
- draftsmanship
- characterization
- satirical power and deep empathy with the human condition

Comparisons: Edouard Manet, Edgar Degas, Claude Monet, Henri Toulouse-Lautrec, Pablo Picasso, Vincent Van Gogh, L. S. Lowry

Glossary terms: academic art, lithography, realism

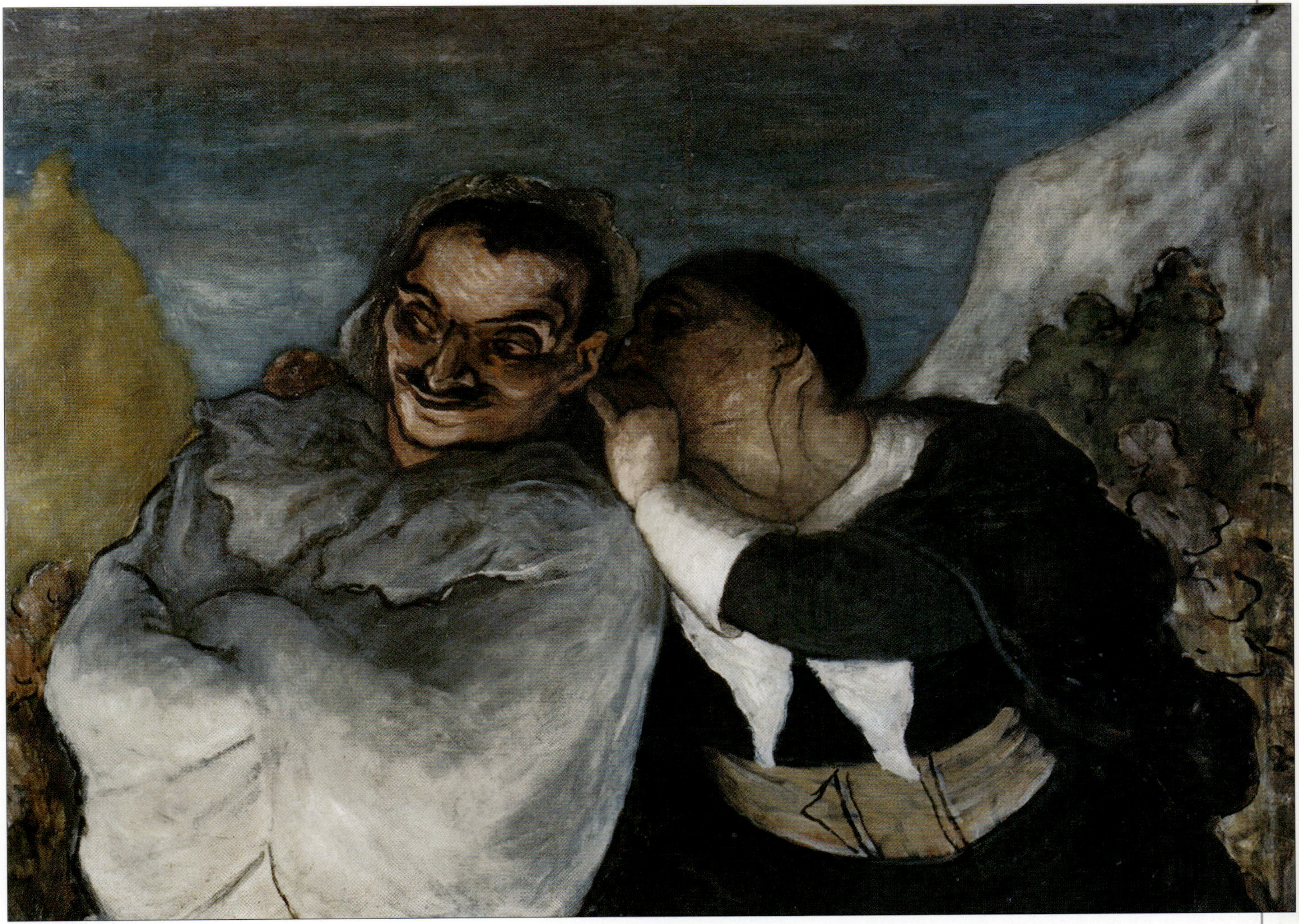

The passionate observer

Daumier's lithographs, paintings, and sculptures helped to define the age in which he lived. He was a prodigious worker; at least 3958 of his lithographs survive, as well as over 60 sculptures—including *Ratapoil* (1850), deemed by many to be one of the most innovative works of the 19th century—300 paintings (mostly unfinished), and 858 watercolors.

All of Daumier's works pulsate with life and are characterized by a feeling for the monumental and the dramatic, however humble the subject matter. His compositions are defined not only by an energetic calligraphic line, but also by his careful, theatrical distribution of light and dark. Daumier's figures are frequently cast in shadow against a luminous background, or vice versa, as in *Crispin and Scapin* (1858–60). His drawing style is fluid and free, with the cursive line covering the paper in a series of overlaying, undulating lines to create silvery grays, clean whites, and deep, velvet blacks.

Figures are characterized by their expressive faces and gestures, and possess a graphic power that renders the accompanying text to his prints redundant. Daumier's prints transcend the merely topical, and his finger was ever on the pulse of Parisian life. Nadar, pictured in *Nadar Elevating Photography to the Level of Art* (c1862), was a friend to many of the artists of the time and became famous for his caricatures, photographs, and for his hair-raising ascents in his hot-air balloon.

Daumier's debt to Michelangelo Buonarroti, Peter Paul Rubens, and Rembrandt, evident in his lithographs, becomes unmistakable in his paintings. He found his lack of technical knowledge frustrating, but it led to an original method. First, he used thin paint to brush in the initial idea. He then overlaid the drawing with pigments and glazes, and finally strengthened the image with line. Layers of paint were applied until a rich, encrusted surface was achieved, transforming observation of the everyday into dramatic narratives charged with atmosphere, movement, and life.

DAVID Jacques-Louis

DELACROIX CALLED HIM "THE FATHER OF MODERN PAINTING." An artist of enormous significance with a far-reaching legacy, Jacques-Louis David had intense personal vision and ambition, living at a time of social and political upheaval. His powerful and direct art, his theories, and his aspirations allied him to the classical school, while his individualism made him influential in initiating the modern art style of Romanticism.

Life and work

Jacques-Louis David was born into a middle-class family in Paris in 1748. From an early age, he decided that he wanted to be an artist. On the advice of his distant relative, the painter François Boucher, he studied with Joseph Vien, a successful French painter who worked in the neoclassical style.

David was resolutely ambitious and sure of his own skill, but it took several attempts for him to win the Prix de Rome that in 1774 took him to Italy. These early setbacks imbued him with an implacable hatred of the Academy that awarded the prize, and at one stage made him contemplate suicide.

David remained in Rome for five years. The revelation of classical antiquity was crucial to him, and he assimilated it into his own style to create art of great dramatic power.

In 1790 he returned to France to paint and teach, and two years later, already well-known and respected (he never had fewer than 40 pupils), he received the commission for *The Oath of the Horatii*. Completed in 1785, it was innovative in its clarity, dramatic characterization, simplicity of composition, and in its narrative and expressive power. The painting depicts the moment when the three warrior brothers of Horatii make an oath to do battle against the three brothers from Alba, the Curatii. The subject may have suggested anti-aristocratic tendencies prevalent at the time, but it also celebrated patriotic valor and self-sacrifice. Acclaimed both in Rome and in Paris, the painting was hailed as the most important example to date of the French neoclassicist style.

With the outbreak of the French revolution in 1789, David threw himself into revolutionary politics, becoming deputy to the convention. He used his position to spearhead an attack on the autonomy of the Academy, and succeeded in helping to end its exclusive privileges, opening the Salon to all artists. He organized a number of great public festivals and pageants to visualize and commemorate the early, idealistic days of the revolution. An active revolutionary, he was also among those who voted for the execution of Louis XVI. In 1793 he produced three paintings of martyrs of the revolution. One of these, *The Death of Marat* (1793), is considered perhaps the greatest piece of revolutionary propaganda ever painted.

With the fall of the left-wing Jacobin party with which David was associated, he came close to losing his life, but escaped with imprisonment. During his incarceration in the

Combining realism and drama

David was, according to Eugène Delacroix, in possession of the great technical secrets of the past. His technique combined drama and realism in a style that was the envy of other artists. Antoine-Jean Gros, Théodore Géricault, Eugène Delacroix, and Jean-Auguste-Dominique Ingres all declared their debt to him.

Much preparation went into his paintings, beginning with black chalk nude studies of the figures. To ensure their anatomical correctness, the basic compositional elements were sketched in and built up with a reddish-brown diluted paint known as bistre. Finally the canvas was covered in thin glazes of color, often rapidly and lightly scumbled. Delicate

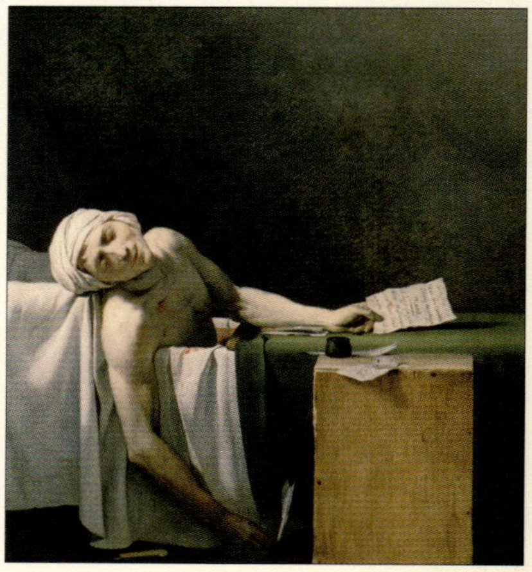

The Death of Marat *1793. Oil on canvas. 65 x 50½ in (165 x 128 cm). Pushkin Museum, Moscow.*

Data file

Full name: Jacques-Louis David

Nationality: French

Style: neoclassicism, Romanticism

Dates: born 1748 in Paris, died 1825 in Brussels, Belgium

Key works:
- *The Oath of the Horatii* 1785
- *The Death of Marat* 1793
- *The Lictors Returning the Bodies of His Sons to Brutus* 1798
- *The Sabine Women* 1799
- *Napoleon on the Saint Bernard Pass* 1801
- *The Coronation* 1805–10
- *Napoleon* 1812

Things to look for:
- drama and monumentality
- propaganda elements

Comparisons: Antoine-Jean Gros, Théodore Géricault, Eugène Delacroix, Jean-Auguste-Dominique Ingres, Pablo Picasso, Fernand Léger, artists of the Third Reich such as Anton Breker

Glossary terms: classicism, neoclassicism, Romanticism, Salon, scumble touches of opaque paint would bring up the effects of light and texture.

Departing from the prevailing rococo style, and inspired by discoveries at Pompeii and Herculaneum, David led a return to the classical styles of ancient Greece and Rome, giving moralistic overtones to his paintings of contemporary historical events. He produced many portraits, some of them monumental and some less formal, culminating in his final work, *The Three Ladies of Ghent* (1818).

The Death of Marat (1793) shows David's ability to use light and space to dramatic effect. Marat was one of the leaders of the French revolution—and a friend of David—who was stabbed to death in his bed.

The sculptural qualities evident in this painting may be seen at their most effective in *Napoleon on the Saint Bernard Pass* (1801). Commissioned to show Napoleon crossing the Alps to conquer northern Italy, the fantastical portrait depicts Napoleon on his horse in a storm. In fact, Napoleon did not cross this pass, and traveled by donkey. (David used a sculpture as a model when he was painting the rearing horse.) But such prosaic truths are not the truths that make history, as David and Napoleon, masters of propaganda, both knew.

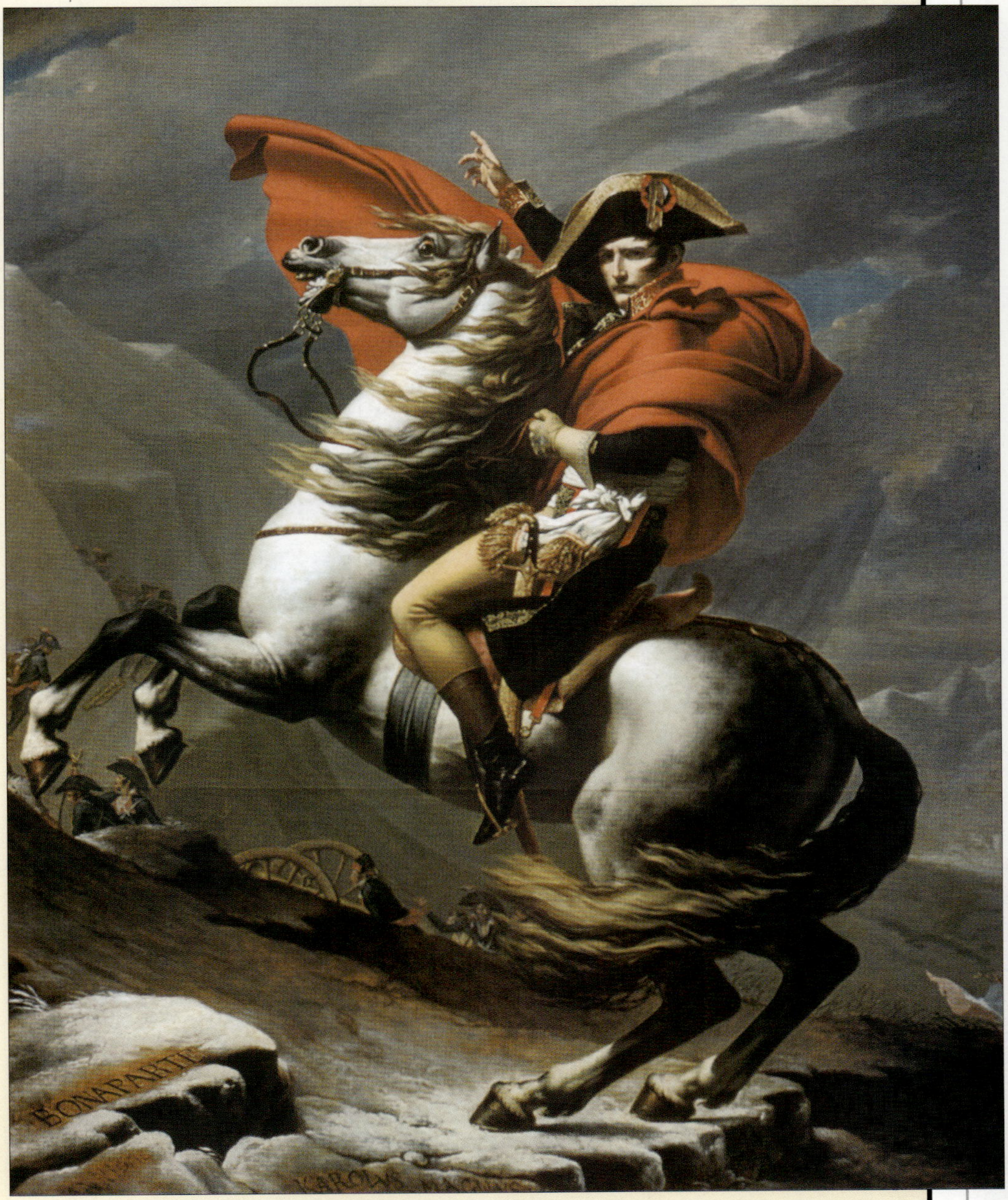

Napoleon on the Saint Bernard Pass
1801. Oil on canvas. 97 x 91 in (246 x 232 cm). Kunsthistorisches Museum, Austria.

Luxembourg prison he painted a sensitive landscape and planned his great canvas of reconciliation, *The Sabine Women*, completed in 1799.

His work was now characterized by a simpler, purer style approaching the simplicity and severity of the ancient Greeks. He sketched a brilliant portrait of the young Napoleon (*Napoleon Crossing the Bridge at Arcole*, c1797), who recognized his usefulness, and David became the major supporter of the Bonapartes.

When Napoleon seized power in 1799, David was made artistic director to the first consul. As a faithful servant of the new regime, he became involved in a wide variety of artistic reforms, and was commissioned to paint many works that would elevate Napoleon's qualities as a leader. He celebrated the coronation of Josephine with a painting in Rubensian style; in a more realist style he painted a portrait of the emperor as a tired but indefatigable bureaucrat (*Napoleon*, 1812).

David's life had parallels with Napoleon's; with the emperor's final defeat at the battle of Waterloo in 1815, David chose exile in Brussels rather than enjoying the favors of Louis XVIII. During these years he produced a brilliant series of portraits and a number of mythological scenes. In 1825, as a result of being struck by a carriage, he died, venerated by some, forgotten by most, but of an enormous influence on the following generation of artists.

DAVIS Stuart

STUART DAVIS WAS A HIGHLY IMAGINATIVE ARTIST whose work made a huge contribution to the development of modern art in the United States. While borrowing stylistic elements from French cubism, his bright, exuberant canvases are quintessentially American and express the vitality of the modern world.

Life and work

Born in Philadelphia in 1894, Stuart Davis had an artistic upbringing. His mother was a practicing sculptor, and his father was the art director of the newspaper *The Philadelphia Press*. In this creative climate Davis soon developed an interest in art.

In 1910 Davis and his family moved to New York City. Here he began studying with the artist Robert Henri and produced numerous paintings that focused on the harsh realities of everyday life in the poorer areas of the city. He also worked as an illustrator for magazines, including the left-wing journal *The Masses*.

The Armory Show of 1913 introduced Davis to the work of such major European modern painters as Paul Gauguin, Vincent Van Gogh, and Henri Matisse. He later said that this experience had had a profound effect upon his own art. Yet Davis's first successful works of the 1920s reveal his passion for all things American, as well as his awareness of European modern art. In such paintings as *Lucky Strike* (1921) and *Odol* (1924), Davis took ordinary, everyday objects and elevated them into the realm of high art. By introducing these consumer goods into his art Davis was clearly influenced by the café still lifes of the cubists Georges Braque, Pablo Picasso, and Juan Gris. These European artists had frequently included references to popular brands of alcohol or cigarettes in their paintings and collages, in order to express modernity and to emphasize the flatness of the canvas. In his works, however, Davis turned specifically to American goods, such as Lucky Strike cigarettes and Odol mouthwash. His emphasis on mass production and consumerism also reflected the industrial and economic boom of the period.

In 1928 Davis visited Paris for the first time. Here he painted many brightly colored scenes of the Parisian streets and squares that he visited, including *Place Pasdeloup* and *Place des Vosges* (both 1928). On his return to New York these works helped him to formulate a new and simplistic style.

Davis was attracted to modern popular music and spent a lot of time in the newly emerging jazz clubs of New York City. Indeed, he saw an affinity between his paintings and jazz; he saw his use of color, tone, and composition as comparable to the use of musical colors, tones, and compositional arrangements in the new musical form. The bright colors and lively forms of Davis's work also suggest the

Data file

Full name: Stuart Davis

Nationality: American

Style: cubism

Dates: born 1894 in Philadelphia, died 1964 in New York, NY

Key works:
- *Lucky Strike* 1921
- *Odol* 1924
- *Place Pasdeloup* 1928
- *Place des Vosges* 1928
- *Eggbeater V* 1930
- *The Mellow Pad* 1945–51
- *Owh! In San Pão* 1951

Things to look for:
- bright, vibrant colors
- representation of objects from the modern world of consumer goods
- inclusion of words and signs

Comparisons: Robert Henri, Georges Braque, Pablo Picasso, Juan Gris, Fernand Léger, Joan Miró, Gerald Murphy

Glossary terms: cubism, purism

Davis and the modern still life

The still-life painting *Eggbeater V* (1930) reveals Davis's dual affection for European modern art and American consumer production. The work was completed shortly after Davis's first visit to Paris, where he encountered for the first time the post-World War I work of such artists as Pablo Picasso, Georges Braque, Juan Gris, and Fernand Léger, the founders of cubist art. At the same time Davis was inspired by the recent works of Amedee Ozenfant and the famous Swiss-born French modernist architect and painter, Le Corbusier. The work of these two artists, known as purism, was a development of cubism into a new, more rational style based upon mathematical principles.

As the cubists had done, Davis takes as his theme objects associated with French café culture: in this case a mandolin, a vase, and a café table. In the middle of this otherwise conventional arrangement, however, Davis included a modern, mechanically produced eggbeater.

Each of these objects is simply drawn and displayed against a bright-blue background. Davis clearly borrows stylistic elements from cubism for his painting. The table top, for example, appears to be tilted, as if it were being viewed from a high angle, while the table leg is seen straight on. Moreover, Davis shows us the internal mechanics of the table leg, as if a section has been cut through the wood, thereby giving an internal and external view of the table.

The objects themselves are all drawn with great clarity and precision, as if they were the work of a technical draftsman or engineer. In both subject and style Davis thus combines his awareness of, and respect for, European modern art with a reference to the modern industrial world that was a symbol of the United States to the rest of the world. The traditional still-life objects are juxtaposed with a modern, machine-made eggbeater, while cubist forms are displayed alongside industrial drawing techniques.

Eggbeater V was the last of a series of still-life works on this theme that Davis produced. In the earlier works, which he created before his trip to Paris, the objects themselves are scarcely identifiable, Davis having abstracted them to the point where they are almost unrecognizable. In *Eggbeater V*, however, he embraced the more austere and orderly style of cubism and purism that was typical of Parisian art of the time, and combined this with the vibrant colors and energy that he believed best characterized life in the modern United States.

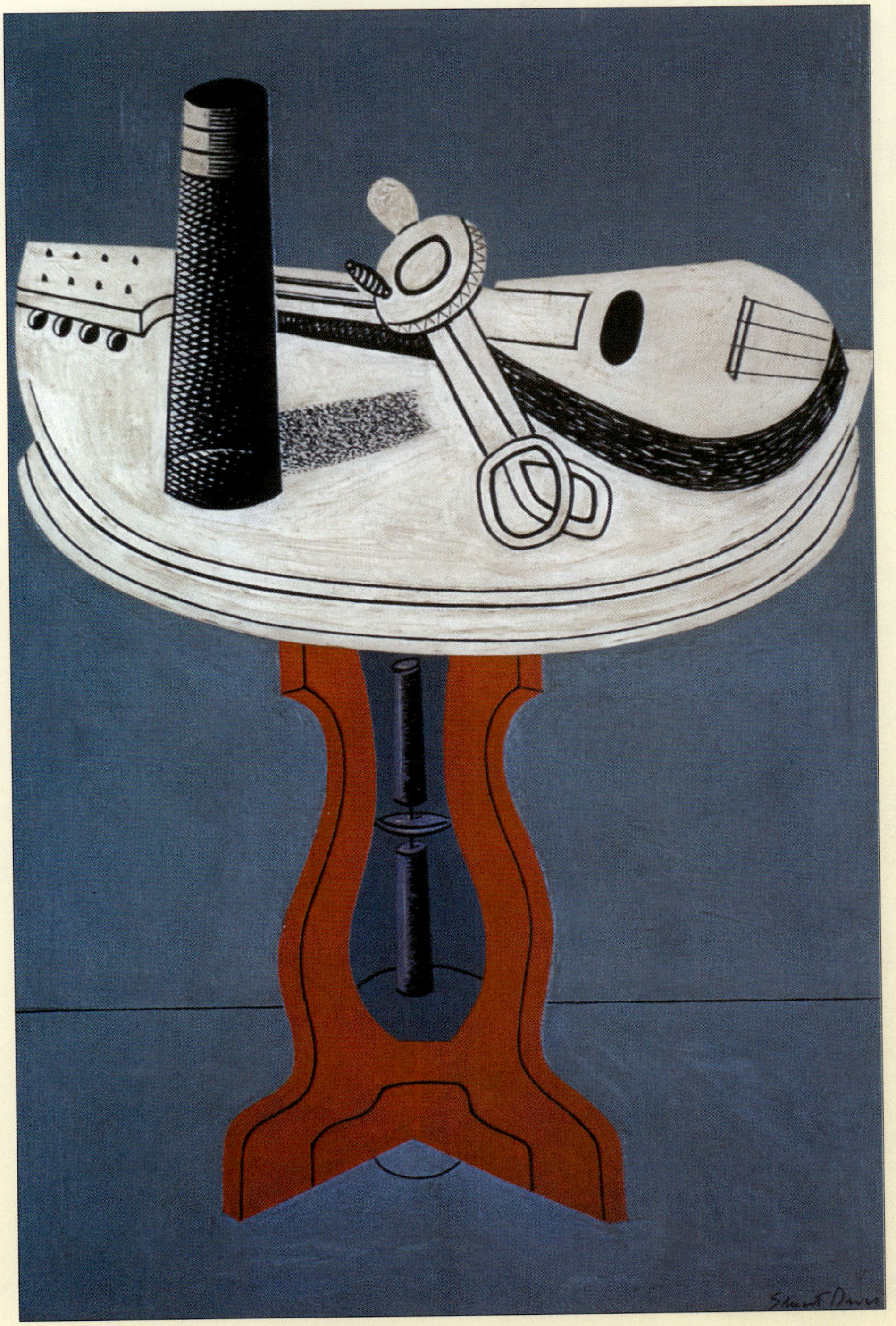

Eggbeater V *1930. Oil on canvas. 50¼ x 32¼ in (127.5 x 82 cm). Museum of Modern Art, New York, NY.*

spontaneity and improvisation of a jazz solo.

During the Depression of the 1930s many American artists turned their backs on European art in favor of focusing on more regionally inspired subject matter. Artists such as Thomas Hart Benton and Grant Wood, for example, rejected modern styles and returned to more traditionally realist forms of painting. Davis, however, continued to support the development of a specifically American type of modern art. His late works, including *The Mellow Pad* (1945–51) and *Owh! In San Pão* (1951), retain the exuberance of his earlier works, fusing colors, forms, and styles reminiscent of Joan Miró and Fernand Léger with the language and rhythm of the modern United States. In combining his awareness of European art with his experience of modern American life Davis created a uniquely American art form.

DEGAS Edgar

EDGAR DEGAS WAS ONE OF THE FOREMOST FRENCH ARTISTS of the late 19th century. He followed an individual path, combining the impressionists' love of light and color with a more rigorous style of figure drawing, and a realist's passion for capturing moments of everyday life.

Life and work

Edgar Degas was born into a well-to-do Parisian banking family. As a student, he gave up law for painting, attending the Ecole des Beaux-Arts in Paris in 1855–56. His early training with Louis Lamothe, a former pupil of Jean Auguste Dominique Ingres, emphasized the importance of studying the human figure, and learning from classical art and the Old Masters by drawing copies. Degas always remained a highly accomplished draftsman.

At the age of 22 he traveled to Italy, where he lived for three years. He visited the art galleries in Naples, Florence, and Rome, where again he drew many copies. While staying with his aunt Laura Bellelli in Florence, he began a group portrait of her family (completed in 1867). This shows his lifelong taste for combining formal poses with unusual compositions (for example, the head of the family, Baron Bellelli, is shown seated with his back to the viewer).

On his return from Italy, Degas settled in Paris. It was in the Louvre in 1862, while making a copy of a work by the great 16th-century Spanish artist Diego Velázquez, that he met the painter Edouard Manet. Like Degas, Manet had formed his own style by studying the Old Masters, and was soon to cause a scandal with his 1863 painting *Déjeuner sur l'herbe*, which showed a nude woman having a picnic with two men in contemporary dress (the nude was considered an acceptable subject only in the context of classical themes). Manet put Degas in touch with the group of progressive young artists who later became known as the impressionists.

At this time, Degas was painting mainly historical works, such as *Young Spartans Exercising* (1860–62), and portraits. By contrast, impressionist painters, such as Claude Monet and Camille Pissarro, painted everyday scenes and places. They aimed to capture the "impression" of a passing moment in the vivid play of light and shadow. Degas was influenced by their choice of modern rather than historical subjects and their fresh use of color.

In 1870 France went to war with Prussia, resulting in the Prussian invasion of eastern France and the siege of Paris. Degas served in the National Guard, and, after the war, went to London and then to New Orleans, where he had relatives. There he painted *The Cotton Market at New Orleans* (1873), extending his interest in subjects taken from modern life. He had already started to produce paintings of horse races, and of musicians and ballet dancers.

In April 1874, when Degas was 39, the impressionists held an exhibition—the first of eight over the following 12 years. Degas contributed to most of these, but he always saw himself (and was seen by the public) as standing apart from the main group. Monet, for instance, was often criticized for his indistinct forms, but Degas' strong grounding in figure-drawing won him the respect even of traditionalists.

In his later career, Degas produced images from the daily life of women. Among the most memorable were his pastel drawings of women bathing.

During his final years he began to lose his sight; he stopped painting five years before his death at the age of 83.

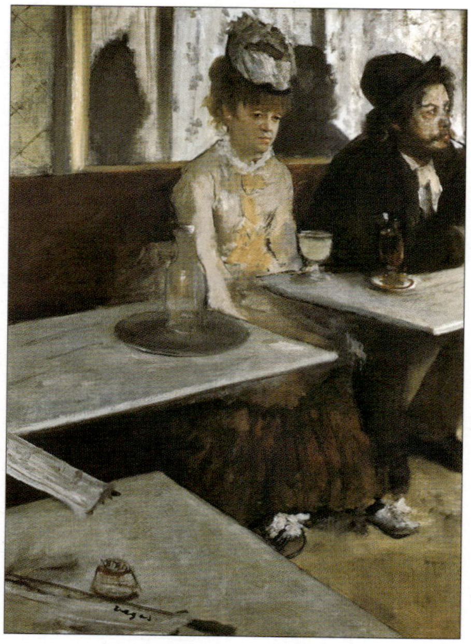

Absinthe *1876. Oil on canvas. 36 x 26 1/2 in (92 x 68 cm). Musée d'Orsay, Paris.*

Data file

Full name: Hilaire-Germain-Edgar Degas

Nationality: French

Style: impressionism/realism

Dates: born 1834 in Paris, died 1917 in Paris

Key works:

Portrait of the Bellelli Family 1858–67

Young Spartans Exercising 1860–62

The Cotton Market at New Orleans 1873

Absinthe 1876

The Little 14-year-old Dancer 1881

Combing the Hair c1896

Things to look for:

- people shown in informal, everyday settings
- figures with clearly defined forms, positioned off-center in the picture
- close observation of movement and gesture
- rich use of color

Comparisons: Jean Auguste Dominique Ingres, Paul Cézanne, Edouard Manet, Claude Monet

Glossary terms: classicism, *en plein air*, figure drawing, impressionism, Old Masters, realism

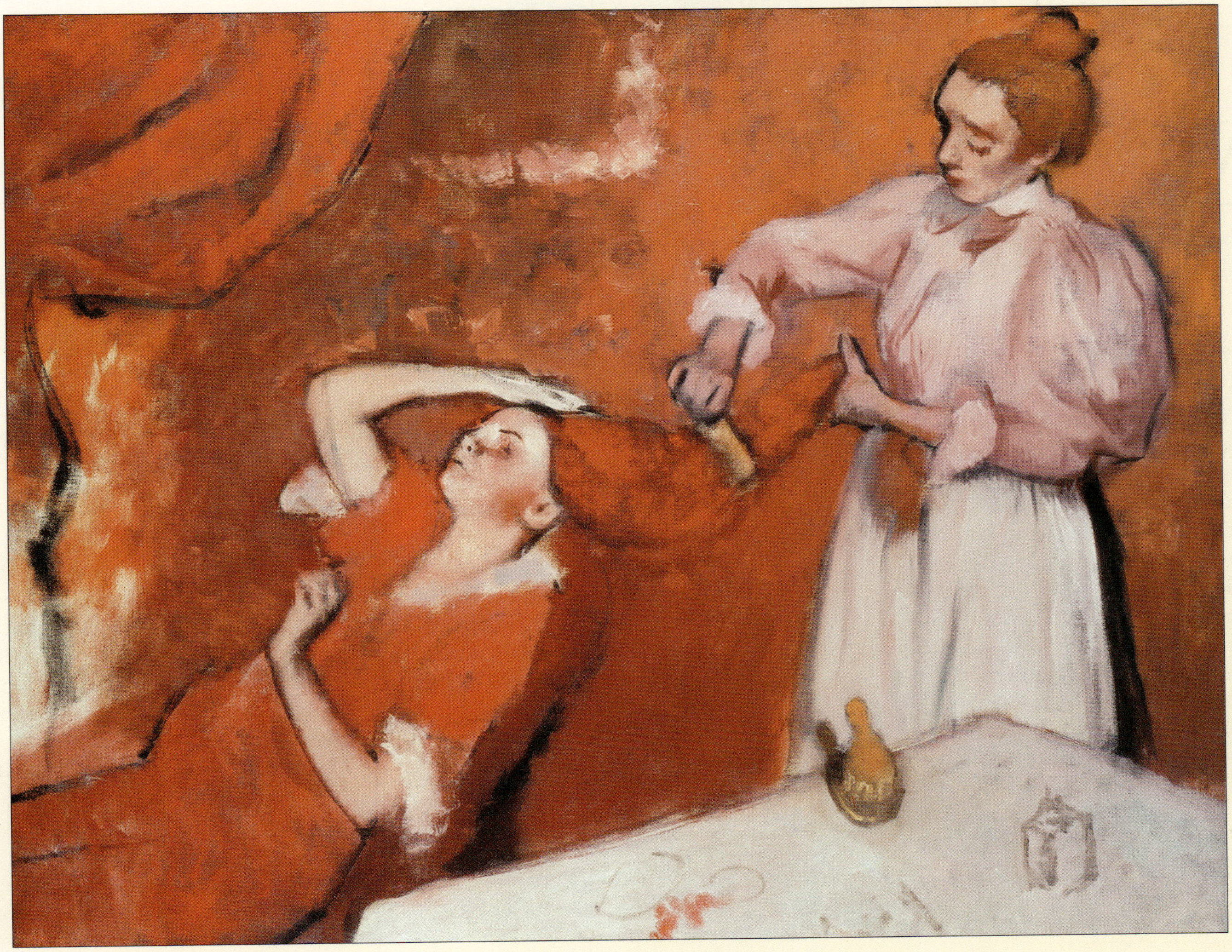

A realist among impressionists

Unlike his fellow impressionists, who became known, above all, for their new vision of landscape, Degas was more interested in the human figure. He studied groups and crowds rather than empty fields, urban interiors rather than open-air scenes. Whereas impressionists liked to paint outside (*en plein air*), from nature, Degas painted in his studio, using drawings that he had made earlier of his subject. He studied closely the way people and animals move, returning repeatedly to the themes of horse racing, ballet dancing, and everyday activities such as ironing and bathing.

In composing his pictures, Degas often combined strongly defined forms with unsettling off-center framing devices. In his *Absinthe* (1876), the picture's human subjects—a woman and a man (at her side but isolated from her) in a bar—are placed in the top righthand corner, while the angular shapes of the empty table tops and floor occupy the foreground.

Degas' own kind of realism (reproducing the actual appearance of things and people, not idealized or picturesque versions) can be seen in his sculpture of *The Little 14-year-old Dancer* (1881). Later cast in bronze, this figure was originally made of wax, with a real tutu and wig, producing a lifelike effect that shocked the public. Many people at the time believed that art should be pleasing and uplifting, and that it had no business presenting ordinary life.

Degas experimented with different media, including oil paints, pastels, printmaking, and sculpture. In his late works his style became freer and his drawing more fluid. *Combing the Hair* (c1896) shows his ability to capture complex, interrelated movements in the apparently simple routine of a maid combing a woman's hair. The strong red coloring gives this scene a dramatic intensity, while at the same time it remains intimate and domestic.

From around the same time, Degas' pastel drawings of women bathing and drying themselves, such as *After the Bath, Woman Wiping Her Neck* (1898), show the human body with the same rich texture of light and color that his fellow impressionists used in their depictions of landscape.

Combing the Hair *c1896. Oil on canvas. 45 x 57½ in (114 x 146 cm). National Gallery, London.*

DE KOONING Willem

WILLEM DE KOONING BECAME ONE OF THE MAJOR FIGURES of the New York-based movement of abstract expressionism. Unlike his contemporaries, however, de Kooning did not restrict himself to abstract images, but included figurative elements; his most famous paintings are of the female form.

Life and work

Willem de Kooning was born in the Netherlands in 1904. He trained as an artist at the Academy in his home town, Rotterdam, for eight years. In 1926 he emigrated to the United States and settled in New York City. Initially, de Kooning's paintings were rooted in the academic tradition of representational art—still-life painting and studies of the human form. However, he was soon influenced by other foreign artists who had settled in the United States. In 1928 he met the Armenian painter Arshile Gorky. Gorky introduced him to many of the avant-garde artists based in New York.

By the mid-1930s, de Kooning had begun to experiment with different styles, and was exploring both abstract and figurative ways of painting.

In 1939 the Museum of Modern Art in New York held a retrospective of Picasso's work. This exhibition had a major effect on de Kooning, not least because Picasso's paintings showed him a possible path for his own work—a path of semiabstraction. Picasso painted figures distorted into geometric shapes. Some features were exaggerated, while other aspects were given a very basic form; this appealed greatly to de Kooning. His work in the mid-1940s owes a great deal to Picasso: *Pink Angels* (1945), for example—one of de Kooning's defining works—clearly derives from Picasso's *Large Nude in a Red Armchair* (1929).

Toward the end of the 1940s, de Kooning's style changed dramatically. He began to paint more figurative works and fantasies. At this time, the artist began a series of monochrome paintings, the *Black and White* series. The works in this series are abstract. Yet elements within them refer to the real world of objects and people—lines and shapes seem to form into doors, chairs, stairs, and body parts, almost unintentionally. "I really think it's sort of silly to do it," de Kooning said of figurative painting, "but the moment you take this attitude it's just as silly not to do it." Toward the end of this series, the artist began to use color once again. This can be seen most subtly in *Attic* (1949), and then with greater vibrancy in *Excavation* (1950) and in *Painting* (1959).

In the early 1950s de Kooning began his famous *Woman* series—his third such series. The controversial work was first exhibited in New York in 1953. It provided a focus for debate between those people who believed in an entirely abstract style of painting and those who believed that figurative

Data file

Full name: Willem de Kooning

Nationality: Dutch (U.S. citizen after 1962)

Style: abstract expressionism

Dates: born 1904 in Rotterdam, died 1997 in East Hampton, NY, United States

Key works:

- *Pink Angels* 1945
- *Attic* 1949
- *Night Square* 1949
- *Excavation* 1950
- *Woman I* (from the series *Woman I–VI*, 1950–53)
- *February* 1957

Things to look for:

- energetic use of paint
- a shift between abstract and figurative painting
- a varied use of color—sometimes vibrant, sometimes very subtle
- an even balance in his compositions, despite the apparent whirlwind of anarchic energy

Comparisons: Chaim Soutine, Arshile Gorky, Pablo Picasso, Jackson Pollock, Francis Bacon

Glossary terms: abstract art, abstract expressionism, avant-garde, cubism, figurative art, semiabstraction, still life, surrealism, Venice Biennale

The anxious image

De Kooning absorbed styles from all around him and reinterpreted them through his own hand and eye. He used the fractured and fragmented view of the world introduced by cubism, and the subconscious, intuitive actions of the surrealists. Through this combination of influences, and the academic training that aided his sense of composition and use of color, de Kooning produced his own version of abstract expressionism.

During his most celebrated period, the 1950s, the artist used every medium at his disposal—oil paint, household enamel paint, crayon, charcoal, graphite, and collage—to achieve his results.

In *Woman IV* (1952–53), we see his most dramatic style. It is an anxious painting, half-obliterated by its own making. In it we see the simultaneous creation and destruction of the image. The painting has been worked over repeatedly with fast, energetic brushstrokes to arrive at this point. In fact, the brushwork seems almost violent. The paint has been layered on thickly, scraped away and, in places, built up again.

As an abstract expressionist, de Kooning always acted in response to the canvas in front of him, rather than carefully planning the composition and theme. The significant communication is between the artist and the medium, the painter and the paint, and the creative process is as much the subject of the work as anything else. Because of this approach—the constant questioning of the painting while working on it—the finished work is always, to some extent, unresolved. In fact, de Kooning himself was often unsure as to whether or not the work was finished.

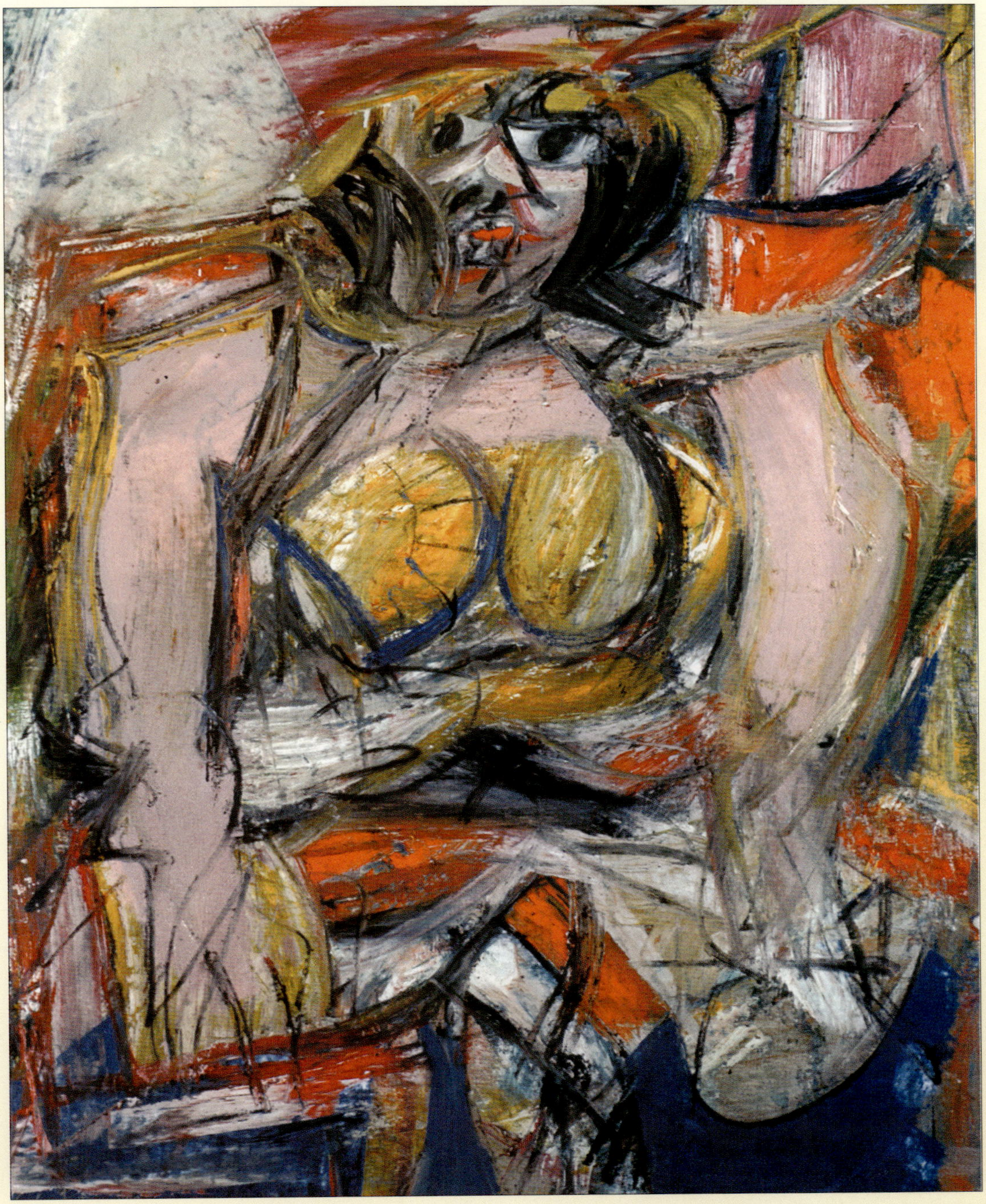

Woman IV *1952–53. Oil and enamel on canvas. 59 x 46¼ in (150 x 117.5 cm). Nelson Atkins Museum of Art, Kansas City, MO.*

work still had a place in modern art. The attention, whether good or bad, helped to promote de Kooning around the world. He was chosen to represent the United States at the 27th Venice Biennale in 1954, and was also included in a major showcase of American painters and sculptors held at the Whitney Museum of American Art in the same year.

After this, de Kooning began to produce abstract landscapes, given a sense of time and place by titles such as *Saturday Night* (1956) and *Suburb in Havana* (1958). His frenetic style gave way to more confident brushstrokes, without producing the tortured atmosphere that comes from continually painting and repainting the subject.

In 1962 de Kooning became a U.S. citizen. Through the following decades he received widespread recognition and many awards, but his best and most influential work was behind him. However, he continued to paint, sculpt, and make prints until the end of his life. He died in East Hampton at the age of 92 after suffering from Alzheimer's disease.

DELACROIX Eugène

EUGÈNE DELACROIX'S WORKS are admired for their sense of movement and drama. He is seen as the leading painter of the Romantic movement in France, and the greatest colorist of his time.

Life and work

Although his early works set him at the forefront of the Romantic movement, Delacroix did not want to be associated with any group of artists; all his life he fiercely preserved his independence. He was taught by Baron Guérin, who also taught Théodore Géricault, a history painter whose work had a profound influence on Delacroix.

Delacroix had grown up in the full glamor of the French Empire led by Napoleon Bonaparte. Like many people of his generation, he carried with him to his death a sense of disillusionment and loss associated with the fall of Napoleon (who was defeated by the British, Dutch, and Prussians at the Battle of Waterloo), and the humiliation of France that followed. His early paintings particularly echo this pessimism and despair: *The Death of Sardanapalus* (1827) is a fantastical image of eroticism, violence, and death. Only art seemed meaningful to Delacroix. "What are most real to me," he wrote in his journal in 1824, "are the illusions I create with my painting; the rest is shifting sand." Literature and music were also important; he felt that reading the Bible, and writers such as Homer and William Shakespeare, was essential to his creativity.

In 1830 revolutionaries in Paris deposed the French king Charles X; the Duke of Orléans was crowned King Louis Philippe in his place. This inspired Delacroix to follow the example of Géricault and to paint a modern allegorical work, *Liberty Leading the People* (1830). Dissatisfied with its reception, and his own artistic direction, he fell into a profound depression, which only lifted when he was offered the opportunity to accompany a diplomatic mission to North Africa in 1832.

The experience proved a turning-point: in Africa he encountered what he called a "living antiquity." He was profoundly moved by the sense of history and the light of North Africa, where the rich colors, bustling everyday life, and heat provided a dramatic contrast to the constraints of 19th-century Europe.

Despite Delacroix's refusal to compromise his own artistic vision, from 1833 he received many commissions to produce large-scale decorative works for some of the most important civic and religious buildings of Paris. He had traveled to England, where he admired the freedom of English painting, to Spain to study Diego Velázquez and Francisco Goya, and to Holland to study Peter Paul Rubens and Rembrandt. But he never visited Italy, despite the fact that the masters of the Renaissance and baroque such as Tintoretto and Paolo Veronese inspired him as a painter of allegory.

Delacroix is often seen as the typical misunderstood genius. He never married, remaining dedicated to his art, though his independent spirit and unconventional techniques went against the approach of the art establishment. He kept a fascinating journal of his personal and professional life, and wrote much on the theory of art. His output was prodigious: he left more than 9000 paintings, pastels, and drawings in his studio.

His final years were dedicated to the decoration of the Chapel of the Angels at Saint Sulpice in Paris, where his *Jacob Wrestling with the Angel* (1861) can be found.

Data file

Full name: Ferdinand Victor Eugène Delacroix
Nationality: French
Style: Romanticism
Dates: born 1798 in Charenton-Saint-Maurice, died 1863 in Paris
Key works:
- *The Death of Sardanapalus* 1827
- *Liberty Leading the People* 1830
- *Women of Algiers* 1834
- *Arab on Horseback Being Attacked by a Lion* 1849
- *Ovid Among the Scythians* 1855–59
- *Jacob Wrestling with the Angel* 1861

Things to look for:
- rich use of color
- biblical, mythical, historical, and literary scenes
- a keen sense of movement

Comparisons: Théodore Géricault, Titian, Paolo Veronese, Henri Matisse, Pablo Picasso
Glossary terms: allegory, baroque, history painting, neoclassicism, Old Masters, Renaissance, Romanticism

Ovid Among the Scythians *1855–59. Oil on canvas. 34 1/2 x 51 1/4 in (87.5 x 130 cm). National Gallery, London.*

Contrasting color

Delacroix was inspired by Peter Paul Rubens' use of color, and by the English landscape painters Richard Parkes Bonington (who was also a friend) and John Constable; in 1825 he saw Constable's *The Hay Wain* (1821), which impressed him strongly with its use of color to create luminosity and vividness.

In 1839 French chemist Michel Chevreul had published a study "On the Harmony and Contrast of Colors." He had discovered that placing complementary colors next to each other makes them seem much more intense, giving them the greatest "simultaneous contrast." Using his knowledge of Chevreul's work, and of past art, Delacroix developed a technique

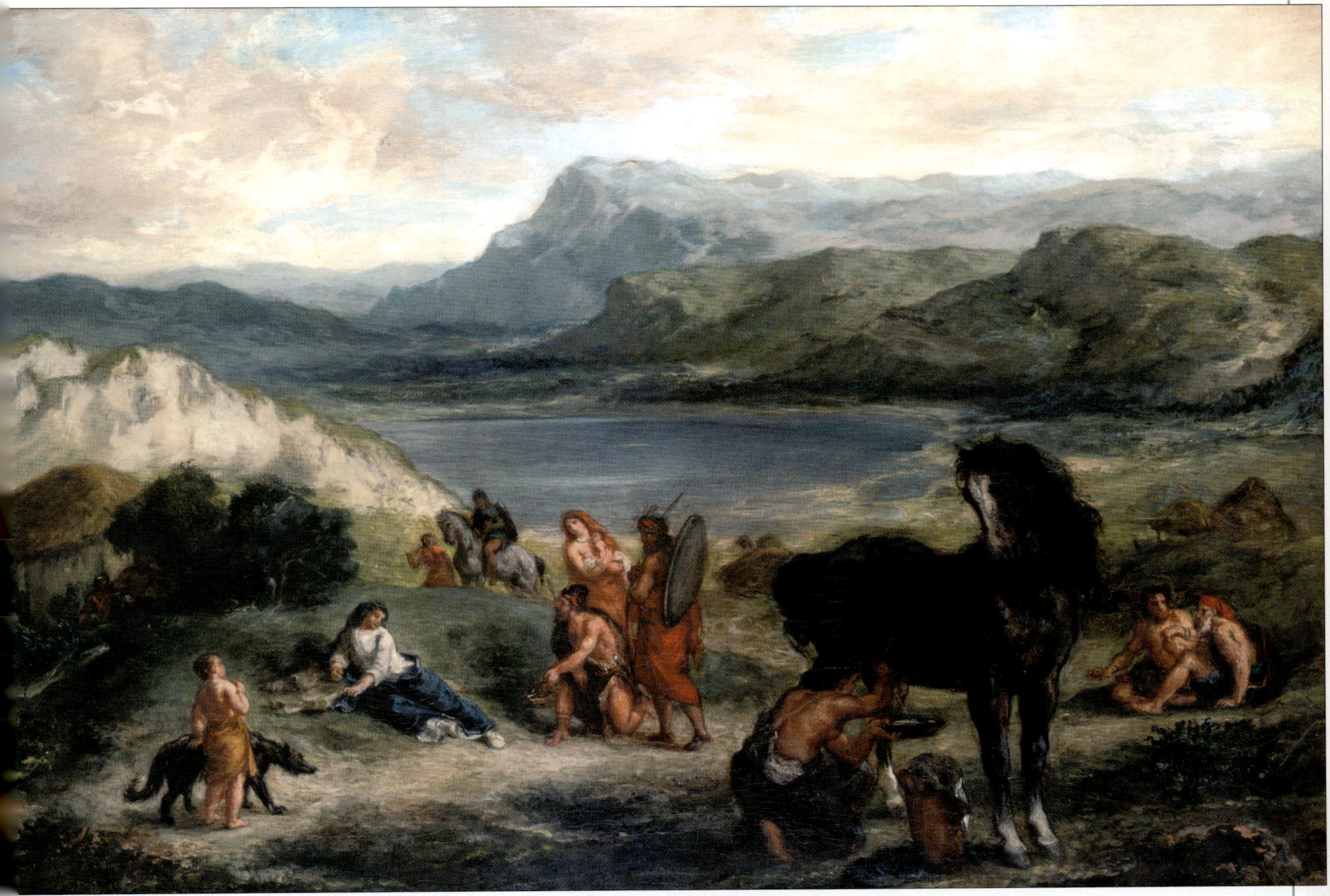

to capture the vividness of what he saw by setting a color against its complementary. This went against the accepted technique of harmonizing colors by using layers of toned varnish.

Delacroix's visit to North Africa stimulated his art, not only because the country inspired him with its color and light, but also in the role memory played in his art: ridding it of extraneous detail and encouraging a personalized expressive interpretation of his chosen themes. In about the mid-1830s, his style softened. The effect can be seen in later works such as *Ovid Among the Scythians* (1855–59). He began to use small touches of broken color, feathering the edges of separate color areas into each other, and building up—as in a tapestry—a surface of great textural and coloristic richness.

As a history painter, Delacroix put a great deal of effort into the planning and research for his pictures, but the finished composition—while displaying clear gestures and a monumental quality—also managed to preserve the spontaneity and energy of the sketch.

Delacroix believed drawing and painting should be a creative harmony. He was happy to change the anatomy of his figures, and distort pictorial space, in order to express his intention more clearly.

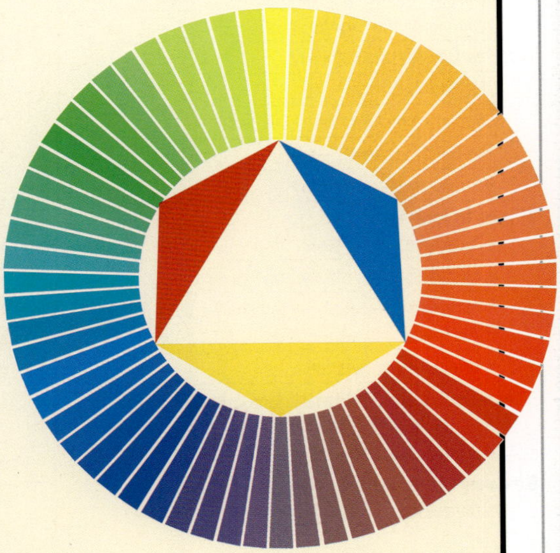

Chevreul's color wheel *The colors opposite each other on the wheel are called "complementary." When placed next to each other these form the greatest "simultaneous contrast." Yellow/violet, blue/orange, and red/green are complementary pairs.*

DELAUNAY Robert

ROBERT DELAUNAY WAS FASCINATED BY COLOR AND LIGHT. He took the color theories of neoimpressionism, the bold handling of fauvism, and the space and form of cubism, and fused these elements into a new style known as Orphism. His bright, highly colored canvases contributed toward the establishment of the modern art style of pure abstraction.

Life and work

Robert Delaunay was an only child born into an aristocratic French family in Paris in 1885. While still in his infancy, however, his parents divorced, and the young Robert was raised by his fashionable, but somewhat neglectful, mother, the Countess Berthe-Félicie de Rose. At school, the young Delaunay was a relatively poor student whose only interests lay in drawing and painting. After leaving school at age 17, he briefly studied decorative painting, but soon left to be an artist.

In 1905 Delaunay discovered impressionism, and produced several early landscapes in the style of Claude Monet. During this period he also saw the work of Henri-Edmond Cross, and began to experiment with neo-impressionism, a style developed by Paul Signac and Georges Seurat which involved the division of the painting into small strokes of pure color. These strokes, according to neoimpressionist theory, would then be mixed not on the surface of the canvas but in the viewer's eye, and would give a more vibrant and authentic image of light and color in nature. By 1909 Delaunay had also become interested in the work of Paul Cézanne and, through his friendship with the artist Jean Metzinger, was becoming increasingly aware of a newly emerging style: cubism.

Delaunay's mature style first emerged in a series of paintings he produced in 1909 representing the interior of the Gothic church of Saint-Séverin in Paris. In these works, Delaunay was fascinated by the effect of light flooding into a darkened interior. His paintings give this light an almost palpable, material quality, and light and color become the primary subject of the works. It was also in 1909 that Delaunay began to work on a series of paintings representing the Eiffel Tower in Paris.

The Eiffel Tower had been a regular feature of the Paris skyline for 20 years when Delaunay first selected it as a motif for his paintings. However, for most Parisians it still symbolized modernity, not least because in 1909 the tower was first used to transmit radio-telegraphic signals across the world. In *The Red Tower* (1911–12), Delaunay distorted the profile of the tower so that the spectator simultaneously sees several views of Eiffel's masterpiece. In this way he suggests the vertiginous effect generated by the sheer scale of the structure dominating the city and reaching into the clouds.

Data file

Full name: Robert-Victor-Félix Delaunay

Nationality: French

Style: Orphism

Dates: born 1885 in Paris, died 1941 in Montpellier

Key works:

Saint-Séverin No. 7 1909

Window on the City No. 4 1910–11

The City of Paris 1910–12

The Red Tower 1911–12

Circular Forms: Sun No. 1 1912–13

The Cardiff Team 1912–13

Homage to Blériot 1914

Things to look for:

- bright, saturated color
- circles, or discs of rainbow-like color
- inclusion of modern city landmarks, such as the Eiffel Tower
- references to aviation

Comparisons: Claude Monet, Henri-Edmond Cross, Paul Signac, Georges Seurat, Paul Cézanne, Jean Metzinger, Albert Gliezes, Sonia Delaunay Terk

Glossary terms: cubism, fauvism, impressionism, neoimpressionism, Orphism

Light and color

One of Delaunay's most successful works, *Homage to Blériot* (1914), reveals the artist's fascination with the modern world and with light and color. The entire painting is awash with disks and spirals of color, intercepting each other and overlapping everywhere. At the top of the image, an orange monoplane rises like an angel into the heavens. On the right, a biplane surrounded by a halo of oranges and purples floats through the sky. Just below the biplane, the red form of the Eiffel Tower can be seen in the background.

Delaunay's emphasis on aviation was making a specific historical reference. Five years earlier, in 1909, the French pilot Louis Blériot was the first man successfully to cross the English Channel in a plane. The feat was regarded as a triumph for the French nation, so much so that Blériot's airplane was processed through the streets of Paris. *Homage to Blériot* acknowledges this triumph. Yet, at the same time, the focus is much more on the prismatic effects of light than on an individual hero. The multiple disks that dominate the image appear as if they are themselves the reflected light of propeller blades turning so fast that all we see is the disturbance they cause in the air. The still propeller in the lower left of the picture reinforces this idea.

The watercolor *Homage to Blériot* was a preliminary work for a large oil painting of the same title, which is now in the Kunstmuseum in Basel.

Homage to Blériot *1914. Watercolor on paper. 30¾ x 26 in (78 x 67 cm). Musée d'Art Moderne de la Ville de Paris, Paris.*

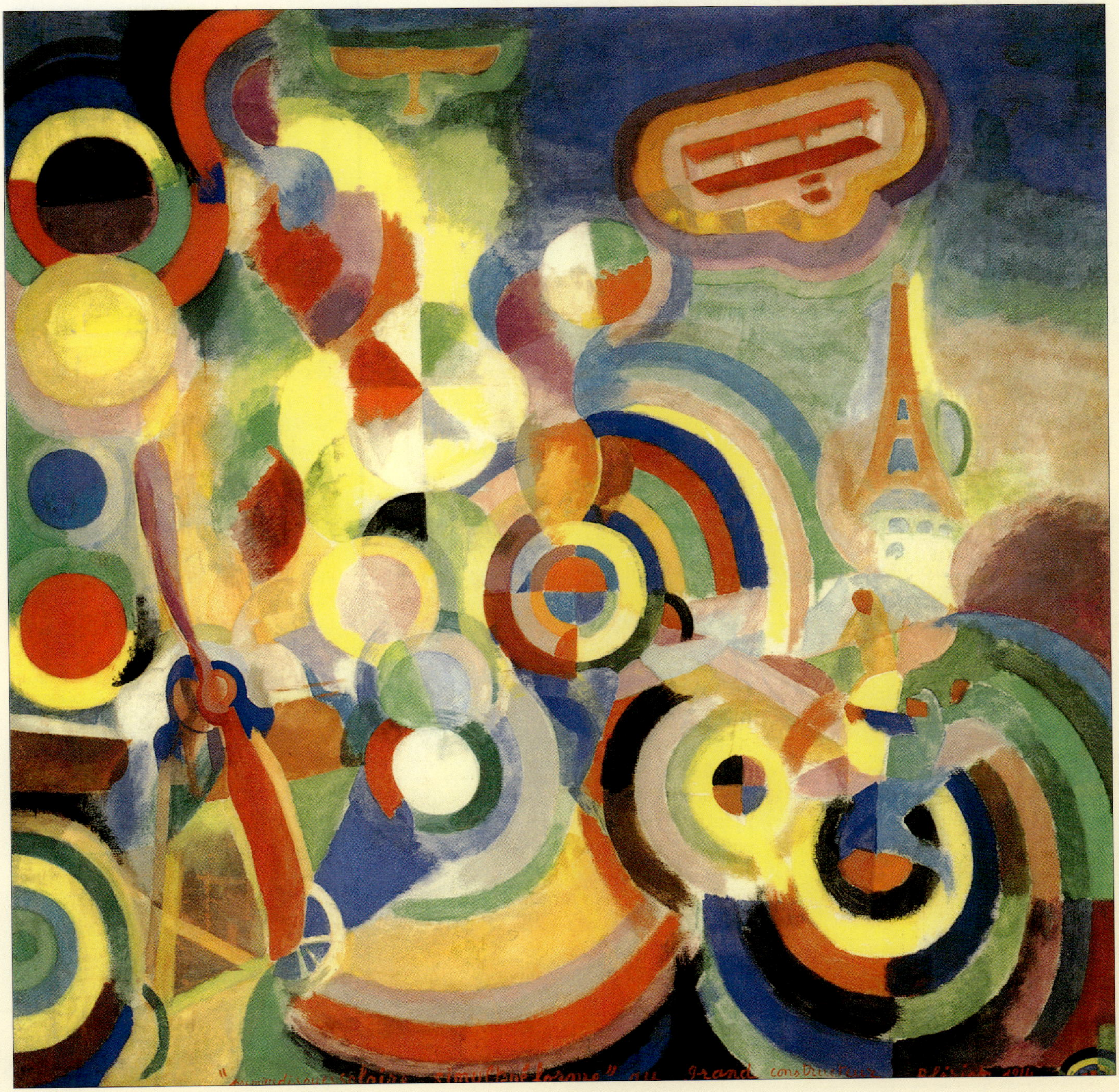

In 1910 Delaunay married Sonia Terk, an artist also fascinated by color and light. Over the next few years both artists developed a new style in which forms were increasingly distorted and abstracted so that all that remains is light and color itself. Delaunay's Window paintings of 1912–14 are a good example of this development. The poet and art critic Guillaume Apollinaire christened this new art form Orphism, referring to his own recent poetry based on the myth of Orpheus, but Delaunay preferred the term "pure painting."

In 1914, on the eve of World War I, Delaunay produced his dramatic *Homage to Blériot*, which focused on the new science of aviation, a theme to which he would return. Delaunay was in Spain when war broke out, and he stayed there until 1921. His last major work was a mural for the Pavilion of Aviation at the 1937 Paris World's Fair.

In 1940 Delaunay and his family fled Paris as the Nazis marched in to occupy the city. Already ill at this point, Delaunay reached Montpellier in the south of France, where he died the following year.

DEMUTH Charles

THE BEST-KNOWN WORKS OF CHARLES DEMUTH were produced in and around the town of his birth. His sharply delineated landscape scenes glorify the modern world and the rise of industrial technology. They made a major contribution to the development of the style known as precisionism.

Life and work

Charles Demuth was born in 1883 in Lancaster, Pennsylvania, where his family had run a tobacco store for over a century. Demuth was deeply attached to his home town of Lancaster; throughout his life it remained his major source of artistic inspiration.

Demuth studied commercial art as a young man before enrolling in the Pennsylvania Academy of Fine Arts. He traveled to London, Berlin, and Paris while he was still a student, and became very interested in the work of the European avant-garde, especially the cubists. In 1912, having completed his studies, he went to stay in Paris, where he met many important supporters of modern European art, including the American writer Gertrude Stein and the American poet Ezra Pound.

After returning to the United States, Demuth made frequent trips to New York, where he got to know many of the major figures in American avant-garde circles. Among them were Alfred Stieglitz, Georgia O'Keeffe, and Marsden Hartley.

By 1914 Demuth's reputation as a notable modern painter earned him his first one-man exhibition in New York. Among his early successful works are a number of watercolors that he had produced while visiting Bermuda with Marsden Hartley. These pictures emphasize interpenetrating planes and dynamic diagonal lines reminiscent of the works of Italian futurism, an avant-garde art movement founded in 1909.

Back in Lancaster, Demuth's stylistic development really took off when he turned his attention toward the mills and factories of Pennsylvania, the cradle of American industry. He portrayed these industrial landmarks in a positive light, giving their association with human labor a heroic quality, although his emphasis was entirely on the buildings; the workers themselves are not shown in these paintings. Demuth presented the factory as a kind of temple, a place of worship in the modern industrial world.

His industrial landscapes are in one sense realistic because they accurately depict scenes that Demuth saw. Stylistically, however, he drastically reduced both the form and details of buildings and illustrated them with all the precision of an architectural draftsman.

Demuth's factory landscapes, along with works by fellow Pennsylvanian artist, Charles Sheeler, came to be regarded as a major force in a new and specifically American style that became known as precisionism. Their work depicted both factory and machine as icons of modernity, symbolizing the progressiveness and vitality of American industry. The fusion of

Data file

Full name: Charles Henry Buckius Demuth

Nationality: American

Style: precisionism

Dates: born 1883 in Lancaster, PA, died 1935 in Lancaster, PA

Key works:

Bermuda No. 2: The Schooner 1917

Church in Provincetown 1919

Flour Mill (Factory) 1921

My Egypt 1927

I Saw the Figure Five in Gold 1928

Buildings, Lancaster 1930

Things to look for:

- scenes of the architecture of Lancaster, PA
- precise linear compositions
- muted, flat tones
- dynamic, diagonal lines and interpenetrating forms

Comparisons: Charles Sheeler, Alfred Stieglitz, Georgia O'Keeffe, Stuart Davis, Marsden Hartley

Glossary terms: avant-garde, cubism, futurism, pop art, precisionism

Temples to modern industry

In *My Egypt* (1927) Demuth depicts a large grain elevator that was situated near his Lancaster studio. He emphasizes the linear qualities of the building, which is viewed from below and starkly lit by precisely defined rays of light.

The title of the work seems to have been carefully considered. During the late 1920s there was widespread interest in ancient Egypt. People's fascination with this culture had been revived and fired by the discovery in 1922 of the treasure-filled tomb of the Egyptian pharaoh Tutankhamun. Demuth's reference to Egypt in the title of his picture alludes to the ancient world and the monumental architecture of the pyramids. The broad columns on the main façade of the building may even recall the Temple of Karnak on the Nile.

By making these references Demuth could also be suggesting that there is no need to travel, in either distance or time, in order to witness architectural wonders. The modern world, he believed, offers buildings that are just as spectacular as those of the ancient world—temples not dedicated to the gods of the past but rather to modern industry and technology.

By fusing the idea of temples with modern industrial buildings, Demuth was echoing a popular view that had been expressed by Calvin Coolidge, the President of the United States from 1923 to 1929: "The man who builds a factory, builds a temple; the man who works there, worships there."

In addition to focusing on these modern "temples" Demuth also developed a style of painting that was intended to reflect their modernity. In *My Egypt*, for example, he concentrates on the geometrical aspects of the scene, reducing all forms to powerful, yet simple shapes. Even the smoke that is emerging from the factory's chimney is given a solid form with well-defined edges.

Precisely constructed with straight, ruler-drawn lines that are reminiscent of architectural drawing, this picture is full of references to the dynamics of futurism and the interpenetrating planes of cubism. For Demuth, the temples of industry have become a blueprint for the modern world.

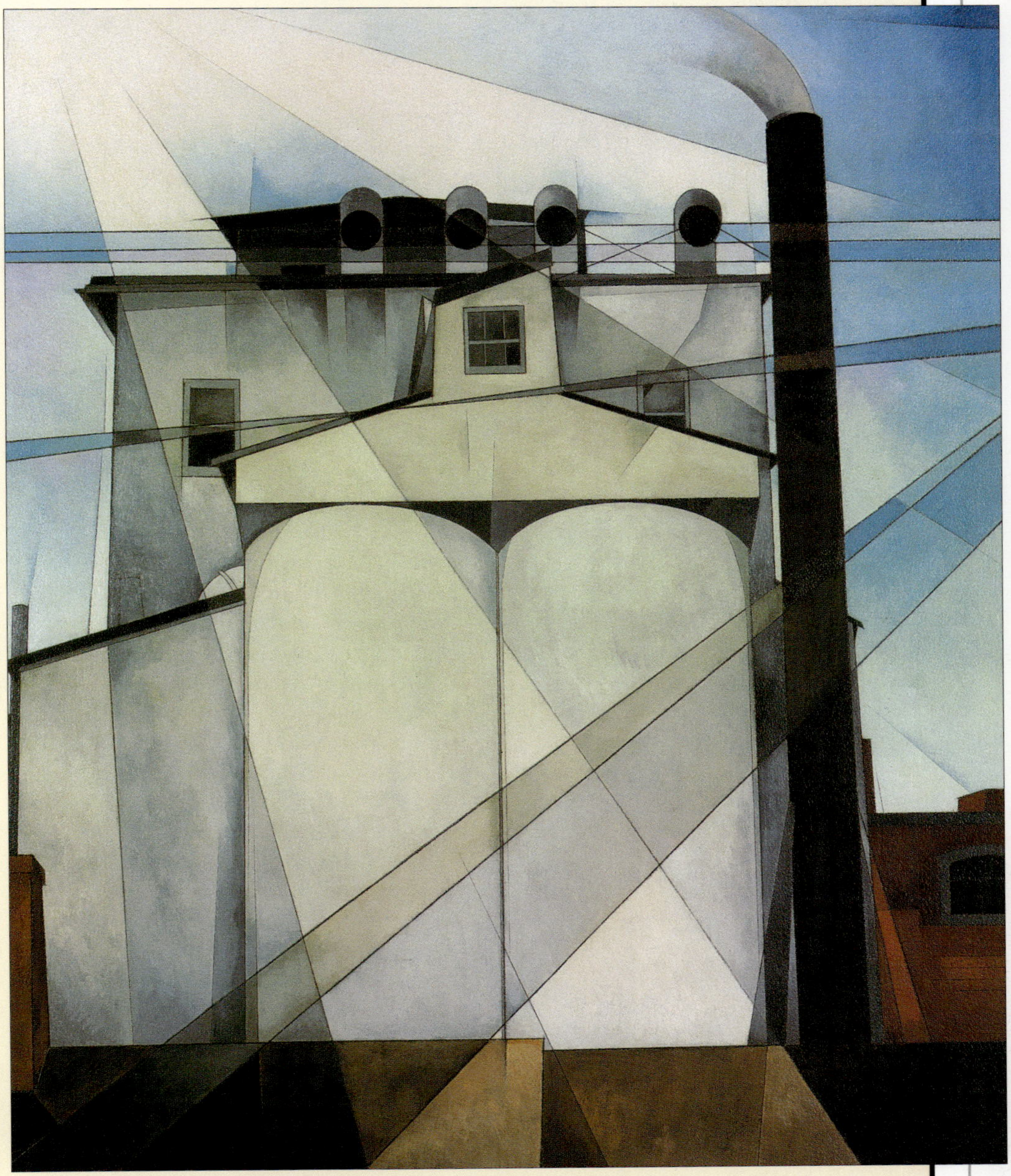

My Egypt *1927. Oil on composition board. 35 3/4 x 30 in (91 x 76 cm). Whitney Museum of American Art, New York, NY.*

Demuth's technical-drawing skills with his fine-art training contributed significantly to the precisionist esthetic.

Although most of Demuth's works focus on the industrial buildings of Lancaster, he did produce one notable image that was based on a more urban setting: *I Saw the Figure Five in Gold* (1928). The piece is a tribute to the poetry of Demuth's close friend, William Carlos Williams. More specifically, the Demuth painting relates to a poem with the same title in which Williams describes the experience of seeing a red fire truck screaming past him on a city street. In common with the poem, the painting does not describe merely a single moment of the truck passing by. Instead, by adopting techniques he had learned from Italian futurism and French cubism, Demuth depicts on one surface several different moments, as if they are actually happening simultaneously. The gold number five emblazoned on the fire truck recurs, diminishing in size as the vehicle recedes into the street beyond.

Later in his career Demuth became increasingly intrigued by the invasion of advertising billboards along the streets and highways. In such works as *Buildings, Lancaster* (1930), such advertisements were a major feature of the scenes he represented.

Demuth's introduction of the objects and images of everyday life into his later pieces both recalls the work of Stuart Davis, his contemporary, and foreshadows the importance that later artistic movements, such as pop art, would accord to popular culture.

DERAIN André

A LEADING FIGURE IN THE FAUVIST MOVEMENT, in his early career André Derain joined fellow artist Henri Matisse in portraying the French Mediterranean in bright colors and a sketchy finish that was reminiscent of children's art. In later life, however, Derain returned to more traditional, figurative painting, inspired by his love for the great artists of the past.

Life and work

André Derain was born and raised in the small town of Chatou, a riverside location near Paris much frequented by impressionist painters. At the age of 15, Derain went to Paris to study engineering. Here, however, he spent more time in the museums and art studios of the city than in his own classes, and he soon rejected engineering for a career as an artist.

Derain particularly enjoyed visiting the Louvre art museum and gallery in Paris, where he developed a love for the work of the Old Masters, and made copies of their paintings. Throughout his career he never lost this interest in traditional art practices. In 1901, however, after visiting an exhibition dedicated to the work of Vincent Van Gogh, his interest in color grew dramatically.

Between 1900 and 1901, Derain shared a studio in Chatou with fellow painter Maurice de Vlaminck. Both artists produced landscapes inspired by impressionism. Then, following a spell of compulsory military service, Derain became increasingly attracted to the work of Henri Matisse.

In 1905, Derain accompanied Matisse to the south of France. Here, in the small fishing port of Collioure, both artists produced powerful canvases, applying bright, pure colors straight from the tube, and leaving whole areas of unprimed canvas bare. In these works they sought to express the simplicity and rawness of life in the Mediterranean, which was then a region still relatively untouched by outsiders. When these paintings were exhibited in 1905 at an exhibition in Paris, their unrestrained use of color and exuberant vitality shocked many critics. One critic even referred to them as the work of "*fauves*" or "wild beasts." The name stuck, and from that point on, the style developed by Derain, Matisse, and their colleagues, including de Vlaminck, Raoul Dufy, and many others, became known as fauvism.

Derain's fauvist paintings owe a considerable debt to both Paul Cézanne and Paul Gauguin, artists whose work Derain had seen in major Paris exhibitions. At the same time, he was influenced by neoimpressionism, a style in which a painting is made up of small dots of color; these fuse in the eye of the viewer when seen from a distance. Derain became familiar with this style through the work of Paul Signac, a major artist whom Matisse had befriended and visited in the southern French village of Saint Tropez.

By 1907 Derain, like the cubist painters Georges Braque and Pablo Picasso, was also showing considerable interest in African sculpture, which could be seen in the ethnographical museum in Paris. His sandstone sculpture *Crouching Man* (1907), for example, rejected traditional modeling in favor of carving, and was highly influential in the development of modern sculptural techniques.

Derain's career was considerably advanced in 1910 when he exhibited with Daniel Henry Kahnweiler, an art dealer already famous for promoting Braque and Picasso. Through Kahnweiler, Derain sold works in Germany and Russia, and exhibited in the United States.

By 1912 Derain's work had become increasingly figurative, drawing upon the tradition of the great religious masters he had studied in the Louvre. After World War I, in which he served, Derain introduced into his work traditional figures from the Italian comic theater, or commedia dell'arte, as in *Harlequin and Pierrot* (c1924). Throughout the 1920s and 1930s Derain's work continued to reflect his interest in traditional themes. He produced many nudes, still-lifes, and scenes from classical mythology.

Derain spent most of World War II in Paris, which was occupied by Nazi troops. Following the war he continued to paint; he also produced stage designs and many book illustrations. He continued to work right up to his death, aged 74, in 1954.

Data file

Full name: André Derain

Nationality: French

Style: fauvism

Dates: born 1880 in Chatou, died 1954 in Garches

Key works:
- *The Golden Age* 1905
- *The Port of Collioure* 1905
- *London Bridge* 1906
- *Crouching Man* 1907
- *The Bathers* 1907
- *Harlequin and Pierrot* c1924
- *The Artist and His Family* c1939

Things to look for:
- bright, pure colors
- areas of bare canvas
- bold strokes of thickly applied paint
- forms inspired by non-European culture

Comparisons: Henri Matisse, Vincent Van Gogh, Maurice de Vlaminck, Raoul Dufy, Othon Friesz, Paul Cézanne, Paul Gauguin, Paul Signac, Georges Braque, Claude Monet

Glossary terms: cubism, fauvism, figurative, impressionism, neoimpressionism, Old Masters

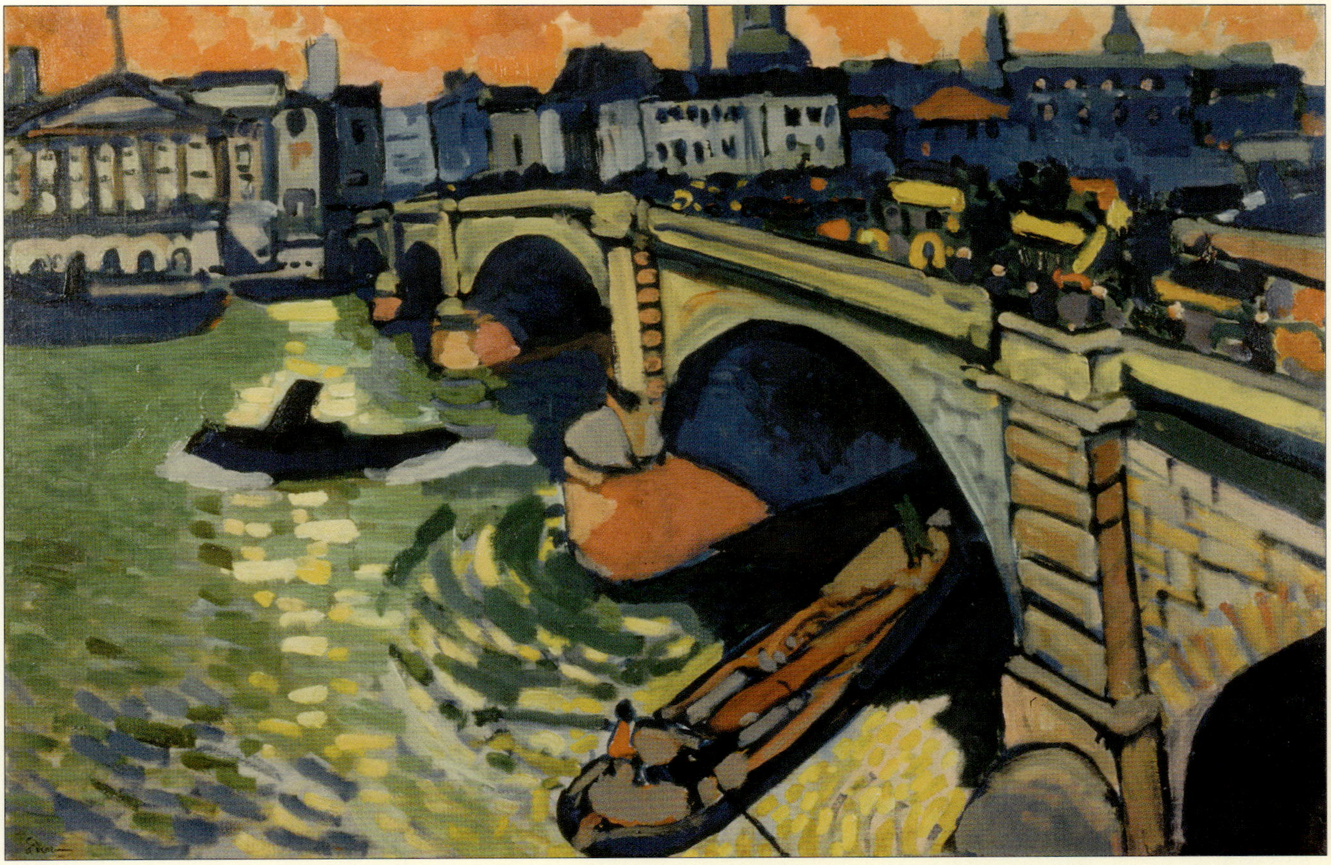

Derain and the vitality of color

Many of Derain's energetic and lively fauvist works were produced on his extensive travels around France in the early 20th century. In *The Port of Collioure* (1905) Derain depicts a small but busy fishing port in the south of France. From a high and commanding viewpoint Derain portrays the numerous boats closely moored along the quayside, with fishermen in the foreground tending to their boats, nets, and sails. Derain has used bold and quickly applied brushstrokes of pure, unmixed color to capture the energy and exuberance of the scene. The use of red and yellow strongly suggests both the bright light and heat of this Mediterranean setting, while the scintillating color contrast between the red-roofed houses on the far side of the bay and the green hill in the distance seems to echo the energetic activity of the foreground scene. Derain's paintings of the small towns and villages of southern France frequently emphasized this harmonious relationship between the landscape and its inhabitants.

Derain's travels also took him farther afield. In the fall of 1905, the art dealer Ambroise Vollard commissioned Derain to produce a series of paintings of London. Thirty-five years earlier Claude Monet had similarly visited London and produced many impressionist paintings of the River Thames. Unlike Monet, however, Derain did not emphasize the atmospheric effects of light. Instead he produced brightly colored, clearly outlined studies of life on the river, as can be seen in *London Bridge* (1906). Here a bright orange sky is contrasted with a vividly green river, while two boats emerge from the densely blue-shadowed arches of the bridge. Derain's specific use of intense and non-naturalistic colors adds a strong sense of vitality and energy to all his landscape scenes.

London Bridge *1906. 26 x 39 in (66 x 100 cm). Oil on canvas. Museum of Modern Art, New York, NY.*

The Port of Collioure *1905. 23½ x 29 in (59.5 x 73 cm). Oil on canvas. Musée Nationale d'Art Moderne, Centre Georges Pompidou, Paris.*

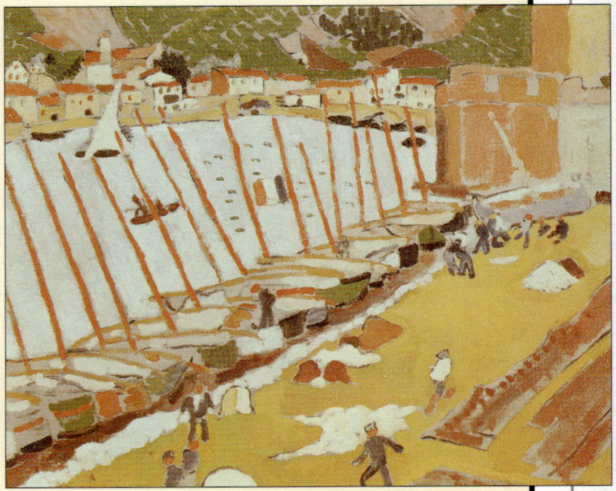

DINE Jim

JIM DINE IS AN AMERICAN ARTIST WHO HAS WORKED IN MANY MEDIA and through many stylistic means, from the happenings that he staged at the start of his career, through the assemblages of the 1960s, to the neoexpressionistic drawings, paintings, and prints that he has produced since the 1970s.

Life and work:

Jim Dine's artistic training began in his home town of Cinccinnati, and continued at the Boston Museum School and Ohio University. He married Nancy Minto in 1957, and they moved to New York, where Dine met artists Claes Oldenburg and Allen Kaprow. Together with the musician John Cage, they pioneered the art events that became known as "happenings."

Dine's first such event was *The Smiling Worker* (1959), a 30-second performance during which he poured paint over his head and jumped through a paper wall on which he had scrawled, "I love what I am doing." It was a crude, chaotic event, but proved a joyous and vibrant contrast to the somber mood of the abstract expressionists, who still held sway in the New York art world. At this point, Dine appeared to share the aspirations of Kaprow and Oldenburg in rejecting the sanctity of "the work of art."

The shared motivation continued through the early 1960s as Dine created his first assemblages, such as *Bedspring* (1960) and *Lawnmower* (1962). In common with Oldenburg, Dine introduced objects from everyday life into the realm of art; because these were mass-produced objects, he was assigned a place in the pop art movement. For a time, Dine enjoyed his critical and commercial success, but underneath suffered artistic turmoil.

In 1967 he moved to London in order to try new ways of working outside the glare of public attention. He stayed until 1971, experimenting with poetry, lithographic printing, and illustration. Back in the States, Dine concentrated on improving his draftsmanship, producing in 1972 a series of drawings of tools, *Fifty-two Drawings (for Cy Twombly)*, and following that with a period of intense figure drawing. In the 1980s he expanded his technical range, with sculpture re-emerging strongly in works such as *Study for Two Venuses* (1983) and *Wheat Fields* (1989). In the last 20 years there has been a gradual shift in the emphasis of his subject matter from the domestic to the natural world.

Data file

Full name: Jim Dine

Nationality: American

Style: pop art/neoexpressionism

Dates: 1935–

Key works:
- *The Smiling Workman* (happening) 1959
- *Green Suit* 1959
- *Car Crash* (happening) 1960
- *Black Bathroom No. 2* 1962
- *Lawnmower* 1962
- *Poulenc* 1971
- *Fifty-two Drawings (for Cy Twombly)* 1972

Things to look for:
- incorporation of everyday objects (particularly tools) in his paintings
- repetition of significant symbols, such as a heart-shape motif
- combination of pop art subject matter with expressionistic means

Comparisons: Marcel Duchamp, Robert Rauschenberg, Jasper Johns, Claes Oldenburg, Allen Kaprow, Robert Indiana, Cy Twombly

Glossary terms: abstract expressionism, aquatint, assemblages, etching, happenings, lithography, neoexpressionism, pop art

The misfit

While Jim Dine's early work was closely identified with pop art in the1960s, Dine was always essentially guided by his own whims rather than those of any movement. His approach, particularly in his representation of ordinary, everyday objects, does not share the cool detachment of many other pop artists' work. Instead, these objects were chosen by Dine because of the personal significance they held for him.

The range of images that Dine uses in his work is limited. It includes items of personal clothing (ties, shoes, and coats); what Dine calls the "tools of the trade" (paintbrushes and palettes); hearts; bathrobes; and handtools. The heart motif is Dine's image for his wife, Nancy, while many of the other images "stand in" for Dine himself.

In 1971, when he began to portray himself, Dine had a heavy beard, so did not appear too dissimilar to the large paintbrushes he used to depict himself! The often solitary images of an "empty" bathrobe with its sleeves akimbo are also Dine's versions of self-portraits. He recalled seeing an advertisement in 1963 for a red bathrobe in the *The New York Times*. "It was headless and it seemed like my whole body was in it. I had searched for some time for a vehicle to label 'self-portrait'," he said.

Dine often uses handtools as inspiration, drawing nostalgically on his childhood experiences in his grandfather's and father's hardware stores. In 1970 Dine wrote: "From the age of nine 'til I was eighteen I worked in these stores.... I found that daydreaming amongst objects of affection was very nice."

Dine constantly seeks out new devices, and experiments in different media, including drawing, collage, and especially print. Dine's first published prints were lithographs, created for a happening called *Car Crash* (1960). In lithography a design is drawn on a metal or stone surface with a greasy crayon, and the surface is wetted and then inked. The wet surface repels the ink, which adheres only to the greasy lines. The inked image can then be printed.

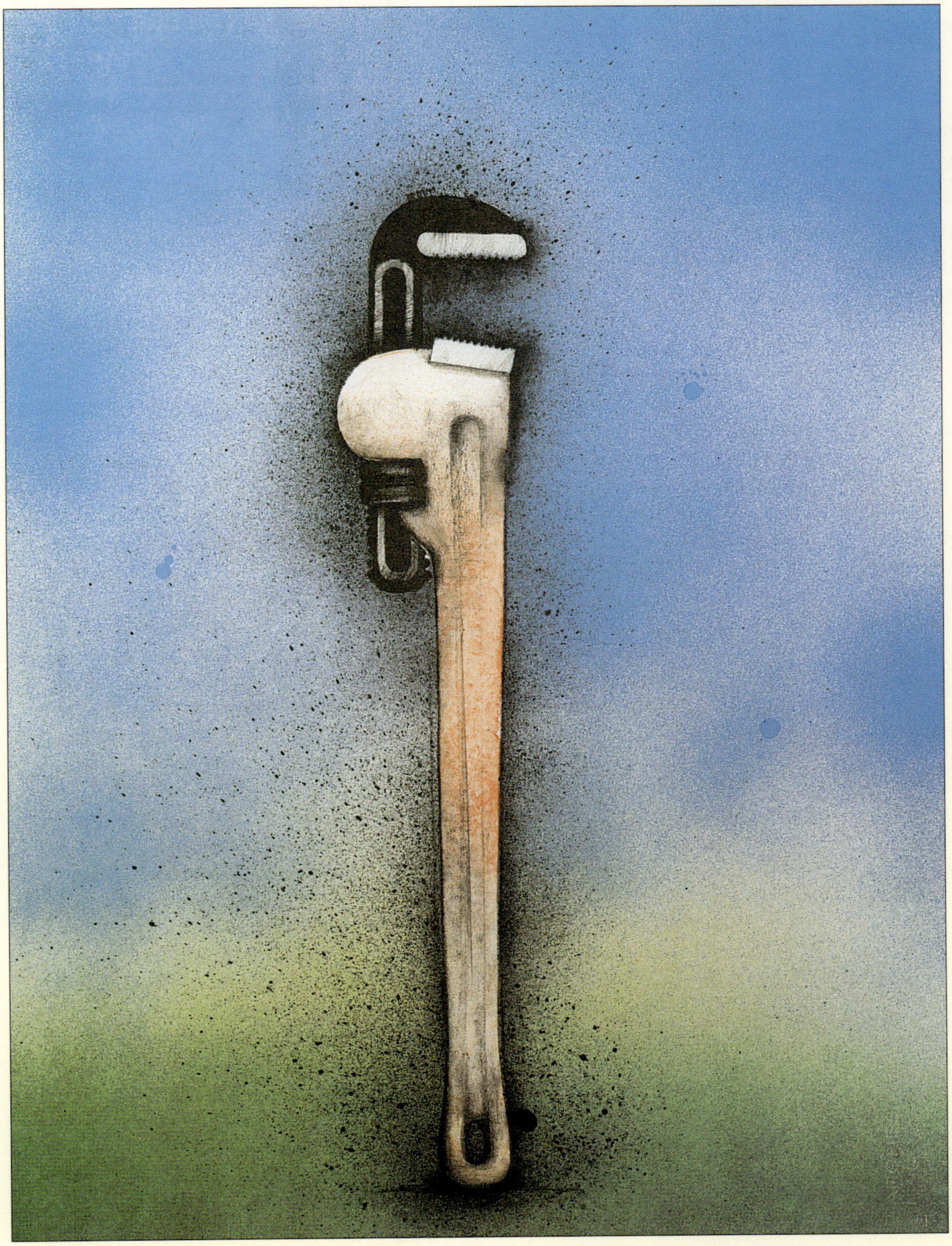

Big Red Wrench in a Landscape *1973. Color lithograph. 30 x 22 1/2 in (76.5 x 57.5 cm). Tate Gallery, London.*

Dine also experimented with other print media, such as etching (engraving using acid), drypoint (engraving using a steel needle), and aquatint (an etching method that produces areas of tones rather than lines). Sometimes he uses more than one print medium in a single print; other times he alters printing plates between editions to produce different states, as in the six "versions" of *Five Paintbrushes* (1972–73).

In *Big Red Wrench in a Landscape* (1973), Dine returned to lithography. This large image of a pipe wrench was printed from five aluminum plates. Dine later took three of these plates—removing the blue sky plate, and replacing the lithographic drawing of the wrench with an etched version of the same drawing—to produce a new series of prints called *The Wrench in Nature* (1973). For the next three years Dine reused the etching plate of *Wrench in Nature* to make three new prints: *Dartmouth Still Life* (1974–76), *Pink Chinese Scissors* (1974–76), and *Piranesi's 24 Colored Marks* (1974–76).

DONATELLO

DONATELLO WAS A FAVORITE SCULPTOR OF THE MEDICI FAMILY. His many works, along with those by his contemporaries Leon Alberti, Filippo Brunelleschi, and Masaccio, embodied the spirit of the Renaissance in Florence, by reinventing the art of antiquity and adding individual and human detail. His work had a major influence on both painters and sculptors of later generations.

Life and work

Donatello began his training as an apprentice to Lorenzo Ghiberti, with whom, from 1404 to 1407, he prepared models for the bronze reliefs on the north doors of the baptistery of San Giovanni in Florence. From Ghiberti he learned about wax and clay modeling, part of the process of modeling in bronze. Donatello probably learned about marble carving in the workshops of Florence Cathedral, and his talents were quickly recognized. He received commissions for patron saints for the cathedral and various guilds in Florence. Each commission required complex consideration of the function of the sculpture and an awareness of the angle from which it would be viewed, as well as a portrayal of the traditional, individual attributes of the saints and their histories.

Donatello began modeling relief scenes that he used to decorate the lintels of his statues as well as to adorn private rooms in patrons' homes. He continued to be much involved with relief carvings over the next 15 years, executing commissions for cathedrals in Siena, Florence, and Rome. Perhaps the most famous of these are the Singing Gallery, or Cantoria, in Florence Cathedral (1433–39), and the Old Sacristy, commissioned for San Lorenzo Church and mausoleum by the Medici family (c1433–43).

Between 1415 and the mid-1430s Donatello also worked on a series of life-size statues of the prophets. Each is treated as an individual, although based on classical models. The interest in individualizing statues of religious figures carried over into Donatello's interest in Roman busts. By reviving this ancient art, in a portrait bust of his contemporary Niccolo da Uzzano, Donatello again embodied the spirit of the Renaissance—a rebirth of the classical past in 15th-century Florence.

Portrait busts remained unusual at the time, but sculpted portraits were common on tombs. Donatello's innovative combination of the effigy of Baldassare Coscia (Antipope John XXIII) with scenes from the scriptures on his tomb inspired many of the tombs that century.

Donatello moved to Padua in 1443, where he remained for 10 years. The

Data file

Full name: Donato di Niccolo (known as Donatello)

Nationality: Italian

Style: early Renaissance

Dates: born c1386 in Florence, died 1466 in Florence

Key works:

- series of Old Testament prophets for the campanile, Florence c1415–1433
- tomb of Baldassare Coscia (with Michelozzo di Bartolommeo) c1424–28
- carvings in the Singing Gallery, Florence Cathedral 1433–39
- carvings in the Old Sacristy, San Lorenzo c1433–43
- *Mary Magdalen* (unknown date)
- *David* c1459
- pulpit at San Lorenzo c1465

Things to look for:

- early carvings with shallow relief
- works combining late-Gothic style, revival of the art of antiquity, and Renaissance thought about perspective and space
- religious scenes and monuments that combine traditional subjects with a new humanist approach and focus on individualism, drama, and expression
- an increasing preoccupation, especially in later years, with realistic figures and often harrowing, emotional subjects

Comparisons: Masaccio, Fra Bartolommeo, Lorenzo Ghiberti

Glossary terms: Gothic, lintel, patron saint, relief, Renaissance

Passionate sculpture

This scene is one from a series of the Passion of Christ made to decorate the pulpit at San Lorenzo, Florence. They were made late in Donatello's career, and reflect many of the innovations in his art, as well as some of the wider concerns of the Renaissance. This particular section shows the three Marys coming to the tomb of the recently crucified Christ.

The biggest innovation that Donatello made in his lifetime was in the field of relief carving. Instead of imitating ancient and medieval carvings by producing figures that stood out prominently against a flatter background, Donatello carved away more deeply into the background of his scenes. Although the figures in the foreground of his works were often modeled only in shallow relief, they appear to stand out very dramatically because of the depth of the indentation behind. In *Marys at the Sepulchre* (c1465), for example, we can see a tomb, comprising columns and a canopy, which is projected out of the bronze. Some of the figures are almost freestanding in real space.

Donatello has used different depths to highlight the narrative aspects of the subject. The dramatic movement of the angel (second from right), who has just appeared, is conveyed by his outstretched arm and the folds of his swirling robe. The three Marys are shown in different positions: one stands with bowed head carrying a jar of ointment, one grasps the column in amazement and shock, and one looks into the tomb, her face showing agony and distress. Each figure is set at a different depth to give the scene more three-dimensionality and realism.

The violence of events and emotions is characteristic of Donatello's later work. This realism has been referred to as

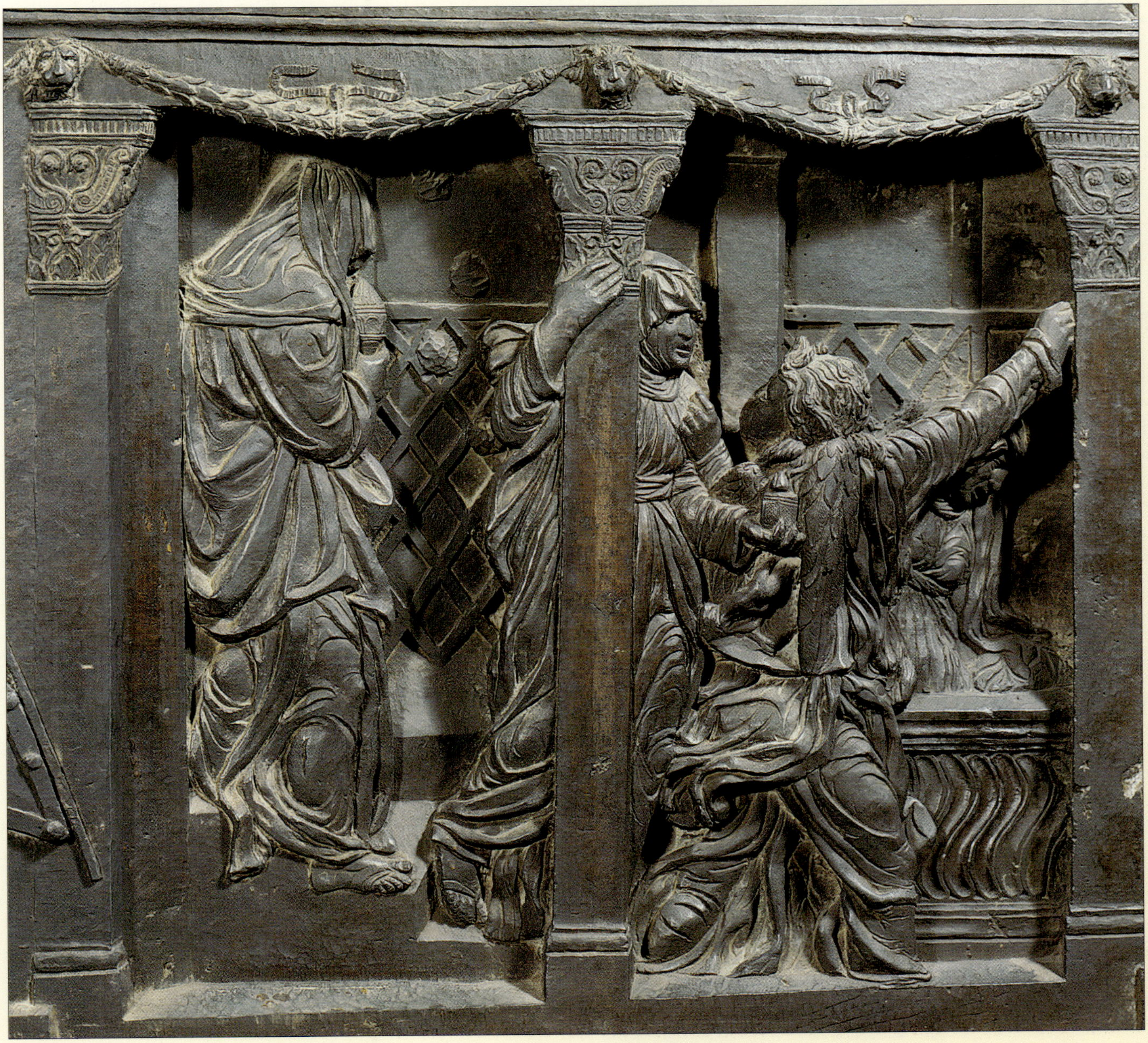

"horrifyingly gripping," and was without comparison in the art of the time. This relief shows Donatello's ability to combine realistic and humanizing touches and a spontaneous modeling of figures within a semiclassical setting. It also demonstrates his adoption of new developments in depicting space and the use of accurate, geometric perspective.

Marys at the Sepulchre *c1465. Bronze. 29 1/2 x 57 in (75 x 145 cm). North pulpit, San Lorenzo Church, Florence.*

most famous works he made there are the bronze crucifix for the basilica of San Antonio and a new high altar, now dismantled. He also created the Gattamelata equestrian monument to a captain-general of the Venetian army—an image of military power that inspired similar monuments for centuries after.

Donatello returned to Florence in 1453. Among his most famous works of this time are his bronze *David* (c1459), which was also unusual for its near nudity, a harrowing painted wood statue of Mary Magdalen, and a series of bronze panels showing scenes from the Passion of Christ and the Martyrdom of Saint Lawrence. Donatello's contribution to the Renaissance was huge and his work was often ahead of the tastes of his time. Donatello was so highly regarded by his Medici patron, Cosimo, that Cosimo left orders for him to be buried in the Medici family vault as a sign of respect for his life and work.

DOVE Arthur

ORIGINALLY A COMMERCIAL ILLUSTRATOR, Arthur Dove did not devote himself fully to painting until he was 50 years old. Dove's work combined imagery drawn from nature with pure, abstract form to create the first American abstract paintings; his 1912 exhibition was the first public showing of abstract art in the United States.

Life and work

Arthur Dove was born in 1880 in Canandaigua in upstate New York. His father was a building contractor, who moved his family to Geneva, New York state, in 1882. After graduating from Geneva High School in 1899, Dove attended Hobart College in Geneva before transferring to Cornell University in Ithaca to study law. He also took classes in art. He graduated with a degree in 1903, and was soon working successfully as a commercial artist, providing illustrations for numerous magazines, including *Collier's Weekly* and *The Illustrated Sports News*.

In 1904 Dove married Florence Dorsey, and in 1907 the couple traveled to Europe, where they spent the next two years. As well as brief trips to Spain and Italy, Dove spent much of his time in and around Paris, then the art capital of the world. There Dove met with other American artists, including Alfred H. Maurer, who introduced him to the art of Paul Cézanne and the fauves, led by Henri Matisse.

Soon after Dove returned to the United States he met Alfred Stieglitz, who ran the 291 Gallery in New York. Stieglitz was responsible for showing—often for the first time in the United States—avant-garde painting and sculpture, as well as pioneering photography, by artists such as Auguste Rodin, Pablo Picasso, Georgia O'Keeffe, and Man Ray. In March 1910, Dove made his New York debut in a group show at 291, displaying just one painting, *The Lobster* (1908), a large still life he had painted in France.

In 1912 Dove had his first solo exhibition at 291; he showed a series of pastel works, collectively called *The Ten Commandments* (1911–12). Brightly colored and filled with bold, curving lines, these images were the first American abstract pictures.

Between 1910 and 1920 Dove was living in Westport, Connecticut. Despite widespread recognition and critical acclaim, Dove's output of new work remained limited during this period, and he supplemented his income by returning to commercial illustration.

Dove left his wife and son William (born 1911), and began living with the artist Helen Torr (known to her friends as "Reds") on a houseboat in New York City. He began painting again, and—from 1924—producing "assemblages." Most were complete by 1926, although

Data file

Full name: Arthur Garfield Dove

Nationality: American

Style: abstract

Dates: born 1880 in Canandaigua, NY, died 1946 in Huntingdon, NY

Key works:
- *The Lobster* 1908
- *The Ten Commandments* 1911–12
- *Portrait of Ralph Dusenbury* 1924
- *Goat* 1935
- *Holbrook's Bridge to Northwest* 1937–38
- *Power Plant* 1938
- *Beyond Abstraction* 1946

Things to look for:
- simplified forms derived from nature
- softened geometric forms of non-natural objects (buildings, machines, etc)
- rhythmic repetitions of broad silhouettes
- earthy colors
- use of mixed media in assemblages: paint, wood, found objects like sheet music, and denim fabric

Comparisons: Georgia O'Keeffe, Wassily Kandinsky, Robert Delaunay, Kasimir Malevich, Pablo Picasso, Frantisek Kupka, Alfred H. Maurer, Milton Avery, Marsden Hartley, John Marin

Glossary terms: abstract art, assemblage, avant-garde, encaustic, fauvism, geometric, pantograph, pastel, still life, tempera

Toward abstraction

In Europe it was the Russian painter Kasimir Malevich and, later, the Dutch painter Piet Mondrian who produced the first entirely non-natural abstractions from about 1918. These featured abstract forms that had been "invented," and did not represent objects or landscapes from the world around. Other European artists such as Robert Delaunay and Pablo Picasso were also exploring abstraction, but they used objects or landscapes as the starting point for their work.

At the same time, independently in the United States, Arthur Dove was creating his own abstract art, and in the 1920s he developed a personal style of painting that laid emphasis on simple, generalized forms that had their origins in the world he saw around him. Selecting a few elements from this environment—a bridge, a tree, or a hill, perhaps—Dove reduced them to flat, abstract patterns.

In his work, Dove often experimented with the materials of painting. From the early 1920s he began to use tempera (powdered color mixed with egg yolk and water), often in combination with oils. After reading Max Doerner's book *The Materials of the Artist* (published in 1934), he also began to experiment with encaustic (a process by which powdered colors are mixed with hot wax) combined with oils. In the 1920s he also experimented with using different supports; instead of canvas he tried wooden or metal panels, and even early plastics.

In the 1930s, Dove returned to canvas, and also began sketching in watercolors out of doors. Many of his subsequent paintings were based on these sketches: sometimes successful watercolor sketches

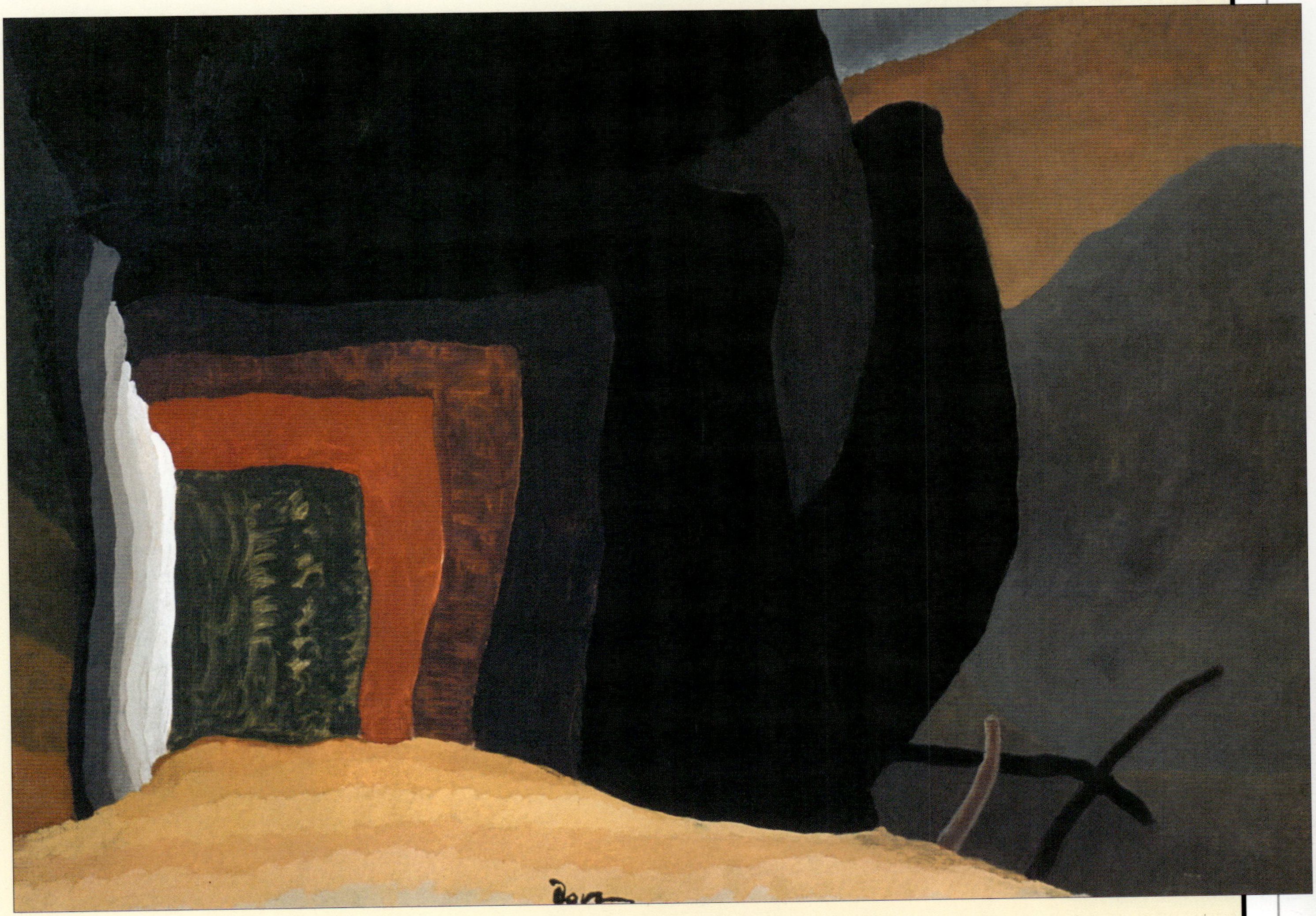

would be transferred and enlarged onto canvas using a device called a pantograph.

While Dove was living in Geneva, New York state, from 1933 to 1938, his subjects were drawn from the landscape around him. Holbrook's Bridge was a motif that Dove returned to on three occasions, first in *Holbrook's Bridge* 1934–35, then in a watercolor of the same name from 1937, and finally in 1937–38, when he painted *Holbrook's Bridge to Northwest.*

Very few of Dove's paintings are dated; the date of this painting is arrived at by a 1938 letter from Dove to Stieglitz, in which he explained that the painting was dedicated to his friend Newton Weatherly, who had died in 1935, aged 100. An important figure in Dove's boyhood, Weatherly was a farmer, amateur naturalist, and painter, who passed on his love of nature and art to Dove. Holbrook's Bridge was a special place for Weatherly, who each year used to pray that he might see it again.

Holbrook's Bridge to Northwest *1937–38. Oil on canvas. 25 x 35 in (63.5 x 89 cm). Private collection.*

the last assemblage was done in 1931. The assemblages include some of his best-known works, as well as his most humorous. *The Critic* (1925) shows a figure made of newspaper wearing a top hat and monocle, whose formal dress is offset by a pair of roller-skates.

Although Dove's work was well received by the critics, it did not attract mass public attention. But he had a powerful influence on other artists: many followed his approach to abstraction by using elements derived from nature that represent different stages—from the "recognizable," to the "completely abstract."

From 1930 onward, Dove received patronage from the art critic and collector Duncan Phillips, and was able to abandon commercial illustration and devote himself entirely to painting. Dove worked steadily on his abstract works, which were now marked by stronger, more simplified forms. At a time when the trend in abstract art was toward creating geometric forms, Dove was creating his own complex and highly personal style based on the living forms and rhythms that he found in nature.

DUCCIO di Buoninsegna

DUCCIO IN SIENA, LIKE HIS NEAR CONTEMPORARY GIOTTO in Florence, heralded the very beginnings of the Italian Renaissance. Both painters took the traditional Byzantine style of the past and recast it. Duccio became famous for his huge two-sided altarpiece, the *Maestà*, for Siena Cathedral.

Life and work

We do not know much about Duccio's life, except that he lived and worked in Siena in Tuscany, and was the leading painter there in the late 13th century. On his death he left behind a prosperous workshop, and he had a huge influence on a younger generation of Sienese painters such as Simone Martini. Duccio himself may have been influenced by his older Florentine counterpart, Cimabue.

All of Duccio's known works were done for religious purposes—either as altarpieces for churches or smaller pictures for private prayer. As most people did not know how to read or write, they relied on such pictures to convey stories from the Bible to them. Like Giotto in Florence, Duccio was a master of storytelling in paint. Stylistically, both artists broke away from the static conventions of Byzantine art. Duccio's additional contribution was the introduction of a greater elegance, of detailed, decorative qualities, and the bold use of color. His emphasis on the decorative links Duccio with the Gothic style. Gothic refers to the style that predominated in art and architecture in northern Europe from the early 12th to the 15th century.

In about 1280 Duccio was commissioned by the Rucellai family to paint a picture now known as the *Rucellai Madonna* to go in a church in the city of Florence. It is not known whether Duccio went to Florence to paint the picture or did it in Siena. Transporting it would have been difficult, as the wooden panel is extremely heavy.

Duccio's only other surviving, documented work is the *Maestà* (translated as the Virgin "in majesty" from *maestà*, Italian for majesty), a huge two-sided altarpiece for Siena Cathedral. A document of 1308 reveals that Duccio promised to work continuously on the altarpiece with his own hands (this means that he would not have his assistants do it for him). In fact, the altarpiece must have been started well before this. It is recorded that on completion in the year 1311 it was carried in a triumphal procession from the painter's workshop through the streets of Siena to be set up above the high altar in the cathedral.

More than 100 years later, in 1450, the altarpiece was described by the Florentine sculptor Lorenzo Ghiberti, who wrote: "The picture was most excellently done and with great skill. It is a magnificent thing, and [Duccio] was a most noble painter."

Data file

Full name: Duccio di Buoninsegna

Nationality: Italian

Style: Gothic

Dates: born 1255 in Siena, died c1319 in Siena

Key works:

Rucellai Madonna, probably for Santa Maria Novella, Florence 1285

Maestà altarpiece 1308–11

Things to look for:

- biblical subjects and altarpieces
- paintings with strong narratives
- extensive use of gold leaf

Comparisons: Cimabue, Giotto di Bondone, Simone Martini

Glossary terms: altarpiece, Byzantine, Gothic, *predella*

Master of skilled narrative

The *Maestà* was a vast altarpiece, originally measuring about 16 ft (5 m) in width. In the late 18th century it was dismantled and parts of it were sold. The main front panel is still in Siena (in the Cathedral Museum). Other panels are in museums throughout the Western world, and some have been lost.

When it was restored in the middle of the 20th century it was discovered that the main panel was quite badly damaged. This was partly because of the way it was broken up, but also because it had been used as an object of veneration and worship in the past and people had stuck nails into it to attach rosaries and other votive objects. This damage was particularly bad in the faces of the Virgin and the Child.

Although most paintings of this subject up to this date were vertical in format, this one, unusually, is horizontal. In most other respects, however, it conforms to tradition. The front of the *Maestà* shows the enthroned Virgin and Child surrounded by a host of angels and saints. The most important figures (such as the Virgin) are larger than the less important ones (such as the saints). The background is pure gold leaf and the whole composition is almost rigidly symmetrical. Each saint can be clearly identified by the clothes he or she is wearing and the objects (or "attributes") he or she is carrying.

Painted in the flat, Byzantine style, the figures are stylish and elegant, but they are not very realistic. Duccio was working at a time when the mathematics of perspective had not yet been applied to art, so the sense of space in a scene was not shown. Also, relatively little was known about the way that the muscles and bones of the body worked, which would later bring greater realism to the representation of people in art.

The back of the *Maestà* was covered with over 30 scenes from the story of Christ, including his miracles, the Crucifixion, and the Resurrection. One of the images on the back (illustrated here)

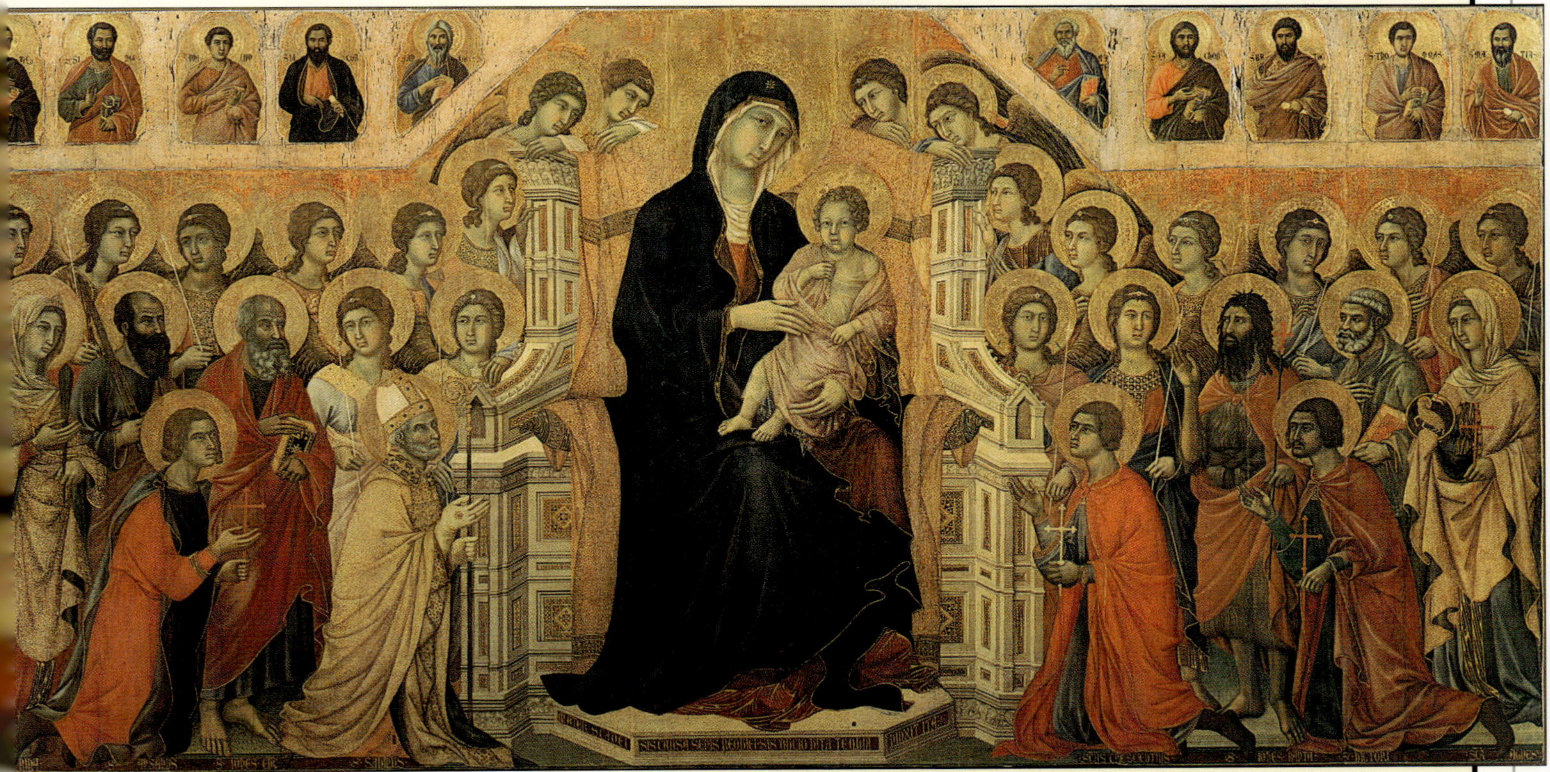

Maestà (front panel) *1308–11. 84¼ x 162¼ in (214 x 412 cm). Tempera on panel. Siena Cathedral Museum, Siena.*

shows Christ restoring a man's sight. Christ, the most important figure, is in the middle and is distinguished from the other men by his halo and the vivid blue of his robe. The man being healed is shown twice: once when Jesus is touching his eyelids, and again on the right when he is able to see. The buildings in the background look like folded cardboard cut-outs rather than stone or brick structures, and the crowd of people watching—Christ's disciples—are equally flat. In spite of this, the picture is a skilled narrative, using the characters and their dramatic settings to tell the story of the miracle that Jesus is performing in a clear and concise way.

Maestà (back panel): Christ Opens the Eyes of a Blind Man *1308–11. 17 x 17¾ in (43 x 45 cm). Tempera on panel. National Gallery, London.*

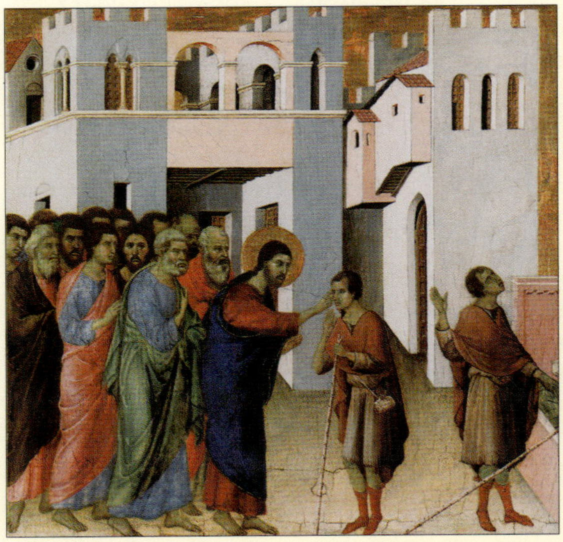

Reconstruction of Duccio's *Maestà* *The two-sided altarpiece (right) was divided on both sides into top panels, a central portion, and a strip of paintings at the bottom called a* predella. *The main front panel showed the Virgin "in majesty" with the baby Jesus. Below, the* predelle *depicted scenes from the early life of Christ (front) and scenes from his later life (back).*

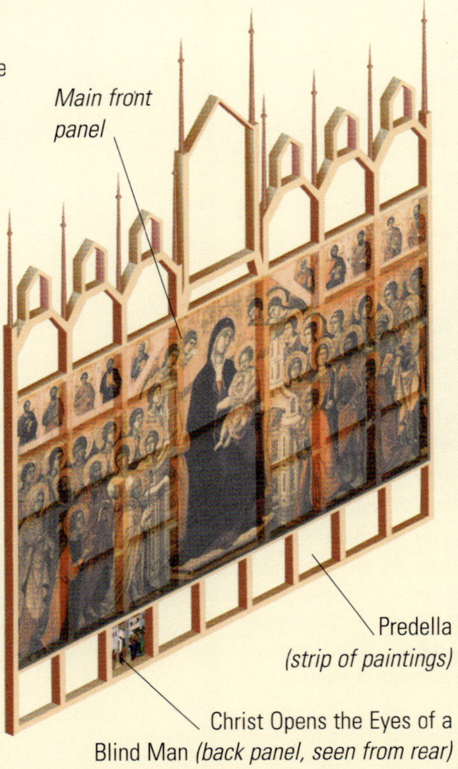

DUCHAMP Marcel

THERE ARE A HANDFUL OF PAINTERS AND SCULPTORS of whom we can say they are like no other; Duchamp is one such artist. Usually categorized as one of the anarchic "dadaists," he challenged traditional preconceptions of what art is, and exerted an individual and powerful influence on modern art.

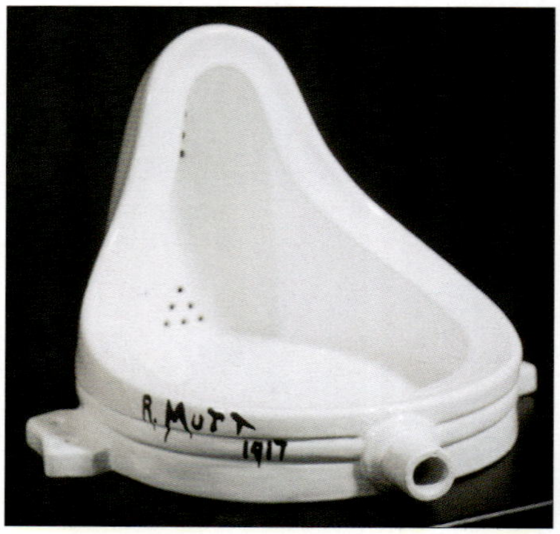

Fountain *1917. Porcelain. 14 in (33.5 cm). Indiana University Art Museum, Bloomington, IN.*

Life and work

As a child, Duchamp grew up in the midst of a family suffused with artistic spirit, and by the age of 15 he was producing passable works. He started in an impressionist style, before moving on to a Paul Cézanne-influenced fauvist period and then, in 1911, embracing the emerging cubist style. One such early work, *Nude Descending a Staircase No. 2* (1912), was the most contentious of all the work shown at the famous Armory Show in New York in 1913. Although it was condemned by most of the American critics, others recognized the originality of the work, and Duchamp sold all three paintings that he had exhibited. At this point, he could easily have capitalized on the notoriety and commercial success that the Armory Show had brought him, but his concerns were greater. He wanted to free himself from the treadmill of artistic production—the necessity to sell work and, by implication, to please an audience. To achieve this aim he took a job unconnected with art.

While working as a library clerk in Paris in 1913, Duchamp created the first of his "readymades," *Rue de Bicyclette*. With this work, Duchamp escaped from the overtly expressive nature of art. He created an artwork out of ordinary materials (in this case a bicycle wheel and a stool); only the idea to do it was his own. Over the next 10 years he created more readymades from time to time, sometimes altering the object and sometimes merely adding a title to a bought object (as in the snow shovel that he purchased in 1915 and titled *In Advance of the Broken Arm*).

Duchamp was unfit for service during World War I, and in 1915 left France for New York. There, he created his most famous readymade: *Fountain* (1917), a porcelain urinal which he bought from a plumbing suppliers in New York. Signing it with the false name R. Mutt, he submitted it to the Society of Independent Artists in order to test their professed belief in artistic freedom represented by the "open to all" exhibition policy. The society rejected *Fountain*: Duchamp proceeded to defend the work on behalf of the fictional R. Mutt. This he did in a one-off magazine that he founded called *The Blind Man*. "Whether Mr Mutt with his own hands made the fountain or not has no importance," Duchamp contended. "He *chose* it. He took an ordinary article of life, placed it so that its useful significance disappeared under the new title and point of view, and created a new thought for that object."

Duchamp's readymade was the precursor of the "found object," an idea that influenced generations of later artists. They initially antagonized much of the art world. They relied on no technical ability or aesthetic judgement, and seemed an affront both to the traditionalists who believed in good and bad taste, and to the avant-gardists who prized the seriousness of their struggle. However, over time, the readymades became accepted by the art world and eventually were venerated as beautiful or meaningful objects (this was not Duchamp's intention at all).

In 1923 he returned to France, where he devoted much of his time to playing chess. At the end of his life, it emerged that for 20 years he had been working on a piece that became known as *Given That...*(c 1948–), a mixed-media work that toyed with the idea of how we look at art.

Data file

Full name: Marcel Duchamp

Nationality: French (U.S. citizen after 1955)

Style: dadaism

Dates: born 1887 in Blainville, died 1968 in Neuilly

Key works:
- *Nude Descending a Staircase No. 2* 1912
- *Rue de Bicyclette* 1913
- *Fountain* 1917
- *Tu m'* 1918
- *The Bride Stripped Bare by Her Bachelors, Even (The Large Glass)* 1915–
- *Given That...* c1948–

Things to look for:
- playfulness
- irreverence
- puns with language
- unusual techniques

Comparisons: Francis Picabia, Man Ray, Andy Warhol, Piero Manzoni, Bruce Nauman, Robert Rauschenburg, Claes Oldenburg

Glossary terms: cubism, dadaism, fauvism, futurism, impressionism, readymade

The anti-art artist

Marcel Duchamp once remarked, "I don't believe in art, I believe in artists." From an early stage in his enigmatic artistic career, Duchamp was interested more in the concept of art than in art techniques and styles. For him, the esthetics of good and bad taste were irrelevant, and a distraction from the creative ideas with which art could experiment. Duchamp did, however, believe strongly in the worth of the artist, so long as the artist was free to think inventively rather than through the restrictions imposed by past and present fashion.

Although he did not belong to any of the avant-garde movements, Duchamp's work was closely allied to that of the dadaists. His method of provoking thought by undermining assumptions about what art could be and what makes sense was akin to the dadaists' impulse to challenge reason.

From 1915 Duchamp worked on a highly complex piece: *The Bride Stripped Bare by Her Bachelors, Even* (also known as *The Large Glass*). He abandoned work on the piece when he left New York in 1923 to return to France. Although it was unfinished, *The Large Glass* was Duchamp's most in-depth work.

Through his many notes and sketches that accompany it (collected together in a file known as "The Green Box"), we can get a pretty good idea of Duchamp's intention for this work. Here, he presents a half-mechanical, half-organic diagram on glass that, through a mysterious, absurd, and poetic science of his own invention, attempts to convey the first sexual encounter between man and woman. The male ("bachelors") domain is the bottom panel; the female ("bride") domain is the upper panel.

In this work and the preceding studies, Duchamp was searching for a way to express his ideas without mediating them through a personalized style. The technical, geometric drawing helped with this, and so also did the elements of chance that he introduced. For instance, the openings in the cloudlike shape in the upper panel are based on three photographs of a sheet flapping at an open window. And below the cloud on the left is a group of small holes, the positioning of which was guided by firing matchsticks dipped in paint at the glass from a toy gun. Through such elaborate acts of what one might call "serious play," Duchamp arrived at a kind of styleless style that allows the internal logic of his work to take precedence over any esthetic concerns.

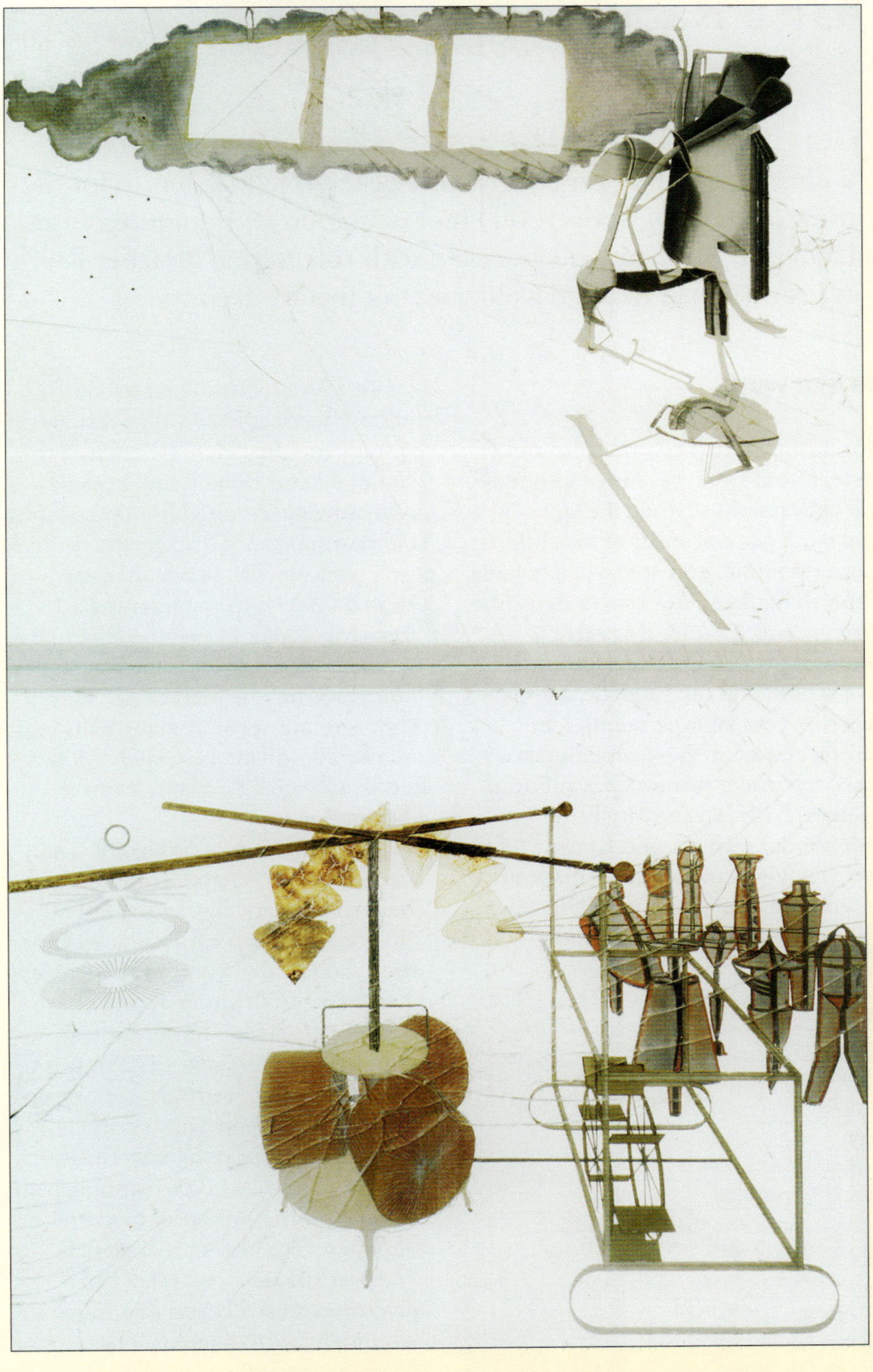

The Bride Stripped Bare by Her Bachelors, Even (The Large Glass)
1915 (unfinished). Oil and lead wire on glass. 109 x 89 in (277 x 226 cm). Philadelphia Museum of Art, PA.

DUFY Raoul

RAOUL DUFY WAS A PROLIFIC ARTIST, as well known for his book illustrations, fashion designs, and decorative interiors as for his paintings. His early works reveal his fascination with impressionism and fauvism, while his collaboration with the fashion designer Paul Poiret contributed to the development of the art-deco style.

Life and work

Born in the French coastal town of Le Havre, Raoul Dufy was raised as one of nine children. His father, a keen musician, encouraged all of his children in art and music, and at the age of just 14 the young Dufy was awarded his first drawing prize. Despite this early success, however, Dufy was forced to leave school and take a job as a bookkeeper. A year later he enrolled in evening classes at the local School of Fine Arts, where he met Othon Friesz. Together, both artists visited the museums of Le Havre and Rouen, where Dufy was particularly struck by the works of Camille Corot, Théodore Géricault, and Eugène Delacroix.

Full name: Raoul Dufy

Nationality: French

Style: fauvism

Dates: born 1877 in Le Havre, died 1953 in Forcalquier

Key works:

The Beach at Sainte-Adresse 1904

Posters at Trouville 1906

woodcut illustrations for *The Bestiary, or The Cortège of Orpheus* 1911

The Racetrack at Deauville: The Start 1929

The Electricity Fairy 1937

Things to look for:

- pure, unmixed colors
- color overlapping line
- bold strokes of thickly applied paint
- strong emphasis on decoration

Comparisons: Henri Matisse, Othon Friesz, Albert Marquet, Georges Braque, Eugène Boudin

Glossary terms: art deco, expressionism, fauvism, impressionism, postimpressionism

Data file

In 1900, following a period of military service, Dufy won a scholarship to study in Paris. Here he entered the studio of Léon Bonnat and became increasingly interested in impressionist and postimpressionist painting. In such early works as *The Beach at Sainte-Adresse* (1904), Dufy presented a brightly colored, loosely sketched image of modern tourists enjoying a day of leisure on the northern coast. This work is reminiscent of many paintings on a similar theme by Claude Monet and by the local Le Havre painter Eugène Boudin.

Within a year of producing *The Beach at Sainte-Adresse*, Dufy's style changed dramatically. In the fall of 1905 he visited an exhibition in Paris where he saw the works of the fauvists. Dufy later recalled how seeing one work in particular, Henri Matisse's *Luxe, Calme, et Volupté* (1905), was to change his whole attitude to painting. With its bold colors and hastily executed, expressive figures, Dufy's *Posters at Trouville* (1906), although still focusing on the subject of modern tourists, reveals this new approach.

Over the next few years Dufy traveled extensively and continued to experiment with different styles, absorbing the influences of Paul Gauguin and Paul Cézanne. In 1909 he visited Munich, where, in emulation of the German expressionist artists, he took up woodcut printing. Two years later he completed a series of woodcut illustrations for *The Bestiary, or The Cortège of Orpheus* (1911) by the French poet, art critic, and champion of cubism Guillaume Apollinaire. In 1910 Dufy joined forces with the fashion designer Paul Poiret. They produced countless textile designs over the next two decades.

After World War I Dufy continued to expand his activities in the decorative arts, designing stage sets for Jean Cocteau and also producing ceramics. His paintings of this period, frequently representing racetracks and

Dufy and the use of color

While traveling around Normandy with his fellow artist Albert Marquet, Dufy produced the painting *Posters at Trouville* (1906). In this work Dufy expressed his fascination with the lively seaside resort of Trouville, with its crowds of tourists and colorful advertising billboards lining the ocean boulevard. Thirty years earlier, the impressionist painter Claude Monet had also painted tourists at Trouville, but Dufy was less inspired by impressionism for this painting than by the fauvist style of such artists as Henri Matisse and André Derain, whose works he had seen on display in Paris the previous year.

In *Posters at Trouville* Dufy introduces bright, unmixed colors rapidly applied in a loose, sketchy manner that is reminiscent of children's art. Color is used randomly and unnaturalistically. The sidewalk along which Dufy's characters are promenading, for example, is described with various shades of red, yellow, and green. Behind these figures the advertising billboards form a rainbow-colored backdrop to the scene while simultaneously revealing the incursion of the modern, urban world into this seaside resort.

Significantly, Dufy's areas of color are not always restricted to the contours of the figures represented, and several are surrounded by halos of bright color. Dufy painted in this free way throughout his career, his colors often overlapping the lines and contours of the subjects that they describe. In *The Racetrack at Deauville: The Start* (1929), for instance, the spectators are sketched in against a background of green and white, suggesting

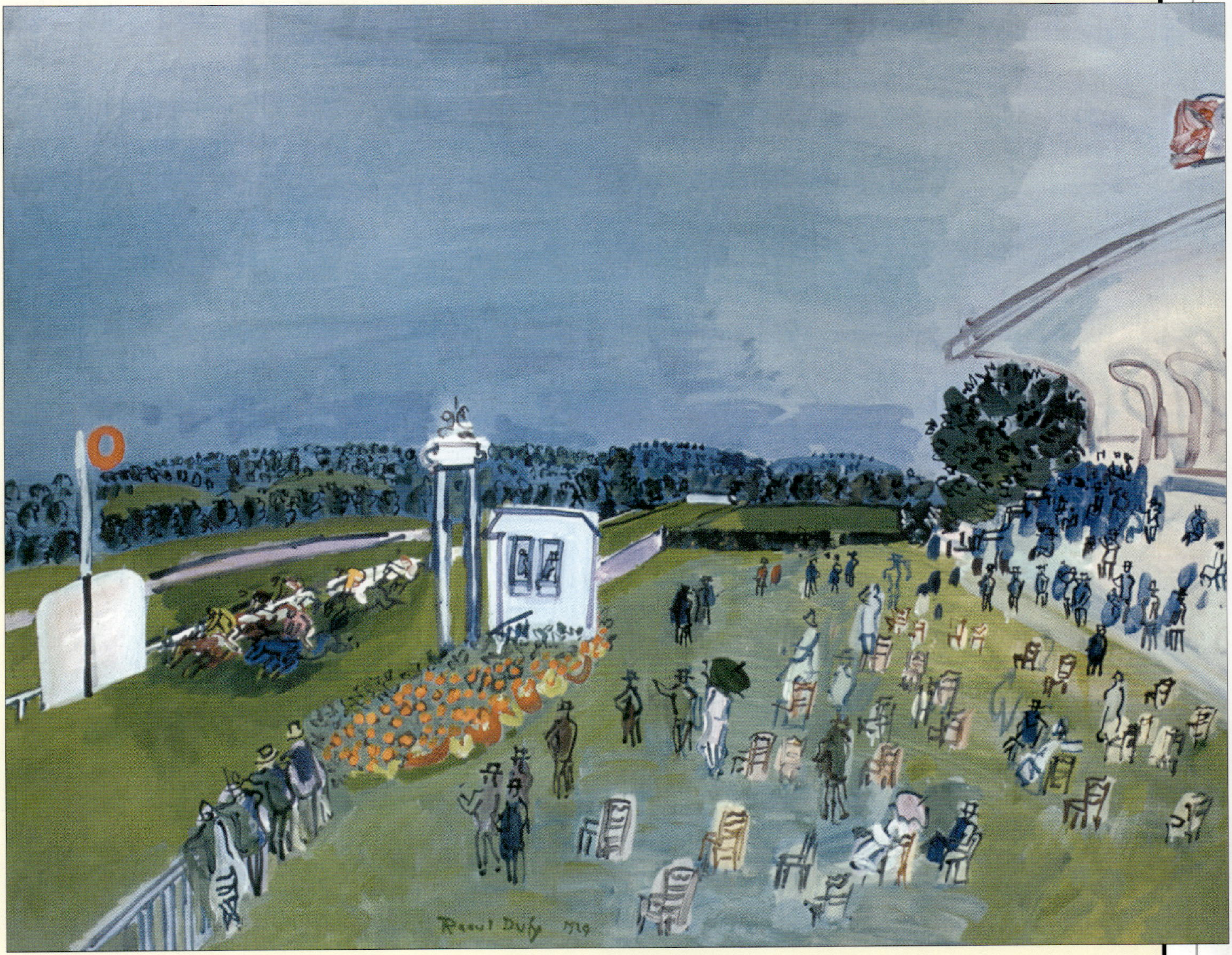

grass and the grandstand. These background colors, however, frequently spill over into the figures themselves, as if the work has been badly colored in. This technique is reminiscent of certain printing practices in which colors, when applied over a line drawing, do not always match exactly. (This "accidental" misalignment can be seen in many cheap 19th-century prints, which were avidly collected during this period.) Dufy's experiences in textile design and printing may well have influenced his use of the technique.

The Racetrack at Deauville: The Start
1929. Oil on canvas. 25¾ x 32¼ in (65.5 x 81.5 cm). Fogg Art Museum, Cambridge, MA.

regattas, also revealed his growing fascination with decoration. In 1925 Dufy was invited to participate in the Paris International Exhibition. Here he exhibited both wallhangings and a ceramic fountain, which, along with other works on display at the exhibition, contributed to the development of the style known as art deco. Twelve years later, when Paris played host to the 1937 World's Fair, Dufy contributed an enormous mural, then the largest painting in the world. The work, entitled *The Electricity Fairy* (1937), is a homage to modern technology and was installed as a backdrop to four electrical generators. In form it is a historical panorama recounting the evolution of scientific developments in the harnessing of nature, ranging from Archimedes to the modern ocean liner.

Although increasingly crippled by arthritis, Dufy continued to produce paintings, textile designs, and book illustrations until his death, in the south of France, in 1953.

DÜRER Albrecht

DÜRER WAS A VISUALLY AND INTELLECTUALLY ARTICULATE ARTIST who brought the esthetic theories of Renaissance Italy to northern Europe. His prints, drawings, and paintings show his compulsive scrutiny of form, as he searched for underlying harmony and order in the natural world.

Life and work

Albrecht Dürer was born in the free town of Nuremberg, the son of a goldsmith. He was initially apprenticed to his father's trade, and his excellent draftsmanship persuaded his father that his talent lay in fine art. He was apprenticed to the painter and book illustrator Michael Wolgemut. Dürer spent four years working in Wolgemut's workshop, where he gained experience in both painting and woodcuts. His ability swiftly flourished; he produced a remarkable painting of his father, *Albrecht Dürer the Elder* (1490), when he was just 19.

In the same year, 1490, Dürer left Nuremberg to travel around the cultural centers of Germany and Switzerland. This was a common practice at the time, and a vital component of a young artist's education. On his travels Dürer sought out the best craftsmen and painters, and worked alongside printmakers in Strasbourg and Basle, who thus helped to develop his skill in making woodcuts in particular.

He returned to Nuremberg four years after he had left to marry Agnes Frey (the marriage had been arranged by their fathers). But Dürer's commitment to art was considerably greater than that to his new wife, and he left for Italy two months after their wedding. He made his way to Venice, a thriving trading center that was home to a vibrant mixture of people and ideas. Dürer was in Venice for six months, and in that time studied the work of Andrea Mantegna and met Giovanni Bellini. It was a formative time for the young Dürer, and instead of hurrying back to Nuremberg he spent time in the countryside on his return journey, honing the painterly skills that he had learned from the Italians. The watercolors that he produced on his homeward trip mix the concentrated detail for which he is particularly known with a looser, sketchy technique that demonstrates the eloquence of his gestures.

Back in Nuremberg, Dürer set up a workshop of his own, in which he concentrated most of his efforts on woodcuts and etchings. The woodcuts in particular, with their strong emphasis on bold lines and deep contrasts, reveal most clearly the Gothic influence on his style. The dramatic *Apocalypse* (1498), for example, radiates with intense, Gothic fantasy, and is almost cartoonlike in its imagery. Yet at the same time Dürer's mind was being drawn elsewhere, and he again became preoccupied with the artistic concerns of Renaissance Italy.

He set off on his travels once more in around 1506, and this time returned from Italy with a more defined method for ascribing set proportions to the human body (which was perhaps derived from Leonardo da Vinci's studies). The human body that the Renaissance artists depicted was not so much real as an idealized concept of perfect human form. This version of humanity thus actually improved upon nature.

By this time Dürer had become a highly successful artist who was lauded both in his home town and abroad. Although he took commissions from far and wide, what is striking about his output is his apparent freedom over subject matter. Many of his works, from studies of animals and plants, such as *Young Hare* (1502) or *The Great Piece of Turf* (1503), to his succession of self-portraits, had no obvious clients. Indeed, they seem to have been fueled purely by Dürer's obsessive desire to extend the limits of art.

One of Dürer's last works was a two-paneled painting, *The Four Apostles* (1526), which Dürer donated to the town of Nuremberg on its completion, perhaps as a call for peace between the Lutheran and Catholic camps that had split the Christian faith in his home town. During the final years of his life Dürer worked on theoretical writings and drawings that would provide a guide for future generations of artists. He produced his *Underweyssung der Messung* (Treatise on Measurement) in 1525, while his *Vier Bücher von Menschlicher Proportion* (Four Books on Human Proportion) were published posthumously in the year of his death, 1528.

Data file

Full name: Albrecht Dürer

Nationality: German

Style: northern Renaissance

Dates: born 1471 in Nuremberg, died 1528 in Nuremberg

Key works:

Apocalypse (woodcut) 1498

Self-portrait 1498

Christ Among the Doctors 1506

Portrait of a Woman 1506

Melancholia 1514

Saint Jerome 1521

The Four Apostles 1526

Things to look for:

- graphic delineation of form and features
- outstanding surface complexion detail

Comparisons: Leonardo da Vinci, Andrea Mantegna, Jan Van Eyck, Giovanni Bellini, Hans Holbein, Mathis Grünewald

Glossary terms: foreshortening, Gothic, Renaissance

Under scrutiny

In this self-portrait (1498) Dürer has turned his scrutinizing eye upon himself and has depicted his facial features with vivid realism. The pose is formal, however, as is his mode of dress, for Dürer is presenting himself as an elegant man rather than as a hard-working painter and printmaker. On his first visit to Venice Dürer had been struck by the greater respect paid to artists in Italy than in Germany, and he was seeking to raise the status of the artist in his homeland with this portrait.

Through the window we can make out a mountain landscape (probably based on one of the watercolor sketches made on his return journey from Venice). The presence of such a view seems to enforce the fact that here is a man of the world who has traveled far and seen much. It is both the work of, and the image of, a highly confident, yet studiously contemplative, artist.

The self-portrait shown here was painted before Dürer's second visit to Italy and therefore before his ideas of proportion and measurement had become dominant factors in his work. But he worked on theories of drawing and painting for most of his career. Along with Renaissance artists in Italy, he strove to perfect the discipline of art and to create images that improved upon the variable, and therefore imperfect, world of nature. He tried to apply a rational, scientific mind to the natural world in the pursuit of universal laws of harmony, proportion, and beauty.

Dürer used many devices to study form. As Leonardo had done, he also drew schematized human forms, with the limb measurements determined by simple geometry, and the division of body parts corresponding to fixed ratios. With such methods he sought to produce a human archetype: an "idealized" form that would become the basis for all of his figures.

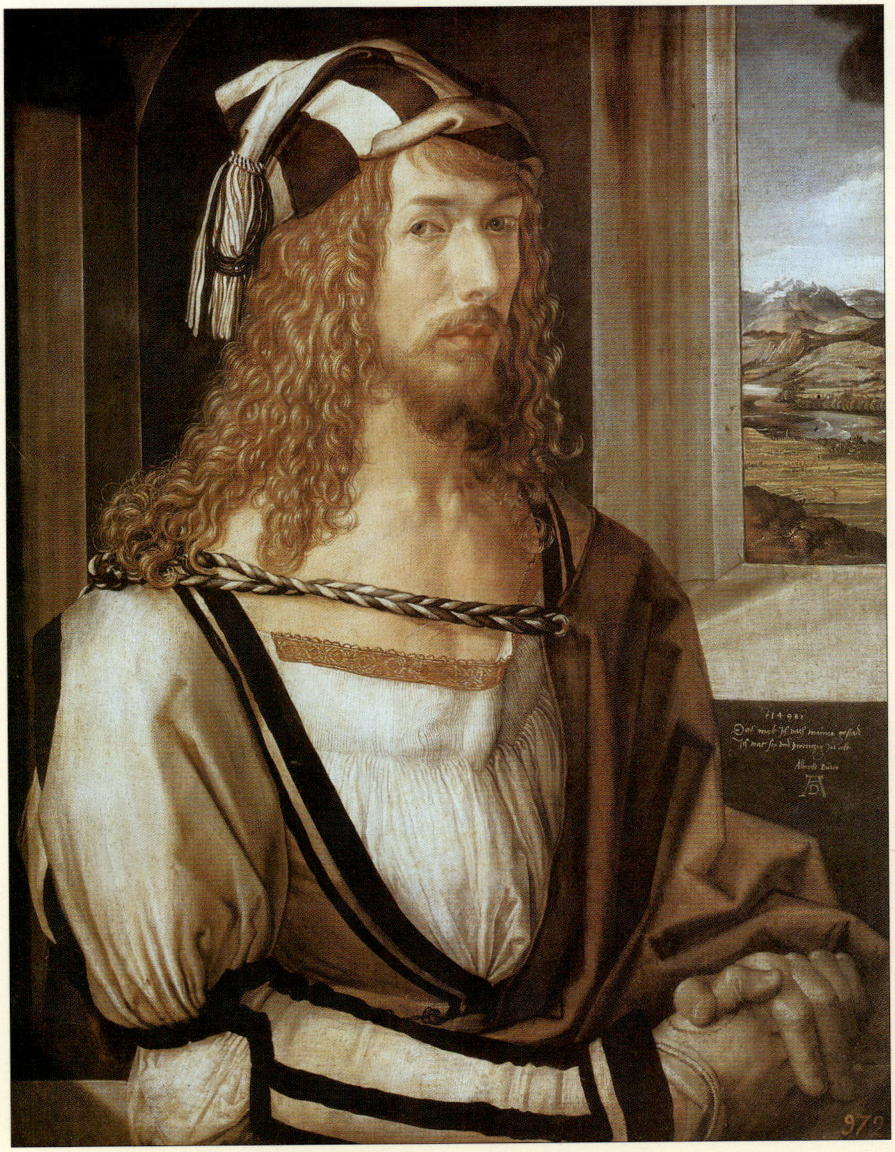

Self-portrait *1498. Oil on wood panel. 20½ x 16¼ in (52 x 41 cm). Museo del Prado, Madrid.*

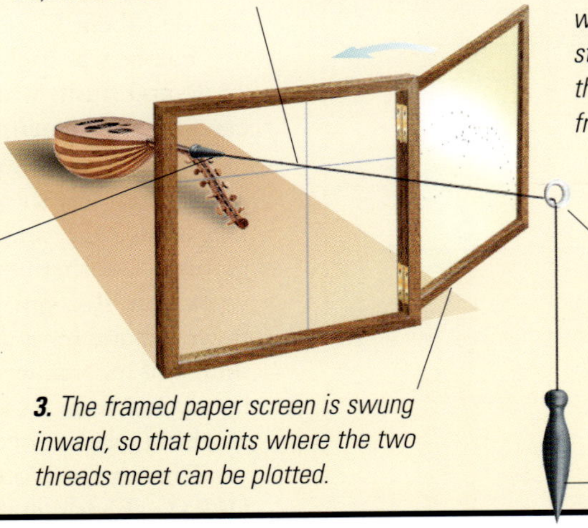

***1.** A string passes from a hook fixed to the wall, through the frame, and ends in a pointer. The string is kept taut by a weight. The pointer is used to mark points on the object.*

***2.** Two threads at right angles to each other are moved so that they cross at the point where the string passes through the frame.*

***3.** The framed paper screen is swung inward, so that points where the two threads meet can be plotted.*

Hook fixed to the wall.

Weight

Dürer's plotting machine *Dürer invented a device for plotting foreshortened objects using a hinged shutter on a wooden frame. The outline of the object was plotted point-by-point onto drawing paper on the frame.*

EAKINS Thomas

ALTHOUGH HIS ART WAS REVILED IN HIS TIME, Thomas Eakins is now widely recognized as the greatest American painter of the 19th century. He is admired above all for his masterly portraits, and for his atmospheric boating scenes.

Life and work

Thomas Eakins was born in 1844 in Philadelphia, the city where he was to spend most of his life, and which was to provide the focus of much of his art.

His father, Benjamin, taught penmanship at a Quaker school and executed the calligraphy on official documents. The qualities of discipline and precision that this job required would later become a feature of Thomas's approach to painting. Benjamin made a number of shrewd investments in the property market, which brought his family financial security. This enabled Thomas to pursue his artistic goals wholeheartedly, even though his pictures were often unpopular with the public.

Data file

Full name: Thomas Cowperthwait Eakins
Nationality: American
Style: realism
Dates: born 1844 in Philadelphia, died 1916 in Philadelphia
Key works:
Max Schmitt in a Single Scull 1871
The Gross Clinic 1875
The Swimming Hole 1883
The Agnew Clinic 1889
Miss Van Buren c1889
Between Rounds 1899
The Thinker 1900
Things to look for:
- dramatic lighting
- boating scenes
- stark realism

Comparisons: Rembrandt, Ashcan school, John Singer Sargent, Gustave Courbet
Glossary terms: academic art, life drawing

Eakins was a good student, earning particularly high grades for his drawing, but his artistic ambitions were slow to develop. Initially he thought of studying medicine, and for a time he taught penmanship with his father. But at the same time he attended life-drawing classes, working from the nude model, and attended lectures on anatomy at the Pennsylvania Academy of the Fine Arts.

Life drawing and anatomy were essential components of academic training, but for American artists of this period there was another requirement: they had to complete their studies in Europe. Eakins chose to study in Paris, which was then regarded as the West's leading art center. He followed this with a trip to Spain.

In 1866, he began working in the studio of Jean-Léon Gérôme, a conventional but highly respected French artist. The meticulous finish in Eakins' pictures may owe something to Gérôme's example, but he was more influenced by the pictures he saw in museums, especially the bold realism of the Spanish artists Diego Velázquez and José de Ribera.

Eakins was back in Philadelphia in 1870, and this is when his artistic career began in earnest. His earliest exhibited work (*Max Schmitt in a Single Scull*) was shown at the Union League in 1871, and he sold his first picture—another boating scene—three years later. Recognition eluded him, however, and for many years his chief source of income would come from his family and from a succession of teaching jobs.

The fate of *The Gross Clinic* (1875), which is arguably his greatest painting, was to be symptomatic of the the artist's lack of popularity. Eakins labored long over this masterpiece, and submitted it for display at the Centennial Exhibition of 1876, hoping that it would help demonstrate how the arts of America could more than match those of Europe. In the end, his picture

Unstinting realism

Eakins produced two large paintings of surgical operations—*The Gross Clinic* (1875) and *The Agnew Clinic* (1889)—which rank among his greatest works. Both received a hostile reception from critics, but both offer fine evidence of the artist's unflinching realism.

The Agnew Clinic started off as a simple portrait commission. In 1889, students and staff from the medical school at the University of Pennsylvania approached Eakins about the painting, intending it as a retirement present for their much-loved professor of surgery, Dr Hayes Agnew. He had been at the medical school since 1871 and was a well-known figure in his field—he was one of the surgeons who attended President Garfield after he was shot by an assassin in 1881.

Eakins was so delighted by the project that, instead of just painting the doctor, he offered to show him at work in his teaching clinic, performing an operation before a group of students. Because he agreed to do all of this for no more than the fee of $750 originally offered, his proposal was gratefully accepted.

Eakins approached the monumental task in his usual, painstaking fashion. He visited the operating theater on several occasions, in order to make preparatory sketches for the general composition. He also invited Agnew into his studio, where he produced a detailed study of him, in the precise pose adopted in the painting. In addition, he had a series of tiered benches constructed so that he could recreate the effect of the hospital amphitheater. It is possible that he also made studies for the other figures, although none of them has survived. All are identifiable portraits. The figure on the far right is Eakins himself, reputedly drawn in by his wife.

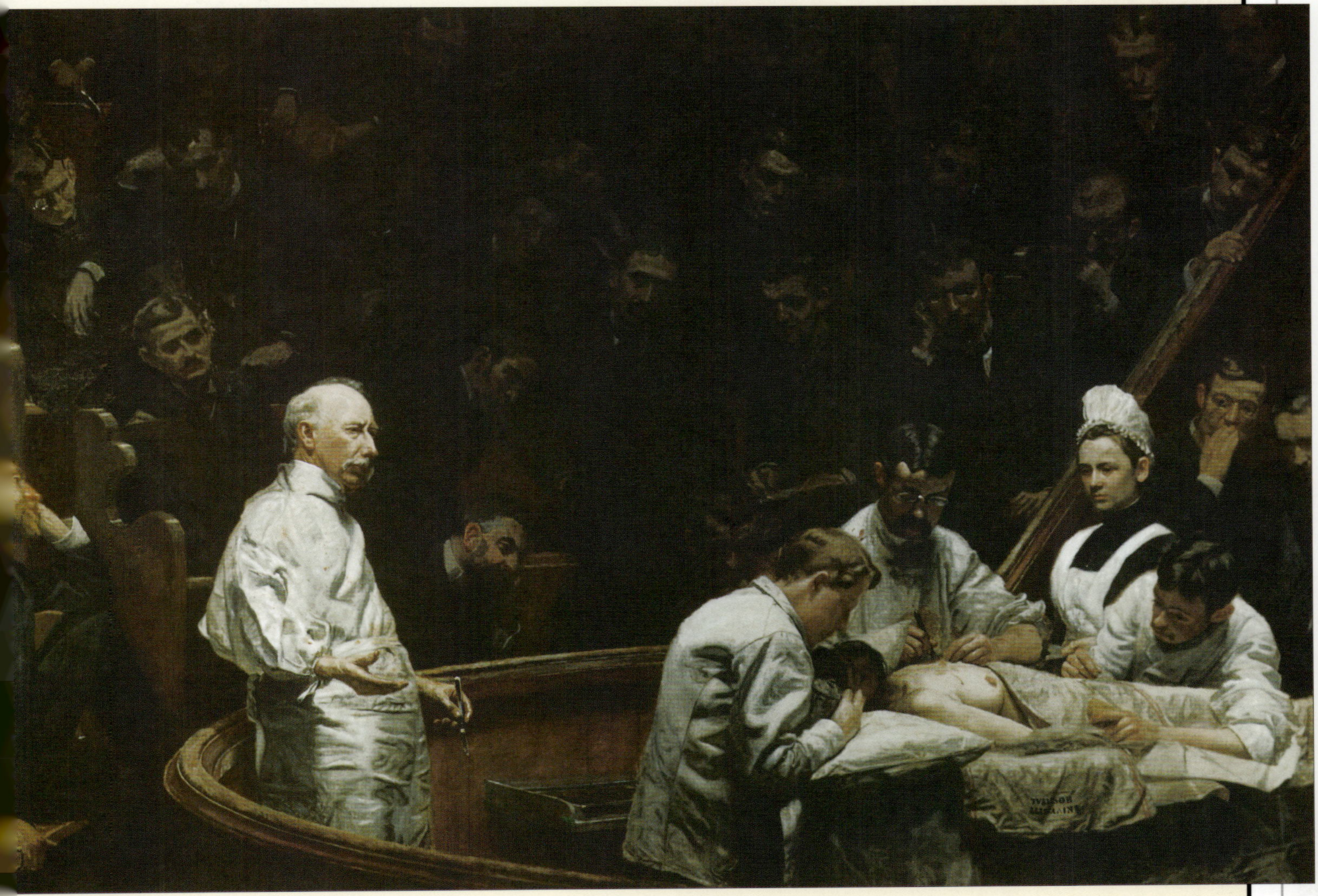

The Agnew Clinic *1889. Oil on canvas. 74 1/2 x 130 1/2 in (188 x 329 cm). University of Pennsylvania School of Medicine, Philadelphia, PA.*

The ultimate inspiration for Eakins' two medical pictures came from Rembrandt's *Anatomy Lesson of Dr. Nicolaes Tulp* (1632). Like the great Dutch master, Eakins was fascinated by the interplay of light and shadow, and this is particularly evident in *The Gross Clinic*, where several different light sources are employed at once.

In *The Agnew Clinic*, Eakins confronted a different problem. Artificial lighting had just been introduced into operating theaters, and here Eakins clearly enjoyed the challenge of contrasting the brightly lit figures in the center with the shadowy figures of the observers sitting on the benches around them.

The American public was shocked by the realistic portrayal of such gruesome subjects. In particular, they were horrified by the bloodstained hands and clothing of the figures in *The Gross Clinic*. At the doctor's request, Eakins avoided this level of detail in *The Agnew Clinic*. The picture still met with disapproval, however. Despite its obvious quality, it was rejected by the exhibition jury at the Pennsylvania Academy.

was rejected by the exhibition committee and it remained unsold for two years. It was eventually bought for a paltry $200, a sum that covered little more than the cost of the picture's frame.

The public took a long time to warm to Eakins' uncompromising brand of realism. He deliberately avoided any narrative or dramatic content in his pictures, preferring to record rather than interpret the scenes before him. To this end, he made use of the latest scientific developments in the fields of anatomical research and motion photography. These efforts were finally rewarded toward the end of Eakins' career. He won prizes at the Pan-American Exposition (1901) and at the Pennsylvania Academy (1904), but his most cherished award was the gold medal for *The Gross Clinic*, which he received in 1904 at the Saint Louis World's Fair.

ELSHEIMER Adam

ADAM ELSHEIMER WAS ONE OF THE MOST INFLUENTIAL ARTISTS of the early 17th century, famed for compressing the essence of an event into a small space, and for capturing a range of light effects. Elsheimer's style would become a point of departure for many other artists including Peter Paul Rubens, Rembrandt, and Claude Lorraine.

Life and work

Adam Elsheimer was born in Frankfurt-am-Main in Germany in 1578. The son of a tailor and one of 10 children, Elsheimer was apprenticed to local artist Philipp Uffenbach. In the second half of 1598, Elsheimer traveled south to Italy. He spent a short time in Venice—no more than 18 months—but during this time he is believed to have painted *The Deluge* (c1599), *The Holy Family* (c1599), and *The Baptism of Christ* (c1598–1600), absorbing the influence of Venetian painters such as Tintoretto and Paolo Veronese.

Why Elsheimer left Venice is something of a mystery. It is possible that he got into trouble with the Venetian guilds. The guilds operated in a manner similar to trade unions, regulating artistic and other professions. As a "foreigner" in Venice, Elsheimer might have found it hard to make a living: the Venetians were suspicious of any outsiders, and the city even employed a small army of private agents who spied on newcomers. Even the great Florentine Leonardo da Vinci, who was in Venice in 1500, could not secure patronage there.

Better opportunities for non-Italian artists existed in Rome. Unlike Florence, Milan, or Venice, Rome did not have its own school of art, but had always been dependent on artists from other regions and from abroad, who were attracted to the powerful courts of the popes, cardinals, and princes. In April 1600 Elsheimer arrived in Rome: artists already established in the Eternal City included Michelangelo Merisi da Caravaggio, and the great Flemish painter, draftsman, and diplomat, Peter Paul Rubens, whom Elsheimer later taught how to etch.

In Rome Elsheimer appears to have found a patron in the figure of Johannes Faber, a doctor from Bamberg, but his fame was established by a painting of *Tobias and the Angel* (1602–03) (known as the "small" *Tobias*, to distinguish it from a later work of the same name). Numerous engravings of the small *Tobias* were made, since lodged in Elsheimer's house was "Henrico pictore" ("Henry the artist"), who has been identified as the engraver Count Hendrick Goudt. The publication of artists' prints spread different styles of art across Europe: Goudt would later produce engravings of Elsheimer's "large" *Tobias* (c1610), an image that was to influence directly the etching *The Flight into Egypt* (c1653) by Rembrandt.

In 1606 Elsheimer married Carla Antonia Stuarda da Francoforte, who was possibly a member of a Scottish family who had moved to Italy, since Stuarda is the Italianized form of the Scottish name, Stuart. Three years later they had a son.

In the earliest landscape that Elsheimer painted in Rome, *Landscape with Bacchus and the Nymphs of Nysa* (c1601), he used a formula developed by Flemish landscape painters who had moved to settle in Frankenthal, near Frankfurt: a group, or "island," of trees in the center of the picture with vistas to either side. Elsheimer's greatest innovation, however, was his rendering of night scenes in works such as *The Burning of Troy* (c1603–04) and *Paul Shipwrecked off the Island of Malta* (c1604).

Elsheimer's small-scale cabinet pictures required a meticulous and painstakingly slow method, so his output was small, but its influence on many artists was great. His work was a constant source of inspiration to Rubens, who owned at least four of his paintings, and to Rembrandt, Claude Lorraine, and Nicolas Poussin. Despite widespread acclaim, however, Elsheimer seems to have lived—and died—in poverty: at one point he was even imprisoned for debt. Contemporary accounts of his character tell of a difficult man, by turns charming and friendly, eccentric and withdrawn.

Data file

Full name: Adam Elsheimer

Nationality: German

Style: High Renaissance

Dates: born 1578 in Frankfurt-am-Main, died 1610 in Rome, Italy

Key works:
- *The Baptism of Christ* c1598–1600
- *Landscape with Saint John the Baptist Preaching* c1599
- *The Deluge* c1599
- *Landscape with Bacchus and the Nymphs of Nysa* c1601
- *Tobias and the Angel* 1602–03
- *The Glorification of the Cross* c1602–03
- *The Burning of Troy* c1603–04
- *Judith Beheading Holofernes* c1607

Things to look for:
- small-scale cabinet pictures on copper panels
- tonal progression from foreground (brown), to middle ground (green), to background (blue), creating effect of depth in landscapes
- atmospheric, sometimes nocturnal scenes
- dynamic play of light and shadow
- use of imaginary architectural features as well as real buildings

Comparisons: Claude Lorraine, Tintoretto, Paolo Veronese, Michelangelo Merisi da Caravaggio, Annibale Carracci, Peter Paul Rubens, Rembrandt, Nicolas Poussin, Albrecht Altdorfer

Glossary terms: baroque, cabinet picture, chiaroscuro, classicism, engraving, etching, high-keyed, mannerism, Renaissance

Dramatic scenes on a small scale

By 1590 the late-Renaissance style of exaggeration, complexity, and grace, known as "mannerism," had largely run its course, and many young artists were turning back to the masters of the Renaissance for inspiration and guidance. From this came the style known as "baroque." Baroque art sought to reinforce religious faith by appealing to the senses and the emotions, rather than to the intellect or reason. Its essence lay in the dramatic use of movement, chiaroscuro (light and shade) and high-keyed colors.

In Rome in 1600, Adam Elsheimer stood at the turning point between the "old" mannerism and the "new" baroque. His stories are told in a simple and straightforward manner, and in this respect he was reacting against the complexity of mannerism. Yet there are mannerist echoes of Paolo Veronese in Elsheimer's use of architectural settings in his early work, while the handling of bodies and the dynamic play of light and shadow demonstrate his awareness of the baroque works by the Carracci brothers and Carravaggio.

The Baptism of Christ (c1598–1600) was the first of his paintings to display what is now regarded as a typical "Elsheimer background." Wooded hills are interspersed with figures, and buildings rise up from the hills in the background. It was also the first painting in which Elsheimer introduced a group of figures into the middle ground. This was characteristic of his later works—the figures often wore turbans or plumed hats, and sometimes rode on horseback.

As in all Elsheimer's paintings, the light source is evident: it is either natural light (from the sun or moon), artificial light (from torches or candles) or, as in this case, supernatural or "divine" light. Depth is achieved by progression through color tones from the dark foreground figures in brown, through the green of the middle distance, to the mostly blue background.

The moment Elsheimer is depicting is from the New Testament, when God declares: "This is my beloved son in whom I am well pleased." (Matthew 3: 17). God the Father is at the top, surrounded by angels. Below is a dove representing the Holy Ghost, surrounded by four putti (cherubs). An angel is descending with a red robe for Christ. At one time it was believed that *The Baptism of Christ* was depicting three different events: Christ's baptism; Christ summoning Saint Peter from his fishing boat (note the two tiny figures and the boat in the left background); and Saint Peter removing a coin from the mouth of a fish. The seated man in the dark shadows of the foreground is, in fact, removing his shoe.

Elsheimer's small but highly detailed paintings—often little larger than a miniature—might have been designed to be inlaid into cabinet doors (these were known as cabinet pictures), and most were painted on small copper panels. On the reverse of *The Baptism of Christ* a vertical division and intersecting arcs were incised into the copper to establish the center of the panel as an aid to the composition. Because painters of the time produced prints from engravings on copper plates, it was natural for them to use copper panels as supports for their paintings as well.

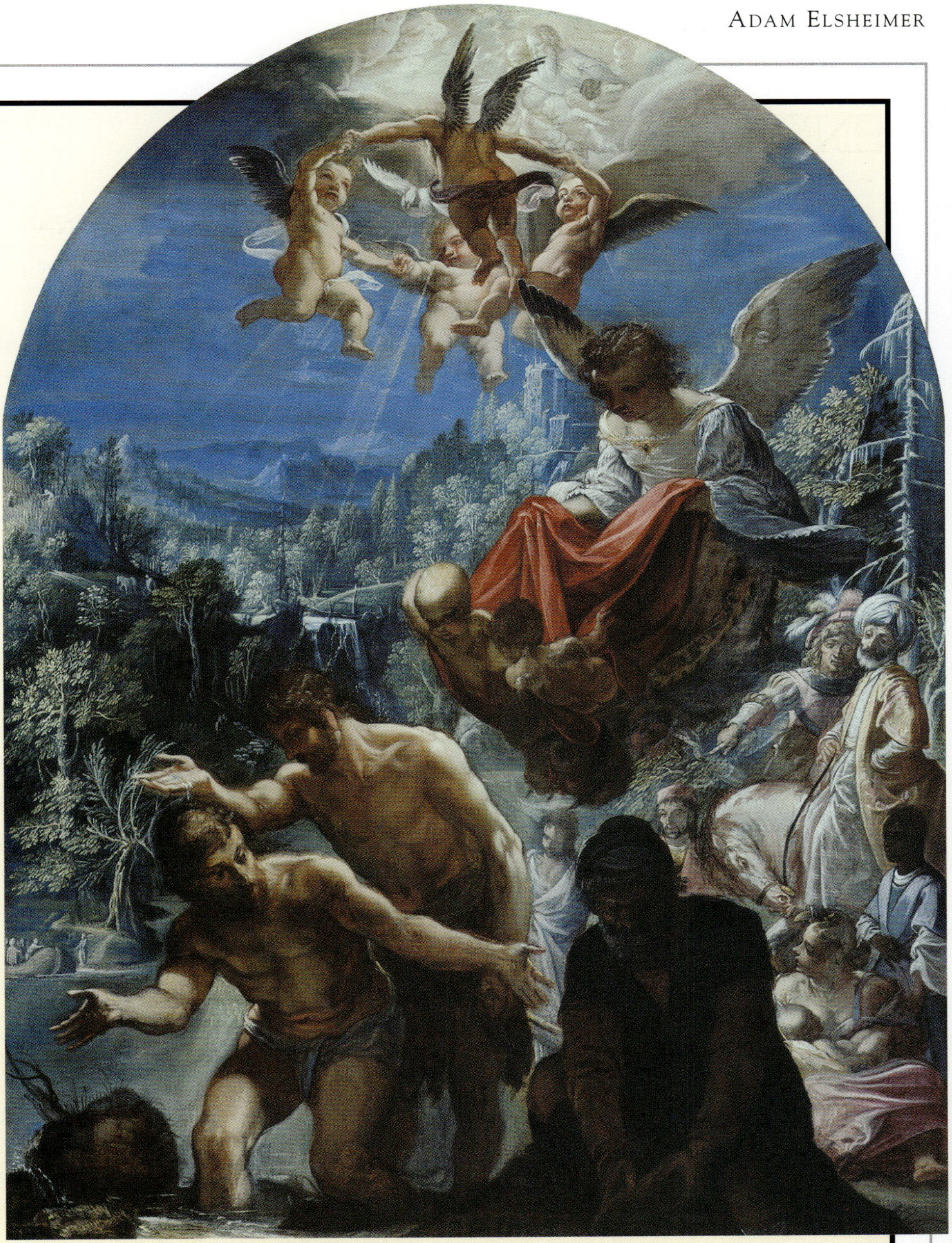

The Baptism of Christ *c1598–1600. Oil on copper panel. 11 x 8 1/4 in (28 x 21 cm). National Gallery, London.*

ENSOR James

JAMES ENSOR DEPENDED ALMOST ENTIRELY ON HIS IMAGINATION for inspiration for his work, which depicted a macabre but strangely colorful world of masks and skeletons. His exaggeration and distortion of form and color can be seen as expressionist before its time.

Life and work

Almost the whole of Ensor's life was spent at his family home in Ostend, a provincial town on the Belgian coast. His parents were moderately prosperous and he was encouraged to develop his artistic skills; he trained for three years from 1877 at the Academie des Beaux-Arts in Brussels. Diligent, but bored by his classically based studies, he soon showed indications of the prickly single-mindedness that would mark his career. His work of the early 1880s also revealed a tendency to move away from the somber form of realism that dominated Belgian art at this time and adopt a much brighter palette of colors.

Although he returned to Ostend, Ensor continued to exhibit regularly in Brussels during the 1880s and 1890s, a period during which the city became an important center for the promotion of artistic innovations taking place abroad, particularly in Paris. In 1883, for example, the influential Belgian critic Octave Maus established Les Vingt ("The Twenty"), a society that exhibited annually and displayed works by impressionists, postimpressionists, and symbolists. Ensor, whose paintings had often been excluded from other exhibitions, became a founding member of Les Vingt; the impressionistic *Women Eating Oysters* (1882) is typical of his work at this time.

However, by the later 1880s he had begun to introduce a type of content and primitive style into his work that even the artists and critics associated with Les Vingt found difficult to accept. Although he continued to paint naturalistic subjects, a strain of fantasy was gradually emerging, leading to frequent rejections of his work.

In his autobiographical writings Ensor not only denied having been influenced by others, but also claimed to have inspired a number of avant-garde ideas, although these in fact owed nothing to his example. During the 1880s many artists, writers, and poets throughout Europe were reacting against the prevailing forms of naturalism, turning instead to an art form that was based on imagination. The birth of the symbolist movement was announced in a manifesto by the poet Jean Moréas in 1886, but the ideas that he presented therein had been circulating for some time. In Belgium, such writers as Maurice Maeterlinck and Emile Verhaeren (both of whom wrote favorably on Ensor), as well as painters like Félicien Rops and Fernand Khnopff were already exploring ideas which, in his own idiosyncratic manner, Ensor was also to pursue.

Although *The Entry of Christ into Brussels* (1888) is regarded as a turning point in Ensor's career, this unusually large canvas contains themes and symbolic forms that had already occurred in his paintings. It also reveals echoes of an earlier Flemish tradition: a diminutive Christ amid a host of masklike faces recalls Pieter Bruegel the Elder and Hieronymous Bosch. Yet Ensor's purpose was to use Christian

Data file

Full name: James Ensor

Nationality: Belgian

Style: expressionism

Dates: born 1860 in Ostend, died 1949 in Ostend

Key works:
- *Women Eating Oysters* 1882
- *The Entry of Christ into Brussels* 1888
- *Astonishment of the Wouse Mask* 1889
- *Skeletons Warming Themselves* 1889
- *Demons Torturing Me* 1895
- *Masks Confronting Death* 1898

Things to look for:
- symbolic subject matter
- savage humor
- expressive brushwork and intense coloring

Comparisons: Hieronymous Bosch, Edouard Vuillard, Félicien Rops, Edvard Munch, Odilon Redon, Emil Nolde

Glossary terms: impasto, surrealism, symbolism, Les Vingt ("The Twenty")

Symbols of life and death

As Ensor became more reclusive, he worked less often from human subjects and more from arrangements of the assortment of props and unusual objects that he kept in his studio. (His descriptions of these recall the curios that his mother sold in her store, as well as his childhood recollection of the strange jumble in his grandmother's "dark and frightening attic.") His works *Studio Props* and *Astonishment of the Wouse Mask* (both 1889) give us glimpses of this studio paraphernalia: exotic fabrics, costumes, vessels, and his collection of carnival masks and skulls.

The subject of death (and therefore images of death, such as skeletons) was often present in symbolist art and literature. Yet Ensor's representations seem less a serious reference to the ultimate mystery and transience of human life than a bitterly ironic commentary on existence. In an etching of 1888, *My Portrait*, for example, he imagined himself as a skeleton.

A year later, in *Skeletons Warming Themselves* (1889), he played with the ideas and stylistic forms that characterize his naturalistic work of the early 1880s. The theme and poverty of the setting is somewhat similar to his earlier work, *Tramps Trying to Get Warm* (1882). The thickly impasted paint, flickering luminosity, and intense coloring can also be found in his earlier paintings of domestic interiors. Here, however, these elements are manipulated in order to draw out the paradoxical humor of the scene, rendering the potentially macabre subject matter pathetic. In the painting, figures emblematic of death and the coldness of the grave engage in simple human acts in the desire to be warm. One wears a top hat at a jaunty angle, while another grins on entering the room. Moreover, all around are symbols of life and the animating power of art, including a lamp, a musical instrument, and a painter's palette.

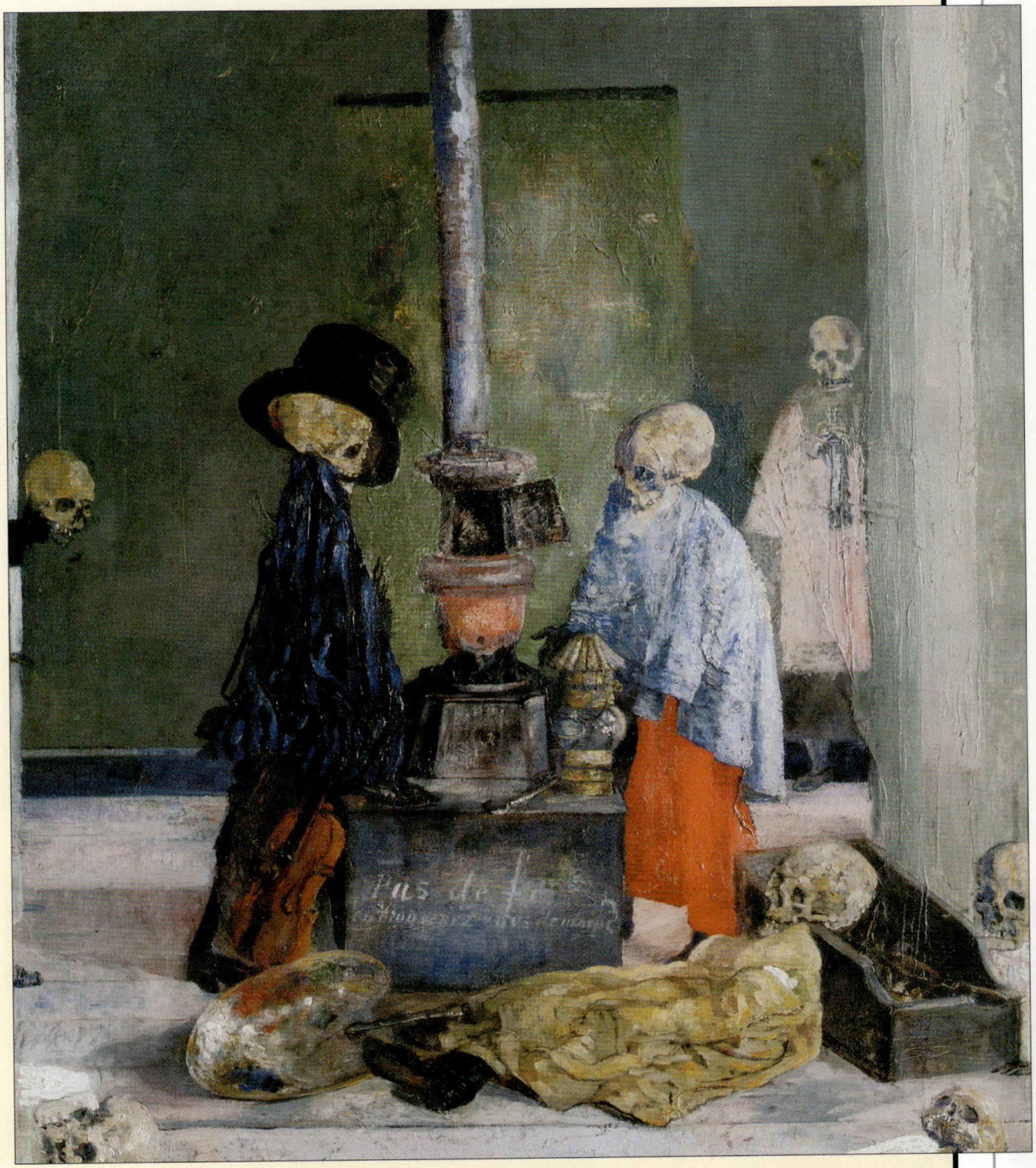

Skeletons Warming Themselves *1889.*
Oil on canvas. 29½ x 24 in (75 x 60 cm).
Kimbell Art Museum, Fort Worth, TX.

iconography to comment on the society in which he lived and to vent his feelings of anger and neglect. In other works of this period he employed the figure of Christ as a symbol for the artist who is reviled in an uncomprehending world. Engravings such as *The Descent of Christ into Hell* (1895), for example, depict Christ surrounded by demonic types. His self-portrait, *Demons Torturing Me*, of the same year, presents this process of identification more explicitly.

Ensor is today primarily remembered for his fantastical work, while his lyrical land- and seascapes of the same period are relatively ignored. His name is linked above all with paintings in which the symbolism of masks is exploited as a metaphor for the hypocrisy and absurdity of the human condition. The symbolist writer Jean Lorrain wrote of the capacity for vice, which "turns our faces into masks." Ensor himself suggested another interpretation: being hounded by his "pursuers," he sought protection behind the mask of a private, imaginative world of "violence, light, and brilliance."

By about 1900 the mainspring of creative anger was less apparent in his work, however, and he began to repeat himself. Ensor's sense of artistic solitude was compounded by his reclusive nature and the suspicion with which the bourgeoisie of Ostend viewed him. It is thus ironic that in later life he was honored by the town of his birth. Ironic, too, is the fact that his status rested mainly on the admiration of artists like the surrealists, whose art he did not understand, but who recognized affinities in the style and grotesque content of his paintings.

ERNST Max

MAX ERNST INTRODUCED DADAISM TO COLOGNE in 1919, but he moved to Paris and became best-known through his association with the French surrealists. He was extremely inventive, and his works combine a wide range of techniques and imagery to create surprising and sometimes disturbing effects.

Life and work

Max Ernst's own account of his birth was that he "emerged from the egg which his mother had laid in an eagle's nest and which the bird had incubated for seven years." This unusual statement gives us an idea of Ernst's playful imagination.

He came from a large family and studied philosophy until the outbreak of World War I in 1914, when he was drafted into military service for four years. He painted when he could, and made friends with some important artists, such as August Macke. In 1919 he became involved in dadaism, and began to explore means of working beyond painting. He pasted together photographs and scraps from books to make images. In Cologne he organized dada exhibitions where unusual "found" objects, such as fish tanks, clocks, and tools were exhibited alongside the collages, paintings, and drawings. The public was confused and the exhibitions were closed down.

In 1922 Ernst moved to Paris, where he became involved with the surrealist group. In 1925, almost by chance, Ernst discovered two techniques that opened up a whole new range of artistic possibilities. While on holiday, he took pencil rubbings from some floorboards and found that the texture of the wood grain produced unusual, fossil-like patterns. Then he found that by scraping away dark oil crayon, which had been laid over color, he could reveal enticing glimpses of the lighter color beneath. He created textured landscapes and strange, organic forms using these techniques, known as "frottage" and "grattage."

Life in France became very difficult for Ernst when World War II broke out. He was imprisoned in southern France, hunted by the Nazis, and eventually escaped to the United States in 1941. During the war he painted large, nightmarish landscapes that look as if they have been burned with acid.

In the United States he met the painter Dorothea Tanning, whom he married in 1946. Ernst finally returned to France and settled on a farm in 1955. Late in life he turned to sculpture, producing large half-human, half-animal figures.

Data file

Full name: Max Ernst

Nationality: German

Style: surrealism

Dates: born 1891 in Brühl, died 1976 in Paris, France

Key works:
- *Elephant of the Celebes* 1921
- *Pietà (Revolution by Night) 1923*
- *Natural History* (series) 1925
- *The Robing of the Bride* 1940
- *Europe after the Rain* 1940–42
- *Capricorn* (sculpture) 1948

Things to look for:
- hybrid creatures
- empty landscapes
- rubbing (frottage) and scraping (grattage) techniques
- collage and photomontage
- dream imagery
- forests and birds

Comparisons: Hans Arp, René Magritte, Giorgio de Chirico, Paul Klee

Glossary terms: collage, dadaism, frottage, grattage, photomontage, surrealism

Dreams and memories:

This striking painting contains both traditional and very unconventional elements. The painting's imagery is cryptic, and its strange title does not immediately help us "logically" to decipher the scene and the relationship between the figures we see. Not surprisingly, it was greatly admired by several important surrealists. Salvador Dalí called it "the point of departure for surrealist experiments" and the leader of the surrealists, André Breton, also regarded it as significant.

The origins of the images in this painting are personal and complex. The first clue is in its title. The "Pietà" is traditionally a Christian image of the dead Christ in the lap of his grieving mother, the Virgin Mary. But what we see here is a stiff, unnatural-looking young man, propped awkwardly on the lap of an impassive, dapper urban gentleman with moustache and bowler hat. This older figure is probably derived from a 1914 painting by Giorgio de Chirico called *The Child's Brain* (now in Stockholm), which was then in Breton's collection and known to Ernst.

However, the image takes on a new significance when we consider three details relating to the artist himself. First, the white-shirted figure has the delicate facial features of Ernst himself. Second, Ernst had badly fallen out with his father a few years previously, in 1920. Third, Ernst's father had once painted his own young son, Max, as the boy Jesus. Bearing these points in mind, we can see the painting as having to do with Ernst himself and his difficult relationship with his father. Perhaps it expresses the artist's wish to be reunited with his father. Perhaps it is concerned with memories and nostalgia, as Ernst reworks his father's earlier image of himself as a Christ-figure.

The young figure seems to be in a trancelike state. The fact that he is wearing socks and a white garment like a hospital-patient's gown perhaps casts him as a sufferer of mental illness. Interestingly, Ernst believed that insane people had special visionary powers. He himself had experienced hallucinations when he was ill with the measles as a

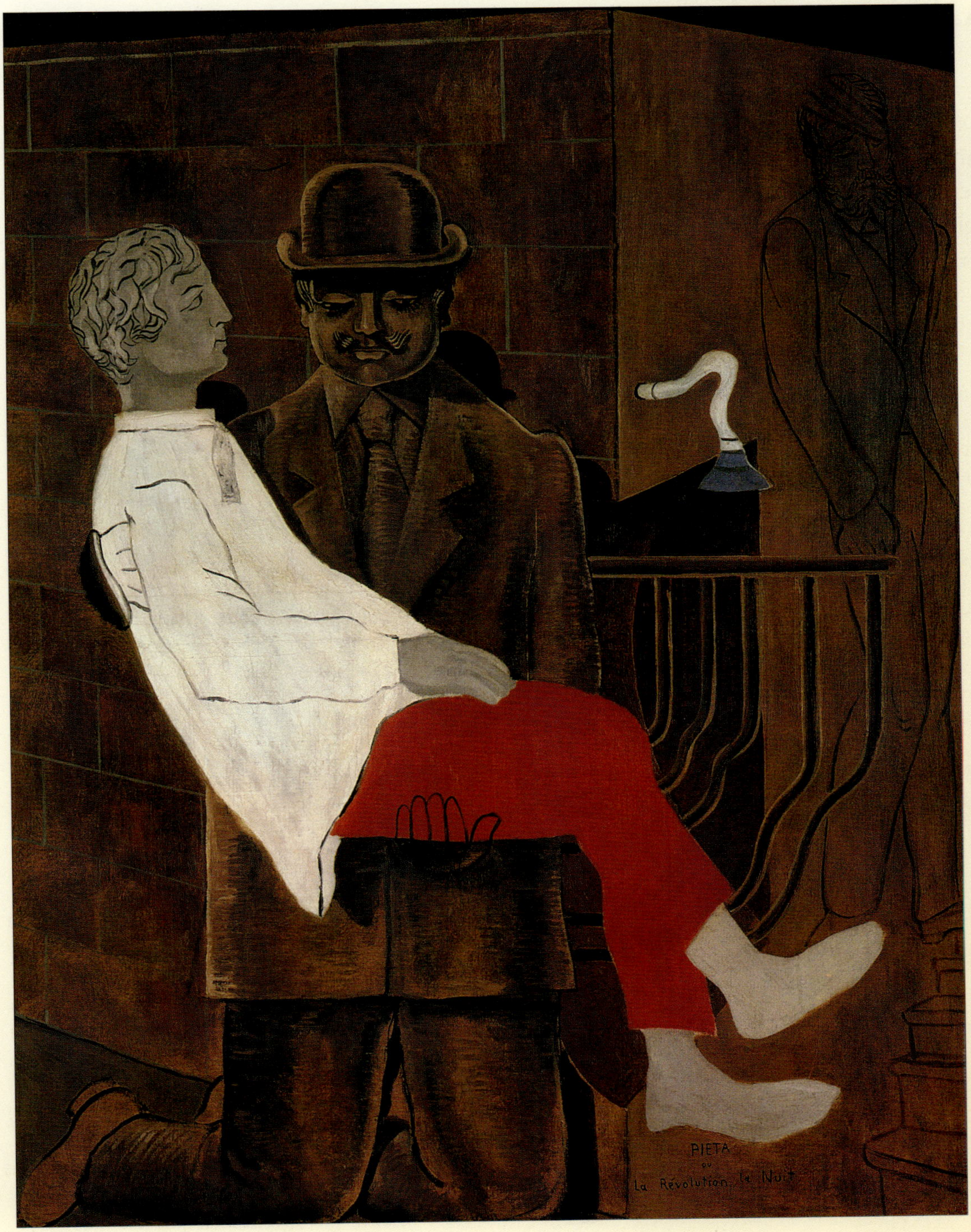

Pietà (Revolution by Night) *1923. Oil on canvas. 45½ x 35 in (116 x 89 cm). Tate Gallery, London.*

child, and later he strove to achieve a "visionlike" quality in his work through unusual combinations of images. Indeed here he has his eyes wide open, (unlike the "father") and looks directly at a third, enigmatic, wounded figure. This third figure appears only sketchily against the wall, looking more like a ghost, or a vision than a solid physical presence. In fact the group is often interpreted as representing the Trinity: the Father, the Son and the Holy Ghost.

No matter how we look at the painting it still seems to resist logical interpretation. The curious curving rails, illogical shadow, steps leading nowhere, and the blue and white funnel seem more like fragments of dream images or random thoughts than explicable objects. It is not that the painting is inept, or that Ernst is trying to confuse us, it is just an early example of surrealist techniques, which emphasized the unconscious rather than the conscious, and rejected "logic" in the hope of accessing the private depths of the human mind.

FRAGONARD Jean-Honoré

JEAN-HONORÉ FRAGONARD THRIVED AS AN ARTIST who catered to the tastes of the French upper classes during the period immediately before the French Revolution of 1789. His paintings convey the carefree lightness that characterized the rococo style, and reflect a social order that was about to be overthrown.

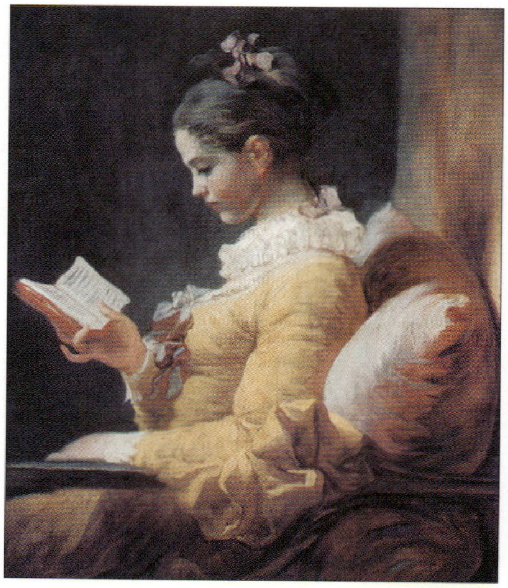

Young Girl Reading *c1776. Oil on canvas. 32 x 25½ in (81 x 65 cm). National Gallery of Art, Washington, D.C.*

Life and work

Fragonard was born in Grasse, in the south of France. From the age of six he lived in Paris, where he later studied art under various masters, but mainly with François Boucher, then the leading exponent of French rococo art. It was as a practitioner of this style that Fragonard was to excel, and it was largely because of Boucher's guidance that in 1752 he won the prestigious Prix de Rome. The prize gave him the opportunity of studying directly the great works of the Italian Renaissance and classical antiquity.

In Rome, Fragonard seems to have struggled with the patient and laborious copying that was required of students; it was thought that the basis of an artist's style should be emulation of the most admired examples of the art of the past. Fragonard preferred a rapid manner of execution, and he continued to be drawn to those earlier artists on which Boucher had formed his style, above all the bold and dynamic compositions of Peter Paul Rubens and Giambattista Tiepolo.

Back in Paris by 1761 and now in his late twenties, Fragonard was obliged to make his own way as an artist. He did not want to follow the traditional methods of intellectual art teaching, nor did he respond to the neoclassicists' purified interpretation of ancient Roman and Greek art, which was becoming increasingly important. Instead, he specialized in a style and subject matter that had been encouraged by the frivolous and sensual tastes of the aristocracy: the rococo.

The democratic ideas that were to lead to the French Revolution of 1789 were already circulating. The art critic had begun to be an important figure in the shaping of a broader public opinion. Leading writers of the Enlightenment, such as the French philosopher Denis Diderot, were very critical of the kind of art that Fragonard and Boucher represented. Instead of pictures of amorous gods and voluptuous goddesses, they called for an art of moral seriousness, an art calculated to both educate and reflect the values of the middle classes.

Fragonard produced a substantial body of work that might be said to conform to such requirements, particularly scenes of humble but harmonious domesticity, often in rustic situations. But the reputation he established in the later 1760s owed more to his semi-erotic paintings of women, either sumptuously clad in costumes of silk and lace, or in states of undress in a boudoir or bed. This was not what Diderot meant when he advocated that painting reflect "the real actions of life."

Because Fragonard had worked for the royal court of Louis XV (though the majority of his admirers were of the lesser nobility and upper middle classes), the French Revolution virtually ruined him financially by removing the privileged patronage on which he had depended. Paradoxically, Jacques-Louis David, the foremost artist of the return to classical ideals following the rococo, recognized Fragonard's merits and aided his appointment to a modestly paid official position to select works of art for the new museum in the Louvre Palace. Nevertheless, in his final years Fragonard was forced to rely on the charity of friends, and he died in relative poverty.

Data file

Full name: Jean-Honoré Fragonard

Nationality: French

Style: rococo

Dates: born 1732 in Grasse, died 1806 in Paris

Key works:

- *The Gardens of the Villa d'Este* c1761–65
- *Coresus Sacrificing Himself to Save Callirhoe* 1765
- *The Swing* c1766
- *The Fête at Saint-Cloud* 1773–76
- *Young Girl Reading* c1776
- *The Good Mother* 1777
- *The Fountain of Love* 1780

Things to look for:

- subjects in idyllic settings
- delicate textures and misty atmosphere
- subtle pastel color harmonies
- vigorous manner of execution

Comparisons: Peter Paul Rubens, Giambattista Tiepolo, Jean-Antoine Watteau, François Boucher, Jacques-Louis David

Glossary terms: Enlightenment, neoclassicism, rococo

"The Good Mother" and the goodness of nature

Much of Fragonard's work can now seem rather slight and superficial, appearing to avoid the harsh realities of existence facing the majority of French people in the 18th century. Paintings of nymphs bathing or robust peasants and shepherdesses were a convenient form of pleasurable escapism fostered by a ruling elite. On the other hand, it was not only the aristocracy who delighted in relaxed scenes of people enjoying themselves in idyllic surroundings.

Writers on Fragonard have often drawn a connection between his artistic temperament and his origins in the Mediterranean south. Furthermore, two extended trips to Italy furnished him with the basis for a type of landscape that owes much to the numerous sketches of picturesque gardens and dilapidated villas he had painted around Rome.

Fragonard's painting *The Good Mother* (1777) combines such a setting with another theme which, apart from his reputation for sensual subjects, had engaged him from the beginning of his career: scenes of family life. The mother might be attractive in a conventional fashion, but she is also watchful and concerned for the care of her children. She represents an ideal of maternity in an idealized natural setting. The abundance of nature spreads around her in the picture. It is significant that Fragonard selected this painting to dedicate to his country in the momentous year of 1789, the year of the French Revolution.

The high regard in which Fragonard was held diminished rapidly during the revolutionary period, and his virtues were not really appreciated again until the middle of the 19th century. The painter and lithographer Honoré Daumier admired him, as did some impressionist artists—Pierre Auguste Renoir, for example, acknowledged a debt to Fragonard—and it is not difficult to see why. Fragonard painted gentle scenes of leisure, and often worked directly onto the canvas without preparatory drawings, and by means of subtly imprecise, broken brushstrokes. His style depended on a consummate mastery of the soft airiness of cloudlike foliage, and of delicately textured drapery and flesh.

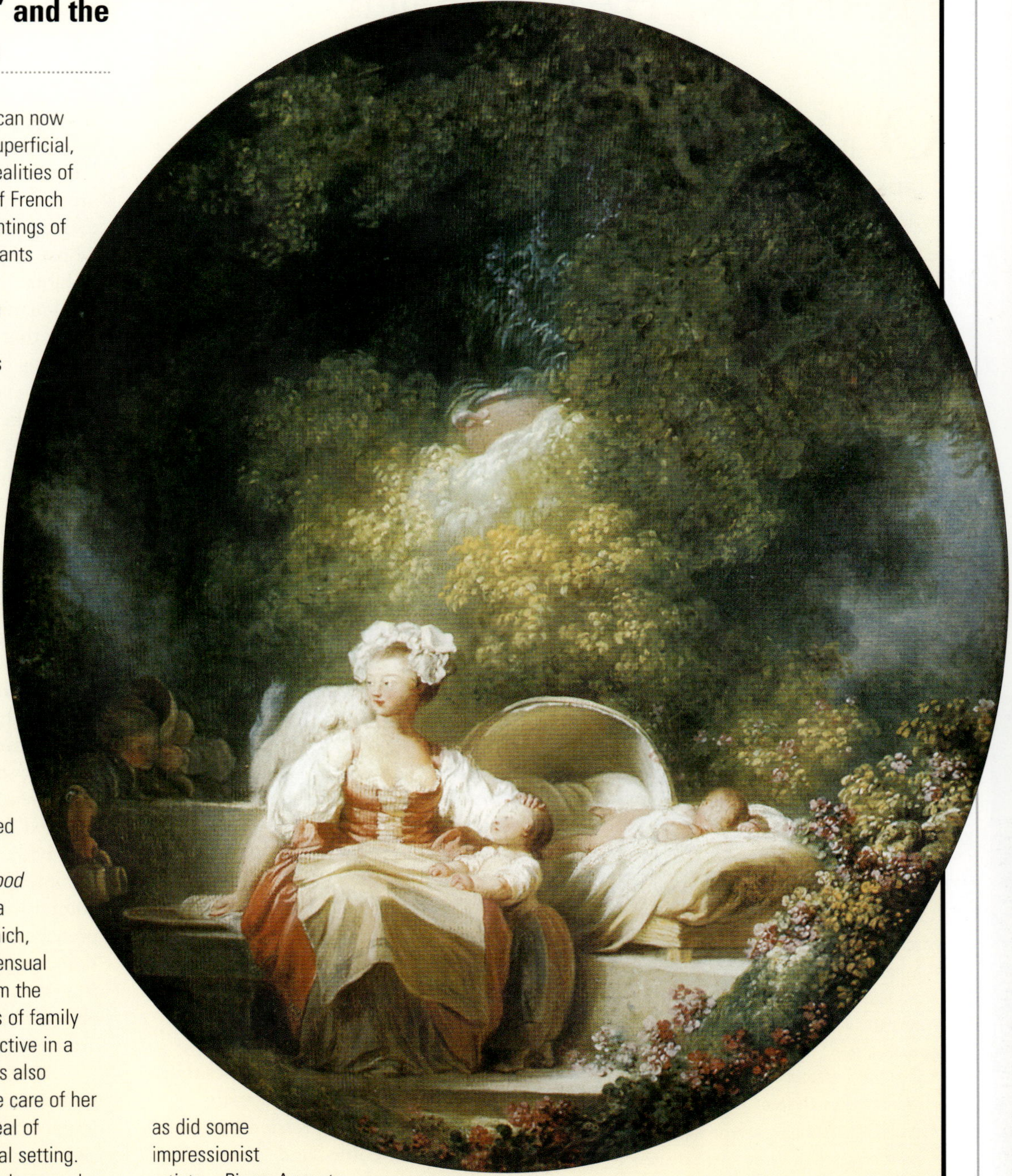

The Good Mother *1777. Oil on canvas. 25 x 20½ in (63 x 52 cm). Museum of Fine Art, Boston, MA.*

FRANKENTHALER Helen

ONE OF THE FIRST OF HER GENERATION to turn from cubist-influenced picture-making to more free constructions, Helen Frankenthaler evolved an individual style of abstraction. Using color washes and pigment stains on unprimed canvas, Frankenthaler explored forms and colors to create a new kind of pictorial space.

Life and work

Helen Frankenthaler was born in 1928 in New York City. In 1945 she graduated from Dalton School, where she had been taught by the Mexican painter and muralist Rufino Tamayo. In the following year Frankenthaler entered Bennington College, where her art training began in earnest under the tuition of Paul Freeley, who encouraged his students to analyze the works of modern artists like Paul Cézanne and Henri Matisse. From Cézanne Frankenthaler learned about the illusion of depth in a painting, and from Matisse how large areas of transparent colors could give the sensation of light and atmosphere. Through Freeley's classes Frankenthaler also became acquainted with the first wave of American modernists—Arthur Dove, Marsden Hartley, and John Marin—as well as with the European pioneers of cubism.

In 1948 Frankenthaler visited Europe, where she saw at first hand the paintings of many of the Old Masters. After returning to New York she completed her final year at Bennington and sold her first painting: a cubist still life in the style of Georges Braque.

Encouraged by the art critic Clement Greenberg, Frankenthaler began spending her summers at Provincetown, a resort town at the tip of Cape Cod, in Massachusetts, where she studied with the painter and former Bauhaus tutor, Hans Hofmann.

By this stage Frankenthaler was painting expressionist landscapes that revealed the influence of Wassily Kandinsky, whose expressive lines, use of transparent colors, and "floating" motifs on open backgrounds are repeated in her own works. Like Kandinsky, Frankenthaler was also interested in the idea of improvising forms out of feelings and memories. Indeed, some of her works, such as *Mother Goose Melody* (1959), refer to her childhood memories.

In addition to landscapes, and under the guidance of Hofmann, Frankenthaler began painting abstractions. Unlike Hofmann, however, Frankenthaler was still primarily interested in drawing, and color was not yet central to her art. At around the same time she became aware of the works of Arshile Gorky, whose highly individual style made use of biomorphic forms painted in a broad, fluid manner. Biomorphic forms are those that look like or suggest the forms of living organisms.

The year 1951 was a pivotal one for Frankenthaler for, in addition to her first solo exhibition of abstractions and landscapes, she was introduced to the paintings of Jackson Pollock. Frankenthaler visited Pollock in his studio and learned from him the technique of dripping paint onto a canvas laid on the floor. Yet she was to develop Pollock's approach further: instead of allowing the pigment to rest on the surface, as Pollock had done, Frankenthaler thinned down her paints so that they soaked through the canvas, creating stained areas. These "improvised" areas of "spilled" and "poured" color were to be the basis for Frankenthaler's paintings as she became less reliant on preliminary compositional sketches. She now preferred to "draw" by manipulating the liquid pigments, rubbing and blotting the pools of color, in order to make her abstractions gestural (emphasizing the artist's movements and brushstrokes).

Although Pollock's influence on Frankenthaler was enormous, the impact that she herself made on 20th-century art was crucial. Such major artists as Kenneth Noland and Morris Louis (key figures in the development of color-field painting) are indebted to her for her development of the techniques of color-staining.

From 1958 to 1971 Frankenthaler was married to the painter Robert Motherwell. In addition to painting and teaching she has continued to exhibit, nationally and internationally, to great acclaim. She lives and works in New York and Provincetown.

Data file

Full name: Helen Frankenthaler

Nationality: American

Style: abstract

Dates: born 1928 in New York, NY

Key works:
- *Mountains and Sea* 1952
- *Mountain Storm* 1955
- *Jacob's Ladder* 1957
- *Basque Beach* 1958
- *Buzzards Bay* 1959
- *Arden* 1961
- *Flood* 1967

Things to look for:
- large-scale, abstract works
- color-staining technique
- intense colors, with variation in values
- use of unprimed canvas with visible weave
- references to landscapes and childhood memories and experiences in forms and titles

Comparisons: Jackson Pollock, Arshile Gorky, Robert Motherwell, Arthur Dove, John Marin, Wassily Kandinsky, Morris Louis, Kenneth Noland, Hans Hofmann, Marsden Hartley

Glossary terms: abstract art, action painting, Bauhaus, color-field painting, cubism, expressionism, gestural, modernism, mural, New York school, Old Masters

Evolving techniques

The first 20th-century group of American artists to achieve international acclaim was the New York school of abstract expressionists, which flourished during the postwar years and tried to find its own form of expression through the physical act of painting. Painted on very large canvases, and usually without preliminary sketches, the final format of its works was determined by the act of painting itself. This approach allowed artists to explore and develop their work by incorporating accidental or "chance" events into it.

There were two distinct tendencies within the New York school. One group, known as action painters (including Jackson Pollock), emphasized spontaneous expression with vigorous brushstrokes. The members of the other group, who were known as color-field painters, concentrated on large areas of flat color, using less aggressive brushstrokes.

Frankenthaler was among the second generation of abstract expressionists to emerge during the mid-1950s. She learned from Pollock to "drip" pigment onto a canvas laid on the floor. In her work *Mountains and Sea* (1952) she poured thinned pigment onto untreated canvas, creating the art of "stain-gesture," in which the diluted colors soak into the fabric. Size was to become another important consideration in Frankenthaler's work. Although large, *Buzzards Bay* (1959), for example, is a relatively small when compared to *Flood* (1967), which measures a vast 124 x 140 in (315 x 356 cm). Because her works were so large she was often unable to see the entire image as she was painting. The viewer is likewise engulfed by the depth and scale of the color areas.

Few of Frankenthaler's colors are pure hues, and she often mixes them from leftover paint. In 1960 she modified her technique in order to produce denser, more brilliant areas of color by priming her canvases to prevent the color from soaking into them. Then, in 1962, she began using synthetic polymers (water-based, acrylic paints). These dried faster than oils and also eliminated the turpentine "halo" at the edge of the color stains that can be seen in her earlier works. The new paints introduced a new palette into her work, too, ranging from dark colors that are close in value, to light-saturated, "hot" colors.

Frankenthaler also uses cropping. She does not "compose" a painting in advance, but imposes a compositional unity on the piece after she has finished painting by cropping forms and areas from canvases that, in her eyes, "don't work." As a result, the framing edge of the work (which marks the boundary between the space within a painting and the space occupied by the spectator) is neutralized, and the images in her paintings seem to flow beyond the confines of the canvas.

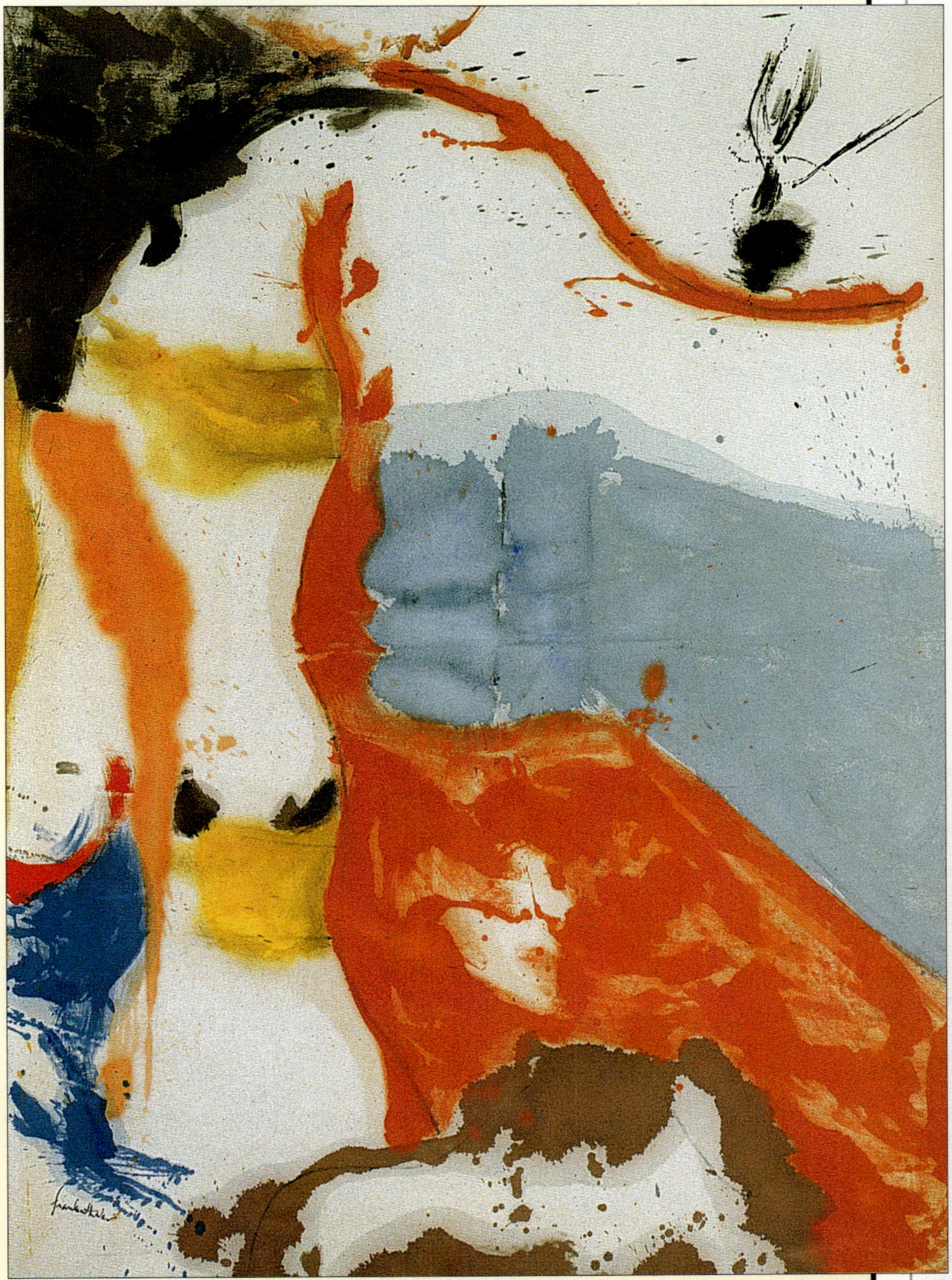

Buzzards Bay *1959. Oil stained into canvas. 60 x 45 in (152.5 x 114.5 cm). Seattle Art Museum, Seattle, WA.*

FREUD Lucian

LUCIAN FREUD IS A LEADING 20TH-CENTURY British figure painter whose portraits and nudes, often pictured in sparse, dingy interiors, reject superficial ideas of beauty. Although they can seem harsh in their realism, they have a humanity and complexity that engages the viewer.

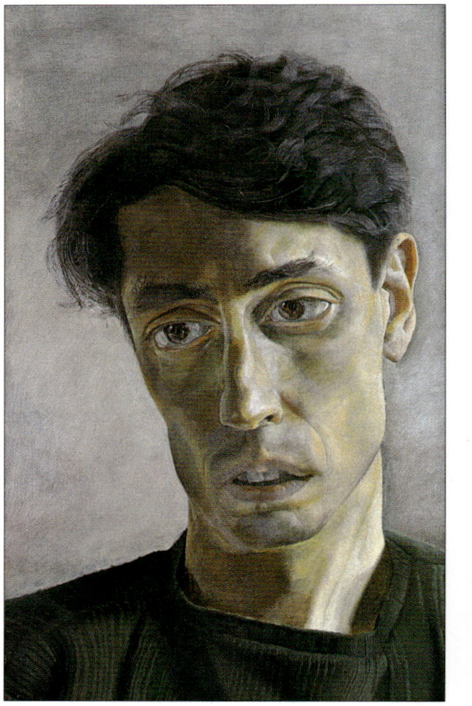

John Minton *1952. Oil on canvas. 15¾ x 10 in (40 x 25.5 cm). Royal College of Art, London.*

Life and work

Lucian Freud was born in Germany in 1922. His father was an architect, and his grandfather was Sigmund Freud, the founder of modern psychoanalysis. In 1931 his family moved to England, and in 1939 he acquired British nationality.

Between the ages of 16 and 18, Freud studied at the East Anglian School of Painting and Drawing under Cedric Morris, an English artist who was in touch with developments in the European art world. Freud's earliest paintings show influences from the German *Neue Sachlichkeit* ("New Objectivity") movement of the 1920s and 1930s, typified by George Grosz's images of human eccentricities and deformities, and surrealist imagery, inspired by dreams or the nonrational.

The Painter's Room, created in 1943 when Freud was 20, shows a boxlike interior containing a tatty sofa, a crumpled red cloth, a spiky yucca plant, and an upturned top-hat. The picture is dominated, though, by the head of a red-striped zebra protruding into the room. These motifs of sofa, plant, and cloth all reappear in later works throughout Freud's career.

After World War II, during which he served briefly in the British merchant navy, Freud settled in Paddington, a rundown district of central London, where he was to live and work for the next three decades.

From the 1950s onward Freud produced many portraits. Most of these were of his friends or relatives, and all are portrayed with great individuality. Some of his best-known portraits are of fellow artists, including *Francis Bacon* (1952, stolen from an exhibition in 1988), *John Minton* (1952), and *Frank Auerbach* (1975–76). He has also produced series of portraits, such as those of his second wife, Caroline (early 1950s), or his elderly mother (1970s–1980s), which explore different poses and moods of the same person.

Many of the recurring themes in his work can be seen in *Large Interior W11 (After Watteau)*, painted in 1981–83. The reference in the title is to the 18th-century French artist, Antoine Watteau, who painted delicate scenes from the leisured lives of the aristocracy that subtly suggest the instability of that life. Freud's interior, by contrast, strikes the familiar note of urban decay, with its damp walls and bare floorboards. No one in the room seems happy, and yet all five—three young women, a young man, and a girl—are strongly present.

The sense of instability is there, however. As so often in his paintings, his sitters seem isolated from each other and about to go off in different directions. He often shows people reclining on a battered old sofa, recalling the one in *The Painter's Room*, or on clinical white sheets.

Another recurring subject is the nude. In Freud's work, these are unflatteringly illuminated by electric light. Some of his most original nude paintings date from the 1980s and 1990s. They include a series featuring the performance artist Leigh Bowery. *Leigh Bowery (Seated)* (1990) and *Nude with Leg Up* (1992) show Freud creating new variations on an old theme.

Data file

Full name: Lucian Freud

Nationality: German, British citizen from 1939

Style: modern realism

Dates: born 1922 in Berlin

Key works:
- *The Painter's Room* 1943
- *Interior at Paddington* 1951
- *Girl with White Dog* 1951–52
- *Man's Head (Self-portrait III)* 1963
- *The Painter's Mother Resting I* 1976
- *Large Interior, W11 (After Watteau)* 1981–83
- *Nude with Leg Up* 1992

Things to look for:
- realism in portraying the human figure
- pictures communicate sense of restlessness or unease
- stark, dilapidated interiors
- muted colors with subtle variations in tone
- series of portraits of same sitter

Comparisons: George Grosz, Francis Bacon, Frank Auerbach

Glossary terms: abstract art, earth colors, *Neue Sachlichkeit*, surrealism

Real lives

Freud was never drawn to abstract art, which has played such an important part in 20th-century art. Instead, like fellow artists Francis Bacon and Frank Auerbach, he concentrated on exploring new possibilities in figure painting, contributing to a strong revival of this art form in Britain after World War II.

Even in work produced during his teens, Lucian Freud's interest in portraiture and the human figure can be clearly seen. *Man with a Feather (Self-portrait)* of 1943 shows the artist standing in a slightly eerie nighttime setting, reminiscent of surrealist art. Freud's expression, with elongated, thoughtful, rather anxious eyes, is echoed in his portraits of other sitters during the 1940s and 1950s, such as that of the painter John Minton (1952). So too is his attention to the detail and the texture of clothing.

In *Girl with White Dog* (1951–52), a woman in a yellow dressing gown sits on a mattress next to a small dog that is resting its head on her legs. The contrasting textures of flesh and fur, upholstery and clothing are closely explored, including their stains and discolorations. This gives the picture a warmth of real life at the same time as the artist seems to be rather coolly observing every minute detail.

Typical of Freud's work of the late 1940s and early 1950s, *Interior at Paddington*, for which Freud won a prize at the 1951 Festival of Britain exhibition, has a high level of detail and finish. It shows a young man with large staring eyes and nicotine-stained fingers. As always with Freud's portraits, there is a strong sense of the subject's physical presence, but the painting also suggests the complexity of his thoughts and feelings. The young man stands in a rumpled coat beside a large, rather shaggy, potted yucca that dominates the foreground. Outside the window, there is a glimpse of a drab street-scene. The picture's mood of restlessness and suppressed anxiety combines with a feeling that the artist and his subject are at home in these surroundings. This feeling is characteristic of much of Freud's art.

From the later 1950s onwards, Freud moved away from the sharp detailing and polish of his earlier work, using broader brushes to make strong, swirling marks, as in several self-portraits painted in 1963. Freud himself said that he wanted "paint to work as flesh.... As far as I am concerned, the paint *is* the person. I want it to work for me just as flesh does." He continued to use a limited range of colors based around grays, reds, and earth colors, but his new technique involved stronger contrasts and highlights.

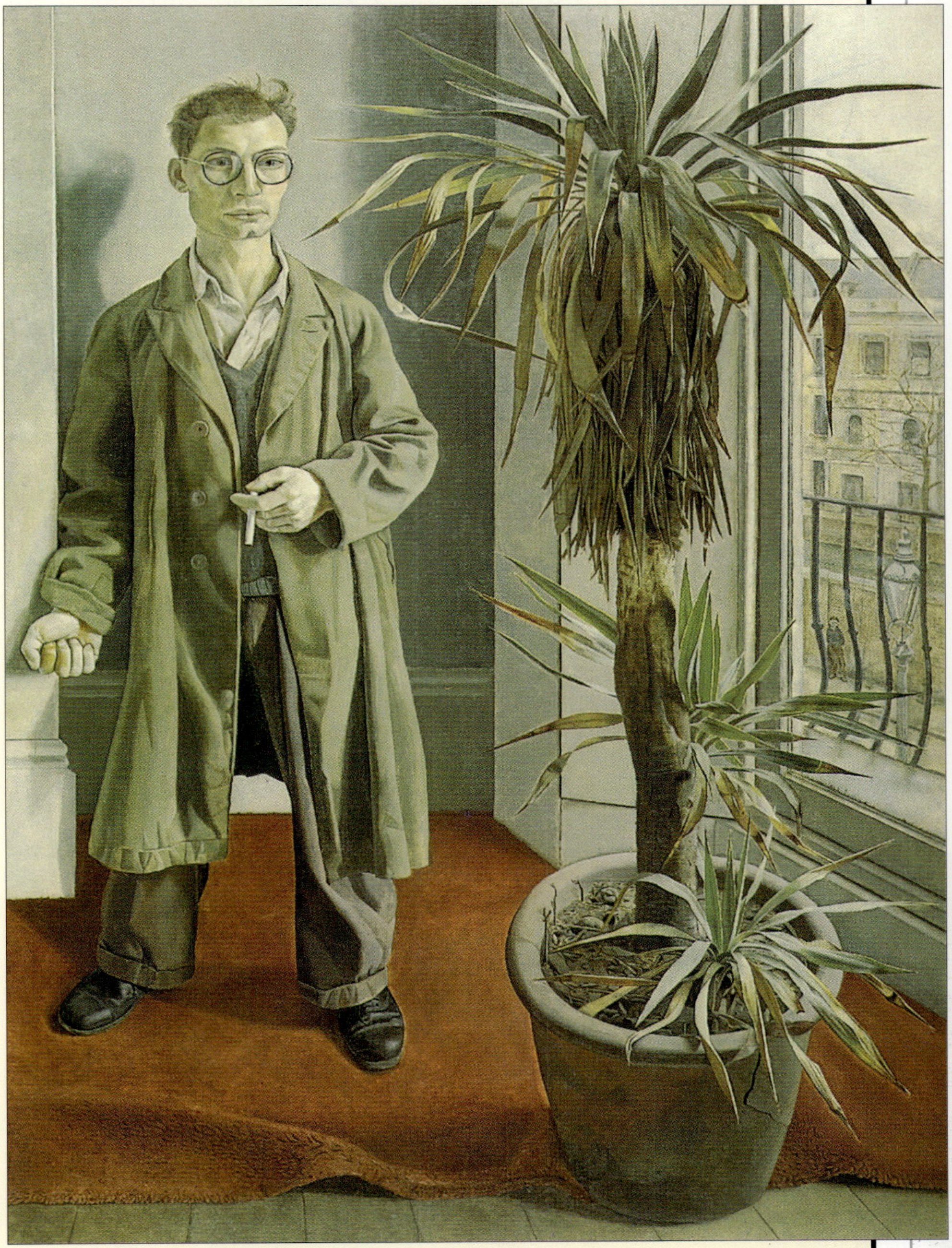

Interior at Paddington *1951. Oil on canvas. 60 x 45 in (152.5 x 114 cm). Walker Art Gallery, Liverpool.*

FRIEDRICH Caspar David

Caspar David Friedrich was a leading figure of the early 19th-century German Romantic movement. His finely detailed, atmospheric landscape paintings emphasized the grandeur and spirituality of nature. Friedrich's works were neglected after his death, but he is now considered a landscape painter of great imagination, whose choice of subject matter and approach was highly innovative.

Life and work

Friedrich was born into a prosperous Lutheran family in the Baltic port of Greifswald. After showing an early interest in art, he began to study drawing at the local university. In 1794 he moved to Copenhagen, the Danish capital, to continue his studies, during which he focused exclusively on drawing. Indeed, he did not begin to paint in oils until he was well into his thirties. This emphasis on draftsmanship influenced Friedrich's work throughout his career.

Data file

Full name: Caspar David Friedrich

Nationality: German

Style: Romanticism

Dates: born 1774 in Greifswald, died 1840 in Dresden

Key works:
- *The Cross in the Mountains* 1807–08
- *Abbey Among Oak Trees* 1809
- *Winter Landscape* 1811
- *Chalk Cliffs at Rügen* 1818
- *Arctic Shipwreck* c1821–23
- *Moonrise Over the Sea* 1822
- *The Stages of Life* c1835

Things to look for:
- finely detailed landscape scenes
- precise drawing
- symbolic details
- soft, muted light
- inclusion of Gothic architecture ruins

Comparisons: Philipp Otto Runge, Johan Christian Clausen Dahl

Glossary terms: Gothic, Romanticism, symbolism

While a student, Friedrich began to take long walks in the countryside and developed a love of nature. It was during these outings that he observed many of the historical sites and ruins that would later appear in his landscape paintings.

After completing his studies, Friedrich moved to Dresden, where he remained for the rest of his life. His early landscape drawings and etchings were created directly from nature. Increasingly, however, Friedrich began to experiment by introducing figures, or emphasizing different times of the day or seasons of the year in his work. He was influenced in this approach by the German Romantic painter Philipp Otto Runge, and in particular by Runge's series of works known as the *Times of Day* cycle (from 1802).

Friedrich's first major oil painting, *The Cross in the Mountains* (1807–08), was based on landscape studies that he had made in northern Bohemia. The work combines attention to realistic detail with a deep spirituality. For Friedrich, the wonders of nature provided evidence of God's glory, and a close study and contemplation of nature could therefore be regarded as a form of spiritual contemplation. Significantly, in view of its spiritual dimension, *The Cross in the Mountains* was used as a devotional altarpiece by its purchaser.

In order to further the religious dimension in his landscapes, Friedrich often included figures marveling at the wonders of nature. This can be seen, for example, in *Chalk Cliffs at Rügen* (1818) and *Moonrise Over the Sea* (1822). In other works he introduced explicitly religious symbols, such as the ruined Gothic church in *Abbey Among Oak Trees* (1809), or the cross in *Winter Landscape* (1811). Even his use of light (a bright, almost heavenly glow emanating from the background) suggests a higher spiritual realm. He first evoked the images he wanted to paint in his mind: "Close your bodily eye, so that you may see your picture first with your spiritual eye," he wrote.

The spirituality of the landscape

The painting *Winter Landscape* (1811), one of Friedrich's best-known works, is simultaneously a representation of the natural landscape and a symbolic allusion to spirituality. At the center of the image a small, barely discernible figure sits leaning against a rock. A cross stands erect before him amid a clump of trees. The figure's hands are clasped in prayer, while two crutches lie nearby. In the background, the façade of a Gothic church emerges from the midst of the snowy landscape like a mystical vision. Notably, the outline of the church precisely echoes the shape of the trees in the foreground. Friedrich thus implies that nature carries as great a religious significance as the building that has been dedicated to God's glory.

But what is the figure doing in this desolate spot in the depths of winter? The clue lies in the crutches that are situated some distance from the praying figure. A miracle must have occurred, because the figure has evidently discarded these crutches and has approached the cross unaided. In gratitude for this transformation in his life he is offering prayers to both the cross and the landscape. Friedrich has also implied a sense of transformation in the landscape itself. In the foreground, blades of grass peek through the frozen, snow-covered ground, while the pale light of dawn rises over the horizon. Winter appears to be turning to spring and night to day.

Friedrich's inclusion of a person with impaired mobility within this work can also

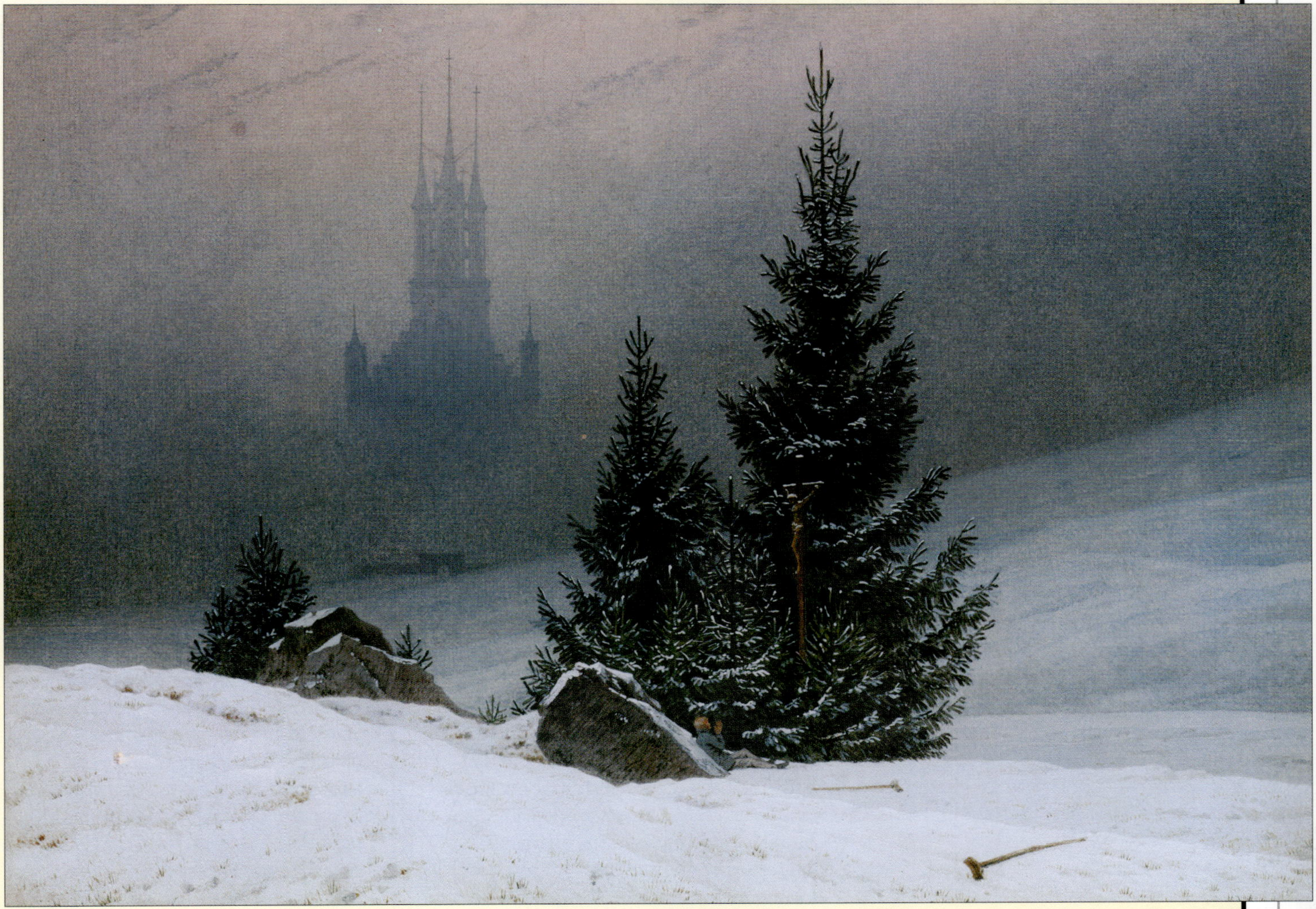

be read as a reflection of the political climate at the time when the work was produced. In 1811 Europe was in the middle of the Napoleonic Wars and Friedrich's native Germany had already been invaded and devastated by the French armies. The figure can therefore be interpreted as symbolizing the damage that had been inflicted upon the German nation and its people. At the same time, however, the healing and salvation of the isolated figure conveys a sense of hope for the future and a message of optimism that a defeated nation can be resurrected from the destruction of war.

Winter Landscape *1811. Oil on canvas. 12 3/4 x 17 3/4 in (32.5 x 45 cm). National Gallery, London.*

In 1818 the Norwegian landscape painter Johan Christian Clausen Dahl arrived in Dresden. The two artists lived, worked, and exhibited together for a period. Influenced by Dahl, Friedrich's colors became much brighter at this stage in his career. By the mid-1820s, however, his work had taken on a new intensity and his colors had become more muted and restrained.

Toward the end of his life Friedrich's art was increasingly rejected by his contemporaries. Friedrich, however, continued to use landscapes as a means with which to convey symbolic messages. In *The Stages of Life* (c1835), for example, he included three generations of figures (children, young adults, and an older man) to suggest both the passage of time and the transience of life. The ships in the distance, receding toward the horizon, reiterate this theme by alluding to the journey of life.

In 1835 Friedrich suffered a stroke and was unable to paint for the last few years of his life. By the time of his death, his highly individual and personal painting style was unpopular, and his works disappeared into relative obscurity. However, the rise of symbolism in the late 19th century, and a revived interest in his works during the early 20th century, helped to restore his reputation as a leading light of the German Romantic movement.

GAINSBOROUGH Thomas

THOMAS GAINSBOROUGH WAS ONE OF THE MOST SOUGHT-AFTER painters of portraits and landscapes in England in the 18th century. His keen eye and occasional irreverence gave his works a freshness often lacking in paintings of the time. He is still admired for his sensitive and lively landscapes, which inspired later artists.

Life and work

Thomas Gainsborough was born in Sudbury, a small town in Suffolk, England. He moved away for several periods, but remained emotionally attached to his native county.

In 18th-century England, portrait and landscape painting were considered of minor importance. The most esteemed form of painting was of historical or religious scenes featuring heroic events and figures. The wealthiest art collectors favored the Old Masters or the work of fashionable French painters. Lower down the hierarchy came portraiture, which was the main means by which painters could make a good income. Landscape paintings or scenes of rural life were generally considered decorative, rather than great art.

Gainsborough, like many other artists, had to devote much of his time to portrait painting in order to earn a living. He clearly resented having to pander to the vanities of the rich and famous, saying that he would rather "walk off to some sweet village where I can paint landscapes and enjoy the fag end of life in quietness and ease."

While still very young, Gainsborough studied art in London. In 1746 he married Margaret Burr. They had two daughters. In 1752 he set up as a portrait painter in Ipswich, Suffolk, and began to find patrons among the merchants of the town and local gentlemen farmers. In 1759 he moved to Bath, a town with a more fashionable society. This move was probably intended to bring him more sitters. Indeed, he was soon in great demand and produced numerous elegant full-length portraits of his rich, sophisticated patrons and their families, posed in imaginary landscapes.

Gainsborough preferred to paint people he knew well. However, he became exasperated with some sitters, especially his actor friends, who were often anxious to be depicted in a flattering way. He was not very tolerant of his sitters' vanity and, when irritated by it, he would sometimes refuse to continue with the painting.

In 1768 the Royal Academy was founded in London and Gainsborough was invited to be a founder member. The president of the Academy was Joshua Reynolds, Gainsborough's greatest rival. They respected one another's work but also competed for the favor of patrons. The British royal family did sometimes seem to prefer Gainsborough. When Gainsborough moved to London in 1774, it was probably with the intention of matching Reynolds' high standing in the capital.

In London Gainsborough was successful and had a prestigious clientele. He seems to have been

Data file

Full name: Thomas Gainsborough
Nationality: English
Style: 18th-century English school
Dates: born 1727 in Sudbury, died 1788 in London
Key works:
- *Cornard Wood* 1748
- *Mr. and Mrs. Andrews* c1750
- *The Artist's Daughters Chasing a Butterfly* 1756
- *Countess Howe* 1763–64
- *The Blue Boy* 1770
- *The Watering Place* 1777

Things to look for:
- portraits in country park settings
- delicate highlights on cloth and foliage
- carefully composed landscape
- influence of Dutch landscape painters

Comparisons: William Hogarth, Joshua Reynolds, Antoine Watteau, Peter Paul Rubens, Anthony Van Dyck, John Constable
Glossary terms: Grand Tour, Old Masters, Romanticism

Painter to the rich

Gainsborough painted his portrait of *Mr. and Mrs. Andrews* (c1750) when he was in his early twenties. The work conforms to a fashion for "conversation pieces," which were popular in England at the time. Such paintings often had more than one figure occupying a relatively small proportion of a landscape setting. In this picture, the couple, Robert and Frances Andrews, are young, newly married, and rich. They pose elegantly on their estate.

Because he needed to establish himself at the beginning of his career as a portraitist, the commission from these wealthy patrons would have been very important for Gainsborough. The portrait is not only very flattering to his sitters, but it also demonstrates his skill as a painter. This is seen in the sensitively painted landscape, the rolling clouds, and the finesse with which the artist represents the rich folds of Mrs. Andrews' skirt.

The painting is also interesting for what it tells us about the wealthy classes in the mid-18th century. It is essentially a display of their wealth, status, and property. By asking a painter to depict them in such a landscape, Mr. and Mrs. Andrews were presenting themselves as nature-loving, cultivated, and sensitive people. They displayed the extent of their wealth by the rich and productive land around them, as well as through the oil painting itself, which was an expensive luxury item.

The abundant fertility of the land suggests that the couple may be equally fruitful in the future, and bear healthy children. The neat rows of harvested corn indicate that the latest agricultural

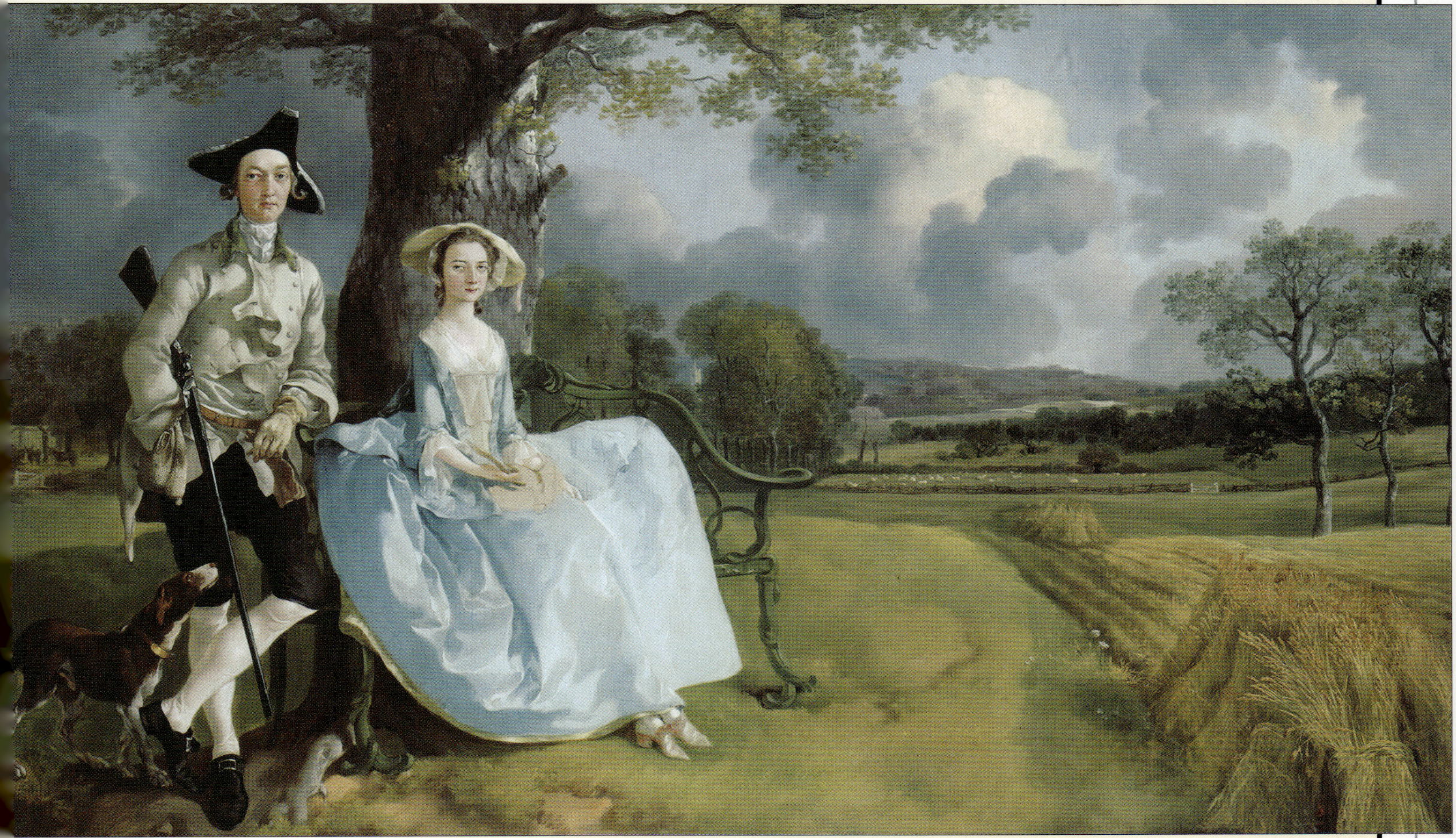

methods have been used to produce a good crop efficiently. In this way, the painting shows that the couple manage their land well and prosper from it. In turn, their wealth ensures that they have the time to enjoy the countryside, and that Mr. Andrews can amuse himself with hunting sports.

The painting was never finished—there is an unpainted patch of canvas on Mrs. Andrews' lap. It is thought that Gainsborough may have intended her to be holding a pheasant, freshly shot by her husband and retrieved by the dog at his side.

Mr. and Mrs. Andrews is not only a masterpiece of its kind, but also very subtly shows something of Gainsborough's humor. The artist learned a great deal from William Hogarth, who had dominated the English art scene in Gainsborough's youth, and who poked fun at his subjects. The prissily crossed and impossibly tiny feet of Mrs. Andrews, the pinched expressions on the faces of the couple, and the ostentatiously ornate bench from which she seems about to slide are perhaps gentle digs at the pretentious aspirations of the provincial rich.

Of his gentleman sitters, Gainsborough once said: "They have but one part worth looking at, and that is their Purse."

Mr. and Mrs. Andrews *c1750. Oil on canvas. 27¼ x 47 in (70 x 119 cm). National Gallery, London.*

remarkably unpretentious, down-to-earth, and sometimes even a little chaotic, however. In this sense, he was not at all like the more serious-minded Reynolds, with whom he is often compared. Gainsborough was known for his lively wit, entertaining company, and his disdain for literary men. He enjoyed drinking with his friends. Apart from painting, music was Gainsborough's great passion. He spent many hours listening to his musician friends as well as trying to play various musical instruments himself (with little success). He did not like reading books, but was a prolific and witty letter writer. His letters show that he cared deeply about his friends and family. He never left England. Unlike many artists of the time, he was not interested in the Grand Tour, or in traveling to Italy to see the works of the great Italian masters. Instead, he studied the beautiful but unassuming landscapes of Dutch 17th-century painters, which he saw in London.

Gainsborough died in 1788, having developed what was probably a cancer on his neck. He was buried at Kew, near London. Before his death he made peace with Reynolds and said that both he and Reynolds would go to heaven in the company of the 17th-century Dutch painter Anthony Van Dyck. Reynolds later paid moving tribute to Gainsborough's greatness as an artist.

GAUGUIN Paul

PAUL GAUGUIN LIVED A VERY ADVENTUROUS LIFE. He was a single-minded and restless man who traveled widely and died poor and lonely on a remote Pacific island. Gauguin's highly original paintings had a powerful influence on modern art, especially in their bold, expressive use of color and form.

Life and work

Gauguin was born in Paris. His father was a French liberal journalist; his mother was the daughter of a Spanish-Peruvian feminist and a French sculptor. Gauguin's family moved to Peru in 1851, but his father died on the journey. Gauguin and his sister returned alone to France in 1855, where they were raised by their mother's family. Gauguin hated his new home. Recalling the color and warmth of Peru, he longed for adventure, and at the age of 17 he went to sea, serving as a merchant seaman and then in the French navy. Returning from the sea in 1871, he took a job as a stockbroker in Paris and married a Danish woman, Mette Sophie Gad, with whom he had five children. Gauguin and his family enjoyed a prosperous, settled life.

After meeting the painter Camille Pissarro and seeing the first impressionist exhibition in 1874–75, Gauguin took up painting in his leisure time. His enthusiasm and dedication grew, and within five years he was showing his own pictures alongside those of the impressionists. The Paris stockmarket crash of 1883 convinced Gauguin to devote all of his time to art. However, his lack of formal training and contacts in the art world meant that his paintings did not sell well and his family quickly ran out of money. They lived briefly with Mette's family in Copenhagen, but her family's disapproval of Gauguin's new career led the artist to return to Paris. Over the next 18 years, Gauguin moved restlessly from one place to another, looking for the ideal location to paint. His estranged family remained in Denmark.

In 1886 Gauguin went to live in the village of Pont-Aven in Brittany, in northwest France. He was fascinated by the Breton peasants, certain that their closeness to nature gave them a deeper understanding of life. He painted some major works here, including *Jacob Wrestling the Angel* (1888). Gauguin returned to Pont-Aven many times over the next few years, and a group of young artists began to admire his paintings and his ideas on art. This group later became known as the Nabis.

Gauguin continued to travel in search of new inspiration. His journeys

Data file

Full name: Eugène Henri Paul Gauguin

Nationality: French

Style: postimpressionism

Dates: born 1848 in Paris, died 1903 in Atuona Hiva-Oa (Marquesas Islands)

Key works:

Jacob Wrestling the Angel 1888

Symbolist Self-portrait with Halo 1889

Yellow Christ 1889

Tahitian Women, or *On the Beach* 1891

When Will You Marry? (Nafea Faa Ipiopo?) 1892

Where Do We Come From? What Are We? Where Are We Going? 1897

Things to look for:

- strong, expressive colors
- large flat areas with clear outlines
- bold patterns and designs
- exotic subjects
- unconventional use of religious symbols

Comparisons: Vincent Van Gogh, Paul Cézanne, Henri Rousseau, Camille Pissarro, Paula Modersohn-Becker

Glossary terms: expressionism, fauvism impressionism, Nabis, postimpressionism, symbolism

Tahitian Women, *or* On the Beach *1891. Oil on canvas. 29 x 39½ in (74 x 100 cm). Musée d'Orsay, Paris.*

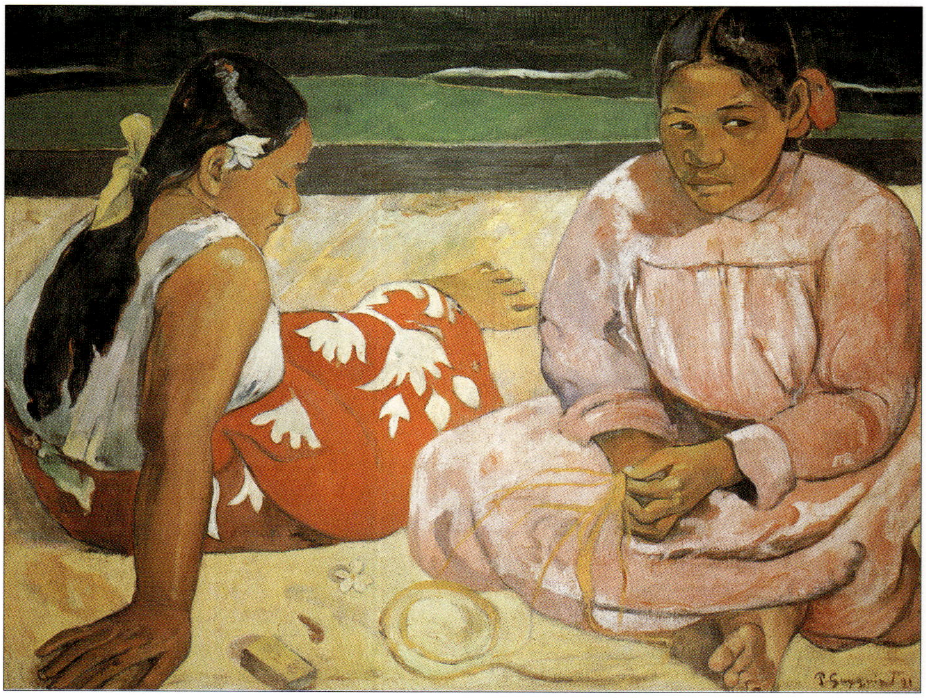

Gauguin's symbolism

Paul Gauguin began his painting career as an impressionist, but grew tired of simply painting a fleeting impression of a person or scene. He wanted his art to make a powerful impact on the people who looked at it. To this end he worked in large expanses of bold color in order to express his own emotions in painting the scene, or the feelings of the picture's subject. He also simplified the shapes in his paintings, often surrounding them with a heavy outline.

These features can be seen in his *Symbolist Self-portrait with Halo* (1889). Two flat areas of bright red and yellow surround the artist's disembodied head, which casts a sad glance out of the picture. There is a hint of martyrdom in the painting—John the Baptist was beheaded, and Gauguin often portrayed himself as a Christlike figure, shunned by society.

The painting also contains various explicit religious symbols: in the artist's hand you can see a small snake, and above his head is a halo and two apples; this could represent the biblical story of Adam and Eve. Gauguin's self-portrait presents the artist as an enigma: is he saintly and pure, or is he just another mortal prone to temptation?

Gauguin's main legacy to the artists who followed him was the freeing of color and form from the depiction of reality in order to use them for expressive purposes instead. These pioneering ideas were later developed by the fauves, who used strong colors and rapid brushwork to convey heightened emotion in their paintings.

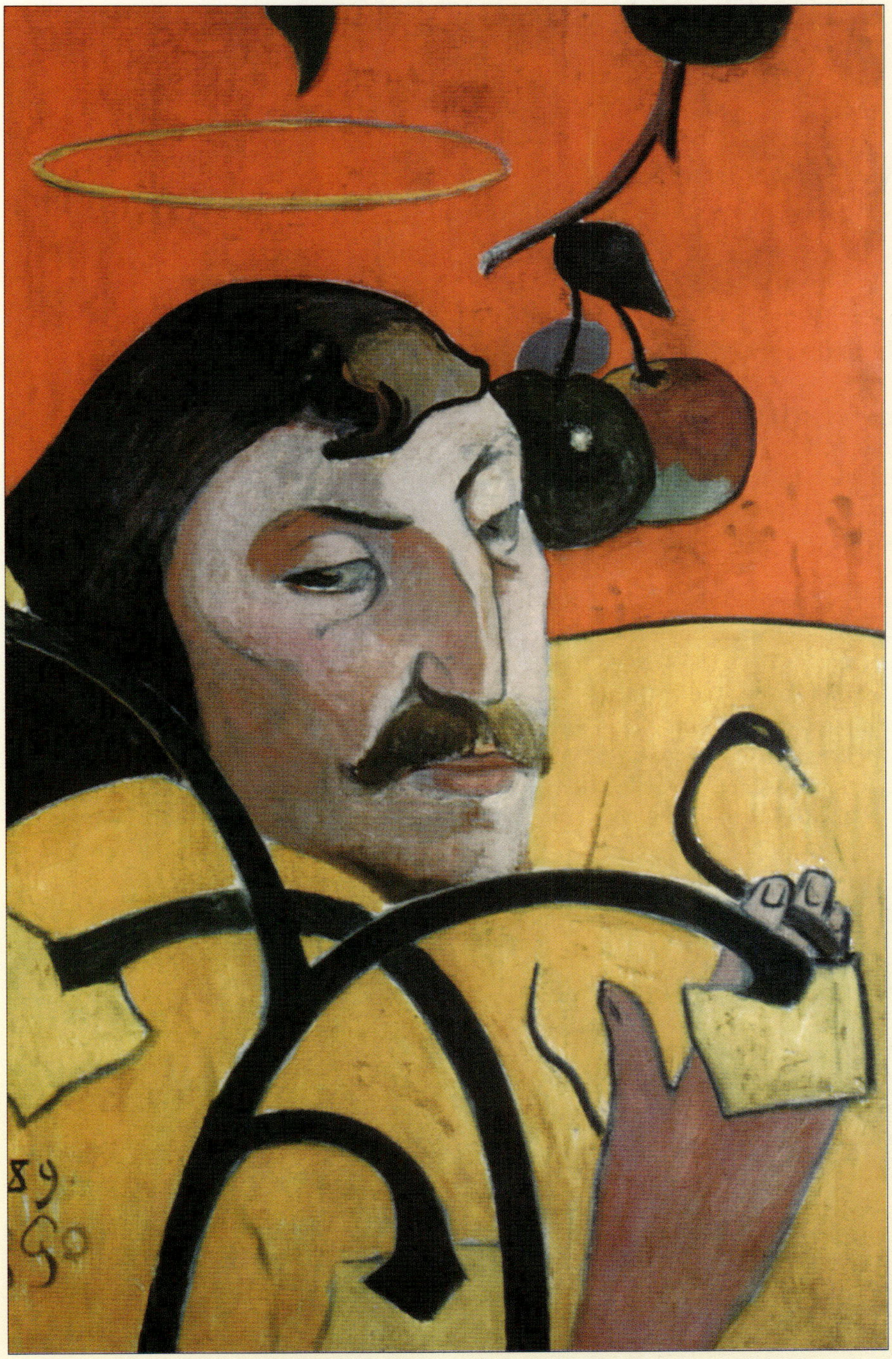

Symbolist Self-portrait with Halo
1889. Oil on wood. 35 x 22 in (89 x 56 cm). National Gallery of Art, Washington, D.C.

were often hazardous; illness and poverty had cut short a visit to Martinique and Panama in 1887. In 1888, Gauguin joined the Dutch artist Vincent Van Gogh in the south of France for a two-month stay.

Gauguin's urge to experience what were then called "primitive" cultures led him to settle on the island of Tahiti in the South Seas in 1891. Its native people seemed to enjoy a "natural" existence, free from the artificiality of Western society. Here, Gauguin painted the works for which he is best known—warm and intimate pictures of Tahitians leading a simple life. The most famous is the huge tableau entitled *Where Do We Come From? What Are We? Where Are We Going?* (1897). The appeal of Gauguin's tropical paradise faded, however, and illness and the death of his daughter drove him to a suicide attempt in 1898. He came to despise the colonial authorities and the other French settlers on Tahiti, and left for the remote Marquesas Islands in 1901, where he died at the age of 54.

GEERTGEN tot Sint Jans

VERY LITTLE IS KNOWN ABOUT GEERTGEN TOT SINT JANS. Early 17th-century records seem to indicate that he died fairly young—at about the age of 28. Only about 15 works have been attributed to him, but these are memorable and distinctive.

Life and work

Geertgen tot Sint Jans took this name while working at the convent of Saint John of the Knights Hospitallers, in Haarlem. It means "little Gerard of the Brethren of Saint John."

Carel Van Mander, a painter and writer who settled in Haarlem in 1583, tells us something about Geertgen in *The Painter's Book* (1604). He was born in Leyden but moved to Haarlem; he was a pupil of a painter called Albert Van Ouwater, and he painted a triptych showing the Crucifixion for the high altar of the church of the convent of Saint John.

It is impossible to say how accurate Mander's information is, as he was writing long after Geertgen had died. The church of the convent of Saint John was destroyed during the 1573 siege of Haarlem, and only the right wing of that triptych now survives (it is in Vienna). It shows the *Lamentation* and *The Burning of the Bones of Saint John the Baptist* (both c1480s).

Typically, these scenes are clear narrative representations; there are many figures, and the compositions are very complex, showing more than one episode from the story in a single picture. These two paintings were once on the front and back of the wing of the altarpiece, but they were sawn apart, in about 1600, so that both sides could be seen at once. Some of the figures in the background are portraits of the artist's patrons, who are skillfully shown mingling with the biblical characters. The paintings have been dated to the 1480s, after examination of the style of the clothes depicted, and the wood of the panels. Altogether about 15 paintings have been attributed to Geertgen.

Geertgen's paintings reflect the art of this period. He painted mostly on oak panels, which were the most common support for pictures in northern Europe at this time. He mixed his color with a drying oil (to make oil paint), using techniques perfected in the Netherlands at the beginning of the 15th century. Oil helped to make the paint stick to the panel, and provided the opportunity to create very subtle, and sometimes dramatic effects of light and texture. The painter could build up layers of paint, one over another. In addition, if the paint was translucent, it allowed the underpainting to glow through the glazes on top.

Data file

Full name: Geertgen tot Sint Jans (also known as Gerrit Gerritsz)

Nationality: Dutch

Style: early Netherlandish

Dates: born c1460 in Leyden, died c1490 in ?Haarlem

Key works:
- *Lamentation* (c1480s)
- *The Burning of the Bones of Saint John the Baptist* (c1480s)
- *Saint John the Baptist in the Wilderness* (date unknown)
- *Nativity at Night* (date unknown)
- *The Raising of Lazarus* (date unknown)

Things to look for:
- complicated compositions
- charming, slender figures with oval heads
- feeling for nature

Comparisons: Jan Van Eyck, Rogier Van der Weyden, Hans Memling

Glossary terms: chiaroscuro, devotional, patron, triptych

A bright nativity

This exquisite little picture, so dramatic in its contrasts of light and shade (known as chiaroscuro), contains two separate scenes. In the foreground the Nativity is the main focus, while the background scene depicts the angel Gabriel appearing to the shepherds in the hills to tell them of the birth of Christ.

The Bible story of the birth of Christ in a stable "because there was no room at the inn" forms the basis of the picture in the foreground. The unclothed baby Jesus lies, possibly on straw, in a stark, boxlike manger, or feeding trough. The infant is emitting a supernatural light: his whole body is glowing and, for added emphasis, Geertgen has painted rays of light radiating from him.

Jesus's mother, Mary, kneels before him, her hands together as if in prayer, as she gazes down in awe at her newborn son. Her face is aglow, reflecting the streaming light. Behind her—very much in the background—stands the shadowy figure of Joseph, his head bowed in respect. Five childlike angels, one still in flight, also cluster around the infant, and they too are touched by the holy radiance.

Behind the makeshift crib you can just make out an ox and an ass looking toward the glowing baby. The awe and amazement of the group of figures in the picture is transmitted to the viewer.

The secondary drama, taking place in the background, is identified by an additional light source. Out on the bare hillside we can just make out a group of shepherds, together with the flock of sheep they have been tending, clustered near a makeshift bonfire. However, their attention is not on the sheep at all, but on an angel, radiating heavenly light, that has appeared in the night sky. The angel, Gabriel, is bringing them the message that Christ the Savior has been born nearby and that they should go and worship him. This story is told in the Bible (Luke 2: 1–20).

This idea that the infant Christ emitted a divine light seems to have originated in the writings of Saint Bridget of Sweden. She lived in the 14th century, and claimed that she had had a vision of the birth of

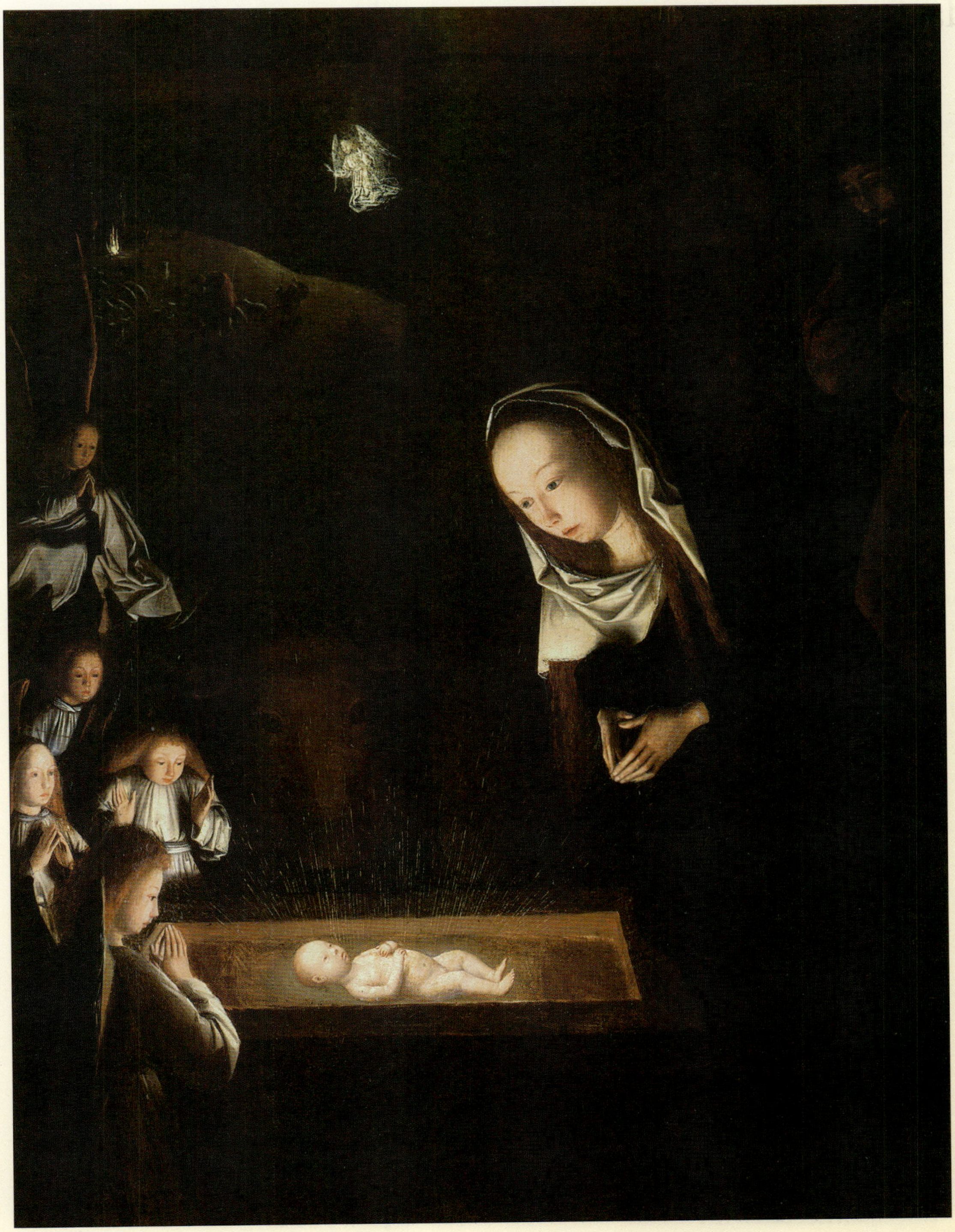

Nativity at Night *date unknown. Oil on panel. 13 1/2 x 9 3/4 in (34 x 25 cm). National Gallery, London.*

Jesus. She wrote that the newborn baby "radiated such an ineffable light and splendor that the sun was not comparable to it." Saint Bridget also said that this divine radiance eclipsed Joseph's candle. In this picture no such candle is visible. However, it is thought that this painting was, at some point, cut down on all four sides, so it is possible that Joseph's candle was in part of the picture that is now lost. Certainly he is holding his right hand in a way that suggests that he may be shielding a candle from a draft. It may seem odd that anyone would want to cut down such a picture; it has been suggested that it was once part of a large altarpiece that was reduced in size to be used in a domestic setting. There is no real evidence for this, though, and it may well be that the picture was always for private devotional use rather than part of a larger work in a public place.

GENTILE da Fabriano

GENTILE DA FABRIANO WAS A LEADING CONTRIBUTOR to the beginnings of what we now think of as the early Renaissance period. His masterly and atmospheric use of light, and the innovations in terms of space and form that he introduced into his compositions, had a profound impact on future artists.

Life and work

Although we know that Gentile di Niccolo di Massio was born in Fabriano, we know little about his youth and early artistic development. The first record of his art is a payment in 1408 for a commission from a Venetian patron for a panel (now lost). Gentile did move to Venice around this time, where he became a member of the School of Saint Christopher of the Merchants. These schools (*scuole*), or confraternities, as they are sometimes known, were often made up of members from several different trades. According to later historical sources, Gentile painted panels for churches during this time, and helped to restore the frescos in the Sala del Maggior Consiglio in the Ducal Palace. These frescos, now destroyed, brought him into contact with many of the great artists of his time, including Jacobello del Fiore and Antonio Pisanello.

During this time Gentile produced his first masterpiece, the Valle Romita altarpiece (c1410), a polyptych showing the Coronation of the Virgin, flanked by scenes from the lives of the saints on either side. This work must have won him wider fame; in 1413 a nobleman from Brescia who had a house in Venice appointed him Court Painter, and in 1414 Gentile moved to Brescia. He spent five years there, working on a decorative scheme of frescos; he also painted a panel as a gift from his patron to the pope, Martin V.

In 1419 Gentile was recorded as traveling to join the pope in Florence, so it is clear that his fame was spreading once more. It was in Florence that he made the *Stigmatization of Saint Francis* (c1420–21), a work now prized for its original and striking use of divine light to provide lighting for the scene depicted. This work also shows the beginnings of the 14th-century Florentine influences on his painting: intricate tooling of gold leaf and more attention given to solid forms. It was also in Florence that Gentile made his most famous work, his first signed altarpiece, the *Adoration of the Magi* (1423), created in a highly decorative but delicate and naturalistic style known as international Gothic.

The influence that Gentile's work had on his contemporaries, and the amount of work he was being commissioned to produce at this stage, tell us something of his status at the time. By the time he produced *Adoration of the Magi*, he was almost certainly the foremost artist in

Data file

Full name: Gentile di Niccolo di Massio da Fabriano

Dates: Born c1385 in Fabriano, died 1427 in Rome

Nationality: Italian

Style: international Gothic

Key works:
- Valle Romita altarpiece c1410
- *Coronation of the Virgin* c1420–21
- *Stigmatization of Saint Francis* c1420–21
- *Adoration of the Magi* 1423
- Quaratesi altarpiece 1425

Things to look for:
- works showing a mixture of the ornate Gothic style and the new Florentine interest in solid forms
- innovative use of illumination in paintings, giving the backgrounds and the figures a more naturalistic appeal
- figures becoming more three-dimensional, in line with the new developments in early Renaissance art

Comparisons: Fra Angelico, Antonio Pisanello, Stefano Sassetta

Glossary terms: international Gothic, polyptych, *predella*, Renaissance, *scuola*, tooling

Towards naturalism

This altarpiece is the greatest surviving masterpiece of Gentile da Fabriano's career. Made in 1423, it was commissioned by one of the Florentine Strozzi family for their private chapel.

Gentile's style is sometimes referred to as international Gothic, because the blend of naturalistic detail, attention to space and light, and courtly elegance were drawn from different areas of Europe. However, Gentile's uniqueness in his use of illumination and simpler, more three-dimensional figures makes him a forerunner of early Renaissance art, with its concentration on a greater naturalism in depictions of space and form.

The main subject of this altarpiece is the arrival of the Magi (the three kings) at Bethlehem. They present their gifts to the infant Christ, who reaches out to touch the head of the kneeling king; the gesture could be a blessing or a natural, babyish touch. The star above the stable glows on the landscape and sets a peaceful mood. In the background three stages of the Magis' journey are shown, but they do not seem separate because of the even tone and the continuing contours of the landscape.

In the three paintings along the *predella*, or lower part of the altarpiece, the artist makes remarkable use of light to create different atmospheres. On the left the light of the moon, the stars, and the angels blend with the divine light of the baby to create a tender and wonderfully realistic Nativity. The middle painting shows the Flight into Egypt. In the right-hand scene—the Presentation in the Temple—Gentile's ability to depict space more naturalistically than his contemporaries is apparent.

Adoration of the Magi *1423. Tempera on panel. 118 x 111½ in (300 x 283 cm). Galleria degli Uffizi, Florence.*

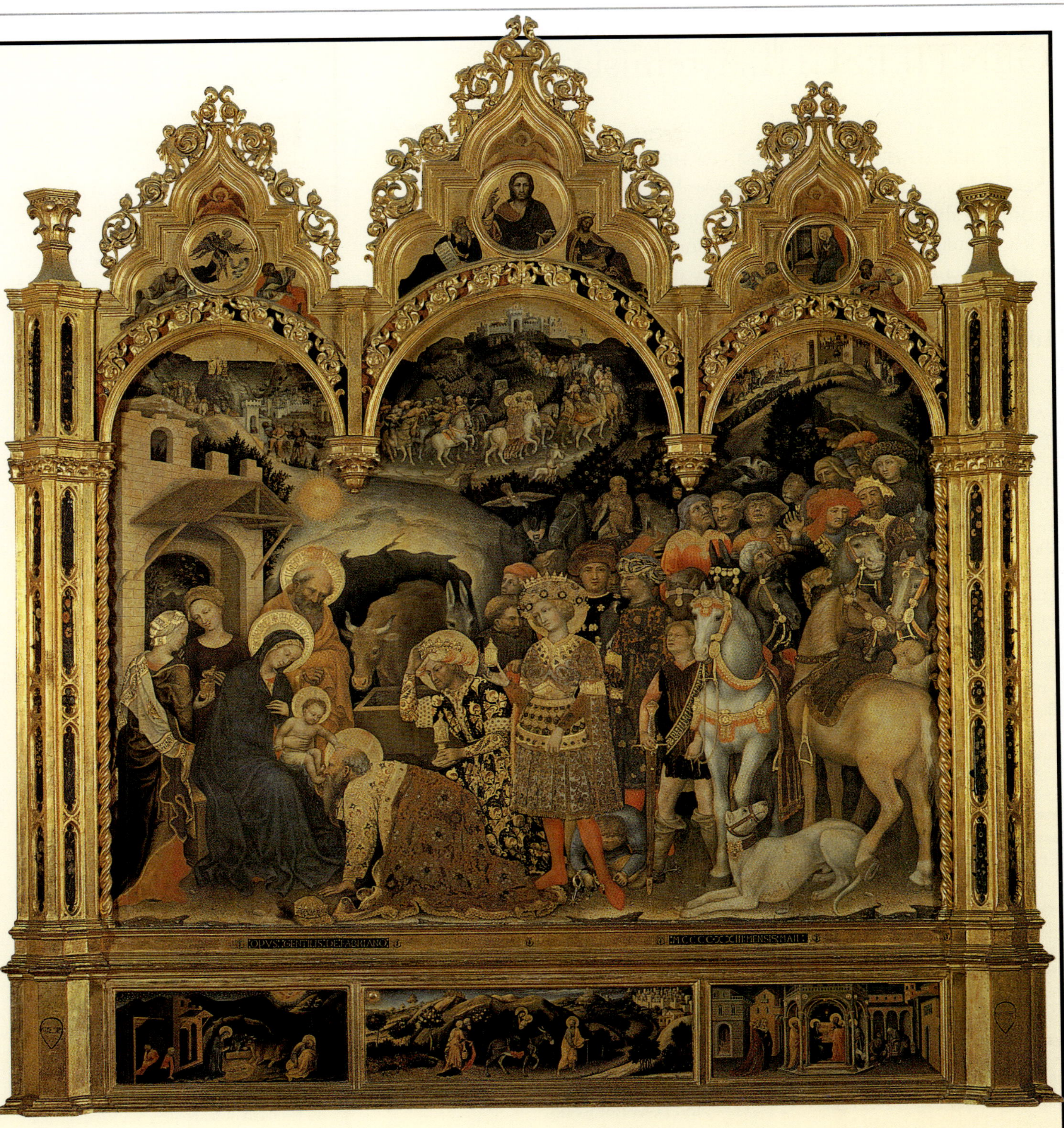

Florence. Another masterpiece completed around this time was the Quaratesi altarpiece (completed in 1425), which inspired artists such as Fra Angelico with its use of light and dark to suggest three-dimensionality. A polyptych he produced in Siena from 1425 had a great impact on the future work of Sienese painters such as Sassetta and Giovanni di Paolo.

In 1427 Gentile traveled to Rome, where he began work on a cycle of frescos for Pope Martin V. These frescos, destroyed in the 17th century, were completed by Pisanello, after Gentile is recorded as having died. Some other works of this time are attributed to him, but none is signed.

GENTILESCHI Artemisia

UNLIKE OTHER FEMALE ARTISTS OF HER TIME, Artemisia Gentileschi did not paint small, domestic-style paintings—thought to be more suitable for women—but attempted large-scale history paintings with dramatic and sometimes shocking subjects. Her powerful works made her a well-known artist in Italy in the 17th century.

Life and work

Born in Rome in 1593, Artemisia Gentileschi was the daughter of a skilled and highly regarded painter, Orazio Gentileschi. Artemisia learned most of what she knew about painting from him, and many of her works show very similar characteristics to his style. Orazio had not studied art in the traditional manner of the era, in which ancient sculptures, the Renaissance masters, and life models were used to help artists understand anatomy. He was trained as a goldsmith, and always favored the sharp edges and clear designs so vital to working in precious metal. Like her father, Artemisia did not have a conventional artistic training, and her figures are sometimes awkwardly positioned. However, her ability to convey textures and materials realistically often concealed her lack of training in anatomy.

Both father and daughter were influenced by Michelangelo Merisi da Caravaggio's dramatically lit subjects, and both used strong contrasts of light and dark (called chiaroscuro, from the Italian words for light and shade) to add atmosphere and realism to their work. Artemisia's first signed painting, *Susanna and the Elders*, dates from 1610, and clearly reveals her powers of dramatic storytelling and individual interpretation.

Orazio hired one of his colleagues, Agostino Tassi, to teach Artemisia about perspective. The move proved disastrous; in 1612 Tassi was brought to public trial for the rape of Artemisia, and sentenced to eight months in prison. In the same year Artemisia was married to a man called Pietro Stiattesi, and moved with him to Florence.

Despite the traumatic events in Rome, Artemisia continued to paint, often choosing—as in the past—strong female heroines as her subjects. With such eminent patrons as Cosimo II de' Medici, she succeeded in establishing a reputation in Florence with striking and powerful works.

With other Florentine artists, Artemisia spent two years painting a tribute to Michelangelo, her *Allegory of Inclination* (1615–17). In 1616 she became the first woman to join the Accademia del Disegno (School of Drawing). In 1620 she returned to Rome and then traveled farther afield to Genoa and Venice.

By 1630 Artemisia had settled in Naples, where her style and subjects changed. She painted fewer female nudes and more biblical subjects, and her work showed less of Caravaggio's

Data file

Full name: Artemisia Gentileschi

Nationality: Italian

Style: Caravaggesque/Italian 17th century

Dates: born 1593 in Rome, died 1652/53 in Naples

Key works:

Susanna and the Elders 1610

Judith Beheading Holofernes c1618

Judith and Her Maidservant with the Head of Holofernes 1625

Self-portrait as an Allegory of Painting 1630

Things to look for:

- dramatic compositions with female nudes or strong female heroines as subjects
- striking contrasts of light and dark (use of chiaroscuro) influenced by Caravaggio
- skillful painting of materials and fabrics, emphasizing and highlighting different textures

Comparisons: Caravaggio, Orazio Gentileschi

Glossary terms: chiaroscuro, history painting, Renaissance

A shocking realism

The story of Judith and the beheading of Holofernes was the subject most often depicted by Artemisia Gentileschi.The story comes from one of the books of the Apocrypha in the Bible, and tells how the Israelite heroine, Judith, gains access to the camp of the enemy Assyrian soldiers and their general, Holofernes. Judith tricks Holofernes, pretending to offer him help, and when he falls asleep after a meal, she severs his head and smuggles it out of the camp to present to her townspeople. Terrified by the death of their leader, the Assyrians are easily defeated.

Although both Caravaggio and Artemisia's father, Orazio, had depicted the same subject, it was never as graphically and explicitly portrayed as in this example. Indeed, the repeated choice of this subject has led many experts to wonder whether Artemisia used it to relieve her feelings about being raped by Agostino Tassi.

The influence of Caravaggio is clear in Artemisia Gentileschi's use of chiaroscuro, and in the realism of the image. However, even Caravaggio does not go so far as to show blood spattering the arms and chest of the heroine. Artemisia makes the viewer very aware of the strength required to carry out the task, and of how messy and horrific it must have been, as blood soaks into the white sheets. Details such as Judith's rolled-up sleeves and her hand clutching the hair of the victim add a graphic realism.

Judith is not an idealized heroine—the look on her face is determined, but not beautiful. She is shown wearing a bracelet on her arm and a low-cut dress, which contrasts her femininity with the gruesome task she is performing. We are shown a reversal of the traditional female role.

A close look at the position of Judith reveals that her arms are not in proportion to her head or body: they are too large and muscular. Her upper body is also strangely positioned. This is not obvious at first,

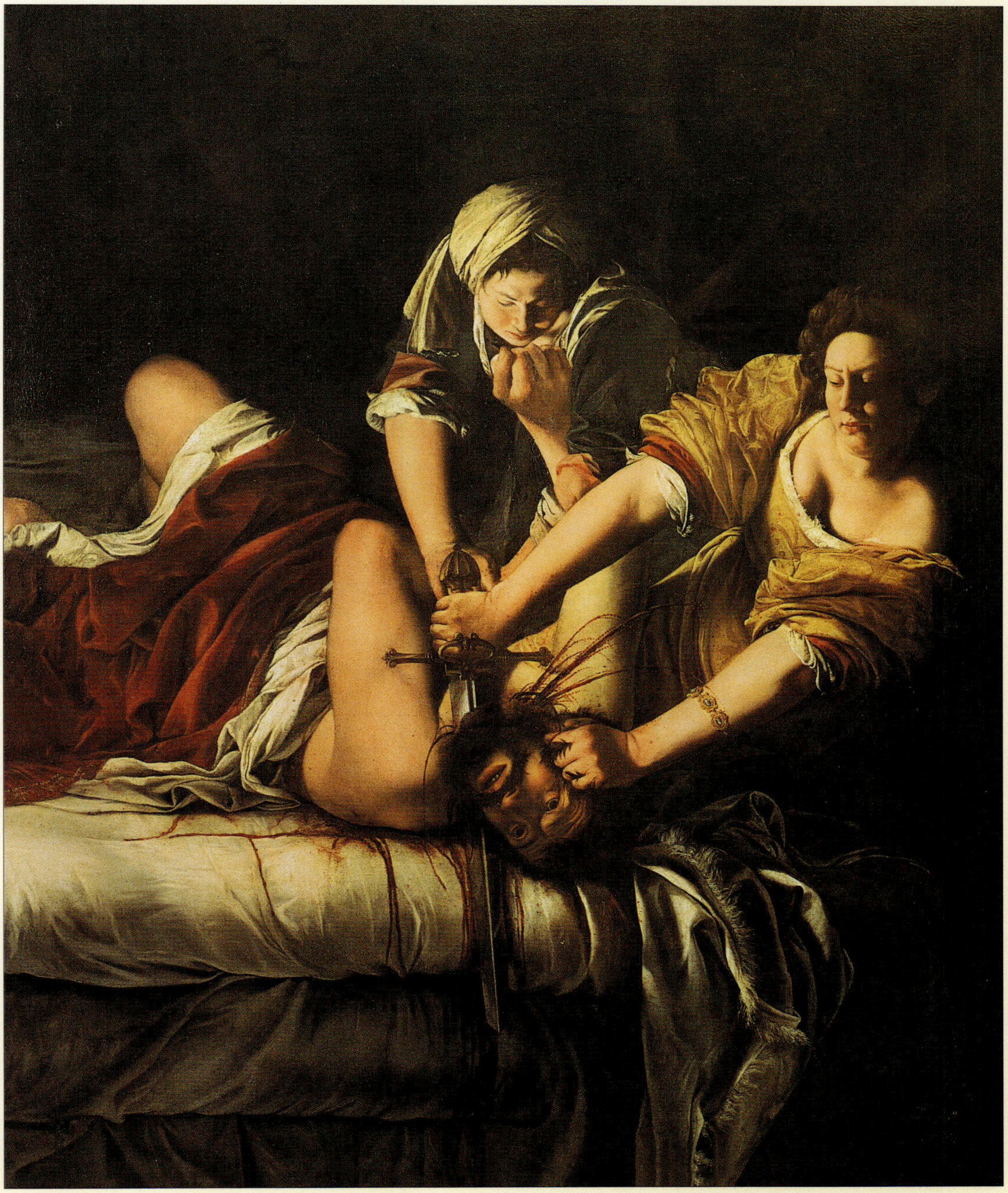

Judith Beheading Holofernes *c1618. Oil on canvas. 78 x 64 in (199 x 162.5 cm). Galleria degli Uffizi, Florence.*

however, as the richness of the fabrics and textures creates a powerful atmosphere that distracts from the awkwardness of the figures.

This painting would have been extremely disturbing for viewers, and it is not known exactly for whom it was made. Some sources suggest that it was for Cosimo II de' Medici. Where previously Judith was depicted in paintings as an innocent young girl and Holofernes as a brute, here the distinction is less obvious. If we did not know the story, we might perhaps wonder who the villain really was. What is certain is that Artemisia wanted to make her mark in Florence, and was not afraid to shock people.

influence. Regardless of this change, her paintings were still appreciated by patrons in Rome and elsewhere.

In 1638 Artemisia traveled to London, where her father had been Court Painter to King Charles I since 1626. Some historians believe she may have helped Orazio with his great masterpiece, the decoration of the Queen's House in Greenwich. She stayed in London until the early 1640s, returning finally to Naples, where she continued to paint versions of her earlier works until her death sometime between 1652 and 1653.

GÉRICAULT Théodore

AFTER GÉRICAULT'S DEATH, many French artists showed their admiration by keeping a cast of his death mask on their studio walls. His expressive style, along with that of Eugène Delacroix, is associated with the rejection of classicism that heralded Romanticism. But Géricault's paintings also contained a sense of realism that influenced later painters such as Gustave Courbet.

Life and work

Théodore Géricault was born in Rouen into a prosperous and well-established family whose wealth derived from commerce, business, and the law. In the mid-1790s his parents moved to Paris, where he received a good classical education, though he showed little interest in his studies. Far more engaging were the two passions that were to dictate the course of his life: art and a love of horses. It is not surprising, therefore, that in 1808 when his father reluctantly gave him permission to train as an artist, he was placed with a specialist in equestrian subjects. Two years later he transferred to the more rigorous discipline of Pierre-Narcise Guerin, an artist whose neoclassical tastes echoed Jacques-Louis David's continuing domination of French art.

Géricault's youth coincided with a turbulent phase in the history of France. His ardent but melancholic character reflects something of the confused condition of a society shaped by the hopes and failures of the French Revolution of 1789, and by the spectacular rise and decline of Napoleon that came after it. In 1812, the year of the disastrous retreat of the French army from Moscow, Géricault first attracted attention at the annual Salon exhibition with a large painting of a cavalry officer, *The Charging Chasseur* (1812). Already it shows a desire to break free from neoclassical restraint. Its brilliance of color and its dynamism of composition and broken, energetic brushstrokes owed much to a preference for the baroque manner of Peter Paul Rubens. Géricault was not alone in this tendency away from a balanced harmony of forms and smoothness of finish. He and Delacroix, particularly, were identified with the emergence of French Romanticism.

This reputation was further established with his work *The Raft of the Medusa* (1819), which soon became a point of reference for younger artists. The large scale of the canvas was normally reserved for heroic subjects, and yet its subject was far from heroic in the ordinary sense of the term. Géricault took the theme from a contemporary political scandal that involved the death of over 100 sailors on an inadequate raft cut adrift after the badly equipped ship, the *Medusa*, had run aground in a storm off the coast of Africa. Most of the officers, who had been appointed under the newly re-established Bourbon monarchy, behaved with callous cruelty. The few sailors who did not drown

Data file

Full name: Jean Louis André Théodore Géricault

Nationality: French

Style: Romanticism/realism

Dates: born 1791 in Rouen, died 1824 in Paris

Key works:
- *The Charging Chasseur* 1812
- *A Horse Frightened by Lightning* c1813
- *Race of the Riderless (or Barberi) Horses* 1817
- *The Raft of the Medusa* 1819
- English lithographs 1821
- Portraits of psychiatric patients 1822–23

Things to look for:
- heroic but also common-life subjects
- dramatic light and shade
- subdued but sometimes vivid coloring
- psychological insight
- emotional sympathy in both human and animal subjects

Comparisons: Peter Paul Rubens, Jacques-Louis David, George Stubbs, Eugène Delacroix, Jean Auguste Dominique Ingres, Gustave Courbet

Glossary terms: baroque, lithography, neoclassicism, realism, Romanticism, Salon

Romanticism with enhanced realism

Throughout his career Géricault painted horses. This was not merely an artistic enthusiasm. Even when short of money he would sometimes buy several horses at a time for the sheer pleasure of owning and riding them. Ironically, his premature death (at the age of 33) came about because of poor medical treatment after a riding accident that damaged his spine.

A Horse Frightened by Lightning (c1813), involves a number of contemporary ideas. It can be associated with Romanticism because of the evident fascination with the power of sublime natural forces to create a psychological effect, albeit in an animal. Géricault had already admired a number of English artists several years before he went to stay in England from 1820 to 1822. Among these was George Stubbs, who had published a book on the anatomy of horses, which Géricault is known to have read. He would also have been aware of Stubbs's paintings of terrified horses being attacked by lions.

From a rather different point of view Géricault was also impressed by a quality of naturalistic realism in other examples of English art. His careful studies of the varied forms, coloring, and textures of different breeds of horses are as meticulously accurate as John Constable's sketches of cloud formations and the structure and foliage of trees. The horse in the painting is set against the darkness of a thundery sky so that an eerie light plays delicately over agitated muscles. The awkward stance of the horse and its anxious expression are also scrupulously recorded in the painting.

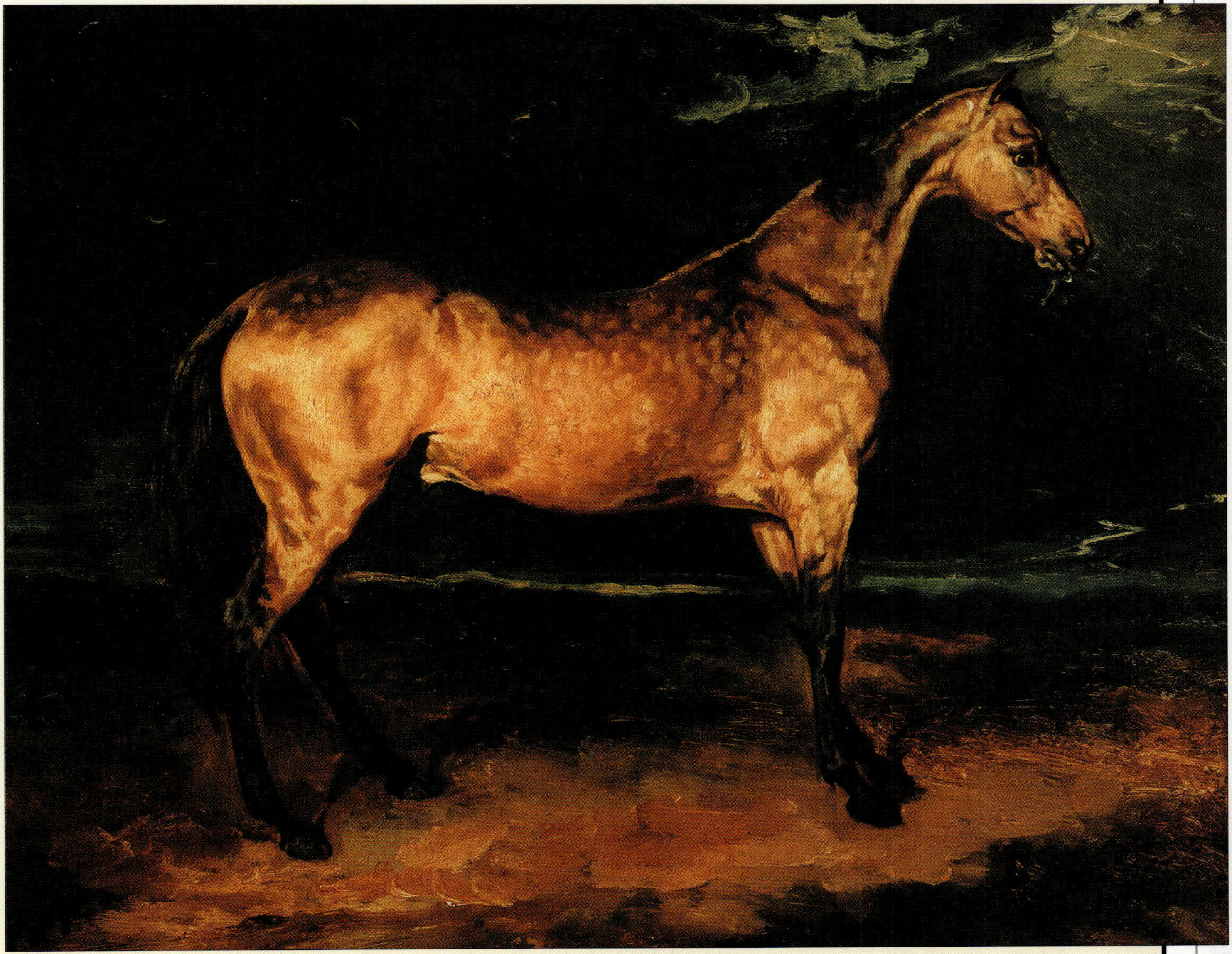

Géricault used a similar curious mixture of analytical scientific detachment and emotional empathy when, in 1822–23, he produced a series of 10 paintings of patients in a psychiatric hospital, only five of which now survive. In these, as in so many of his paintings, Géricault anticipated the attention to detail, realism, and documentary attitude towards situations that preoccupied so many artists during the century that followed.

A Horse Frightened by Lightning
c1813. Oil on canvas. 19¼ x 23½ in (49 x 60 cm). National Gallery, London.

were reduced to delirium and to eating human flesh to survive.

Géricault went to tremendous lengths in order to reconstruct the dreadful reality of the tragedy. He studied emaciated patients dying in hospitals, and corpses in the morgue. He painted portraits of the survivors and questioned them so as to be able to build a model of the raft in his studio. In the finished painting the figures are as accurately observed as those of Michelangelo whose work Géricault had studied in Rome.

During his stay in England, from 1820 to 1822, Géricault painted the common sights to be seen in the streets: men at work, beggars, and fashionable ladies. Frequently he included horses, sometimes elegant thoroughbreds, but more often, heavy draft-horses in somber industrial settings. In some cases, drawings were worked up in the recently invented medium of lithography, to be sold as folios of prints. That they failed to sell well was probably because he treated his subjects with seriousness rather than trivializing them with humor for a middle-class audience.

GHIBERTI Lorenzo

LORENZO GHIBERTI WAS AN OUTSTANDING SCULPTOR, and also a painter, architect, and writer. His most famous work was the design and casting of two sets of bronze doors for the baptistery of San Giovanni. The second set surpassed all expectations in its display of skill and beauty; the doors became known as the Gates of Paradise.

Life and work

Lorenzo Ghiberti learned the art of goldsmithing from his stepfather. This experience of working in intricate detail with precious materials gave him an excellent training as a sculptor, especially for work in bronze.

In 1400 artists were invited to compete for the prestigious project of making bronze doors for the San Giovanni Baptistery in Florence. Ghiberti's winning entry showed his mastery of designing and casting reliefs in bronze. The subject was the Old Testament story of the Sacrifice of Isaac, presented in a quatrefoil, following the pattern of an earlier set of doors made by Andrea Pisano. Ghiberti combined all the required specifications (a rocky landscape, animals, and people involved in dramatic action) in a beautifully balanced composition. The only element cast separately was the body of Isaac, inspired by a classical Roman sculpture, which was then fixed seamlessly into the rest of the relief.

Ghiberti began work on the doors in 1403 and continued on the project for the next 20 years. It was a huge task, involving 28 quatrefoil reliefs: 20 scenes from the life of Christ (a change from the original plan of scenes from the Old Testament), the four Fathers of the Church (Augustine, Gregory, Jerome, and Ambrose), and the four Evangelists (Matthew, Mark, Luke, and John). Ghiberti included portraits of himself and his son Vittorio in the decorated borders between the reliefs.

In addition to a team of assistants, Ghiberti employed several young Florentine artists to work with him. They included Donatello, Paolo Uccello, and Benozzo Gozzoli, all of whom gained valuable experience in Ghiberti's workshop, for his designs made use of all the latest developments in picture-making.

Ghiberti soon established a reputation as the best sculptor in bronze in the city. In 1413 he was asked to produce an over-life-size statue of Saint John the Baptist to stand in a niche on the outside of the guildhall of Orsanmichele in Florence. This was the first large-scale bronze statue made since classical times, and again Ghiberti demonstrated his technical ability by casting the saint in one piece. The influence of classical sculpture is seen in the strong modeling of the head and the standing pose in which the saint's weight is concentrated on one leg. Ghiberti's feeling for pattern and graceful line comes out in the cascading folds of the cloak. He cast a similarly sized and equally impressive bronze statue of Saint Matthew in 1419, again for Orsanmichele. This time Ghiberti made the saint appear to twist slightly at the waist. He also designed the

Data file

Full name: Lorenzo Ghiberti

Nationality: Italian

Style: early Renaissance

Dates: born 1378 in Florence, died 1455 in Florence

Key works:
- North Doors, San Giovanni Baptistery 1403–24
- *Saint John the Baptist* 1413
- *Saint Matthew* 1419
- *Saint Stephen* 1425
- Gates of Paradise, San Giovanni Baptistery 1426–52
- Shrine of Saint Zenobius 1432–42

Things to look for:
- well-balanced compositions in relief
- influence of classical sculpture
- variety of lifelike detail
- sense of flowing movement in drapery

Comparisons: Filippo Brunelleschi, Donatello, Fra Angelico, Masaccio, Paolo Uccello

Glossary terms: bronze casting, gilding, quatrefoil, Renaissance

The art of storytelling in bronze

Ghiberti applied to relief sculpture many of the innovations found in the work of Florentine Renaissance painters, such as Masaccio and Fra Angelico. These are especially clear in the panels of the Gates of Paradise, where he moved away from the restricting quatrefoil shape framing the scenes in his first doors. He used perspective with greater clarity to describe space both indoors and outdoors, and even increased the effect in relief by making the people in the foreground more solid than those in the background. The appearance of people and buildings was clearly influenced by examples from the classical past and from his own observations from life, which contribute to the variety of detail and action in each scene.

In several panels Ghiberti included more than one episode from the story. This required considerable skill because each episode had to be clearly identifiable and to contribute to the pleasing effect of the scene as a whole. In the *Story of Joseph* panel the most eye-catching feature is the round, arcaded building that occupies two-thirds of the picture space and frames a lively group of men, women, and children collecting sacks of grain. The elegant poses and gestures are emphasized by the graceful folds and sweeping lines of their classically inspired clothes. The three episodes telling the story of Joseph are arranged around the edges of the panel. At the top right we can see Joseph's jealous brothers selling him to merchants. Ghiberti depicts the group in very shallow relief,

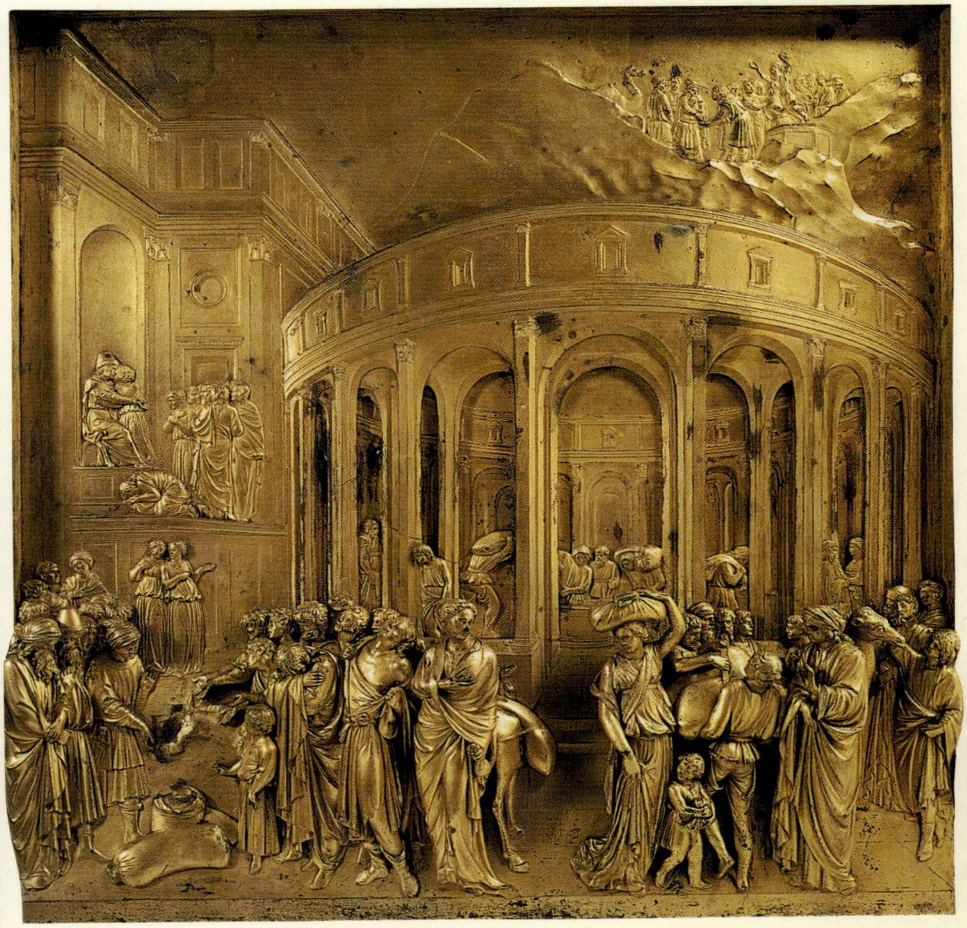

made his design in wax on a clay core, the wax was melted and replaced by metal. The casting was carried out in a foundry; the sculptor and assistants then refined and polished the cast piece. The bronze reliefs on the baptistery doors was further enriched by gilding. Michelangelo was so impressed that he called them the Gates of Paradise.

Story of Joseph (detail), Gates of Paradise *(left) 1426–52. Gilt bronze. 31 x 31 in (79.5 x 79.5 cm). Baptistery of San Giovanni, Florence.*

Gates of Paradise *(below) 1426–52. Gilt bronze. 102 x 43 in (259 x 109 cm). Baptistery of San Giovanni, Florence.*

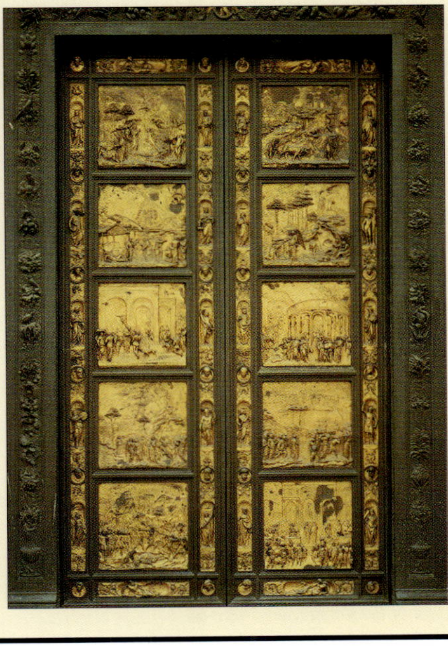

which helps suggest the distance of this episode from the others both in place and time. This hilly setting is placed appropriately high up in the panel. The next episode, at bottom left, shows the scene where Joseph's silver cup is found in the sack belonging to Benjamin, his younger brother. (Joseph has ordered it placed there so that he can accuse Benjamin of theft and force his brother to stay with him.) The final episode in which Joseph is happily reunited with his brothers takes place on the left-hand side, halfway up the panel. Again the architecture provides a fitting frame that helps separate this episode from the rest of the action.

The subtlety of the relief and the exquisite detail of the modeling illustrate Ghiberti's technical mastery. He cast his relief panels and statues by a process called the "lost wax" method. When Ghiberti had

architecture of the niche in which the statue still stands.

Ghiberti's interest in architecture extended to the design and the construction of the dome of Florence Cathedral. Filippo Brunelleschi was its chief architect, but Ghiberti's advice was sought at various stages from about 1406 onward. He also collaborated with Jacopo della Quercia and Donatello in designing bronze reliefs for the font in Siena's baptistery in the 1420s.

Ghiberti's first baptistery doors were installed in 1424 and were such a success that he was immediately commissioned to make a second pair based on scenes from the Old Testament. He could design these as he wished and decided upon 10 almost square panels with more figures and heads included in the borders between them. The outer frame was just as richly decorated as the first, with animals, birds, and plants. The doors were finally completed in 1452, and were acknowledged as his masterpiece.

Ghiberti was also a collector of classical sculptures and a writer. In about 1447 he started on his *Commentarii*, writings on the history and theory of art. Although these were unfinished when Ghiberti died, they nevertheless provide a unique and fascinating account of the history of Western European art from the point of view of a Renaissance artist.

GHIRLANDAIO Domenico

BY PUTTING RECOGNIZABLE PLACES AND PEOPLE IN HIS LIFELIKE frescos, Domenico Ghirlandaio excelled at making scenes from the Bible come to life. Michelangelo Buonarroti was among his pupils in one of the busiest and most successful painting businesses in 15th-century Florence.

Life and work

Domenico Ghirlandaio was the eldest son of a family of artists. His father was a goldsmith, and like many Renaissance artists, the young Domenico trained as a goldsmith before becoming a painter. He learned the art of mosaic from Alesso Baldovinetti, who may also have taught him painting.

Building on the achievements of earlier Florentine artists, Ghirlandaio is noted for making his paintings appear lifelike. He was also influenced by Netherlandish painting, especially in his landscapes and portraits.

In 1470–71 he painted frescos for the influential Vespucci family in the Florentine church of All Saints. His *Madonna of Mercy* shows the Virgin Mary standing with arms and cloak outstretched to shelter the kneeling Vespucci family at her feet. A flair for portrait painting is seen in the striking individuality of the faces.

From 1475 to 1476 Ghirlandaio collaborated with his brother David on frescos for the Vatican Library in Rome. He made designs for painted busts of the church fathers and philosophers from classical antiquity. These incorporated rich decorative patterns based on classical ornamental detail. David probably did most of the painting. The brothers continued to collaborate on their return to Florence.

Ghirlandaio's first fresco cycle (his first series of frescoed scenes) was in the Saint Fina Chapel in the collegiate church of San Gimignano. The chapel itself had been designed by Giuliano da Maiano. Ghirlandaio made sure that the painted architecture and sculpture within and around his scenes fitted in perfectly. In the scene of Saint Fina's funeral Ghirlandaio had plenty of scope for portraits among the crowd of officials and townspeople gathered around her. The distinctive tall towers of San Gimignano formed a backdrop.

Ghirlandaio was summoned to Rome in 1481–82 to join Sandro Botticelli, Cosimo Rosselli, and Pietro Perugino, working on frescos in the Sistine Chapel. This prestigious project consisted of scenes from the lives of Christ and of Moses, and portraits of popes. Ghirlandaio was assigned two scenes from the life of Christ, but only one survives. In *Christ Calling Saints Peter and Andrew* (1481–82), the Sea of Galilee looks more like a view of the Tiber than the Middle East. On either side of the central group—Christ and his two new disciples—are prominent Florentines then living in Rome. These include Giovanni Tornabuoni, head of the Medici bank in Rome, who was to become one of Ghirlandaio's most important patrons.

On returning to Florence Ghirlandaio contributed to the fresco decoration of the Palazzo Vecchio, Florence's seat of government. He employed several assistants to carry out the work to his designs. He also began the fresco cycle in the Sassetti Chapel in Santa Trinità (the church of the Holy Trinity). Francesco Sassetti, a wealthy banker, required scenes from the life and miracles of Saint Francis. Ghirlandaio blended past and present successfully. His use of recognizable places and people would have brought the scenes vividly to life for contemporary Florentines.

Among the paintings he produced are *The Nativity*, an altarpiece for the Sassetti Chapel (1485) and two portraits, one of Giovanna Tornabuoni in 1488 and another entitled *An Old Man and Boy* (c1485), in which he conveyed the gentle relationship between grandfather and grandson as well as their contrasting appearances.

Tornabuoni commissioned Ghirlandaio to decorate his family chapel in the church of Santa Maria Novella in 1485. The large expanses of wall were to be covered in frescos with scenes from the lives of the Virgin Mary and Saint John the Baptist. Ghirlandaio's assistants included his brothers David and Benedetto, his eldest son Ridolfo, and possibly the young Michelangelo Buonarroti. The chapel, completed at the end of 1490, was Ghirlandaio's last major work and undoubtedly his masterpiece. No other artist gives such a lively insight into late 15th-century Florence and its eminent citizens.

Data file

Full name: Domenico Ghirlandaio

Nationality: Italian

Style: Renaissance

Dates: born 1448/49 in Florence, died 1494 in Florence

Key works:
- *Christ Calling Saints Peter and Andrew* 1481–82
- *The Confirmation of the Franciscan Rule* 1485
- *The Adoration of the Shepherds* 1485
- *An Old Man and Boy* c1485
- *The Birth of the Virgin Mary* 1485–90
- portrait of Giovanna Tornabuoni 1488

Things to look for:
- biblical stories depicted in 15th-century costume
- many contemporary portraits included in scenes
- decorative detail

Comparisons: Alesso Baldovinetti, Benozzo Gozzoli, Sandro Botticelli, Antonio and Piero Pollaiuolo, Andrea del Verrocchio

Glossary terms: cartoon, composition, fresco, silverpoint

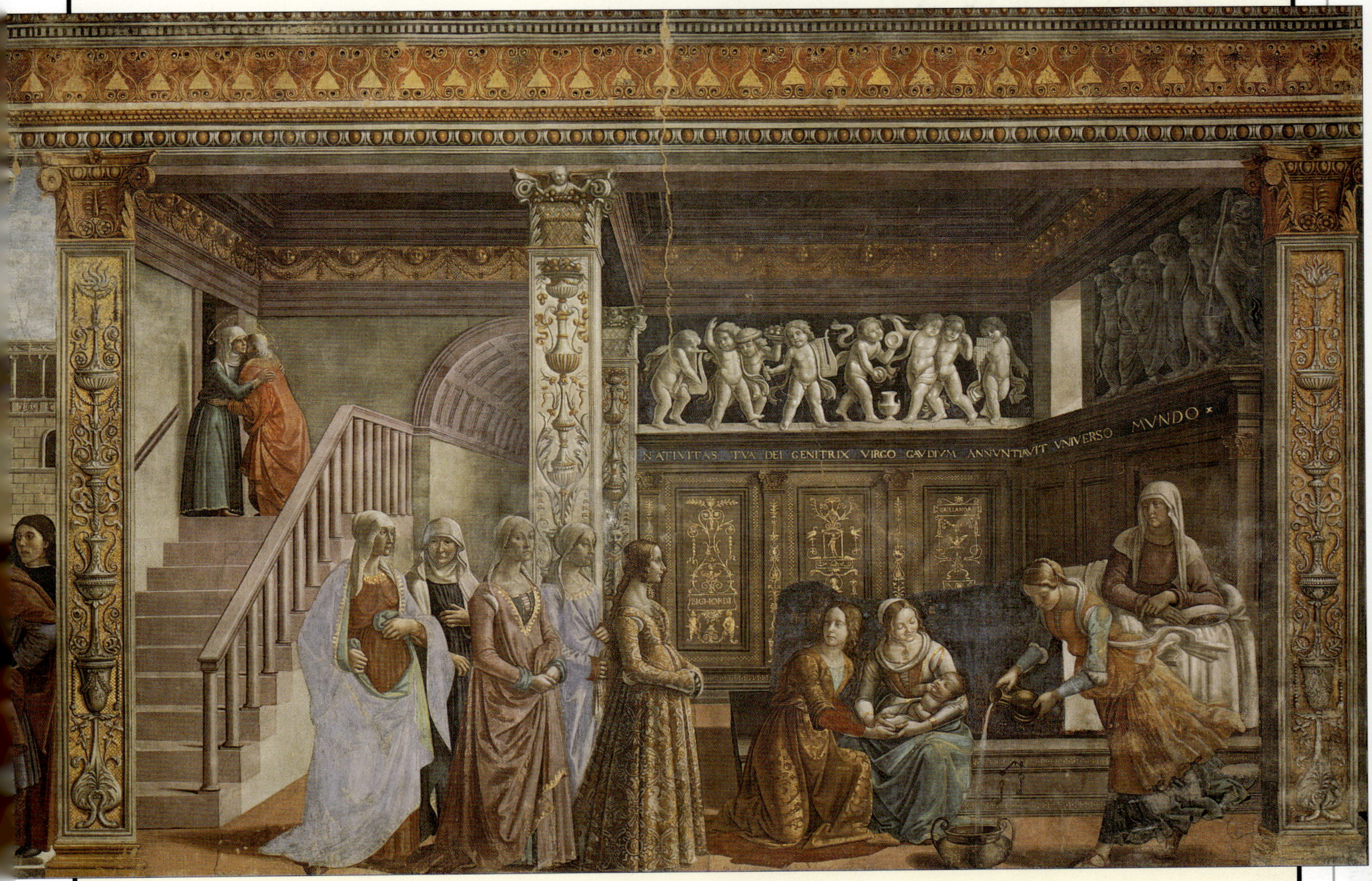

Historical themes, contemporary detail

Ghirlandaio's method of working followed the established practice of 15th-century Florentine artists, which included making numerous preparatory drawings. Many of these have survived, and they provide fascinating information about the various stages involved in designing his extensive fresco cycles. An excellent example is the scene of *The Birth of the Virgin Mary* (1485–90) in the Tornabuoni Chapel in the church of Santa Maria Novella.

The preliminary pen-and-ink sketch of the whole composition was used to establish the general character of the scene. It outlines the architectural features and perspective of the room and the people who will appear.

The drawing shows that from the outset Ghirlandaio planned to combine the scene of Mary's birth with an earlier one—the meeting at which Joachim and Anna share the news (brought to each of them by angels) that Mary will be born. Traditionally, Mary's father, Joachim, and mother, Anna, meet, share their visions, and embrace in the street, under Jerusalem's Golden Gate, but here the episode has been brought inside to occur at the top of the stairs. Interestingly, the three female visitors in the sketch became five in the finished scene, presumably at the request of Ghirlandaio's patron, Giovanni Tornabuoni.

Ghirlandaio made separate studies of some of the people in silverpoint, black chalk, or pen and ink. He used small sketches to work out positions and to record details of costume. He then drew portrait heads to the size required in the painting so that they could be used as cartoons to transfer specific facial characteristics accurately from paper to wall.

The Birth of the Virgin Mary *1485–90. Wall fresco. Church of Santa Maria Novella, Florence.*

Ghirlandaio also made a beautiful drawing of the girl pouring water on the right in the painting, in which he explored the angle of her movement and the playful folds of her dress. She provides a dynamic contrast to the stately female visitors led by Giovanni Tornabuoni's daughter.

The inclusion of Tornabuoni family members in the scene as well as its setting in a wealthy Florentine bedroom must have increased the immediacy of its impact for contemporaries. The use of gold and elaborate decoration, reflecting contemporary taste, added to its richness.

GIACOMETTI Alberto

FAMOUS BOTH AS A SCULPTOR AND A PAINTER, from the earliest days of his career this Swiss artist was profoundly interested in the human figure. He was also inspired by African art and artifacts, and by European surrealism. His late sculptures, representing tall, emaciated figures isolated in space, reflect the doubts and anxieties that were sweeping postwar Europe.

Life and work

Alberto Giacometti was born on the Swiss-Italian border in 1901, the son of the successful impressionist painter Giovanni Giacometti. At the age of 10 he was already actively drawing and painting, but later turned his attention to sculpture, the medium for which he has become best known.

In early 1922 Giacometti moved to Paris to study under the famous sculptor Emile-Antoine Bourdelle. Giacometti's early sculptures were inspired by the cubist works of Jacques Lipchitz and Henri Laurens. Like many of his contemporaries, however, he was also fascinated by the African sculptures he was able to see at the ethnographical museum in Paris. Many of Giacometti's early works borrowed the forms of African works and applied them to his own, frequently figurative works, as can be seen in *The Spoon Woman* (1926).

During the late 1920s, Giacometti met the surrealist artists André Masson and Max Ernst. Intrigued by their interest in the psychoanalyst Sigmund Freud's theories about dreams and the subconscious mind, Giacometti introduced dark themes of sexuality and violence into his work.

This perhaps reached its most controversial and disturbing level in his *Woman with Her Throat Cut* (1932). In this abstracted work, Giacometti emphasized sharp, spiky forms in the splayed limbs and rib-cage of a dying female figure, suggesting that a gruesome murder has taken place. At the same time, however, the long, thin limbs and bulbous torso are reminiscent of an insect. The suggestion of a metamorphosis, in which a creature appears to have changed from one form of being into another, was a common device of surrealist artists and one that Giacometti regularly used.

Throughout the first half of the 1930s Giacometti continued to produce works inspired by surrealism. In *The Palace at 4.00 AM* (1932–33), for example, he juxtaposed a strange assortment of unrelated objects—a female figure, a spinal column, a bird—all situated within the skeletal structure of a building. This accumulation of the weird and the wonderful is reminiscent of the experience of dreams in which seemingly unconnected objects or ideas come together.

By the mid-1930s Giacometti's interest in surrealism began to wane, and in 1935 he was officially expelled from the surrealist group. With the outbreak of war in 1939, he remained in Paris, but in 1942 returned to his native Switzerland to escape the Nazis. During this period Giacometti worked and reworked a series of small plaster figures. Some of them were just a few centimeters high.

After his return to Paris in 1945 he began to develop these figures into a series of tall, elongated, emaciated sculptures. Whether they are presented singly—as in *Walking Man II* (1960)—or in groups, these figures convey a sense of anonymity and isolation. In 1948 the French writer Jean-Paul Sartre described Giacometti's new works as existentialist. Sartre associated Giacometti's sculptures with his own literary and philosophical works, in which he tried to express the sense of anxiety, loss, and despair experienced by many in the wake of the war.

During this period, Giacometti also returned to painting and produced a number of works representing individuals such as the French writer Jean Genet. Interestingly, he created them in a similar fashion to his sculptures, building up and reworking the image until the surface was scarred and pitted with the artist's constant efforts. Giacometti's works in this way expose the long and arduous process of producing art, and reveal the artist's doubts and uncertainties. This doubt and uncertainty was an integral aspect of Giacometti's art.

Giacometti died in 1966 after developing stomach cancer. The paintings and sculptures he left behind reflect the changing moods, attitudes, and anxieties of the turbulent period of European history through which he lived and worked.

Data file

Full name: Alberto Giacometti

Nationality: Swiss

Style: surrealism/existentialism

Dates: born 1901 in Stampa, died 1966 in Chur

Key works:
- *The Spoon Woman* 1926
- *Suspended Ball* 1930–31
- *Woman with Her Throat Cut* 1932
- *The Palace at 4.00 AM* 1932–33
- *Head of Diego* 1954
- *Portrait of Jean Genet* 1955
- *Walking Man II* 1960

Things to look for:
- strangely juxtaposed objects and figures
- tall, thin, and emaciated sculptural figures
- scarred and pitted surfaces
- drawings and paintings with heavily incised lines and overworking

Comparisons: Jaques Lipchitz, Henri Laurens, André Masson, Max Ernst

Glossary terms: cubism, existentialism, surrealism

Isolation and anxiety in Giacometti's sculptures

The work entitled *Walking Man II* (1960) was one of a large number of figurative sculptures that Giacometti produced after World War II. The figure was built up by applying small pieces of plaster to a wire armature. When this process was complete the figure was cast in bronze.

A tall, more than life-sized figure stares straight ahead as it strides forward. The thin, almost skeletal body looks emaciated, while the scarred and pitted surface makes the figure appear both vulnerable and damaged. Furthermore, the heavy base of the work seems almost to imprison the individual, not allowing him to advance despite his obvious attempt to stride forward.

Walking Man II is a later version of a work originally produced in 1947, shortly after the end of the war. At this time, the gauntness and pathos of Giacometti's figures reminded contemporary viewers of the horror and destruction of the conflict through which they had just lived. In particular, the frailty and despair of Giacometti's isolated and anonymous figures inevitably recalled the tragic victims of Hitler's concentration camps. The shocking film footage of prisoners at the camps at the time of the liberation continued to haunt the world throughout the postwar period, and Giacometti's sculptures provided a sad evocation of the traumatic experiences of the war and its aftermath.

The original *Walking Man* was designed for a plaza in front of the Chase Manhattan Bank in New York. It was to be one of three Giacometti sculptures for the site. The other two were to be a standing female figure and a large bust. Giacometti produced numerous models but was dissatisfied with them, so they were never installed. *Walking Man II*, however, was cast in bronze as a separate work and is now in a museum in the Netherlands.

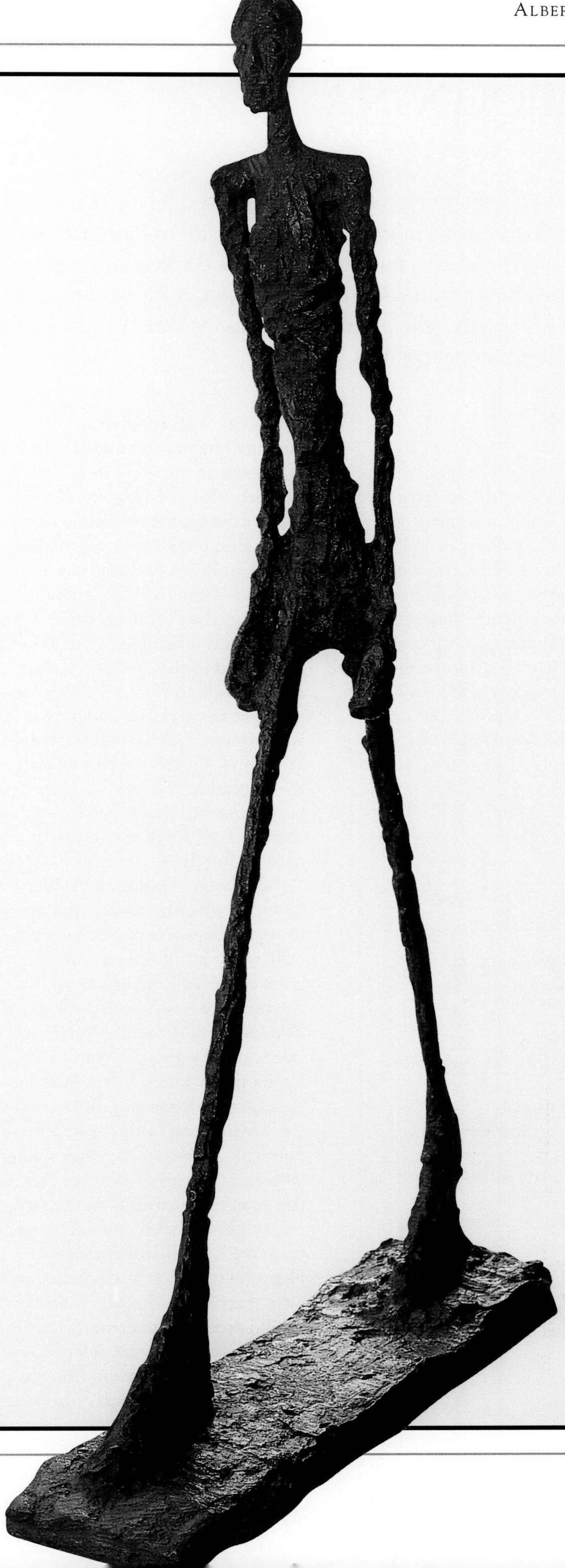

Walking Man II *1960. Bronze. 75 in (190 cm). Kröller-Müller Museum, Otterlo.*

GIAMBOLOGNA

ONE OF THE MOST INVENTIVE AND INFLUENTIAL mannerist sculptors, Giambologna spent most of his working life in Florence in the service of the great Medici family. His style was spread throughout Europe by the many young assistants employed in his workshop and by the bronze statuettes themselves, given as diplomatic gifts by the Medici to other European rulers.

Life and work

Giambologna is the shortened, Italianized version of the sculptor's real name Jean Boulogne. The artist was born in Douai in Flanders in 1529. During his training under the sculptor Jacques Dubroeucq, Giambologna mastered the techniques of carving and modeling. His apprenticeship complete, around 1550 Giambologna traveled to Rome to make models of Greco-Roman and Renaissance sculpture. But he became interested in Hellenistic sculptures, with their writhing, entwined figures in motion. The rebirth of interest in ancient Greek and Roman cultures during the Renaissance had encouraged early archaeology. Major discoveries of ancient Greek statues in Rome included the Laocoon (c50 BC), found in 1506 in Nero's palace on the Esquiline, while a group known as the Farnese Bull had been discovered in the Baths of Caracalla in 1546. While in Rome, Giambologna also met the greatest artist of the High Renaissance, Michelangelo Buonarroti. From him, Giambologna was to learn the important lesson of finalizing the basic poses of figures in sketch models (*bozzetti*) of clay or wax before considering the final finish.

On his way home to Flanders, Giambologna visited Florence in order to study the works of Michelangelo as well as the art of the city, which was a great center of Renaissance culture and the home of artists such as Giotto di Bondone, Fra Angelico, Sandro Botticelli, Andrea del Verrocchio, and Leonardo da Vinci. It was in Florence that Giambologna was introduced to the Medici, one of the most powerful political families of the time, and great patrons of the arts. They encouraged the young artist to stay in the city.

In Florence, Giambologna made his name with a full-scale model of Neptune (now lost), which he made for a competition to see which artist should produce the centerpiece for a fountain for the Piazza della Signoria. Although he did not win the competition, the success of his entry led Francesco de' Medici to commission him to carve *Samson Slaying a Philistine* (c1561–62), the first of Giambologna's group sculptures in marble.

In 1563 Giambologna was commissioned to make the bronze sculptures to decorate the Fountain of Neptune in Bologna. In this work he incorporated elements influenced by Hellenistic art and by Michelangelo. During his stay in Bologna, he also produced the first of his many versions of the "flying" figure of Mercury. The youthful, athletic figure of the winged messenger of the gods standing on tip-toe, with one hand pointing to the sky, appearing as if he is about to lift off the ground, is a technical and artistic tour de force. It is visually effective from every angle. Giambologna also solved the problem of balancing a freestanding figure supported only on a single point. By choosing a figure in flight as the theme—a motif that had previously only appeared in two-dimensional art—he broke away from the static forms of earlier works, and was to influence the development of sculpture well beyond his own period.

Once Giambologna had returned to Florence, Francesco de' Medici commissioned *Florence Triumphant over Pisa* (1575), a political allegory designed to accompany Michelangelo's sculpture, *Victory* (c1532–34). The third great marble group was *The Rape of a Sabine*, carved in about 1581, which was the climax of Giambologna's career as a figure sculptor. A masterpiece of immense energy and movement, this sculpture consists of three figures, extreme *contrappostos* (curving human figures with shoulders, hips, and legs in different planes), their limbs entwined in a fierce struggle.

Another major achievement was the bronze equestrian statue of Duke Cosimo I de' Medici (1595). The monarch mounted on horseback became the model for statues celebrating the achievements of nearly every ruler in Europe.

Data file

Full name: Jean Boulogne or Giovanni Bologna (known as Giambologna)

Nationality: Flemish

Style: mannerism

Dates: born 1529 in Douai (now in northern France), died 1608 in Florence, Italy

Key works:
- *Samson Slaying a Philistine* c1561–62
- *Fountain of Neptune*, Bologna 1563–66
- *Flying Mercury* c1565
- *The Rape of a Sabine* c1581
- equestrian statue of Cosimo I de' Medici 1595

Things to look for:
- exaggerated *contrapposto*
- compact compositions, often with twisting outlines
- arrangement of figure groups requiring more than one viewpoint
- compositions repeated in different sizes and materials

Comparisons: Michelangelo Buonarroti, Andrea del Verrocchio, Benvenuto Cellini

Glossary terms: *bozzetti, cire perdue, contrapposto,* Hellenistic, mannerism, Renaissance

Casting beauty in bronze

By 1561, Giambologna was in the service of the Medici family in Florence, and his workshop, staffed with a number of assistants, was busy producing a variety of sculptures in bronze and marble, both for private and public display. In addition to crucifixes and religious reliefs, the workshop also produced numerous small bronze statuettes which were designed to be displayed in the cabinets of private collectors. Popular designs included lions, bulls, horses, and birds—the latter were often designed as decorations for grottos (artificial caves), which were a popular feature of garden design at the time.

Sometimes bronzes were given by the Medici family as gifts to political allies across Europe. The Vienna *Venus after the Bath* is believed to have been presented by Cosimo I de' Medici to Emperor Maximilian II in 1565. Cosimo was in the process of arranging his son Francesco's marriage to the emperor's sister, the Archduchess Johanna, and no doubt the theme of the Roman goddess of love seemed most appropriate.

This bronze statuette of a woman bathing is regarded as an early work by Giambologna and is the only one of the Venuses to be signed. Other statuettes were often the work of his assistants, in particular Antonio Susini and Pierto Tacca. The goddess is shown here standing on a shallow base with her left foot resting on a pedestal. In her right hand she holds a towel which is in danger of slipping down across her legs, while with a cloth in her left hand, she dries herself.

The statuettes were made using the *cire perdue* ("lost wax") method of casting, so named because a layer of wax was melted off (or "lost") and molten bronze poured into its place. Once cooled, the rough bronze cast was returned from the foundry to the Giambologna workshop for finishing—hammering, chiseling, and filing the surface of the bronze. During busy periods in the workshop, Giambologna would delegate this part of the production to an assistant; the quality of the finish in such statuettes is a reflection of the involvement of the master in undertaking or supervising this stage.

Only one or two of the numerous bronze statuettes from Giambologna's studio are believed to have been finished by Giambologna himself. Even after his death, his assistants continued to produce copies of popular original models.

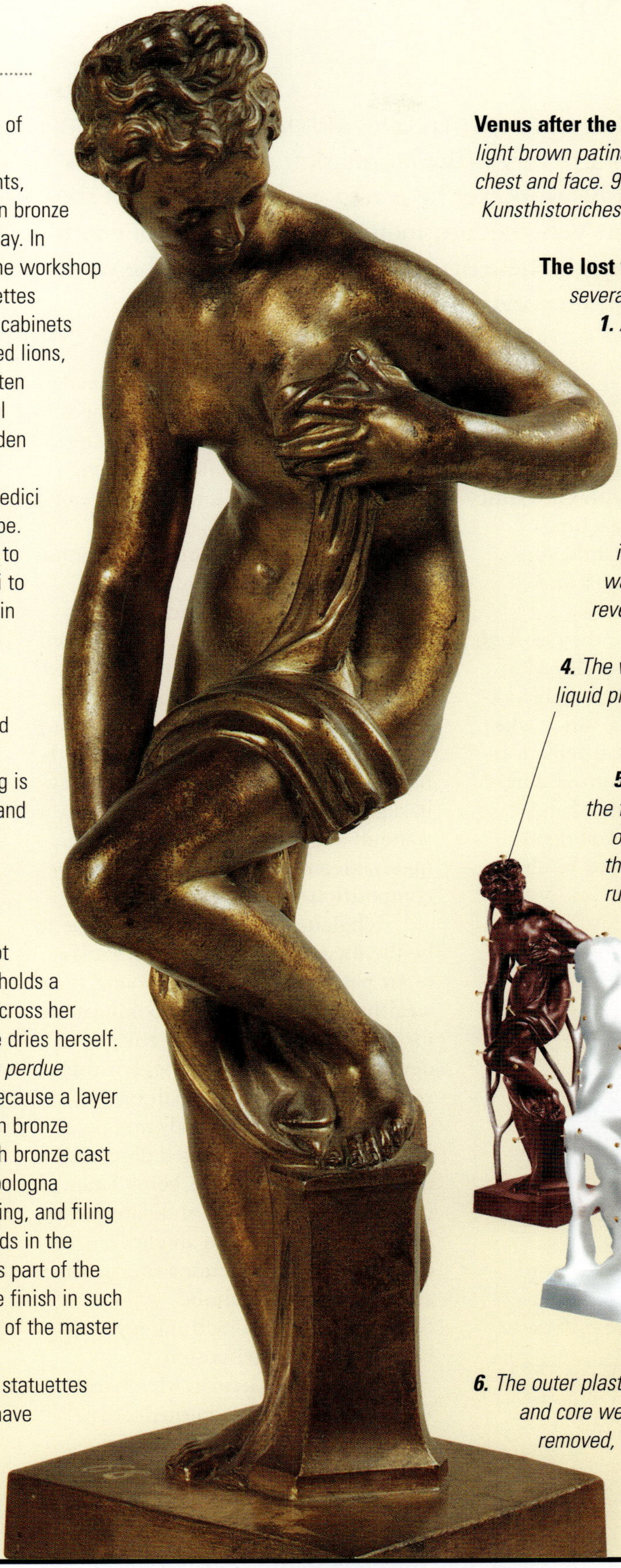

Venus after the Bath *1565. Bronze, with light brown patina and golden varnish on chest and face. 9¾ in (25 cm). Kunsthistoriches Museum, Vienna.*

The lost wax process *involved several stages.*
1. *A model was made, typically of clay.*
2. *A cast of this model was made.*
3. *The inside of the cast was coated with the wax to the thickness of the intended bronze. The cast was then removed to reveal a hollow wax figure.*

4. *The wax figure was filled with liquid plaster to form a core. Wax "runners" were attached.*

5. *Plaster was poured over the figure. When heated in an oven, the plaster dried and the wax ran out through the runners. Molten bronze was then poured into the plaster cast to replace the "lost" wax.*

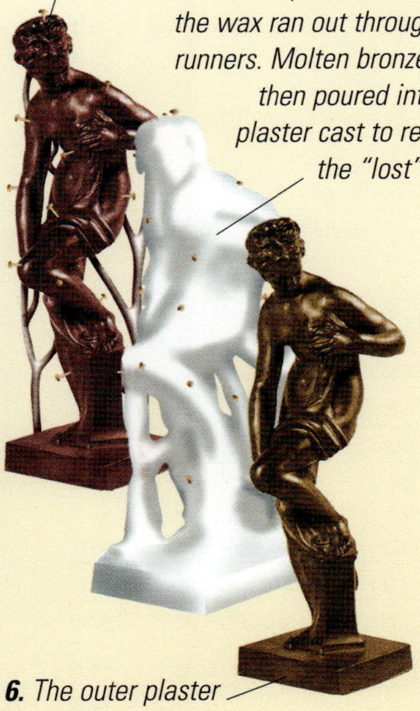

6. *The outer plaster and core were removed, and the runners sawn off before the finishing process.*

GIORGIONE

GIORGIONE IS ONE OF THE MOST ELUSIVE AND MYSTERIOUS ARTISTS in the history of art. Very little information remains about his relatively short life or his work, yet he is responsible for many of the greatest innovations in Venetian art, including his creation of poetic and evocative landscapes. These developments lived on in the work of his most famous contemporary, Titian.

Life and work

Giorgione is believed to have moved from his native town, Castelfranco, to Venice in 1488 to study with Giovanni Bellini, who had a large teaching workshop there. Bellini's landscapes were known for their breadth and harmony of color and the contemplative atmosphere they evoked, and these qualities were developed in Giorgione's work. Another possible influence was Leonardo da Vinci, who showed great interest in the depiction of landscape and natural surroundings in paintings, creating mystical and moody settings for his central figures. Giorgione's concerns grew to be almost the reverse—he used figures to populate his intense and emotional landscapes. Leonardo had also pioneered a softer way of painting nude flesh, *sfumato*, which appealed to Giorgione's love of subtle tones.

Giorgione painted many Madonnas at first. One of these Madonnas is thought to be the Castelfranco altarpiece, made around 1504 for a lord in Giorgione's native town. The seated Madonna, raised high upon her throne above the saint on either side, seems to be lost in a dreamlike daze as she holds her sleeping infant. This, and the hazy background landscape, lend the scene a tranquil and somewhat wistful mood, quite different from any contemporary compositions for an altarpiece.

Religious works did not continue to be the focus of his career. A new class of art patron was emerging: young, wealthy, and interested in looking at art for pleasure rather than for any devotional or moral purpose. For these collectors Giorgione specialized in small paintings with moody and poetic landscapes. He also painted portraits, perhaps the most famous being *Laura* (1506), his only signed and dated work. Even his portraits have an elusive quality; the sitters seeming to gaze in enigmatic or melancholic contemplation of something just beyond our comprehension.

In 1505 the German Merchant's Warehouse in Venice burned down. Along with Titian, Giorgione was commissioned to decorate the new building in fresco. Sadly, nothing of this scheme of classical nudes in intense colors remains. The Venetian climate does not support fresco painting; because of the humidity caused by the canals and lagoon, they slowly crumbled off the walls. In 1507 a commission for the Doge's Palace in

Data file

Full name: Zorzi da Castelfranco; Giorgio Barbarelli

Nationality: Italian

Style: Venetian 16th Century

Dates: born c1477 in Castelfranco, died 1510 in Venice

Key works:
- *Castelfranco Madonna* c1504
- *Laura* 1506
- *The Tempest* c1508
- *The Three Philosophers* 1508
- *Sleeping Venus* 1509–10

Things to look for:
- small-scale works with subjects and themes from mythology and secular literature
- importance given to the role of landscape
- creation of poetic and evocative mood whether in portraits or subject paintings

Comparisons: Giovanni Bellini, Leonardo da Vinci, Titian

Glossary terms: allegory, altarpiece, classical, devotional, fresco, *sfumato*

Mood and mystery

Giorgione's works often depict particular atmospheric or temporal conditions, such as sunsets and storms. *The Tempest* (c1508) is his most famous work and one of the few that are known for certain to be by him. It is typical of his style in that it is a small-scale work with an elusive and mysterious subject. Who is the woman with her child? Who is the soldier in the bottom left-hand corner of the painting? Are they part of an invented allegory? We do not know for certain. In fact, x-ray examination of the painting has shown that the soldier was originally a seated female nude. This radical alteration shows that neither the figures, nor the story they are telling, was the artist's central concern.

Although the breastfeeding woman could be taken to represent fertility and nature at its most tender and intimate, Giorgione is more interested in the landscape. Despite the fact that the woman looks out and catches our eye, we are led beyond her by the river, through the reflected light, into the shadow, and to the town and the tempestuous sky. The flash of lightning casts a strange luminosity over the landscape and we can visualize the stormy scene—humid, dark, and dramatic.

Giovanni Bellini, who almost certainly influenced Giorgione, would sketch every form before adding the color. Giorgione, however, did not use preparatory drawings, but painted directly onto canvas with color, using tone—the darkening or lightening of color and the smooth transition from one color to the next—to make his creations evolve. The figures, the buildings, and the natural world blend with one another in a way that was original at that time.

The Tempest *c1508. Oil on canvas. 31 1/4 x 28 3/4 in (79.5 x 73 cm). Galleria dell'Accademia, Venice.*

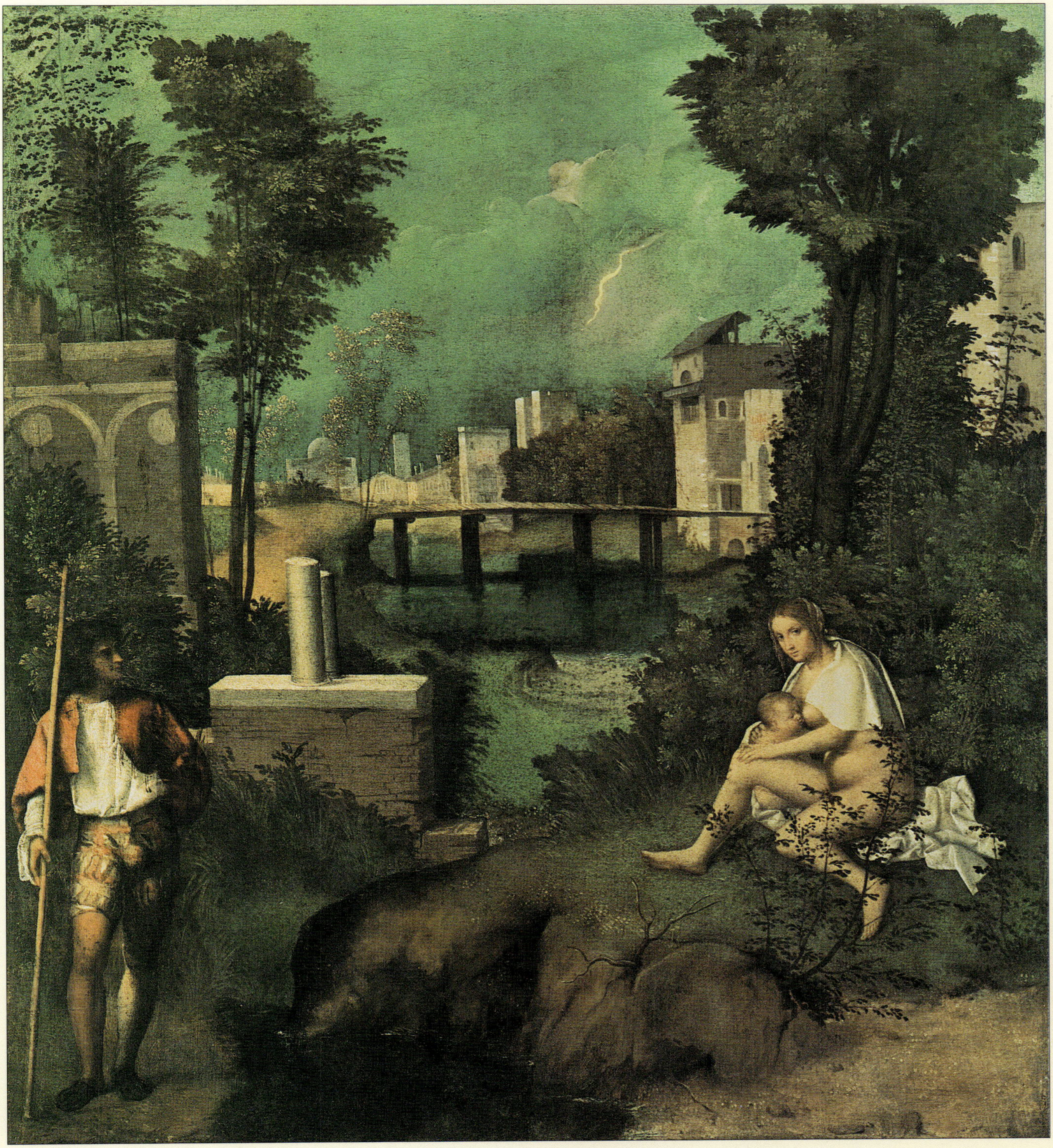

Venice is recorded, but again, the work perished, this time probably in a fire. In 1510 the plague swept through Venice and Giorgione fell victim to it. At the time of his death, although only 32 years old, Giorgione was the foremost painter in Venice, and his works were so sought after that a rich noblewoman collector, Isabella d'Este, recorded her dismay at the fact that none of his works was available for purchase. It was left to his close associate Titian to complete some of Giorgione's work, and to carry on his stylistic and compositional innovations.

GIOTTO di Bondone

GIOTTO IS USUALLY considered to be one of the most important artists of all time. Instead of producing flat, decorative works similar to those created by his predecessors, he made pictures that looked much more lifelike, real, and natural—and unlike anything that anyone had seen before.

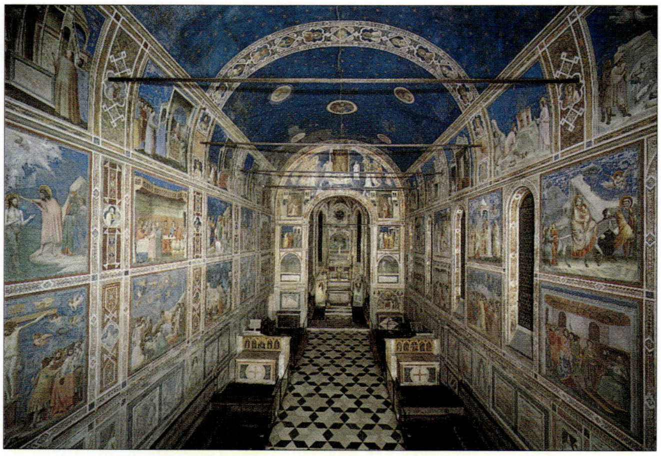

Arena Chapel
1303–06. The chapel was built for a wealthy merchant, and decorated by Giotto. Scenes from the life of the Virgin and the life of Christ adorn the upper walls, while the lower part is decorated with figures representing Virtues *and* Vices, *which are painted to look like marble statues.*

Life and work

Giotto's importance as a painter was recognized in his own time, as well as in the centuries after his death. He was mentioned in Dante's *The Divine Comedy* as having superseded his master, Cimabue. The painter and biographer Giorgio Vasari, who wrote about Giotto over 200 years later, has many stories to tell about him, though we do not know how many of them are true. He tells us that at the age of 10, Giotto had been sent to look after some sheep by his father. He was drawing a sheep from life on a stone, when Cimabue happened to pass by. Cimabue recognized the child's gift for drawing, and asked to take him to Florence as his pupil. Vasari also claims that Giotto once painted a fly on a person's nose in a drawing by Cimabue; the insect apparently looked so realistic that, when Giotto's master returned to his work, he tried to swat the fly away with his hand.

There are no surviving signed pieces by Giotto, so experts have spent many years trying to find out which paintings he worked on. He probably worked on the frescos in the Upper Church of San Francesco at Assisi; these were painted by several artists, including Cimabue, between about 1297 and 1305. The paintings show scenes from the life of Saint Francis.

Giotto almost certainly produced the frescos in the Arena Chapel (so-called because it is built on the site of a Roman arena) in Padua, because his work on them is mentioned in documents written at the time. The chapel was built between 1303 and 1306 for Enrico Scrovegni. Enrico's father had made his fortune by lending money to other people and charging them high rates of interest, and Enrico thought that if he spent a lot of money building a grand chapel, God might forgive his father his sins.

By this time Giotto would almost certainly have been the most eminent painter of the day. He was paid to decorate the walls of the Arena Chapel with 39 scenes from the life of the Virgin and the life of Christ. These are remarkable in the way they break with the Byzantine tradition of painting, showing the stories in a very sensitive, human, and naturalistic way that seems to be based on personal experience and observation. The lower parts of the chapel walls—the parts within reach of the congregation—were painted to look like marble, with imitation statues of seven *Virtues* along one side and seven *Vices* along the other side. Illusionistic painting like this was virtually unknown at the time.

He painted many other famous works, including the walls of two chapels in the Church of Santa Croce in Florence, and a very large painting on wood of *The Madonna Enthroned* (c1307). Although this is not signed, it is attributed to Giotto because it is so similar in style to his other works.

Giotto worked in Rome, and, from 1329 to 1333, in Naples, where he was Court Painter to the King of Anjou. All the work he did there is now lost, however. By 1334 he had returned to Florence, where he oversaw building works on the cathedral—he is often credited with the original design of the famous belltower (or *campanile*)—and on the town's fortifications.

Full name: Giotto di Bondone
Nationality: Italian
Style: early Renaissance
Dates: born 1266/67 in Florence, died 1337 in Florence
Key works:
- frescos in the Upper Church of San Francesco, Assisi c1297–1305
- frescos in the Arena Chapel, Padua 1303–06
- *The Madonna Enthroned* c1307
- frescos in the Church of Santa Croce, Florence c1312–28

Things to look for:
- solid, bulky-looking figures
- clear storytelling

Comparisons: Cimabue, Duccio di Buoninsegna
Glossary terms: Byzantine, fresco, illusionism

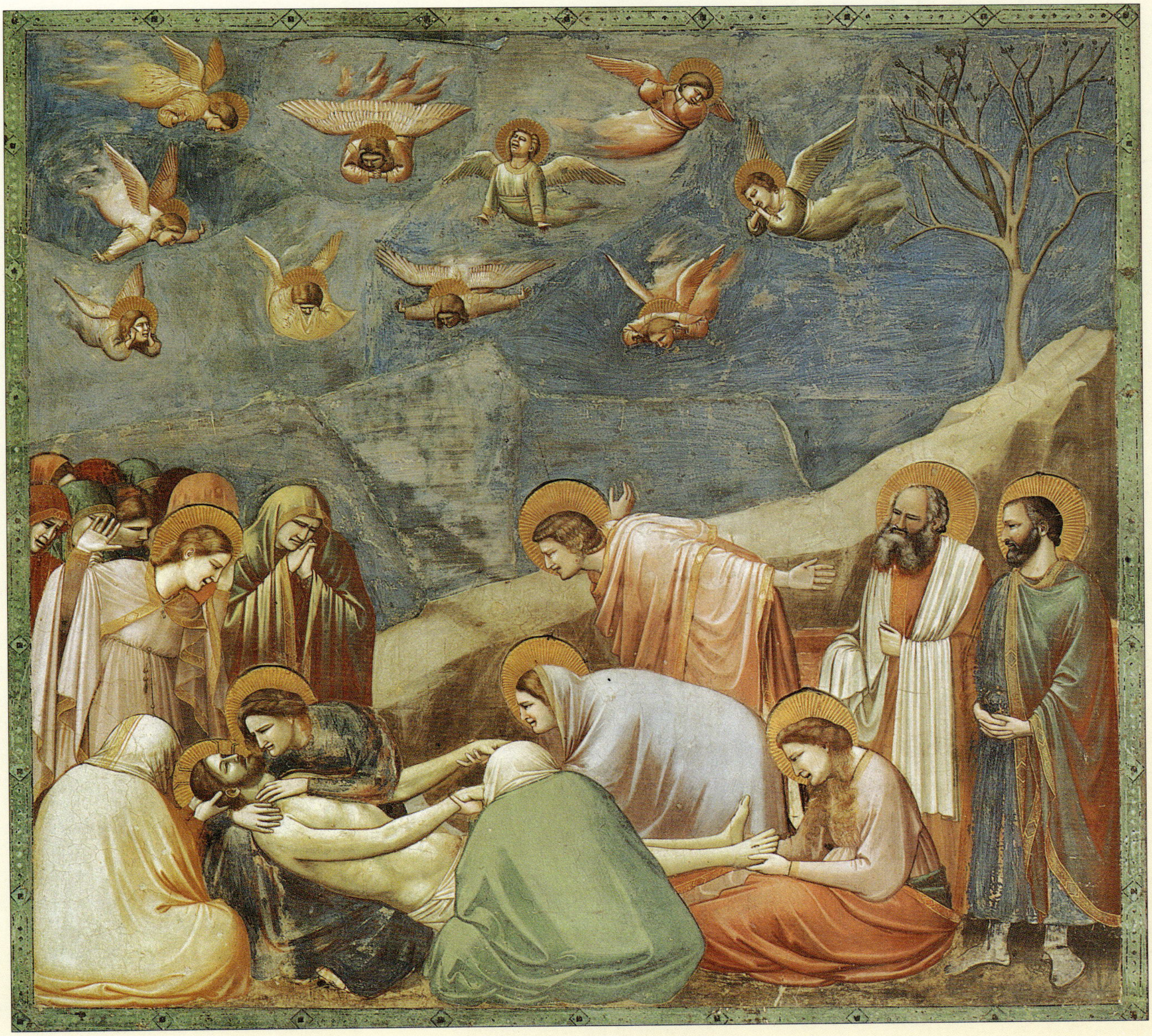

A lamentation

This is one of the scenes from the life of Christ. *Lamentation Over the Dead Christ* (1303–06) is one of the frescos on the upper walls of the Arena Chapel. The patches that now appear in the painting (particularly in the sky) are due to wear.

When viewed together, the pictures tell a story in a sequence of images; they were meant to be easy to "read" and understand. Giotto therefore chooses carefully what to include, and (very importantly) what to leave out. Every figure in his pictures is there for a reason, every gesture is important. Even the backgrounds, the buildings, or landscapes are designed to help make the story clearer.

This painting shows a group of people mourning, or lamenting, that Jesus is dead. (A picture of this subject is called a "lamentation.") This is one of the most expressive pictures in the chapel because the grief of the people has been so carefully observed. Some of the women gently cradle the rigid corpse, while others look on as if unable to believe what has happened.

The barren landscape is broken by a hill, which slopes down towards Christ's head, almost as if it is pointing us toward the most important part of the painting. In the sky 10 angels are wracked by every possible gesture of grief. The two figures who complete the circle around the dead body are particularly poignant. Hunched, and with their backs towards us, they give us a sense that we are outsiders, excluded from the scene; that we are onlookers witnessing the private grief of others.

Lamentation Over the Dead Christ
1303–06. Fresco. 78½ x 73 in (200 x 185 cm). Arena Chapel, Padua.

GIOVANNI di Paolo

GIOVANNI DI PAOLO WAS AN IMPORTANT ARTIST IN SIENA in the mid-15th century. His work paid little heed to innovations in art, such as the use of perspective and more accurate proportions, being introduced by artists in Florence at the time. Largely neglected by art historians until the 20th century, his paintings are intriguing for their distinctive, whimsical figures.

Life and work

Giovanni di Paolo (sometimes called Giovanni dal Poggio after the part of Siena where he lived) was one of the last practitioners of traditional medieval painting. Little is known of his life. Several small-scale religious paintings have been identified as showing his distinctive style, and his work in Siena is documented from 1426 to 1475. But few of his paintings are signed and dated, and the works that survive are often part of much larger pieces.

Like many artists of the time, Giovanni di Paolo mainly produced religious paintings such as altarpieces for churches. These were solid, heavy, wooden structures (usually of poplar), often consisting of several panels.

Giovanni di Paolo, with his near contemporary Sassetta (Stefano di Giovanni) was one of the leading painters of the Sienese school. The cities of Siena and Florence had long been rivals, and each developed its own distinctive style of painting. In the 15th century, Florentine artists developed a new realism in terms of how they depicted space and people in their paintings, and made references to works of art from the ancient Roman civilization centuries earlier. In Siena, artists looked back to their local, more recent predecessors, and used works by painters such as the Sienese artist Duccio di Buoninsegna as models. Giovanni di Paolo and Sassetta were aware of the innovations in Florence, but blended these with the traditions of their own city to produce distinctive, colorful, and lively paintings.

Giovanni di Paolo is known to have been working by 1417 and his earliest dated painting, *Madonna and Child with Angels*, was done in 1426. He produced his most important work in the 1450s, including the *Presentation of Christ in the Temple* altarpiece (1447–49) and an altarpiece depicting scenes from the life of Saint John the Baptist (c1453).

After his death Giovanni di Paolo was for many years rated as an inferior artist because his style was idiosyncratic. Many of the altarpieces have been broken up, and small parts are now to be found in museums and art galleries all over the world.

Data file

Full name: Giovanni di Paolo (also known as Giovanni dal Poggio)

Nationality: Italian

Style: late Gothic

Dates: born c1403 in Siena, died 1482 in Siena

Key works:

Madonna and Child with Angels 1426

Christ, Suffering and Triumphant 1426

Flight into Egypt c1436

Presentation of Christ in the Temple 1447–49

scenes from the life of Saint John the Baptist c1453

Assumption 1475

Things to look for:

- religious pictures, including miniatures
- a colorful, distinctive style with whimsical figures and odd angles

Comparisons: Duccio di Buoninsegna, Stefano Sassetta, Masaccio, Gentile da Fabriano

Glossary terms: altarpiece, Gothic, mannerism, perspective, *predella*

Scenes from the life of Saint John the Baptist

Many of Giovanni di Paolo's works feature the natural world and the landscape, with whimsical, distorted figures. *Saint John the Baptist Retiring to the Desert* (c1453) was part of the *predella* (lower part or platform) of an altarpiece containing scenes from the life of Saint John the Baptist, and probably would have stood in a chapel or church dedicated to the saint. The other pictures alongside it showed significant moments from the saint's life, including the birth of Saint John the Baptist, the Baptism of Christ (where the adult Saint John baptizes Christ in the River Jordan), and the feast of Herod (where the saint's decapitated head is presented to Herod on a plate).

Saint John the Baptist Retiring to the Desert illustrates Giovanni di Paolo's distinctive style and his skill in storytelling. The painting shows an extensive landscape: well-cultivated fields dotted with farmsteads in the foreground, a fearsome wilderness with great mountains clawing at the sky in the distance and, beyond that, a hazy blue horizon. On the left is a town complete with defensive walls and a gateway, and it is through this that Saint John strides as he leaves the protection of the civilized world to spend time on his own in the wilderness. He is dressed in a short pink robe, and carries a bundle on a stick over his shoulder.

Strangely, Saint John appears twice in the picture: once in the foreground as he leaves the town, and once again in the background as he enters the wilderness. If Giovanni di Paolo was obeying the newly devised rules of perspective, he would have painted the background figure considerably smaller than the foreground figure, to make him seem farther away. Similarly, the fields and the farmsteads close to us are much too small for their position in the picture.

This reflects the artist's choice to put the narrative function of the picture first. If the distant figure of Saint John were smaller, it would be obscured by the mountains, so the meaning of the story

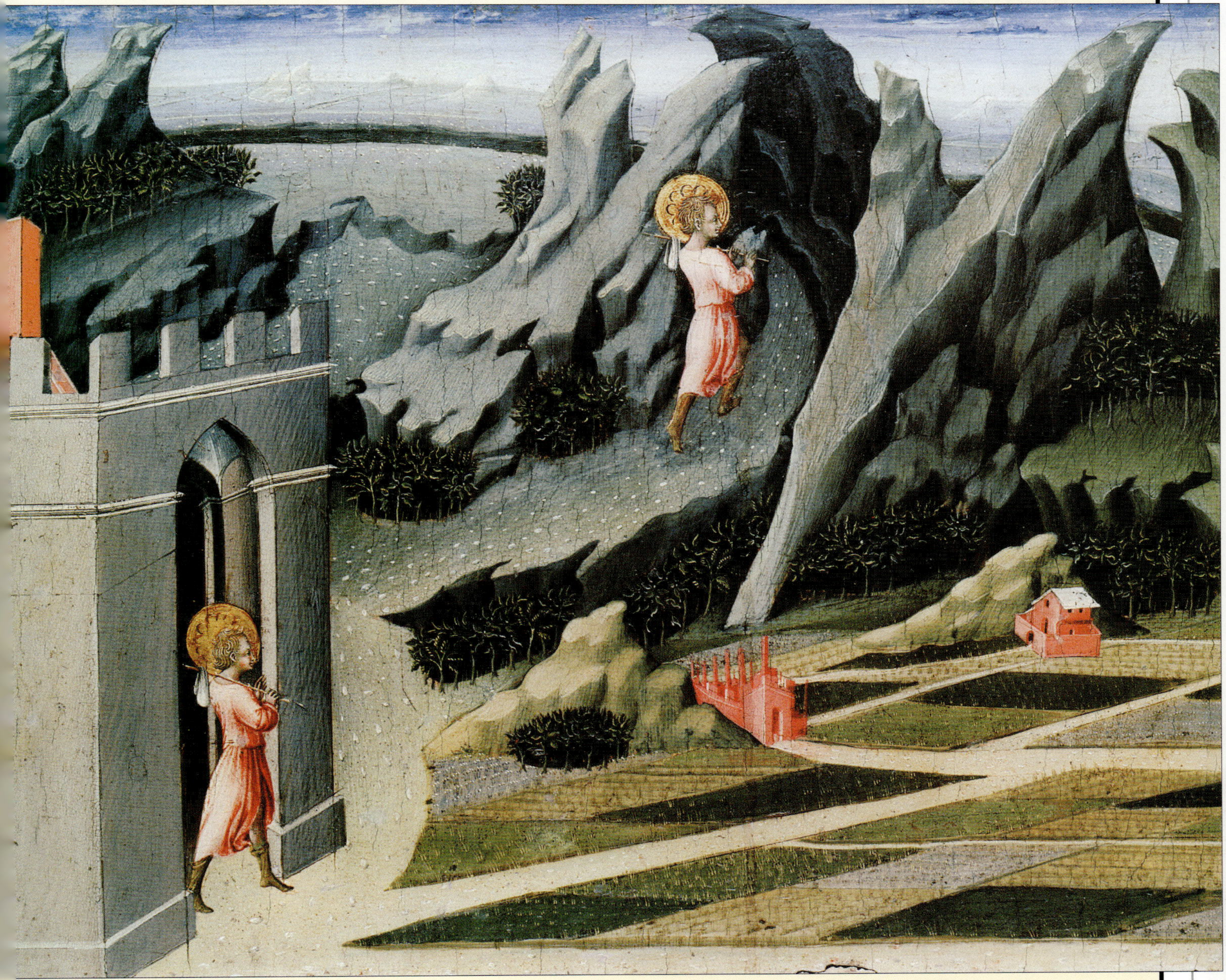

would not be so clear. Perspective was not Giovanni di Paolo's main concern; he wanted his pictures to tell the story clearly.

Giovanni di Paolo's style was regarded as old-fashioned; it was conservatively Gothic at a time when the trend among Tuscan painters was toward greater naturalism. However, from about 1920 Giovanni di Paolo's works aroused considerable interest, and were reassessed by some art critics as heralding the mannerist style of the 16th century, characterized by its bright colors and bold, exaggerated forms.

Saint John the Baptist Retiring to the Desert *c1453. Tempera on panel. 12 x 14 in (30.5 x 35.5 cm). National Gallery, London.*

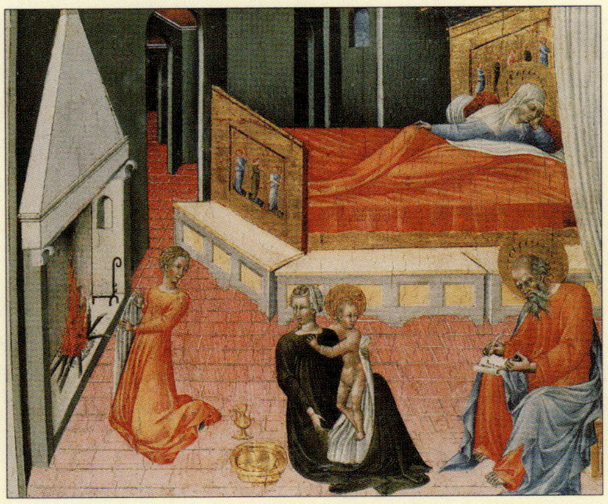

The Birth of Saint John the Baptist *c1453. Tempera on panel. 12 x 14 in (30.5 x 35.5 cm). National Gallery, London.*

GONCHAROVA Natalia

NATALIA GONCHAROVA WAS A MAJOR FIGURE in the early 20th-century Russian avant-garde, whose interest in Russian folk art contributed to the development of a neoprimitivist style. She left Russia in 1915, spending the rest of her career in Paris, where she contributed stage designs to Sergei Diaghilev's Ballets Russes.

Life and work

Natalia Goncharova was born into a prosperous family in provincial Russia. After leaving school she moved to Moscow to study sculpture, where she also met her life partner, the artist Mikhail Larionov. Having abandoned sculpture in favor of painting, Goncharova began exhibiting in Moscow in 1904. Two years later, she participated in Sergei Diaghilev's exhibition of Russian art in Paris.

Like many Russian artists at that time, Goncharova was fascinated by modern European art, particularly the work of Paul Cézanne, Paul Gauguin, and Henri Matisse, which could be seen in Russia in exhibitions and publications. Although she adopted the stylistic features of modern European painting, she was more interested in what inspired modern artists (not least the so-called "primitive" art forms). Goncharova was particularly fascinated by Russian folk art, icons, and popular prints (known as *lubki*). Indeed, she regularly used both icons and *lubki* as sources of inspiration for her own works, such as *Madonna and Child* (1905–07), *The Evangelists* (1910–11), and *Peasants* (1911). Goncharova's work in this style was soon dubbed "neoprimitivism."

In around 1912, together with Larionov, she also developed a new style of painting, known as "rayonism." In this colorful, linear style, objects are described through a series of intersecting lines crisscrossing their way across the surface of the painting. These lines, described as "reflected rays of light," break up the appearance of objects and thus become almost abstract. While rayonism was certainly a style that was unique to Goncharova and Larionov, it also recalled the work of the German artist Franz Marc.

Between 1912 and 1914 Goncharova was involved in a number of avant-garde activities. In 1913, for example, she took part in theatrical performances alongside Vladimir Mayakovsky, and even acted in a movie. Along with other members of the Russian futurist group, she also produced illustrations for experimental book publications. Like her fellow artists Kasimir Malevich and Vladimir Tatlin, she was aware of cubism in Paris, and introduced cubist techniques into her work. This can be seen in the canvas entitled *The Laundry* (1912), in which Goncharova uses the multiple viewpoint of the cubist still life while simultaneously introducing fragments of words to suggest the subject of the painting and to emphasize the flatness of the canvas. Goncharova and her

Data file

Full name: Natalia Sergeyevna Goncharova

Nationality: Russian

Style: cubism (cubofuturism/rayonism)

Dates: born 1881 in Ladyzhino, died 1962 in Paris, France

Key works:

- *Madonna and Child* 1905–07
- *Haycutting* 1910
- *The Evangelists* 1910–11
- *Peasants* 1911
- *The Laundry* 1912
- *The Green and Yellow Forest* 1912
- *Spanish Woman* 1920

Things to look for:

- motifs from Russian folk art
- simple drawing, with bold outlines
- broad, flat areas of strong color
- sharp, diagonal forms

Comparisons: Mikhail Larionov, Paul Gauguin, Franz Marc, Kasimir Malevich, Vladimir Tatlin

Glossary terms: avant-garde, cubofuturism, futurism, neoprimitivism, rayonism

Goncharova's version of folk art

Goncharova's large canvas entitled *Peasants* is part of a series of nine works representing grape harvesting that she produced in 1911. In this painting Goncharova presents two Russian peasants (identified as such by their beards and smocks) carrying an abundant harvest of grapes from the fields.

The monumental peasant figures dominate the image and are barely contained within the margins of the painting itself. In using such an approach Goncharova was making a stylistic reference to the popular prints, or *lubki*, that were attracting considerable attention in Russia at that time. These cheaply made prints were distributed throughout the countryside by peddlers and traveling salesmen. The *lubki's* outline drawing was typically crude and childlike, while color was roughly applied, either by hand or by a simple printing process, which often resulted in the colored area not matching its designated space accurately. During the late 19th century, Russian museums began to collect these *lubki* and to praise them for their "primitive," direct style. They were also regarded as displaying an authentically Russian style, in contrast to the abundance of European ideas and styles that had been introduced to Russia during the previous century.

Goncharova not only recognized this widespread interest in *lubki*, but also adopted some of the genre's stylistic features. The forms of her peasants are thus described by clear outlines, filled in with simple, flatly applied colors. There is no attempt to introduce perspective, as can be seen in the way in which the peasants' boots are depicted sideways, in profile, while their torsos are painted facing the viewer. Even the background is reduced to two simple areas (green for the ground and blue for the sky), divided by a low horizon.

In adopting the stylistic elements of the so-called "primitive" Russian *lubki*, Goncharova was attempting to develop a new, modern style of painting. By drawing her inspiration specifically from emblems of Russian folk art, however, she was also proclaiming the validity of Russian culture alongside that of the West.

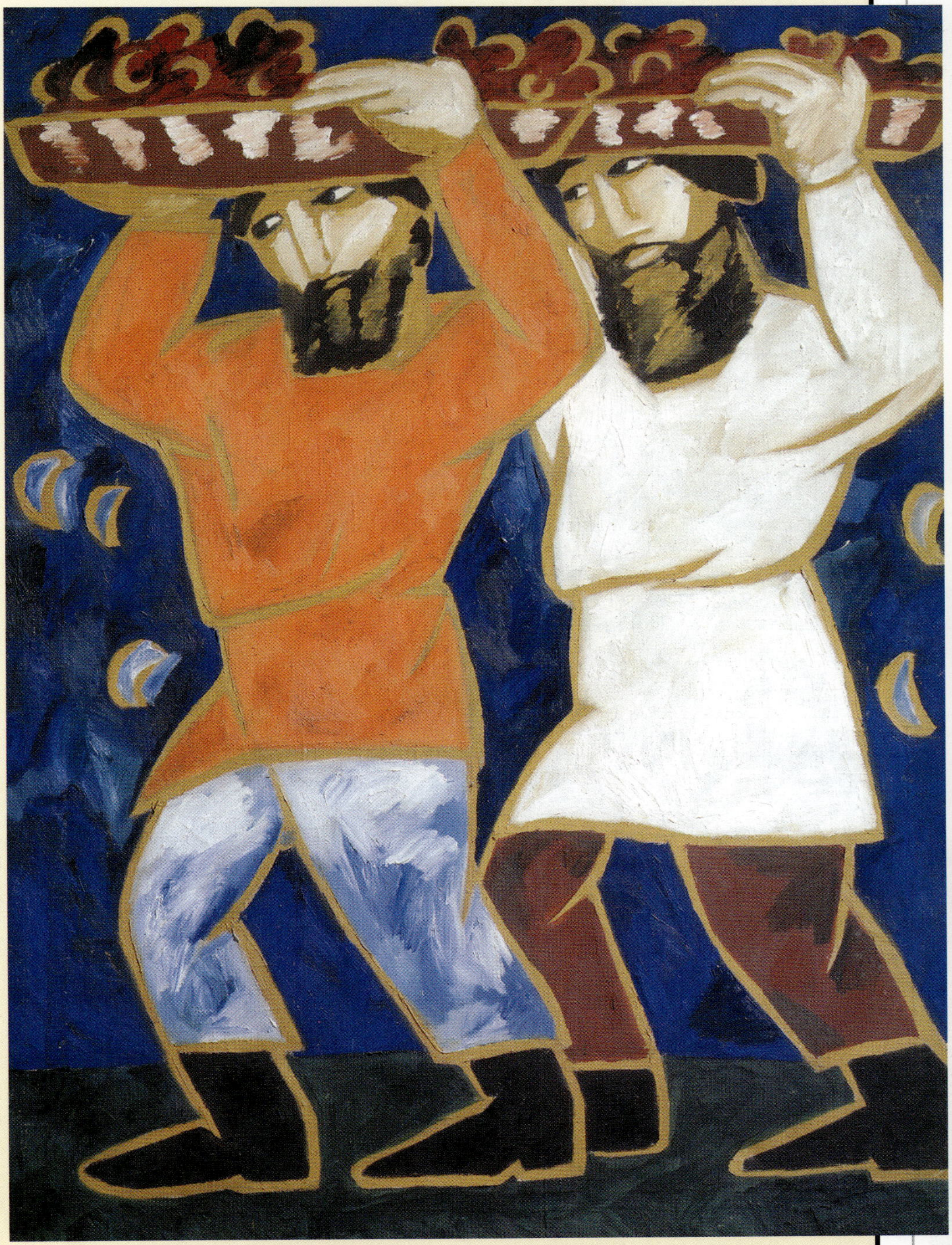

Peasants *1911. Oil on canvas. 51 1/2 x 39 1/2 in (131 x 100.5 cm). State Russian Museum, Saint Petersburg.*

Russian colleagues referred to their work as "cubofuturist," in order to distinguish it from its Parisian sources.

In 1914 Goncharova traveled to Paris to produce theatrical designs for the Ballets Russes. On the outbreak of World War I in 1914 she was forced to return to Russia, but in 1915, together with Larionov, she joined Diaghilev in Switzerland. Following the Russian Revolution of 1917 she settled in Paris.

After Diaghilev's death in 1929 Goncharova produced less and less work, although she continued to work as a painter and theatrical designer. Her best-known work of this period often represents women in Spanish costume, which had been a fascination of Goncharova's ever since her first trip to Spain in 1916.

Goncharova died in Paris, in poverty, in 1962. Her companion Larionov died two years later.

Despite having been exiled from her native Russia, Goncharova's reputation remains that of one of the most influential of Russian artists.

GORKY Arshile

VIRTUALLY SELF-TAUGHT, Arshile Gorky blended elements of cubism and surrealism to create a unique style of painting that anticipated abstract expressionism, making him a vital link between European avant-garde and modern American art. He began to develop his style first by imitating the artists he admired.

Life and work

In order to avoid conscription into the Turkish army, Gorky's father emigrated alone to the United States when his son was four. Gorky learned about art through his mother, who came from a family of priests who knew the sacred texts and art treasures of the churches and cathedrals of Armenia.

During the massacres of Turkish Armenians in World War I, Gorky's mother fled with her children to Russian Armenia. Two older sisters set off for the United States. Gorky, his younger sister, and their mother were supposed to join them later, but in 1919 his mother died of starvation.

In 1920 the 16-year-old Gorky made his own way to New York and joined his father in Providence, Rhode Island. He had a year of junior high school; his father, not believing the boy could make a living as an artist, encouraged him to take a factory job.

In 1922, however, Gorky enrolled at the New School of Design in Boston. There his skills were recognized, and he became a part-time instructor. His paintings from this period show the influence of impressionism. After a move to New York, a postimpressionist phase, influenced by Paul Cézanne, resulted in paintings such as *Landscape in the Manner of Cézanne* (1927) and *Landscape, Staten Island* (1927–28).

Late in the 1920s Gorky began experimenting with cubism, in still lifes and in self-portraits. Then he became interested in surrealism. His most complex work from the 1930s is a series entitled *Nighttime, Enigma, Nostalgia* (1930–34). Using a variety of media, including pen and ink on paper, and pencil and oil on canvas, he did 13 versions, as well as mural studies. Each is based on the same composition and imagery: a tabletop, on which he placed a number of abstract, organic forms. The fluid lines and curving shapes suggest the influence of Pablo Picasso and the surrealists Joan Miró and Max Ernst. The series won Gorky public attention. A work based on it, *Painting* (1936–37), was acquired by the Whitney Museum of American Art in New York.

His work now appeared in several exhibitions. Like many artists during the Depression, he often went without food in order to buy paints. In 1933 he joined the Public Works of Art Project. Two years later, he joined the mural division of the Federal Arts Project, and designed 10 large panels based on air travel. These were installed in 1937 in the Newark Airport Administration Building in New Jersey, but disappeared during World War II—the building was under military control and the panels were painted over. During restoration in 1972, only two could be recovered.

By the end of the 1930s, after more than 15 years as a professional artist, Gorky's work finally began to demonstrate his own unique style. New experiences played a part: for the first time since he had arrived in the United States he began to explore outside New York; and, after 15 years of living alone, he married Agnes Magruder in 1941.

A cross-country trip to California, and vacations in Virginia reawakened an interest in landscapes. Encouraged by his friend, the Chilean artist Matta Echaurren, Gorky painted in a more fluid style. His pigments were greatly diluted and accidental drips, runs, and splashes of paint were exploited for their painterly qualities. In this, his mature style, Gorky anticipated the abstract expressionism of Jackson Pollock and Willem de Kooning.

In 1945 a fire in his studio destroyed about 30 of Gorky's paintings. In 1946 he had surgery for cancer, and in June 1948 broke his neck in a car crash that left him paralyzed for several months and in constant pain. Shortly afterward his wife left him. In despair, Gorky hanged himself in his studio, aged 44.

Data file

Full name: Vosdonik Manuk Adoian (known as Arshile Gorky)

Nationality: Armenian American

Style: abstraction

Dates: born 1904 in Khorkom Vari, Armenia, died 1948 in Sherman, CT, United States

Key works:
- *Landscape in the Manner of Cézanne* 1927
- *Landscape, Staten Island* 1927–28
- *The Artist and His Mother* c1926–34
- *Abstraction with Palette* c1930
- *The Pirate I* 1942
- *Waterfall* 1943
- *The Liver Is the Cock's Comb* 1944
- *The Plow and the Song* 1947

Things to look for:
- images flat on the surface of the canvas
- abstract forms suggesting living organisms
- early works with smooth surfaces
- cubist-influenced works with pigments applied in layers up to half an inch thick
- in later works, pigments that become translucent color stains
- thin, clear lines in black pigment produced by a long, pointed signwriter's brush

Comparisons: Paul Cézanne, Joan Miró, Pablo Picasso, Jackson Pollock, Willem de Kooning, Wassily Kandinsky, Max Ernst, Matta Echaurren

Glossary terms: abstract expressionism, abstraction, avant-garde, biomorphic, collage, cubism, impasto, impressionism, mural, organic, postimpressionism, surrealism

Painting from within

Despite the abstract appearance of his paintings, Gorky always considered himself to be a "traditional" painter. The techniques he used—even though they changed across time—were always based on those of the European masters.

In the early 1920s, Gorky's works were mainly small in size. Like Cézanne, who was a major influence on him at this time, he used a palette knife and brush to build up his pigments into solid forms on the surface of the canvas.

From about 1926–34 a series of portraits and self-portraits culminated in two huge canvases, both called *The Artist and His Mother.* In one of them, acquired by the Whitney Museum, Gorky used a technique that produced a smooth, polished surface with few traces of brushstrokes. Between applications of paint, he would scrape away the surface with a razor blade and wipe off the excess paint with a damp cloth.

In his cubist-inspired paintings of the 1930s, Gorky continued the process of layering paint, but instead of scraping it away, he now allowed the paint to build up into thick impasto. Yet despite his obvious interest in synthetic cubism—the movement that introduced collage into fine art—Gorky made only one known collage himself. He also made very few mixed-media works and sculptures.

Gorky was influenced by the surrealist Joan Miró's biomorphic forms and Wassily Kandinsky's "improvisations" (created in 1912–13 but seen for the first time by Gorky at the Guggenheim Museum when it opened in 1939). Another influence were his friend Matta Echaurren's "inscapes"—paintings that equated the human body with landscape, and merged images seen in the real world with those of the imagination.

As Gorky's own personal style began to emerge, pigments became thinner; line and color became more pronounced. *Waterfall* (1943) demonstrates Gorky's approach. Here, turpentine has been mixed with oil colors to produce thin, gauzelike stains that are both absorbed into the canvas and appear to float above its surface. As well as a change in style, *Waterfall* also demonstrates a thematic change in Gorky's work. This change took place during a vacation at his friend Saul Schary's home in Connecticut. There the surrounding landscape stimulated Gorky to draw and paint directly from nature. *Waterfall* is said to have been inspired by a real waterfall on the Housatonic River in Roxbury. But Gorky is not presenting a specific waterfall at a specific time. Instead the painting is about "what a waterfall is." Gorky said: "I do not paint in front of, but from within nature."

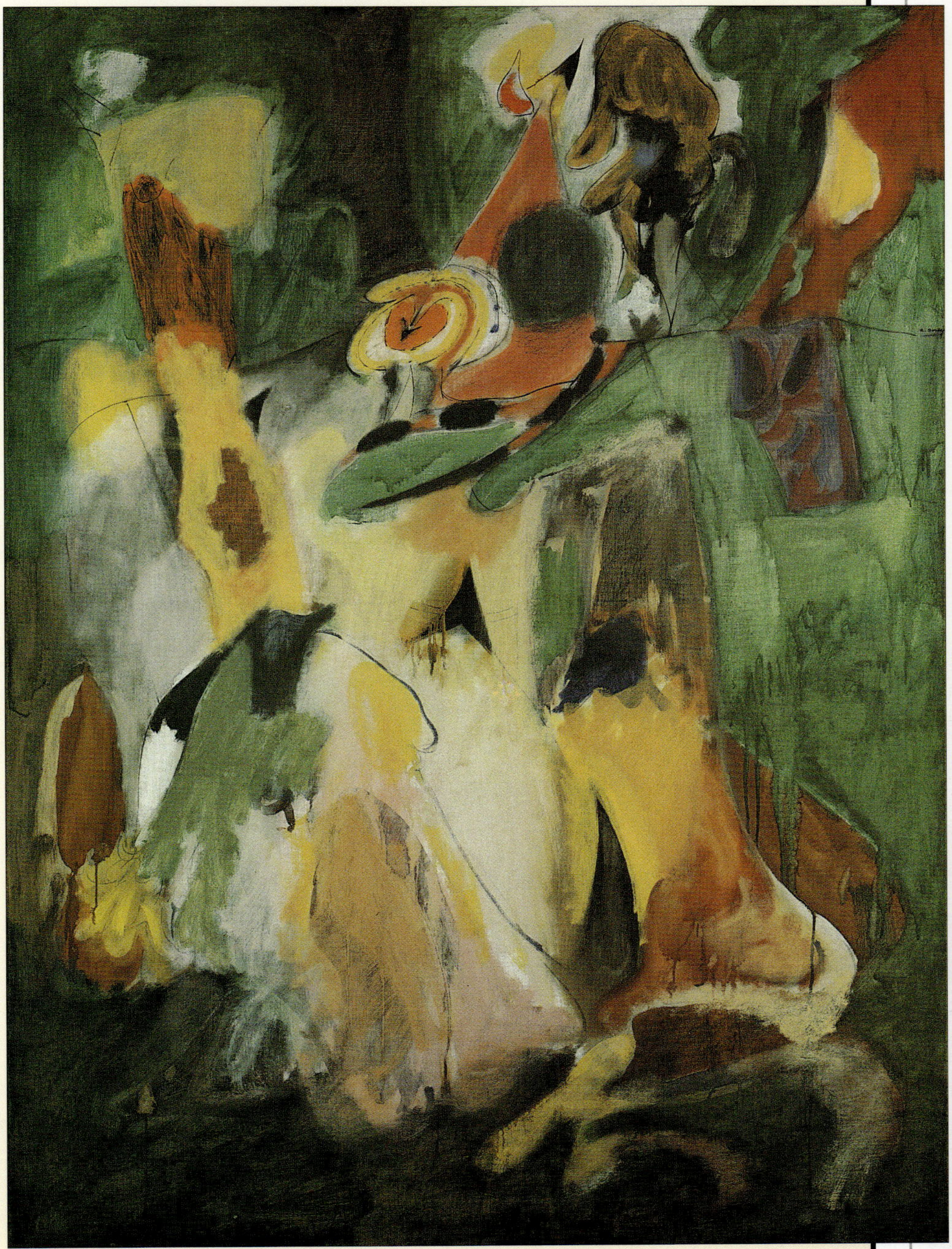

Waterfall *1943. Oil on canvas. 61 x 44 1/2 in (154 x 113 cm). Tate Gallery, London.*

The colors range from dark green, yellow, orange, and red, to cool, tinted whites. The loose brushstrokes and thin pigments run into each other, creating a sense of cascading water. Lines appear and disappear, suggesting the rocks that would themselves appear, disappear, and reappear under the flow of water.

GOYA Francisco

GOYA WAS AN ARTIST OF EXTREMES. He created glowing portraits of members of the late 18th-century Spanish court, and colorful tapestry designs. He also produced horrifying records of wartime atrocities, and nightmarish imaginings. No other artist has suggested so powerfully the thin line that separated the Enlightenment world of reason and its dark opposite of madness and violence.

Life and work

Francisco Goya was born in 1746 in the region of Aragon, eastern Spain. His father was a master gilder, who applied gold leaf to picture frames and furniture. In 1774 the family moved to the city of Saragossa. There Goya studied with the painter José Luzán Martínez, mainly copying engravings, a practice that might have sparked Goya's lifelong interest in printmaking.

In 1770 Goya traveled to Rome to paint and study. In Italy he won second place in a competition at the Parma Academy for a history painting of Hannibal; the prize gave him confidence as a serious professional artist.

Returning to Saragossa, in 1773 Goya married Josefa Bayeu, the sister of Francisco, Manuel, and Ramón Bayeu, who had studied with him at Luzán's academy. In 1774, aged 28, Goya went to Madrid, where, under the direction of his brother-in-law Francisco, he produced designs for the Royal Tapestry Factory. These designs, or cartoons, were large-scale oil paintings from which the weavers took the images for their tapestries. They included hunting scenes, and scenes of amusements and celebrations, such as *The Picnic* (1776).

In the late 1770s, Goya began to make prints of works by the 17th-century Spanish artist Diego Velázquez, as well as original etchings. In the 1780s he undertook several important religious commissions. At the same time, he was becoming sought-after as a portraitist; his eminent patrons included the Duke of Altamira, whose five-year-old son, dressed in red, is the subject of one of the most memorable child portraits ever painted.

In 1789, now in his early forties, Goya became Court Painter to the new king, Charles IV. Around the same time he experienced an unexplained illness that left him completely deaf. While recuperating, he began to experiment with "fantasy" pictures that developed into an extraordinary series of prints, *Los Caprichos* (1799). Created through a striking combination of the etching and aquatint methods, these images show a world of gross human folly. Particular targets for Goya's satire included the Catholic Church, attitudes to sexuality, and pretentions.

By the age of 50, Goya had reached the heights of his profession: in 1800–01 he painted *The Family of Charles IV*, his most celebrated group portrait, which portrays the family members in an incisive, even unflattering way. In the background, Goya can be seen at his easel.

In 1808 Napoleon Bonaparte of France invaded Spain, crowning his brother Joseph as king. Goya remained the chief Court Painter, but at the same time produced a disturbing visual record of the horrors of the French occupation. His print series, *The Disasters of War* (1810–13), contains enduring images of the casual brutality brought about by war. It was not published until long after his death.

In 1812 Goya's wife, Josefa, died. In the same year the Duke of Wellington, commander of the British army, sent to help liberate Spain from Napoleon, entered Madrid. In 1814, under the restored Spanish king, Ferdinand VII, Goya painted two of his most famous works, *The Second of May, 1808* and *The Third of May, 1808*, which show inhabitants of Madrid resisting the French invasion and, the next night, being executed by their conquerors.

From the age of about 70, Goya retired from public life, living in the Quinta del Sordo ("House of the Deaf Man") outside Madrid. He decorated the interior with 14 large wall paintings (the so-called "Black Paintings") containing some of his most terrifying images, such as *Saturn Devouring One of His Sons* (1820–23).

Caught up in the conflict between the old monarchy and new liberals, in 1824 Goya left Spain for France. He continued to paint and produce prints, and was even granted a full pension after resigning as Court Painter in 1826. Two years later, in 1828, he died in his adopted home of Bordeaux.

Data file

Full name: Francisco José de Goya y Lucientes

Nationality: Spanish

Style: early Romanticism and realism

Dates: born 1746 in Fuendetodos, died 1828 in Bordeaux, France

Key works:
- *The Picnic* 1776
- *The Naked Maja* c1798–1800
- *The Clothed Maja* c1798–1805
- *Los Caprichos* (series of prints) 1799
- *The Family of Charles IV* 1800–01
- *The Colossus* c1812–16
- *Saturn Devouring One of His Sons* 1820–23

Things to look for:
- highly perceptive portraits of Spanish ruling class
- contrasts between glowing color and shadow
- powerful satirical images
- preoccupation with world of fantasy and nightmare

Comparisons: Rembrandt, Diego Velázquez, Joshua Reynolds, Edouard Manet, Pablo Picasso

Glossary terms: aquatint, cartoons, engravings, Enlightenment, etchings, realism, Romanticism

Glowing portraits and nightmare visions

No one knows for certain the identity of the woman in *The Clothed Maja*, which Goya painted around 1798–1805. There is no evidence to support the story that she represents Goya's patron and lover, the Duchess of Alba—at that time one of the most influential women in Spain—whom Goya depicted in grand, formal portraits and many ink drawings.

The word "*maja*" meant a type of young woman of the lower classes who had a certain colorful style and personal freedom (the male equivalent was *majo*). These women had a definite "street credibility" that middle-class and aristocratic women admired and imitated. In Goya's painting, the maja wears Turkish costume, which was highly fashionable at the time.

The strong artificial lighting of the figure against a plain, dark background is typical of Goya's portraits. The increasing freedom of his brushwork at this stage in his career can be seen in the dabs of black paint on the maja's short sleeves and the sweeping brushstrokes that form her dress and sash.

The painting belonged to Manuel Godoy, a powerful and unpopular political figure, and one of Goya's leading patrons. He also owned its companion piece, *The Naked Maja* (c1798–1800), which shows the same model in an identical pose, but unclothed. Images of the naked human body were banned by the Spanish Inquisition, which was set up to ensure people conformed with the teachings of the Spanish Catholic Church. In 1815 *The Naked Maja* led to Goya's being interrogated by the tribunal of the Inquisition, although he seems not to have been punished further.

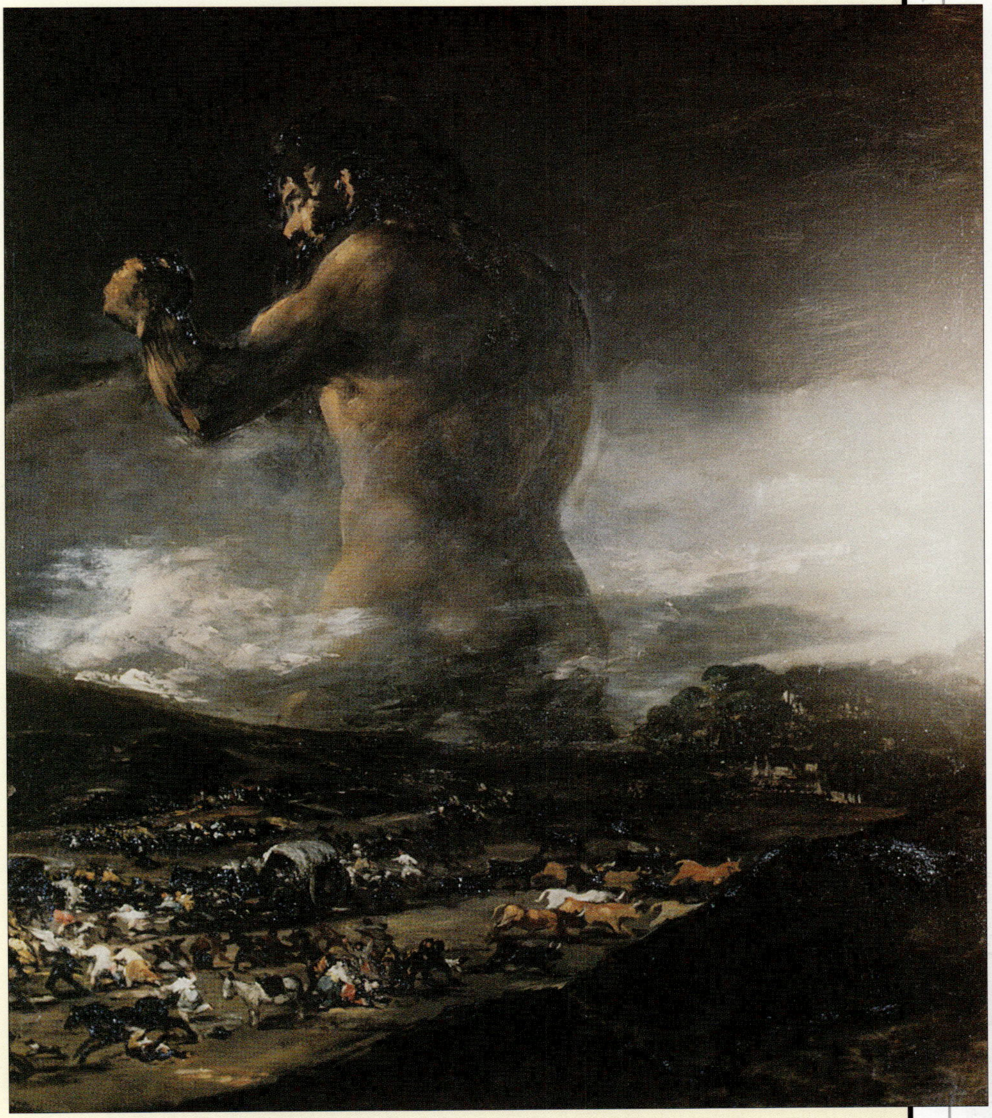

The Colossus *c1812–16. Oil on canvas. 46 x 41 in (116 x 105 cm). Museo del Prado, Madrid.*

The Colossus (c1812–16) is a very different work. It shows a valley landscape, seen from above, through which people and animals are fleeing in terror. Although they are only sketchily painted against the dark, threatening background, there is a strong sense of panic in the picture. The landscape is dominated by a giant male figure, who either could be striding away or about to turn and pounce. Compared to the tiny figures below, his size is overwhelming.

Painted at the time of the French occupation of Spain (1808–14), this image conveys the total helplessness of people in the shadow of war. While Goya must have witnessed scenes of flight like this, the giant is a nightmare fantasy figure, a combination of the fairytale ogre and the giants and gods of Greek myth.

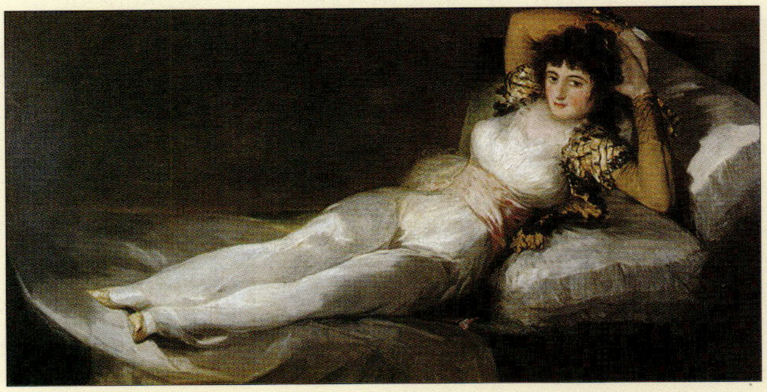

The Clothed Maja *c1798–1805. Oil on canvas. 38½ x 75¼ in (95 x 188 cm). Museo del Prado, Madrid.*

GOZZOLI Benozzo

BENOZZO GOZZOLI ENJOYED A LONG AND SUCCESSFUL CAREER as a painter of frescos, working on projects for eminent people throughout central Italy. His most famous paintings now are the colorful, crowded scenes of *The Procession of the Magi* (1459–61) in the Medici-Riccardi Palace in Florence.

Life and work

Benozzo Gozzoli probably trained with Fra Angelico in Florence. From 1445 to 1447 he worked on Lorenzo Ghiberti's Gates of Paradise in Florence. Then, in 1447, he was Fra Angelico's chief assistant on the decoration of the chapel of Pope Nicholas V in the Vatican Palace, Rome.

These were key experiences in Gozzoli's development. In particular, they taught him how to compose narrative scenes. They also stimulated his interest in architecture and decorative ornamental detail. He adopted Fra Angelico's style of painting people and reused similar poses and gestures throughout his own work.

Gozzoli's first independent projects were in the Umbrian town of Montefalco. These included, in 1452, the fresco cycle of 12 scenes from the life of Saint Francis in the church of Saint Francis. He used architecture and landscape to enhance the dramatic action of each scene and also ensured that the painted light and shadow corresponded with the fall of natural light from the chapel window. This—together with the predominant pale greens, pinks, and whites—contributed to the vividness of the whole cycle.

He painted frescos and altarpieces in Viterbo, Perugia, and Rome before returning to Florence in 1459. There he worked in the private chapel of the Medici-Riccardi Palace on frescos of *The Procession of the Magi* (1459–61). Three walls are covered by separate processions of the magi, which wind through rocky yet lush landscapes toward the fourth wall, painted with a paradise garden and rows of kneeling angels who look toward the altarpiece by Filippo Lippi.

In 1461 Gozzoli painted an altarpiece of the *Virgin and Child Enthroned with Saints and Angels* (the "Purification" altarpiece) in the Florentine convent of Saint Mark's. The contract stipulated Fra Angelico's high altarpiece for Saint Mark's as a model, which Gozzoli followed rather loosely. He enjoyed greater freedom and invention in the small-scale stories of the saints in the *predella* panel below.

Gozzoli's next significant work was in the Tuscan hilltop town of San Gimignano. Here, beginning in 1463, he painted a fresco cycle of 17 scenes illustrating the life of Saint Augustine in the church of Saint Augustine. The compositions are more elaborate than his earlier Franciscan scenes, with richly ornamented architecture framing each episode. Scenes set in landscape strongly echo the character of the Medici Chapel frescos, especially the procession of Augustine leaving Rome for Milan. He completed work on these frescos in 1465.

Work on the chapel was briefly interrupted when an outbreak of the plague prompted commissions for two frescoed altarpieces of Saint Sebastian, to whom people prayed for protection from the plague. Gozzoli painted one in the church of Saint Augustine, showing Sebastian protecting the people of San Gimignano under his outstretched cloak, and another—depicting the saint's martyrdom—in the collegiate church in San Gimignano. He employed several assistants, who also painted frescos for chapels in other Tuscan towns, following his designs.

Gozzoli began his most ambitious project in 1468: the completion of the 14th-century fresco decoration of the Campo Santo in Pisa. The approval of his trial piece, *The Drunkenness of Noah* (1468–69), led to a further 24 scenes from the Old Testament, which occupied him and his assistants for the next 16 years.

Changing tastes led to the neglect of the frescos, which were also damaged by a bomb in World War II. Fortunately, colored engravings made in the 19th century record their appearance and something of their character. The detailed compositions often combined more than one episode in a scene, but were unified through Gozzoli's use of color. In form and content they were similar to the contemporary frescos of Domenico Ghirlandaio, Cosimo Rosselli, and Sandro Botticelli.

Gozzoli's renown died with him, and his work was not rediscovered by artists and historians until the 19th century.

Data file

Full name: Benozzo di Lese (known as Benozzo Gozzoli)

Nationality: Italian

Style: Renaissance

Dates: born c1420–22 in Florence, died 1497 in Pistoia

Key works:
- *The Birth and Youth of Saint Francis* 1452
- *The Procession of the Magi* 1459–61
- "Purification" altarpiece 1461
- *The Conversion of Saint Augustine* 1464–65
- *The Drunkenness of Noah* 1468–69

Things to look for:
- crowded compositions
- studies from nature
- portraits included in narrative scenes
- repetition of poses and gestures

Comparisons: Fra Angelico, Lorenzo Ghiberti, Alesso Baldovinetti, Sandro Botticelli, Domenico Ghirlandaio

Glossary terms: fresco, *predella*, *sinopia*

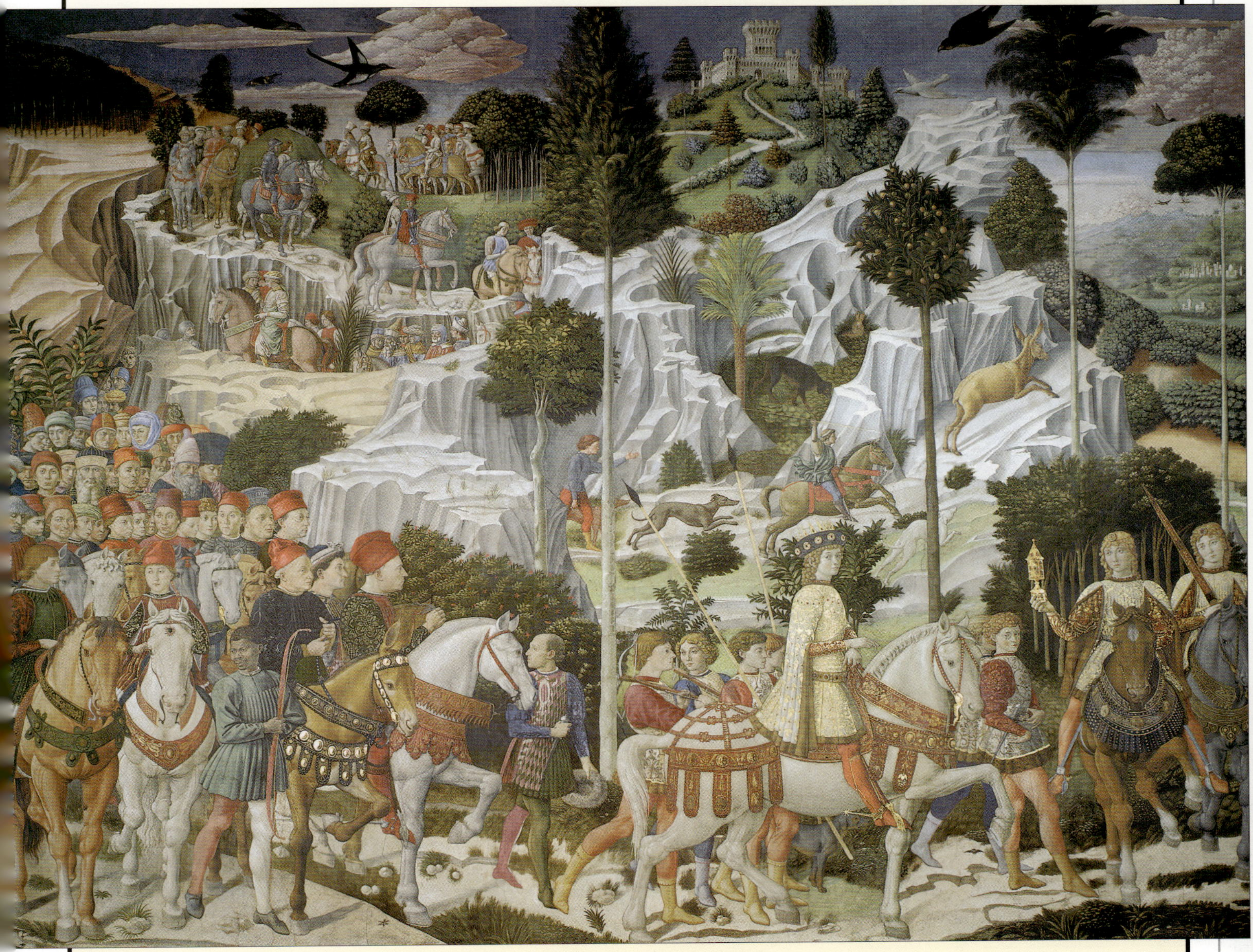

Procession of the Magi *1459–61. One of three wall frescos. Medici-Riccardi Palace, Florence.*

Detail and decoration

Gozzoli's *Procession of the Magi* frescos depict the journey of the magi—the wise men, or kings—who, in the Bible story, came from the East to pay homage to the infant Jesus. Gozzoli painted the magi according to the well-established tradition of each representing one of the three ages of man: youth, middle age, and old age.

Gozzoli adapted his style to meet the demands of his patrons. For example, in these frescos he used rich colors such as azure (a deep sky blue), vermilion (a bright red), and gold, which were appropriate to the subject, and which also reflected the taste of Piero de' Medici, who commissioned the frescos. Their tapestry-like appearance, with high horizon levels, naturalistic details of plants and animals, and the decorative costumes of the processing crowds, suited their location and the Medici family's desire to rival earlier paintings of the magi, such as Gentile da Fabriano's 1423 altarpiece for the Strozzi family. Gozzoli introduced many portraits into the scenes. Piero and his father Cosimo de' Medici are pictured following the youngest magi on his white horse. Gozzoli has even painted himself, with his name in gold letters around the base of his red cap, several rows behind the Medici family members.

Gozzoli's mastery of his materials and quick, efficient painting methods enabled him to complete many projects. He usually worked in true fresco, drawing his designs straight onto the prepared wall. A number of these drawings, called *sinopie*, have come to light during restoration work, and in some cases they include brief written instructions for his assistants.

GRECO El

El Greco was a highly original artist from Crete who established his reputation in Spain during the late 16th and early 17th century. He combined his awareness of traditional Byzantine art with the Venetian Renaissance emphasis on color to create religious paintings and portraits of great individuality and imagination.

Life and work

Domenikos Theotokopoulos, popularly known as El Greco, or "The Greek," was born in Candia (which was later renamed Heraklion), on the island of Crete. His father worked as a tax collector for the Venetian Republic, at that time the colonial ruler of Crete. Although little is known of El Greco's early artistic training, he was probably taught in the traditional Byzantine style. By 1563 he had established himself as a master painter, and left his native Crete for Venice four or five years later. Here he worked under the influence of the great Venetian painter Titian, and also saw the work of Tintoretto and Paolo Veronese. His contact with these artists had a huge impact on El Greco, who quickly adopted the colorist tradition of Venetian art in his work.

El Greco had left Venice for Rome by 1570, by way of Verona, Palma, and Florence. On arrival in Rome he entered the Academy of Saint Luke, and also established a workshop with the financial support of Cardinal Farnese. Although the reputation of the recently deceased Renaissance master Michelangelo was still greatly respected in Rome at this time, El Greco was more interested in the work of artists, such as Parmigianino, who were reworking the accepted Renaissance style into a style that would later be known as mannerism.

By 1577 El Greco was on the move again, this time traveling to Spain. The reasons why he chose to leave Rome for Spain are unclear. He may not have received sufficient commissions in Rome, or perhaps he was attracted by the possibility of participating in the decoration of the Spanish king Philip II's newly built El Escorial Palace in Madrid. El Greco settled in Toledo, a cultural center that had also attracted some of the greatest poets and philosophers of the age.

El Greco's first major commission in Toledo was to produce a painting for the sacristy of the main cathedral. This work, which is known as *El Espolio (The Disrobing of Christ)* (1577–79), depicts Christ being humiliated by the Roman soldiers before his execution. In the painting El Greco contrasts the dignity and solemnity of Christ with the anger and brutality of the crowd of onlookers. Shortly after completing *El Espolio*, El Greco received the commission that he had been hoping for: to create a painting on the theme of the martyrdom of Saint Maurice for the El Escorial Palace in Madrid. He then spent two years completing *The Martyrdom of Saint Maurice* (c1580–82), but ultimately was disappointed when it was rejected by King Philip.

Following this setback El Greco returned to Toledo, where he remained for the rest of his life. He produced his best-known work, *The Burial of the Count of Orgaz*, in 1586. After it was installed in the Church of Santo Tomé, the painting attracted flocks of visitors to Toledo, as well as significantly increasing El Greco's reputation and fame.

In many of his religious works, such as *Christ Driving the Money-changers from the Temple* (c1600) and *The Resurrection* (1605–10), El Greco compressed the pictorial space and elongated the human figure. These distortions of the natural world gave his works a less earthly, more spiritual mood that was appropriate to his depictions of intensely religious subjects that were intended to encourage piety. Indeed, his works were in keeping with the devoutly religious atmosphere of Counter-Reformation Spain.

El Greco had an extensive library, and befriended many great intellectuals of the day, such as the historican Salazar de Mendoza and the poet Don Luis de Góngora y Argote, who became chaplain to King Philip III of Spain. El Greco's *Portrait of Fray Hortensio Felix Paravicino* (1609–10) takes as its subject another of El Greco's friends, the monk and well-known orator and poet. Painted in black, white, and red, the portrait conveys the wisdom, sensitivity, and intellectual authority of the Dominican.

Data file

Full name: Domenikos Theotokopoulos (known as El Greco, "The Greek")

Nationality: Cretan

Style: Renaissance

Dates: born c1541 in Candia (now Heraklion), died 1614 in Toledo

Key works:
- *El Espolio (The Disrobing of Christ)* 1577–79
- *The Martyrdom of Saint Maurice* c1580–82
- *The Burial of the Count of Orgaz* 1586
- *View of Toledo* 1597–99
- *Christ Driving the Money-changers from the Temple* c1600
- *The Resurrection* 1605–10
- *Portrait of Fray Hortensio Felix Paravicino* 1609–10

Things to look for:
- elongated figures
- brightly colored, flowing robes
- compressed space and foreshortening
- translucent, cloudlike forms

Comparisons: Titian, Tintoretto, Paolo Veronese, Antonio Correggio, Parmigianino

Glossary terms: baroque, Byzantine, Counter-Reformation, mannerism, Renaissance

Depicting heaven and earth

The Count of Orgaz was a benefactor of the Church of Santo Tomé in Toledo. According to legend, the saints Augustine and Stephen made a miraculous appearance at his burial in 1323, in honor of the sanctity of the count's life. In his famous painting *The Burial of the Count of Orgaz* (1586), which was designed for the Church of Santo Tomé, El Greco depicts the specific moment at which the soul of the Count of Orgaz leaves his body and ascends to heaven.

In the lower half of the painting two figures in richly embroidered church vestments lower the count's body into his grave. These figures represent Saint Augustine and Saint Stephen. Behind this central group a crowd of men witnesses the miracle. Interestingly, El Greco's witnesses can be identified as notable Toledan citizens of his own time. The dead count similarly wears contemporary, 16th-century armor, even though his funeral took place more than two-and-a-half centuries earlier.

Heaven is represented in the upper half of the painting, with Christ, the Virgin Mary, and Saint John the Baptist presiding over an entourage of angels and saints. Beneath this group a winged angel can be seen encouraging a white form (representing the count's soul) toward its heavenly destination.

The two spheres of heaven and earth are depicted in different ways. The earthly sphere appears dark and heavy, and is defined by a strongly horizontal composition. In contrast, the heavenly sphere is both lighter and more colorful, and is inhabited by a multitude of figures floating on ethereal clouds.

El Greco's visionary representation of the two realms of heaven and earth reflects the popular climate of religious fervor that prevailed in Spain at the time when the work was painted. During the Counter-Reformation artists were encouraged to produce paintings that celebrated religious devotion in this life and its rewards in the next. The story of the Count of Orgaz's funeral and the visitation of the saints provided El Greco with a suitable subject with which to depict both a miraculous event and the ascension of the human soul into heaven.

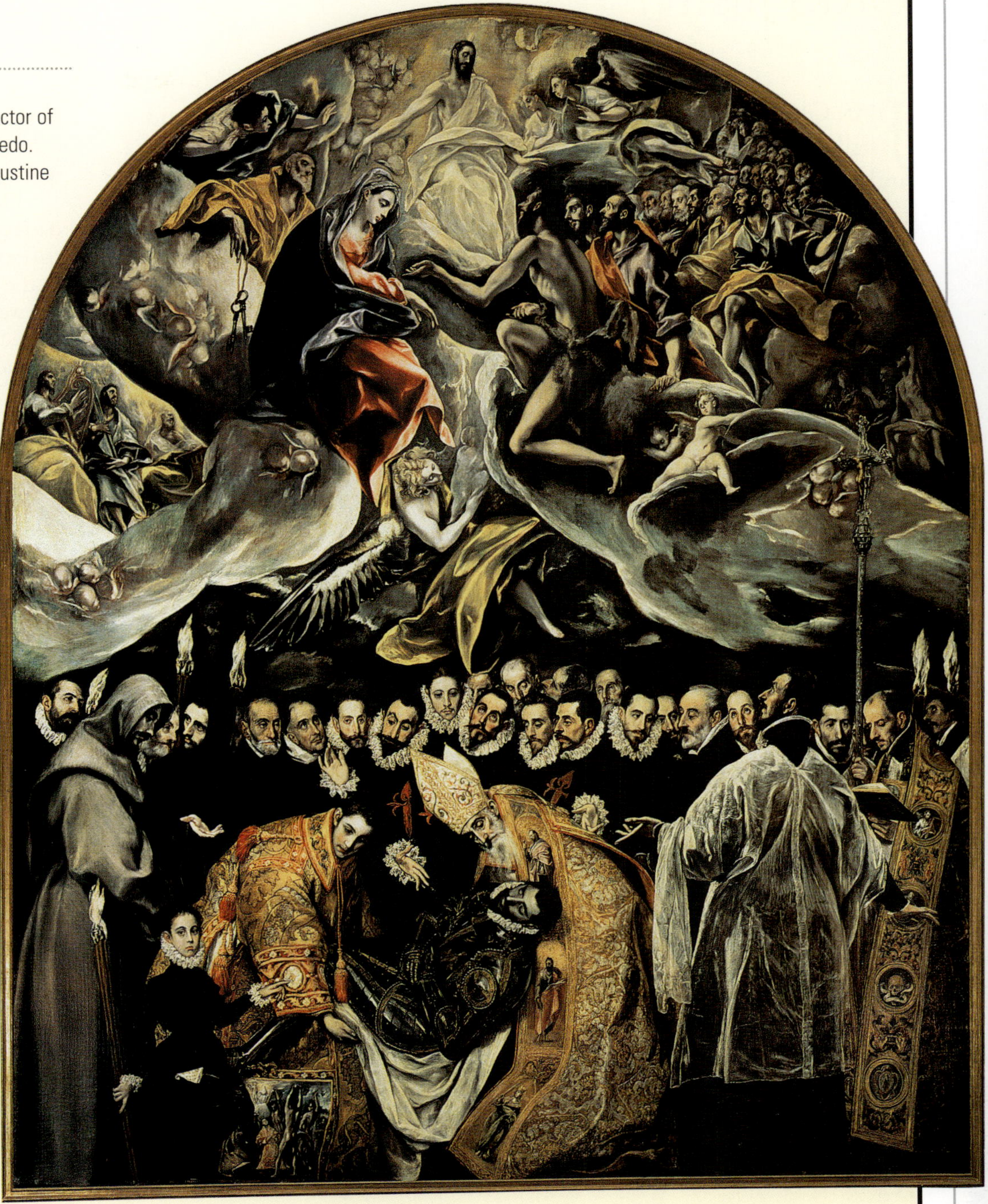

The Burial of the Count of Orgaz *1586. Oil on canvas. 15¾ x 11¾ ft (5 x 3.5 m). The Church of Santo Tomé, Toledo.*

GRIS Juan

JUAN GRIS'S EARLY WORKS—CAREFULLY COMPOSED PORTRAITS and still lifes—helped advance the cubist style introduced by Braque and Picasso. His later emphasis on Harlequins and clowns contributed to the development of a neoclassical style often referred to as the "return to order."

Life and work

Juan Gris was the 13th of 14 children born into a merchant family in Madrid, Spain, in 1887. He was christened José Victoriano Carmelo Carlos González Pérez, but adopted the name Juan Gris shortly before his arrival in Paris, France, in 1906.

After leaving school Gris entered the Madrid School of Art and Industry to study mathematics, sciences, and engineering. In 1904, however, he trained as an artist with the Spanish academic painter José Moreno Carbonero. By 1905, when he was still only 18 years old, Gris was producing drawings and illustrations for magazines. In the following year he set off for Paris, and remained in France for the rest of his life.

During his first years in Paris, Gris worked as an illustrator for popular journals. By 1908 he had befriended Pablo Picasso, a fellow Spaniard, and was renting a studio in the same building as Picasso's in Montmartre, where he soon became a familiar face among Montmartre's artistic circles. In 1912, he produced a portrait of his friend and compatriot entitled *Homage to Pablo Picasso*.

Gris's early paintings owed a considerable debt to both Georges Braque and Picasso, who had invented and developed the cubist style. By 1913 he was also producing collage works, known as *papiers-collés*, in which he attached pieces of newspaper or bottle labels to the surface of his canvases. Although this technique had also been developed by Braque and Picasso, Gris was equally aware of the work of such artists as Jean Metzinger and Albert Gleizes, as can be seen in his *Still Life With Oil Lamp* (1911–12) and *Man in a Café* (1912).

Metzinger and Gleizes constituted the public face of cubism in about 1912. Whereas Picasso and Braque rarely exhibited their works, instead selling them directly to their dealer, Daniel Henry Kahnweiler, Metzinger and Gleizes showed their cubist-inspired paintings at the Paris Salon des Indépendants. Moreover, the works of these so-called "Salon cubists" were frequently brightly colored and sharply delineated and thus more in keeping with Gris's own style.

Gris remained in France at the outbreak of World War I. As a foreign national he was not required to enlist in the French Army, and spent most of the war years in Paris. In 1916 he visited a country château at Beaulieu, central France, where he painted many of the local peasants and created the work entitled *Woman with a Mandolin (After Corot)* (1916). Although executed in a cubist style, this piece was based upon a traditional genre scene painted by the early 19th-century French artist Camille Corot. Gris was by now increasingly turning his attention to more traditional subjects, a preoccupation that would emerge more prominently after 1920 with his numerous representations of Harlequins and Pierrots (characters from the Italian commedia dell'arte who were popularly represented in 18th-century paintings).

Even Gris's still lifes, such as his late work *The Musician's Table* (1926), increasingly relied on the grand tradition of French 18th-century painting. Indeed, his frequent inclusion of musical instruments in his works alluded both to the cubism of Picasso and Braque and the work of the 18th-century still-life painter Jean-Baptiste-Siméon Chardin. Gris was not alone in his emphasis on a new, or neoclassical, style: many French artists at this time were also looking to the art of the past to guide their own future development. This promotion of traditional artistic values and subjects has frequently been termed the "return to order."

Gris fell ill in 1920. Following a period of convalescence he returned to painting, working on stage designs for Sergei Diaghilev's Ballets Russes between 1922 and 1924. In 1925, however, his health deteriorated again and he died two years later, only 40 years old, in Boulogne-sur-Seine.

Data file

Full name: José Victoriano Carmelo Carlos González Pérez (known as Juan Gris)

Nationality: Spanish

Style: cubism

Dates: born 1887 in Madrid, died 1927 in Boulogne-sur-Seine, France

Key works:

Still Life with Oil Lamp 1911–12

Homage to Pablo Picasso 1912

Man in a Café 1912

Still Life and Townscape (Place Ravignon) 1915

Woman with a Mandolin (After Corot) 1916

The Two Pierrots 1922

The Musician's Table 1926

Things to look for:

- broken and fragmented forms
- inclusion of words or letters
- use of newspaper or other collage materials
- musical instruments in still-life arrangements
- characters from the Italian commedia dell'arte

Comparisons: Pablo Picasso, Georges Braque, Albert Gleizes, Jean Metzinger

Glossary terms: Academy, Ballets Russes, commedia dell'arte, cubism, fauvism, neoclassicism, *papiers-collés*, return to order, Salon des Indépendants

Gris and the cubist still life

Juan Gris's cubist still lifes focus on ordinary, everyday objects seen in ordinary, everyday settings. Through his art, however, Gris transformed these mundane scenes into paintings of great harmony and beauty. His *Still Life and Townscape (Place Ravignon)* (1915) provides a prime example of his cubist still-life work. The painting was produced during World War I, a time of great difficulty and privation for Gris, despite the fact that he was not required to serve as a soldier at the front (Spain was neutral). With its careful composition and rich textures and colors, the work nonetheless captures a sense of peacefulness, lyricism, and optimism, qualities that were possibly inspired by Gris's love of the poetry of Pierre Reverdy.

In the painting, Gris presents us with a simple still-life arrangement of a fruit bowl, an assortment of bottles and glasses, and a newspaper entitled *Le Journal*, all laid out on a table. In typical cubist style, Gris depicts the objects as if they are being viewed from different angles while the viewer moves through time around them.

The objects were arranged in Gris's Montmartre studio, in front of a window overlooking the Place Ravignon. Behind the table we can see the patterns of the window's cast-iron balustrade, and beyond that trees, a lamppost, and the shutters of the windows of the building opposite. This simultaneous presentation of interior (the studio) and exterior (the street) spaces was a notable feature of the work of the fauvist painter Henri Matisse, with whom Gris had been working in the south of France a few months before he completed this work.

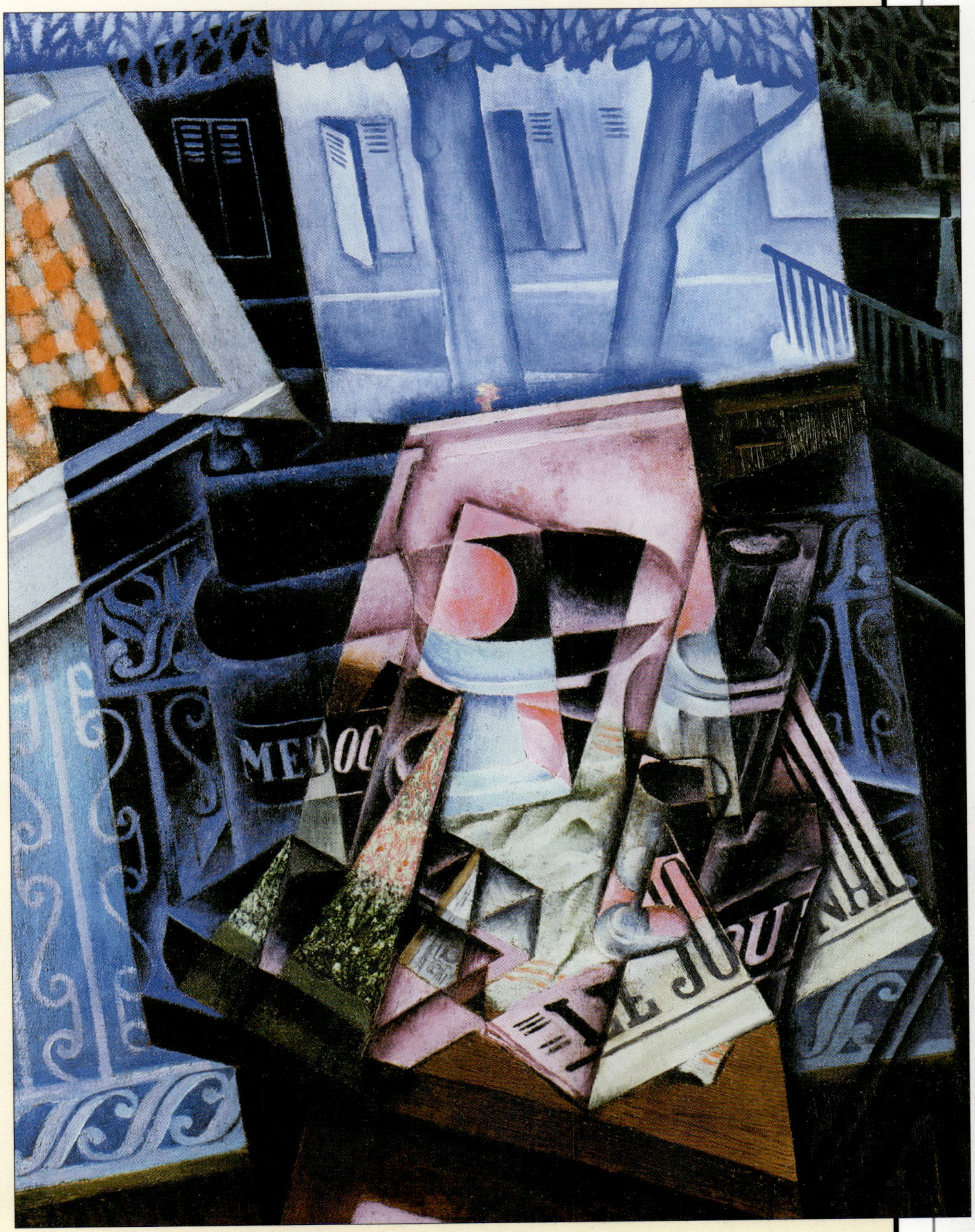

Still Life and Townscape (Place Ragivnon) *1915. Oil on canvas. 45 x 35 in (114.5 x 89 cm). Philadelphia Museum of Art, Philadelphia, PA.*

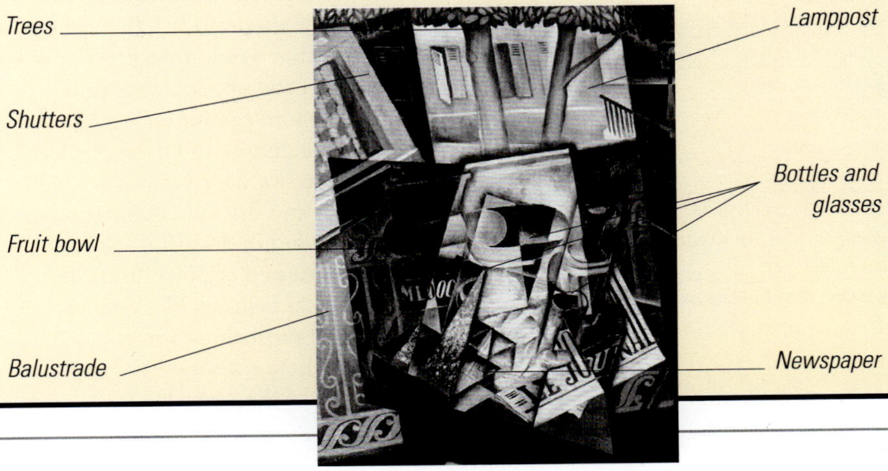

The still life transformed *Traditional still-life objects are presented anew in this cubist work by Gris.*

GROSZ George

GEORGE GROSZ IS KNOWN BOTH FOR HIS DRAWINGS AND PAINTINGS. In them he satirized the world around him between the two world wars. Important for dadaism and expressionism, Grosz's images retain their appeal today as blackly comic exposures of the weakest aspects of human nature.

Life and work

Grosz was born in Berlin, but he spent many childhood years living in remote rural Germany. Possibly as a result of this, big cities, especially Berlin and New York, fascinated him. He volunteered for army service in 1914. Although he only saw the front line very briefly, he became dangerously ill in 1915; he was kept in a military hospital and then moved to a psychiatric hospital. He described this as a hellish experience, and his hatred of the military and of authority in general may be related to this time.

Data file

Full name: George Grosz (born Georg Groß)

Nationality: German (U.S. citizen after 1938)

Style: expressionism

Dates: born 1893 in Berlin, died 1959 in Berlin

Key works:

Dedicated to Oskar Panizza 1917–18

Fit for Active Service 1918

Daum Marries 1920

Gray Day 1921

Ecce Homo (series) 1923

Eclipse of the Sun 1926

Pillars of Society 1926

Things to look for:

- exaggeration and caricature
- montage and collage
- thin black outlines
- political subjects
- violent images
- distorted perspective
- a sense of irony and satire

Comparisons: Otto Dix, John Heartfield, Marcel Duchamp, Man Ray

Glossary terms: dadaism, expressionism

As a protest against his German roots and his country's hatred of the enemy during World War I, the artist anglicized his name from Georg Groß to George Grosz.

He produced many political and anti-war illustrations. Although he is seen as an expressionist painter, he was contemptuous of the typical view of expressionist artists, whom he saw as self-centered and ignorant of the ugliness of real life.

Grosz was attracted to the irreverent protests of the dadaists in Berlin. The dada movement, founded in Zurich in 1916, rebelled against traditional values, and spread their ideas through public demonstrations and literature designed to disrupt public complacency. An important member of the group, Grosz fitted in well as a "savage boxer, fighter, and hater," as one colleague described him. At this time he made many collages and photomontages, using fragments of photographs, words cut from magazine articles, and paint, to produce comic, anarchic, and disturbing effects.

Shortly after the war ended, Grosz joined the German Communist Party on the day it was founded, hoping for a revolution that would take power out of the hands of the upper classes and establish a more egalitarian society. But he was to be disappointed. In postwar Germany he saw deprivation, corruption, and disease. The streets of Berlin were full of destitute soldiers who had returned crippled from the war, as well as beggars, black-market dealers, and prostitutes. Grosz illustrated these scenes with sharp irony and a sense of the absurd.

Grosz's drawings, which were widely reproduced in serial form in books and magazines, have a cartoonlike quality. We see fat, skinny, old, and young people and animals in the city streets. They depict scenes of life in the "underworld" of criminals, gangsters, murderers, and their victims, and we see the ugly details in the private lives of ordinary people. The drawings often have short, ironic captions to make their satirical meaning even clearer.

Grosz's work was very popular, especially abroad, with those who could appreciate its biting wit, and his drawings gained him an international reputation. But in Germany he was prosecuted several times for blasphemy and his work was banned.

In the 1920s Grosz painted large, detailed oil paintings. These did not sell well, so he was often forced to produce more commercial work.

Grosz fled Germany in 1932, the year before the National Socialist German Workers' Party (Nazis) seized power under Adolf Hitler. They later banned and burned his drawings.

With his wife, Eva, whom he had married in 1920, Grosz emigrated to the United States. It was a land he had always dreamed of; the romance of the Wild West had intrigued him. When he arrived, he was famous as a political satirist, but he had lost his subject—German life—and felt that he could not satirize what he did not know. He became bitter, renounced his Communist past, and supported himself through teaching at the Art Students' League in New York. Eventually he moved to Long Island.

In 1959 Grosz returned with Eva to Berlin. He was now prone to mood swings and bouts of heavy drinking. In the end, his drinking may have caused his death; after just a few months back in Germany, he collapsed one night in the entrance to his apartment and died shortly afterward.

Biting satire

Grosz described himself as a "natural scientist" of German society. His paintings are a dissection of modern life, and an attempt to show that crime and corruption lie beneath the veneer of "respectability" in all sorts of people, including judges, clergymen, and businessmen.

This painting's title, *Pillars of Society,* is sarcastic. It is a large, detailed painting, made with all the care of a traditional religious altarpiece. But in it we see Germany in chaos. Fighting and destruction are visible in the top part of the image, and below we see the human "pillars" on which this society is built.

From the top, there is a thuggish army officer in steel helmet with telltale blood on his sword. Then there is an unhealthy-looking priest in mid-sermon. Next, we see a politician, who has a steaming pile of dung where his brains should be. In the foreground are a nationalist journalist or editor, clutching his precious newspapers (with a chamber-pot for a hat), and a beer-swilling Nazi whose open, hollow head shows he is dreaming of military victory.

These are all the figures Grosz hated most in German society. Grosz's depiction of their grotesque physical features—large heads, bloated, red cheeks, and small, unresponsive eyes—conveys the sense that they are mean-spirited and blind to the injustices of the society they uphold.

Like much of Grosz's work, this is a portrayal of the gluttony and corruption in society, and it reflects the mood of disillusionment in Germany after World War I.

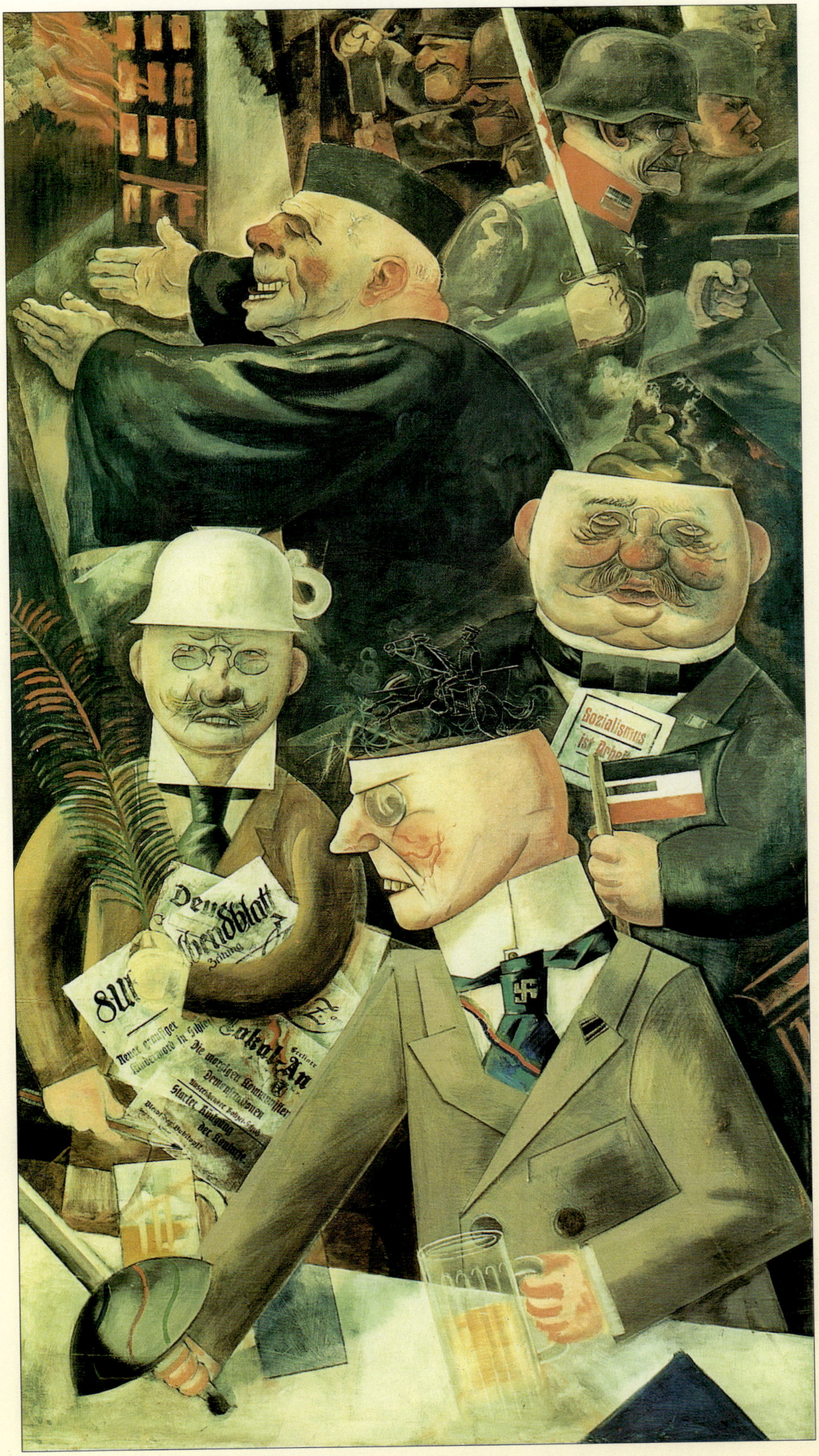

Pillars of Society *1926. Oil on canvas. 79 x 42½ in (200 x 108 cm). Nationalgalerie, Berlin.*

GRÜNEWALD Mathis

GRÜNEWALD BECAME FAMOUS FOR HIS RELIGIOUS PICTURES, which displayed a powerful blend of high emotion and unstinting realism. Along with Albrecht Dürer and Lucas Cranach the Elder, he was among the greatest German painters of the Renaissance.

Life and work

The painter known today as Mathis Grünewald was actually called Mathis Gothardt. The error was introduced by the artist's first biographer, writing in 1675, who may have mixed him up with another painter, Baldung Grien. The confusion was exacerbated by the artist's use of his adopted son's name, Neithardt, and because many records refer simply to "Master Mathis."

There is little information about Grünewald's career. He was probably the "Master Mathis" recorded as working in 1501 at Seligenstadt, near Frankfurt. This fell within the diocese of Mainz, and Grünewald appears to have spent several years (1508–14) in the service of its influential archbishop, Uriel Von Gemmingen. Records show that, as well as painting, Grünewald worked as an architect and hydraulic engineer, supervising the construction of fountains.

During his employment with Von Gemmingen, Grünewald created the Isenheim altarpiece (c1512–15), the masterpiece that forms the basis of his reputation. Isenheim Abbey was dedicated to Saint Anthony, the patron saint of plague-victims; the monks of the Anthonite Order spent their lives tending the sick. The misery of their ordeal was reflected in Grünewald's gruesome image of *The Crucifixion*, while the radiance of *The Resurrection*—on the same altarpiece—offered hope for a release from suffering in the afterlife.

Grünewald was retained by Von Gemmingen's successor, Albrecht of Brandenburg, who became a cardinal in 1518. Accompanying Albrecht to the coronation of Emperor Charles V in 1520, the artist had the opportunity to meet Albrecht Dürer. The latter generously gave Grünewald a series of his engravings, as a token of admiration for his work.

Grünewald's reputation was at its peak during these years, but his private life was wretched: he had an unhappy marriage, and was melancholy. After Lutheran reformers were linked with the Peasants' Revolt of 1525, Grünewald, a known Protestant sympathizer, was dismissed from his post. He spent his final years in Frankfurt and Halle, struggling to earn a living, and died of the plague in 1528. After his death, his reputation plummeted, and by the end of the century his work was all but forgotten.

Data file

Full name: Mathis Gothardt (known as Mathis Grünewald)

Nationality: German

Style: northern Renaissance

Dates: born c1470/80 in Würzburg, died 1528 in Halle

Key works:

The Mocking of Christ 1504–05

Christ on the Cross with the Three Maries, John the Evangelist, and Longinus c1505–10

Isenheim altarpiece c1512–15

The Little Crucifixion c1520

The Disputation of Saint Erasmus and Saint Maurice c1520–23

Things to look for:

- heightened emotions
- distorted limbs
- gloomy backgrounds

Comparisons: Albrecht Dürer, Lucas Cranach the Elder

Glossary terms: altarpiece, foreshortening, perspective

Expressive power

Grünewald's paintings bridge two very different styles of art. In terms of pure technique, he belonged to the Renaissance. He had a firm grasp of both anatomy and perspective. He had the ability to position his figures convincingly within their environments, and to construct landscapes. He also demonstrates an obvious delight in displaying the tricks of foreshortening—a technique that produced an accurate depiction of a figure tumbling forward or a book shown at an oblique angle.

Despite this, Grünewald's art was rooted in the past. His versions of biblical scenes were not portrayed like real historical events. Instead, they were shown as symbolic, spiritual experiences. Here, for example, Christ is depicted on a larger scale than the other figures. This was a typically medieval practice, in which the size of painted figures was directly related to their importance. As a result, Christ would invariably appear larger than the Virgin or the disciples, who would in turn overshadow other figures.

Throughout the Middle Ages, the main patron of artists was the Church, and the most popular subject was the Crucifixion. It was portrayed so frequently, however, that its treatment became formulaic. Lesser artists would follow a set pattern, producing versions that were virtually identical, apart from a few minor details. Grünewald managed to create a vision of the scene that was totally unique.

For Western artists, the key dilemma presented by the Crucifixion was whether to focus on the human suffering of Christ, or the glory of His divine sacrifice. Grünewald opted wholeheartedly for the former. No artist has ever portrayed the tortures of the Crucifixion so graphically. Christ's discolored flesh is flecked with a host of sores and tiny wounds; His feet are stretched and distorted; the fingers of His nailed hands curl up in agony. The sense of tragedy is reinforced by the somber coloring. Grünewald translated the biblical description of the scene quite literally ("and there was darkness over all the earth until the ninth hour," Luke 23: 44). The foreground details of the landscape are

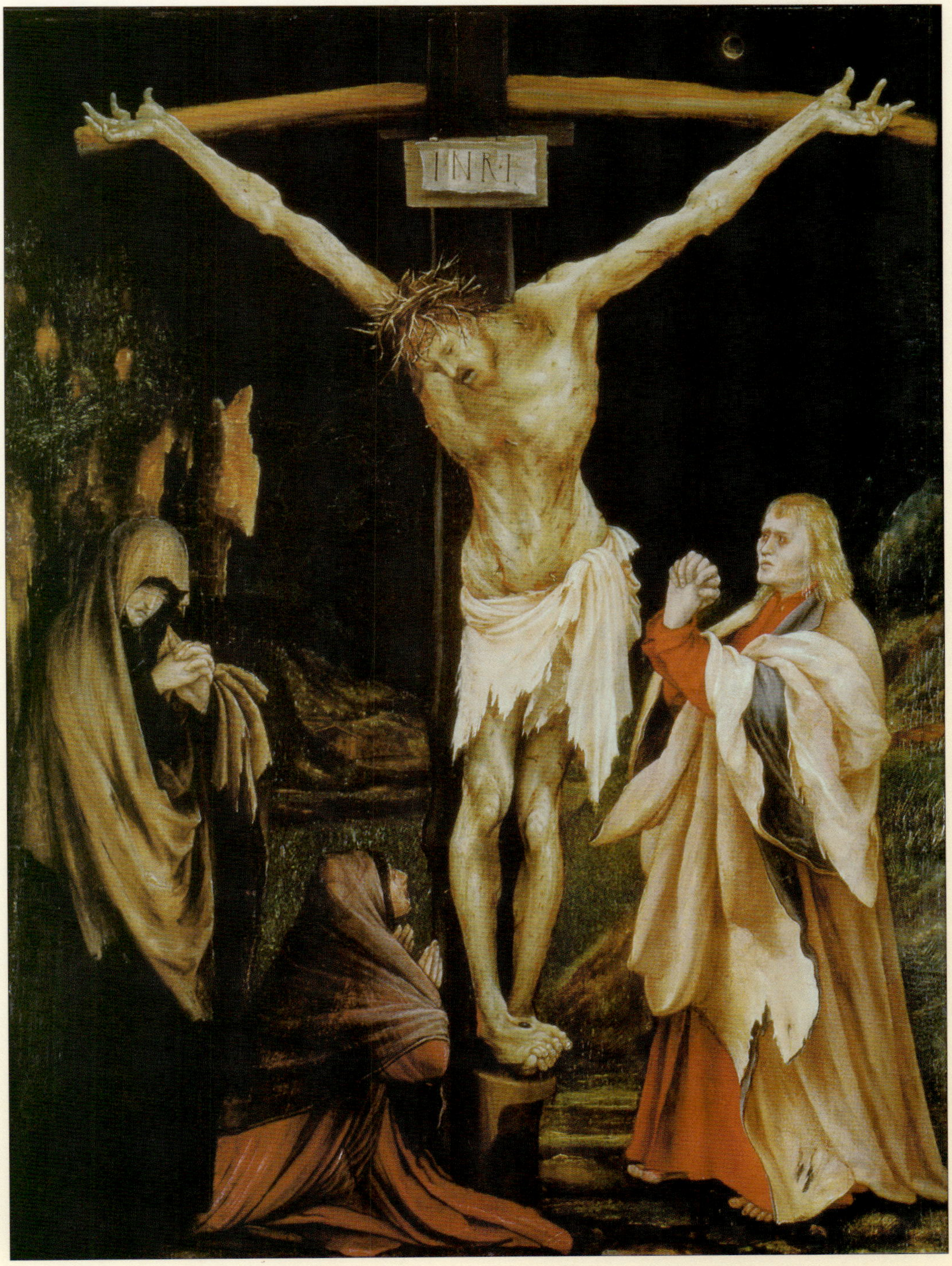

The Little Crucifixion
c1520. Oil on panel.
24 1/2 x 18 in (62 x 46 cm).
National Gallery of Art,
Washington, D.C.

barely visible, and the background melts away into the gloom.

Grünewald's definitive version of *The Crucifixion* (c1512–15) appeared on the Isenheim altarpiece, but he reworked it for a number of smaller pictures. *The Little Crucifixion* (c1520) is a compressed version, but it retains some hints of the original's power. Christ's body hangs limply, on the point of death. Its weight is emphasized by the sagging beam of the cross. On the right, Saint John holds Jesus's ragged cloak and wrings his hands in anguish, while on the left the Virgin bows her head. The crying woman at the foot of the cross is Mary Magdalene. The orb in the sky (on the right) has led one critic to suggest that Grünewald was drawing on his memory of the solar eclipse of 1502.

The austerity of Grünewald's vision is usually ascribed to his reformist (Protestant) beliefs and, in particular, to the writings of Saint Bridget of Sweden (1303–73). In her *Revelations,* she dwelt at length on the physical torments suffered by Christ.

HALS Frans

ALTHOUGH FRANS HALS PAINTED A FEW DOMESTIC AND RELIGIOUS pictures, the vast majority of his paintings were portraits. He is regarded as one of the best painters of this genre, and he is admired for his ability to capture both the character of his sitters and a sense of momentary movement and expression.

Life and work

Frans Hals is now a very famous artist, but from the time of his death until the middle of the 19th century his work went out of fashion, with the result that many of his paintings have been lost. His surviving paintings are not dated, so it is hard to work out when and in which order they were made.

The exact date of Hals's birth is not known, nor exactly where he came from, but it seems that he was born in Antwerp in Flanders (modern-day Belgium). In 1591 his family moved to Haarlem in Holland, where he became a pupil of a well-known painter named Karel van Mander. It was here that he joined the Guild of Saint Luke (an organization for professional painters) in 1610, and became one of the first artists of what became known as the 17th-century Dutch school.

It is thought that Hals's family moved to Holland for religious reasons, but also possibly to take advantage of the new prosperity there. In 1581 seven united provinces (the richest of which was Holland) in the Low Countries, which for years had been known as the Spanish Netherlands and ruled by Spain, had declared their independence. Spain was a Catholic country, while the rebels were Protestants. The city of Antwerp had fallen to the Spanish in 1585. In 1609, however, a 12-year truce ended hostilities between the Dutch and the Spanish, and a Dutch republic was established, giving the Dutch independence. There were new opportunities for bankers and merchants, shippers, and manufacturers to make a lot of money. As a result, Holland (and the other provinces) began to enjoy a period of great prosperity. Rich people wanted nice things to put in their new houses and many artists began to produce paintings to meet the new demand.

As with many painters of the day, Hals was a specialist—he chose portraiture as his genre—and he quickly established a reputation for capturing the character of his sitters and bringing them to life on the canvas, providing a "speaking likeness" rather than flattering them.

In 1616 he painted the first of a series of large-scale group-portraits of a group of militia (military men) at a banquet—a type of painting for which he became well known. During the 1620s and 1630s, when he was at the height of his popularity, Hals painted five large group-portraits of these civic guards at meetings and banquets. These remarkable paintings are about life size. Hals's lively brushstrokes give the sitters an appearance of movement, and his depiction of their wrinkled red

Data file

Full name: Frans Hals

Nationality: Dutch

Style: Dutch baroque

Dates: born c1580–85 in Antwerp, died 1666 in Haarlem

Key works:
- *The Laughing Cavalier* 1624
- *Portrait of a Young Man with a Skull* c1626–28
- *The Gypsy Girl* 1628–30
- *The Merry Drinker* 1628–30
- *Regents of the Old Men's Almshouses* c1664
- *Regents of the Old Women's Almshouses* c1664

Things to look for:
- portraits and large group-portraits
- rapid brushwork

Comparisons: Rembrandt, Jan Vermeer, Peter Paul Rubens

Glossary terms: baroque, genre

Capturing a glance

The effect of movement and the impression of life that Hals gives his sitters is achieved by the apparent looseness and spontaneity of his brushwork. If you look closely, it seems as though the artist has almost flicked on the paint—a dab of white to make a nose shine, a blob to give texture to a lace collar, a dash of color to give movement to a hand or arm. As no drawings by Hals survive, it seems that he worked straight onto the canvas. But however quick the paintwork may seem to be, in fact it was very tightly controlled. Many of the subtle effects he achieved were the result of adding highlights at the last stage of making a painting—he is said to have described this final process as "putting in his handwriting."

It is not just his way of putting the paint on that was so unusual; it was also the way that he chose to portray his figures. They seem to have been caught almost unawares—as they turn their head, or in mid-sentence, or while gesturing during a conversation. This spontaneous pose is something that we take for granted with snapshot photography, but in those days it was very rare.

All the elements of Hals's style are reflected in *Portrait of a Young Man with a Skull* (c1626–28): the sense of movement, the lively brushstrokes, the way we are glimpsing a moment in time. But perhaps the most arresting element is the human skull the boy is holding. Here it acts as a symbol of mortality, and a reminder of the shortness of human life, a theme often found in Dutch still-life paintings of the same period.

Portrait of a Young Man with a Skull
c1626–28. Oil on canvas. 36 x 32 in (92 x 81 cm). National Gallery, London.

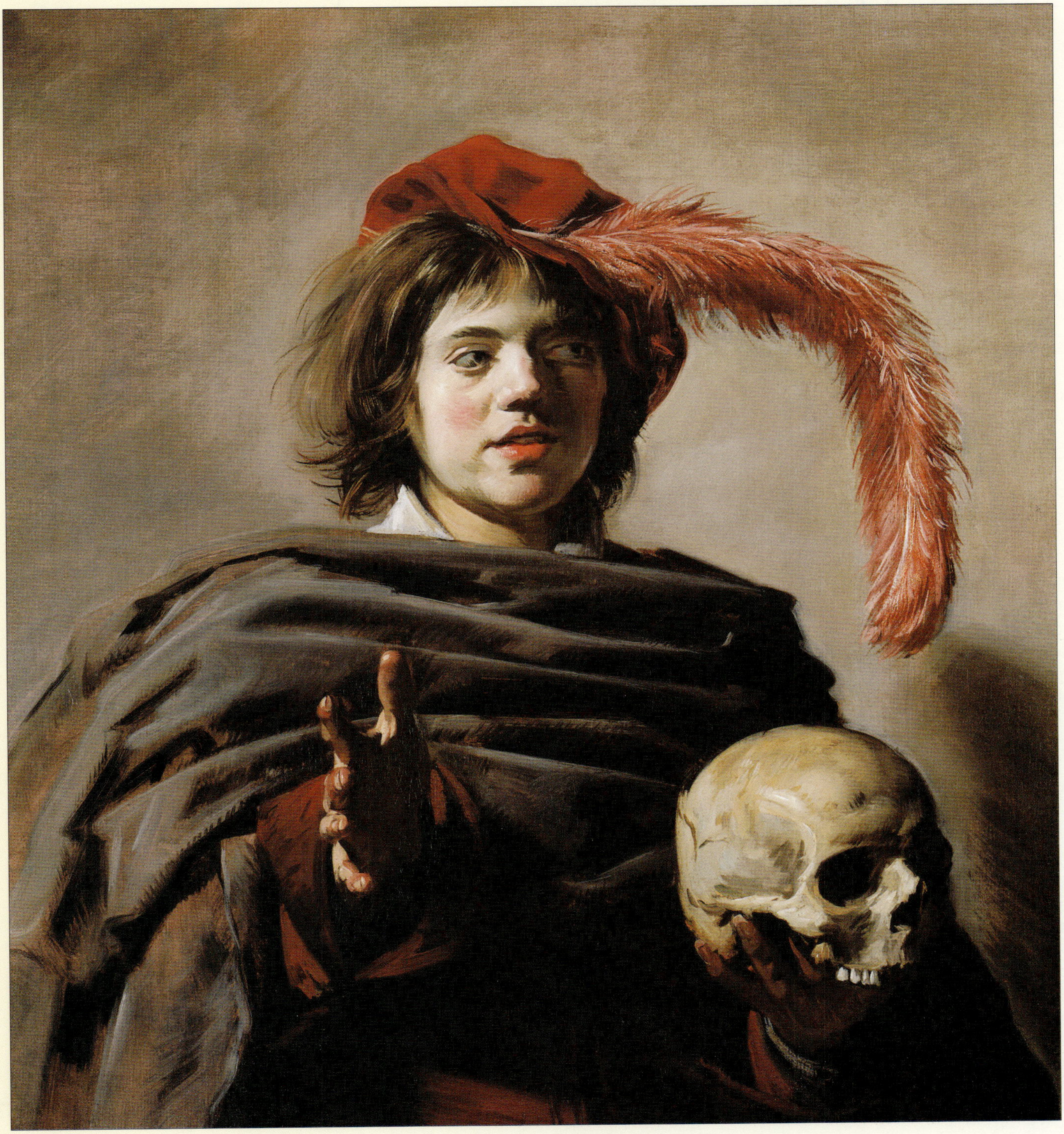

faces, crumpled clothes, and portly bodies is acutely realistic. It may be that this realism was the reason his work fell from fashion in the 1640s, when sitters wanted portraits that made them look stately and elegant. However, Hals's informal style was to become a great influence on Manet and the impressionists.

At the age of 86 Hals painted two group-portraits of the governors of Haarlem's almshouses. His own dependence on charity in his old age may have contributed to the compassion displayed in these late portraits, in which Hals's ability to capture character and likeness is still extraordinarily acute.

HASSAM Childe Frederick

CHILDE HASSAM, ONE OF THE FOUNDERS OF "THE TEN" and the most successful member of the group, is, after Mary Cassatt, the American painter most closely associated with French impressionism. Best known for his paintings of light-dappled gardens, Hassam also documented the changing contemporary urban New York scene.

Life and work

Born in Massachusetts, Hassam studied in Boston. In 1883, like many young American artists, he traveled to Europe to study. In 1886 he enrolled at the Académie Julian in Paris, and it was his stay in this city that proved to be the turning point for his art. Before this trip, Hassam had specialized in dark-toned scenes of Boston streets. In Paris he began to adopt the lighter-toned palette and touch of the impressionists. This is evident in his painting *Grand Prix Day* (1887), which won him a gold medal at the 1888 Salon.

Encouraged by this success, Hassam returned home the following year and moved his studio from Boston to New York's Fifth Avenue. Hassam quickly became celebrated for his seasonal views of the city, a body of work that has helped make these American places as recognizable as Claude Monet's garden at Giverny. In *Washington Arch in Spring* (1890), Hassam shows us a cross-section of American urban life. The aerial view of *Union Square in Spring* (1896) demonstrates how close in both subject and style Hassam's work is to the street scenes of his French contemporaries—in particular, Camille Pissarro's *Avenue de l'Opera: Sun on a Winter Morning* (1898) and Edouard Manet's *Boulevard des Capucines* (1873).

Following his return to the United States in 1889, Hassam spent many of his summers at a small hotel run by the poet and gardener Celia Thaxter at Appledore, a small island off the New Hampshire coast. Hassam's friendship with Thaxter dated back to the early 1880s, when she had been a pupil in his watercolor class in Boston. While Thaxter celebrated her "natural" (as opposed to "formal") flower garden and the Appledore landscape in poetry, the same scenery inspired some of Hassam's best works of the 1890s, such as *Celia Thaxter in Her Garden* (1892). For Thaxter's last published book of poems, *An Island Garden* (1894), Hassam was commissioned to produce watercolor illustrations. In a sense, Hassam returned to his origins in this project; he had begun his artistic career as a magazine illustrator.

After Thaxter's death in 1894, Hassam worked in Old Lyme and Cos Cob, Connecticut, before settling in

Data file

Full name: Childe Frederick Hassam

Nationality: American

Style: impressionism

Dates: born 1859 in Dorchester, MA, died 1935 in New York, NY

Key works:
- *Horse and Carriage on Columbus Avenue* 1885
- *Grand Prix Day* 1887
- *Gathering Flowers in a French Garden* 1888
- *Washington Arch in Spring* 1890
- *Celia Thaxter in her Garden* 1892
- *Union Square in Spring* 1896
- *Old House and Garden, East Hampton, Long Island* 1898
- *Allies Day, May 1917* 1917

Things to look for:
- contemporary scenes
- flat, broken brushstrokes capturing the effects of sunlight and season
- light, shining colors
- oblique viewpoints
- close attention to subject matter. Forms do not completely "dissolve" into light and color
- illusion of distance created by diminishing size of brushstrokes

Comparisons: Edouard Manet, Claude Monet, Camille Pissarro, John Twachtman, Theodore Robinson, J. Alden Weir, Robert Vonnoh

Glossary terms: *en plein air*, impressionism, palette, Salon, Salon des Réfusés, The Ten

City lights

The most significant group of painters in the evolution of American impressionism were "The Ten," an exhibiting group that was founded in 1897. Like their French counterparts, who rebelled against the academic traditions and values of the Salon and set up their own Salon des Réfusés in response, The Ten (who included Hassam) seceded from the Society of American Artists. The society, they complained, was exhibiting too many paintings that ranged too widely in quality and style.

Also like their French counterparts, each of The Ten developed a distinct personal style, but it is Hassam whose paintings come closest to French impressionism. Like the impressionists, Hassam was uninterested in painting the lofty, historical scenes or picturesque views of rustic life that had occupied the previous generation of artists. Instead, he was interested in exploring the modern life around him, and his subject matter included views of the contemporary city. This led one critic to describe Hassam as "a sort of Watteau of the Boulevards, with unlimited sparkle and gaiety, movement and animation...he gives you the color of the street and the tone of the city."

As in many of Hassam's city views, *Horse and Carriage on Columbus Avenue* (1885) shows a lively cross-section of urban humanity. The compositional format, with the diagonal sweep of the road crossed in the foreground by an intersection, conjures up a sense of the world continuing beyond the painting's edges.

In general, Hassam used loose, sketchy brushstrokes: it was the development of the metal ferrule on paintbrushes, which hold the bristles flat, that gave rise to the characteristic brushstroke of the

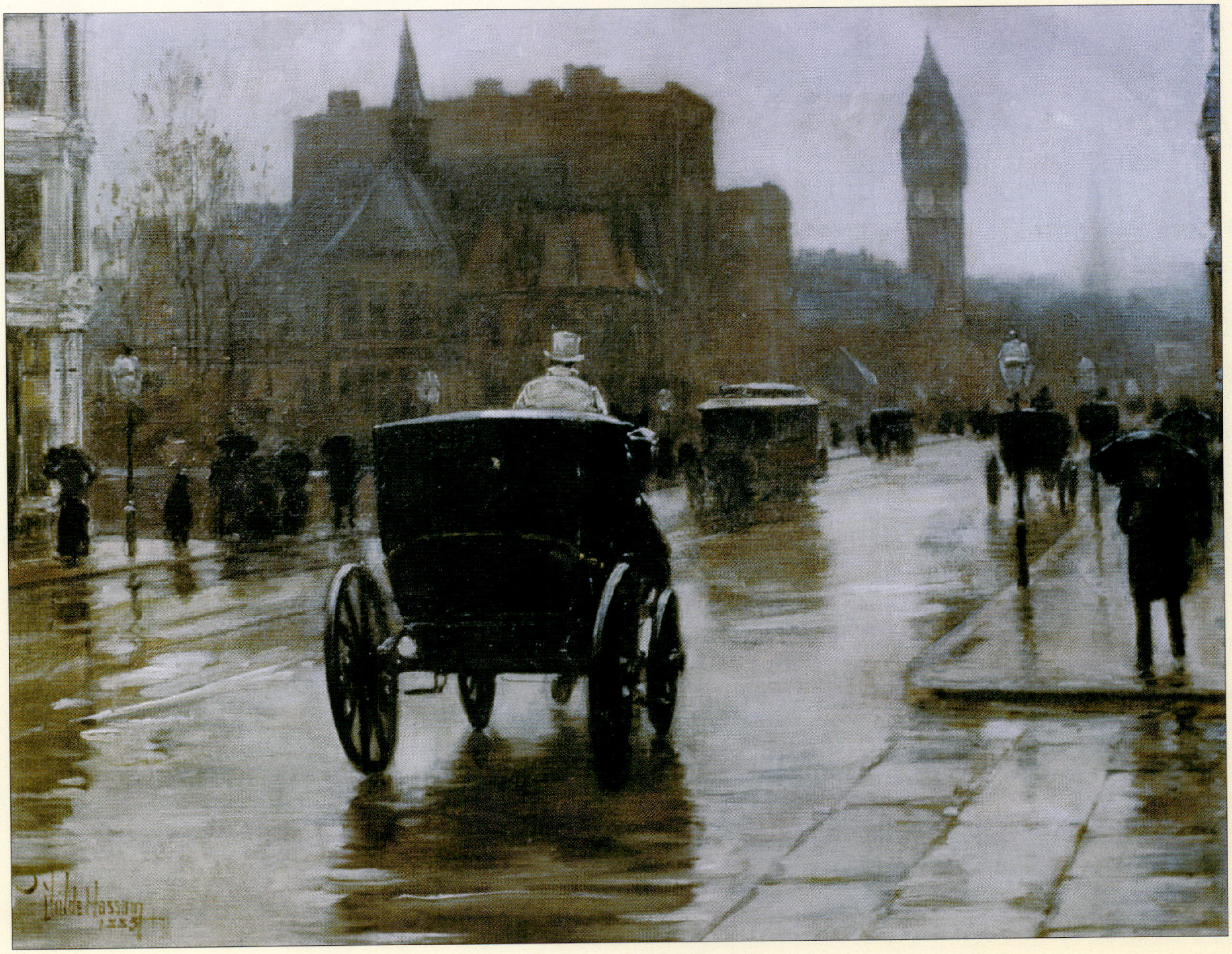

impressionists. The painterly style gives the illusion of immediacy and suggests that the city is not static and fixed, but constantly changing and in motion. The best way to approximate the effects of air, light, and color was to paint *en plein air*—in the open air—and artists were aided in this by the advent of easily transportable paints contained in the now familiar collapsible metal tubes.

Industrial processes also meant that colors were now stable and that a new palette of colors (including cobalt blue, emerald green, and chrome yellow, which were first used in the textile industry) was available to give impressionist paintings their shimmering quality. The brilliancy of the new colors was preserved by laying them directly onto the canvas rather than "muddying" them by mixing them on the palette.

Horse and Carriage on Columbus Avenue *1885. Oil on canvas. 25 x 28 in (63.5 x 71 cm). Private collection.*

East Hampton, Long Island. In all three places Hassam continued to paint garden scenes, delighting in the contrast between the brightness of the blooms and the weathered clapboard buildings against which they were set, as in *Old House and Garden, East Hampton, Long Island* (1898).

Hassam's later period is marked by his series of flag paintings—about 24 pictures—commemorating the festive events connected with World War I. The paintings depict the changing display of flags that decked Fifth Avenue, earning the street the name "The Avenue of the Allies." The series allows us to trace the United States' involvement in the war, from support of the Allies, through entry into the hostilities, to final victory. Decorative as well as political, Hassam's flag paintings have their antecedents in works by the French impressionists Manet, Monet, and Pissarro.

HENRI Robert

As the driving force behind The Eight, a group of artists working in the United States, Robert Henri organized independent exhibitions, paving the way for the 1913 Armory Show, which was the first major exhibition of avant-garde art in the United States. Henri was also an influential teacher, encouraging his students to seek inspiration in the contemporary scene.

Life and work

Throughout his life Robert Henri was secretive about details of his family background and childhood. This was because his father, John Cozad, had killed a man in self-defense and was, for years, a fugitive from the law.

Data file

Full name: Robert Henry Cozad (known as Robert Henri)

Nationality: American

Style: realism

Dates: born 1865 in Cincinnati, OH, died 1929 in New York, NY

Key works:

Girl Seated by the Sea 1893

Fourteenth of July: Boulevard Saint-Michel 1898

The Rain Storm: Wyoming Valley 1902

Derricks on the North River 1902

Antonio Banos (Calero), Picador 1908

Herself 1913

Ruth Saint Denis in "The Peacock Dance" 1919

Things to look for:

- impressionistic influence in early works
- darker palette adopted during the 1890s, along with rapid, slashing brushstrokes
- scenes of everyday, urban life, as well as landscapes and seascapes
- portraits of ordinary people from Ireland, Spain, Mexico, and the southwestern United States
- in portraits, the sitter's eyes appear to peer out at the spectator

Comparisons: Frans Hals, Rembrandt, John Constable, Thomas Eakins, Edouard Manet, Diego Velázquez, Childe Hassam, William Glackens, John Sloan, Ernest Lawson, Everett Shinn

Glossary terms: academic, Armory Show, avant-garde, *en plein air*, impressionism, modernism, Nabis, picturesque, realism, The Eight

Assuming a new name in 1883, the family moved to Atlantic City, New Jersey. Here Henri began painting, enrolling in 1886 at the Pennsylvania Academy of Fine Art, where he was taught by Thomas Anshutz. Anshutz passed on to his students the ideas of American painter Thomas Eakins, in particular that American art should be independent of European styles and traditions and that students should look at the everyday world for their inspiration and paint what they saw in a dramatic, realist style.

In 1888 Henri arrived in Paris, France, where he enrolled at the Academie Julian. Here he came into contact with the work of the group of French artists known as the "Nabis," while in the museums he discovered the works of Diego Velázquez and Rembrandt. The following year Henri went to Concarneau, on the Brittany coast, where he painted portraits of the local fishermen, as well as *en plein air* landscapes and seascapes in an impressionistic manner.

Back in Philadelphia, in 1892 he began teaching at the Philadelphia School of Design for Women. In addition, he organized weekly meetings of artists, including John Sloan, William Glackens, Everett Shinn, and George Luks. Together they formed the nucleus of the group that would later be called The Eight.

As a result of Henri's growing influence, Philadelphia was to become the center for a new realism in art. Those working under Henri rejected the light-toned palette of the impressionists, instead adopting a much darker one that was coupled with rapid brushstrokes in order to capture the essence of everyday, urban life.

Between two further trips to Europe Henri exhibited 87 of his paintings in Philadelphia, thus firmly establishing his reputation. In 1900 he moved to New York City, where he taught at the New York School of Art.

By now a feud was developing between Henri and the National Academy of Art, to which he had been elected as a jury member, concerning

Progress, freedom, and experimentation

For 15 years prior to the Armory Show in 1913, Henri had been vocal in his criticism of the conservative, academic art system and had fought for the right of all artists to exhibit their works free of the constraints imposed by selection juries. He achieved his aims with the success of The Eight's independent exhibitions and the Armory Show, which opened American eyes to European avant-garde art.

As one of the United States' foremost artists he now considered himself free to return to his own work and to reassess his painting in the light of the new artistic forces that he had helped to promote. Because he believed in the artist's need for independence and experimentation, he painted in several different styles, often at the same time. Because he found that his subject matter suggested different styles, Henri's landscapes were influenced by the impressionists and John Constable, his portraits by Frans Hals, and his figure studies by Edouard Manet and Velázquez.

Henri made painting trips every summer. He became fascinated by the culture of the Native Americans in the American southwest, and returned to Santa Fe to paint during the summers of 1916, 1917, and 1922. In 1913 Henri made his first visit to Achill Island, off the west coast of Ireland. Here he painted some of the best-known works of his career: landscapes like *Menaune Cliffs* (1913), as well as portraits of the local people, like *Patrick* (1913). During subsequent yearly trips from 1924 to 1928 Henri devoted himself largely to painting portraits of children, including those of Mary Ann Cafferty in *The Pink Pinafore* (1926) and *Blonde Bridgett Lavelle* (1928).

Herself (1913), one of a pair of portraits of Johnny Cummings *(Himself)* and his wife, dates from Henri's first trip to Achill Island. Originally from the mainland, the pair had eloped. During the course of 55 years of marriage, the couple had raised 13 children, entertaining the islanders with both their arguments and their declarations of devotion.

Recalling the spirit of the 17th-century Dutch artist Frans Hals, under Henri's brush such ordinary people are depicted with dignity and respect. In 1915 Henri wrote in the *Craftsman* magazine: "The people I like to paint are 'my people,' whoever they may be, wherever they may exist."

His spontaneous, rapid brushstrokes give a sense of lively vitality and immediacy. This sense of vitality is enhanced by Henri's use of one of his favorite devices, in which the sitter's eyes seem to peer out at the spectator. Henri also encouraged artists to work at great speed, because, as he wrote in *The Art Spirit*, "The most vital things in the look of a face...endure only for a moment."

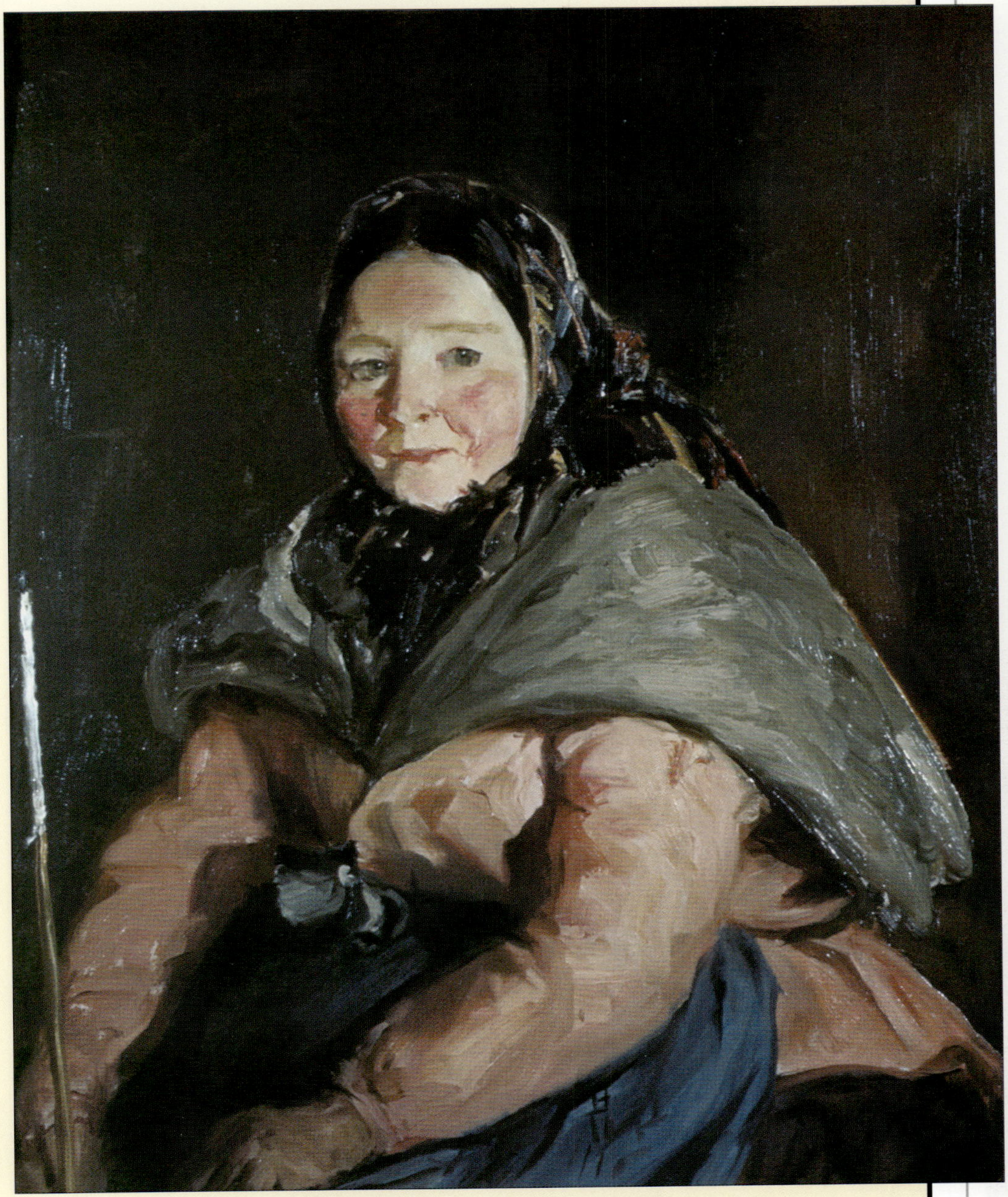

Herself *1913. Oil on canvas. 32 x 26 in (81.5 x 66 cm). H. Schulze Memorial Collection, Art Institute of Chicago, ILL.*

the Academy's constant rejection of works by young, progressive artists for exhibition. As a result Henri decided to stage his own exhibitions, along with Arthur B. Davies, Maurice Prendergast, Ernest Lawson, Sloan, Glackens, Shinn, and Luks—together The Eight. Their 1908 exhibition at Macbeth's Galleries on Fifth Avenue was a commercial and critical success, encouraging Henri to plan a second show for 1910. This was the Exhibition of Independent Artists, the first large, unrestricted, nonjury-selected exhibition of American art. In 1911 the breakaway artists re-formed as the Association of American Painters and Sculptors, helping to stage annual exhibitions of modern European and American art.

Henri's philosophy toward art was simple: progress, freedom, and experimentation; the seminal 1913 Armory Show represented a visual illustration of his philosophy.

Henri himself continued to paint, producing portraits and finding inspiration for figure studies in picturesque characters (like gypsies and bullfighters) during his frequent trips to Europe. His teaching and writing were equally important to him, however: he ran his own school from 1909 and also taught at the Art Students' League from 1915 to 1928. Having developed pseudoscientific theories of color and composition, Henri published *The Art Spirit*, a collection of his letters, lectures, and articles on art, in 1923. He died of cancer in 1929.

HESSE Eva

IN SPITE OF A SHORT CAREER, prematurely ended by a brain tumor, Eva Hesse's work made her one of the most original and influential artists of the 1960s. She opened up new frontiers in the form, materials, and content of sculpture.

Life and work

Born in Hamburg, Germany in 1936, Eva Hesse was only two when she and her sister Helen boarded a train to Amsterdam, The Netherlands, to escape Nazi persecution. They were later reunited with their parents. In 1939 the Hesse family emigrated to the United States, settling in Washington Heights, New York. Hesse's mother never recovered from her war experiences, however, and was hospitalized. By 1945 Hesse's parents were divorced; the following year her mother committed suicide. Hesse's resulting fear of mental illness became a persistent feature of her life thereafter.

Determined to become an artist, Hesse began studying at the High School of Industrial Arts in New York, and the Pratt Institute of Design. She was unhappy at the school, however, and left in the middle of her second year, instead taking evening classes at the Art Students' League while working as an intern at *Seventeen Magazine* during the day. In 1953 the magazine featured three of Hesse's watercolors, a drawing, and a lithograph.

Between 1954 and 1957 Hesse studied at Cooper Union before accepting a scholarship as a painter to Yale University School of Art and Architecture, where she was taught by former Bauhaus master Josef Albers. Hesse found her time at Yale difficult: she was attracted by abstract expressionism, which was at odds with Albers's more formal, theoretical approach to painting. This conflict, between the emotional and formal concerns of art, would only later be resolved in Hesse's work.

After Yale Hesse still believed that her goal as an artist was to paint, and it was not until 1962 that she made her first three-dimensional construction, a costume for a series of "happenings," or spontaneous theatrical events. By this time it was her drawings—with their combinations of collage, ink, pencil, gouache, and watercolor—and not her paintings that were attracting critical acclaim.

Disheartened by her paintings' poor reception, and now both an artist and the wife of an artist (she married the sculptor Tom Doyle in 1961), Hesse's work developed little until 1964, when she made a return visit to her native Germany. She began making sculptures, working with discarded materials and plaster. She also began to investigate the potential offered by grid forms, into which she threaded and knotted her materials.

Hesse's personal life was troubled following her return to the United States (her marriage to Doyle had

Data file

Full name: Eva Hesse

Nationality: American (U.S. citizen after 1945)

Style: minimalism/process art

Dates: born 1936 in Hamburg, died 1970 in New York, NY

Key works:

Ringaround Arosie 1965

Several 1965

Hang Up 1966

Sequel 1967–68

Repetition Nineteen III 1968

Sans II 1968

Accession II 1969

Tori 1969

Things to look for:

- nontraditional materials, such as industrial latex, rubberized fabrics, wire mesh, and ropes
- themes of sequences and serials
- use of grid forms, spheres, and layering
- references to "viscera": the internal organs of the human body

Comparisons: Claes Oldenburg, Robert Rauschenberg, Jackson Pollock, Carl Andre, Donald Judd, Sol LeWitt, Robert Morris, Richard Serra, Louise Bourgeois

Glossary terms: abstract expressionism, Bauhaus, collage, gestural painting, gouache, happening, lithography, minimalism, process art, relief

Themes and processes

Hesse's sculpture is sometimes classified as minimal art, and sometimes as process art. The term "process art" was first introduced to the public in Lucy Lippard's 1966 exhibition called "Eccentric Abstraction," which featured Hesse's work. Process art was a reaction against the anonymous, machine-finished—and expensive—industrially produced materials that were the components of the minimalists' work . Process artists replaced these with the by-products and even the waste of modern industrial society.

Process artists incorporated all kinds of materials into their work, including wood, rubber, and felt, as well as grass, fat, and yeast. Not only was the use of these materials unusual in the history of art, but the works into which they were incorporated were unstable, impermanent, prone to decomposition, and extremely fragile. While the minimalists believed that the anonymously produced, industrial materials that they used were free of emotional and subjective content, the process artists created pieces that were personal, tactile, and powerfully suggestive, although they continued to use an abstract, formal language. The forms used in process art tended to be organic and amorphous, because the emphasis was placed on the actual processes involved in the making of the sculptures.

Despite its labeling as process art, Hesse's work nevertheless shares some links with that of the minimalists. Like them, she was interested in repetition and the serial potential of elements. Several of

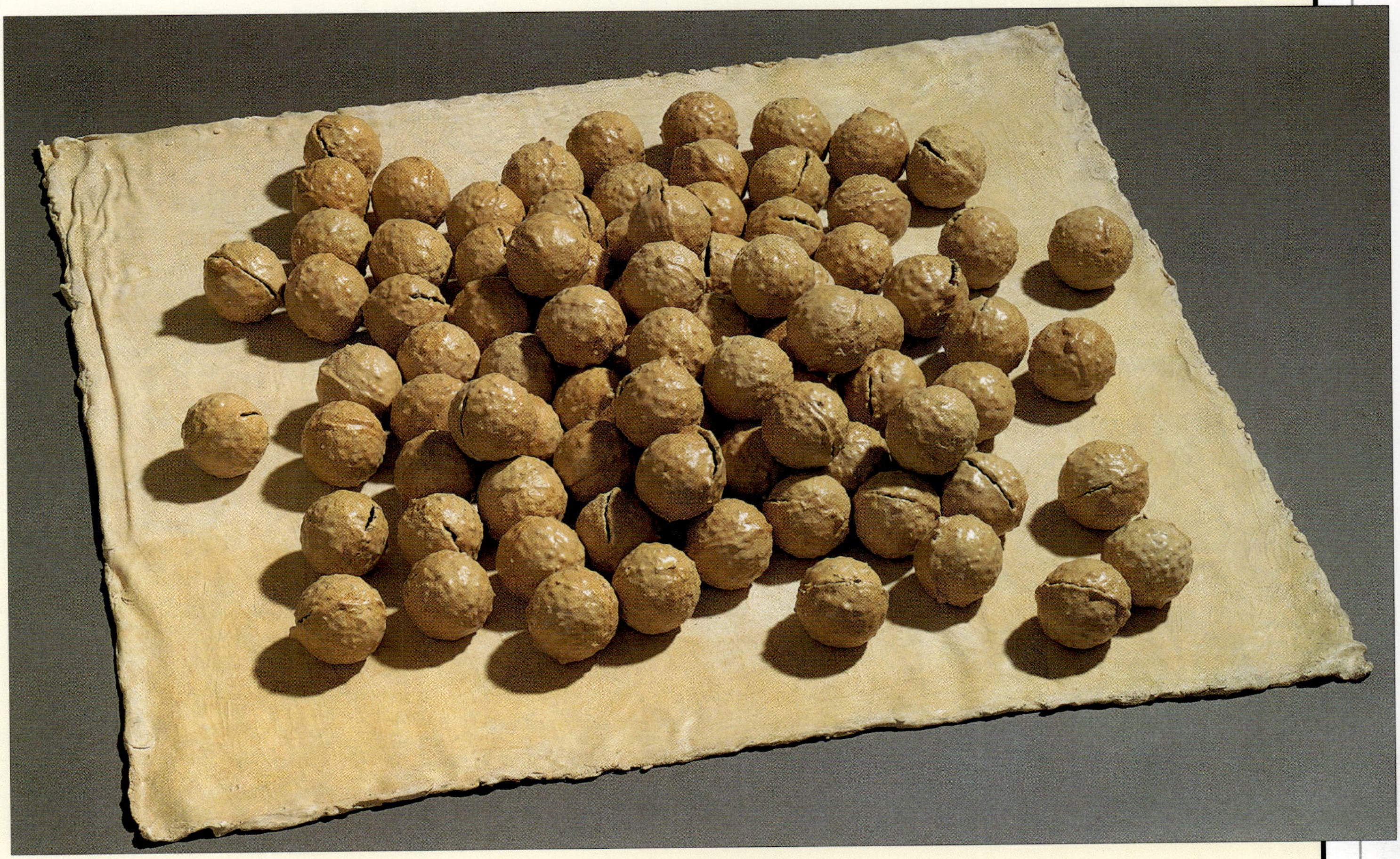

Sequel *1967–68. Latex mixed with powdered white pigment. 30 x 32 in (76 x 81 cm). Lannan Foundation, Los Angeles, CA.*

her works' titles illustrate this interest, such as the *Accession* series (1967–69), and *Repetition Nineteen III* (1968). For Hesse, repetition could either be neat and orderly or untidy and chaotic: in *Schema* (1967), for example, 144 latex spheres are laid out in neat rows, while in *Sequel* (1967–68), some of the spheres that are piled up on a sheet appear to be in danger of rolling off it.

Sequel also indicates Hesse's fascination with the passage of time, an interest that may have developed as her health declined, but that is reflected, too, in the unstable nature of the materials that she often used. Although materials like latex were prone to disintegration, fiberglass was more permanent, yet its translucent quality accorded a central role in her sculpture to an infinitely variable element: light itself.

Some of Hesse's works deal with the mutability of the body and have been interpreted as references to Hesse's own illness. More characteristic of her mature work, however, are *Sequel* and *Hang Up* (1966), in which a thin, flexible rod loops out from, and back to, a rectangular frame. Like *Sequel*, however, such sculptures refuse to communicate their meaning to the spectator, or, indeed, to demonstrate any "inner truth."

ended), but her work now entered a new phase, and she completed her first relief, *Ringaround Arosie*, in 1965, which she named for her pregnant friend Rosalyn Goldman.

Hesse's use of grid forms, combined with layers of material and string, led many American feminist critics to discern "female imagery" (evocations of women's bodies, especially their internal organs) in what were essentially abstract works. Furthermore the "stringy" nature of her sculptures caused them to be likened to three-dimensional versions of Jackson Pollock's gestural paintings (also called action paintings).

In 1968 Hesse began to experiment with fiberglass and polymer resins, attracted by their translucent qualities. *Repetition Nineteen III* was her first piece in fiberglass, followed by *Accretion*, and *Sans II* (all 1968). She staged her first solo sculpture show in the same year, but indications of her illness appeared alongside the first fruits of her success. In April 1969 Hesse collapsed, and was admitted to the hospital, where she underwent brain surgery. She continued to work, although weak and wheelchair-bound, producing some of the most important sculptures of her career. Further surgery, radiation, and chemotherapy proved ineffective; in May 1970 Hesse fell into a coma and died, at the age of only 34.

HICKS Edward

EDWARD HICKS WAS THE GREATEST OF THE SELF-TAUGHT American folk artists, or "primitives," of the 19th century. He was a member of the Society of Friends (the Quakers), and his paintings were the expression of his religious convictions of faith, love, and peace, as well as a literal belief in the words of the Bible.

Life and work

The folk artist Edward Hicks was born in 1780 in Longhorne, Pennsylvania, but he would spend most of his adult life around Newtown, Pennsylvania. Shortly after his birth, Hicks's mother died, and he was raised by neighbors. In 1803 he married, and joined the Quakers. An eloquent speaker, he became a preacher.

Preaching was unpaid work, but his sign- and carriage-painting business flourished, and he was able to afford preaching trips to New Jersey and New York and around New England.

As well as signs and carriages, he painted landscapes, farmscapes, and biblical scenes, but he gave most of them as gifts to friends and relatives. In his day, Hicks would not have been considered—or even have considered himself—an artist. He was a self-taught amateur, far removed from the art world. Furthermore, he was a Quaker.

The Quakers did not hold art in high esteem: music was a distraction, drama was shunned, and painting positively reviled. Consequently, few paintings by Quakers exist (Benjamin West was raised as a Quaker, but he gave up his faith before pursuing serious artistic training). The only artist to live and die a Quaker was Edward Hicks, and even he wrote in his diary that painting was a trifling and insubstantial art that offered no real advantage to mankind.

Hicks's imagination may have been wide but, like many folk artists, his vision remained firmly rooted in the world around him. In his scenes from the Bible, the landscapes look more like "home" than the ancient Near East. The composition of *Noah's Ark* (1846) is based on an 1844 lithograph by Nathaniel Currier, but Hicks has transformed the ark into a sturdy, floating, Pennsylvania barn.

Hicks painted numerous views of the farms and livestock of David Twining and James C. Cornell. *The Residence of David Twining, 1787*, painted around 1846, echoes the early American tradition of painting plantation views. It is like a domestic example of his versions of *The Peaceable Kingdom* (1820–48), and contrasts with the theological and social visions of the many paintings of that name. The fruits of industry and domestic harmony are seen in the prosperity and peace enjoyed by a Quaker family.

Echoes of Hicks's business often crept into his paintings. One view of

Data file

Full name: Edward Hicks

Nationality: American

Style: folk art

Dates: born 1780 in Longhorne, PA, died 1849 in Newtown, PA

Key works:
- *The Peaceable Kingdom* (60–100 versions) 1820–48
- *Noah's Ark* 1846
- *The Residence of David Twining, 1787* c1846
- *Cornell Farm* 1848

Things to look for:
- landscapes, historical scenes, and farm scenes, as well as religious themes
- inscriptions at bottom of canvas or around the frame, sometimes paraphrasing biblical texts
- main theme often combined with vignette of a historical event to provide a parallel
- flat colors, stylized forms, and decorative patterning
- neatly applied pigments
- clearly defined contours

Comparisons: Grandma Moses, Horace Pippin, Erastus Salisbury Field, Francis Guy, Sheldon Peck, Charles C. Hofmann, Paul A. Siefert, Susan Merrett

Glossary terms: engraving, folk art, lithograph, primitive

The ideal visualized

The theme of the painting shown here preoccupied Hicks throughout his life. It is estimated that he painted between 60 and 100 different versions. They mix Old Testament prophesy and American Quaker history and are best described as painted sermons. They are colorful, lively, and sound in craftsmanship and design.

Isaiah prophesies a day when "The wolf shall lie down with the lamb, and the leopard shall lie down with the kid; and the calf and the young lion and the fatling together, and a little child shall lead them" (Isaiah 11: 6). In the foreground of the painting is the entire assembly of animals as listed by Isaiah, organized into a pyramidal group. Each animal has an individual, naïve charm, and projects a quality of divinely inspired innocence.

If animals can live in peace and harmony, so can mankind. In the middle ground, Hicks has depicted William Penn's treaty with the Indians. In 1861 Penn led his congregation to the Delaware River to build a community of Christians there. This "Holy Experiment" was to encourage Quakers and other Protestant settlers to live in harmony. As a Quaker, Penn could not swear to an oath, yet as the French writer Voltaire observed, Penn's treaty was the only one between Christians and Indians that was "never sworn to and never broken."

Hicks often painted a frame around the edge of his works, and on this 1826 version of *The Peaceable Kingdom* it includes a paraphrase of Isaiah's words, as well as a reference to Penn's treaty with the Indians. The carefully lettered inscription in gold is in the same style that Hicks would have used for the sign painting by which he earned his living.

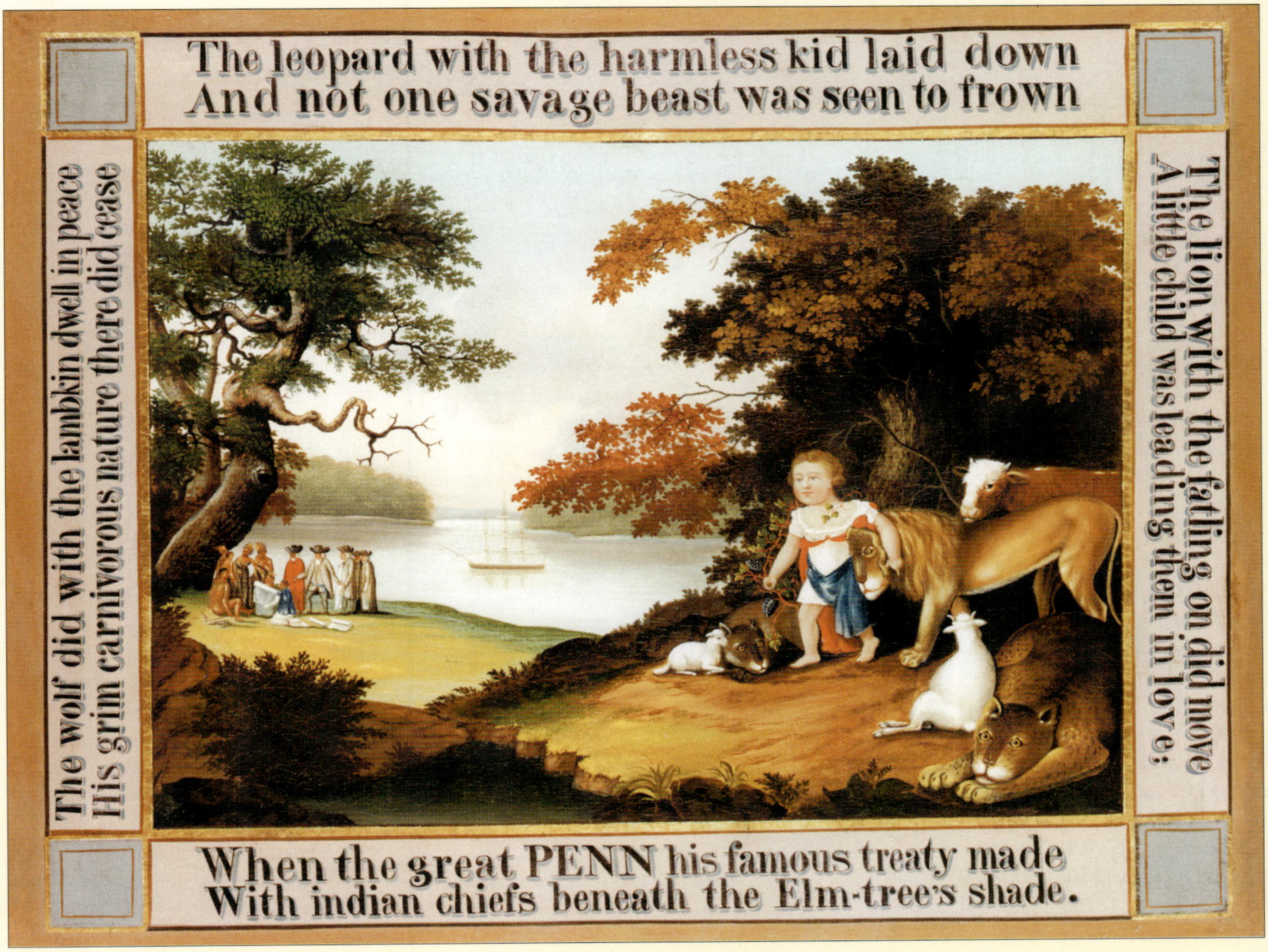

In this "Peaceable Kingdom," under the branches of the great elm tree, Penn and his colleagues, in their broad-brimmed black hats, present a large scroll to the Indians. As a basis for this part of the composition, Hicks used an engraving of Benjamin West's painting of 1771 depicting the same event. Like many folk artists, Hicks made regular use of popular prints and engravings as source material. It is possible that he was referring to this use of prints when he wrote in his diary the rhyme:

> Inferior folks with only monkey's art
> May imitate but never life impart.

In the distance, Hicks gives us a view of the Delaware Water Gap as a sign of nature's wonders and God's gifts to mankind. In other versions, he depicts the Natural Bridge in Virginia.

The Peaceable Kingdom *1826. Oil on canvas. 32¾ x 41¾ in (83.5 x 106 cm). Philadelphia Museum of Art, Philadelphia, PA.*

The combination of two different scenes within one picture area is a nonrealistic approach to the subject that is typical of primitive artists, who did not feel in any way restricted by artistic conventions of what constitutes reality.

the Cornell farm painted in 1848 is inscribed with the words: "An Indian Summer view of the Farm & Stock of James C. Cornell of Northampton Bucks County Penn. That took the Premium in the Agricultural Society, october the 12th, 1848," and is signed "Painted by E Hicks in the 69th year of his age."

Hicks stands apart from many other amateur American folk artists of his generation. Despite being self-taught, he treats space three-dimensionally. Colors recede atmospherically as the landscape merges with the sky on the horizon. When watercolors were the preferred medium of the amateur, he was painting in oils.

Hicks was distressed by divisions in the Society of Friends, caused by separatists led by one of his own relatives, and painting made him feel he was in conflict with religion. His numerous versions of *The Peaceable Kingdom*, the earliest of which dates from around 1820, may have been an attempt to counter these disharmonies.

HILLIARD Nicholas

NICHOLAS HILLIARD TOOK THE ART OF MINIATURE PAINTING to unsurpassed levels. The tiny portraits he made, small enough to be held in the hand, have a jewel-like exquisiteness that is as astonishing to us today as it must have been when they were first made in the late 16th century.

Life and work

Nicholas Hilliard was born about 1547 in Exeter in south-west England. His father was a successful goldsmith. At that time it was customary to educate middle-class children by placing them in a family of rank, and it seems that from about the age of nine Nicholas was living with the Bodley family. The Bodleys had to flee to (Protestant) Geneva for religious reasons after the (Catholic) Queen Mary came to the throne in 1553.

Hilliard was back in England by 1562, and he gained himself an apprenticeship of seven years to a goldsmith/jeweler, Robert Brandon, who was jeweler to Queen Elizabeth I. In 1569 he set up in business with his brother John, and by 1570 Hilliard is recorded as a member of the Goldsmiths' Company. From the outset he was both a limner (a painter of miniatures) and a goldsmith, and when he entered the service of Queen Elizabeth I around 1570 it was in both these capacities.

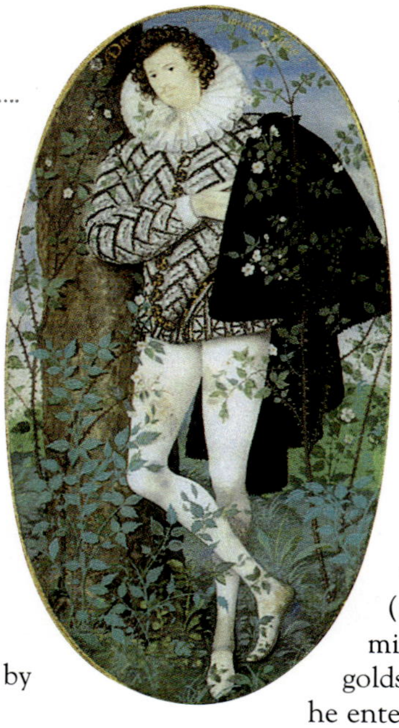

Young Man Leaning Against a Tree
(portrait miniature) c1590. Watercolor on vellum. 5 1/4 x 6 3/4 in (13 x 7 cm). Victoria and Albert Museum, London.

Hilliard married Robert Brandon's daughter Alice in 1573. Having earned a reputation for his work, he went to France around 1577, hoping to make a good living there. He stayed two years in France, mostly in Paris, mingling with rich and educated people. However, by 1597 he was back in England, not having made the "piece of money" he had hoped for, and it seems that he had financial problems for the rest of his life. Over the next 10 years his wife, Alice, gave birth to four sons and three daughters.

Hilliard lived and worked in the city of London for the next 35 years. His fame was such that the English poet John Donne mentioned him in his 1597 poem "The Storme":

A hand, or eye
By Hilliard drawn, is worth an history
By a worse painter made…

While he was in service to Queen Elizabeth I Hilliard developed miniature painting to new levels of intimacy and subtlety. An important painter, Francisco Pacheco, in Seville, Spain, somehow saw one of Hilliard's miniatures and wrote: "The head is done with so much skill, that (in my opinion) it leaves far behind all of this kind I have ever seen. I say truly that

Data file

Full name: Nicholas Hilliard
Nationality: English
Style: Elizabethan
Dates: born c1547 in Exeter, died 1619 in London
Key works:
Young Man Leaning Against a Tree c1590
Miniature portraits of Queen Elizabeth I and other prominent Elizabethans, including Sir Walter Raleigh and Sir Francis Drake
Things to look for:
- miniature portraits of exquisite beauty
- avoidance of the use of shadows

Comparisons: Hans Holbein, Isaac Oliver
Glossary terms: limning, miniature

Jewels fit for a queen

This jewel was painted in 1588 for Queen Elizabeth I. It commemorates a famous English victory at sea: the destruction of the Spanish Armada (fleet). The Queen gave the jewel as a present to Sir Thomas Heneage. We do not know whether all the gold and enamel was actually crafted by Hilliard himself, but he would have designed it. The loop at the top of the frame indicates that this almost certainly had a chain and would have been worn around the owner's neck.

The Armada Jewel was made of enameled gold and has a hinged lid. Shown here is the jewel itself, with a portrait of Queen Elizabeth, and the inside lid of the case. Hardly surprisingly, the portrait is slightly damaged.

The red enameled rose on the inside of the case has an inlaid inscription in Latin, which reads "Alas that virtue endued [provided] with so much beauty should not be uninjured and enjoy perpetual life." The outside case was also decorated, with a tiny ark and a Latin inscription meaning "Calm though stormy seas."

It is the painting inside the jeweled case, however, which is so astonishing for its sensitivity and fine detail. Hilliard's style avoided the use of shadow, which he wrote was in accordance with Queen Elizabeth's taste. The portrait shows the queen in a huge collar or ruff, which was fashionable at the time, with jewels in her hair, on her clothing and around her neck. The date 1588 appears in gold lettering on the blue background (after *Anno*, Latin for "year.")

In *The Arte of Limning* Hilliard tells us that such miniatures should be done on the finest parchment (vellum) stuck onto card (often a playing card was used, for these

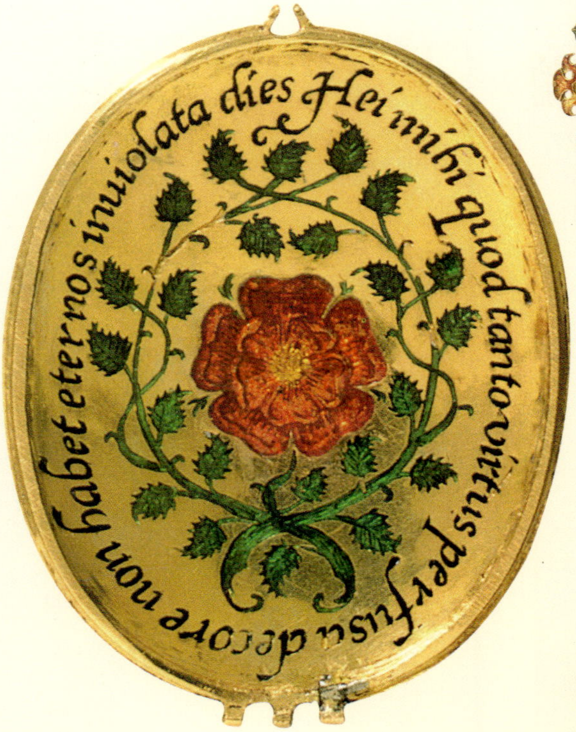

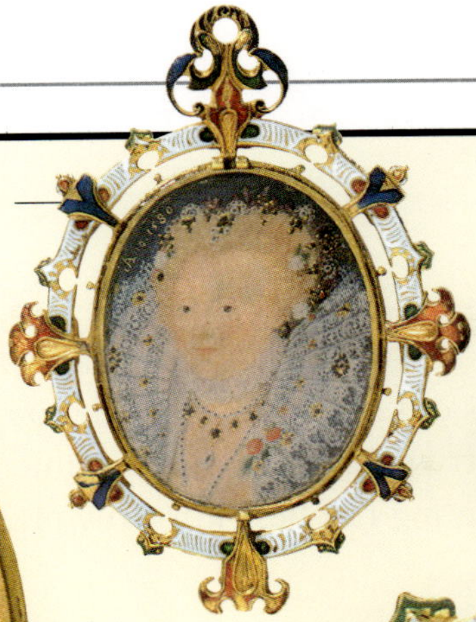

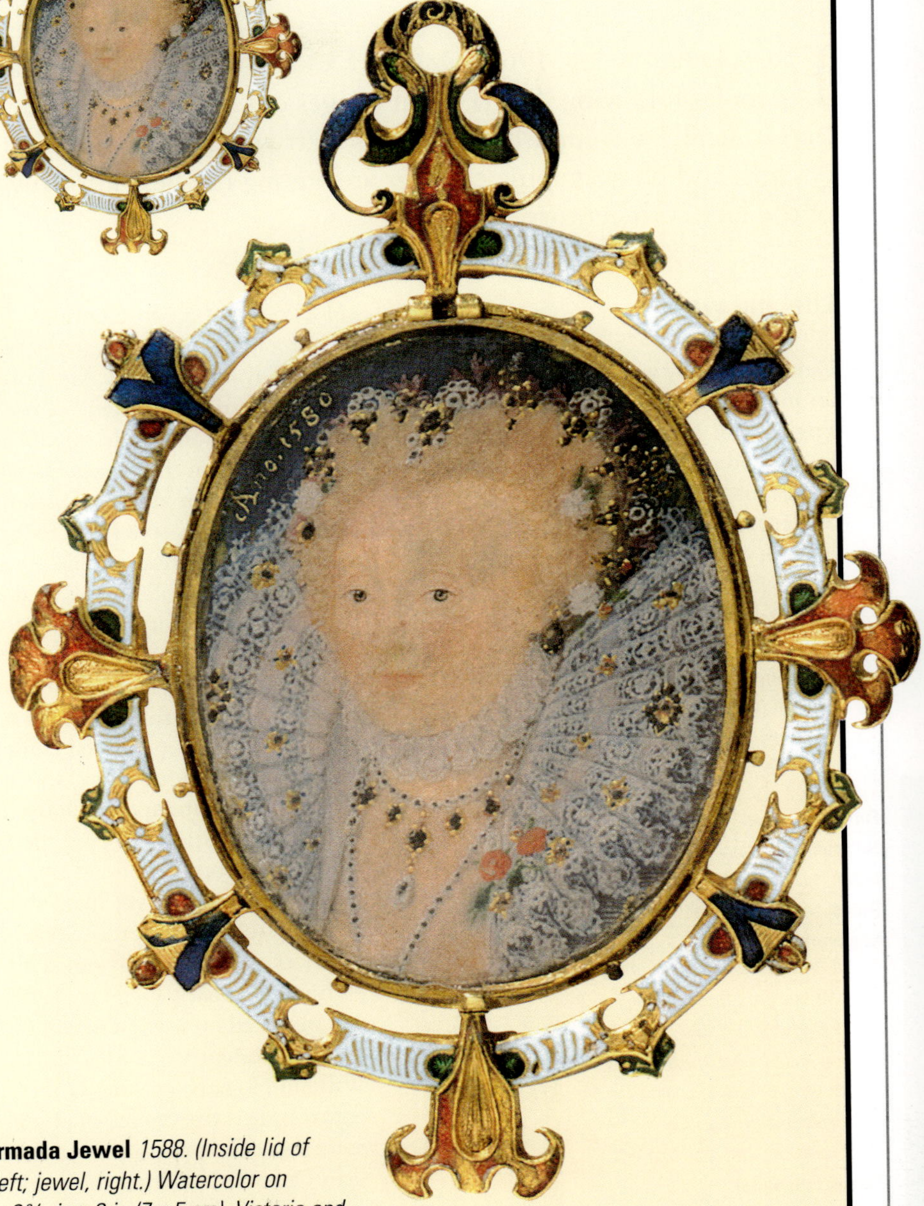

were of fine quality). Hilliard worked with the sitter about two yards in front of him. He used very fine brushes (which were called "pencils" in those days) made of hairs taken from squirrel tails. The colors were mixed with a thin water-based gum to make them stick, and sometimes a little sugar was added to prevent them from cracking when they dried.

Hilliard's colors came from a number of sources: earths, plants, and minerals. Some of these are very sensitive to light, but fading was slowed because many miniatures were kept in lockets and cases. Even so, this portrait of Elizabeth I looks quite pale and the pinks almost certainly have faded.

The Armada Jewel *1588. (Inside lid of case, left; jewel, right.) Watercolor on vellum. 2¾ in x 2 in (7 x 5 cm). Victoria and Albert Museum, London.*

methinks Limning could go no farther; and that there the art reached perfection."

Hilliard's work is perhaps most famously epitomized in the miniature *Young Man Leaning Against a Tree* (c1590), which may have been commissioned by a man as a gift to a woman to show her that his love was sincere. At the top of the painting is a motto reading "My praised faith causes my suffering."

After the death of Elizabeth I, Hilliard also worked for James I, but his style began to go out of fashion. He continued to have money problems, and in 1617 was briefly imprisoned for guaranteeing a debt.

Hilliard would be remembered not only for his exquisite miniatures but for his treatise *The Arte of Limning*, written around 1600. In this he makes it quite clear that painters of miniatures ranked above other painters, as they produced works of art that were fit for gentlemen, and the finest enameled and bejeweled lockets worn by courtiers. His book also covered practical matters, such as his advice to wear silk while painting, as inferior clothes made dust.

HOCKNEY David

FROM EARLY IN THE 1960S DAVID HOCKNEY'S WORK has won a wide popular following. His colorful images of California poolside life, his classically accomplished drawings, witty prints, set and costume designs, and photographic collages are among the best-known works of the late 20th century.

Life and work

David Hockney was born in Bradford, an industrial town in northern England, in 1937. From the age of 16 he studied at Bradford School of Art, where his talent as a draftsman became evident. His earliest works, such as a portrait of his father painted at the age of 17, show the influence of the Euston Road school of artists of the 1940s, known for their naturalistic rendering of urban subjects in muted colours.

In 1959, after two years' national service spent working in hospitals (Hockney was a conscientious objector), he began postgraduate study at the Royal College of Art, London. He was a brilliant student whose confident personal style rapidly gained attention. From the outset Hockney demonstrated an ability to assimilate and develop new styles and techniques, and explore different media.

The Royal College was a center of pop art in Britain in the early 1960s. Artists such as Peter Blake and R. B. Kitaj employed modern, figurative imagery in works that often made reference to mass-produced commercial graphic art. Although Hockey's ironic handling of contemporary subjects gave him the reputation of being the "golden boy" of the pop art generation, Hockney himself never liked this label.

His student work took its cue from a variety of sources. His series of etchings, *A Rake's Progress* (1961–63), was modeled on a sequence of pictures with the same title produced by William Hogarth around 1735. By contrast, it is the expressive figure paintings of the postwar French artist Jean Dubuffet, evoking the crude technique and emotional immediacy of children's art, that can be sensed behind *We Two Boys Together Clinging* (1961). This shows two childlike figures hugging; it is roughly inscribed with various words and phrases. These, together with the painting's title, are taken from a poem by the American poet Walt Whitman. The poem celebrates homosexual love—one of Hockney's primary themes throughout his career. It is taken up explicitly in his print series, *Illustrations for Fourteen Poems by C. P. Cavafy* (1967), which provides another fine example of the interplay of literary sources and artistic ideas in much of Hockney's work.

From his early twenties onward, his work had enormous popular appeal. To a public accustomed to thinking of 20th-century art as being difficult and demanding, his sharply defined, colorful images struck viewers as both original and approachable.

By the early 1960s Hockney yearned to escape from the "gloominess" of English art into the colorful excitement that he associated with American art. It was also the promise of greater personal freedom in a more tolerant and extrovert culture that prompted Hockney's decision in 1963 to leave Britain for California. The world he found there seemed to

Data file

Full name: David Hockney
Nationality: English
Style: modern
Dates: born 1937 in Bradford
Key works:
- *A Rake's Progress* (series of etchings) 1961–63
- *We Two Boys Together Clinging* 1961
- *A Bigger Splash* 1967
- *Mr. and Mrs. Clark and Percy* 1970–71
- designs for Mozart's opera *The Magic Flute* 1978
- *Pearblossom Hwy* 1986
- *Fourth Very New Painting* 1992

Things to look for:
- vibrant color
- accomplished draftsmanship
- exploration of different media
- contemporary and autobiographical themes
- strong sense of the pleasure of visual experience

Comparisons: Jean Dubuffet, Henri Matisse, R. B. Kitaj, Peter Blake, Pablo Picasso
Glossary terms: abstract expressionism, acrylic, collage, cubism, Euston Road school, figurative, pop art

Removing the distance

David Hockney has written that "Art is about sharing.... I am constantly preoccupied with how to remove distance so that we can all come closer together, so that we can all begin to sense...that we are one." His portraits, in particular, can be viewed in these terms, since they are mostly of the artist's friends and convey a sense of relaxed intimacy.

From 1967 Hockney produced a number of large double portraits in a highly realistic idiom. *Mr. and Mrs. Clark and Percy* (1970–71) shows Hockney's friends Ossie and Celia Clark, with their cat, Percy, in what appears to be a fashionable London interior. The couple's carefully chosen possessions and clothing suggest their shared tastes, but their separation by the strong vertical lines of the window and shutters strikes a note of distance.

The white cat, a symbol of domestic warmth but also wildness, seems mesmerized by something in the bright sunlight beyond the window. It subtly suggests the presence of restlessness and unpredictability in this otherwise very coolly poised portrait.

Mr. and Mrs. Clark and Percy *1970–71. Acrylic on canvas. 84 x 120 in (213 x 305 cm). Tate Gallery, London.*

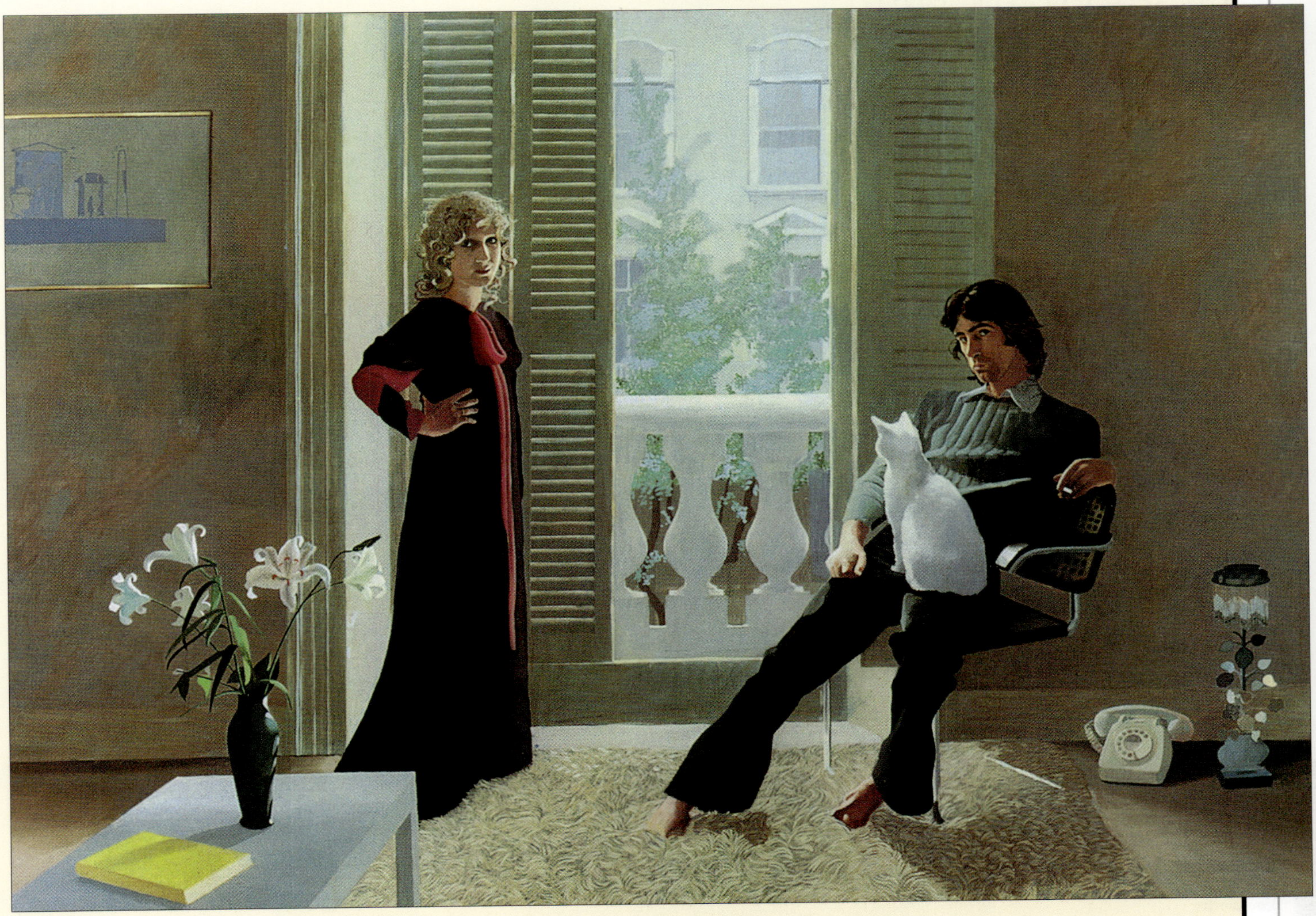

be a perfect match for his artistic temperament. Hockney's exuberant, memorable pictures of Los Angeles poolside life have come to symbolize the carefree, pleasure-seeking lifestyle that many people aspired to in the new consumer culture of the 1960s.

A Bigger Splash, which Hockney painted in 1967, delights in the strong blues of the sky and water, the green of the palm tree, whose sprouting form is echoed by the explosion of the water following a swimmer's dive. Made in the relatively new medium of acrylic paint, which produces a quicker-drying, flatter surface than oil paint, the painting has the instantaneous feel of a snapshot.

In 1967 Hockney returned for a time to Europe, where he lived in London and Paris. From his student days, Hockney's personality had been an important part of his fame, and in 1974 a biographical film about him, called *A Bigger Splash*, reached a wide cinema audience.

Hockney had once referred to his figure paintings as "being really dramas," and during the 1970s he became involved in stage design, producing set and costume designs for operas and ballets, such as his 1975 designs for *The Rake's Progress* by Igor Stravinsky, and his 1978 designs for Mozart's *The Magic Flute*. Stage design has continued to play an important part in his career.

Hockney has also continued to experiment with new approaches, both in painting and in other media, notably photographic collage. In the 1980s he began assembling composite images, called "joiners," made up of many photographs of the same subject. The effect resembles the fragmented forms of early 20th-century cubist art.

In the late 1980s Hockney began to explore different styles of landscape painting—both naturalistic and highly schematized. In the 1990s he developed an abstract style in his sequence of *Very New Paintings*, which he came to regard as "internal landscapes."

In the same period he also painted more intimate, domestic subjects, such as still lifes and portraits of his cherished dachshunds. Together, these works show that, even in his fifties and sixties, Hockney's work retains its irrepressible variety.

HOGARTH William

HOGARTH WAS ONE OF ENGLAND'S GREATEST PAINTERS, but it is only recently that the key role he played in the story of British painting has been recognized; during his lifetime he never achieved the recognition he felt was due to him. Hogarth was a highly skilled painter and engraver, and an astute observer of people's foibles. His wit and liveliness shine through his vivid and fluent portraits.

Life and work

William Hogarth was born in London in 1697. He had a difficult start in life: his father fell into debt, and from 1708 to 1712 William and the rest of his family were held in a debtors' prison. In 1713, at the age of 15, Hogarth was apprenticed to a silver engraver. He did not enjoy the craft, and in his twenties he turned to painting.

Hogarth was largely self-taught, but in 1724 he joined a drawing school at the house of Sir James Thornhill, Serjeant Painter to King George I. Hogarth eloped with Thornhill's daughter Jane in 1729, but the couple were forgiven by Jane's father.

To his irritation, Hogarth found that wealthy English patrons preferred artworks by foreign painters, but there was some demand for portraits, so Hogarth began painting small, informal portrait groups called conversation pieces. He found them time-consuming to produce and not very lucrative; though *The Beggar's Opera* (1728), showing a scene from the popular play by John Gay, was so successful that he had to produce several copies of his original picture to satisfy demand.

Further success followed when he developed a new and highly original idea—the "modern moral subject." These were pictures designed to be seen in a series, which told a moral story in a humorous way. As a skilled engraver he was able to make engravings of the paintings from which prints on paper could be made. This was much cheaper and quicker than copying the paintings by hand each time. The first six-episode series (*A Harlot's Progress*, c1732) told the story of the downfall of an innocent country girl.

The prints were an instant success, and many inferior copies were soon in circulation. In an attempt to stop this pirating, Hogarth delayed the printing of his next series, *A Rake's Progress*, until 1735, when a law on copyright was passed. Known at the time as Hogarth's Act, the law was introduced largely because of his campaigning.

Although Hogarth was annoyed by the popularity of foreign painters, he also envied them. His attempts to rival Italian and other European painters by producing grand pictures of serious historical subjects were unsuccessful, however, and in the early 1740s he returned to portraiture, though this time on a grand scale.

In 1745 he persuaded his artist friends to donate paintings for the first public exhibition of contemporary art. In the same year he produced his finest modern moral series, *Marriage à la Mode*, which satirized arranged upper-class marriages. *The Breakfast Scene*, one of six in the series, shows a couple in chaos. The wife has been up all night playing cards, and her husband has just got home after being with another woman, whose bonnet is in his pocket; the dog is sniffing it. On the far left, their steward is leaving the room in despair, holding a pile of unpaid bills.

Throughout the 1750s Hogarth produced further satirical engravings, but he became increasingly involved in disputes with patrons and politicians and his popularity declined.

Marriage à la Mode (The Breakfast Scene)
c1745. Oil on canvas. 28 x 36 in (71 x 91 cm). National Gallery, London.

Data file

Full name: William Hogarth

Nationality: English

Style: rococo

Dates: born 1697 in London, died 1764 in London

Key works:
- *The Beggar's Opera* 1728
- *A Harlot's Progress* c1732
- *A Rake's Progress* 1735
- *Captain Coram* 1740
- *Marriage à la Mode* c1745
- *'O the Roast Beef of Old England!' (Calais Gate)* 1748
- *The Election* 1754

Things to look for:
- small-scale group portraits
- pictures (paintings or engravings) in a series telling a story
- modern (i.e. 18th-century) life
- large-scale portraits
- lively (often humorous) style

Comparisons: Arthur Devis, Thomas Gainsborough, Joshua Reynolds, Jean Baptiste Chardin

Glossary terms: conversation piece, copyright, engraving, modern moral, rococo

Paintings as stories

Hogarth's portraits, whether on a small or large scale, are full of life and informality. The sitters are often engaged in some characteristic activity (such as having tea), or shown with objects that reflect their lives or interests. In his large-scale portrait of *Captain Coram* (a retired sea-captain who set up the Foundling Hospital for orphaned children), painted in 1740, the sitter holds the seal of the royal charter granted to the hospital, and there is a globe and a view of ships at sea.

Hogarth's modern moral subjects are more busy than his portraits, and are full of amusing details to make the narrative as

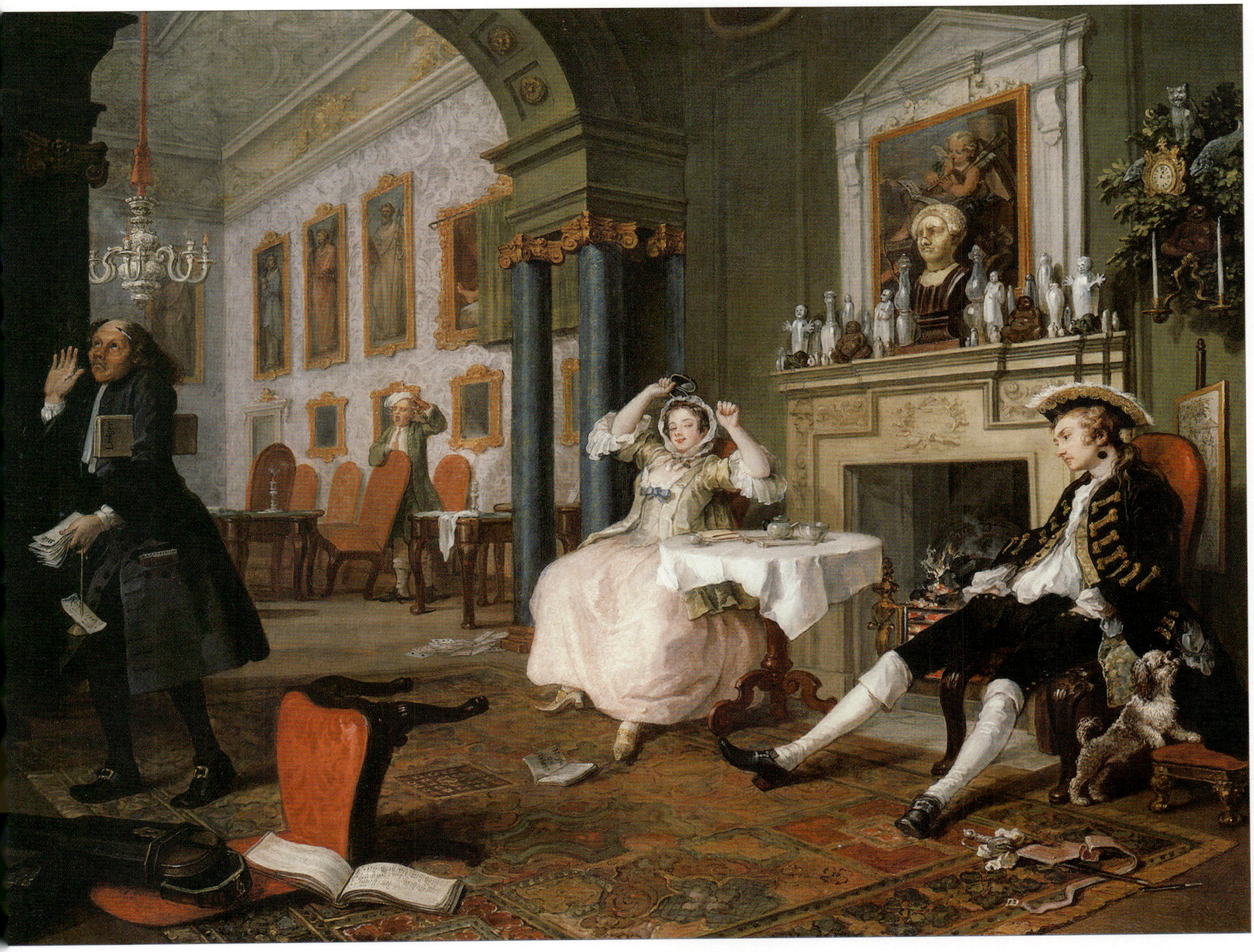

witty, lively, and varied as possible. These pictures are designed to be read almost like a book, with one scene leading to the next as the story unfolds.

Hogarth's first modern moral series, *A Harlot's Progress* (c1732), showed the downfall of a country girl under the influence of corrupt Londoners. Eighteenth-century audiences would have recognized characters and understood the significance of places depicted. For example, the portrait hanging in the background of *A Harlot's Progress (scene 1)* depicts a well-known seducer named Colonel Charteris, while the Bell Inn, also shown, was where coaches from York arrived in London.

In his treatise on art, called *The Analysis of Beauty* (published in 1753), Hogarth draws parallels between the beauty of certain kinds of dance and art, which both depend upon a variety of "chiefly serpentine," or snakelike, lines. This is a characteristic of his pictures; the composition, storyline, and characters take the viewer on an entertaining meander through the image.

Hogarth's style, full of curves and movement, has sometimes been called rococo, a term that is more commonly applied to French art of the period. Ironically, he was rabidly anti-French, and in 1748 was arrested as a spy for drawing the fortification of Calais.

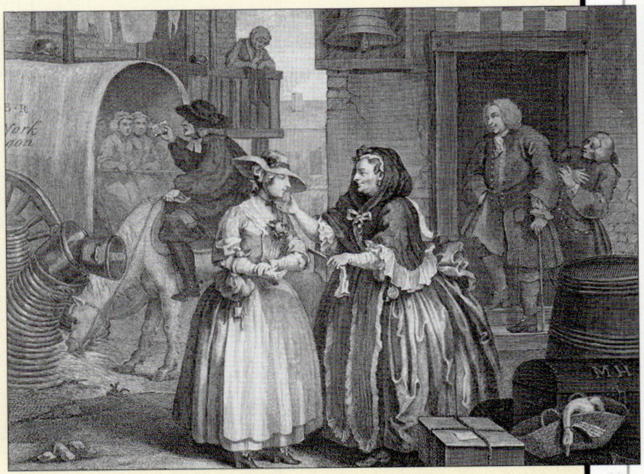

A Harlot's Progress (scene 1) *c1732. Engraving. 12 x 15 in (30 x 37.5 cm).*

HOLBEIN Hans

HOLBEIN WAS THE PRE-EMINENT PORTRAIT PAINTER OF HIS DAY. His most significant works were painted in Switzerland and England, where he lived from 1532, eventually working his way into the position of Court Painter to King Henry VIII.

Life and work

Hans Holbein was born in the German town of Augsburg, the son of a famous and respected painter (Hans Holbein the Elder), who was particularly noted for his religious works. Having moved with his family in 1514 to the Swiss town of Basle, Hans the Younger assisted his father in the decoration of houses, and in 1519 became a master in the town's guild of painters. This position brought him into contact with the famous humanist philosopher Erasmus. Holbein painted a succession of portraits of Erasmus, the best-known of which is *Erasmus Writing* (1523–24).

Although Holbein is prized above all else for his portraiture, many of his early commissions in and around Basle were for works of a religious nature, such as the four-panelled *Passion* altarpiece (1525–26). *Christ in the Tomb* (c1521–22) is the most remarkable of his religious works, and depicts the thin, pale, grubby body of Christ enclosed within a narrow panel that refers to the confines of his tomb. It was recognized as a concentrated and deeply expressive work.

In 1526 Holbein made his first trip to England, using the friendship of Erasmus as an introduction to the statesman and future lord chancellor to Henry VIII, Sir Thomas More. Holbein painted a group portrait of the More family (destroyed 1752), which was exceptional, for no artist had until then painted a group portrait of full-length figures in their home. In 1528 he returned to Basle, where he worked on a commission to decorate the town hall with scenes from classical history.

Four years later he returned to England. It was a precarious time for the nobility. More was out of favor with the king (and would later be executed), and many of the people Holbein had painted were now dead or in political exile. Undeterred, he sought out new patrons, such as the chief adviser to the king, Thomas Cromwell, and by 1536 he was Painter to the English Court. Holbein remained in the service of Henry VIII for the rest of his life, completing some of the best portraits of the age, such as those of the monarch and his third wife, Jane Seymour. He was also sent abroad to paint portraits of prospective wives for Henry VIII. Through his many commissions, Holbein became very wealthy man. He died in London from the plague.

Data file

Full name: Hans Holbein the Younger

Nationality: German

Style: portrait painting

Dates: born 1497/98 in Augsburg, died 1543 in London, England

Key works:

- *Christ in the Tomb* c1521–22
- *Erasmus Writing* 1523–24
- *Portrait of a Lady with a Squirrel and a Starling* 1526–28
- *Sir Thomas More* 1527
- *The Ambassadors* 1533
- *Henry VIII* 1536
- *Queen Jane Seymour* 1536–37
- *Christina of Denmark* c1538

Things to look for:

- graphic depiction of character
- economy of compositional detail

Comparisons: Albrecht Dürer, Jean Clouet, Jan Van Eyck, Robert Campin, Frans Hals

Glossary terms: anamorphosis, perspective, vanishing point

Stretching reality

In building up a rounded picture of a person, Holbein made use of objects that either pointed toward character traits or symbolized universal truths about humanity. Nowhere is this more evident than in *The Ambassadors* (1533), a double portrait of Jean de Dinteville, French ambassador to England, and his friend George de Selve, Bishop of Lavaur.

The physical characteristics of the two men are clearly presented by Holbein, but it is what surrounds them that attracts so much of our attention. The table against which they lean is crammed with a fascinating array of objects: terrestrial and celestial globes, mathematical books and instruments, as well as navigational tools and religious manuscripts. These are placed within the composition to indicate that the subjects are learned men, who have an understanding of science as well as the arts (acknowledged by the lute, the flutes, and a musical score).

But amid this material, intellectual, and spiritual wealth Holbein has included more subtle elements that call to mind the mortality of humanity. For instance, in the upper left-hand corner of the painting is a crucifix, half revealed behind the green curtain; it is a reminder of the transience of worldly objects and knowledge. The other symbol of death is hidden: the strange, elongated shape across the base of the painting is a human skull. Holbein used the technique of anamorphosis (the Greek word meaning "to transform") so that the image is only clear when viewed from a certain angle. In this case, the viewer must stand at the right of the painting and look at it almost straight on to see the skull—a traditional memento mori (reminder that we all must die).

In using anamorphosis, Holbein was displaying his ability to play tricks with perspective. The device also makes us aware that looking is not just a passive activity, but an exercise in which we engage with the world.

The Ambassadors *1533. Oil and tempera on panel. 81½ x 82½ in (207 x 209 cm). National Gallery, London.*

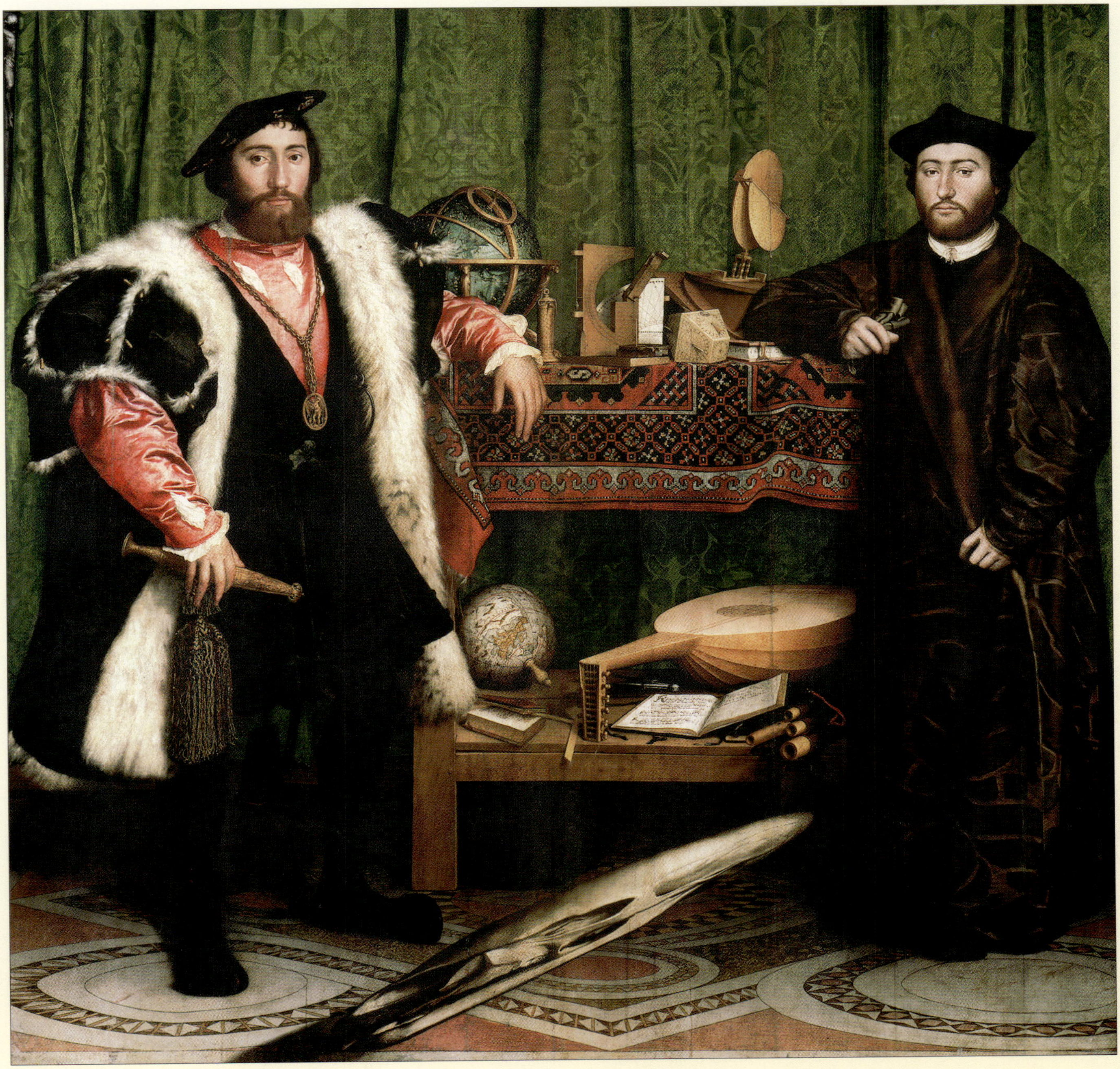

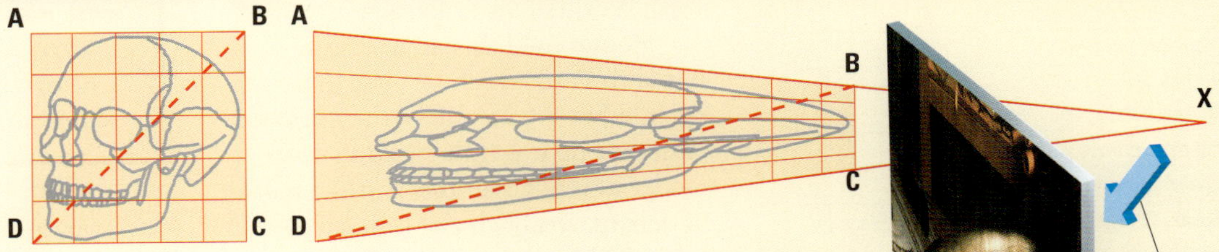

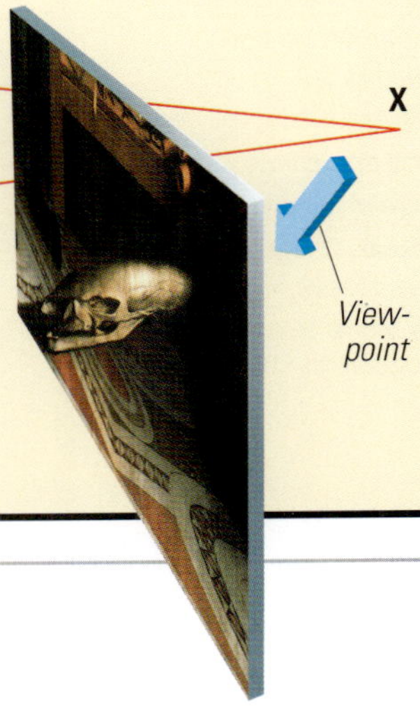

Creating anamorphosis *A squared grid is placed over the image, the line B–D fixing the scale of the image. To distort the image, a vertical line (A–D) is drawn alongside the original image, and the point X (the vanishing point) is placed at some distance to the right. Lines are then drawn to connect A, D, etc. to X and "stretch" the image. The amount of distortion is decided by the placement of B–C. The other vertical grid lines can now be plotted at the points where line D–B crosses the horizontal lines, and the image is drawn to the grid.*

HOMER Winslow

WINSLOW HOMER IS BEST REMEMBERED for his vigorous oils and watercolors of marine life and hunting scenes. Originally a commercial illustrator, he made the transition to fine art with ease, but rejected the public attention that followed his success.

Life and work

Winslow Homer was a very private man. Throughout his career, he avoided publicity, keeping outsiders away from his studio, and steering clear of all public debate about his work. As a result, comparatively little is known about his private life.

Born the son of a businessman in Boston, Massachussetts, Homer's artistic interests appear to have been fired initially by his mother, who was a keen amateur watercolorist. His parents had intended to send him to study at Harvard, following in the footsteps of his elder brother, but Homer preferred to develop his drawing skills. So at the age of 19 he was apprenticed to John H. Bufford, manager of the principal lithographic firm in Boston. Homer soon came to excel in this relatively new printmaking technique. He found the work at Bufford's—mainly producing illustrations for sheet music covers—extremely dull. Nevertheless, it gave him a firm grounding in commercial art, enabling him to set up as a freelance illustrator in 1857.

Homer was to remain in this field for nearly 20 years, designing illustrations of contemporary life for magazines such as *Harper's Weekly* and *Ballou's Pictorial.* He still harbored ambitions of becoming a professional artist, though. Accordingly, he took evening classes at the National Academy of Design, and also studied with a minor painter named Rondel.

The opportunity to put his newly acquired skills into practice came in 1861, with the outbreak of the American Civil War. *Harper's* sent Homer to the war zone to record images of the conflict, which he did with unsentimental realism. The events that he witnessed inspired some of his earliest paintings. One, *Prisoners from the Front* (1866), made quite an impact, and was selected as one of the American exhibits at the 1867 World's Fair in Paris.

Homer used this as an excuse to travel to Paris which, at that time, was regarded as the capital of the art world. Whether he was influenced by any modern French painters is still a matter of debate, although the influence of Edouard Manet—particularly his use of broad tonal contrasts—can be detected in works such as *Long Branch, New Jersey* (1869). The trip also appears to have confirmed Homer's commitment to painting *en plein air* ("in the open air"), an interest he shared with many impressionist artists.

During the 1870s Homer produced his best work during summer stays in the Adirondack Moutains, the White Mountains, and at Gloucester, Massachussetts. In 1873 he painted his

Data file

Full name: Winslow Homer

Nationality: American

Style: naturalism

Dates: born 1836 in Boston, MA, died 1910 in Prout's Neck, ME

Key works:

Prisoners from the Front 1866

Long Branch, New Jersey 1869

Snap the Whip 1872

Breezing Up 1876

Hunter in the Adirondacks 1892

The Gulf Stream 1899

Things to look for:

- vigorous hunting and marine subjects
- bold color effects
- watercolors with robust brushwork

Comparisons: Edward Hopper, George Caleb Bingham, Edouard Manet, Hudson River school

Glossary terms: *en plein air,* Hudson River school, impressionism, lithograph, naturalism

Battling against the elements

As his style matured, Homer became increasingly interested in scenes that showed humanity pitting its wits against the forces of nature.

In the 1870s this struggle was implied rather than shown. In *Waiting for Dad* (1873), a family stand by the seashore, anxiously awaiting the return of a fisherman, while in *Breezing Up* (1876) Homer depicts a change in the weather, suggesting that the young sailors are in for an exhilarating but rough ride. During the 1880s, the threat from the sea became more explicit. Paintings such as *The Fog Warning* (1885) and *Undertow* (1886) portray scenes of genuine danger. This sequence would eventually culminate in *The Gulf Stream* (1899), Homer's famous picture of a lone seaman surrounded by a group of sharks.

The theme of man against nature appeared in other works as well. Although the sea was Homer's favorite subject, in the early 1890s he produced a remarkable series of hunting scenes, mostly set in the Adirondack Mountains of upper New York State. Homer visited the area on regular fishing trips, using these as an opportunity to study and paint different kinds of huntsmen, isolated in the wide open spaces of the American landscape. In working this way he was following in the tradition of George Bingham and the painters of the Hudson River school (c1825–75), who had excelled at capturing the fearless "frontier spirit" of the American people.

During his career as a professional artist, Homer alternated frequently between watercolor and oils. The later watercolors, with their bold composition and vivid coloring, have an impact with the

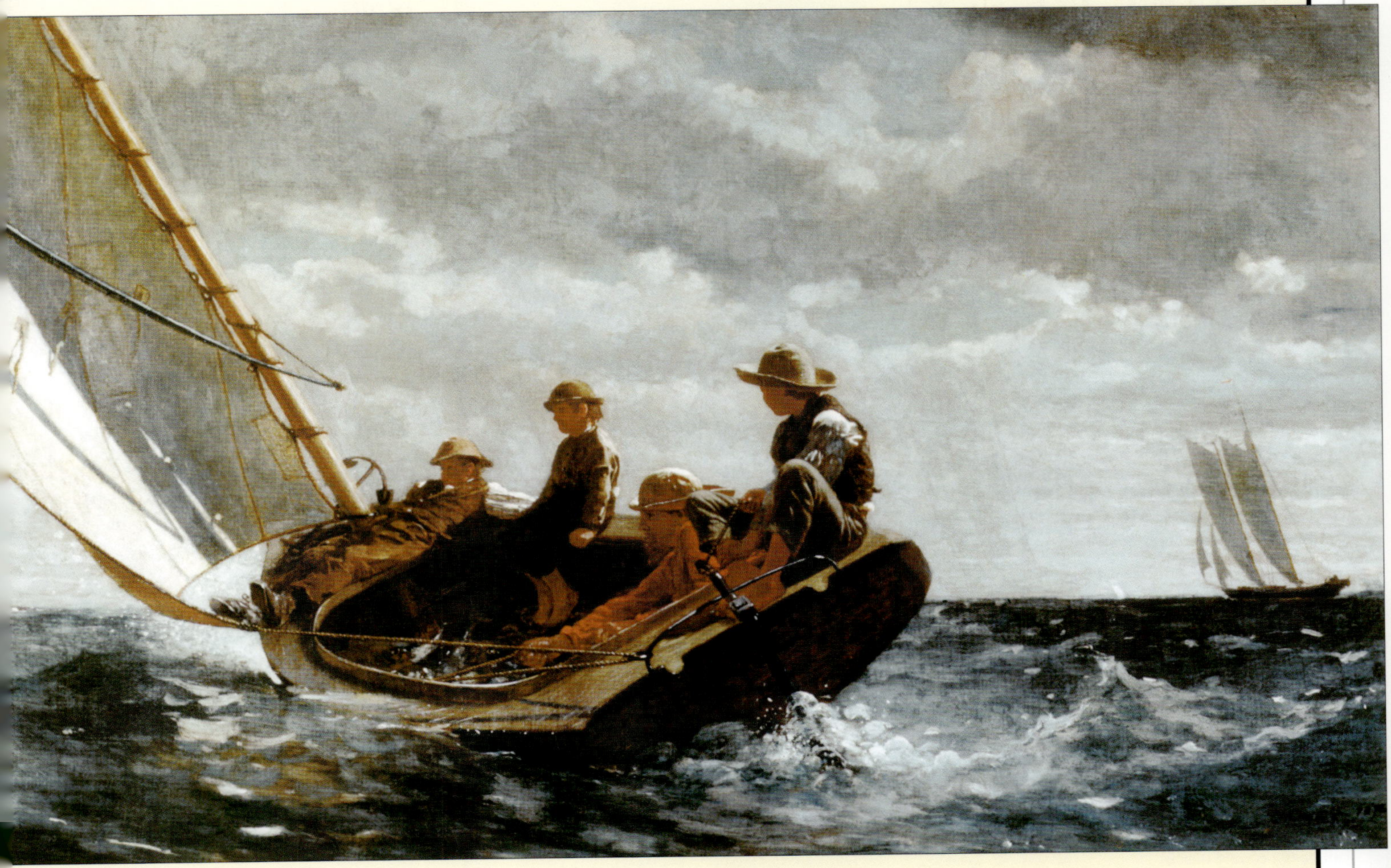

force of oil paintings, and are regarded by many as his finest works. In the 1870s, however, Homer was more conscious of their low reputation: watercolors were widely viewed as the medium of the amateur painter, and he tended to use them in a more subsidiary role. *Breezing Up*, for example, is closely based on one of his earliest watercolors, *Sailing the Catboat* (1873). Homer painted this while spending the summer at Gloucester, Massachussetts (the place is commemorated in the name of the boat). He was evidently pleased with the results, deciding that the scene was worth reproducing on a larger scale in oils. The two scenes are virtually identical, apart from on the right-hand side, where Homer has echoed the tilt of the *Gloucester* in the slanting sails of two other boats, and in the wings of a lone seagull.

In both pictures the composition displays the influence of Japanese prints; this influence can be seen in many of Homer's works of the 1870s. During the 1860s in Europe there was a craze for all things Japanese. It is likely Homer would have seen many Japanese-styled items during his stay in Paris. In this painting, the dominant diagonal at the left-hand edge of the painting, the placement of the main subject close to the picture surface, and the vacant space on the right are all typical of the fresh approach adopted by Japanese printmakers. To Western traditionalists, these elements might have seemed jarring, destroying the overall balance of the scene, but in reality they lend a dynamic thrust and compelling immediacy to the composition.

Breezing Up *1876. Oil on canvas. 24 x 36 in (61 x 96.5 cm). National Gallery of Art, Washington, D.C.*

first watercolors, and their success may finally have prompted him to abandon his job as an illustrator in 1875 and take up painting full time.

Increasingly, Homer retreated from city life, preferring to isolate himself in remote, coastal locations, where he could work in peace. In 1881–82 he moved to live near Tynemouth, on the northeastern coast of England, before returning to the United States and settling permanently at Prout's Neck in Maine in 1883, where he became a virtual recluse. Dubbed "the hermit of the brush" by a bemused public, he devoted himself to creating scenes of lonely huntsmen dwarfed by immense landscapes, fishermen threatened by a cruel sea, and vividly naturalistic works evoking images of the American pioneer spirit.

HOPPER Edward

ONE OF THE GREAT AMERICAN REALIST PAINTERS, Edward Hopper was often out of step with the prevailing tide of modernism and experimentation. He has been hailed as a precursor of pop art and superrealism.

Life and work

For many years, Hopper worked as an illustrator. Although he later disregarded his commercial work, it was in this field that he initially received recognition and praise. He had been coerced into studying illustration by his parents, who were anxious that he should enter a more financially secure profession than painting.

In his final year at the New York School of Art (1906), he did manage to switch to a full-time course in painting, but on leaving he immediately took up work as an illustrator at an advertising company in New York. He was unhappy with the restrictions imposed by his commercial work, but the salary did afford him the opportunity to make trips to Europe—and in particular to Paris. There, he produced some impressionistic works, as well as a humorous collection of watercolor portraits and caricatures of Parisian stereotypes—red-cheeked, glossy-lipped women at café tables, a fat concierge, a mustachioed policeman.

Back in New York, he continued to work as an illustrator while pursuing his own artistic ambitions. One of his paintings, *Sailing* (1911), was selected for the famous Armory Show in 1913, and he managed to sell it. But this was a false dawn—it would be more than 10 years before he sold another painting. His reputation as an illustrator and etcher continued to grow, and in 1918 he won a prize for a wartime poster entitled *Smash the Hun*—a patriotic portrayal of American strength.

In 1924 Hopper married Jo Nivison, who had been a fellow student at the art school, and she encouraged him to work with watercolors. He would produce works in this medium right through his career. They are less well known than the oil paintings, but particularly the earlier watercolors from the mid-1920s to the late 1930s have an easy, relaxed style, with a warmth and spontaneity that is purposefully drained from his oil paintings.

Hopper had critical and commercial success with his early watercolors, but he did not abandon the medium of oil, and in 1925 he painted the first of his most famous images, *House by the Railroad*, in which a sense of loneliness and isolation pervades. From the late 1920s this mood of isolation became a consistent force in his work, whether the depiction was of buildings in a rural setting, such as *Cobb's Barns, South Truro* (1930–33), or of a lonely figure in a city interior, as in *Night Windows* (1928) or *Automat* (1927).

In some ways, Hopper's style would seem to connect him more to American writers than to the artists of his time. He was economic and spare, not allowing great complexity or sophistication. It was a plain and

Data file

Full name: Edward Hopper

Nationality: American

Style: realism

Dates: born 1882 in Nyack, NY, died 1967 in New York, NY

Key works:
- *House by the Railroad* 1925
- *Automat* 1927
- *Early Sunday Morning* 1930
- *Gas* 1940
- *Nighthawks* 1942
- *Hotel Lobby* 1943
- *Excursion into Philosophy* 1959

Things to look for:
- isolated figures
- simple compositions
- atmospheric use of light

Comparisons: Jan Vermeer, Edgar Degas, Edouard Manet, Thomas Eakins, Andrew Wyeth, Eric Fischl, Alex Katz

Glossary terms: abstract expressionism, Armory Show, impressionism, pop art, realism, superrealism

A brooding silence

Edward Hopper's style of painting changed little over the years, from the emergence of his particular vision of the American psyche in the mid- to late 1920s until his death in the mid-1960s. Hopper's figures are frequently contemplative and sad, as if caught in a brooding silence following a quarrel or tragedy. Hopper seems to capture moments when words and emotions have been used up—when there is nothing more to be said. The silence is frequently palpable, especially in works such as *Automat* (1927), shown here, with its lonely, downcast figure, and *Nighthawks* (1942), where the people are behind a window and, it seems, in no mood for conversation. His paintings could be described as the antithesis of expression, but, ironically, it is the very absence of emotion—the banality of the images —that is their most compelling feature; they contain no drama, only the tension of the atmosphere.

Automat, completed during Hopper's formative period, is reminiscent of many works from the more distant past, and particularly Edouard Manet's *The Plum* and Edgar Degas' *Absinthe* (both c1877). But in these works, the mood is more of weary boredom, whereas Hopper concentrates on the isolation of the seated woman. A sense of absence is stressed by the empty chair facing the young woman and the large expanse of the marble tabletop. The background is greatly simplified, with a series of lights reflected in the large glass window that serves to stress the echoing void that surrounds the figure. The simplification of the background and

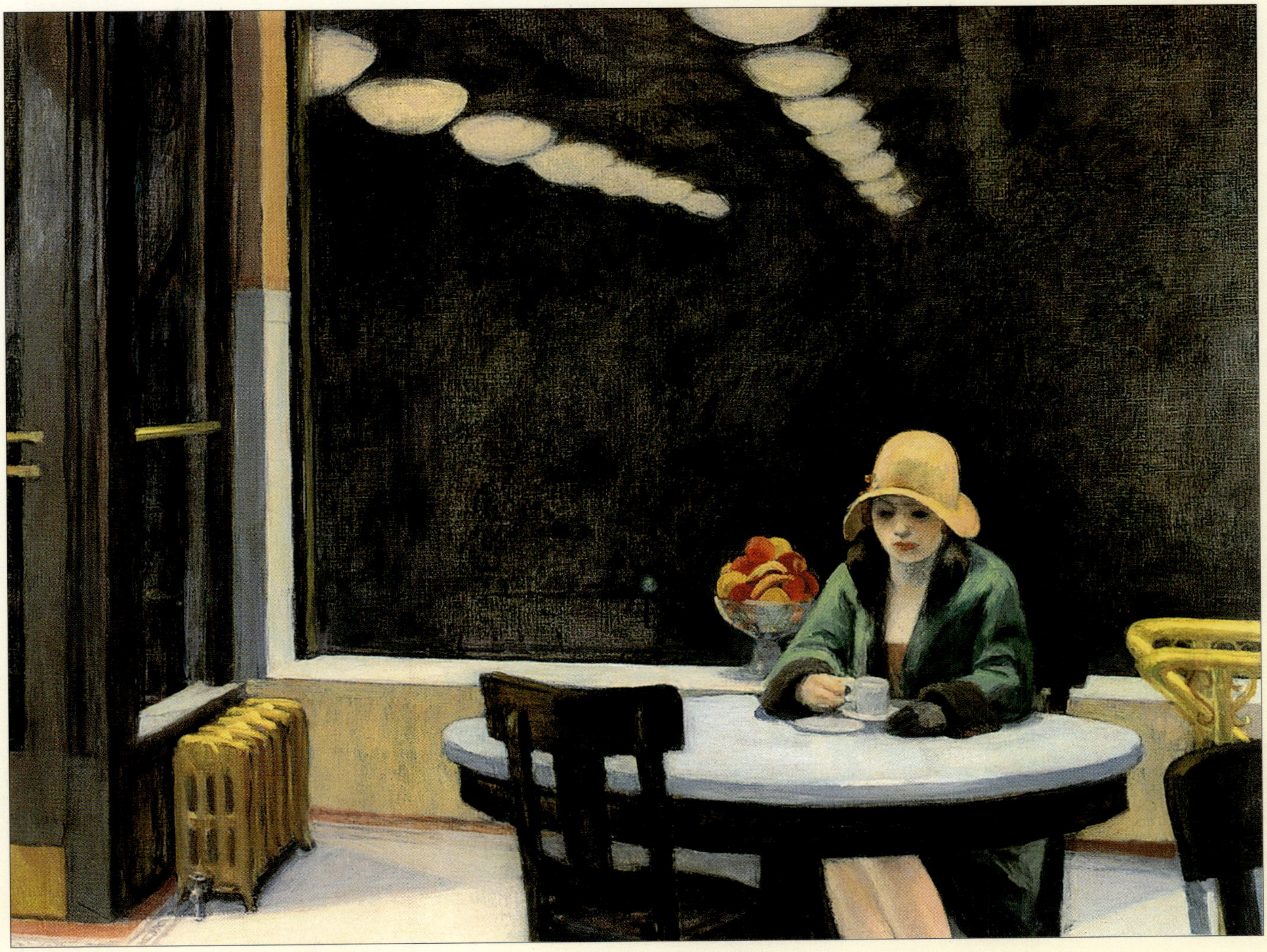

attention to the fall of light and shadow owes a debt to the example of Jan Vermeer, an early master at capturing the subtle effects of light on interior surfaces.

Yet in *Automat*, as in all Hopper's work, there is also something entirely of its time. His paintings seem to capture a slice of 20th-century American life with a detached, deadpan style that—despite Hopper's refutation of any similarity—would later recur with pop artist Andy Warhol. Both artists understood and accepted American life, and their work reflected it with a cool and steady eye.

Automat *1927. Oil on canvas. 28 x 36 in (71 x 91.5 cm). Des Moines Art Center, Des Moines, IA.*

simple style, and as such seemed to express something of the same American straightforwardness that is evident in the writing of Ernest Hemingway or Norman Mailer.

One of his later works stands out for its title, *Excursion into Philosophy* (1959). It is a title unlike any of his others and it seems to encourage a more complex interpretation of his work. It is remarkable as an exception, however, and as his wife pointed out in a letter to the art critic Lloyd Goodrich, "It may be that Edward won't stand for naming the new picture 'Excursion into Philosophy.' You know E. Hopper. He'll call it 'Sunlight on the Floor' or something." This was, perhaps, his one moment of pretension in his career.

With the emergence of abstract expressionism, Hopper fell out of favor with the New York art world, but he obstinately continued with his comparatively conservative realist style. Then, as abstract expressionism waned and pop art emerged to take its place in the 1960s, he came to be regarded as an influential precursor of pop art and superrealism.

Hopper himself held such claims in disdain, but it remains true that his influence has affected many painters from the 1960s to the present day, including Eric Fischl and Alex Katz, as well as filmmakers such as David Lynch and Martin Scorsese.

INGRES Jean Auguste Dominique

By the end of his long life, Jean Auguste Dominique Ingres had become the most honored artist in France, celebrated for his imposing classical scenes and dazzling portraits. During his career, however, he experienced both the highest praise and absolute rejection from critics.

Life and work

Ingres was born in Montauban in southwest France in 1780. He studied drawing with his father, a sculptor, and attended the Toulouse Academy before going to Paris to study with Jacques-Louis David in 1799. David was the most celebrated artist and teacher of the period, and the young Ingres became his prize pupil, winning the Prix de Rome in 1801. This enabled him to study in Rome. Before taking up this scholarship in 1807, he exhibited his portrait of Napoleon (see opposite), to heavy criticism, at the Paris Salon. It was with some relief that Ingres finally went to Rome, away from the unforgiving critics in Paris. He vowed not to return to France until his work was fully recognized.

In Rome Ingres studied the works of Raphael, Hans Holbein, and Titian. He began at this time to paint pictures such as the *Valpinçon Bather* (1808) and oriental-style nudes such as *La Grande Odalisque* (1814), intended for rich collectors; these subjects remained popular with him throughout his life and are some of his best-known works.

His aim was to paint scenes of classical and historic importance that would both please and educate their viewers. However, he also painted portraits for wealthy patrons and produced pencil drawings of tourists in Rome. Although he detested this kind of work and considered it beneath his talents, the money enabled him to continue painting his more ambitious works. Ironically, his portraits are now considered some of his greatest works.

Ingres lived in Rome until 1820, when he moved to Florence. There, in addition to his usual portraits and smaller paintings, he worked on a large-scale history painting, *The Vow of Louis XIII*, for Montauban Cathedral. After its exhibition in Paris in 1824, where it received very favorable reviews, he returned triumphant to the French capital after nearly 20 years. Ingres was celebrated as the new leader of neoclassicism. He was concerned with a traditional style of painting and opposed to Romantic artists such as Delacroix, who used dramatic color contrasts and looser brushstrokes.

Ingres decided to stay in Paris and concentrate on his history paintings. He opened his own teaching workshop

Data file

Full name: Jean Auguste Dominique Ingres

Nationality: French

Style: neoclassical

Dates: born 1780 in Montauban, died 1867 in Paris

Key works:

- *Napoleon on His Imperial Throne* 1806
- *Valpinçon Bather* 1808
- *The Countess of Tournon* 1812
- *La Grande Odalisque* 1814
- *The Vow of Louis XIII* 1824
- *The Apotheosis of Homer* 1827–33
- *Odalisque with Slave* 1839–40
- *Madame Moitessier, seated* 1856

Things to look for:

- large-scale paintings of historical, mythological or religious significance
- richly painted portraits of wealthy and important society figures
- meticulous attention to detail and polished appearance of the painted surface
- attention to long lines and curves in paintings of exotic and oriental female nudes
- subtle elongations of limbs and hands

Comparisons: Jacques-Louis David, Eugène Delacroix, Raphael

Glossary terms: Academy, antique, classical, Gothic, history painting, neoclassicism, northern Renaissance, Prix de Rome, Romanticism, Salon

Portraits in the neoclassical style

Ingres is thought of as a neoclassicist painter because of his subject matter, his attention to drawing and composition, and his preference for clear lines and classical forms, as modeled on the works of the ancient Greeks and Raphael.

This early work, *Napoleon on His Imperial Throne* (1806) shows Ingres' interest in the classical world. The pose is modeled on a famous antique sculpture of the ruler of the Olympian gods, Jupiter. Ingres' deliberate reference to Raphael, who painted famous images of the Madonna and Child, can also be seen in the bottom left-hand corner on the carpet; he has used a Raphael Madonna and Child for the zodiacal symbol of Virgo, the Virgin.

Just as Ingres was drawn to the beauties of line and curve in his numerous paintings and drawings of the female nude, here too he shows his interest in distorted

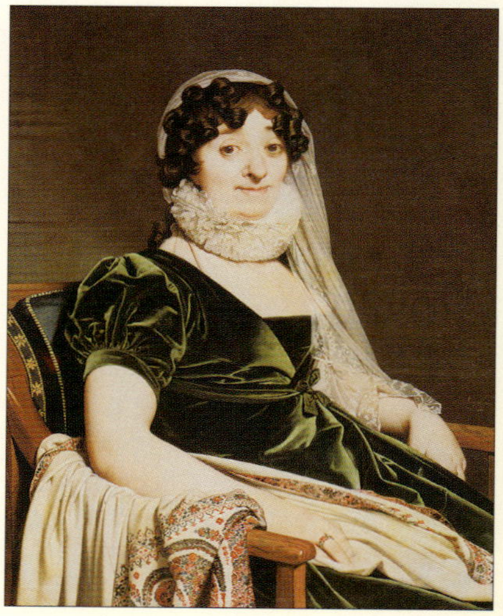

The Countess of Tournon *1812. Oil on canvas. 36 1/4 x 28 3/4 in (92 x 73 cm). Philadelphia Museum of Art, Philadelphia, PA.*

shapes and in the fluid sweep of line: look, for example, at the raised, elongated arm of Napoleon. Ingres' delight in depicting different materials and textures also shows the influence of northern Renaissance artists such as Jan Van Eyck.

The painting was criticized for its meticulous attention to the robes and finery of the emperor, to the point that they detract from his face. It was also attacked for copying the art of the past, and because the stylized pose and attention to decorative effect made Napoleon seem more like a symbol or a medieval icon than a real person. Some critics thought that the flatness of Napoleon's face contributed to this effect.

The portrait of the Countess of Tournon (1812) was done for a private commission. It is unusual in that the female sitter is an older woman, aged about 60. Ingres has delighted in the smooth curves of the countess's arms and hands, just as he delighted in the bold lines of his grand imperial portrait.

The countess was an extremely influential client, and Ingres captures her likeness while also flattering her. The folds of her cashmere shawl and the sumptuous velvet of her dress display her wealth and good taste. The delicate ruff and her dark curls frame her face. Although she has rather plain features, her eyes are enlarged and her skin is made smooth so that she appears more youthful—an effect that would have pleased her.

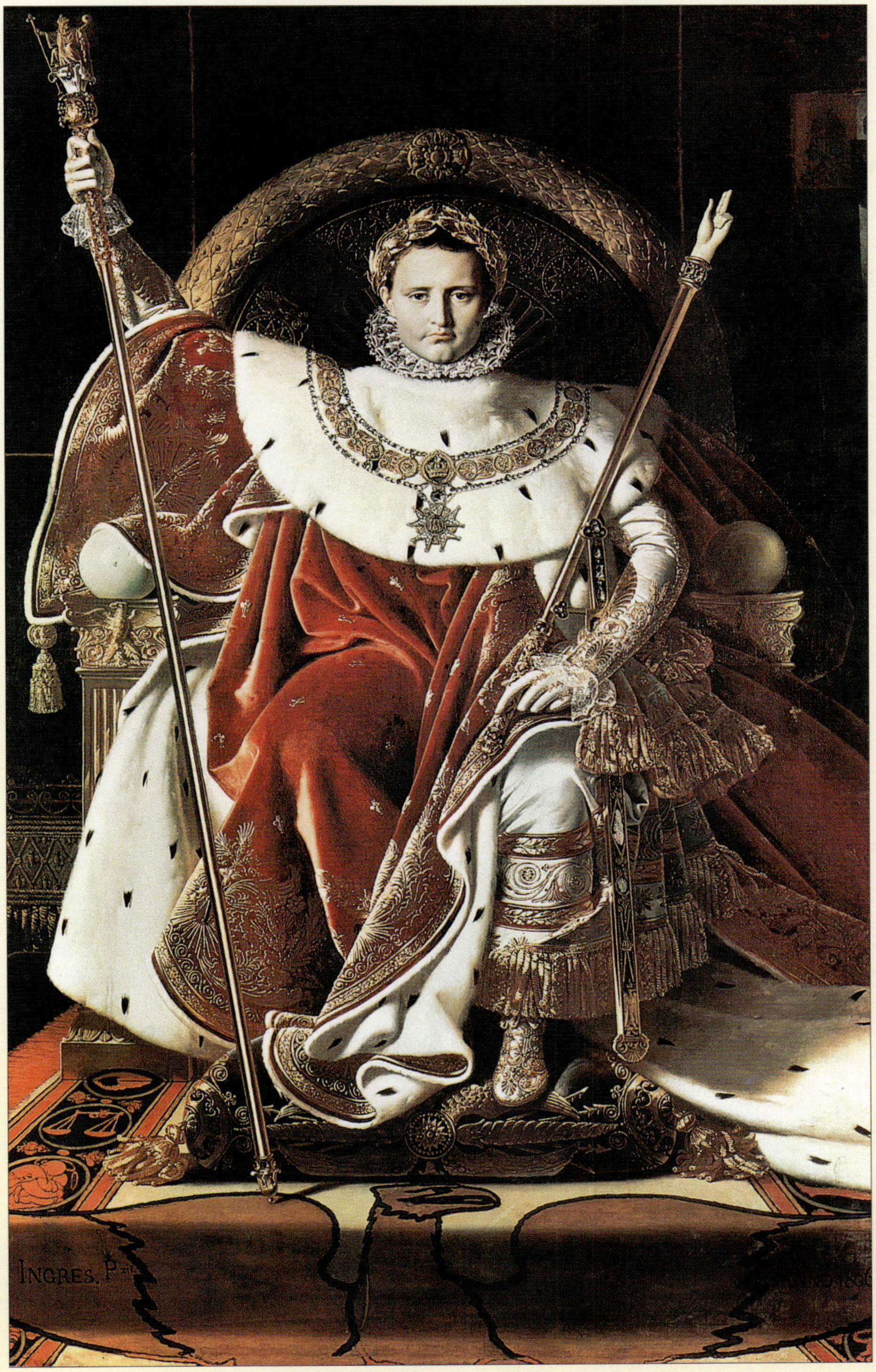

Napoleon on His Imperial Throne
1806. Oil on canvas. 102 x 63¾ in (259 x 162 cm). Musée de l'Armée, Paris.

in 1826. During this period he painted *The Apotheosis of Homer* (1827–33), which contained all of the figures from history, music, literature, and painting, who had inspired his own art. He also painted a remarkably original portrait of Louis-François Bertin (1833), which was widely discussed and praised for the individuality and character of the newspaper owner it portrayed.

From 1834 to 1841 he was back in Rome, this time as the director of the French Academy where he had first been a student. In 1841 he returned to Paris where he became president of the Ecole des Beaux-Arts. Commissions for large paintings and portraits continued until the end of his life.

INNESS George

When George Inness began to paint, landscape painting was a relatively new phenomenon in the United States, dominated by the Romantic movement and the Hudson River school. Today, Inness ranks as one of the greatest of all 19th-century landscape artists, and as the one who independently anticipated impressionism in his country.

Life and work

Born on a farm in Newburgh, a few miles from New York, Inness spent his early years in Newark, New Jersey. Largely self-taught, he served a year's apprenticeship with a New York firm of map engravers, and, in 1846, received his only formal art training—a month's study with Regis Gignoux, who had been a pupil of the history painter Paul Delaroche in Paris. When Gignoux arrived in the United States, he became allied with the Hudson River school, a name loosely applied to a number of American Romantic landscape painters who worked mainly, though not exclusively, in the area around the Catskill Mountains and the Hudson River in New York state. While the Hudson River school was never really an organized group, the artists involved shared a sense of marvel at the newly discovered American landscape. Inness, however, remained largely independent of the major art movements at home and abroad.

The titles of Inness's paintings that were shown at the National Academy and the Art Union from 1844 onward demonstrate that he was actively painting from nature and studying the landscape around Newark as well as at the home of his brother James, who lived in Pottsville, Pennsylvania. Inness's talent was such that he soon attracted a wealthy patron, Ogden Haggerty, who sponsored Inness's first trip to Italy in 1847.

Inness was already familiar with the paintings of the great 17th-century landscape artists Claude Lorraine and Nicolas Poussin, and, after his Italian trip, the influence of the Hudson River painters, as witnessed in Inness's tight, literal depictions of nature, gradually gave way to classical influences. Further visits to Europe followed: Inness was in Rome between 1851 and 1853, and in 1854 he visited Paris, where he was deeply influenced by the artists of the Barbizon school, who painted details of the countryside and peasant life. It was this influence that altered Inness's style dramatically, for in his later paintings he attempted to come to terms with visual forms in the same way as the impressionists. Inness, however, bristled at being compared to the impressionists: he felt that they were far too attached to the material world. Inness was, in fact, a follower of the mystic Emanuel Swedenborg; consequently, in his paintings, he sought to reveal the "invisible" and "spiritual" truths within matter. Inness believed that "the subject was nothing," and that art's true purpose was to "arouse the emotions."

Nevertheless, Inness was still concerned with the physical, material world around him, and he continued to concentrate on accurately rendered surface details right through the 1860s, as demonstrated in paintings such as *Shades of Evening* (1863).

In 1859 Inness moved to Medfield, Massachusetts, and one of his best-known canvases, *Peace and Plenty* (1865), dates from this period. After the Civil War, Inness returned to New Jersey to live at Eagleswood. He now entered a highly productive phase in which he painted *Harvest Scene on the Delaware* (1867), *Hudson River Valley* (1867), *Near Eagleswood, NJ* (1869), and *Lake Albano, Italy* (1869).

A lengthy stay abroad from 1870 saw Inness in Perugia and Albano in Italy and Etretat in France, where he produced many fine paintings, including *Tivoli* (1871) and *Rainbow over Perugia* (1875). In 1875 he returned to the United States. By now Inness's brushstrokes were becoming softer, his forms less architectural, and his outlines more fluid. A new and more personal vision was emerging; it is the works of his last years that have largely led to his being considered an American impressionist. From 1886 until his death in 1894 while on a trip to Scotland, Inness's work grew more monotone, and the solid, classical forms gave way to atmospheric landscapes shrouded in mists.

Data file

Full name: George Inness

Nationality: American

Style: associated mainly with Hudson River school in his early period, then influenced by Barbizon painters, and later associated with impressionism

Dates: born 1825 in Newburgh, NY, died 1894 in Bridge-of-Allan, Scotland

Key works:
- *The Old Mill* 1849
- *Peace and Plenty* 1865
- *Rainbow over Perugia* 1875
- *Short Cut, Watchung Station, New Jersey* 1883
- *Niagra Falls* 1885

Things to look for:
- literal depictions of nature, especially of American landscape
- accurate rendering of surface details
- influence of classical Italian landscape artists from 1847
- increasing abstractionism, near monotone palette, and atmospheric style in later works

Comparisons: Claude Lorraine, Nicolas Poussin, Jean-Baptiste Corot, James Abbot McNeill Whistler

Glossary terms: Barbizon school, classicism, Hudson River school, impressionism, plastic, Romanticism

Emotions awakened

According to Inness, the true use of art was to cultivate the artist's own spiritual nature, and his role as an artist was to reproduce in the spectator's eye the impressions that a scene had made on him. For Inness, the aim of a painting was not to instruct, but to awaken the emotions.

While the Hudson River painters produced flamboyant panoramas, Inness's work is best described as quiet, or even understated. For him nature was not a stage set. It was the world seen by him on a daily basis, which he captured during changing seasons in a continually evolving style. Like the Barbizon painters he greatly admired, Inness painted gentle, undramatic views of country life.

Painted at a time when the very landscape of the United States was being transformed, Inness includes the image of a steam locomotive in the background of *Short Cut, Watchung Station, New Jersey* (1883). His paintings are modest expressions—in spite of their sometimes large scale—and these qualities can be noted in the colors, the angle of view, and the subordination of the figures and buildings within the total scheme. The figures in *Short Cut* are plastic but subsidiary elements in the painting, and the aerial distance and perspective are subtle and delicate.

Although primarily a landscape painter, Inness was interested in the human figure, and the problems of capturing the effects of light on the flesh. He is known to have made many life studies, including the nude, but it is believed that he destroyed most of these works. This behavior was typical of his somewhat eccentric nature. Other quirks included his insistence on wearing old clothes in order to appear poverty-stricken—even when he was financially secure—and maintaining that a painting belonged to him even after he had sold it. There are also many stories of outraged collectors who found that the painting delivered to them was completely different from the one they had originally purchased from the artist: it was Inness's practice to take a still-wet canvas—even one he had just sold—and paint over it. Often six or seven paintings were laid over each other.

In 1889 *Short Cut* was shown at the Paris International Exposition. Inness objected strongly to its inclusion without his permission. Characteristically he argued that he still owned the painting; he also believed that it was not representative of his recent work. His numerous protests asking for the picture to be withdrawn were ignored and, ironically, it was awarded a gold medal.

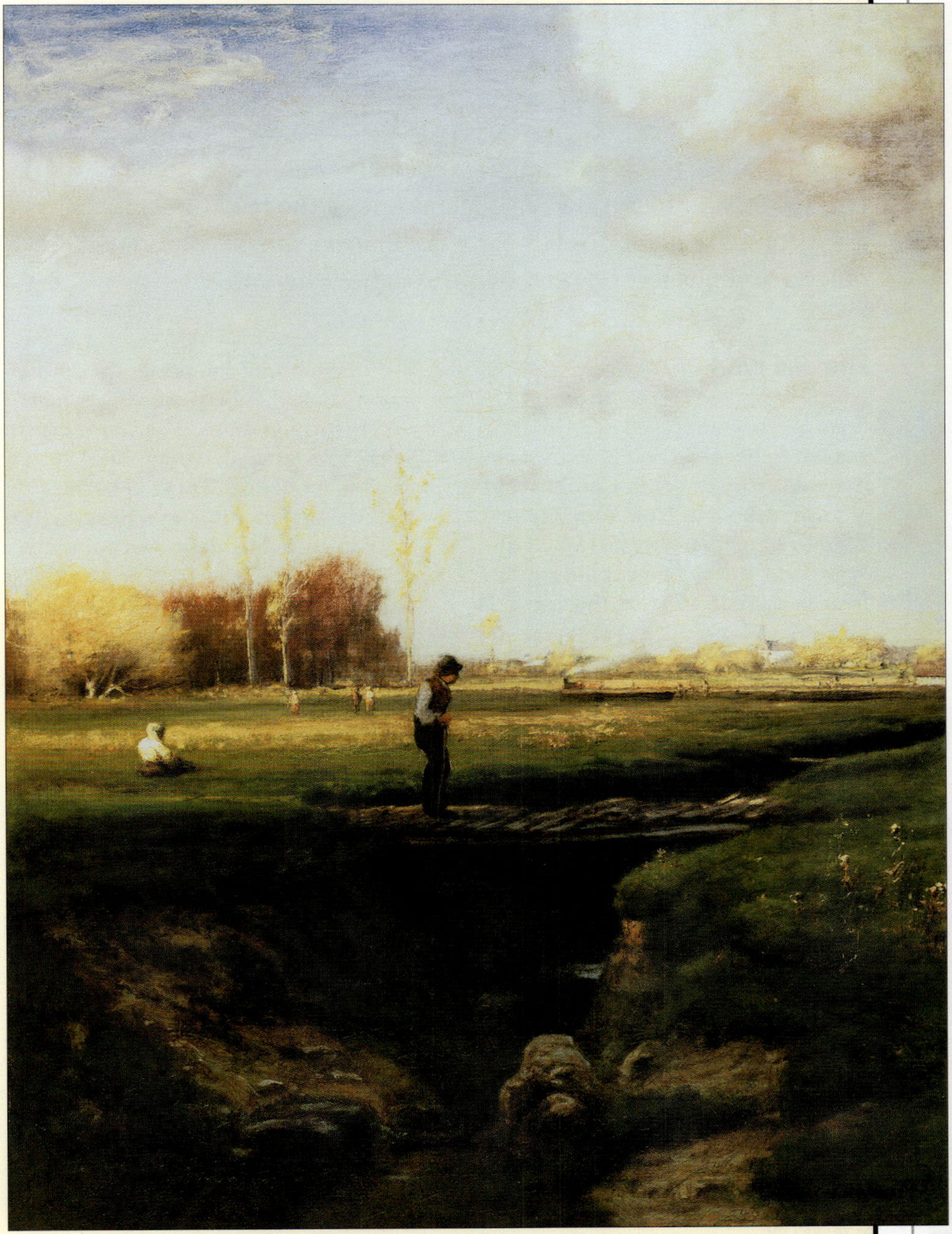

Short Cut, Watchung Station, New Jersey *1883. Oil on canvas. 37¾ x 29 in (96 x 74 cm). Philadelphia Museum of Art, Philadelphia, PA.*

JOHNS Jasper

JASPER JOHNS'S WORK COMBINES EXPERIMENTAL VIGOR AND DRAMATIC visual impact. His paintings first came to public attention in the late 1950s, and he is now regarded as one of the leading American artists of his generation. His early fascination with commonplace objects and imagery has endured throughout his career.

Life and work

From a very young age Jasper Johns wanted to be an artist. He studied art at the University of South Carolina and at an art school in New York, but completed neither course. Details of Johns's early development are hard to trace because in 1954, at the age of 24, he destroyed most of his work. He was determined to pursue originality: "I decided to do only what I meant to do, and not what other people did. When I could observe what others did, I tried to remove that from my work."

In New York Johns met the painter Robert Rauschenberg, who encouraged his artistic ambitions. The young artists worked together, designing window displays for department stores. They used the opportunity to promote their work by including their own paintings in the displays.

In 1957 Johns showed *Green Target* (1955) at a group exhibition where his work was noticed by the art dealer Leo Castelli. Soon afterward, three of his paintings were bought by the Metropolitan Museum of Art, signaling that Johns had arrived on the New York art scene. From this time onward his work was avidly collected and continually debated.

Johns has always asserted that he is not a colorist and that gray is his favorite color, but in 1959–60 color took on a fresh importance in his work. In *False Start* (1959) the names of colors were stenciled onto fiery patches painted with rapid brushstrokes. *Painting with Two Balls* (1960) used a similar palette, plus optical illusion and objects attached to the painting.

Many other works from the 1960s include attachments such as wires, hinges, rulers, cups, and a broom. His massive 1964 canvas, *According to What* (which measures 88 x 192 in/223.5 x 488 cm), combined a number of Johns's favored techniques—collage, readymade lettering, and attached objects (including a chair and cast of a human leg)—in a virtuoso display.

At the age of 33 Johns was hailed as "probably the most influential young painter in the world," by *Newsweek* magazine. From the mid-1960s onward his work assumed a questing, self-referential quality. He revisited earlier motifs, such as the flag, light bulb, and target. At the same time, large new works such as *Harlem Light* (1967) combined abstract forms with references to actual spaces and places.

Johns continued to experiment with different media, producing lithographic prints and creating "drawings" of his own body made by

Data file

Full name: Jasper Johns

Nationality: American

Style: pop art/modern figurative

Dates: born 1930 in Augusta, GA

Key works:

- *Target with Plaster Casts* 1955
- *Green Target* 1955
- *Target* 1958
- *False Start* 1959
- *Painting with Two Balls* 1960
- *According to What* 1964
- *Dancers on a Plane* 1979
- *Untitled* 1991

Things to look for:

- use of "readymade" images, e.g. target, flag, map
- choice of unusual media, e.g. encaustic, sculp-metal
- incorporation of actual objects into paintings
- interest in optical illusions and visual puns

Comparisons: Willem de Kooning, Marcel Duchamp, Robert Rauschenberg, Andy Warhol

Glossary terms: abstract expressionism, encaustic, figurative, lithograph, pop art

Target practice

During his twenties, before Johns came to public attention, two distinctive features of his work emerged with great strength and clarity. The first was his interest in readymade images—"things the mind already knows"—such as circular targets, the American flag, and standard numerals. This process began after a dream in 1954, in which Johns saw himself painting the American "Stars and Stripes" flag. Historically, this interest in everyday objects can be linked to the work of Marcel Duchamp, a French artist who famously exhibited a urinal in 1917.

Johns's use of bold, recognizable images, such as *Target* (1958), represented a startling break from the dominant post-war art style of abstract expressionism—the first American art movement to achieve an international following. His paintings showed actual objects rather than abstract forms, and he chose objects that had become so familiar that people no longer thought about their meaning. This fascination with the commonplace led to Johns being linked to the emerging pop art movement, which took mass-produced commercial images, such as soup cans or soap boxes, as inspiration.

The second major feature of Johns's work was his readiness to experiment with media and techniques that were not being used by other artists. In his early flag and target paintings, for example, he developed the use of encaustic—a medium that almost became his personal trademark. Encaustic is a difficult technique, in which pigment mixed with hot wax is applied. It was used in the ancient world and revived in the 20th century as something of a

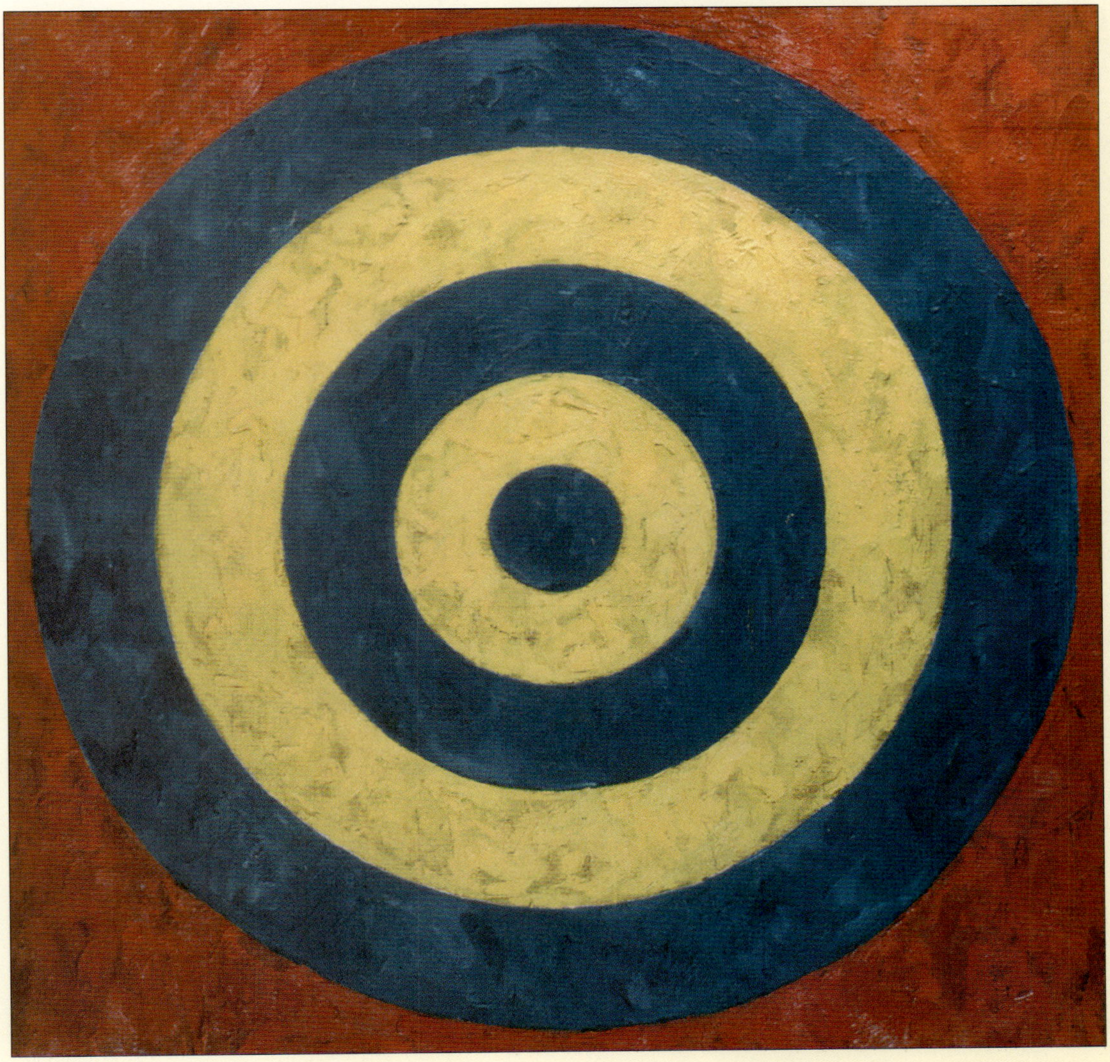

Target *1958. Oil and collage on canvas. 36 x 36 in (91.5 x 91.5 cm). Private collection*

curiosity. In paintings such as *Target with Plaster Casts* (1955), Johns applied encaustic over a collage of newsprint pasted onto canvas, creating textured areas of strong color through which jumbled fragments of printed text can be seen. Above the hypnotic target shape is a line of nine wooden boxes containing plaster casts of body parts (ear, hand, foot, etc.). The boxes can be opened or closed independently, changing the appearance of the picture.

Johns also experimented with sculp-metal, a quick-drying modeling material produced for amateur crafts enthusiasts rather than "serious" sculptors. Again Johns combined ordinary objects with an unusual medium. This lifelong interest in the physical qualities of different media sets Johns apart from the pop art mainstream, which was always more concerned with the graphic qualities of images.

coating himself in oil and charcoal, then rolling on a sheet of paper.

In the 1970s Johns based many of his paintings on a crosshatching design (crisscrossed parallel lines), sometimes in somber tones, sometimes more brightly colored.

Some of his large works from the 1980s seem autobiographical: Johns's bathroom wall—decorated with his own flag paintings—was repeatedly painted in these years. These paintings also included optical illusions: a vase was both a white vase and two dark profiles facing each other (here Johns was using a well-known "trick" image). Similar illusory images were featured in his works of the 1990s. In *Untitled* (1991), human heads, eyelike forms, and lips tease the viewer in their resistance to a simple, single interpretation.

In Johns's paintings, the viewer is confronted by images that are both boldly assertive and subtly humorous. Both his critics and admirers respond with feelings of uncertainty. In interviews about his work, Johns reinforces the impression that the meaning of his works cannot be pinned down. His saying, "You can see more than one thing at a time," seems to apply to all of his work.

KAHLO Frida

THROUGH HER SELF-PORTRAITURE, Frida Kahlo created images of a personal reality that was remembered, experienced, and imagined. Her images seem to have a surrealistic quality, but hers was an intuitive surrealism that was allied to Mexican culture rather than learned from abroad. In fact, to Kahlo it was not surrealism at all, but merely her own realism.

Life and work

Frida Kahlo, the daughter of a Mexican mother and a German father, was born in a suburb of Mexico City. She had intended to embark upon a career in medicine, but in her late teens she was badly injured in a road accident, which permanently disrupted her studies. She had been traveling on a bus that collided with a trolley car, and in the ensuing disintegration of the vehicles she had been impaled upon a metal pole. The bus had exploded on impact, ripping off her clothes, and in an image as surreal as one of her own paintings, her blood-soaked body had been scattered with the gold dust that a fellow passenger had been carrying. Kahlo's injuries were so severe that she was in near-constant pain for the rest of her life and endured over 30 operations in an attempt to repair her fractured spine. It was during her first spell of convalescence following the crash that Kahlo began to produce paintings.

She had received no formal training in painting, and just as her subject matter was rooted in herself, so her style and technique were self-taught. Her artistic ability did not take long to surface, however, and when she showed her work to Mexico's foremost painter, Diego Rivera, in 1929, he was immediately and deeply impressed. Rivera's opinion was almost certainly sincere, but his admiration extended beyond Kahlo's painting ability. Within a year the two were married, beginning a turbulent partnership that lasted until her death.

If the crash had provided the initial impetus for her art, both Rivera's support and intermittent infidelity became the motivation for much of her work from then on. This is most evident in a series of pictures painted at the time of their divorce in 1939, which expose her emotional pain with an extraordinary calmness and honesty. One such painting, a double self-portrait called *The Two Fridas* (1939), displays a stark symbolism: her heart is exposed and her lifeblood drips from an artery that has been severed from Rivera's body. However, the couple remarried in 1940.

By this stage Kahlo had achieved a degree of recognition and success, both in Mexico and abroad. In 1938 she had her first solo exhibition in New York and also showed work in an exhibition in Paris organized by the leader of the surrealist movement, André Breton. Interest in her work, as well as occasional exhibitions of her paintings, continued throughout the 1940s, but

Data file

Full name: Frida Kahlo

Nationality: Mexican

Style: primitivism, surrealism

Dates: born 1907 in Mexico City, died 1954 in Mexico City

Key works:

My Birth 1932

My Parents, Grandparents, and I 1936

Self-portrait with Monkey and Necklace 1938

The Two Fridas 1939

Self-portrait with Thorn Necklace and Hummingbird 1940

The Broken Column 1944

Without Hope 1945

Viva La Vida (Long Live Life) 1954

Things to look for:

- the portrayal of internal anatomy as an expression of emotional and physical pain
- surrealistic juxtapositions and scenarios
- strange, metamorphic subjects

Comparisons: René Magritte, Giorgio de Chirico, Diego Rivera, Paul Delvaux

Glossary terms: primitivism, surrealism

Painting with a purpose

Through portraying her experiences, Kahlo found a way in which to express her struggle for life in an emphatic way, at times joyful, but frequently also alarming and raw with pain.

Although her initial point of reference was the road accident and its effect upon her, her acute portrayal of herself as a sensitive and emotional being became a working method that she used throughout her life. She expressed her identity in relation to the events, people, culture, and history that surrounded her through self-portraiture. Her paintings therefore had purpose and represented a function within her life. She used them particularly to express the physical and emotional hurt that she was suffering, and by doing so apparently was able to confront and survive her pain.

In both her individual paintings and throughout the body of her work she created a very strong sense of self-identity, picturing her interior world as clearly as she depicted her sensuous exterior image.

Mexican folklore does not shy away from the imagery of violence and death, and Kahlo's work melds into this tradition, through the reality of her own experience, in which physical pain was a daily occurrence and the shadow of death was a constant presence. Although the imagery within her work is frequently of a dramatic nature, its scale is often small enough to lend the paintings a certain intimacy. In some senses this distances the horror of her more gruesome paintings from the viewer, but it also means that she painted such works with tremendous control and in fine detail. Kahlo painted very close to the canvas, in a position that enabled her directly to confront the emotional and physical life that she portrayed. In technical terms her work is simple, diagrammatic, and undertaken with a high degree of control. The expressiveness of her paintings is not the result of her technique, however, but of the imagery that she invoked, be it the exposure of her blood and organs, or, as here, through the striking twinning of Kahlo and her pet monkey.

Although Kahlo painted many self-portraits, no two are alike. They seem to convey more than an exploration of personality, and each seems to be entirely connected to a significant moment, summing up something of her life at that time. In *Self-portrait with Monkey and Necklace* (1938), for example, the artist is represented as being closely allied to the natural world, surrounded as she is by leaves and their stems. Yet it is not an easy relationship that is being depicted for, like her pet monkey, she, too, is bound, in her case by a simple bone necklace that seems more oppressive than decorative. One of the monkey's arms is wrapped around her neck in a gesture that suggests not only comfort and support, but also possession and dependency. It is a simple painting of a complex relationship, and, as such, is typical of Kahlo's work.

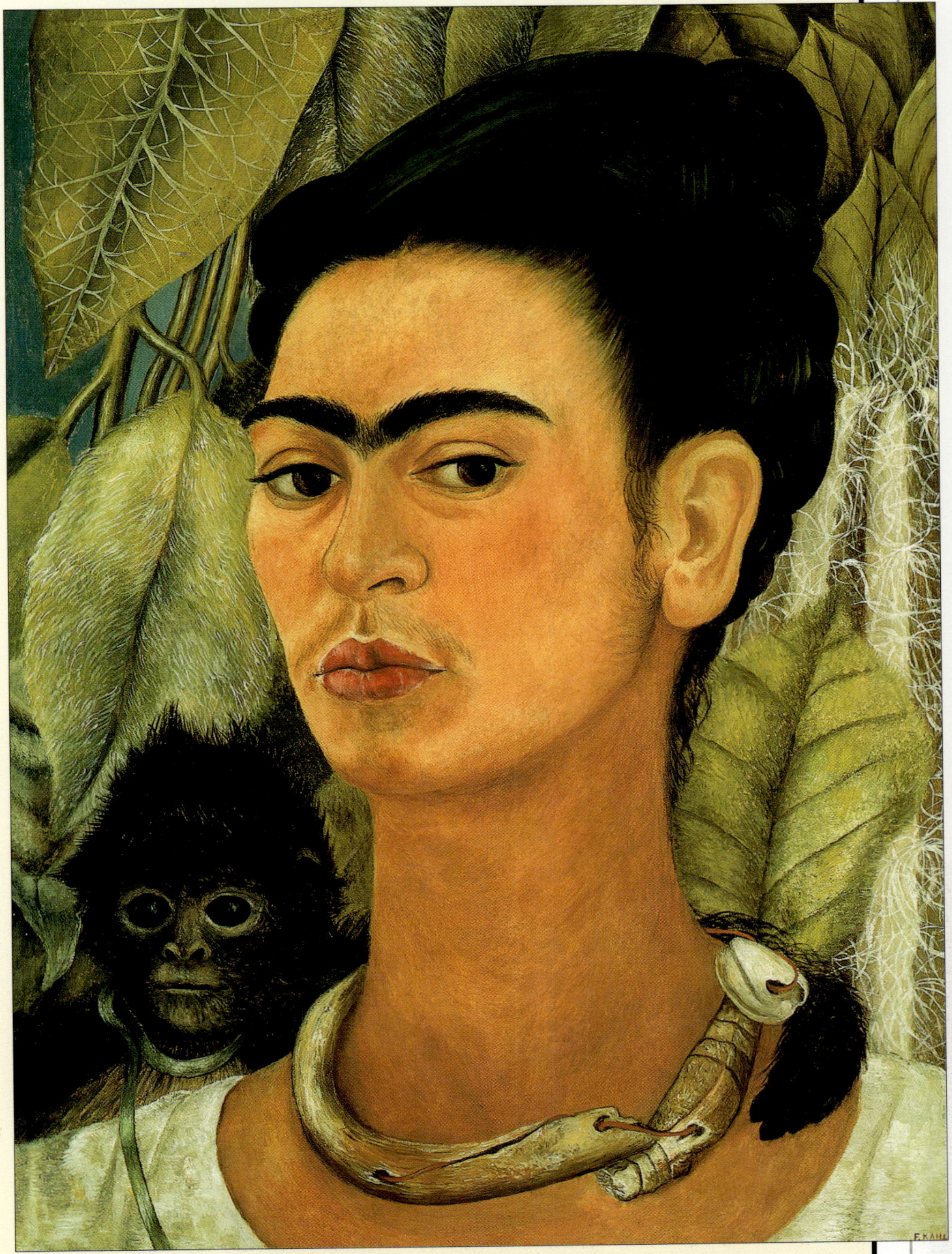

Self-portrait with Monkey and Necklace
1938. Oil on masonite. 16 x 12 in (40.5 x 30.5 cm). Albright Knox Art Gallery, Buffalo, NY.

during this period her back problems got worse. Paintings like *The Broken Column* (1944) and *Without Hope* (1945) graphically express her physical discomfort, her sense of bodily impermanence, and her resigned reliance upon surgery and medical care for her future survival. In 1950 she was hospitalized for nine months as her doctors tried to alleviate her spinal condition, but their efforts were largely unsuccessful. A gangrenous foot caused further difficulties for Kahlo in 1953, resulting in the amputation of the lower portion of her leg. That her health had deteriorated greatly is evident in her paintings of the 1950s. In order to dull the pain Kahlo had begun to take alcohol and drugs, which meant that her painting technique lost its clarity, instead becoming sketchy and uncertain, as can be seen in one of her final works, *Self-Portrait with Ixcuintle Dog and Sun* (1953–54). Her last painting, of 1954, was a simple still life of succulent, red-fleshed watermelons against a blue-and-white, windswept sky. Kahlo spelled out the title of the painting on one of the slices of fruit: *Viva La Vida (Long Live Life)*.

KANDINSKY Wassily

WASSILY KANDINSKY WAS ONE OF THE FIRST ARTISTS ever to make abstract paintings. He was a leading member of the Blaue Reiter group, and later taught at the Bauhaus. Although he spent many years in Germany and France, Kandinsky never forgot his Russian roots.

Life and work

Kandinsky was 30 years old and well on his way to a successful legal career in Moscow when he decided to move to Munich and become an artist. He had been profoundly inspired by the experience of seeing one of Claude Monet's paintings in a Moscow exhibition. Kandinsky studied art in Munich until 1901, when he co-founded the Phalanx Exhibition Society and School. There he met Gabriele Münter. She was one of his students, who later lived and worked with him for several years, becoming an important painter in her own right.

At this time Kandinsky was producing decorative, jewel-like paintings of imagined or half-remembered Russian scenes. They seem to glitter with color, and they often combined fairy-tale figures and the distinctive cupola domes of traditional Russian churches. For a time he traveled in Europe with Münter. Then, in 1909, she bought a house in the small mountain town of Murnau, near Munich. Over the next five years the couple spent their summers there with friends, painting from the local landscape; many of the mountain forms in Kandinsky's abstract works can be traced back to Murnau.

Kandinsky began to explore a range of new possibilities in painting. He was always extraordinarily sensitive to color, but he also looked for inspiration in many other art-forms, past and present. For example, he was inspired by traditional Russian folk art, and also painted on glass after seeing old glass paintings in local churches. Yet he was also fascinated by the most contemporary music, philosophy, and by ideas about modern art and abstraction.

In 1911 and 1912, together with his friend Franz Marc, Kandinsky developed plans for publishing a book, called the *Blaue Reiter* ("Blue Rider"). The name came from Kandinsky's idea of the artist as a heroic knightlike figure, and from his love of horses and the color blue. Combining poetry, prose, and modern art with children's drawings, medieval artefacts, Chinese paintings, African sculptures, Russian folk art, and other images, the book, or almanac, sought to inspire and document innovative art. Artists including Münter, Marc, August Macke and later Paul Klee formed a group with Kandinsky and exhibited their vibrant, colorful works under the Blaue Reiter name, alongside other important modern European artists. For two years, this was a crucial focus for expressionism in Germany.

When World War I broke out in 1914, Kandinsky and Münter left

Full name: Wassily Kandinsky

Nationality: Russian

Style: expressionism

Dates: born 1866 in Moscow, died 1944 in Neuilly-sur-Seine, France

Key works:
- *Couple on Horseback* 1906–07
- *Railway near Murnay* 1909
- *Composition V* 1911
- *Small Pleasures* 1913
- *Blue Crest* 1917
- *Black Spot* 1921
- *Composition VIII* 1923

Things to look for:
- bright colors
- abstract images
- horses and riders
- religious themes
- geometric shapes

Comparisons: Paul Klee, Franz Marc, August Macke, Robert Delaunay

Glossary terms: abstraction, Bauhaus, Blaue Reiter, constructivism, expressionism

Data file

Abstraction and the Apocalypse

Like so many of Kandinsky's paintings, *Blue Crest* (1917) is both an abstract composition and a landscape. The title refers to the visual shape of a blue arch and to the ridge of a hill or mountain; indeed, we can detect blue mountainous shapes in the center of the canvas.

In 1911 Kandinsky had put his own complex theories on art into writing, in a long essay entitled "Concerning the Spiritual in Art." He felt strongly that true art was an expression of the artist's "inner world" of needs and emotions. He set himself a hard task: paintings should contain no trivial details, but should both express and uplift the spirit through form and color. If it did this, true art could affect a sensitive viewer in the way that the most moving piece of music could.

Kandinsky believed that colors were like different musical tones; a bright yellow was like a shrill, high note, for example, and a deep blue "sounded" like a low bass note. However, the rich colors and energetic lines here also originate in nature, and in some of Kandinsky's earlier paintings.

Horses and riders appear over and over again in Kandinsky's work. In the top left corner we can make out a form like a galloping horse. The lively black curving lines above the "horizon" are also characteristic Kandinsky "shorthand" for horses. Topping the mountainous central shape, angular lines refer to the towering buildings of Kandinsky's favorite city—Moscow. The whole scene appears at first to be lit by a radiant sun in the top right corner, but then we notice the crashing, wavelike forms in the lower part of the picture. The "sun" is a blowing gale, and the force that whips the scene into action. Many of Kandinsky's works draw on the imagery of the Apocalypse and the Last Judgment—the end of the world—as it is prophesied in the Bible. Floods, storms, saints, and angels fill his canvases.

Kandinsky painted *Blue Crest* in Russia in September 1917. It was a turbulent time: Europe was at war, the Russian Revolution was brewing, and this was also the month in which his new wife, Nina, gave birth to his son. If we bear all this in mind, this is a painting as much about destruction and creation as it is about abstract art. And we can now even see the riders as the Four Horsemen of the biblical Apocalypse—symbolizing death, famine, war, and pestilence.

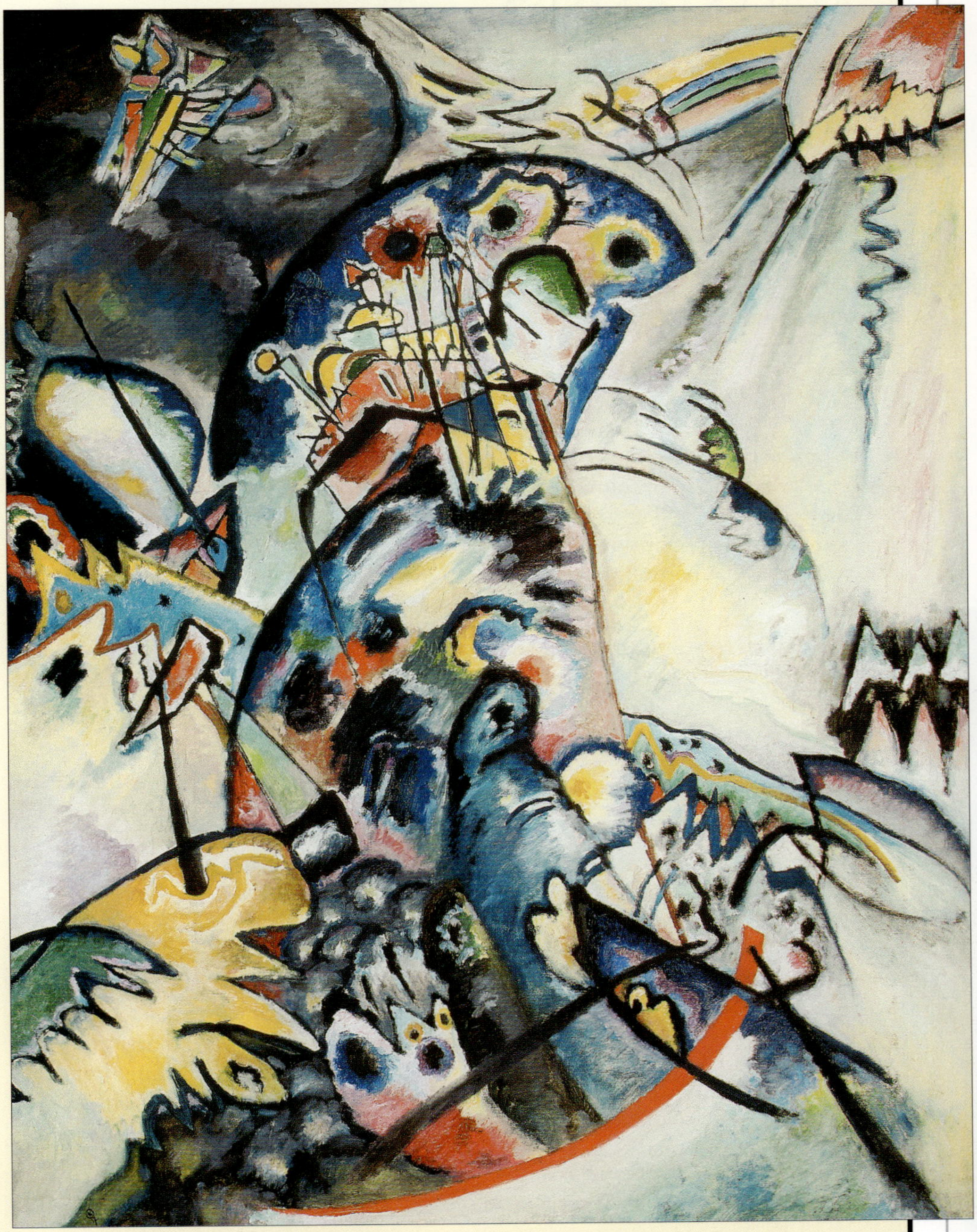

Blue Crest *1917. Oil on canvas. 52½ x 41 in (133 x 104 cm). State Russian Museum, St Petersburg.*

Germany for Switzerland. But their affair ended unhappily, and in the same year Kandinsky moved back to his beloved Moscow. He was involved in plans for new artistic institutions in Russia, but in 1922 left for Germany where he was invited to teach painting and theory at the new Bauhaus School of architecture and applied arts.

Kandinsky had seen the work of the Russian constructivists, and this influenced his art; during the 1920s it became more geometric and its lines sharper and shapes more regular.

At the Bauhaus he showed students how to produce abstract wall-paintings to bring color to and complement the new crisp, white modernist architecture for which the Bauhaus School was famous. He was, however, wary of severe geometric abstraction, fearing that it lacked emotional depth. His work always retained the distinctive combination of abstraction and individual expression.

Kandinsky led a truly cosmopolitan life. He became a German citizen in 1928, and continued to travel widely, even in old age. Forced to leave Nazi Germany in 1933, and stripped of his German passport, he finally settled in France; by that time he was an internationally recognized artist.

KAUFFMANN Angelica

IN AN AGE WHEN MOST FEMALE ARTISTS WERE AMATEURS, Angelica Kauffmann was unusual in being a professional artist. Although she painted decorative interior schemes, as well as many fine portraits and allegories, it was in the highly prestigious and competitive field of history painting that Kauffmann achieved critical acclaim and international status.

Life and work

Angelica Kauffmann began her career assisting her father, a painter of ecclesiastical murals and portraits, but she soon received commissions in her own right. Her first portrait, of Monsignor Nevroni, Bishop of Como, was painted before she was 12 years old.

Kauffmann was a talented woman: she was fluent in several languages and showed a great aptitude for music and singing. She was encouraged to pursue a musical career, but opted for the visual arts. She later depicted her dilemma in *Self-portrait Hesitating Between Painting and Music* (1794).

Kauffmann's early style was influenced by Antonio Correggio and the Carracci family; she copied the works she saw by them in museums and churches while traveling with her father. Later she was influenced by rococo, a lighter and more playful version of baroque, which continued to pervade her work, even when the style gave way to neoclassicism.

In 1762 Kauffmann and her father were in Florence. She met many of the young artists who were working in the new neoclassical style, including the American painter Benjamin West and the German etcher J. F. Reifferstein.

The following year Kauffmann traveled to Rome. Her linguistic and artistic skills helped her enter the social and cultural milieu there, and soon she was receiving commissions for portraits.

After a visit to Naples, Kauffmann returned to Rome to paint her first subject pictures: *Penelope* and *Bacchus and Ariadne* (both 1764). She was elected to Rome's Academy of Saint Luke in 1765. The same year, in Venice, after studying the works of Titian, she produced numerous etchings and drawings. She was befriended by Lady Wentworth, the wife of an English diplomat, who persuaded her to leave her father for a while and travel to England.

Kauffmann arrived in London in 1766. There she painted several portraits, including one of the famous English painter Sir Joshua Reynolds. While most women artists were content

Data file

Full name: Angelica Maria Anna Catharina Kauffmann

Nationality: Swiss

Style: neoclassicism

Dates: born 1741 in Chur, died 1807 in Rome, Italy

Key works:

Bacchus and Ariadne 1764

Venus Directing Aeneas and Achates to Carthage 1769

Mary, Duchess of Richmond 1775

four ceiling decorations for the Royal Academy: *Color, Design, Composition, Genius* 1778

Cornelia, Mother of the Gracchi 1785

Virgil Writing His Own Epitaph 1785

Self-portrait Hesitating Between Painting and Music 1794

Portrait of a Lady c1795

Things to look for:

- large history paintings and allegorical works
- portraits of aristocratic women in neoclassical poses but painted in "softer," more rococo manner
- gestures and expressions of figures based on classical motifs and Renaissance paintings
- figures arranged near the picture plane
- subjects chosen give female figures the prominent roles

Comparisons: Joshua Reynolds, Benjamin West, Gavin Hamilton, Jacques-Louis David, Anton Mengs, Nathaniel Dance, Elizabeth Vigee-Lebrun

Glossary terms: academic, allegory, baroque, classical, etching, genre, history painting, linear, pastel, picture plane, neoclassicism, rococo

Artistic delicacy

For wealthy women in the 18th century, artistic training was an essential part of their education. However, practical art instruction was usually limited to watercolor and pastel drawing. The few women who were professional artists tended to concentrate on decorative art, such as designs for porcelain dinner services. Even Kauffmann produced works for the Meissen china factory.

Kauffmann was unusual for a woman in deciding to produce history paintings. In history painting, artists represented human actions based on themes from history, mythology, literature, and the scriptures. This required extensive knowledge of the classics and the Bible, as well as formal academic art training. However, female artists were not allowed to study in the art academies, as this would entail study of the male nude.

Kauffmann was able to produce history paintings successfully because she avoided the "problem" of the male subject (nude or clothed), instead selecting scenes in which female figures such as Cleopatra and Venus dominate. The figures are arranged near the picture plane (the surface of the picture, just behind the frame's glass). They are posed in neoclassical stances, with their gestures based on classical motifs and Renaissance paintings.

Stylistically, Kauffmann's history paintings can also be said to be softer than the more linear work of similar artists such as Jacques-Louis David or Anton Mengs. This style, coupled with the central role she gave to female characters, was attractive to many patrons.

The neoclassical style was popular, but most English patrons preferred portraits of themselves, their families, and even their horses rather than historical subjects. Kauffmann therefore had to paint portraits

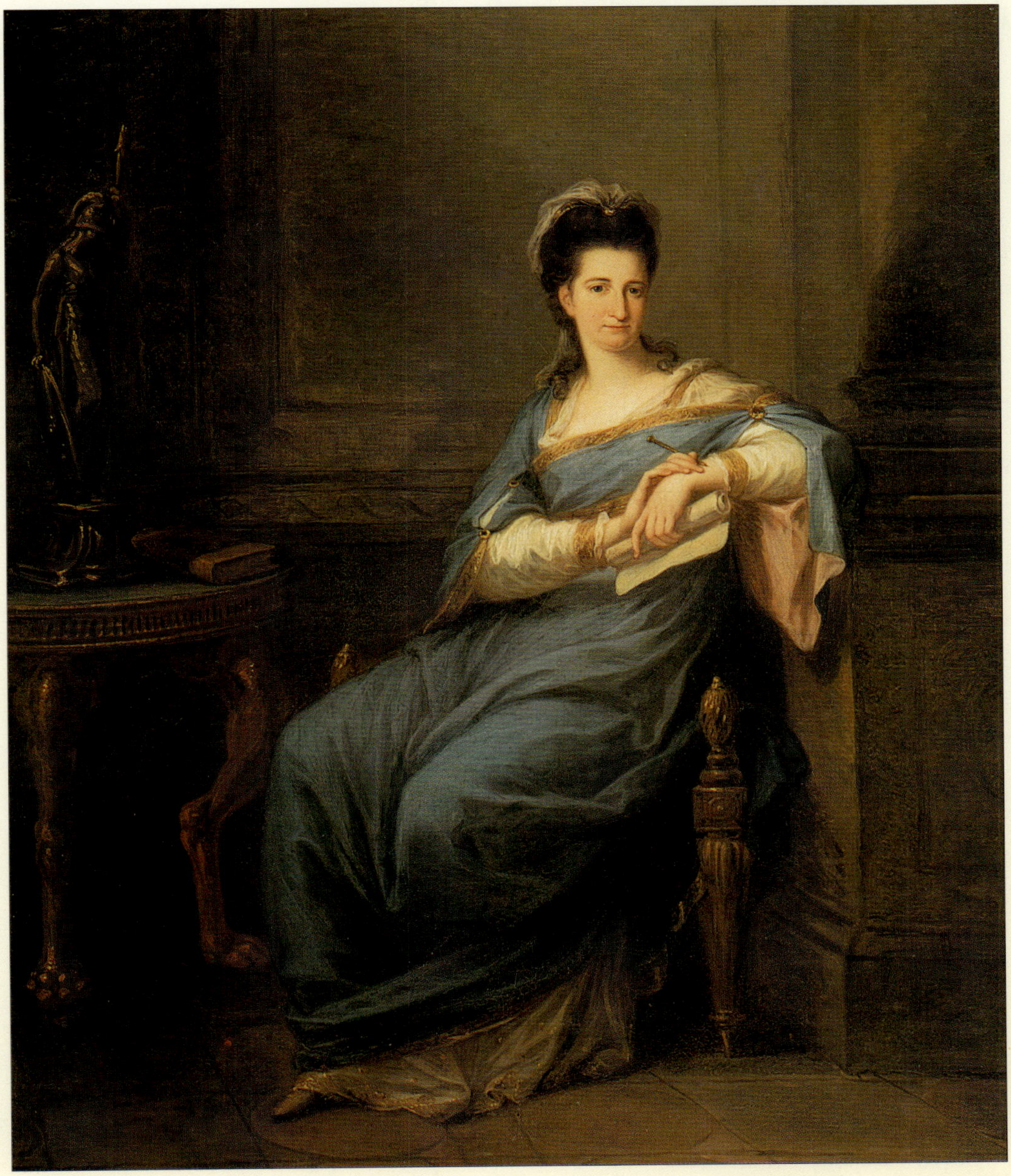

Portrait of a Lady *c1795. Oil on canvas. 31 x 25 in (79 x 63.5 cm). Tate Gallery, London.*

to earn her living. While she did paint portraits of men, most of her sitters were women: the Duchess of Richmond and Marchioness Townshend are two examples. In all these portraits of society women—as in *Portrait of a Lady* (c1795)—Kauffmann has turned the subjects into classical allegories. Draped in classical finery, with ancient-looking jewels, seated on Roman-style chairs and surrounded by statuary, they are nevertheless engaged in solitary, suitably feminine pursuits like needlework or reading.

Portrait of a Lady was painted late in her career when Kauffmann was producing fewer works. While the subject might have been well-born, the absence of her name in the portrait's title suggests that she was not a member of the nobility.

with genre painting and portraiture, Kauffmann's own preference was for history painting, considered to be the highest artistic genre and the preserve of male artists.

Kauffmann's paintings of classical mythology, history, and allegories brought her not only wealth but critical acclaim as well. She was a founder member of the Royal Academy in 1768 and in 1778 she decorated the ceiling of its lecture hall at Burlington House.

In 1781 Kauffmann married Italian painter Antonio Zucchi, and the couple returned to Italy. In Rome she was once again at the center of artistic society, enjoying the patronage of European nobles such as Emperor Joseph II of Austria. When she died in 1807, two of her paintings were carried in triumph in her funeral procession.

KIRCHNER Ernst Ludwig

ERNST LUDWIG KIRCHNER LED A BOHEMIAN LIFE, painting lively scenes of city life and nature. He is known for his many graphic works, especially woodcuts, and for his bright, expressive paintings. The self-appointed leader of the artistic group Die Brücke, he was one of the most important and influential German expressionists.

Life and work

Kirchner was the son of a paper technician, and in 1901 he began studying architecture in Dresden. He quickly became bored by the conventional teaching methods at the school, so along with a small group of friends, including Erich Heckel and Karl Schmidt-Rottluff, he organized separate painting and drawing sessions. Working closely together, the students made rapid, spontaneous drawings from live models, and developed a free, expressive style. In 1905 they found a name for their group, Die Brücke ("The Bridge"), and began to exhibit together. Looking at the work of Vincent Van Gogh, Edvard Munch, and the French fauves, they were inspired to use color freely and inventively. Kirchner also greatly admired the German masters, especially Albrecht Dürer and Lucas Cranach the Elder, and woodcarvings from Africa and the South Seas. Energetic marks and intense color, quickly applied to paper, canvas, or printing blocks, became important features of what was later known as German expressionism.

From 1906, Die Brücke artists worked together in a little studio, which they decorated themselves with colorful murals and unusual, "primitive" artifacts. The work Kirchner produced in Dresden has a lush, youthful exuberance; his canvases and prints are full of relaxed, happy models and friends. Wearing bright, exotic clothes, or no clothes at all, we see them picnicking, lounging around the studio, playing with children, animals, bows and arrows, or splashing around in the lakes outside Dresden, which Die Brücke painters often visited in the summer. They would often work outside. This young group wanted to live a free and unconventional life, as well as painting in a free and unconventional manner.

In 1911 Kirchner left Dresden for Berlin, and the following year he met Erna Schilling, who became his model and lifelong companion. In 1913 Die Brücke split up. The other artists had been annoyed by Kirchner's attempts to present himself as the most important member of the group.

Kirchner now found his subjects in the hectic center of Berlin, Germany's biggest, loudest, and most modern city. He was fascinated by urban life, and expressed its rapid tempo through sharp, spiky lines and exaggerated perspective. He painted and drew the fashionable women parading up and down the busy streets in their furs and heavy make-up, circus performers, dancers, and all aspects of city nightlife. Gradually, Kirchner's style became

Data file

Full name: Ernst Ludwig Kirchner

Nationality: German

Style: expressionism

Dates: born 1880 in Aschaffenburg, died 1938 in Davos, Switzerland

Key works:

Girl with a Japanese Umbrella 1909

Bathers at Moritzburg 1909–26

Striding into the Sea 1912

Five Women in the Street 1913

Modern Bohemia 1924

Painters of the Group Die Brücke 1925

Things to look for:

- bright, unnaturalistic colors
- jagged forms
- rough, thick brushstrokes
- graphic works, especially woodcuts

Comparisons: Erich Heckel, Karl Schmidt-Rottluff, Emil Nolde, Vincent Van Gogh, Edvard Munch, Lucas Cranach the Elder

Glossary terms: Die Brücke, expressionism, fauvism, perspective

Kirchner's view of expressionism

By the time Kirchner finished this large group portrait, expressionism had long become part of the mainstream of modern art, literature, music, theater, and dance in Germany. It was even rather commercial. There were expressionist-style posters, advertisements, and fashions. Many artists now disowned expressionism. Nonetheless, Kirchner clearly wanted to commemorate the artists who were among the innovators of the early, idealistic movement, even though the group itself had long since splintered.

The painting is a good example of Kirchner's later style. There are the typical bold, simplified forms and colors, and the paint applied to the large canvas in broad brushstrokes. The flattened perspective—the apparent shallowness of the picture space—is characteristically modern. But this painting is already rather muted and controlled in comparison with Kirchner's earlier works, and gives us an indication of how art after World War I in Germany was gradually becoming more "objective," sober, and realistic.

We see four men in a studio. Interestingly, there are signs both of the youthful, bohemian exuberance that characterized the Die Brücke group in its early years, and of the professional formality that befits established, successful artists. Their poses are casual, but this is also very much a portrait of professionals. The large size of the painting alone implies this.

Squatting on a low stool, smoking his pipe contemplatively, is Otto Müller, who was sometimes associated with Die Brücke, and is best known for his sensitive paintings of gypsies in the landscape. Peering in profile from behind the curtain is Kirchner himself. In contrast to his many earlier self-portraits, his facial features here are especially realistic; he can be recognized easily by comparing the painting with photographs of the artist. As in his writings, in this painting Kirchner seems to be presenting himself as the most dynamic member of the group, even as its leader. He is the only figure in an animated posture. He holds a poster, or perhaps one of the well-known expressionist art magazines, and his gestures suggest that he is explaining something to his colleagues. Next to him stands Heckel, who of all the artists had been closest to Kirchner.

Standing with his back half toward us, bearded and bespectacled, is Karl Schmidt-Rottluff. Other members of the old group have been left out; most noticeably Max Pechstein, who had distanced himself from his old friends some years earlier.

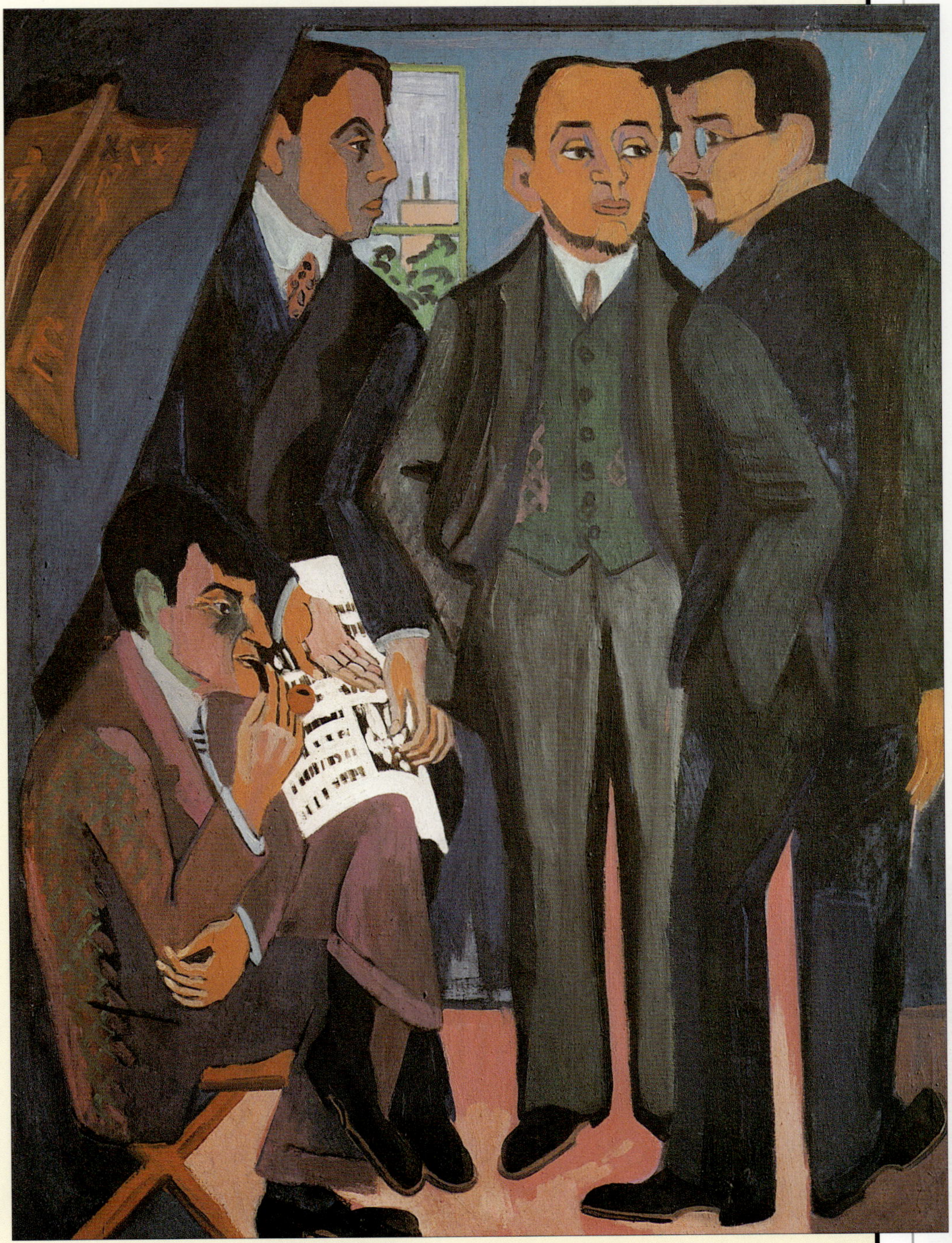

Painters of the Group Die Brücke *1925. Oil on canvas. 66 x 49½ in (168 x 126 cm). Wallraf-Richartz Museum, Cologne.*

more angular, appearing to express the tension and nervousness of modern life, and of the artist's own anxieties.

In May 1917, following his very traumatic experience of war, and unable to cope with the constant fear of having to return to military service, Kirchner left Germany and moved into a little mountain hut near the beautiful village of Davos, high up in the Swiss Alps. Davos must have been a welcome retreat; indeed, he remained there for the rest of his life. In Davos Kirchner painted mountain landscapes, simple peasant scenes and portraits of his friends. His style here became calmer, his forms more simplified. As one of the first expressionists, he continued to inspire younger artists in the 1920s, and his reputation grew.

By 1938 Kirchner was suffering acute depression, caused partly by political events in Germany, where the Nazis had banned his work. Over 600 of his pieces had been removed from museums and many were destroyed. On June 15, Kirchner shot himself.

KLEE Paul

PAUL KLEE'S WORK CHANGED greatly over the years, but it was always highly imaginative, often strange, and sometimes playful. He was greatly admired by Pablo Picasso and the surrealists. Much influenced by his background in graphic art, Klee defined his own art as "taking a line for a walk."

Life and work

Klee's life began and ended in Switzerland, but he spent most of his working years in Germany. There he came into contact with many of the leading modern artists of his generation, and with ideas that changed art and design forever.

Klee developed an extraordinary range of techniques and styles. These can be traced to his many interests.

Data file

Full name: Paul Klee
Nationality: Swiss
Style: expressionism
Dates: born 1879 near Berne, died 1940 in Muralto-Locarno
Key works:
Virgin in a Tree 1903
Marianne 1925
Fish Magic 1925
Black Prince 1927
Ad Parnassum 1932
Marked Man 1935
Death and Fire 1940
Things to look for:
- unusual combinations of creatures and objects
- ambiguous space
- glowing colors
- dots and lines

Comparisons: Wassily Kandinsky, Franz Marc, August Macke, Robert Delaunay, Max Ernst
Glossary terms: abstract, Bauhaus, Blaue Reiter, expressionism, mural, surrealism, symbolism

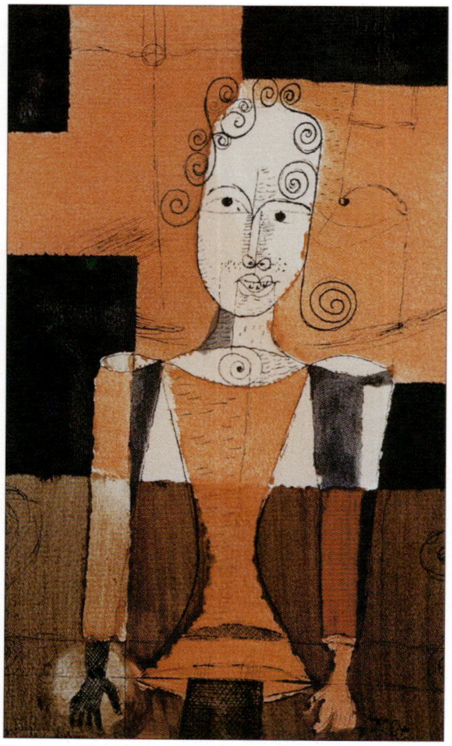

Marianne *1925. Oil and watercolor on muslin mounted on board. 14 x 8¼ in (35.5 x 21 cm). Private collection.*

Klee wrote poems when he was young and drew inspiration from them years later for his paintings. He was interested in theater, and seriously considered music as a career. In fact, his paintings have been likened to music. Some, such as the portraits, have a theatrical quality; in others, objects look like floating notes from a page of sheet music. Even when he finally settled on art as a career, Klee continued to write extensively. He was always a deep thinker as well as a painter. His large number of works were part of an attempt to discover what he called "the reality that is behind visible things."

In 1906, the year he married, Klee decided to move to Munich, which was an important place for international as well as German art. There, in 1911, he made friends with the expressionist artists Wassily Kandinsky, August Macke, and Franz Marc of the Blaue Reiter school. They encouraged Klee to develop the visionary, mystical aspects of his work. Like them, Klee admired children's drawings for their creativity and unexpected combinations of objects. In 1914, just before war broke out in Europe, Klee took a trip with Macke to Tunisia. He had rarely worked in color, but the strong North African light, lush foliage, painted roofs, and colorful local fabrics made a powerful impression on him. He had been inspired already by Robert Delaunay's use of color in his vast murals. Now, a whole new world of color opened up for Klee. Back in wartime Munich, the artist turned to his memories, and produced a stunning series of vibrant watercolors that evoked the towns and landscapes of Tunisia. Mediterranean or Arabian motifs—domes, palms, and camels—resurfaced in Klee's work, even in the last years of his life.

In 1921 Klee was invited to teach at the new Bauhaus School of art and design in the German city of Weimar. When he arrived, the bearded, quiet family man, who loved cats and classical music, did not immediately fit in with the avant-garde spirit of the Bauhaus. But he was serious about teaching, and soon gained the respect of many staff and students through his lectures and educational writings, which are still regarded as important today. Taking his wife and son, Klee moved with the Bauhaus to Dessau in 1926, where he stayed until 1931.

When the Nazis came to power in Germany in 1933, they censored modern art; more than 102 of Klee's works disappeared from German museums. Klee returned to Switzerland.

Even at the end of his life, suffering from illness, Klee produced bold, simplified images that remind us of prehistoric cave paintings or ancient hieroglyphics. Their titles referred to ancient myths and powerful emotions, and the images were now darker and more morbid. Klee died of heart failure in 1940, leaving about 9000 works.

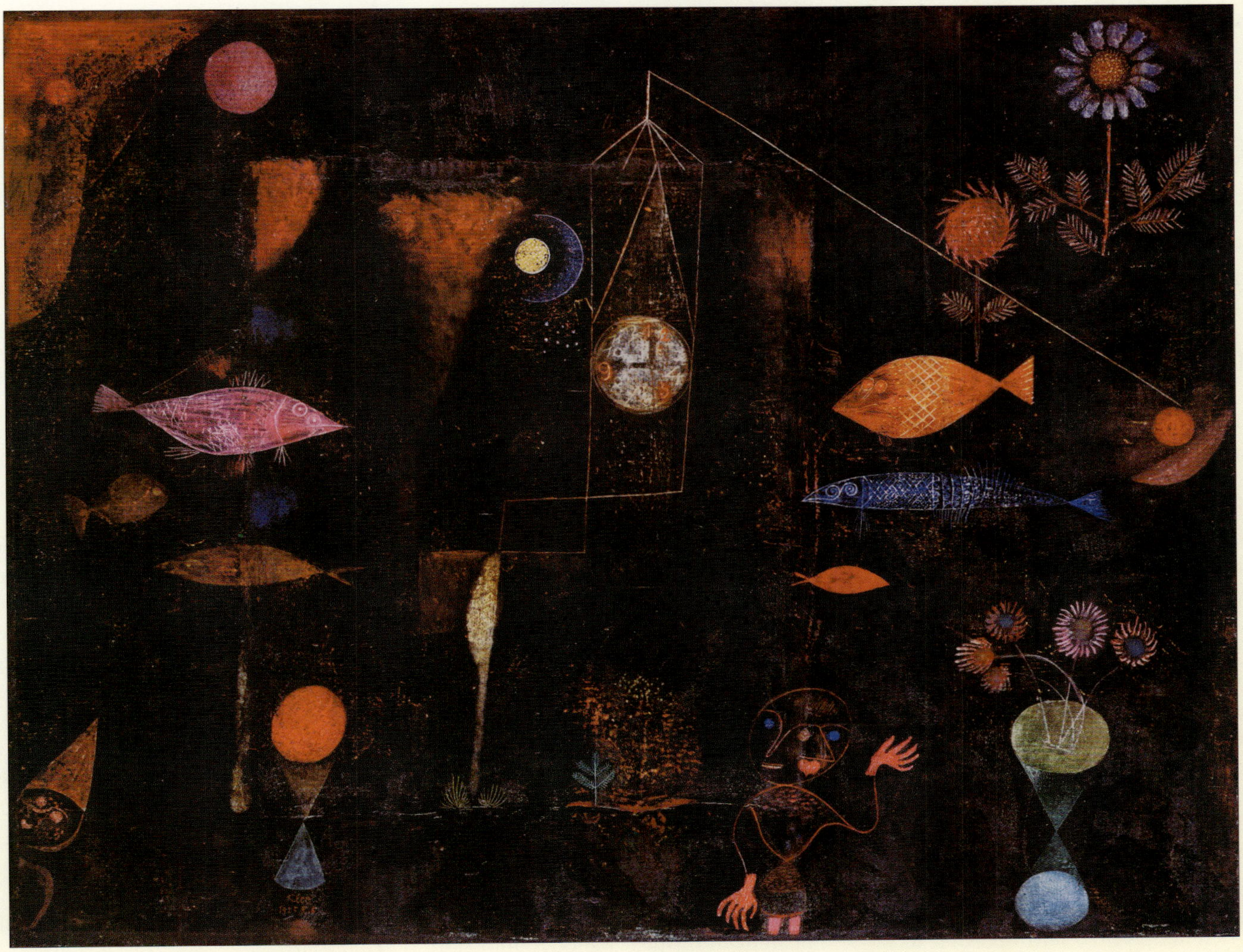

Different worlds

Klee's background in graphic art was significant in all his work. He understood how simple lines, dots, and spaces could be expressive, and provoke new and unusual associations. For Klee, the artist was like an explorer taking a trip to "the land of deeper insight." For example, by means of scattered dots the artist-explorer could discover stars; in zigzag lines could be lightning; in curves, bridges; in wavy lines, boats; in spirals, a child with curly hair, and so on.

Like his old friend, the German expressionist painter Franz Marc, Klee searched for meaning and wisdom in the animal kingdom. But in Klee's work, animals live in strange worlds where the laws of gravity and nature are turned upside down.

Fish Magic, an unusually large painting for Klee, demonstrates well the meeting of "worlds" in his work, as well as his playful use of scale and composition. Looking at the pale clock face and glowing moons, we might see the picture's inky blackness as a night sky and glittering cosmos. But then we observe the fish swimming languidly across the canvas, and the space becomes a deep ocean. Then again, at the bottom left of the picture we notice the grinning face of a clown, and above him a hint of a curtain is pulled back to reveal the scene. Suddenly it all becomes theater, complete with a tragic-comic figure waving to us from the stage.

Looking carefully, we can see that the picture is painted on two canvases. One tall rectangle has been sewn on top of the other, and plants seem to be growing from inside its base. If space is ambiguous here,

Fish Magic *1925. Oil on canvas, mounted on board. 30 x 38 in (77 x 96.5 cm). Philadelphia Museum of Art, Philadelphia, PA.*

so is time. There are two hour-glass shapes—one acts as a vase for flowers—and the church clock face shows an unusual four numbers: 1, 2, 5, and 9. Slowly we come to realize that Klee has used the numbers to tell us the "time" of the picture's creation: 1925.

Klee's pictures are often described as "dream-images," and their mysterious, "otherworld" quality appealed greatly to artists in the surrealist movement. More than mere fantasies, however, these images came about after years of philosophical reflection on the nature of art and life. Today, Klee is recognized as one of the most poetic and original artists of modern times.

KLIMT Gustav

KLIMT'S ART EVOKES BOTH THE SPLENDOR AND THE DECADENCE of Vienna at the end of the 19th century. After conventional beginnings, he became the leader of the Austrian avant-garde movement, producing paintings that were admired for their sumptuous beauty but notorious for their erotic content.

Life and work

Gustav Klimt came from an artistic but impoverished background. His father, an immigrant from Bohemia, was a goldsmith and an engraver. He had little success, however, and the seven Klimt children were brought up in terrible poverty.

At the age of 14, Gustav left school to train at the Viennese School of Applied Arts, where his talent soon became obvious. He formed a partnership with his brother Ernst and another student, Franz Matsch. By the end of the 1880s they were firmly established, winning great acclaim for their decorations at the city's new theater (1886–88) and at the Kunsthistorisches Museum (1890–91).

Klimt appeared set to become a pillar of the art establishment. However, he was unsettled by his brother Ernst's premature death in 1892, and this coincided with his growing interest in various avant-garde movements such as impressionism and symbolism. Increasingly he became dissatisfied with the conservative nature of Austrian art and, in 1897, he and a group of friends took a momentous step, resigning from the traditional artists' association, and setting up a new body to promote modern art. In this they were following the lead of other groups of artists who had resigned from their associations and formed Sezessionen (the German word for "secessions"). Klimt was appointed the first president of the Vienna Sezession.

Klimt's change of outlook became apparent in his next major commission, a series of murals for Vienna University. Some of the professors were horrified when they saw what he was producing, and accused Klimt of creating art that was both chaotic and pornographic. The scandal was taken up by the press until, in 1905, Klimt felt obliged to abandon the project. The paintings were destroyed by a fire in 1945.

The loss of work from public institutions did not really damage Klimt's career, and he was soon in great demand as a portraitist. Rich businessmen were keen to have him paint their wives, because of his ability to create stunning images of beautiful women. Some of these portraits were fairly conventional, while in others the sitter's face and hands were virtually engulfed in swathes of rich, decorative patterns. Klimt's model for these daring artistic experiments was his sister-in-law, Emilie Flöge. She ran a fashion shop and was the artist's close companion for more than 20 years.

Klimt also continued to paint murals. In 1902, he executed *The*

Opulent eroticism

Klimt's most celebrated painting is *The Kiss* (1907–08). He produced it at the peak of his "golden period," when he successfully managed to blend the various elements of his style into a unique fusion of visual splendor and eroticism. This fusion was made up of three basic components: art nouveau, symbolism, and early mosaics.

The most obvious links with art nouveau (a movement at its height in the 1890s) stem from the artist's use of sinuous, flowing lines and exuberant pattern-making. With both of these features, decoration takes precedence over physical accuracy. At first glance, for example, there might seem to be nothing inaccurate about this rapturous embrace. However, the woman's protruding feet show that she is kneeling down, while the man appears to be standing. If this image were interpreted realistically, then the difference in their sizes would be quite considerable, but in fact the mechanics of the embrace are unimportant. They take second place to the overall, poetic impression of the scene.

The "Embrace" or the "Kiss" was a very common theme in symbolist art. It figured prominently in the art of Norwegian Edvard Munch, among others. The theme had also been explored by Klimt in a number of paintings prior to *The Kiss*. There were embracing couples in *The Beethoven Frieze* (1902) and in *Fulfillment*, which formed part of *The Stoclet Frieze* (1909–11). In the latter, the lovers wore elaborate, patterned gowns, which Klimt developed still further in *The Kiss*. Here, the shapes of the cloaks are more vague, and they have been transformed into a kind of cocoon, separating the lovers from the world around them. One key feature of the symbolist movement was its emphasis on suggestion and evocation, rather than on representation of the concrete world.

Data file

Full name: Gustav Klimt

Nationality: Austrian

Style: symbolism, art nouveau

Dates: born 1862 in Vienna, died 1918 in Vienna

Key works:

Music I 1895

The Beethoven Frieze 1902

Danäe 1907–08

The Kiss 1907–08

The Stoclet Frieze 1909–11

Death and Life 1911–15

Things to look for:

- opulent coloring
- highly charged eroticism and sinuous lines

Comparisons: Egon Schiele, Edvard Munch

Glossary terms: art nouveau, avant-garde, frieze, mosaic, Sezession, symbolism

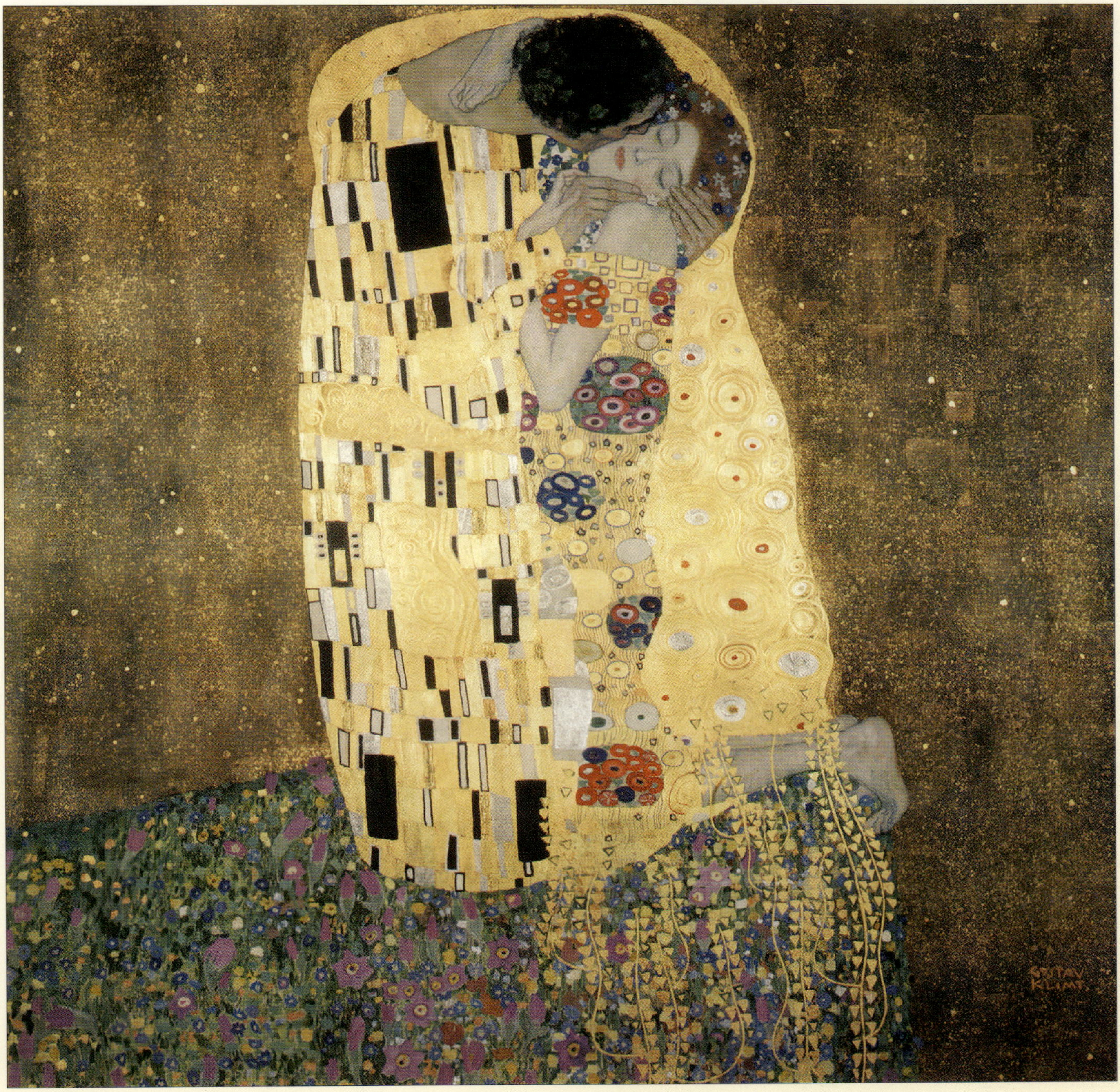

Here, for instance, the lovers' environment is quite ambiguous.

The prolific use of gold paint and the sumptuous appearance of *The Kiss* owes much to Klimt's fondness for mosaics. Klimt had seen some spectacular examples of this art form in Ravenna, Italy, in 1903, and he adapted the technique for use in his work.

The Kiss *1907–08. Oil on canvas. 71 x 71 in (180 x 180 cm). Osterreichische Galerie, Vienna.*

Beethoven Frieze, as part of the refurbishments at the Sezession building. Then in 1904, he received one of his most important commissions, to provide decorations for the Stoclet Palace in Brussels. This striking mansion had been designed by Josef Hoffmann, a fellow member of the Vienna Sezession, and Klimt was asked to design a frieze for its dining room. With its three elaborate mosaics, composed of precious stones, coral, and mother-of-pearl, this proved to be his most lavish project. The frieze was completed in 1911.

KOKOSCHKA Oskar

OSKAR KOKOSCHKA HAD A LONG AND VERY EVENTFUL LIFE marked by both success and tragedy. A writer as well as a painter, he was an important expressionist who drew largely on personal experience. His unique style and imagery made him one of the most original artists of the 20th century.

Life and work

Oskar Kokoschka's childhood was not easy. He was born into a family that had once been rich, but had fallen on hard times. He grew up in Vienna, the spectacular capital city of Austria, but his family lived in the poorer suburbs. Even later in life, when Kokoschka was a successful artist, most of his money went to support his mother, brother, and sister.

Kokoschka began his training at the School of Arts and Crafts in Vienna, hoping to become an art teacher. Initially, he lacked the confidence to develop his own style, but by 1908 he was becoming more sure in his work, painting predominantly landscapes, and using strong flowing lines and color to express emotion. His first exhibition that year attracted a lot of attention and controversy. Gustav Klimt, the most famous painter in Vienna, called him "the greatest talent of the younger generation."

Kokoschka was also a playwright, and penned some of the earliest expressionist plays. These included his 1907 work, *Mörder, Hoffnung der Frauen* ("Murderer, Hope of Women"). He later said that it "contrasted the callousness of our male society with my basic conception of man as mortal and woman as immortal...."

In 1909 Kokoschka met the modern architect and writer Adolf Loos. He painted his portrait, and the two became friends. Loos paid for smart new clothes for Kokoschka and encouraged him to paint more portraits.

Over the next few years, some of the most important people in Vienna sat for him. A great portraitist throughout his life, Kokoschka's ability to capture the essence of his sitters' character, through line and through color, was remarkable. We can see it even in his 1969 portrait of the great English crime novelist Agatha Christie—made to honor her 80th birthday—by the artist who was himself then aged 84.

Much of Kokoschka's personal life was extremely turbulent. He was unruly by nature, but also popular and attractive, and had several affairs with women. He was very nearly killed in World War I by a shot to the head and a bayonet wound, and he was later severely shell-shocked. He suffered great emotional pain, too, with the breakdown of his three-year-long relationship with Alma Mahler, the widow of the Austrian composer Gustav Mahler.

These experiences had brought Kokoschka to the brink of despair. But by 1919 he was becoming established as an artist. His work was much better received in Germany than it had been in more conservative Austria, and he

Data file

Full name: Oskar Kokoschka

Nationality: Austrian (British citizen after 1947)

Style: expressionism

Dates: born 1886 in Pöchlarn, died 1980 in Montreux, Switzerland

Key works:
- *Portrait of Adolph Loos* 1909
- *The Tempest* 1914
- *The Knight Errant* 1914–15
- *Polperro* 1939
- *Agatha Christie* 1969

Things to look for:
- uncompromising portraits
- jagged, uneven lines
- thick paint
- sharp color contrasts

Comparisons: Egon Schiele, Max Beckmann, Chaim Soutine, Edvard Munch

Glossary terms: expressionism

Visionary expressionism

The Tempest (1914) is considered by many to be the greatest painting Kokoschka ever made. The title is literary, but the image relates directly to his intense love affair with Alma Mahler. The two met in 1912. Alma was already famous, having married the eminent composer and conductor Gustav Mahler in 1902. Widowed in 1911, she remained a central figure in Viennese society. She was older and more sophisticated than Kokoschka, and he worshiped her. He wrote her hundreds of love letters, desperately wanted to marry her, and was insanely jealous of her dead husband and of the other men he believed pursued her.

He painted *The Tempest* at a time when the relationship was beginning to show signs of breaking down. Kokoschka shows himself, taut, awake, and looking troubled, his hands clasped, while Alma rests peacefully against his shoulder. All around there are imagined stormy waves or clouds. The setting suggests a dreamlike vision and a relationship that transcends ordinary life. It also clearly expresses the tempestuous nature of his love for Alma, for he was plagued by the fear that she might leave him.

Indeed, when the war broke out and Kokoschka went away to fight, Alma quickly lost interest in him, and instead pursued the famous young architect Walter Gropius, whom she married in 1915. Traumatized already by his war experience, Kokoschka was left broken-hearted and obsessed by his lost love.

When Kokoschka began *The Tempest*, it contained more warm reds than we now see. The cold blue and green hues of the figures and the setting in the finished painting suggest a love growing cold.

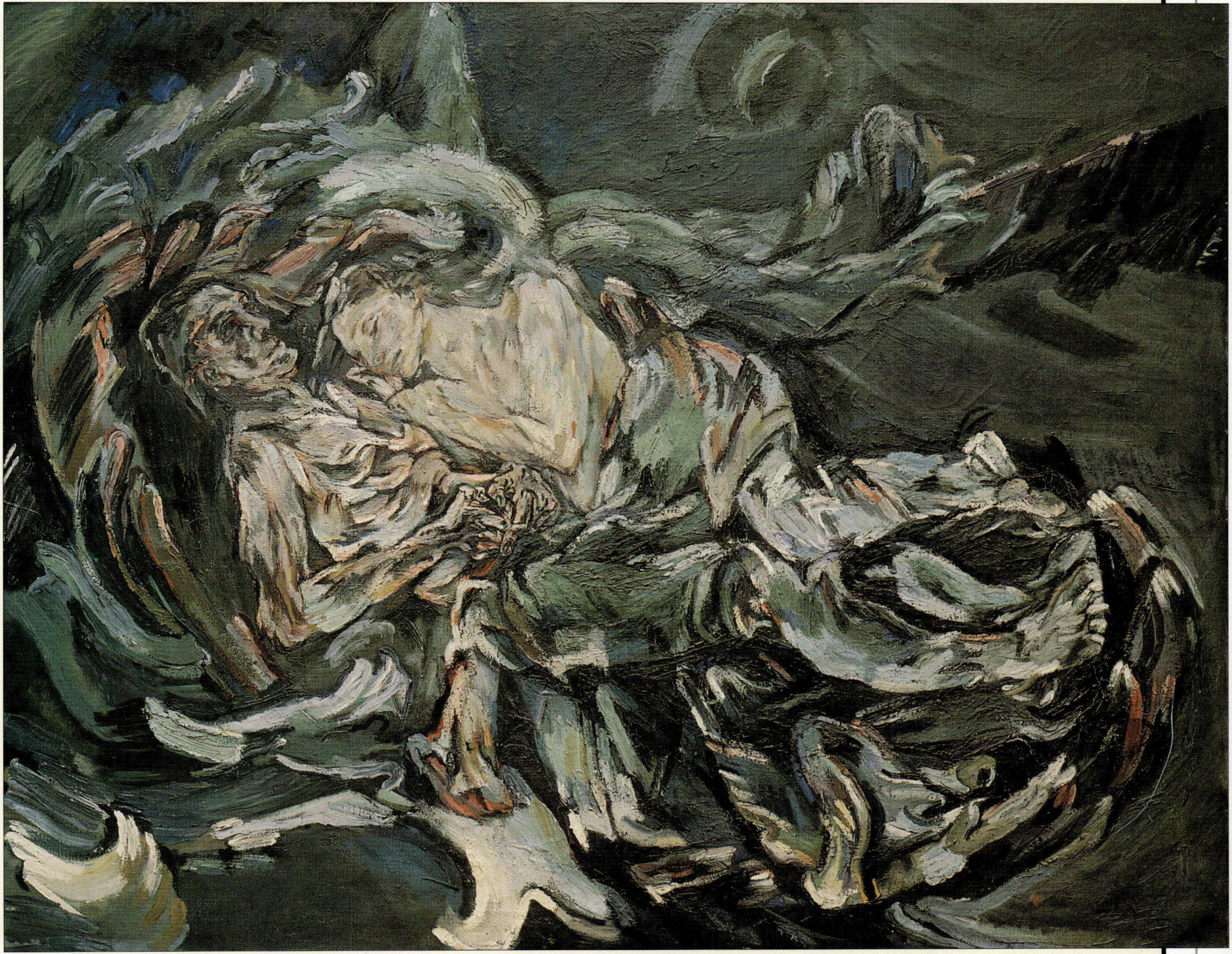

One of Kokoschka's largest paintings, *The Tempest* sealed the artist's international success when he exhibited it in 1914. One famous critic pronounced it the most important painting in the exhibition and praised its "visionary" quality. A wealthy German collector bought it for 400 crowns; enough money for Kokoschka to buy himself a horse.

In 1937 this painting was one of the many confiscated from collectors by the Nazis. They sold it to the Kunstmuseum in Basel, Switzerland, where it can be found today.

The Tempest *1914. Oil on canvas. 71 x 86 1/2 in (181 x 220 cm). Kunstmuseum, Basel.*

moved to Germany to take up a post as Professor of Fine Arts at the Dresden Academy. However, this settled life did not really suit him; in 1924 he packed his bags, leaving a short letter of explanation, and set out on a journey. He spent some years traveling through Europe, North Africa, and the Middle East, before returning to Vienna.

When Germany and then Austria were taken over by the Nazis in the 1930s, life became dangerous for Kokoschka. He had become involved in politics, speaking out in protest against Nazism. He fled to Prague, where he met and fell in love with Olda Palkovsky. In 1938, when it was no longer safe to stay in Prague, the couple fled to England. In 1941, during World War II, Kokoschka married Olda in an air-raid shelter in London.

Kokoschka continued to paint in London; in 1947 he became a British citizen. He and Olda moved to Switzerland in 1953, but they kept close links with Britain until his death, just a week before his 94th birthday.

LA TOUR Georges de

ALTHOUGH LITTLE IS KNOWN ABOUT LA TOUR'S LIFE, and few of his works can be dated, he was a popular and successful painter in his day. His nocturnal scenes featuring simple, religious subjects and dramatic contrasts of light and shadow, are reminiscent of the work of the Italian master Michelangelo Merisi da Caravaggio.

Life and work

Georges de La Tour spent most of his life in the war-torn duchy of Lorraine, which is now a part of France. Although we know that he worked in a town called Lunéville and was the son of a baker, it is difficult to be certain of the events of his life or the dates of his paintings because few records survived the local political upheavals of the 17th century.

When La Tour was growing up in the early 1600s, the established style of painting in his part of Europe was mannerism. Mannerist works were highly stylized, with stiff figures posed in unnatural positions. La Tour may have studied with Jacques Bellange, a mannerist painter, but his surviving works do not show this influence. Instead, it is more likely that La Tour's style was influenced by a much smaller school of contemporary realist painters, including the Dutch painter Henrich Terbrugghen and the Italian painter Caravaggio. Scenes from everyday life, known as genre painting, appear in La Tour's early works.

One surviving record tells us that La Tour married Diane Le Nerf, the daughter of a nobleman, in 1617. Later, in 1620, La Tour would argue that as he had married a noblewoman, and as painting was a noble profession, he ought to be allowed the privileges of the nobility, particularly exemption from certain taxes. Some art historians have found his preoccupation with finance and social status difficult to reconcile with the often deeply moving religious subjects of his later paintings.

In the 1620s La Tour was known to be prospering, employing apprentices in his workshop, and buying property. His son, Etienne, trained in the workshop and helped with the paintings. It is partly La Tour's workshop practices that make it difficult for us to identify paintings that are definitely by him, as his style was so carefully copied by his apprentices. Even a signature does not guarantee the hand of the artist, for a master would often sign "studio copies" of a work. Copies of many of La Tour's compositions still exist, even though the originals have been lost or destroyed. The large number of these poorer quality replicas proves that La Tour's works were very much in demand. His paintings are relatively small in size, suggesting that his market consisted mainly of private clients

Data file

Full name: Georges de La Tour

Nationality: French

Style: French 17th century

Dates: born 1593 in Vix-sur-Seille, died 1652 in Lunéville

Key works:
- *The Payment of Dues* c1618–20
- *The Musicians' Quarrel* c1625–27
- *Saint Sebastian Tended by Saint Irene* c1630–33
- *The Fortune Teller* c1630–38
- *Christ with Saint Joseph in the Carpenter's Shop c1635–40*
- *The Magdalen with the Smoking Flame* c1636–38
- *The Newborn Child* c1645
- *The Dice Players* c1650

Things to look for:
- early paintings: scenes from everyday life
- later works: religious subjects
- a sense of contemplation or a moving atmosphere
- candles or torches lighting dark spaces and creating subdued colors
- geometric and monumental figures with smooth features and outlines

Comparisons: Michelangelo Merisi da Caravaggio, Gerrit Van Honthorst, Henrich Terbrugghen

Glossary terms: chiaroscuro, genre painting, mannerism

The emotional balance of light and dark

La Tour's greatest innovation was in the production of night scenes, or "nocturnes," which invoke a reflective and calm mood, helping the viewer to contemplate religious subjects. The most famous painter of dramatic contrasts of light and dark, or chiaroscuro, was Caravaggio, who influenced much of the painting in Europe at this time. La Tour is considered a follower of Caravaggio, even though he may not actually have seen any of Caravaggio's original paintings, and has his own distinctive style.

We could read light and dark in La Tour's paintings as representing good and evil, a theme common in the religious writing of the time. However, a dramatic light source also creates atmosphere and helps us concentrate on the expressions of the subjects. It allows us to respond to what is going on more directly than if we were distracted by surrounding objects.

Christ with Saint Joseph in the Carpenter's Shop (c1635–40) is typical of La Tour's nocturnes. It uses little color—the shadows lend the whole painting an almost black-and-white quality, perhaps making it seem more realistic to us. The setting is also very plain, again concentrating the viewer's mind on the figures. The details of Joseph's toes, and of his wrists straining as he struggles with the tool he is using, provide realistic touches that contrast with the smooth, idealized face of the child. The composition of the painting places the young, innocent face of Christ beside the old, honest face of his father, to reinforce the difference between the humble, laboring carpenter and his saintly child.

The most striking example of La Tour's skill as a painter is shown here in the hand of the young Christ. La Tour makes us believe that the light is shining through the child's fingers, as he cups his hand around the flame. We cannot fully see the flame, but we really believe it is there.

La Tour created perfectly balanced compositions that add to a sense of harmony within the work and help us reflect on the subject. Nothing jars or upsets our viewing of this peaceful scene. Instead, the figures have a calm solidity, with smooth, rounded limbs and idealized features.

The harmonious world pictured in La Tour's paintings may have appealed to a population so often in the midst of violent or dangerous political and social situations. The subject of this painting would also have found favor with those trying to reform the Catholic Church at the time, and the Jesuits, who believed in the importance of education. Many of La Tour's other works, such as *The Education of the Virgin* (c1650), also take this theme.

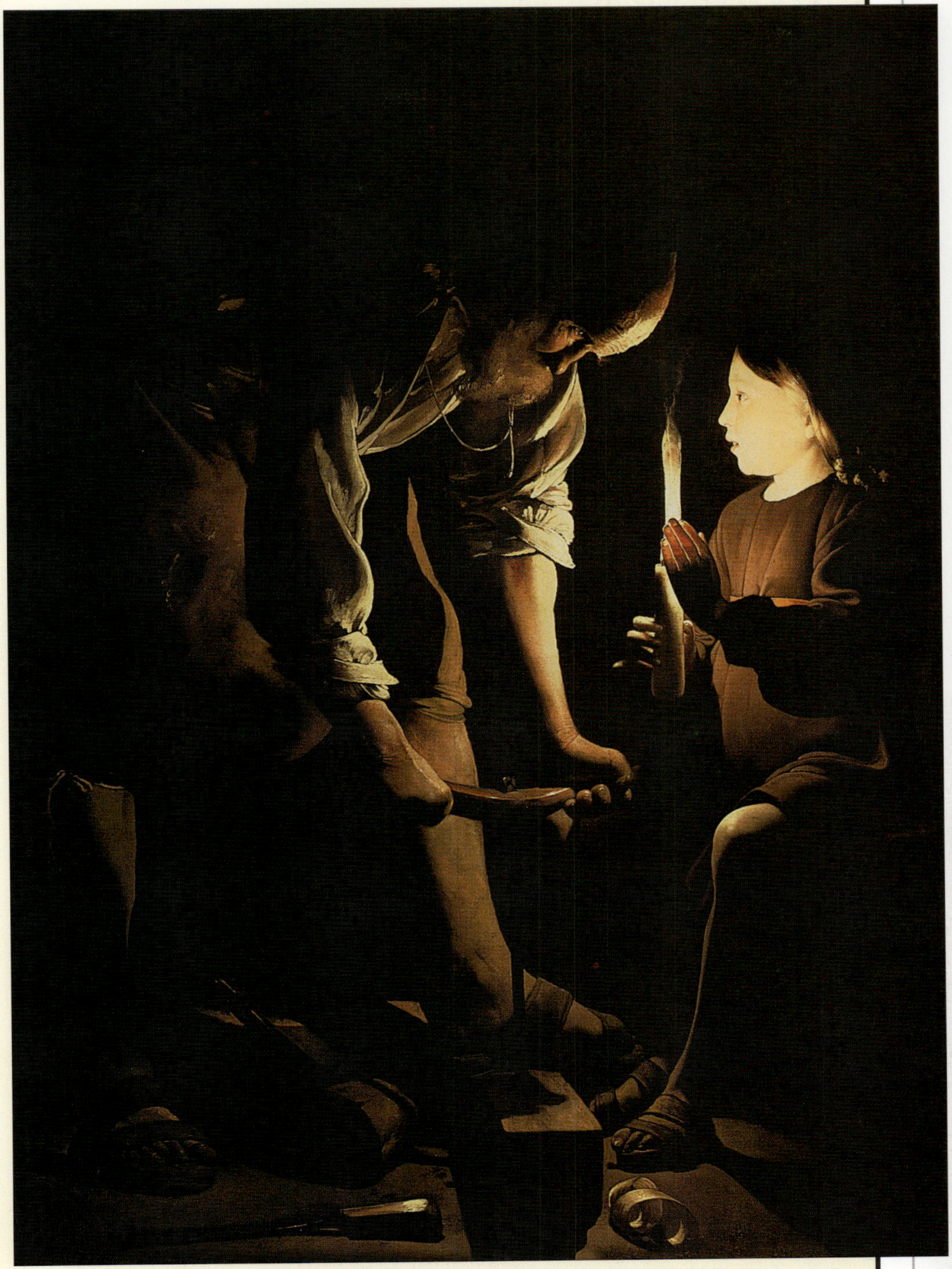

Christ with Saint Joseph in the Carpenter's Shop *c1635–40. Oil on canvas. 54 x 40 in (137 x 102 cm). Musée du Louvre, Paris.*

wanting paintings for their homes, rather than patrons commissioning large-scale or public works.

At the end of the 1630s, a decade of war and plague in the duchy of Lorraine, La Tour traveled to Paris and was granted the title of King's Painter. The French king, Louis XIII, owned at least one of La Tour's attributed works, *Saint Sebastian Tended by Saint Irene* (c1630–33), which was presented in the early 1630s. The influential Cardinal Richelieu also owned a painting by La Tour. From the 1640s until his death, La Tour produced works for the local government of Lunéville to use as diplomatic offerings to the French governor of Lorraine, who had invaded the independent duchy.

Despite the obvious popularity of La Tour's works in his lifetime, the lack of information about him meant he was largely forgotten by art historians until the 20th century.

LAWRENCE Thomas

LAWRENCE COMBINED THE GRANDEUR of 18th-century portraiture with the dash and vigor of the Romantic era. He was endowed with an instinctive feeling for color and an extraordinary sense of touch that made him the greatest English portrait painter of his generation.

Life and work

Thomas Lawrence's artistic gifts became apparent at a very early age. He was the son of an innkeeper and, while he was still a boy, his father encouraged him to draw the inn's customers. These pencil portraits were greatly admired, and Lawrence's father wasted no time in promoting his son's precocious talent. He took Lawrence to Oxford to sketch the masters of some of the university colleges there. By 1780 the family had settled in Bath, in southwest England, where Lawrence made portraits of the many society figures who came to visit the fashionable spa town. Lawrence was then working in pastel rather than pencil, and had even produced his first oils. Further advancement, however, could only be achieved by moving to London and showing his work at the Royal Academy of Arts.

Lawrence moved to London in 1787, and exhibited his first full-length portrait in 1789. This attracted the attention of Queen Charlotte, who offered him his next commission. In 1790 Lawrence submitted several pictures to the Academy. Two portraits—*Queen Charlotte* (1789) and *Miss Farren* (1789)—met with particular acclaim, confirming his reputation.

Lawrence's appearance in London was well timed. Thomas Gainsborough died in 1788, and Joshua Reynolds was nearing the end of his career. Lawrence soon became the capital's leading portraitist. In 1792 he succeeded Reynolds as King George III's official artist, and in 1794 he became a full member of the Royal Academy.

Artistic success came easily to Lawrence, but his private life was troubled. He was often in debt, and only the help of a friend saved him from ruin. His love life was tangled. He had romances with two daughters of Mrs. Siddons (a famous actress), but neither relationship led to marriage.

Despite these setbacks, Lawrence's career went from strength to strength. He was knighted in 1815, and three years later received his most important commission: to paint the military and political leaders who had just defeated the French emperor, Napoleon. On his return to England in 1820, Lawrence was honored with the presidency of the Royal Academy, a position he held until his death.

Data file

Full name: Thomas Lawrence

Nationality: English

Style: Romanticism

Dates: born 1769 in Bristol, died 1830 in London

Key works:

- *Queen Charlotte* 1789
- *Miss Farren* 1789
- *Pinkie* 1794
- *Kemble As Hamlet* 1801
- *Mrs. Wolff* 1815
- *The Duke of Wellington* c1815
- *The Windsor Portraits* 1818–20
- *Charles Lambton* 1825

Things to look for:

- fluid brushwork
- lush coloring
- sweeping landscape backgrounds

Comparisons: Joshua Reynolds, Thomas Gainsborough, John Singer Sargent, Henry Raeburn

Glossary terms: Academy, classical, Old Masters, pastel, Romanticism

A virtuoso portraitist

Lawrence became an instant celebrity in the art world following the huge success of his portraits of *Queen Charlotte* and *Miss Farren* (both painted in 1789). Lawrence was a handsome and charming man; these attributes attracted the interest of London's fashion-conscious socialites, and brought him more recognition and prestigious subjects. Over the next few years, members of high society clamored to sit for him, and Lawrence could barely keep up with the commissions. This is particularly impressive because his rates were astonishingly high for a young artist.

This young girl is typical of Lawrence's wealthy clientele. Her name was Sarah Goodin Barrett Moulton, better known by the nickname "Pinkie." She came from a family of plantation owners, who lived in Jamaica and made money from sugar and slaves. Like most children of colonial families, Sarah was sent back to Britain to be educated. In 1792 Sarah and her younger brother crossed the Atlantic, and she attended a school in Greenwich, near London. The following year, Sarah's mother commissioned this portrait of her daughter, specifying that Lawrence was to portray the girl "in an easy, careless attitude."

Sarah's mother may have hoped that a portrait painted by a fashionable artist would make an impact at the Royal Academy, and that her daughter's status in society would increase as a result. Sadly, though, Sarah's health could not withstand the change to the damp climate of England: she died of tuberculosis just a few weeks before the picture was exhibited at the Academy in 1794. Sarah's brother, incidentally, later gained notoriety as the domineering father of Elizabeth Barrett Browning, the celebrated poet.

It is easy to see why Lawrence's portraits were held in such high esteem. Lawrence strove to inject his pictures with high emotion, or a dynamic sense of movement. Although his style is dashing, he often made a detailed drawing of the subject on the canvas before beginning a painting. His skilled draftsmanship brought him a stream of commissions for portraits in pencil and chalk, as well as oils.

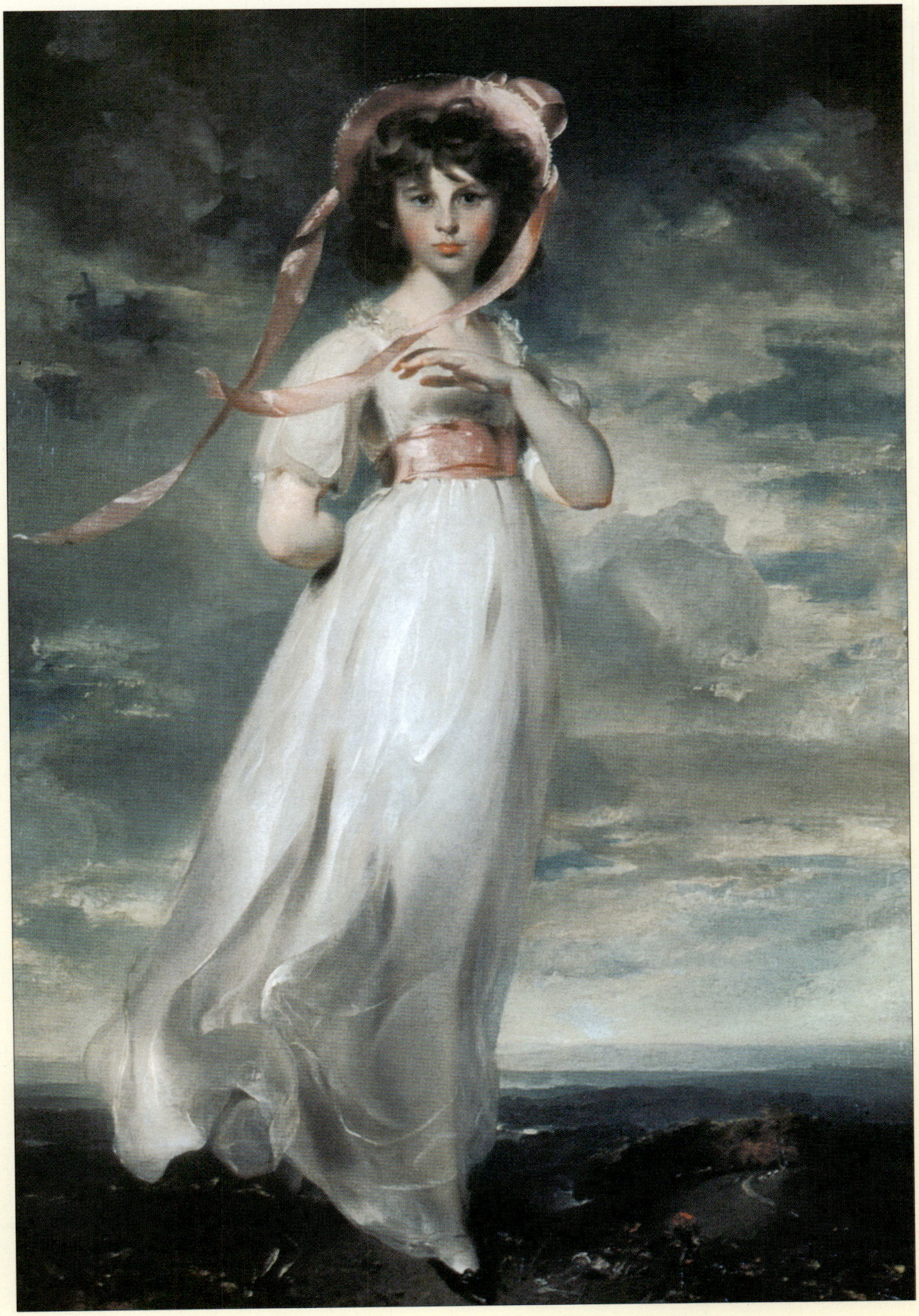

Pinkie *1794. Oil on canvas. 57 x 39 in (145 x 99.5 cm). Henry E. Huntington Library and Art Gallery, San Marino, CA.*

Landscape backgrounds had appeared in portraits by earlier artists but, as in *Pinkie*, Lawrence achieved a more dramatic mood by depicting his sitter at a dizzying height, with a sweeping panorama below. He also made the picture more lively by suggesting a gentle breeze, which wafts the hem of the girl's dress and tugs at the ribbons of her bonnet.

Lawrence's work formed a bridge between the grandiose paintings of Joshua Reynolds and the fiery spirit of the budding Romantic movement. Reynolds had often borrowed the poses of his sitters from classical statues or Old Master paintings. Lawrence sometimes adopted this practice: his portrait of *Mrs. Wolff* (1815) was based on one of Michelangelo Buonarroti's sibyls (female prophets) in the Sistine Chapel.

LÉGER Fernand

FERNAND LÉGER WAS A PIONEERING FRENCH ARTIST working in the first half of the 20th century. His early cubist-inspired works emphasized fragmented forms reminiscent of machine components. In his later career he adopted a more figurative style characterized by the heroic representation of ordinary citizens at work and at play.

Life and work

Léger was raised in the countryside of Normandy, in northern France. At the age of 16 he traveled to Caen, where he was apprenticed to a local architect, before moving to Paris three years later to work as an architect's draftsman. In 1903 he began his studies at the School of Decorative Arts in Paris; soon afterward he attended the highly respected Académie Julian.

By 1908 Léger had become a familiar face among the artistic community of Montparnasse, in the south of Paris, and was working in a neoimpressionist- and fauvist-influenced style. Few of his early works survive, however, because he destroyed most of them around 1910 when he abandoned these styles in favor of the newly emerging cubism. In such works as *The Wedding* (1910–11) Léger prioritized form and volume over color, even giving such non-material substances as smoke a solid appearance.

During World War I Léger was drafted into the army and sent to the front. His experiences in the trenches, not least being gassed at Verdun, as well as the deep affinity that he felt for his fellow soldiers, were to change his entire attitude toward life. The war also changed Léger's art, inspiring him to produce such images as *The Card Players* (1917), which represented life in the trenches. Léger became particularly fascinated by the mechanization of war, claiming to find a strange beauty in machine-guns and the barrels of howitzers shining in the sun. The soldiers whom he represented also took on the quality of machines with shiny, metallic bodies and component parts.

After his return from the front Léger continued to emphasize machinelike forms in his works. In *The Three Women* (1921), for example, he adapted the traditional theme of the female nude by representing three figures whose bodies, with their solid, metallic flesh and hair, and blank, anonymous expressions, emerge like automatons from their starkly geometric, interior setting. Léger's wartime experiences also changed his attitude toward the role of art in society. He increasingly adopted new techniques and worked in media that he believed to be more appropriate for the "masses." Thus he experimented with printmaking and book illustration. He designed for the Swedish Ballet in 1921–22, worked for the cinema and even produced his own abstract movie in 1924, entitled *Mechanical Ballet*, in which he presented a sequence of images emphasizing ordinary, everyday objects. By juxtaposing these images and animating the objects, Léger presented a strange and eerie world

Data file

Full name: Fernand Léger

Nationality: French

Style: cubism

Dates: born 1881 in Argentan, died 1955 in Gif-sur-Yvette

Key works:
- *The Wedding* 1910–11
- *The Card Players* 1917
- *The City* 1919
- *The Mechanic* 1920
- *The Three Women* 1921
- *Leisure (Homage to Jacques-Louis David)* 1948–49
- *The Constructors* 1950

Things to look for:
- ordinary, everyday objects
- bold outlines, bright colors, and machine forms

Comparisons: Robert Delaunay, Albert Gleizes, Jean Metzinger

Glossary terms: cubism, fauvism, neoimpressionism, surrealism

Léger and mechanized forms

Léger's *The Card Players* (1917) was inspired by the artist's personal experiences in the trenches during World War I. Although they are at first difficult to identify in the paintng, three soldiers sit around a hastily erected table, playing cards. The most prominent figure, on the left, can be identified as a soldier by his costume details. He wears a medal pinned to his chest and the traditional red cap of the French Army, although Léger presents it simultaneously from two different angles, in cubist style. His head, torso, and arms, however, are depicted as though they are parts of a geometrical machine, alluding to both the mechanical nature of trench warfare and to the anonymity of the soldiers. The second card player, in the center of the painting, can be identified as a sergeant from the stripes on his uniform. He also wears a red cap and smokes a pipe while holding his cards in his left hand. The third figure, on the right, is depicted in darker tones and wears a helmet rather than a cap. Although the smoke billowing from his pipe blends with that of the central soldier, it is represented as having a solid, geometrical volume rather than being a vaporous gas.

In depicting his soldiers playing cards Léger was referring to the work of Paul Cézanne, whose images of peasants playing cards were then well known. By representing his figures as geometrical forms (cones and cylinders, for example) Léger may also have been literally following the advice (often ascribed to Cézanne) given to artists: to represent the world in terms of geometrical forms.

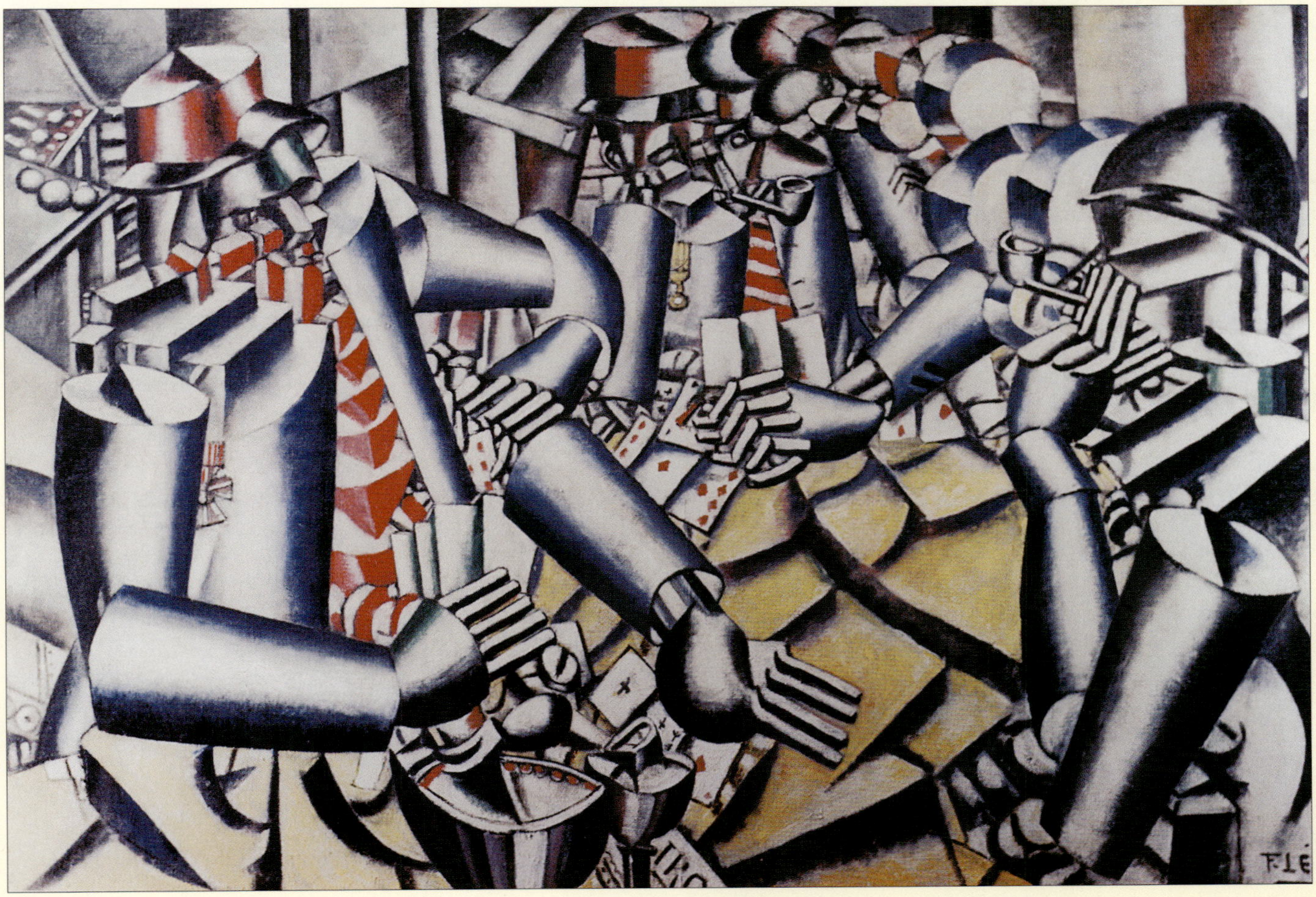

The Card Players *1917. Oil on canvas. 50 1/4 x 76 in (128 x 193 cm). Kröller-Müller Museum, Otterlo.*

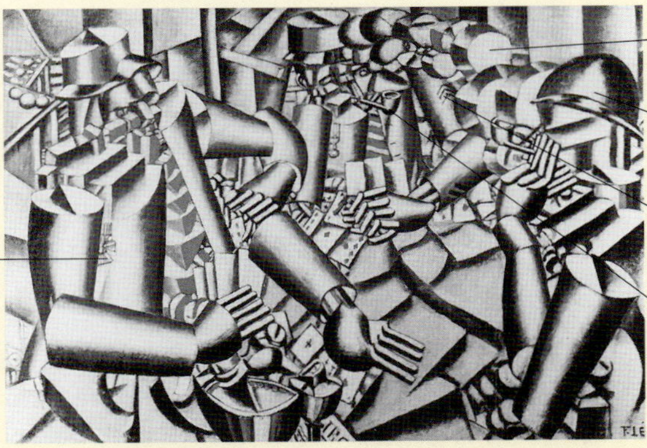

Discovering everyday objects in Léger's art *By carefully examining the image, it is possible to discern a medal, a helmet, sergeant's stripes, a pipe, and smoke.*

dominated by dynamic mechanical movement, a theme that inevitably attracted the attention of the emerging surrealist group.

Throughout the 1930s Léger continued to include everyday objects in his work. Yet despite the obvious affinities between his pieces and those of the surrealists, he moved toward a greater realism in his paintings, believing that this made his work more accessible to the public.

On the outbreak of World War II Léger abandoned France for the United States. Inspired by the bright lights of New York's Broadway, his works became brighter, bolder, and more highly colored, often featuring acrobats and cyclists. After his return to France in 1946, he entered the last great phase of his career. Influenced by his Communist sympathies, Léger produced monumental canvases representing ordinary French people, whether enjoying a leisurely day in the countryside, as in *Leisure (Homage to Jacques-Louis David)* (1948–49), or at work on construction projects to rebuild war-torn towns, as in *The Constructors* (1950). Léger died in 1955.

LEONARDO da Vinci

LEONARDO DA VINCI COMPLETED SURPRISINGLY FEW WORKS OF ART. Nevertheless, with that of Raphael and Michelangelo, his work is considered to epitomize the High Renaissance, a period in the early 1500s of supreme self-confidence in art and ideas. He was recognized as extraordinary in his own time, not only for his art but also for his creativity in science, engineering, and music.

Life and work

Leonardo spent his early years living in the humble peasant home of his mother's family before moving to Florence to be apprenticed to the artist Andrea del Verrocchio. Verrocchio's workshop was one of the largest and busiest in Florence, and Leonardo continued to be connected with it until at least 1476.

Florence was the most progressive artistic center in Italy at that time, so it is not altogether clear why Leonardo should have attached himself to the court of Ludovico Sforza, duke of Milan, in 1482. Whatever the reason, the duke's patronage gave Leonardo the freedom to develop his personal inclinations far beyond the limits that were normally allowed to artists.

Leonardo was fascinated by the mystery and the divine spirit that united and harmonized nature's elements. He had a wide knowledge of traditional and contemporary scientific theories and systematically tested them by observation and experimentation.

He recorded his ideas in notebooks that included hundreds of sketches and text in "mirror" writing (back-to-front) for secrecy. He examined human anatomy in an attempt to discover how the body works in motion, and was fascinated by flight; his notebooks contain studies of flying machines long before the age of aircraft. His analyses of the principles of motion in flowing water and cloud formations are echoed in his studies of curling hair, folds of drapery, the growth of plants, and even the way in which figures within groups interact with each other.

Leonardo did more than any other individual to establish the practice of art as an intellectual, rather than a manual, profession. He did this by applying the results of his broad scientific investigations to every aspect of painting. He was not content to follow conventions of style or technique. Indeed, throughout most of his career he had a reputation for not working to deadlines stipulated in his contracts with his patrons. He was also a restless artist, and frequently left his work unfinished.

Among Leonardo's most famous works are *The Last Supper* (c1496–98), painted on the wall of Santa Maria della Grazie in Milan, and two versions of *The Virgin of the Rocks* (c1483 and c1506). These paintings seemed to tell the Christian story from a more human

Data file

Full name: Leonardo da Vinci

Nationality: Italian

Style: High Renaissance

Dates: born 1452 in Vinci, died 1519 in Cloux, France

Key works:
- *The Adoration of the Magi* 1481
- *The Virgin of the Rocks* c1483
- *Vitruvian Man* (sketch) c1487
- *The Last Supper* c1496–98
- *The Virgin and Child with Saint Anne and Saint John the Baptist* c1498
- *The Battle of Anghiari* c1502–05
- *Mona Lisa* c1503–06
- *The Virgin of the Rocks* c1506

Things to look for:
- carefully balanced groups of figures
- coordinated gestures and emotions of figures
- softly modeled forms
- atmospheric perspective
- attention to detail (such as plants, rocks, and water)

Comparisons: Andrea del Verrocchio, Sandro Botticelli, Pietro Perugino, Raphael, Michelangelo Buonarroti, Titian

Glossary terms: perspective, Renaissance, *sfumato*

Divine proportions and the enigmatic smile

Scientific inquiry and a better understanding of classical times brought about a change in the way the world was perceived during the Renaissance. Leonardo's education gave him only a limited knowledge of the authors of the ancient world. However, his drawing *Vitruvian Man* (c1487) shows that he worked directly from the only surviving Roman text on architectural theory: *De Architectura*, written by the Roman architect Vitruvius in about 27 AD.

Like Piero della Francesca and Albrecht Dürer, Leonardo was preoccupied with the idea that the whole of creation was governed by the principles of geometry,

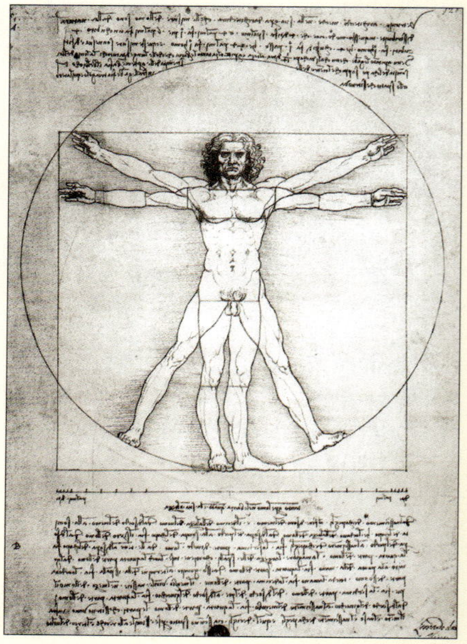

Vitruvian Man *c1487. Pen and ink. 13 x 9½ in (34 x 24.5 cm). Galleria dell'Academia, Venice.*

symmetry, and proportion. In his writings and drawings he frequently explored the ratios that he discerned in everything from the ordered motions of the planets to the anatomical structure of bodies, and that he believed were also applicable to musical and architectural harmony.

Vitruvian Man demonstrates a classical formula that Vitruvius had devised, in which the human body can be taken as a model for a set of relationships; this was then used by architects as a basis for the harmonious design of buildings. The ratios between the parts of the body and mathematical proportion were thought to have a direct link with beauty. Leonardo wrote that even the beauty of the human face depends upon the "divine proportionality" of its parts.

The *Mona Lisa* (c1503–06) is Leonardo's most famous work, and the sitter's enigmatic smile has become a legend in art. In the portrait Leonardo used a technique of oil painting called *sfumato*, the blending of colors so that they create a misty effect (*sfumato* is Italian for softened or shaded off). He also conveyed an impression of deep space by the use of atmospheric perspective: the strength of colors is muted toward the horizon.

Leonardo thought that portraits should convey the inner vitality of the mind. The timeless appeal of the *Mona Lisa* is perhaps partly due to a feeling that we are engaging with a real person with an inner vitality that is nevertheless elusive.

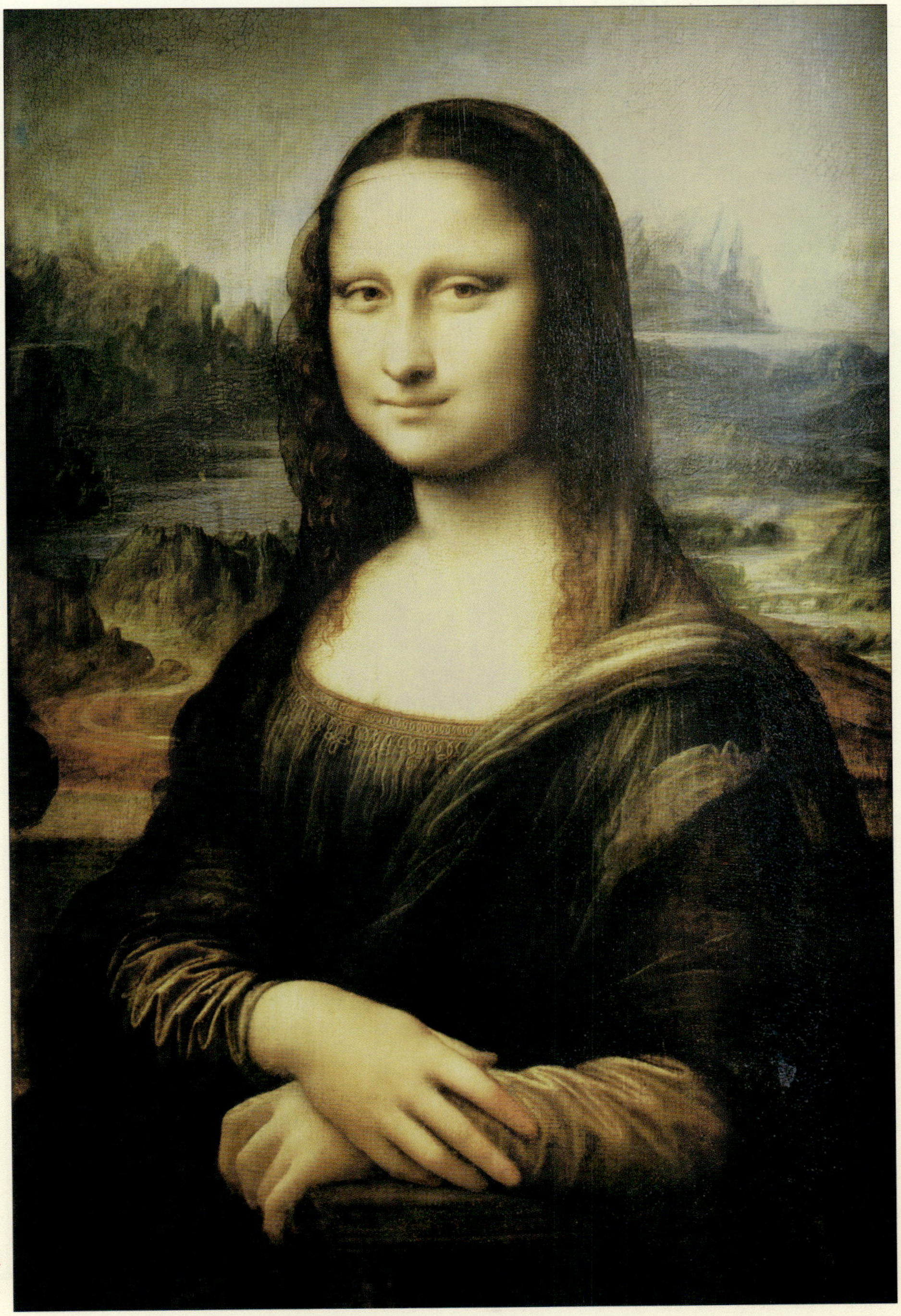

Mona Lisa *c1503–06. Oil on panel. 30¼ x 21 in (77 x 53 cm). Musée du Louvre, Paris.*

point of view, and set new precedents in painting.

In about 1503–06 Leonardo produced the *Mona Lisa*, a portrait of an unknown woman often identified as Lisa Gherardini, the wife of a wealthy Florentine merchant. The enigmatic ambiguity of the woman's smile fascinated people, and it became the best-known image in Western art and the most enduring legacy of any artist.

Having being obliged to leave the Sforza court in 1499, Leonardo's later years were restless as he traveled back and forth between Florence, Milan, and Rome before ending his days at Amboise as an honored guest of the French king François I.

Leonardo da Vinci's work came to be seen as the high-point of the High Renaissance, a time of "rebirth" when the place of mankind in the world was celebrated. Yet to many, both in his time and later, he seemed a strange individual, more a magician than an artist, who was isolated by the novelty of his ideas.

LICHTENSTEIN Roy

LICHTENSTEIN IS ONE OF THE KEY FIGURES OF AMERICAN POP ART. His most famous paintings are enlarged and repainted comic-book images that challenge us to question the esthetic hierarchies in art and to reconsider mass-produced images.

Life and work

A New Yorker by birth, Roy Lichtenstein trained and worked as a designer in Ohio. In the late 1950s he returned to New York City and taught painting at the state university while also working on his own canvases. His work went through many stylistic changes, but by the late 1950s he had adopted the then prevalent style of abstract expressionism.

He next turned his attention to pop art, a movement that derived inspiration from mass-produced objects and mass-media techniques, and elevated these images themselves to the field of fine art. The paintings that became Lichtenstein's signature works were representations of images taken from comic books and magazines. They were isolated and enlarged onto giant canvases, emphasizing both the apparently trivial subject matter and the process of their manufacture. Bright, primary colors were used, and the coarse, half-tone screen used for printing images was imitated as painted dots. Sometimes the paintings appeared as one "frame" from a comic-book sequence, complete with thought-bubble or speech balloon, the clichéd text becoming part of the process of magnifying the trivial, and contributing to a sense of irony conveyed by the painting.

It is said that Lichtenstein's technique was initially prompted by one of his children, who challenged him to paint a picture as good as the images in the comic he had been reading. Lichtenstein would develop this style throughout the rest of his career. Ironically, perhaps, the mass-produced, stylistically bland images for a popular medium (comics) became associated with Lichtenstein's individual art.

The first works that Lichtenstein painted in this unmistakable style were exhibited in New York in 1961, with great success. He developed his technique with *Whaam!* (1963), a painting that imitates the highly stylized depiction of intense action in comic books.

In the mid-1960s Lichtenstein used this same technique to pastiche the works of painters from the canon of art history. Works included *Picasso with Flowered Hat* (1963) and *Mondrian with Non-objective I* (1964). In paintings such as *Yellow and Green Brushstrokes* (1968), he played a comical game with the creative process, especially as it was used by the abstract expressionist painters, whose every mark had come to be seen in some quarters as expressive of artistic genius. Lichtenstein reduced abstract expressionism to a few bold gestural paint strokes that typified the style, and meticulously painted these brushstrokes using small dots, as if they had been

Data file

Full name: Roy Lichtenstein

Nationality: American

Style: pop art

Dates: born 1923 in New York, NY, died 1997 in New York, NY

Key works:
- *Forget It! Forget Me!* 1962
- *Whaam!* 1963
- *OK Hot-shot* 1963
- *Picasso with Flowered Hat* 1963
- *Mondrian with Non-objective I* 1964
- *Big Painting VI* 1965
- *Yellow and Green Brushstrokes* 1966

Things to look for:
- comic-book style images, imitated and isolated on large canvases
- references to fine art in later work (traditional, art-historical themes and compositions)

Comparisons: Jasper Johns, Andy Warhol, Stuart Davis, Fernand Léger, Charles Demuth

Glossary terms: abstract expressionism, pastiche, pop art

Taking art seriously

In *Forget It! Forget Me!* (1962) Lichtenstein was attempting to subvert the meaning of the original image in the comic. He has isolated it and enlarged it, drawing (undue) attention to it. By doing this, he encourages the viewer to question the significance of the image. Why should we take it seriously? What kind of relationship is being portrayed? Who invents these characters? Do they have an esthetic value of their own? Lichtenstein's role is to provoke these questions.

"I am nominally copying, but I am really restating the copied thing in other terms," Lichtenstein said in 1983. The images are immediately striking because of their deadpan coolness. They were highly stylized but expressionless—a style that is graphic and entirely subservient to the image. In other words, there is no trace of the artist trying to express himself through his painting.

At the time when Lichtenstein first painted such images as *Forget It! Forget Me!* and *Whaam!* (1963), abstract expressionism was still the dominant style of painting in the United States. In abstract expressionism, the very process of making art was the subject of the work. It was characterized by the subjective emotion that had been seen throughout work in the 1950s—in Jackson Pollock's splattering of paint, Willem de Kooning's angst-ridden contortions of the human form, and Mark Rothko's emotive use of color and tone. Lichtenstein's apparent denial of the "artist's voice" marked a dramatic shift in American postwar art.

Pop art privileged the material world and the reality of everyday life for the masses over the rarefied experience of an individual, and especially an isolated artist. Lichtenstein sought to make use of the visual clichés of comic books—square-jawed heroes and emotionally wrought women, along with comic-book typography and exclamation marks to indicate moments of action. What appealed to him was the contrast between the emotionally charged subject matter—such as love, despair, war, and fear—and the highly controlled methods of representation. Here was a clear gap between the subject and the painting process.

The motives of pop art are still disputed: was it a celebration of the commercial world or was it a criticism of that highly commercialized system? Whereas abstract expressionism was supposedly profound and sincere, pop art was transient and witty. It was playful, but that playfulness could be humorous and light or edged with a darker irony.

Lichtenstein himself believed that his own work was in some sense critical. "The heroes depicted in comics are fascist types," he once said, "but I don't take them seriously in these paintings—maybe there is a serious point in not taking them seriously, a political point."

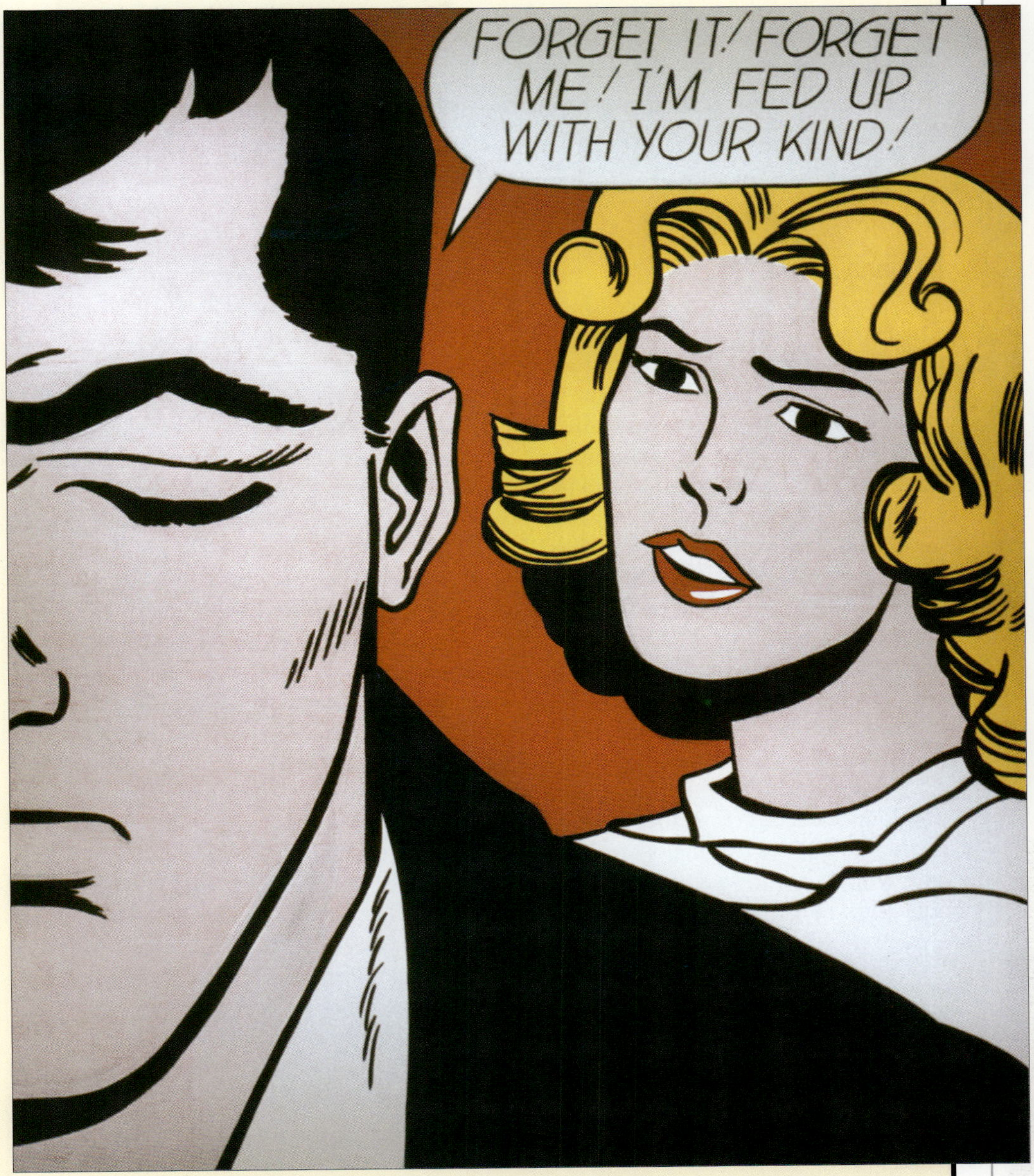

Forget it! Forget Me! *1962. Oil and magna on canvas. 80 in x 68 in (203 x 172.5 cm). Rose Art Museum, Brandeis University, Waltham, MA.*

reproduced by the same printing process used for the comic strips. As with the comic-strip pictures, the brushstrokes were rendered in a highly stylized way—as a gesture devoid of meaning, but merely reproduced mechanically, and repetitively. This was almost certainly a criticism of what he felt abstract expressionism had become: no longer an expressive style, but merely a stylistic convention.

In the 1970s and 1980s Lichtenstein pursued the reworking of artists' paintings, and indeed entire genres of painting, in the comic-book style, making pop art versions of cubist, expressionist, and surrealist paintings. During this time, his technique reached the peak of its sharpness and clarity, though the focus of his work lacked the impact, immediacy, and shock value of his 1960s paintings.

Intermittently throughout his career, Lichtenstein turned his hand to sculpture, and this became an increasingly significant part of his output in the later years. Most of his work was in polished brass. He received his first public sculpture commission in 1979, producing *Mermaid for Miami Beach*, and in 1984 he completed *Brushstrokes in Flight* for Columbus International Airport in Ohio.

LIMBOURG BROTHERS

ALTHOUGH THEY WERE ACTIVE FOR ONLY A BRIEF, 14-YEAR PERIOD at the beginning of the 15th century, the Limbourg Brothers left as their legacy two illuminated manuscripts that are among the very finest examples of the art. In terms of acuteness of detail and vibrancy of color, these works are unsurpassed to this day.

Life and work

The early 15th century was a turbulent time in Europe: the Black Death had ravaged the land; the intermittent Hundred Years War (between France and England) dragged on, draining resources and fostering hatred and fear; and revolts against the punitive taxes imposed by the warring nations added to the atmosphere of uncertainty and anger. Yet against this backdrop of turmoil and violence, the Limbourg Brothers, Paul, Jean, and Herman, created small, delicate works of immense beauty, the making of which required great patience and devotion.

Although the brothers came from the Low Countries (now the Netherlands), the two major works with which they are associated were created in Paris. The brothers arrived there during the first years of the 15th century (possibly through a connection established by their uncle, the painter Jean Malouel), and were commissioned by the powerful and wealthy dukes of Burgundy. Philip the Bold was the first of the dukes to engage the talents of Paul and Jean when he commissioned them to produce a finely decorated Bible. Philip died before the book was completed, however, and although the art historian Millard Meiss has suggested that the Limbourgs' Bible is synonymous with a manuscript known as the *Bible Moralisée* (c1402–04), there are insufficient records to identify this work with certainty.

The patron of the Limbourg Brothers' two most famous illuminated manuscripts (*Les Belles Heures du Jean, Duc de Berry*, c1405–08, and *Les Très Riches Heures du Jean, Duc de Berry*, c1411–16) was Jean, Duke of Berry, the brother of Philip the Bold. The duke was a great patron of the arts who surrounded himself with works from across the European continent. While in the service of the duke, the brothers would have come into contact with a fantastic array of art, especially from Italy and France. It is not known whether one or all of the brothers ever traveled to Italy, but it is possible that they could have accompanied the duke on his frequent travels. Equally, they may have come under the influence of Italian painters working at the court of the duke. Either way, the Italian influence imbued the brothers' work with an expressive style, not so much imitative of the Italians' paintings as of the Italian flair for invention. Rather than strictly adhering to the traditional Flemish way of representing people and landscapes, they drew upon their personal experience, depicting places that they would have known (albeit in a stylized fashion) and portraying people with a greater degree of emotional expression.

Data file

Full names: Pol (Paul), Hennequin or Jacquemin (Jean), and Herman Limbourg

Nationality: Netherlandish

Style: late Gothic (illumination)

Dates: born c1375–85 in Nijmwegen, died 1416 in Bourges

Key works:
- *Les Belles Heures du Jean, Duc de Berry* c1405–08
- *Les Très Riches Heures du Jean, Duc de Berry* c1411–16

Things to look for:
- use of intense colors
- paintings with acute detail

Comparisons: Ambrogio Lorenzetti, Melchior Broederlam, the Boucicault Master, Master of the Rohan Book of Hours, Jan Van Eyck

Glossary terms: Book of Hours, gold leaf, illumination, miniature

Painting the world in miniature

The Book of Hours, *Les Très Riches Heures du Jean, Duc de Berry* (c1411–16), consists of about 200 folios (double pages) of illuminated script and miniatures. The first section presents the calendar, month by month, including devotional times and days, and is followed by psalms from the four gospels. Finally, there is a section of masses devoted to the year's religious festivals.

Each calendar page is a fine miniature painting connected to the month—showing, for example, sowing seeds in fall, feasting in the new year, and harvesting crops in late summer. The arch above the miniature contains the signs of the zodiac circling a chariot conveying the sun. Here we find the phases of the moon set against the days of the month. The painting of the zodiac for each month was undertaken independently of the miniatures, and it seems that the brothers died before completing all 12 months.

As we can see here, *Janvier* (January) is one of the incomplete pages. The miniature itself, however, is perfectly complete, and portrays the work's patron, Jean, Duke of Berry. He can be seen seated at the table, wearing a fur hat and with his head turned toward a humble clergyman. The scene is a New Year's Day feast where greetings and gifts would have been exchanged. Behind the table men line up to greet and give thanks to the duke. *"Aproche, Aproche"* ("Approach, Approach") has been inscribed in the space between the duke and his acquaintances, indicating his benevolence on such a day. A decorated section above the chimney bears his coat of arms: golden *fleurs-de-lis*, which are surrounded by swans, another of the duke's emblems. The background intermingles with the feasting scene, rather confusingly bringing a battle to the banqueting table. The battle is, in fact, a tapestry hanging behind the feasting friends, and it has been suggested that the scene depicts events from the Trojan War brought into the medieval world.

The Limbourgs' miniatures are characterized by an astonishing degree of detail. We can see it in the woven floor covering, for instance, or in the inclusion of a man feeding a white dog in the bottom right-hand corner. Such elements add intimacy to the scene, giving a sense that the painters really witnessed the events they depict. The other characteristic element of their illuminated manuscripts is an intensity of color that, as the term indicates, lights up the page with a similar effect to that of a stained-glass window.

It is thought that each miniature would have been built up in sections, beginning with an underdrawing. Gold leaf would then have been applied to some parts and burnished (made shiny). The background and landscape surrounding the figures would have been laid down next, followed by clothing, and finally the flesh tones of individual faces. It is not known whether each of the brothers specialized in certain aspects or whether each undertook different pages. Certainly a work containing such a quantity of detail would have required the time and skill of many craftsmen, their talents guided and led by the Limbourg Brothers.

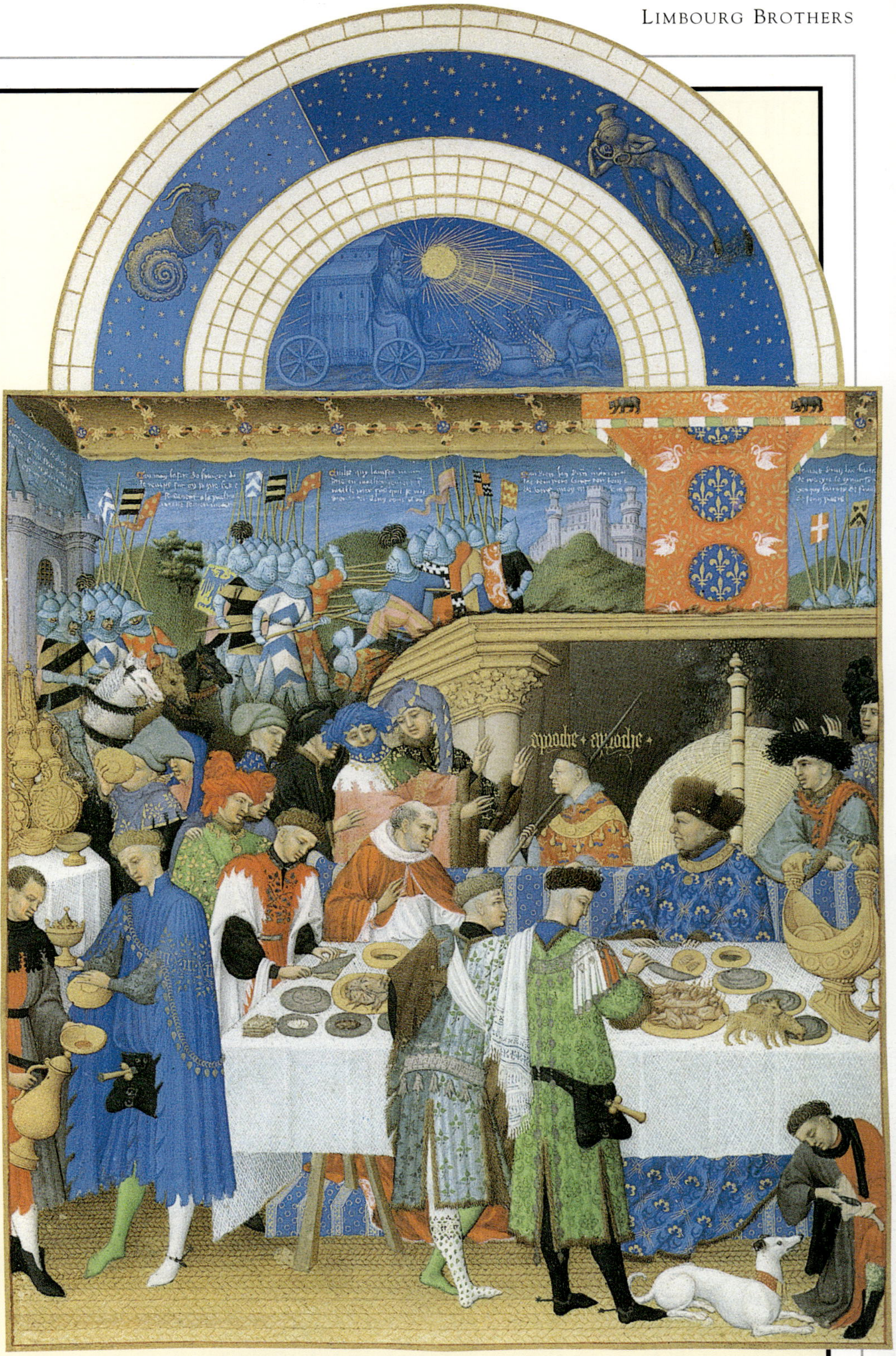

Les Très Riches Heures du Jean, Duc de Berry: Janvier *c1411–16. Illumination on vellum. 9 x 6 in (24 x 15 cm). Musée Condé, Chantilly.*

The two works created for Jean, Duke of Berry, were Books of Hours (books used for private worship, containing prayers appropriate to certain hours, days, weeks, months, or seasons). The brothers were sensitive to this greater freedom of artistic style. Compared to specific or complete religious texts, such as the Bible commissioned by Philip the Bold, a Book of Hours offered more adaptability with regard to content. As long as it incorporated a comprehensive calendar of prayers for the year, the miniatures allowed a great scope for the artistic imagination to flourish.

All three brothers died within eight months of each other in 1416. The proximity in date of their deaths has led to the speculation that they were the victims of a plague epidemic.

LIPPI Fra Filippo

FRA FILIPPO LIPPI WAS A FLORENTINE PAINTER who was strongly influenced by the great master Masaccio. He applied the innovative use of perspective pioneered by his contemporary, but also developed many new and imaginative ways of depicting the subject of the Madonna and Child. Lippi's unconventional and scandalous behavior as a friar led to numerous myths about his life.

Life and work

Lippi entered the Carmelite monastery in Florence in 1421, when he was probably aged 15. Nothing is recorded of his life prior to this, but over the next 10 years his name appears in the records of the monastery.

The young Lippi must surely have been influenced by the great works of art that surrounded him, such as the magnificent frescos in the Brancacci Chapel of the church of Santa Maria in Florence, painted by Masaccio in the 1420s. Lippi's interest in the three-dimensionality of figures, and his attempts to show perspective in space, all reveal his appreciation of Masaccio's work. The attention to detail, and use of various materials and textures in his work, seen for example in *Annunciation* (c1450), suggest that he was also influenced by painters from northern Europe, such as Jan Van Eyck and Rogier Van der Weyden.

By the 1430s, Lippi's career as a painter was well established. He had undertaken several major commissions, including the Barbadori altarpiece (1437–39) for the Barbadori family chapel in the church of Santo Spirito, and the *Coronation of the Virgin* (1439–47) for the church of Saint Ambrogio. Among his patrons were the powerful Medici family, who supported and encouraged many of the leading artists of the time. During this period Lippi started to paint portraits, and the Madonna and Child subjects for which he is now best known.

By 1442 Lippi had been installed as the rector of San Quirico, Legnaia, outside Florence. The work he produced began to show the influence of another great contemporary artist: the Dominican friar Fra Angelico. Bright colors and smooth, elongated figures draped in flowing clothes appeared in Lippi's work, recalling the decorative style of late Gothic painting.

Lippi began work on a series of expensive frescos for Prato Cathedral near Florence in 1452, but these were not completed until 1466. It is possible that Lippi's involvement in several legal problems between 1450 and 1455 interrupted his work. The disputes were regarding payments for work and the role of Lippi's assistants in undertaking commissions. Some of these he won, others he lost after admitting his guilt under torture. The culmination of all this came in 1455 when, after overcharging a client, he was stripped

Data file

Full name: Fra Filippo di Tommaso Lippi

Nationality: Italian

Style: late Gothic/early Renaissance/15th-century Florentine

Dates: born c1406 in Florence, died 1469 in Spoleto

Key works:

- Barbadori altarpiece 1437–39
- *Coronation of the Virgin* 1439–47
- *Annunciation* c1450
- cycles of frescos for Prato Cathedral 1452–66
- *Madonna and Child with Scenes from the Life of Saint Anne* 1453
- *Madonna and Child with Two Angels* c1466

Things to look for:

- use of perspective influenced by Masaccio
- the influence of Fra Angelico in the colors and forms of later works
- decoration, flowing lines, sharply delineated figures
- the Madonna and Child in *tondo* form

Comparisons: Sandro Botticelli, Fra Angelico, Masaccio, Jan Van Eyck, Rogier Van der Weyden, Donatello

Glossary terms: Gothic, perspective, Renaissance, *tondo*

Line and expression

Lippi is most famous for his Madonnas—gentle, maternal figures painted in many different ways; these Madonnas became the greatest influence on Lippi's pupil, Sandro Botticelli.

Madonna and Child with Scenes from the Life of Saint Anne (1453) was made as a round painting, known as a *tondo*, from the Italian word for "round." The idea of using a round form probably originated from the round or octagonal painted birth-plates, which were decorated trays on which food was presented to women after childbirth. This is the first example of a Madonna and Child to be painted as a *tondo* in Florence.

In this *tondo*, Lippi broke with convention by placing his Madonna and Child in a familiar, domestic environment. Usually a religious subject such as this would be placed against a heavily gilded background, signifying an unearthly, spiritual realm, such as heaven, and the Madonna would be seated on an ornate throne. Here Lippi refers to this by showing the carved back and arm of the chair on which the Virgin is sitting in her home.

The Virgin's face shows tender gentleness, but it also has a quality of sorrow, as if in some way she knows what the fate of her child will be. The infant Jesus has his eyes raised toward his mother, but this could also be read as looking up to heaven. He is holding some pomegranate seeds, which he shows to his mother. The pomegranate is a traditional symbol of the Passion (Christ's suffering between the Last Supper and his death).

Jesus looks as if he might be about to eat the pomegranate seed—his mouth is open, showing some baby teeth—and he playfully curls his toes. This touch of naturalism sets Lippi's painting apart from

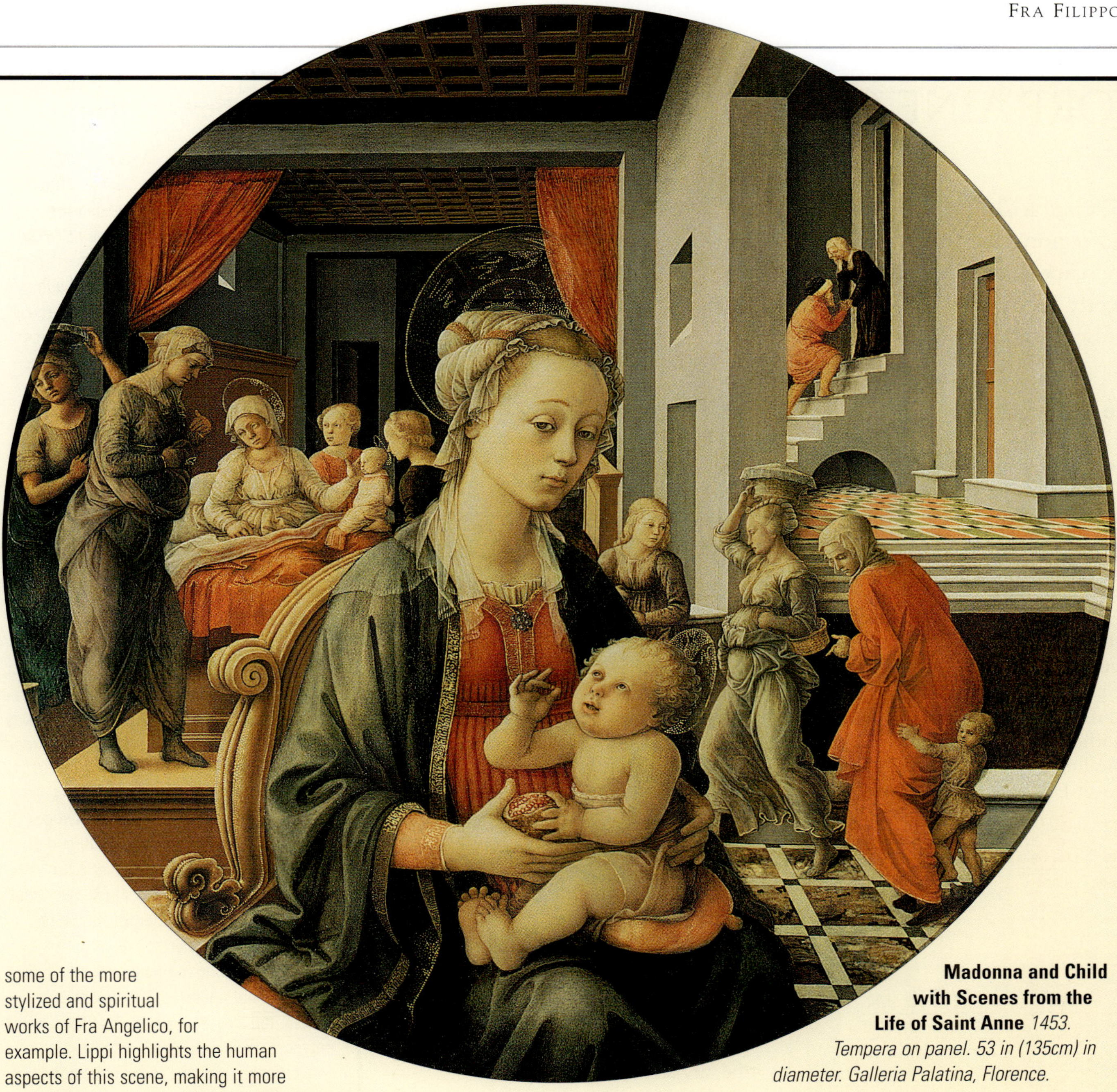

Madonna and Child with Scenes from the Life of Saint Anne *1453. Tempera on panel. 53 in (135cm) in diameter. Galleria Palatina, Florence.*

some of the more stylized and spiritual works of Fra Angelico, for example. Lippi highlights the human aspects of this scene, making it more appealing to us. Lippi's Madonna is pretty and the baby is sweet and lively. This playful mood is also evident in the pose of the child in the background to the right of Jesus, who clings on to the skirts of the woman in front, as children often do.

Lippi's interest in perspective is obvious in this painting: he uses the walls and receding lines of the geometric floor pattern to give a sense of depth, and to mark a division between the different scenes from the life of Saint Anne, mother of the Virgin Mary. Lippi is very concerned with lines, both straight and flowing, which often make his works seem like a relief carving, yet they are full of life and movement.

of his post at San Quirico and sent to the Augustinian convent in Prato.

More scandal was to follow. In 1456 Lippi ran away with a young nun, Lucrezia Buti, who became the model for some of his Madonnas. A year later they had a son, Filippino, who also became a famous painter. No official action was taken at the time, but in 1461 Lippi was publicly denounced, and by 1465 he had been stripped of his church duties. He was allowed to stay with Lucrezia, who later bore him a daughter, Alessandra.

Lippi was a highly sought-after artist. His works were not only used for religious purposes, but they were also given by the Medicis to influential contacts in royal courts and within the Church, including the pope.

Lippi's assistants included Sandro Botticelli, who developed Lippi's painting techniques and became Filippino Lippi's teacher.

LORRAINE Claude

CLAUDE GELLÉE, KNOWN AS CLAUDE LORRAINE after his native region, spent most of his life in Italy. His paintings of ideal landscapes, often based on studies of the Italian countryside, were eagerly acquired by wealthy collectors. He greatly influenced later landscape artists.

Life and work

Claude Gellée was born in the village of Chamagne in the Duchy of Lorraine, now part of eastern France. Perhaps when he was as young as 12 years old, he traveled to Italy, where he studied art in Rome and Naples.

In the 17th century, an essential part of the education of all serious young artists was a visit to Italy, where the greatest artworks of the classical age and the Renaissance were to be seen. Another attraction was the possibility of finding a good teacher. Artists from all over Europe worked in Italian cities, and Claude may have become a pupil of a well-known landscape painter from the Netherlands, Goffredo Wals. He also worked in Rome as an assistant to the painter Agostino Tassi; according to one story, he was first employed by Tassi as a pastry cook.

Claude returned to France in 1625. Two years later he left for Rome, where he remained for the rest of his life. At this time Rome was an exciting center of the arts. The pope, Urban VIII, led the way in encouraging writers and artists. Claude soon found work decorating the palaces of members of the Roman nobility with frescos showing beautiful rural scenes (few, if any, of these works survive) and producing the easel paintings of landscapes for which he became internationally known.

He also had opportunities to explore the countryside around Rome, which he recorded in many drawings, and to examine the impressive ruins of ancient Roman buildings that stood in the city and the open fields.

Landscape paintings were popular with wealthy collectors at this time. In their great town houses and country villas, away from the cut-and-thrust of politics or business, they liked to dream of a peaceful pastoral world, where shepherds and villagers lived a simple, happy life, and which was the setting for events in history or mythology.

Claude's pictures, like those of many other artists, conjured up this world. But he soon became celebrated for one quality in particular—his hauntingly beautiful treatment of light. These two facets of his work are memorably combined in such paintings as *The Marriage of Isaac and Rebecca* (also known as *Landscape with Dancing Figures*) of 1648.

From the age of about 25, Claude's reputation grew rapidly. Among his patrons during the 1630s were the most influential men in Rome—aristocrats, cardinals, and the pope himself. King Philip IV of Spain commissioned Claude to produce several paintings for his new palace of Buen Retiro.

His success was not without problems. Other artists began to copy his work and sell their paintings as

Data file

Full name: Claude Gellée (known as Claude Lorrain(e))

Nationality: French

Style: ideal landscape

Dates: born 1600 or 1604 in Chamagne, died 1682 in Rome, Italy

Key works:

Coast Scene with Europa and the Bull 1634

Landscape with Tobias and the Angel c1640

The Marriage of Isaac and Rebecca (Landscape with Dancing Figures) 1648

Landscape with a Sacrifice to Apollo 1662

Landscape with Pysche at the Palace of Cupid (The Enchanted Castle) 1664

Things to look for:

- picturesque and poetic interpretation of landscape
- effects of light (e.g. at sunrise, sunset)
- presence of classical and Renaissance architecture in landscape
- references to classical mythology, biblical stories, and other literary sources

Comparisons: Adam Elsheimer, Nicholas Poussin, Richard Wilson, J. M. W. Turner

Glossary terms: fresco, pastoral, picturesque

The poetic landscape

Throughout his career, Claude's response to natural beauty was reflected in his paintings. In Naples, he had been deeply impressed by the beauty of the coastline, and this influence can be seen in much of his later work.

All his landscapes, however, show his mastery of effects of light in different places and at different times of day—sunrise and sunset, the light filtering through leaves or reflecting off water, and the subtle contrasts between the clear foreground and the fading, misty distance.

Claude often based his paintings on stories from literature, including the Bible and classical mythology, as in his early work, *Coast Scene with Europa and the Bull* (1634).

Landscape with Psyche at the Palace of Cupid, also known as *The Enchanted Castle* (1664), which Claude painted when he was in his sixties, is based on a story recounted by the 2nd-century Roman writer Lucius Apuleius. It tells how a beautiful girl, Psyche, was married to an unknown god, who later turned out to be Cupid, god of love. After living for some time in his palace, attended by invisible servants, she finally discovered his identity, at which point he deserted her.

In the painting the pale sun, low in the sky, does not penetrate the darkness among the trees. It just touches the topmost walls of Claude's imaginary enchanted castle and the waves in the

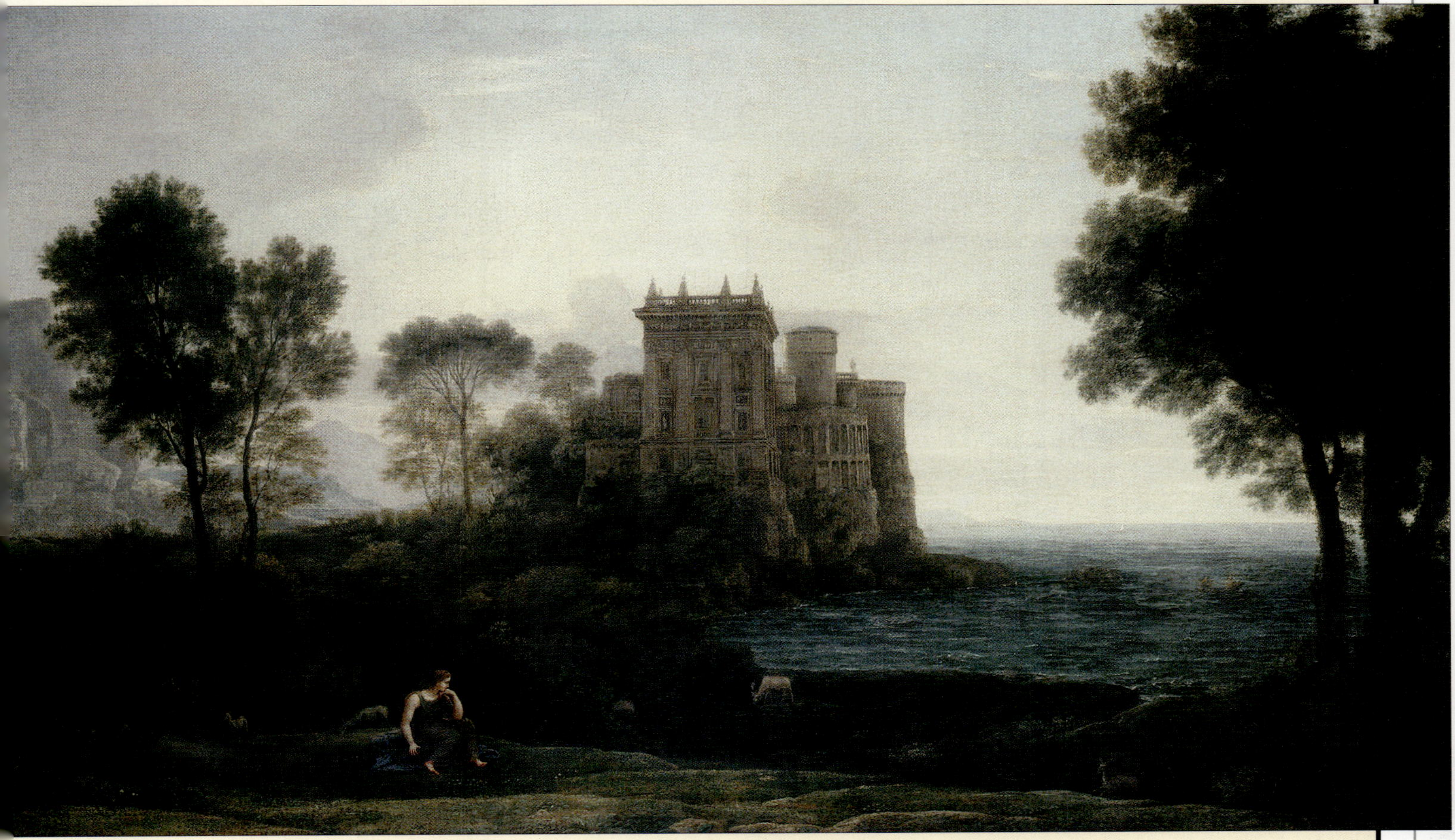

little bay. Clouds drift in the wind, which also catches the almost-invisible sails of boats far out at sea.

It is not absolutely certain whether Claude meant this as a dawn or evening scene (the events of the story suggest evening, but the sky lacks the red tints of sunset). Either way, its atmosphere, midway between sleeping and waking, is one of gradual sensual awakening, mirroring what is happening in the story to Psyche herself.

Claude took great trouble to make his landscapes appear fresh and natural. He worked out-of-doors, creating preliminary ink drawings, and perhaps preliminary paintings, too. The strong brushwork of his ink drawings is striking, and has been compared to Chinese ink paintings.

Landscape with Psyche at the Palace of Cupid (The Enchanted Castle) *1664. Oil on canvas. 34 1/4 x 59 1/2 in (88 x 151 cm). National Gallery, London.*

genuine "Claudes." He countered this by making copies of almost every picture he painted in his *Liber Veritatis* or *Book of Truth*. This contains 195 detailed drawings in pen and ink, arranged in chronological order, and now provides a useful record of Claude's work from 1634 to his death.

By the mid-1640s Claude was considered one of the leading artists in Europe. There was a long waiting list for his work, and even rich collectors could be shocked by his high prices. Despite his wealth and reputation, Claude seems to have lived quietly in Rome. He never married and raised a family, and friends recalled his total devotion to his art.

In his later years Claude suffered badly from gout, but he continued to work until his death in 1682. His last paintings take themes from the *Aeneid*, the epic poem written between 42 and 37 B.C. by the Roman poet Virgil, which tells the story of the founding of Rome by the Trojan prince Aeneas. Claude's final painting, *Landscape with Ascanius Shooting the Stag of Silvia* (1682) is unfinished—he had no time to copy it into his *Book of Truth*.

Claude had an enormous influence on later landscape painters, including the English artists Richard Wilson and J. M. W. Turner. The idea of the picturesque landscape—one that resembles a picture in its qualities of light and composition—owes much to him. Claude's work also informed the ideas of natural beauty that were reflected in literature, and inspired changes in English landscape gardening in the middle of the 18th century.

LOTTO Lorenzo

ALTHOUGH LORENZO LOTTO TRAINED IN VENICE, living alongside such great artists as Giorgione and Titian, he remains distinct, both in his style and his choice of diverse, often innovative, subjects. His work appeals to a modern audience particularly because of the way he identifies with his subjects, effectively conveying their feelings as well as their status.

Life and work

Lotto was born in Venice in the early 1480s, and the first record we have of him working as a painter dates from 1503, when he was in Treviso. Unlike most other artists of his time, who lived and worked in Venice, the great commercial and artistic center of the region, Lotto chose to travel around the provinces. His work consisted mostly of devotional paintings, some altarpieces for local churches, and portraits for important private patrons. Many of his religious works depict the Holy Family and saints positioned side by side in a genre known as a *sacra conversazione*—literally, "sacred conversation." Lotto painted these throughout his life. In his compositions and subjects he often added realistic details gleaned from observing people's behavior. In some ways he created paintings that are more like dramas than conventional representations. For example, his depictions of the young Christ often show him behaving more like a real baby, with an innate curiosity and playful nature. Lotto really seemed to understand and sympathize with characters he was portraying, whether he was painting portraits or religious scenes.

In 1509 there is a record of Lotto's being paid for work done in the Vatican palace. He *did* paint some of the pope's rooms, but his efforts seem to have been dwarfed by those of Raphael, who soon took over most of the commissions in the Vatican. Leaving Rome in 1511, Lotto went to Recanati, but by 1513 he had settled in Bergamo. In the period 1513–25, Lotto made six altarpieces there, before moving back to Venice. Lotto's propensity for travel has led some art historians to suggest that he was not as successful as many of his contemporaries. However, it would appear that he simply preferred the provinces to Venice, and that he had many supportive patrons there.

Throughout his time in Venice (1525–32), Lotto continued to paint religious works and altarpieces, but since there were wealthy patrons there, he more often painted privately commissioned portraits. By 1532 Lotto had moved outside Venice again, this time to an area of Italy called the Marches, to work on similar commissions. He returned to Venice at

Data file

Full name: Lorenzo Lotto

Nationality: Italian

Style: 16th-century Venetian

Dates: born c1480 in Venice, died 1556 in Loreto

Key works:
- *Allegory of Virtue and Vice* 1505
- *Madonna and Child Enthroned with Saints* 1506–08
- Martinengo altarpiece 1513–16
- *Marsilio and His Wife* 1523
- portrait of Andrea Odini 1527
- *Saint Nicholas in Glory with Saints John the Baptist and Lucy* 1527–29
- *Adoration of the Shepherds* 1534
- *Saint Antoninus* altarpiece 1542

Things to look for:
- early works showing the use of bright colors and clearly painted forms
- interest in emblems, symbols, and plays on words in his paintings
- an ability to convey mood, even in religious works
- later use of muted colors and tones along with softer edges in his forms

Comparisons: Giovanni Bellini, Titian

Glossary terms: northern Renaissance, *sacra conversazione*

Portrait of the moment of marriage

This double portrait was commissioned in 1523 by Giovanni Cassotti to celebrate the marriage of his son, Marsilio. Lotto has created a composition that, through the positions of the characters, the details surrounding them, and the depiction of their expressions, provides a penetrating, psychological, gently humorous record of the solemn vows of marriage. Both sitters look very serious, and it has been suggested that, by commissioning this portrait, Giovanni Cassotti was probably making fun of their solemnity, while at the same time reminding them of the responsibility of marriage. Marsilio was about 21 years old at his wedding, rather young to be married in this period.

The painting is rich with symbols. Marsilio and Faustina are about to be joined together by Cupid, the Roman god of love, who carries a yoke. The yoke, usually used to keep oxen together when plowing, symbolizes the fact that the two young people will be bound together in marriage for life. Interestingly, the word "conjugal," meaning relating to marriage, derives from the Latin word for yoke, *jugum.* The laurel leaves that Cupid is wearing, and which also sprout from the yoke, are used in paintings to symbolize fidelity. Cupid appears to be curious to see Marsilio's reaction to the yoke.

The portrait shows us the moment just before Marsilio places the ring on Faustina's finger—seconds before they are actually married. Marsilio and Faustina look directly out at the viewer, their faces composed. The directness of the portrait makes us feel as if we are witnesses to the marriage. Lotto evidently relished painting all the details of clothing and jewelry, paying much more attention to them than

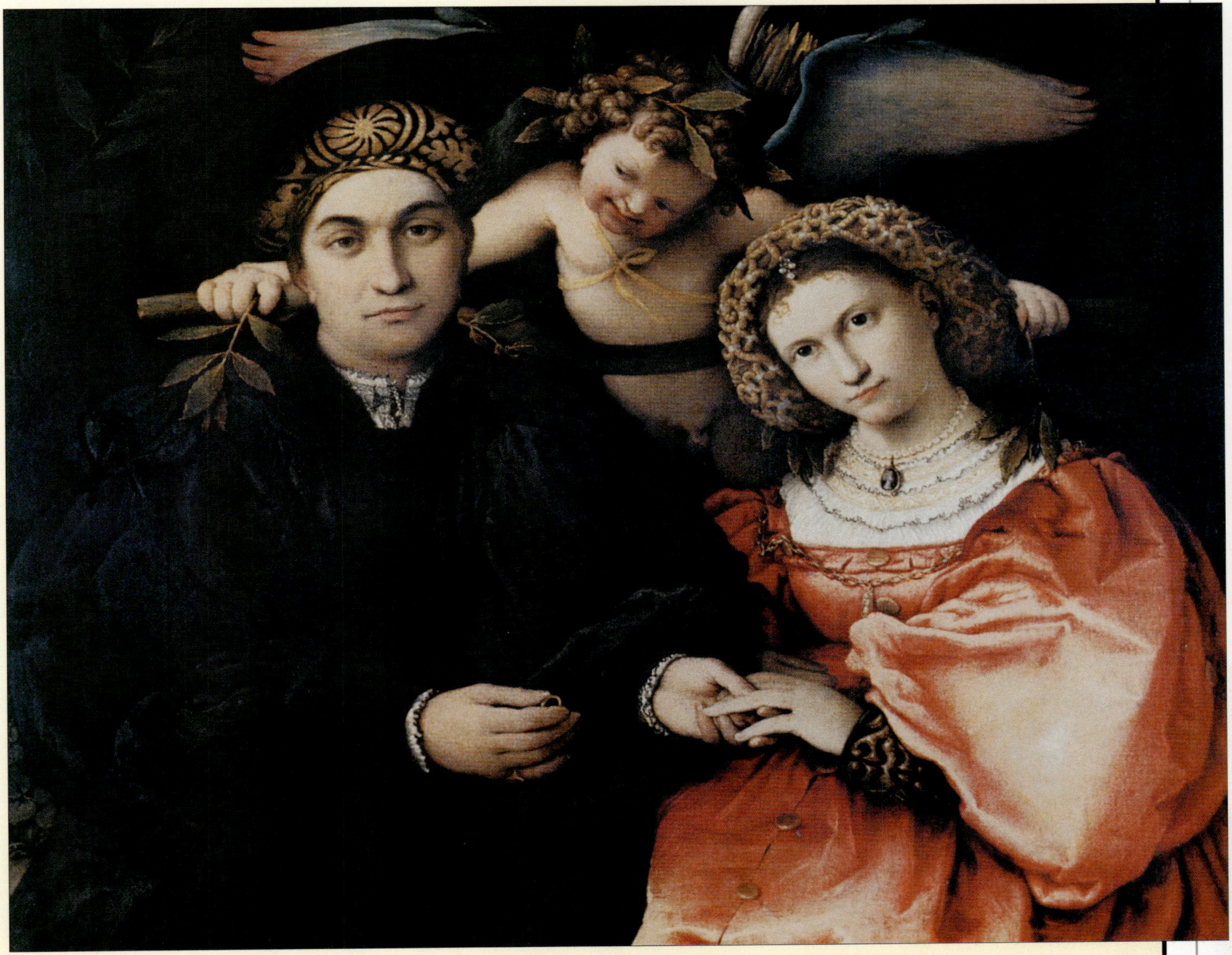

many of his contemporaries in Italy would, and reminding us of the northern Renaissance painters. However, this work is more interesting for the way the feelings and personalities of the characters are revealed. Lotto had a gift for capturing the way people related to one another. In this painting, Marsilio is shown sitting up straight, while Faustina inclines her head sympathetically toward him.

Early paintings by Lotto show very bright, pure colors and strong contrasts of light and dark. By 1523, the date of this work, he was painting with more subtle, moody tones, but the interest in color is seen here in the bride's vivid dress.

Marsilio and His Wife *1523. Oil on panel. 28 x 33 in (71 x 84 cm). Museo del Prado, Madrid.*

the end of his career, intending to stay there, but commissions from the provinces encouraged him to travel once more.

Having developed close links with the religious community of the Santa Casa in Loreto (for whom he had painted an altarpiece), he chose to become a lay brother and remained there until his death in 1556. In an early will he described himself as "old, alone, and anxious" but by this stage, when he made a new will, he may have found solace in the Santa Casa.

Lotto's life is extremely well documented. More than 40 letters survive, and a personal account book, detailing the various commissions and materials used, has helped to reconstruct his life and work, despite his mobile lifestyle.

LOWRY L. S.

BEST KNOWN FOR HIS EVOCATIVE AND IDIOSYNCRATIC PAINTINGS of the industrial north of England, L. S. Lowry was a painter of surprising breadth, producing landscapes, seascapes, and figure studies of great dramatic power and expressive intensity.

Life and work

L. S. Lowry has a claim as one of Britain's best-known and best-loved 20th-century painters. Along with David Hockney and Henry Moore he has become a household name and a national institution. This has led to oversimplification of the subtleties of his artistic achievement. To some degree Lowry himself was responsible for this—he professed to be "a simple man." Despite outward appearances, however, his life and art were complex.

He was an only child, and lived with his parents until their deaths. Following in his father's footsteps as a rent collector and cashier for a Manchester-based property company, he retired on a full pension at the age of 65, 14 years after he began to attract national attention as an artist.

Determined from his earliest years to become an artist, he attended evening classes intermittently for about 25 years, first at the Manchester Municipal Art College and then at Salford School of Art. His national reputation only began to develop with his one-man exhibition, when he was over 50, at the Lefevre Gallery in London in 1938. He would keep his job as a rent collector a closely guarded secret until his death 38 years later.

His father had died in 1932 and his mother, who had never held a high opinion of her son's artistic activities, died in 1939, a few months after his belated discovery by the art world. This was the central tragedy of Lowry's life—not having the opportunity to prove to his mother that, at least in the world's eyes, he was a success. He never recovered from her death, and after his bereavement his work became more and more expressive of his own sense of isolation (he never married) and the purposelessness of existence.

He had gained his reputation as a painter of mill scenes, and was mistakenly understood as a "primitive" painter. In fact, he was a sophisticated artist whose inspiration was fueled by his great love of the theater and music hall.

His thorough knowledge of the history of art included the writings of the 17th-century theoretician C. A. du Fresnoy, but above all he had a special admiration for the Pre-Raphaelite painters. He particularly liked Ford Madox Brown and the late, sexually alluring paintings of Dante Gabriel Rossetti. Honoré Daumier and Vincent Van Gogh were also very important to him, as was the example of Rembrandt and, later in life, the surrealists.

It is a measure of the power of Lowry's personal vision that these influences on his work are sublimated into a highly original style of painting. A fundamental element in the development of his style, however, was the example of his life-drawing teacher, the little-known French artist Adolphe Valette. In the years when Valette taught at Manchester Municipal Art College, he painted some extraordinary images of the urban center of Manchester.

Lowry was a remarkably complex man. His ambition, he said, was to paint himself into the scenes that absorbed him, and to some degree all his work may be regarded as extended self-portraiture, manipulating reality to suit his own needs.

His paintings of the industrial community in which he lived and worked reduce the complexity of the urban worker to a puppet-like creature—a fitting and suggestive metaphor for the dehumanizing processes of the industrial revolution. He always denied any such agenda in his work, although in the second half of his career he concentrated his efforts not so much on the declining cotton industry as on the unfortunates, the outcasts, and the down-and-outs with whom he increasingly identified.

He painted cold and sterile images of the hills and valleys of the north of England, which he called his "lonely landscapes," and extraordinary seascapes with vigorous power and imaginative force.

Lowry resisted the modernist movement with its emphasis on abstaction and spirituality. He preferred to root the majority of his work in everyday life. His public continues to embrace him as a provider of nostalgic images, a chronicler of a disappearing industrial way of life.

Data file

Full name: Laurence Stephen Lowry

Nationality: English

Style: independent

Dates: born 1887 in Manchester, died 1976 in Glossop

Key works:

- *Coming Out of School* 1927
- *Coming From the Mill* 1930
- *Head of a Man (Man with Red Eyes)* 1938
- *The Landmark* 1938
- *In the Park* 1949
- *The Funeral Party* 1953
- *The Sea* 1963
- *The Beggar* 1965

Things to look for:

- a vivid sense of atmosphere
- texture and luminosity

Comparisons: Honoré Daumier, Edvard Munch, Giorgio de Chirico, Maurice Utrillo, Stanley Spencer, René Magritte, Leon Kossoff

Glossary terms: classical, Pre-Raphaelite, primitive, surrealism

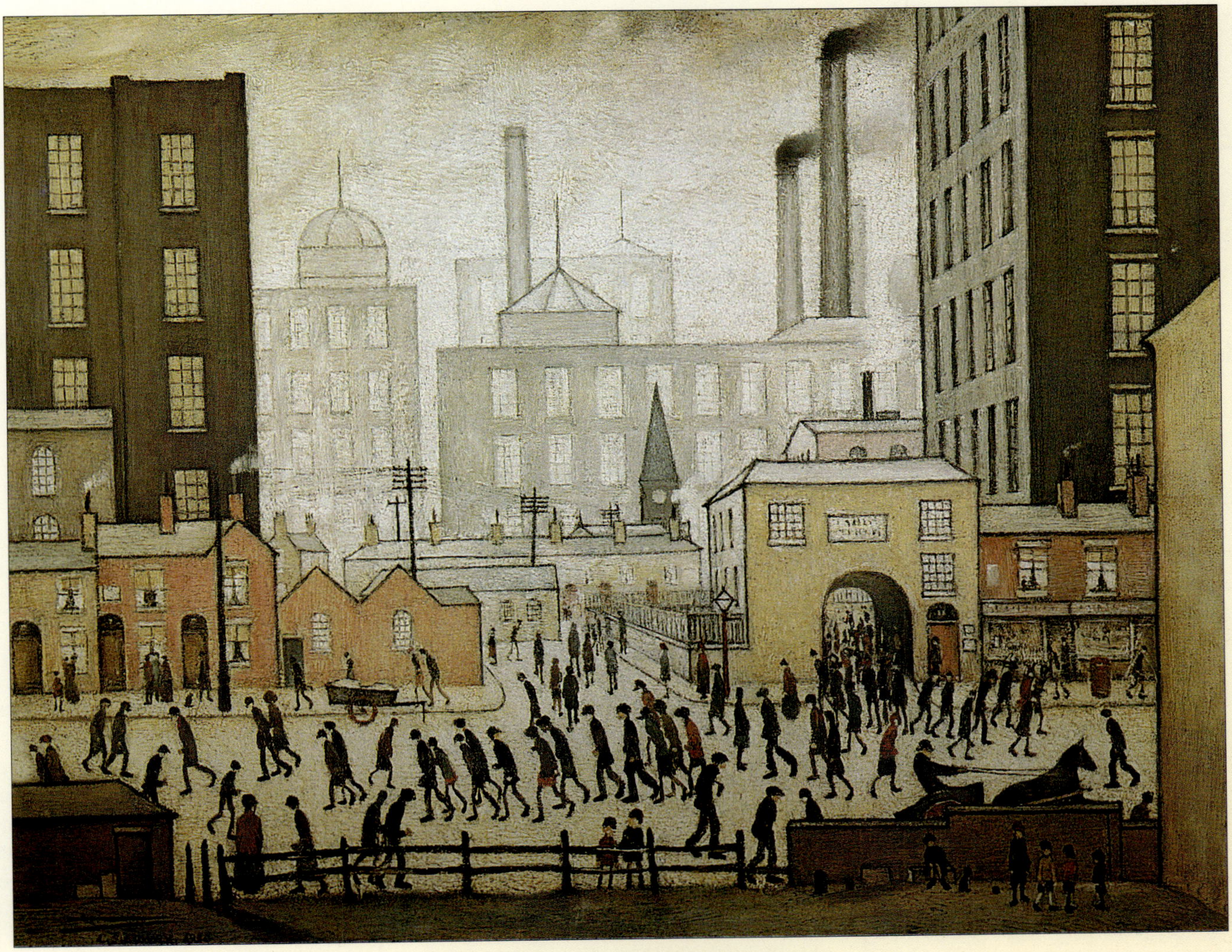

A private beauty

Lowry's unique style is based on just five colors—ivory black, flake white, scarlet vermilion, yellow ochre, and prussian blue. He painted on a ground of thick white oil paint, building up a highly worked, textured finish, and cutting into the surface with a pocket knife or a nail, scratching, gouging, and overpainting.

His paintings of working life, such as *Coming From the Mill* (1930), reveal a classical sensibility that endows the industrial architecture of the north of England with an unexpected unity. Colors, tones, lines, and shapes work together to create an almost musical harmony.

Set against this ordering principle are works like his 1938 painting *Head of a Man (Man with Red Eyes)*. Based on a self-portrait, and painted at a time of great tension and stress, when his mother was terminally ill, it reveals him as a painter of great expressive power who, like Edvard Munch, could create stark, haunting images that evoke shared human emotions.

Painting and drawing were a necessary activity for this compulsive but sensitive draftsman, and he painted his largely imaginary scenes over long periods of time, in the evenings after work, or on weekends. Although he was ambitious, his subjects always had a deep personal relevance to him. Despite the fact that he gained many honors in his lifetime, they all came too late to give him real pleasure.

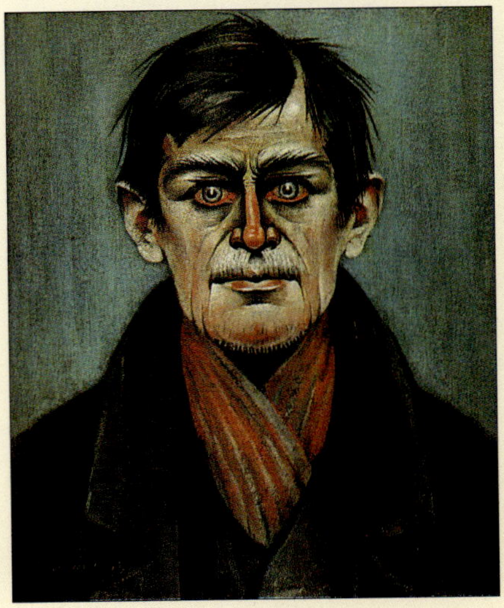

Head of a Man (Man with Red Eyes) *1938. Oil on canvas. 20 x 16 in (50.5 x 41 cm). Museum and Art Gallery, Salford.*

Coming From the Mill *1930. Oil on canvas. 16 1/2 x 20 1/2 in (42 x 52 cm). Museum and Art Gallery, Salford.*

MACKE August

AUGUST MACKE DIED YOUNG, but in his short life he produced a remarkable range of work in many media. Influenced by modern artists in both France and Germany, Macke developed a distinctive style, characterized by intense, bright colors. He was one of the most important artists associated with the Blaue Reiter movement.

Life and work

August Macke spent most of his childhood in Cologne. He showed little interest in schoolwork, preferring to spend his time drawing. When he was 16 he met a young girl, Elisabeth; he eventually married her. In 1904 he was accepted into the Art Academy at Düsseldorf, but found it too old-fashioned; he much preferred the evening classes he went to at a more progressive school in the city. There he was encouraged to experiment with many printing and drawing techniques.

In 1910 Macke met the artist Franz Marc and the two became close friends. The following year, by now married with a baby son, Macke became involved with the newly formed Blaue Reiter group, led by Wassily Kandinsky. Echoing Kandinsky, Macke believed that art was an "expression of man's inner life." However, Macke's letters show that he was skeptical about Kandinsky and unconvinced by the Russian artist's "spiritual" abstraction. Macke's work developed in a different, more figurative direction. Some of his paintings, with their interlocking, geometric forms, show that Macke had been influenced by cubism and Italian futurism.

In 1912 Macke went to Paris and met Robert Delaunay. He was enormously impressed by Delaunay's Orphistic paintings (relating to a mystery religion of ancient Greece). In Macke's oil or watercolor paintings we often see luminous, interlocking colors, formed into gentle curves. Sometimes these are abstract patterns, but more often they describe human figures or plant forms. They clearly show Macke's admiration for the French painter, and indeed, Delaunay came to admire Macke's work, too. There is often a strong sense of calm and order in Macke's art, and his work has been described as "gentle" expressionism.

Macke was a prolific and very versatile artist. Like Kandinsky, he sometimes painted on glass, but he also made embroidered pictures and decorated ceramics. For his paintings, Macke usually chose scenes from everyday life, but he often managed to bring out an enticing, exotic quality, even in the ordinary settings he chose. His canvases often show couples strolling in the park or children playing, the kinds of subjects that had been painted by the French impressionists. But he surrounded his figures with brightly colored foliage, violet or turquoise skies, and patches of intense yellow, suggesting strong sunlight. He painted women window-shopping, looking at the elaborate displays, and wearing hats adorned with extravagant feathers, making urban and suburban life look lush and exotic.

Data file

Full name: August Robert Ludwig Macke

Nationality: German

Style: expressionism

Dates: born 1887 in Meschede, died 1914 on the Western Front, France

Key works:
- *Portrait of Franz Marc* 1910
- *Indians* 1911
- *Zoological Garden I* 1912
- *Hat Shop* 1913
- *The Tightrope Dancer* 1914
- *Turkish Café I* and *II* 1914
- *Colorful Life* 1914

Things to look for:
- bright colors
- simplified, curving forms
- exotic figures and animals
- park scenes

Comparisons: Franz Marc, Wassily Kandinsky, Robert Delaunay, Paul Klee

Glossary terms: Blaue Reiter, cubism, expressionism, futurism, impressionism, Orphism

A colorful spectacle

August Macke painted *The Tightrope Dancer* early in 1914 when he and his family were staying by Lake Thun in Switzerland. At this time, Macke was trying to free himself from the fashionable "isms" of modern art. He wanted to make a fresh start and to paint honestly and directly from nature. He took none of his old paintings with him, so that he could concentrate purely on looking afresh at his surroundings. In Switzerland he continued to paint his favorite subjects of people wandering in the city, but he also discovered a wonderful new source of imagery—circus life.

Macke's wife, Elisabeth, remembered that, late in 1913, when the evenings were still mild enough, a famous troupe of circus performers would put on open-air shows in the town's marketplace. The tightrope was strung up across the square and lit by little colored lamps, illuminating the spectacle of the dancers, in their colorful silk costumes, balancing on the wire. In the painting we can see the crowd, wrapped up warm on the autumn evening, the tightrope, and the old town's houses in the background. The scene is warmly lit by the lamps against a dark sky. Macke has simplified the roofs and walls especially, so that they have a flattened, patternlike quality, adding to the festive look of the scene.

The painting also shows us Macke's sensitive use of color; for example, the walls illuminated here and there show how cleverly he could play with lighting to enliven the image, and the predominant reds of the scene are skillfully offset by the blue skirt in the crowd. Macke made many sketches showing clowns, acrobats, and bareback riders from the circus, but it was the tightrope act that fascinated him most. Here, the painting's sense of stillness and the carefully balanced composition matches perfectly the taut wire, the hushed excitement in the crowd, and the precarious balancing act being performed by the dancer.

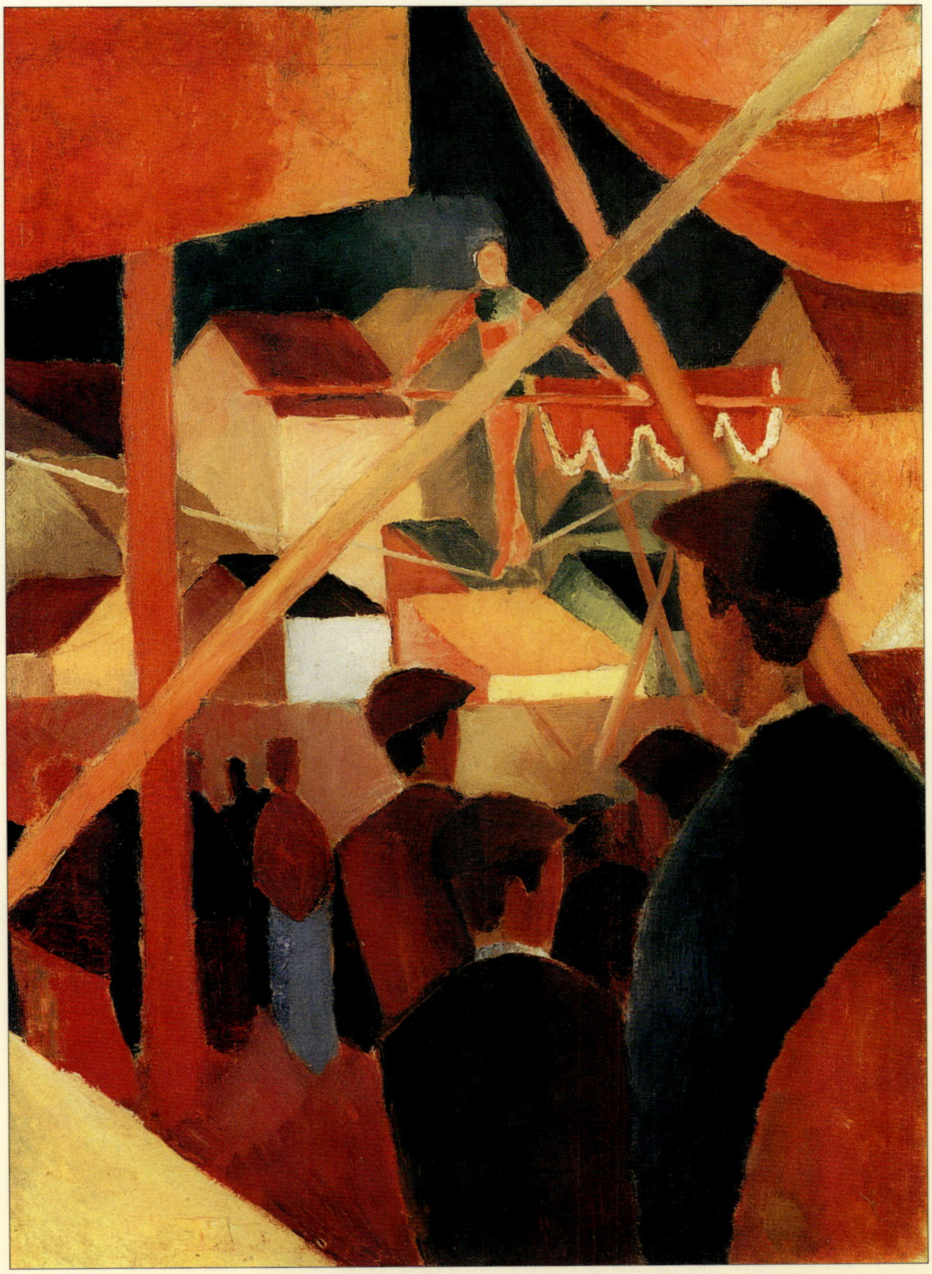

The Tightrope Dancer *1914. Oil on canvas. 32 x 23½ in (82 x 60 cm). Kunstmuseum, Bonn.*

It is not surprising that he was drawn especially toward the zoological gardens in Cologne, where he painted visitors strolling amongst parrots, flamingos, ostriches, and deer. These paintings seem to show a kind of modern paradise within the city, where people can be reunited with nature.

In 1913 Macke had a second son, and the family moved to a picturesque lakeside house in Switzerland. But in spring 1914 Macke went farther afield to seek out exotic, colorful subject-matter. Together with Paul Klee and another artist friend, he traveled to Tunisia. The three were greatly inspired by the strong light and colorful surroundings of North Africa, and spent every day in the hot sun, sketching the mountains, palms, camels, and whitewashed villages they saw. Macke was especially interested in the people of Tunisia. He drew and painted the Arab merchants selling their wares in the streets and souks (markets), busy harbor life, and men relaxing in cafés. Macke made hundreds of sketches in just over two weeks, and later turned them into some of his best oil paintings.

A few months later, war broke out. Macke was called into the army. He wrote to his wife that he feared he may never see his two young sons again, and indeed, tragically, after just a few weeks, he was killed in action.

MAGRITTE René

René Magritte was a surrealist artist whose meticulously detailed and highly finished paintings frequently represent eerie, dream-like worlds in which inanimate objects metamorphose into living beings. Alternatively, they challenge our very sense of reality by presenting ordinary objects accompanied by texts that claim the opposite of what we see.

Life and work

René Magritte was born in Hainaut in Belgium in 1898. As a teenager he regularly visited the local cinema, where he immersed himself in the movies of his day, and avidly read detective stories published in popular magazines. In 1912 Magritte's world was devastated by the suicide of his mother, who was found drowned in a local river, an event that haunted him for the rest of his life.

In 1916 Magritte entered the Brussels Academy of Fine Arts where, after experimenting with impressionism and cubism, he turned his attention toward the graphic arts. By 1918 he had set himself up as a commercial artist. Magritte's approach to painting changed dramatically in 1922, however, when he encountered a reproduction of *The Song of Love* (1914) by the famous Italian painter Giorgio de Chirico. At this time, de Chirico was known for his representation of weird and eerie spaces frequently inhabited by an assortment of inanimate objects. His work profoundly affected Magritte, who adopted many of his stylistic features, as seen in *The Difficult Crossing* (1926).

By the late 1920s, Magritte's work began to incorporate an increasing sense of mystery and horror, as can be seen in *The Threatened Assassin* (1927). Such works attracted the attention of the newly formed surrealist group that had gathered around the poet André Breton in Paris. In 1927, Magritte left Belgium and spent three years living near Paris, where he came into contact with artists such as Max Ernst, Jean Arp, and Yves Tanguy. Yet, while Magritte's works were regularly exhibited at surrealist exhibitions throughout the late 1920s and 1930s, his relationship with the Parisian surrealists remained tense; by 1930 he had returned to Belgium.

It was also during this period that Magritte's works reflected a fascination with the illusionism of art—visible in *The Human Condition* (1933)—and with the use of words in paintings. In *The Betrayal of Images* (1929) Magritte presented the image of a pipe alongside the seemingly contradictory words *"Ceci n'est pas un pipe"* (This is not a pipe). Yet Magritte's claim is essentially correct. What we see is not a pipe, but the image of one, which can neither be lifted nor smoked.

Data file

Full name: René François-Ghislain Magritte
Nationality: Belgian
Style: surrealism
Dates: born 1898 in Hainaut, died 1967 in Brussels
Key works:
Blue Cinema 1925
The Difficult Crossing 1926
The Threatened Assassin 1927
The Lovers 1928
The Betrayal of Images 1929
The Human Condition 1933
Red Model 1935
Things to look for:
- highly detailed finish
- juxtaposition of strange, seemingly unrelated objects
- strange objects that appear to metamorphose into living beings
- ordinary, expressionless characters, frequently in bowler hats

Comparisons: Giorgio de Chirico, Max Ernst, Jean Arp, Yves Tanguy, Salvador Dalí
Glossary terms: cubism, expressionism, impressionism, pop art, realism, surrealism

Mystery and illusion in Magritte's art

Magritte's early fascination for mystery can, in part, be traced to his love of detective stories in the popular journals and movies of his youth. At the same time, however, incidents in his own personal life also affected his art. While Magritte was still a boy, his mother tragically committed suicide. A story soon emerged that when the body was recovered from the local river, the head was shrouded in the white nightgown that Magritte's mother was wearing at the time of her death. Furthermore, when this shroud was removed, the face was said to be bearing an expression of great calm and tranquility.

Whether this incident actually occurred or not, the story of the shrouded face struck a deep note in Magritte's imagination and helps to explain the obsessive inclusion of shrouded heads in such key paintings as *The Lovers* (1928). Many of Magritte's works seem to thrive on this sense of mystery, an incongruity of elements and narrative reminiscent of the strange disorientation experienced in our dreams.

Magritte's fascination for mystery also extended into the realms of visual illusion. In *The Human Condition* (1933), for

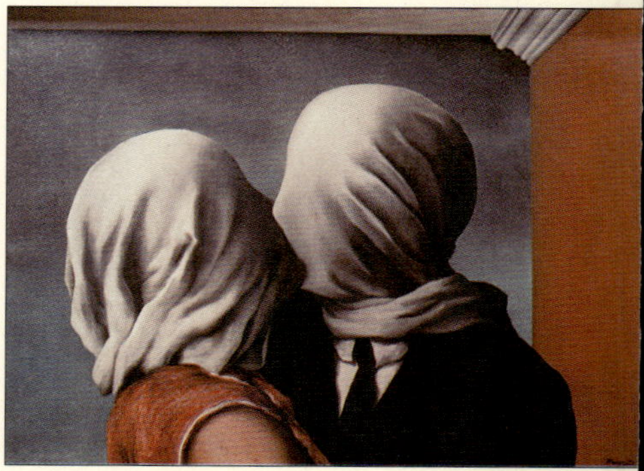

The Lovers *1928. Oil on canvas. 24 x 32 in (61 x 81 cm). Private collection.*

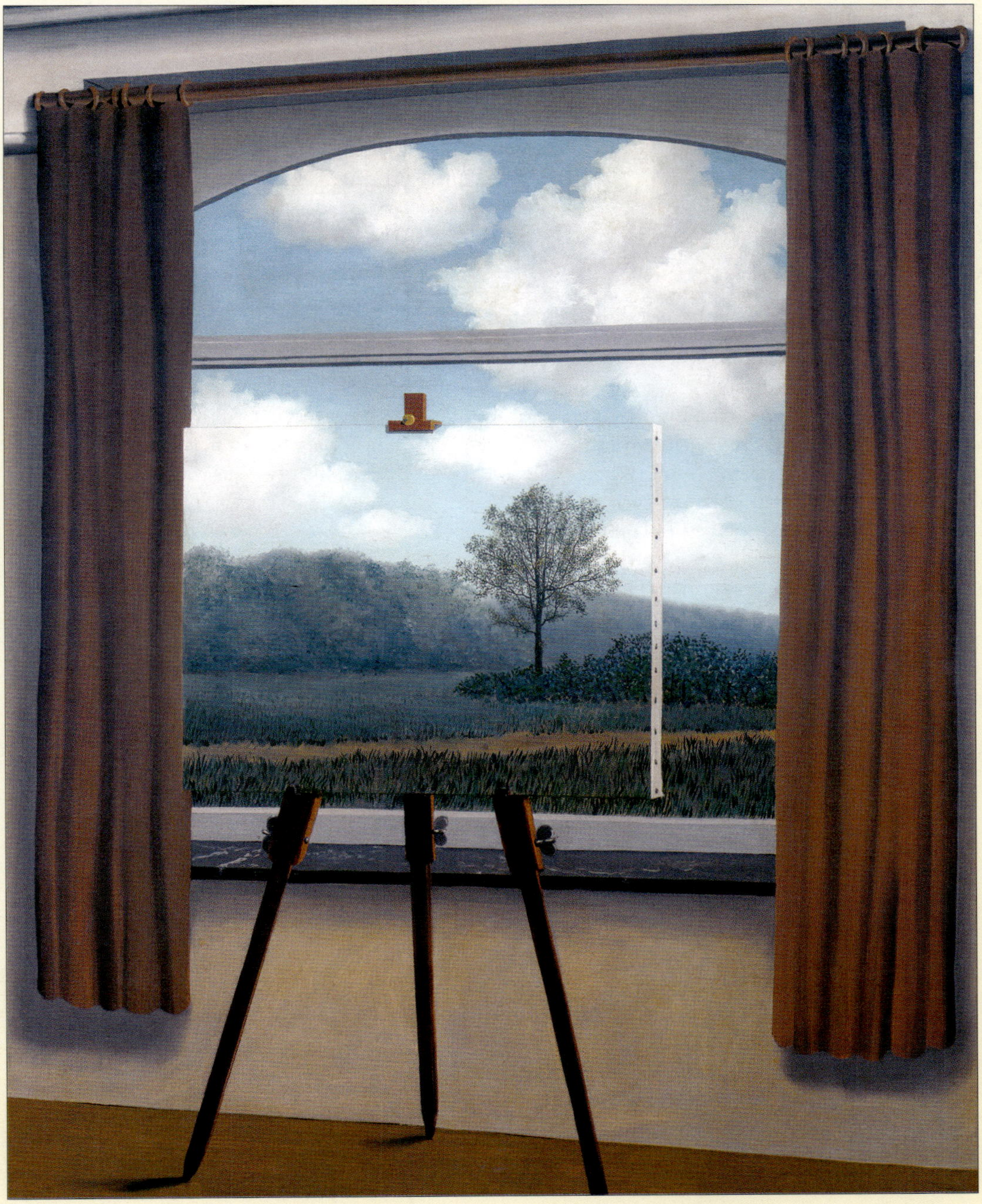

The Human Condition
1933. Oil on canvas. 39½ x 32 in (100 x 81 cm). National Gallery of Art, Washington, D.C.

example, Magritte presents a still scene in an empty room. A painted canvas stands on an easel placed before a window. The image painted on this canvas appears to coincide with the scene visible in the surrounding window. Here Magritte is asking us what it is that we actually see. Is this an actual landscape, or an illusionistic representation of a landscape? How do we know that the scene that exists behind the canvas actually corresponds to the painted image? Magritte's paintings question the way we experience the world around us. They deliberately invite us to examine our own perceptions, but never provide us with concrete answers.

From the 1940s, Magritte experimented with new styles. In 1943, for example, in the midst of World War II, he produced impressionist-inspired paintings reminiscent of the work of Claude Monet and Pierre Auguste Renoir. By 1947 his work had become more expressionist. The works were not well received, however, and Magritte returned to painting strange scenes in a detailed manner, which continued until his death in 1967. By this time his works were being embraced by a new generation of artists who would soon launch the movement called "pop art."

MALEVICH Kasimir

BETWEEN 1915 AND 1920 KASIMIR MALEVICH was a key figure in the development of pure abstraction, taking abstract painting to its most extreme form. As a painter, printmaker, teacher, and theorist, his influence has been felt throughout the 20th century in the fields of art, design, and architecture.

Life and work

Malevich's childhood was spent in Kiev in Ukraine. In his late teens, however, his family moved to Kursk in Russia, where he worked for a local railroad company. After eight years he had saved enough money to enable him to enroll at an art school in Moscow, where he absorbed and imitated the then prevalent styles of post-impressionism and symbolism.

The revolutionary ideas that were influencing Russian politics in the early 20th century were echoed in Russian culture. Malevich joined a succession of artistic groups whose ideologies were influenced by fauvism, futurism, and cubism. This pushed him toward ever more extreme forms of abstraction. Although Malevich was still producing figurative pieces, his figures were increasingly being formed from a collection of tubular, geometrical shapes, in a style that was greatly reminiscent of the work of the 20th-century French artist Fernand Léger.

In 1913 Malevich designed the set and costumes for an avant-garde opera, *Victory over the Sun*. This experience with design affected his work as an artist by freeing him to structure his paintings with bolder simplicity. He began to leave large areas of the canvas painted in a single color, uncluttered by extraneous detail.

At some point between 1913 and 1915 Malevich discarded any trace of figurative representation from his work and instead set out to explore the then uncharted territory of pure abstraction. During this period he experimented with paintings that were composed of elemental shapes (mainly squares, circles, and rectangles), at times restricting himself to monochrome tones, but occasionally reintroducing color into his repertoire. *Black Square* (1915)—simply a black square on a white background—was the most extreme work of this kind, and signaled the arrival of a new, modern movement: suprematism. In 1919 he showed some of the results of his experimentation at an exhibition in Moscow called "Objectless Art and Suprematism," and staged his first solo exhibition in the same year.

Data file

Name: Kasimir Malevich
Nationality: Russian
Style: suprematism
Dates: born 1878 in Kiev, died 1935 in Leningrad
Key works:
- *Black Square* 1915
- *Red Square: Painterly Realism of a Peasant Woman in Two Dimensions* c1915
- *Black Circle* c1915–20
- *Black Cross* c1915–20
- *Suprematist Painting* 1916
- *White Square on White* 1918

Things to look for:
- simplicity and strength of form
- subtle deviations in geometry
- the relationship of forms and colors
- the physicality of the painting itself (rather than looking through the picture plane to an artificial image: a picture)

Comparisons: El Lissitzky, Alexander Rodchenko, Lyubov Popova, Wassily Kandinsky, Piet Mondrian, Ad Reinhardt, Mark Rothko, Barnett Newman

Glossary terms: abstract art, avant-garde, cubism, fauvism, futurism, icon, postimpressionism, socialist realism, suprematism, symbolism

Black and white

Suprematism is the style of painting that Malevich originated, and he painted his most famous works in this style during a period between 1913 and 1920. *Black Square* (1915) illustrated the extreme position of suprematism more clearly than any of Malevich's previous works.

When *Black Square* was first exhibited, Malevich published a booklet called "From Cubism and Futurism to Suprematism: the New Realism in Painting." This announced the arrival of suprematism, a new movement in art, which advocated the exploration of visual language through the interplay of significant shapes and colors rather than by means of representation.

By rejecting the traditional elements of painting, such as theme, narrative, and the portrayal of objects as they appeared, Malevich indeed achieved a "new realism in painting." Instead of being a depiction of something else, something drawn from the natural world, the painting became an object to look at in itself. According to Malevich, suprematist painting was no longer imitative in style, and because it was not imitative it therefore had to be real. "Painting is paint and color," Malevich declared, and suprematist paintings "will not be repetitions of living things in life but will themselves be living things."

With *Black Square*, however, Malevich appeared to have reached an end point, in that it seemed that he had reduced visual language to its simplest form. From this point he began producing variations, for example by exchanging the square for a circle or cross, and by subtly altering the geometry of his shapes. He also started to expand his visual vocabulary by combining simple, geometrical shapes in increasingly complex relationships and compositions,

Having formed an artists' group UNOVIS (Advocates of the New Art) during the 1920s, Malevich became a highly influential teacher and theoretician. He encouraged his students to work in a wide range of media, and his influence also extended into the field of design. By the late 1920s, however, the policies of the

White Square on White *1918.*
Oil on canvas.
31 1/4 x 31 1/4 in
(79 x 79 cm).
Museum of Modern Art, New York, NY.

also introducing colors to fill the void between the extremes of black and white in such works as *Suprematist Painting* (1916).

Between 1917 and 1919, returning to the simplicity of *Black Square*, Malevich produced a series of white-on-white compositions, including *White Square on White* (1918). For many critics, this work represents the epitome of pure abstraction, in which Malevich's palette is reduced to two subtle modulations of white, and the barely visible form is a lopsided square on a rectangular canvas. The paint is applied quite thickly, revealing the brushstrokes that created the work and thereby stressing its physical presence. However minutely, these brushstrokes nevertheless betray a trace of expression that would later be extinguished in the abstract works of American minimalist artists such as Ad Reinhardt and Donald Judd.

dictator Josef Stalin had begun to affect the artistic life of Russia and the other Soviet states, curbing the influence and expression of avant-garde movements, which were regarded as subversive. A retrospective exhibition of Malevich's work was held in Kiev in 1930, but it was immediately closed down. Malevich was detained by the Soviet authorities and called to account for the ideology of the new forms of art with which he associated himself. He was released after two months, but his artistic freedom was constantly under threat.

During the 1930s Malevich's paintings became a curious hybrid of the state-imposed, socialist realist style, and the loose, painterly brushwork of impressionism. It is clear that his most important contribution to art—his creation and exploration of suprematism—had already been made.

In 1933 Malevich was diagnosed with cancer and he died in 1935. He had earlier designed his own casket, which had a black square and a circle painted on the lid.

MANET Edouard

EDOUARD MANET WAS ONE OF THE MOST INFLUENTIAL ARTISTS of the 19th century. Inspired by the ideas of the poet Charles Baudelaire, Manet challenged traditional artistic conventions by introducing modern-life, urban subjects into his painting. His sketchily finished canvases also challenged traditional academic values and paved the way for many subsequent artists.

Life and work

Edouard Manet, the son of an eminent member of the French Ministry of Justice, was born in Paris. As a youth his artistic leanings were encouraged both by his uncle and his schoolfriend, Antonin Proust. In his late teens he joined the studio of the artist Thomas Couture, where he learned traditional painting techniques and developed his more sketchy style of finish. Manet traveled widely at this time, visiting many of the museums of Europe before setting up his own studio in 1856.

Manet's early works were inspired by Diego Velázquez and Peter Paul Rubens and are often dark in tone. His subjects, however, as in *The Old Musician* (1862), were based on modern urban figures—the poor, beggars, and street entertainers—many of whom had been forced off the city streets during the rebuilding of Paris in the 1850s and 1860s.

Manet was much inspired by the writings of the French poet Charles Baudelaire, who had called upon artists to reject the traditional emphasis on history painting in favor of representing the "heroism of modern life." Manet's respect for Baudelaire was revealed by his inclusion of the poet in his *Music in the Tuileries* (1862), which represented an elegant Parisian crowd parading in the city's public gardens.

Manet's reputation took a major step forward in 1863, when several of his works, including the famous *Déjeuner sur l'herbe* (1863), were submitted to the major exhibition held in Paris, known as the Salon. Although Manet's works were rejected, they caused a scandal when they were later exhibited at the Salon des Refusés, an exhibition of work refused by the Salon. In particular his representation of a female nude figure seated alongside two modern bourgeois men in a wooded glade shocked contemporary audiences more familiar with the nude in the guise of a nymph or goddess.

Two years later Manet again gained public notoriety when his painting *Olympia* (1865) was exhibited at the Salon. Based upon Titian's famous *Venus of Urbino* (1538), *Olympia* substituted a modern-day courtesan for the Renaissance master's mythological goddess. Despite its overt reference to traditional art, Manet's nude figure, which stares directly at the viewer in a blatantly sexual way, was regarded by many as an affront to decency.

In 1867 Manet produced several versions of a notorious event of the same year: the execution of the Emperor Maximilian of Mexico by Mexican revolutionaries. The French

Data file

Full name: Edouard Manet

Nationality: French

Style: impressionism

Dates: born 1832 in Paris, died 1883 in Paris

Key works:
- *The Old Musician* 1862
- *Music in the Tuileries* 1862
- *Déjeuner sur l'herbe* 1863
- *The Execution of Emperor Maximilian* 1867
- *The Balcony* 1868–69
- *A Bar at the Folies-Bergère* 1882

Things to look for:
- modern subjects
- loose, sketchy finish
- contrasts of dark and light
- direct gaze of the model

Comparisons: Thomas Couture, Berthe Morisot, Gustave Courbet, Claude Monet, Edgar Degas, Gustave Caillebotte

Glossary terms: history painting, impressionism, realism, Salon, Salon des Refusés

The painter of modern-life subjects

Throughout his career, Manet's work placed much emphasis on the representation of modern-life subjects. In *The Balcony* (1868–69), for example, three modern Parisians gaze outward toward the public space of the street. Each figure gazes in a different direction, although the seated female on the left seems to be staring most intensely. Interestingly, the model for this figure was Manet's fellow-artist and sister-in-law Berthe Morisot. For many contemporary critics, this work made little sense. They could not deduce what was happening, nor did they feel comfortable with the powerful and authoritative gaze of the female who, according to the social strictures of the

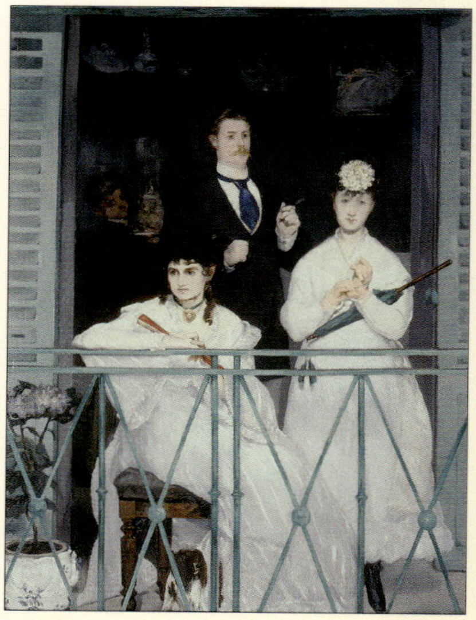

The Balcony *1868–69. Oil on canvas. 67 x 49 in (170 x 124.5 cm). Musée d'Orsay, Paris.*

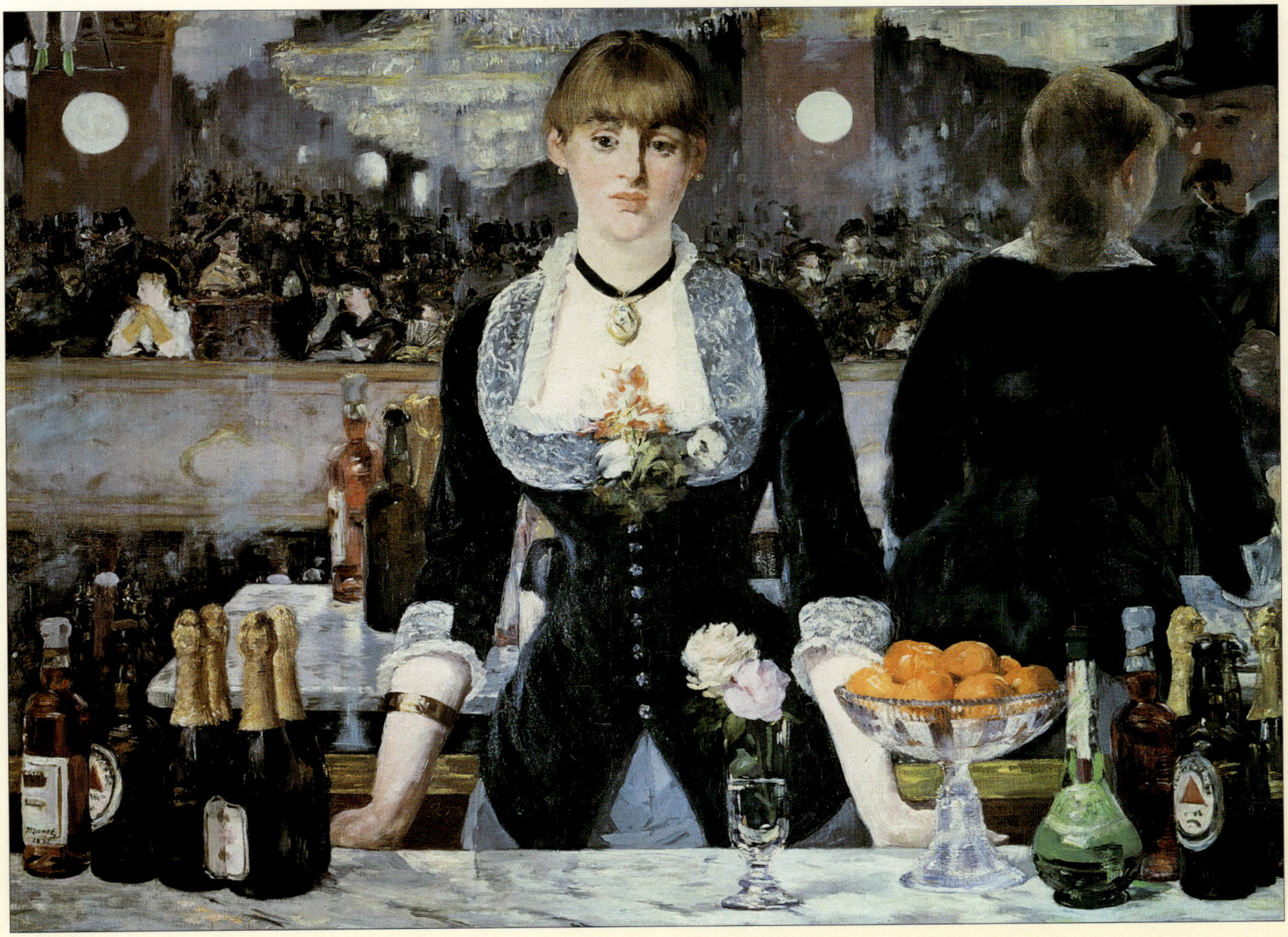

day, should not have been staring so brazenly into a public street. Manet, however, was unwilling to accept these limitations, either on his art or on his understanding of social roles.

Even in his last major painting, *A Bar at the Folies-Bergère* (1882), Manet presented a challenge to the viewer. Here the spectator confronts a barmaid standing behind a marble-topped counter and in front of a mirror which reflects the space of the Folies-Bergère nightclub. In the top left corner we see a tiny detail—the legs of a trapeze artist—suggesting the kind of entertainment that took place in the club. On the right we can also see the reflection of the barmaid herself, although Manet has moved this reflection into an artificial space, thus allowing us to see two views of the same figure. Here the enthusiastic manner in which the reflected figure leans forward to serve the top-hatted customer seems contradicted by the evident tiredness of the centrally positioned barmaid, perhaps suggesting the difference between the façade and the reality of life in 19th-century Paris.

A Bar at the Folies-Bergère *1882. Oil on canvas. 38 x 51 in (96 x 130 cm). Courtauld Gallery, London.*

government's failure to save him was seen by many as a public scandal. Manet's representation of this event was deemed to be so politically sensitive that it was banned from public exhibition.

During the early 1870s, Manet worked in Argenteuil, a popular riverside resort just outside Paris, where Claude Monet was also producing some of the earliest impressionist works. Although frequently associated with impressionism, Manet kept his distance from the main impressionist group and never exhibited with it, preferring instead to show his works at the annual Salon. His influence upon the group's later representation of modernity was, however, notable. In turn the impressionists' bright use of color and loose handling, as well as their practice of painting outside, had an influence on Manet's own work.

Manet died a year after completing his last major painting, *A Bar at the Folies-Bergère* (1882), a work that captured the excitement and complexity of the modern urban world, and confirmed his lifelong interest in the representation of modern subjects.

MANTEGNA Andrea

Andrea Mantegna was inspired by the classical, or antique, world and its art. He was original in his style of painting, particularly in creating dramatic effects of foreshortening and in manipulating perspective to underline the meaning or emotional content of his works.

Life and work

Andrea Mantegna was the son of a carpenter. Even as a young boy, his artistic talent was obvious, and by the age of 10 he had been apprenticed to Francesco Squarcione, the most influential teacher of the time in Padua. Squarcione adopted Mantegna, not because he specially preferred him, but simply in order to avoid paying his most brilliant pupil for any work he might do for Squarcione's workshop.

By the time he was 17 Mantegna sought independence, and fought a legal battle with Squarcione to gain the freedom to undertake commissions independently. Mantegna had already developed an individual style characterized by sharply defined lines, light, and colors, with inspiration often drawn from classical art and architecture. He was also intensely interested in the new science of perspective.

In 1448 Mantegna was one of several artists to receive a commission to paint frescos in the Ovetari Chapel of the Eremitani Church in Padua (destroyed in 1944). One of the other artists, Pizzolo, became a great influence on Mantegna; he showed him how to paint figures in a more three-dimensional way, almost as if they were sculpture. Mantegna also learned about perspective and creating illusions in space. However, while Mantegna became interested in idealized, classical figures based on the art of antiquity, Pizzolo's work remained more realistic.

The other artists completed their works, and Pizzolo was killed in 1453, so Mantegna took over sole responsibility for the unfinished chapel frescos. Even though all the scenes were biblical, he gave free rein to his interest in representing the settings, architecture, and sculptural figures of antiquity, while also experimenting with new and dramatic viewpoints and perspectives. The most famous are those from the life of Saint James, in particular *The Trial of Saint James*, and *Saint James Led to Martyrdom.*

Around the end of the decade, Mantegna received an invitation to be Court Painter for the ducal Gonzaga family at Mantua. Between 1460 and 1488 he worked exclusively for the Gonzagas, decorating the chapel of San Giorgio, producing portraits of the family and, perhaps most importantly, creating a scheme of murals in the Camera Picta or Camera degli Sposi (Bridal Chamber) of the palace.

Data file

Full name: Andrea Mantegna

Nationality: Italian

Style: Italian Renaissance

Dates: born c1430 in Isola di Carturo, died 1506 in Mantua

Key works:

- frescos in the Eremitani Church in Padua 1448–57
- *The Presentation in the Temple* 1455
- San Zeno altarpiece 1456–59
- decoration of the Camera Picta or Camera degli Sposi at the Ducal Palace in Mantua 1465–74
- *The Triumphs of Caesar* late 1480s–1505
- *The Dead Christ* c1480–90

Things to look for:

- inspiration drawn from ancient Roman sculpture and classical art
- monumental and sculptural figures
- dramatic use of perspective and foreshortening to "deceive" the eye of the viewer and create expressive effects
- later works use little very color to achieve the effects of sculpture or relief carving

Comparisons: Giovanni Bellini, Donatello

Glossary terms: foreshortening, *grisaille*, perspective, Pietà, *trompe l'oeil*

Tricks of the eye

Both these works, although showing very different subjects, are typical of Mantegna's style and his interests.

The Dead Christ (c1480–90), below right, shows a very inventive way of looking at a subject. This is Christ after the crucifixion, but rather than seeing him draped across his mother's knees in a traditional Pietà pose, we see his body from the foot of the table or slab where he is lying. We can see the marks of crucifixion on his feet and hands. However, if this view were really supposed to be true to life and the rules of perspective, the feet would be much larger than they are, and we would not be able to look down on his body and his face.

The dramatic foreshortening is a way of awakening our emotions and heightening the expressive power of his subject. It is a shocking way to view the dead Christ, and also a very intimate one. We can see the face of his mother and another Mary mourning at the side, and feel almost that we are part of a family group. This would have been the purpose of such a private devotional painting: viewers would feel drawn into the image and better able to contemplate what they saw.

Mantegna also uses dramatic effects of foreshortening in his decoration of the Camera Picta (1465–74), although here the subject was not religious but a mixture of historical and mythological subjects, and portraiture. The detail shows the ceiling, where the legs of cherubs are seen from below, as if disappearing up into the skies. The next circular band (the outer ring of people) contains the curious onlookers who seem to be peering over a balcony to see what is going on in the room down below. Below these figures were decorative painted scenes showing Mantegna's patron Ludovico II Gonzaga, his

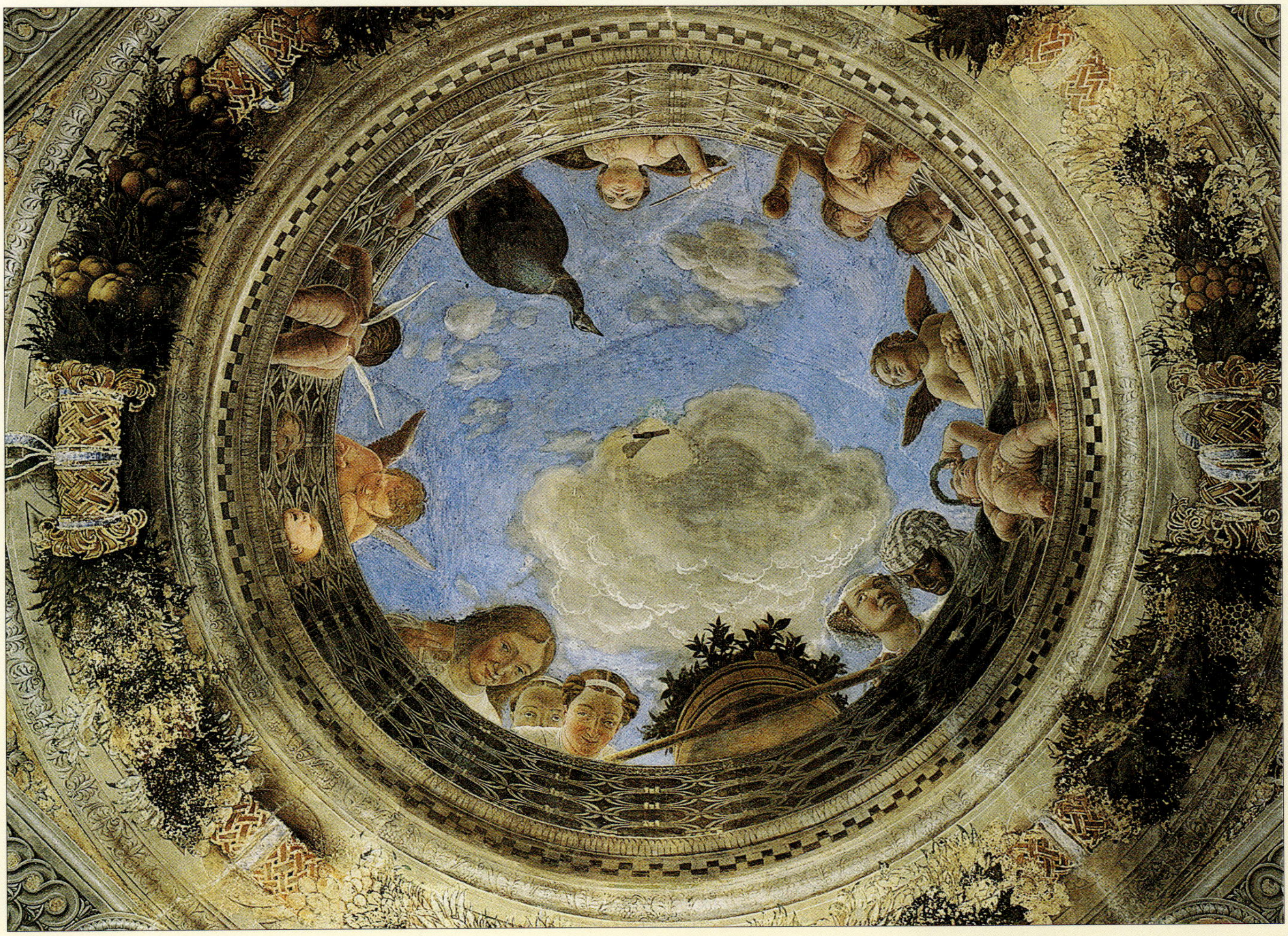

wife, and children engaged in their daily pursuits; they are shown meeting important people and are also depicted in mythological settings. Mantegna includes his own self-portrait as well.

This kind of effect is known as *trompe l'oeil,* which literally means "deceiving the eye." The term refers to the fact that we are convinced by the foreshortening that the figures really are leaning out over a balcony, and the cherubs really are ascending into the sky, even though everything is painted onto the ceiling: a two-dimensional surface.

Camera Picta (Camera degli Sposi) *1465–74. Ceiling fresco. Palazzo Ducale, Mantua.*

The Dead Christ *c1480–90. Tempera on canvas. 26 x 32 in (66 x 81 cm). Pinacoteca di Brera, Milan.*

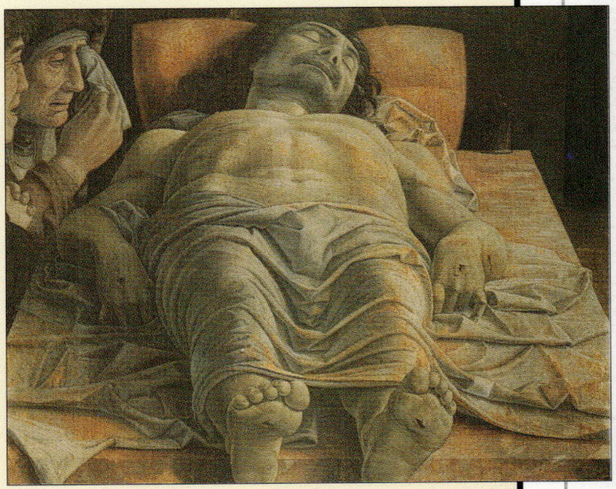

Whether painting a private devotional work, an altarpiece, or a grand decorative scheme for public view, Mantegna's work is always concerned with what the viewer sees and, just as importantly, how they see it.

In 1488 Mantegna was summoned to Rome by the Pope, where he painted frescos in the Belvedere Chapel in the Vatican (now destroyed). He returned to Mantua in 1490 and continued work on *The Triumphs of Caesar*—a series of nine huge paintings using classical subjects as their main inspiration. He also painted mythological scenes for Isabella d'Este's private room or "*studiolo*," and became interested in producing works in *grisaille*—works with very little or no color that were meant to represent stone, bronze, or marble. Once again Mantegna turned to the classical era for his subjects and styles.

Mantegna was buried in Mantua in 1506, in a chapel decorated with his own work, including a self-portrait, and with the work of his son.

MARC Franz

A MAJOR FIGURE IN GERMAN EXPRESSIONISM in the early 20th century, Franz Marc was a co-founder, with Wassily Kandinsky, of the Blaue Reiter (Blue Rider) art group. His brightly colored, expressive canvases, often representing the world of animals, made him a unique artist among his contemporaries.

Life and work

Franz Marc was born in 1880 in Munich, then a thriving artistic center. The son and grandson of artists, he also took up a career as a painter. Art, however, was not his first calling. Adopting the Christian views of his parents, he first studied theology with the intention of becoming a priest. During his studies he became fascinated with literature and philosophy, and in 1900 turned his attention to painting. Marc's spiritual interests were to stay with him throughout his career, profoundly influencing his art.

From the outset he focused on representing the natural world. His early works, depicting birds, sheep, and horses, were relatively somber in mood and color. In 1907, however, he visited Paris and encountered the work of the French postimpressionists Paul Cézanne, Paul Gauguin, and Vincent Van Gogh. On his return to Munich Marc adopted brighter colors, and more vivid and simplified forms.

Despite his engagement with postimpressionist styles, he retained his interest in nature and its capacity to suggest a higher spiritual world. Here Marc was drawing heavily on the German Romantic tradition of Caspar David Friedrich. Like Friedrich, Marc viewed contact with nature as a spiritual experience. Moreover, he feared that, as the world of cities, factories, and modern transportation encroached into the landscape, humans were losing contact with nature.

In 1910 he produced a large-scale painting entitled *Horse in the Landscape*. Using bright, non-naturalistic colors, he made no distinction between the horse and its landscape environment, suggesting that both the animal and its natural surroundings were deeply integrated. That same year, Marc met fellow German expressionist August Macke, who introduced him to the work of Henri Matisse and the fauve group in France. This contact further fired Marc's enthusiasm for the use of bright colors.

The year 1911 marked a major transition in Marc's brief career. He had recently married and was now living in the natural surroundings of a farmhouse in the Bavarian mountains. His sense of exuberance and joy at this time is perhaps best expressed in the painting entitled *Yellow Cow* (1911).

It was also in 1911 that Marc joined with the Russian artist Wassily Kandinsky to form a new artistic group known as the Blaue Reiter (Blue Rider). Kandinsky, like Marc, was seeking a new, spiritual approach to art. Together, the artists produced a journal, the *Blaue Reiter Almanach* (Blue Rider

Data file

Full name: Franz Marc

Nationality: German

Style: German expressionism

Dates: born 1880 in Munich, died 1916 in Verdun, France

Key works:
- *Horse in the Landscape* 1910
- *Blue Horse I* 1911
- *Yellow Cow* 1911
- *Fate of the Animals* 1913
- *Fighting Forms* 1914

Things to look for:
- bright primary colors
- affinity between animals and landscape
- sharp diagonal lines

Comparisons: Caspar David Friedrich, Vincent Van Gogh, Paul Cézanne, Paul Gauguin, Wassily Kandinsky, August Macke

Glossary terms: Blaue Reiter, expressionism, fauves, futurism, postimpressionism, Romanticism

The meaning of color

Marc was influenced by a wide range of modern artistic styles, such as postimpressionism, fauvism, and futurism, but he used these stylistic elements to his own personal ends. His works are particularly distinctive in the way they use simplified forms and bright colors.

Color plays an especially vital role in his paintings. Each color carries a specific symbolic meaning. Red, blue, and yellow are the most important, with red representing the material world; blue, spiritualism and masculinity; and yellow, sensuousness and femininity.

In 1911 Marc produced a large-scale painting entitled *Blue Horse I*. He depicted the body of the horse in a strikingly non-naturalistic blue amidst a multicolored landscape of reds, violets, blues, and greens. A yellow mist shrouds the hills that form the scene's background. Marc's young horse stands boldly upright, dominating the foreground and the natural landscape setting. Yet its gently tilted head and neck, and its gaze away from the viewer, also impart a peacefulness and tranquility to the image. The animal is clearly at one with its surroundings. Marc specifically depicted the body of the horse in a vivid blue to express its spirituality and nobility. For Marc, the animal kingdom was superior to the human race precisely because it had maintained this close contact with nature.

In his later works, such as *Fate of the Animals* (1913) and *Fighting Forms* (1914), Marc increasingly moved toward the use of darker, more threatening color combinations to suggest the growing conflict between the natural world and encroaching modernity. These works foreshadow the tragic events of World War I, including the artist's own death on the Western front.

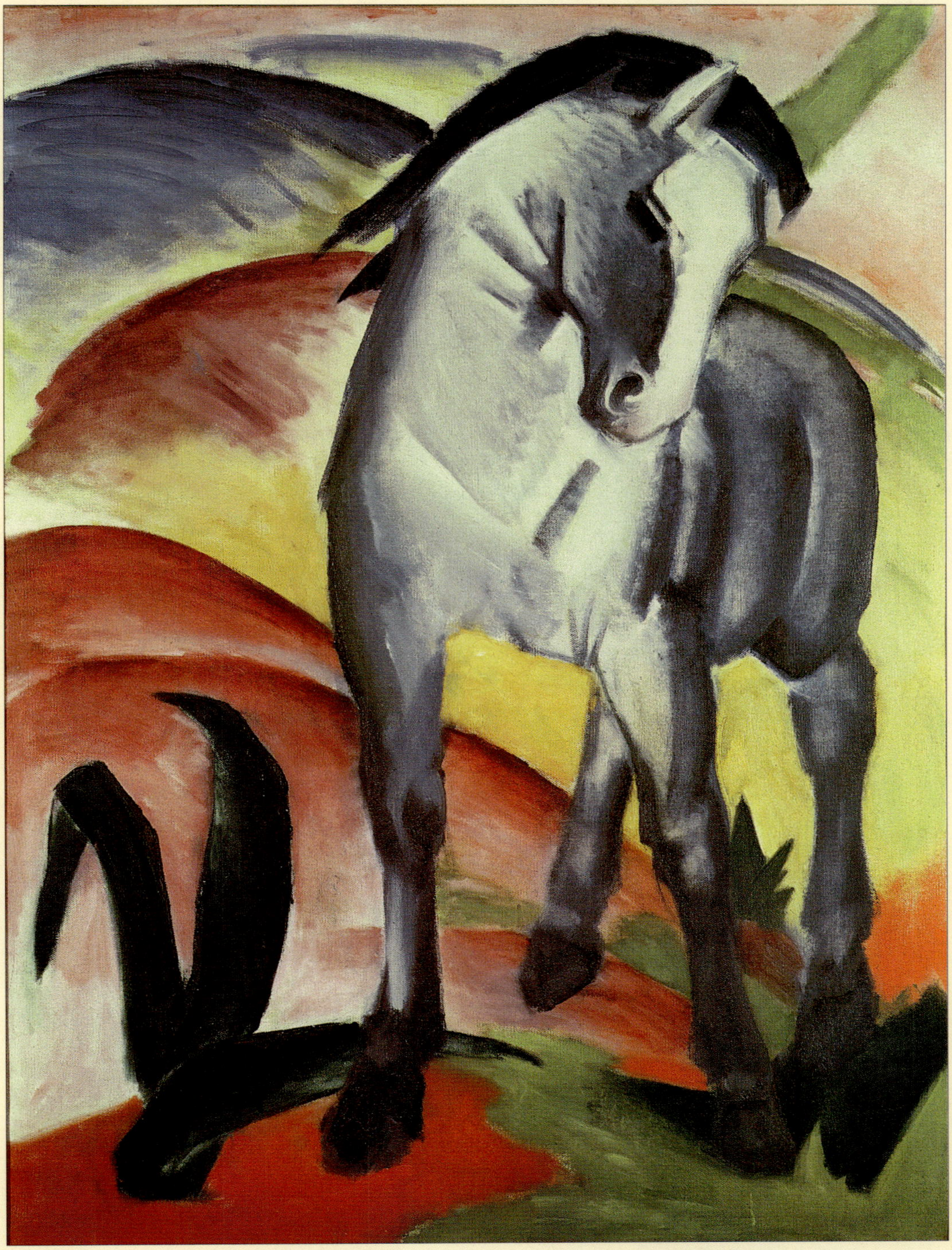

Blue Horse I *1911.*
Oil on canvas. 44 x 33 in (112 x 84.5 cm). Galerie im Lenbachhaus, Munich.

Almanac), that expressed their interests in a wide range of cultural activities, including music, theater, literature, and popular illustration. The motivation behind this venture was to promote the idea that art was central to all cultures and marked a major contribution to well-being.

By 1913, however, with increasing political tensions in Europe, Marc's initial faith that nature could revitalize humankind was beginning to fail. At this time, works such as *Fate of the Animals* (1913) reveal his acceptance of a coming apocalypse. Significantly, he expressed this destruction not through images of human conflict, but through a natural catastrophe—a violent storm destroying nature and the animals in its midst. A year later, when World War I broke out, Marc joined the German troops on the front line in France. He died on the battlefield at Verdun at the age of just 36 years.

MARIN John

PRINCIPALLY FAMED FOR HIS SEMIABSTRACT WATERCOLORS, John Marin took as his inspiration locations such as New York City and the rugged Maine coast. In his seascapes, coastal images, and city scenes Marin used powerful, cubistlike, fractured forms, vigorous, slashing lines, and bold patterns of color with which to communicate the energy and movement of the world around him.

Life and work

Because Marin's mother died only a few days after his birth, his father took him to live in Weehawken, New Jersey, where he was brought up by his two maiden aunts. Although he began painting when he was around 18 years old, at his father's insistence he studied commerce and eventually became a freelance architect.

Realizing that Marin would never make a successful architect, however, his aunts persuaded his father to finance his studies at the Pennsylvania Academy of Fine Arts in Philadelphia. Here Marin demonstrated his skill, and was awarded a prize in 1901 for his sketches of Weehawken. From 1901 to 1903 Marin studied at the Art Students' League in New York City, where he became familiar with the works of the impressionists and the American artists who had come under their influence.

Marin traveled to Europe in 1905 to continue his artistic education. Apart from a brief visit home in 1909, he remained abroad, living mostly in Paris, until 1910. There he was impressed by the works of James Abbott McNeill Whistler; like him, Marin developed a keen interest in oriental art.

In addition to selling etchings, Marin was now also exhibiting and selling paintings. From 1907 to 1909 he exhibited at the Salon d'Automne in Paris; his painting *The Mills of Meaune* (1906) was bought by the French government. Marin showed his work at the Salon des Indépendants in 1909, the year in which he was also introduced to the photographer Edward Steichen. Steichen sent some of Marin's watercolors to Alfred Stieglitz in New York, who exhibited them at his 291 Gallery. Later that year Marin returned briefly to the United States to meet with Stieglitz and arrange his first one-man show, which was held at 291 in 1910.

It was Marin's return to New York, as well as his association with Stieglitz and his circle of artist friends, that enabled him to make his first real contact with European avant-garde styles after impressionism. By the time of the 1913 Armory Show (which introduced avant-garde art to New York

Data file

Full name: John Marin

Nationality: American

Style: abstraction

Dates: born 1870 in Rutherford, NJ, died 1953 in Cape Split, ME

Key works:
- *Brooklyn Bridge* 1910
- *Woolworth Building No. 31* 1912
- *Pertaining to Stonington Harbor, Maine, No. 4* 1926
- *Movement in Brown with Sun* 1928
- *Region Brooklyn Bridge Fantasy* 1932
- *Movement—Sea or Mountain—As You Will* 1947
- *Off the Cape, Cape Split, Maine* 1952

Things to look for:
- images of New York City and the Maine coast
- majority of works in watercolor
- areas of paper or canvas left blank
- use of color bars in works dating from the 1920s
- use of straight, gridlike lines
- irregular "frame-within-a-frame" device surrounding central subject
- elements taken from nature are freely transformed in color and shape

Comparisons: Wassily Kandinsky, Robert Delaunay, Stanton Macdonald-Wright, Arthur Dove, Georgia O'Keeffe, Morgan Russell, Marsden Hartley, Max Weber, Alfred H. Maurer, Joseph Stella

Glossary terms: abstraction, Armory Show, avant-garde, cubism, etchings, expressionism, futurism, impressionism, Orphism, Salon des Indépendants

The modern city in modern art

Although Marin made etchings and painted in oils, it is for his watercolors that he is best known.

Under the influence of James Abbott McNeill Whistler, Marin's emphasis in his early watercolors from around 1887 was on the atmospheric qualities produced by hazy, tonal landscapes. Indeed, when Marin exhibited at the Salon d'Automne from 1907 to 1909 he was still producing atmospheric scenes, causing one of the leading art critics of the day, James Huneker, to call him the "master of mists."

In 1910 Marin began his first paintings of scenes of New York City. These pictures represent his search for a new language of color and form with which to express his emotional response to what he saw; this would lead him to break from the restrictions of purely representational art. Gone is the impressionist approach, and in its place are fragmented and distorted scenes used for expressive purposes.

Marin incorporated the subject matter of New York City into his art in two ways. In some of his works he portrayed the city as seen from a distance, from across the Hudson River, emphasizing the irregular contours of the skyline. In others he depicted scenes from within the city itself. By repeating motifs, blurring forms, and using strong, diagonal lines, Marin captured the speed and rhythms of the bustling city.

Marin painted his first image of Brooklyn Bridge in 1910. Not only was it a motif to which he would return in subsequent decades, but it was also painted by many other American artists, most notably Joseph Stella in 1917 and Georgia O'Keeffe in 1947.

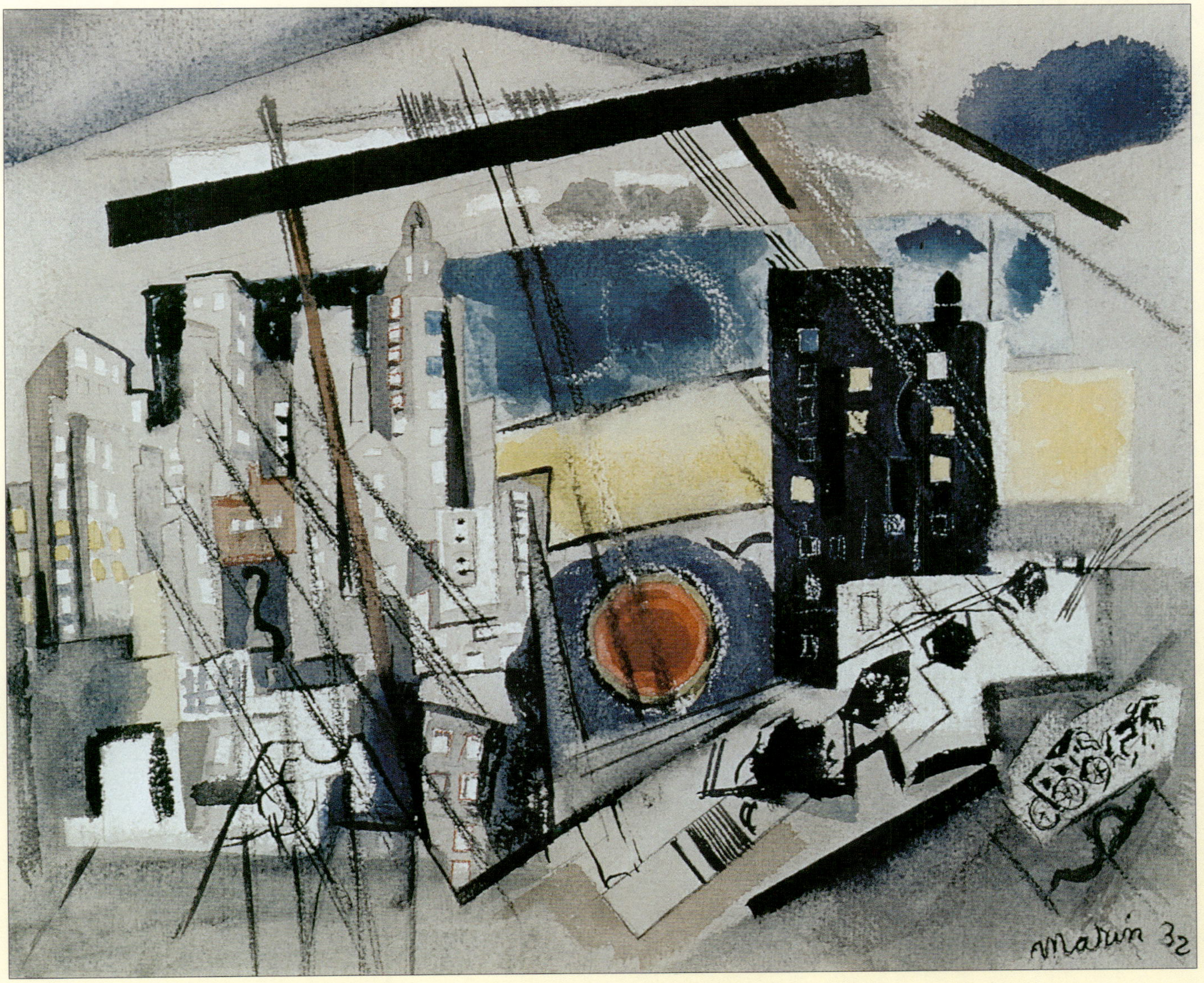

In *Region Brooklyn Bridge Fantasy* (1932) Marin gives the spectator the sense of viewing New York from the bridge. The only parts we can see of the bridge itself are the suspension cables (suggested by black, gridlike lines). The roadway is indicated by the highly stylized horse and carriage in its own little space at bottom right. The blue of the river, the image of the sun, and the skyscrapers complete the composition.

From the 1920s Marin frequently used a "frame-within-a-frame" (an internal framing device) to impose structure upon his work. It also emphasizes his paradoxical treatment of space, which is both illusionistic and flat. Here the lines of the bridge are the "frame-within-a-frame." These form a flat plane through which we are dropped into the more illusionistic space of the view beyond.

Region Brooklyn Bridge Fantasy *1932. Watercolor on paper. 18¾ x 22¼ in (46 x 56.5 cm). Whitney Museum of American Art, New York, NY.*

audiences), his earlier, impressionistic style had been replaced in his series of drawings and watercolors of New York by fragmented lines and turbulent masses inspired by Robert Delaunay's Orphist abstractions of the Eiffel Tower, and echoed the futurists' ideas about the dynamism of the city.

From 1914 onward Marin spent most of his summers in Maine, bringing to his paintings of the state's rugged coastline the same expressionistic approach. He also continued to develop his distinctive, semiabstract style.

Although Marin is best known for his watercolors, during the late 1920s he began working extensively in oils, producing such paintings as *Movement in Brown with Sun* (1928). Although he was one of the United States' leading modern artists, by the 1950s his small-scale paintings were being overshadowed by the sensational large-scale works of the abstract expressionists.

MARTINI Simone

SIMONE MARTINI BECAME AN OUTSTANDING PAINTER in the city of Siena in the first part of the 14th century, and developed a highly decorative and colorful style. He worked for some of the most important patrons of his day, and produced paintings of unusual realism for his time.

Life and work

Simone Martini (often referred to as Simone) was almost certainly a pupil of Duccio di Buoninsegna, and is regarded, with Duccio, as the most important painter of the Sienese school. His first known work is a huge fresco, the *Maestà*, commissioned for Siena town hall in 1315 (and reworked in 1321), which is comparable to Duccio's great *Maestà* (1311) in Siena Cathedral. It shows the Virgin enthroned surrounded by angels (or "in majesty," which is what *maestà* means in Italian).

Simone's next important work was a portrait of Saint Louis of Toulouse (1317), who had died in 1297 and recently been canonized. Louis had been heir to the throne of Naples, but had given up his claim to the throne in favor of his younger brother Robert. Louis then became a priest, and was later made a bishop for the diocese of Toulouse, but instead of living in the sumptuous bishop's palace, he chose to live in poverty. Simone was asked by Robert (Saint Louis's brother) to paint this picture. It shows the saintly Louis, large, enthroned, and richly robed, bestowing his crown on his brother to show that Robert not only had come by his power legitimately, but also that it was God-given.

Simone went on to paint many altarpieces and further frescos in Siena town hall, including a dramatic equestrian portrait of a soldier named Guidoriccio da Fogliano riding his elaborately harnessed horse through a barren landscape of fortified hilltop towns and the tents of an army encampment. He also worked in the famous church of Saint Francis of Assisi, where many famous artists, such as Cimabue and Giotto, had worked before him. There he did some notable paintings showing scenes from the life of Saint Martin (1312–17).

His best-known work is the *Annunciation* (1333), which he worked on in collaboration with his brother-in-law Lippo Memmi. It was common in those days for more than one painter to work on an individual picture, and there were always lots of assistants in a painter's workshop—young men and boys in training who would help, for example, to prepare the wooden panels for painting and to grind up the colors to make the paint.

Simone developed what was essentially a court art. His paintings, particularly those done on panel, sparkle with tooled gold leaf and fresh, vivid, brilliant colors that give the paintings a jewel-like quality, while the figures are refined, decorative, and elegant. On the one hand he produced works of traditional subject matter in a conventional way—for example, his religious panel paintings on wood featured extensive use of gold leaf, a very traditional way of executing backgrounds, halos, and so on. Even in his portrait of Saint Louis of Toulouse, he sticks to the traditional idea that

Human reaction

Simone Martini's *Annunciation* (1333) shows the moment when the Angel Gabriel appears to the Virgin Mary to announce that she will give birth to the Son of God. This message appears as text on the gold background in the scene.

In the context of the Gothic art of the period, Martini's figures are unusual in their sense of individuality and emotion. For example, the Virgin Mary cringes at Gabriel's message, drawing her robe across herself in a self-protective gesture. It is as if the painter has considered how it would actually feel to be visited by an angel and given this news.

There is also an unusual sense of realism in the work. The angel is shown as having just arrived—his cloak is still billowing out behind him—and both the vase of lilies in the background and the book Mary has been holding look convincingly real.

The figures have an extraordinary elegance, with their lithe and sinuous bodies clad in rich fabrics that loop, swirl, and ripple around them. This, together with Simone's vivid use of bright, jewel-like colors, make his works fine examples of the Gothic style.

Annunciation *1333. Tempera on panel. $72\frac{1}{2}$ x $82\frac{3}{4}$ in (184 x 210 cm). Galleria degli Uffizi, Florence.*

Data file

Full name: Simone Martini

Nationality: Italian

Style: Gothic

Dates: born c1284 in Siena, died 1344 in Avignon

Key works:

- *The Life of Saint Martin* 1312–17
- *Maestà* 1315 (reworked 1321)
- *Annunciation* 1333

Things to look for:

- frescos of religious subjects in Gothic style
- use of gold leaf and bright colors

Comparisons: Duccio di Buoninsegna, Giotto di Bondone, Fra Angelico

Glossary terms: altarpiece, fresco, Gothic, polyptych

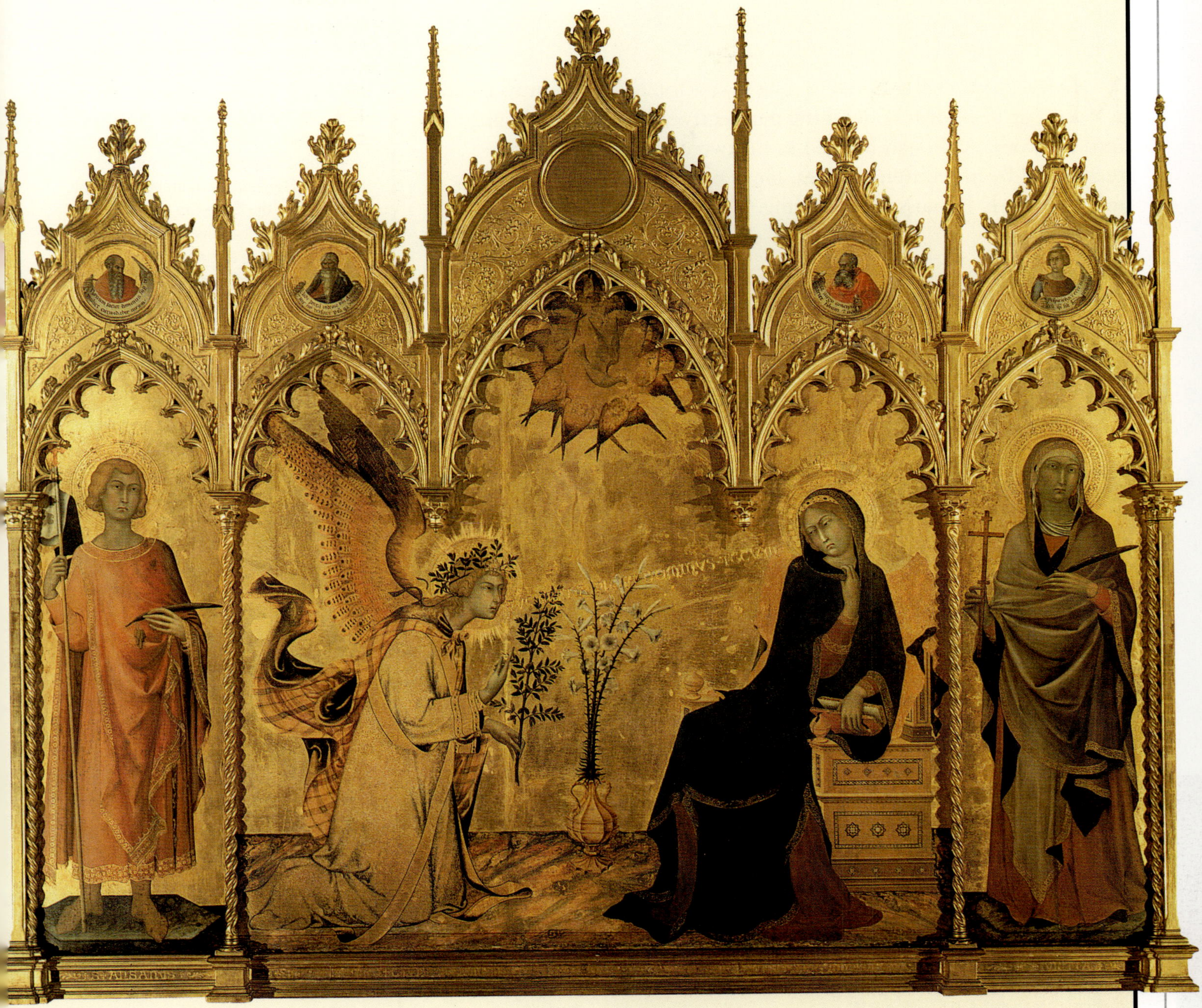

important people in a painting should be shown larger than unimportant ones —so Saint Louis, as a holy person, is depicted considerably larger than his brother, who was merely an earthly king. However, within these restrictions (which were probably largely due to his patron's wishes) his work, such as the *Annunciation*, showed moments of startling originality.

Toward the end of his life, in 1339, at the invitation of Pope Benedict XII, Simone settled in Avignon in France. He may have gone on official business and not as a painter at all, but while he was there he certainly produced some paintings (though these are largely lost). He was still in Avignon when he fell sick and died in 1344. Four years later, Europe was in turmoil from the plague (Black Death), which killed about a third of its population. The economic and social problems that resulted also meant that developments in painting were not followed up as quickly as they might otherwise have been. However, by the 15th century the sculptor and author Lorenzo Ghiberti wrote that the Sienese regarded Simone as their greatest painter.

MASACCIO

MASACCIO WAS A PAINTER OF GREAT ORIGINALITY who introduced many new ideas concerning perspective, anatomy, and light into his work. Although he died in his twenties, his talents were recognized by his contemporaries. He is now considered the great master of early Renaissance painting.

Life and work

The nickname Masaccio has been translated as "Big Tom," or "hulking Tom," indicating that the artist was probably a large man. The first records of Masaccio as a painter date from 1422, when he entered the guild in Florence; a 1429 tax return states that "he is said to have died in Rome" in 1428, so his working life was only of about six years' duration. Masaccio introduced so many innovations during that time, however, that he is regarded as one of the greatest painters of the 15th century.

Masaccio's first major work for which documentary evidence exists is a large polyptych painted in 1426 for the Carmelite church in Pisa. Unfortunately, this altarpiece was dismantled, probably in the 18th century, and most of it is now lost.

Although the painting was created using established techniques—the background of gold leaf, for example—and traditional subject matter—the Virgin enthroned with the baby Jesus in her lap, surrounded by saints and angels—it was the distinctive way in which Masaccio painted these things that set him apart from both his predecessors and his contemporaries.

Masaccio died—it is not known how—at the age of about 27, only two years after he painted this groundbreaking picture. During those two years he completed his famous fresco of *The Holy Trinity* (c1428) on the nave walls of the church of Santa Maria Novella in Florence. Again, the subject is traditional, but Masaccio placed the figures in a painted architectural setting. The perspective is so skillfully executed that, when you stand in front of the painting in the church, it looks as if there is another chapel opening up in the wall where the holy figures stand.

However, it was not just Masaccio's understanding of perspective that was new: he also introduced Roman-style architecture, such as classical columns and decoration, to his paintings. This must have seemed startlingly modern to Masaccio's contemporaries, who were used to the Gothic style that had dominated in the preceding centuries.

New ideas abounded in Masaccio's other great work from around this time, the frescos in the Brancacci Chapel in the church of Santa Maria del Carmine in Florence. Although several artists worked on the frescos simultaneously, it is generally agreed that the most competent and modern-looking ones are the work of Masaccio, notably *The Expulsion of Adam and Eve from Paradise* (1427) and *The Tribute Money* (1427).

Data file

Full name: Tommaso di Ser Giovanni (known as Masaccio)

Nationality: Italian

Style: early Renaissance

Dates: born 1401 in San Giovanni Valdarno (Arezzo), died 1428 in Rome

Key works:
- frescos in the Brancacci Chapel of Santa Maria del Carmine, Florence 1425–28
- polyptych for the Carmelite church in Pisa 1426
- *The Holy Trinity* fresco in Santa Maria Novella, Florence c1428

Things to look for:
- early use of perspective
- use of realistic human figures
- influence of ancient Roman remains

Comparisons: Giotto, Piero della Francesca, Donatello

Glossary terms: altarpiece, classical, fresco, gold leaf, Gothic, perspective, polyptych, Renaissance

Groundbreaking techniques

Although *The Virgin and Child* (1426) illustrated here is just a fragment of the original, it demonstrates all of the innovations introduced by Masaccio. It is the central and most important part of the polyptych for the Carmelite church in Pisa, Masaccio's first major work.

Compared to other paintings of the time, such as the *Santa Trinità Madonna* (c1260–80) by Cimabue, this picture was revolutionary in its realism. Masaccio's Virgin is a solid-looking person rather than an idealized figure. He has draped the blue fabric of her robe across her knees in a way that makes her legs seem to project toward us.

On her lap, the infant Christ is grasping the grapes his mother is holding with one hand, and with his other hand he is stuffing them into his mouth. His head is quite large, a realistic reflection of baby proportions, but was unusual in paintings at that time; babies were generally given the same proportions as adults. The Virgin's face is a strange color because the picture is damaged—what we can now see are the underlayers of paint; most of the top layers have gone.

The Virgin and Child are sitting on a throne inspired by ancient Roman remains—it is clearly made of stone or marble, is adorned with a number of paired classical columns, and has none of the more usual Gothic arches.

Both the throne and the figures seated on it are bathed in light coming from the top left of the painting. The shadows all fall the same way, one corner of the throne is lit and the other remains in shade, and the light falls on the baby, modeling his limbs to make him seem three-dimensional.

The light is also used to enhance the perspective of the painting, which is dramatically executed. Note, for example,

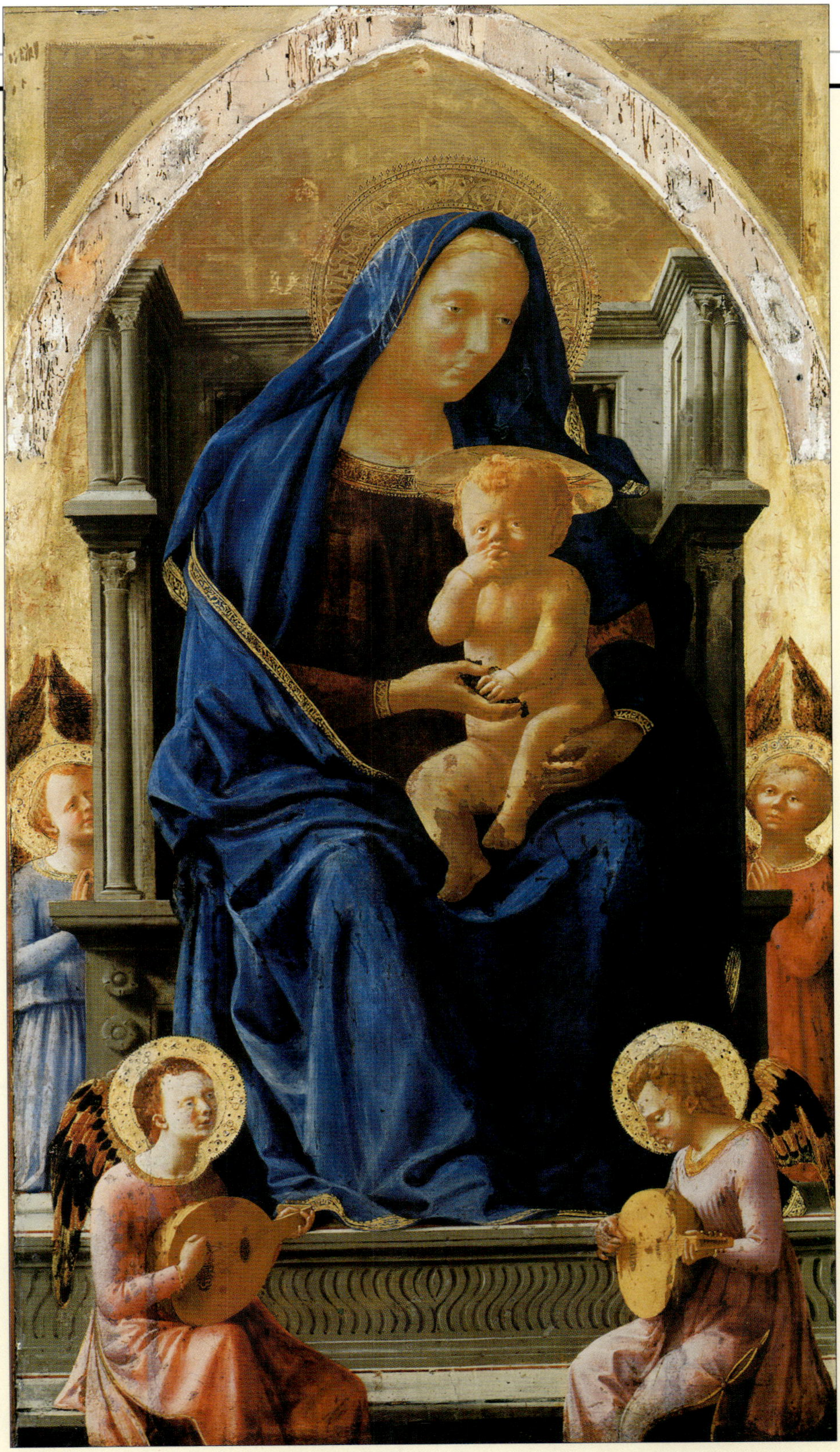

how Masaccio has skillfully shown the musical instruments at a difficult angle.

Perhaps the most spectacular example of perspective is Christ's halo, which, instead of being shown in the traditional manner as a circle behind the head (as it is with the Virgin), is shown above Christ's head and seen from the edge. No artist had done this before. Masaccio's work would inspire many later artists such as Fra Filippo Lippi, Piero della Francesca, Raphael, and Michelangelo Buonarroti.

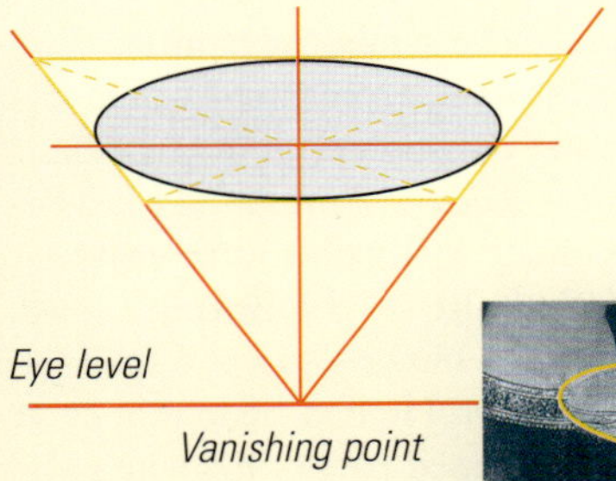

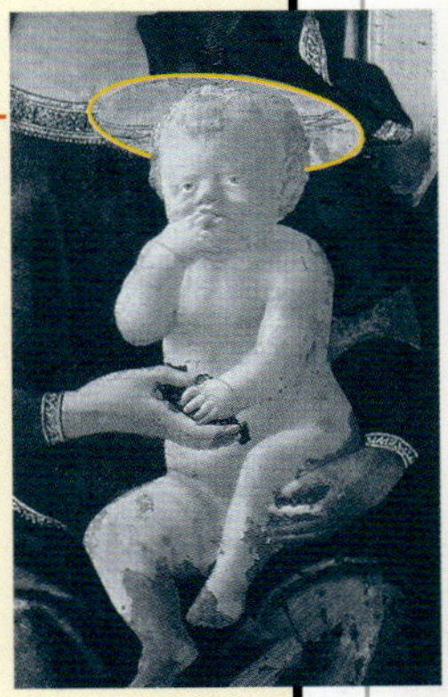

Circle in perspective *Masaccio took the unprecedented step of painting the halo on the infant Christ as an ellipse, the shape a circle takes on when seen from an angle. This can be achieved by first drawing a square in perspective (shown in yellow on the diagram) and then constructing the ellipse mathematically within the square. Masaccio left the other halos in the painting two-dimensional.*

The Virgin and Child (fragment of Pisa polyptych) *1426. Tempera on panel. 53¼ x 28¾ in (135.5 x 73 cm). National Gallery, London.*

In these frescos—and in all his works—Masaccio's figures are anatomically convincing and well-proportioned. He again uses perspective and a single light source to make them appear solid and three-dimensional. Masaccio's figures also seem to convey genuine human emotion, whereas in more traditional, religious pictures of the time, the figures appeared flat and unrealistic.

For his innovations in approach and subject matter, Masaccio stands at the forefront of the Renaissance in art, alongside the sculptor Donatello and the architect Brunelleschi.

MATISSE Henri

THROUGH COLOR, LINE, AND FORM, this visionary artist set out to achieve a pictorial expression of what he termed the "almost religious feeling I have toward life." In a career absorbed by this ambition, he created a vision of harmony, balance, and serenity.

Life and work

Matisse came late to art. It was only at the age of 20, recovering from an illness, that he began to paint, and found himself transported into what he called "a kind of paradise." In 1892 he gave up law clerking to study painting in Paris, where he attracted the attention of the symbolist painter Gustave Moreau, an inspired teacher.

Among the sources of inspiration that appear to have stimulated Matisse to experiment with color were visits to Corsica, Belle-Ile on the Brittany coast, and London, where he saw the work of J. M. W. Turner. He had little money at this time, but used part of his wife's dowry to purchase paintings, including a small picture of bathers by Paul Cézanne. In the early 1900s Matisse looked to Auguste Rodin and sculpture for rhythm, expressive strength, and power in the body; to Cézanne for color and structure; and to Vincent Van Gogh for expressive power in oil paint and for draftsmanship.

The art of Matisse is marked by a deep affinity with painters of the past, such as Jean-Baptiste-Siméon Chardin, Jean Auguste Dominique Ingres, and Eugène Delacroix. Also deeply important to him were the decorative values he saw in the art and artifacts of Africa and the Islamic countries.

By 1901 he was working in a modified pointillist style in the south of France, with Georges Seurat's friend Paul Signac. He spent the summer of 1905 at Coullioure with André Derain, and, with Maurice de Vlaminck, they became identified with fauvism.

Matisse set out his ideas in *Notes of a Painter* (1908), after his painting *The Joy of Living* (1905–06) had made him the leader of the avant-garde. By 1908, however, this title had already been ceded to Pablo Picasso, the leading innovator of cubism. The rivalry instigated at this time remained the driving force of their relationship.

Matisse followed his art with tenacity and vision through drawing, printmaking, and sculpture. Visits to North Africa in 1910–11 and 1913 had a profound and lasting impact upon him. Together with the example of the radical cubist canvases of Picasso and Georges Braques, they stimulated him to create extraordinarily diverse and challenging works through the years of World War I.

In 1917 Matisse settled in the south of France and painted beautiful women in luxurious hotel interiors. These works have an opulent, languorous splendor, but to many his art had lost its direction and ambition. After traveling to the United States and, following in Gauguin's footsteps, spending three months in Tahiti, he began once more to work on large-scale decorative compositions, producing two further versions of *The Dance*.

From 1943 he lived in Vence, near Nice, where he began to work on *papiers découpés*—arrangements of shapes cut from colored paper and stuck down. "Cutting directly into color reminds me of the direct carving of the sculptor," he said.

Matisse's design of the Dominican chapel at Vence brought together the various aspects of his art into one harmonic structure—he designed the building and decoration single-handedly, working with simple black line drawings on white ceramic tiles. His stained-glass windows and brilliantly patterned church vestments allowed him to achieve his lifelong ambition—to integrate color, space, and movement into a united whole.

Data file

Full name: Henri Emile Benoît Matisse

Nationality: French

Style: fauvism, expressionism

Dates: born 1869 in Cateau-Cambrésis (now Le Cateau), died 1954 in Vence

Key works:

The Joy of Living 1905–06

The Dinner Table (Harmony in Red) 1908

Nasturtiums and "The Dance I" 1912

The Open Window 1914

Pink Nude 1936

The Chapel at Vence late 1940s

Things to look for:

- simplified form, line, and color (from about 1910)
- emphasis on harmony and balance

Comparisons: Paul Cézanne, Paul Gauguin, Pierre Bonnard, Pablo Picasso, Max Beckmann

Glossary terms: cubism, fauvism, *papiers découpés*, pointillism

The Dinner Table (Harmony in Red) *1908. Oil on canvas. 71 x 97 in (180 x 246 cm). Hermitage Museum, St Petersburg.*

Construction by colored surfaces

In 1929 Matisse summarized his artistic program as "construction by colored surfaces. Search for intensity of color, subject matter being unimportant. Reaction against diffusion of local tone in light. Light is not suppressed, but expressed by a harmony of intensely colored surfaces."

From the very beginning of his career, Matisse's art had been governed by these principles, which can be seen in his 1908 painting, *The Dinner Table (Harmony in Red)*. A reworking of a subject he painted with great success as a student in Gustave Moreau's studio, this canvas displays the

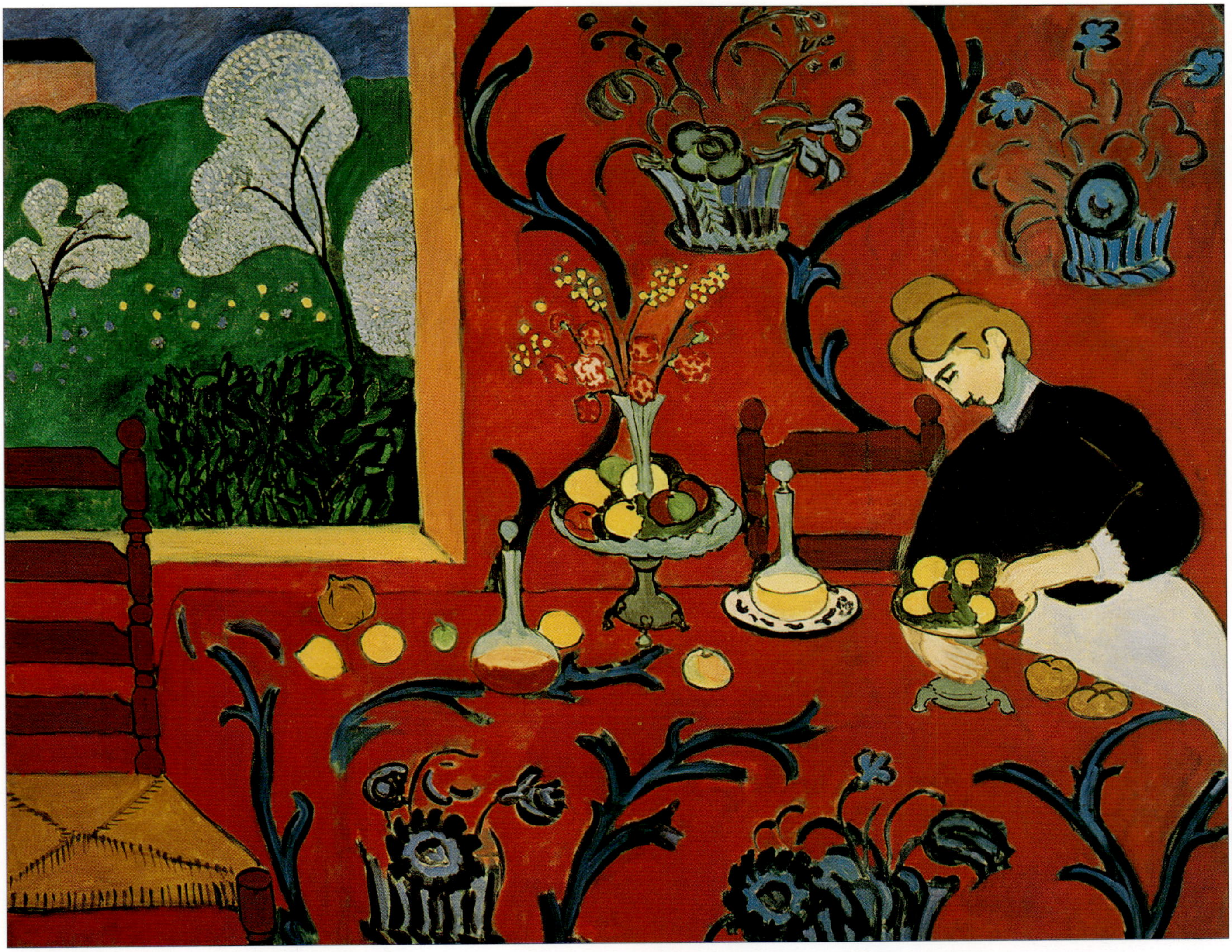

vibrant balance of line, form, and color that is typical of his output.

Like so much of Matisse's work, the final form of the painting gave an impression of spontaneity and simplicity, but was the result of arduous working and reworking. At a late stage in its production, Matisse—probably influenced by Edgar Degas' picture *Combing the Hair* (c1896), which Matisse then owned, and which is characterized by strong red coloring—completely repainted the background color of *The Dinner Table.*

Matisse's paintings make no direct reference to the world beyond his artistic concerns; both world wars go unnoticed in his work, unless the ominous black night in *The Open Window* (1914) can be interpreted as a reference to the dark years of war ahead. His art is narrow in its subject matter in order to express the almost religious reverence that Matisse felt for the female body.

One of the most powerful aspects of Matisse's art is his channeling of his love for the alternating physical energy and peacefulness of the female form into the abstract *papiers découpés*, or paper cut-outs, that he produced during his last years. The spirit of these paper cut-outs can be seen in his earlier painting *Nasturtiums and "The Dance I"* (1912), which depicts the enclosed world of the artist's studio.

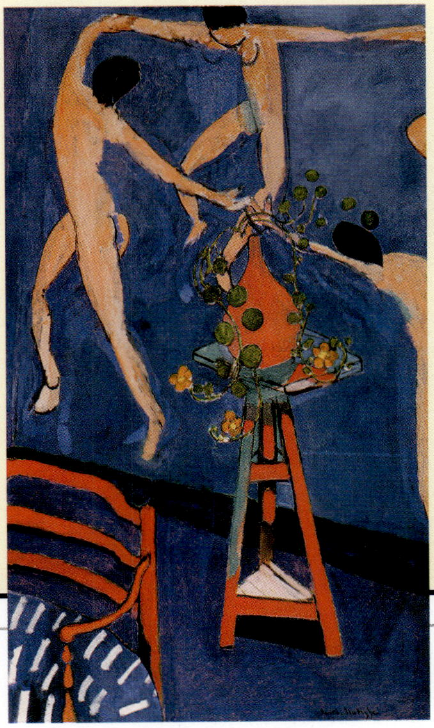

Nasturtiums and "The Dance I" *1912. Oil on canvas. 75 x 45 in (190.5 x 114 cm). Pushkin Museum, Moscow.*

MEMLING Hans

HANS MEMLING WAS THE INHERITOR of Rogier Van der Weyden's mantle as the leading Netherlandish painter of the mid-15th century. He extended the scale and scope of his teacher's work, painting poignant religious pictures and serene portraits.

Life and work

Hans Memling was born in the German town of Seligenstadt, near Frankfurt, but artistically his influence was almost entirely from the Netherlandish tradition. It is thought that he was apprenticed to the workshop of Rogier Van der Weyden in Brussels, and that, following Rogier's death in 1464, Memling left for the town of Bruges. At the time, Bruges was a significant port and a key point for various trading routes running between England, Germany, France, Spain, and Italy. As merchants came to the town to trade in cloth, metalwork, and other decorative arts, paintings of the Netherlandish tradition were also bought and sold, and lucrative commissions were undertaken. Memling's work was particularly prized, and his paintings became sought after throughout Europe, especially in Italy.

It was an important Italian—Angelo Tani, an employee of the Medici bank—who gave Memling one of his first commissions in Bruges: the *Triptych with the Last Judgment* (1467–71). The painting was destined for a new chapel in Florence dedicated to Saint Michael, but the continual movement of wealth and power during this period of vigorous international trade provided treacherous times. En route to Florence, the ship carrying the painting was caught up in a dispute between the trading centers of England and Poland. It was attacked by a Polish vessel, and the booty, including Memling's *Last Judgment*, was taken off to the Polish town of Gdansk.

The Italian connection with the Medici bank provided a rich flow of commissions for Memling. Through Tani's successor in Bruges, Tommaso Portinari, Memling was paid to paint more works, including a pair of portraits of the banker and his wife, Maria Baroncelli, in about 1470. The bank eventually withdrew its Bruges operation in 1480, but by then Memling had become a member of a religious association known as the Confraternity of Our Lady of the Snow. The members of this pious organization included the wealthiest citizens of the region as well as influential members of the clergy. The confraternity would have provided Memling with important connections for commissions.

Memling prospered with the good fortunes of Bruges until the 1480s, when the ruler of the region, Charles

Full name: Hans Memling (or Memlinc)
Nationality: Netherlandish
Style: Netherlandish/early Renaissance
Dates: born c1435 in Seligenstadt, Germany, died 1494 in Bruges
Key works:
- *Triptych with the Last Judgment* 1467–71
- *Portrait of an Elderly Couple* c1470–72
- *Tommaso Portinari and his wife* (pair of portraits hung either side of a central panel) c1470
- *The Virgin and Child with Saints and Donors* (the John Donne triptych) 1479–80
- *Portrait of a Young Woman* 1480
- *Saint Ursula Shrine* c1480s
- *Triptych with the Virgin and Child Enthroned* c1480–88
- *Virgin and Child with Two Angels Playing Music* c1490–1500

Things to look for:
- serene expressions in his portraiture
- a completeness of composition
- subtlety in flesh tones
- richness of hue in clothing

Comparisons: Rogier Van der Weyden, Jan Van Eyck, Robert Campin, Dieric Bouts, Hugo Van der Goes, Michel Sittow
Glossary terms: Netherlandish school

Beyond time and place

Unlike artists of the previous generation such as Jan Van Eyck and Robert Campin, Memling seems to have been less concerned with everyday reality. He did not make use of the townscape that surrounded him, as Campin had done; nor did he concentrate his efforts on the precise details of an interior, as Jan Van Eyck had done with his painting *The Arnolfini Marriage* (1434). More in an Italian style, Memling drew upon imaginary landscapes in which to set his works, and this is particularly true of the religious paintings. Memling wanted, with each painting, to achieve a unified image, where detail would be less important than overall impact. With Memling's work, there is a sense that the physical world—as important as it clearly is to his work—means less to him than the world of the imagination and spirit.

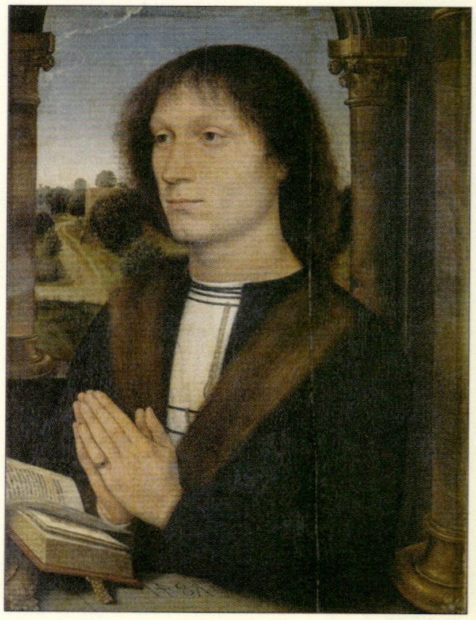

Tommaso Portinari *(one of a pair) c1470. Oil on panel. 17½ x 13 in (44.5 x 33 cm). Galleria degli Uffizi, Florence.*

In his portraits, any trace of facial expression is very slight, and character is represented almost entirely by attention to the qualities of the face. It is the soul in its most solemn sense that Memling sought to convey, rather than the emotional character. In the portraits of Tommaso Portinari and Maria Baroncelli (twin portraits thought originally to have hung either side of a central panel), the sitters lightly clasp their hands in prayer, their faces a picture of serene devotion. In other works, such as *Portrait of an Elderly Couple* (c1470–72), the sitters' heavy eyelids suggest that a quiet tiredness has descended upon them. In all such works, in which Memling concentrates closely on the human condition, a slight sense of sadness or melancholy is invoked.

In many of Memling's paintings there are striking similarities with the work of Rogier Van der Weyden (under whom he studied). This can be seen particularly in the composure of the figures and modeling of faces, though in Memling's case their expressions are almost blank, as if they are hiding emotion.

His paintings—particularly the portraits—seem to absorb our gaze. Only in a few paintings, such as *Christ Giving His Blessing* (two versions, 1478 and 1481) and *Portrait of a Man with a Roman Coin* (c1480–90), do the eyes stare back at us, returning and confronting our gaze. Elsewhere, the eyes look to the side and are frequently downcast, the solemn countenance of the sitters absorbing our inspection passively.

With his religious works, Memling frequently returned to the theme of the Virgin and Child. The composition used in *Virgin and Child with Two Angels Playing Music* (c1490–1500) is one that he used on at least three occasions. Again, the composition is resolved to a point where all action seems to have ceased; the atmosphere of the painting is both stately and sedate. Beyond the symmetrically arranged group, the background is of a timeless landscape, slightly paler and more vaguely defined than the foreground, and denying a sense of place.

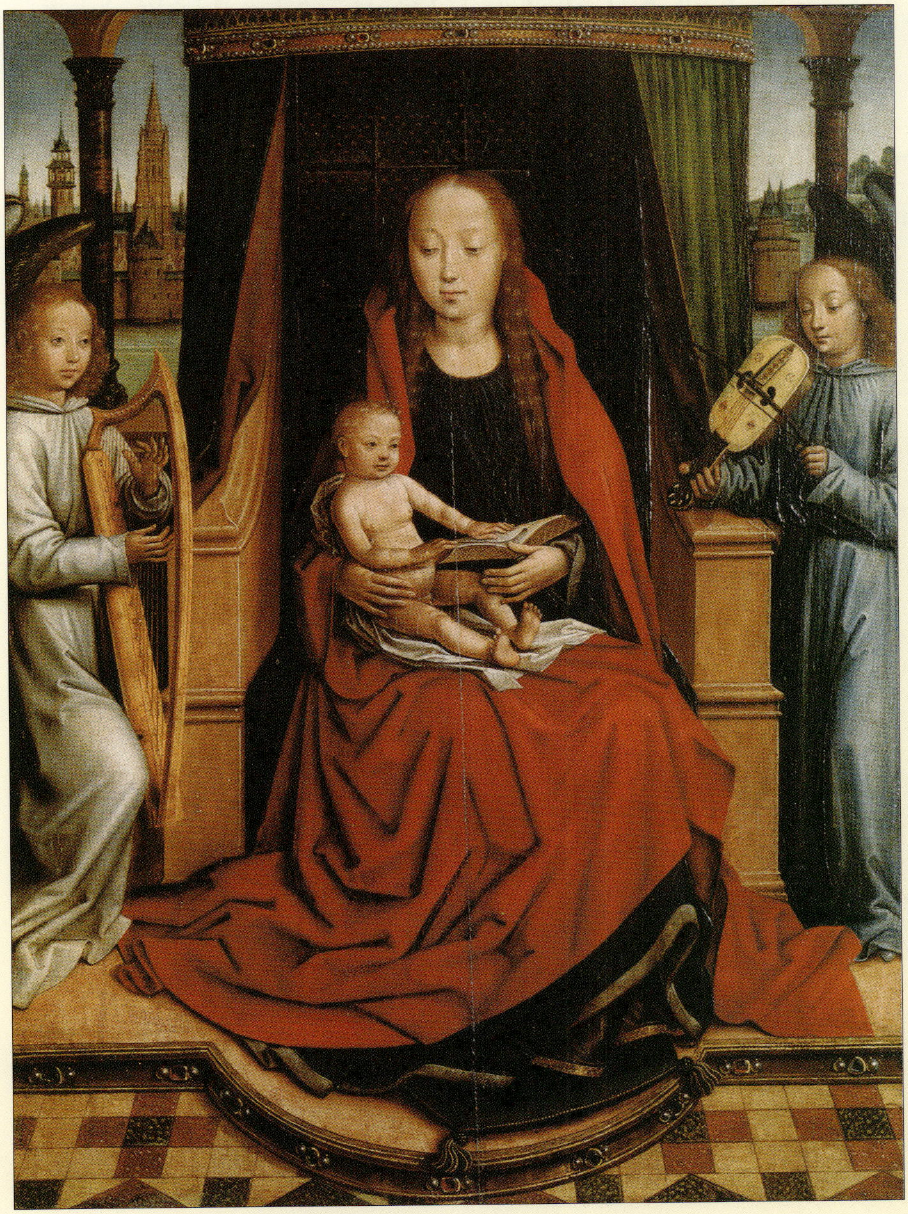

Virgin and Child with Two Angels Playing Music *c1490–1500. 32 x 17 in (59 x 44 cm). Oil on panel. Galleria e Museo Estense, Modena.*

the Bold, was killed in a battle with the Swiss. Revolts within the trading towns ensued as merchants and craftspeople fought for greater control over their destinies. Ultimately, however, this served only to alienate the town from other centers of trade, and Bruges then fell into a downward spiral, both economically and culturally. Surprisingly, these dramatic events did not seem to be reflected in Memling's output or style.

Throughout the 1480s Memling worked on many portraits and religious paintings, often returning to the theme of the Virgin and Child. He continued to paint, producing ambitious works until his death in 1494.

MICHELANGELO BUONARROTI

SCULPTOR, ARCHITECT, AND PAINTER, Michelangelo was one of the most influential artists of the Renaissance. He is chiefly remembered for his frescos on the altar wall and ceiling of the Sistine Chapel, which represent some of the greatest feats of painting ever undertaken.

Life and work

Michelangelo once described himself as he thought others regarded him: "strange and obsessed," a melancholic only occasionally able to escape from the weight of responsibility that his art imposed. His admirers saw in his work a disturbing conflict of human emotions. Many tried to emulate his muscular, figurative style, but few, if any, caught his brooding psychological depth.

He was the son of an impoverished nobleman; in later life, when his fame as an artist was without equal, he fostered the impression that he had been largely self-taught. However, he did receive something of the education usual for artists, as the apprentice, briefly, to the painter Domenico Ghirlandaio in 1488. He was also to learn from the example of his older contemporary Leonardo da Vinci. These two artists, who did so much to establish the heroic figurative style associated with the High Renaissance, seem to have approached each new work as if it were a problem to be solved. Consequently, Michelangelo often broke away from the conventions of tradition. However, from surviving drawings and other sources, we know he valued the qualities of artists of earlier times, such as Giotto di Bondone, Masaccio, and Donatello.

Strong-willed and gifted, Michelangelo soon attracted the attention of Lorenzo de' Medici, head of the Florentine banking family. Lorenzo was a passionate enthusiast of humanist culture and the study of antiquity. The young Michelangelo was given access to his collection of Roman sculptures, and from the age of 15 he lived within the Medici household. He thus absorbed an early understanding of classical ideas, and was encouraged by the Latin scholar and poet, Angelo Poliziano. Michelangelo's earliest known sculpture, a carved relief depicting the mythical battle between Greeks and centaurs, reflects this literary and artistic atmosphere. It also indicates the main aspects of his future artistic interests, being entirely composed of nude, mainly male figures in a dynamic composition involving a rich variety of interrelated poses.

Michelangelo was one of the first artists to be allowed a much greater freedom in the choice and interpretation of his commissions. Nevertheless, he frequently suffered from the ambitions of powerful patrons keen to have their names commemorated by him. In 1505, for example, he was summoned to Rome by Pope Julius II to provide him with a monumental tomb featuring about 40 large sculpted figures. The project, like so many of Michelangelo's endeavors, was never finished, and was to cause him much anxiety for years to come.

Subsequent popes also imposed their own demands on him. In the meantime, Pope Julius II decided that Michelangelo should devote his efforts to the painting of the huge ceiling of the Sistine Chapel in the pope's headquarters, the Vatican. "I am no painter," Michelangelo complained, but in vain. He was not satisfied with his work on the project: "I am here, wasting my time, of which I have little enough, with these paintings," he wrote. Nevertheless, the ceiling won him recognition, at the age of 37, as the greatest artist of his day.

In the decades that followed, Michelangelo was often employed on projects of a similarly dramatic scale. The Catholic Church was feeling under threat from the spreading effects of the Protestant Reformation, and used the arts to emphasize its abiding power. Michelangelo made impressive contributions to the symbolic restructuring of the city of Rome, particularly in his designs for the dome of the basilica of Saint Peter's. The Capitol in Washington and Saint Paul's Cathedral in London are echoes of his achievement as an architect. As a painter and sculptor, his influence on mannerist, baroque, and Romantic artists was also profound. When he died in 1564, he was honored with a funeral far grander than any normally staged for an artist.

Data file

Full name: Michelangelo di Lodovico Buonarroti Simoni

Nationality: Italian

Style: High Renaissance

Dates: born 1475 in Caprese, died 1564 in Rome

Key works:

- *Pietà* 1497–1500
- *David* 1501–04
- ceiling of the Sistine Chapel (including *The Creation of Adam*) 1508–12
- tomb sculpture of the Medici Chapel, San Lorenzo, Florence 1519–33
- *The Last Judgment* altar wall of the Sistine Chapel 1536–41
- design for the dome of the basilica of Saint Peter's, Rome 1546–64

Things to look for:

- heroic scale of figures and paintings
- muscular, figurative style
- a sense of troubled or turbulent emotion

Comparisons: Giotto di Bondone, Masaccio, Leonardo da Vinci, Raphael, Tintoretto, Gianlorenzo Bernini, Auguste Rodin

Glossary terms: fresco, High Renaissance

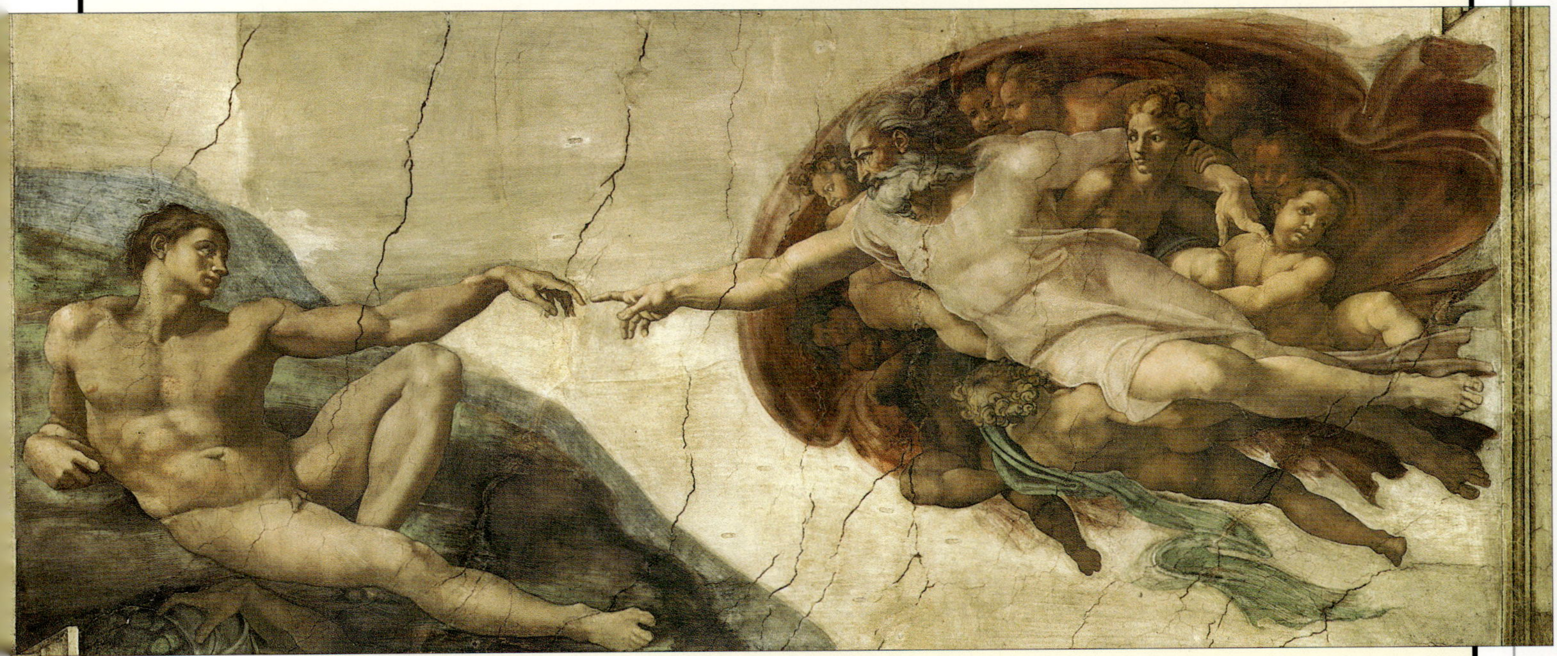

Renaissance masterpieces

Michelangelo's *David* (1501–04) presented him with particular problems because the 14-foot block of marble had already been worked by other hands for an earlier commission. The slenderness of the figure in relation to the largeness of the head and the hands has been attributed to the subject: the youthful stature of the boy David about to engage in combat with the giant Goliath. But Michelangelo also had to calculate a figure to fit the material he had been given. The body and its carefully balanced posture are indications of how much he had absorbed from his study of anatomy and antique sculpture, but the face, with its deeply furrowed brow and tense expression, introduces a dramatic psychological dimension rare in classical art.

Many of Michelangelo's sculptures are, for various reasons, unfinished. They give us a special insight into his eventual method of working into the block from the frontal plane of the figure only. He began to conceive of the idea of the sculpture as existing somehow simultaneously in the artist's mind and within the marble block. Michelangelo's friend and biographer, Giorgio Vasari, famously described his approach: it was as if the figure were gradually emerging fully formed from a vessel of water, some parts smoothly finished, others waiting for the artist's final touch.

Principally a sculptor, Michelangelo's expertise in the difficult practice of painting in true fresco was limited, and the task of painting the Sistine Chapel was enormous. He made about 300 preliminary drawings for the scheme, which were then enlarged and transferred to the ceiling. He worked on a high scaffold, painting awkwardly in an unfamiliar medium above his head. (It was said that he spent so long in this position that afterward he had to tilt his head back in order to see clearly.) The figurative style he developed during the 10-year process was immediately recognized, like the task itself, as superhuman.

The Creation of Adam *(detail from the Sistine Chapel) 1508–12. Ceiling fresco. The Sistine Chapel, the Vatican, Rome.*

The Creation of Adam (1508–12) conveys an idea of the mystery of existence, as the strong but languid body of the first man is brought to life by contact with the touch of divine energy. Here Michelangelo's background in sculpture was evident, as was the influence of classical art. The image became one of the most famous in Western art, particularly, the detail of God's and Adam's fingers, outstretched and nearly touching. It has become a metaphor for the transfer of physical and spiritual energy, and has overtones of an almost electrical magnetism.

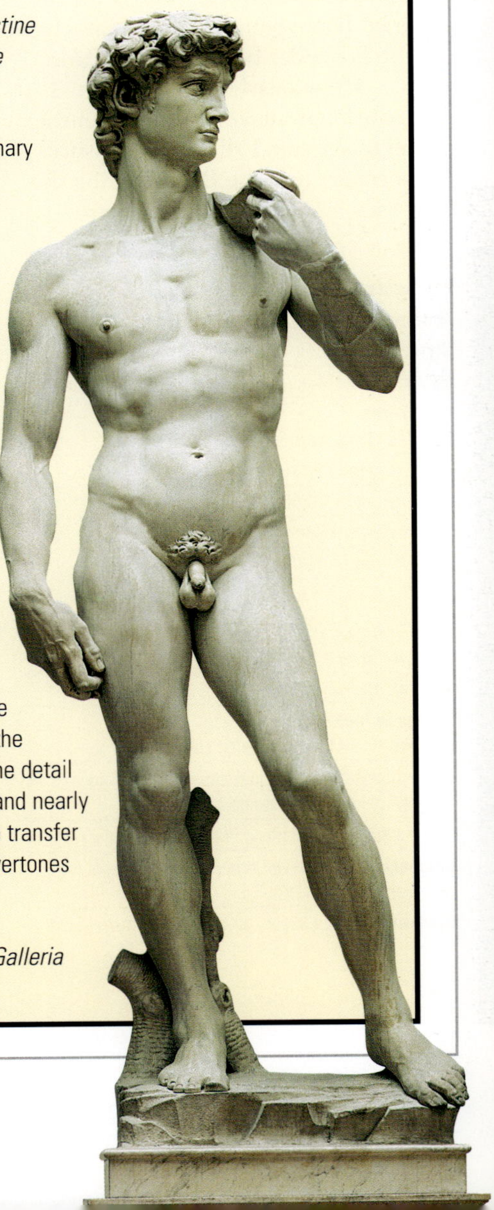

David *1501–04. Marble. 170 in (434 cm). Galleria dell'Accademia, Florence.*

MILLET Jean-François

JEAN-FRANÇOIS MILLET WAS A REALIST PAINTER who specialized in atmospheric figure paintings and landscapes of rural French life. His peasant paintings are bathed in a golden light, granting their humble subjects an epic grandeur. Millet has been interpreted as a painter of hardship, as well as of timeless religious and natural cycles.

Life and work

Jean-François Millet, the son of affluent peasants, was born in Gruchy, on the Normandy coast in France. As a young man he divided his time between studying with a local portrait painter and helping on his family's farm. Then, in 1836, the city of Cherbourg gave him a scholarship to study with the great figure painter Paul Delaroche at the Ecole des Beaux-Arts in Paris.

Millet's early works portrayed traditional subjects drawn from the mythology and allegory of classical antiquity and the Bible. During the 1840s he moved back and forth between Paris and Cherbourg, occasionally receiving portrait commissions. From 1839 he tried to have his paintings and pastels accepted by the Paris Salon, the annual, state-sponsored exhibition at which he hoped that potential patrons might see and purchase his work.

Millet then became friendly with a circle called the Barbizon painters, landscape artists who painted near the village of Barbizon on the outskirts of the Fontainebleau forest. Among others, the artists Constant Troyon, Narcisse Virgile Diaz de la Peña, and Théodore Rousseau were committed to painting French landscapes in changing weather conditions rather than the classical allegories and Italianate landscapes that were most popular with the Salon. Their small, thickly painted forest and river scenes appealed to many middle-class Parisians, who missed the countryside and could now afford to purchase paintings of it.

At around this time, too, Millet met Alfred Sensier, a government employee who would become his most loyal patron and agent, providing him with materials and payment in return for paintings, which Sensier then encouraged other collectors to buy.

In 1848 France was swept by revolution, and a republic was declared. Millet had now turned to rustic subjects as his inspiration, and in the same year he exhibited a peasant scene, *The Winnower*, at the Salon. Such subject matter was seen as revolutionary, and Millet attracted much criticism. He moved to Barbizon in 1849, where he would stay for the rest of his life, occasionally returning to Gruchy.

Data file

Full name: Jean-François Millet

Nationality: French

Style: realism

Dates: born 1814 in Gruchy, died 1875 in Barbizon

Key works:
- *The Winnower* 1848
- *Going to Work* 1850
- *The Sower* c1850
- *Harvesters Resting* 1851–53
- *The Angelus* 1855–57
- *The Gleaners* 1857
- *Woman Pasturing Her Cow* 1858
- *Man With a Hoe* 1860–62
- *Fall: the Haystacks* 1868–74

Things to look for:
- peasant life as a realist subject
- palette of earth tones coupled with bold contrasts of light and dark
- biblical associations in titles and imagery

Comparisons: Gustave Courbet, Pieter Bruegel the Elder, Camille Corot

Glossary terms: allegory, antiquity, patronage, Salon

Somber earth tones and bold contours

The Sower (c1850) captures the epic naturalism of Millet's peasant painting. He painted and drew several versions of this theme, which Vincent Van Gogh later copied. Millet often drew upon biblical narratives with which to grant an epic quality to the world around him. The title of this painting invokes the biblical parable in which the sower casts his seeds on different grounds: rocks, on which they cannot flourish; open land, on which birds will eat them; and fertile earth, in which they will grow. The fertile ground symbolizes the true heart that can hear and heed the word of God.

Although Millet's title alone refers to this parable, he portrays it through the image of a monumental male peasant sowing a field, with another peasant, who has harnessed a colossal ox, plowing furrows in the distance. In this painting Millet presents the peasantry and countryside as being part of a timeless rural world, as well as a particularly modern, French experience. The figure's shaded eyes, crude mouth, sweeping throwing gesture, and sinewy strength are slightly threatening. Millet is thus inviting us to think about the life of the peasant, who, by working the land, is closest to the cycles of nature and traditional life. Yet he also reminds us that the forces of nature are hugely powerful, as well as nurturing.

The painting is executed in Millet's typical manner, in somber earth tones and with bold contours and minimal detail. His subjects are simultaneously ordinary and heroic, poor farm laborers who symbolize both dignity and the human condition.

By the 1850s Millet had established an international reputation, receiving commissions from the United States and Britain, and exhibiting in both countries. His success enabled him to collect prints and drawings by painters whom he admired, such as Eugène Delacroix and the 16th- and 17th-century Dutch masters Pieter Bruegel the Elder and Rembrandt. The humble

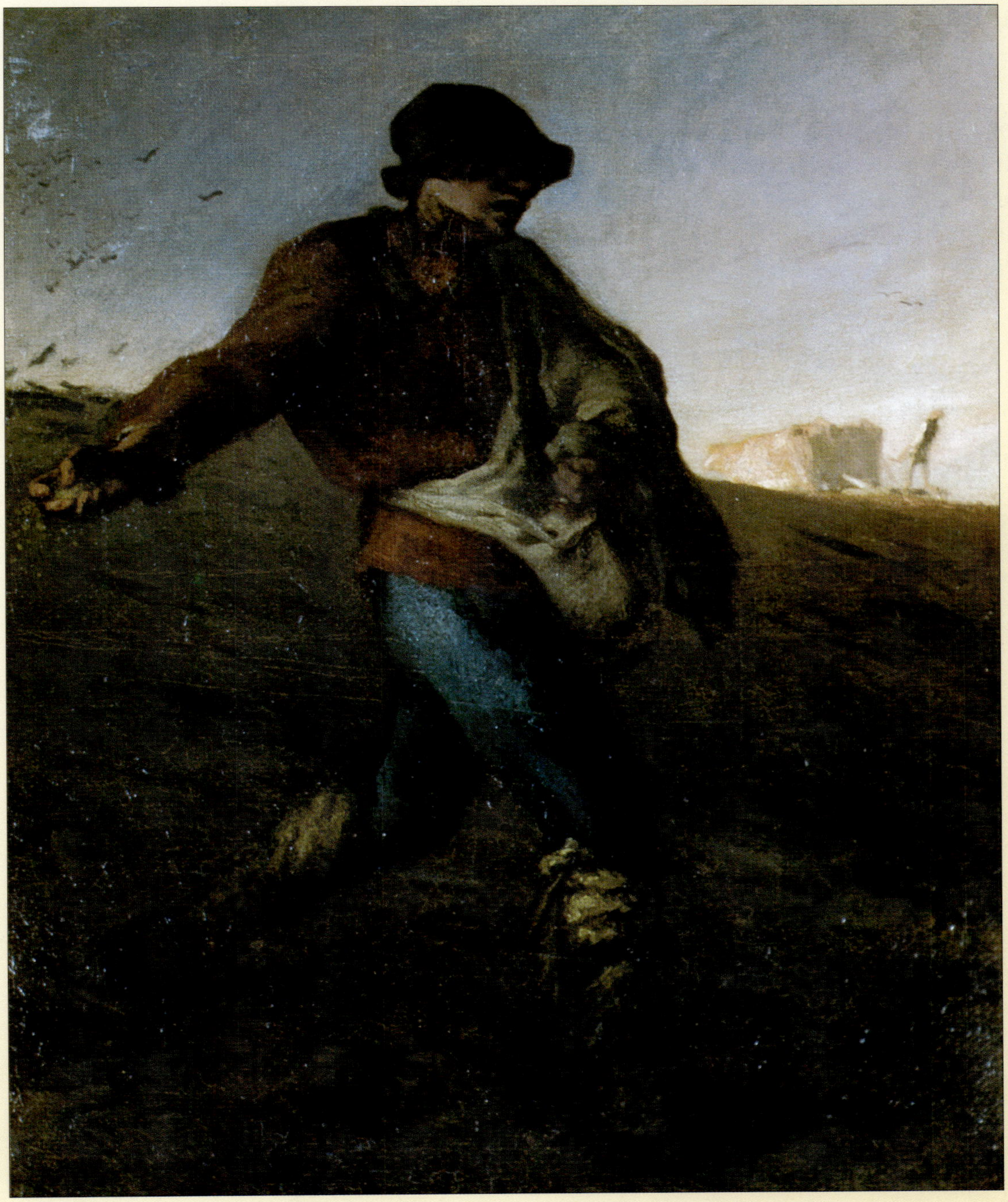

The Sower *c1850.*
Oil on canvas.
40 x 32½ in
(101.5 x 82.5 cm).
Museum of Fine Arts,
Boston, MA.

subjects and detailed realism of these artists' works were great inspirations for Millet's peasant paintings. He was also an avid collector of photography (then a new medium) and asked his friends to give him photographs of artworks that they had seen on their travels, as well as unposed images of local people.

Millet's sympathy with the hard working life that was endured by most peasants has often led to his work being compared with that of Gustave Courbet. Unlike Courbet, however, Millet rejected the revolutionary politics of the Paris Commune of 1870, and fled to his native Normandy when France was defeated in the Franco–Prussian War. (He sent his paintings to the dealer Durand-Ruel, who sold them in England.)

Millet's first wife, Pauline-Virginie Ono, died of consumption three years after their marriage in 1841. He had nine children (six daughters and three sons) with his common-law wife, Catherine Lemaire, whom he married on his deathbed in 1875. He was buried in the cemetery at Chailly, next to his friend and fellow Barbizon painter Théodore Rousseau.

MIRÓ Joan

Although Miró did not consider himself to be a member of the surrealist movement, he was nevertheless a surrealist at heart. In his paintings, prints, and sculpture, he drew upon the subterranean realm of his personality to create works that moved between abstraction and a rudimentary—some would say primitivist—style.

Life and work

Joan Miró was born in Barcelona into a family with a strong craft tradition—he was the son of a goldsmith and grandson of a blacksmith and carpenter. As a young man, Miró studied at the School of Fine Art in Barcelona, combining art with business studies. In 1911 he contracted typhoid fever and had a nervous breakdown.

When he continued his studies, following a spell of convalescence in the Spanish countryside, Miró concentrated solely on art. During and immediately following his student days, he worked in a style that he described as fauvist because of the expressive rather than representational use of color. But his technique was also clearly influenced by Paul Cézanne and the cubist style of fellow Spanish artists Juan Gris and Pablo Picasso (who was also a friend).

Miró's subject matter was not particularly inspired at this time. He concentrated mostly on portraits and academic nude compositions. However, from a very early age Miró enjoyed sketching in the countryside, and the open landscape offered great scope for his vivid imagination. His works from around 1918, such as *House with Palm Tree*—with its simplified arrangement of nature, allowing every element its own separate space—gave some idea of the direction in which the artist was now heading.

Miró's style continued to evolve with more crisply delineated forms, as in *The Farm* (1921–22), a painting that he worked on in Barcelona and in his new wintertime home of Paris. The following year he began a work that took him to the border of representational landscape painting and complete abstraction. In *The Tilled Earth* (1923–24) there is a mix of highly stylized representations of animals, ploughed fields, and invented shapes that do not bear any relation to the natural world.

Landscape became an increasingly imaginative realm for Miró, as the subject of his paintings crossed from the natural into the psychological world. He signed the surrealist manifesto in 1924; the attempt to free the mind from logic and reason that is associated with surrealism is reflected in his paintings from then on. The sinuous objects and images in paintings such as *Maternity* (1924) seem less of the real, physical world and more the imaginary creatures of dreams, nightmares, or of a fevered mind. Indeed, Miró said that the collection of insectlike forms and fishlike fantasies that make up *Harlequin's Carnival* (1924–25) was the result of "hallucinations brought on by hunger."

Miró was influenced by the ideas and poetry of surrealism. In the late 1920s, he began a cycle of "dream paintings," which were loose and freely formed works. Some incorporated text into the compositions, as in *This Is the Color of My Dreams* (1925). Others, such as *Head of Catalan Peasant IV* (1925), were practically free of compositional structure, concentrating on color and spontaneous marks. Despite the surrealist nature of these paintings, the primitivism and playfulness of Miró's work set him apart from other artists in the movement.

During World War II, Miró returned to Spain to avoid the German invasion. From then on he lived mainly in Majorca. There he worked on some of his most intense paintings: the *Constellation* series (1940–43).

From the late 1940s Miró began to take commissions for murals and other public works in Europe and the United States, including ceramic murals for the Unesco building in Paris. His reputation grew steadily with his continuous output in other fields, which included printmaking, ceramics, and sculpture.

Miró continued to experiment with style and technique into old age, and some of his later works are among his most expressive.

Data file

Full name: Joan Miró

Nationality: Spanish

Style: surrealism

Dates: born 1893 in Barcelona, died 1983 in Majorca

Key works:
- *The Farm* 1921–22
- *The Tilled Earth* 1923–24
- *Maternity* 1924
- *Harlequin's Carnival* 1924–25
- *This Is the Color of My Dreams* 1925
- *Composition* c1933
- *Constellation* series 1940–43
- *Painting (Personage and Moon)* 1950
- *Wall of the Sun* and *Wall of the Moon* (ceramic murals for the Unesco building in Paris) 1958
- *Man and Woman* 1962

Things to look for:
- subtle color variation
- repetition of motifs such as stars, crescent moon, and heavily outlined circular shapes
- simple, primitive, or cartoonlike figuration
- undercurrent of sexual imagery

Comparisons: Pablo Picasso, Wassily Kandinsky, Jean Arp, Salvador Dalí, Henry Moore, Clyfford Still, Willem de Kooning, Jackson Pollock, Robert Motherwell

Glossary terms: abstract expressionism, academic art, automatism, cubism, fauvism, motif, mural, primitivism, surrealism

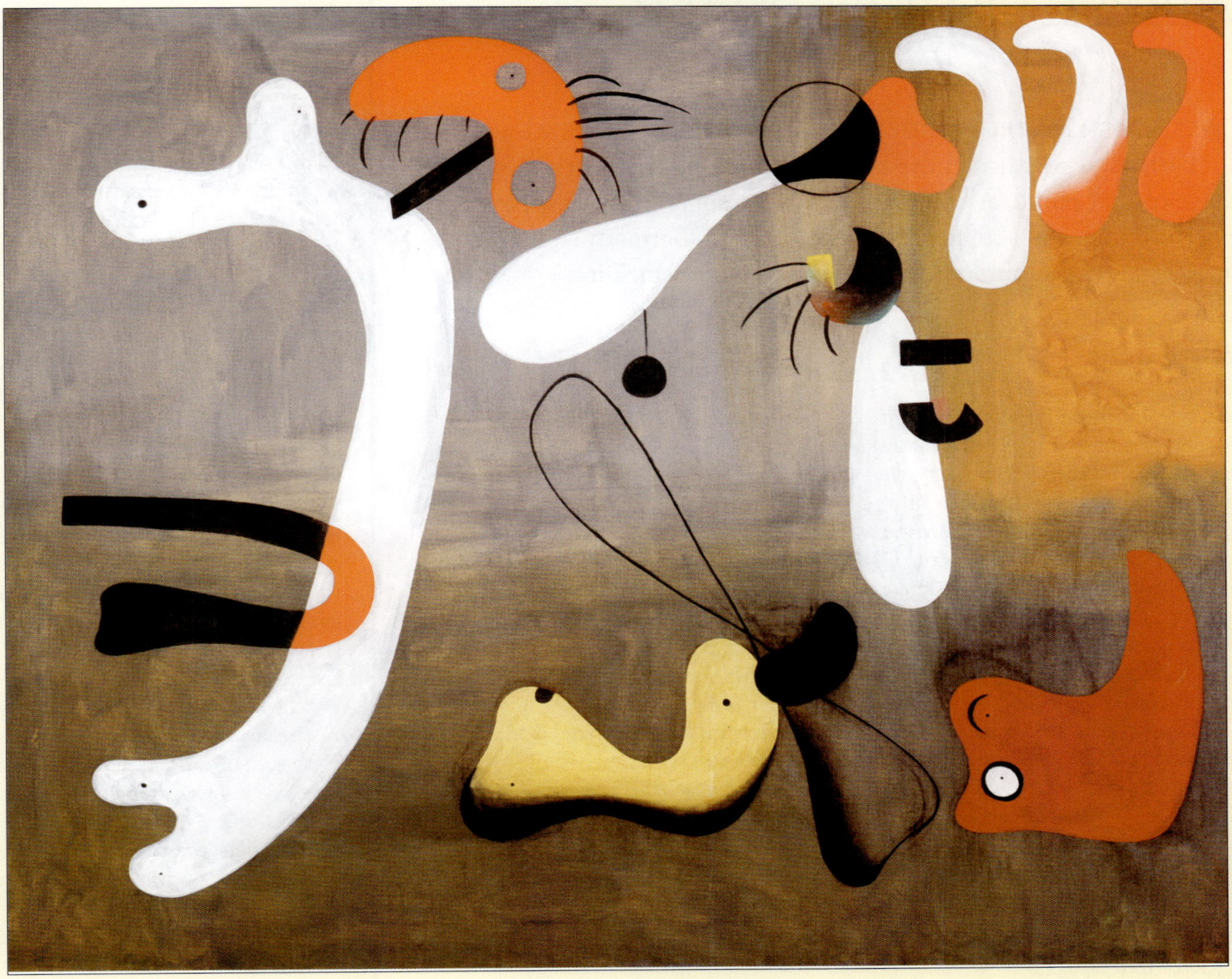

A fluid world

Miró's style resisted inclusion in any one movement. He was, however, closely associated with surrealism and also with the more general realm of abstract painting. In many ways, his work seemed to straddle the boundary between the surrealists of Europe and the abstract expressionists of the United States. The link to both groups was the automatic process (automatism)—a method by which the artist tries to disengage with the rational, conscious mind in order to freely express the deeper emotions and thoughts of the human psyche.

Miró did not talk at length about his working process, but did refer to inspiration coming from hallucinatory-like experiences. This may be true of Miró's sketches, which were quickly executed, as if he had been absentmindedly doodling. However, his finished works, despite their sense of playfulness, seem to have been created with considerably more regard to structure and harmony. Elements from his sketches are introduced rhythmically and with great consideration for balance and color harmony in Miró's paintings. Even the "dream paintings" of the late 1920s and the murals of the 1960s were not immediate and spontaneous creations. They were based on preliminary sketches, comprising a few small, simple marks on scraps of paper.

Composition (c1933) contains many of the elements that recur throughout Miró's work, particularly that of the late 1920s to 1960. Here we see figurative elements in a

Composition *c1933. Oil on canvas. 62 x 51½ in (163 x 130.5 cm). Philadelphia Museum of Art, Philadelphia, PA.*

highly abstract form: a lopsided head, the suggestion of hair, bonelike structures, eyelike circles centered with pupil-like dots, the recurrent crescent shape, and vague suggestion of body parts, such as breasts that appear to be changing into eyes. Everything is suggestive rather than literal, and presents us with a fluid world—a psychedelic vision perhaps. There is a sense of primitivism about the painting. There is also, however, a sense that Miró is honing images from the subconscious mind and placing them on the canvas with the control of a technically accomplished, intuitive artist.

MODERSOHN-BECKER Paula

PAULA MODERSOHN-BECKER BELONGED TO THE WORPSWEDE SCHOOL of artists, who painted the landscapes around the north German village of that name. Although she died young and sold few paintings in her lifetime, she is today regarded as one of Germany's most important artists, a forerunner of German expressionism.

Life and work

Paula Becker, the third of seven children, was born into a cultured and intellectual family. In 1888 the Beckers moved from Dresden to Bremen, in the far north of Germany. After spending a short time at art school in London, England, and undergoing two years of teacher training, Becker left home in 1896 to attend the School of Berlin Women Artists, visiting Worpswede for the first time shortly afterward.

Worpswede, a rural village in the countryside near Bremen, was a small, closeknit community. It had been colonized by a group of young painters during the early 1890s, who were attracted by its wild, moorland scenery, and by the "unspoiled" simplicity of its peasant life. The Worpswede artists painted the landscape, farmers, and scenes depicting village customs. Their work could sometimes be bold and earthy, like that of the French painter Gustave Courbet, but was more often rather sentimental, even romantic. Worpswede would become important to Becker, who studied with Fritz Mackensen (a painter of popular peasant scenes), and also met her future husband, the artist Otto Modersohn, there.

Several women artists worked at Worpswede. At a time when it was difficult for women to make careers as artists, it was often easier for them to work in such rural settings rather than in the academies of the big cities. Poets and friends of the artists also came to Worpswede, and the many surviving descriptions of the colony give the impression that it was an idyllic, creative community.

Becker made her first trip to Paris in 1900, staying there for six months to train at the Académie Colarossi. She also met other artists in Paris, including Emil Nolde, as well as studying the Old Masters in the Louvre and seeing the work of Paul Cézanne and Paul Gauguin, which impressed her enormously. On returning to Worpswede she became engaged to Otto Modersohn, becoming Paula Modersohn-Becker on their marriage the following year.

Modersohn-Becker, who was both a determined woman and completely dedicated to her work as an artist, often felt the need to live and work independently from her husband. Paris must have provided the excitement and stimulation that Worpswede could not give her, for she returned to the city, and to the Académie Colarossi, in 1903. This time she was impressed by Japanese art as well as by the work of such modern French artists as Edgar Degas and Auguste Rodin, whose studio she visited. Although she then returned to Worpswede for a while, she was soon drawn to Paris again. In 1906, for example, she spent a whole year there (even though her husband often begged her to come home), writing to her sister that this was the "most intensely happy period" of her life.

Data file

Full name: Paula Modersohn-Becker

Nationality: German

Style: postimpressionism/expressionism

Dates: born 1876 in Dresden, died 1907 in Worpswede

Key works:

Trumpeting Girl in the Birch Wood 1903–05

Reclining Mother and Child 1906

Self-portrait with Amber Necklace 1906

Poorhouse Woman with Glass Bowl 1907

Kneeling Mother and Child 1907

Nude Girl with Flowers 1907

Things to look for:

- earthy colors
- flat, rough areas of color
- peasant images
- strong, dark outlines

Comparisons: Paul Gauguin, Paul Cézanne, Emil Nolde

Glossary terms: Academy, expressionism, Old Masters, postimpressionism, tempera

Portraits of poverty and old age

This 1907 portrait, *Poorhouse Woman with Glass Bowl*, was one of Modersohn-Becker's last major works, and shows a subject she treated many times in her working life. The woman depicted was from the poorhouse at Worpswede, in northern Germany, and was one of several inhabitants painted by the artist. In fact, Modersohn-Becker had noted in her diary some years before that the old women in the poorhouse vied with one another to be selected as models because of the money they were paid in return.

Unlike many other artists who depicted farmers and villagers, Modersohn-Becker did not idealize her subjects, but was particularly drawn to locals with uneven or unusual physical features. Here, the woman's bulbous nose and protruding lower lip add interest to the portrait, without disturbing its quiet, solid quality.

The painting clearly demonstrates Modersohn-Becker's originality, as well as her ability to give her subjects great presence. The lighting is especially distinctive. The striking, ornamental shapes of the poppies and their seed-pods, the oddly formed glass bowl in the rear left of the picture, and the large bulk of the old woman's frame are all silhouetted against a glowing evening sun. This makes the glass of the bowl opaque. It also casts the woman's face in darkness, although we can still make out her features.

Another striking feature is the way that particular shapes or forms are echoed over and again throughout the picture. The manmade materials appear here to exist in harmony with nature: the glass bowl echoes the seed-pods of the poppies; the pattern on the woman's skirt echoes the flowers. Even the colors of her dress are in harmony with those in nature around her.

There is a sense of the cycle of life here. Fruit, foliage, and seeds symbolize fertility and birth; the artist Paul Gauguin often used fruits and flowers in his pictures of beautiful young Tahitian women. But this woman is old, poor, and perhaps sick. It is an indication of Modersohn-Becker's interest in and respect for all stages of life—early and late—that she consistently painted the very old and the very young with such sensitivity.

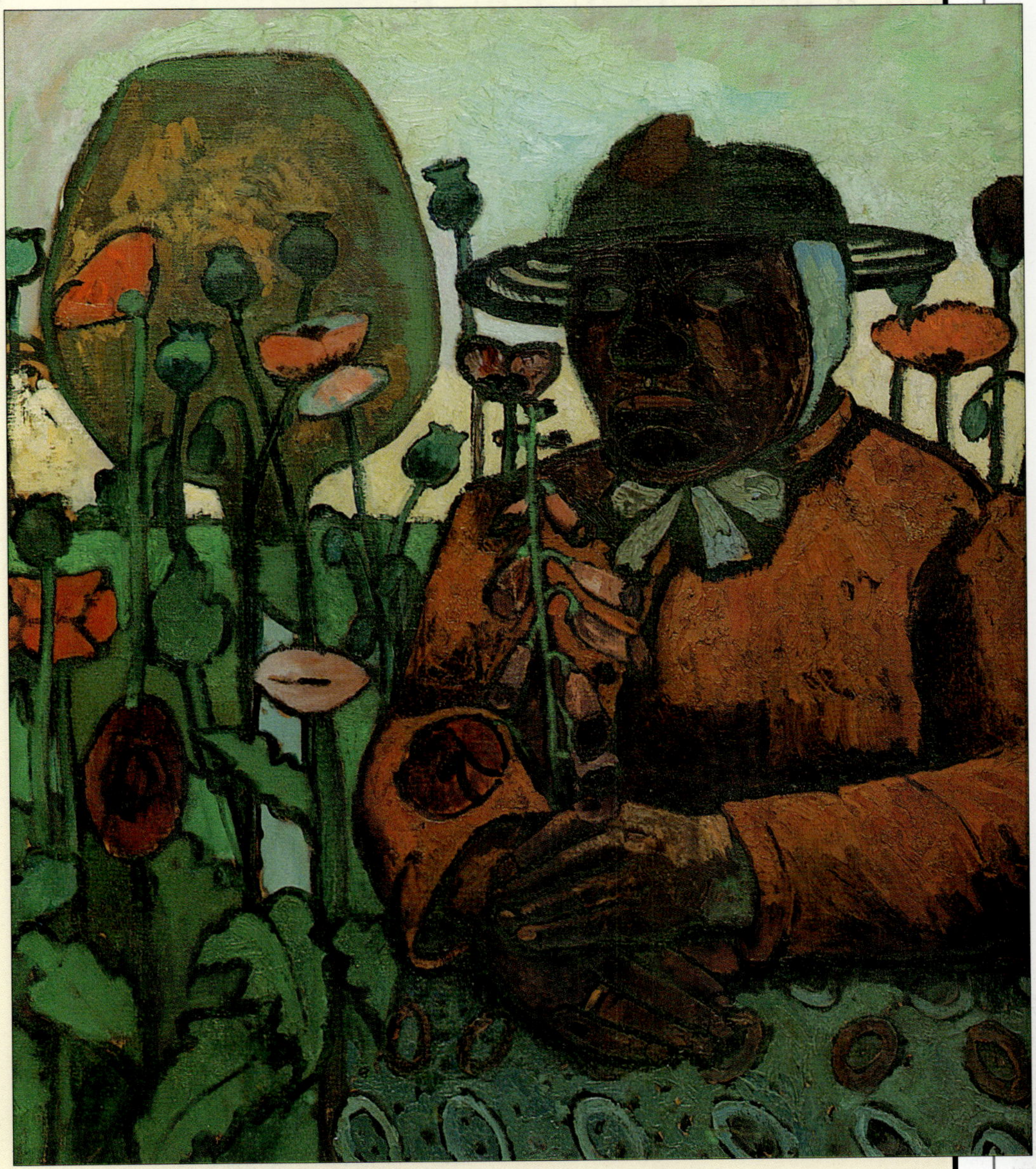

Poorhouse Woman with Glass Bowl
1907. Oil on canvas. 38 x 31 1/2 in (96.5 x 80 cm). Kunstsammlungen Böttcherstrasse, Bremen.

The modern influences that Modersohn-Becker absorbed in Paris stimulated her to aim for a radical, simplified style in painting. Like Cézanne and Pablo Picasso, she worked through her artistic problems by using simple, still-life subjects. Admiring what she called their "great biblical simplicity," as well as their resilience in enduring the hardships of peasant life, Modersohn-Becker most often turned to the people and natural landscape of Worpswede in her search for subjects. She seems to have been especially fascinated by the oldest, youngest, and poorest residents of Worpswede. Indeed, some of her most powerful images are portraits of the old people from the local poorhouse, or of the skinny village children with whom she frequently played. In order to achieve a comparably rough simplicity in her work, she frequently used tempera (colored pigment blended with another medium, usually egg yolk) rather than oil paint.

Modersohn-Becker died on 20 November 1907, 18 days after giving birth to her daughter, Mathilde. It was only after her death that the full extent of her work was discovered: in her short working life Modersohn-Becker had produced over 400 paintings and about 1000 graphic works.

Although she was by nature a loner, the sensitivity with which she treated her subjects shows that she had a great interest in both individuals and human relationships. She is an artist whose work is difficult to categorize: although it has much in common with French postimpressionism, its quality of expressive boldness means that she can also be regarded as an early German expressionist.

MODIGLIANI Amedeo

AMEDEO MODIGLIANI'S UNIQUE BODY OF WORK reveals influences from both modernity and traditionalism. A major painter and sculptor working in Paris in the early 20th century, he was inspired simultaneously by the monuments of ancient Egypt and Greece, Italian Renaissance painting, and African tribal art.

Life and work

Amedeo Modigliani was the youngest of four children born into a Jewish family in Livorno, northern Italy. He began his studies with the Italian landscape painter Guglielmo Micheli in 1898. They were interrupted, however, when Modigliani developed pleurisy, a condition which left him with a tubercular lung. In 1902 he entered the Academy of Fine Arts in Florence. From there he moved to Venice, where he continued his studies until 1905.

In 1906 he moved to Paris, settling in the Montmartre district and enrolling at the Colarossi Academy, where he studied life drawing and painting. He focused primarily on portraiture and the nude. Montmartre at this time sustained a thriving artistic community. The young Modigliani came to know many of the major artists of the period, including the cubist painters Pablo Picasso and Georges Braque, and the sculptors Jacques Lipchitz and Constantin Brancusi.

Modigliani's early work was heavily influenced by postimpressionism. He was particularly drawn to the work of Paul Cézanne, specifically his portraits and figure studies. Many of these were exhibited in Paris following Cézanne's death in 1906.

Modigliani's emphasis on portraits and figure studies was, in many respects, traditional, and drawn from his affinity to Italian Renaissance art. His stylistic approach, however, was drawn from more diverse sources. During the first decade of the 20th century, many artists developed a fascination with the arts of non-Western nations. This interest was inspired by an increasing knowledge of the culture of nations that had been colonized by the major European powers during the 19th century.

Artifacts from the colonies were on public display at the Trocadero, a major ethnographical museum in Paris. The exhibits on African art, in particular the tribal masks, captured the attention of many avant-garde Parisian artists, including Picasso, André Derain, and Modigliani himself. Along with ancient Greek and Egyptian sculptural monuments, African art would prove a powerful influence on Modigliani's future work.

Although remembered as a painter, Modigliani was also a major sculptor. His sculptural interests were fired by a meeting with the Romanian sculptor Brancusi, who encouraged Modigliani to carve directly into wood and stone rather than model in plaster or clay. Despite producing relatively few finished sculptural works—poor health

Data file

Full name: Amedeo Clemente Modigliani

Nationality: Italian

Style: primitivism

Dates: born 1884 in Livorno, died 1920 in Paris, France

Key works:

Head c1911

Paul Guillaume 1916

Seated Nude c1916

Jacques Lipchitz and His Wife 1916

Reclining Nude with Blue Cushion 1917

Leopold Zborowski 1918

The Little Peasant c1918

Things to look for:

- forms inspired by non-European art
- masklike faces and features
- bold brushstrokes

Comparisons: Paul Cézanne, Pablo Picasso, Jacques Lipchitz, Chaïm Soutine, Constantin Brancusi

Glossary terms: avant-garde, cubism, postimpressionism, Renaissance

Masklike individuality

Amedeo Modigliani produced dozens of portraits throughout his lifetime. Many of them represent his friends from the Parisian art world of the early 20th century, including such notable figures as Jean Cocteau, Juan Gris, and Chaïm Soutine. *Jacques Lipchitz and His Wife*, shown here, was the result of a commission offered to Modigliani by the famous sculptor Jacques Lipchitz in 1916.

About this time Lipchitz, a Jewish immigrant from Lithuania, was establishing his reputation as a sculptor. He had recently married, and to commemorate the event, he asked Modigliani to produce a double portrait of himself and his bride. It may well be that Lipchitz was trying to help Modigliani at a time of financial difficulty for the painter; it was the middle of World War I, and difficult to earn a successful living.

The portrait of the newlyweds is casually posed, with Lipchitz dressed in a loose-fitting jacket worn over an informal sweater. His right hand is thrust into his pocket, while his left hand rests on the shoulder of his more elegantly dressed wife. Both figures look directly toward the viewer.

While the facial details seem to suggest individual traits—the elegant smile and rouged cheeks of Madame Lipchitz, and the broad forehead and cropped hair of Lipchitz himself—the features are flat, elongated, and masklike. The eyes in particular are reduced to a single color, with no iris or pupil distinguishable. These very reduced features appear in his sculptures and, after 1910, in many of his portraits and figure studies. Like other Parisian artists of his generation, Modigliani took inspiration for his approach from African tribal masks and other non-Western art.

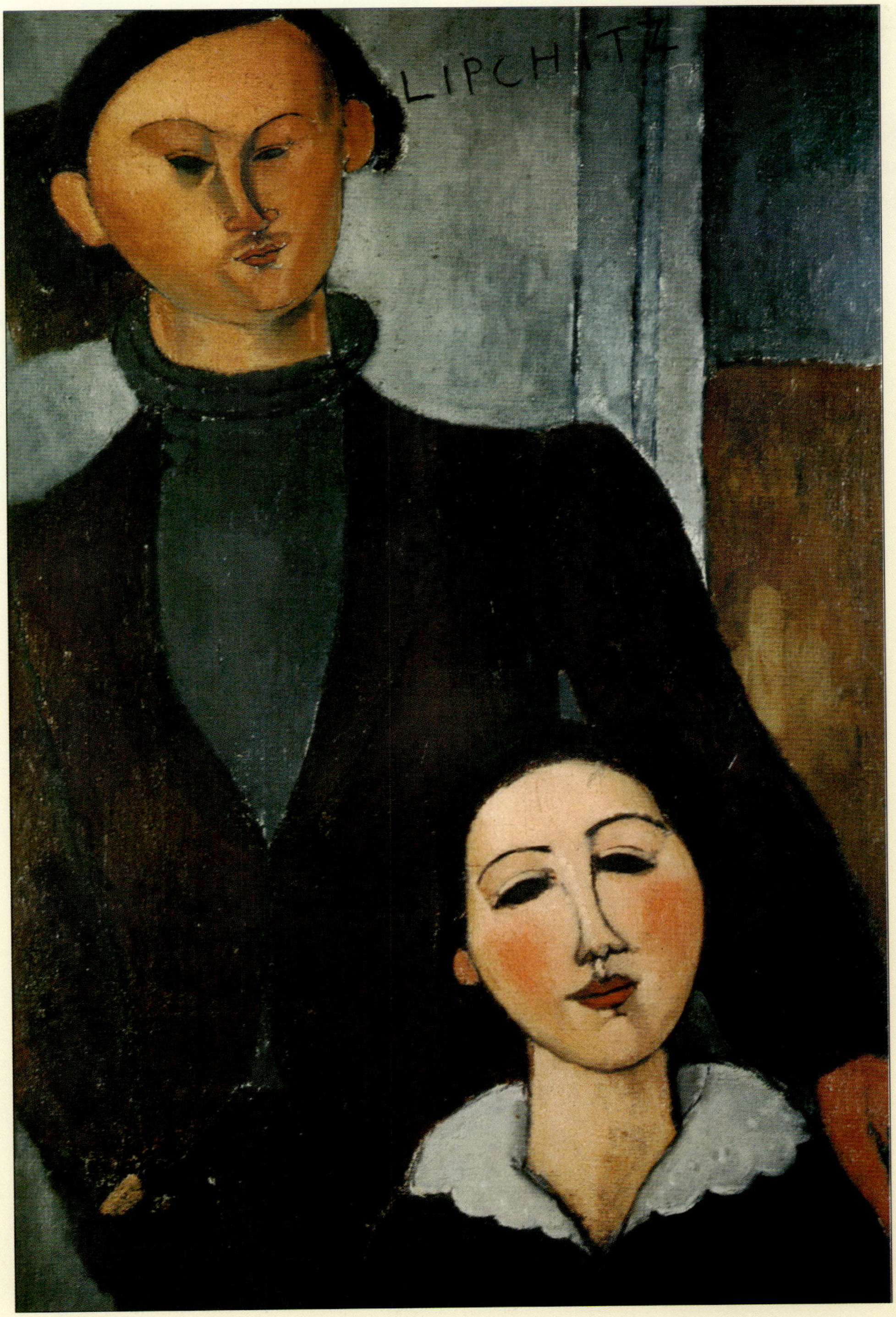

Jacques Lipchitz and His Wife
1916. Oil on canvas. 31 1/2 x 21 in (80 x 53.5 cm). Art Institute of Chicago, Chicago, IL.

hampered him in this physically demanding activity—he completed several works in both wood and stone.

He worked throughout World War I and began to exhibit and sell his work regularly. His contacts with two major art dealers, Paul Guillaume and Leopold Zborowski, helped him greatly, and their portraits (Guillaume's in 1916 and Zborowski's in 1918) are among his most striking paintings.

By 1918 Modigliani's health began to decline. Always an unconventional figure, and now troubled by a turbulent relationship with his partner, Jeanne Hébuterne, he increasingly turned to alcohol and drugs for solace. In 1920, despite convalescence in the south of France, his condition worsened, and he died a lonely and tragic figure at the age of 35 years.

MONDRIAN Piet

PIET MONDRIAN WAS A LEADING MEMBER of the De Stijl movement. It was not until he was almost 50 years old that he discovered the style of painting—abstraction—for which he is known.

Life and work

Piet Mondrian was born in the town of Amersfoort, just outside Utrecht in the Netherlands. His father was an amateur artist and his uncle was a professional artist. The two men, together with a retired drawing teacher, taught Mondrian painting techniques. He later studied at the Rijksakademie in Amsterdam, where his early work was unexceptional.

In 1911, Mondrian moved to Paris, where the influence of cubism and a growing interest in theosophy—a semi-religious movement—gave his work a new direction. Mondrian at first saw his role as one of combining the spiritual essence and physical appearance of the world. This led to a variety of work that drew on natural subjects, such as flowers, trees, and human forms. The style of his work veered from expressionism to symbolism, and began to resemble the more abstract style of cubism.

In 1914, at the outbreak of World War I, Mondrian returned to the suburbs of Amsterdam. By this time, through progressively more extreme forms of cubism, he had almost eliminated curved lines from his painting. Yet there were still underlying traces of representation in his work.

The next few years were formative in his career as he ventured toward the pure and austere style of abstraction for which he is best known. With the encouragement of fellow Dutch painter Theo van Doesburg and the De Stijl group, Mondrian set out a philosophy for the future of painting, which was published in a series of articles in the *De Stijl* magazine in 1917. He called his vision of rigorous, geometrical, abstract painting "neoplasticism." He wanted to express universal truths and would use the most simple methods to do so: reducing forms to geometrical shapes, line to its vertical and horizontal axes, and color to the three primary colors

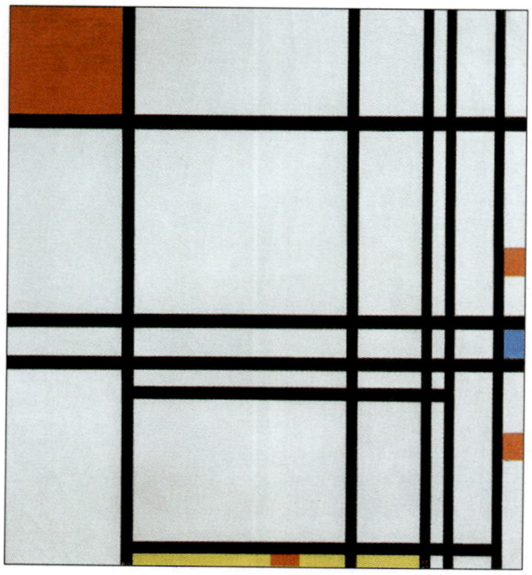

Composition No. 8 *1939–42. Oil on canvas. 26¾ x 29½ in (68 x 75 cm). Kimbell Art Museum, Fort Worth, TX.*

Data file

Full name: Piet Mondrian

Nationality: Dutch

Style: pure abstraction

Dates: born 1872 in Amersfoort, died 1944 in New York, NY, United States

Key works:
- *Apple Tree in Bloom* 1912
- *Composition No. 10* (from the *Pier* and *Ocean* series) 1915
- *Composition with Gray, Red, Yellow, and Blue* 1920
- *Composition with Blue and Yellow* 1931
- *Composition with Red* 1939
- *Composition No. 8* 1939–42
- *Broadway Boogie-Woogie* 1942–43
- *New York City II* 1942–44

Things to look for:
- compositions that appear harmonious
- use of vertical and horizontal lines and variation in line weight
- limitation of colors to the primaries (red, blue, and yellow) plus black, white, and shades of gray

Comparisons: Theo van Doesburg, Kasimir Malevich, El Lissitzky, Barnett Newman, Ad Reinhardt, Ellsworth Kelly

Glossary terms: abstraction, cubism, De Stijl, neoplasticism

Toward abstraction

Like many of his contemporaries, Mondrian was searching for a new role for art—one that was not visually dependent on its relation to the natural world. He was progressing toward an art form that was independent of comparisons, that functioned on its own terms, and that broke away from traditional ideas of beauty. He wanted to create works that were harmonious, but did not simply seek to please the eye; works that resonated with what one might call the "heartbeat of life itself." The term he coined for this was "neoplasticism," a word that comes to us in translation from the Dutch to English via French, which we can take to mean "new image creation," or "structuring."

One of the primary forces behind Mondrian's work was his interest in theosophy. Followers of this semireligious movement believed in a unified spirit behind the physical dimensions of life. Mondrian believed in an art that tapped into that all-pervasive spirit and occurred in many different areas of society, rather than an art that was only the preserve of museums and galleries.

Mondrian's work from 1900 until about 1920 shows a progression from representational art to more abstract forms. *Apple Tree in Bloom* (1912)—one of a series of paintings on the theme of a tree—is midway through this transition. We can just make out the form of a tree, but the painting reflects Mondrian's new geometrical abstract style.

Mondrian worked in a cubist style from 1912 to about 1915–16, when the

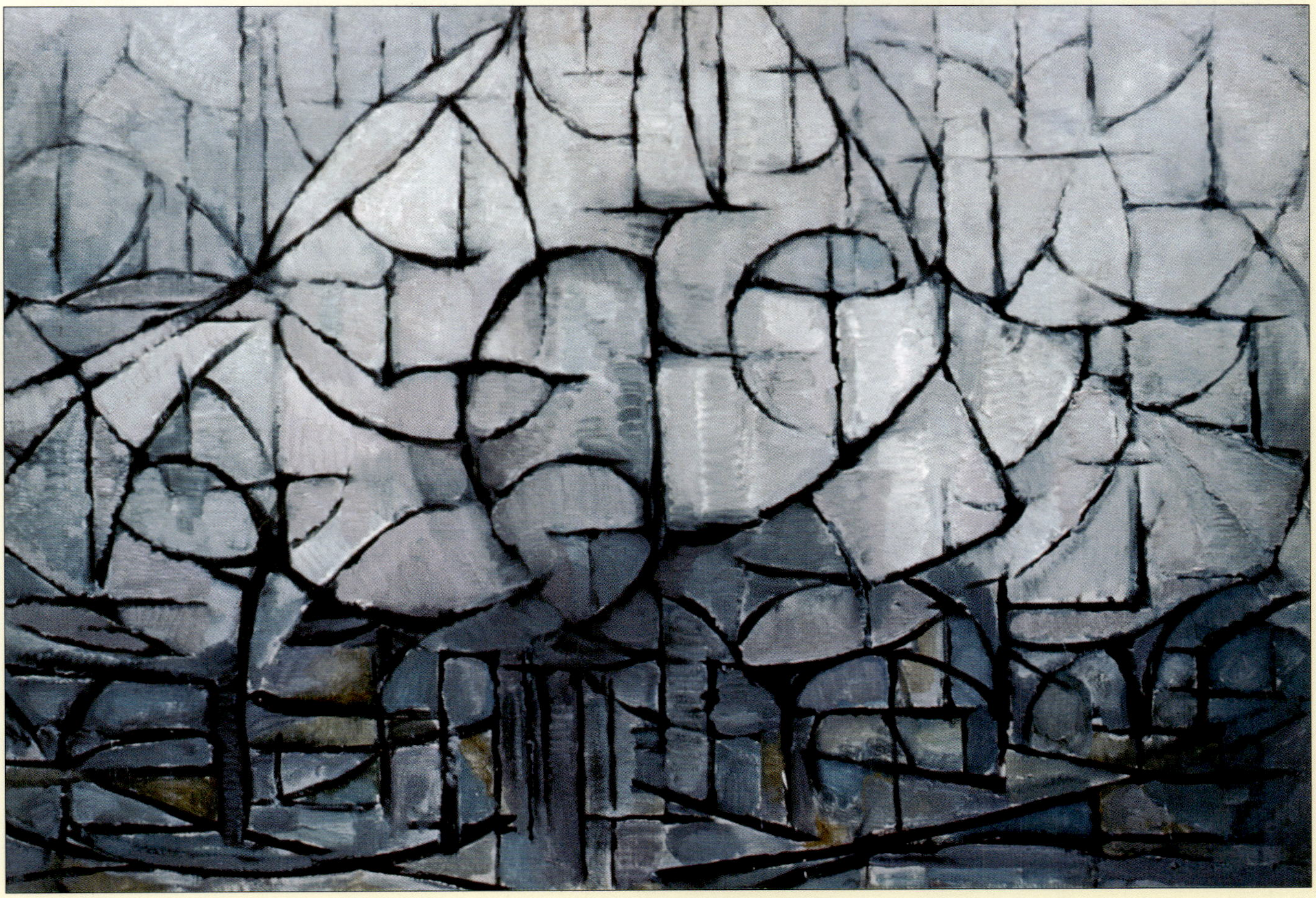

separation of forms on his canvases increased further the level of abstraction in his paintings. By 1921, Mondrian was using only the three primary colors plus black, white, and shades of gray, and the compositional building blocks offered by a strict regime of vertical and horizontal linear divisions. Now he had assembled the means to create purely abstract art, and for his remaining 24 years he worked through countless variations of this linear geometry. Sometimes the color would be reduced to just one small section of the canvas, as in *Composition with Red* (1939). At other times the color became dominant—as in his final works in New York, such as the vibrant *Broadway Boogie-Woogie* (1942–43). From 1920 to the end of his career, however, Mondrian remained committed to the principles of pure abstraction.

Apple Tree in Bloom *1912. Oil on canvas. 33½ x 23½ in (85 x 60 cm). Private collection, New York, NY.*

with white and black, or gray.

Mondrian returned to Paris in 1919. The work that he produced over the next few years consolidated his style of abstraction. For years he had struggled to make a living. But now, after showing his work in France, the Netherlands, and Germany, Mondrian's international reputation grew steadily. In 1936, when he was 64, his work was shown in the United States for the first time. The exhibition, entitled "Cubism and Abstract Art," was held at the Museum of Modern Art in New York.

In 1938 Mondrian left Paris and moved to England, and after the outbreak of World War II he settled in New York. He had always had an interest in music, and in New York he came upon the newest developments in jazz—the fast and furious "bebop" style. This, and the dynamism of the city, had a major influence on Mondrian's later works, in which his familiar black lines are replaced by a vibrant medley of primary colors, and the rhythm is more complex than before.

Composition No. 8 (1939–42), however, is more representative of Mondrian's work. It is highly restrained, with color restricted to the primaries, and structure defined by a grid of horizontal and vertical lines. Harmony is achieved not by symmetry, but by the line widths, the division of space, and the small blocks of color.

MONET Claude

MONET WAS ONE OF THE FOUNDERS OF THE IMPRESSIONIST STYLE, a term derived from one of his works. His paintings explore the effects of light and color, and reflect the area in which Monet lived, as well as his private contemplation of the coasts, mountains, rivers, and meadows of France.

Life and work

The son of a French grocer, Monet grew up in Le Havre, Normandy, where his mentor, the painter Eugène Boudin, encouraged him to paint landscapes "*en plein air*" (in the open air). In 1859 Monet went to Paris and enrolled as a pupil of the academic painter Charles Gleyre at the Ecole des Beaux-Arts. He also frequented the Académie Suisse, an "open" studio where artists could use models for free. He became a friend of Camille Pissarro, as well as of Pierre Auguste Renoir, Frédéric Bazille, and Alfred Sisley; they would later form the core of the impressionist group.

During the 1860s Monet made painting trips to the forest of Fontainebleau and the Normandy coast. Inspired by the controversial paintings of Edouard Manet, he also painted scenes of Paris, where Baron Haussmann was modernizing the capital into the city of boulevards and elegant buildings that we know today.

Monet fled to London during the Franco–Prussian War (1870–71). Between 1873 and 1878 Monet, with his wife, Camille, and their son, Jean, settled in the village of Argenteuil, near Paris. Many of their friends, Renoir, Sisley, Gustave Caillebotte, and Manet among them, visited Argenteuil to paint boating and swimming scenes, as well as the river cafés, villas, and factories in the area.

During the art-market slump of the 1870s, Monet, Sisley, Pissarro, and Renoir decided to mount independent exhibitions to draw attention to their work. The first exhibition was staged in April 1874. A contemporary critic called the group the "impressionists," after Monet's gray, blue, and orange view of the port of Le Havre entitled *Impression, Sunrise* (1874). Others joined the group, including Berthe Morisot and Mary Cassatt.

In 1876, Monet met Ernest Hoschedé and his wife, Alice, who commissioned Monet to paint four panels for their home. In 1878 Hoschedé was declared bankrupt, and the Monets' second son, Michel, was born; the two couples (who had eight children between them) decided to form a joint household in Vétheuil. When Camille died the following year, Alice and Monet became partners, and married after Ernest's death in 1882. In 1883 the new family moved to Giverny.

Monet made many painting trips throughout France during the 1880s. He returned several times to the Normandy and Brittany coasts, focusing on remote sites rather than the tourist-filled resorts of Trouville and Saint-Adresse. Among other scenes, he painted the rough seas and rock pools of Fécamp and Pourville, the isolated,

Data file

Full name: Claude Oscar Monet
Nationality: French
Style: impressionism
Dates: born 1840 in Paris, died 1926 in Giverny
Key works:
- *Women in the Garden* 1866–67
- *Bathers at La Grenouillère* 1869
- *The Beach at Trouville* 1870
- *Impression, Sunrise* 1874
- *Gare Saint-Lazare, the Normandy Train* 1877
- *The Poplars, the Four Trees* 1891
- *Grain Stacks at Sunset* 1891
- *Waterlily Pond* 1899

Things to look for:
- paintings that capture the moment, or "impression"
- individual brushstrokes of different colors
- an exploration of the effects of light and season
- use of a specific motif in a series of paintings at different times, from different viewpoints

Comparisons: Eugène Boudin, Edouard Manet, Pierre Auguste Renoir, Alfred Sisley, Camille Pissarro
Glossary terms: Barbizon school, *en plein air*, impressionism

From darkness to light

Monet painted *The Beach at Trouville* (1870) while he and his first wife, Camille, were on honeymoon in Trouville, a resort on the Normandy coast. The painting includes Camille and Madame Boudin, wife of his mentor Eugène Boudin, at the beach, their parasols casting their faces in dark shadows. The painting marks a transition from Monet's early figure paintings to his mature, landscape subjects.

The ultimate *en-plein-air* sketch (embedded in the paint are specks of sand that blew onto the canvas), Monet executed *The Beach at Trouville* rapidly, and on a small scale, revealing only the scene's main shapes and color notes. He derived the abrupt brushwork and relatively traditional palette of this early painting from the work of such realist painters as Gustave Courbet, the artists of the Barbizon school, and the *en-plein-air* techniques of Eugène Boudin and Johan Barthold Jongkind. Monet later abandoned the use of dark and bright contrasts, instead creating a sense of depth and volume through color relationships alone. He enhanced his bright palette by painting on canvases that had first been primed with either white or light beige tones.

Waterlily Pond (1899) is typical of Monet's later work, and is one of several works showing the water garden at Giverny, capturing the changing colors of light on the water. The bold color and curve of the bridge reflects the influence of the Japanese prints that Monet collected.

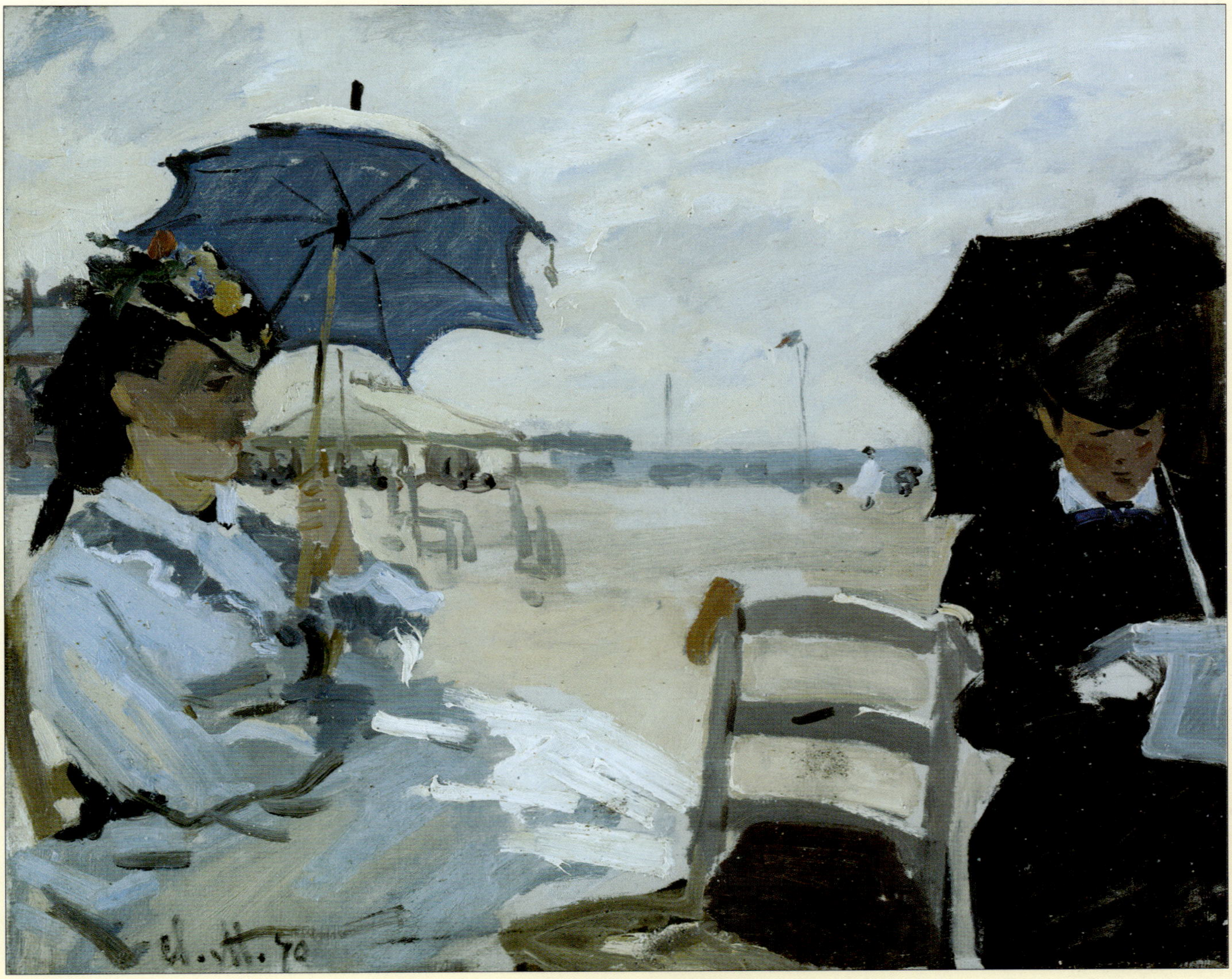

The Beach at Trouville *1870. Oil on canvas. 14½ x 18 in (37.5 x 45.5 cm). Wadsworth Atheneum, Hartford, CT.*

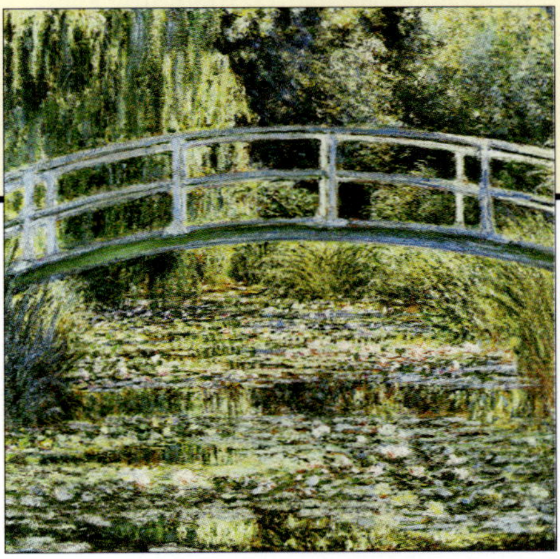

Waterlily Pond *1899. Oil on canvas. 34¾ x 36¼ in (88.5 x 93 cm). National Gallery, London.*

hilltop church at Varengeville, and the dramatic cliffs and needles of Etretat. Monet also explored the Dutch tulip fields and the sunlit brilliance of the Mediterranean, his travels inspiring his monumental and decorative series-paintings. He would select a subject, such as grain stacks, poplar trees, or Rouen Cathedral, and then paint a series of paintings portraying it under different conditions of light and season.

Monet's last, and longest, artistic project was the creation of the water garden by his house at Giverny. He first created an elaborate flower garden that incorporated every shade and variety of bloom in a veritable palette of flowers. In 1893 Monet purchased a second plot of land, which lay on the opposite side of the road and railroad track that ran through the property. There he enlarged an existing pond and added a red, arched, Japanese-style bridge.

Monet built a special studio to work on murals inspired by the garden. The waterlily paintings were Monet's last works, done to commemorate the dead of World War I. They are now housed in the Orangerie Museum in the Tuileries Gardens in Paris.

MOORE Henry

THE 20TH-CENTURY BRITISH SCULPTOR HENRY MOORE is best known for his monumental public sculptures, which can be seen in cities around the world. His work combines a modernist simplification of form and surface, much influenced by non-Western art styles, with a deeply felt humanity.

Life and work

Henry Moore was brought up in the coal-mining town of Castleford in northern England, the seventh child of a miner. Moore later recalled the moment, at the age of 11, that he first realized he wanted to be a sculptor: when a schoolteacher told the class a story about Michelangelo Buonarroti.

In 1917, at the height of World War I, Moore joined the army. He served on the Western Front and was badly injured in a gas attack. In 1919, aged 21, he gained an ex-serviceman's grant to study sculpture at Leeds School of Art, then won a scholarship to the Royal College of Art in London.

The academic approach favored by the Royal College, with its emphasis on ancient Greek and Renaissance art, was not to Moore's taste. He discovered alternative sources of inspiration in the British Museum, where he was powerfully drawn to the stone and wood carvings of ancient Egypt, Mesopotamia, and Africa, and to the art of Pre-Columbian Mexico. At the same time he read *Vision and Design* (1920) by the artist and critic Roger Fry, who championed the expressive strength of "primitive" art. The concept of "truth to materials" (allowing the qualities of the materials used to influence the final form of a sculpture) was another formative influence on Moore's early work. This preoccupation was shared by other artists of the European avant-garde, including the sculptors Constantin Brancusi and Henri Gaudier-Brzeska.

In 1923 Moore visited Paris in order to see original paintings by Paul Cézanne, which made a deep impression on him, as did the early Italian art he saw on his first visit to Italy in 1924. He later said that ancient Mexican and Italian art represented two opposing aspects of his own artistic nature: the "tough" and the "tender."

During the 1920s Moore taught at the Royal College and began to gain a reputation in avant-garde circles. His *Mother and Child* (1924–25) and *Reclining Figure* (1929), both carved in stone, show the influence of ancient Mexican art, but also introduce subjects to which Moore repeatedly returned throughout his career. In 1928, aged 30, he had his first one-man show.

In 1933 Moore joined a group of avant-garde artists and architects called Unit One. The group took its cue from developments in European modernism, in particular the exploration of abstract art. Other members included the painter Ben Nicholson and Nicholson's wife, the sculptor Barbara Hepworth. Moore's work during this period reveals the influence of contemporary European sculptors such as Jean Arp and Alberto Giacometti. *Recumbent Figure* (1938) has smooth curves and bulging forms that suggest hills and rocks as well as human features; it also shows Moore introducing the motif of holes pierced through his sculptures, so that the viewer could see right into and through the sculptural form.

Soon after the outbreak of World War II, Moore's Hampstead studio was bombed. He moved to Much Hadham, a village in southern England, where he lived for the rest of his life. He was appointed an official war artist, and made many drawings of Londoners sheltering in subway tunnels during the German bombing raids. It was his "shelter drawings," rather than his sculptures, that established Moore's reputation with a wider public. Their vulnerable human subjects are echoed in the sculptures *Madonna and Child* (1943–44) and *Family Group* (1948–49), in which Moore returned to a more naturalistic rendering of the body.

Moore's *Reclining Figure*, commissioned for the 1951 Festival of Britain, began a series of prestigious public sculptures. Moore produced these in bronze rather than by direct carving. He collected natural objects such as pebbles and flints, which stimulated ideas for sculptures. *King and Queen* (1952–53) was privately commissioned for a remote moorland site in Scotland; the couple's heads, with their through-pierced eyes, recall the shapes of flints.

Data file

Full name: Henry Spencer Moore

Nationality: English

Style: modernism

Dates: born 1898 in Castleford, died 1986 in Much Hadham

Key works:
- *Mother and Child* 1924–25
- *Reclining Figure* 1929
- *Recumbent Figure* 1938
- *King and Queen* 1952–53
- *Knife-edge* 1962
- *Reclining Figure* 1969–70
- *Large Four-piece Reclining Figure* 1972–73

Things to look for:
- use of natural materials (stone and wood), and interest in natural shapes of rocks, bones, etc.
- preoccupation with human form, especially reclining or seated
- placing of sculpture in relation to landscape
- simplified monumental forms, recalling ancient Mexican or early European sculpture, for example

Comparisons: Michelangelo Buonarroti, Auguste Rodin, Alberto Giacometti, Barbara Hepworth

Glossary terms: abstract art, avant-garde, modernism, primitive art

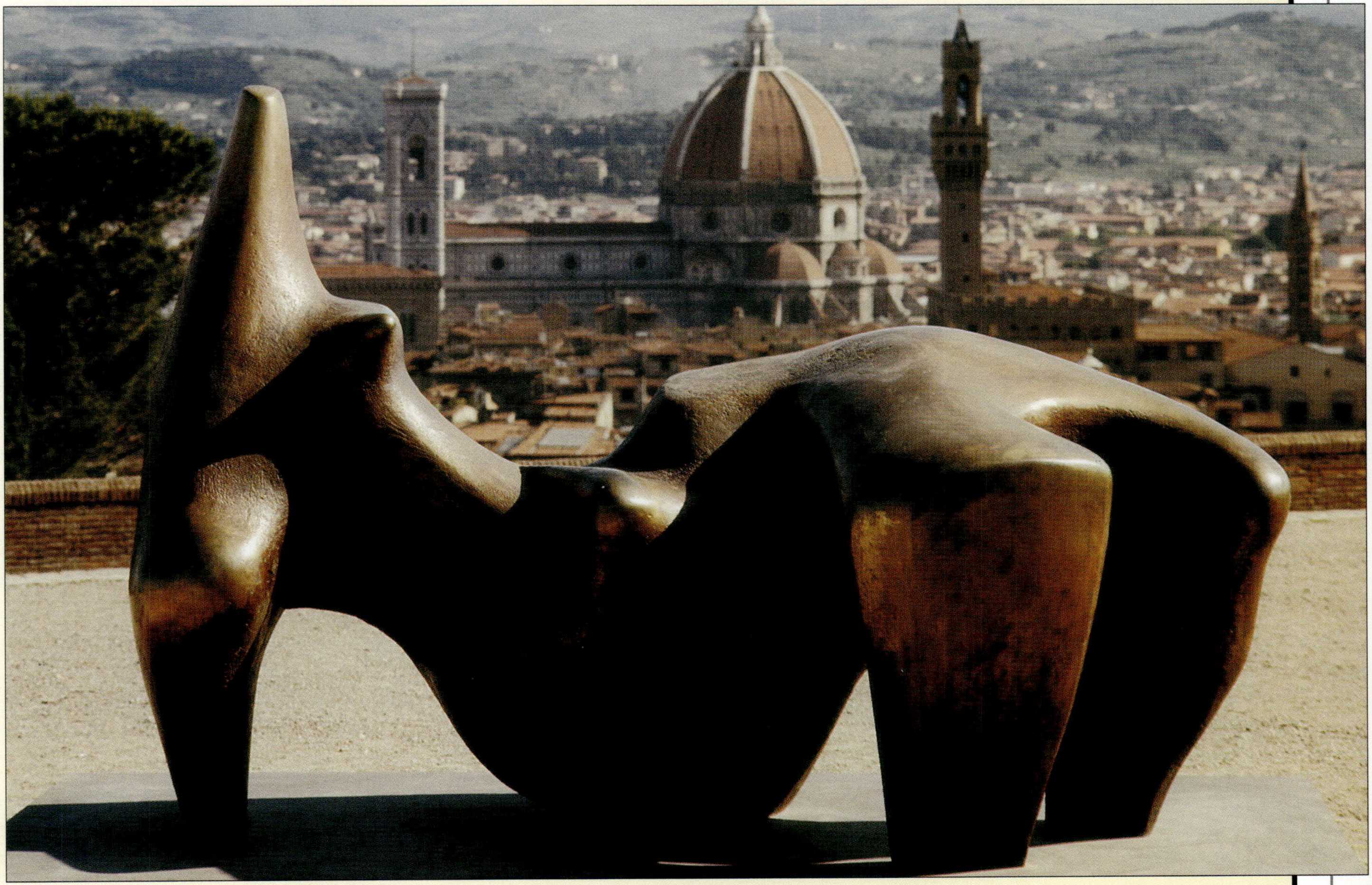

"A sculpture must have its own life"

Moore has always emphasized the centrality of the human form to his art, and of the way this relates to natural forms—landscapes, rock formations, trees, and seaworn stones. Even in his most abstract sculptures, these elements are present. He spoke of striving for "a sense that the form...is trying to give off the strength from inside itself," rather than being shaped from outside by the sculptor.

He habitually made many preparatory drawings for his sculptures. "Drawing keeps one fit," he claimed, "like physical exercises." Every so often he would devote several weeks to life drawing.

One of the motifs that Moore especially made his own is the reclining figure. His early interest in this way of representing the body was aroused by a picture of an ancient Mexican chacmool figure (a fallen warrior lying on his back with head and knees raised), and by his admiration for Michelangelo Buonarroti's *Night* (begun c1520) in the church of San Lorenzo, in Florence, Italy. His variations on this theme represent every stage of his artistic development, from the 1920s through the comparatively naturalistic *Draped Reclining Figure* of 1952–53 to the schematic *Large Four-piece Reclining Figure* of 1972–73.

Reclining Figure *1969–70. Bronze. Length 135 in (343 cm). Forte Belvedere, Florence.*

The bronze *Reclining Figure* (1969–70), pictured on the site above Florence where a major retrospective exhibition of Moore's work was staged in 1972, shows clearly how Moore's human forms relate to landscape. The figure's curves are echoed by the hills beyond the city and the dome of the cathedral. The verticals of the legs, arms, and neck are echoed by the Renaissance towers. "Sculpture gains by finding a setting that suits its mood," said Moore, "and when that happens, there is a gain for both sculpture and setting."

Pared down to essentials, the human body combines with a feeling for exposed, weathered landscape forms in Moore's large public sculptures of the 1960s and 1970s. Some of these, such as *Knife-edge* (1962), and the *Reclining Figure* (1963–65) located in the pool outside the Lincoln Center, New York, are in two or more pieces.

Moore continued to be active throughout his eighties, when he increasingly concentrated on drawing and printmaking. By this time he was internationally acknowledged as one of the foremost artists of the 20th century.

MOREAU Gustave

GUSTAVE MOREAU created an intensely personal body of work of great imaginative power. He was associated with the symbolist movement, whose painters derived inspiration from literary or mythological sources. This leaning toward otherworldliness stood in stark contrast to the realist tendencies of most avant-garde art movements of the time, notably impressionism.

Life and work

The son of a successful Parisian architect, Moreau studied at the Ecole des Beaux-Arts, but left after twice failing to win the prestigious Prix de Rome. In 1848, he became friendly with the Romantic French painter Théodore Chassériau, whose untimely death, aged only 37, had a profound effect upon him. Chassériau had been a favorite pupil of the classical painter Jean Auguste Dominique Ingres, and was an admirer of Eugène Delacroix's Romantic style. Moreau, inspired by the same ideals, stayed in Italy from 1857 to 1859, where he pursued his independent training. He met the young Edgar Degas in Rome in 1858. On his return he gained success at the Salon in 1864 and 1866 with paintings that completely contrasted with the work of Gustave Courbet and Jean-François Millet, then at the height of their popularity. Like Degas, Moreau cherished a deep regard for history paintings based on classical themes but, unlike his young friend, he remained faithful to the belief that the artist's role was to express his inner thoughts in complex allegorical form.

Always deeply sensitive to criticism, Moreau remained somewhat apart from the artistic establishment, although he was honored and respected. His work became much valued and borrowed by artists and writers of the symbolist movement and later the "decadent" movement. Both eclectic and independent, he looked to the artists of the Renaissance for inspiration, and to the exotic art and artifacts of Asia. Much of his work is centered on stories from Greek mythology, and his interest in science and comparative religion also played a part in his thinking.

Moreau never married, but was content with his long-term companion, who lived separately from him, and a small circle of friends. The death of his beloved mother in 1884 affected him greatly, and he left his last works largely unfinished, which only adds to their evocative power.

For Moreau, the world of the idea was superior to that of perceptual reality, and true reality is veiled, inaccessible to all but a few, although it can be hinted at in works of art. "I believe only in what I cannot see and only in what I feel...my interior feeling seems the only thing that is eternal and incontestably certain," he said. These ideas also inspired Paul Gauguin, Wassily Kandinsky, and Piet Mondrian.

His painting is characterized by conflict: between the world of material reality and that of the ideal; order and chaos; life and death; sexuality and spirituality; these ideas find their greatest expression in his paintings of the biblical *femme fatale* Salome. He encouraged viewers to have their own responses to his work: "It embodies an idea.... One can make of it what one wishes, although I attach a very specific meaning to it."

Moreau's watercolors have a freedom, vitality, and openness often missing in his more heavily, even obsessively overworked oil paintings. But even these obey the precepts he thought necessary for a successful painting, which he felt should contain what he called "necessary richness" and "beautiful inertia," qualities that can be seen, very differently interpreted, in the work of Henri Matisse.

Moreau was elected to the Ecole des Beaux-Arts in 1892, where he proved himself to be a liberated and inspirational teacher. His students included Matisse, Albert Marquet, Henri Manguin (all three of whom would be involved subsequently in the short-lived fauvist group), and Georges Rouault, who would become the first director of the Moreau Museum (the artist's house) on rue Rochefoucauld in Paris.

Moreau's work appealed not only to these artists, but to the surrealists, who, like Moreau, celebrated the liberating qualities of art. One of the early visitors to the Moreau Museum was the young André Breton, the so-called "pope of surrealism," who claimed that the encounter was one of the formative events of his life.

Data file

Full name: Gustave Moreau

Nationality: French

Style: symbolism

Dates: born 1826 in Paris, died 1898 in Paris

Key works:
- *The Suitors* (unfinished) begun 1852
- *The Athenians Delivered to the Minotaur in the Labyrinth on Crete* 1855
- *The Young Man and Death* 1865
- *Orpheus* 1865
- *The Apparition* c1874–76
- *Sappho* c1884
- *Jupiter and Semele* 1889
- *Orpheus at the Tomb of Eurydice* c1891–97

Things to look for:
- allegorical and mythological themes
- expressive rather than descriptive meaning

Comparisons: Edgar Degas, Georges Rouault, Henri Matisse, Marcel Duchamp, Max Ernst

Glossary terms: allegory, decadent art, fauvism, impressionism, Romanticism, surrealism, symbolism

Scenes from mythology and the mind

Moreau developed his complex paintings from his studies and reading, making numerous meticulously drawn studies from a wide variety of sources. An unusual feature of his work is his use of spontaneously painted oil sketches to suggest the color and compositional structures of his chosen subjects. Gradually, through a number of different stages, which included the construction of beautifully modeled wax figurines, the final picture would be brought into being, as Moreau used paint to create canvases of great richness.

Orpheus (1865) was a sensation when it was shown at the Salon of 1866, and is typical of the artist's early style. The story is Moreau's own invention, based on the figure of Orpheus, the poet and lyre-player of Greek mythology. In the picture, the head and lyre of the murdered Orpheus are being recovered from the river Hebron by a beautiful Thracian maiden. The young girl intuitively recognizes the significance of the dead poet's remains.

Although they are tied to complex allegorical narratives, Moreau intended his works to operate primarily as mysterious and evocative poems of color, line, and imagery. *Orpheus* embodies the qualities that appealed not only to Moreau's pupils but also to the surrealists of the 1920s, who, like Moreau, were interested in the subconscious powers of the mind and the ability of art to convey fantasies, dreams, and nightmarish visions.

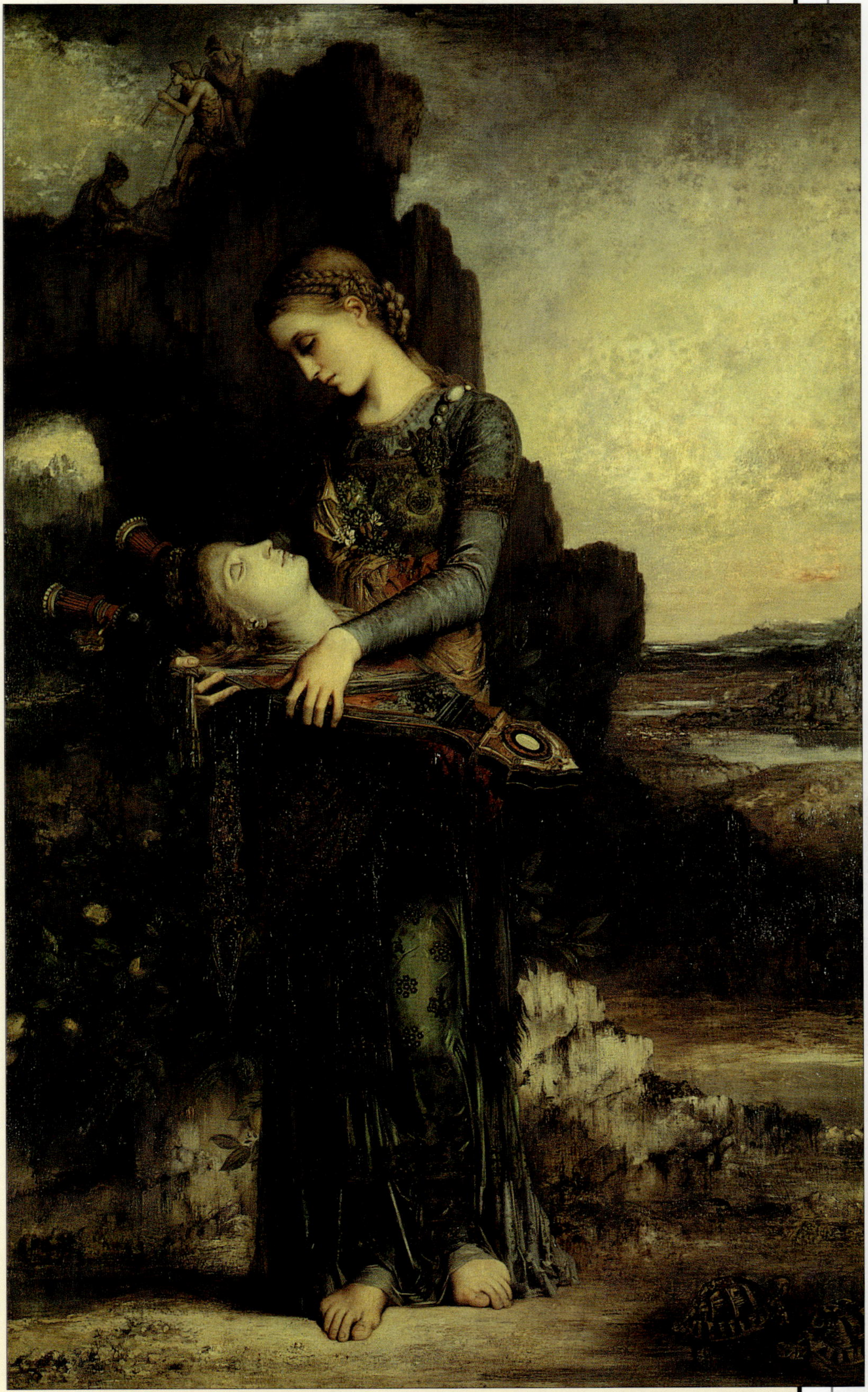

Orpheus *1865. Oil on canvas. 60 x 39 in (154 x 99.5 cm). Musée d'Orsay, Paris.*

MORISOT Berthe

BERTHE MORISOT PAVED THE WAY for subsequent generations of women to develop professional careers as artists. The leading female member of the 19th-century French impressionist movement, her landscapes and portraits were a unique record of life in suburban Paris, and of her family.

Life and work

One of four children of a provincial civil servant, Berthe Morisot was born in Bourges in 1841. Her supportive and affluent family traveled around France before settling in Passy, a leafy suburb of Paris, in 1852. Berthe and her two sisters, Yves and Edma, were taught by Geoffroy-Alphonse Chocarne before Joseph Guichard showed them the colorful Romanticism of Eugène Delacroix and the merits of copying the Old Masters in the Louvre. The atmospheric light and delicate, airy brushwork in the sunlit landscapes of her final teacher, Camille Corot, helped Morisot to formulate her own form of impressionism. Her experiences during the Franco–Prussian War (1870–71), however, when Paris was bombarded during the siege and its citizens were subjected to starvation, interrupted her artistic development and affected her health for the rest of her life.

Both the River Seine and more distant parts of France inspired Morisot's landscapes. Many of her idyllic figure and landscape sketches were inspired by the green parkland of the Bois de Boulogne in Passy, and later in Bouvigal. Regular family visits to Normandy, southern France, the Isle of Wight, and Guernsey inspired her many views of shipping and promenaders in coastal ports. In works such as *The Harbor at Lorient* (1869) Morisot often placed a single figure in the foreground, isolated by a bold, diagonal motif, such as a bridge or balustrade. As viewers, we identify with such a figure, who is both removed and protected from the active world beyond the barrier, thus creating a mood of isolated reverie. Her family and domestic servants were the principal models for her figure paintings, including *Madame Morisot and Her Daughter, Madame Pontillon* (1869–70) and *The Psyché* (1876), which were set in the elegant interiors of her various homes in Paris and its suburbs.

Morisot married Edouard Manet's brother, Eugène, a painter, novelist, and civil servant, in 1874, and their daughter Julie was born in 1878. Julie became one of Morisot's favorite models, whom she portrayed in every phase of her life, from toddler, as in *Eugène Manet and His Daughter Julie at Bouvigal* (1881), to adolescence.

Morisot was encouraged by her friendships with many contemporary writers and painters, such as the symbolist poet Stéphane Mallarmé, who was godfather to Julie, Edgar Degas, Pierre Auguste Renoir, and

Full name: Berthe Morisot

Nationality: French

Style: impressionism

Dates: born 1841 in Bourges, died 1895 in Paris

Key works:

The Harbor at Lorient 1869

Madame Morisot and Her Daughter, Madame Pontillon 1869–70

Views of Paris from the Trocadero 1871–72

The Cradle 1872

Laundresses Hanging Out the Wash 1875

Eugène Manet and His Daughter Julie at Bouvigal 1881

The Cherry Tree 1891–92

Things to look for:

- loose, sketchy finish and delicate, pastel palette
- averted gazes
- bold, diagonal compositions and fluid contours
- women's and children's lives as subjects

Comparisons: Camille Corot, Mary Cassatt, Edgar Degas, Edouard Manet, Pierre Auguste Renoir

Glossary terms: etching, impressionism, Old Masters, palette, Romanticism, Salon, symbolism, (Les) Vingt

Pastel, palette, and the fluid line

Morisot's technique and subject matter celebrate the experiences of 19th-century women and children. She usually worked on a small scale, and her main artistic tools were a delicate, but rich, pastel palette, fluid lines, spontaneous brushstrokes, and unusual compositions. In her early works, such as *The Cradle* (1872), she used a higher degree of finish than in her later works.

The Cradle portrays one of Morisot's favorite motifs: the close bond between mother and daughter, and is a portrait of her sister, Edma, and Edma's baby daughter, Blanche. The baby and mother mirror each other's gestures by raising one hand, yet the two figures are contrasted in their different degrees of finish. The mother's fascinated, loving face is painted in careful detail, whereas the gauzy screen of the canopy intervenes between the viewer and infant, underlining the unformed features and personality of this newborn life.

Morisot, a sensitive and vibrant colorist, uses a subtle range of hues in the loosely rendered drapery of the cradle's canopy, in which areas of white and gray are punctuated by bursts of pink. She also uses black, which she avoided in her later work.

Morisot was a prolific artist in watercolor and pastel, media that encourage the use of vibrant colors and rapid, unblended brushstrokes. She experimented with techniques in these forms before applying them to her oil paintings. In later life she began to make prints, translating her pencil drawings into etchings and color lithographs.

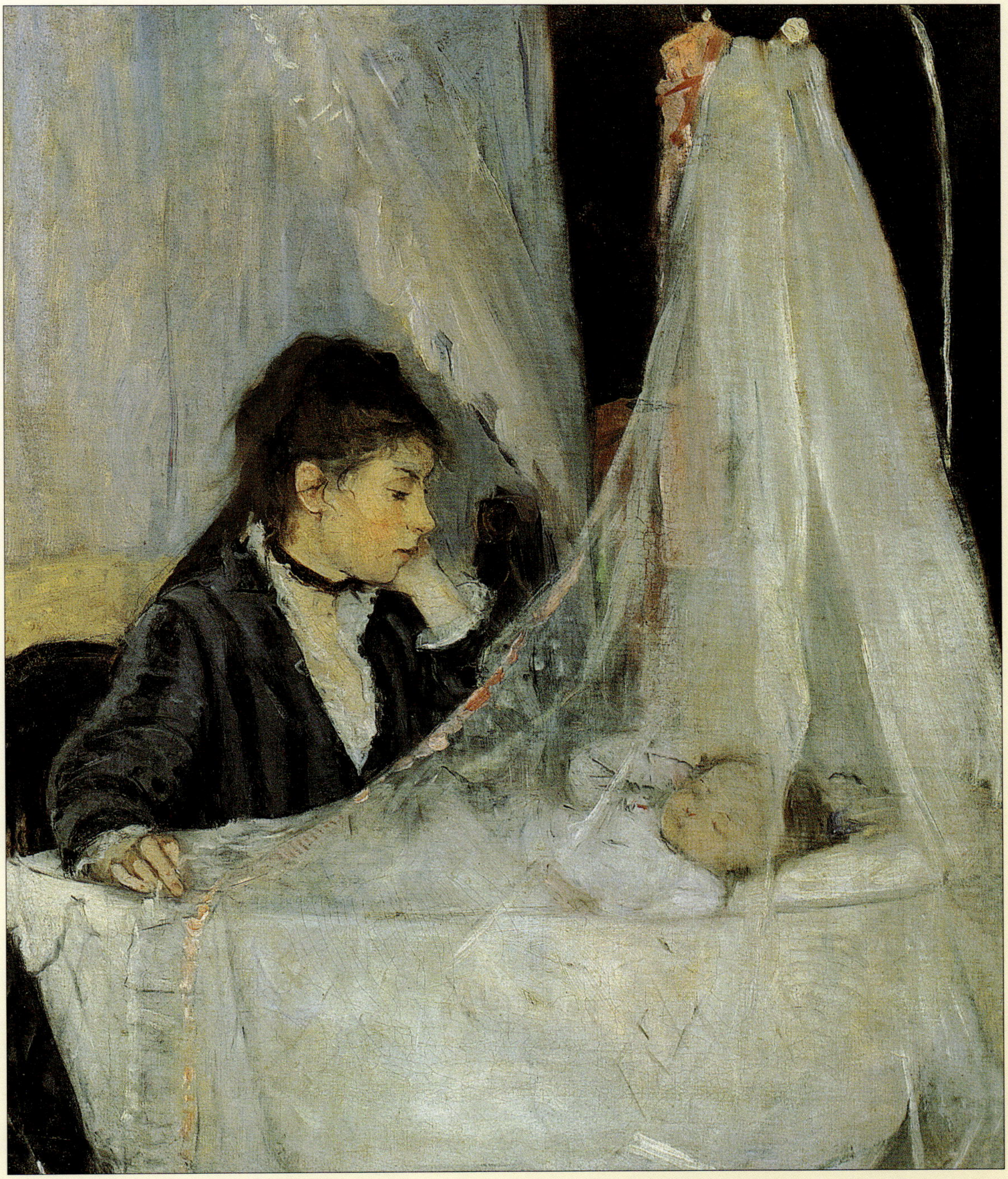

The Cradle *1872.*
Oil on canvas.
22 x 18 in
(56 x 46 cm).
Musée d'Orsay,
Paris.

Pierre-Cécile Puvis de Chavannes. She was also often painted by fellow artists.

Morisot was committed to achieving a career as a professional artist. She made her exhibiting debut in 1864, at the annual Salon. She also showed her work at all but one of the eight independent exhibitions of the Société Anonyme. Various members of the impressionist group selected and organized these shows between 1874 and 1886; Morisot and her husband played an active role in the later ones. She also exhibited with other artistic societies, such as the New English Art Club in London, as well as with Les Vingt ("The Twenty"), and the Association for Art in Belgium. A one-woman show in Paris in 1892 confirmed her reputation.

During the last years of her life Morisot shifted from landscapes and family interiors to intimate studies of hired models resting and dressing. Following her husband's death she left the chateau at Mesnil where the couple had intended to spend their final years, and moved into a Parisian apartment with Julie, where they painted together until Morisot's death in 1895.

MORRIS William

WILLIAM MORRIS WAS AN ARTIST, DESIGNER, WRITER, POET, and committed socialist. He created an interior decoration company, and designed stained glass, embroidery, wallpaper, furniture, tapestry, and books. Morris's work in literature and design inspired the next generation of Arts and Crafts designers, who sought to revive medieval craftsmanship, and found followers in the United States.

Life and work

Morris was born in Walthamstow, near London. He came from a large, well-off family and had an idyllic childhood. He developed his life-long fascination with the Middle Ages at an early age by reading novels set in the period and studying local monuments. When his father died, Morris was sent off to boarding school, and the family moved to Water House in Walthamstow (now the William Morris Museum).

Morris entered Exeter College at Oxford University in 1853. There he met the group of undergraduates who would become close friends. Among them was Edward Burne-Jones, the painter and stained-glass designer who was part of the Pre-Raphaelite Brotherhood, an association of painters and writers founded in 1848. The group immersed themselves in the writings of the contemporary art critic John Ruskin, who championed the Gothic Revival and saw a connection between art and moral aspects of society.

Morris and Burne-Jones traveled to northern France and to Belgium to study the medieval paintings and Gothic architecture. After graduating from Oxford, Morris joined a local architecture firm, while Burne-Jones apprenticed himself to a leader of the Pre-Raphaelite painters, Dante Gabriel Rossetti. The three men shared a flat in London. Morris abandoned architecture for painting, and in 1857 the three decorated the Debating Hall at Oxford University with frescos inspired by Thomas Malory's poem, *Le Morte d'Arthur* (completed in 1470).

In 1859 Morris married an Oxford girl, Jane Burden. She frequently posed for Rossetti, who also fell in love with her. Morris commissioned the architect Philip Webb to design their first home, the Red House, in Bexleyheath near London. The interior decoration was carried out by Morris and his friends.

In 1861 Morris, Webb, Rossetti, Ford Madox Brown (an artist), P. P. Marshall (a surveyor), and Charles Faulkner (an accountant) formed the interior decoration firm of Morris, Marshall, Faulkner, and Company. Their designs got a mixed reception when shown at the London World's Fair, but did get them noticed. Among the firm's first commissions were stained-glass windows for churches, and the decoration of rooms in the South Kensington Museum (now the Victoria and Albert Museum) in London.

The firm's aim was to make objects through individual craftsmanship, an idea that ran counter to notions of progress brought about by the increasing mechanization and industrialization of the time. Morris advocated the importance of good design and workmanship in life, and wanted to create objects of "beauty and utility" for the home. In 1875 Morris bought out the other partners and renamed the firm Morris and Co. From then on, working only with Burne-Jones and Webb, Morris specialized in wallpaper and textile designs, opening a shop in London in 1877. That year he also founded the Society for the Protection of Ancient Buildings, to help protect original craftsmanship from the extensive restoration of medieval cathedrals.

Morris helped to form the Art Worker's Guild in 1884, and the Art and Craft Exhibition Society in 1888. From these emerged what came to be called the Arts and Crafts movement.

Morris visited Iceland in 1871 and 1873, admiring the simple life of the people there. A committed socialist, he formed the Hammersmith Socialist Society, and briefly edited *Commonweal*, a socialist periodical. Morris was also a talented writer. Among his works were an epic poem, *The Earthly Paradise* (1866–67), and a futuristic utopian novel, *News from Nowhere* (1891).

In 1891 Morris set up the Kelmscott Press, a private printing press that published lavishly illustrated editions of the great works of English literature. Its finest edition was *The Works of Geoffrey Chaucer* (1896) with 87 woodcuts by Burne-Jones and decorative borders by Morris.

Data file

Full name: William Morris

Nationality: English

Style: Arts and Crafts

Dates: born 1834 in Walthamstow, near London, died 1896 in London

Key works:
- *La Belle Iseult* (oil painting) 1858
- Saint George's cabinet 1861
- hand block-printed wallpapers, including *Fruit* 1866
- Sussex armchair c1868
- *Honeysuckle* chintz wallpaper 1876
- stained-glass windows for Trinity Church, Boston, England 1883–87
- *Woodpecker* high-warp tapestry 1885
- Kelmscott Press edition of *The Works of Geoffrey Chaucer* 1896

Things to look for:
- works in a variety of media: tapestry, wood, stained glass, manuscript illumination
- traditional materials and methods of production

Comparisons: Edward Burne-Jones, Dante Gabriel Rossetti, John Ruskin

Glossary terms: Arts and Crafts movement, Gothic Revival, Pre-Raphaelite Brotherhood

Beauty, utility, and nature: a Morris wallpaper

Morris is best known for his flat patterns, which were made into wallpapers, tapestries, and carpets. In his designs, individual details of birds or flowers remain closely related to an accurate depiction of living nature, but are woven into a more abstract overall structure. Morris himself described his ambition: "to combine clearness of form and firmness of structure with the mystery which comes of abundance and richness of detail."

Fruit of 1866 was one of Morris's first wallpaper designs. It captures the different rounded shapes and colors of fruits in each stage of their development, from bud to bursting flesh. The fruits are interspersed among leaves and branches, which create a series of opposing diagonal lines. This double focus allows us to enjoy both the minute detail of each fruit or leaf and the repeated diagonal pattern that harmonizes these elements into a whole.

In addition to a close study of nature, Morris developed his patterns from the history of ornamental design. He studied and helped to collect the large and diverse textile collection in the Victoria and Albert Museum. He learned from the elaborate interlacing of Arab and Indian design, the stylization of Greek ornament, and the elaborate continuity of Byzantine art, to develop his own visual rhythms.

Wallpapers such as this were made using wooden blocks produced in craft workshops, which looked to the medieval craft guilds as the ideal model. All the goods sold by Morris and Co. showed attention to craft methods, such as hand block-printing for wallpapers, rather than the mechanized production of factories, which Morris saw as dehumanizing.

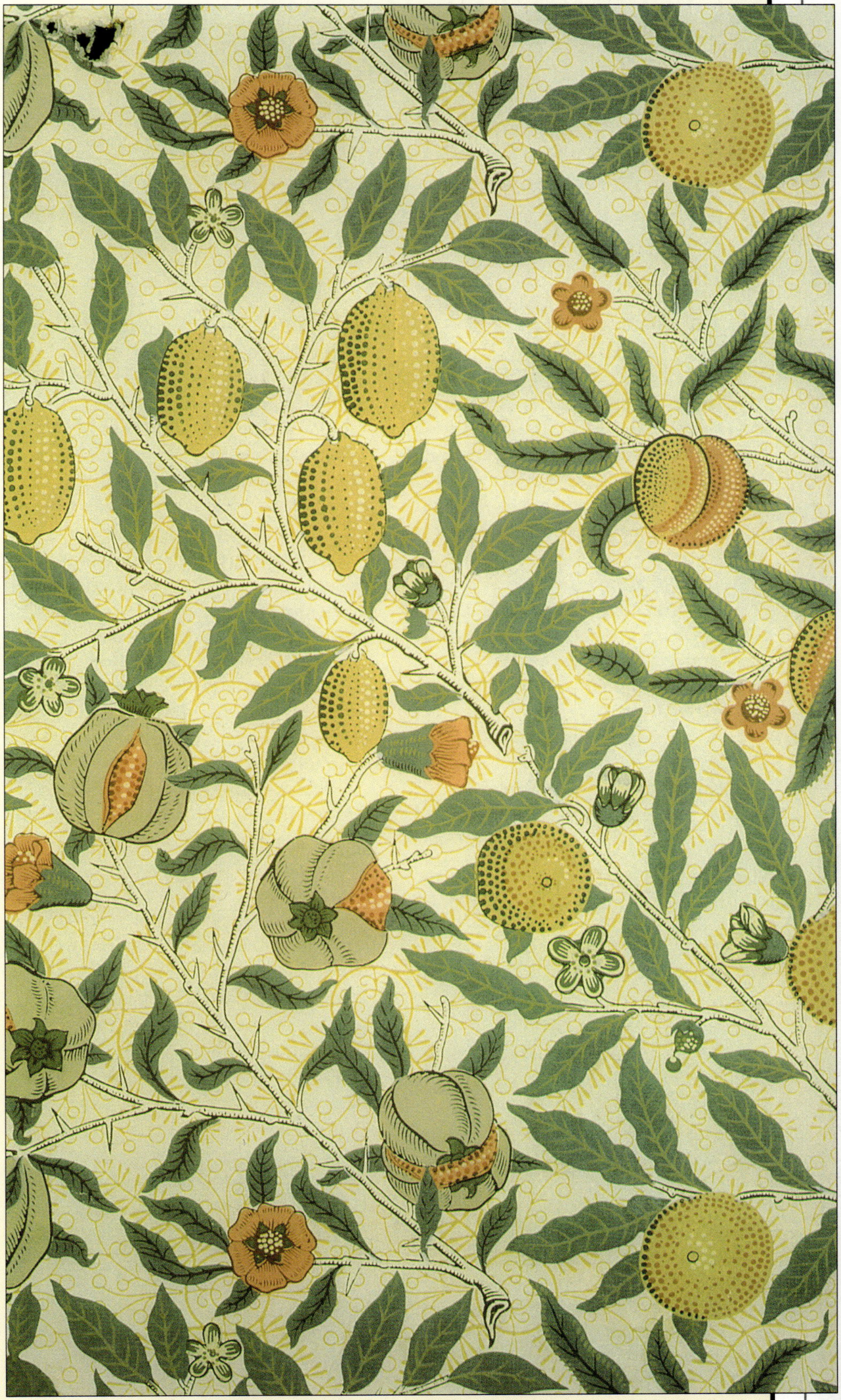

Fruit *1866. Hand block-printed wallpaper. Victoria and Albert Museum, London.*

MOTHERWELL Robert

ROBERT MOTHERWELL BROUGHT AN INTELLECTUAL BEARING to abstract expressionism. Along with Jackson Pollock and Willem de Kooning, he helped the movement achieve dominance in the United States in the 1950s. He was also influential in the art world as a writer and a teacher.

Life and work

Motherwell studied philosophy at Stanford University and then esthetics at Harvard University. His studies took him to Europe in the 1930s, where he was exposed to the developing and competing factions of modern art. Surrealism, particularly in its more abstract manifestations, was the movement that had the most profound effect on him and inspired him to create works of his own, first in Paris and then back in New York during a period of art history study at Columbia University.

Most artists associated with abstract movements—even painters such as Piet Mondrian, Kasimir Malevich, Wassily Kandinsky, and Jackson Pollock—progressed to abstraction gradually, having first worked in more traditional styles of representational, or figurative, painting. Unlike these artists, however, Motherwell began working in an abstract style immediately. He was strongly influenced by the automatic process (automatism) practiced by many of the surrealists. It was a method by which they endeavored to suppress conscious control over the creative process, hoping to achieve a freer, more emotional style of drawing and painting. Motherwell borrowed this approach from the surrealists and applied it to the emerging style of abstract expressionism.

Much of Motherwell's early work was small-scale—spontaneous sketches and collages of disparate elements, arranged to produce expressive compositions. For such collages he began to use fibrous paper, torn and soaked in ink or paint. Paper saturated in black liquid proved to be of immense appeal to Motherwell, and black became a constant element in his art throughout his life.

Motherwell frequently worked on themed series of paintings, collages, and prints. The most famous of these is the *Elegy to the Spanish Republic* series. The first work, *Elegy to the Spanish Republic No. 1* (1948), was a small composition in ink on paper; one of the last, *Elegy to the Spanish Republic No. 172 (With Blood)* (1990), was a canvas of over 78 x 117 in (200 x 300 cm).

Through the late 1940s and early 1950s, Motherwell spent a great deal of time teaching and theorizing on the nature of modern art. He edited a series of publications entitled *Documents of Modern Art* and wrote many essays for contemporary art journals. Following the breakup of his second marriage, he produced the *Je T'aime* series of paintings (1954–58), which demonstrate the very personal nature

Data file

Full name: Robert Motherwell

Nationality: American

Style: abstract expressionism

Dates: born 1915 in Aberdeen, WA, died 1991 in Provincetown, MA

Key works:
- *Elegy to the Spanish Republic* series 1948–90
- *Je T'aime No. 8 (Mallarmé's Swan: Homage)* 1957
- *Beside the Sea* series 1962
- *In Plato's Cave No. 1* 1972
- *Yellow Wall* from the *Open* series 1973
- *Hollow Men* 1983

Things to look for:
- recurrent shapes, especially ovals and verticals
- extensive use of black as a principal color

Comparisons: Joan Miró, Barnet Newman, Willem de Kooning, Jackson Pollock, Helen Frankenthaler

Glossary terms: abstract art, abstract expressionism, automatism, collage, esthetics, surrealism

Reflecting a sense of the individual

Motherwell began making paintings at a time when the idea of individual creative will had never been stronger. Acknowledging this, he once wrote, "Anyone can paint blue and put a line on it...the real test is if you'll stake your life and your reputation on it.... The only virtue I have over any other painter is I'm the only person who can make 'Motherwells.' This is a very different situation from the Renaissance or the Middle Ages, in which the virtue was to make a specific kind of thing, and who made it was a matter of inconsequence so long as it was well made...."

The *Elegy to the Spanish Republic* series (1948–90), consisting of more than 100 pictures, exemplifies how Motherwell created personal expression out of simple means. All the works make use of two principal motifs: a rough oval shape and a slightly longer vertical bar or post. The shapes are repeated two or three times in each composition and are never precise. They are, however, recognizable, in much the same way that a scribbled signature, in which the individual letters are illegible, can still be recognized.

It is difficult to understand the significance of such shapes for Motherwell, and their meaning for him seems almost impossible to put into words—there is something almost primeval about the insistence of the shapes. Their significance surely grew more profound for the artist over the years—he returned again and again to paint these shapes, and they must have taken on a special status for him over time.

Motherwell's art seeks to express *from* the artist rather than communicate *to* the viewer. His works are therefore very much

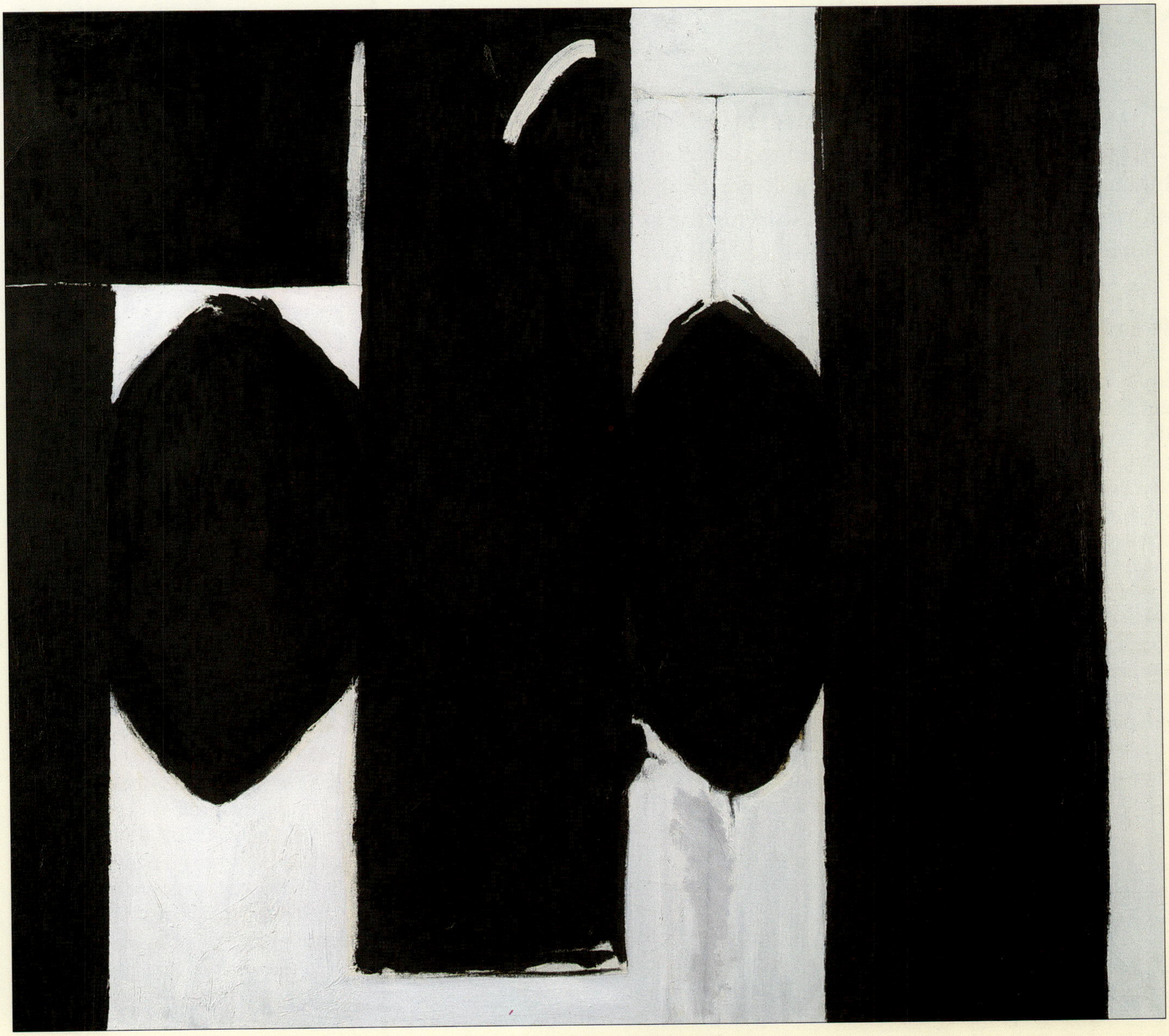

open to the viewer's interpretation. Their meaning—what they are about—arises jointly from the artist's expression and the viewer's reaction to it. Perhaps strangely, the simplicity of Motherwell's paintings makes them obscure and impenetrable for some viewers. His main aim, however, was simply to let the visual form evolve before the idea—to paint before deciding what to paint. He believed that some kind of meaning could be conveyed through the visual language of gesture and form.

Elegy to the Spanish Republic No. 55
1955–60. Oil on canvas. 70 x 76 in (179 x 193 cm). Cleveland Museum of Art, OH.

of his work. Here—as with the *Elegy* series—there is the insistence of repetition; in this case, the declaration "Je t'aime" (I love you).

Motherwell was married to the artist Helen Frankenthaler from 1958 to 1971. In the 1960s they moved to the coastal location of Provincetown, MA, which inspired Motherwell's *Beside the Sea* series, over 60 works in which he splashed oil paint onto paper using as much physical strength as he could muster. His intention was not to represent the appearance of the waves, but rather to imitate their action. *Hollow Men* (1983), was Motherwell's last major series, in which he brought together stylistic elements of the *Elegy* series and the more sensuous, color-filled *Open* series produced in the late 1960s and early 1970s.

MUNCH Edvard

EDVARD MUNCH IS NORWAY'S MOST FAMOUS ARTIST. A founder of expressionism, which attempted to convey deep feelings in art, Munch produced work that was highly personal, and sometimes very disturbing. He devoted most of his working life to painting every facet of human emotion in what he called his "Frieze of Life."

Life and work

Born in Lote, Norway, Edvard Munch spent his early years in Christiania (later renamed Oslo), the Norwegian capital. He grew up in a conservative, rather puritanical household, but his friends were unconventional bohemians interested in anarchy and "free love." Munch studied at the School of Drawing, and was regarded as one of Norway's most gifted young painters before he was 20. Famously, he said, "I paint not what I see, but what I saw," meaning that he was interested in memories and emotions rather than stories or the material world. His themes are universal—the stages of life, love, and death.

Data file

Full name: Edvard Munch

Nationality: Norwegian

Style: expressionism/symbolism

Dates: born 1863 in Lote, died 1944 in Ekely

Key works:

- *The Sick Child* 1885
- *The Scream* 1893
- *Puberty* 1894–95
- *The Madonna* 1894
- *Self-portrait with Cigarette* 1895
- *The Dance of Life* 1900
- *Between the Clock and the Bed* 1940–42

Things to look for:

- sinuous lines
- themes of death and sickness
- themes of love and jealousy
- large dark shadows

Comparisons: Ernst Ludwig Kirchner, James Ensor, Oskar Kokoschka

Glossary terms: expressionism, symbolism

Sickness and death in Munch's work are sometimes blackly humorous, represented with dancing skeletons or menacing vampires. However, there was a profoundly personal and serious side to this apparent morbidity. Munch's own life was touched by death and disease. His mother died of tuberculosis when Munch was five years old, after giving birth to his sister, Ingar. His brother died in 1895, aged 30. But it was the death of his sister Sophie, when Munch was 14 and she only a year older, that made the greatest impact on him. She suffered a long time with the tuberculosis that had already taken their mother. Munch watched Sophie's decline and later produced several works, such as *The Sick Child* (1885), in which she appears, pale and weak on her deathbed, in an atmosphere of bleak despair. We sense that Munch was both fascinated and terrified by death. He must have understood something of his sister's ordeal, as he too contracted the disease, suffering fever and hallucinations.

In 1889 Munch went to Paris to study at the Ecole des Beaux-Arts. Committed to working true to intimate human experience, he wrote: "We will not paint interiors any longer, no people reading, no women knitting. We must paint living beings who breathe and feel, suffer and love."

Ironically, Munch's success as an artist was brought about, in part, by negative criticism. In 1892 Munch was invited to show his work in Berlin. His images of sex, death, and violence outraged so many important people—including the German Kaiser himself—that the exhibition was closed after only six days. But the publicity did wonders for Munch's career, making him famous overnight.

"Frieze of Life" was the collective title Munch gave to a large group of his paintings dealing with many aspects of love and death. Several are set against the distinctive Norwegian coastline of

Anxiety and expression

The Scream (1893) is the picture for which Munch is best known. One of the most arresting images in his "Frieze of Life," it represents what Munch called the "terror of life." He made about 50 different versions in several different media.

A figure stands on a bridge or coastal path, reminiscent perhaps of the shoreline near Oslo. He appears to be screaming silently, his isolation emphasized by the indifference of the other figures.

Munch's own statements about the painting provide the key to understanding it. In 1892, in the south of France, Munch recorded in his diary a memory of a sensation he had experienced back in Norway. He wrote: "I was walking along the road with two friends. The sun set. I felt a tinge of melancholy. Suddenly the sky became bloody red. I stopped, leaned against the railing, dead tired, and I looked at the flaming clouds that hung like blood and a sword over the blue-black fjord and the city. My friends walked on. I stood there, trembling with fright. And I felt a loud, unending scream piercing nature."

The scream is sensed by the figure, and it is nature that screams. This intense and frightening psychic experience has been translated by Munch into a bloody landscape to convey the artist's extreme anxiety, distorted reality, and isolation.

The Scream has been interpreted as expressing a fear of losing one's identity, of being "swallowed up" by the environment. Some thought Munch was mad; others saw his work as expressing universal fears. It is certainly true that painting expressed his own anxieties, and was sometimes therapeutic for him. Munch later said he had been suffering from agoraphobia—the acute fear of open spaces—when he painted *The Scream*.

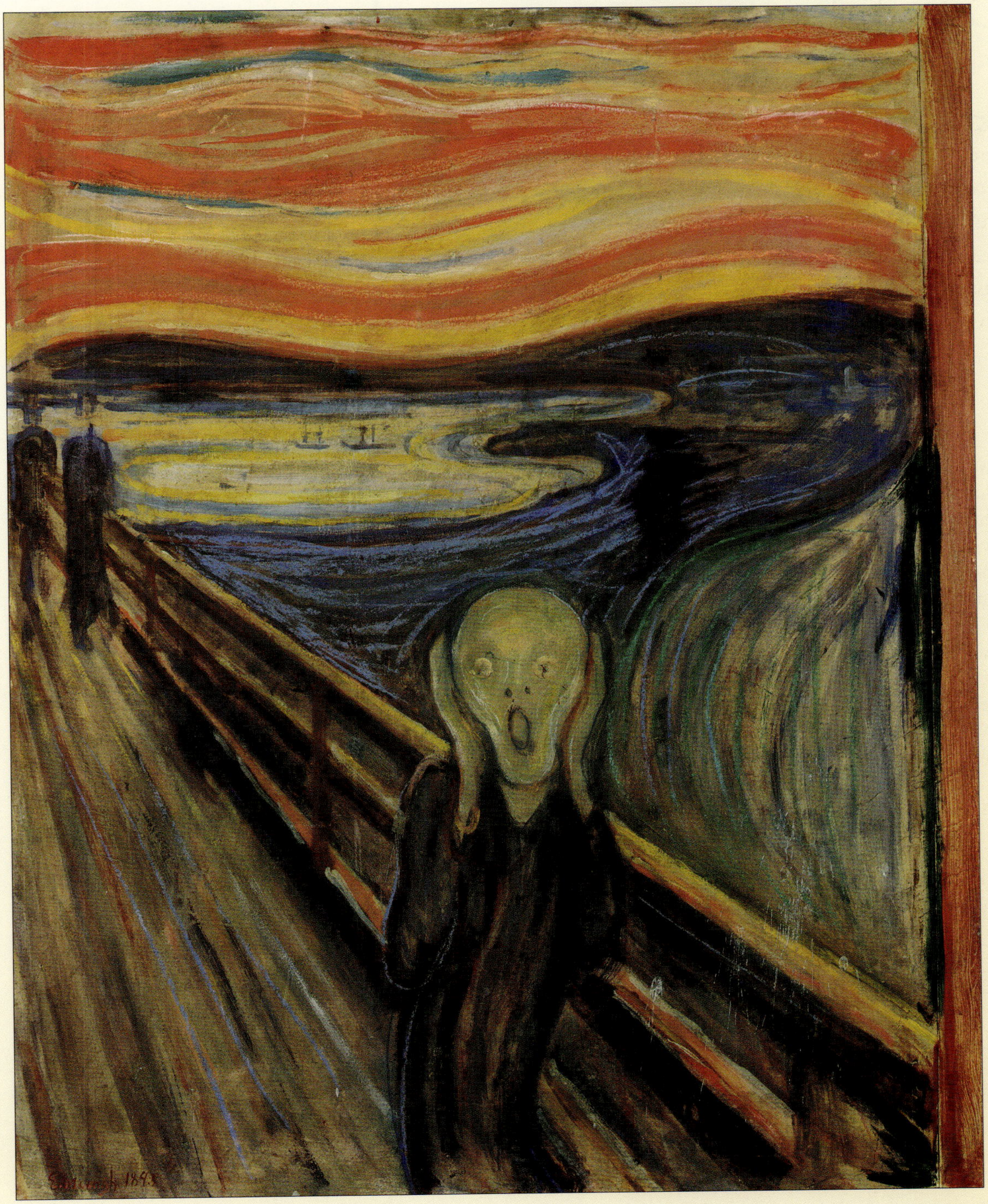

The Scream *1893. Oil, pastel, and casein on cardboard. 35¾ x 29 in (91 x 73.5 cm). Nasjonalgalleriet, Oslo.*

Asgardstrand, where Munch spent his summers. In pictures such as *Jealousy* (1894), Munch explored the dark side of love. Jealousy was an emotion he knew well through a passionate affair he had had with a married woman. The painting is set in an Eden-like garden and expresses a troubled love-triangle poisoned by temptation. A couple, like a modern Adam and Eve, are absorbed in one another, while a haunting third figure faces us, tormented by the thought or memory of the woman.

Munch was lively and sociable by nature, and had a sharp wit. However, he also suffered from bouts of depression. He drank heavily, but this made him violent and culminated in a nervous breakdown, for which he was treated in a clinic in Copenhagen.

In old age he was almost completely blind. In the years before his death in 1944, he helped persecuted artists fleeing Nazi Germany.

MURILLO Bartolomé

THE MOST IMPORTANT RELIGIOUS PAINTER OF 17TH-CENTURY SPAIN, Murillo was one of the few painters, with Velázquez, to be widely known outside his own country during his lifetime. Spending much of his life in his native Seville, he concentrated on religious painting. He produced images of the Virgin Mary and parables that were studies of everyday life. Murillo was also father of a large family, and his love of children is apparent in much of his work.

Life and work

Bartolomé Murillo spent most of his life in Seville, the rich and ancient city in southern Spain where he was born. As a boy he applied to travel to the New World, where he had many relatives, but it does not seem that he ever made the journey. From 1645 he became established as Seville's most important religious artist. Many of his commissions were carried out for monasteries and churches in the city, and some of them remain in their original setting.

Murillo worked as a painter for the whole of his career and achieved a very respected position. He only once made a major journey away from Seville, and his art is strongly influenced by the character of this highly religious city. He also played an important part in civic life and in artistic education. For example, he was concerned with the reputation of painters and with their possibilities for advancement. In 1660 he helped to found the Academy of Seville, where artists could be trained, although he later transferred his teaching to his own studio.

In his earlier work, Murillo used a naturalistic style that was popular in Spain at the time and was being developed by Diego Velázquez. His *Prodigal Son* series (c1660–70) tells the story of a young man who led a wild life but was finally welcomed back home by his loving father (a parable for the erring Christian being welcomed to heaven). Murillo used contemporary dress and settings to bring the events alive for his audience. He loved painting street life: his *Flower Girl* (c1670) affectionately depicts a young girl selling flowers, which are scattered in her shawl, but also offers a reminder of the brevity of youth and beauty.

Murillo's largest works were his religious scenes, generally intended to be displayed above the altar in a church and used for devotional purposes by worshippers. Where his works survive in the buildings for which they were intended, one can see how much thought he gave to using the existing light to create sympathetic lighting effects to illuminate his compositions.

Data file

Full name: Bartolomé Esteban Murillo
Nationality: Spanish
Style: naturalism/religious
Dates: born c1617 in Seville, died 1682 in Seville
Key works:
- *Four Figures on a Step* c1655–60
- *Immaculate Conception of the Escorial* c1660–65
- *The Prodigal Son* series c1660–70
- *Self-portrait* c1670
- *The Flower Girl* c1670

Things to look for:
- strong religious feeling
- naturalistic detail
- humorous depiction of street life and of the poor
- soft, rich paint

Comparisons: José Ribera, Diego Velázquez, Thomas Gainsborough
Glossary terms: devotional, earth colors, genre painting, low life scenes

Murillo's portraits and genre paintings

The art of self-portraiture was practiced by many artists in the 17th century, in very different ways. Only two self-portraits by Murillo have survived. This portrait (below) is dated about 1670 and shows the artist aged just over 50. As the inscription beneath the oval frame reveals, it was commissioned "to fulfill the wishes and prayers of his children." The picture uses the device of a frame within a frame, which was popular at the time. Here we are led to think that the portrait is itself a painting set within a larger picture space, but the idea is questioned by the way in which the sitter's hand emerges from the inner picture space to rest on the frame. The tools of the artist's trade lie on the shelf in front of him: his palette and brushes, the paper he has used for sketching the figure of a male nude, and a ruler and compass.

Murillo is shown as a self-assured and calm individual, richly dressed and confident of his abilities. This revealing

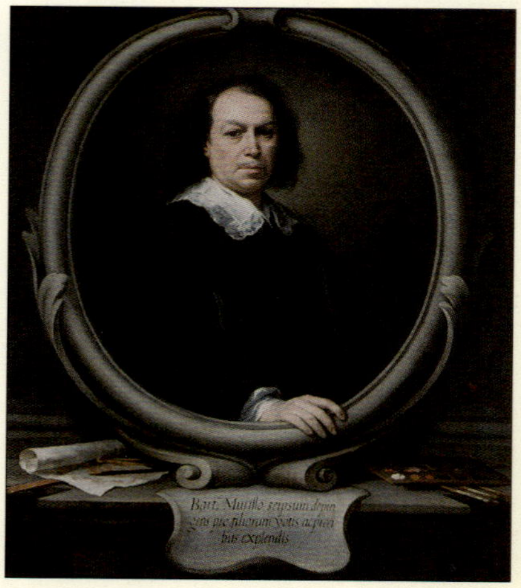

Self-portrait *c1670. Oil on canvas. 48 x 42 in (122 x 107 cm). National Gallery, London.*

He painted numerous depictions of the Immaculate Conception, showing the moment when the Virgin Mary conceived Jesus Christ through divine power. In the *Immaculate Conception of*

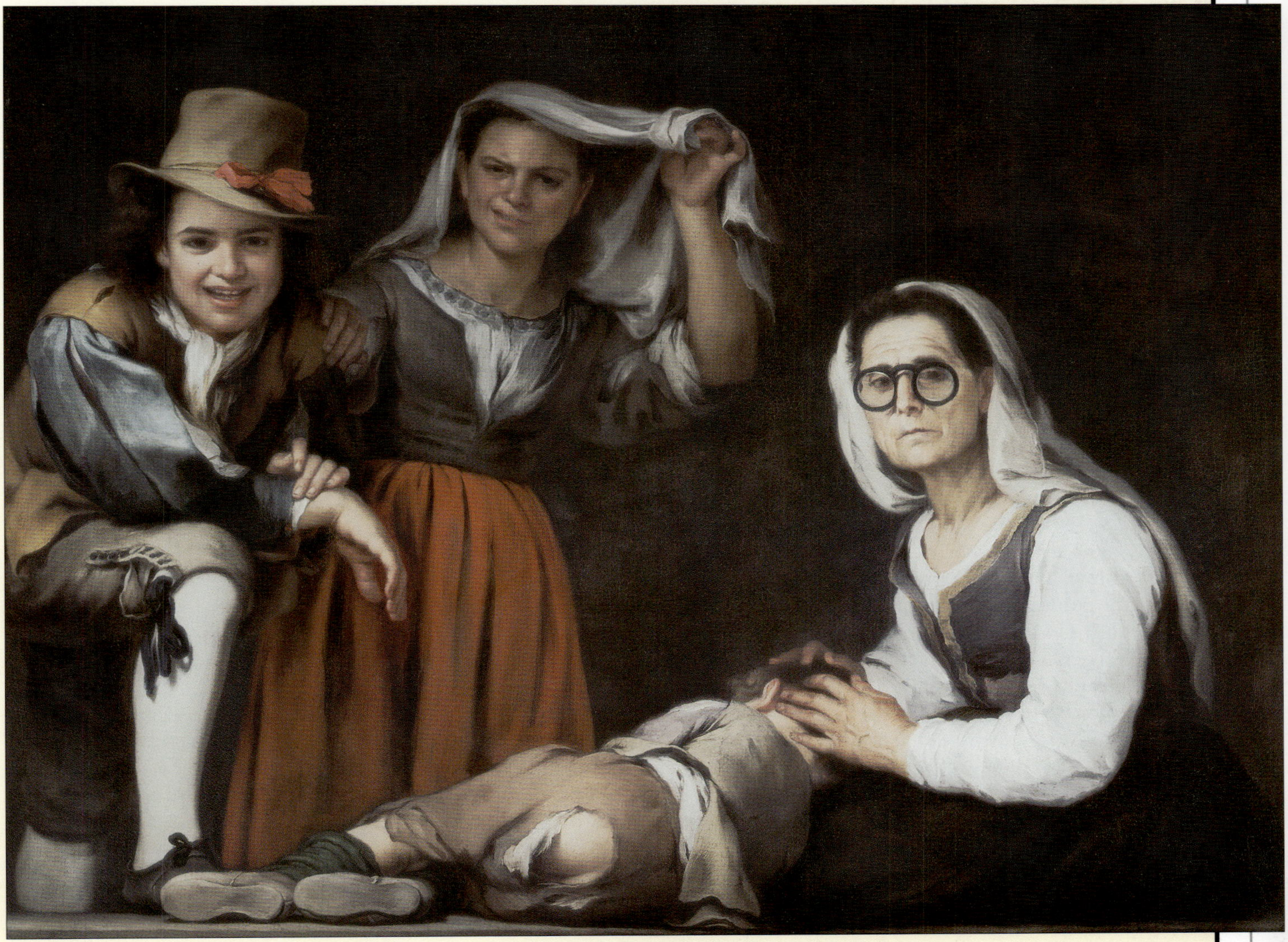

painting stresses the growing status and respect shown to painters in the 17th century, when they were attributed with an important social role and unique abilities. Here, the artist shows self-understanding: he does not conceal the effects of age, such as the slightly receding hair and the loosening of his chin, nor the melancholy in his eyes.

Murillo is remembered for his portraits (of which only a few exist), for his religious paintings, and also for his depictions of everyday life. This last type of picture is often called "genre painting." He gained a great reputation for work of this type. His *Four Figures on a Step*, painted between about 1655 and 1660, is a good example of this genre painting. Painted in the dark, earth colors that the artist favored for his "low life scenes," it shows three adults—including a woman wearing glasses; though not often depicted in paintings, these were already being used in the Middle Ages. The woman in the glasses soothes the head of a young boy who is lying asleep, with his torn trousers and the soles of his feet firmly in the foreground of the picture. All the sitters are gazing out from the picture. This tendency to depict the figures as though they are trying to communicate directly with the spectator, the simple naturalism of the costumes, and the sense of alertness of the figures' mood, are typical of Murillo.

Four Figures on a Step *c1655–60. Oil on canvas. 43 1/4 x 56 1/2 in (110 x 143.5 cm). Kimbell Art Museum, Fort Worth, TX.*

the Escorial (c1660–65) the youthful Mary is shown rising on a cloud, communing with heaven, and surrounded by angels bearing such symbols as the martyr's palm.

Murillo's home town of Seville was a major port, and his work appealed to merchants and sea captains from the north, who bought his paintings.

His soft, melting colors, command of lighting effects, the dramatic compositions of some of his paintings, and his feeling for children, influenced later artists, such as the English painter Thomas Gainsborough.

NEWMAN Barnett

BARNETT NEWMAN'S LIFE WAS CONSUMED by his passion for art, which he regarded as the highest achievement of humanity. His paintings, among the most restrained abstract-expressionist works, using pure color and stripes, were influential for painters during the 1960s, when he finally received recognition.

Life and work

Barnett Newman, the eldest son of Russian-Polish émigrés, was born in New York. From an early age he mixed his school studies with frequent visits to the city's galleries and museums, and when he was 18 he began taking drawing classes at the Art Students' League. Although he was not naturally gifted in the academic style of drawing that was taught at the school, he nevertheless persevered until he had attained a reasonable standard. Encouraged by his tutors, he pursued his art training alongside studies in philosophy, and eventually graduated from City College. Newman agreed to work for a brief period in his father's clothing business in order to earn enough money to support his fledgling art career. The plan backfired, however, due to the stock-market crash and subsequent Depression of the 1930s, which almost bankrupted his father. The young and idealistic artist then found an alternative way in which to support himself: teaching in the city's high schools.

Throughout the early part of his career Newman occasionally gave up painting, at one stage making an unsuccessful bid to become the mayor of New York, and embarking upon the study of bird and plant life during the early 1940s. It was not long before he returned to the easel, however, and by the mid-1940s he was beginning to develop his characteristic style in such works as *The Beginning* and *Moment* (both 1946).

In 1948 came the first signs of a breakthrough for Newman. This was the year in which he painted *Onement I*, a work that in its simplicity, richness of color, and poetry of title has come to be seen as Newman's defining work. It was this small painting that seemed to provide the key for all of the work that followed it throughout the remaining 22 years of Newman's life. In 1948, too, Newman published an article entitled "The Sublime is Now" in the art journal *Tiger's Eye*. This article was, in a sense, a prescription for his work: "The image we produce is the self-evident one of revelation, real and concrete, that can be understood by anyone who will look at it without the nostalgic glasses of history," he wrote.

It was cunning way of telling people how to look at his paintings, but it was largely ignored by the critics, who went to his first two solo exhibitions, which were staged at the Betty Parsons Gallery in New York in 1950 and 1951. Both shows were badly received by critics and by artists—even his fellow abstract expressionists.

Data file

Full name: Barnett Newman

Nationality: American

Style: abstract expressionism

Dates: born 1905 in New York, NY, died 1970 in New York, NY

Key works:
- *Onement I* 1948
- *Be I* 1949
- *Abraham* 1949
- *Eve* 1950
- *Adam* 1951–52
- *Stations of the Cross* 1965–66
- *Who's Afraid of Red, Yellow, and Blue III* 1966–67

Things to look for:
- vertical sections that divide the color field
- saturation of color
- monumental scale that encompasses the viewer

Comparisons: Mark Rothko, Clyfford Still, Ad Reinhardt, Kasimir Malevich, Yves Klein, Donald Judd, Robert Motherwell

Glossary terms: abstract expressionism, color-field painting, esthetics, sublime

Esthetics and the artist

During a panel discussion entitled "Esthetics and the Artist" in 1952, Newman commented, "Esthetics is for the artist as ornithology is for the birds." This statement succinctly summed up his opinion that esthetics (a method with which to prescribe and order our ideas of beauty) had no place in the mind nor heart of the artist. The artist's role, as Newman saw it, was to search for ways in which to express the state of being. He wanted to make the viewer profoundly aware of existence in a way that could not be stated or illustrated visually. In short, he wanted to express what is inexpressible.

Because of the difficulty of this concept, it is frequently hard to make a connection between what we see in his paintings and his lofty aspirations. Newman had an extremely high opinion of the role of art: to him, a painting was not merely an object with physical attributes that can be appreciated or not, but rather a means with which to invoke a sense of the sublime. Newman worked for many years before he felt that he had created a form that was sufficient for his task, and even after he had created that initial work, *Onement I* (1948), he still spent months considering it before accepting it as his archetype for the paintings that followed.

Adam (1951–52) contains many of the same qualities as *Onement I*, including similar colors, but Newman's confidence had grown considerably in the three years between the two paintings, and with that came a dramatic increase in the scale of his work. With *Adam* he clearly wanted to create a work that was impressive and imposing. Seen up close, it is a painting

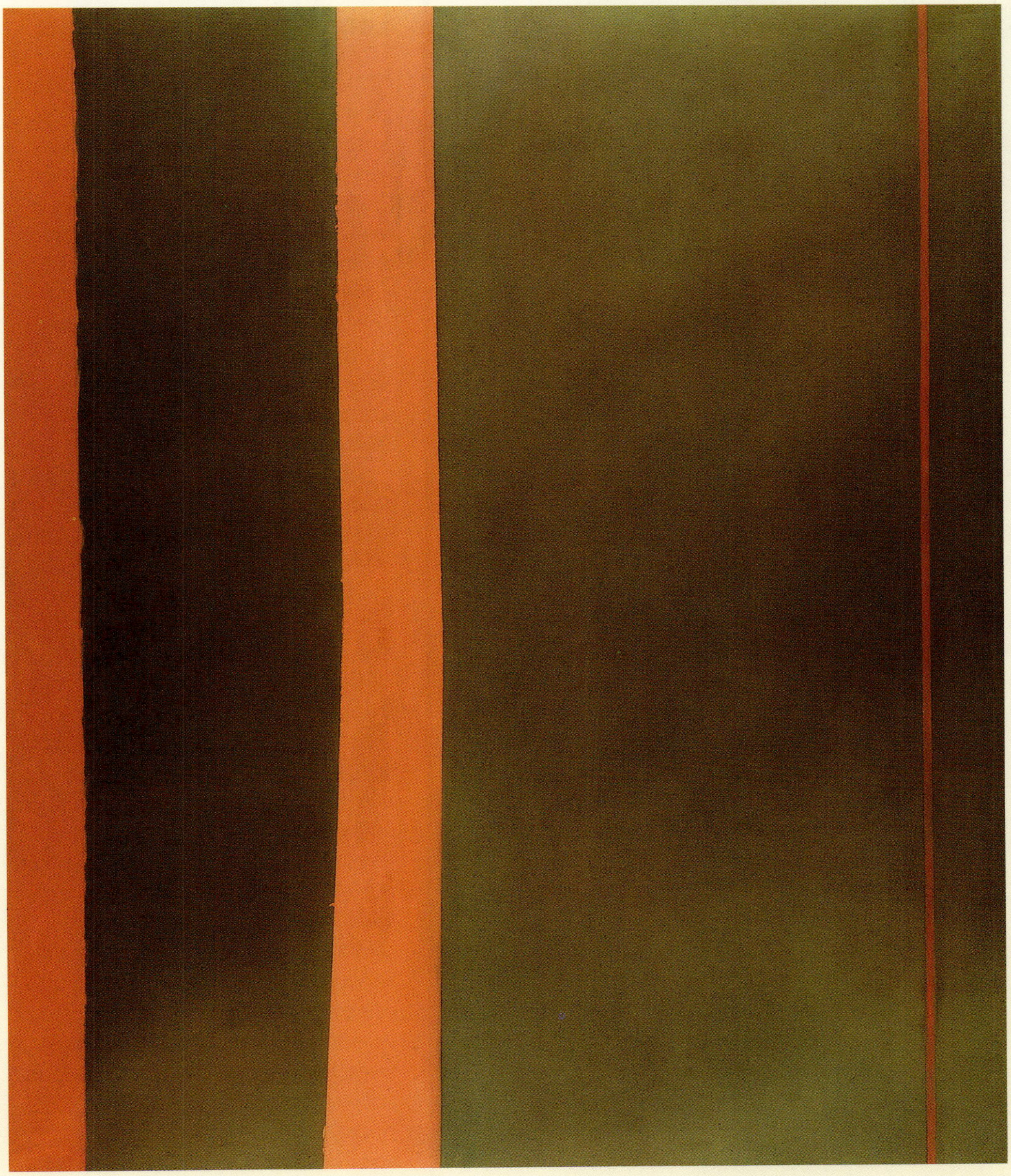

Adam *1951–52. Oil on canvas. 96 x 80 in (244 x 203.5 cm). Tate Gallery, London.*

that dominates and consumes the viewer's vision with a saturation of color, divided by vertical bands that mirror and overwhelm the standing spectator. It is an invitation to the viewer to engage with the painting in a mood of introspection that is usually reserved for a spiritual experience. There is nothing light-hearted or casual about Newman's work, for his efforts are earnest, considered, and very deliberate. Whether they achieve his desired effect, however, is ultimately up to the perception of the viewer.

Such vehement criticism confounded Newman, who vowed never to exhibit his work again. He did, however, but it was not until 1959 that there was another substantial show of his work. By that time the mood of the art world had changed: having grown tired of the approach of many abstract expressionists, it was more prepared for the cooler, restrained, and more contemplative work of Newman, in which color was the principal expressive force.

His most successful and productive period now began, a period which included his major work *Stations of the Cross* (1965–66), a series of 14 monochromatic paintings. During the 1960s Newman also made steel sculptures, the forms of which, in works such as the *Here* series and *Broken Obelisk*, recall the vertical strips (or "zips," as he referred to them) on his canvases. At the end of this decade, and at the height of his success, Newman had a fatal heart attack and died on July 4, 1970.

NOLAN Sidney

SIDNEY NOLAN, AN INTERNATIONALLY ACCLAIMED AUSTRALIAN painter, was one of the most widely traveled artists of his generation. For more than 50 years he worked in an imaginative, highly personal expressionist style. He produced vivid, semiabstract interpretations of the Australian landscape, and of legendary figures from the country's history.

Life and work

After leaving school in 1932, Sidney Nolan took evening classes at the art school of the National Gallery of Victoria in Melbourne. His parents hoped he might become a teacher, but he was determined to be an artist.

In 1938 he met John Reed, who in the 1940s helped publish the avant-garde journal *Angry Penguins*. Reed and his wife lived in Heidelberg, near Melbourne. In the 1880s Heidelberg had been a center for Australian impressionists such as Arthur Streeton, Charles Conder, and Tom Roberts; it remained a magnet for young Australian artists in the 20th century.

Nolan became a founding member of the Contemporary Art Society, which urged artists to give expression to contemporary thought and life, and to break the restrictions they felt the "official" Australian art world imposed. In 1940 Nolan staged his first one-man show. His early abstract works, such as *Boy and the Moon* (c1939–40), betray a debt to the modernist European art he had been able to study only through reproductions in books.

In 1942, conscripted into the army, Nolan was posted to Wimmera in Victoria. The countryside, with its black-soil plains, stunted trees, and granite and sandstone cliffs, compelled him to paint landscapes. When he could not paint because of his military duties, he made pages of small drawings in colored chalk. Nolan regularly sent his work to his friends, the Reeds, in Heidelberg, and in return they sent him painting materials.

In 1944, sick with fever, and unwilling to be posted to the front line in New Guinea, he went absent without leave. John Reed arranged false papers for him, and Nolan hid out at "Heide." That year he began the first of his Ned Kelly paintings, and he made his first visit to "Kelly country."

Further journeys were to follow: in 1947 he visited Queensland and explored the island where, generations before, the shipwrecked Eliza Fraser had seen her sea-captain husband killed by hostile Aborigines before making her way back to civilization with the help of an escaped convict, David Bracefell. Nolan drew the landscape, birds, and flowers, and began a series of paintings based on Mrs. Fraser.

In 1948 Nolan set off to travel by road, rail, air, and sea to some of the remotest parts of Australia. The trip

Data file

Full name: Sidney Nolan

Nationality: Australian

Style: highly personal with touches of expressionism and surrealism

Dates: born 1917 in Melbourne, died 1992 in London, England

Key works:
- *Boy and the Moon* c1939–40
- *Ned Kelly* 1946
- *Kelly, Spring* 1956
- *Glenrowan* 1956–57
- *Camel and Figure* 1966
- *Sydney Harbour* 1978
- *Burial of Burke* (triptych) 1985

Things to look for:
- landscape, historical incidents, and legendary figures of Australia: Ned Kelly, Burke and Wills, Eliza Fraser
- imaginative style with surreal backgrounds
- early works more abstract in nature
- use of Ripolin enamel
- scratched-out details in paintings
- paintings on smooth surfaces of hardboard, steel, and sometimes glass

Comparisons: Arthur Boyd, Russell Drysdale, Albert Tucker, John Perceval, Fred Williams

Glossary terms: abstract, avant-garde, expressionism, modernism, naïve, surrealism

Landscapes and legends

The story of the 1870s outlaw Ned Kelly was to occupy Nolan throughout his career. His earliest Kelly-related studies date from 1944.

During Nolan's absence without leave from the army, when he himself was a fugitive from the law, this interest became a preoccupation. In this first series of Kelly paintings (1945–47), each picture represents a particular episode in the Kelly story. Large in scale and "naïve" in execution, they capture the spirit of the Australian outback.

Glenrowan (1956–57) comes from a series begun in the1950s, when Nolan was in England. The style is more abstract, the atmosphere more powerful, and darker.

All the paintings include the stark silhouette of Kelly's trademark—his home-made armor and plowshare helmet. In fact, Kelly wore this outfit only once, at his last stand, in Glenrowan, a town in Victoria. There Kelly planned a siege in the summer of 1880 as the start of a popular revolt for reform of the land acts and police policies.

The plan went badly wrong. Kelly and his gang found themselves holed up in Mrs. Jones's hotel along with some 60, mostly sympathetic, "hostages." When Kelly confronted the police, his armor proved to be his downfall: it weighed nearly 100 pounds, and offered no protection to his arms and legs, where he was shot many times. He stood trial and was hanged. His last words were, "Such is life."

In *Glenrowan* Nolan presents the lone figure of Kelly, his wounded arm holding his shotgun aloft. Through the square helmet we can see through to a window in Mrs. Jones's hotel. The bloodied face in

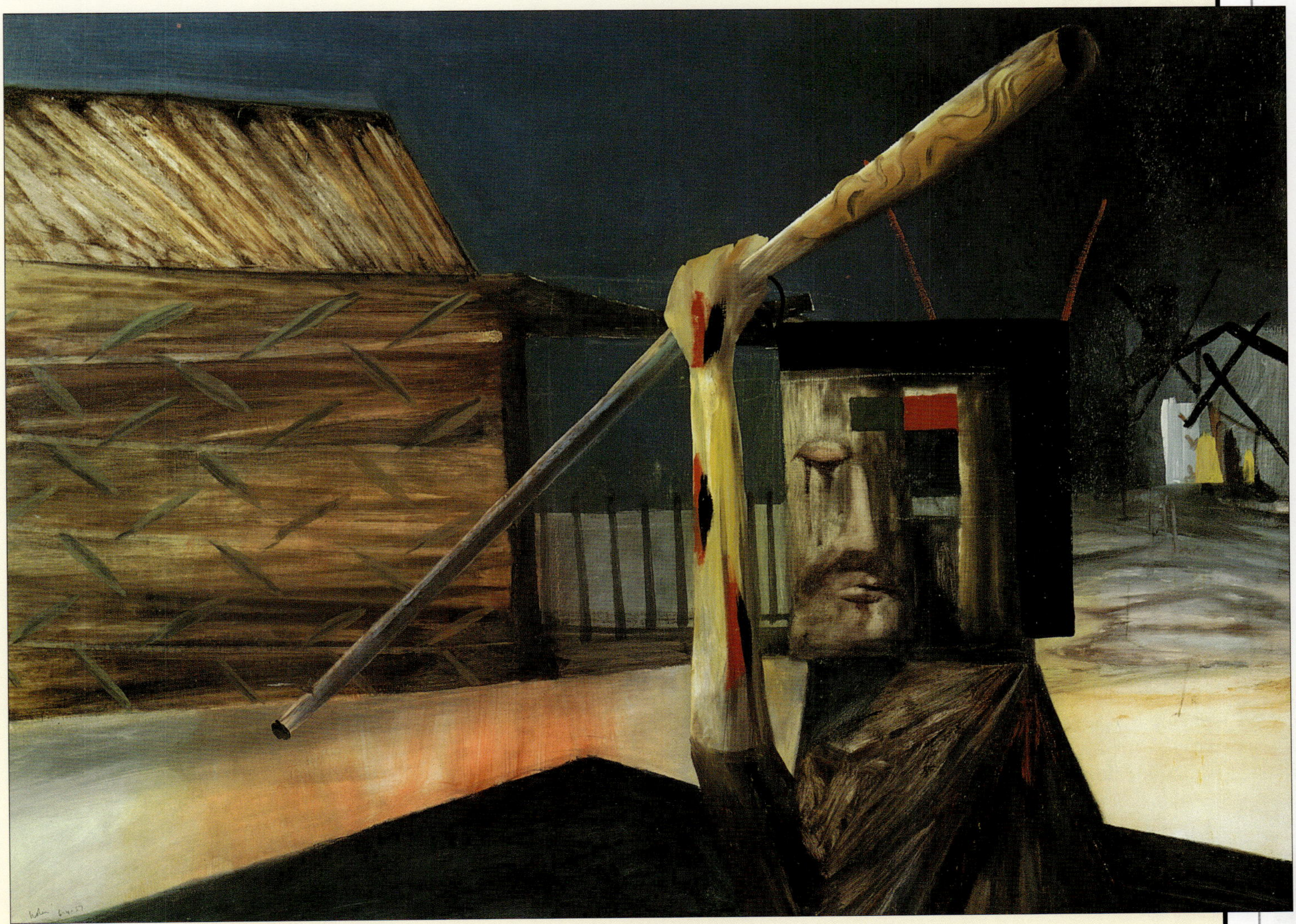

the helmet appears almost Christlike. When Nolan was painting this series, he was also working on Crucifixion scenes, and a number of his paintings of the head of Christ are related in style and treatment.

In his early paintings, Nolan almost invariably used Ripolin, a fast-drying, high-grade enamel normally used for painting boats and houses. An extremely fluid medium, it had to be applied quickly to the board or canvas lying flat. In the 1950s he began using oils. Nolan mixed them with PVA (polyvinyl acetate), a fast-drying synthetic glue that allowed the paints to be either thick or thin and, like the earlier enamels, to be very fluid—ideal for depicting surreal, atmospheric landscapes.

Glenrowan *1956–57. Oil on hardboard. 36 x 48 in (91.5 x 122 cm). Tate Gallery, London.*

inspired some of his most impressive works: remarkable landscapes, studies of gold mines and miners, and paintings of the ill-fated 1861 expedition on which the explorers, R. O. Burke and W. J. Wills, died of starvation.

In 1951 he had his first one-man show in London, and in 1956 his first in New York. The same year he was commissioned by the Australian airline Qantas to fly around the world gathering material for paintings to decorate their offices. He traveled extensively: to the United States, South America, Europe, China, Southeast Asia, Africa, and even to Antarctica.

The new experiences helped to develop a new theme, the mythological story of Leda and the swan: 75 works based on this theme were exhibited in London in 1960. The show was a huge success. Almost single-handedly, Sidney Nolan had put modern Australian art on the map.

Knighted by Queen Elizabeth II in 1981, in 1988 Nolan was made a Companion of the Order of Australia. He began experimenting with a computerized Quantel paintbox to create a series of prints celebrating Australia's bicentenary. He died in London in 1992.

NOLDE Emil

EMIL NOLDE LED A TURBULENT LIFE marked by professional difficulties and illness. His striking paintings of strange subjects in unusual settings have a mysterious, visionlike quality. They helped to establish expressionism throughout the world and have continued to inspire generations of artists.

Life and work

Emil Nolde was born Emil Hansen, but in 1902 took the name of his birthplace, the village of Nolde, in Schleswig-Holstein, northern Germany. He felt a special closeness to particular places and to nature, and all his life he remembered the impression made on him by the sun, the flowers, and the little trees he planted as a child on his parents' farm. His earliest paintings were most often of flowers and gardens. It was through these that he began to develop his distinctive style, which was characterized by rich, intense colors.

Nolde began his career teaching industrial design in Switzerland and painting conventional watercolors. In 1897 he became restless, gave up his job, and traveled to Munich and Paris. In 1901 he met a young Danish actress, Ada Vilstrup, in Copenhagen. She became his wife and closest companion. They moved to the island of Als (now Danish, then Prussian), where Nolde built a hut on the beach as a studio. In spite of his love of the coast, from 1905 he spent most winters in Berlin, taking a studio there in 1910. The artists of Die Brücke saw his work and invited him to exhibit with them.

In his native Schleswig-Holstein, few people liked or even understood Nolde's work. In the city too he met hostility. He had a prickly personality, often antagonized others, and attacked older, respected artists. He was expelled from Berlin's most important artists' association in 1910.

Nolde cultivated a rather romantic, idealized image of himself as a "pure," instinctive artist rather than a sophisticated intellectual. He had little time for art history. Instead, he read Norse legends, folk tales, and biblical stories. His paintings often blend images from these sources and from his imagination and the local landscape.

In 1911, Nolde visited the painter James Ensor in Belgium. There he would have seen Ensor's famous mask paintings. They obviously inspired him, for he painted masks many times, a subject that suited his taste for mystery. He also painted exotic still lifes based on artifacts from around the world, which he sketched in a Berlin museum.

Nolde found even greater creative stimulus two years later when he and Ada set out across Russia, Japan, China, and the South Seas to Papua New Guinea. There he sketched exotic landscapes, brilliant sunsets over wild seas, and the inhabitants of the tribal villages he visited. By the time of their return journey, war had broken out. At Port Said, in British-controlled Egypt, Nolde's baggage and many paintings were confiscated. (After the war Nolde was, remarkably, able to track down the missing pictures and eventually recovered them, in 1921, from Plymouth in England.) In Germany, Nolde painted oils and watercolors based on his memories of the South Seas, and these pictures were successful enough to pay the costs of the trip.

Ada was often ill now, and Nolde's angry dissatisfaction with his own work led him to destroy many of his own paintings. However, by the 1920s he was a highly respected artist, one of the most important of the expressionists. An entire room was devoted to him at Berlin's National Gallery, and by the late 1920s he was rich enough to build a house to his personal requirements at Seebüll, on the north coast.

Nolde developed stomach cancer in the 1930s and was often in the hospital. By 1937 the Nazis had removed more than 1000 of his paintings, which they deemed "degenerate," from museums. In 1941 he was banned from painting at all. A proud German, he was deeply hurt by this rejection, and by the restrictions imposed upon him. He even tried to convince the authorities that his art was well-suited to Nazi beliefs and ideals. The police watched him carefully, but from 1941 to 1945 he secretly painted more than 1000 watercolors on small pieces of scrap paper. He called them his "unpainted pictures." Drawing almost solely on his imagination, they are some of the most beautiful works he ever made.

Nolde's studio in Berlin and its entire contents were destroyed in an air raid in 1944, but many of his best works have survived. His Seebüll house is now a permanent museum for his work.

Data file

Full name: Emil Nolde (born Emil Hansen)

Nationality: German

Style: expressionism

Dates: born 1867 in Nolde, died 1956 in Seebüll

Key works:
- *Wildly Dancing Children* 1909
- *Christ Among the Children* 1910
- *Still Life with Masks* 1911
- *The Life of Christ* 1911–12
- *Mary of Egypt* 1912
- *The Prophet* 1912
- *Tropical Sun* 1914

Things to look for:
- religious or fantasy subjects
- seascapes, flowers, and gardens
- use of bright colors
- use of thick pigment

Comparisons: Edvard Munch, Ernst Ludwig Kirchner, Oskar Kokoschka, James Ensor

Glossary terms: Die Brücke, expressionism

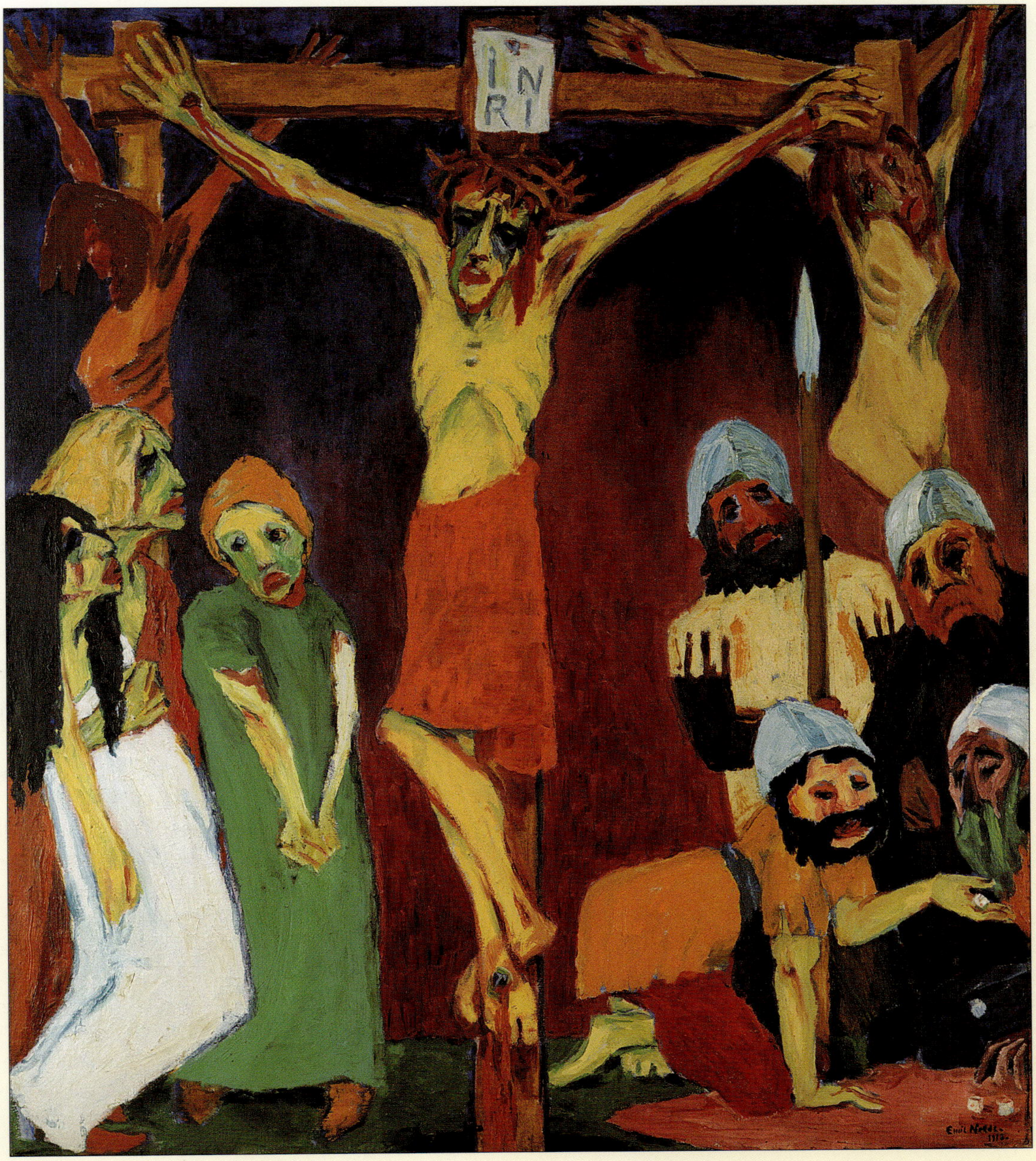

The Crucifixion *from* **The Life of Christ** *One of nine panels. 1911–12. Oil on board and canvas. 87 x 77 in (220.5 x 193.5 cm). Nolde Stiftung, Seebüll.*

Religious expression

Nolde's *Life of Christ* (1911–12) is a very large and complex work. Consisting of nine panels, it depicts the life of Jesus Christ from birth to the Resurrection.

The painting is at once modern and very traditional. The striking composition, bright colors, and thick, expressive brushwork, mark it clearly as a modern, expressionist painting. Yet its subject and format remind us of altarpieces made by painters and craftsmen in the Middle Ages to instruct illiterate medieval churchgoers in the teachings of the Bible. Like other expressionists, Nolde must have looked at old German masterpieces such as Mathis Grünewald's Isenheim altarpiece (c1512–15).

This series of panels is a remarkable combination of storytelling and expression. Each scene depicts an event in Christ's life, but also expresses the intense human passions of love, joy, and pain. The faces of Christ and some of the figures at the base of the crucifixion have "primitive," masklike features and may even be based on tribal masks from Nigeria that Nolde worked from in 1911. The exaggerated gestures and heightened color all amplify the intensity of this powerful story. In other panels Nolde shows the drama of the emotional and physical experiences of birth, wounding, and death. We see the joy and wonder of childbirth as Mary holds up her newborn baby, still covered in blood. We see the terror of the witnesses to Christ's fiery rising from the tomb. But most harrowing is the central panel, where Christ's exhausted and strained body hangs from the cross.

O'KEEFFE Georgia

ACKNOWLEDGED AS A PIONEERING FORCE in modern American art, and as one of the first artists to express a woman's viewpoint on canvas, Georgia O'Keeffe is best known for her unique, highly personal visions of the landscape and nature of the United States. Her paintings include bold, vibrant flowers, bleached-bone still lifes, city scenes, and landscapes.

Life and work

After graduating from high school in Wisconsin in 1905, Georgia O'Keeffe enrolled at the Art Institute of Chicago. A year later, she moved to New York to study at the Art Student's League under William Merritt Chase. Her diligent studies paid off when she won the top still-life prize for her painting of a rabbit beside a copper pot.

Data file

Full name: Georgia Totto O'Keeffe

Nationality: American

Style: largely independent of main stylistic movements, but her work displays elements of precisionism, realism, abstraction, and surrealism. Her style has also been referred to as "magic-realism"

Dates: born 1887 in Sun Praire, WI, died 1986 in Santa Fe, NM

Key works:

Evening Star No. V 1917

Red Cannas 1924

Radiator Building 1927

Black Cross, New Mexico 1931

Cows Skull: Red, White, and Blue 1931

From the Faraway, Nearby 1937

It Was Blue and Green 1960

Sky Above the Clouds VI 1965

Things to look for:

- exotic colors
- close-up views
- plants and flowers taken out of their natural context, sometimes juxtaposed with bleached animal bones
- subjects subordinate to line and color

Comparisons: Wassily Kandinsky, John Marin, Arthur Dove, Charles Demuth, Charles Sheeler

Glossary terms: abstraction, magic-realism, precisionism, realism, surrealism

Financial difficulties caused O'Keeffe to move back to Chicago in 1908; there she worked for two years as a commercial artist in the newly emerging advertising industry.

In the summer of 1912, O'Keeffe took a course at the University of Virginia in Charlottesville, marking a new direction in her career. Here, she studied with Aloon Bement, a disciple of Arthur Wesley Dow. Dow's innovative and unorthodox methods were based on the principles of abstractionism. He rejected realism and emphasized simplified, flat patterns in art exercises that used lines and stressed rhythms and balance. While in Charlottesville, an old school friend helped O'Keeffe to secure a teaching job in Amarillo, Texas. The Texan countryside made a lasting impression on O'Keeffe and inspired her painting.

In 1914 O'Keeffe returned to New York to study with Arthur Wesley Dow himself at the Teacher's College of Columbia University. In 1915, however, she broke with her academic training to experiment with abstractionism, drawing images from direct observation of nature and emphasizing the formal qualities that she discerned in organic things. As O'Keeffe began to develop her own means of expression, her style underwent many influences, from precise realism to pure abstractionism.

In 1916 O'Keeffe met the photographer Alfred Stieglitz. She had gone to his Gallery 291 in New York to protest about his display of some of her charcoal drawings, which a friend had shown him without O'Keeffe's knowledge. The following year Stieglitz organized the first of many "one-man" shows of O'Keeffe's work. Their personal relationship also developed, and in 1924 they were married.

In the 1920s O'Keeffe began producing paintings based on magnified botanical subjects, especially flowers. The exotic colors and forms of the plants and flowers are heightened by their being out of their natural context. While living in New York, O'Keeffe also painted a number of cityscapes, views of the changing appearance of the city from her apartment windows.

In 1929 O'Keeffe visited Taos, New Mexico. From then on, she spent most of her summers in the southwest, where she was inspired by the majestic landscape and became fascinated with the forms of sun-bleached animal bones that she found scattered across the desert floor. *Cows Skull: Red, White, and Blue* (1931) is among the first of her isolated studies of bones. Later works have skulls or bones that seem to float in a surrealist manner.

When Stieglitz died in 1946, O'Keeffe decided to settle in New Mexico. She retreated into isolation at her home in Abiquiu, where she continued to paint obsessively and prolifically, constantly experimenting and refining her ideas. In 1960 she was persuaded back into the public eye with a major exhibition at the Worcester Art Museum, Massachusetts. *Newsweek* heralded her as "the grand old lady of painting," and her reputation as the United States' greatest woman painter was celebrated with her election to the American Academy of Arts and Letters—as one of only five women members and the only painter among them. In her 60-year career, O'Keeffe executed over 900 works.

O'Keeffe often said that she would live to be 100. She very nearly made it: she died aged 98. At her request, her ashes were scattered in New Mexico, over the landscape she so loved.

Bright lights, big city

Although O'Keeffe's work is primarily nature-oriented, architectural forms also appear in her paintings. Paintings depicting New York City skyscrapers come from the period when O'Keeffe lived at the Shelton Hotel (now the Marriott East Side) in 1925. The rapidly changing panorama of Manhattan was clearly visible from her top-floor apartment windows. As she became familiar with a place, O'Keeffe's paintings of it became less representational and more interpretive, concerned with her own responses to what she saw. "You paint *from* your subject, not what you see.... I rarely paint anything I don't know very well," she once said.

New York was a subject that O'Keeffe did indeed know well: she lived in one of the busiest parts of the city on and off for over 30 years. Considering the length of her residency, however, O'Keeffe focused on the city as her subject for a relatively short period, between 1925 and 1929. The only time she returned to the theme was for two later commissions in 1932 and 1948.

Alfred Stieglitz objected to O'Keeffe's attempts to paint the city, arguing that it was essentially "alien" to her and that nature was the more "appropriate" and "feminine" sphere. Fiercely independent, O'Keeffe was undaunted and carried on with her work. One of the buildings that particularly interested her was the American Radiator Building, which she depicted in *Radiator Building* (1927). Its pinnacle, decorated with gold leaf, was dramatically illuminated at night. The neon sign (shown on the left of the picture) flashed the words "Scientific American," but O'Keeffe has mischievously replaced this with the word "Stieglitz," a reference to her husband.

Many of O'Keeffe's paintings of New York dramatize the perpendicularity of the buildings. In *Radiator Building*, the geometric rendering of the building recalls the precisionist approach that can be seen in the works of painters such as Charles Demuth and Charles Sheeler, both of whom were among the close circle of artist-friends whose work Stieglitz exhibited. Many of the Manhattan paintings give the viewer the sense of claustrophobia that O'Keeffe herself often felt in New York. In *City Night* (1926), the tiny sphere of the moon appears between the black walls of buildings. She painted many dramatic night scenes; in *New York, Night* (1928–29), for example, a seemingly people-free city is lit by the eerie glow of electric lights.

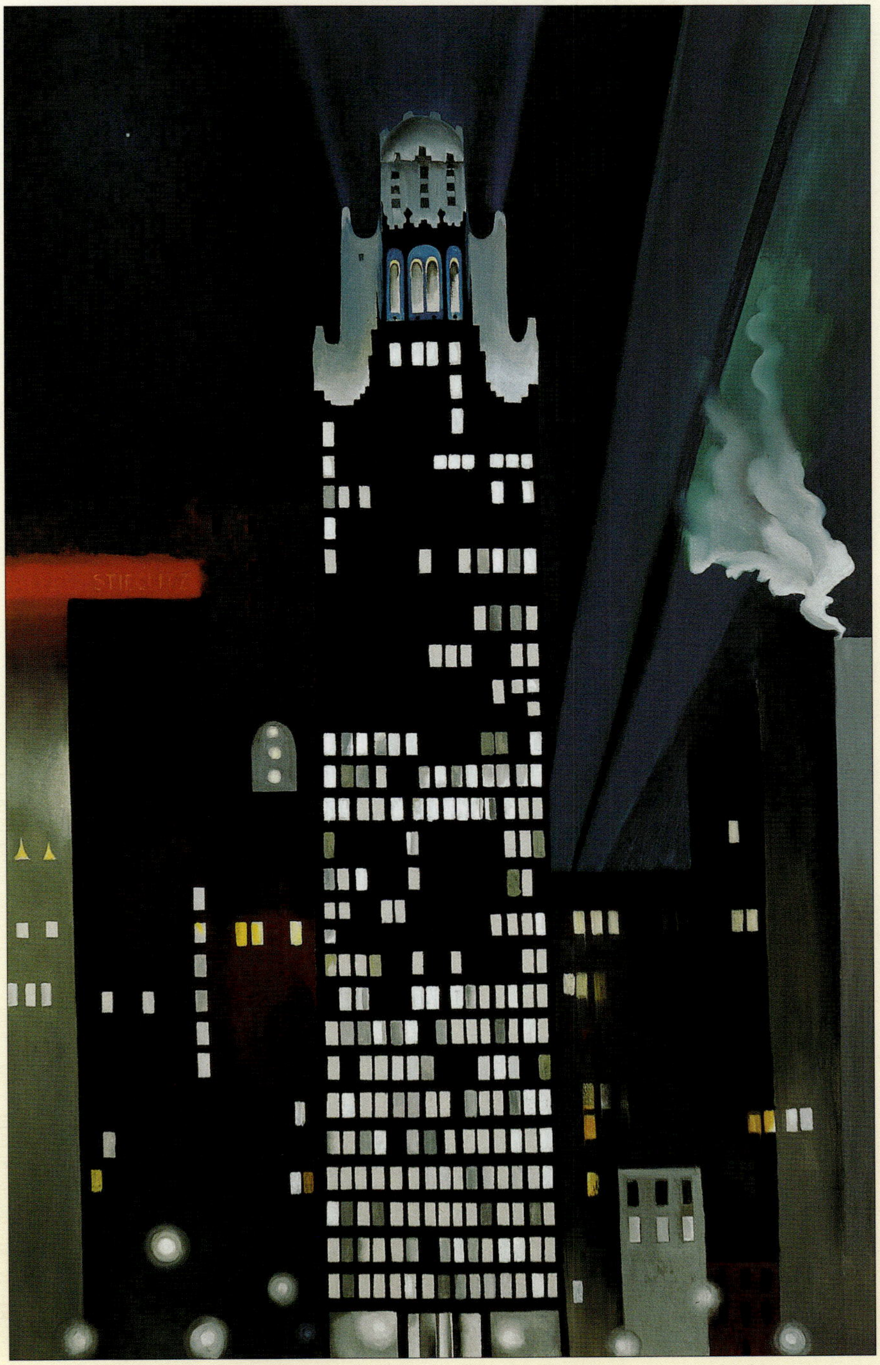

Radiator Building *1927. Oil on canvas. 48 x 30 in (122 x 76 cm). Fisk University, Nashville, TN.*

OLDENBURG Claes

CLAES OLDENBURG IS A PIONEERING ARTIST, who from the late 1950s and early 1960s, began to direct art away from the accepted traditions of painting and sculpture, and beyond the space of galleries and museums. He wants art to become more democratic, so that everyone can become more actively involved.

Life and work

Although he was born in Sweden, Claes Oldenburg has lived in the United States since he was about six years old. He grew up in Chicago, and studied art and literature in New York. Following another period in Chicago, where he worked as a reporter for the City News Bureau, he settled permanently in New York in 1956.

In New York Oldenburg met a group of young artists, including Allen Kaprow, Jim Dine, and George Segal, who shared a common goal: they all wanted to destroy the notion of art being the private preserve of the artist. Instead they aimed to bring art to the public, and to use the material of city streetlife culture for their inspiration and subject matter. In particular they wanted to strip away the impenetrability that had grown up around abstract expressionist artists, who had become revered for their "artistic genius." They did adopt the spontaneity and natural drama of action painting, however.

Oldenburg staged his first public one-man show in 1959; the following year, in his second show, *The Street* (an exhibition with Dine), Oldenburg incorporated trash that he had found outside, such as newspapers, cardboard, old bits of cloth, and wooden pallets. Torn, frayed, and partly blackened with paint, this raw material was scattered throughout the gallery, and was sometimes also covered with the random words and letters of graffiti.

It was in this installation that Oldenburg staged his first "happening," called *Snapshots from the City*. In it, he was clothed in the trash that he had collected, and many of his actions were improvised. His aim was to stimulate the audience with the excitement of the moment and the importance of the everyday, urban environment.

Much of Oldenburg's work concentrates on his promotion of everyday objects. One of the earliest such pieces was *White Shirt and Blue Tie* (1961), a rough plaster portrayal of a shirt and tie, crudely painted with shiny enamel paint in a splattered style that mocked the abstract expressionists' technique. He made many similar pieces during the early 1960s, some of which he displayed in his environment *The Store* (1961), a disused storefront in New York that he filled with the painted plaster casts of many mass-produced objects, in particular clothes and cakes. Through making objects for performances and environments Oldenburg began to develop his technique for creating soft sculptures of familiar objects (like hamburgers, typewriters, and bathroom appliances). He began to construct these on a grand scale, in cloth that was loosely stuffed to make the sculptures sag with the force of gravity.

From the mid-1960s Oldenburg's work became more ambitious, and he exhibited such proposals as *Lipsticks in Piccadilly Circus, London* (1966), as well as a giant popsicle: *Proposed Colossal Monument for Park Avenue, New York: Good Humor Bar* (1965). These works existed for a long time only as rather elegant sketches, collages, and watercolor drawings, but in 1969 the first of his large-scale outdoor works was constructed. *Lipstick (Ascending) on Caterpillar Tracks* was situated in Beinecke Plaza at Yale University.

Oldenburg's work has followed two distinct paths since the late 1960s. *Lipstick (Ascending) on Caterpillar Tracks* opened up the possibility of further, and more adventurous moves into public sculpture, while he also began to create smaller sculptures as multiples. He frequently produced editions of around 30 to 100 sculptures, once even producing an edition of 36,000 *Airflow Boxes* (1966), reflecting his ambition to destroy the preciousness that is attached to unique pieces of art.

Since 1976 Oldenburg has collaborated with the Dutch writer Coosje van Bruggen, whom he married in 1977. They have concentrated mainly on public commissions for large-scale works—such as *Binoculars* (1991) at the Chiat/Day Building in California—which has brought wide public attention to their work.

Data file

Full name: Claes Thure Oldenburg

Nationality: Swedish (U.S. citizen after c1935)

Style: pop art

Dates: born 1929 in Stockholm

Key works:
- *The Street* 1960
- *The Store* 1961
- *White Shirt and Blue Tie* 1961
- *Floor Burger (Giant Hamburger)* 1962
- *Soft Toilet* 1966
- *Giant Pool Balls* 1967
- *Bathroom* 1969
- *Lipstick (Ascending) on Caterpillar Tracks* 1969
- *Extinguished Match* 1987

Things to look for:
- huge scale
- soft forms
- everyday objects

Comparisons: Marcel Duchamp, Jim Dine, George Segal, Allen Kaprow, Christo

Glossary terms: abstract expressionism, action painting, environmental art, happening, installation, multiple, pop art

Soft boiled

"I am for an art that takes its form from the lines of life itself, that twists and extends and accumulates and spits and drips, and is heavy and coarse and blunt and sweet and stupid as life itself…."

"I Am For an Art…" was a declaration of his aspirations for art, written by Claes Oldenburg in 1961. As is clear from this brief extract, Oldenburg works in a manner that resists easy categorization. Although he has worked in various media, including sculpture, environments, and performance/happenings (spontaneous events or displays), there are common features of his character and concerns that are apparent throughout his work.

Soft Toilet (1966) is typical of the "soft sculptures" that Oldenburg originally made for his performances. It is fabricated from shiny vinyl and stuffed with a light filling that is not sufficient to support the outer skin. The result is a half-collapsed form, in effect an exhausted toilet. It is a funny sculpture, rather like a cartoon creature or a glove puppet (without a supporting hand). Using an apparently simple technique Oldenburg manages to mine a rich seam of associations. In this soft sculpture, for example, we can recognize either the sagging effects of age and gravity, or view it as a drunken toilet that is unable to stand up anymore.

However we think of the sculpture, Oldenburg is encouraging us to relate to this everyday object in a new and imaginative way. As with all his work, he is giving a monumental character to an object that we might disregard because it seems so ordinary to us. This is even more true of his large-scale public works, in which he enlarges screws, matches, shuttlecocks, and bicycle parts to giant proportions. The enlargement echoes the way in which society honors war heroes, statesmen, and royalty by erecting monumental statues to them.

Perhaps Oldenburg's most imaginative and humorous works are those that remain as proposals. These include *Proposed Colossal Monument in the Form of Knees, on the Victoria Embankment, London* (1969) (inspired by the sight of power-plant cooling towers), and a proposal to sail a huge bar of soap down the Ohio and Mississippi rivers from Cincinnati (the home of a well-known soap manufacturer) to Baton Rouge. In such instances, Oldenburg's inventiveness, untethered by practicalities, enters a more surreal world.

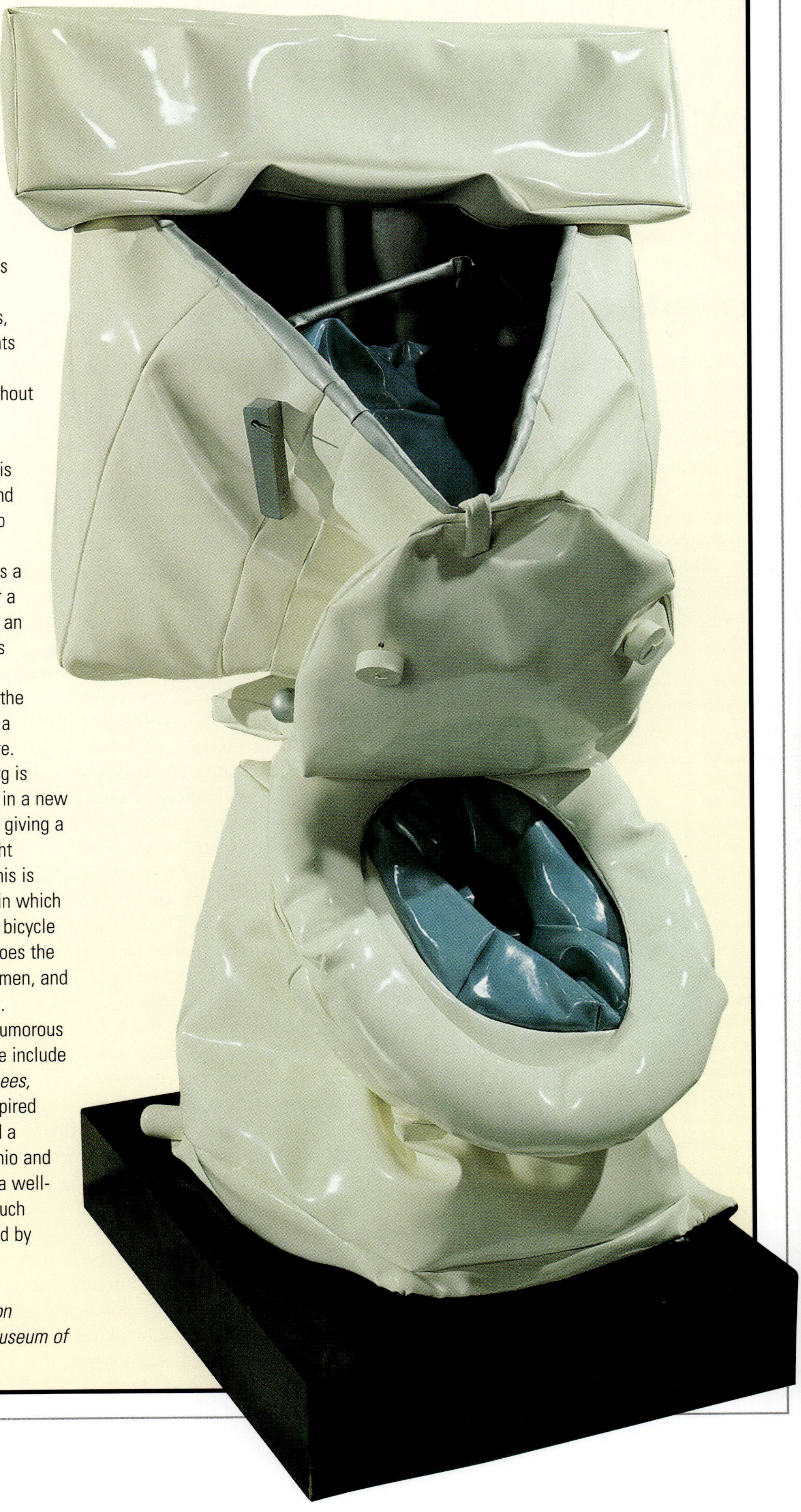

Soft Toilet *1966. Vinyl, plexiglass, and kapok on painted wood base. 57 in (145 cm). Whitney Museum of American Art, New York, NY.*

OROZCO José

A POLITICALLY AND SOCIALLY COMMITTED PAINTER, the muralist José Clemente Orozco was a dominant force in modern Mexican art. Using the history and culture of the Americas as his subject matter in large-scale frescos, he expressed the universal themes of freedom and justice and the futility of war.

Life and work

It was in Guadalajara, where he spent most of his childhood, that Orozco first became interested in art. On his way to school he would pass the print shop of the graphic artist José Guadelupe Posada, who distributed satirical cartoons on political and social issues to the poor and illiterate.

Orozco's middle-class family did not want him to study art, and instead enrolled him at agricultural college. It was only after a science experiment went wrong and he lost his left hand that he finally began studies at the San Carlos Academy of Fine Arts in Mexico City. Among his teachers was Dr Gerardo Atl, who had studied the Renaissance frescos in Italy. He was to urge the Mexican government to sponsor public mural projects.

Orozco's early work included *The House of Tears* (1912), a series on local brothels and prostitutes. They were influenced by Pablo Picasso's early drawings and paintings of the same subjects. Orozco also drew caricatures and cartoons, which newspapers printed during the revolution of 1910.

In 1917 he made his first visit to the United States. He worked as a sign painter in San Francisco, then in a New York factory, painting the faces on dolls. Returning to Mexico City in 1920, he joined the emerging mural painting movement. In 1923–24, along with artists such as Diego Rivera and David Alfaro Siqueiros, he helped create murals for the National Preparatory School. Mainly reworkings of traditional themes, the bold symbolic images used by the artists aroused protest; a group of conservative students defaced many of them. Two years later Orozco overpainted them, and the only original mural to survive intact is *Maternity* (1923–24).

In 1930 Orozco painted the *Prometheus* fresco at Pomona College in Claremont, California, and the four-wall mural cycle for the canteen of the New School of Social Research in New York. In 1932 he began work on the mural cycle for the Baker Library of Dartmouth College in Hanover, New Hampshire. It is his interpretation, in epic narrative terms, of the evolution of civilization in the United States from ancient migration to modern industrial man. Halfway through the Dartmouth murals, Orozco visited Europe. The scale and the power of Michelangelo Buonarroti's frescos in the Sistine

Data file

Full name: José Clemente Orozco

Nationality: Mexican

Style: (in manner) expressionism, (in subject) realism

Dates: born 1883 in Cuidad Guzman, died 1949 in Mexico City

Key works:

The House of Tears 1912

Maternity and other murals 1923–24

Omniscience 1925

Prometheus 1930

mural cycle for Dartmouth College, New Hampshire 1932–34

Guadalajara fresco cycle 1936–39

Things to look for:

- large-scale dramatic murals
- subjects from the culture and history of Mexico
- themes of war, justice, and liberty, expressed through symbols and symbolic colors
- motifs of fire, destruction, and chaos
- political and social comment

Comparisons: Michelangelo Buonarroti, El Greco, Diego Rivera, David Alfaro Siqueiros, Jean Charlot, Juan O'Gorman, Pablo O'Higgins, Fernando Leal, Ramon Alva de la Canal

Glossary terms: easel painting, expressionism, fresco, mural, narrative, Renaissance, social realism

The real and the ideal

While the murals of David Siqueiros and Diego Rivera celebrated struggles to achieve dignity and freedom, Orozco's monumental works are concerned with a darker theme—man's seeming inability to realize his noble ideals. That is not to say that Orozco did not believe in the value of freedom, it was simply that he did not see any signs of it around him. Instead, he saw people oppressed and enslaved by politics, poverty, technology, and machines.

In the Pomona College frescos of 1930, Orozco depicted the figure of Prometheus, who in Greek mythology stole fire from the gods and gave light to man on earth. To punish him for bringing enlightenment to man, Zeus had Prometheus chained to a rock, where each day an eagle tore at his liver. Eventually he was freed by Hercules.

In the Guadalajara frescos (1936–39) Orozco would return again to this theme of the rebel who pits himself against authority and sacrifices himself for mankind. The Guadalajara frescos consist of three fresco cycles on three different sites. One, *Creative Man and the People and its False Leaders* (begun in 1936) was for the assembly hall of the city's university. Another cycle, in the deconsecrated chapel of the former orphanage of the Hospicio Cabañas, was painted from 1938–39 and dealt with the historical and cultural development of Mexico. Between these two, in 1937–38, Orozco painted a complex cycle over the main staircase in the Palacio de Gobierno.

This staircase scheme consists of three sections. On the left-hand wall is the mural entitled *The Phantasms of Religion in Alliance with the Military.* It concerns the historical role that, together, the Catholic Church and the army played in Mexican history; despite their devotion to the faith,

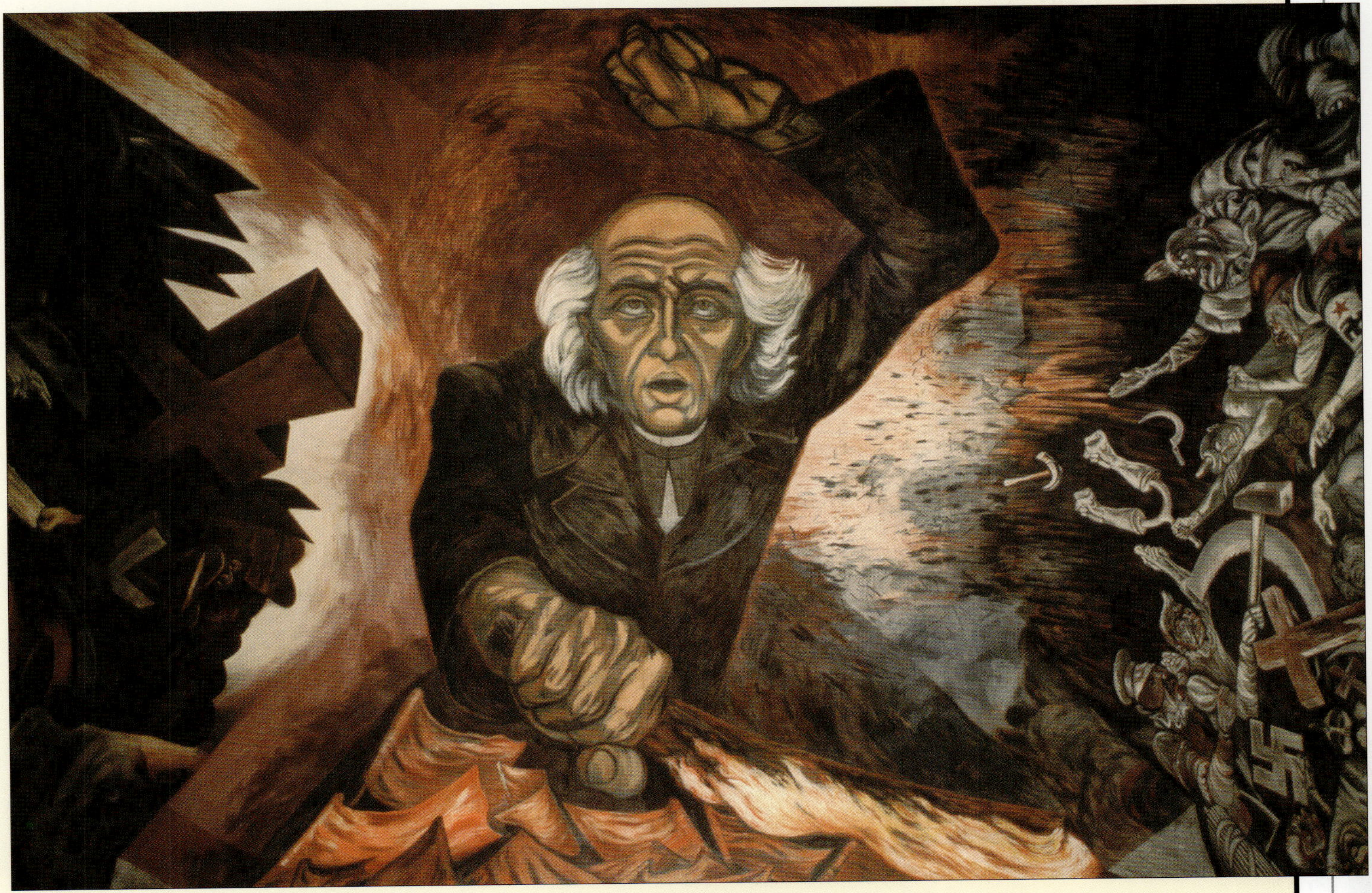

many Mexicans felt that the Church had often supported the wrong side in the country's turbulent history.

On the right-hand wall is *The Carnival of the Ideologies,* a satirical representation of the conflicting philosophies of the 20th century, in which controversial world leaders such as Adolf Hitler and Josef Stalin appear as grotesque clowns.

The central wall, which arches over the staircase, contains the gigantic, towering figure of a modern Prometheus, the Jesuit priest, Father Miguel Hildago. Hildago was a champion of the Indians, the poor, and the oppressed. In 1810 he became the leader of an uprising against Church-supported Spanish rule. Like Prometheus, the rebel priest Hildago was punished for challenging the powers that be. The Catholic Church excommunicated him.

In Orozco's mural, Hildago appears armed with a flaming brand, which he thrusts out over a struggling mass of fighting and dying bodies that are surrounded by a sea of red flags and flames. Fire is common throughout the Guadalajara murals, and it is a central

Hildago *(detail) 1937–38. Wall fresco. Palacio de Gobierno, Guadalajara.*

motif in Orozco's mature works. He uses it to symbolize oppositions: pain and purification, conflict and enlightenment.

The bodies of the struggling masses in the lower section of the mural are painted in dark, gloomy colors, to suggest mankind struggling in a world of darkness. Farther up the mural, toward the figure of Hildago, the colors become brighter and lighter, symbolic of the ideals of freedom.

Chapel in Rome, and the dark, brooding intensity of El Greco's paintings in Toledo, impressed him immensely.

He returned to Mexico City in 1934, and began work on the mural *Catharsis* for the Palace of Fine Arts. In 1936 he returned to his childhood home of Guadalajara. The murals he would paint here include the image of Father Miguel Hildago (1937–38).

In the 1940s Orozco was beginning to concentrate on easel paintings. A commission in 1940 from the Museum of Modern Art in New York, however, resulted in another mural, *Dive Bomber and Tank*, depicting powerful forces—human and machine—overwhelming ordinary people. Three enormous human heads, weighted down by chains and surrounded by bolts, twisted metal shapes, and iron girders, appear against a background of flames. The six large panels can be arranged in any order.

PERUGINO

PERUGINO WAS A RENAISSANCE PAINTER who was important enough to be commissioned by Pope Sixtus IV to paint frescos in the Sistine Chapel in Rome. His paintings, often with landscape backgrounds, featured graceful, elongated, and sentamentalized figures. Perugino is best known as the teacher of Raphael, whose early works show his influence.

Life and work

Perugino was born in Umbria in central Italy. He was known as "Il Perugino," or "the Perugian" in his lifetime, although he was not from the City of Perugia, but the nearby Città della Pieve. His early works in the 1460s suggest that he was influenced by Piero della Francesca—the Umbrian artist who was a pioneer of perspective, color, and geometric orderliness in fresco painting—and it is thought he may even have been Piero's pupil.

In 1472 Perugino moved to Florence, then a great center for artists, and here he learned the newly popular technique of oil painting, probably from the painter and sculptor Andrea del Verrocchio, who ran a workshop training goldsmiths, sculptors, and painters (and is known to have taught Leonardo da Vinci).

Perugino was married in Florence; in 1478 he moved to Rome. By 1481 he was sufficiently well known to receive a very important commission from the papal court to paint frescos in the newly built Sistine Chapel in the Vatican in Rome. (The word Sistine comes from the Italian *Sistino*, relating to Sisto Sixtus (Pope Sixtus IV), for whom the chapel was built.) Perugino worked alongside other eminent artists of the day: Cosimo Rosselli, Domenico Ghirlandaio, and Sandro Botticelli. He painted scenes from the life of Moses and from the life of Christ. One of his frescos in the Sistine Chapel—*Christ giving the Keys to Saint Peter* (c1482)—was particularly admired because of the clarity, control, and organization of the composition, and the skilled use of perspective, perhaps reflecting the influence of Piero della Francesca. It was this painting that established Perugino's reputation.

Perugino went on to receive many other important commissions in and around Perugia and Florence, and elsewhere, and between 1490 and 1505 he was generally considered to be the finest painter in Italy. In 1494–95 he painted his *Pietà* for the church of San Guisto near Florence. A Pietà is a work that shows the Virgin Mary holding the body of her dead son, Jesus, while she contemplates and mourns his death. Perugino's version is a superb example of his mature style. As with most of his paintings, the composition is balanced and symmetrical, and all the figures are in the foreground. The space is severely defined by the architecture.

From about 1500 to about 1504 the young Raphael was a pupil of Perugino, and may have helped him with his largest work in fresco, created in the Audience Chamber in the Sala del Cambio in Perugia (c1499).

In 1506 Perugino retired to Perugia. By now his style, which had hardly developed during his long career, was considered old-fashioned by the people of Florence.

Throughout his life Perugino was hardworking and prolific—many of his works are in galleries all over the world. In addition to his religious works, he painted portraits and mythological subjects.

Many of his works have a sentimental style that is very easy to recognize. The young Raphael adopted this style in his early works, but soon developed it into something much more robust and exciting.

Data file

Full name: Pietro Vannucci (known as Perugino)

Nationality: Italian

Style: Renaissance

Dates: born 1445–50 in Città della Pieve, died 1523 in Fontignano

Key works:
- frescos in the Sistine Chapel, primarily *Christ Giving the Keys to Saint Peter* c1482
- *Crucifixion* in the Chapter House of Santa Maria Maddalena dei Pazzi, Florence 1493–96
- *Pietà* 1494–95
- *Lamentation over the Dead Christ* 1495
- frescos in the Audience Chamber in the Sala del Cambio, Perugia c1499

Things to look for:
- paintings of Christian subject matter; altarpieces
- elegant, sentimentalized figures, often in balanced groupings
- landscape settings reflecting the Umbrian countryside

Comparisons: Domenico Ghirlandaio, Sandro Botticelli, Cosimo Rosselli, Luca Signorelli, Piero della Francesca

Glossary terms: fresco, perspective, Pietà, Renaissance

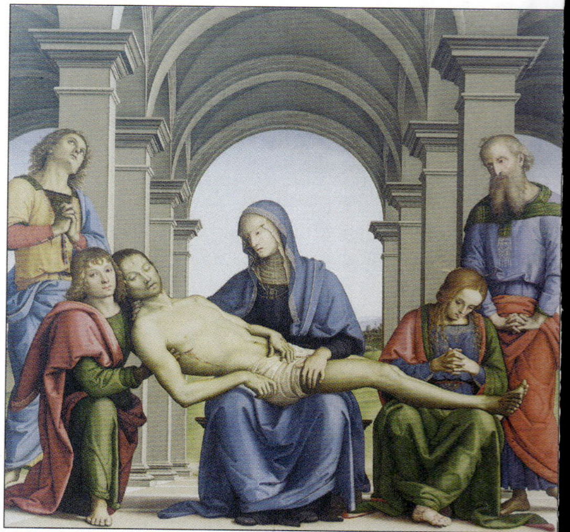

Pietà *1494–95. Oil on panel. 69 1/4 x 66 1/4 in (176 x 168 cm). Galleria degli Uffizi, Florence.*

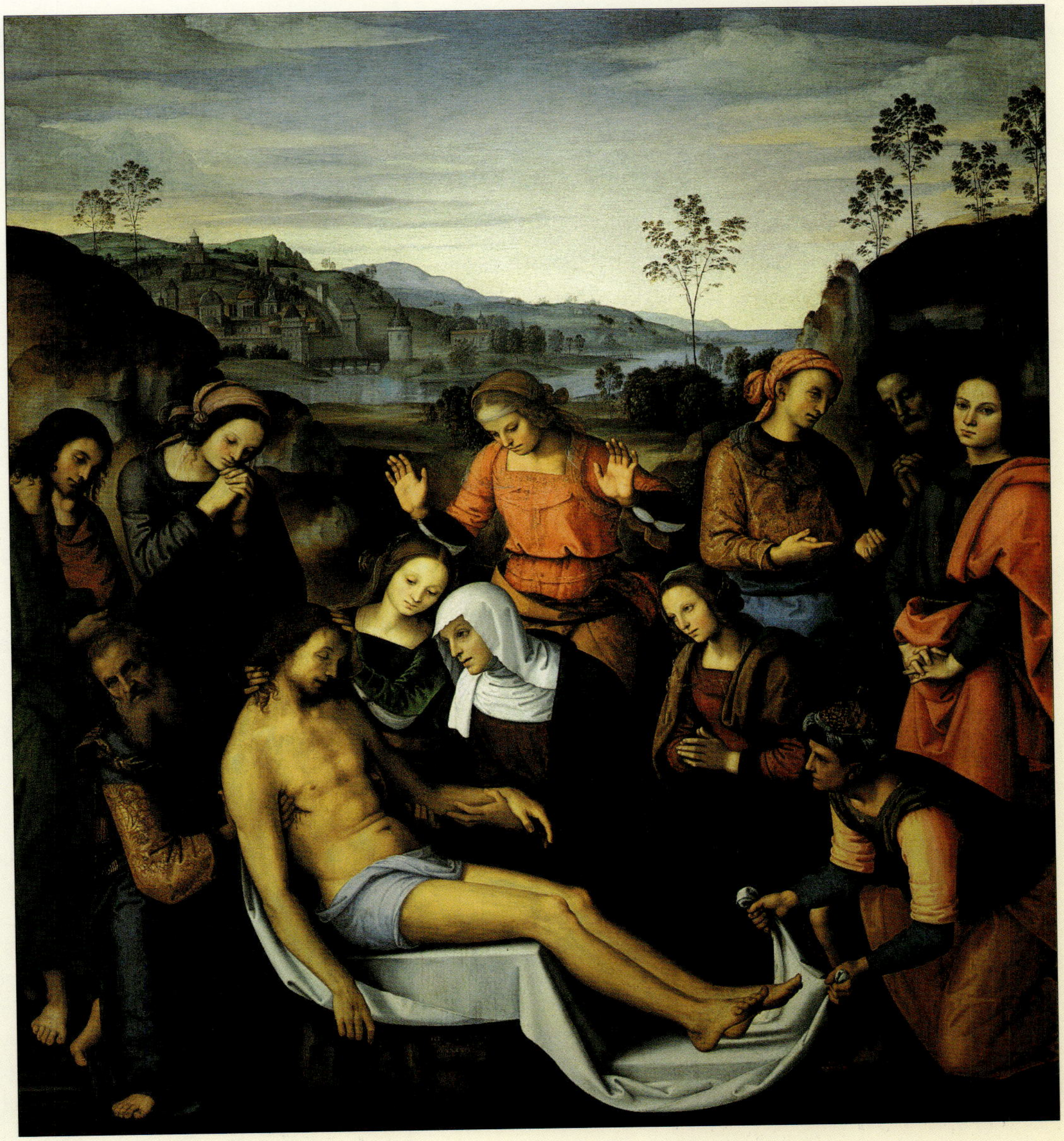

Lamentation over the Dead Christ *1495. Oil on panel. 84 1/4 x 77 in (214 x 195 cm). Galleria Palatina, Florence.*

An Umbrian scene

Perugino's *Lamentation over the Dead Christ* (1495) is one of many religious pictures, created for churches, that helped the viewer to imagine scenes from the Bible. Such paintings were an important aid to prayer, and encouraging devotion.

The theme of the Lamentation was a common one. The painting shows a scene in which Jesus has been crucified by the Romans and his dead body returned to his family and friends, who are grieving. The body is only partly clothed and it is slumped on a white cloth, displayed to the viewer. The old man supporting Christ's shoulders stares out at us, challenging us to look, and join the group of mourners.

The painting has a fairly simple and symmetrical composition. The scene is set out of doors in a luscious landscape more reminiscent of central Italy, where the artist lived, than of the Holy Land, where the story is set. The treatment of the landscape—using subdued rather than vivid colors—is in itself typically Umbrian.

The people gathered around Christ in the picture are clearly grieving, but not in a dramatic way. Their gestures are restrained and thoughtful rather than realistic (this is in contrast to the emotionally convincing *Lamentation* of c1305 by the Florentine artist Giotto di Bondone). The women are not characterized in a way that gives any indication of an individual personality, and the same, perhaps to a lesser extent, goes for the men. The body of Christ does not display distinctive or individual features either: he is neither tall nor short, and not very muscular; he is not particularly handsome, but not ugly either.

Perugino worked from drawings he made of his assistants. Some of these drawings survive, and he is known to have used them repeatedly by adapting the poses or taking elements of them to use again. The result is that the figures in his paintings often look very similar to one another.

PICASSO Pablo

PABLO PICASSO WAS ARGUABLY THE SINGLE MOST IMPORTANT and influential artist of the 20th century. With Georges Braque, he was the cofounder of cubism. He also played a significant role in many other movements, including surrealism, throughout his career. Highly prolific, he was proficient in a wide range of media, including painting, sculpture, graphic art, and ceramics.

Life and work

Picasso was born in Malaga, Spain, in 1881, the son of a teacher at the local art school. He learned to draw at an early age, and in his mid-teens, entered the School of Fine Arts in Barcelona. Soon afterward Picasso moved to Madrid, where he studied the Old Masters in the Prado Museum.

During this time, Picasso frequently visited Paris, where he settled permanently in 1904. His early works can be categorized into two distinct phases: his Blue Period and his Rose Period. During the first of these, from about 1901 to 1904, Picasso produced melancholy images representing outcasts from society such as beggars and prostitutes. By 1904, however, these had given way to representations of harlequins and clowns, painted in warmer pink and flesh tones.

During this stage of his career Picasso was drawn to the work of Paul Cézanne and Paul Gauguin. At the same time he developed a fascination for non-Western art, especially African tribal masks. This interest is most evident in *Les Demoiselles d'Avignon* (1906–07), a ground-breaking work that marked a major turning point in Picasso's career, not least through its representation of form in a flatter, more compressed space.

Picasso was first introduced to the painter Georges Braque in 1907. Over the next few years both artists worked intensely together, simultaneously developing the style known as cubism. Picasso's first cubist works were mostly landscapes produced on trips back to his native Spain. By 1910, however, he was producing portraits and still lifes.

Following Braque's lead, Picasso also introduced fragments of words into his paintings, both to emphasize the flatness of the canvas and to evoke a sense of playfulness and mystery. This approach, in which natural forms are analyzed and fragmented, is described as analytical cubism. Between 1912 and 1914 Picasso began to stick newspaper cuttings and labels onto the surface of his works, thus producing collages, or *papiers-collés*. This stage of Picasso's work is known as synthetic cubism.

During World War I Picasso remained in France. From 1916 he was involved with the theater, producing stage designs for Sergei Diaghilev's *Ballets Russes* (Russian Ballets). By the early 1920s he had adopted a more classical style, characterized by scenes of figures in Mediterranean landscapes.

Data file

Full name: Pablo Ruiz y Picasso

Nationality: Spanish

Style: cubism

Dates: born 1881 in Malaga, died 1973 in Sorgues, France

Key works:

Les Demoiselles d'Avignon 1906–07
Portrait of Uhde 1910
Ma Jolie 1911–12
Glass and Bottle of Suze 1912
Glass of Absinthe 1914
The Three Musicians 1921
The Three Dancers 1925
Guernica 1937
Massacre in Korea 1951
The Maids of Honor (after Velázquez) 1957

Things to look for:

- use of multiple viewpoints
- fragmented forms
- inclusion of words and musical signs
- real newsprint and labels attached to the canvas

Comparisons: Paul Cézanne, Paul Gauguin, Henri Rousseau, Georges Braque, Juan Gris

Glossary terms: analytical cubism, *Ballets Russes*, cubism, *papiers-collés*, Renaissance, surrealism, synthetic cubism

Picasso: from portraits to politics

Picasso's *Portrait of Uhde* (1910) represents a young gentleman dressed in a jacket and tie with a wing-collared shirt. The sitter, Wilhelm Uhde, was a young German art dealer who supported Picasso during his early career.

Although the figure of Uhde is easy to distinguish, the space he inhabits seems far less recognizable. Small clues, such as the inclusion of a drawer to the right of the figure, imply that he is situated in an interior. Besides this, however, the space fragments into myriad intersecting planes and surfaces, simultaneously suggesting depth and flatness. Moreover, the figure of Uhde himself also offers visual contradictions. For example, the left side of his face is seen as if in profile, with the left eye looking out to the right, but the right side of his face is represented as if it is seen from the front. In doing this, Picasso has abandoned the single viewpoint used by artists since the Renaissance. Instead, he represents Uhde from several different views at once, as if moving through space and time.

One of Picasso's best-known works is *Guernica (1937)*, produced during the Spanish civil war. In 1937 fascist Germany supported the Spanish nationalists led by General Francisco Franco. In an effort to destroy the morale of Franco's republican enemies, German bombers mounted a four-hour-long attack on Guernica, the capital of the northern Basque region of Spain. The town was almost completely destroyed.

Earlier in the year Picasso had been invited to produce a mural for the Spanish

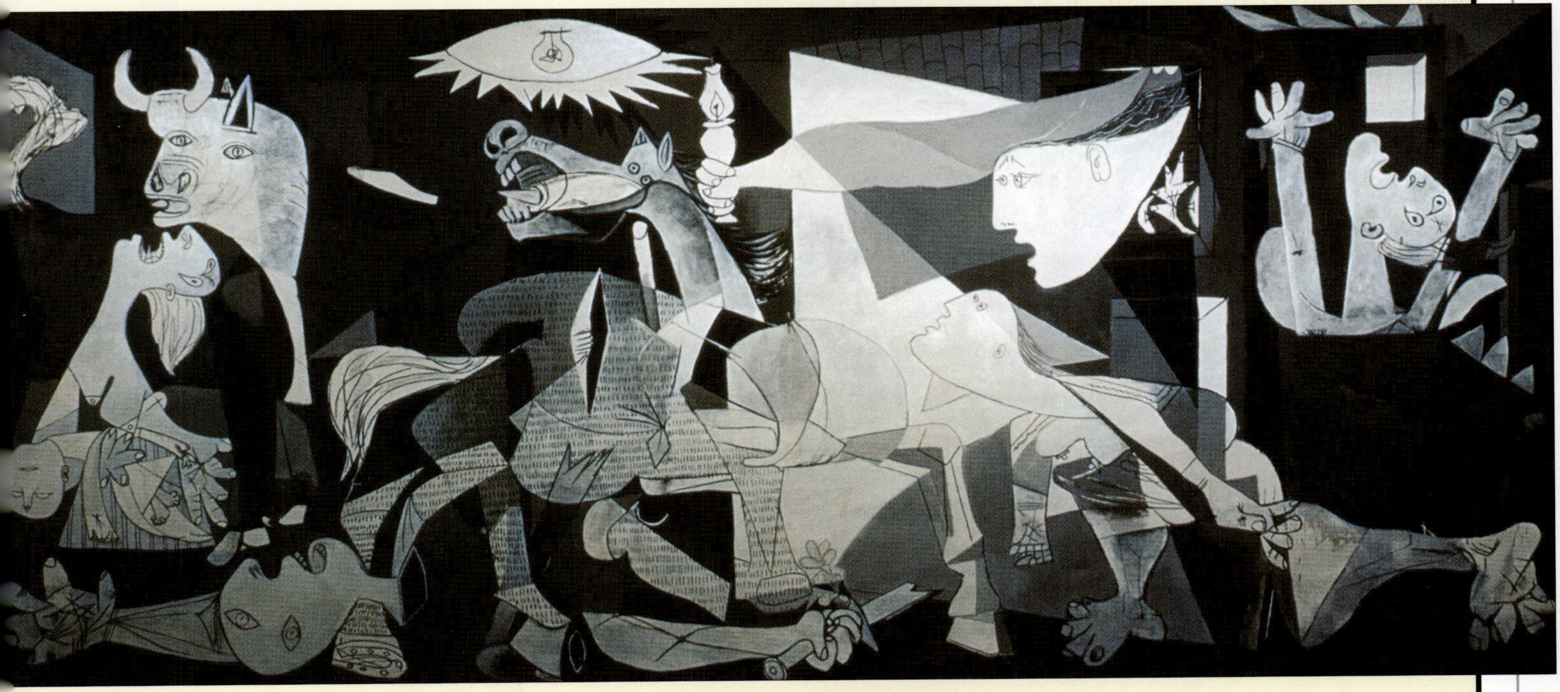

pavilion at the forthcoming International Exhibition in Paris. Horrified by events in Guernica, Picasso set to work on a large mural, entirely in black and white, depicting the bombing. In the center a horse, a symbol of republican Spain, screams as it is speared through its chest. On the right, figures flee from a burning house; on the left, a mother carries a dead infant in her arms. The scene is watched over in the top left-hand corner by a rampant bull, signifying the military aggression of General Franco and his Spanish nationalists.

Picasso once said that painting "is not done to decorate apartments; it is an instrument of war against brutality and darkness." *Guernica* vividly expresses war's cruelty and destructiveness, and is now regarded as one of the most powerful political paintings of the 20th century.

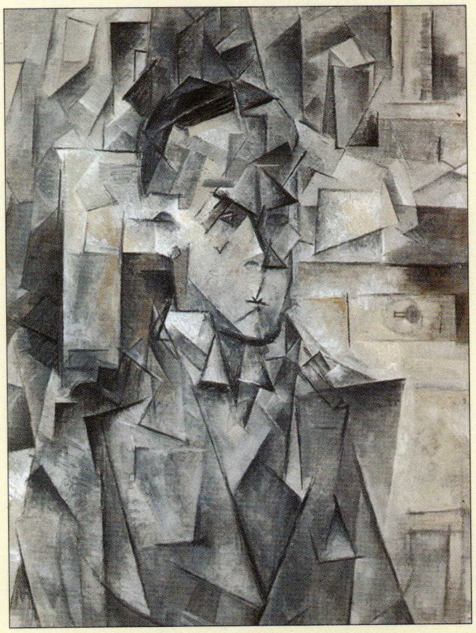

Guernica *1937. Oil on canvas. 137 1/2 x 306 in (349 x 777 cm). Museo del Prado, Madrid.*

Portrait of Uhde *1910. Oil on canvas. 31 x 23 1/2 in (81 x 60 cm). Joseph Pulitzer Collection, St Louis, MO.*

During the 1920s and 1930s Picasso's work drew the attention of the surrealist group. Yet, while he exhibited with the surrealists, Picasso maintained an independence from them. This is particularly evident in many of his works from the late 1930s, particularly his political works such as *Guernica* (1937).

The German invasion of France in 1940 forced many artists to flee Paris, but Picasso remained there throughout the occupation. The often dark and somber works he produced at this time reflect the hardships of life in occupied Paris during World War II. After the war, Picasso's fame spread worldwide. He attended numerous peace conferences and produced antiwar works such as *Massacre in Korea* (1951). He also became a prominent member of the Communist Party.

Many of Picasso's late works are based on famous paintings by Old Masters such as Diego Velázquez, Nicolas Poussin, Eugène Delacroix, and Edouard Manet, though he continued to impose his own unique style. As well as paintings, he produced countless drawings, sculptures, ceramics, and collages. His 85th birthday was celebrated by a major retrospective in Paris; he died in 1973 aged 92.

PIERO DELLA FRANCESCA

PIERO DELLA FRANCESCA WAS RENOWNED IN HIS DAY, and, along with his predecessor Paolo Uccello, was seen as one of the earliest masters of perspective in painting. But after his death he was almost completely forgotten. It was only in the 20th century that he was recognized as one of the greatest painters of the early Renaissance.

Life and work

Piero della Francesca was born in the small hill town of Borgo San Sepolcro in Umbria, northern Italy. His father was a leather-tanner and shoemaker. Nothing is known of Piero's upbringing, or his early artistic education.

We do know, however, that in 1439 he became an assistant to the artist Domenico Veneziano, who was painting frescos in Florence. The city was a bustling center of trade, and wealthy merchant families offered many opportunities for young artists. Yet, for reasons unknown, Piero did not stay there. Most of his career was spent working in other, smaller towns throughout northern and central Italy, and for the last 20 years of his life he lived in his home town.

It was probably his knowledge of and trips to Rome (we know that he was there in 1459), however, that fueled his love of classical architecture and his fascination with geometry. He applied his mathematical knowledge to his paintings in his attention to proportion, his careful placement of figures, and his use of perspective.

He began his first work as master rather than assistant in about 1445 in Borgo: a religious society paid him to paint an altarpiece made up of 23 separate paintings. The centerpiece of this series is known as the *Madonna of Mercy*. Piero seems to have been a slow and methodical painter; although his first commission was supposed to be finished in three years, records of payment for it show that it was probably only completed in 1462, some 17 years later.

In the 1450s Piero went to Urbino in northern Italy. His association with Urbino was to last for the rest of his life. At this time—the late Middle Ages—Italy was not a single country as it is today, but a collection of small states and independent cities. Some of these had their own courts. Urbino was ruled by the soldier and scholar Federico da Montefeltro. Federico invited writers, artists, and architects to his city-state, which soon became one of the leading cultural centers of early Renaissance Italy.

It was probably during his first visit to Urbino that Piero painted his famous work *The Flagellation of Christ* (mid-1450s). This painting, like his earlier work *The Baptism of Christ* (late 1440s), is characterized by strongly modeled figures standing in a setting that gives the viewer a powerful impression of depth, and is his most enigmatic work.

During the 1450s and 1460s Piero created a masterpiece for which he became famous, *The History of the True Cross*, in the church of San Francesco

Data file

Full name: Piero da Benedetto de'Franceschi (known as Piero della Francesca)

Nationality: Italian

Style: early Renaissance

Dates: born between 1415 and 1420 in Borgo San Sepolcro, died 1492 in Borgo San Sepolcro

Key works:
- *Madonna of Mercy* c1445–c1462
- *The Baptism of Christ* late 1440s
- *The History of the True Cross* c1452–c1465
- *The Flagellation of Christ* mid-1450s
- *The Resurrection* after 1458
- *Battista Sforza and Federico da Montefeltro* c1472
- *Madonna and Child with Federico da Montefeltro* c1472–75

Things to look for:
- use of perspective
- balanced composition with calm, still figures
- mastery of clear, soft colors

Comparisons: Domenico Veneziano, Paolo Uccello, Sandro Botticelli

Glossary terms: altarpiece, composition, early Renaissance, fresco, perspective

Order and serenity

Piero's *The Flagellation of Christ* (mid-1450s) depicts the whipping of Christ before the Crucifixion. This punishment was ordered by the Roman governor of the region, Pontius Pilate, who is shown seated on the left. What makes this scene strange is the fact that Christ is shown as a small figure in the background, while the three much larger men on the right seem far more important. It is not clear who these men are, though it is thought the two older men are important political or religious figures from Piero's day, and that the young man in the center is an angel. The richly dressed figure on the far right may well be the man who commissioned the painting, Ludovico Gonzaga, the ruler of Mantua.

Despite the violence of the subject, this painting conveys a sense of harmony, dignity, and calm. The figures and the architecture are sharply depicted, the scene lit by a cool, clear light. Moreover, the men on the right are not watching Christ's punishment, but seem engaged in quiet conversation; even the man whipping Christ seems to be striking a pose.

Piero's use of perspective in this picture is also unusual. In religious paintings at this time the vanishing point, the visual focus of the picture, was often the face or figure of Christ. Diagram ***A*** shows what the picture would have looked like if Piero had done this. Instead, he made the vanishing point in the middle of the picture, focusing on nothing in particular: ***B***. It is unclear why he did this, though composition ***A*** would have made Christ even farther away. Also, use of the central vanishing point ***B*** creates a strong impression of balance and stability—always one of Piero's concerns.

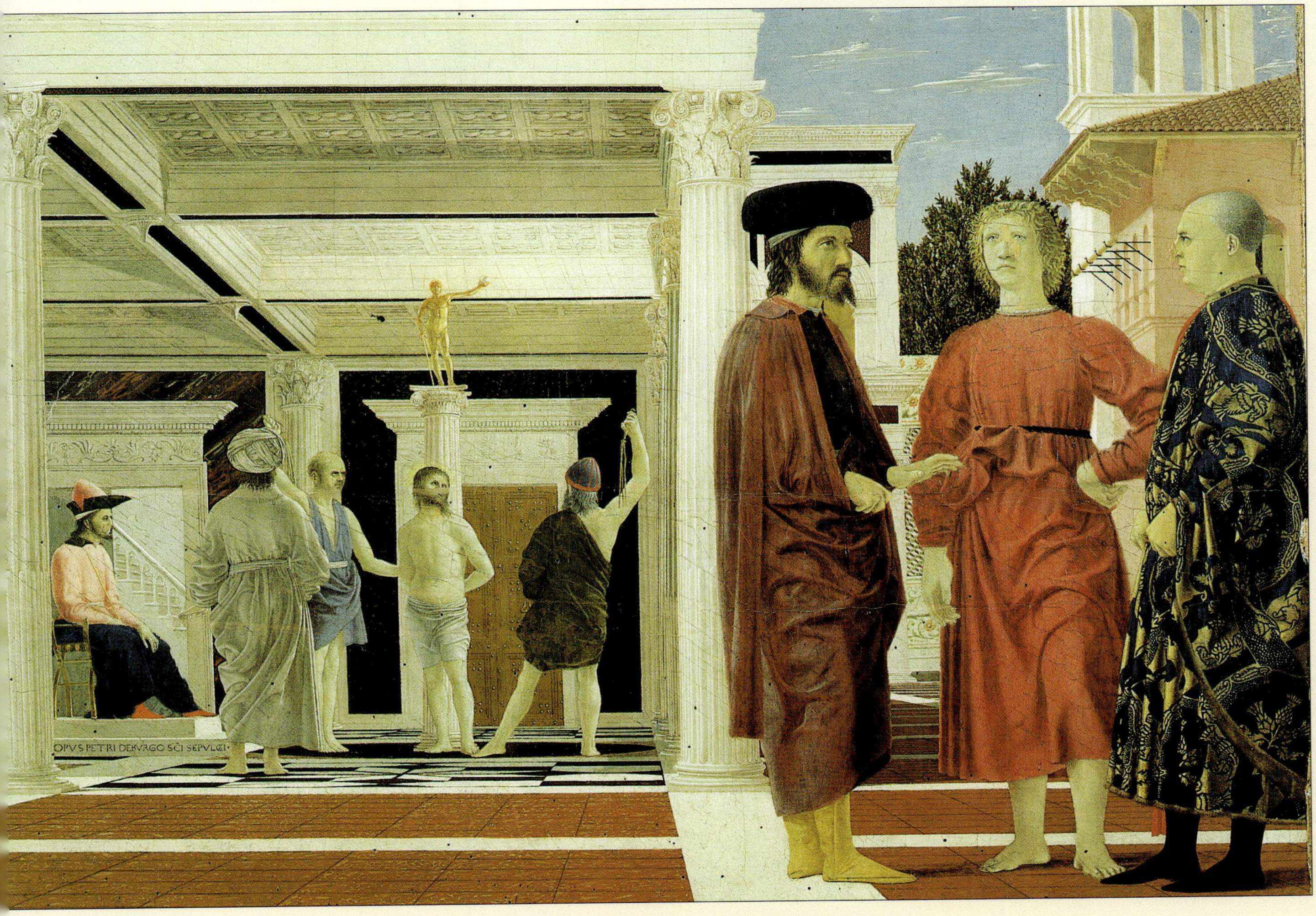

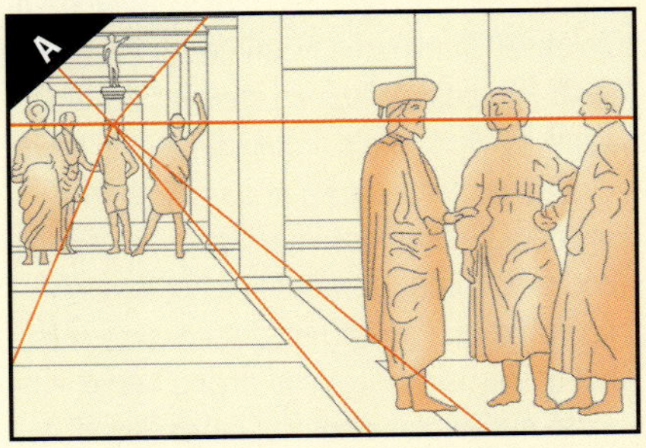

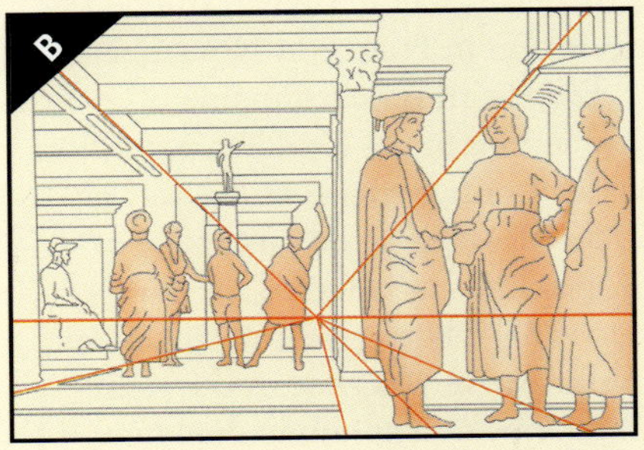

The Flagellation of Christ *mid-1450s. Oil on panel. 23 x 32 in (58 x 82 cm). Galleria Nazionale della Marche, Urbino.*

The vanishing point *is where the lines of perspective meet. The vanishing point, and hence the visual focus of the picture, would traditionally be the figure of Christ (**A**) but here it is in the middle of the picture (**B**).*

in Arezzo near Florence. It is a series of frescos portraying stories from the Bible and from medieval legends. Some images in the scenes attempt to symbolize Christianity's loss of (and urge to regain) the city of Constantinople, which had fallen to the Turks in 1453, the year after Piero had begun working on the painting.

One of the most outstanding pictures from Piero's later career is his double portrait of Duke Federico da Montefeltro and his wife (c1472). Piero painted his patrons in profile against their home landscape of Urbino. Interestingly, the duke is seen from the left; he had lost his right eye in battle and did not like that side of his face to be shown. The portraits were innovative in that they presented their subjects in an unidealized way in a natural setting; combining portrait and landscape was unusual at the time. By this stage Piero was using a system known as aerial perspective. This was based on the observation that objects in the far distance are hazier and their color less vivid than those in the foreground.

Piero may have become blind as he got older, and spent much of his later life writing treatises about the use of mathematics in painting.

PIPPIN Horace

HORACE PIPPIN IS ONE OF SEVERAL MODERN ARTISTS WHOSE WORK is identified as "naïve," for it does not conform to traditional or avant-garde standards of western painting. His paintings are simple, colorful, powerful, and imaginative evocations of Black American life and experiences, as well as moving representations of his own private visions.

Life and work

Born in West Chester, Pennsylvania in 1888, Horace Pippin began drawing with pencils and crayons at the age of seven. Following the death of his father, Pippin and his mother moved to Goshen, New York. He often referred to his life there in his early paintings.

Data file

Full name: Horace Pippin

Nationality: American

Style: naïve

Dates: born 1888 in West Chester, PA , died 1946 in West Chester, PA

Key works:

The End of the War: Starting Home 1931

Buffalo Hunt 1933

The Woman at Samaria 1940

John Brown on His Way to His Hanging c1942

Domino Players 1943

Mr Prejudice 1943

Victorian Interior 1946

The Park Bench 1946

Things to look for:

- naïve style of painting
- near symmetrical compositions
- representations of Black American life and experience: themes inspired by the Bible, literature, and memories of World War I
- bright areas of color and concentrated areas of intricate linear patterns
- colors laid on thickly but with tiny brushstrokes
- non-naturalistic (non-scientific) perspective

Comparisons: Grandma Moses, Morris Hirschfield, John Kane, Joseph Pickett, Edward Hicks, J.O.J. Frost, Olaf Kraus, Henri Rousseau

Glossary terms: impasto, naïve

Many of Pippin's first works in crayon and watercolor depicted scenes from the Bible, on squares of muslin, the edges of which were frayed to imitate the appearance of doilies or antimacassars. Both the Bible and the doily were continuing motifs in his works. In *My Life Story*, published in 1946, Pippin told how a buyer became angry with him after the colors washed out of the paintings when laundered!

When Pippin was 15 he left school to support his ailing mother. He worked in various jobs before settling as a porter in a hotel. Drafted in July 1915, soon after the United States had entered World War I, Pippin trained as an infantryman and joined the renowned Black American 369th Infantry Regiment. He was shipped into action in France in November.

For the next year Pippin documented life as a soldier, recording the devastating effects of the war on the people, cities, and landscape of Europe. The war affected Pippin profoundly—both psychologically and physically. He was shot in the right shoulder by an exploding dumdum bullet from a German sniper. Army surgeons attached his shattered shoulder to the upper part of his arm with a steel plate. The wound left Pippin unable to raise his right hand above the level of his shoulder.

Discharged from the army in May, 1919, Pippin returned to the United States, where he met and married Jennie Ora Featherstone, a widow with a young son. Returning to his native West Chester, Pippin supported his new family with a variety of jobs that supplemented his army pension.

After experimenting with charcoal drawings on wooden boxes, in 1929 he started applying a hot poker to wood panels. Using this method he made 17 "drawings" some with spots of primary color added to the burnt incisions. He began to paint in the last six years of

Horrors of war

Pippin did not paint or draw for nine years after being discharged from the army. When he did, he started using charcoal, held in his left hand, and drew pictures on the tops of wooden cigar boxes. He was both encouraged and dismayed by the results. With his interest in drawing reawakened, the boxes proved too small to develop ideas and the charcoal kept rubbing off.

The turning point came in 1929, when Pippin tried using a hot poker. Balancing it between his right hand and his knee, he began to burn a design onto a table top. Pippin was happy to have discovered a method that enabled him to draw, and it had the benefit of helping to strengthen his right hand and arm as well.

Pippin returned to painting; his first work was *The End of the War: Starting Home* (1931). It took him three years to complete, and in his effort to create the desired effects, he applied nearly a hundred coats of paint.

Having drawn the outlines on the canvas in pencil, Pippin applied the paint to the canvas with tiny brushstrokes, moving from one side to the other and composing elements in the foreground before painting the background. Working on small canvases, Pippin painted mostly at night, at an easel illuminated by an unshaded 200-watt lightbulb. When an element did not seem to work in a painting, he would paint over it, building the paint up to a thick impasto. Sometimes Pippin used oil paints, and other times he would use ordinary house paints, which had the advantage of being less expensive and drying faster.

In his autobiographical notes Pippin commented: "The pictures I have already painted come to me in my mind, and if to me it is a worthwhile picture, I paint it. I go

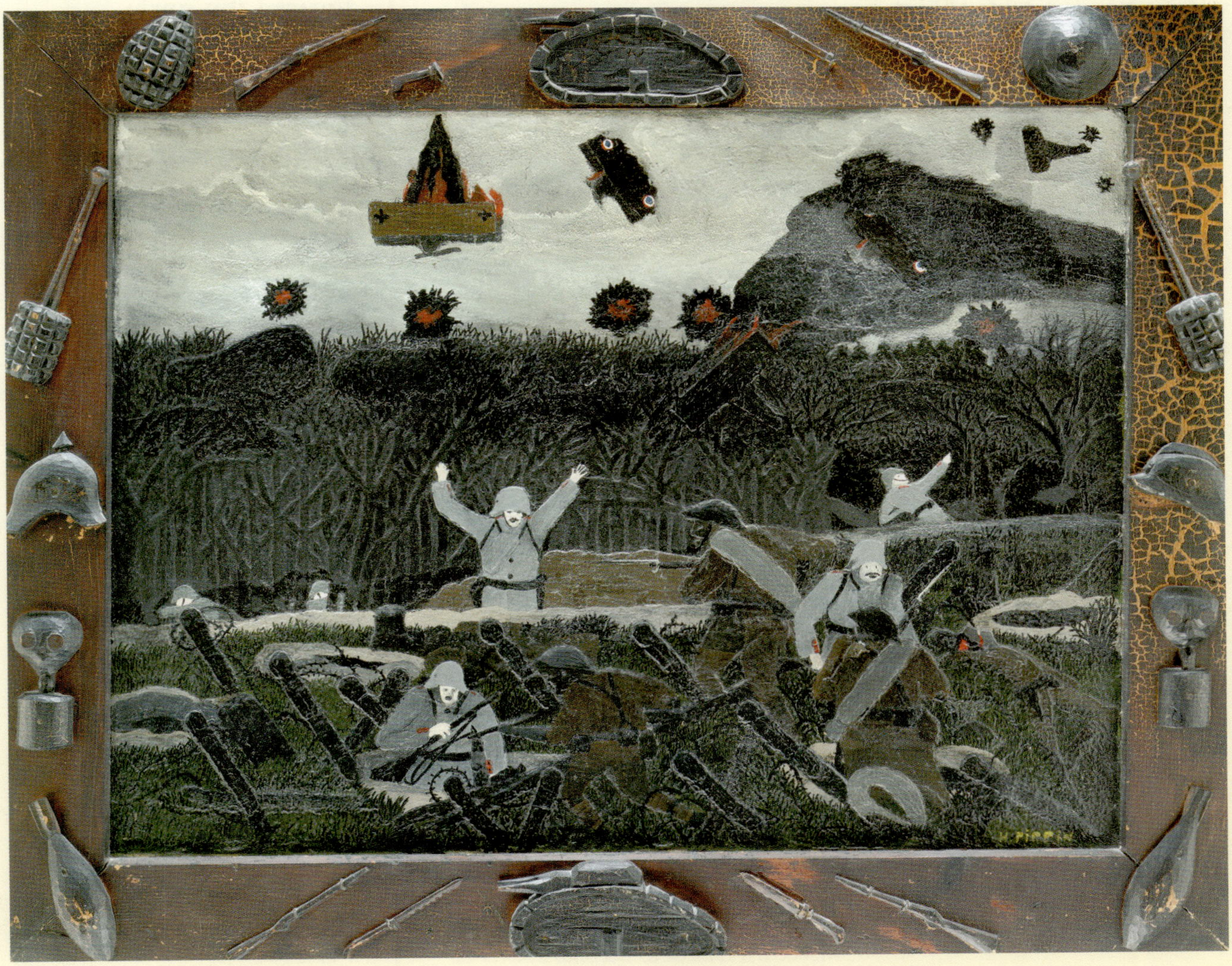

over that picture in my mind several times and when I am ready to paint I have all the details that I need."

The End of the War: Starting Home (1931) is Pippin's attempt to come to terms with World War I. He was one of the first to paint convincingly the horrors of modern war. He conveys a sense of violent movement, of the ground racked by explosions. Instead of depicting a cheerful event—the end of war—Pippin gives us expressionless soldiers, emerging from trenches into a landscape of barbed wired and anti-tank defences. Above the soldiers, airplanes dodge ground-fire. On this last day of war, one plane falls from the sky in flames. A lack of parachutes suggests the crew will not survive. The deathly theme is echoed in the soldiers, who rise like corpses from graves on the Day of Judgment.

The End of the War: Starting Home
1931. Oil on canvas. 25 x 32 in (63.5 x 81 cm). Philadelphia Museum of Art, Pennsylvania, PA.

Pippin remained self-taught and true to his vision. He wrote: "My idea of art is that one must have a love for it, for I think a man paints from his heart and from his imagination."

his life, producing 75 works. The first painting he completed was *The End of the War: Starting Home* (1931).

In 1937 Pippin was "discovered" by local art critic Christopher Brinton. He had his first solo exhibition in the summer, and in 1938 four of his paintings were included in the "Masters of Popular Painting" exhibition at the Museum of Modern Art, New York. After his one-man show in 1940, drug manufacturer and art collector, Albert C. Barnes, stated that Pippin was the first Black American painter of his generation whose work displayed "the most individual and unadulterated painting, authentically expressive of the American spirit."

Further exhibitions followed, and it was in his last years that Pippin created some of his best-loved works. While working on a fourth painting in the *Holy Mountain* series in 1946, Pippin suffered a stroke and died, aged 58.

PISANO Andrea

THE WORKS FOR WHICH ANDREA PISANO IS NOW MOST FAMOUS are the south doors for the baptistery in Florence, Italy. In these the artist shows a new concern for depicting real space, and for creating a more organic human figure, which marks him as a forerunner of early Renaissance art.

Life and work

Andrea Pisano was born in Pontedera in Italy, which explains why he is sometimes known as Andrea da Pontedera. His father was a notary, or clerk. Andrea became a goldsmith and sculptor by trade; later he would also take on the role of Master of the Cathedral Works in both Florence and Orvieto.

The only documented works by Andrea Pisano are the south doors of the Florence Baptistery. These doors are signed by him and dated 1330 (they were completed in 1336). For this reason he is considered the founder of the school of sculpture in Florence. Famous 15th-century sculptors such as Lorenzo Ghiberti and Donatello would look to his work in the future. Ghiberti would later create the north doors of the Florence Baptistery (1403–24).

Pisano was influenced by the Florentine painter and architect Giotto di Bondone. What Giotto did for painting, Pisano achieved in sculpture. This was to break away from the traditional Gothic or Byzantine style in art that was stylized, flat, and decorative. Both artists created figures that were more naturalistic—figures that looked more three-dimensional and realistic.

By 1340 Andrea Pisano had succeeded Giotto to become Master of the Cathedral Works in Florence. His works of this period are relief carvings and statues for the lower part of the new cathedral bell tower, or campanile. Altogether, eight sculptors were employed on this project, including Andrea's son, Nino. Andrea's works, although not signed, are recognizable: the natural poses of the figures and the attention to details and "real" space are distinctive. Andrea was also responsible for the supervision of the campanile building plans designed and begun by Giotto. One writer at the time tells of Andrea's eventual dismissal from this project because he deviated too much from Giotto's original plans.

In 1341 Andrea Pisano went to Pisa. He set up a workshop there and continued to work on religious commissions. There he executed a series of sculptures including *Virgin Suckling the Infant Christ* (1342–43) and statues of the Virgin and Child with other saints (early 1340s). He also sculpted a Virgin and Child for the façade of the cathedral in Pisa.

Data file

Full name: Andrea Pisano (sometimes known as Andrea da Pontedera)

Nationality: Italian

Style: Gothic/early Renaissance

Dates: born c1290 in Pontedera, died c1348/9 in Orvieto

Key works:

relief on the bronze doors of the south portal of the Florence Baptistery 1330–36

reliefs and sculptures for the lower part of the campanile in Florence 1337–41

Virgin and Child with Saint Peter and John the Baptist early 1340s

Virgin Suckling the Infant Christ 1342–43

Things to look for:

- figures that show a concern for depicting the three-dimensional body as well as the patterns of line and drapery
- an attention to fine detail, reminiscent of the art of a jeweler or a goldsmith
- clear and harmonious lines in relief compositions

Comparisons: Giotto di Bondone, Masaccio, Donatello, Duccio di Buoninsegna, Lorenzo Ghiberti

Glossary terms: *cire perdue* (lost wax), early Renaissance, Gothic, relief sculpture

Toward the early Renaissance

The baptistery in Florence is named for John the Baptist, patron saint of Florence. Pisano was commissioned to make the south doors of the building, which show 20 scenes from the saint's life.

The full image of the doors (right) shows bronze sculptures that are not freestanding but projected out against a flat background. This is known as relief sculpture, from the Italian verb *rilevare,* "to raise." First Pisano modeled the different scenes in wax. The wax models were then covered with either plaster or terracotta clay, which hardened around the soft wax. Molten-hot bronze was then poured into the plaster or clay, melting the wax, which ran out through a special hole. When the liquid bronze had been cooled and was solid, the plaster or clay layer was broken away to reveal the bronze model. This is known as the *cire perdue*, or "lost wax" method of casting.

After the doors had been cast in bronze, Andrea and his assistants polished them and rubbed away any rough edges. Sometimes the very fine details were chiseled into the metal at this stage. Gold highlights (gilding) were also added. These highlights have now worn away.

In *The Transportation of the Baptist's Body* (detail, above right), we can hardly see the figure of John the Baptist, whose dead body lies horizontally, carried by his followers. Only his head and feet are visible. A gentle rhythm is created by the harmonious lines of the smooth and flowing drapery, which echo each other in a curving pattern across the scene. This gentle "rocking" motion of the draperies helps to convey the tenderness of the followers for the dead Baptist. Some of them incline their heads over his face, again suggesting concern and grief. The

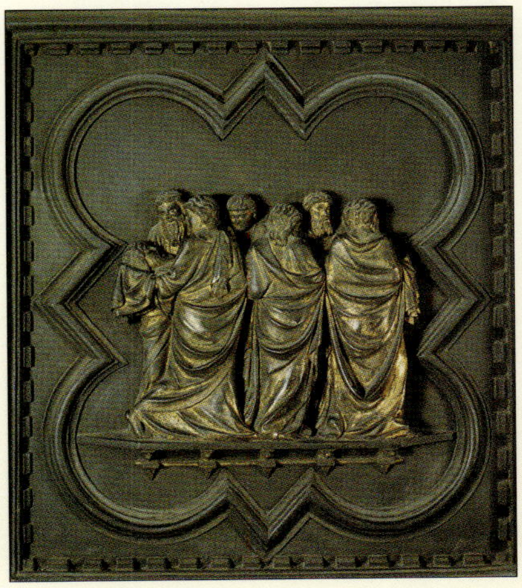

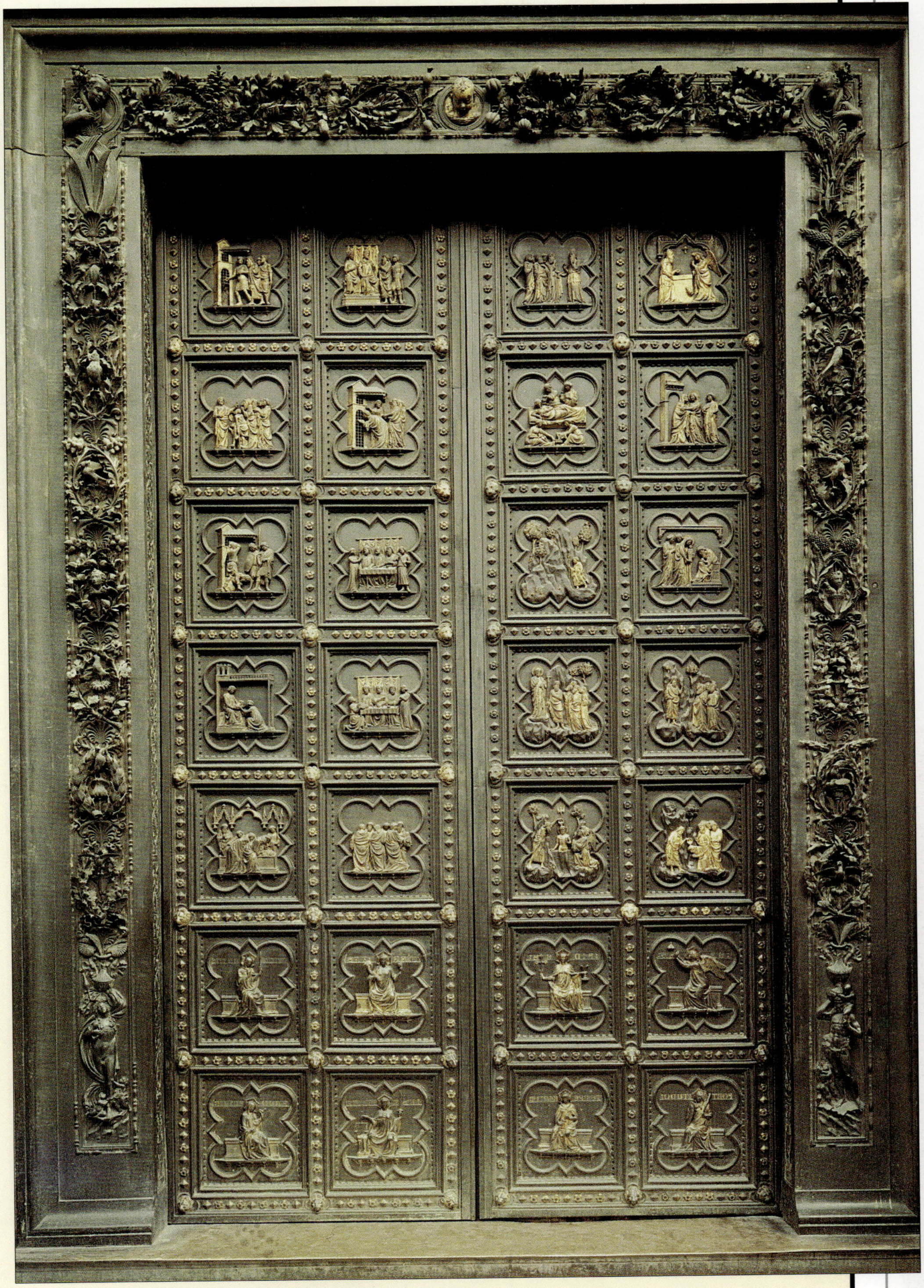

The Transportation of the Baptist's Body *(above). Scene from the south doors (right). 1330–36. Bronze. Height 222 in (564 cm). Florence Baptistery.*

draperies also suggest the moving of feet as the followers process.

The scene is divided into layers: the three figures closest to us are more three-dimensional than the three who, we imagine, stand on the other side—though in fact only the heads of those figures have been modeled. By using different depths in the relief, Andrea has convinced us that he is depicting real space.

Although the drapery is important, we have a sense of a solid form in the figures underneath. For example, the shoulders of the middle figure nearest us hunch up with the weight of the body he is bearing. This is one of the basic changes from Gothic art—in which figures are ornate, finely detailed, and very light—to the early Renaissance. Early Renaissance artists were more interested in depicting the heavier, more organic, three-dimensional body beneath the drapery and ornament.

Although some art historians have found it difficult to distinguish the works of Andrea and his son, in fact their styles are quite distinct. Andrea was more concerned with the naturalistic proportions of his figures.

In 1347 Andrea became Master of the Cathedral Works at Orvieto. He kept his workshop in Pisa as a base, and delivered works to Orvieto from it. Other fragments of works produced for the cathedral in Orvieto remain there.

Andrea Pisano is thought to have died in Orvieto in 1348/9, possibly a victim of the plague epidemic that ravaged the city at the time. His son, Nino, succeeded him as Master of the Cathedral Works at Orvieto.

PISSARRO Camille

CAMILLE PISSARRO WAS A PAINTER AND PRINTMAKER who experimented with a number of different styles in his landscapes, cityscapes, and figure paintings. Sometimes called "the painter's painter," he was a friend and mentor to two generations of artists, playing a part in the creation of impressionism and neoimpressionism.

Life and work

Born in St Thomas in the Virgin Islands, Pissarro was one of six children in a prosperous French-Portuguese Jewish family that ran a general store. He began by working in his father's business, but he left the island in 1852 and traveled with his friend, the Danish artist Fritz Melbye, to Caracas, Venezuela, where they set up a tropical studio, in a move that would be echoed by Paul Gauguin's Tahitian voyages.

In 1855 Pissarro went to France and settled in Paris. There he made many copies of the French art on display in the World's Fair, and also of the Old Masters in the Louvre, and developed an admiration for the landscape paintings of Camille Corot. He also shared a studio with the Danish artists Anton Melbye and David Jacobsen.

In 1856 Pissarro enrolled at the Ecole des Beaux-Arts and the Académie Suisse, where he met the friends who would later join together to create impressionism: Paul Cézanne, Claude Monet (who would become a lifelong friend), and Armand Guillaumin. Unlike some of the impressionist painters, Pissarro had many works accepted for the annual state-sponsored Salon exhibition, where his large-scale panoramic landscapes won him acclaim. Pissarro was the only painter to show his work at all eight of the exhibitions held by the impressionists between 1874 and 1886. He also exhibited with the Belgian independent group, Les Vingt ("The Twenty") in Brussels in the 1890s.

In 1870 the Franco–Prussian war broke out and Pissarro fled to London. There he was influenced by the work of English landscape painters such as John Constable and J. M. W. Turner. He also met his future wife.

In 1872 Pissarro returned with his wife to Pontoise, France, where the couple developed friendships with Cézanne and Edgar Degas. An outstanding teacher, Pissarro was greatly admired by his contemporaries, but he also learned from his talented peers. Largely as a result of Cézanne's influence, Pissarro decided to break up his brushstrokes more and to apply paint more thickly and systematically. Degas encouraged Pissarro to explore the possibilities of printmaking. Their work in etching, in particular, helped to elevate printmaking from a means of copying other artworks to an original art form in itself. In the 1880s, Pissarro began to focus upon the figure subjects within his landscapes and interiors, inspired by Degas and Paul Gauguin.

In 1885 Pissarro met Paul Signac and Georges Seurat, who inspired the

Data file

Full name: Jacob Abraham Camille Pissarro

Nationality: French

Style: impressionism/neoimpressionism

Dates: born 1830 in St Thomas, died 1903 in Paris

Key works:

- *Côtes des Boeufs, Pontoise* 1877
- *The Poultry Market, Gisors* 1885
- *View from My Window, Eragny-sur-Epte* 1888
- *The Gleaners* 1889
- *Turpitudes Sociales* (drawings) 1890
- *Le Grand Pont, Rouen* 1896
- *Avenue de l'Opéra* 1898

Things to look for:

- use of the pointillist technique
- depiction of effects of light and seasonal climate

Comparisons: Paul Cézanne, Camille Corot, Paul Gauguin, Paul Signac, Georges Seurat, Claude Monet, Alfred Sisley, Edgar Degas

Glossary terms: Barbizon school, impressionism, neoimpressionism, Old Masters, palette, pointillism, Salon, (Les) Vingt

From landscape to cityscape

Camille Pissarro had one of the most varied and experimental careers of all the impressionist artists. His early work reflects an awareness of the Barbizon landscape painters and the great mid-19th-century peasant painters. He assimilated Gustave Courbet's bold brushwork, Charles Daubigny's panoramic compositions, and Corot's airy, atmospheric light. Pissarro's palette was rich, though somber, during this period, with dark greens and warm russet earth tones.

In the late 1870s, when he was working closely with Paul Cézanne, Pissarro adopted a new constructive system of even touches in his brushwork. He also employed a lighter, more restricted palette. In the 1880s, Pissarro's empathy with the younger neoimpressionist painters led him to adopt a pointillist technique, in which bright colors were juxtaposed in tiny dots. In his last works, however, Pissarro returned to the looser impressionist brushwork of his middle age.

Pissarro's willingness to experiment with technique was paralleled by the breadth of his subject matter. Perhaps best known as a landscape painter, Pissarro also created powerful figure paintings. One of his main concerns was to examine the different lives experienced in the city and in the countryside. His groups of peasants harvesting fruit or planting crops imply a collective consciousness in rural areas that was felt to have died in the metropolitan centers, while his heroic images of peasants at rest show the importance of time for personal reflection.

Pissarro's last great series of paintings, depicting the boulevards of Paris, takes up

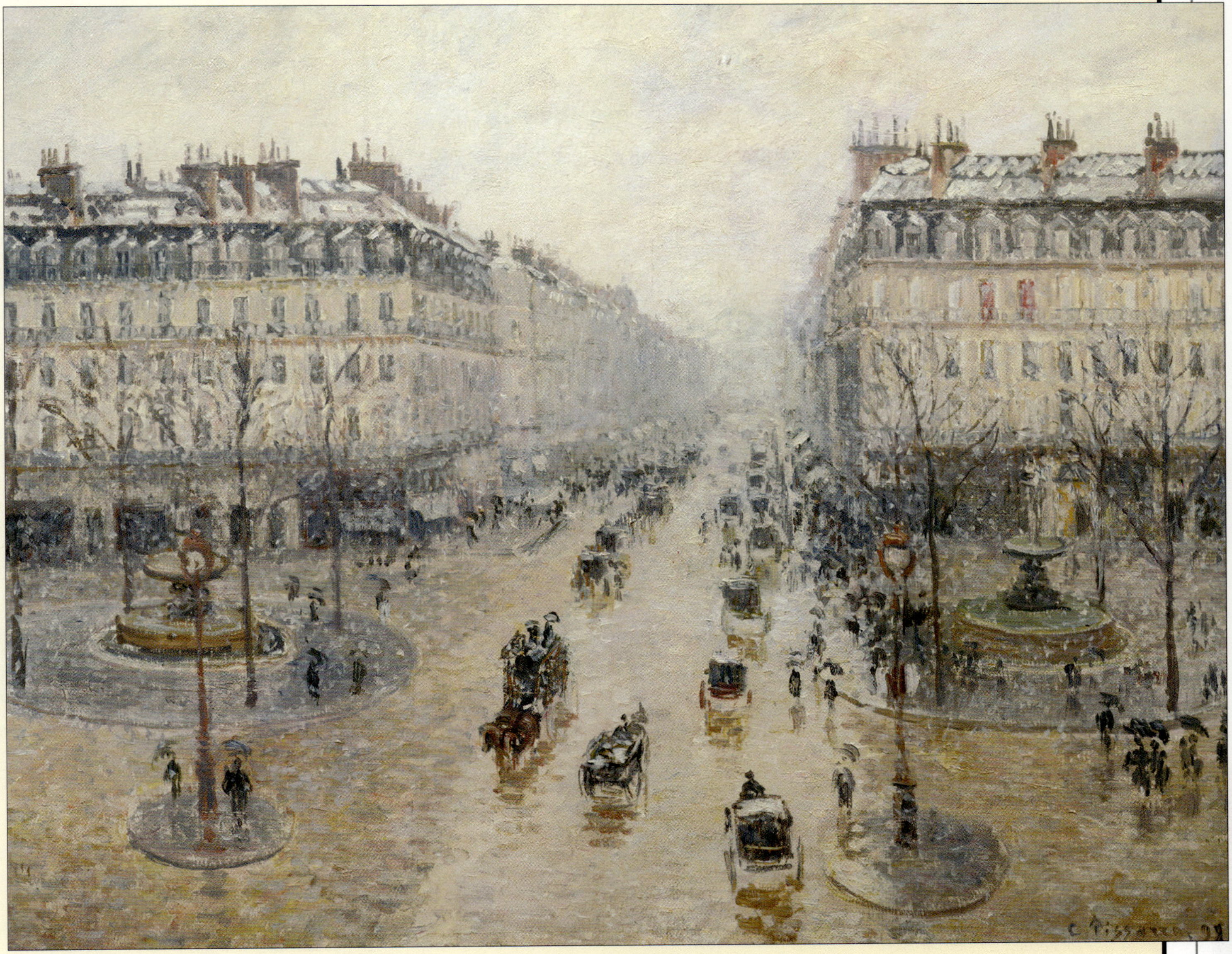

a classic impressionist theme, but with a new perspective. Instead of the viewer being immersed in the crowd or inside cafés and theaters, as one is in the paintings of Edgar Degas and Edouard Manet of the 1860s and 1870s, Pissarro looks down on the mass of humanity and carriages of Paris from the safety of a balcony. Like Gustave Caillebotte, Pissarro emphasizes the plunging depth of these huge thoroughfares, but he dissolves the architecture of this vertiginous perspective in brilliant light or rainy mud.

Avenue de l'Opéra *1898. Oil on canvas. 25 1/2 x 32 1/4 in (65 x 82 cm). Pushkin Museum, Moscow.*

artist's use of the pointillist technique and his search for luminosity, which would dominate his work through the 1890s. He used vibrant color and applied his paint in dots. Late in life, Pissarro returned to the looser impressionist touch of his earlier work.

Always a man of the left, Pissarro became deeply committed to the anarchist cause, financing and illustrating anarchist journals such as Jean Grave's *Temps Nouveaux* ("New Times"). In his depictions of the verdant suburb of Eragny-sur-Epte, his last home (from 1894), Pissarro created a utopian world of collective labor and rest amidst abundant food, clean air, and sunlight.

Pissarro's last works, like Monet's, were series of paintings, depicting scenes in different seasons and at different times of day. From 1893 Pissarro produced 24 canvases of the boulevards of Paris as seen from hotel windows, as well as views of Rouen (where he stayed from 1896 to 1898), Dieppe, and Le Havre.

POLLOCK Jackson

POLLOCK'S CONTRIBUTION TO ART has been ridiculed and praised in approximately equal measure. Some critics have described his work as uncontrolled and ultimately empty, while others have seen his fluid, paint-splattered canvases as bearing witness to an explosion of semifocused creative energy.

Life and work

Jackson Pollock is often described as an all-American artist; he was the first U.S.-born painter to achieve international recognition. Artists who had been successful in the United States before him were either émigrés from Europe or had been far more indebted to European art.

Pollock came to the New York art world from the farmlands of Wyoming, Arizona, and California; he was influenced as much by the landscape, romance, and pioneering spirit of the American West as by the avant-garde movements of the early 20th century. He was the youngest of five brothers, born to parents who struggled to farm land throughout the Western states.

One of Jackson's earliest influences was his eldest brother, Charles, who went to New York in the 1920s to study art. A few years later Jackson followed him, initially training with his brother's tutor. Then, in the early 1930s, as part of a government scheme for artists, Pollock came into contact with the Mexican muralist David Alfaro Siqueiros. The scale of Siqueiros's work, as well as his expressive techniques—carried out quickly with commercial paints rather than oils—made a lasting impression upon Pollock.

Another important influence upon him was psychoanalysis. From his teenage years, Pollock had struggled to control his appetite for drink, and in 1937 he went into sessions with a psychoanalyst in an attempt to cure his alcoholism. Pollock's sketches were used and encouraged as a focus for the patient's and doctor's exploration of Pollock's subconscious. The treatment had only limited success, but the semicreative, semianalytic technique provided a new approach for Pollock; it was similar to the spontaneous doodles, practiced by the surrealists, known as automatism. However, his paintings of the early 1940s, such as *Moon Woman Cuts the Circle* (1944–45), were still imitative of the dominating figure of modern art, Pablo Picasso. But whereas Picasso drew on African, Iberian, and classical forms, Pollock's imagery seems to derive from Native American or Mexican mythology.

In 1943 the art dealer and patron Peggy Guggenheim began to show his work at her gallery, and also offered him a degree of financial security. Through this important art world connection, Pollock came into greater contact with other abstract expressionists, such as Willem de Kooning, Robert Motherwell, and Mark Rothko. The style of these painters varied considerably, but they all aimed to find a highly personal and intuitive form of expression.

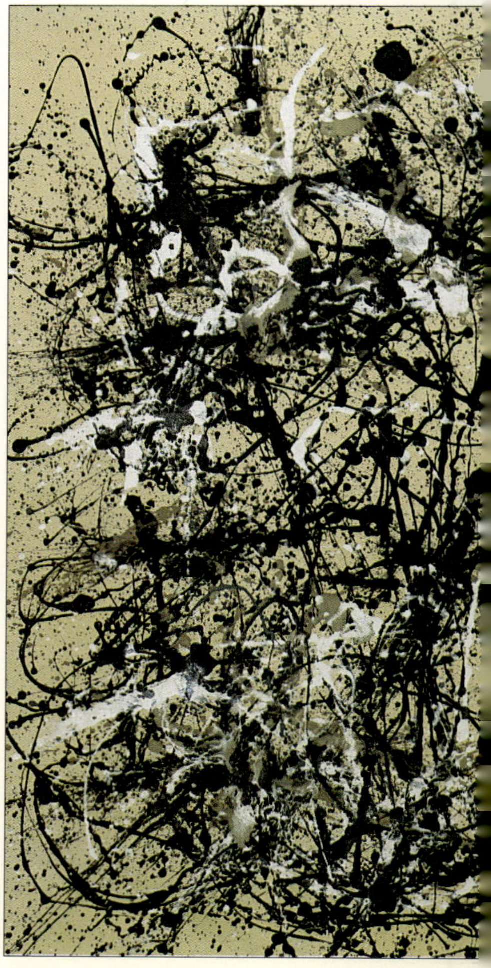

Beyond the brush

The action painting for which Jackson Pollock became famous is essentially basic: Pollock dripped, splashed, smeared, flicked, and poured paint onto canvas laid out on the studio floor, until a complete visual field had been built up into a sinuous and impenetrable chaos. But what governs the action—the gesture of the arms and, in

Data file

Full name: Jackson Pollock

Nationality: American

Style: abstract expressionism

Dates: born 1912 in Cody, WY, died 1956 in Springs, NY

Key works:
- *Untitled (Composition with Pouring II)* 1943
- *Lucifer* 1947
- *Number IIa* 1948
- *Summertime: Number 9a* 1948
- *Lavender Mist: Number I* 1950
- *Autumn Rhythm: Number 30* 1950
- *Convergence: Number 10* 1952

Things to look for:
- dynamic use of paint; rhythmic gestural traces
- even coverage across the canvas
- large scale

Comparisons: David Alfaro Siqueiros, Wassily Kandinsky, Joan Miró, Lee Krasner, Willem de Kooning, Franz Kline, Robert Motherwell

Glossary terms: abstract expressionism, action painting, automatism, gestural art, impressionism, mural, surrealism

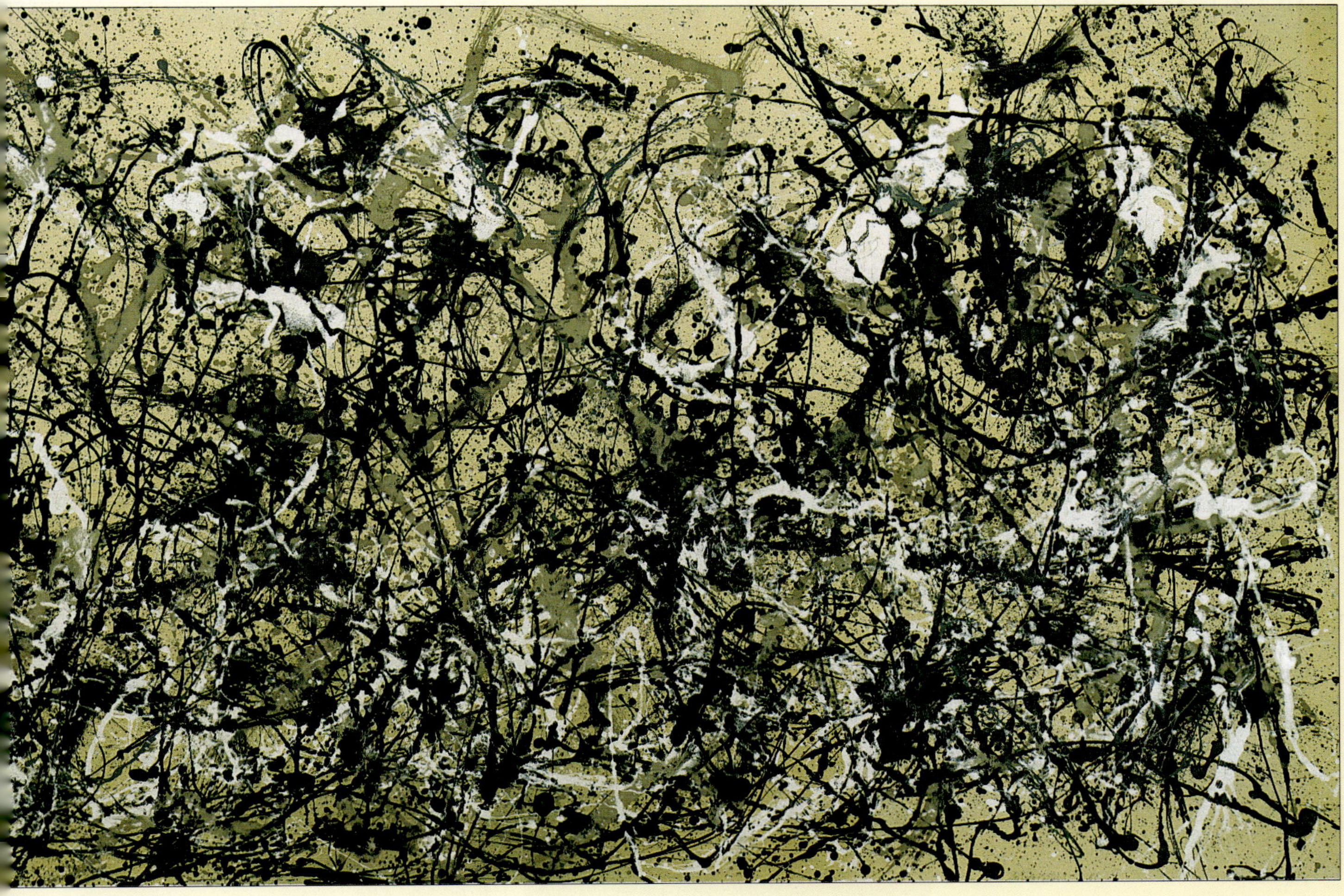

fact, the whole body—continues to be a matter of debate. What control is exerted by the artist? Is the action unconscious and haphazard, or is it governed by an artist trained in the use of color, tonal range, and compositional structure? Is it a reaction against controlling forces, or an extreme expression of them?

Even concentrating only on Pollock's most spectacular and original period (from 1947 to 1952), there is a huge variation in his work. Some works have great intensity (his 1948 painting *Number Ia*, for example), while others are looser and more fluid (*Number IIa*, 1948). Pollock's use of color can be vibrant and pervasive, or subtle, as in the almost impressionistic *Lavender Mist: Number I* (1950). He produced great works, with a sophisticated tonal and color balance, and he produced paintings that lost that control.

Autumn Rhythm: Number 30 *1950. Oil on canvas. 105 x 207 in (267 x 526 cm). Metropolitan Museum of Art, New York, NY.*

As an action painter, Pollock acted, performed, and expressed emotion physically, but he also concentrated on pushing painting toward a new form—an extreme form—and the object, the painted canvas, mattered to him entirely.

By the mid-1940s Pollock had moved from Manhattan to Long Island, where he lived with his wife, the painter Lee Krasner. In 1947, in a series of works including *Lucifer* and *Alchemy*, Pollock abandoned figuration and formal composition, and worked purely with color, tone, and rhythm—a kind of visual equivalent of improvised jazz.

Despite the fact that Pollock had created a new and exciting form—his own style—continuation from this point was no easy matter. In 1950 film-makers Hans Namuth and Paul Falkenberg made a documentary of Pollock at work, which laid bare his (physical) working methods. Perhaps the resulting film made the process look too easy to Pollock himself; in any case the film's effect was to detonate a kind of paranoia inside him. He became unable to carry the burden of his most original and contentious paintings, retreating to the symbols and figures he had labored with in the early 1940s. In the last years of his life he drank more and worked less.

Pollock died at the wheel of a car, while driving home at speed and under the influence of alcohol. This dramatic end cemented his reputation as a wild and reckless man, driven by competing passions for creation and destruction.

PONTORMO

ALTHOUGH OVERSHADOWED BY THE WORK of his more famous contemporaries, Pontormo's art nevertheless possesses rare qualities of vision and design. By temperament he was melancholy and self-absorbed, even neurotic. Yet through his art he responded sensitively to the political and religious tensions that affected Florentine society during the first half of the 16th century.

Life and work

Jacopo Carucci was nicknamed "Pontormo" after the village of his birth. Following the death of his mother and his painter father, he was apprenticed to train as an artist in Florence. He seems to have worked under a succession of masters, with the result that his emerging style reflected the influence of a number of artists active in Florence during this time, notably Fra Bartolommeo, Andrea del Sarto, and Piero di Cosimo.

Data file

Full name: Jacopo Carucci (known as Pontormo)
Nationality: Italian
Style: mannerism
Dates: born 1494 in Pontormo, died 1557 in Florence
Key works:
- *Joseph with Jacob in Egypt* 1515–19
- *Portrait of Cosimo de' Medici* c1518
- *Vertumnus and Pomona* 1520–21
- scenes from the Passion of Christ 1522–25
- *Deposition* 1526–28
- *Portrait of a Halberdier* c1527
- *The Three Graces* (date unknown)

Things to look for:
- complex and almost decorative approach to figurative compositions
- occasionally exaggerated gestures and intensity of emotion
- elongated elegance of anatomical forms
- bright, even sharp, coloring and clarity of line
- refined aloofness of portrait figures

Comparisons: Piero di Cosimo, Michelangelo Buonarroti, Andrea del Sarto, Agnolo Bronzino, Rosso Fiorentino
Glossary terms: High Renaissance, mannerism

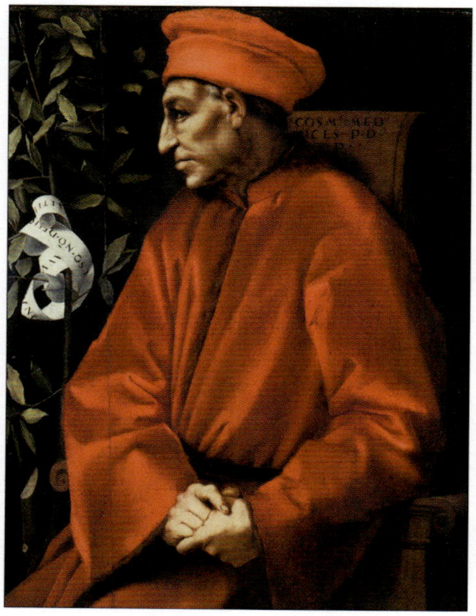

Portrait of Cosimo de' Medici *c1518. Oil on panel. $34\frac{1}{4}$ x $25\frac{1}{2}$ in (87 x 65 cm). Galleria degli Uffizi, Florence.*

Florentine art was undergoing a process of profound change at this time, and no artist could ignore the innovations of Leonardo da Vinci, Michelangelo Buonarroti, and Raphael. Florence was experiencing social turbulence, too: although the Medici family had been expelled from the city in 1494, the election of a Medici pope, Leo X, in 1513, returned the family to power. Pontormo himself benefited from the Medicis' patronage throughout his career. From 1519 to 1521, for example, he was engaged in decorating rooms in the Medici family's rural villa, Poggio a Caiano.

Pontormo's *Portrait of Cosimo de' Medici* (c1518), a posthumous likeness of the man who established the power of the Medici family, was one of a series commissioned to illustrate the kindly aspects of Medici rule. Working with Pontormo on the project was Giorgio Vasari, an artist, architect, and biographer of Pontormo; his work is still used as a reference about the artist.

The beauty of nature and the beauty of art

Writers on Pontormo often link the eccentricities of his character with his unusual mature style. Yet Pontormo's distortions of anatomy, perspective, and spatial arrangement were also features of mannerism, a general stylistic tendency of the period. Indeed, Pontormo was one of the earliest artists to use the mannerist style. This evolved from, yet in some ways also rejected, the classical principles of harmony and balance that had been established by High Renaissance artists.

The composition of *Joseph with Jacob in Egypt* (1515–19) is strange. Pontormo uses an old-fashioned narrative device by including two separate scenes within a single image. Joseph is portrayed in the lower left of the picture, presenting members of his family to the pharaoh, while in the upper right-hand corner of the picture Joseph's father, Jacob, is depicted blessing his sons on his deathbed. The architectural setting creates a sense of depth, but it is hard to relate this to the figures that it contains. This element of confusion is increased by the fact that the statues appear to be on about the same scale—and almost as alive—as the real people that surround them.

Although mannerism is characterized by an emphasis on details of posture and gesture in order to intensify a concept, this can result in what appears to be meaningless theatricality. The shapes of the elongated and elegantly posed figures, for example, appear to have been painted to fit within a compositional pattern, rather than to express normal, or even extreme, human emotions. In other words, the artist's concern with creating beauty in the

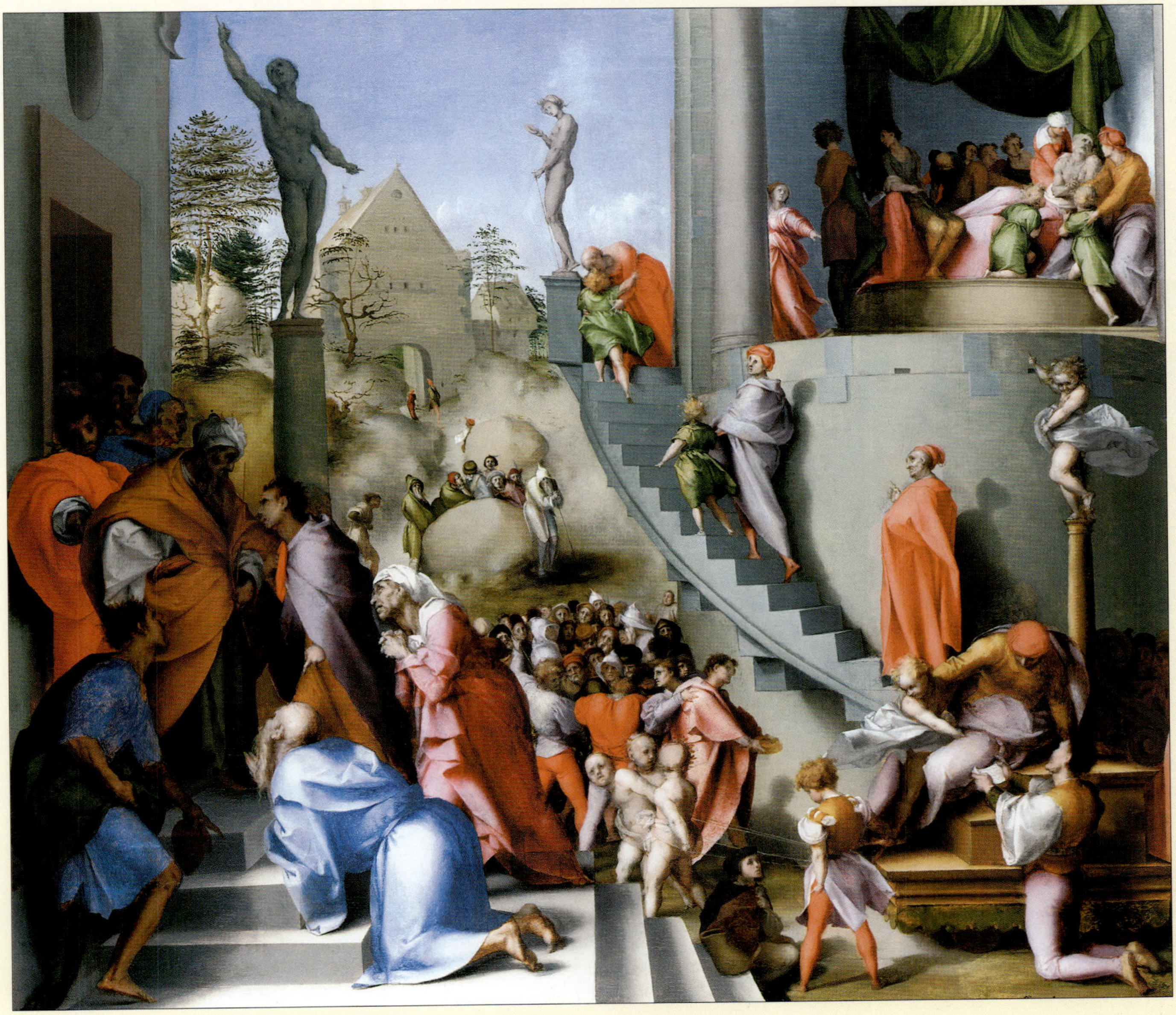

overall design prevails over his desire to produce a more accurate representation of natural forms. This is true of both his structuring of the figure groups and his use of color, which is bright and hardly modified by the effects of light and shade.

Yet Pontormo did not entirely turn his back on the truths of natural perspective. His portraits, as well as his numerous surviving drawings, combine his exquisite compositional refinement with his ability to observe and reproduce reality accurately.

Joseph with Jacob in Egypt *1515–19. Oil on panel. 37¾ x 43 in (96 x 109 cm). National Gallery, London.*

By his mid-20s Pontormo was regarded as one of the most promising artists of his generation in Florence. Although Vasari stressed his diligence and superb draftsmanship, he also drew attention to Pontormo's perceived failings. In particular he criticized the influence on Pontormo's style of the German artist Albrecht Dürer, whose engravings had become well known in Florence.

Vasari also linked the increasing strangeness of Pontormo's style with certain neurotic and melancholic character traits in the artist, especially his reclusiveness and obsessional, solitary, and prolonged way of working. Between 1554 and 1556 Pontormo kept a daily record of his life; from this diary we gain the impression of an old man living very humbly, in hermitlike seclusion, striving all the while to produce beauty beyond the limits of natural appearances.

POUSSIN Nicolas

NICOLAS POUSSIN WAS A 17TH-CENTURY PAINTER whose work contains some of the greatest examples of formal harmony and control. He had an impressive ability to convey emotion and expression within the perfect lines and patterns of his compositions. He was inspired by the classical past of ancient Greece and Rome, turning later to a more meditative approach toward the natural world.

Life and work

After some early training from Quentin Varin, a visiting painter to his native Normandy, Poussin went to Paris. He spent 11 years there, during which he was commissioned to do paintings for the Luxembourg Palace, and to illustrate *Metamorphoses* by the 1st-century Roman poet Ovid.

In 1624 Poussin traveled to Rome; the following year Cardinal Barberini, the pope's nephew, began to support him. The cardinal's secretary, Cassiano dal Pozzo, was an extremely influential man, who advised his master on all aspects of the arts. Through him, Poussin was able to meet other artists, such as Giovanni Bellini and Titian. He also learned more about the art of antiquity from the cardinal's large library, and from Cassiano himself.

Poussin married Anne-Marie Dughet in 1629; her brother, Gaspard, was a landscape painter. Together with Gaspard and the artist Claude Lorraine, Poussin explored and sketched the countryside around Rome. Many of the paintings done by Poussin at this time show an interest in nature, landscape, and light, as well as a continuing passion for the art and literature of the classical past. Inspired by Titian, he used warm, harmonious colors.

His success in working for the cardinal led to commissions for altarpieces and church decoration. Although these are perhaps not his finest works, and he decided to paint only for private commissions afterward, this work on such a large and public scale taught him about painting individual figures while also expressing movement and emotion. The drama of the human forms in paintings such as *Massacre of the Innocents* (1628) contrasts with the calm backgrounds of landscape or classical architecture.

After 1630 Poussin returned to private commissions, working on mythological and religious paintings. His interest in harmonizing human forms with almost scientific patterns of color, light, movement, and setting continued. He tried to imbue his work with the purity and simplicity of the art of the classical past so as to provoke direct, true emotions in the viewer.

From 1635–36 Poussin worked on a series of Bacchanals—scenes of revelry from the ancient world—for Cardinal Richelieu of the French court. Poussin's vigorous, perfectly balanced classicism is obvious in these works. In 1640 he

Data file

Full name: Nicolas Poussin

Nationality: French

Style: classical

Dates: born 1594 in Les Andelys, died 1665 in Rome, Italy

Key works:

Massacre of the Innocents 1628

Echo and Narcissus 1630

Dance to the Music of Time 1634–36

The Arcadian Shepherds 1638–39

Self-portrait 1650

The Four Seasons 1660–64

Things to look for:

- classical settings and moral content
- figure drawing based on ancient Greek and Roman sculptures, and therefore perfectly proportioned
- increasingly atmospheric depictions of idealized landscape surroundings, peopled with mythological or historical figures

Comparisons: Claude Lorraine, Raphael, Peter Paul Rubens, Titian

Glossary terms: allegory, classicism, golden section

A perfect balance

Poussin's interest in the classical past and in figure painting is combined in this painting with his reflections on life and death. The scene is set in an atmospheric landscape, known as Arcadia, where some shepherds have found a tomb. Arcadia is actually a rather barren, mountainous region of Greece, but through references made to it by the Roman poet Virgil, Arcadia became idealized as a blissful pastoral paradise. The crouching figure is tracing the letters chiseled into the stone, "Et In Arcadia Ego," usually translated as "even in Arcadia, I am there." The message on the stone has been left by Death, and the shepherds are coming to realize that this means that even in happiness there is death, that life is not everlasting. The female figure already understands this truth, and she looks on sympathetically.

Some critics also think that the action of the crouching shepherd is a reference to the origins of painting, which were said to be in the tracing of a shadow on a wall. Perhaps the artist wanted to convey that painting is one of the only ways to record this state of perfect happiness. It is possible that the red, yellow, and blue robes of the group on the right might represent the primary colors of painting and be a sign of hope. They do stand out against the shadowy surroundings. Certainly this is a complex work in which Poussin was trying to deal with very difficult philosophical and moral questions.

From left to right, the figures grow in understanding. The two stooping shepherds pointing to the letters help us to focus on the central message of this work, while their knees and elbows balance each other. They are also echoed in the shadows. The woman, who could be an allegorical figure (representing an abstract idea), looks like a

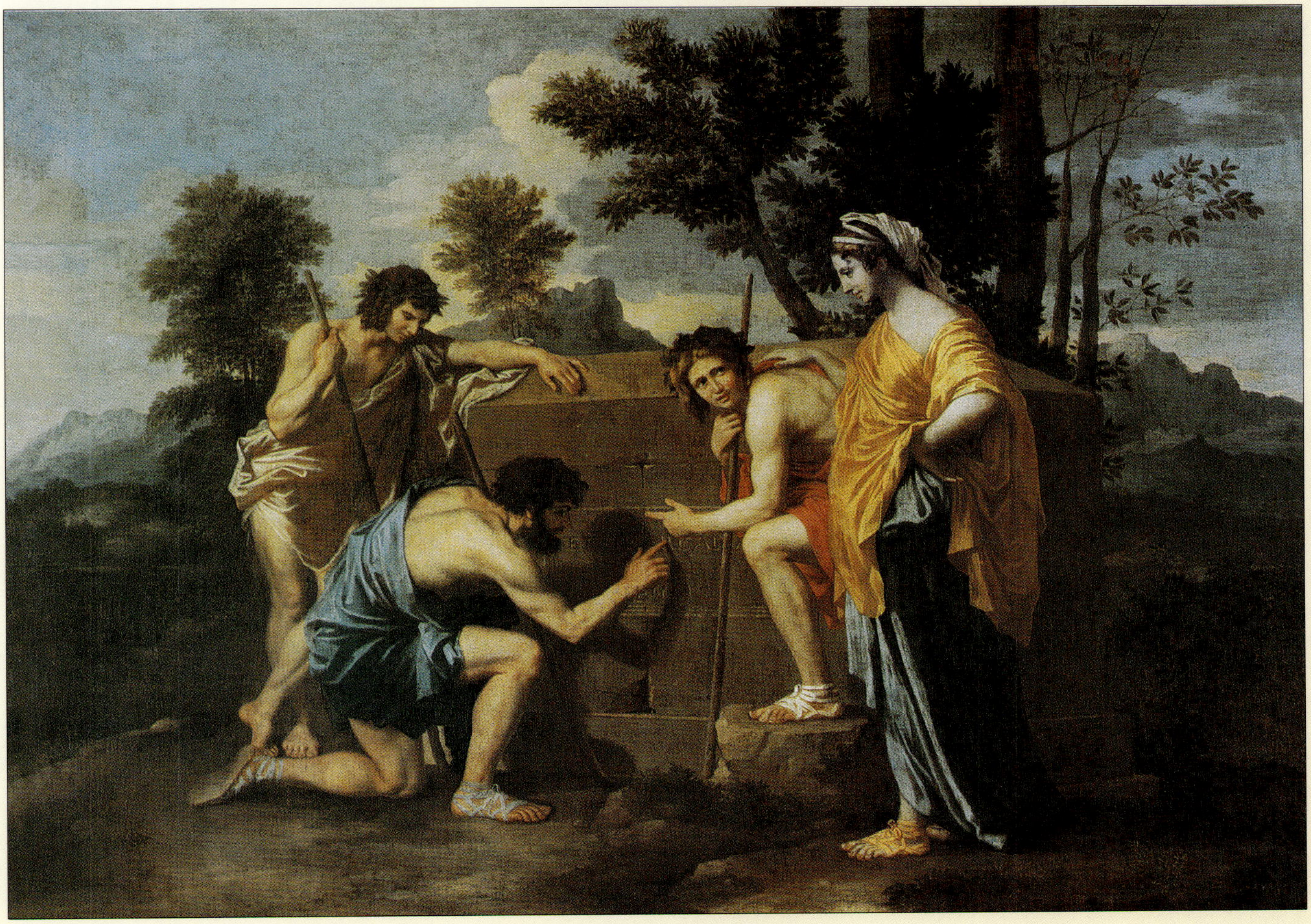

figure from the classical past. Her face is in profile, recalling a Roman bust or statue, and her pose is as motionless as a marble carving.

The Arcadian Shepherds *1638–39. Oil on canvas. 33½ x 47½ in (85 x 121 cm). Musée du Louvre, Paris.*

The golden section *Poussin often built up his compositions on geometric principles such as the "golden section." The golden section is the division of a line so that the shorter part is to the longer as the longer is to the whole.*

A rectangle whose sides are in the golden section can be divided into a square and a rectangle. Here line C–D splits the rectangle of the painting into a square to the left and a rectangle to the right. Line A–B creates, in the lower left, another rectangle of the same proportions as the original rectangle (the painting). This new, smaller rectangle could be further split in the same way. The golden section can be used to position key elements. Here the trees and female figure lie on division C–D, while the line A–B runs along the top of the tomb.

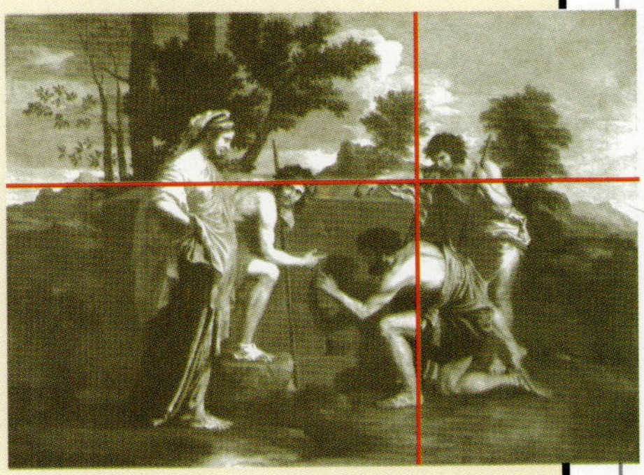

was persuaded to go and work for King Louis XIII in France. He did drawings for a decorative scheme for the Louvre, but he did not enjoy the work and in 1642 he returned to Rome.

Poussin believed that the subject and mood of a painting should have an appropriate visual language; in the mid-1640s he began to develop this idea. He aimed to show that everything could be worked out, measured, and constructed by certain rules and principles derived from the classical past. Works of this period such as *The Seven Sacraments* series (1644–48) show a geometrical, ordered, and simplified world.

In later life, Poussin returned to landscapes, moving towards a more poetic, warmer atmosphere. Nature and humankind's place within the universe interested him, and paintings such as *The Four Seasons* (1660–64), shows the natural environment as an almost mystical emotional force.

RAPHAEL

NO OTHER ARTIST represents the transition from the early to the High Renaissance style quite as well as Raphael. Nor did any other artist contribute as much to the style that would be promoted by academies of art from the 16th to the 19th centuries.

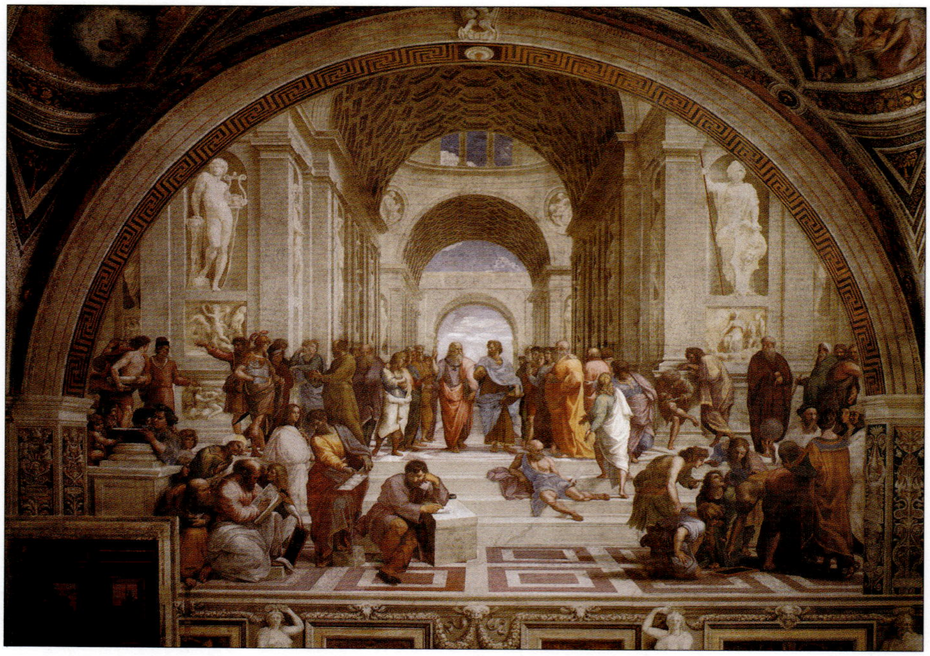

School of Athens *c1510–12. Wall fresco. Stanza della Segnatura, Vatican Palace, Rome.*

Life and work

Raphael was fortunate in being able to pass the early years of his life in the cultured atmosphere of the court at Urbino, an Italian city that was an important center of intellectual and artistic thought. The city's duke, Federico da Montefeltro, had used the wealth he had accumulated as a successful soldier to build one of the most beautiful palaces in Italy, as well as to attract scholars and artists. In fact, Raphael's father, who died when his son was 11, had been a minor but respected painter in Urbino, and Piero della Francesca, famed for his orderly and harmonic compositions, had been employed by the duke in the 1460s.

It was normal at this time for young artists to improve by imitating the style of their master, who would educate them in all aspects of artistic practice, and Raphael's earliest work is so close to the style of Pietro Perugino that it has sometimes been thought that he trained with him. This is not necessarily the case, however; throughout his life Raphael showed a remarkable ability to adopt the characteristics of other artists' work.

In 1504 Raphael traveled to Florence, carrying a letter of recommendation from the mother of the heir to Urbino's dukedom. Raphael's timing was fortunate, since in Florence Leonardo da Vinci and Michelangelo Buonarroti were producing works that resolved many artistic problems that had occupied their predecessors. Having absorbed their solutions, Raphael established himself as a leading exponent of the monumental, figurative, High Renaissance style. In 1508 Raphael was summoned to Rome by Pope Julius II.

School of Athens (c1510–12) is one of the frescos that Raphael created to decorate a series of apartments in the Vatican, the pope's headquarters in Rome. The fresco celebrates the seriousness of classical philosophy. Although few of the individuals depicted can be identified, they represent a philosophical debate being conducted around the central figures of Plato (who points upward, toward the realm of pure ideas) and Aristotle (who gestures downward, toward the world of earthly experience).

Raphael was respected within the intellectual circles of Rome, and his work was greatly sought after by powerful patrons of the arts. As a result, he was obliged to delegate much of his work to a growing band of assistants. As well as being commissioned to produce altarpieces and portraits, he was also appointed architect in charge of the basilica of Saint Peter and chief surveyor of the antiquities of Rome. Although it has been suggested that his premature death was brought on by overwork, it is more likely that he died after having caught a feverish chill.

Data file

Full name: Raffaello Sanzio (known as Raphael)

Nationality: Italian

Style: High Renaissance

Dates: born 1483 in Urbino, died 1520 in Rome

Key works:

Crucifixion with Saints Mary Virgin, Mary Magdalene, John, and Jerome c1503

Madonna of the Meadow c1505

School of Athens c1510–12

Galatea 1512

Portrait of Baldassare Castiglione c1514–15

The Transfiguration 1518–20

Things to look for:

- Christian subjects, but also themes from classical mythology
- powerful, figurative style, but often within an atmosphere of calm
- compositions in which all elements are harmonized
- keen attention to classical architectural detail

Comparisons: Piero della Francesca, Pietro Perugino, Leonardo da Vinci, Michelangelo Buonarroti, Nicolas Poussin, Jean Auguste Dominique Ingres

Glossary terms: Academy, figurative, fresco, perspective, Renaissance

Geometry and the harmony of creation

At the time when Raphael was working, geometry was associated with both the harmony of God's creation, the universe, and with the learning and philosophy of the classical world. All these elements come together in Raphael's portrayal of the *School of Athens* (c1510–12), pictured left. Although the composition of the *School of Athens* is quite complex, Raphael has clarified what might otherwise have appeared to be a confused mass of bodies by incorporating into his painting simple, triangular forms.

The two foreground groups in the *School of Athens*, for example, revolve around two small blackboards on which geometrical diagrams have been drawn. This may be intended to evoke Pythagoras (the 6th-century Greek philosopher and mathematician), and Euclid (the 4th-century Greek mathematician).

If they are looked at separately, some of the figures in the *School of Athens* seem to be engaged in agitated discussion or to be having troubling thoughts, yet the overall impression is again one of calm and balanced order. This is partly due to the perspective of the architectural setting in which the figures are portrayed. Along with others, Raphael was in the process of rediscovering the beauty and geometrical logic of the classical buildings that had survived in Rome. He also took inspiration from the architecture of his friend Donato Bramante, who also came from Urbino.

Many scholars believe that Raphael's own face looks out from the lower right-hand corner of the painting, almost hidden by the two figures holding spheres.

Madonna of the Meadow (c1505) is one of a series of similar subjects in which the young Raphael tried to follow Leonardo da Vinci's principles in creating compositions of this kind. Although the geometry within this composition is not immediately apparent, the triangle reminds us of the Holy Trinity (God the Father, God the Son, and God the Holy Spirit), as well as of the cross, subtly reminding us that the adult Christ would suffer death by crucifixion.

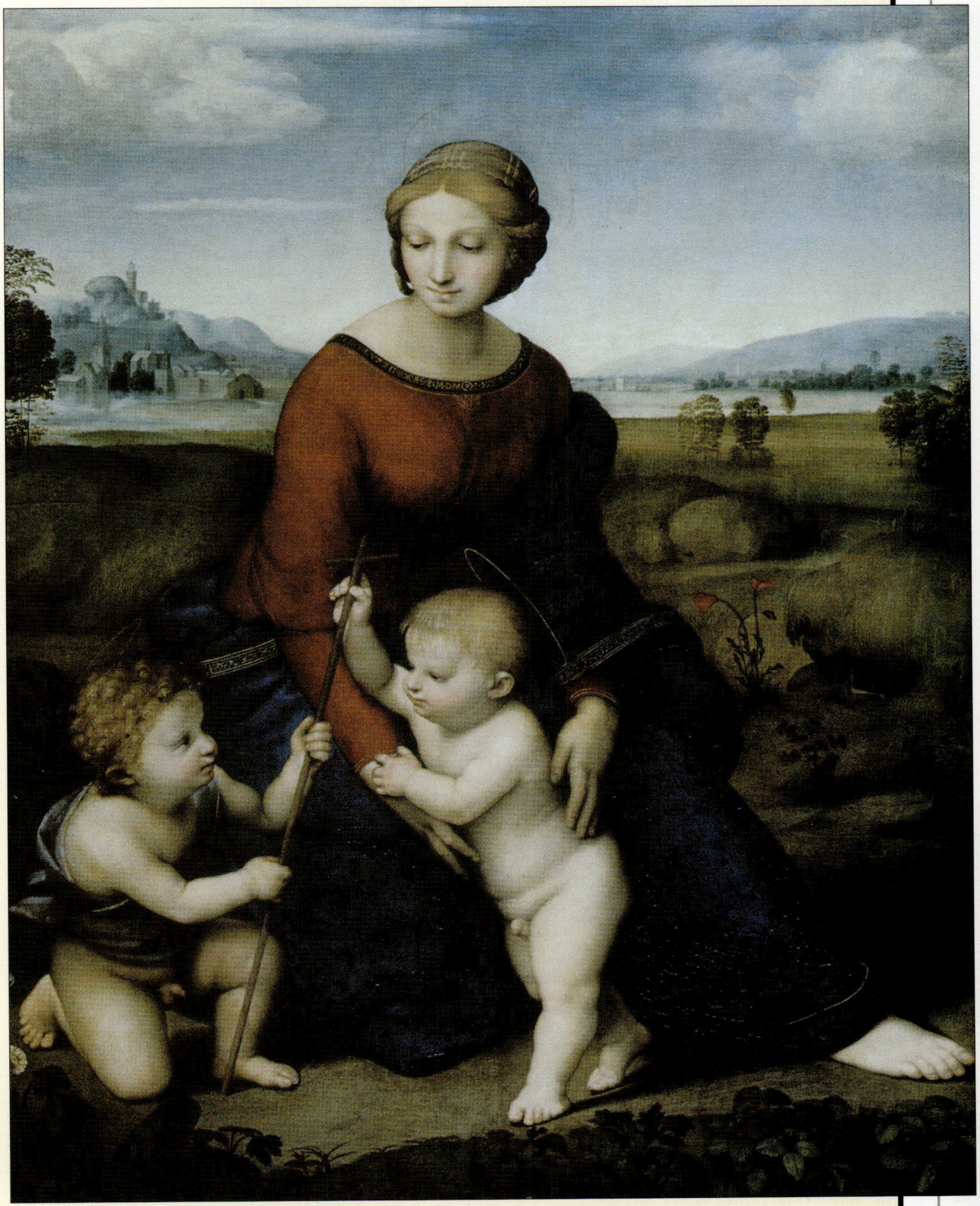

Madonna of the Meadow *c1505. Oil on panel. 44 1/2 x 34 1/4 in (113 x 88 cm). Kunsthistorisches Museum, Vienna.*

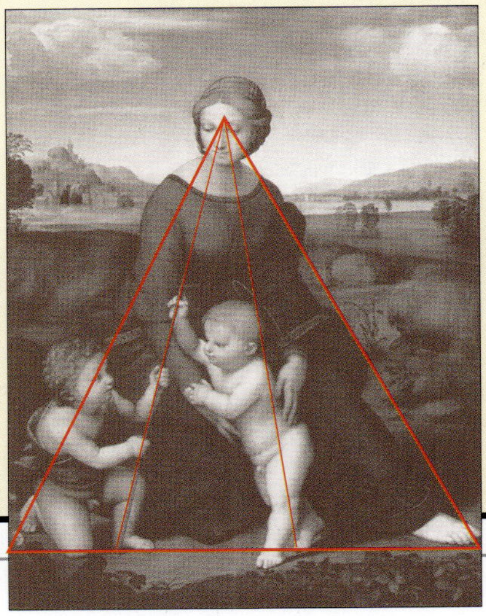

Triangular harmony *The figure of the Virgin Mary forms a large triangular or cone shape. Within this a narrower triangle links the infant Saint John the Baptist to the baby Jesus on the right. The cross held by the babies bisects this smaller triangle, leading the viewer's eye back up to the face of the Virgin Mary.*

RAUSCHENBERG Robert

THROUGHOUT HIS CAREER ROBERT RAUSCHENBERG has worked in a host of media, from painting and printmaking to performance art and photography. His work does not belong to one particular style, but occupies the ground between a form of expressionism and the more reflective pop art of the late 1960s.

Life and work

Rauschenberg served in the U.S. Navy during World War II, gaining his first serious introduction to art in 1942 when he visited an art gallery. From 1947 to 1952 Rauschenberg studied at Kansas City Art Institute and the Académie Julian in Paris, as well as other institutes in the United States. The most significant was Black Mountain College, in North Carolina, where Rauschenberg came into contact with the avant-garde musician John Cage and the dancer Merce Cunningham. Their ideas for an art of performance—not limited to the confines of their respective disciplines—had a significant effect on Rauschenberg, and their example freed him to work across disciplines and with a variety of media.

Much of Rauschenberg's early work was created in response to abstract expressionism, the most important movement in 20th-century American art, which had begun in the late 1940s. *Automobile Tire Print* (1953), for instance, was made by running a tire through ink and then across a roll of paper. The ease of the piece's creation parodied the inner turmoil associated with the works of the abstract expressionists. It also took to an extreme the approach of such action painters as Jackson Pollock, who wanted to reveal overtly the process by which their work was made.

In *Erased de Kooning Drawing* (1953), he showed irreverence toward a great pillar of the abstract-expressionist movement, Willem de Kooning, by obtaining a drawing from the artist and then simply erasing it, leaving only a faint trace of the original drawing below the smudges. This action challenged accepted notions of creativity, the artistic process (a major preoccupation at that time), and value.

During the mid- to late-1950s Rauschenberg started to build what are now referred to as his "combines." These were works in which discarded objects he had gathered (including printed images and words from newspapers, stuffed animals, bottles, and, most famously, a bed cover and pillow) were incorporated into complex and freely arranged collages or assemblages. One such work, *Monogram* (1959), consisted of a stuffed goat with a rubber tire around its middle. These works were somewhere between paintings and sculptures, hence the term "combines." Through the incorporation of "found objects" and discarded material into works that would occupy gallery space, he was attempting to plug the gap, as he perceived it, between art and life.

A playful approach to art

During the 1960s Rauschenberg developed ways in which to layer two-dimensional images over the top of one another, initially by transferring newspaper pictures onto paper by dissolving the ink with spirit. He then adopted the more refined method of silk-screen printing, in which photographic images can be printed onto canvas (or, indeed, virtually any other material). Many of his silk-screen prints have the sense of having been randomly arranged; they were further embellished with oil paint that was applied with the sketchy dynamism of the abstract expressionists. This loose, abstract-expressionistic style, combined with imagery from everyday life that was more often associated with pop art (such as street signs, buildings, and forms of transport), seemed to play one movement off against the other.

The use of ordinary objects, which is seen throughout Rauschenberg's "combines," was influenced by the "anti-art" dada movement, and in particular by Marcel Duchamp's invention of "readymades." These were everyday objects, taken out of their context, retitled, and exhibited as art; the artist thereby created, as Duchamp described it, "a new thought for [an] object."

Duchamp famously used a great painting from the annals of art history—Leonardo da Vinci's *Mona Lisa* (1503–06)—to create an altered readymade (what he called a "readymade aided"), by adding a

Data file

Full name: Robert Rauschenberg

Nationality: American

Style: expressionism/pop art

Dates: born 1925 in Port Arthur, TX

Key works:
- *Automobile Tire Print* 1953
- *Erased de Kooning Drawing* 1953
- *Bed* 1955
- *Dante's Inferno* 1958–60
- *Monogram* 1959
- *Black Market* 1961
- *Persimmon* 1964
- *The Quarter-mile or Two-furlong Piece* 1981–present

Things to look for:
- layering of images, through either collage or printing
- references to the history of art mixed with references to modern popular culture

Comparisons: Jasper Johns, Jim Dine, Claes Oldenburg, Andy Warhol, Kurt Schwitters, Marcel Duchamp

Glossary terms: abstract expressionism, action painting, assemblage, collage, dadaism, found objects, Old Masters, performance art, pop art, readymade, silk-screen printing moustache and a new "caption." Rauschenberg adopted a similarly provocative approach in some of his silk-screen works.

Persimmon (1964) typifies his playful approach to art, using objects and images from everyday life and an iconographic image from history. A painting by Peter Paul Rubens, *Venus at the Mirror* (c1615), was the inspiration for and basis of the piece. In creating it, Rauschenberg first printed a copy of the Rubens painting and then overlaid it with contemporary imagery. He then gave it the title *Persimmon,* the name of the sweet orange-red fruit of a type of tropical tree. The work seems to question the hallowed art of the Old Masters, the esthetics of modern consumerism, and the nature of art itself.

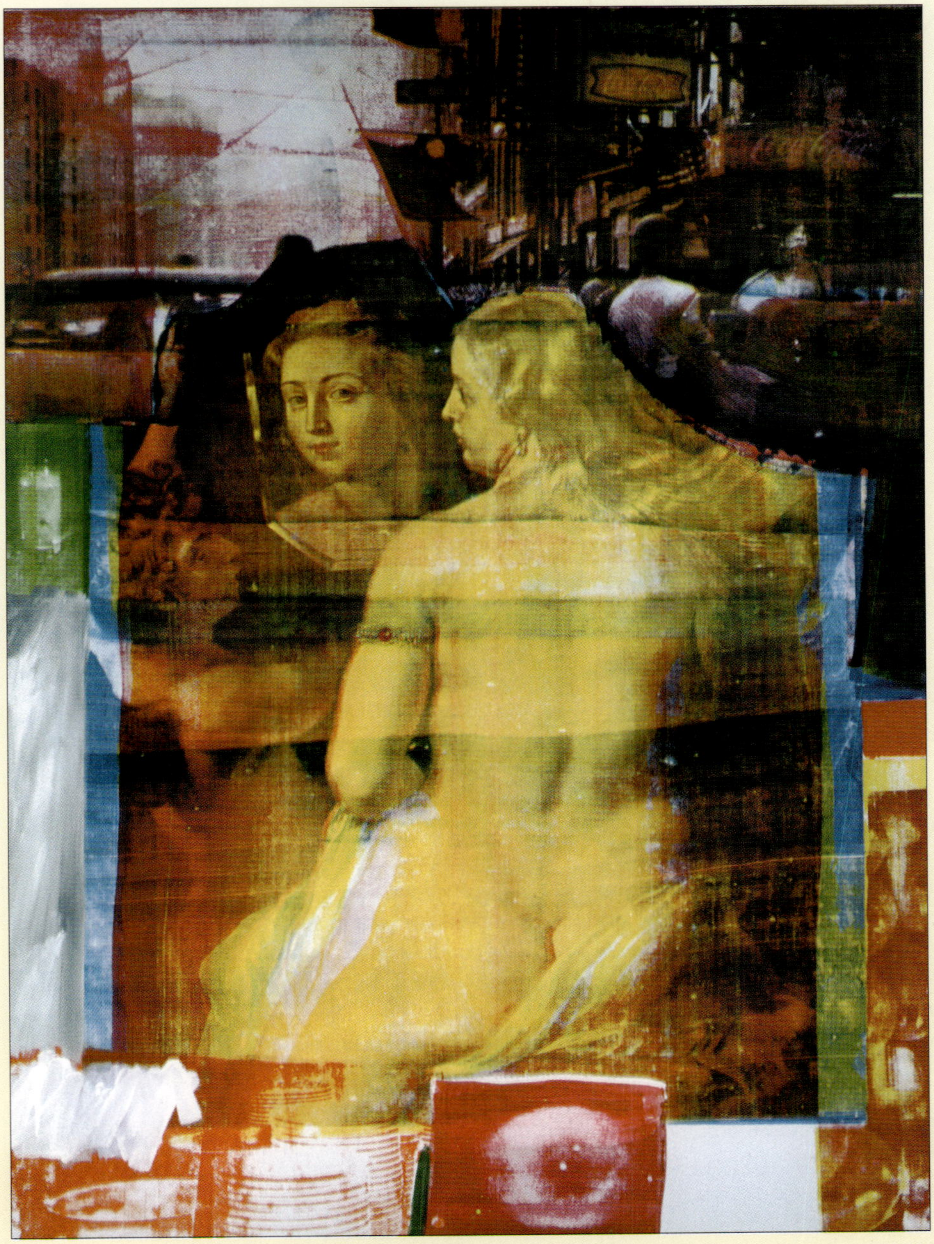

Persimmon *1964. Oil and silk-screen print and ink on canvas. 66 x 50 in (168 x 127 cm). Private collection.*

Rauschenberg started to experiment with silk-screen printing during the 1960s. Throughout his career he has also intermittently worked on stage design and choreography, sometimes with Cunningham, but also for his own performance projects, such as *Pelican* (1963). His inclination toward performance has been evident in certain works that have involved an interaction between the viewer and the piece. One such piece was *Black Market* (1961), which comprised a "combine" painting with a case attached to it, into which a small selection of objects was placed. Viewers were encouraged to exchange these objects for objects of their own; they were also asked to make sketches of the objects on clipboards attached to the painting. These simple invitations put some of the responsibility for making art into the public's hands.

Rauschenberg has also been interested in combining art with new technological developments in fields such as engineering. In recent years his efforts have been primarily focused on the ever-growing *The Quarter-mile or Two-furlong Piece* (1981–present). This consists of a huge sequence of works, printed and assembled, which together represent a visual assessment of the United States at the end of the 20th century. Rauschenberg describes the work as the largest painting in the world, and it may eventually exceed even the quarter-mile of its title.

REDON Odilon

Odilon Redon was a symbolist artist whose favorite themes were drawn from his own imagination, mythology, folklore, and the operas of Wagner. His most famous works are black-and-white drawings and lithographs known as the *"Noirs,"* but after 1900 he also began to work in richly colored oils and pastels.

Life and work

Odilon Redon was born on his family's estate, Peyrelebade, near Bordeaux, in the Médoc region of France. The extraordinary natural beauty and rich folklore of this area had a formative influence on the young artist. Although he eventually settled in Paris in order to pursue his artistic education, he returned to Peyrelebade every summer until his family sold the property in 1897.

Redon received his earliest artistic training in Bordeaux from Stanislas Gorin, a local painter. He was befriended by the botanist Armand Clavel at this time, who introduced him to both the wonders of the natural world and contemporary literature, in particular the poetry of the symbolists. These interests would influence Redon's choice of subject matter throughout his life.

In 1864 he enrolled at the studio of Jean-Léon Gérôme in Paris but soon returned to Bordeaux, where he met another local artist, Rodolphe Bresdin, who convinced Redon that art was his calling. An extraordinary draftsman, Bresdin not only opened Redon's eyes to the world of the imagination but also taught him the necessary technical skills needed for producing etchings and engravings.

After serving in the French Army during the Franco–Prussian War (1870–71), Redon moved to Paris in order to have access to the city's art and literature. Here he began to produce large charcoal drawings of fantastic creatures and imaginary landscapes. It was in Paris, too, that he befriended Henri Fantin-Latour, who encouraged Redon to produce his drawings as lithographs.

In 1879 Redon published his first album of lithographs, *Dans le Rêve (In the Dream)*. This was the first of Redon's famous series of 12 albums known as the *"Noirs"* (black ones), which he created between 1879 and 1899. The astonishing lithographs portray a world of marsh flowers with human faces, eyeballs that turn into hot-air balloons, giant smiling spiders, and mythological monsters. The lithographs often illustrate symbolist poems. Redon's *La Tentation de Saint-Antoine* ("The Temptation of Saint Anthony") of 1888 illustrates Gustave Flaubert's 1874 poem of the same name.

Redon showed his charcoal drawings at exhibitions held at the offices of popular newspapers. He also helped to found the Salon des Indépendants in 1884, participated in the last impressionist exhibition in 1886, and showed works with the independent group Les Vingt ("The Twenty") in Brussels, Belgium. At the turn of the century, the dealer Paul Durand-Ruel included Redon's work in shows of younger artists. During this time Redon also exhibited his work at

Data file

Full name: Odilon Bertrand Jean Redon

Nationality: French

Style: symbolism

Dates: born 1840 in Bordeaux, died 1916 in Paris

Key works:

Dans le Rêve 1879

La Tentation de Saint-Antoine 1888

Closed Eyes 1890

Red Screen 1903

Things to look for:

- mythological narratives
- graphic media

Comparisons: Rodolphe Bresdin, Albrecht Dürer, Henri Fantin-Latour, Gustave Moreau, Pierre-Cécile Puvis de Chavannes

Glossary terms: charcoal, engraving, etching, Gothic, lithograph, Salon des Indépendants, symbolism, (Les) Vingt

From nightmarish dreams to soothing harmonies

Stylistically, Odilon Redon had a dramatically divided career. Between the 1870s and early 1890s he worked only in black and white. Then, around 1900, he imbued his palette with rich pastel colors and never worked in black and white again. Similarly, the type of media in which he worked can be divided into two very distinct phases. During the first period he almost exclusively produced work on paper: charcoal drawings, etchings, and lithographs. During the second period he created much more decorative work: murals and screens, as well as small-scale pastels and paintings.

Closed Eyes (1890) represents an interesting transition between these two phases. In its monochromatic tones of beige and brown, the central oval (which contains the image of a woman with closed eyes) seems to relate to Redon's early graphic work. The outer field of saturated pastel colors and flowers that surrounds the oval like a halo, on the other hand, suggests the vibrant color decorations of his late work.

The painting's subject matter, the world of dreams and imagination, also indicates a transition between the two phases of Redon's work. Whereas the dreams of the *"Noirs,"* with their monsters and mournful creatures, verge upon the nightmarish, the late works portray the imagination as a place of serenity and soothing color harmonies. Thus when this beautiful young woman closes her eyes, she enters a world of exquisite color and floral perfumes.

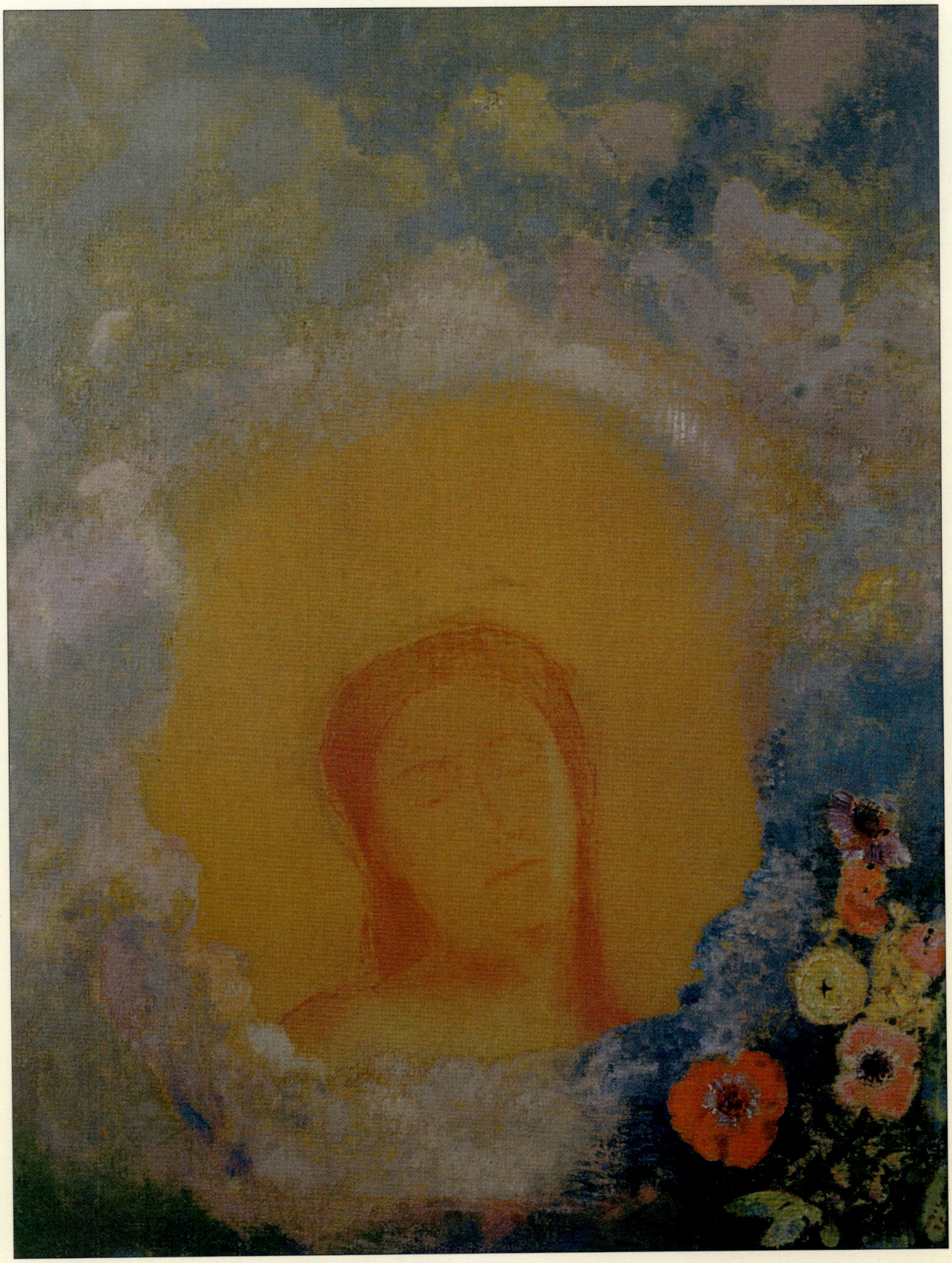

Closed Eyes *1890. Oil on canvas. 25 x 19¼ in (63.5 x 49 cm). Wildenstein & Co., New York, NY.*

the Salon d'Automne and the Armory Show of 1913 in New York.

Many writers and critics admired Redon's work. Joris Karl Huysman, for example, included a description of Redon's *"Noirs"* in his 1884 novel *A Rebours* ("Against the Grain"). Redon's closest friendship was with the symbolist writer, Stéphane Mallarmé. Redon worked on an illustrated version of Mallarmé's 1897 poem *Un Coup de Dés* ("A Throw of the Dice") in 1898 but never completed it. A generation later, the playwrights André Gide and Jean Cocteau also supported Redon.

During the 1890s Redon began to create works in color alongside his startling black-and-white drawings and prints. By 1900 he was working in color alone, using oil paints and pastels. Although he remained fascinated by flowers, Redon also began to portray the human figure in his paintings. He was commissioned to complete decorations, both on movable screens and on the walls of buildings, such as those for the Font-froide Abbey library near Narbonne, and he received numerous commissions from private patrons as well.

REGO Paula

PAULA REGO IS PORTUGUESE BY BIRTH. Drawing strongly on her memories, emotions, or half-forgotten experiences, she paints and draws finely crafted images of people and animals. At first sight they might appear banal, but they often have disturbing undertones. Her distinctive style and unusual subjects fascinate the public and have greatly impressed art critics.

Life and work

Paula Rego was born in Lisbon, the capital of Portugal, the first and only child in her family. Throughout Rego's life she has always had strong connections with England, and has spent many years living and working in London. However, her Portuguese background has always been a very important influence on the character of her work.

When Rego was very young, her parents went to England, leaving Paula behind in Portugal with some relatives. As a child she was educated at home by a private tutor who mistreated her. She maintains that these early, troubling experiences in her life affected her deeply. When we look at the figures in her work, especially the many women and girls that she paints, there is often a powerful sense that, beneath their well-mannered exterior, these women are strong and rebellious, or sometimes bitter and cruel. Rego is very interested in struggle, and even in violent relationships, but what makes her work remarkable is that these tensions are not always immediately obvious. Instead, they are often hinted at by the subtlest of gestures or postures displayed by her figures.

At the age of 17 Rego went to the Slade School of Art in London. She was an enthusiastic moviegoer, sometimes attending the movie theater three times a day. Some of her work draws on images from movies she has found particularly memorable. Recently she has even used animation by American artist and film producer Walt Disney as inspiration for her work.

By the mid-1960s Rego's standing as an artist had grown. She was enjoying her first public success, and was chosen to represent Portugal in important international exhibitions. At this time she was working largely with collage, cutting up painted paper and using the fragments to discover new and unexpected combinations. In this way she echoed some of the techniques of the surrealist artists.

Although Rego's work has been very popular and widely accepted for some time, she has always been an artist who swims against the tide. For example, in the 1970s Rego was unusual in that she was still painting figurative pictures, while many other artists at the time believed that painting was dead, and were occupying themselves with conceptual art.

In 1981 Rego abandoned collage to concentrate fully on painting and drawing. Her best-known work has been made since then, beginning with a disconcerting group of images called the *Red Monkey* series (1981), in which a remarkably humanlike monkey carries out a range of actions, some banal, others violent and shocking. In their combination of both comic and grotesque elements, there is a similarity between these pictures and those of the 18th-century Spanish artist Francisco Goya.

In recent years Rego has concentrated on the human figure, often using her favorite model, a Portuguese woman named Lila. She has also explored, in particular, the medium of pastel. In 1994 she produced a remarkable series of pastels of so-called "dog women," in which the model howls, snarls, and rolls on the floor like a dog. Although these images seem highly original, we can also see similarities with the pastel nudes of impressionist/realist Edgar Degas, and with the oil paintings of contemporary British artist Lucian Freud.

Rego's paintings are about storytelling. For her subject matter she often draws directly on fairytales, and on traditional Portuguese folk stories, effectively creating a sense of drama in apparently simple scenes. Looking at them, we often feel that something dramatic is about to happen, has already happened, or is happening just outside the frame of the canvas. Rego has often said that she cannot explain the way her pictures evolve. But it is significant that Portugal has a strong tradition of storytelling. In many ways, Rego's paintings are also like stories that are not planned or fixed, but evolve with the telling. She herself has said that "by not trying to do art, I get better at what I do."

Data file

Full name: Paula Rego

Nationality: Portuguese

Style: postwar figurative painting

Dates: born 1935 in Lisbon

Key works:

Stray Dogs (The Dogs of Barcelona) 1965
Red Monkey series 1981
The Policeman's Daughter 1987
The Family 1988
The Dance 1988
Dog Women series 1994

Things to look for:

- stocky figures
- dramatic lighting
- animal-like humans and humanlike animals
- undercurrents of violence

Comparisons: Edgar Degas, Max Ernst, Lucian Freud, Francisco Goya

Glossary terms: collage, conceptual art, figurative, surrealism

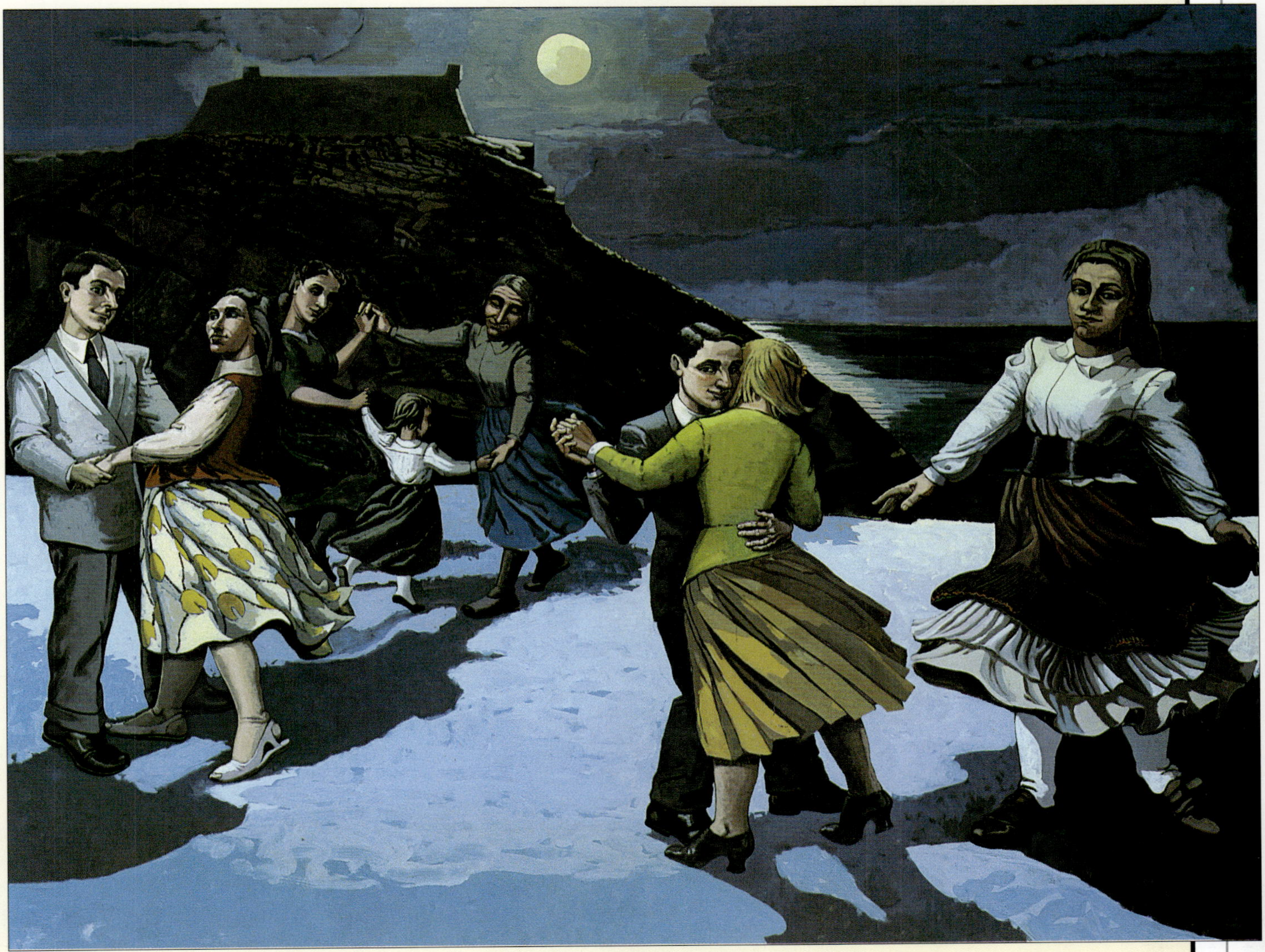

Human relationships

The Dance (1988) is an important painting for Rego in many ways. It is very large and the figures in the foreground are almost life-size. Typically, it is a simple, and yet at the same time rather mysterious image. However, it also has a more personal significance. Like many of Rego's works, the painting deals with human relationships and family ties. This was the painting Rego was working on when her husband died after a long illness. The idea for the work had come from him; he had suggested that she "paint people dancing."

Set on the Portuguese coast, *The Dance* has a nostalgic atmosphere, less menacing than many of her other works, and seems to convey a sense of farewell. We know that soon the luminous moon in the night sky will wane or disappear behind the clouds, and that the light illuminating the dance will be gone. We can notice, too, something very typical of Rego's work: the timelessness of the scene. Nothing we see indicates that this is 1988. Rego's paintings seem always to be set sometime within living memory, but we can never pin them down to a particular time or era (there are never televisions or cars in her work, for example). This helps to explain why her paintings seem so often to be evocations of memories from somewhere in the past. The eight figures dancing on the beach are stocky and chunky, yet still graceful. This is another distinctive characteristic of Rego's work. The figures are grouped so that they seem to represent what we might call "the dance of life," and the three female figures represent the links between three generations. (Rego's first grandchild had recently been born.) There are also more traditional couples, dancing romantically close or in friendship, but the single woman seems to remind us that we are sometimes alone in life. In this sense the painting is a good example of the way Rego is often able to convey the touching poignancy of people's relationships with one another through her use of strong, simple subjects.

The Dance *1988. Acrylic on paper laid on canvas. 84 x 108 in (213 x 274 cm). Tate Gallery, London.*

REMBRANDT

REMBRANDT'S PAINTINGS ARE CHARACTERIZED by luxuriant brushwork and dramatic contrasts of light and shade. His painted and etched portraits, genre scenes, and landscapes provide a vivid record of life in 17th-century Amsterdam. Despite his fame, and the volume of work he produced, he died in poverty.

Life and work

Rembrandt was born in Leiden, where his father was a miller. Around 1624 or 1625 he set up as a painter in Leiden, and in 1631–32 he moved to Amsterdam because he was so much in demand there. His large-scale group portrait of the Amsterdam surgeons' guild, known as the *Anatomy Lesson of Dr. Nicolaes Tulp* (1632) was an instant success; for some years he was one of the most successful portrait painters in the city.

In 1634 he married Saskia Van Uylenburgh; between then and 1641 they had four children, only one of whom, Titus, survived. Rembrandt used Saskia as a model for many of his paintings and drawings. His works from this period are characterized by strong contrasts of light and shade. This technique, used to make pictures more dramatic, was known as chiaroscuro; it shows the influence on Rembrandt's work of the Italian artist Michelangelo Merisi da Caravaggio.

During the middle years of his career Rembrandt was very active, producing large, dramatic works. These included some featuring Old Testament stories such as *The Blinding of Samson* (1636). He painted numerous portraits and landscapes as well. Between 1628 and 1661 he also produced many prints using etching (engraving using acid), and drypoint (engraving using a steel needle without acid); these were so well received that they were collector's items during his own lifetime.

In 1642 Rembrandt's wife, Saskia, died, and he began to get into financial difficulties. In 1647 Hendrickje Stoffels joined his household as a maidservant, and in 1654 she and Rembrandt had a baby daughter, Cornelia. By the mid-1650s Rembrandt's house was auctioned to pay some of his debts; the artist was later declared insolvent. In 1660 his son, Titus, and companion, Hendrickje, employed him as an art dealer to avoid creditors; he did get some commissions, but they were not all well received.

Rembrandt died in 1669, leaving behind a vast volume of work: about 600 paintings, 300 etchings, and 1400 drawings. Of these works about 60 are self-portraits, providing a unique record of his appearance and state of mind throughout his career.

Data file

Full name: Rembrandt Harmensz van Rijn

Nationality: Dutch

Style: Dutch

Dates: Born 1606 in Leiden, died 1669 in Amsterdam

Key works:
- *Anatomy Lesson of Dr. Nicolaes Tulp* 1632
- *The Blinding of Samson* 1636
- *"Night Watch"* 1642
- *The Mill* 1650
- *Aristotle Contemplating the Bust of Homer* 1653
- *Self-portrait, aged 63* 1669

Things to look for:
- many different types of subject: biblical, mythological, landscapes, portraits, and still lifes
- images that convey the complexity of human emotion through facial expressions
- paint applied in thick strokes, built up with glazes
- brilliant handling of light and shade

Comparisons: Michelangelo Merisi da Caravaggio, Frans Hals, Peter Paul Rubens

Glossary terms: chiaroscuro, drypoint, engraving, etching

Chronicler of contemporary life

Rembrandt can be seen at his most inventive in *The Company of Captain Frans Banning Cocq and Lieutenant Willem Van Ruytenburgh ("Night Watch")* which he completed in 1642. At the time Rembrandt produced this painting there were 20 companies of civic guardsmen in Amsterdam. These military groups had served an important function in the 16th century, when the United Provinces of the Netherlands had been fighting the Spanish.

Many of these militias commissioned artists to paint group portraits of them. Usually each individual was given equal emphasis, but here Rembrandt has given more prominence to some and less to others. It has been said that the people who paid him the most were given most prominence in the picture, but he was probably more concerned with creating an illusion of movement and realism.

The man in black with the red sash is the company leader, Captain Frans Banning Cocq; his lieutenant, Willem Van Ruytenburgh, is beside him as they lead their men out of company headquarters. The work is popularly known as the *"Night Watch,"* because to generations of viewers it appeared that the company was setting out for a night patrol. It was only when it was cleaned in the 1940s that its brilliant colors were revealed.

Rembrandt might have painted this picture to commemorate a visit by Marie de' Medici, mother of the French king Louis XIII, to Amsterdam in 1638. Although the painting was cut down to fit a new location in Amsterdam Town Hall, it still reveals Rembrandt's mastery. Not only does he portray a complicated group of individual company members, but he also conveys a mass of activity. The scene is full of life; the viewer can almost hear the noise and bustle: the man beating a drum, the dog barking. Splashes of color draw our attention to unexpected details, such as children running among the militiamen. Strong contrasts of light and shade, movement and stillness, pose and gesture all combine to animate the entire scene.

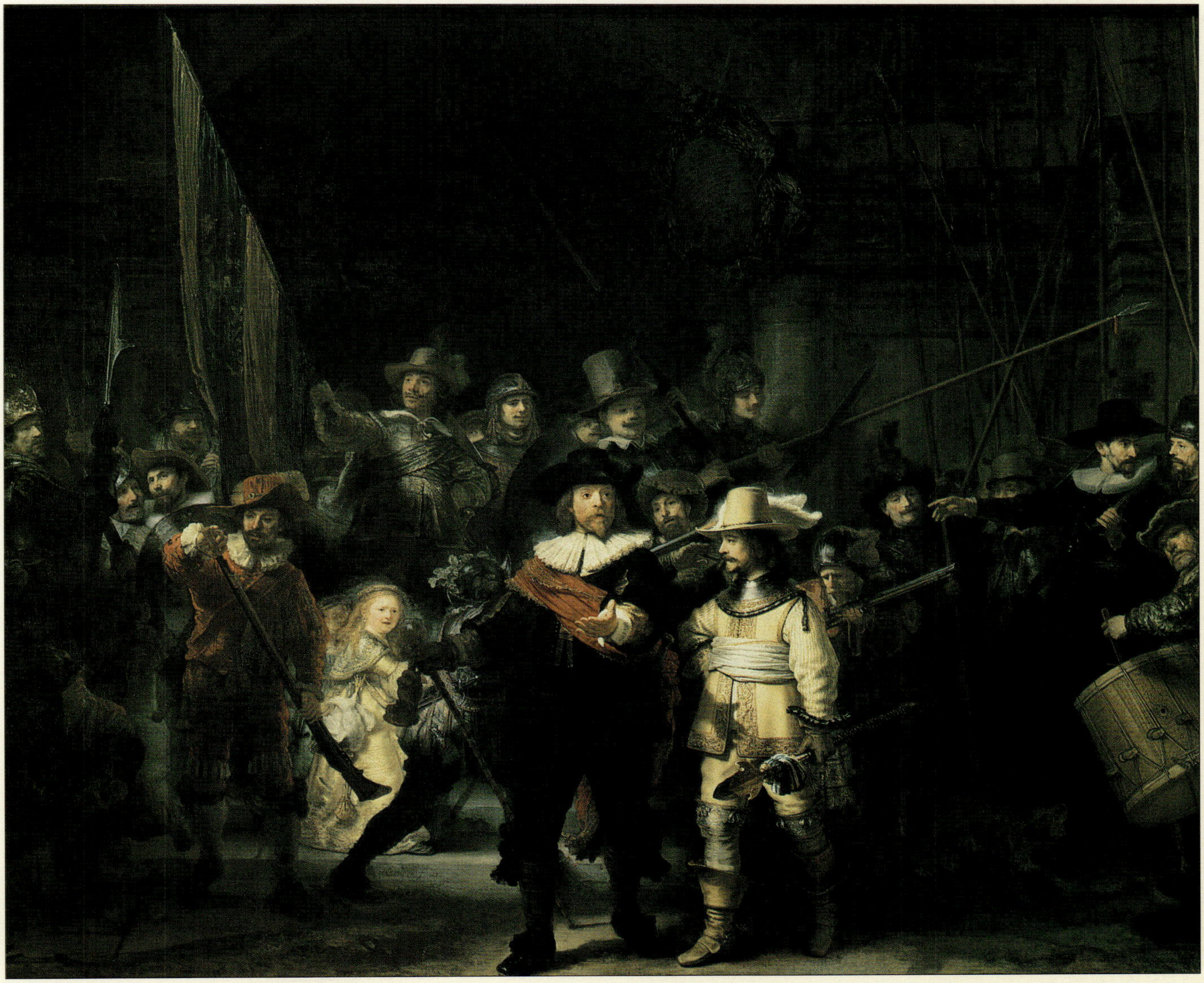

"Night Watch" *1642. Oil on canvas. 143 x 172 in (363 x 437 cm). Rijksmuseum, Amsterdam.*

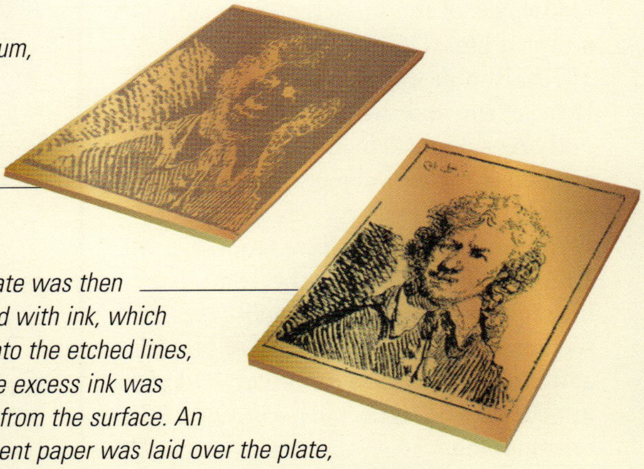

The art of etching

Rembrandt drew with a fine point directly onto a wax-coated copper plate, cutting away the wax and exposing the copper. The plate was then treated with an acid solution. The acid ate into the copper where the wax had been removed, etching the lines of Rembrandt's drawing into the plate.

The plate was then covered with ink, which sank into the etched lines, and the excess ink was wiped from the surface. An absorbent paper was laid over the plate, and the two were inserted in a press. The paper drew the ink up from the lines to create the etched image; this was a mirror image of the original drawing.

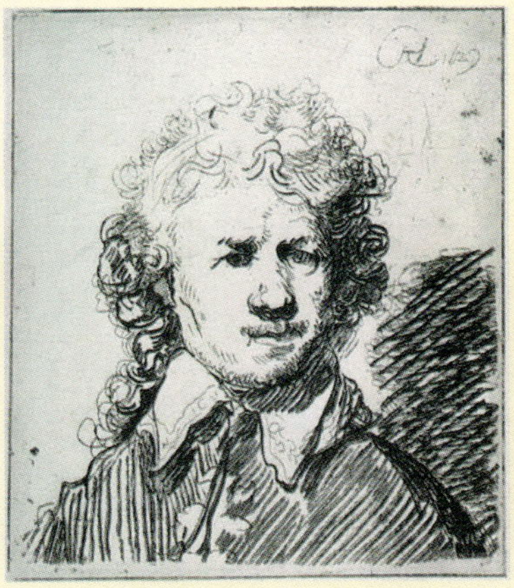

Self-portrait *c1650s. Etching. 9 x 8 in (23 x 20 cm). Private collection.*

RENOIR Pierre Auguste

RENOIR WAS A PAINTER, SCULPTOR, AND PRINTMAKER, who became a leading figure in the impressionist movement. His joyous, sunlit images of young Parisians at leisure on the banks of the River Seine, and the portraits of his own family are some of the most cherished and familiar of impressionist paintings.

Life and work

One of seven children of a French tailor, Renoir was first apprenticed to a porcelain painter. He studied on his own in Paris's Louvre museum, making copies of famous Old Masters, before entering the studio of Charles Gleyre at the Ecole des Beaux-Arts in Paris in 1862. There he met the artists with whom he would create impressionist painting: Frédéric Bazille, Claude Monet, and Alfred Sisley. They made day trips to the forest of Fontainebleau to sketch landscapes *en plein air*.

Although Renoir had several paintings accepted by the state-sponsored Salon exhibition, many of his works, like those of Monet and Sisley, were refused. These artists decided to form an independent exhibiting group, the *Société Anonyme* ("Anonymous Society"), which held eight exhibitions between 1874 and 1886. Renoir exhibited at the first three shows, but after 1877 decided to try again for success at the Salon. During the 1880s and 1890s the efforts of art dealers such as Paul Durand-Ruel and Ambroise Vollard helped to build his international reputation.

Renoir is best known as a figure painter; indeed, he was fascinated by the human body in all its forms. He often painted scenes of the day-to-day life of women and children, frequently using members of his family as models. His brother, Edmond, appears in *La Loge* (1874), for example, while his wife, Aline, his three sons, and his favorite model, the family's nanny and friend Gabrielle Renard, were his main subjects in his later years.

Renoir also painted views of Paris, landscapes of the French countryside, and still lifes. During the 1860s and 1870s, Renoir was inspired by both Parisian life and the pleasure spots of its outlying suburbs. He and Monet often painted the same subject side by side; each artist, for example, created several versions of *La Grenouillière* around 1869. His travels during the 1880s led him to paint more exotic landscapes, such as Morocco and the Bay of Naples, and during the 1890s he began working in other media, especially sculpture and printmaking.

Just as Renoir began to achieve his greatest success, his health suddenly deteriorated drastically. He died at Cagnes-sur-Mer in 1919.

Data file

Full name: Pierre Auguste Renoir

Nationality: French

Style: impressionism

Dates: born 1841 in Limoges, died 1919 in Cagnes-sur-Mer

Key works:
- *La Grenouillière* c1869
- *Le Moulin de la Galette* 1876
- *Luncheon of the Boating Party* 1881
- *The Umbrellas* 1881–86
- *Nursing (Aline and Her Son Pierre)* 1886
- *The Great Bathers* 1887

Things to look for:
- use of color
- bold brushstrokes

Comparisons: Frédéric Bazille, François Boucher, Eugène Delacroix, Peter Paul Rubens, Raphael, John Singer Sargent, Alfred Sisley, Claude Monet

Glossary terms: Barbizon school, *en plein air*, impressionism, motif, Old Masters, Renaissance, rococo, Salon

From impressionism to Raphael

Renoir experimented with a number of different styles over his long career. His brightly colored earliest works, for example, reflect the sharp-edged impressionism of Edouard Manet. When he was closest to Monet, however, during the late 1860s and 1870s, he began to develop a much more blurred and spontaneous touch, exploring the effects of light on the surfaces of fabrics and faces. His travels to Italy led to a drastic change of technique during the 1880s, when he began focusing intensely on bold draftsmanship. His late works are warmer and more feathery in style, resuming his impressionist manner.

Le Moulin de la Galette (1876), which was shown at the Third Impressionist Exhibition of 1877, typifies Renoir's most vigorous early impressionist brushwork. It is a painting that conveys the spontaneous experience of an outdoor dance hall in Montmartre, captured in both the passing lamps and shadows of afternoon light. No face, lamp, or bench is clearly defined; instead, a flurry of brushstrokes summarizes the overall effect of light upon each element of the composition.

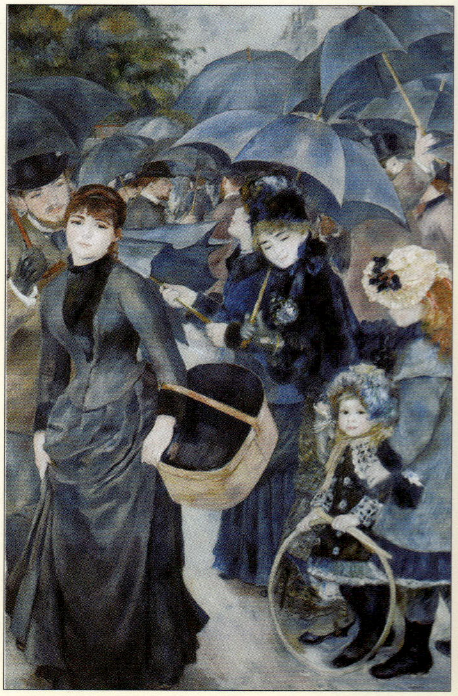

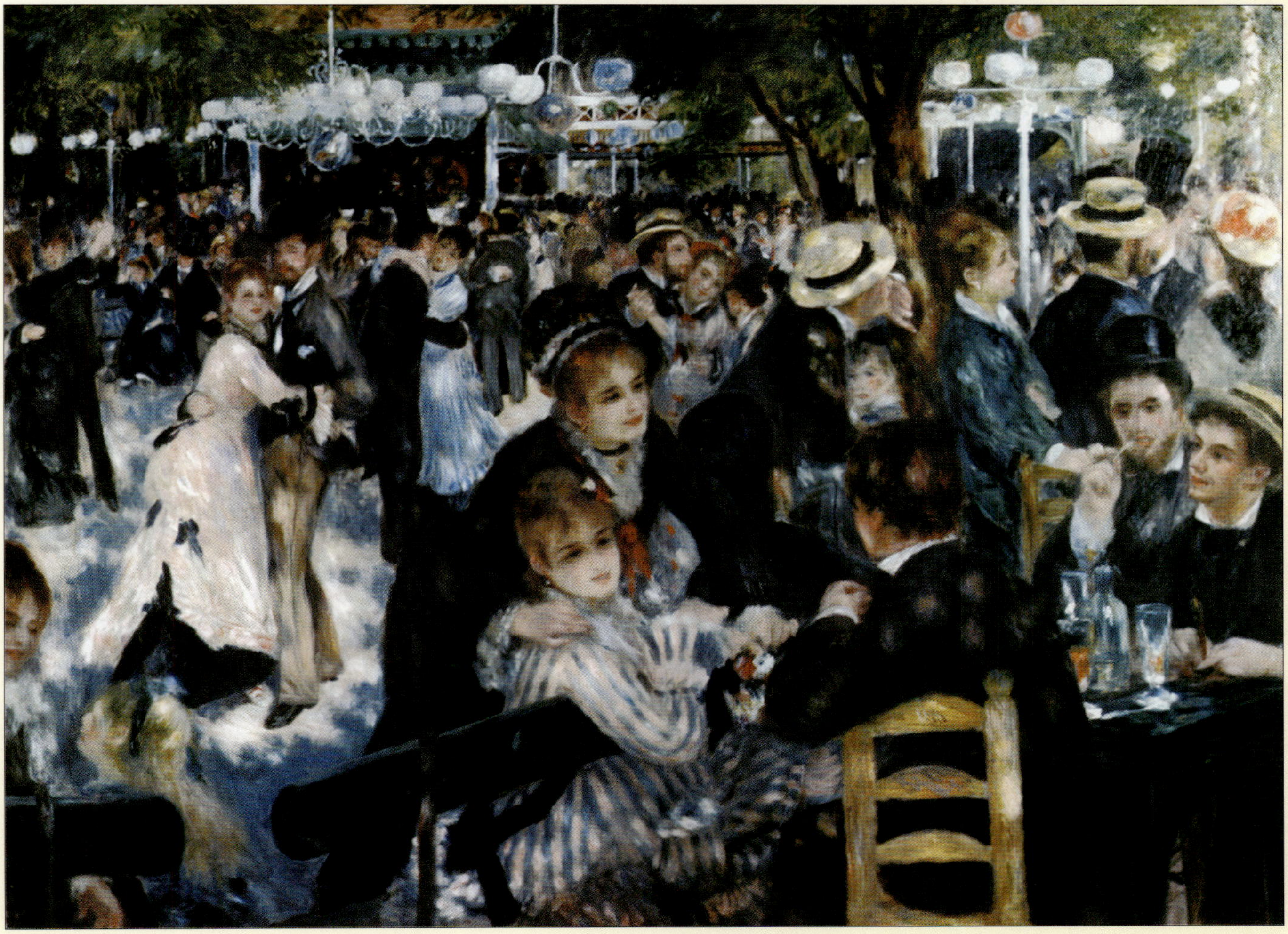

During the 1880s Renoir traveled extensively. He first visited North Africa, as Eugène Delacroix had done, then the islands of Guernsey and Jersey, and finally traveled from Marseilles along the Mediterranean coast to Genoa. Of all the countries that he visited, Italy had the greatest impact upon Renoir. His encounters with the supreme draftsmanship of Raphael and the harmonious forms of classical sculpture in that country led him to abandon his feathery, impressionist touch in favor of a more careful delineation of contours.

The Umbrellas (1881–86) provides a unique testament to this stylistic transformation. On the right-hand side of the composition the women and children emerge in a flurry of tiny strokes of paint. The light in the figures' eyes and the textures and colors of their blue costumes (which combine many shades of blue, built up in layers of paint) all sparkle. However, the figures on the left, in particular the bareheaded young woman in the foreground, are executed in much more highly finished detail. The colors of her features and costume are flatter, focusing the viewer's attention on drawing, line, and volume rather than the surface effects of color and brushstroke. Renoir has also meticulously distinguished the fashions of two different decades in the painting's halves. The woman in the foreground on the left, for example, wears a bustle, which only came into fashion during the 1880s.

During his final years Renoir readopted, to some extent, the looser brushwork and warm palette of his early impressionism. His last works, especially the "Bather" paintings and still lifes, reflect his interest in rococo painters such as François Boucher, as well as the grand tradition of such Renaissance colorists as Titian and Peter Paul Rubens.

Le Moulin de la Galette *1876. Oil on canvas. 51 1/2 x 69 in (131 x 175 cm). Musée d'Orsay, Paris.*

The Umbrellas *1881–86. Oil on canvas. 71 x 45 1/4 in (180 x 115 cm). National Gallery, London.*

REYNOLDS Joshua

JOSHUA REYNOLDS WAS THE LEADING BRITISH PORTRAITIST of his day, specializing in grand, life-sized depictions of important people, often in heroic, classical poses. An intellectual, cultured man, his theories about art greatly influenced future generations of artists.

Life and works

Joshua Reyonds was born in Plympton, on the southwest coast of England, the son of a schoolteacher. From 1740 to 1743 he was apprenticed to Thomas Hudson, a well-known portrait painter in London, after which he set up as a portraitist, working first in Plymouth and then in London.

It was common for aristocratic young men of the time to make a "Grand Tour" of Europe to complete their classical education. The Grand Tour was an extended cultural journey, often made with a tutor, to learn about history, art, and architecture. In 1749 Reynolds was invited to Italy as the guest of his life-long friend, the English naval commander and aristocrat Augustus Keppel. The opportunity that Keppel gave the young artist was to contribute greatly to his later success by broadening his experience and knowledge, and helping him understand the tastes of his clients.

Reynolds stayed in Italy for two years, mostly in Rome, making studies of and notes on the art he saw. Along with the ancient Roman art and architecture that he would have seen there, it is known that he was impressed with the works of the Renaissance artists Raphael and Michelangelo Buonarroti, and Venetian painters such as Titian.

By 1753 Reynolds was back in London. His reputation as a portraitist was established by his dramatic, life-size, full-length painting, *Commodore Keppel* (1752). The painting showed Keppel striding across a seashore, every bit the commander, apparently controlling the storm raging behind him. Reynolds took Keppel's pose from a famous ancient Roman statue of Apollo (known as the "Apollo Belvedere") that he had seen in Italy, a pose that gave his subject great dignity.

Commodore Keppel was typical of the intellectual approach that Reynolds took to his painting, which greatly appealed to his educated and wealthy clients. He often placed his subjects in noble surroundings and in classical poses, wearing classical or semiclassical clothing, their physical imperfections disguised. Reynolds's ability and cultured approach brought him great success: in 1759 more than 150 clients sat for portraits for him, and he had to employ several studio assistants to meet the demand for his work.

In 1768 the prestigious Royal Academy was founded to exhibit the work of contemporary artists in public. Its full title was the "Royal Academy in London for the Purpose of Cultivating and Improving the Arts of Painting, Sculpture, and Architecture." Reynolds was one of its founding members, and his reputation was so great that he was appointed its first president. It was this appointment that led to his knighthood

Data file

Full name: Joshua Reynolds

Nationality: English

Style: English 18th-century/Venetian

Dates: Born 1723 in Plympton, died 1792 in London

Key works:
- *Commodore Keppel* 1752
- *Nellie O'Brien* 1763
- *Self-portrait* 1773
- *Three Ladies Adorning a Term of Hymen* 1774
- *Colonel Sir Banastre Tarleton* 1782

Things to look for:
- grand portraits
- sitters sometimes in classical dress

Comparisons: William Hogarth, Thomas Gainsborough

Glossary terms: Academy, classicism, Grand Tour, history painting

Classicism, grandeur, and drama

There are many paintings by Sir Joshua Reynolds in existence, but not all of these are his work alone. As a successful artist he was in great demand, and he employed studio assistants to help him complete his commissions. His own paintings give a clear sense of the values and interests of the people he painted. Most of his paintings are portraits of prominent and wealthy citizens—professional people, aristocrats, and royalty—but he was also enthusiastic about "history paintings" (historical scenes of important or significant events), although there was not the same demand for these and fewer exist.

This painting of Colonel Sir Banastre Tarleton is a good example of a Reynolds portrait (although the background may have been painted by an assistant). Records tell us that Tarleton—who became a member of Parliament, a general, and a baronet—sat nine times for Reynolds. The sitter is depicted about life size (he was a short man), and is exhibiting a cool and confident response to the battle raging behind him in the background. The smoke from the cannon fire and the frenzied horses contrast dramatically with his nonchalance. The battle is an imaginative rendering of an episode in the American War of Independence (1775–83), in which Tarleton distinguished himself on the British side. He returned from the war in 1782 a popular 28-year-old hero, and this picture was painted in the same year. Reynolds exhibited the painting at the Royal Academy, where it was well received by the public.

In the painting Tarleton seems to be about to draw his sword, using both hands, oblivious to the danger he is in. The pose is

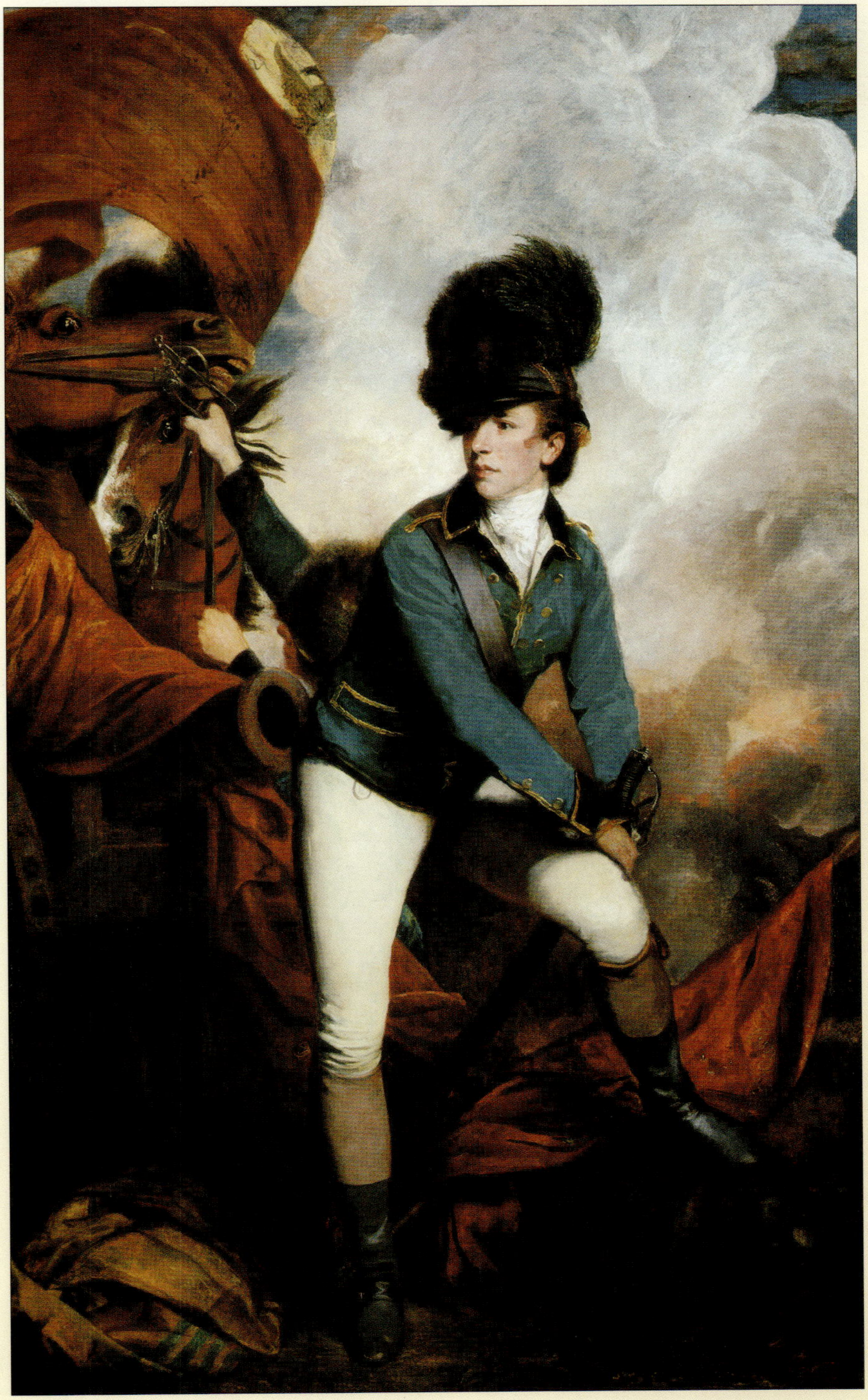

a subtle one and was probably chosen for two reasons. Firstly, Tarleton had lost two fingers on his right hand the previous year, and his position cleverly disguises this fact, while the awkward angle also explains why he needs two hands to draw the sword. Secondly, and more importantly, the pose is taken from a well-known ancient statue of Hermes, one cast of which was in the Royal Academy in London. This reference to a well-known classical sculpture is typical of Reynolds, and would have been recognized and appreciated by the educated people who saw the painting.

Like many of Reynolds's paintings, this one is in quite a poor condition. Many of the techniques he used were experimental and have not stood the test of time. In particular he used two pigments which are now known to cause long-term problems. One was carmine, a red color made from insects, which gradually fades and has given some of Reynolds' faces a ghostly pallor. The other was a dark-brown, tarry substance called bitumen that never dries properly and tends to blacken with age. No one is sure whether there is bitumen in this painting, or if its poor condition stems from another cause.

Colonel Sir Banastre Tarleton *1782. Oil on canvas. 93 x 57 1/4 in (236 x 145 cm). National Gallery, London.*

in the same year. Between 1769 and 1790 he delivered a series of 15 highly influential "Discourses on Art" (lectures which were later published) to students and Academy members. In the lectures Reynolds outlined the principal functions of the Academy: to teach students, to exhibit works of a suitably high standard, and to "form a repository for the great examples of the Art." He also expanded on his theory that to be a great artist it was essential to study the art of the past.

Reynolds visited Flanders and Holland in 1781, where he was impressed by the work of the 17th-century artists Peter Paul Rubens and Rembrandt. In 1784 he was appointed Portrait Painter to King George III. After his death in 1792 he was buried in Saint Paul's Cathedral in London.

RIVERA Diego

DIEGO RIVERA PAINTED MONUMENTAL MURALS that were inspired by his revolutionary ideals. His early experimentation with cubism gave way to realist depictions of Mexico's turbulent past.

Life and work

Diego Rivera was one of twin brothers born in Guanajuato, Mexico in 1886. Tragically, his brother died at the age of only 18 months. Rivera's parents were both teachers; by the age of three, Rivera could read and draw proficiently. (He once recalled that his earliest memory was of himself drawing.) By the age of 12 he had started evening classes at the San Carlos Academy of Art in Mexico City.

In 1907 Rivera left Mexico for Madrid. Two years later, he went to Paris, where he became acquainted with the leading cubist artists Pablo Picasso, Juan Gris, and Fernand Léger. He also met Amedeo Modigliani, who became a good friend. He was drawn to cubism and produced works in this style, including *Sailor at Lunch* (1914). By this time, he was living with a Russian emigré artist, Angeline Beloff, with whom he had a son.

Although Rivera rarely returned to Mexico during this period, he was nonetheless aware of political developments in his native country. Since 1910, when Porfirio Díaz had been unseated from his presidency, farmers and laborers had been demanding reforms and the country was in turmoil.

In 1921 Rivera returned to Mexico, where a program to decorate public buildings with large-scale murals had begun under the reformist and art-loving new president, Alvaro Obregón. Rivera was commissioned to paint murals for the National Preparatory School and the Ministry of Education, both in Mexico City, and the National Agricultural School in Chapingo. He had already visited Italy to study the frescos of the Renaissance. Now he also made a trip to the Yucatan to explore Mexico's early heritage from before the Spanish conquest in the 16th century.

Rivera and fellow muralists David Siqueiros and José Orozco, were dubbed *Los Tres Grandes* ("The Big Three"). Their work soon attracted international attention. American photographers Edward Weston and Tina Modotti visited Rivera and, over the next few years, countless artists and critics traveled to Mexico to witness Rivera's work.

An active communist, Rivera was invited to the Soviet Union in 1927, where he worked with a group of Moscow artists.

In 1929 Rivera married the Mexican artist Frida Kahlo. Despite a stormy relationship, both were to play a large role in each other's lives until Kahlo's death in 1954.

Rivera's first mural commission for the United States was in 1930, when he was invited to make *Allegory of California* (1931) for the San Francisco Stock Exchange. While there, he also painted a mural for the California

Data file

Full name: José Diego María Rivera

Nationality: Mexican

Style: cubism/realism

Dates: born 1886 in Guanajuato, died 1957 in Mexico City

Key works:

- *Sailor at Lunch* 1914
- *Allegory of California* mural for San Francisco Stock Exchange 1931
- murals for National Preparatory School and Ministry of Education, Mexico City 1931–37
- *Man at the Crossroads* mural for Rockefeller Center, New York 1932 (destroyed); redone for National Palace, Mexico City 1934
- *The Fecund Earth* mural for National Agricultural School, Chapingo 1936

Things to look for:

- large-scale murals for public buildings
- complex compositions of figures

Comparisons: Juan Gris, Pablo Picasso, Robert Delaunay, David Siqueiros, José Orozco

Glossary terms: cubism, realism, surrealism

Capitalism and communism collide

Man at the Crossroads (1934) is Rivera's most controversial mural. The work was originally commissioned in 1932 to decorate the interior of the RCA building in the Rockefeller Center in New York. The following year, Rivera began work on the mural, making several alterations to the sketch he had originally provided. By early May he had completed two-thirds of the work, which now included a labor leader figure who bore a striking resemblance to Lenin (see A in the diagram). Rockefeller objected and asked Rivera to replace this figure with an anonymous character, but Rivera refused to make any alterations. Infuriated by his attitude, Rockefeller canceled the commission and immediately had the mural destroyed. Two years later, Rivera reproduced the mural in the Palace of Fine Arts in Mexico City, where it can still be seen.

Man at the Crossroads represents Rivera's view that society in the 1930s had two choices, capitalism or socialism. On the left-hand side of the painting Rivera presents the world of capitalism, characterized in his view by gambling and dancing (B), soldiers at war (C), and policemen beating workers (D). The world of socialism on the right includes proudly marching workers (E), and fit, young sportswomen (F). At the center of the image is a worker operating a huge machine (G). Two large elliptical forms intersect the worker, the first (H), representing the world as seen through a microscope and the second (I), the cosmos as seen through a telescope.

In Rivera's vision, technology, as characterized by the large machine

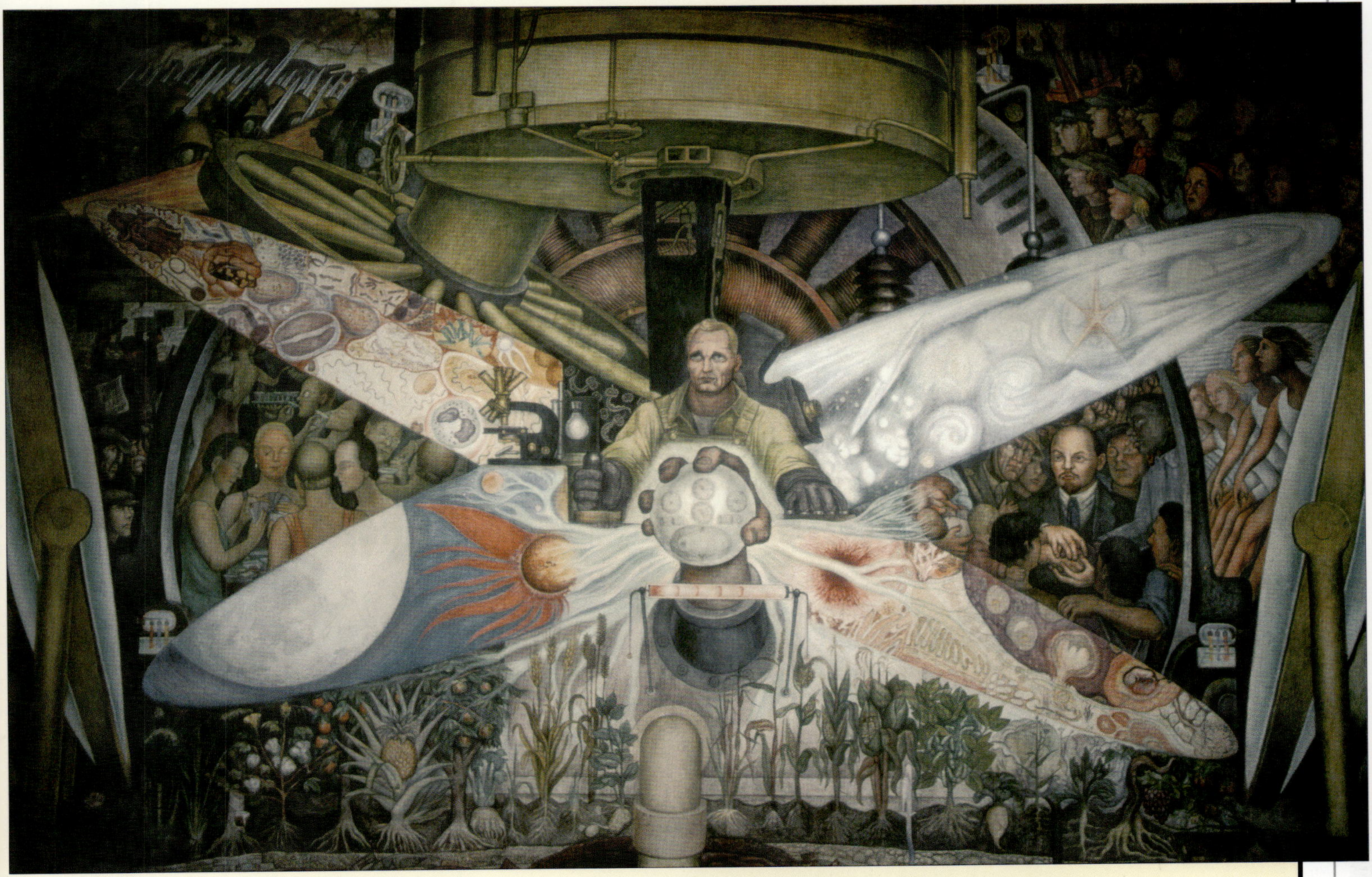

Man at the Crossroads *1934. Fresco. 191 x 450¾ in (485 x 1145 cm). Museo del Palacio de Bellas Artes, Mexico City, Mexico.*

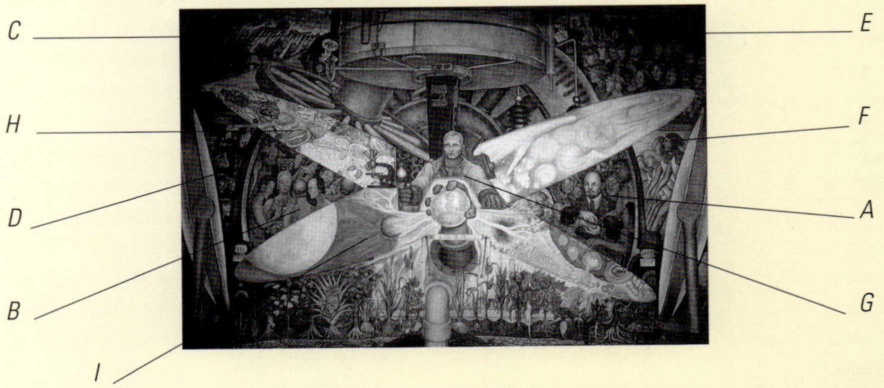

operated by the worker, will transform the world. As a supporter of communism, Rivera used his art to present the positive aspects of socialism and contrast them with the negative side of capitalism. By expressing his political views in the public form of mural painting, he hoped to spread his message to a wider audience.

School of Fine Arts, which included an illusionistic portrayal of artists seated on a scaffold and working on the mural.

Diego Rivera's most prestigious commissions in the United States were for the Detroit Institute of Arts and the new RCA building in the Rockefeller Center in New York. In the latter, Nelson Rockefeller was outraged by the inclusion of a representation of the Russian leader Vladimir Ilyich Lenin and cancelled the project.

Rivera returned to Mexico in 1934, where he produced a mural for the Palace of Fine Arts in Mexico City based on the RCA building mural. He was visited by the exiled Soviet leader Leon Trotsky, and by André Breton, founder of the surrealists.

After World War II, Rivera developed a reputation as a portraitist. When he died, his last work, a mural on the history of Mexico for the National Palace, was still not complete.

ROBBIA Luca della

LUCA DELLA ROBBIA GAINED WIDE ACCLAIM for his blue-and-white terracotta figures, which he created in his thriving family workshop using a secret process. Admired throughout Europe, he produced figures for churches in France and Spain as well as Italy.

Life and work

Luca della Robbia was born in Florence, where he spent most of his career. He came from a family of prosperous wool merchants, but little else is known about his early life, although it is frequently assumed that he received his initial training from Lorenzo Ghiberti. It is also quite possible that he was taught how to work in marble by Nanni di Banco. Ghiberti and Nanni di Banco were both Florentine sculptors.

The first documented reference to Luca dates from 1431, when he began work on his Cantoria ("Singing Gallery") for Florence Cathedral. This remarkable work was a marble organ loft, decorated with rows of child musicians, who were depicted singing or playing instruments. The Cantoria is the most monumental and impressive of all Luca's sculptures, even though it differs greatly from his usual style.

The warm praise that the Cantoria attracted brought della Robbia further commissions for work in stone. By the late 1430s, however, he was already experimenting with glazed terracotta. In 1442–45 he created a lunette of the Resurrection in polychrome enameled terracotta for the northern sacristy of Florence Cathedral.

A welter of other commissions soon followed and, within a short space of time, the bulk of Luca's orders were for terracotta figures. By 1446, he needed larger premises, so he purchased a sizeable house on the Via Guelfa. Here, he built a kiln and established a flourishing workshop, which gained an international reputation. The chief demand was for images of the Virgin and Child. In catering to this market, Luca emphasized Mary's strong maternal feelings, becoming one of the first artists to focus on her humanity rather than on her divine status.

Luca continued working until he was in his seventies, when the business was gradually taken over by his nephew, Andrea. By this stage, the sculptures of della Robbia were so famous that they seemed in many ways to symbolize the Florentine Renaissance. "I suppose nothing brings the real air of a Tuscan town so vividly to mind," wrote one later commentator, "as those pieces of blue-and-white earthenware, by which he [Luca] is best known, like fragments of the milky sky itself, fallen into the cool streets, and breaking into the darkened churches."

Data file

Full name: Luca della Robbia
Nationality: Italian (Florentine)
Style: Renaissance
Dates: born 1399/1400 in Florence, died 1482 in Florence
Key works:
- Cantoria 1431–38
- *The Apostles* c1444
- *Labors of the Months* c1455
- *Madonna of the Apple* 1462
- *Crucifixion* c1465
- *Madonna of the Stonemasons* 1475–80

Things to look for:
- sculptures in glazed terracotta
- portraits of the Virgin and Child
- decorative borders

Comparisons: Donatello, Lorenzo Ghiberti, Filippo Brunelleschi
Glossary terms: glaze, kiln, polychrome, sweet style, terracotta

A talent for graceful decoration

In his treatise, *Della Pittura*, one of the most important texts written on the Renaissance, the Italian architect Leon Battista degli Alberti cited Luca della Robbia as one of the founding fathers of the movement, along with Filippo Brunelleschi, Donatello, Lorenzo Ghiberti, and Masaccio. It is highly unlikely that any modern art historian would make such an extravagant claim for Luca, but it does indicate just how popular and respected a figure he was in his own lifetime.

Stylistically, della Robbia is normally classified as one of the chief exponents of the "sweet style" in Florentine sculpture. His work was very decorative and charming and, as such, it made a striking contrast with the carvings of Donatello, which were rather more challenging and dramatic. Luca did not owe his fame to his style, however, but to his pioneering work in a new medium—glazed terracotta.

The use of terracotta (the word is Italian for baked clay) had been revived by Brunelleschi and Donatello, but it remained a fragile medium, particularly when sculptures were placed outside and left exposed to the elements. This problem could be overcome, however, by coating the terracotta in a glaze, a transparent, protective coating made out of tin, fired clay, antimony, and a variety of other minerals. The process had been known since antiquity, but della Robbia brought it to a new peak of refinement.

It was possible to obtain colored glazes by adding certain substances. Cobalt would produce a blue pigment, copper would produce green, and so forth. Some colors were more successful than others. It was particularly difficult, for example, to achieve a satisfactory shade of red—it usually came out as a dirty violet tone. Della Robbia spent a great deal of time experimenting with color schemes before deciding on the ideal combination. Most of his sculptures follow the pattern adopted in this *Crucifixion* (c1465). The central section is colored blue and white, while the border contains a slightly wider selection of hues.

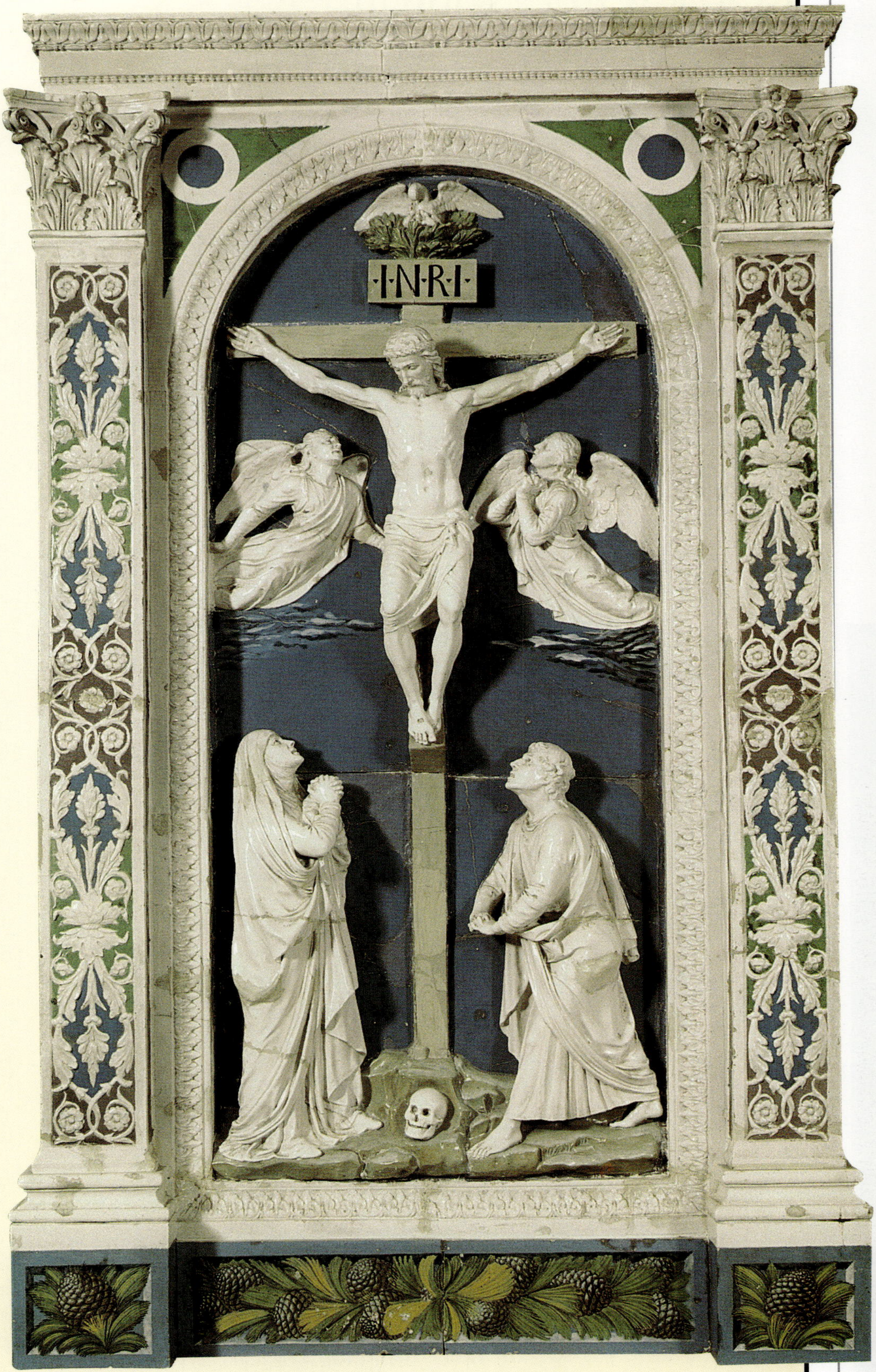

Some prestigious commissions were unique items, but the majority of carvings produced in the della Robbia workshop were standardized pieces. Even so, the process was a lengthy one. First, a segment of the composition was modeled in clay (either by hand, or using one of the workshop molds). Then it was left to dry and fired in a kiln. In most cases, it took three separate firings, at different temperatures, in order to produce the right color and consistency. Finally, the individual pieces were packaged up and sent to their destination, where they were assembled into the finished article.

The entire process was shrouded in secrecy, especially the recipe for the glaze itself. Contemporaries whispered that the della Robbias had a magic formula, which they guarded jealously. According to a local legend, they wrote it down on a scrap of paper and hid it inside the head of one of their terracotta Madonnas.

Luca was best known for his sculptures of the Virgin and Child, although he did tackle a wide range of religious subjects. This *Crucifixion* was one of a series of works that he produced for the Chapels of the Virgin and the Cross in the parish church at Impruneta. The commission appears to have come through his contacts with a member of the Medici family. The composition itself was influenced by a Brunelleschi sculpture in Florence, but Luca added the unusual feature of the nesting pelican at the top of the cross. Traditionally, the bird was thought to feed its young with blood, by pecking at its own breast. For this reason, it was sometimes used as a symbol of the Crucifixion, where Christ shed His own blood in order to save humanity.

Crucifixion *c1465. Glazed terracotta. 59 x 25½ in (150 x 65 cm). Church of Santa Maria, Impruneta.*

ROCKWELL Norman

FEW ARTISTS HAVE ENJOYED GREATER POPULARITY or influenced more illustrators than Norman Rockwell. For more than 50 years, Rockwell's instantly recognizable style—paintings featuring idealized depictions of small-town and rural life in the United States—illustrated covers of major national magazines, and were used for war posters and calendars.

Life and work

Norman Rockwell was born in 1894 in the suburb of Flushing in New York City. He lived and worked there for some 30 years. However, unlike many of his contemporaries who drew upon city life for their subject matter, Rockwell chose to depict subjects with which he was far less familiar: the picturesque scenes of small-town and rural life in the United States. Rockwell said in his autobiography that he doubted whether he would have idealized the countryside in the way that he did if he had actually grown up in a rural area. In fact, Rockwell's only experience of rural life came during summer vacations when his family went to stay on a farm. However, it was these happy childhood experiences that formed the basis of Rockwell's nostalgia and that he later used as inspiration for his art.

As a youngster, Rockwell was encouraged to draw. After dropping out of high school in 1909, he enrolled at the National Academy of Design before transferring to the Art Students League in 1911, where he studied under George Bridgman and Thomas Fogarty. In order to finance his studies, Rockwell did odd jobs in the evenings, but in 1911 Fogarty found Rockwell his first commercial assignments—before he was 18 years old, Rockwell had produced a series of illustrations for the children's book *Tell Me Why Stories*, for which he was paid $150.

Soon Rockwell was regularly contributing illustrations to children's publications, and in 1913 he was appointed art editor of the magazine *Boy's Life*. Rockwell's ambition, however, was to produce a cover for the *Saturday Evening Post*, the illustrated weekly magazine that had been founded in 1728 by Benjamin Franklin.

Despite his ambitions, Rockwell was modest and often insecure regarding his own talent: throughout his career, he was plagued by doubts about his ability as an artist. It was not until 1916 that he plucked up enough courage to make the journey to Philadelphia to see the *Post*'s editor, George Horace Lorimer. For the interview, Rockwell took two paintings and three sketches. Lorimer liked all five and bought the paintings for $75. More importantly, he told Rockwell to develop the sketches into three more covers for the *Post*. This was the start of Rockwell's long and unbroken relationship with the *Saturday Evening Post*, which lasted until 1963; he produced a total of 322 covers.

While the covers of the *Post* established Rockwell as the United States' greatest illustrator, they are not the only works for which he is known. Rockwell also produced illustrations and covers for publications such as *Collier's*, *Life*, *Literary Digest*, and *Look*, as well as advertising art for Maxwell House coffee, Pan American World Airways, Massachusetts Mutual Life Insurance company, and the *Encyclopedia Britannica*.

From 1924 to 1976, Rockwell also produced artwork for Bigelow & Brown, the United States' foremost publisher of calendars. For them, and in association with the Boy Scouts of America, Rockwell produced illustrations for an annual calendar on the theme of scouting, as well as a calendar each year from 1947 to 1964 on the theme of the four seasons. Both series were highly popular. Just two years before his death in 1978, Rockwell produced his last magazine cover, for the bicentennial celebration issue of *American Artist* magazine.

Rockwell said that his work depicted "ordinary people in everyday situations." In his biography, *My Adventures as an Illustrator* (1960), he described painting with his left hand, and even with a brick. This, he believed, stopped him from destroying the spontaneity of his paintings: "You can't be clever with a brick; you have to paint loosely."

Data file

Full name: Norman Rockwell

Nationality: American

Style: realism

Dates: born 1894 in New York, NY, died 1978 in New York, NY

Key works:
- illustrations for *Tell Me Why Stories* 1911
- 322 covers for the *Saturday Evening Post* 1916–63
- scouting calenders 1924–76
- illustrations for *The Adventures of Tom Sawyer* and *The Adventures of Huckleberry Finn* 1935
- *The Four Freedoms* posters 1943
- *The Four Seasons* calendars 1947–64
- *American Artist* bicentennial issue cover 1976

Things to look for:
- acutely observed images of small-town and rural American life
- ordinary people in everyday situations
- semiphotographic, realistic style
- "historical" works including authentic antique props
- views from different angles afforded by the use of photographic aids

Comparisons: Grant Wood, Andrew Wyeth, Edward Hopper, Thomas Hart Benton, Maxfield Parrish, James Montgomery Flagg, J. C. Leyendecker, John Held Jr

Glossary terms: picturesque, realism

Freedom paintings

Freedom of Speech (1943) is one of four paintings that Rockwell executed to explain to Americans what World War II was about. Inspired by Franklin Roosevelt and Winston Churchill's Atlantic Charter, which proclaimed "four Freedoms"—Freedom of Speech, Freedom from Fear, Freedom of Worship, and Freedom from Want—these paintings quickly became some of Rockwell's best-known works of the era. While the U.S. Treasury Department took the original oil paintings on a nationwide tour to encourage the sales of war bonds, the paintings were also reproduced in the *Saturday Evening Post*, accompanied by short essays explaining what Rockwell was saying in the pictures. Later, they were reproduced as posters.

In his autobiography, Rockwell wrote that *Freedom of Speech* took longer than the others to "get right." Early ideas were abandoned because there were too many standing figures. Finally, Rockwell recalled a town meeting in Arlington, Massachusetts, where a neighbor, Jim Edgerton, had stood up and said something of which the rest of the meeting disapproved. Nevertheless, Jim was allowed to have his say. It was this incident that Rockwell captured on canvas, inspiring millions of people.

While most artists hired professional models, Rockwell was more interested in "types." In the early part of his career, he often walked several miles in search of the right type, or character, who was willing to pose for him. Later in his career, when Rockwell lived in small New England communities and, from 1953, in Stockbridge, Massachusetts, he knew the townsfolk individually and used them repeatedly for his illustrations.

Eventually Rockwell turned to photographs as compositional aids. Later he realized that photography could free him from straight, "head-on" views from his easel, and allow him to depict scenes outside his studio. For each *Saturday Evening Post* cover, Rockwell used between 75 and 100 photographs—from each photograph, only one small detail might be used. Sometimes Rockwell also made a model of the scene he was painting. In this miniature stage set, he was able to rearrange the position of figures, move around the props, and adjust the lighting to help him find the best composition.

Once Rockwell had made his selection of elements from the photographs, he used an epidiascope (an optical device like a slide projector) to magnify and project each detail onto his canvas. He then blocked in the outlines of the projected image in charcoal, repeating the process with each photographic detail until the whole composition was completed. After fixing the charcoal to prevent it from smudging, Rockwell stained the canvas with a coating of oil paint thin enough to allow the charcoal drawings underneath to show through. When this was dry, he added a violet-colored underpainting to the figures' faces to give the skin tones a warm glow. He then applied the rest of the colors to the canvas.

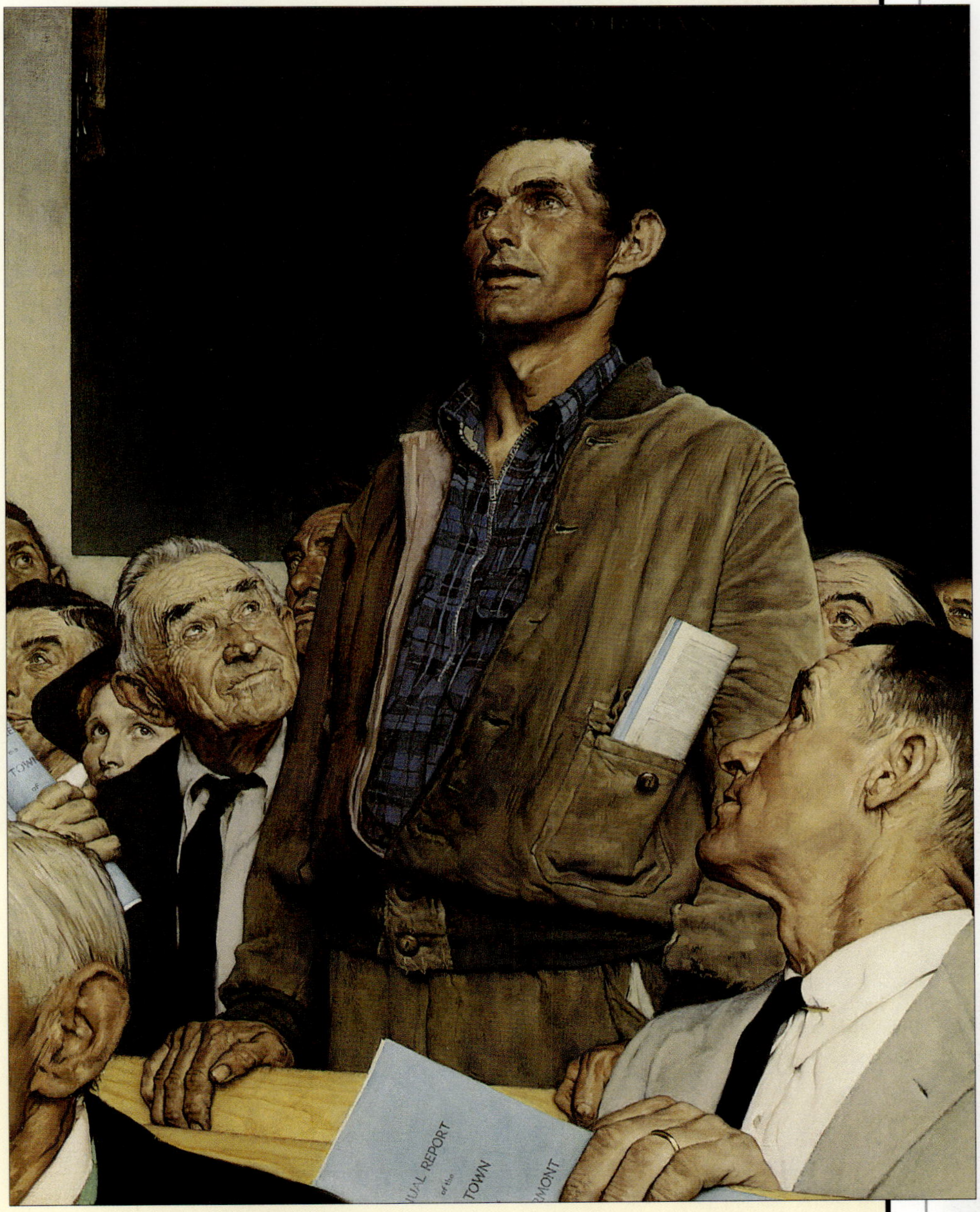

Freedom of Speech *1943. Oil on canvas. 45¾ x 35½ in (116 x 90 cm). Norman Rockwell Paintings Trust, Stockbridge, MA.*

RODIN Auguste

AUGUSTE RODIN REVITALIZED SCULPTURE AT A TIME when it was becoming outmoded and repetitive. Regarded by some as the greatest sculptor since Michelangelo, he was the most influential sculptor of modern times. His powerful and sensuous works are today among the best known and most admired in the world.

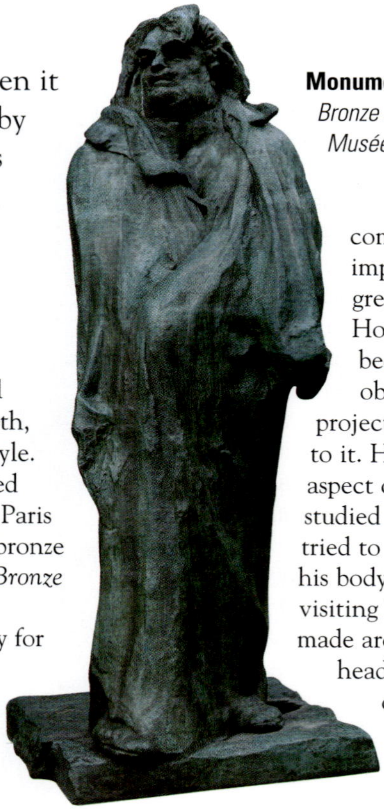

Monument to Balzac *1891–98. Bronze sculpture. 106 in (269 cm). Musée Rodin, Paris.*

In 1891, Rodin was commissioned to create an important monument to the great French novelist, Honoré de Balzac. Rodin became deeply, almost obsessively attached to the project, devoting seven years to it. He researched every aspect of Balzac's life. He studied photographs of him and tried to discover exactly what his body had looked like, even visiting Balzac's old tailor. He made around 50 studies of the head and body. Rodin considered the final, towering, robed figure, "the logical outcome of my whole life."

However, when the full-scale, 17-foot-tall plaster version was exhibited at the Salon in 1898, it was badly received because it did not conform to what was expected from a great monument. The society that had commissioned the sculpture rejected it, and it was not cast in bronze until 13 years after Rodin's death.

Life and work

Auguste Rodin came from a working-class Parisian background. He worked as a decorative stonemason in the 1860s, but in 1875, when he was in his thirties, he scraped together enough money for a trip to Italy to see the work of Donatello and Michelangelo Buonarroti. The self-taught Rodin said that Michelangelo liberated him as a sculptor. We can see this in the dynamic, muscular forms that are typical of Rodin's works.

He rarely used professional models, often preferring to work from dancers. He even worked from an 82-year-old model, whose sagging and wrinkled body fascinated him. This was adventurous at a time when sculpture was still dominated by the smooth, idealized neoclassical style.

In 1877 he exhibited for the first time at the Paris Salon. His piece was a bronze male nude, *The Age of Bronze* (1875–77). Rodin had worked on it intensively for nearly two years, and was devastated when, instead of winning praise for his lifelike figure, he was accused of casting it from the model's body.

In 1884 Rodin won an important competition to design a monument to the medieval heroes of Calais who, in 1347, had offered their heads to Edward III of England. The gesture was intended to save other citizens of Calais from being killed as punishment for resisting Edward's successful siege. The result was *The Burghers of Calais* (1884–89), six figures who powerfully express the anguish of the moments before their reprieve.

As Rodin's success grew, so did his workshop. He employed a tightly organized team of technicians to help produce his sculptures. His technique was most often to model in clay, using his hands, rather than to carve. He worked on a very small scale to produce the first models; from these larger versions could be made. He often used photographs of his work to develop his ideas, and reproduced favorite figures again and again in different combinations, sizes, and materials.

Rodin was not a sophisticated figure. He was short, with coarse hair, and a yellowing beard. But, by the turn of the century, he was a celebrity. In 1900 a major exhibition secured his fame, and he received commissions from all over the world—more than he could complete.

Rodin's most famous mistress was the talented young sculptress Camille Claudel, who began as his pupil. However, he spent most of his life with Rose Beuret, whom he had met while he was young and poor. Rose modeled for Rodin, and was one of his most trusted assistants. They married only in old age, in 1917. She died two weeks later, and Rodin died later that year.

Data file

Full name: Auguste Rodin

Nationality: French

Style: modern sculpture

Dates: born 1840 in Paris, died 1917 in Meudon

Key works:
- *The Age of Bronze* 1875–77
- *The Thinker* 1880–1904
- *The Gates of Hell* 1880–1917
- *The Burghers of Calais* 1884–89
- *The Kiss* 1886
- *Monument to Balzac* 1891–98

Things to look for:
- broken or unfinished surfaces
- traces of working process left
- dynamic figures
- muscular bodies

Comparisons: Michelangelo Buonarroti, Edgar Degas, Camille Claudel

Glossary terms: neoclassicism, Salon

Monumental expression

In 1880, Rodin received a commission that occupied him for the rest of his life. It was to produce a monumental pair of doors for a museum of decorative arts. They were never completed or put in place, but most of Rodin's creative output is related in some way to figures for *The Gates of Hell* (1880–1917), as he called the work. The sculptures adorning the gates are figures from a famous story about tragic love and damnation to hell, called the *Divine Comedy*, written by the 14th-century Italian poet Dante Alighieri. Rodin presented the terrible, hopeless spectacle of figures falling, embracing, screaming, and clinging to the gates. The whole hellish scene is watched over from above by a pensive male figure. He is often interpreted as representing the writer or the artist himself. So powerful was the image of this figure that Rodin reproduced it on a greatly enlarged scale, seated upon a massive pedestal, as a single monument. He called it *The Thinker* (1880–1904).

This sculpture is a fine example of Rodin's ability to express the human psyche through the human form. Everything about the figure embodies deep immersion in thought. It appears almost to topple forward, as if the head is heavy with the weight of thought. The right hand clenched before the mouth silences it, and the eyes are empty holes that do not see. This emphasizes all the more the figure's concentration. Although the pose is static, the figure seems still to ripple with energy. There is a strong sense of tensed muscles and pent-up force in the body. Rodin summarized the effect well himself when he said: "What makes my *Thinker* think is that he thinks not only with his brain, his distended nostrils, and compressed lips, but with every muscle of his arms, back, and legs, with his clenched fist and gripping toes."

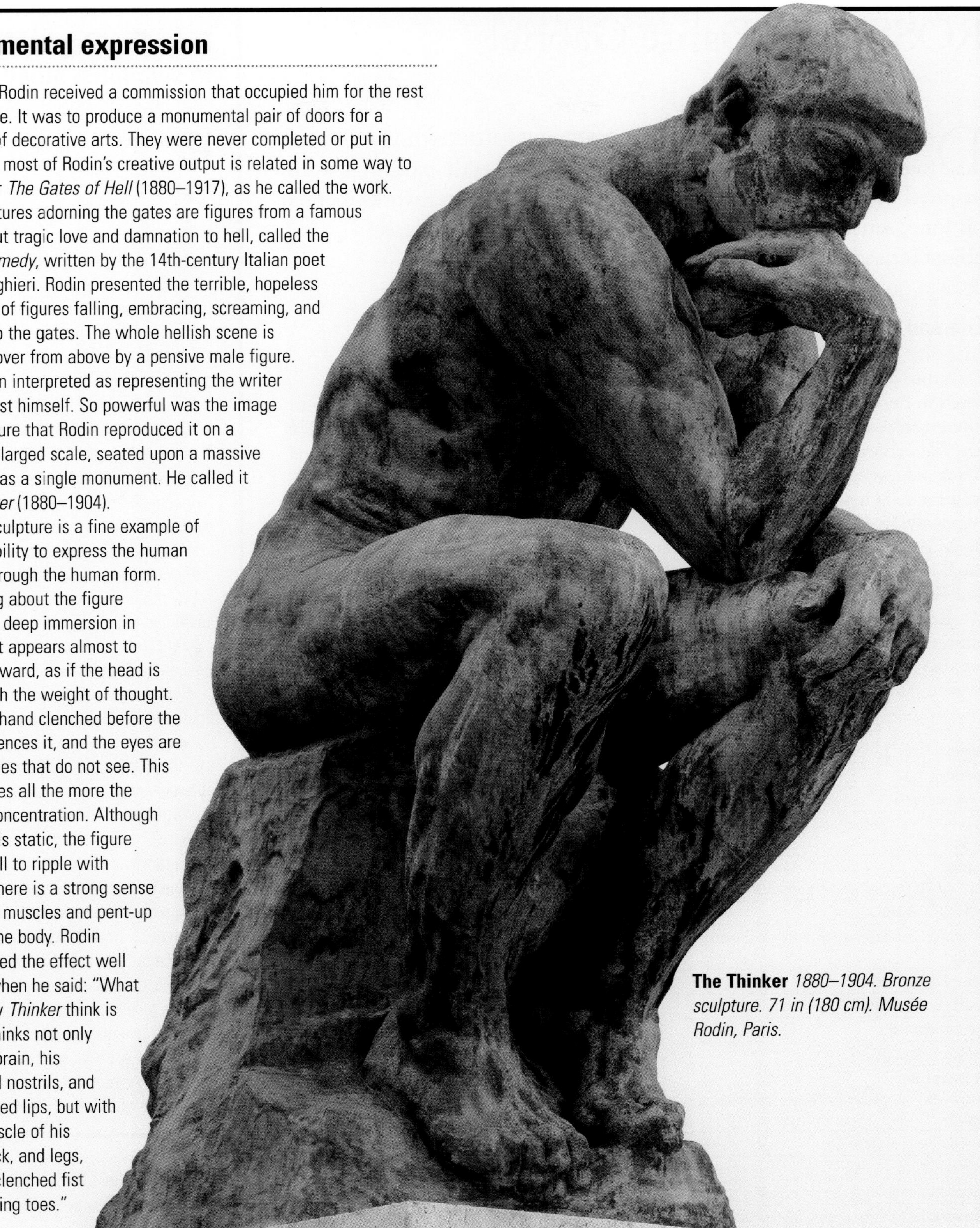

The Thinker *1880–1904. Bronze sculpture. 71 in (180 cm). Musée Rodin, Paris.*

ROSSETTI Dante Gabriel

DANTE GABRIEL ROSSETTI WAS A POET AND ARTIST who helped to found the Pre-Raphaelite Brotherhood. His early paintings were inspired by the legendary British king, Arthur; his later works focused on lone, sensual women in contemplative poses. His style is characterized by prolific detail and rich color.

Life and work

Born into an artistic Italian family based in England, Rossetti showed an interest in poetry and art from an early age, but achieved little success in his formal education. From 1841 to 1845 he attended Henry Sass's Drawing Academy; in 1846 he went on to the Royal Academy Schools, where he met English painters John Everett Millais and William Holman Hunt.

Rossetti soon tired of copying plaster casts of classical sculpture, and became a private pupil of Ford Madox Brown. As a young man, Rossetti was known more for his poetry than his painting, producing his famous translations of Italian lyric poetry which, with the help of art critic John Ruskin, were published in 1861 as *The Early Italian Poets*. His sister, Christina Rossetti, was also an important poet.

In 1848 Rossetti, Hunt, and Millais created an art group, known at first to the public just by its initials, called the Pre-Raphaelite Brotherhood. The group shared a love for the tradition of art "before Raphael," admiring the simple authenticity of pre-Renaissance Italian art, with its careful portrayal of nature. In 1850 Rossetti founded a magazine, *The Germ*, to further this cause, but only four issues were printed.

Many critics attacked Rossetti's paintings from this period, most famously *The Girlhood of Mary Virgin* (1849) and *Ecce Ancilla Domini! (The Annunciation)* (1850), for the clumsiness of their execution. Rossetti decided never to exhibit in public again. However, Ruskin continued to admire and support the young artist, commissioning work from him regularly and encouraging him to teach.

From the 1850s, Rossetti devoted his talents principally to watercolors. His preferred themes were drawn from the legend of King Arthur, classical and medieval narratives, and the poetry of English writer Robert Browning. Rossetti's early works use meticulous detail in their depiction of historical costume and setting.

In 1856 Rossetti met artists Edward Burne-Jones and William Morris, and the three became close friends. They undertook many projects of interior design, including the decoration of the Debating Hall at Oxford University. Because Rossetti was unaware of the technical complications of fresco painting, though, the color of these murals has been greatly damaged by time. Rossetti also contributed stained-glass designs to Morris's interior decorating firm.

Data file

Full name: Gabriel Charles Dante Rossetti

Nationality: English

Style: Pre-Raphaelite

Dates: born 1828 in London, died 1882 in Birchington-on-Sea

Key works:
- *Ecce Ancilla Domini! (The Annunciation)* 1850
- *Arthur's Tomb* 1855
- murals for the Debating Hall at Oxford University 1856
- *Bocca Baciata* 1859
- *Beata Beatrix* c1864–70
- *The Beloved* 1865
- *Astarte Syriaca* 1877

Things to look for:
- subjects from medieval romance and classical legend
- highly detailed style
- rich color
- women with flowing hair in decorative settings

Comparisons: Ford Madox Brown, Edward Burne-Jones, William Holman Hunt, John Everett Millais, William Morris

Glossary terms: fresco, Pre-Raphaelite, symbolism

From Pre-Raphaelite detail to symbolist mood

Rossetti combined a meticulous evocation of detail and a vibrant palette in order to create a mood of mystery and romance. Many of his early works, usually painted in watercolor, portray angular knights and ladies in historical interiors or carefully described forest settings. The later paintings, mostly in oil, used sensual colors to capture the voluptuous, fleshy features of monumental, beautiful women.

Beata Beatrix (c1864–70) marks a turning point between these two manners. This painting was both a highly personal response to the death of his wife, Elizabeth Siddal, in February 1862, and a universal meditation on death and afterlife. Siddal appears in a mood of reverie with her eyes half-closed. A bird with a halo bears a poppy to Siddal's hands, symbolizing the laudanum which took her life, but which also set her soul free from the world of time and care represented by the sundial.

Siddal is poised between two shadowy figures in the background: one, in radiant red drapery, represents peace after life's toil; the clothed, darker figure reminds us of two Dantes, the medieval poet and Rossetti himself, both traveling into the circles of hell searching for their lost loves. In the far distance a hazy view of London and the bridges of the River Thames invokes the modern world that Siddal has left and that Rossetti will choose to abandon in favor of his private world of legend and romance, far from the pain of Siddal's loss and critics' disdain.

The tragic themes of the painting, and its detailed yet atmospheric technique, were greatly admired by a subsequent generation of artists, the symbolists.

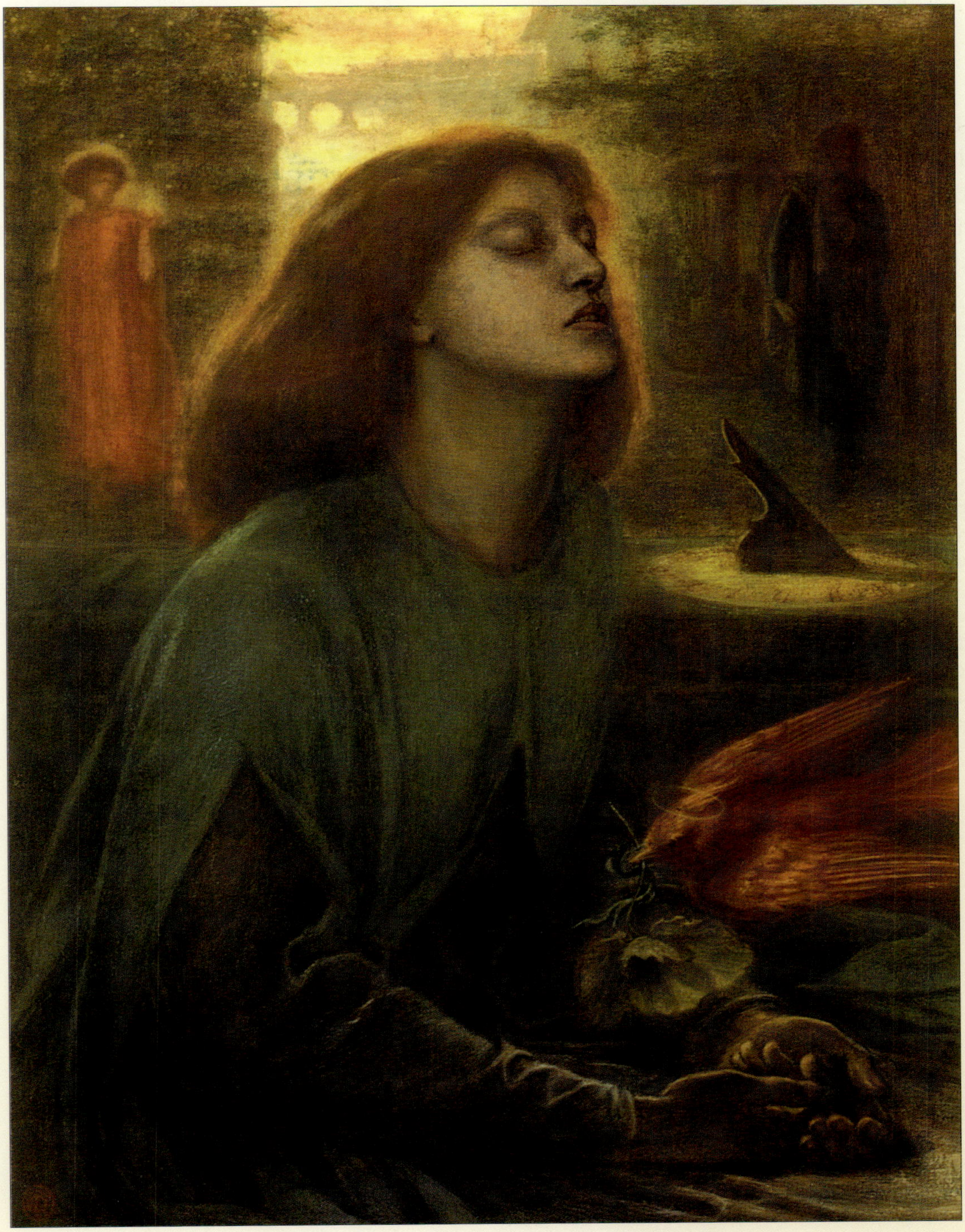

Beata Beatrix
c1864–70. Oil on canvas.
34 x 26 in (86.5 x 66 cm).
Tate Gallery, London.

In 1860 Rossetti married Elizabeth Siddal, his chief model of the 1850s, but she died two years later from an overdose of the tranquilizing drug laudanum. Rossetti was devastated. He moved to a house in Chelsea, London, where he kept a menagerie of exotic animals in his large garden.

Rossetti's later work focused mainly on oil paintings of single female figures in decorative settings. These were very popular with the public, and Rossetti achieved new heights of financial and social success. From the 1870s onward, however, attacks on his poetry and chronic insomnia led him to become dependent upon alcohol and sedatives.

His passion for Morris's wife, Jane, provided some escape from his anxieties; she appears as the epitome of voluptuous beauty in his works between 1871 and 1874. Rossetti's last years were spent as a recluse at his Chelsea house, although he died in Kent, southeast England.

ROTHKO Mark

MARK ROTHKO'S PAINTINGS OF HUGE RECTANGLES OF COLOR that seem to float and shimmer on the canvas made him one of the leaders of abstract expressionism, the movement that began in New York during the 1940s and placed great emphasis on spontaneous expression in art. Unlike the movement's most famous artist, Jackson Pollock, Rothko conveyed a sense of restraint and contemplation in his work, but was nevertheless evocative.

Life and work

Mark Rothko was born Marcus Rothkowitz in the Russian town of Dvinsk, but emigrated to the United States with his parents when he was 10. He was an intelligent child who studied literature and music. Having enrolled at Yale University, he became dissatisfied with academic education and dropped out of college to make his way to New York in 1923. There he studied for a while at the Art Students' League of New York, a school in the then-current modernist tradition with a liberal entrance policy and an informal structure to its classes. He is nevertheless usually regarded as a self-taught painter.

At the end of the 1920s Rothko began teaching while also experimenting with expressionist and surrealist influences. This learning process continued throughout the 1930s as he gradually developed his own style and methods. Such experimentation proved more fruitful during the 1940s, when Rothko began to create large, rectangular works built up with layers of paint, some thin and heavily diluted, others opaque, first with watercolor on paper and then with oil on canvas. His work of this period, such as the untitled pieces dating from between 1946 and 1948, *Untitled* (1946) and *No. 1 (Untitled)* (1948), for example, appear both watery and highly atmospheric. They convey a sense of infinite depth, and in this respect Rothko's style is reminiscent of the English landscapist J. M. W. Turner, whose luminous landscapes appeared approximately a century earlier.

By the end of the 1940s Rothko began to develop a more distinctive style by soaking areas of color into the fabric of the canvas. During the 1950s he structured his colors more formally, frequently stacking two or three soft-edged blocks of color vertically, in proportions that created a harmonious composition.

Rothko's position as one of the leading lights of abstract expressionism was secured during the 1950s, although commercial success only came at the end of the decade. A major retrospective exhibition of his work at the Museum of Modern Art in New York in 1961 increased Rothko's reputation. Along with Barnett Newman and Helen Frankenthaler, he came to be seen as

Data file

Full name: Mark Rothko

Nationality: American

Style: abstract expressionism

Dates: born 1903 in Dvinsk, died 1970 in New York

Key works:

No. 15 1952

No. 7 (Dark over Light) 1954

Black Area in Reds 1958

Black on Maroon 1958

No. 18 1961

Red, Orange, Orange on Red 1962

Rothko Chapel murals and related paintings, Houston, TX 1965–67

Untitled 1967

Untitled (Black on Gray) 1969–70

Things to look for:

- large blocks of color with soft edges that give them a shimmering quality
- recurrent rectangular shapes

Comparisons:

Jackson Pollock, Barnett Newman, Helen Frankenthaler, Adolph Gottlieb, Robert Motherwell, Ad Reinhardt, Robert Ryman, Richard Serra

Glossary terms: abstract expressionism, color-field painting, modernism, surrealism

Color and heightened emotion

Despite evidence to the contrary, Rothko maintained that he was not an abstract artist, and the boundaries between representational and abstract art meant little to him. "I'm not interested in the relationship of color or form or anything else," he declared. "I'm interested only in expressing basic human emotion—tragedy, ecstasy, doom, and so on." Rothko took pride in the fact that some viewers broke down in tears while looking at his work. For him this confirmed that he had communicated these "basic human emotions" and that viewers were experiencing the same heightened senses that he had felt when painting. He wanted the viewer to commune with the work, and he assumed that his paintings were imbued with an individual identity—even that they had personality.

Rothko hoped that his art would go beyond everyday experience to tap into a profound connection between us all. He had the highest aspirations for his art, and he viewed its creation as a spiritual or magical experience. He attempted to achieve this with the very simplest of means, however: through the use of large canvases of intense color. In a publication entitled *Possibilities I* (1947), Rothko writes: "The most important tool the artist fashions through constant practice is faith in his ability to produce miracles when they are needed. Pictures must be miraculous: the instant one is completed, the intimacy between the creation and the creator is ended. He is an outsider. The picture must be for him, as for anyone experiencing it later, a revelation, an unexpected and unprecedented resolution of an eternally familiar need."

Untitled *1967. Oil on canvas. 80 x 69 in (203 x 175 cm). Empire State Plaza Art Collection, Albany, NY.*

The scale of Rothko's paintings has a parallel in the theatricality that is often associated with large-scale classical and modern architecture (in the use of vast entrances and lofty ceilings, for example). His paintings fill the viewer's field of vision with an overbearing and awe-inspiring presence.

Untitled (1967) is one of the black-and-gray works that Rothko painted toward the end of his life as his depression escalated. The solemnity of this, and of all Rothko's later work, can be compared with the capacity of images in religious art, such as the image of Christ on the cross, to evoke emotion. Rothko wanted to invoke the intense feelings that are often associated with such subjects in a new way and without recourse to figurative representation.

one of the leading creators of color-field painting, the name given to abstract paintings featuring large expanses of color. But the concentration on color theory and the formal qualities of his pieces neglects the strong emotional simplicity of his work ("I paint large paintings because I want to create a state of intimacy," he once said). It distressed Rothko to have his work discussed in ways that did not connect with his intentions.

His depression is, superficially at least, paralleled in the progress of his work from the 1950s onward. The bright colors of his earlier paintings, such as *No. 15* (1952), and *Orange and Yellow* (1956), gave way to darkened tones, as in his cycle of paintings for the non-denominational chapel in Houston, Texas, or his black-on-gray paintings, including *Untitled* (1967). Rothko took his own life in his New York studio in 1970.

ROUAULT Georges

LIKE HIS CONTEMPORARY HENRI MATISSE, GEORGES ROUAULT explored the expressive possibilities of line, color, and form. In Rouault's work, however, these combine with a uniquely intense moral feeling to create images that are both visually striking and gently compassionate.

Life and work

Rouault was born in 1871 into a country and city in turmoil. France had just suffered humiliating defeat in its war with Prussia, and factional fighting had erupted in Paris. Rouault often recalled how his mother had given birth to him in the cellar of a house under shellfire.

Although his parents were not well off (his father worked as a piano varnisher), Rouault's artistic abilities were encouraged, especially through his grandfather's interest in modern artists such as Gustave Courbet and Honoré Daumier. His first job, at the age of 14, was as an apprentice in a firm of stained-glass makers. In 1890 Rouault entered the Ecole des Beaux-Arts, the state art school in Paris, and the following year became a pupil of the symbolist painter Gustave Moreau.

Moreau was a gifted teacher (his other pupils included Henri Matisse and Albert Marquet), whose work was very different from the prevailing impressionist style of the day. He painted mystical imaginary scenes with sensuous, glittering color. The young Rouault was highly receptive to the idea that art should present inner truths rather than external reality. His *Infant Jesus among the Doctors* (1894) clearly shows Moreau's influence, as well as Rouault's new commitment to Christianity in his twenties.

The master and his favorite pupil had become close friends and, when Moreau died in 1898, Rouault felt bereft. He sought new subjects in the streets, nightlife, and law courts of Paris, and himself lived in poverty. In 1901, aged 30, he spent a few months at a monastery near Poitiers, where the novelist Joris-Karl Huysmans was trying to form a spiritual and artistic community. He was also influenced by the call for social justice in the writings of Léon Bloy. Rouault's *The Meal* (1900), with its mysterious group listening to lute music by candlelight, suggests the artist's dream of a meeting of kindred spirits.

In 1903 Rouault became the first curator of the Gustave Moreau Museum, established in Moreau's former home in Paris, which gave him a small salary and somewhere to live. He also helped to set up a new annual exhibition, the Salon d'Automne, where his work was regularly exhibited. His paintings during the following decade concentrate on an impassioned exploration of several clearly defined themes: circus performers, prostitutes, and judges.

In March 1908, at the age of 36, Rouault married Marthe Le Sidanier, sister of the artist Henri Le Sidanier. He and Marthe went on to have four children. In 1910 he had his first one-man exhibition, showing 121 paintings, as well as ceramics and drawings. He had begun to paint landscapes and the human figure. His work was taken up by the influential art dealer Ambroise Vollard, who in 1913 bought up Rouault's entire studio.

Vollard ensured Rouault a regular income, and also supported new projects, such as the illustration of his own 1932 book *Les Réincarnations du Père Ubu* ("The Reincarnations of Father Ubu"). Rouault's ink and gouache "Ubu" sketches, like the nudes he produced around the same time, show a free handling of thick, fluid lines and washes that has been compared to Rembrandt's drawings in its economy and expressive power.

In the period between the two World Wars, Rouault's work was widely exhibited and his reputation grew. In addition to painting, he undertook a range of commissions, including print series, cartoons for tapestries, and stage design for the ballet *The Prodigal Son* by Sergei Prokofiev (1929), produced by the great Russian impresario Serge Diaghilev. His earlier preference for watercolor and gouache was superseded by a renewed interest in oil painting, and he often returned to earlier images, reworking them in rich, dense color. *The Old King* (1937) combines the fiery red tones of Rouault's earlier paintings of judges with the mood of resignation found in his circus pictures.

Rouault remained in France during the German occupation of World War II (in 1940 German troops raided his

Data file

Full name: Georges Rouault

Nationality: French

Style: expressionism

Dates: born 1871 in Paris, died 1958 in Paris

Key works:
- *Infant Jesus among the Doctors* 1894
- *The Meal* 1900
- *Clown with Puppet* 1903–08
- *At the Mirror* 1906
- *Judges* 1908
- *The Old King* 1937
- *The Holy Countenance* c1946

Things to look for:
- compassionate vision of suffering humanity
- expressive use of colors
- free handling of line and contour
- personal, non-naturalistic interpretation of human figure and landscape

Comparisons: Gustave Moreau, Honoré Daumier, Paul Cézanne, Henri Matisse

Glossary terms: expressionism, gouache, icon, impasto, symbolism

A compassionate vision

Rouault has the reputation of an artist who returned repeatedly to the same themes: clowns and circus people, judges, Christian imagery, the lives of the poor and oppressed. In fact, his subject matter also extended to landscapes and townscapes, self-portraits, nudes, and still lifes. What gives his work a particularly unified feeling is the artist's serious and compassionate interpretation of his subjects.

From his teacher, Gustave Moreau, he learned how to use line and color to express eloquently an inner vision without resorting to sensational effects. Rouault's long career could be viewed in terms of his handling of paint and graphic media to achieve this aim, from the delicate, blurred pastel and charcoal of *The Meal* (1900) to the built-up layers of oil paint in *The Holy Countenance* (c1946).

Clown with Puppet (1903–08) shows the lifted, deeply lined head of a male clown confronting the sketchy, almost ghostlike head of a puppet. The painting conveys tension—the pain of trying to salvage dignity from a life spent making others laugh. *The Wounded Clown* (1939) is also melancholy in mood. The theme of warm companionship, embodied in the central figure's red tunic, is outweighed by cooler tones suggesting sadness and isolation. These clowns belong inside the rowdy, sociable atmosphere of the big top, yet appear like exiles in a chilly landscape. The picture does not tell a story, or make a statement; instead it invites meditation of a kind that can lead the viewer far away from any idea of its apparent subject. This was characteristic of Rouault's art: he wanted viewers to see the emotions and vulnerabilities that lay behind the act he was portraying.

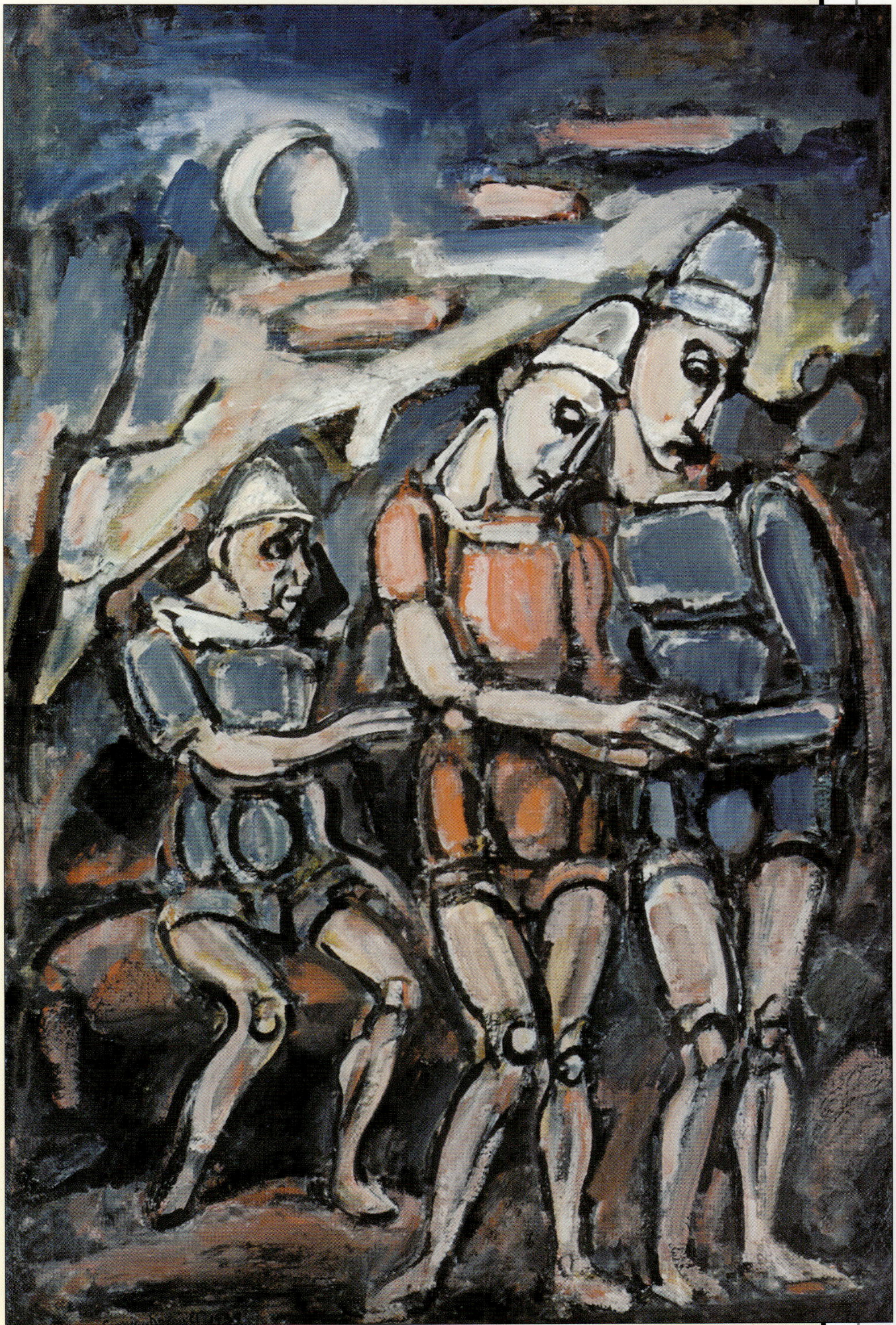

The Wounded Clown *1939. Oil on canvas. 18½ x 12 in (47 x 30 cm). Private collection.*

home). After the war his paintings often adopted simplified forms—almost iconlike in the case of *The Holy Countenance* (c1946), a head of Christ done in thick, luminous impasto.

In the later 1940s and 1950s major retrospective exhibitions of Rouault's work were held worldwide, and he was finally recognized by the Catholic Church as one of the great religious artists of his time. Characteristically, he seems not to have felt easy with fame: "How I miss my peaceful obscurity," he remarked. Rouault continued to paint into his eighties; he died in 1958.

ROUSSEAU Henri

ALTHOUGH ROUSSEAU DID NOT RECEIVE ANY FORMAL TRAINING, his innovative style impressed such famous contemporary painters as Pablo Picasso and Wassily Kandinsky. He pioneered an artistic style—later called "naïve"—that was entirely original for its time.

Life and work

Henri Rousseau was born in Laval in northwest France in 1844. Though he attended the lycée, Rousseau did not have any specialist training in art and was first employed by the French military. Later, he claimed to have traveled as far as Mexico, involved in battle and heroic adventure. However, it is now known that he probably never even left France—his adventures were the product of a vivid imagination!

By 1871 Rousseau had a job at one of the municipal toll booths at the gates in the Paris city walls, where he earned the nickname "Le Douanier" (customs officer), although he was never promoted to this position. It has been suggested that he painted and drew during the long shifts, and certainly by 1884 he regularly visited the Louvre, where he had a permit to copy works of the Old Masters.

In 1885 Rousseau exhibited two works in the Salon, the annual art exhibition in France. Because the jury held conservative views on the subject of paintings and the way they were painted, most of the critics mocked his work. Rousseau was not discouraged, and in 1886 he showed his work with the breakaway group the Salon des Indépendants; other exhibitors included Paul Signac, Paul Gauguin, Edgar Degas, and Odilon Redon. He continued to show his work with this group until his death in 1910. Critics did not change their opinions quickly, however.

At the age of 40, Rousseau took early retirement from his job with the municipal toll service and devoted his time to art. Though his paintings never altered much from their original style—featuring flat, stiff figures in odd imaginary or dreamlike settings—Rousseau did come to be highly regarded by other important artists, if not by the critics. In 1908 Picasso held a banquet in his honor in Paris; Picasso owned some of Rousseau's paintings (and later gave them to the Louvre).

Rousseau's work had begun to gain popularity by this time, but he died two years later. In 1910 an exhibition of his work was held in New York, and the following year a retrospective exhibition was held at the Salon des Indépendants in Paris.

Data file

Full name: Henri Julien Félix Rousseau

Nationality: French

Style: naïve

Dates: born 1844 in Laval, died 1910 in Paris

Key works:

- *Myself, Portrait Landscape* 1890
- *Tiger in a Tropical Storm (Surprised!)* 1891
- *War* 1894
- *The Sleeping Gypsy* 1897
- *The Football Players* 1908
- *The Jungle: Tiger Attacking a Buffalo* 1908
- *The Dream* 1910

Things to look for:

- a particular interest in painting the jungle or other densely vegetated areas; careful attention to the details and different shapes of leaves
- a simple, childlike style using bright colors and strong bold patterns
- figures that seem more like puppets or dolls
- later scenes with a strange, dreamlike quality and an exaggerated scale of plants and flowers

Comparisons: Eugène Delacroix, Wassily Kandinsky, Pablo Picasso

Glossary terms: naïve, Old Masters, Salon, Salon des Indépendants

A childlike vision of the world

Tiger in a Tropical Storm (1891), the first of Rousseau's jungle scenes, was exhibited at the Salon des Indépendants in 1891 with the title *Surprised!* Rousseau claimed that scenes like this, and others such as *The Jungle: Tiger Attacking a Buffalo* (1908), were painted from his memories of Mexico. It is now known that he never traveled to Mexico but instead studied the exotic plants and animals in the botanical gardens in Paris, where there was a tropical hothouse. He also studied prints, journals, newspapers, and illustrated books.

Interestingly, the plants that seem most magical and exotic in Rousseau's paintings are often ordinary house plants, exaggerated in scale and placed in a wild environment—the rubber plant in the bottom right-hand corner and the sansevierias along the foreground in this painting both illustrate this tendency. It has been suggested that Rousseau copied the tiger from a children's book or from a drawing by Eugène Delacroix, who also enjoyed depicting wild and exotic animals.

Although the tiger is stylized and the environment seems more like a greenhouse

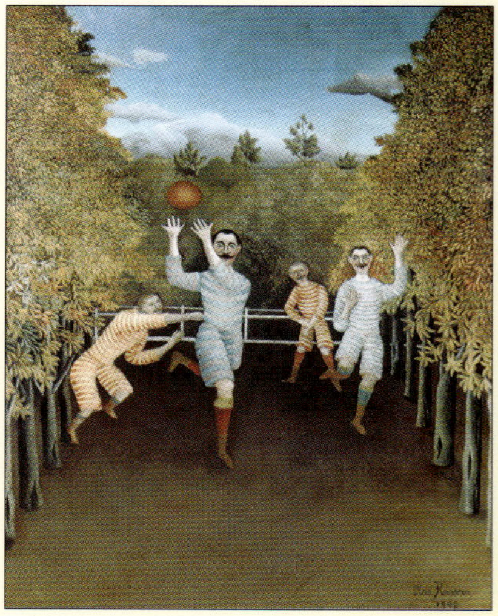

The Football Players *1908. Oil on canvas. 40 x 32 in (101.5 x 81 cm). The Solomon R. Guggenheim Museum, New York, NY.*

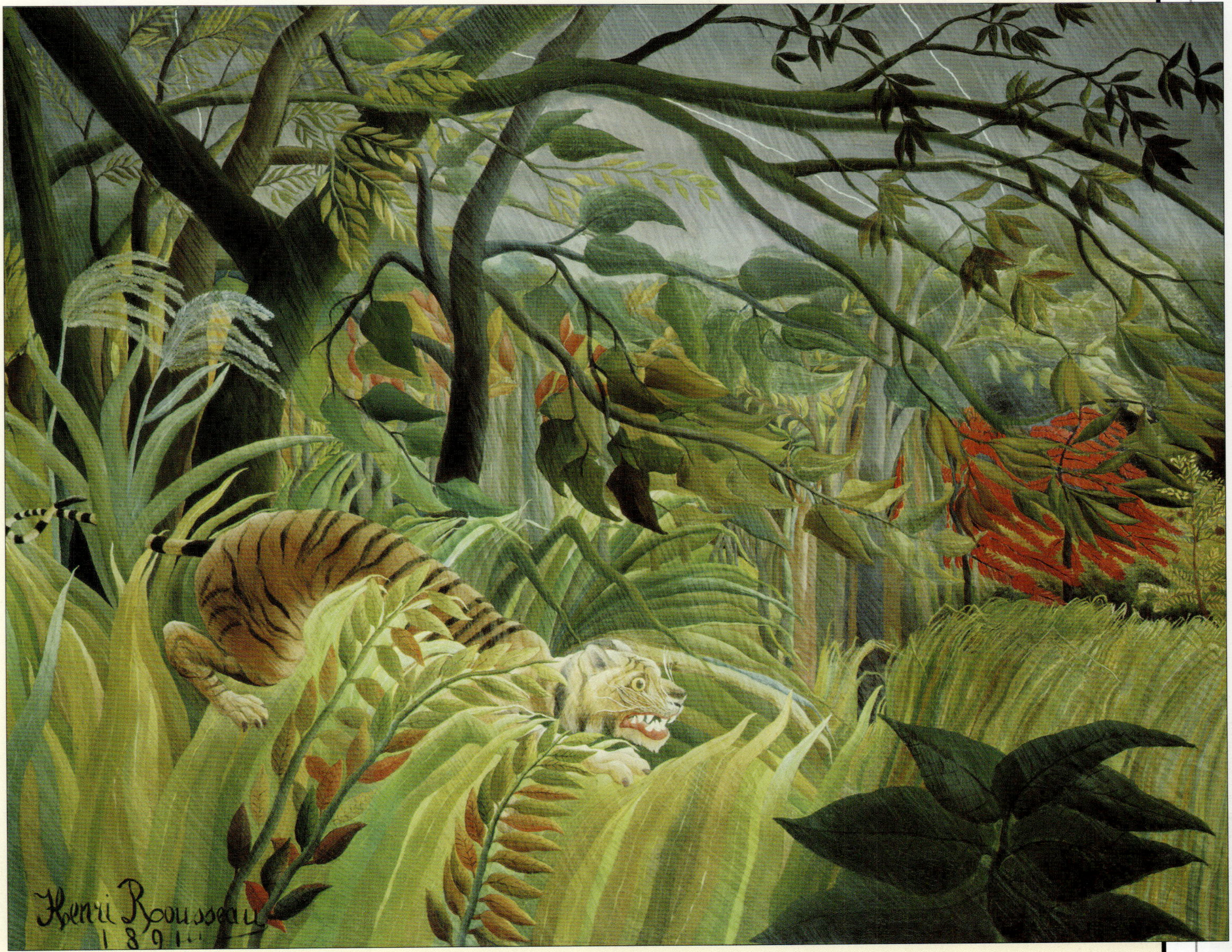

Tiger in a Tropical Storm (Surprised!)
1891. Oil on canvas. 51 x 63 1/2 in (130 x 162 cm). National Gallery, London.

than a jungle, something of the wildness and adventure of the jungle is nevertheless conveyed to us by the tangled vegetation and violent downpour. The tiger's stripes contrast with the lines of the grasses and trees; its diagonal position is echoed in the branches above it, which sweep along with the rain in a diagonal direction. Aside from a burst of vibrant red in the background, the colors are mainly greens, browns, and yellows (Rousseau once claimed to have used up to 22 different shades of green in one painting), with fine glazes of white and gray for the rain. The red is echoed in the tiger's mouth. We wonder whether it is about to pounce on an unsuspecting explorer outside the painting who has not noticed it camouflaged in the grasses, or whether the surprise is the sudden storm itself, with lightning streaking across the sky. The pattern of the leaves and branches looks like woodcarving or superimposed cut-outs.

In Rousseau's later work *The Football Players* (1908) we see men running toward us with a ball but remaining curiously static. The costumes, the number of players, their movements, and the setting are not reminiscent of any "real" soccer game. The anatomies of the men, particularly the crouching figure on the left, are exaggerated and out of proportion, and they seem more like puppets. Critics often judged this as a reflection of Rousseau's lack of formal artistic training. One journalist wrote of this painting: "The amusing Monsieur Rousseau will not abandon his attempts at infantile art, which recalls toys, the laughable shapes of wooden or gingerbread figures."

Rousseau transposed the most prosaic subject matter into the realm of foreign lands and dreams. His art was referred to as "naïve" or "childlike," and the simplicity of his style was rarely praised. It was only after his death that his talent was acknowledged.

RUBENS Peter Paul

DESCRIBED BY A CONTEMPORARY AS "THE PRINCE OF PAINTERS," Rubens was the leading northern European artist of the 17th century. He painted portraits of the great and the humble, religious and historical scenes, and landscapes of the areas he lived in. He not only executed major artistic commissions for the crowned heads of Europe, but he also became an international diplomat.

Life and work

Rubens was born in Germany, where his Flemish family had taken refuge for political reasons. When his father died in 1587, the family returned to Flanders, and Rubens spent the early part of his life in Antwerp, where he trained as an artist. He always regarded Antwerp as his home.

In 1600 he embarked on a long series of international journeys. He first traveled to Italy, remaining there, apart from one trip to Spain, until 1608. During all these travels he was able to study works of art in princely collections (there were no public museums at the time). He was much influenced by the Spanish royal collection, with its magnificent pieces by the Venetian artist Titian.

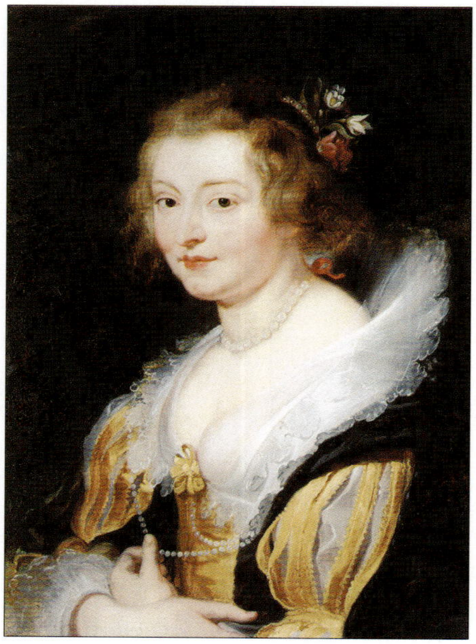

Portrait of Catherine Manners, Duchess of Buckingham *c1630. Painted panel. 25 x 18 in (64 x 46 cm). Pitti Palace, Florence.*

On his return to Antwerp, Rubens gained the patronage of Albert and Isabella, the viceroys of Spain, which ruled Flanders. From them and from the Church he received numerous commissions, which he carried out with the help of his large studio of assistants. Many of these works were altarpieces for such buildings as the Jesuit church in Antwerp and Antwerp Cathedral. Some remain in the buildings for which they were originally intended.

In addition to his large works, Rubens executed rapid oil sketches in which he worked out his ideas in paint, showing extraordinary natural feeling for the possibilities of the medium. He also produced *modelli* (finished sketches) for his patrons, and these are of the highest quality.

Rubens was very interested in architecture. The home he built for himself in Antwerp (which still survives) was intended to house his extensive collection of paintings, sculptures, books, and medals. It was also intended to illustrate the advantages of classical architecture to his northern contemporaries.

Data file

Full name: Peter Paul Rubens
Nationality: Flemish
Style: baroque
Dates: born 1577 in Siegen, Germany, died 1640 in Antwerp
Key works:
- *Marie de' Medici* cycle 1620s
- *Peace and War* 1629
- *Portrait of Catherine Manners, Duchess of Buckingham* c1630
- *An Autumn Landscape with a View of Het Steen in the Early Morning* c1636

Things to look for:
- use of pure color
- study of light
- large-scale scenes with numerous figures
- panoramic landscapes

Comparisons: Pieter Bruegel the Elder, Anthony Van Dyck, Jacob Jordaens, Antoine Watteau
Glossary terms: allegory, baroque, impressionism, *modelli*

Master of color

Although some of Rubens's allegorical paintings, with their large fleshy nudes and complicated narratives, may be hard to understand today, his acutely observed and detailed landscapes still convey the pleasure that the Flemish countryside gave him when he painted it more than 350 years ago.

Rubens spent much of his later life at Het Steen, the castle he bought in 1635 in the Flemish countryside. In *An Autumn Landscape with a View of Het Steen in the Early Morning* (c1636), painted for his own delight, he studies the effect of the light, showing it delicately rising from the right-hand side of the picture and touching every part of the landscape, including his house behind the trees to the left. A few figures can be seen, but the main interest lies in the countryside itself. Rubens is fascinated both by the great panorama, with the broad view related to the shifting clouds above, and by such details as the water, to which he gives life by the use of bold strokes of paint. This is a realistic scene, and many of the plants, such as blackberries, are recognizable.

One of the great problems of landscape painting is that of creating an effect of distance. In this landscape, Rubens places a dark mass at the front of the picture, setting the more distant areas in relief. He also arranges a series of strong linear emphases, receding into the picture space, so that the viewer's eye is gently led into the distance.

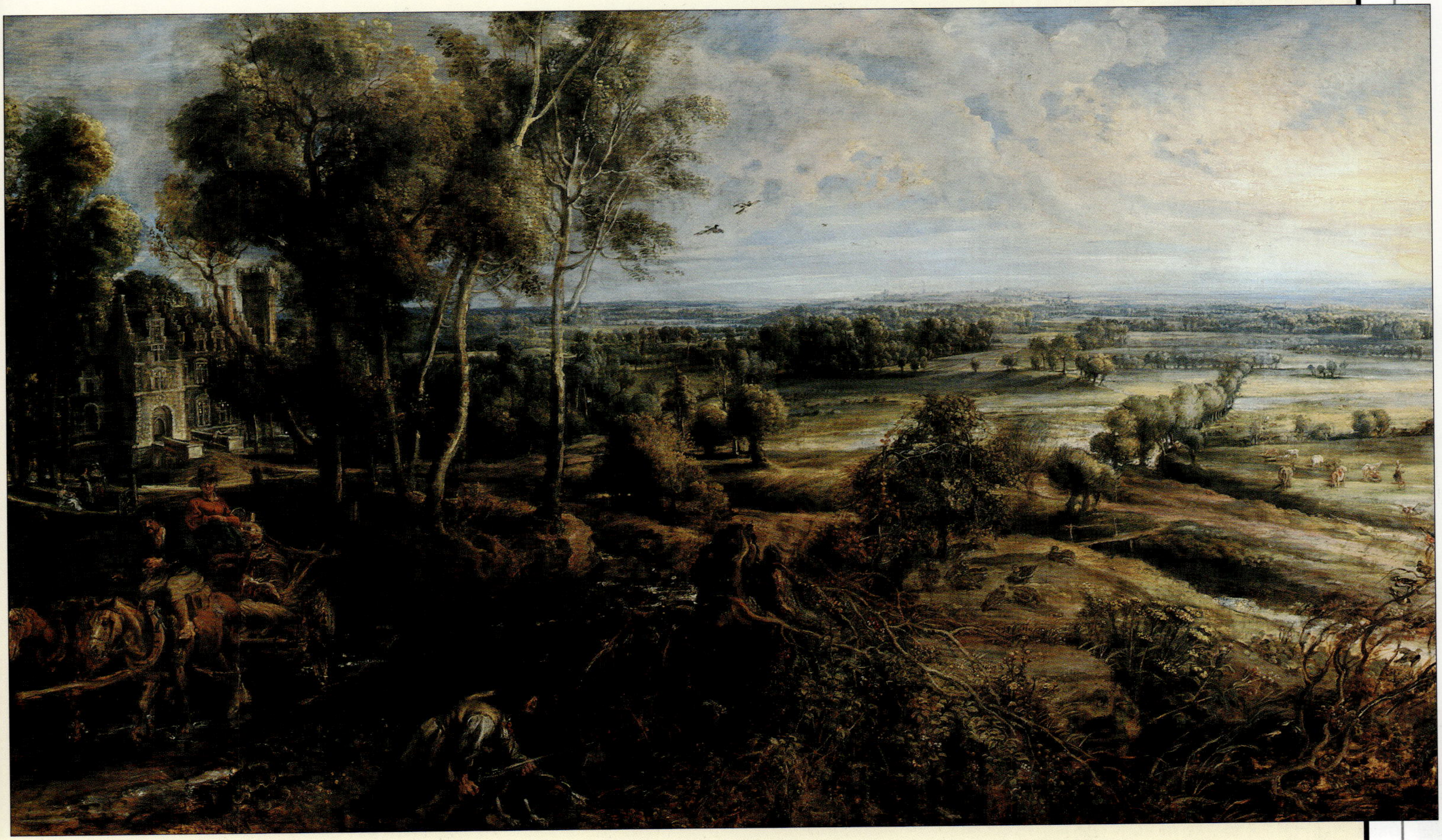

Rubens has always been admired for his mastery of color. Unlike many of his contemporaries, who created flat, demarcated areas of color, Rubens allowed his brushstrokes to remain visible. He explored the contrast of primary and complementary shades in a way that was not fully understood until the work of the impressionists in the 19th century. As a result, his finest paintings (when he was working on his own, without assistants) have an extraordinary freshness and liveliness, so that the colors sing out from the background. When art criticism emerged from the 17th century onward, Rubens was regarded as the master of color, with Nicolas Poussin as the master of design.

An Autumn Landscape with a View of Het Steen in the Early Morning *c1636. Oil on panel. 51½ x 90 in (131 x 229 cm). National Gallery, London.*

The artist was given a number of major commissions by Europe's rulers. In 1622 he was asked to paint a series of canvases celebrating the life of Marie de' Medici, the mother of the king of France. Even though her career had been inglorious, he portrayed the events of her life in a series of ambitious allegories as though they had been triumphantly successful. He also executed numerous paintings for the king of Spain, including a set intended for the king's bedroom.

But Rubens was not only an artist: he was a public figure, a friend of many of the most important people of the time. He was employed as a diplomat by the king of Spain, who, in 1629, sent him as an ambassador to King Charles I of England. This journey led to his important allegorical painting, *Peace and War* (1629), which depicts the glories of peace. He also created the ceiling paintings for the Banqueting House at Whitehall Palace. Completed and installed in 1633, this series praises the Stuart monarchy and the union of England and Scotland.

Rubens had two happy marriages and frequently painted both his wives. His first wife, Isabella Brant, died in 1626, and in 1630 he married Hélène Fourment, with whom he had a large family. In celebration of this marriage, throughout the 1630s, Rubens painted numerous portraits of his young wife and their children in family settings filled with the joy of life.

Primarily for his own pleasure, he also painted a large number of landscapes, concentrating on the countryside of Flanders. These works, which he executed without studio assistance, are some of his greatest achievements.

RUBLEV Andrei

ANDREI RUBLEV WAS A RELIGIOUS PAINTER of frescos and icons (representations of Christ, the Virgin Mary, or a saint). His special ability was to invest the figures in his works with a serenity and an intense spirituality. He achieved this through the use of delicate, flowing lines and "misty" colors.

Life and work

The facts surrounding Andrei Rublev's life are fragmentary: he is thought to have been born around 1370. As a religious painter he carried a great deal of moral authority. Icon painters were particularly revered at the time.

The production of religious icons and frescos was centered in workshops, usually attached to princes' courts or to the monasteries. Though there were some variations in style, on the whole Russian icon painting from the 11th to the 15th century remained attached to its traditional Byzantine roots, and was governed by rules regarding color, composition, and technique. Until the 16th century Russian painters did not usually sign their work, so historians have had to study styles to decide which works belong to which artist.

We know that, as a young man, Andrei Rublev became a monk at the Holy Trinity-Saint Sergius Monastery at Zagorsk, north of Moscow. Here he came under the influence of the statesman and scholar Sergius of Radonez, the founder and superior of the monastery.

While at the monastery, it is likely that Rublev became a pupil of the painter Prokhor of Gorodet. In 1405 Prokhor and Rublev are documented as assisting Theophanes the Greek, an artist newly arrived in Moscow, on paintings for an iconostasis, the richly decorated screen that separates the eastern, altar end of a Byzantine church from the nave, where the congregation sits. The iconostasis was for the cathedral of the Annunciation in the Kremlin in Moscow. Three icons from the iconostasis, now in the Tretyakov Museum, Moscow, are believed to be the work of Rublev: the *Nativity*, the *Baptism*, and the *Transfiguration* icons.

Rublev's earliest monumental works, dated around 1407–10, are two frescos in the cathedral of the Annunciation on Gorodok in Zvenigorod. The cathedral had been erected around 1400 by Prince Yury of Zvenigorod, and Rublev's frescos decorate the altar pillars. On the upper part of the south pillar is a half-length figure of Saint Laurus, and on the north pillar is a fragment of a half-length figure of Saint Florus. Both are depicted as warriors because, although they were actually the patron saints of horse-breeders, they were also, by extension, regarded as protectors of the soldiers of the cavalry.

In 1408 Rublev and his close friend Daniil Chorney (known as "Daniel the Black") were at work on decorations for the cathedral of the Annunciation in Vladimir, east of Moscow. They had been asked to replace the earlier 12th-century frescos, which had fallen into disrepair. Regrettably, most of the Rublev-Chorney frescos have also perished, though a few fragments depicting scenes from *The Last Judgment* remain; these are attributed to Rublev. In contrast to Chorney's heavy figures, Rublev's works demonstrate more precise draftsmanship, flowing lines, and elegant, delicate figures.

While at Vladimir, Rublev also painted his version of the icon of *The Virgin of Vladimir* (c1408) and the icons in the iconostasis of the church of the Savvin-Storozhevsk Monastery. It is possible that Rublev also painted the three panels depicting the figures of Saint Michael, Saint Paul, and Christ. These were only discovered in 1918 in a storeroom near the cathedral, and have been attributed to Rublev on stylistic grounds.

In about 1422 Rublev was asked to return to Zagorsk to redecorate the walls of the cathedral of the Trinity, which had been rebuilt following a fire. It was here that Rublev painted his most famous icon, the *Old Testament Trinity*. This icon is considered Rublev's masterpiece; it was painted in memory of his superior, Saint Sergius of Radonez, who had died in 1411.

Towards the end of his own life, Rublev returned to a monastic life. He entered the Andronnikov Monastery, where he died around 1430.

Data file

Full name: Andrei Rublev

Nationality: Russian

Style: late Byzantine iconographic

Dates: born c1370 in Moscow (?), died c1430 near Moscow

Key works:
- *Nativity, Baptism,* and *Transfiguration* icons for the cathedral of the Annunciation in the Kremlin, Moscow c1405
- *Saint Laurus* and *Saint Florus* frescos for the cathedral of the Annunciation on Gorodok, Zvenigorod c1407–10
- *Last Judgment* frescos for the cathedral of the Dormition at Vladimir c1408
- *The Virgin of Vladimir* c1408
- frescos and *Old Testament Trinity* icon for the cathedral of the Trinity, Holy Trinity-Saint Sergius Monastery, Zagorsk, near Moscow c1422

Things to look for:
- figures reduced to flat, silhouette-like outlines
- use of flowing lines
- soft mist appearing to overlie the paintings
- harmonious colors

Comparisons: Theophanes the Greek, Dionisius, Daniil Chorney, Prokhor of Gorodet, Aleksa Petrov

Glossary terms: Byzantine, fresco, gesso, icon, tempera

The art of the icon

The true place for an icon was on the iconostasis, the screen separating the altar in a Byzantine church from the part where the congregation gathered. Icons were placed on the screen in a set order.

First came representations of Christ and of the Virgin. These were followed by the most important scenes in the life, Passion, and Resurrection of Christ. Next came the archangels, martyrs and saints, theologians and prophets, and, finally, the apostles. The central group of the iconostasis is formed by the "deesis," which showed Christ flanked by the Virgin and Saint John the Baptist.

Rublev's *Old Testament Trinity* (c1422) icon was painted in honor of Saint Sergius of Radonez, the founder of the Holy Trinity-Saint Sergius Monastery. It was first displayed on the grave of the saint in the cathedral of the monastery. It is believed that the angel on the left symbolizes God the Father, the middle angel is God the Son, and the right-hand angel is God the Holy Ghost.

While Rublev took the scheme for the composition of his icon from Byzantine prototypes, it is his technical, artistic, and stylistic rendering of the theme that makes this icon a masterpiece. It is believed that Rublev painted his icons outdoors, in natural light. This innovation makes Rublev's colors appear more natural and transparent; the light appears to come from within the icon.

The technique of icon painting was devised to support and enhance this inner luminosity. A piece of non-oily wood was cut to the desired size and the area to be painted was hollowed out. The surface of the hollow was then roughened with a grater; side supports were placed on the reverse to keep the wood from warping. The rough surface was covered with a layer of gesso (an absorbent white base, such as chalk), and a piece of linen was laid on top. This was covered with *levkas* (a fine plaster), which formed the painting surface.

The outlines were either drawn onto the surface or could be incised into it. When that was completed, the painting proper could begin. The layers of colors (*plav*) always consisted of tempera (colored pigments mixed with a binding agent, usually egg and water), and the artist worked using a blending technique, in which dark tones were overlaid with lighter ones. When dry, the *plav* was given a coating of oil. This soaked into the *plav* and made the colors and forms softer in appearance. Because the oil absorbed dust and incense smoke over the years, the surfaces of icons grew dark.

The condition of Rublev's *Old Testament Trinity* icon is poor, and there is little remaining of the original painting: whole layers of tempera have been scraped off over the years, and the faces of the angels have been overpainted. Nevertheless, the composition remains unaltered.

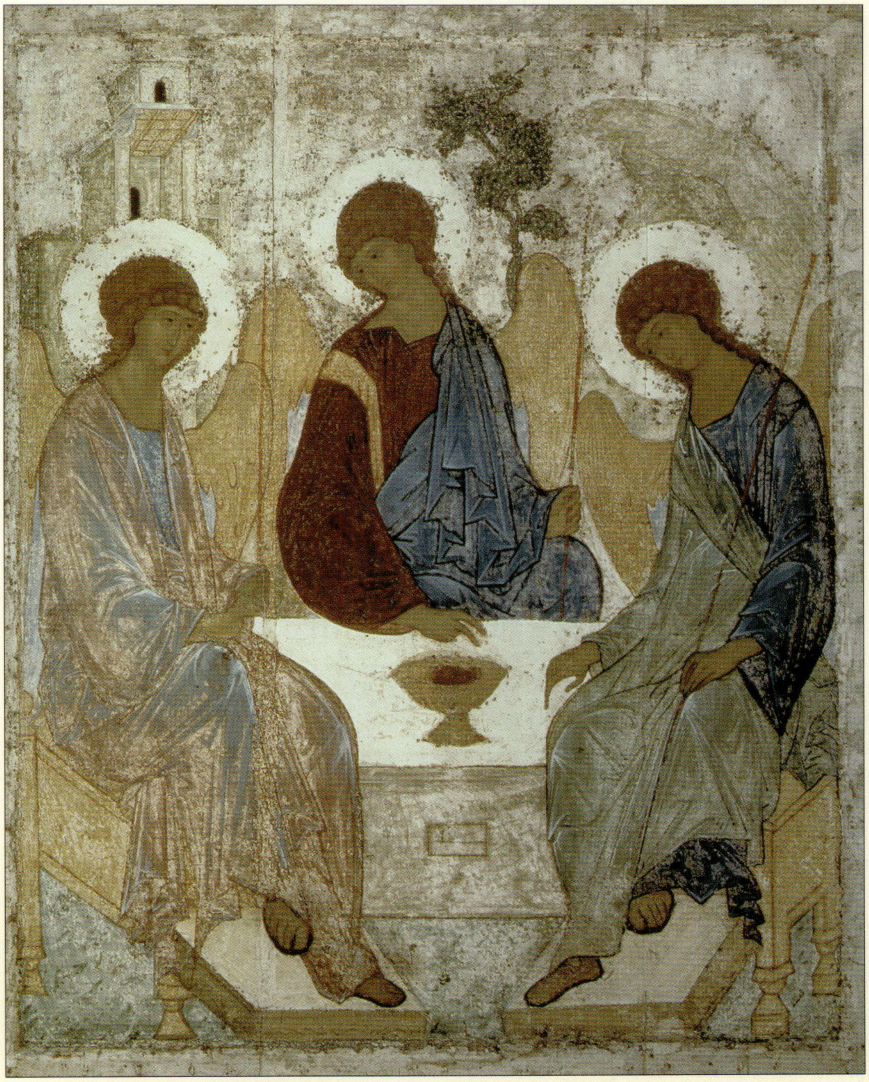

Old Testament Trinity *c1422. Tempera on panel. 56 x 45 in (142 x 114 cm). Tretyakov Gallery, Moscow.*

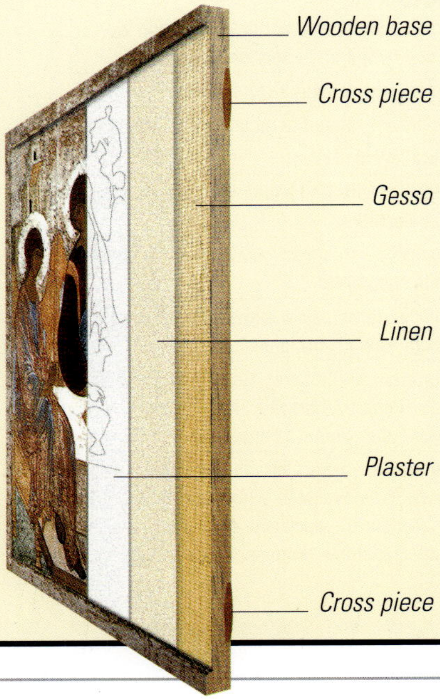

RYDER Albert Pinkham

THE LAST OF THE HIGH ROMANTICS IN AMERICAN ART, Albert Pinkham Ryder was a self-taught painter with a passionate love of color and an intensely personal style. He was one of the most original artists of his time and, decades after his death, he came to be regarded as a pioneer of modernism.

Life and work

Because of poor eyesight, Albert Ryder left school early and had no formal training in art. His first pictures, small landscapes, were painted out-of-doors in the 1860s around his birthplace, the thriving Massachusetts whaling port of New Bedford.

Data file

Full name: Albert Pinkham Ryder

Nationality: American

Style: Romanticism

Dates: born 1847 in New Bedford, MA, died 1917 in Elmhurst, NY

Key works:

Evening Glow, the Old Red Cow c1870s

Moonlight Marine c1870–90

Siegfried and the Rhine Maidens c1881–91

Toilers of the Sea before 1884

Jonah c1885–90

Macbeth and the Witches c1890–1908

Death on a Pale Horse (The Race Track) c1910

Things to look for:

- small paintings of marine scenes and works inspired by literature and the Bible
- colors laid on with a palette knife
- colors not related to natural atmospheric effect
- thick layers of paint
- organic forms and lines that relate to others in the composition
- images painted from memory and imagination, details eliminated
- familiar forms represented like elements from dreams, seen in soft, glowing light

Comparisons: Camille Corot, George Inness, Elihu Vedder, Robert Albert Blakelock, Thomas Dewing, George Fuller, John La Farge, J. Alden Weir

Glossary terms: abstract art, abstract expressionism, Armory Show, Barbizon school, engraving, Grand Tour, modernism, narrative, naturalism, Old Masters, pastoral, Romanticism, symbolism

In 1870 he moved to New York to live in the hotel his brother had opened. He applied to study at the National Academy of Design. Rejected, he had informal teaching from a New York portrait painter, William E. Marshall, and joined part-time classes in drawing from life and from antique casts. He also studied engravings, and the pastoral scenes of the Barbizon school of painters, a group of French landscape artists. Ryder began to develop an intensely personal style, marked by a childlike simplicity and an individual sense of form and color. In 1873 he showed paintings at the National Academy and met Daniel Cottier, who became his dealer and agent. Cottier secured him commissions for decorations on mirrors, cabinets, and screens.

Encouraged by Cottier, Ryder visited England in 1877, staying in London, but for only one month. Five years later, in 1882, he made a Grand Tour in the company of Cottier and the sculptor Olin Warner. Ryder's close friend J. Alden Weir noted that the artist's best memories were of crossing the Alps and returning home! In 1887 and 1896 he made two further trips to Europe. He sailed with a friend, Captain John Robinson, who recalled that Ryder spent most of his time—night and day—on deck, so that he could watch the sea and the sky.

Around 1880 Ryder began to turn away from pastoral themes to those inspired by literature, mythology, the Bible, and Richard Wagner's operas. *Siegfried and the Rhine Maidens* (c1881–91) was painted after a New York performance of Wagner's *Götterdämmerung*, while *The Temple of the Mind* (c1885) was inspired by Edgar Allen Poe's poem "The Haunted Palace" from his story "The Fall of the House of Usher" (published in 1840).

Nature still had a part to play: to Romantics like Ryder, nature was the embodiment of man's subjective self, a

Slowly ripening images

The condition of many of Ryder's paintings today is poor. In his pursuit of the jewel-like effects and deep layering of color he admired in the Old Master paintings, he would paint "lean over fat." In this method, a slower-drying layer of oily or "fat" paint was applied first, followed by a quicker-drying "lean" layer thinned with turpentine. This combination is unstable, and the surface cracks. His attempts to imitate the appearance of Old Masters also led him to use strange, unsuitable materials such as wax, candlegrease, and alcohol, held in place by copious amounts of thick varnish.

Ryder's concepts took shape slowly: he said that he carried the ideas for some of his pictures in his mind for five years before beginning to put them on canvas. He would then alter his compositions over many years, often leaving them, as he called it, "ripening" in his studio. Most of his 160 paintings remain unfinished.

Death on a Pale Horse (The Race Track) was inspired by the suicide of a waiter who worked at Ryder's brother's hotel. Sometime around 1888, the waiter had gambled and lost his life-savings on a race. The earliest record of the painting dates from about 1895, but Ryder continued to work on it until about 1910.

In *Death on a Pale Horse* we can see Ryder's creative use of symbolism. He has combined the theme of a horse running on a deserted racetrack with the more profound image of the mounted Grim Reaper (death) riding as one of the Four Horsemen of the Apocalypse (war, famine, pestilence, and death). The racecourse seems familiar, but in fact it is more like a dreamscape than a landscape. The leafless tree indicates the desolation of this place, while the serpent slithering on the ground

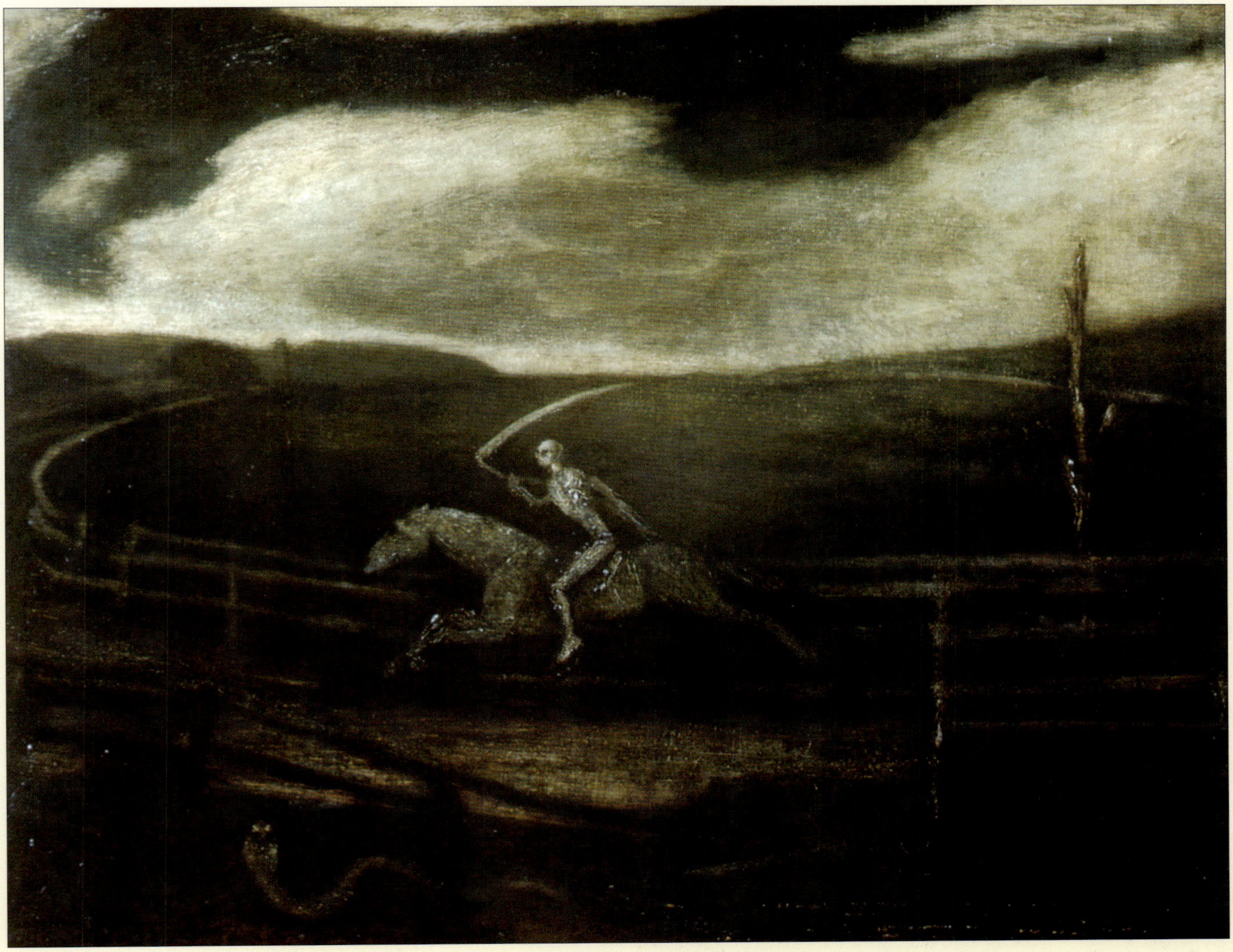

reminds the viewer of the temptations that lure men into foolhardy ventures.

Everything in this painted world is barren or inverted—the leafless tree, the fleshless horseman, the deserted track, and the bridleless horse whose hooves do not appear to touch the ground as it circles clockwise—the wrong way. We cannot even tell if it is day or night. Details that might tie the painting to an actual place, or even to reality, are obscured, and the colors are not related to any natural atmospheric effect.

In many ways, Ryder's approach to his painting foreshadowed developments associated with modernism in art. He abandoned the objective "true to nature" approach in favor of portraying subjective emotions. He was more concerned with forms and colors than with narratives. He was deeply interested in the physical properties of his materials, and he concentrated on the processes of painting.

Early pioneers of modernism and—later—abstract expressionists greatly admired Ryder's visionary work.

Death on a Pale Horse (The Race Track)
c1910. Oil on canvas. 27¾ x 35 in (70.5 x 89 cm). Cleveland Museum of Art, Cleveland, OH.

reflection of his own emotions. Except in his early years, though, he rarely painted directly from nature. It is possible that his poor vision persuaded him to rely on his "mind's eye." In paintings such as *Jonah* (c1885–90), and in the seascapes *Moonlit Cove* (c1890–1900), *Moonlight Marine* (c1870–90), and *Toilers of the Sea* (before 1884), Ryder simplified nature and made it obey the rhythms of his designs.

Ryder was a poor money manager and couldn't cope with housekeeping. His home was dirty and he slept on a piece of carpet that was rolled up in the day. He was a lover of poetry, though, and a poet himself; he never wrote for publication, however. Instead his poems were composed to accompany paintings.

In spite of his reclusive lifestyle, Ryder's work became well known. In 1913 six paintings were included in the Armory Show in New York, and in later life he saw his paintings imitated.

SARGENT John Singer

JOHN SINGER SARGENT'S WORK is reminiscent of that of the impressionists, although he was not a member of this circle of painters. After he settled in London, he painted portraits of members of Edwardian high society; his sitters are depicted wearing the most elegant fashions and within lavish interiors. He also painted landscapes, and was employed as a war artist during World War I.

Life and work

The son of an American expatriate medical doctor, Sargent was born in Florence, Italy. His family traveled around Europe throughout Sargent's childhood. When he was 18 he enrolled in the studio of Carolus-Duran, a famous Parisian portrait painter, and at the Ecole des Beaux-Arts in Paris.

Sargent achieved initial success with paintings of exotic corners of Europe. Both *Oyster Gatherers of Cancale* (1878), which depicts Breton fisherfolk at work, and *El Jaleo* (1882), which captures the drama of Spanish dancing, confirmed his reputation in Britain and France. Sargent also returned almost every year to Italy. He was particularly inspired by Venice, with its golden light, picturesque local costumes, and historical architecture. Indeed, throughout his life he traveled for several months each year, not only in Britain, Europe, and the United States, but also the Middle East.

During the 1880s Sargent began to specialize in portraiture. *Madame Gautreau* (1884), his provocative portrait of a woman wearing a *risqué* black evening gown, caused a scandal when it was exhibited at the Paris Salon of 1884. As a result Sargent left for London, where he later settled permanently. Although he was not immediately accepted by the British art world, by the 1890s Sargent had established a reputation as a portraitist of British high society. Among others, his sitters included members of the Marlborough and Wertheimer families. Sargent also painted artists such as the Shakespearean actress Ellen Terry, painters Claude Monet and Paul Helleu, and writers Robert Louis Stevenson and Edith Sitwell (as a child, with her aristocratic family). He painted many notable Americans too, including the financier J. D. Rockefeller, society beauties, and philanthropists such as Isabella Stewart Gardner.

Sargent's popularity as a society portraitist also helped him to gain several important commissions to decorate civic buildings in the United States. Alongside Pierre-Cécile Puvis de Chavannes, he was invited to create a mural decoration for the upper gallery of the Boston Public Library, which he completed in 1919. The decoration

Data file

Full name: John Singer Sargent

Nationality: American

Style: impressionism

Dates: born 1856 in Florence, Italy, died 1925 in London, England

Key works:
- *Oyster Gatherers of Cancale* 1878
- *The Daughters of Edward D. Boit* 1882
- *El Jaleo* 1882
- *Madame Gautreau* 1884
- *Carnation, Lily, Lily, Rose* 1885–86
- *Ellen Terry as Lady Macbeth* 1889
- *Lady Agnew of Lochnaw* 1893
- murals for the Boston Public Library 1895–1919
- *Gassed* 1919

Things to look for:
- paintings that convey the character of the sitter
- paintings that capture textural effects
- free brushwork and a rich palette of colors

Comparisons: Paul Helleu, Frederic Lord Leighton, Edouard Manet, Pierre-Cécile Puvis de Chavannes, James Abbott McNeill Whistler

Glossary terms: *belle époque*, chiaroscuro, impressionism, Salon

Sargent's evocative portraiture

The Daughters of Edward D. Boit (1882) exemplifies the technical virtuosity and powerful atmosphere of Sargent's portraits. This large, square painting portrays the four daughters of Edward Darley Boit and his wife, Mary Louisa Cushing Boit, prominent Bostonians who had settled in Paris. Florence (aged 14), Jane (12), Mary Louisa (10), and Julia (4), are all posed in a reception room in the family's elegant apartment in Paris. In terms of furnishings, the main features of the room are the Persian carpet and a pair of huge Japanese vases.

The composition of the painting makes it an especially fascinating portrait. Its unusual square format may have been inspired by *Las Meninas* (1656), by the Spanish Old Master painter Diego Rodriguez de Silva y Velázquez, which Sargent had copied when he visited Madrid. The placement of the four girls within the room is very striking, for they appear to be both together and apart from each other. Although their glowing, white smocks and the similarity of their faces and long, flowing hair unite them, each girl is looking in a slightly different direction and there are large expanses of open space between them. Sargent balances the feeling of freedom created by childhood's sense of endless time, but also conveys a sense of waiting, perhaps for the girls' parents to come home.

Sargent often constructed his portraits around a bold contrast of light and dark. In *The Daughters of Edward D. Boit* he achieves this contrast both through color and lighting. The Boits' daughters wear highly contrasted dark dresses and white smocks, while in the room itself, which is half-lit by the suggested window on the left and half-dark in its background depths, he has created chiaroscuro light effects.

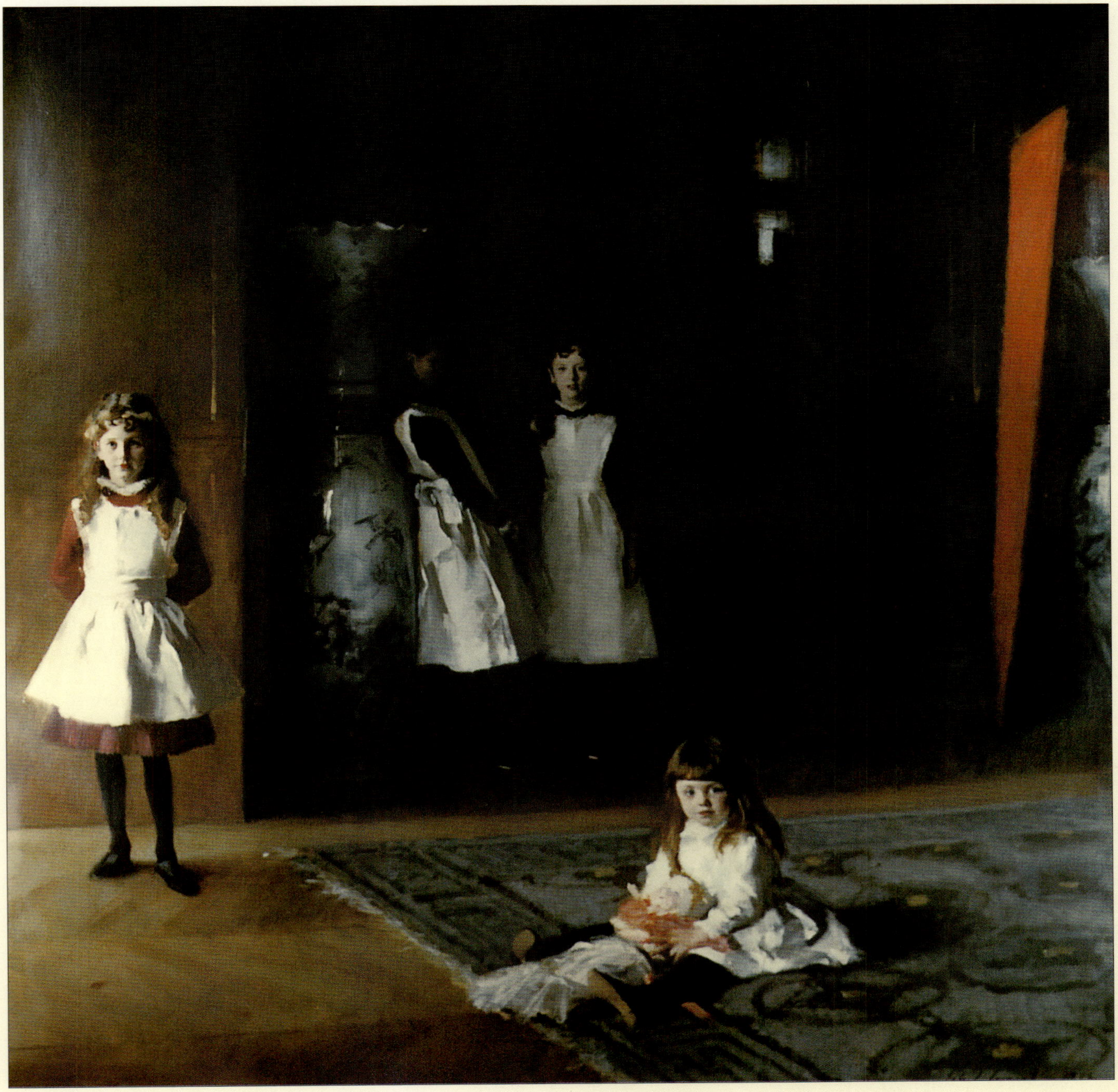

Sargent's portraits both reveal the identity of their sitters and offer thoughts about shared human experience, such as a time of life or a profession. *The Daughters of Edward D. Boit* is a meditation upon the transition from childhood to womanhood, as well as a record of the life of four sisters, each at a different stage of this journey.

The Daughters of Edward D. Boit *1882. Oil on canvas. 87 x 87 in (221 x 221 cm). Museum of Fine Arts, Boston, MA.*

represents the contribution of ancient Egypt, the Old Testament, and Christianity to literature. He spent his last years creating murals for the Boston Museum of Fine Arts.

In 1918 Sargent traveled to northern France as an official war artist. His painting *Gassed* (1919) remains a unique testament to the horror of the conflict. The vast scale and the statuesque grandeur of this, Sargent's last great work, captures the tragedy of World War I as eloquently as his portraits express the *belle époque*, the comfortable period before 1914.

SASSETTA Stefano

AN HEIR TO RICH GOTHIC TRADITIONS, Stefano Sassetta was the leading artist, with Giovanni di Paolo, in the Italian city of Siena, and was closely in touch with the ideas of Renaissance artists in Florence, Siena's great rival city. He received one of the highest fees recorded for a painting in the 15th century for his altarpiece in the church of San Francesco at Borgo San Sepolcro.

Life and work

Sassetta may have been born in Siena or in Cortona, his father's native town. It is probable that he trained as an artist in Siena, although little is known about his early life. He was certainly living and working in the city by the time he was 26. The dearth of information about the beginning of his career is not helped by the fact that many of his paintings, especially altarpieces, have either been lost or broken up.

His earliest known painting was an altarpiece painted for the Sienese guild of wool merchants in about 1426. Although the main panel is now lost, it was described in a later manuscript as showing two musician angels holding a monstrance (a special receptacle for a blessed communion wafer). The altarpiece was traditional in its Gothic shape, with several painted pinnacles above and a *predella* (plinth) with small scenes below. From the surviving *predella* panels it is clear that Sassetta was strongly influenced by Sienese painters of the 14th century—for example, Simone Martini and Ambrogio Lorenzetti. People in his paintings are long and slender, with clothes designed to emphasize elegant curling folds.

Sassetta continued the Gothic legacy through his use of rich color and pattern. However, he also demonstrated his awareness of linear perspective, which he used to define architectural space, and an interest in natural light effects, particularly in scenes showing landscapes.

The influence of contemporary developments in Florentine painting toward lifelike effects is even clearer in his next major work, a large altarpiece for a chapel in Siena Cathedral, known as *The Madonna of the Snow* (1430–33). The central panel was of the *Virgin and Child Enthroned with Saints and Angels*, but its title comes from the *predella* scenes illustrating the miracle of the snow and the building of the church of Santa Maria Maggiore in Rome.

A crucifix painted for the church of Saint Martin in 1433 was destroyed by the community of monks there in the early 19th century when they sawed it up and used the wood to make doors. This is a fate that was shared by the paintings of many other artists when tastes changed and earlier pieces were dismissed as old-fashioned and dispensable.

Sassetta received commissions for work from outside Siena. These included an altarpiece of the *Virgin and Child* with two musician angels (c1435) for the church of Saint Dominic in Cortona. His most famous work was destined for the Tuscan town of Borgo San Sepolcro: a double-sided altarpiece painted for the church of San Francesco. A contract was drawn up in 1437 and Sassetta delivered the altarpiece seven years later in 1444. Although it is no longer in one piece, most of the panels have survived so it is possible to imagine how sumptuous it must have appeared.

In overall shape it conformed to a traditional polyptych. On the front Sassetta painted the Virgin and Child with Angels flanked by four saints, two on each side, and a *predella* below. On the back he showed Saint Francis in Glory flanked on either side by a total of eight scenes from the life of Saint Francis, again with a *predella*. The amount of work required and the high quality of materials contributed to the agreed fee of 510 florins, which made it one of the most expensive altarpieces of its day. Sassetta painted it in Siena then traveled to Borgo San Sepolcro to supervise its construction on the altar.

He also worked on other projects from 1437 to 1444, including work for Siena's main institutions, such as the cathedral and the comune (the city's government). Unfortunately these do not seem to have survived. Nothing is left of his last works, which were decorative frescos for the city's new gates. The scope of the commissions that Sassetta received nevertheless confirms his high esteem among his contemporaries.

Data file

Full name: Stefano di Giovanni (later known as Sassetta)

Nationality: Italian

Style: Renaissance

Dates: born c1400 in Siena or Cortona, died 1450 in Siena

Key works:
- altarpiece for the Siena wool merchants' guild c1426
- *The Madonna of the Snow* 1430–33
- *Virgin and Child* altarpiece, church of Saint Dominic, Cortona c1435
- *Saint Francis* altarpiece for the church of San Francesco, Borgo San Sepolcro c1437–44

Things to look for:
- tall, slender figures
- richly painted clothing with cascading folds
- variety of light effects
- use of gold and silver leaf in decorative details

Comparisons: Masaccio, Fra Angelico, Paolo Uccello

Glossary terms: Gothic, linear perspective, polyptych, *predella*, Renaissance, *sgraffito*

Richness and luminosity

Sassetta's panels of scenes from the life of Saint Francis (c1437–44) are excellent examples of his assured mastery of traditional painting materials and techniques. They also show his skillful response to pictorial demands of the time.

The first panel depicts two separate episodes, which Sassetta combines, making the most of the prescribed shape. On the left Saint Francis gives his coat to a poor knight. The two men stand in the foreground on a road, which leads the eye to a walled town in the distance. The proportions of the men and the horse are reminiscent of Gothic paintings. Yet his depiction of the beautiful light of the sunset and the attention to architectural perspective indicate Sassetta's Renaissance concerns.

On the right, the architecture of the saint's bedroom frames the episode of his dream. The fact that the floating castle in the sky above is related to the dream and not the previous episode is clarified not only by its appearance but also by the pointing hand of the angel hovering over the sleeping saint. The angel confirms to Saint Francis that his dream was about his future crusade, not as a soldier but as the founder of the Franciscan order of friars.

Saint Francis is dressed as a rich youth, but his tunic would originally have looked even more luxurious. Sassetta used the technique of *sgraffito,* which involved painting over a layer of gold or silver leaf and then scraping through the paint to make a pattern revealing the shimmering metal beneath. He used maroon and silver for the saint's tunic and blue and gold for the star-studded bed canopy. Sassetta's delight in color and pattern is evident too in his painting of the bed cover, the angel's dress, and the cascading folds of the saint's coat.

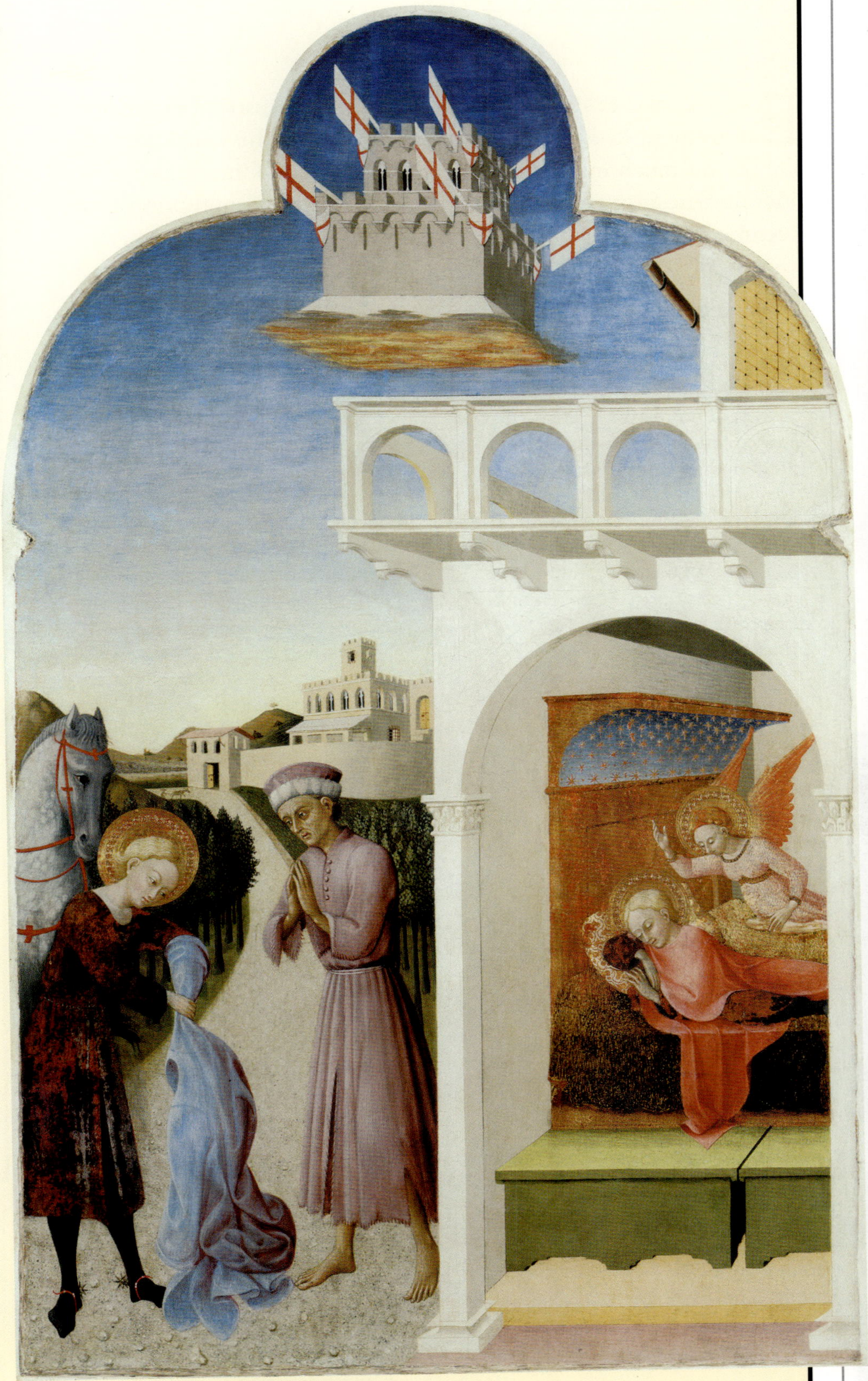

The Wish of the Young Saint Francis to Become a Soldier
c1437–44. Painted panel. 34¼ x 20½ in (87 x 52 cm). National Gallery, London.

SCHIELE Egon

EGON SCHIELE WAS A LEADING FIGURE in the Austrian expressionist movement in the early 20th century. During his tragically short life he was much inspired by the work of Gustav Klimt and the Vienna Sezession group. His work as both a painter and printmaker became highly influential on later artists.

Life and work

Egon Schiele was born the son of a railroad worker in the small Austrian town of Tulln in 1890. Schiele first showed promise as an artist during his childhood, when he regularly got into trouble for drawing during his school lessons. Following encouragement from his drawing teacher, Schiele decided to take up art as a career, and in 1906 passed the entrance examination for the prestigious Academy of Fine Arts in Vienna.

Initially Schiele's approach was fairly traditional, gaining him much praise from his teachers. However, he soon came into contact with many young artists keen to reject traditional art practices in favor of the emerging art nouveau style, known in Vienna as Jugendstil. This decorative style, characterized by an emphasis on flowing lines and organic forms, was popular throughout Europe. However, it was also rejected by many academic painters, and Schiele's adoption of Jugendstil soon brought him into conflict with many of his teachers.

At this stage Schiele was becoming increasingly fascinated by the work of fellow Austrian artist Gustav Klimt. In 1897, Klimt had been a major figure among the artists associated with the Vienna Sezession.The Sezessionen were groups of artists that abandoned the established art institutions and set up their own exhibiting societies to promote modern art.

In 1909, together with several fellow students, Schiele left the Academy of Fine Arts and established a group known as the New Art Group. Despite its brief existence, the New Art Group enabled Schiele to exhibit his work from an early age. Schiele's early works drew heavily from Klimt, whose own decorative paintings were influenced by a number of sources, including the art of Japan and the Byzantine Empire. Klimt also used unusual decorative materials, including metallic paint. Schiele soon adopted a similar approach, as can be seen in his portrait, *Arthur Roessler* (1910).

By 1911 Schiele had left Vienna for Krumau, his mother's home town, where he produced several works representing local scenes. In these he exaggerated the forms of the buildings, elongating their facades and giving an impression of tension and claustrophobia. The images resembled those of the German expressionists. By introducing contorted forms, Schiele hoped to convey a sense of individual emotional intensity, as if the inner

Data file

Full name: Egon Schiele

Nationality: Austrian

Style: expressionism

Dates: born 1890 in Tulln, died 1918 in Vienna

Key works:

- *Grimacing Man (Self-portrait)* 1910
- *Arthur Roessler* 1910
- *Eduard Kosmack* 1910
- *The Poet (Self-portrait)* 1911
- *The Self-seers II (Death and Man)* 1911
- *Transfiguration (The Blind II)* 1912
- *Self-portrait with Chinese Lantern Plant* 1912

Things to look for:

- bold, expressive brushstrokes
- dramatic, convulsive gestures
- masklike faces with haunted expressions
- figures set against vague, undefined backgrounds

Comparisons: Gustav Klimt, Vincent Van Gogh, Edvard Munch, Oskar Kokoschka

Glossary terms: Academy, art nouveau (Jugendstil), expressionism, Vienna Sezession

Haunted and haunting images

One of Schiele's most powerful and haunting images is *The Self-seers II (Death and Man)* (1911). The painting depicts the figure of a man, possibly the artist himself, seen from the front. His body, cloaked in black, seems thin and emaciated, and his face is gaunt and sickly. The deeply set eye-sockets and sunken cheeks are reminiscent of a skull rather than the head of a living being. Behind this figure floats the ghostly apparition of Death. This shadowy figure is represented in pale tones, yet is a replica of the man himself. The arms of Death are wrapped around the living being, as if in an embrace. Here Schiele seems to foresee his own death, representing his own sickly self and its future ghostly condition.

Schiele uses several stylistic devices to emphasize this mood of somberness and anxiety. Both figures are exaggerated and elongated, giving them an unreal appearance. Their faces are masklike, and the arms of Death are dramatically posed in a wild, convulsive gesture. The brush-strokes in the picture are frenetic and full of energy, as if the artist is experiencing emotional turmoil while painting. The background is depicted in dark, earthy tones and seems insubstantial and ethereal.

Many of Schiele's figure studies and portraits emphasize this sense of sickness and decay. In this way they are reminiscent of the paintings of Norwegian artist Edvard Munch, whose haunting work has been linked to the social anxieties that prevailed at the turn of the century.

The Self-seers II (Death and Man)
1911. Oil on canvas. 31¾ x 31½ in (80.5 x 80 cm). Leopold Collection, Vienna.

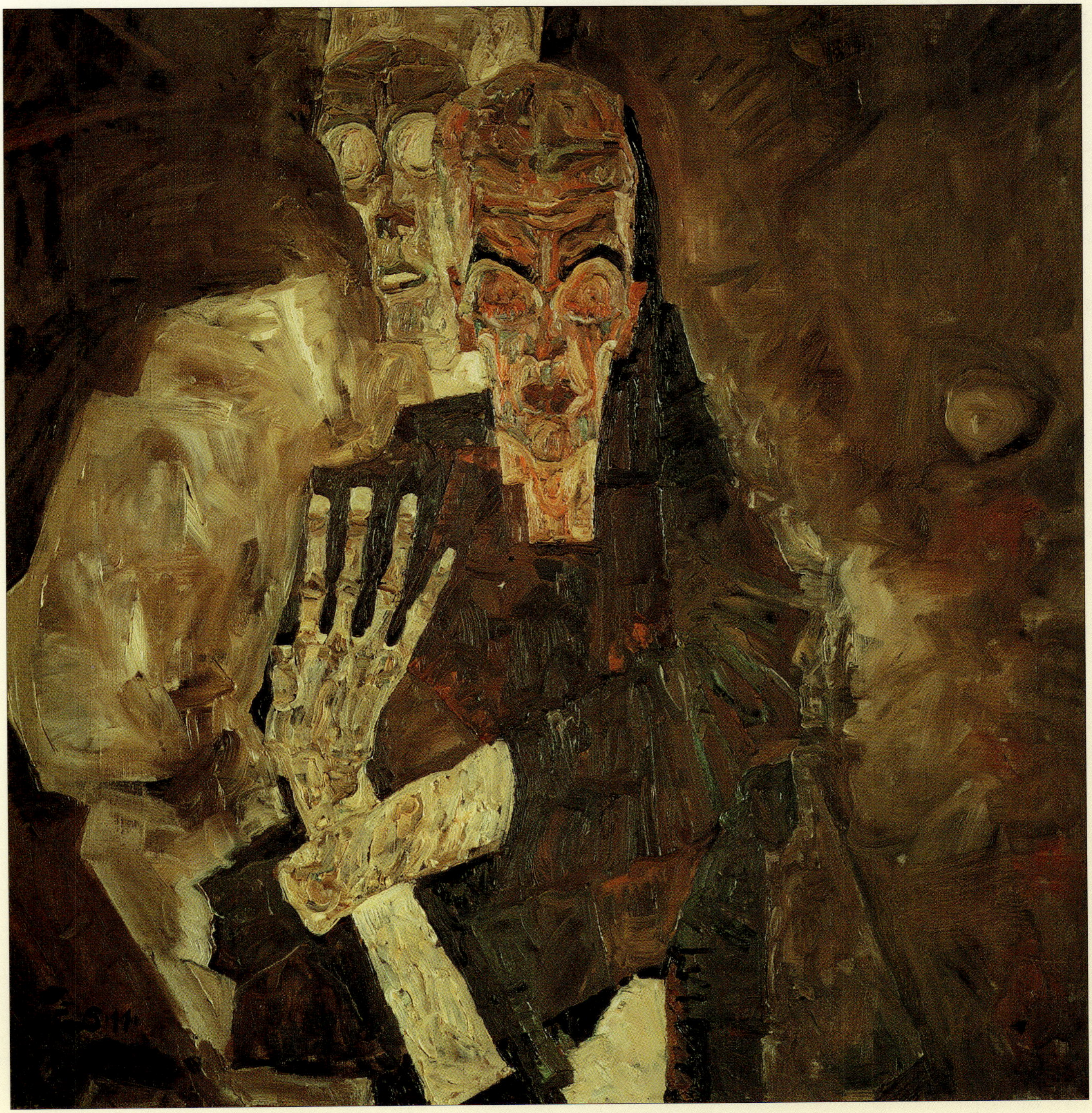

feelings of the artist could be seen in the forms of the physical world. These tense, contorted forms were also present in his numerous portraits and self-portraits from this time, in which the sitter is shown grimacing or staring into space, holding his hands in clumsy, awkward postures that indicate alienation and anxiety. Schiele usually leaves the background to these portraits blank, suggesting loneliness and isolation.

By 1912, Schiele had moved back to Vienna. The start of World War I inevitably restricted his opportunity to paint, and in 1915 he joined the army. Toward the end of the war, Schiele was beginning to secure both financial security and critical success after several major European exhibitions. In 1918, however, during the epidemic of influenza that followed World War I, the artist contracted the virus and died aged only 28.

SEGAL George

George Segal came to prominence during the early 1960s, when he began making roughly sculpted casts of the human body. His figures were set in mundane situations, yet it was their very ordinariness that provoked perplexed, even outraged, reactions from those who saw his work.

Life and work

Although he was born in 1924, it was not until the early 1960s that Segal had any impact on the art world. He had a lengthy, but intermittent, artistic training at the Cooper Union, Pratt Institute of Design, New York University, and Rutgers University. He also studied literature and philosophy. His artistic training principally centered on painting, which he began to teach during the 1950s (he also farmed chickens in New Jersey in order to make a living).

Although the style of his work at this time was a form of figurative painting, he began to try to incorporate a greater physicality and spatial sense into his work. This change of style was partly due to the influence of Allen Kaprow and Claes Oldenburg, who were regularly staging "happenings" and creating "environments" by the end of the 1950s.

It was at this stage in his career that Segal came up with his first stylistically original sculpture, *Man at a Table* (1961). The work involved the use of medical bandages soaked in plaster, which Segal wrapped around either his own, or a model's, body in much the same way as a broken limb is bound after it has been set.

Segal's choice of subject matter is significant, if only for its apparent insignificance. He typically opted to focus on a single figure or a group of people in the most commonplace of situations, in works such as *Man at a Table*, *The Bus Riders* (1962), and *The Laundromat* (1966–67). Although actions such as sitting at a table, in a bus, or in a laundromat take up much of our lives, they are often dismissed as insignificant. Yet just as psychoanalysis had focused on such details of everyday life earlier in the 20th century, so Segal's concentration on mundane activities mined a rich seam of artistic potential. Such daily activities had not been artistically "frozen" in this manner before, without pretensions to grander themes or a greater sense of drama. Segal's work separated a moment of everyday life from its wider context and then set it apart for contemplation and study.

Throughout the 1960s and early 1970s, Segal continued to explore a seemingly inexhaustible supply of everyday scenarios in pieces such as *The Dancers* (1971–73) and *Hot Dog Stand* (1978). His repetition of banal events assumed increasing significance as his output grew, and between 1971 and 1972 a major retrospective exhibition of his sculptural work was shown throughout Europe.

In 1973 Segal started working on public commissions, which necessitated the use of a more permanent medium than plaster, such as bronze. These pieces were the most contentious when

Data file

Full name: George Segal

Nationality: American

Style: pop art

Dates: born 1924 in New York

Key works:

Man at a Table 1961

The Bus Riders 1962

Cinema 1963

The Laundromat 1966–67

The Dancers 1971–73

The Holocaust 1982

Things to look for:

- oversized, leaden bodies
- rough surfaces
- the banality of his figures' activities

Comparisons: Claes Oldenburg, Tom Wesselmann, Edward and Nancy Kienholz, Gilbert and George, Duane Hanson, Kiki Smith

Glossary terms: assemblage, environment, happening, impasto, pop art

Art in plaster and bandages

During his early career, Segal's figurative paintings had grown out of the influence of abstract expressionism, the abstract art movement that grew in the United States in the 1940s. By 1958, however, Segal had become increasingly frustrated by the constraints of working in two dimensions. He turned his attention to the process of assemblage, in which the art object is built up from three-dimensional "found" materials.

Inspired by shop-window mannequins, Segal began to make three-dimensional figures from armatures (supporting frameworks) of wire mesh covered in burlap dipped in plaster. In 1962 he turned to casting from live models (he usually used his friends or relatives) using bandages soaked in plaster. When dry, the thin plaster layer was removed in sections, reassembled and painted white. The resulting figures are not smooth like a cast, but have a rough and uneven surface that is similar, in fact, to the impasto paintings of Segal's earlier career. The true likeness of the model is invisible, appearing on the inside of the casts, while the rough monochrome of the exterior surface of the figures reduces their naturalism. This makes them anonymous, heightening the sense of human isolation in modern urban life that is at the heart of Segal's work.

The life-size figures are posed as if they are caught in the act of performing everyday, mundane activities. Sometimes these activities are private ones, such as bathing; other times, as in *The Bus Riders*, or *Cinema* (1963), the figures are depicted in a public setting. Segal closely observed how people move. In a 1964 interview with the *New York Herald Tribune*, Segal spoke of how the human body was capable of an infinite number and variety of gestures and attitudes: "My job is to select and freeze the gestures that are most telling," he said. "I try to capture a subject's gravity and dignity."

Segal placed his finished figures alongside real objects, such as the soda fountain, coffee cups, and fluorescent light of *Diner* (1964–66), the Coke machine and tires of *The Gas Station* (1963), or the illuminated Plexiglas of *Cinema*. This was to emphasize the fact that the figures were also "manufactured." The spaces Segal created have distinct fronts and backs, rather like a stage set. Unlike conventional sculpture, Segal's work is more an extension of painting and relief.

The white-painted figure of a man arranging letters on the front of a movie house in *Cinema* is eerie and anonymous. His actions have been frozen, and he seems unaware that he is being observed. The figure contrasts strongly with—and seems strangely insubstantial within—the environment constructed from real, architectural elements. Like the actions of the figure, the setting is equally everyday, impersonal, and manufactured, and it competes for the viewer's attention.

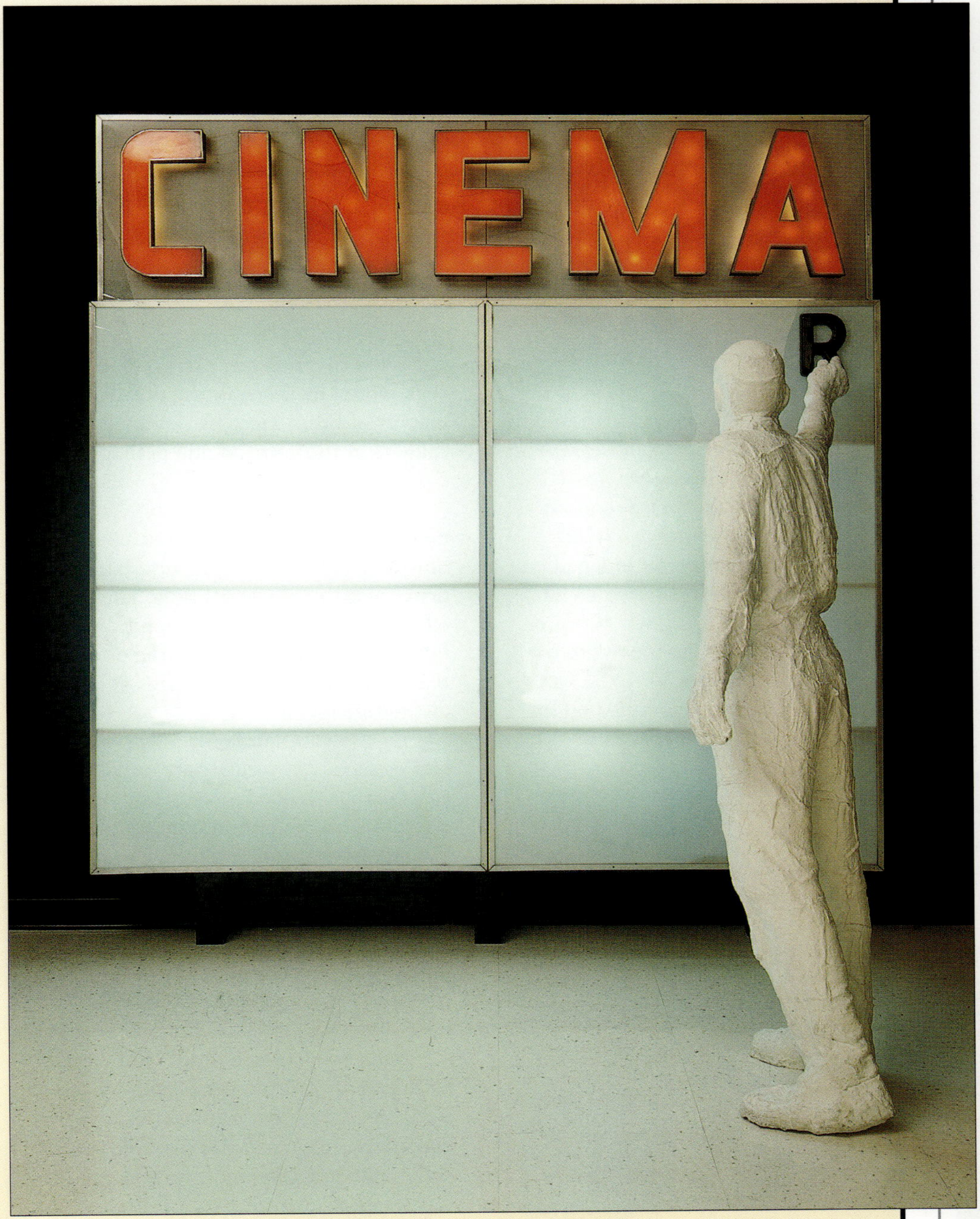

Cinema *1963. Plaster, illuminated Plexiglas, and metal. 118 x 96 x 30 in (300 x 244 x 76 cm). Albright-Knox Art Gallery, Buffalo, NY.*

they depicted religious themes in relation to contemporary events. Such works included *The Sacrifice of Isaac* (1973), a theme that he returned to in *In Memory of May 4, 1970, Kent State: Abraham and Isaac* (1978), a memorial to students who had been killed by the National Guard when staging an anti-Vietnam War demonstration in 1970. His sculpture *Gay Liberation* (1980), a public work intended for a park in New York, incited hostility on all sides. Some people were opposed to what they regarded as its celebration of homosexuality, while others believed Segal had produced a narrow and somewhat timid representation of sexuality, as the piece featured two young, Caucasian couples, one male and one female.

Segal's most successful public work is arguably *The Holocaust* (1982), which stands in Golden Gate Park in San Francisco. Recalling the horrific events that occurred at the Nazi concentration camps, it depicts a pile of prone bodies lying behind a barbed-wire fence with a lone survivor standing by dejectedly. The abiding connection between this late work and his earlier pieces is the consistent isolation of the human figure. It is this that imbues all of his work with a degree of sadness.

SEURAT Georges

DURING THE 10 YEARS BEFORE HIS EARLY DEATH IN 1891, Seurat developed and refined a distinctive new painting technique. Through his theory of divisionism, he combined impressionist light and color with a rigorous intellectual approach, creating images that are both calmly monumental and luminously vivid.

Life and work

Georges Seurat was born into a middle-class Parisian family. His father was a *huissier,* or bailiff; his astute financial management meant that Seurat always had a small private income, which allowed him to pursue an independent path in his art. At the age of 15 he entered a local drawing school; three years later, in 1878, he moved to the Ecole des Beaux-Arts.

In 1879 Seurat was called up for military service. He managed to commute his three-year term to one year, which he spent in the northern seaport of Brest. Here he sketched soldiers in the garrison and perhaps conceived his feeling for seascapes.

After returning to art school, Seurat concentrated for two years on drawing, using conté crayon (a hard, dry crayon) to create subtle tonal effects. His portrait of his friend Edmond Aman-Jean, exhibited at the Salon in 1883, exemplifies this very distinctive technique.

By the 1880s impressionism, which had seemed so revolutionary only 10 years earlier, needed a new sense of direction. Seurat consciously adopted the airy freshness of impressionist color, applied in short, light brushstrokes, and gave it a more intellectual dimension through the application of color theory. He saw himself as a pioneer whose carefully thought-out painting style would open up new possibilities for art.

After producing a series of oil paintings of country scenes and landscapes, by 1883 Seurat was ready to embark on his first major painting. He made numerous preparatory drawings and small oil paintings for his *Bathers at Asnières*, but nothing quite anticipates the scale and impact of the finished picture, which measures over 6 feet by 9 feet. It shows workers relaxing on a summer's day by the banks of the River Seine as it flows through the industrial suburb of Asnières outside Paris. The shimmering, monumental stillness of Seurat's work announced the arrival of a formidable new talent when it was exhibited in 1884.

Almost immediately Seurat began work on a second large work, *A Sunday Afternoon on the Island of La Grande Jatte* (1884–86). It was praised by the critic Félix Fénéon, who coined the term "pointillism" to describe Seurat's technique. (This, rather than Seurat's own term, "divisionism," became most often used).

A trip to Honfleur in 1886 resulted in *Harbour Entrance, Honfleur,* and

Data file

Full name: Georges Pierre Seurat

Nationality: French

Style: neoimpressionism/pointillism

Dates: born 1859 in Paris, died 1891 in Paris

Key works:

Bathers at Asnières 1883–84

A Sunday Afternoon on the Island of La Grande Jatte 1884–86

Harbour Entrance, Honfleur 1886

The Models 1886–88

The Parade 1887–88

The Circus 1890–91

Things to look for:

- distinctive "shadowy" drawing technique using conté crayon
- impressionist subject matter, including open-air scenes, landscapes, seascapes, and popular entertainments
- development of "pointillist" painting technique, using small touches of pure color
- strong, static compositions

Comparisons: Claude Monet, Paul Signac, Paul Cézanne, Vincent Van Gogh

Glossary terms: conté crayon, divisionism, impressionism, neoimpressionism, pointillism, realism

A luminous mingling

Two major traditions in 19th-century French art, realism and impressionism, took their cue from painters' direct observation of the world around them. From the start, Seurat's approach was different. His "divisionism" was based on complex theoretical interpretations of the workings of color and line.

Painted early in his career, the large works that established his reputation, *Bathers at Asnières* (1883–84) and *A Sunday Afternoon on the Island of La Grande Jatte* (1884–86), show how he made the transition from impressionistic blending of colors on the canvas toward a full expression of the divisionist principle of "optical mingling," in which small touches of pure color are not mixed but placed side by side on the canvas. When the picture is viewed from a certain distance the colors blend together. The critic Fénéon described the effect: "Isolated on the canvas, these colors recompose on the retina...." This method was supposed to make the colors appear much more luminous than if they had been mixed on the palette. Earlier artists had been aware of this process, but Seurat was the first to exploit it systematically in his work.

Whereas the impressionist art of Seurat's contemporaries was concerned with passing, momentary perceptions, these scenes of ordinary Parisian life have a timeless quality. They invite the viewer to inspect the picture carefully, as Seurat painted every detail with equal attention.

The divisionist technique is more evident in *A Sunday Afternoon on the Island of La Grande Jatte,* which also has several puzzling features. For example, the wind on the river seems to be blowing in two different directions, judging by the

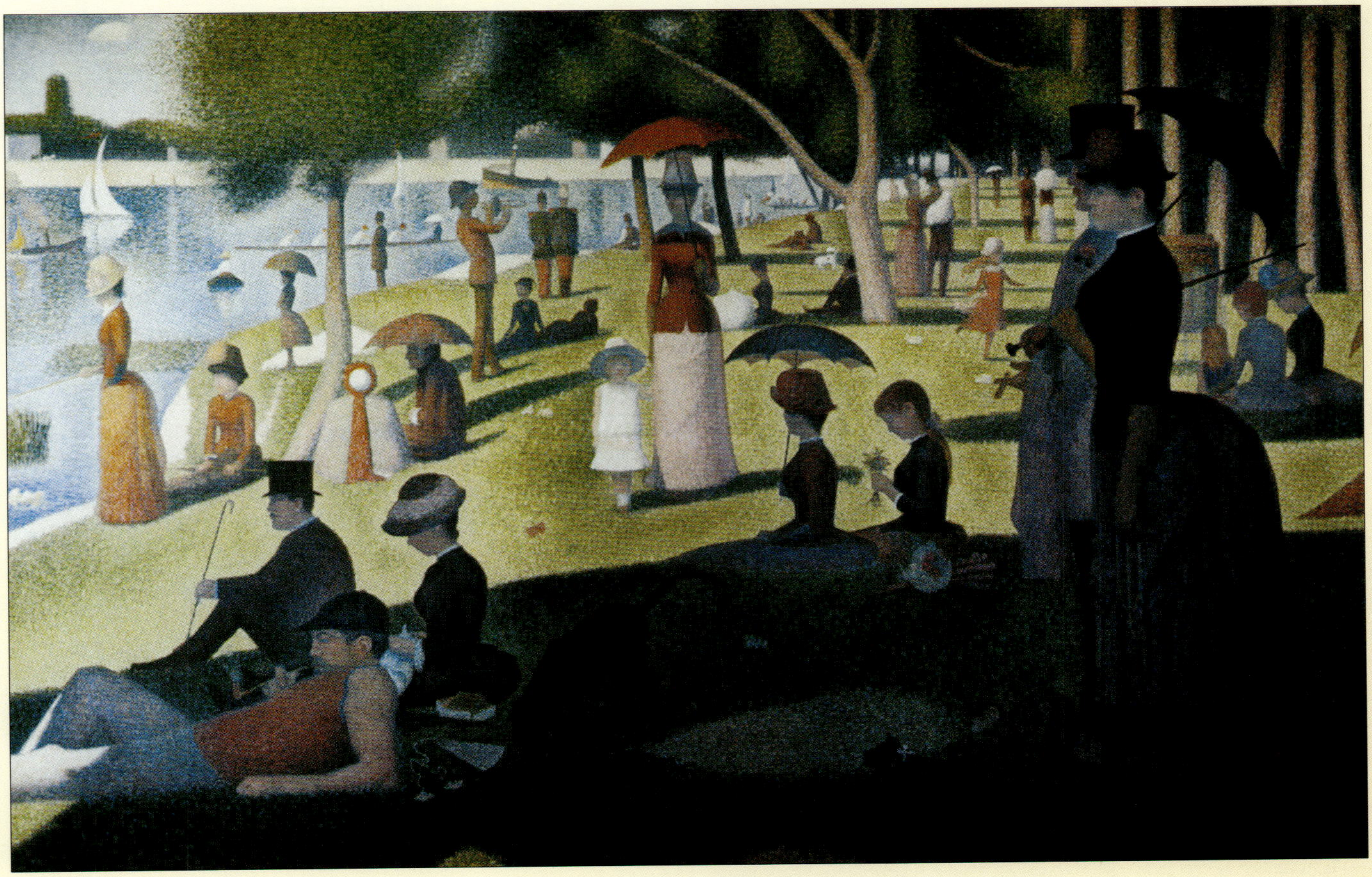

A Sunday Afternoon on the Island of La Grande Jatte *1884–86. Oil on canvas. 81¾ x 121¼ in (207.5 x 308 cm). Art Institute of Chicago, Chicago, IL.*

sails and the smoke from the steamers; and the couple standing in the foreground are huge compared to the seated woman and man in a top hat in front of them. These discrepancies cannot be accidental, as we know how thoroughly Seurat prepared these works. In fact they embody the startling truth, central to his work, that the eye and brain respond to visual stimuli quite independently of reason.

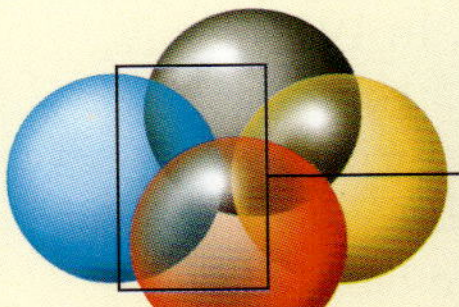

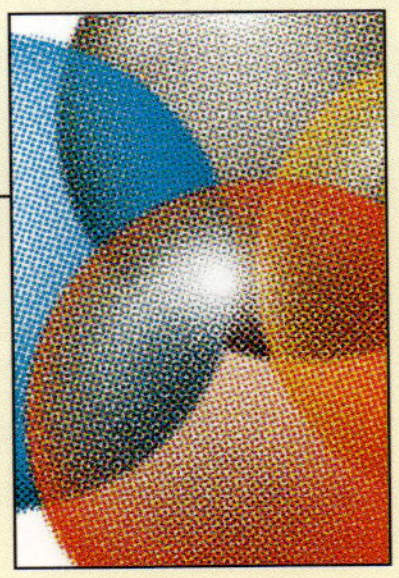

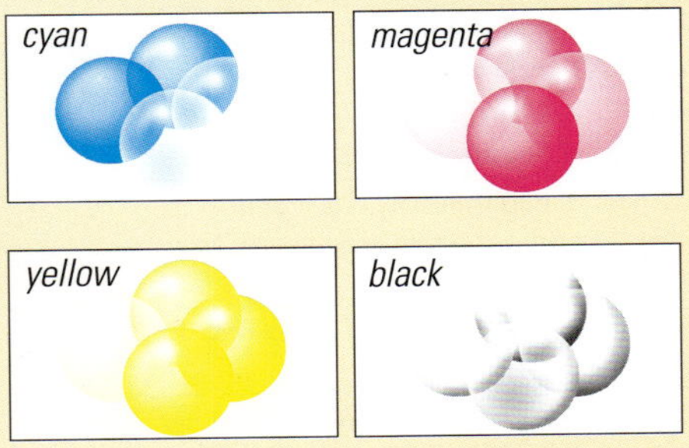

Halftone color printing *In his use of "optical mingling," in which pure dots of color are juxtaposed and merge in the viewer's eye, Seurat anticipated the method later used to print color images. In color printing, the image is converted into a series of dots of different sizes (halftone) to convey different densities of tone. A halftone image is then produced for each of the four basic printing colors: cyan, magenta, yellow, and black. When printed, the colored dots combine in the viewer's eye to create the effect of a full color image.*

other works composed with multitudes of distinct dots of color, his most determined application of divisionism to date. Seascapes continued to absorb Seurat in the last three years of his life, culminating in a masterly series of paintings of the shipping channel at Gravelines. During this time he also produced three major paintings of circus and cabaret scenes: *The Parade* (1887–88), *The Uproar* (1889–90), and *The Circus* (1890–91, unfinished). In these Seurat balances light and dark forms, and vertical, horizontal, and curving lines; he believed that line, like color, could be employed to achieve very precise effects. The upward curves of the acrobats' limbs in *The Circus*, for example, were probably intended to convey gaiety.

It is impossible to be certain of his thoughts, however. Seurat was intensely secretive about both his art and his personal life. At his sudden death in 1891, hardly anyone in his circle was aware that he had a mistress, Madeleine Knobloch, and a young son.

SHAHN Ben

ONE OF THE MAJOR FORCES IN AMERICAN REALIST PAINTING, Ben Shahn alternated between symbolism and a form of realism that used exaggerated figures. Shahn took as his subject the human experience: his frescos, easel paintings, and posters express his concern for social reforms, making his works powerful protests against injustice and inhumanity.

Life and work

Born in Lithuania in 1898, Ben Shahn emigrated with his family to the United States in 1906 and settled in Brooklyn, New York. Between 1913 and 1917 Shahn attended high school at night and worked as an assistant to a lithographic printer during the day. Until around 1930, Shahn continued to support himself through lithography.

Data file

Full name: Ben Shahn

Nationality: American

Style: social realism

Dates: born 1898 in Kovno, Lithuania, died 1969 in New York, NY, United States

Key works:

The Passion of Sacco and Vanzetti 1931–32

fresco mural in the community center of a federal housing development in Roosevelt, New Jersey 1937–38

fresco mural in the Bronx Central Annex Post Office, New York 1938–39

fresco mural in the Federal Security Building, Washington, D.C. 1940–42

Red Stairway 1944

Allegory 1948

The Lucky Dragon (series) 1960–62

Things to look for:

- depictions of contemporary life
- heightened colors for emotional impact
- exaggerated features, almost to the point of caricature, and distorted physical scale

Comparisons: George Grosz, Diego Rivera, Francisco Goya, Philip Evergood, Peter Blume, Jack Levine, Reginald Marsh, Moses Soyer

Glossary terms: abstraction, allegory, expressionism, easel painting, fresco, gouache, lithography, magic-realism, realism, social realism, tempera

Shahn traveled to Europe and North Africa in 1925 and again in 1927. Back in New York in 1929, he exhibited his watercolors of North African scenes and completed a series of 12 border illustrations for an edition of a *Haggadah*, the book containing the liturgy of the Seder service for the Jewish festival of Passover.

In 1931 Shahn came to public attention through a series of 23 gouaches and two large panel paintings that took as their subject the two Italian-American anarchists Nicola Sacco and Bartolomeo Vanzetti, whose trials and executions in 1927 caused worldwide indignation. In 1932 he completed a group of 15 gouaches and a tempera panel on the case of labor leader Tom Mooney, who was accused of involvement in a bombing.

Shahn's work was admired by the Mexican mural painter Diego Rivera, who asked Shahn to assist him on a fresco for the lobby of the RCA Building in the Rockefeller Center, New York. Although the fresco was destroyed soon after completion because of its political content, Shahn became fascinated with the medium.

In 1937 Shahn was commissioned by the Farm Security Administration to paint a large, single fresco in the community center of a federal housing project for garment workers in Roosevelt, New Jersey. The fresco depicts the arrival of immigrants to the United States—including Albert Einstein—after fleeing persecution in Europe; scenes of sweatshop labor and the disastrous Triangle Shirt factory fire; and images of social reform symbolized by new homes and better working conditions.

For a commission from the U.S. Treasury in 1938, Shahn—with his wife, Bernarda Bryson—painted 13 large fresco panels on the theme of industry and agriculture for the main lobby of the Bronx Central Annex Post Office in New York. From 1940 to 1942, Shahn concentrated on frescos for the main corridor of the Federal Security Building in Washington, D.C.

In 1941, after the United States' entry into World War II, Shahn joined the graphic arts division of the Office of War Information. He produced a number of outstanding posters and painted several works in which he demonstrated his sympathy for the plight of the ruined countries and people involved in the war.

After the war, Shahn turned to allegory and symbolism and became more interested in what he called "personal realism." In 1948 *Harper's* magazine asked Shahn to illustrate an account of a Chicago tenement fire in which a tenant called Hickman had lost four children. Hickman had then killed his landlord, who he believed had deliberately started the fire. Unlike the more realist documentation of the Sacco–Vanzetti case, in *Allegory* (1948) Shahn symbolized the tenement fire as a raging beast under whose belly lie Hickman's dead children.

In 1962 Shahn completed what many regard as his finest series, collectively known as *The Lucky Dragon*. The numerous drawings and 11 oils were inspired by the tragedy in 1954 of the Japanese fishing boat *Fukuryu Maru* (*Lucky Dragon*), which unwittingly sailed into the Bikini Atoll in the North Pacific where H-bombs were being tested. The *Lucky Dragon* and her crew were showered with radioactive dust. Shahn represented the radioactive cloud above the boat as a flying monster in *We Did Not Know What Happened to Us* (1960).

Personal realism

Ben Shahn led the American social realist group of painters, who rejected abstraction in favor of real, recognizable subjects. The styles they used to depict these subjects were diverse; some are described as expressionist, others as magic-realist. Shahn himself preferred to call his style "personal realism." He pointed out that while social realism was "dictated" from the outside, his work was the result of his own personal responses to what he saw. None of Shahn's paintings is, in fact, strictly realist: features are often exaggerated; physical scale is distorted for effect; figures are flattened and backgrounds simplified.

The *Sacco–Vanzetti* series of paintings, consisting of 23 gouaches and two large panels, are works by which Shahn became known as a painter of social protest. Sacco and Vanzetti were two Italian immigrants executed in 1927 for committing murder during a hold-up in Boston. Both defendants were avowed anarchists, and in the midst of a "Red Scare," a jury found them guilty despite flawed prosecution and questionable eyewitness evidence.

In one large panel painting from 1932, Shahn depicted all the main protagonists in the drama: protesters demanding that the prisoners be freed; Alvin Fuller, the governor of Massachusetts who refused to stay the execution; and Sacco and Vanzetti. Shahn often reworked the right-hand section of the painting and the variation pictured here is perhaps his most famous image. Standing over the dead men's coffins (Vanzetti's coffin in the foreground) is the "committee of prominent men"—a judge and the presidents of Harvard University and Massachusetts Institute of Technology—who investigated the trial, declared it fair, and upheld the death sentence. They hold white lilies, symbols of purity and martyrdom. In the background hangs a portrait of the trial judge, Webster Thayer, who denied all motions for a new trial in the six years between trial and execution.

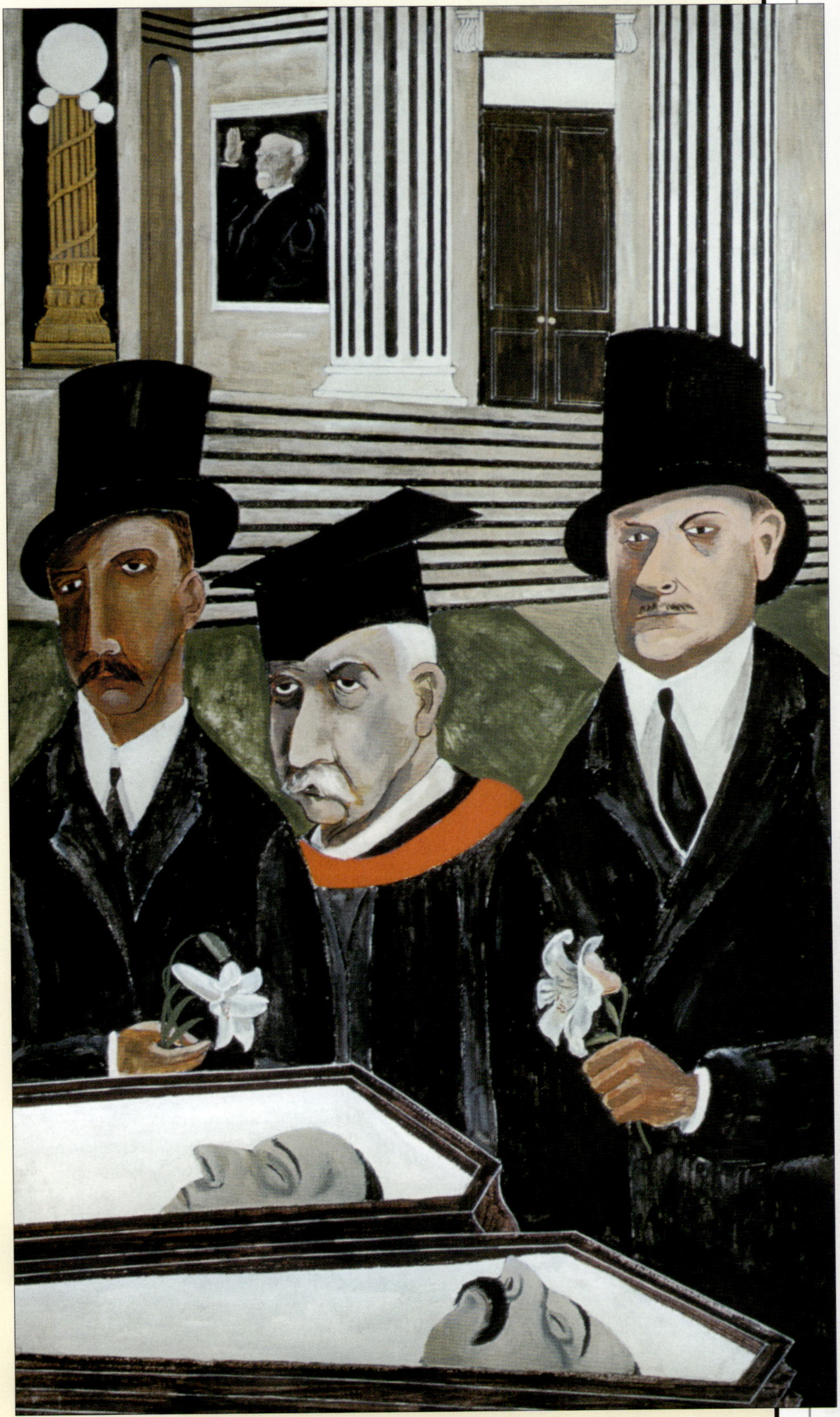

The Passion of Sacco and Vanzetti
1931–32. Tempera on canvas. 84 1/2 x 48 in (214.5 x 122 cm). Whitney Museum of American Art, New York, NY.

SISLEY Alfred

ALFRED SISLEY WAS A LEADING MEMBER of the impressionist movement and was strongly influenced by his friend Claude Monet. His works were almost exclusively landscapes, painted in both northern France and southern England. Today they are admired for their delicate touch and richness of tone.

Life and work

Alfred Sisley was born into a wealthy English family that had settled in Paris, the second of four children. He went to London at the age of 18 to study commerce, with a view to entering the family's artificial flower business. He soon found that this was not for him, and decided to devote himself entirely to painting. During his four years in London (1857–61), he was no doubt influenced by seeing the works of the great English landscapists John Constable and J. M.W. Turner in the city's fine museum collections.

Upon his return to Paris in 1863, assured of family support, Sisley entered the studio of the Swiss painter Charles Gleyre, where he met and became lifelong friends with Claude Monet, Pierre Auguste Renoir, and Frédéric Bazille. Sisley and Renoir became particularly close friends; Renoir painted portraits of both Sisley and his father. The two young artists shared an apartment and went on sketching trips to the forest of Fontainebleau together.

Although Sisley's first recorded landscape dates from 1865, there are only 18 works painted before 1871 that are known to be by him. This reflects the financially comfortable circumstances of his youth; he did not have to paint for a living.

His lifestyle changed abruptly in 1870, the year of the Franco–Prussian War, with the death of his father and his family's financial ruin. He was then compelled to turn to painting as a means of supporting himself. From this time on his correspondence to friends and patrons is dominated by pleas for financial aid and support. During the Siege of Paris of 1871, Sisley moved to Louveciennes. He spent the rest of his life living in picturesque villages along the banks of the Loing and Seine rivers, which were to be the main subjects of his paintings.

Sisley was the only impressionist to paint almost exclusively landscapes, only very occasionally producing a still life. His chief interest was in trying to represent the mood and atmosphere of nature. He did studies of the changes in color and form that different seasons and times of day brought to a particular place. Water always played an important role in Sisley's work, giving his paintings a joyous vibrancy and purity of tone. His landscapes of the 1870s and 1880s capture the essence of impressionist technique and subject matter.

Like Monet, Sisley began to explore the particular effects of light and climate upon a single motif in his late series paintings. Both painters were inspired by churches. In 1893–94, just

Data file

Full name: Alfred Sisley
Nationality: French
Style: impressionism
Dates: born 1839 in Paris, died 1899 Moret-sur-Loing
Key works:
- *View of the Canal Saint-Martin* 1870
- *Snow at Louveciennes* 1870
- *The Bridge at Hampton Court* 1874
- *Watering Place at Port Marly* 1875
- *Boat in a Flood 1876*
- *Haystacks at Moret: Morning Light* 1891
- *The Church of Moret-sur-Loing* (series of 14 paintings) 1893–94

Things to look for:
- climate and light effects
- the representation of water
- English and French landscapes

Comparisons: Claude Monet, Camille Pissarro, Pierre Auguste Renoir, Camille Corot
Glossary terms: impressionism, Salon, Salon des Refusés

The splendor of natural light

Boat in a Flood (1876) is a perfect example of Sisley's impressionism. In that year the area around the village of Port-Marly, just outside Paris, was extensively flooded when the Seine burst its banks. This dramatic event inspired Sisley to create a whole group of paintings of the village while it remained under water. Whereas in several of the later versions he portrays the inconvenience and even potential dangers of the flooding, in *Boat in a Flood* he captures the initial excitement and sheer oddity of finding the village's streets turned into rivers. This is one of six works painted in 1876 in which Sisley portrays the effects of the flood from different viewpoints and at different times of day.

The painting is artfully constructed through four main motifs. The foreground is dominated by a road which has become a canal with its own makeshift "gondoliers." The wine shop on the left-hand side, recognizable by its painted board and suspended sign, is unchanged by the tumult raging beyond its doors. An avenue of chestnut trees in the distance on the right-hand side of the painting is the only remaining marker of the presence of an adjacent street, now completely lost to view. Lastly, a glorious, sunlit sky unifies all these elements into a picturesque calm after the tempest.

Boat in a Flood marks a transition in Sisley's painting technique. In his early works he used an evenly applied, more uniform brushstroke, but in this painting he explores the expressive possibilities of using different sizes of brushstroke to create different textures and patterns. He also employs a wider range of colors than

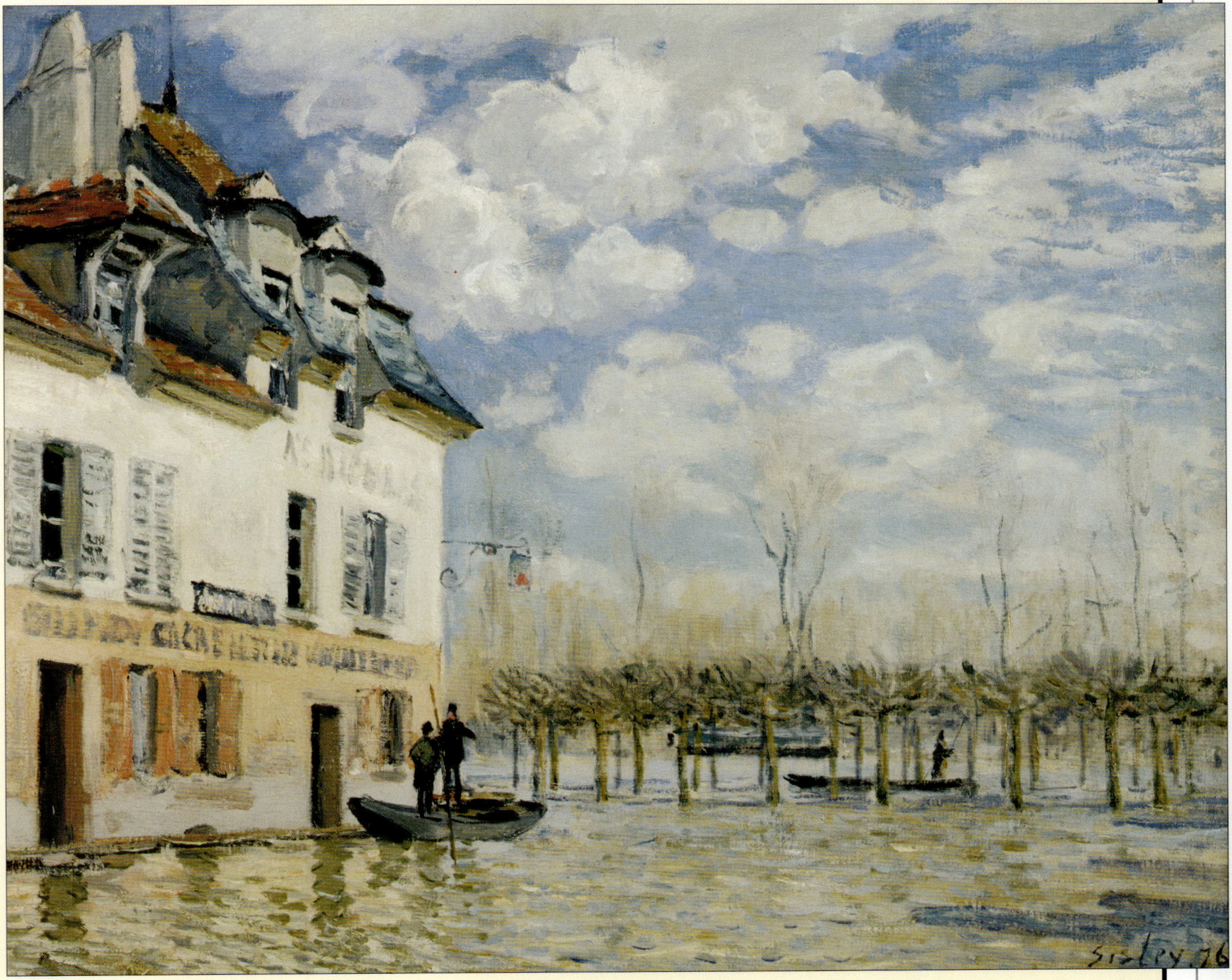

in previous paintings to create an intense effect of tone.

Typical of his impressionist technique is Sisley's application of paint in lively, hatched brushstrokes which instantly draw attention to the surface of the painting, animating the canvas. His colors are vibrant, and seem to fill his paintings with a celebratory glow. He became adept at the difficult art of capturing water on canvas, and among his favorite subjects were the riverbanks southwest of Paris.

Boat in a Flood *1876. Oil on canvas. 23 1/2 x 32 in (60 x 81 cm). Musée d'Orsay, Paris.*

after Monet had painted his famous series of views of Rouen Cathedral, Sisley painted 14 views of the parish church in the village of Moret-sur-Loing. Whereas Monet dissolved the details of Rouen cathedral's elaborate façade into masses of color, Sisley sought to combine the vibrancy of light effects while maintaining a clearer sense of the architecture of the church. Both artists also painted a series of paintings inspired by haystacks.

Sisley exhibited at the Salon des Refusés in 1863, at the Paris Salon in 1866, and contributed to four of the impressionist group exhibitions held between 1874 and 1886. Despite a successful one-man show given by the dealer Durand-Ruel in 1883, Sisley's paintings did not find many buyers during his lifetime. In 1897, at a large retrospective exhibition held at the Georges Petit Gallery, not one painting was sold.

SLUTER Claus

CLAUS SLUTER WAS ONE OF THE MOST ORIGINAL SCULPTORS of the late 14th century. He formulated the Burgundian style and introduced a new realism into northern Renaissance sculpture. He is noted for his expressive treatment of draperies and his portrayal of human emotions through facial expressions and postures.

Life and work

"Claes de Slutere van Haarlem" first appears in history as a member of the Guild of Stone-Cutters and Masons in Brussels in about 1379. Sluter probably received training in stone cutting in his family's workshop in Haarlem in the Netherlands. He seems to have had his formal artistic training in Brussels.

From March 1, 1385, Sluter was in Dijon in eastern France. There he worked for the court sculptor, Jean de Marville, in the workshop supplying sculpture for Philip the Bold, Duke of Burgundy. The duke's accounts show that Sluter was paid more than any other assistant and in 1389, following de Marville's death, became master.

Sluter's first major project was the portal of the charterhouse (Carthusian monastery) of Champmol, not far from Dijon. Documents from 1377 record that Marville was planning the charterhouse, but it was not until 1383 that the foundation stone was laid.

When Sluter assumed control, he redesigned the portal to accommodate his own sculptural program. In Sluter's new scheme the figures of Duke Philip the Bold and his wife, Margaret of Flanders, kneel on each side of the portal. Their patron saints, Saint John the Baptist and Saint Catherine of Alexandria, are presenting them to the Virgin and Child, who occupy the *trumeau* (the pillar dividing the portal). Sluter also incorporated into his design figures of prophets holding scrolls. These were conceived and in position in about 1390, after new stone from a local quarry at Asnières had arrived.

While the Virgin as a *trumeau* figure is traditional, the life-size kneeling portraits of the duke and duchess are innovative in their free-standing poses and naturalistic approach. The charterhouse was largely destroyed during the French Revolution, but the portal survived and was incorporated into the chapel of a psychiatric hospital built on the grounds in the 19th century.

In about 1393 Sluter worked on decorations for Margaret of Flanders' castle at Germolles, near Chalon-sur-Saône. They included his only known secular work (now lost), installed near the entrance of the castle. It was a pastoral scene with life-size figures of Philip and Margaret under a tree, accompanied by a flock of sheep.

From 1390 to 1396 Sluter produced a number of statues for the oratory at Champmol, including figures of the Virgin, Saint John the Baptist, and Saint Anthony. (These were also destroyed, probably in about 1792, during the French Revolution.) In 1395 Sluter traveled to the Netherlands to buy stained glass for the oratory; in the same year he was also commissioned to work on a great font, known as *The Moses Well*, for the center of the charterhouse cloister.

Sluter's last work was the tomb of Philip the Bold. It was originally commissioned from Jean de Marville, who probably devised the overall scheme. In 1392 Sluter traveled to Paris to collect alabaster blocks for the duke's effigy, but work on the tomb took place mostly after the duke's death in 1404.

When Duke Philip died, a contract between Sluter and the new duke, John the Fearless, specified the effigy figure, 54 small angels (now lost), and "40 *ymages pleurants*." These are the famous "weepers"—mourner figures around the sides of the tomb. Each is treated in a different way. Some appear to be turning, some are pausing in the funeral procession, while others stand still and weep in profile, three-quarter, or frontal views. The realism and drama of the weepers are the products of Sluter's acute observation. Each weeper reflects Sluter's concern with realistic portraiture. He accurately renders facial details such as beards, stubble, and wrinkles, as well as clothing, the dramatic folds of which seem to echo the grief of the mourners.

When Sluter died in about 1406, the tomb was completed by his nephew, Claus de Werve.

Data file

Full name: Claus Sluter (also known as Claux Celoistre; Claes de Slutere; Claves de Slutere, or Claux Slutre)

Nationality: Flemish

Style: international Gothic

Dates: born c1360 in Haarlem, died c1406 in Dijon, France

Key works:
- portal of the charterhouse of Champmol c1391–93
- tomb of Philip the Bold c1392–1406
- pastoral scene for the castle of Germolles c1393
- oratory statues at Champmol c1395–96
- *The Moses Well*, Champmol c1395–1406

Things to look for:
- sculptures often life-size
- statuesque, freestanding figures
- dramatic carving reproducing the effects of heavy woolen cloth
- remains of original painting on the sculptures
- concern with portraiture: facial details used to convey emotions
- close attention to details, such as buttons on clothes and fur linings in coats

Comparisons: Jacopo della Quercia, Lorenzo Ghiberti, Donatello, Claus de Werve, Jean de Marville, Jean Michel, Georges de la Sonnette

Glossary terms: Gothic, Renaissance, *trumeau*

Expressive features

On his marriage to Margaret of Flanders in 1369, Philip the Bold, duke of Burgundy, was lord of the counties of Flanders, Artois, Burgundy, and Nevers. Philip wanted lasting testaments to his power and wealth in the form of buildings, sculptures, and paintings. In the 1360s he began rebuilding the largely derelict cathedral in Dijon, where he had his court. As a result of his marriage, he invited Flemish artists into his service. They brought the new vigor of Flemish realism, balancing the largely Italianate influence that had dominated the French court style of the 14th century. The name "Burgundian school" is given to the Flemish artists who worked for the duke between 1390 and 1420. Claus Sluter is acknowledged as the artist who initiated their style.

In 1385 Philip the Bold established a charterhouse (Carthusian monastery—the Carthusians were an austere monastic order) at Champmol, near Dijon. This was also to be a monument and mausoleum for himself. With the exception of his tomb, the complex of buildings was completed before his death in 1404.

The Moses Well (c1395–1406) is the only existing work at the charterhouse known to have been conceived and executed by Sluter. It was commissioned as a great baptismal font for the center of the cloister. Based on a hexagonal stone, the font was originally topped by a calvary scene (a representation of Christ's crucifixion). This appears to have perished when the monastery was destroyed during the French Revolution. The calvary figures were carved and installed by 1399, but today only fragments survive from this part of the composition.

Rising from columns at corner pillars on the base of the font are six weeping angels, whose outspread wings lead the spectators' eyes up past the cornice to the space that would have held the calvary scene. Each side of the pier is occupied by a life-sized and individualized figure of a prophet: Moses, Jeremiah, David, Daniel, Isaiah, and Zachariah (illustrated here).

The prophets' features and stances are expressive of the prophesies inscribed on the scrolls they are holding. The shortness of the figures and the carving of the heavy wool garments are hallmarks of Sluter's style. There is a tension between the static framework and the expressive carving of the bodies and their draperies. The naturalism was enhanced further by the use of colored paint, only traces of which now survive.

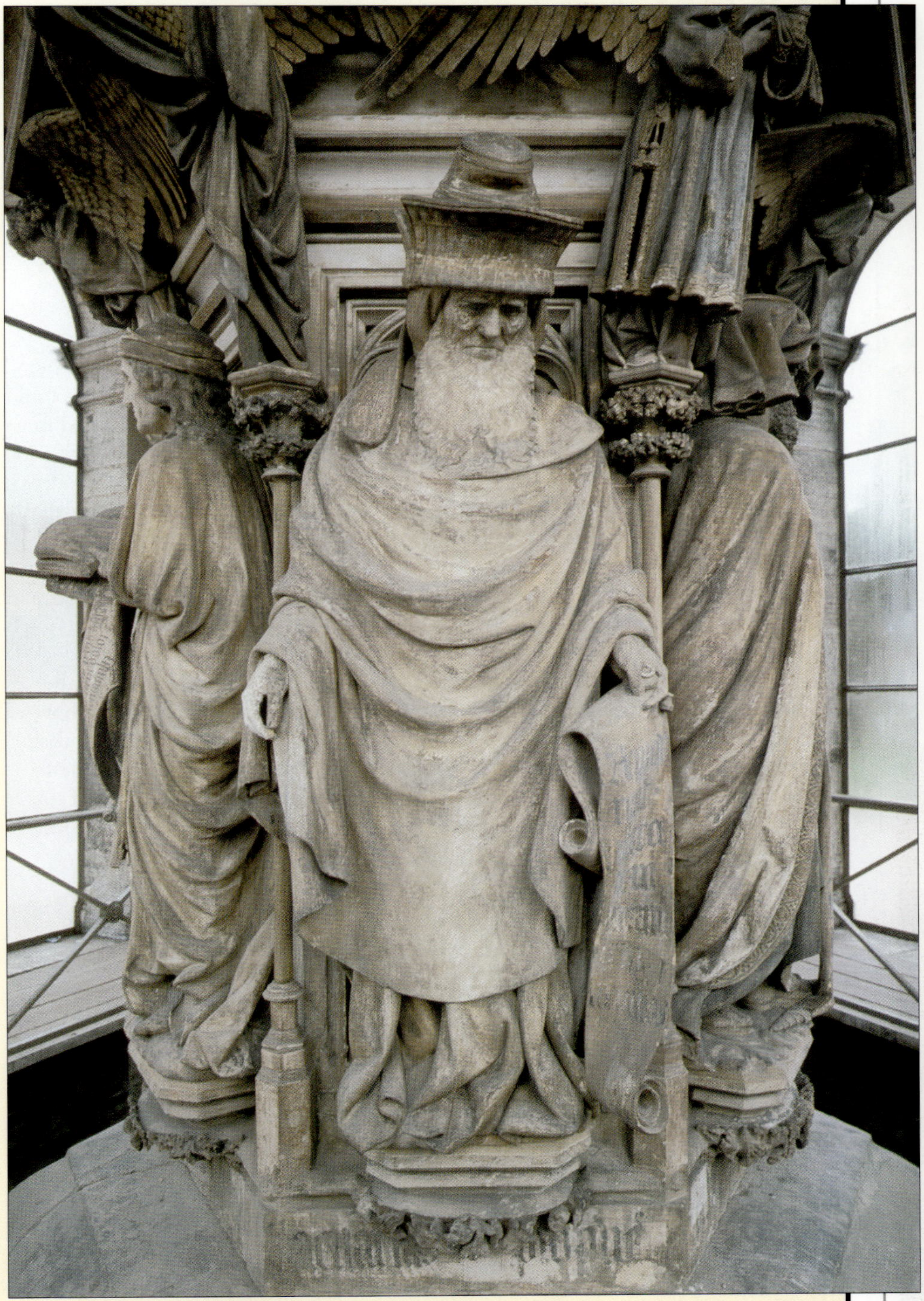

The Moses Well *c1395–1406. Marble. Figures 6 ft (1.83 m) high. Charterhouse, Champmol.*

SOUTINE Chaïm

CHAÏM SOUTINE CAME FROM A RUSSIAN BACKGROUND of miserable rural poverty, but he moved to Paris where his striking paintings were eventually "discovered," and he achieved sudden fame and success. Close to expressionism in style, his paintings convey a strong sense of vitality, but have an underlying, uneasy morbidity.

Life and work

Chaïm Soutine was born into a large, impoverished Jewish family in the tiny village of Smilovitchi, in Belorussia. This was a harsh environment. Not only was he surrounded by poverty, but the traditional Jewish belief that making images was sinful meant that Soutine was regularly punished—sometimes severely—because of his love of drawing. In 1909 he left for the city of Minsk. After studying art in Vilna in Lithuania, Soutine went to Paris in 1913; from then on he never returned to his native country.

In 1913 Paris was the liveliest and most important center for modern art, but Soutine did not immediately blend in: he was scruffy, unsophisticated, and could not speak French. He lived in squalor, surrounded by filth, damp, and bedbugs in "La Ruche" (The Beehive). This was a bohemian settlement that in the early 20th century was home to nearly 200 artists, including, at times, Marc Chagall, Amedeo Modigliani, and Robert Delaunay.

Soutine was inspired by the paintings of the Old Masters in the Louvre. The artist he admired above all others was Rembrandt; it is said that Soutine once traveled all the way to Amsterdam just to sit in front of Rembrandt's *Jewish Bride* (c1665) in the Rijksmuseum.

Soutine found much modern art, especially cubism, too coldly intellectual, and preferred instead to paint with intense colors, which he applied with free, energetic brushstrokes. In this sense his work was closest to that of Vincent Van Gogh, and to expressionists such as the Austrian painter Oskar Kokoschka. He disliked using new canvases, and instead would search Parisian flea-markets for paintings, preferably two or three centuries old, to paint over.

Soutine's subjects are at first glance conventional: portraits, landscapes, and still lifes. However, he brought to them a raw intensity, stemming from his practice of painting directly in front of the object, often in a single sitting. He did not work from sketches or photographs, relying instead on his direct, emotional response. His paintings are often "imperfect," yet this is also the key to their powerful expressiveness.

In 1915 Soutine became close friends with Modigliani. They would drink heavily together, but Soutine suffered from intensely painful stomach ulcers, and soon had to give up alcohol. Modigliani introduced Soutine to his first dealer, Leopold Zborowski, who sent Soutine to Céret in the French Pyrenees. Soutine stayed in the mountains for three years and painted many rough, angular, almost abstract landscapes in thick impasto.

In the winter of 1922–23, Soutine's life changed completely. He was "discovered" by the immensely wealthy American collector of modern art, Albert C. Barnes. Barnes immediately bought about 100 of Soutine's works for the enormous sum of 60,000 French francs. He also had Soutine clothed in fine tailored suits, and provided him with a comfortable new studio. In the past Soutine had sworn not to forget his poor artist friends, but from this moment on he did everything he could to sever all contact with his impoverished past. He became almost maniacally obsessed with his own earlier paintings; he would hunt them down and buy them, often for high prices, only to attack the canvases violently, slashing them beyond repair.

In 1925 Soutine worked on one of his most impressive series of paintings, using as his subject a slaughtered cow. The inspiration came from Rembrandt's *Slaughtered Ox* (1655), which Soutine had seen in the Louvre. Soutine acquired a cow's carcass from an abattoir, hung it up in his studio and, working directly from it, made several rich and visceral paintings. These were on a much larger scale than usual, indicating that he considered it an important subject.

Dead creatures, especially rayfish, fowl, ox, and rabbits feature repeatedly in Soutine's still-life compositions. When we consider that almost all kinds of food except milk caused Soutine to suffer excruciating stomach pains, it

Data file

Full name: Chaïm Soutine
Nationality: Russian
Style: central European expressionism
Dates: born 1893 near Minsk, died 1943 in Paris, France
Key works:
Little Girl with a Doll 1919
The Rayfish 1922
The Groom 1925
Large Choirboy 1925
Small Town Square, Venice 1929
Maternity 1942
Things to look for:
- sharp contrasts
- thick paint
- exaggerated gestures
- meat, poultry, and fish in still life
- portraits of workers in uniform

Comparisons: Vincent Van Gogh, Amedeo Modigliani, Rembrandt, Gustave Courbet, Oskar Kokoschka
Glossary terms: abstract art, cubism, expressionism, impasto, realism

Portraiture and the body

Soutine painted many portraits of workers in uniform during his life, including cooks, hotel porters, and choirboys. *The Groom* (1925) is one of his most powerful portraits. The groom sits against an indeterminate background, hands on hips, his body spread out to the sides of the canvas. The most striking feature is the intense red of his clothes; it is likely that Soutine was attracted to painting figures in uniform precisely because their clothing was often of one distinctive color. Soutine's portraits have been described as being like "autopsies" (examinations of dead bodies) in paint. It is true that there is something very fleshlike about the groom's blood-red suit, while his splayed body even seems to echo the beef carcass painted by Soutine in the same year.

At first sight the image seems simple, and even rather mundane, but the portrait conveys a powerful sense of the sitter's physical and psychological presence. The viewer cannot escape the sense that the artist is looking at this man exactly as he looks at beef, fish, and poultry. There is a strong sensitivity to the man's anatomy. We can see, for example, how the gold buttons of his uniform follow the line of his spine, his hands rest on his hips, and the brushstrokes across the chest even seem to echo the ribcage.

The painting is a good example of the way in which Soutine exaggerates the features of his sitters to an extent that gives them a great expressive, and even slightly unnerving force, though this exaggeration never slips into the realm of caricature. The groom's face is lopsided, his nose appears to be broken, his eyes are swollen, and his lips half-pouting, half sneering. We can also see a trademark feature of Soutine's portraits—the sitter's left ear protrudes almost comically. Soutine liked to go to boxing matches, and if the groom were not sitting so nonchalantly, we could almost imagine that this man had just been beaten to a pulp in the ring. The subtle balance between a sense of violence and an objective, factual painting was surely what caught the eye of early collectors of Soutine's art, as well as those who view his work today.

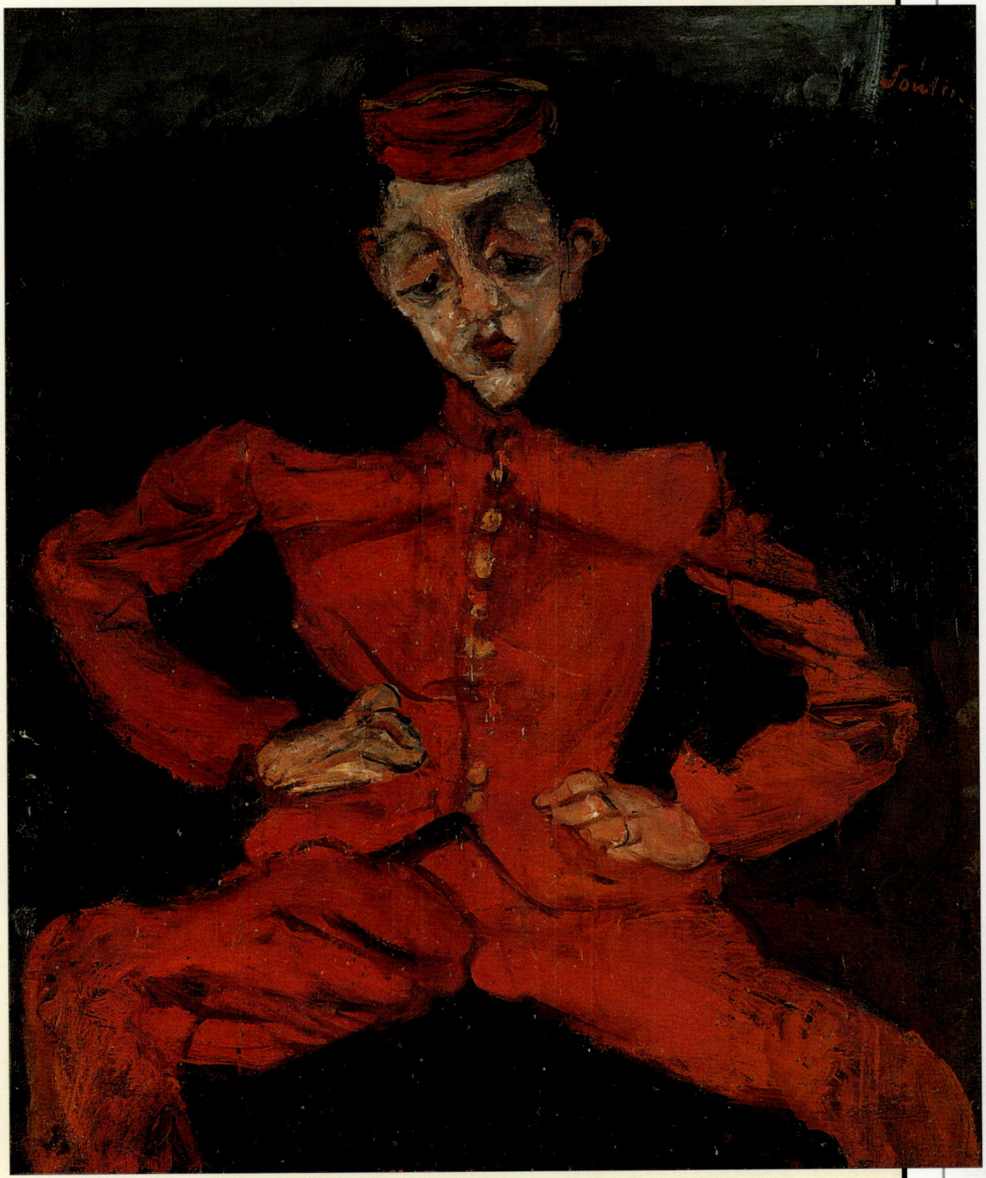

The Groom *1925. Oil on canvas. 38 1/2 x 31 1/2 in (98 x 80 cm). Musée National d'Art Moderne, Centre Georges Pompidou, Paris.*

adds an extra dimension to such subjects, since for Soutine they must clearly have had associations both with inaccessible pleasures and with terrible pain.

At the end of the 1920s, Soutine suffered both health and financial problems, and his ulcers became so bad that he could no longer work. In the 1930s, in between periods of illness, he returned to painting, taking as his subject workers who wore uniforms, such as waiters and cooks. He began to admire the realist style of the 19th-century French artist, Gustave Courbet, who believed painting should "concern itself with things seen…."

In 1943 Soutine's pains became so agonizing that he was rushed to the hospital for an operation on his stomach from which he never awoke.

SPENCER Stanley

STANLEY SPENCER WAS A SPIRITUALLY INSPIRED ARTIST who played a leading role in early 20th-century British art. Greatly influenced by early Italian painting, as well as by postimpressionism, Spencer created unique, figurative paintings of biblical scenes. Many of these scenes, however, were set in the modern world, in Spencer's native village of Cookham, southeast England.

Life and work

Stanley Spencer was born in 1891 in Cookham, in the county of Berkshire in England. The small village was to provide a constant source of inspiration for the artist throughout his life. The son of a church organist, he grew up in a household dominated by literature, music, and religion. Spencer turned to art, however, and in 1908 entered the Slade School in London. His fellow students at the art school nicknamed him "Cookham," because he commuted to London by train from his home every day.

Data file

Full name: Stanley Spencer

Nationality: British

Style: primitivism

Dates: born 1891 in Cookham, died 1959 in Cliveden

Key works:

- *The Nativity* 1912
- *Travoys with Wounded Soldiers Arriving at a Dressing Station* 1919
- *The Last Supper* 1920
- *Resurrection, Cookham* 1922–27
- Sandham Memorial Chapel at Burghclere, Hampshire 1923–32
- *Saint Francis and the Birds* 1935
- *Resurrection, Port Glasgow* 1945–50

Things to look for:

- simple drawing style
- religious scenes set in the modern world
- complex figural compositions

Comparisons: Giotto, Masaccio, Fra Angelico, Paul Gauguin, William Roberts

Glossary terms: Academy, figurative, postimpressionism, primitivism

In 1912 Spencer left the Slade and returned to Cookham, where he rented a studio. During his studies he had become fascinated by early Italian painting, which was then called "primitivist." However, he combined his interest in the works of 14th- and 15th-century artists, such as Giotto, Masaccio, and Fra Angelico, with a love of the paintings of the 19th-century French artist Paul Gauguin. Like Gauguin, who regularly set biblical scenes in the modern landscape of Brittany, Spencer began to paint religious subjects set in Cookham.

The outbreak of World War I in 1914 shattered Spencer's tranquil life, and within a year he had enlisted in the army. Toward the end of the war Spencer was appointed an official war artist, and in 1919 produced the large-scale *Travoys with Wounded Soldiers Arriving at a Dressing Station*, a vivid recollection of his experiences.

After the war Spencer returned to Cookham. In 1924 he started work on a huge canvas entitled *Resurrection, Cookham* (1922–27), a work that established his reputation as a major British artist.

During this period memories of the war continued to haunt Spencer, and he started to sketch ideas for a proposed war memorial. The opportunity to fulfill this project came in 1923, when he was commissioned to decorate a chapel dedicated to the memory of a man killed in the war, Henry Willoughby Sandham. Spencer worked on the Sandham Memorial Chapel at Burghclere, Hampshire, for the next nine years. Much inspired by Giotto's Arena Chapel in Padua, Italy, he ultimately produced one of the most powerful and fitting memorials to the victims of World War I.

As he increasingly focused on erotic subjects throughout the 1930s, Spencer's work fell out of public favor. He was also in conflict with the Royal Academy, who had elected him a

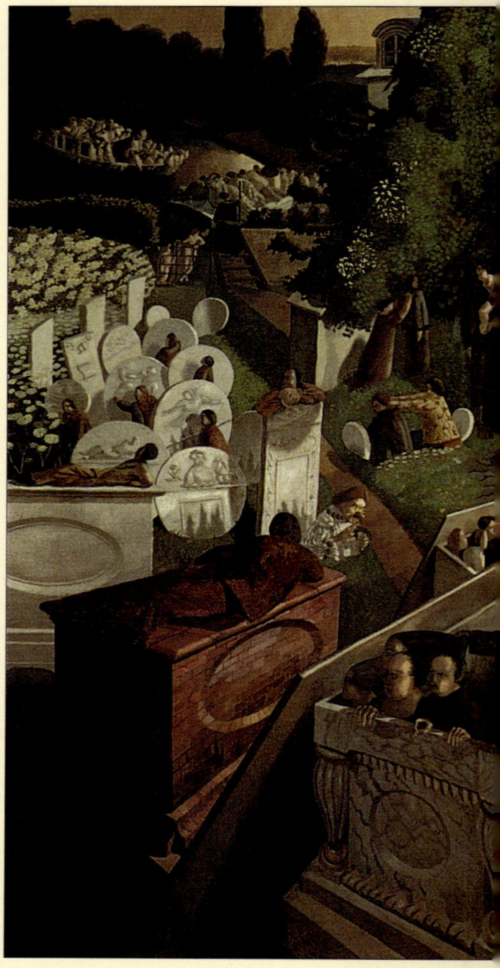

Spencer's modern biblical scenes

Resurrection, Cookham (1922–27) was one of Spencer's largest and most important early works, which proved a huge success when it was first exhibited in London in 1927. In the work Spencer portrays Cookham's churchyard, with the River Thames in the background. This is not a simple landscape scene, however, for

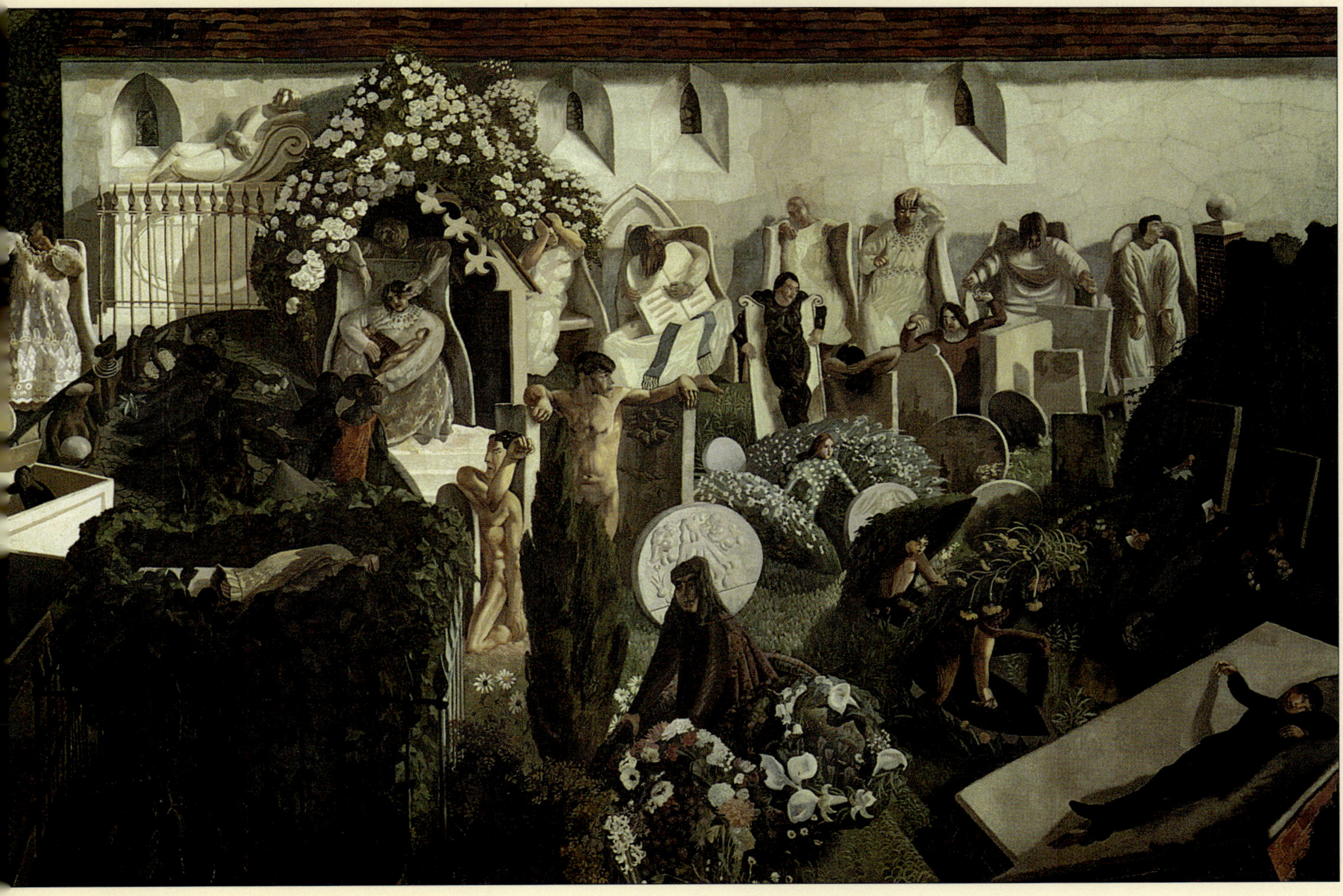

Spencer depicts the dead rising slowly from their graves into a modern paradise. God the Father and His Son, Jesus Christ, can be seen at the center of the image, beneath a flower-covered porch. Behind these divine figures, along the church wall, Spencer has painted a row of prophets (Moses can be seen holding the stone tablets that conveyed God's law to the Israelites).

Along with these religious figures Spencer has also included some modern characters, including many of his friends and relatives. Spencer himself appears twice in the painting, firstly emerging from between two gravestones at the center of the image, and then again on the surface of two tombs in the lower right-hand corner. Spencer also gives the work an international dimension by portraying a group of African people rising from the sunbaked soil of their native land.

Some of the figures that are emerging into Spencer's paradise are being punished. These include the two groups in the tombs in the foreground, who are being rounded up to

Resurrection, Cookham *1922–27. Oil on canvas. 108 x 216 in (274 x 549 cm). Tate Gallery, London.*

await their final judgment. Yet even this mild retribution does not diminish the joyous and celebratory mood of the work. This is best expressed in the top left-hand corner of the painting, where the resurrected can be seen climbing aboard boats and drifting down the river. Indeed, Spencer presents heaven as if it were Cookham.

member in 1932. Two of Spencer's works, including *Saint Francis and the Birds* (1935), were rejected from a Royal Academy exhibition, and Spencer handed in his resignation in protest at the decision.

During World War II Spencer was once again called upon to serve as an official war artist. He was sent to Glasgow, Scotland, to sketch the building of warships in the shipyards of the River Clyde. Between 1945 and 1950 Spencer produced a series of monumental canvases entitled *Resurrection, Port Glasgow*, in which he transported the modern shipbuilding community into scenes drawn from the Bible.

During the last years of his life Spencer was reconciled with the Royal Academy and was once more recognized as a major British artist. At the time of his death in 1959 he was still working on a painting that represented Christ preaching to a modern crowd at a regatta. Once more, the setting was his native Cookham.

STUBBS George

GEORGE STUBBS WAS THE BEST-KNOWN ANIMAL PAINTER in the 18th century. He was a keen scientist and carefully studied the anatomy of the animals he painted. His famous illustrated book, *The Anatomy of the Horse* (1766), established his reputation and gained him many commissions to portray the racehorses of the English aristocracy.

Life and work

George Stubbs was born the son of a leather-worker, in Liverpool in 1724. He was largely a self-taught artist, having spent only a few weeks studying with a little-known painter when he was just 15 years old. At this time, the study of anatomy was regarded as an essential element of artistic training. Stubbs was fascinated by anatomy and, in the early 1750s, went to work in a hospital, where he assisted in the dissecting room. His skill in depicting the human form surpassed that of many of his contemporaries and Stubbs was soon asked to produce a number of anatomical illustrations for publication in medical texts.

In 1754 Stubbs, like many British artists during this period, traveled to Italy to study the art of ancient Rome and the Italian Renaissance. Although he was later to claim that this experience had little impact upon his art, Stubbs nonetheless adopted a more balanced and harmonious approach to composition clearly derived from classical sources. After his return to England, Stubbs once again turned to the study of anatomy, and in 1756 began to examine the anatomy of horses. He moved to an isolated village in central England, where he dissected dead horses, producing highly detailed drawings of each stage in the process. Stubbs believed that the knowledge gained in this endeavor would greatly assist him in representing live horses. He later published these drawings in his famous book, *The Anatomy of the Horse* (1766), which became a great success because of its beauty and anatomical accuracy.

When Stubbs moved to London in about 1758, he soon attracted the attention of the English aristocracy. During this period, many English aristocrats bred and raced horses; indeed the 1750s saw a great expansion in the sport of horse racing with the establishment of the Jockey Club and the development of race courses such as Goodwood and Newmarket. Many aristocrats, including the duke of Richmond, the earl of Grosvenor and the marquess of Rockingham, were impressed by Stubbs's anatomical drawings of horses and subsequently commissioned him to produce portraits of their most successful racehorses. His work is notable not only for the beauty and grace with which he depicted his equine subjects, but for its lack of sentimentality.

In addition to these commissions, Stubbs also included horses in more dramatic compositions, producing several paintings, drawings, and engravings on the theme of a horse being attacked by a lion. A fascination

Data file

Full name: George Stubbs

Nationality: English

Style: neoclassicism/early Romantic

Dates: born 1724 in Liverpool, died 1806 in London

Key works:

Whistlejacket 1762

Horse Attacked by a Lion 1762

Cheetah with Two Indian Attendants and a Stag c1764

Gimcrack on Newmarket Heath with a Trainer, Jockey and Stable-lad 1765

Kangaroo from New Holland c1773

Reapers 1785

Haymakers 1785

Hambletonian, Rubbing Down 1799

Things to look for:

- paintings of horses and exotic animals
- close attention to anatomical detail
- balanced, harmonious compositions
- scenes of conflict between animals

Comparisons: Thomas Gainsborough

Glossary terms: neoclassicism, Renaissance, Romanticism

Stubbs and the exotic animal

Throughout his career, Stubbs produced numerous representations of exotic animals. His first wild animal painting was the precisely executed *Zebra* (c1760–62). This was followed by the first of the illustrations showing mortal combat between a horse and a lion. His highly realistic and detailed works particularly appealed to early zoologists because the works rendered the individual characteristics of each species with great accuracy. Many of Stubbs's patrons came from the scientific community.

Cheetah with Two Indian Attendants and a Stag (c1764) is the largest exotic animal painting produced by Stubbs. Here the artist represents the cheetah in profile, showing its body shape, musculature, and the markings on its fur in great detail. Significantly, however, the animal is also seen wearing a hunting hood and lead, and is about to be released by two attendants. Stubbs has also included a stag, seen on the right. Clearly the stag is here offered as prey about to be hunted by the cheetah once it is released. Stubbs may well have been inspired by an event that took place in the summer of 1764, when the duke of Cumberland released a cheetah to hunt a stag in Windsor, near London.

Cheetah with Two Indian Attendants and a Stag was commissioned by George Pigot, the governor of Madras in the British Raj. According to family tradition, the painting commemorates Pigot's gift of a cheetah to King George III in 1764.

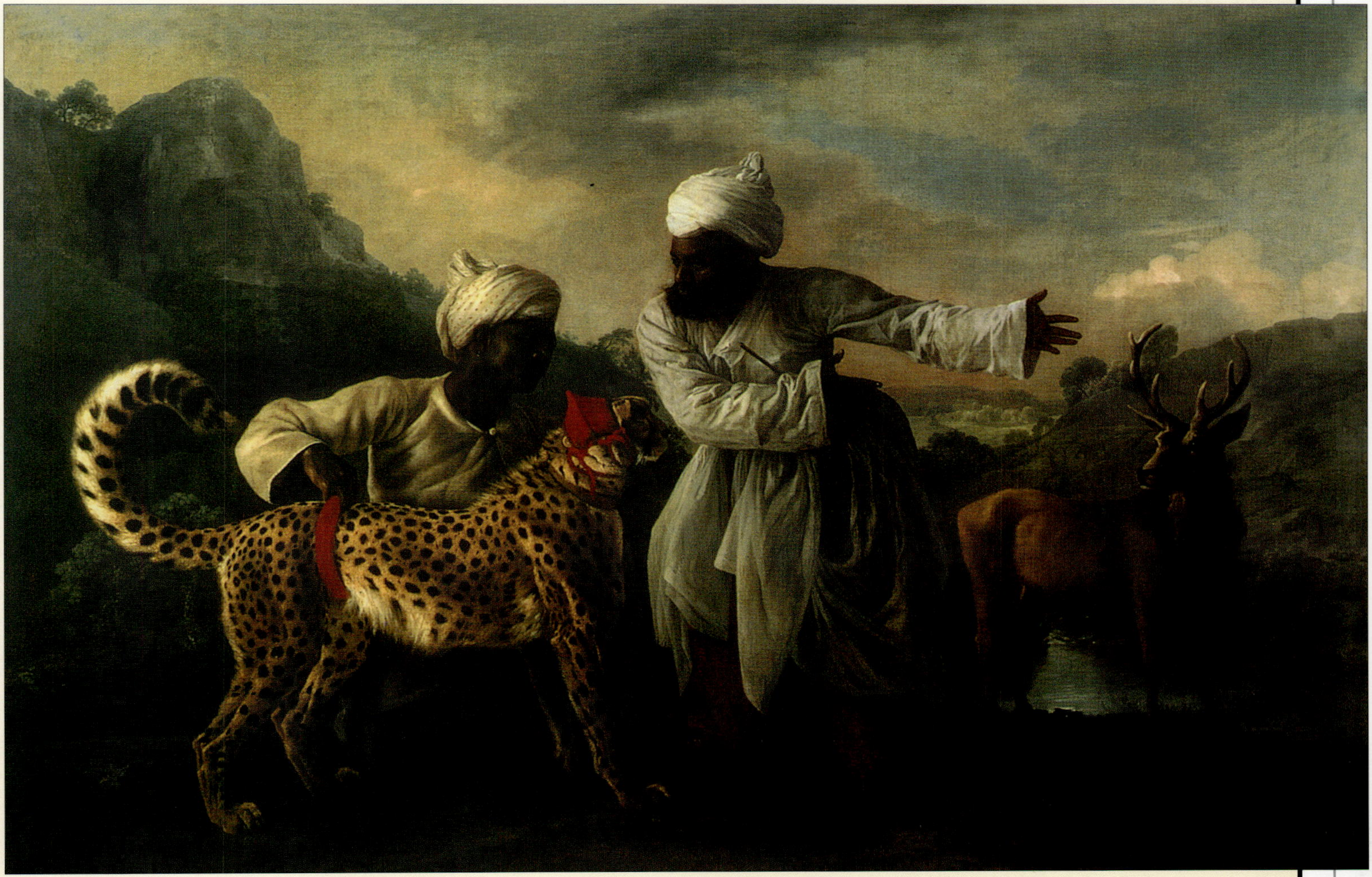

Significantly, Stubbs has also included two Indian attendants dressed in full native costume to increase the sense of exoticism in the work and to allude to Pigot's own connections with British India. However, these Indian figures are presented as if they themselves are examples of an exotic species to be recorded and classified.

During the 1880s, the painting was notably altered when the stag was painted over, thus removing the sense of a hunt. The work remained in this condition for over half a century until restorers cleaned it and revealed the stag once more.

Cheetah with Two Indian Attendants and a Stag *c1764. Oil on canvas. 81 x 107 in (206 x 272 cm). Manchester City Art Gallery, Manchester.*

with the animal kingdom also drew Stubbs to paint other more exotic species, including tigers, leopards, monkeys, lemurs, a zebra, and a rhinoceros. In about 1773 he even produced a painting of a kangaroo; the work was based on a stuffed specimen, for the animal was rarely seen outside of its native Australia.

Stubbs constantly questioned painting techniques and, in an attempt to avoid the inevitable deterioration of works of art, experimented with many different materials. During the 1770s he started to use enamel paint and, instead of canvas, tried different supports, including copper and ceramic. He even asked the famous ceramic manufacturer Josiah Wedgwood to produce large-scale ceramic panels specifically for him.

By the 1780s, scenes of rural labor, such as those produced by Thomas Gainsborough, were attracting much popular attention. Stubbs responded to this trend by producing a pair of paintings entitled *Reapers* (1785) and *Haymakers* (1785). Toward the end of his life, however, he reverted to the themes that had most interested him throughout his illustrious career.

In 1795 he began a series of anatomical studies contrasting the human body with that of a tiger and a common fowl. His last great work, however, *Hambletonian, Rubbing Down* (1799), shows Stubbs at his best, representing in exquisite detail a racehorse, with its trainer and stable-lad. Stubbs died in London in 1806.

TIEPOLO Giambattista

TIEPOLO'S WORK IS CHARACTERIZED BY ITS LUMINOSITY and its joyous, rococo style. A painter of numerous schemes for church ceilings in Venice, he was heir to the traditions both of Venetian High Renaissance art, and the legacy of baroque illusionistic painting.

Life and work

The family into which Giambattista Tiepolo was born in 1696 had a prestigious background, and was connected with the hereditary aristocrats (patricians) who dominated Venice during the 18th century. The advantages of birth no doubt helped him in the acquisition of his early commissions. These formed the foundation of his reputation, first in Italy and then elsewhere in Europe.

Unlike his fellow Venetians, Giovanni Canaletto and Francesco Guardi, Tiepolo was not from an artistic background. However, evidence of a precocious artistic talent led him to be trained as an artist by Gregorio Lazzarini, from about 1710. By the age of 21, in 1718, he was earning enough money from his vocation to marry Guardi's sister, Cecilia. In the 1720s a series of commissions from members of the Dolfino family, for oil paintings and—more significantly—for frescos, established him as a leading exponent of Venetian mural decoration.

The city had become famous as a center for this branch of art. Tiepolo's early style shows the influence of Giovanni Antonio Pellegrini and Sebastiano Ricci, each of whom had been in demand with foreign patrons. Both these artists worked in a light, impressionistic style, using pale iridescent colors; like Tiepolo, they also both openly tried to emulate the great 16th-century Venetian muralist Paolo Veronese.

Once the center of a vast and influential maritime republic, by the 18th century Venice was no longer the prosperous city it had been. Many aristocrats lived in genteel poverty, and opportunities for major decorative projects were few. It is a measure of Tiepolo's success that he became the principal painter of large-scale frescos at a time when patronage for such work was in decline.

Tiepolo's works sometimes contain elements of humorous observation; he had a fascination with the exotic, and his exaggeration of facial types bordered on caricature. His depictions of humanity generally share the sensuousness and frivolity of the age. However, his treatment of sacred subjects indicates a depth of spiritual feeling not always evident in the works of his contemporaries.

Data file

Full name: Giovanni Battista (Giambattista) Tiepolo

Nationality: Italian

Style: rococo

Dates: Born 1696 in Venice, died 1770 in Madrid, Spain

Key works:
- *The Finding of Moses* c1740
- *The Banquet of Cleopatra* c1740s
- *The Family of Darius Before Alexander* 1743–44
- series: *Apollo and the Continents* 1750–52, *An Allegory of Venus and Time* c1754, *The Coronation of the Virgin* 1754–55

Things to look for:
- large-scale mural and ceiling frescos
- dynamic compositions
- figures floating in expanses of sky; luminosity of colors and tones
- exotic details, theatrical figures, and costumes

Comparisons: Paolo Veronese, Pietro da Cortona, Tintoretto, Giovanni Canaletto, François Boucher, Francesca Guardi, Giovanni Antonio Pellegrini, Sebastiano Ricci

Glossary terms: baroque, High Renaissance, illusionism, perspective, rococo

Grand illusions and iridescent colors

Throughout his life Tiepolo worked energetically. Fresco, the medium in which he excelled, allowed little room for corrections or reworking, as it involved painting directly onto damp plaster. It required an imaginative breadth, and decisiveness of execution from the artist.

To work on such a grand scale necessitated assistants, and in his Venetian workshop Tiepolo employed two of his sons, as well as Girolamo Mengozzi Colonna, a specialist in perspective illusionism. Tiepolo was also highly accomplished in this respect; hundreds of his drawings survive, displaying a mastery of anatomy and an ability to represent the human figure from every conceivable angle. The style of the drawings suggests a very rapid way of working, and much of this energy is retained in the larger finished works. Details and textures are sometimes conveyed by a few brisk strokes of the paintbrush.

The Coronation of the Virgin (1754–55) is painted in oil on canvas rather than fresco, though it was intended to be part of a ceiling decoration. Tiepolo painted it for the church of Santa Maria della Visitazione (known as La Pietà) in Venice, and it was one of the last works of this kind that Tiepolo produced there.

The painting clearly shows his skill in placing large numbers of figures floating effortlessly, and convincingly, apparently in space. Here, with a religious subject, as in similar schemes dealing with allegorical and mythological themes, Tiepolo shows how much he learned from the traditions of illusionism, put to such spectacular effect for church festivals and on the operatic stage.

Typical of Tiepolo's paintings on a spiritual or moral theme is *An Allegory of Venus and Time* (c1754). In this, as other paintings, there are marked contrasts of color, enhancing the interplay of the symbolic themes. The whole composition is infused by a sense of airiness and luminosity.

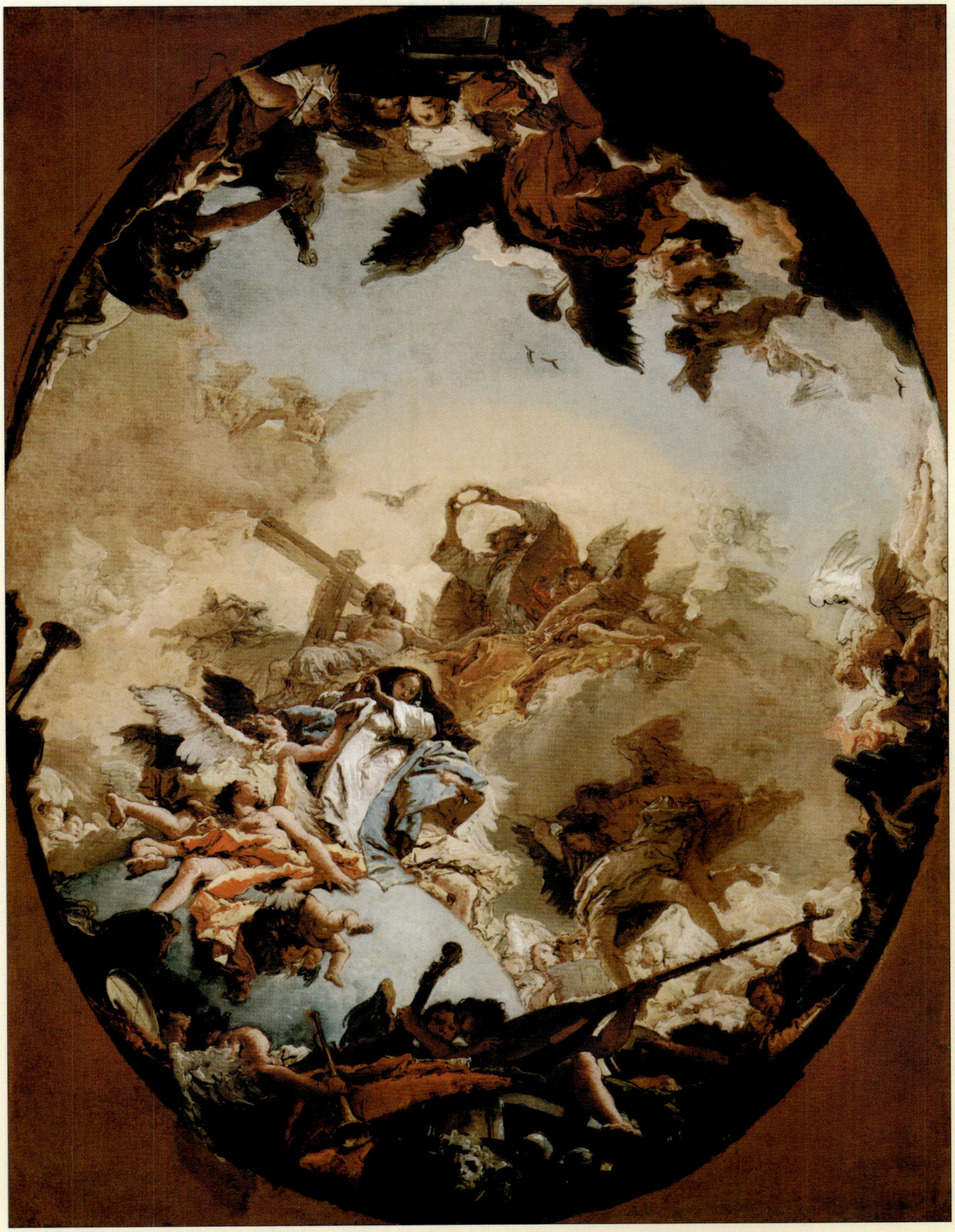

The Coronation of the Virgin *1754–55. Oil on canvas. 40½ x 30½ in (103 x 77 cm). Kimbell Art Museum, Fort Worth, TX.*

In 1750 Tiepolo was appointed by Carl Phillip Von Greiffenklau, prince-bishop of Würzburg, to produce lavish murals for his newly built Residenz. Tiepolo's sons Giandomenico and Lorenzo helped him paint frescos and some altarpieces there over the following three years.

This prestigious commission was followed by further honors; in 1755 he became first president of the Venetian Academy. The last years of Tiepolo's life were spent reluctantly, but no less productively, in Madrid, serving as a kind of pawn in a diplomatic arrangement. The Venetian Republic was regularly in conflict with Spain, and obliged Tiepolo to work for the Spanish king, Charles III, who had applied pressure to acquire his skills as a mural painter. Tiepolo lived long enough to see the tide of European opinion and taste turn against the style he presented so magnificently.

TINTORETTO

TINTORETTO'S WORK DISPLAYS A VARIETY OF INFLUENCES. He drew on diverse sources to create a personal style that combined overwhelming effects with closely observed detail. He lived and worked entirely in Venice, but his influence spread throughout Europe, and helped to shape the development of numerous baroque artists after his death.

Life and work

Born Jacopo Robusti, the artist was given the nickname "Tintoretto" because of his father's trade as a cloth dyer ("*tintore*"). Little is known of his early life, but Carlo Ridolfi, a biographer, claimed that as an apprentice in Titian's workshop, Tintoretto was expelled after a few days, either for disrespect, or for showing too much talent for his master's liking. The latter situation is often reported in accounts of artists' lives at this time, and is almost certainly a myth, possibly encouraged by the artist himself. Tintoretto was extremely ambitious: he often undercut rivals and frequently used devious means to get commissions.

His style borrowed heavily from others. He employed the rich coloring and luminosity of Titian, then the most admired painter in a city abounding in artistic talent. His figures were copied from Michelangelo Buonarroti, whose works were known from engravings. Even so, his style was unique, and in the latter decades of the century he was considered one of the most important Venetian artists.

By 1539 Tintoretto was registered as an independent artist. *Christ and the Woman Taken in Adultery* (c1545) is an

Uniting line, color, and composition

Tintoretto's aim in art was to combine "the drawing of Michelangelo and the coloring of Titian." At the time there were conflicting opinions regarding the relative merits of Florentine and Venetian painting styles, represented respectively by Michelangelo and Titian. Tintoretto was stating his ambition to combine the best of both. His success extends beyond a fusion of these two technical aspects of his art—however, his later style, though much influenced by the heroic grandeur of Michelangelo's figures and compositions, retains something of the realism of the Venetian tradition, exemplified by Titian.

In his long career Tintoretto's principal theme and purpose was an examination of the meaning of the life of Christ. He was working at a time when Protestant reformers were questioning the very validity of holy images, and the Catholic Church had to justify its promotion of Christian art. It is perhaps significant that, even in his largest paintings, full of movement and incident, the central idea is sometimes presented by a simple human action conveyed without elaboration.

Tintoretto's compositions were often unorthodox in their organization of groups

Data file

Full name: Jacopo Robusti (known as Tintoretto)
Nationality: Italian
Style: High Renaissance
Dates: Born 1518 in Venice, died 1594 in Venice
Key works:
- *Christ and the Woman Taken in Adultery* c1545
- *The Miracle of Saint Mark Rescuing a Slave* 1548
- *Venus, Vulcan, and Cupid* c1550
- *Presentation of the Virgin* 1551–52
- *Christ Washing His Disciple's Feet* c1555–60
- *Paradise* after 1588

Things to look for:
- diagonal compositions using depth of space
- dramatic use of light and shade
- active figures in complex groupings
- vivid coloring and boldness of brushstrokes
- profound religious sentiment

Comparisons: Giovanni Bellini, Titian, Paolo Veronese, Michelangelo Buonarroti, El Greco
Glossary terms: baroque, engraving, fresco, High Renaissance, *scuola*

Christ and the Woman Taken in Adultery
c1545. Oil on canvas. 46 x 66 in (117 x 168 cm). Galleria Nazionale d'Arte Antica, Rome.

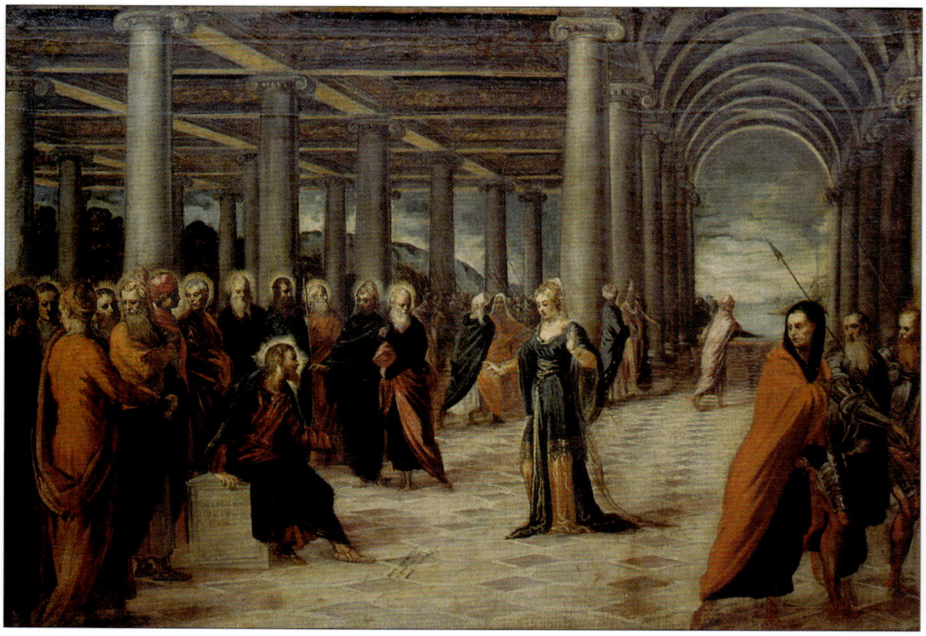

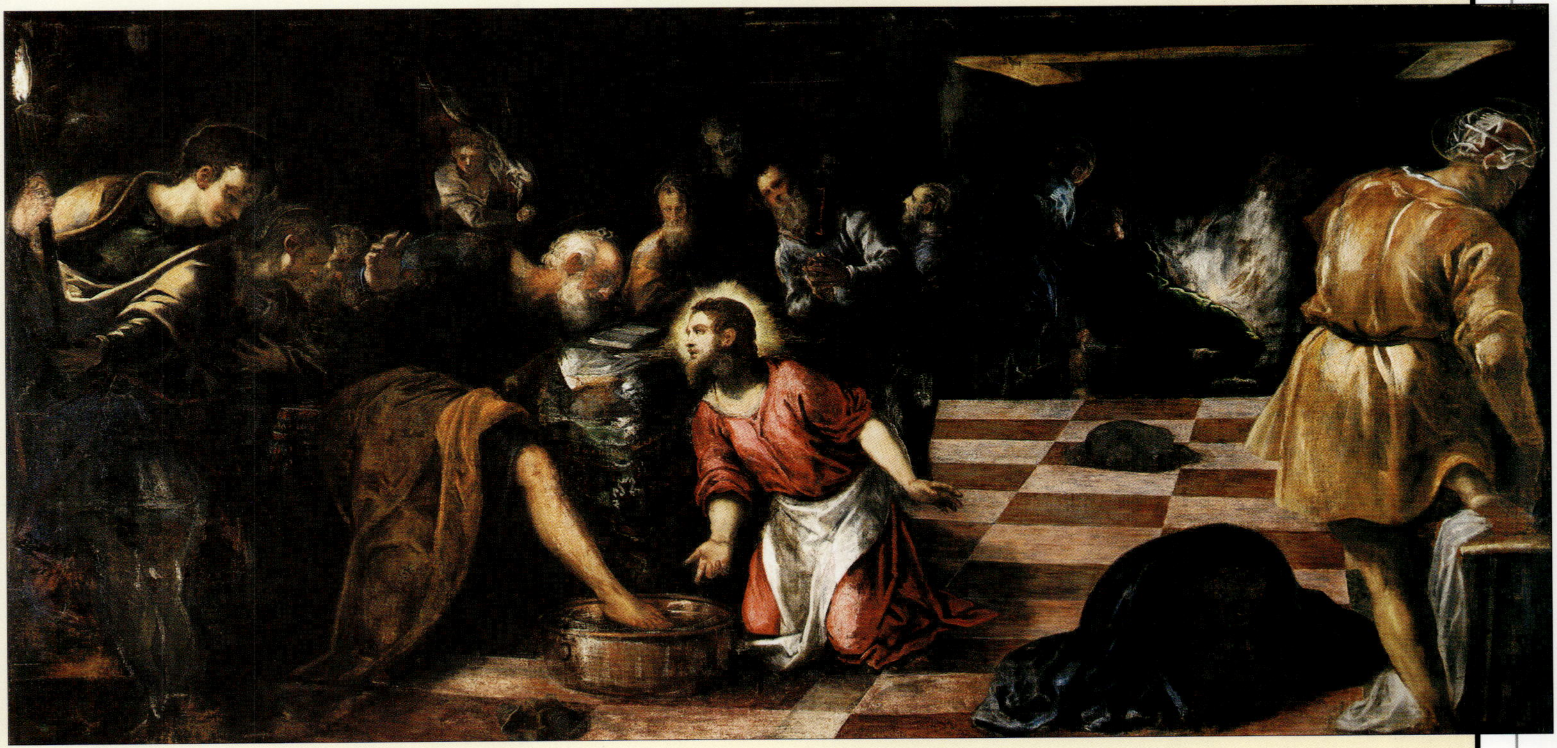

of figures in a confined space. He achieved such effects, in part, by building small architectural models in which he arranged figures, and then tried out different light effects until satisfied with the result. Here, the oblique angle of the work, so often seen in his pictures, focuses on the glowing fire, directed by the posture of the figure on the right, who is engaged in removing a sandal.

The subject of *Christ Washing His Disciple's Feet* (c1555–60) was one Tintoretto painted on a number of occasions. It offered the chance to explore the nature of Christ's character, and His message. The act of humility astonishes the surrounding disciples, not least Saint Peter, whose feet are being cleansed. Nevertheless, the profound event is shown taking place in a modest room, with others present warming themselves by the fire, seemingly oblivious to the incident.

Christ Washing His Disciple's Feet
c1555–60. Oil on canvas. 79 x 160¾ in (201 x 408 cm). National Gallery, London.

early work, with some elements of uncertainty in the handling of figures in relation to the surrounding space. However, it includes features that were to become characteristic of his style: the setting of the scene in deep perspective with a diagonal rather than central orientation is typical.

Tintoretto was well established by the 1550s, and was regularly employed, mostly by churches and religious societies in Venice, providing paintings on sacred themes. He occasionally used mythological themes, and, like Titian and Paolo Veronese, received commissions from aristocratic patrons, and from the Republic of Venice itself.

In 1564 a turning point occurred in his career when he was engaged by the Scuola di San Rocco to produce a series of Old and New Testament works, beginning with the huge *Crucifixion* (1565). This project occupied him, though not exclusively, for over 20 years. Rarely were artists given a chance to display their talents in a single location: Michelangelo at the Vatican and Giotto di Bondone at Padua are comparable examples. In the rooms of the *scuola*, Tintoretto demonstrated his genius for interpretation of Christian narrative. The scheme details were probably dictated by religious advisers, but the presentation of the subject was uniquely his own.

During his long career, Tintoretto's output was huge, requiring the support of a large and well-organized workshop. Three of his children joined his assistants, who were allowed great freedom in the translation of his designs. His style depended on working rapidly, in sweeping strokes of color, which often only briefly delineate figures emerging from dramatic areas of light and shade. This approach should be considered in context: his works were up to 17 feet high and 80 feet long. These were painted in oils on canvas attached to the walls; the damp Venetian climate was not very suitable for true fresco technique.

At his death in 1594 Tintoretto was still busy. He left instructions in his will for his son Domenico to finish his incomplete paintings. Ridolfi noted that his funeral was attended by "many painters who wept for the death of their master, and by notables, and those who loved him."

TITIAN

TITIAN EXCELLED WITH ALL HIS SUBJECTS during his lengthy career, but gained particular renown for his lifelike portraits and his sensuous nudes. He was accomplished in every branch of painting, and is regarded as the finest artist ever produced by the city of Venice, and one of the supreme masters of the Italian Renaissance.

Life and work

Titian was born in the Dolomites, a mountainous region of northern Italy, but moved to Venice while still a child. He came from a line of lawyers and civil servants, inheriting financial skills and a careful approach to business.

In Venice he trained initially as a mosaic artist before turning to painting. His teacher was Giovanni Bellini, a leading figure in the field, but Titian was more impressed with the poetic style of Giorgione, and became his assistant. After Giorgione's premature death, Titian took over his uncompleted projects, and soon acquired a considerable reputation for himself.

In 1516 Bellini died, and Titian assumed his role as Official Painter of the Venetian Republic. At the time, Venice was a powerful city state, with territories as far away as Cyprus, so the honor was an important one. It led to a number of prestigious commissions, most notably *The Assumption of the Virgin* (1516–18), a huge altarpiece for a local church. In addition, Titian began to receive offers of work from Italian princes. The rulers of Mantua and Urbino approached him, but it was the Duke of Ferrara who supplied the most tempting commission—for a series of colorful Bacchanals.

Titian's private life did not run as smoothly as his professional career. He married Cecilia Soldano in 1525, but she died five years later, shortly after giving birth to their third child. Titian never remarried, preferring to bury himself in his work. By now he had built up a well-organized workshop that could deal with the routine pictures, while he attended to his most illustrious patrons, including the two most influential figures in the Western world—Pope Paul III and Charles V, the Holy Roman Emperor.

Titian met Charles V in 1530, and rapidly became an imperial favorite. Over the years, he received many commissions from him, the most famous of which was a sumptuous equestrian portrait. In gratitude, the emperor made Titian a Count Palatine and Knight of the Golden Spur, a unique honor for a painter.

Titian continued working into old age. At the time of his death, he was still busy creating a Pietà, intended to decorate his own tomb.

Data file

Full name: Tiziano Vecellio (known as Titian)

Nationality: Venetian

Style: Renaissance

Dates: born c1485 in Pieve di Cadore, died 1576 in Venice

Key works:

- *The Assumption of the Virgin* 1516–18
- *Bacchanal (The Andrians)* 1518–19
- *Bacchus and Ariadne* c1522–23
- *Venus of Urbino* 1538
- *Danaë* c1549–50
- *Allegory of Prudence* 1566

Things to look for:

- bold brushwork
- rich coloring
- dynamic composition

Comparisons: Giorgione, Paolo Veronese, Tintoretto, Giovanni Bellini, Jacopo Bassano

Glossary terms: *contrapposto,* mosaic, Pietà, Renaissance, sarcophagus

A dashing colorist

In the course of his long career, Titian tackled a variety of subjects—portraits, religious pictures, mythologies—and excelled at them all. Over the years, his style developed, but he was always acknowledged as a master of color. He reflected a tradition that held Florentine painters to be best at drawing, while the Venetians placed greater emphasis on coloring. After seeing Titian's latest picture in 1545, Michelangelo Buonarroti (a Florentine) declared that he was much impressed with the lavish coloring, but thought it "a pity that in Venice men did not learn to draw well from the beginning."

Both of the works illustrated were painted in the early part of Titian's career, when the style of his composition was particularly dynamic. *Portrait of a Man* (c1512) bears all the hallmarks of an artist who is aware of his exceptional talent and keen to flaunt it. It is hard to look at the man's face for long, because your eye is drawn to the virtuoso depiction of the enormous blue sleeve. Titian accentuated this effect by placing the man's arm on a ledge, with part of the sleeve hanging over it. The arm appears to project beyond the picture surface toward us, creating an odd sense of immediacy. The sitter may have

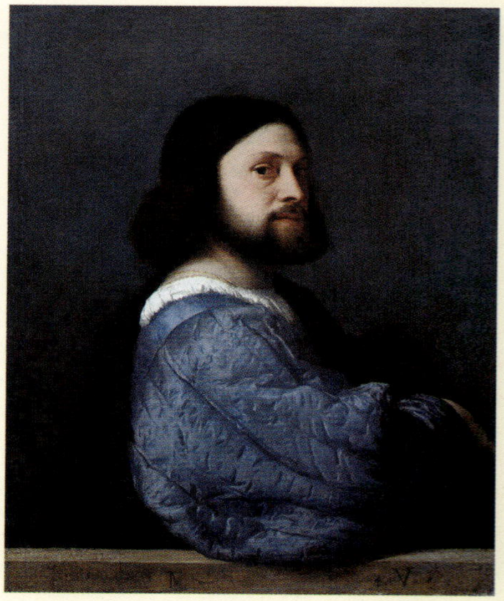

Portrait of a Man *c1512. Oil on canvas. 32 x 36 in (81 x 91 cm). National Gallery, London.*

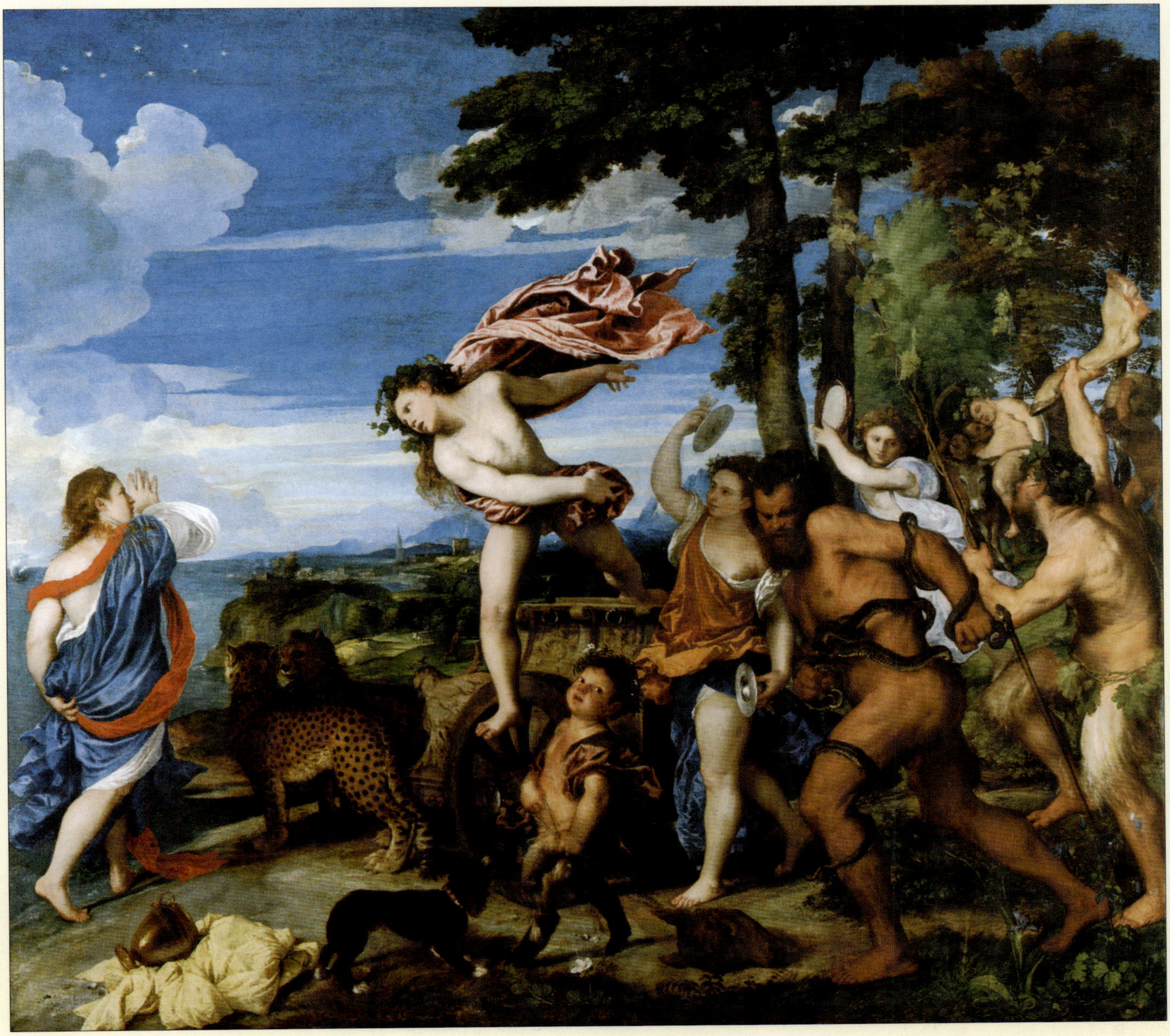

been the poet Luduvico Ariosto, or this may be a self-portrait. Both Rembrandt and Anthony Van Dyck knew the picture and modeled their own self-portraits on it.

In this, as in many of his works, Titian introduced an element of *contrapposto* (a pose that involves a twisting movement). His painting of *Bacchus and Ariadne* (c1522–23) contains far more dramatic examples. This is one of a trio of mythological scenes that Titian produced for the alabaster pleasure chamber of Alfonso d'Este, the duke of Ferrara. Inspiration came from the images on ancient sarcophagi and statuary, and from the written accounts of classical authors, such as Ovid and Catullus, but Titian breathed new life into these sources in a remarkable piece of visual storytelling.

Ariadne (left) has been abandoned on the island of Naxos by Theseus, in spite of her vital assistance in defeating the minotaur. As she watches her lover's ship depart, her grief is interrupted by the arrival of a noisy procession. The savage revellers have just torn apart an animal (its head is on the ground and a leg is waved aloft by one of the satyrs), but Bacchus, the god of wine, leaps down from his chariot and declares his love for Ariadne. Promising to be a more faithful companion than Theseus, he offers her a constellation of stars, the Cnossian crown (visible top left) as a wedding gift. Titian managed to extract the maximum amount of drama out of this tale, largely through the dynamic poses of his two main actors. Equally notable are the swirling draperies with their shimmering blue and rose tones, the artist's two favorite colors.

Bacchus and Ariadne *c1522–23. Oil on canvas. 69 x 75 in (175 x 190.5 cm). National Gallery, London.*

TOULOUSE-LAUTREC Henri de

MORE THAN ANY OTHER ARTIST, Toulouse-Lautrec captured the atmosphere of Paris during the closing decades of the 19th century. And yet there is a darker side to his art, which conveys something of the tragic circumstances of his life and the sometimes harsh reality of the bohemian world he chose to inhabit.

Life and work

Henri de Toulouse-Lautrec was born in southwest France in 1864. He was the son of a nobleman and a descendant of the counts of Toulouse and the viscounts of Lautrec. As a child he showed a talent for drawing, being especially adept at depicting horses in motion. However, he suffered a series of accidents, including breaking both legs, that had a major effect on his future, stunting his growth and leaving him deformed. He used the long periods of convalescence that followed to develop his artistic skills.

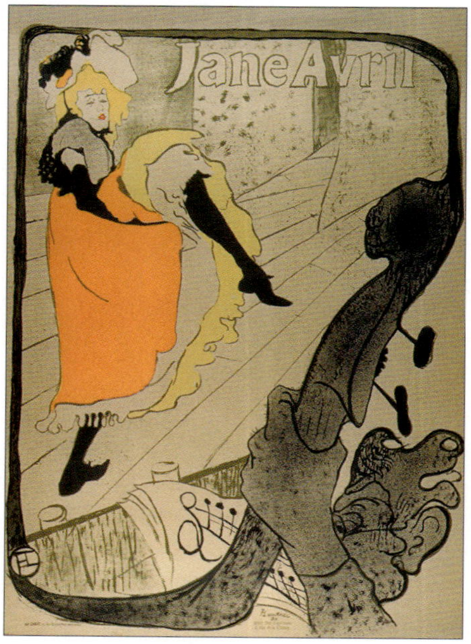

Jane Avril at the Jardin de Paris
Lithograph. 1893. 49 x 36 in (124 x 91.5 cm). Metropolitan Museum of Art, New York, NY.

In 1882 Toulouse-Lautrec moved to Paris to study with the academic painter Léon Bonnat. Bonnat was a highly regarded portrait painter who exhibited at the Salons. He encouraged his young pupil to paint animals.

In 1883 Toulouse-Lautrec joined the school of another academic, Fernand Cormon, who painted religious pictures and imaginary scenes of primitive life. Here, at Cormon's studio, he came into contact with many impressionist and postimpressionist artists. He was especially influenced by Vincent Van Gogh and Emile Bernard, whose ideas were developing in opposition to the officially approved styles of the time. Yet he did not attach himself to any particular theory or movement. His personal style, first apparent in his work of the late 1880s, adapted a range of contemporary influences to his own rapid approach to image-making. His speed of hand and eye was at odds with the patience required for the style of academic drawing practiced at Cormon's studio.

Toulouse-Lautrec's style also reflected his great interest in the theaters, music halls, and cafés of Paris,

Full name: Henri Marie Raymond de Toulouse-Lautrec
Nationality: French
Style: postimpressionism
Dates: born 1864 in Albi, died 1901 in Malromé
Key works:
- *At the Moulin de la Galette* 1889
- *At the Moulin Rouge: The Dance* 1890
- *Moulin Rouge: La Goulue* (poster) 1891
- *At the Moulin Rouge* 1892
- *Jane Avril at the Jardin de Paris* 1893
- *The Salon in the Rue Des Moulins* 1894
- *Elles* (series of lithographic prints) 1896

Things to look for:
- scenes of Paris nightlife
- highly simplified, strong, and expressive outlines
- sketchlike finish
- rapid movement showing the whole atmosphere of a scene with a few strokes

Comparisons: Edgar Degas, Vincent Van Gogh, Emile Bernard, Georges Seurat, Paul Gauguin
Glossary terms: academic art, art nouveau, expressionism, impressionism, lithography, neoimpressionism, postimpressionism, Salon

Form and movement

Toulouse-Lautrec especially admired the impressionist Edgar Degas, who not only specialized in similar social situations, but also used a number of methods to increase the sense of momentary action and interaction, including cutting off figures at the edge of the picture and placing them, as if by accident, behind one another, as if in a photograph. His ability to combine large numbers of separately studied individuals in an apparently spontaneous scene is shown in the painting *At the Moulin Rouge: The Dance* (1890). The arrangement is complicated, and yet there is no confusion in the diverse groupings of people. In a seemingly spontaneous composition, the figures focus around movements of the celebrated dancer La Goulue and her partner Valentin le Désossé. In the background are faces recognizable as friends of Toulouse-Lautrec. The grinning mask of a skull is an example of Lautrec's bitter humor.

The clear, expressive outlines and rough stippling of color illustrate the artist's admiration for Vincent Van Gogh and, possibly, some of the less formal followers of Georges Seurat's neoimpressionism. Toulouse-Lautrec wanted to capture a figure as quickly as possible, and to achieve this, he developed a method that enabled him, in effect, to draw in paint. By diluting oil colors and working on absorbent cardboard, he allowed the background to show through slashes of color. On canvas, the effect in places was similar. The variable application of paint in clearly visible strokes adds to the impression of combined vigorous motion.

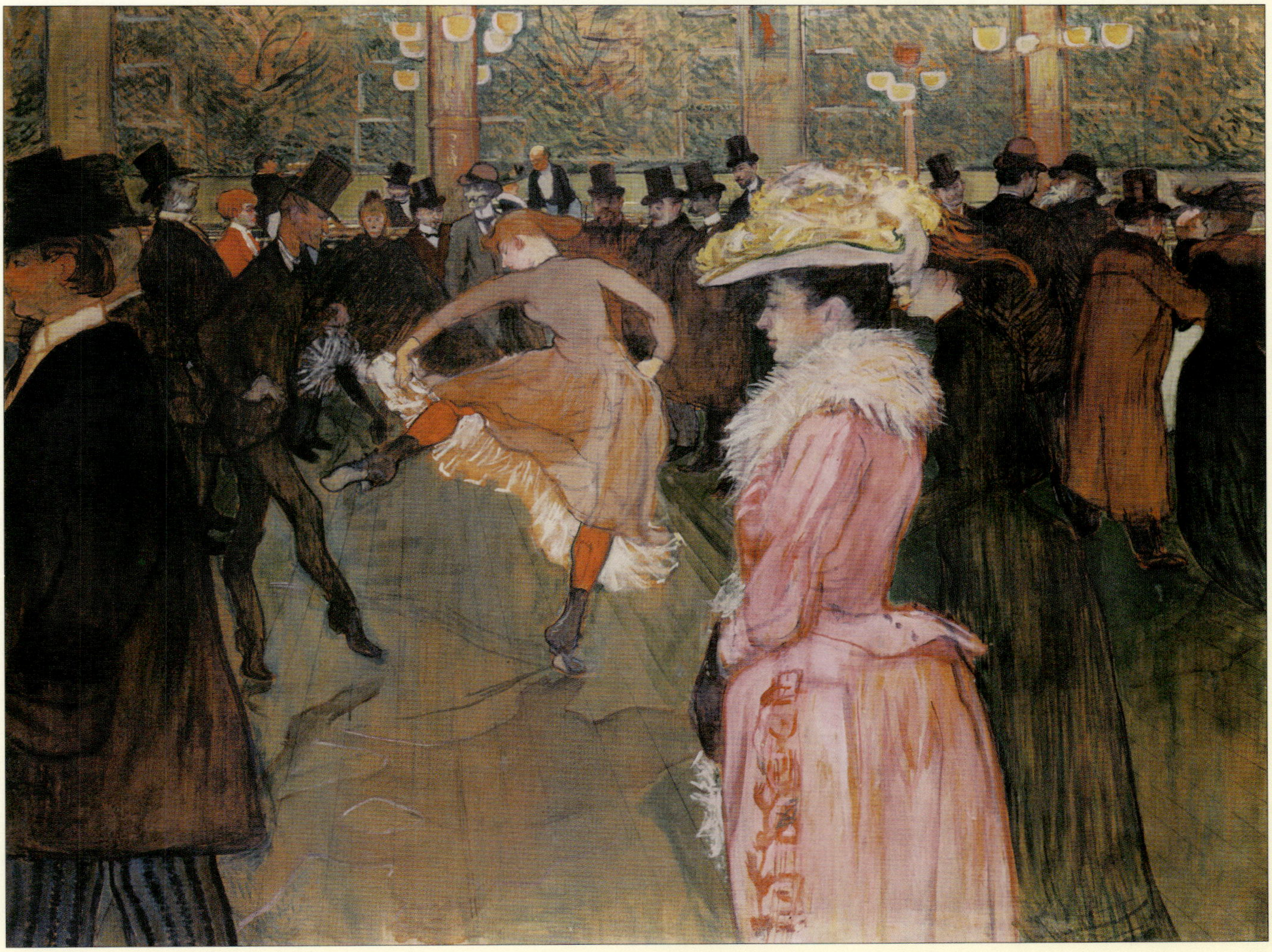

In 1888 Lautrec came into contact with Paul Gauguin. His admiration for the artist's work, and shared enthusiasm for Japanese art, encouraged a tendency toward large areas of flat color contained within clear outlines.

In his graphic work, Toulouse-Lautrec was able to exploit even further the directness of transcription of the original sketch. His apparently simple style and bold images have often been compared to contemporary art nouveau posters. But his strong reputation was due particularly to the marked contrast of his style with the complicated character of poster design at the time.

At the Moulin Rouge: The Dance
1890. Oil on canvas. 49½ x 59 in (77 x 89 cm). Philadelphia Museum of Art, Philadelphia, PA.

especially those in the district of Montmartre, with its busy nightlife. His art largely depended upon drawings done on the spot. Some consist of a few very hastily sketched lines. Worked up afterwards in the studio, the paintings often retained a sense of the vibrant spontaneity of the original.

From 1891 Toulouse-Lautrec established his reputation as a poster artist, with works such as *Jane Avril at the Jardin de Paris* (1893), which features a dancer he greatly admired. For the rest of his life, Toulouse-Lautrec produced posters and paintings of dancers, singers, and prostitutes, all of whom he treated as friends.

Toulouse-Lautrec's work received some critical praise and was included in important exhibitions, such as the Salon des Indépendants. Although, unlike other major postimpressionists, he had little influence as a painter, his impact on modern art was significant. He made both lithography and the poster into major art forms.

Alcoholism was only one of the excesses that led to Toulouse-Lautrec's early death. His weakened physical and mental condition was apparent in the uneven quality of his later work. Yet he continued almost throughout to be prolific, and occasionally brilliant. Friends found in him an unfailing, albeit bitter humor about the virtues and vices of human beings.

TURNER J. M. W.

FROM TERRIFYING NATURAL CATACLYSMS AND GRAND SCENERY to misty sunrises and calm sunsets, Turner's work epitomizes the Romantic feeling for landscape. He was a commanding presence in early 19th-century British art, and his huge and varied output set new standards for landscape painting.

Life and work

Turner's artistic talents were recognized when he was a young boy; his earliest signed drawings date from the age of 12. After working for a time in architects' offices, he entered the Royal Academy Schools in London, which had been established in 1768 to provide a national school for British artists. Turner's close involvement with the Royal Academy lasted throughout his career: it was here that he exhibited his first watercolor in 1790, aged just 15, and where he showed his last great oil paintings some 60 years later.

In the early 1790s Turner undertook the first of his sketching tours. These would eventually take him through Britain and Europe. Works such as *Tintern Abbey, Monmouthshire* (1795), depicting the overgrown ruins of a medieval abbey, reflect a close attention to natural and historical detail, as well as the contemporary taste for the picturesque. Landscape painters such as Richard Wilson had helped to create a demand for this art form, which was collected by wealthy patrons and which also, through engraved copies of paintings, reached a wider public.

The first oil painting that Turner exhibited, in 1796, was a seascape, *Fishermen at Sea*. Moonlight breaks dramatically through the clouds as the fishing boats move toward the dark expanse of open sea. In the following years his paintings continued to explore the grand dramas of nature. *Calais Pier, with French Poissards Preparing for Sea*, painted after his first trip to France in 1802, draws the viewer into the scene as a deep swell lifts giddily from the lower right of the picture.

This was the kind of effect for which, by the 1800s, Turner was becoming famous. In the Romantic era the public wanted art to have a direct, emotional impact, and Turner's paintings aroused a thrilling sense of awe. At the same time, he continued to paint in a quieter manner. Scenes such as *The Thames near Walton Bridges* (c1807), an oil sketch produced out of doors in broad, confident brushstrokes, are closer in mood to the peaceful landscapes of John Constable.

Data file

Full name: Joseph Mallord William Turner

Nationality: English

Style: Romanticism

Dates: born 1775 in London, died 1851 in Chelsea (now a district of London)

Key works:
- *Tintern Abbey, Monmouthshire* 1795
- *Calais Pier, with French Poissards Preparing for Sea* 1802
- *Snow Storm: Hannibal and His Army Crossing the Alps* 1812
- *Dido Building Carthage* 1815
- *The Fighting Téméraire* 1839
- *Snow Storm—Steam-Boat off a Harbor's Mouth* 1842
- *Sunrise with Sea Monsters* c1845

Things to look for:
- dramatic treatment of landscape
- wide range of landscape subjects
- interest in atmospheric effects of light and weather
- increasingly free, gestural handling of paint

Comparisons: Claude Lorraine, Richard Wilson, John Constable, Claude Monet

Glossary terms: Academy, classical, gestural, perspective, picturesque, Romanticism

Dramas of nature

Turner was very fond of this painting, which he never agreed to sell. It shows the warship *Téméraire* being towed to a shipbreaker's yard on the River Thames. The *Téméraire* had fought beside Admiral Lord Nelson's flagship, the *Victory*, at the Battle of Trafalgar in 1805, where the French navy was decisively defeated.

Produced more than 30 years later, *The Fighting Téméraire* (1839) contains one of Turner's great sunsets. The low sun turns the clouds red and gold; the light effects are balanced by the plunging reflections of the two vessels in the water. Turner's sunsets are often connected with the presence of death, however. The old warship, heroic survivor of battle, is shown on her last voyage. Her pale, ghostly form, echoed by the moon just visible in the upper left, contrasts strongly with the steamer—part funereal black, part fiery red where the sunlight catches the hull and sparks spurt from the smokestack.

The *Téméraire* embodies a heroic, Romantic past—the age of sail—while the steamer is a modern machine, part of the rapid industrialization of the time. Turner's grasp of history, both the classical and (as here) the more recent past, is an important element in many of his landscapes.

The Fighting Téméraire *1839. Oil on canvas. 35¾ x 48 in (91 x 122 cm). National Gallery, London.*

In 1802, aged 27, Turner was elected a full member of the Royal Academy. His work was beginning to attract important patrons, and in 1804 he opened his own gallery on Harley Street, London. In 1807 he was appointed professor of perspective at the Royal Academy, a post he held for 30 years. He was now a senior figure in the British artistic establishment; but at the same time his work seemed to embody the individualistic, Romantic spirit of the age. Also in 1807, he began to issue a vast series of prints of his paintings, entitled the *Liber Studiorum* after Claude Lorraine's celebrated *Liber Veritatis* (*Book of Truth*), in which the

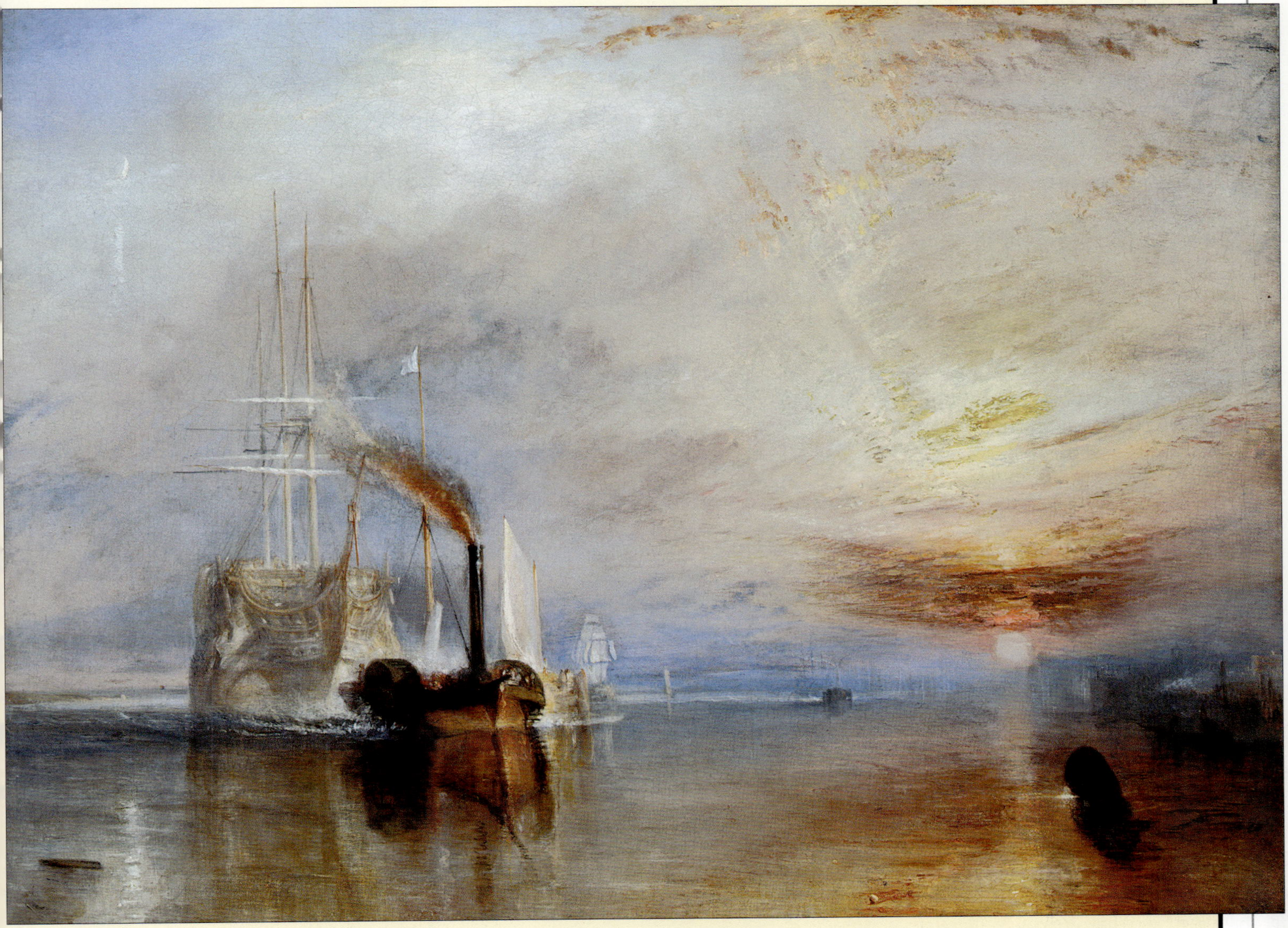

17th-century French master recorded every painting he made.

After traveling in northern Europe in 1817, Turner made his first visit to Italy in 1819. His response to the sparkling Mediterranean light can be seen in a changed tonality in his paintings. The beautiful watercolors in his Venice sketchbooks are full of airy yellows, blues, and rosy reds. From this time his preoccupation with rendering light as refracted through different atmospheric conditions became more marked. The Italian landscape and its classical past encouraged him to create tranquil settings painted in warm, rich colors.

In the 1820s and 1830s Turner made several further visits to Europe. From 1827 he also spent much time at Petworth Park in Sussex, the country house of his foremost patron, the Third Earl of Egremont. Here, from a studio provided by his host, he produced paintings of the house and the estate.

Egremont died in 1837; in the same year Turner resigned from his Royal Academy professorship. He continued to travel, making repeated visits to Switzerland. When in England he lived an increasingly reclusive life in Chelsea (then just outside London), calling himself Mr. Booth, after his mistress, Sophia Booth.

Turner's style had always been controversial, and by the 1840s it seemed to many people puzzlingly eccentric. His work found a champion, however, in the young writer and artist John Ruskin. Through his book *Modern Painters* (first volume published 1843), Ruskin secured Turner's reputation, but also went too far in protecting it by destroying many of Turner's erotic drawings after his death in 1851. Turner bequeathed a huge collection of his works—more than 20,000 in all—to the nation. It was finally housed in the Clore Gallery, built for that purpose, which opened as part of the Tate Gallery in London in 1987.

UCCELLO Paolo

UCCELLO WAS SKILLED NOT ONLY AS A PAINTER but also as a mosaicist and craftsman. His pictures reflect a fascination with perspective—one of the major preoccupations of Florentine painters during the 15th century—but include curiously stylized details.

Life and work

No one knows exactly when Paolo Uccello was born, but his approximate date of birth has been calculated from his tax returns. "Uccello" was the nickname given to him because of his love of birds (*uccello* is Italian for "bird"). His father, Dono di Paolo, was a surgeon who was married in Florence in 1387. Uccello spent most of his life in Florence, apart from visits to Venice, Padua, and Urbino. He married rather late in life and had a son in 1453 and a daughter in 1456.

From about 1412 to 1416 Uccello was apprenticed to the sculptor Lorenzo Ghiberti, one of the main Florentine exponents of the decorative late-Gothic style, and he is recorded as having been in the workshop where Ghiberti's baptistery doors were made. Uccello was being referred to as a painter in his own right in 1415. Between 1425 and 1427 he was in Venice working as a mosaicist in Saint Mark's Basilica, but the full extent of his work there is not known.

In 1436 Uccello was commissioned to paint a commemorative fresco of the English soldier Sir John Hawkwood. This is still on the north wall of Florence Cathedral. Like other works by Uccello, it illustrates an interest in perspective.

Uccello made three designs for stained glass to go below the cupola of Florence Cathedral, a project started in the early 1430s, in which other artists, notably Ghiberti, Donatello, and Andrea del Castagno, were involved.

Uccello's paintings of the 1440s and 1450s reveal his determination to come to terms with recent developments in Florentine art, particularly regarding the representation of space. He was familiar with a celebrated book by Leon Battista Alberti: *Della Pittura (On Painting)* of 1436, in which a system of perspective is described. He painted frescos in the Chiostro Verde (Green Cloister) of the church of Santa Maria Novella in Florence, and the most famous of these (dating from between 1445 and 1455) illustrate the story of Noah. The scene showing the flood and the recession of the waters is remarkable for its use of perspective to show acute depth and a sense of movement.

In the mid-1450s Uccello was commissioned by Piero de' Medici to paint three large panels illustrating the Battle of San Romano for the new Medici Palace in Florence. (These are now scattered: one is in London, one in Florence, and one in Paris.)

Data file

Full name: Paolo di Dono (known as Paolo Uccello)

Nationality: Italian

Style: Renaissance

Dates: born c1397 in Florence, died 1475 in Florence

Key works:

Sir John Hawkwood 1436

The Flood 1445–55

The Battle of San Romano c1450s

Saint George and the Dragon c1460

The Hunt in the Forest 1460s

Things to look for:

- experimental use of perspective
- frozen, wooden appearance of figures

Comparisons: Donatello, Masaccio, Gentile da Fabriano, Andrea del Castagno

Glossary terms: fresco, Gothic, perspective

A sense of the pageantry of war

This picture is one of the three that Uccello painted to commemorate the Battle of San Romano. Originally they were part of a decorative scheme in the newly built Medici Palace in Florence. Seen in a book, or even in an art gallery, paintings such as this lose impact; we have to imagine them high up (about seven feet above the floor) on the walls in a grand chamber in the palace.

The foreground space of the picture is narrow, though it would have seemed much deeper when viewed from below. Candlelight and firelight by night would have caught the shine of the silver and gold leaf (now dulled but originally bright) picking out the armor and the horses' trappings. The colors, pattern, and rhythm of the composition add to the sense of sumptuousness that pervades the picture, which would have had the same impact as a rich, decorative tapestry.

The Battle of San Romano took place in 1432 as part of an ongoing war between Florence and the town of Lucca. Uccello painted these pictures years after the actual event, from his imagination and perhaps from descriptions by people who had been there.

The painting shows the Florentine commander Niccolò da Tolentino (in the red turban), directing an attack on the Sienese, who had joined forces with the enemy town of Lucca. The outcome of the battle was inconclusive and both sides claimed victory. Because the picture was painted for a Florentine who was a personal friend of Niccolò da Tolentino, it is hardly surprising that all except one of the soldiers shown are on the Florentine side.

The painting has the sense of pageantry associated with a jousting match rather than the bloodiness of war. This is a strange battle indeed, for there is no blood,

Uccello's later works included *Saint George and the Dragon* (c1460) and *The Hunt in the Forest*. The latter, probably done in the 1460s, is one of his best-known works. Here he organized the

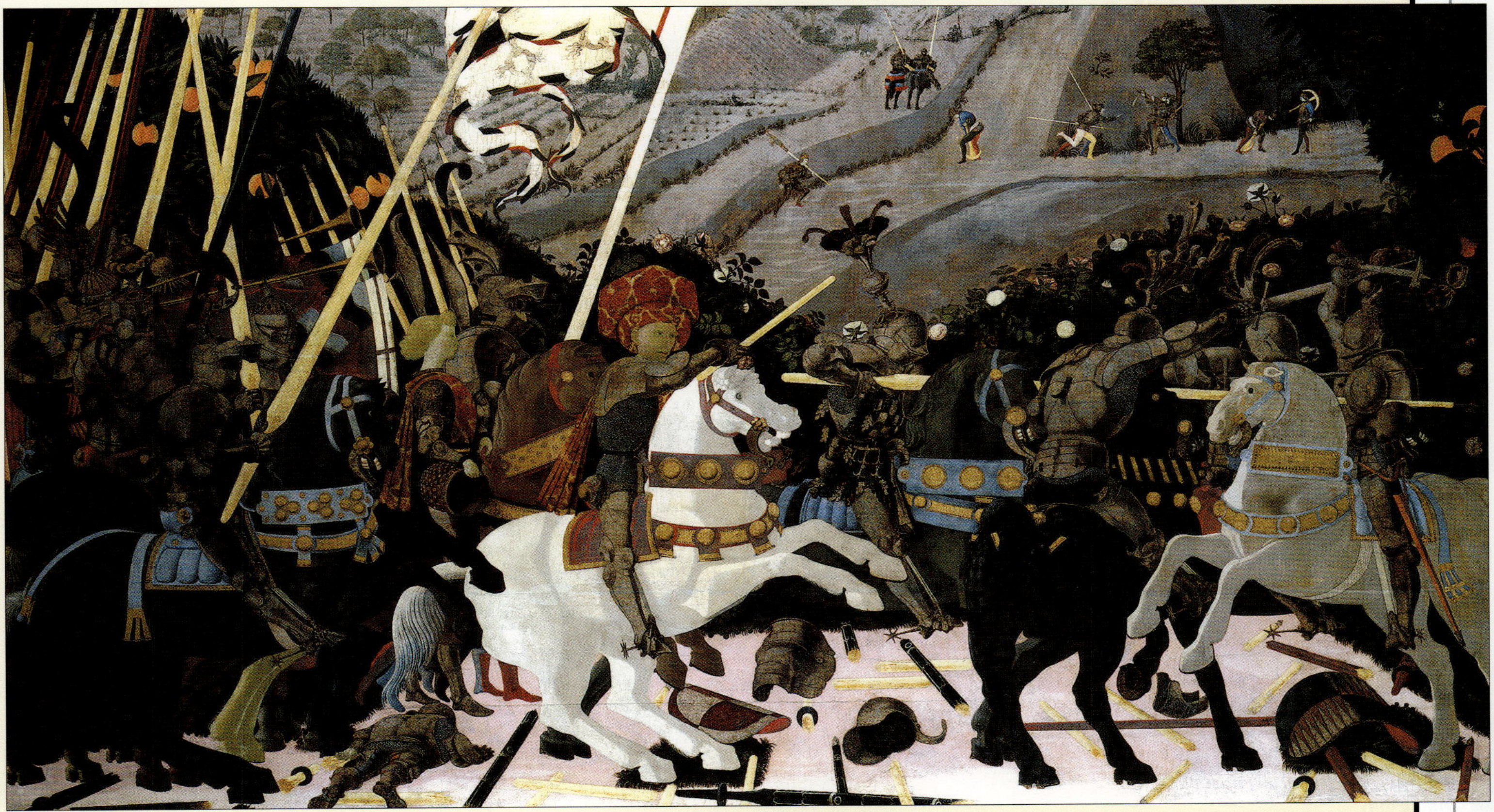

The Battle of San Romano *c1450s. Tempera (perhaps with some oil) on panel. 71 1/2 x 126 in (182 x 320 cm). National Gallery, London.*

and there seems to be only one casualty: a man is lying prostrate on the ground.

Other details reinforce the sense of unreality. Niccolò da Tolentino wears a glorious red and gold turban rather than a helmet, which is being held by his young squire beside him. He carries a baton rather than an ax or sword, and seems to be conducting an orchestra rather than leading his soldiers into battle. His horse (light-colored to make him the most prominent figure in the painting), and the other horses, are strangely wooden in appearance.

The middle ground of the painting is taken up by a hedge bearing oranges and roses, another decorative and stylized detail.

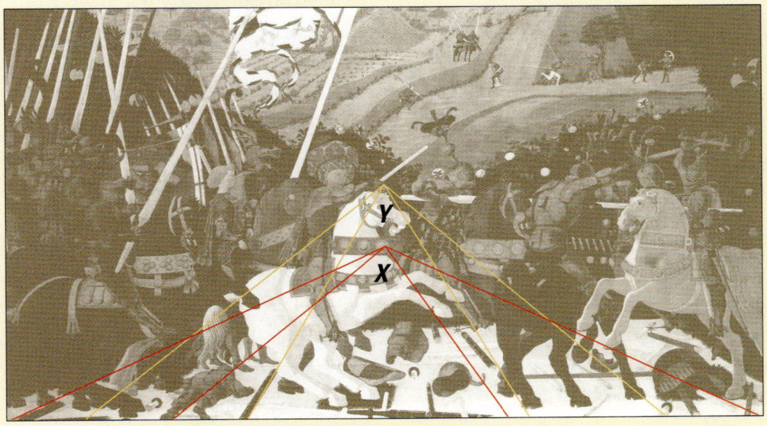

The perspective of the painting is by no means straightforward. The debris of battle and the wounded man are arranged in such a way that the receding lines of perspective, or "orthogonals," meet in at least two vanishing points in the foreground of the painting.

Orthogonals *direct the viewer's eye to at least two vanishing points (see X and Y), both focusing on Niccolò da Tolentino's rearing horse, while the background, separated emphatically by the hedge, has a different perspective scheme.*

picture with such precision that it almost turns into an abstract pattern. The area is neatly divided into equal parts; elements such as trees, fleeing stags, and galloping hounds, lead the eye back into the space. Within this structure, the pursuing huntsmen, many dressed in scarlet, create a river of color winding in and out of the trees. The image has a strong sense of movement.

Uccello is said to have become a hermit, and seems to have had a sad old age. On his 1469 tax return, he wrote: "I find myself old and ailing, my wife is ill, and I can no longer work."

UTRILLO Maurice

THE PAINTER PAR EXCELLENCE OF PARISIAN SCENES, Maurice Utrillo began painting as a therapy to combat alcoholism. He went on to enjoy popular and commercial success with numerous interpretations of the streets, churches, and houses around Montmartre, the area forever associated with bohemian artistic life.

Life and work

Maurice Utrillo's mother was the artist and artist's model Suzanne Valadon; the identity of his father is unknown. When Utrillo was seven years old, the Catalan art critic Miguel Utrillo y Molins adopted him. Utrillo signed his early works as Maurice Valadon, later changing to Maurice Utrillo.V. (the "V" in honor of his mother).

Data file

Full name: Maurice Valadon (changed his name to Maurice Utrillo.V.)

Nationality: French

Style: realism

Dates: born 1883 in Paris, died 1955 in Dax

Key works:

The Roofs of Montmagny 1906–07

Renoir's Garden 1909–11

Cottin Dead End 1911

Reims Cathedral in Flames 1914

Holiday Fair c1922

Le Sacré-Coeur, Montmartre, and Rue Saint-Rustique c1927–28

Windmills of Montmartre 1949

Things to look for:

- simple compositions: horizontal, vertical, and diagonal lines establish the framework
- high-keyed colors
- views of churches and the streets of Paris and Montmartre
- often views of empty streets, but when figures do appear, they are anonymous and seen from behind
- locations are identifiable by inscriptions on the painting in the artist's handwriting

Comparisons: Camille Pissaro, Alfred Sisley, Vincent Van Gogh, the fauves

Glossary terms: *catalogue raisonné*, cubism, *en plein air*, high-keyed, impressionism, realism

Utrillo suffered the first of many alcohol-induced breakdowns at the age of 18, and spent two months in a sanatorium. On the advice of his physician and his mother, he began to paint. By 1903 he had painted hundreds of views of Montmagny, a suburb of Paris. Utrillo's oil paintings from 1903 to 1907—known as his *Periode Montmagny* (Montmagny period)—were usually completed in one or two hours.

At a time when Pablo Picasso was attracting attention with his experiments in cubism, Utrillo took little interest in any art style newer than impressionism. His early paintings betray the influence of Camille Pissarro and Alfred Sisley in particular. The only contemporary painter Utrillo is known to have admired is the little-known Jean François Raffaëlli, who was also a painter of Parisian scenes.

In 1909 Utrillo's work was included in the Salon d'Automne exhibition. Around this time he stopped painting *en plein air* in the impressionist manner, and began working from picture postcards, enlarging and altering the compositions onto his canvases. In this, his *Periode Blanche* (white period), Utrillo concentrated on depicting white buildings, mixing glue and plaster into his white paint in order to reproduce the textures of their walls.

After the white period came his *Periode Colorée* (colored period), marked by bright colors and a greater emphasis on line, which replaced the rich brushwork of his earlier periods. A new theme also emerged in Utrillo's work: women walking in the streets, always with their backs to the viewer.

Memories of Paris

For the most part, Utrillo's paintings fall into two major groups: images of churches, and the *petit patrie*, the local places he knew best—these were the streets of Montmartre and northern Paris. Like many of Utrillo's paintings, *Le Sacré-Coeur, Montmartre, and Rue Saint-Rustique* (c1927–28) was painted from memory and from black-and-white picture postcard references. In the manner of picture postcards, Utrillo identifies the location with an inscription in the bottom left of the painting.

Before the 19th century, Montmartre was just one of many small villages outside Paris. Here, the locals on the Butte Montmartre (the Holy Hill) grew vines and quarried the local stone. In the 19th century, as Paris grew, the area was discovered by painters and poets. Today, the streets are largely unchanged, and look much as Utrillo painted them. Some 300 feet above the right bank of the River Seine, the summit of the Butte is reached by a maze of steep, winding streets, including the rue Rustique. In many of these streets wheeled traffic cannot pass, but pedestrians can continue their ascent to the top of the hill and the white domes of the church of Sacré-Coeur via steep flights of steps.

While this church often seems to be a timeless feature of the Montmartre scene, its construction did not begin until 1878. Its image, however—with the great dome crowned by the lantern, the four smaller domes, and the square bell tower—came not only to dominate the Butte, but also to appear in paintings by many artists. It was a frequent motif in Utrillo's work: sometimes the image of Sacré-Coeur rises in the distance like a ghostly presence; at other times the church's monumental scale

In 1912 Utrillo was included in an exhibition of modern French art, in Munich, Germany. His first one-man show came the following year, and the price of his paintings rose significantly. Fame did not rest easily on Utrillo's shoulders, however: he continued to wear old clothes despite financial

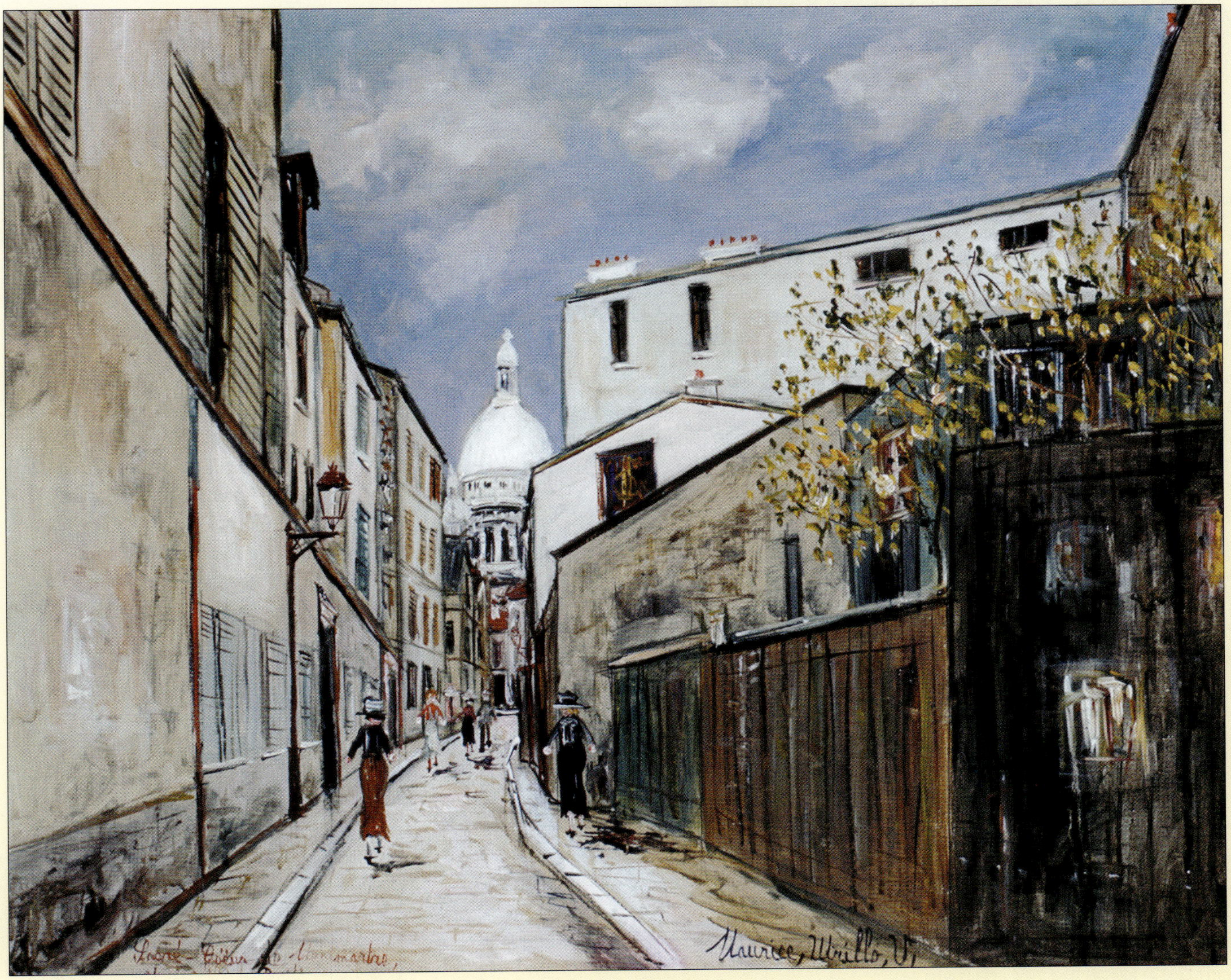

dwarfs the surrounding buildings; and on other occasions the dome appears hemmed in by the mass of foreground buildings.

The painting's loose brushstrokes and high-keyed colors, which contrast with the white dome of Sacré-Coeur, are characteristic of Utrillo's work after 1927. In all his paintings, the composition is simple: horizontal, vertical, and diagonal lines establish the framework in which the sky, street, and houses occupy separate areas.

Although this was a relatively stable period in Utrillo's personal life (he was acclaimed for his work, he had largely controlled his alcoholism, and had turned to religion), there is a sense of the artist's isolation in the anonymous, almost caricatured figures that appear to recede.

Le Sacré-Coeur, Montmartre, and Rue Saint-Rustique *c1927–28. Oil on canvas. 19½ x 24 in (49.5 x 61 cm). Museum of Fine Arts, Boston, MA.*

security, and by 1924 he was drinking so heavily that he was often arrested and jailed. On one occasion, while in jail, he even tried to commit suicide. Suzanne Valadon decided to move her son away from the temptations of Montmartre: with money from the sale of her son's paintings she bought the Château de Saint-Bernard near Lyons, where Utrillo was able to avoid alcohol. He began to paint again.

Despite frequent periods of drunkenness, often followed by seclusion and even hospitalization, Utrillo's output—in sheer numbers of paintings, even if they are not all of a consistently high quality—was huge. In the four years of World War I alone, he produced some 1200 oils. The posthumous *catalogue raisonné* lists more than 3500 oils that have survived—and there may be many more, since it is known that Utrillo often exchanged a painting for wine.

VAN DER WEYDEN Rogier

LITTLE SURVIVES OF ROGIER VAN DER WEYDEN'S WORK, but he was held in high esteem in mid-15th-century Flanders. The paintings that have been attributed to him reveal a subtle talent on a level with that of his more famous contemporary, Jan Van Eyck.

Life and work

The two towns in which Rogier Van der Weyden is known to have lived suffered widespread destruction in the 17th and then the 20th century, and records that may have shed light on his life have been lost.

It is known that Van der Weyden was born in Tournai around the beginning of the 15th century, where his father worked as a successful maker and seller of cutlery. His childhood and early training as an artist are a mystery, but we do know that by his mid-twenties he had married a woman called Elisabeth Goffaert, who was the daughter of another prosperous tradesman. Some degree of financial security provided by the families allowed Van der Weyden to make investments, and throughout his life he was reasonably wealthy.

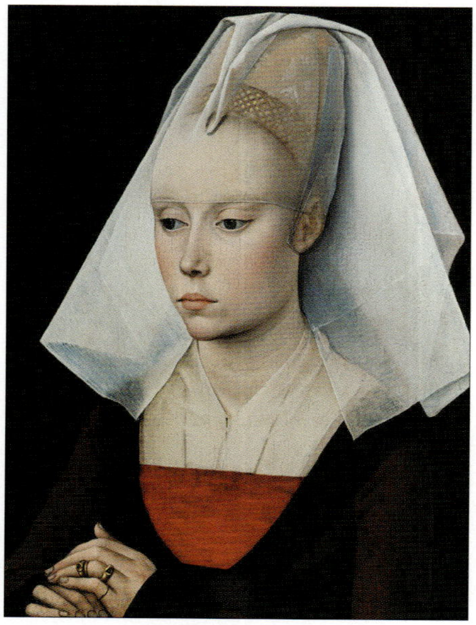

Portrait of a Lady *c1460. Oil on panel. $14\frac{1}{4}$ x $10\frac{1}{2}$ in (36 x 26.5 cm). National Gallery, London.*

Another great early Flemish painter of the period, Robert Campin, was also living in Tournai, and records suggest that Rogier was employed in Campin's workshop, either as an apprentice or as a journeyman (a craftsman who is qualified to work at his trade in the employment of another). An apprenticeship would have lasted for four years, by which time Rogier would have been in his early thirties—rather a late age for someone to complete their training.

Van der Weyden became a master in the town's guild of painters soon afterward, and would probably have undertaken his first commissions in Tournai in the early 1430s. In about 1435, however, Van der Weyden moved to Brussels, although he is thought to have maintained connections with Tournai (and perhaps even kept a workshop there). He was at least as talented as Campin, and soon found himself the official town painter in Brussels. Unfortunately, one of his

Expressive religious images

As was a common practice of the time, Van der Weyden established a large workshop, where he employed many assistants. This fact complicates the already difficult process of attributing works to him, since he never signed or dated his work.

The majority of Van der Weyden's commissions were either for religious paintings, or for portraits of the Flemish nobility. But, whatever the subject matter, there is a level of detail and a subdued, thoughtful mood that runs through almost all his work. The colors that Van der Weyden used are less rich and glowing than those of his contemporary Jan Van Eyck; he seems to have preferred subtler hues, which lend his work a cooler atmosphere.

Regardless of the subject or the sitter, there is great similarity in the faces that Van der Weyden painted, and sometimes it seems as if all his models and sitters belonged to one great family. He had a preference for well-balanced, even decorative compositions, and favored idealized forms over absolute reality, and so he imposed his artistic preferences upon the world he painted. Faces are defined with a graphic clarity, as are the features upon them. Noses tend to have a long and noble bearing, eyelids frequently hang heavy over downcast eyes, and the mouths hold a quiet serenity.

As is typical of the early Flemish artists, Van der Weyden's work displays a devotion to detail. *The Magdalen Reading* (c1445) is alive with complexity and subtle variations in surface texture. We can see it in the

Data file

Full name: Rogier Van der Weyden

Nationality: Netherlandish

Style: early Netherlandish

Dates: born c1399 in Tournai, died 1464 in Brussels

Key works:

- *Saint Luke Drawing a Portrait of the Virgin* c1430s
- *Miraflores Triptych* c1435
- *Deposition* c1435
- *The Descent from the Cross* c1438
- *The Magdalen Reading* (fragment from *The Virgin and Child with Six Saints)* c1445
- *The Columba Triptych* c1455
- *Portrait of a Lady* c1460

Things to look for:

- detailed facial expressions
- highly contrived figurative compositions

Comparisons: Jan Van Eyck, Robert Campin, Hugo Van der Goes, Gerard David, Jacques Daret, Hans Memling

Glossary terms: guild, impressionism, master, Renaissance delicate feathering that creates the fur-lined effect on her dress, and in the rich, raised decoration on her golden underdress. The eyes of the woman lead us to the carefully drawn illuminated lettering of a linen-covered Bible. This is a very crisp level of detail as if seen through a microscope, but, through the window beyond, we see a freer brush technique that has produced a small figure by the edge of a river and her reflection in the rippling water. Close up, this tiny section of the painting is almost impressionistic.

The magdalen (a courtesan who has repented her sins) is a demure figure symbolizing repentance and a new life dedicated to holy work. The jar next to her contains myrrh, used in worship.

The Magdalen Reading is a fragment from what is thought to be a much larger work, known as *The Virgin and Child with Six Saints*. One or two other fragments survive, such as the head of what is possibly Saint Catherine, and the quizzical face of Saint Joseph, and from sketches and copies of the work an approximate composition can be determined.

The level of detail in this one panel indicates the amount of work that would have gone into the complete painting. At first the painting seems rather oddly composed, but this is because *The Magdalen Reading* occupied only a small part of the entire work. This is why the upper body of the standing figure is abruptly cut off, as is the top of the cabinet behind the magdalen, and, on the left of the painting, toes poke out from beneath hanging folds of cloth.

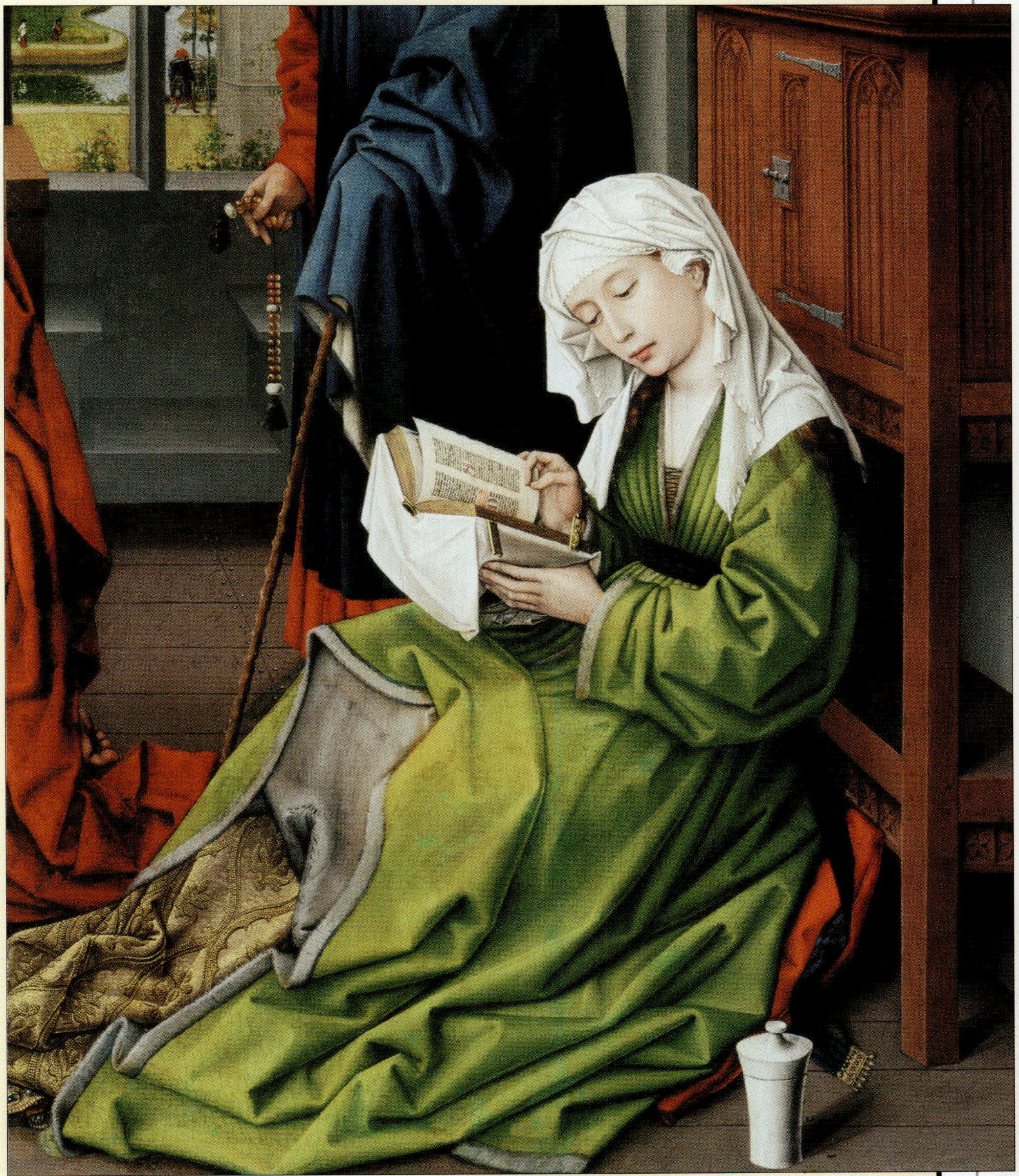

The Magdalen Reading *c1445. Oil on panel. 24 1/4 x 21 1/2 in (61.5 x 54.5 cm). National Gallery, London.*

largest works—a series of paintings on the theme of justice, which he produced for the Golden Chamber in Brussels' town hall—was destroyed in the 17th century. Several of his other works that do survive, however, show that he was able to convey a strong emotional atmosphere in his paintings, which is seen as the key progression from the work of his early mentor, Campin. The depiction of subtle emotion can be seen in the pensive concentration of the *The Magdalen Reading* (c1445), for example, or in the sighing expressions of the two figures bending to support the dead body in *The Exhumation of Saint Hubert* (c1440).

Van der Weyden became known as far away as Spain and Italy, where he was described in glowing terms by theologians and noblemen. He is thought to have made one notable excursion from Brussels: a pilgrimage to Rome, where he is said to have seen—and been highly impressed by—the work of one of the early Renaissance artists, Gentile da Fabriano.

Van der Weyden died in 1464 in Brussels. The painters' guild in Tournai held a funeral service in his honor.

VAN DYCK Anthony

ANTHONY VAN DYCK WAS ONE OF THE GREAT FLEMISH PAINTERS of the 17th century, second only to Rubens. During his short but brilliant career, he traveled through Europe working for the rich and famous. From 1632 he lived and worked in London, painting at the court of King Charles I. Still in great demand, but exhausted, he died in 1641, aged just over 40.

Life and work

Anthony Van Dyck was born in 1599 in Antwerp, a large, prosperous town in Belgium, which was then ruled by Spain. It had a flourishing artistic community in which Peter Paul Rubens played a leading part. Van Dyck's exceptional skill as a painter was recognized at an early age, and he was apprenticed to an artist when he was just 10 years old. Later he entered the workshop of Rubens, who called him "my best pupil."

In about 1616 Van Dyck set up his own studio, but continued to work with Rubens, carrying out such important works as *Samson and Delilah* (1619).

Early self-portraits of Van Dyck show him as elegant, handsome, and self-assured. In 1620 he embarked on the first of many journeys that were to be an important part of his career, with a trip to London. There he studied private collections and spent some months in the service of King James I. Among his commissions was *The Continence of Scipio* (1620–21) for the duke of Buckingham.

Between 1621 and 1627 Van Dyck lived in Italy. He was well received and painted many portraits of the nobility, showing them as tall, magnificent individuals in sumptuous pillared settings, as in *A Genoese Noblewoman and her Son* (c1625). Here he refined the style that would be characteristic of his work from then on. In many of his portraits he produced the effect of comfortable elegance: creating a timeless image of the aristocracy. Among his surviving drawings and watercolors are some that demonstrate the freshness and spontaneity with which he responded to nature.

In 1627 Van Dyck returned to Antwerp, where he received the patronage of Archduchess Isabella Clara Eugenia. There he painted many impressive religious pictures that were intended as altarpieces for churches, as well as portraits of the local people, who tended to be shown in sober, dark clothing. An invitation to work for the court of King Charles I, one of the great patrons of the 17th century, took him to London in 1632. He would stay in England for the rest of his life.

Data file

Full name: Anthony Van Dyck

Nationality: Flemish

Style: baroque

Dates: born 1599 in Antwerp, died 1641 in London, England

Key works:

Samson and Delilah 1619

A Genoese Noblewoman and Her Son c1625

Charity c1627

Queen Henrietta with Jeffrey Hudson and an Ape 1633

Triple Portrait of Charles I 1635

Lady Elizabeth Thimbleby and Viscountess Andover c1637

Things to look for:

- elegant portraiture of the aristocracy
- paintings evoking the personality of the sitters
- dramatic composition
- brilliant use of color

Comparisons: Peter Paul Rubens, Gianlorenzo Bernini, Thomas Gainsborough, John Singer Sargent, Titian

Glossary terms: allegory, baroque

The changing face of portraiture

Van Dyck was fortunate to grow up in Antwerp, one of the great artistic centers of 17th-century Europe. He was greatly influenced by the large-scale baroque compositions of Rubens, but even as a youth showed great individuality in the execution of his paintings. He often used a fairly rough technique, in which the strokes of the brush are clearly visible, and some of the forms are only suggested, rather than meticulously finished, as was the custom of the time. He was much influenced by Italian art, and especially by Titian.

While many of his contemporaries were fine portraitists, Van Dyck was supreme in creating a style of fashionable portraiture that influenced many artists well into the 20th century. For instance, he was unusual for his time in using landscape as a background to his portraits. His approach changed from the tall, imposing portrayals of the Italian nobility of about 1620 to the

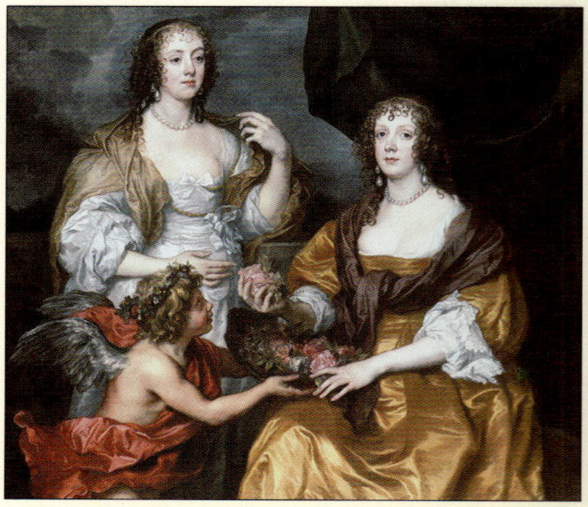

Lady Elizabeth Thimbleby and Viscountess Andover *c1637. Oil on canvas. 53 x 59 in (132 x 149 cm). National Gallery, London.*

Van Dyck was well supported by the king. He painted numerous portraits of the royal family, including the *Triple Portrait of Charles I* (1635). This was sent to Rome so that a sculpture of the king could be made by the famous Italian sculptor Gianlorenzo rather sober depictions of Flemish citizens of about 1630.

While in England, Van Dyck painted a remarkable set of portraits of the royal family, in which he showed the king and queen as dignified yet humane people. This reflected the king's ideas about the importance of the monarchy (which he thought were appointed by God). Van Dyck depicted the royal family and the nobility in a variety of lively and elegant poses and costumes, creating an ideal vision of the aristocracy. His portrait *Lady Elizabeth Thimbleby and Viscountess Andover* (c1637) is a good example of his allegorical pictures: Cupid, the winged god of love, offers roses (which are associated with love) to a young woman who is about to be married.

In his portraits of women and children, Van Dyck showed sensitivity and sympathy. *Charity* (c1627), for example, shows the spirit of loving kindness in the form of a mother with her children, who cluster around her. He depicted young people with dignity and humor, often showing them clutching their possessions, or with their pets (usually dogs), to set them in context.

The artist was also celebrated for his religious paintings, both from the Old Testament (such as *Samson and Delilah,* 1619) and the New Testament. He clearly developed the bold technique of his youth to produce grand and impressive works, in which all the leading figures are swept into the painting's narrative.

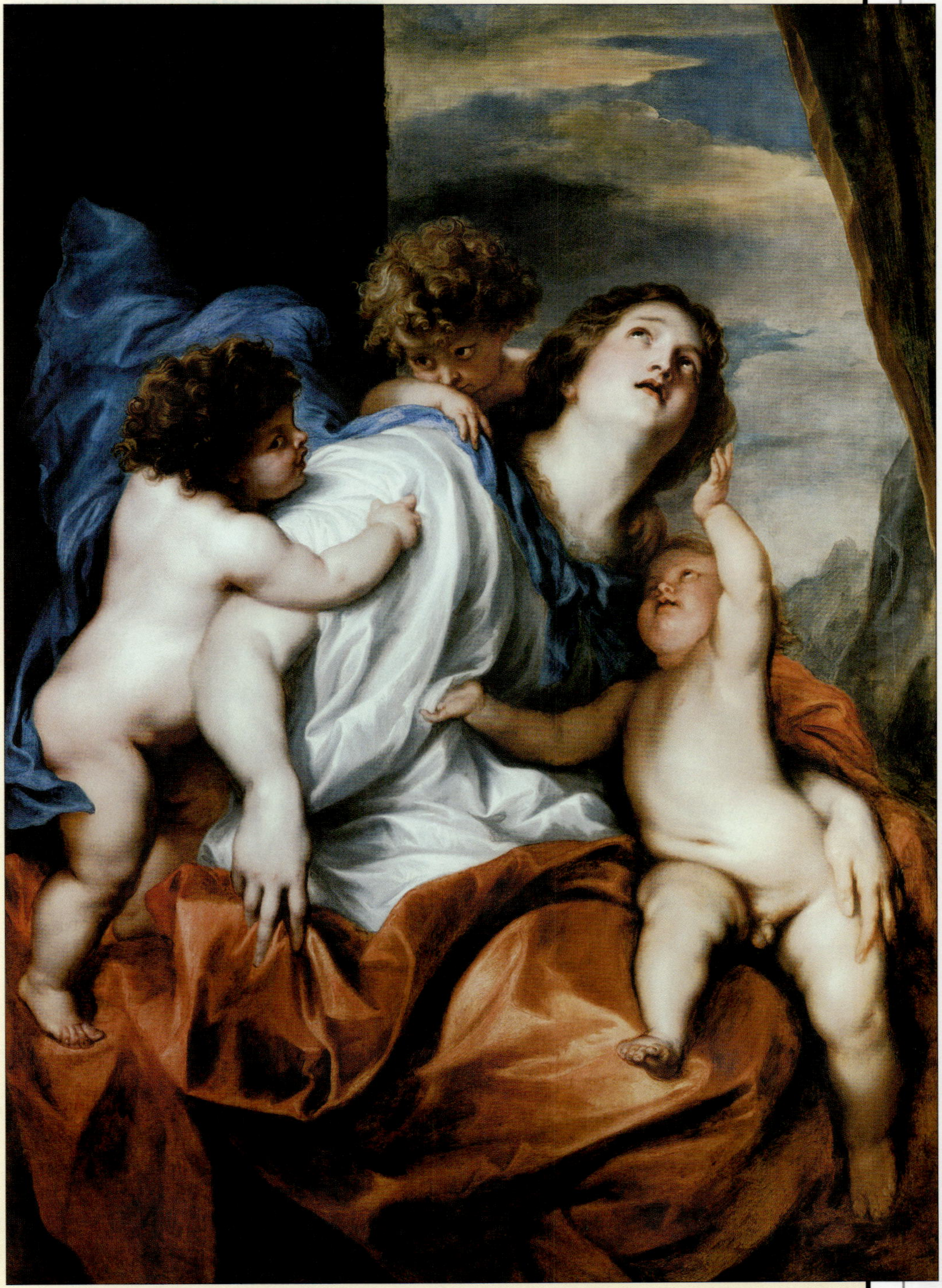

Charity *c1627. Oil on panel. 58 1/4 x 42 1/4 in (148 x 108 cm). National Gallery, London.*

Bernini. Van Dyck also painted many portraits of the queen and the royal children. He generally flattered his sitters: his study of Queen Henrietta Maria with the dwarf and ape shows her as a fine, dignified lady, although in reality she was far from attractive.

The artist's popularity and the royal family's favor earned him a knighthood from Charles I. This led to more commissions from leading members of the aristocracy, and huge pressure on Van Dyck. Exhausted, he died in London in 1641.

Van Dyck had a lasting influence on portraiture, and his work was well known. In the 18th century, when 17th-century clothing was regarded as the most elegant and suitable costume for a formal portrait, some sitters chose to be painted in "Van Dyck dress."

VAN EYCK Jan

JAN VAN EYCK WAS AN EARLY NETHERLANDISH PAINTER whose mastery over the newly established technique of oil painting was extraordinary. The medium allowed greater depth of tone and subtle variations of color, giving his work an intense realism that is awe-inspiring.

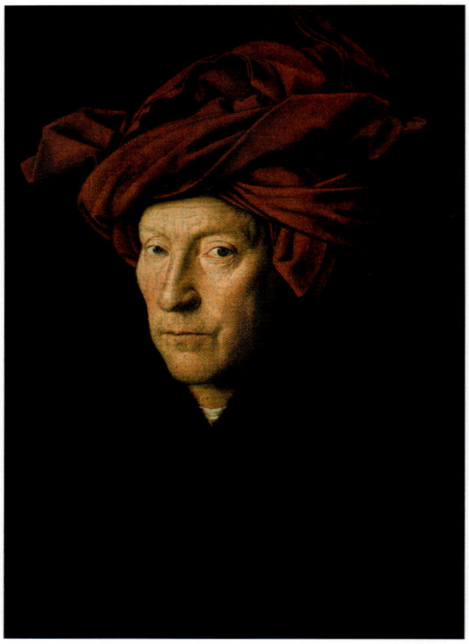

Man in a Red Turban *1433. Oil on panel. 13 x 11 in (33 x 26 cm). National Gallery, London.*

Life and work

Little is known about the early life of Jan Van Eyck. It is thought that he was born in the town of Maaseik (in present-day Belgium), but the first record that can be found of him as an artist is not until 1422, when he was established as a painter in The Hague, working for John III, Count of Holland.

When John died in 1425, Van Eyck made his way to the prosperous trading town of Bruges, where he became Court Painter to Philip the Good, Duke of Burgundy. As Court Painter, Van Eyck traveled between various ducal palaces in Lille, Tournai, and Bruges; in addition, he was also trusted with making secret diplomatic trips for the duke to Spain and to Portugal.

While we may assume that Van Eyck would have produced many works to commemorate significant events in the life of the court, few such works can be traced. One of the earliest surviving paintings that can be attributed to him is the *Virgin and Child with Nicolas Rolin* (c1428). Van Eyck's incredible eye for detail, and his ability to rearrange structure for esthetic and dramatic effect, is absolutely evident in the work, as is his mastery of surface texture. Van Eyck was able to paint fur-lined collars, gold-braided cloth, and translucent, patterned glass in the windows in fantastic detail and extremely realistically—these features recur in his 1434 portrait, *Giovanni Arnolfini and His Wife Giovanna Cenami (The Arnolfini Marriage)*.

Van Eyck's brother Hubert was also a great painter of the time. Hubert died in 1426; during the late 1420s and early 1430s Van Eyck's time was partially taken up with completing one of his brother's great, unfinished works, the Ghent altarpiece *(Adoration of the Lamb)* (c1424–32). Both artists had immense technical virtuosity, and scholars have been unable to detect any deviation in the brushwork that would suggest that two different artists had worked on the painting. The dedication on the frame of the Ghent altarpiece declares that the work was begun by Hubert and completed by Jan, but says that Hubert was the greater artist: Jan is described as "second to him in art." It seems likely that Jan was being rather modest. The scale of the multipaneled work and the limited amount of time that Hubert spent on it before his death means that Jan must have been responsible for by far the larger part of the painting.

Although Van Eyck worked primarily for the Duke of Burgundy, he was also able to undertake commissions from other patrons, particularly from the community of Italian merchants who were resident in Bruges. Among the works he did for them, the most famous is *The Arnolfini Marriage* portrait. Giovanni Arnolfini was a merchant who supplied cloth to Philip's court.

Van Eyck also produced a handful of single portraits. Some would have been commissioned, but others seem to have been painted for his own pleasure, such as the painting of his wife, *Portrait of Margaret Van Eyck* (1439), and *Man in a Red Turban* (1433), which is generally taken to be a self-portrait.

Data file

Full name: Jan Van Eyck

Nationality: Netherlandish

Style: early Netherlandish

Dates: born probably c1395 in Maaseik, died 1441 in Bruges

Key works:

- Ghent altarpiece *(Adoration of the Lamb)* c1424–32
- *Virgin and Child with Nicolas Rolin* c1428
- *Man in a Red Turban* 1433
- *Giovanni Arnolfini and His Wife Giovanna Cenami (The Arnolfini Marriage)* 1434
- *Virgin and Child with George Van der Paele* 1434–36
- *Triptych with the Virgin and Child* 1437

Things to look for:

- intense, luminous colors
- visual tricks that show off his technical ability
- graphic, almost photographic, attention to surface details
- subtle gradations of light and shade

Comparisons: Rogier Van der Weyden, Hugo Van der Goes, Robert Campin, Hubert Van Eyck

Glossary terms: esthetic, tempera

Clarity of purpose

The style of Jan Van Eyck's work is intrinsically tied to the technique of oil painting. Oil was not an entirely new ingredient for making paint, but the main medium from the early 13th century until the time of Van Eyck was tempera, in which colored pigments were mixed with a binding agent, usually egg and water. Tempera functioned well, producing bright colors that adhered to the wooden panels on which pictures were usually painted. But oil had more effect on the pigment, and was more adaptable. It could be built up in thin layers (glazes), to produce subtle gradations of tone and more gradual variations in color.

In this 1434 portrait of the Arnolfinis (Giovanni Arnolfini was a merchant based in Bruges), we can see how Van Eyck's mastery of the techniques of oil painting has enabled him to produce an image of outstanding clarity and realism.

Jan Van Eyck has created not just the elements in the picture, but also the illusion that there is something beyond the confines of this frame. We can believe in a world outside the window, and can imagine spinning around in this room to inspect each wall and a second window—out of the scope of this image—through which light falls on the wooden boards at the feet of Giovanni and the small dog.

For all the naturalness achieved by this realism, the scene is carefully constructed and full of signs and symbols. Some we can interpret and others remain a mystery. The couple's hands are joined, suggesting that this painting may well be portraying their marriage. (Although the woman looks as though she is pregnant, it was fashionable at the time to have a rounded stomach, which is emphasized by the thick folds of her dress.) The man's right hand is poised in a gesture that defies a precise meaning. Is it raised to take a vow, or held up as a sign of abstinence? If the painting does have one complete meaning, it has been—at least partially—lost through the years.

Centrally placed on the back wall is a convex mirror, which cleverly reflects the entire scene. Close up, in its reflection, we can see the couple from behind. The reflection also shows two other figures standing at the doorway to the room. One of them seems to be Jan Van Eyck himself. Above the mirror is an inscription, which reads *Johannes de eyck fuit hic* ("Jan Van Eyck was present"), possibly indicating that the artist was a visitor or even a witness at the wedding ceremony. The chandelier has a single candle burning, which has been interpreted as the candle traditionally put in the home of newly-weds.

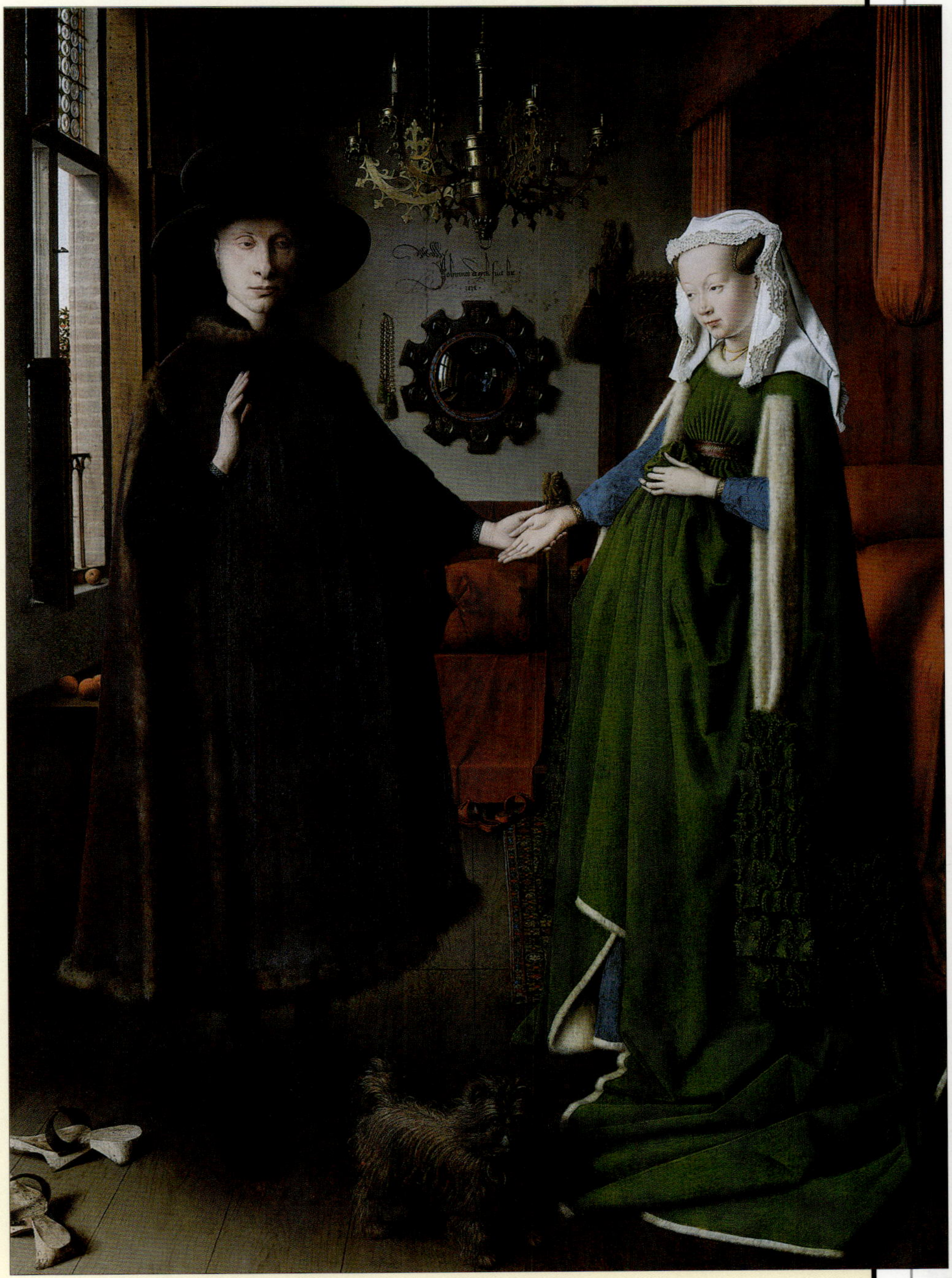

Giovanni Arnolfini and His Wife Giovanna Cenami (The Arnolfini Marriage) *1434. Oil on panel. 33 x 25 in (84.5 x 62.5 cm). National Gallery, London.*

VAN GOGH Vincent

ALMOST IGNORED BY THE ART WORLD IN HIS LIFETIME, in the 20th century Vincent Van Gogh became one of the most famous names in the history of art. His work has been reproduced widely and traded for huge sums, and his life-story has come to symbolize the sufferings and aspirations of creative genius.

Life and work

Vincent Van Gogh was the eldest son of a pastor in North Brabant. At 16 he became an apprentice art dealer, but in his early twenties an unrequited love for his landlady's daughter, the first of many painful failures in relationships, disrupted his work. He turned to religion for support, and came to despise the world of art dealing. In 1876 he was dismissed from his job.

He worked as a teacher in England and as a bookseller in Dordrecht, then studied for the ministry. From 1878 to 1880 he was a missionary in mining communities in Belgium, giving all his possessions away in order to live a life of Christian poverty. He lost this post too, and at the age of 27 decided to become a painter.

At first he followed Jean-François Millet, using muted colors to depict the lives of peasants. Supported by his brother, Theo, an art dealer, he evolved a style from fairly crude and clumsy beginnings. *The Potato Eaters* (1885), showing a peasant family at table, is his most famous work from this period.

In the winter of 1885–86 he studied art in Antwerp before moving to Paris to live with Theo, who was dealing in impressionist art. In Paris he saw paintings that were full of sunlight and color, the work of artists such as Claude Monet and Pierre-Auguste Renoir. He especially admired the pointillist paintings of Georges Seurat. Another influence was Paul Gauguin, who was developing a flatter, expressive use of strong color. He was fascinated by Japanese *ukiyo-e* prints, several of which can be seen in the background in *Portrait of Père Tanguy* (1887–88).

Color became central to his work. He used it boldly and deliberately to express emotions. His handling of paint also became freer. He combined the pointillist-style dabs seen in *Self-portrait before Easel* (1888) with the curving brushstrokes of *Sunflowers* (1888) and *The Sower* (1888). These were painted after he moved to Arles, in the south of France, in February 1888, hoping to find the sunlit colors of the impressionists and the peasant subjects that had first inspired him. Van Gogh worked furiously, producing hundreds of landscapes, portraits, and still lifes, but he could sell none of them.

Gauguin joined him, planning the formation of an artists' colony. The two were temperamentally incompatible, however, and, after a violent quarrel, Van Gogh cut off part of his own ear. While recovering in the hospital, he experienced his first severe attack of a

Data file

Full name: Vincent Willem Van Gogh
Nationality: Dutch
Style: postimpressionism
Dates: born 1853 in Zundert, died 1890 in Auvers-sur-Oise, France
Key works:
- *The Potato Eaters* 1885
- *Portrait of Père Tanguy* 1887–88
- *Self-portrait before Easel* 1888
- *Sunflowers* 1888
- *The Sower* 1888
- *Self-portrait* 1889
- *A Cornfield, with Cypresses* 1889
- *Cornfield with Crows* 1890

Things to look for:
- landscape and peasant life
- expressive handling of paint, often with highly visible brushstrokes
- vivid color used to create strong contrasts
- clearly defined forms with emphasis on simplified outline and contour

Comparisons: Rembrandt, Jean-François Millet, Georges Seurat, Paul Gauguin, Paul Cézanne
Glossary terms: impressionism, pointillism, postimpressionism, *ukiyo-e*

Terrible passions

About his picture *The Night Café* (1888), Van Gogh wrote, "I have tried to express with red and green the terrible passions of the human heart." Van Gogh attributed a special significance to color, and he could make any subject, no matter how ordinary—even a café interior—a vehicle for expression.

Unlike impressionists such as Claude Monet, in whose landscapes natural features—cliffs, trees, rivers—seem to merge with the light-drenched atmosphere, Van Gogh always depicted clearly identifiable subjects defined by strong contours. His many self-portraits document the rapid development of his painting style, from the pointillist method he was exploring in 1887 to his 1889 *Self-portrait*, in which the swirling background and modeling of the jacket introduce a visionary, non-naturalistic element.

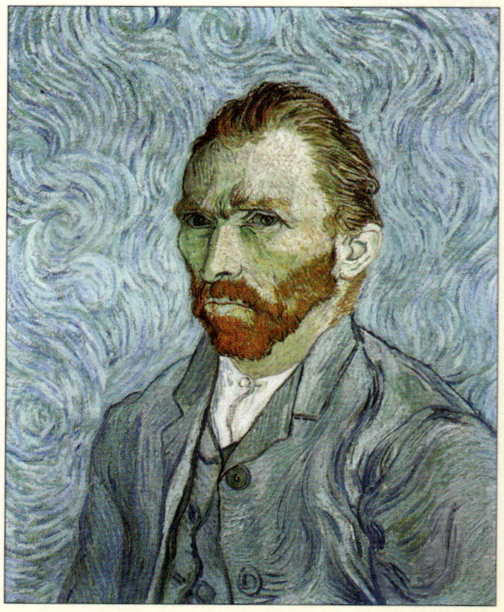

Self-portrait *1889. Oil on canvas. 25 1/2 x 21 1/4 in (65 x 54 cm). Musée d'Orsay, Paris.*

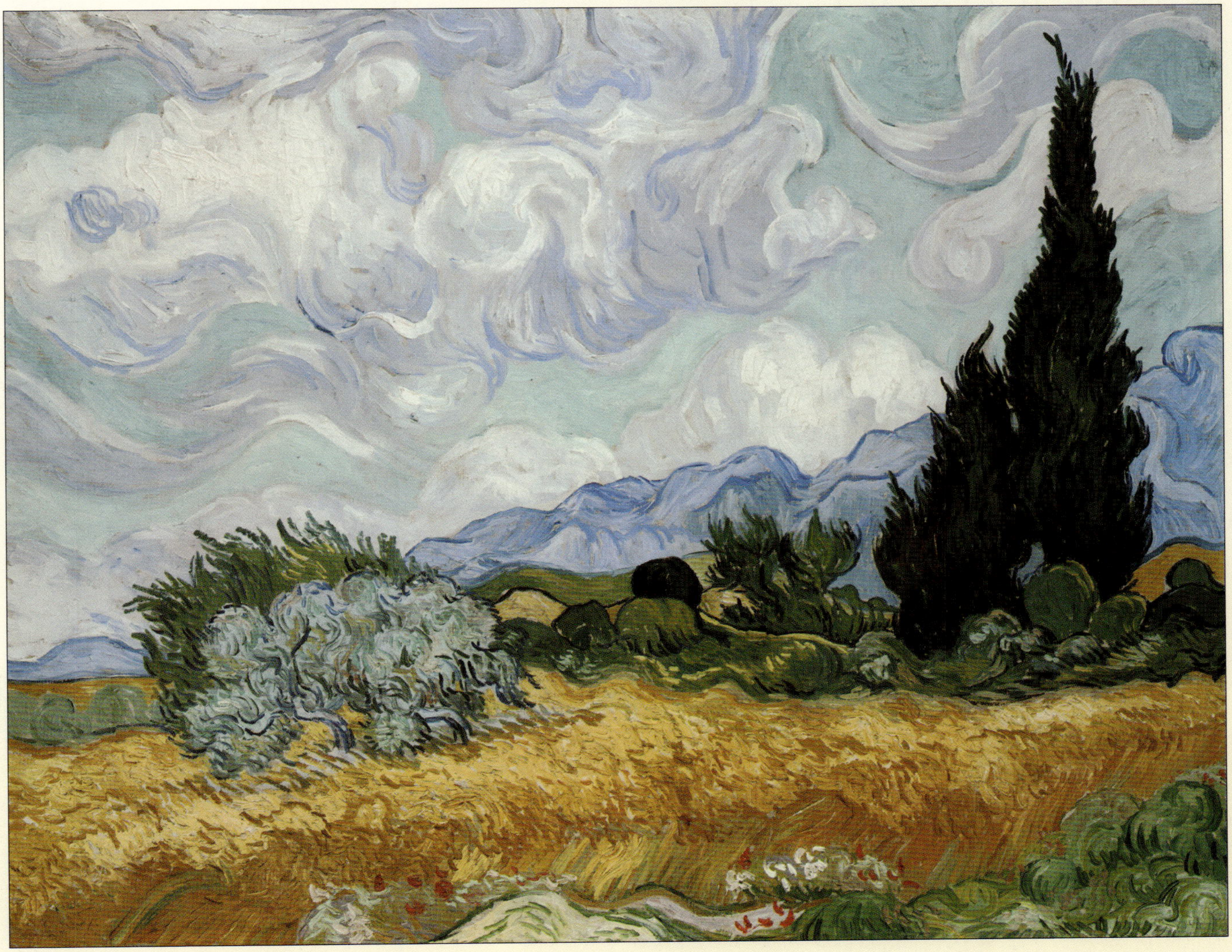

A Cornfield, with Cypresses (1889) shows the view from Van Gogh's window in the asylum at Saint-Rémy. Like the self-portrait, it employs a relatively cool color range dominated by greens and blues. The whole scene—crops and trees, the distant mountains, and the cloudy sky—is animated by a turbulent, fluid movement.

This vision contrasts again with the impressionists' delicate play of light. Van Gogh seems to be looking beyond nature into the symbolic significance of the landscape. The golden grain suggests warmth and plenty; but it will soon be harvested, as summer turns into fall. The leaping forms of the cypresses, like a dark flame, are very vigorous, but at the same time they carry associations with death—dedicated by the Romans to Pluto, god of the underworld, cypresses are still often found in cemeteries.

A Cornfield, with Cypresses *1889. Oil on canvas. 28 1/2 x 35 3/4 in (72 x 91 cm). National Gallery, London.*

recurrent mental illness. In May 1889 he had himself admitted to an asylum in Saint-Rémy-en-Provence, and painted in and around the asylum. Works such as *Cornfield with Reaper* (1889) have a quieter, more subdued coloring than those of the previous year, with a greenish tinge softening the strong southern light, but the restless, swirling movement of his brushstrokes is more pronounced. In May 1890, aged 37, Van Gogh moved to Auvers-sur-Oise, near Paris, to live near Theo and be treated by Dr. Paul Gachet. An amateur artist, Gachet encouraged him in his work. Once again, Van Gogh responded to new surroundings with a burst of creativity, averaging one painting every day. Despite their vivid colors, the paintings of 1890 convey anguish and an "unending forlornness" that Van Gogh endured at this time.

Early in 1890 he began to achieve recognition, with his first sale at an exhibition, and an article about him in a French newspaper. He continued to suffer acute depressions, however, and on 27 July he shot himself in the chest and died two days later.

VAN RUISDAEL Jacob

JACOB VAN RUISDAEL CAPTURED THE DISTINCTIVE CHARACTER of the flat, 17th-century Dutch landscape in his accomplished and atmospheric paintings. He later incorporated elements of both German and Scandinavian scenery into his works, inspired by fellow Dutch painter Allart Van Everdingen, and by a visit to Germany.

Life and work

Jacob Van Ruisdael was born in Haarlem, Holland, in 1628, the son of a picture framer. His uncle was the distinguished painter, Salomon Van Ruysdael. The young Jacob showed early artistic talent, and it is likely that he was taught to paint by both his father and his uncle. Confusingly, the surname Ruisdael appears with several different spellings but "Ruisdael" is the spelling that Jacob used when he signed his pictures.

The 17th century was a time of great prosperity in Holland, and consequently the arts flourished. Dutch artists of the time tended to specialize in one particular genre of painting such as portraiture or landscape. This was due partly to demand from the newly rich merchants. They built themselves grand houses and wanted the paintings that adorned their walls to reflect the pride they felt in their country. These paintings tended to be small in scale, unlike those produced for churches or grand palaces.

The mass of specialist painters who emerged at this time often produced works for "the market" rather than commissions, painting the types of pictures that were appropriate to domestic settings, such as still lifes, scenes of home life, and animals. Jacob Van Ruisdael's specialty was landscape. His earliest known dated works are from 1646; he became a member of the Haarlem Guild of Painters in 1648.

In 1650 Ruisdael visited Germany with his great friend and fellow painter Nicholas Berchem. This visit influenced the style and content of Ruisdael's later works. By 1657 he had settled in Amsterdam, where he remained until his death in 1682.

There is some confusion about the latter part of Ruisdael's life. Although he clearly continued painting, few dated works after 1653 are known. There are records of a Jacob Van Ruisdael in Amsterdam practicing as a doctor. It was not unknown for artists in Holland at this time to have more than one job; however there is no evidence that the artist and the doctor were one and the same person.

In the flat landscape of Holland, tall buildings such as churches and windmills provide essential landmarks. These types of features occur prominently in many of Ruisdael's paintings, helping to capture the character of the land. He did not always position the landmarks exactly as he saw them, however. At this time it was considered perfectly proper to move things around in a painting to improve the overall composition. Indeed, in the late 1650s Ruisdael painted a number of scenes that really do not look Dutch at all—they contain hills and rocky outcrops, dramatic gushing waterfalls, and conifers. It seems likely that he saw such natural features on his visit to Germany in

Data file

Full name: Jacob Van Ruisdael

Nationality: Dutch

Style: 17th-century Dutch

Dates: born 1628 in Haarlem, died 1682 in Amsterdam

Key works:

- *The Jewish Cemetery* c1660
- *Windmill at Wijk* c1665
- *A Landscape with a Ruined Castle and a Church* c1665–70

Things to look for:

- landscapes showing the flat Dutch countryside
- landscapes with hills, rocks, pine trees, and waterfalls

Comparisons: Allart Van Everdingen, Aelbert Cuyp, Meindert Hobbema

Glossary terms: esthetic, golden section, perspective

Dramatic skies

The painting illustrated shows a panoramic view of the flat Dutch landscape. It is thought to be based on an area in Gooiland, a district to the east of Amsterdam where Ruisdael was living at the time. Expansive views of this sort were not invented by Ruisdael, but he became famous for them, and was one of their best exponents. Notice how low the horizon is, and the way that at least two-thirds of the picture is sky.

This is a typical Dutch scene; a great sweeping view of the flat terrain, much of which had been reclaimed from the sea. The viewer is treated to a pattern of fields and waterways dotted with figures and buildings. The whole view, set under an overcast, threatening sky, is typical of northern Europe. Small gaps in the clouds give us a glimpse of the blue sky above and allow patches of pale sunshine to illuminate areas of the distant fields. This enormous cloudy sky is full of movement—far more so than the static panorama beneath it.

If you look carefully on the horizon you may just be able to make out the sails of a windmill—one of the principal man-made features of this country and frequently included in landscapes of this period. The sky and land seem almost to be pinned together by the pointed church tower, which breaks the continuum of the horizon. In the foreground is a ruined castle.

It is possible that a hidden meaning is intended here, suggesting political and religious change. The castle would have formed part of the country's defense system before the Dutch achieved independence from their Spanish rulers. By the time of this painting it was unused. In contrast, the church in the background stands out boldly near the center of the

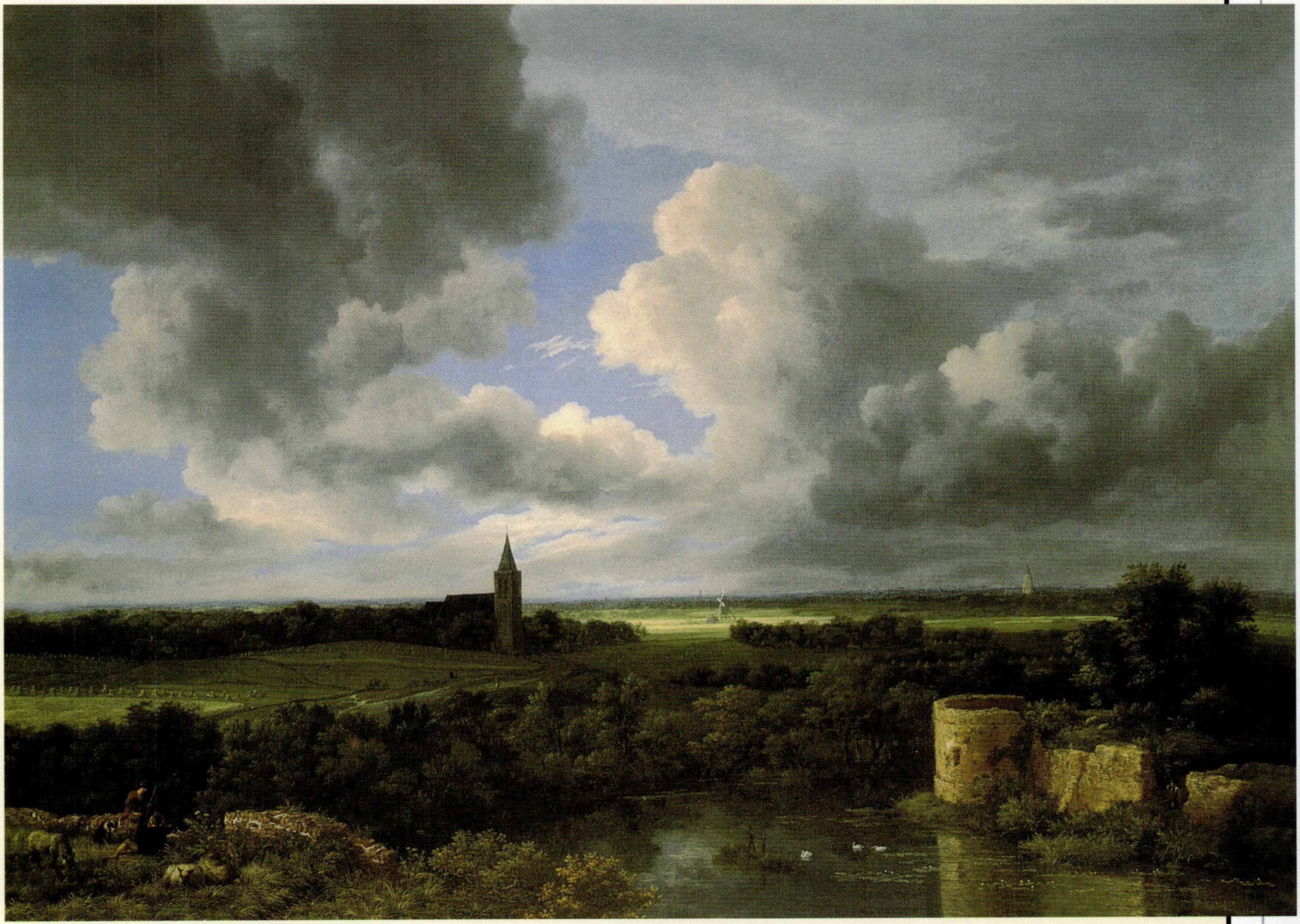

composition. This is probably a converted Catholic building, now a Protestant church, and might represent the rise of Protestant Calvinism as the officially recognized religion in Dutch society. The swans and the small figure of man standing among the castle ruins in the right foreground are painted by Ruisdael himself, while the two peasants and their animals on the left were painted by Adriaen Van de Velde.

Ruisdael probably used a system of mathematical proportion called the golden section or golden mean to position the church. Known since the time of the Greek mathematician Euclid, this proportion was thought to possess a hidden harmony and esthetic virtue.

Ruisdael would frequently paint several versions of the same scene, each one slightly different, and this view of a church and castle is a case in point. At least one of the known copies of this picture is much smaller than the original, and it is tempting to guess that it was commissioned for a patron whose house (or budget) was too small to accommodate the larger version.

A Landscape with a Ruined Castle and a Church *c1665–70. Oil on canvas. 43 x 57 in (109 x 146 cm). National Gallery, London.*

1650. More importantly, around this time he came into contact with the work of another Dutch artist, Van Everdingen, who had visited Scandinavia and whose paintings also included these dramatic elements.

There are parallels between this Scandinavian influence and the effects that other Dutch artists introduced following visits to Italy. These artists brought to their works the idea of adding warm sunlight to landscapes. There is no golden Italian light in Ruisdael's scenes, however. He was a master of cold views of Holland and other northern places, and his cloudy skies always seem to threaten rain. Ruisdael's works rarely include people or animals; in fact, such was his honesty about his own artistic strengths that, when figures were required in his pictures, he would frequently ask other artists, such as Nicholas Berchem, to paint them in for him.

VELÁZQUEZ Diego

VELÁZQUEZ ROSE FROM PAINTING KITCHEN SCENES to becoming an important member of the court of King Philip IV of Spain. He was an extraordinarily gifted artist who painted with a bold and confident style, and became the most famous Spanish painter of the baroque period.

Life and work

Diego Velázquez's most important influence was his second master, Francisco Pacheco. He was apprenticed to him for six years from 1611. Master and pupil became good friends, and Velázquez married Pacheco's daughter, Juana, in 1618.

After serving his apprenticeship, Velázquez was allowed a licence to practice as an independent painter, opening up his own shop and taking on students himself. Velázquez's early work is a mixture of religious subjects and genre, or domestic scenes. These scenes were known as "bodegones" after the Spanish word for an inn or tavern. They scenes show low-life subjects—servants at their work, cooking, eating, socializing—painted with great naturalism. Often, however, he would include a religious element by placing a painting of a biblical story within these tavern scenes. This shows the beginnings of his interest in looking at frames within frames, paintings within paintings, and the illusions a painter can create.

Velázquez was also a skilled portrait painter. Through Pacheco he had made many influential contacts, and he painted many members of the Spanish aristocracy. In 1623 he was asked to paint a portrait (now lost) of King Philip IV; this was so successful that Velázquez was appointed King's Painter the same year. In addition to this position, he held other positions of responsibility at court, and became an important member of the royal household. He was keen to travel to Italy, however, and in 1629 the king granted him permission to do so.

In Italy he stayed with the friends and acquaintances of Philip IV, and studied both the Old Masters and the new developments in Italian art, returning to Madrid in 1631. Here he continued to paint royal portraits, including some of his most famous works of sitters on horseback. He also devised and painted grand decorative works for the royal palaces and apartments. At this time he was also asked to organize the complete redecoration of the Alcazar Palace; he decided that he should return to Italy to buy works of art for that purpose.

In 1649 Velázquez was back in Rome; in between purchasing art and finding artists to help decorate the palace, he also painted portraits. Many

Data file

Full name: Diego Rodriguez de Silva Velázquez

Nationality: Spanish

Style: baroque

Dates: born 1599 in Seville, died 1660 in Madrid

Key works:
- *Old Woman Cooking Eggs* c1618
- *Philip IV in Brown and Silver* 1631–32
- *Surrender at Breda* 1634
- *Infante Baltasar Carlos on Horseback* c1636
- *Toilet of Venus* (the *Rokeby Venus*) c1649
- *Pope Innocent X* 1650
- *Las Meninas* 1656

Things to look for:
- early works showing kitchen or everyday scenes with realistic observation
- strong contrasts between light and dark (chiaroscuro), influenced by Caravaggio
- swift, deft brushwork, called virtuoso or bravura, to create seemingly effortless effects
- portraits of aristocratic sitters that display a great ability to capture character, likeness, and the details of costume
- an interest in playing with what the viewer sees and what is really there

Comparisons: Francisco de Zurbarán, Michelangelo Merisi da Caravaggio, Peter Paul Rubens

Glossary terms: baroque, bravura, chiaroscuro, Old Masters

Realism, illusions, and atmosphere

If Velázquez's subject matter was influenced by his teacher, Francisco Pacheco, his earlier style was perhaps more influenced by the dramatic light and dark contrasts (chiaroscuro) in the art of Michelangelo Merisi da Caravaggio and his followers, moving later to the brilliant works of Titian and other Venetians whose work he had seen in the Spanish royal collection. These works and those of Peter Paul Rubens, whom he met in 1628, had a great influence on his use of color and his painterly technique. *Las Meninas (The Maids of Honor)* (1656) is seen as bringing together many of the approaches to and techniques of painting that Velázquez had absorbed throughout his life.

The small blonde-haired child is the king's five-year-old daughter, the Infanta Margarita, who is surrounded by her maids of honor, a dwarf, a young jester figure, and some servants. The figures seem small compared to the large, dark room, but they stand out quite brilliantly. With his deft, virtuoso brushwork, Velázquez has depicted all the finery and suggested all the details of their clothing, as well as conveying its shiny satin texture. On the left, behind the group of girls, stands the artist himself, posed in front of a huge canvas.

This is where Velázquez starts to play with what we are seeing. Is he painting the picture we now see before us, or is he painting something else? After all, we can only see the back of the canvas. Almost directly in the center of the composition, a framed image on the wall stands out behind the head of the young princess and her maid. Within this frame are the faces of the king and queen of Spain. This is not a painting, though, but a mirror, and in the

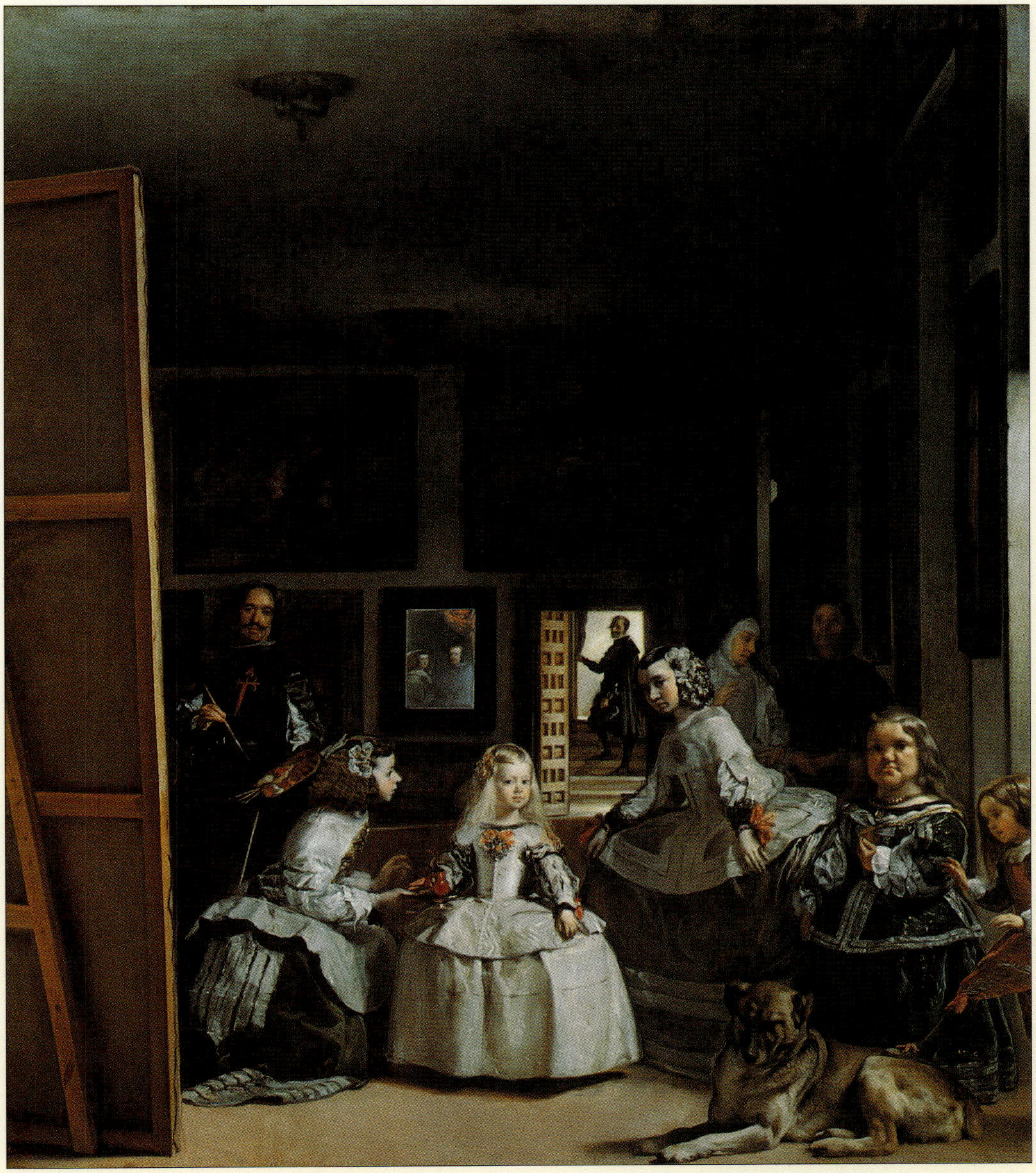

Las Meninas (The Maids of Honor) *1656. Oil on canvas. 127 x 108½ in (318 x 276 cm). Museo del Prado, Madrid.*

mirror the viewer can see the real subject of the huge canvas—it is a portrait of the king and queen. If we imagine where they must be standing in order to pose for Velázquez, it is where we, the viewers, are also standing in order to see this picture. This composition ensures that simultaneously we can see what Velázquez is doing, what the princess and maids are doing, what the king and queen are doing, and what they can see.

Viewers at the time marvelled at the portraits that Velázquez painted; they seemed so original in their technique and in the characterization of the sitters. Velázquez also displays bravura technique—the free, bold, quick, suggestive brushstrokes that later 19th-century painters greatly admired and tried to copy.

historians believe that he painted his famous *Toilet of Venus* (the *Rokeby Venus*) at this stage. This is the first known example of a female nude in the history of art in Spain. He also produced a masterful portrait, *Pope Innocent X* (1650), that the pope considered "too truthful."

Velázquez returned to Madrid in 1651. When he was appointed palace chamberlain in 1652, his duties at court became so time-consuming that he was scarcely able to paint. However, in 1656 he produced possibly his most famous work, *Las Meninas*. Velázquez was knighted in 1658: his ambassadorial services to the Spanish court and his great gifts as a painter were recognized in this final honor. He died in 1660, having arranged and witnessed the marriage of Louis XIV to Philip IV's daughter, Infanta Maria-Theresa, a union that also ended the war between Spain and France.

VERMEER Jan

TODAY JAN VERMEER IS ONE OF THE MOST CELEBRATED DUTCH painters, but for over two centuries following his death he was little known. Vermeer's skill in rendering the qualities of daylight flooding into interior spaces produced compelling works with a quiet, contemplative stillness.

Life and work

Vermeer's interest in art may well have stemmed from his father, a craftsman from Amsterdam who became an art dealer in Delft. After training and serving his apprenticeship, in 1653 Vermeer was admitted as a master to the Delft Guild of Saint Luke (the town's guild of painters).

His first works were in the genre of history painting, which takes themes from the Bible, classical mythology, and various significant historical events. Two works in this style survive: *Diana and her Companions* (c1655) and *Christ in the House of Mary and Martha* (c1654–56), the latter probably Vermeer's oldest surviving painting.

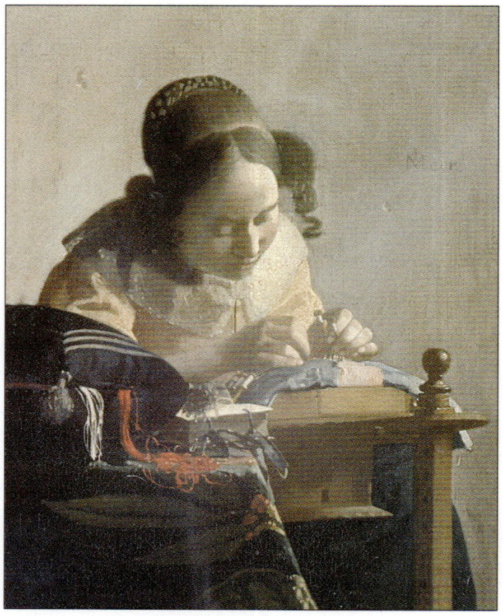

The Lacemaker *c1669–70. Oil on canvas over panel. $9\frac{1}{2}$ x $8\frac{1}{4}$ in (24 x 21 cm). Musée du Louvre, Paris.*

The style of these works is close to that of the Italian baroque, and in them the influence of the Flemish painter Peter Paul Rubens (another northern European artist with Italian leanings) can be seen.

Vermeer's dalliance with history painting is represented only by these two paintings, however. Soon his work began to depict domestic scenes of everyday life in the Dutch home. Paintings from this period, including *Woman in Blue Reading a Letter* (c1662–64) and *The Lacemaker* (c1669–70) are those for which Vermeer is best known today.

Pieter de Hooch, a contemporary and fellow resident of Delft who is now recognized as one of the finest Dutch genre painters, probably exerted a significant influence on Vermeer at this time. De Hooch's paintings (such as *The Courtyard of a House in Delft*, 1658, and *The Pantry*, c1658) featured the subtle effects of light and depicted tranquil and domestic scenes, and he painted surface textures—particularly bricks and tiles—with great care and attention. Some of Vermeer's works dating from the period around 1660, such as *Soldier with a Laughing Girl* (c1658–60), bear a striking similarity to the work of de Hooch. Vermeer's paintings, however, reveal a greater

An allegory of painting

Like so many of Vermeer's works, the setting for *Allegory of Painting* (c1666–67) is domestic: the painting depicts a curtain drawn back to show an artist (seen from the back and possibly a shy self-portrait) at work in his studio. However, unlike in some of his simpler compositions, such as *The Lacemaker* (c1669–70), there are references here to the larger world, beyond the time and place depicted. Unusually for Vermeer, he has taken on a grander theme: the relationship between art and life. The woman in the painting is dressed as the muse of history and fame, standing in front of a map of the Netherlands. As a result, the picture can be interpreted as the painter taking pride in the history of his nation.

Yet the painting is also more complicated than this. The woman looks down with a slightly bemused expression, as if unable to maintain the seriousness of her role. Furthermore, the painter is dressed in very old-fashioned clothes (even for the 17th century), while the map shows the Netherlands as it was in the past, before religious disputes led to its division between Catholic- and Protestant-dominated regions.

Given that Vermeer abandoned history painting early in his career, one could assume that the painting depicts the plight of the artist who struggles to paint history while neglecting the present-day reality.

Data file

Full name: Jan Vermeer

Nationality: Dutch

Style: Dutch genre painting

Dates: born 1632 in Delft, died 1675 in Delft

Key works:

- *Christ in the House of Mary and Martha* c1654–56
- *Diana and Her Companions* c1655
- *Little Street* c1658
- *The Music Lesson* c1662–64
- *Woman in Blue Reading a Letter* c1662–64
- *Allegory of Painting* c1666–67
- *The Lacemaker* c1669–70
- *A Young Woman Standing at a Virginal* c1670

Things to look for:

- photographic realism
- subtle depiction of light and shadow

Comparisons: Pieter de Hooch, Carel Fabritius, Samuel Van Hoogstraten, Emmanuel de Witte, Pieter Saenredam, Peter Paul Rubens, Rembrandt

Glossary terms: camera obscura, genre painting, history painting

This is speculation, however, and whatever the enigmas of the painting's subject matter, the overriding brilliance of the work lies in its evocative rendering of an interior scene. As is so often the case with Vermeer's interiors, light is used to dramatic effect and is shown flooding in from windows (hidden by the curtain) to the left of the scene.

Vermeer took great care over the spatial arrangement of his paintings; here vertical and horizontal lines (the edges of the map, the ceiling, and the folds of the curtain) form a linear framework for the picture. He also became increasingly interested in the rules of perspective; in *Allegory of Painting* he makes use of the gridlike effect of the tiled floor to contribute toward the illusion of depth in the painting.

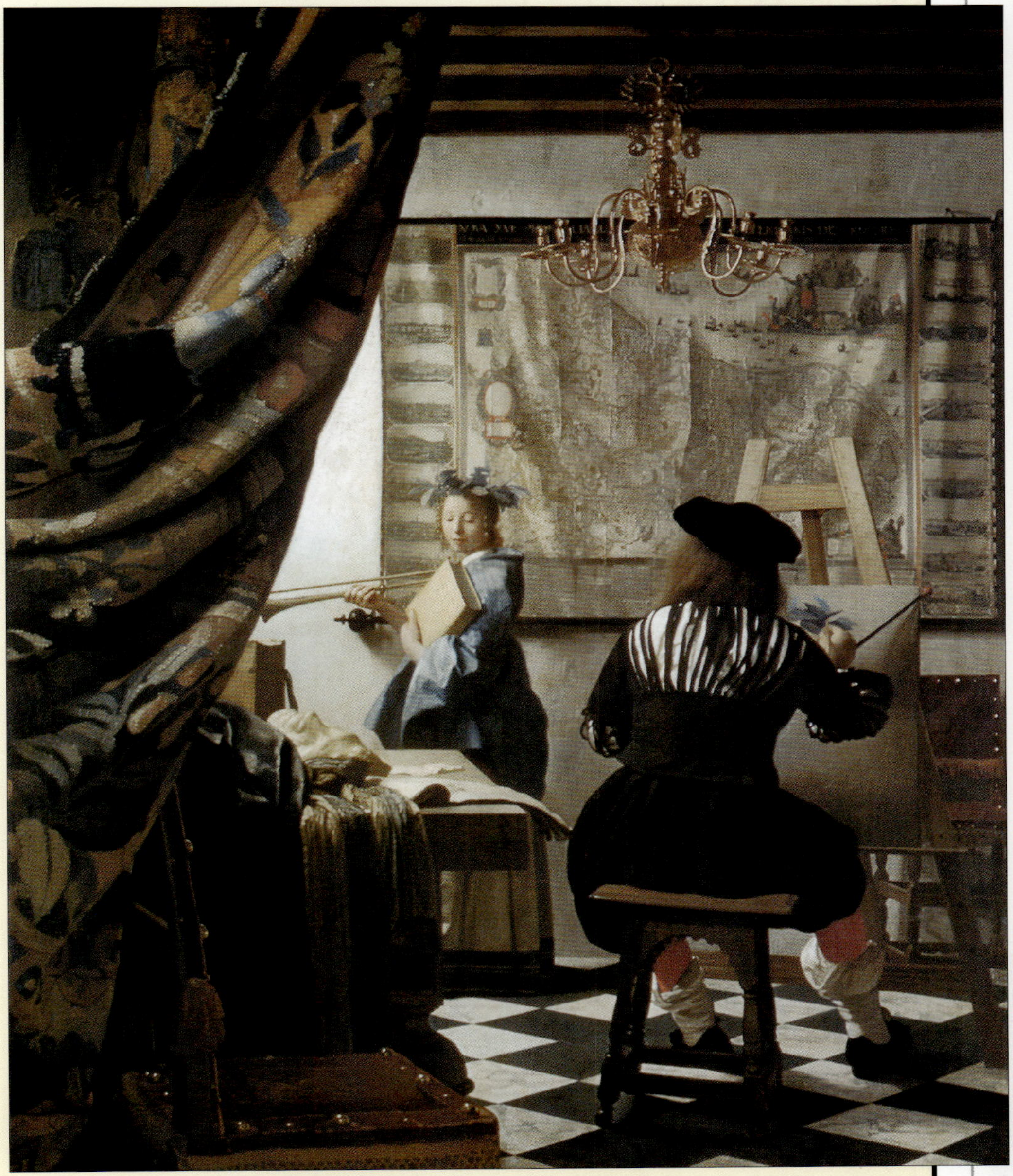

Allegory of Painting *c1666–67. Oil on canvas. 51 1/4 x 43 1/4 in (120 x 100 cm). Kunsthistorisches Museum, Vienna.*

technical rigor and a more sublime handling of color and tone.

Vermeer came to be admired for his ability to depict the effect of light and shade. Little is known of Vermeer's technique, but it has been suggested that he used a camera obscura, an apparatus with a lens with which he would project the image of a scene onto a surface, making it appear in miniature. This also intensified the effects of light and shade. (Canaletto is also thought to have used this device.) In some of Vermeer's paintings, small dots of bright pigment can be seen, as if he had recreated the small, gleaming, jewel-like highlights seen in the camera obscura image. This is evident in *The Lacemaker*, in which the effect is to make the painting appear as if it were an image reflected in glass.

Although not internationally known, Vermeer was held in high regard by other artists in Delft; in 1662 he was made head of the painters' guild, a great honor for the 30-year-old.

From the mid-1660s onward, Vermeer began to place figures farther back in many of his pictures, thereby giving the interior space greater presence.

Vermeer not only sold his own work, but also that of other artists, as his father had done before him. However, war between the Netherlands and France, and the resultant financial collapse of his country, made it impossible for him to continue with this trade, which caused him considerable hardship. As a result, the last years of Vermeer's life were burdened by poverty.

VERONESE Paolo

VERONESE WAS OUTSTANDING AMONG THE PAINTERS of High Renaissance Venice who specialized in large-scale decorative works. His canvases and frescos are among the largest and most theatrical ever painted in Italy. He spent almost all his career in Venice, or in the Veneto, the surrounding countryside. His work can still be found in the palaces, villas, and churches that survive there.

Life and work

Veronese's real name was Paolo Caliari, but he is generally known by the name "Veronese," reflecting his birth in Verona, a major town close to Venice. Having trained there, he moved to Venice, then a rich and powerful city-state, around 1550. Much of his work would celebrate the great city.

His first major commission dated from 1555, when he was asked to decorate the church of San Sebastiano in Venice with a series of paintings. Here he already showed the skill in foreshortening that was to become one of his most remarkable gifts. It was ideal for commissions in which the relationship between painting and architecture was especially important. He often included simulated architectural details in his work.

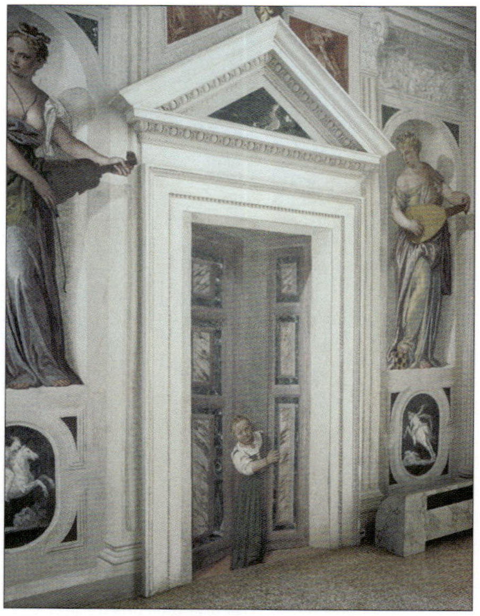

Door with Girl *c1560. Trompe l'oeil wall decoration. Villa Maser, Italy.*

During the 1560s Veronese was employed by many of the Venetian nobility to paint the walls of their country villas, which called for a less grand, more relaxed and playful style. At the Villa Maser, a house designed by the leading Venetian architect, Andrea Palladio, he covered the walls with colorful, lively figures set against *trompe l'oeil* architectural details and landscapes—backgrounds so skillfully painted that they deceive the eye into believing they are real.

From the 1560s onwards Veronese became extremely popular and was offered numerous commissions, often for large-scale works. One of the best known, *The Marriage at Cana* (1562), began a new style of huge, sumptuous paintings, filled with animated figures and painted in rich colors that were a

Data file

Full name: Paolo Caliari (known as Paolo Veronese)
Nationality: Italian
Style: High Renaissance
Dates: born c1528 in Verona, died 1588 in Venice
Key works:
- decorations at the church of San Sebastiano, Venice 1555
- decorations at the Villa Maser, near Verona c1560
- *The Marriage at Cana* 1562
- *The Family of Darius before Alexander* c1570
- *The Adoration of the Kings* 1573
- *The Triumph of Venice* c1585

Things to look for:
- huge, multifigured paintings
- rich colors
- dramatic organization of figures
- vivid, humorous details

Comparisons: Tintoretto, Titian, Giambattista Tiepolo
Glossary terms: foreshortening, fresco, High Renaissance, *trompe l'oeil*

Dramatic paintings

In his painting of *The Adoration of the Kings* (1573) Veronese shows one of the most important moments in the early life of Jesus Christ. It illustrates the biblical story of the Three Wise Men, or "kings," who were led by a star to the stable in Bethlehem where the infant Jesus had been born. They brought gifts anticipating his life and death.

In this enormous painting the three kings are shown kneeling in front of Jesus, who is held by his mother, Mary. The eldest king, Caspar, kneels directly in front of Jesus, offering his gift of gold, expressing the kingship of Jesus. Mary's husband, Joseph, stands behind the child. The painting is filled with other figures, including the king's attendants, while a shaft of sunlight, surrounded by angels, descends from Heaven upon the infant.

Veronese's gifts are well illustrated in this painting. The numerous figures are set in a boldly organized setting, which gives a glimpse of the sky beyond but focuses attention on the leading participants, whose importance is established by their places within the composition as well as by their poses. The scene is set within battered palace walls, which are in the classical style and suggest the period of Christ's birth. The palace symbolizes the Old Testament, which is giving way to the Christian faith in the birth of Christ, and the beginning of the New Testament.

Veronese organizes the scene as though it were the stage of an opera or play. The almost life-size figures are arranged to maximum effect, so that the most important participants, Mary and the infant Jesus, whom she holds, are placed at a greater height than the kneeling kings.

The Adoration of the Kings *1573. Oil on canvas. 140 x 126 in (355.5 x 320 cm). National Gallery, London.*

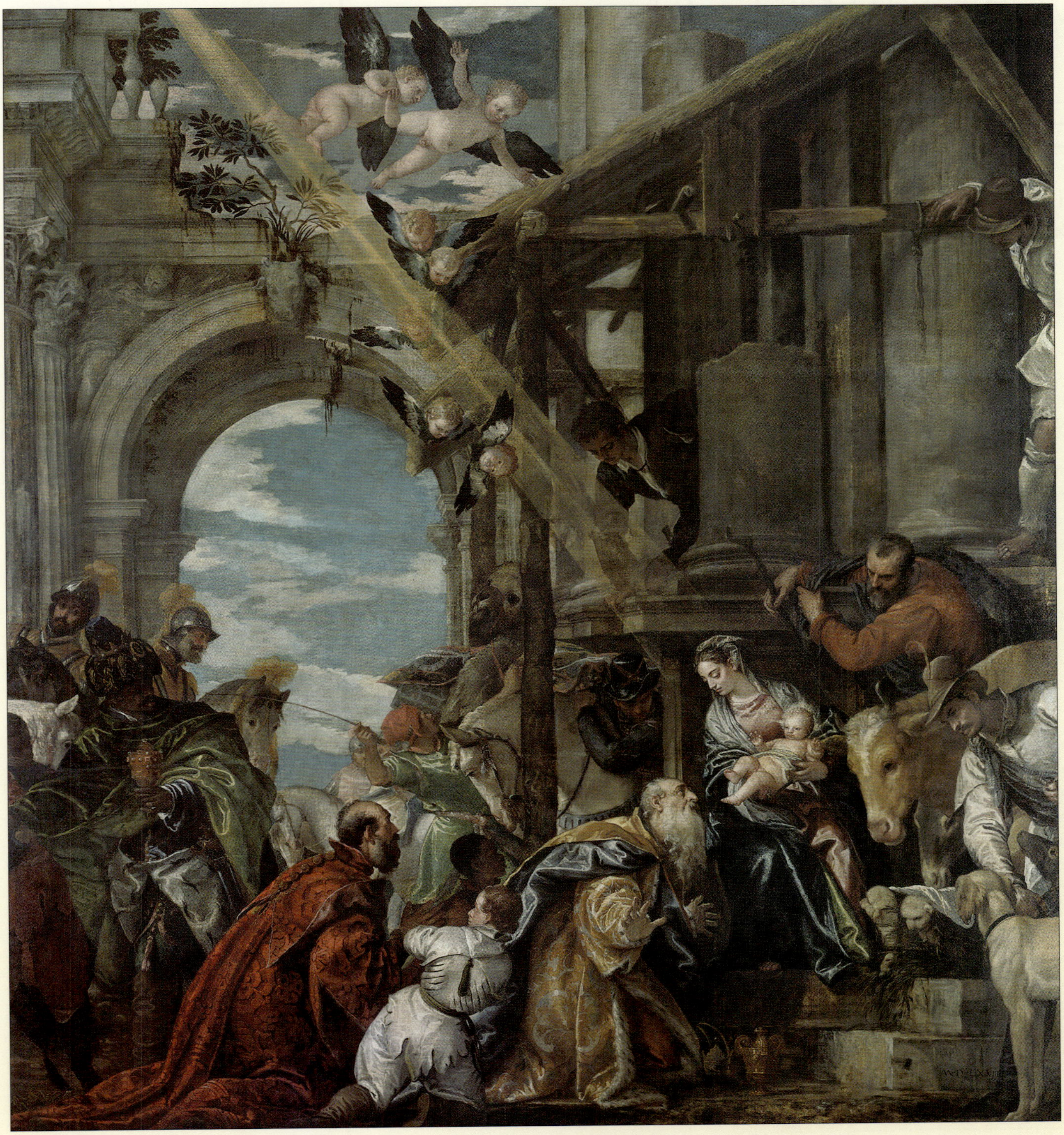

Venetian trademark. Although he was often helped by members of his large workshop (including three sons), Veronese sometimes painted pictures almost entirely by himself. *The Family of Darius before Alexander* (c1570) is a good example of his ability to arrange figures as though on a stage, creating a sense of high drama and courtly luxury.

From 1577 onward Veronese worked at the Ducal Palace in Venice. One entire wall of the Audience Chamber is occupied by his celebratory painting, *The Triumph of Venice* (c1585). His work was an important influence on Venetian painting in the 18th century, and particularly on the work of Giambattista Tiepolo.

VUILLARD Edouard

EDOUARD VUILLARD WAS A PAINTER AND A CRAFTSMAN whose favorite themes were the lives of women and children in interiors or public parks. A leading member of the Nabis group of artists, who advocated an antinaturalist style of painting, he designed theater scenery, prints, and series of decorative panels for private residences.

Life and work

Edouard Vuillard was a lifelong bachelor who lived with his sister and mother, both of whom were dressmakers, until his mother's death in 1928. He went to school at the respected Lycée Condorcet, where he met many of the young artists and musicians who were to influence his art.

With his close friend Ker Xavier Roussel, Vuillard studied at the Académie Julian, where he was a pupil of Tony Robert Fleury, and then at the Ecole des Beaux-Arts, the foremost art school in Paris. However, he was perhaps most influenced by copying Old Master paintings in the Louvre.

At the Académie Julian, Vuillard met a circle of artists who were inspired by the flat color techniques and symbolist subject matter of Paul Sérusier and Paul Gauguin, who are also often referred to as the "synthetists." They advocated painting from memory rather than attempting to record nature by direct observation. By filtering what they saw through their imaginations, these artists strove to paint the essence of things as much as their appearance.

From 1888 Vuillard formed a group with Roussel, Maurice Denis, and Pierre Bonnard, known as the "Nabis," the Hebrew word for prophets. They exhibited with the art dealer Le Barc de Bouteville in the 1890s. Vuillard went on to exhibit with another dealer, Ambroise Vollard, who commissioned albums of color lithographs from him. Vuillard had his paintings rejected by the official Salon exhibitions when he was a young man, but he helped to found the Salon d'Automne in 1903, and he exhibited regularly at the Salon des Indépendants.

Vuillard drew on a wide variety of influences as an artist, including the techniques of Japanese printmaking and the experimental theater of the day. He worked with his schoolfriend, Aurélien Lugné-Poe, in avant-garde theaters, where actors performed the experimental plays of Maurice Maeterlinck, Henrik Ibsen, and August Strindberg. Vuillard was fascinated by the emotional intensity of these plays, and designed programs and scenery for numerous productions.

Data file

Full name: Edouard Vuillard

Nationality: French

Style: Nabis

Dates: born 1868 in Cuiseaux, died 1940 in La Baule

Key works:

Coquelin Cadet 1890

Self-portrait 1891

La Causette 1892

Public Gardens 1894

Figures and Interiors 1896

Landscapes and Interiors (print album) 1899

Théodore Duret in His Study 1912

Things to look for:

- decorative pattern effects
- unusual picture formats
- a variety of media: distemper, graphics, prints, decorative arts
- the lives of women and children as subject

Comparisons: Pierre Bonnard, Maurice Denis, Félix Vallotton, Antoine Watteau

Glossary terms: distemper, fresco, lithography, matt, Nabis (Les), Old Masters, rococo, Salon, Salon des Indépendants, symbolist, synthetists

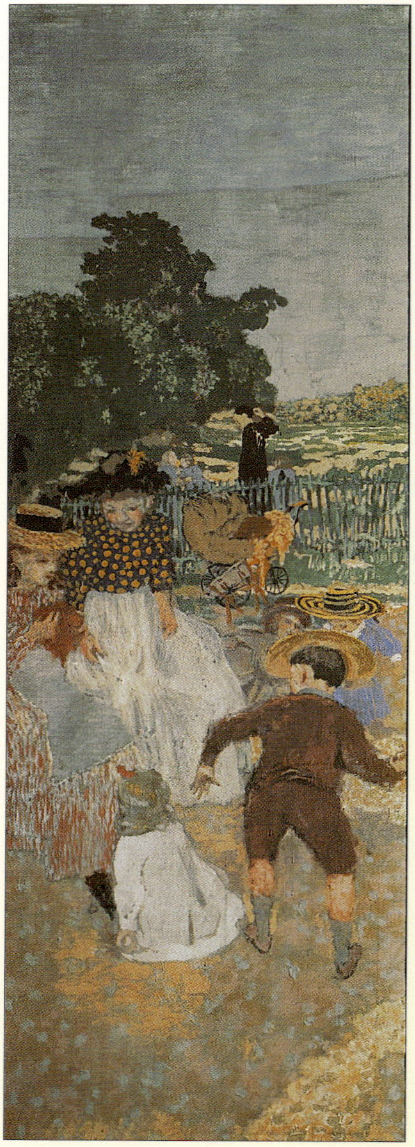

Decorative gardens

Vuillard's early paintings were usually intimate studies on a very small scale, but he also created large decorative panel series for private mansions and public buildings. *Public Gardens* (1894) was the first of his larger ensemble projects, and was commissioned by Vuillard's friend and patron Alexandre Natanson. The complete

In the 1890s, Vuillard became close to the Natanson brothers who edited the art journal, *La Révue Blanche*. Various members of the Natanson family commissioned decorative panels

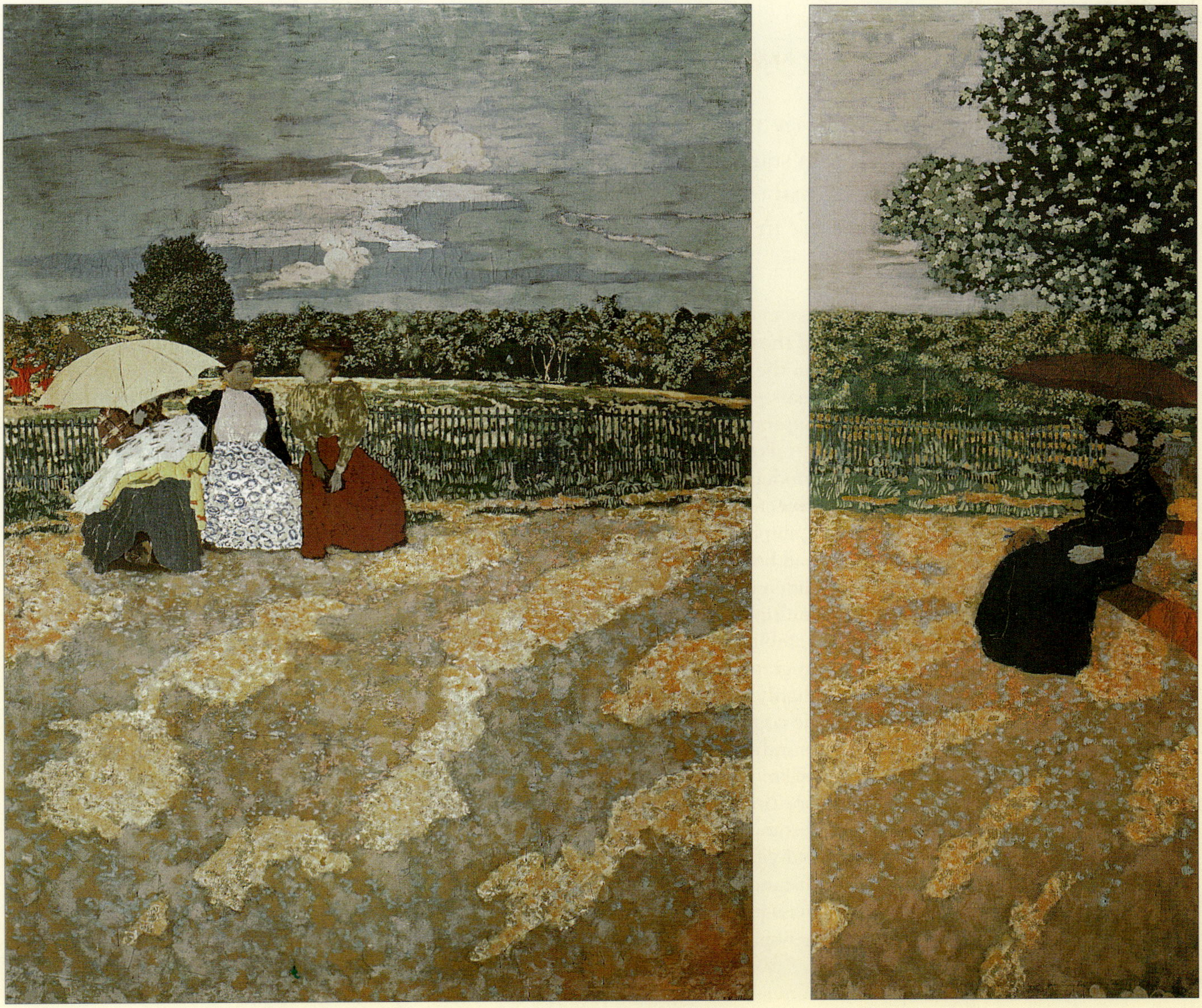

Public Gardens *(three of original nine-panel series) 1894. Distemper on canvas. 84 x 95 in (213 x 242 cm). Musée d'Orsay, Paris.*

decoration (of nine panels in total) was designed for the drawing room of Natanson's house in Paris.

In creating this decoration Vuillard drew upon several artistic precedents and traditions. The theme of elegant ladies and children enjoying nature is a familiar one in Vuillard's work, and echoes the garden paintings of the 18th-century rococo painter, Antoine Watteau.

Vuillard also borrowed from the techniques and conventions of Japanese art. He used unusual and varied canvas sizes, copying the format of Japanese folding screens. The composition also uses a high horizon line and a large, empty, open space in the foreground that is typical of Japanese prints.

These paintings were executed in Vuillard's preferred medium, distemper, a water-based medium in which the pigment is suspended in glue. Distemper has a distinctive dry appearance, and produces pale, matt colors. It dries quickly, so Vuillard could apply many layers of paint to create a dense picture surface.

for their rooms at home. In addition to private commissions, Vuillard produced mural ensembles for public buildings. In 1913 he created a series for the Champs-Elysées Theater; he also produced a decoration called *Peace Protecting the Muses* for the Palace of the United Nations.

In the 1920s Vuillard became a highly popular portrait painter. He painted much larger works; the claustrophobic, highly patterned interiors of his early work gave way to the more expansive, comfortable apartments of his well-to-do sitters.

WARHOL Andy

ANDY WARHOL WAS AT THE CENTER OF THE POP ART phenomenon, rendering images of pop and film stars, and of everyday consumer objects. His attempts to avoid individual expression in his art ironically encouraged immense interest in him and his work.

Life and work

Andy Warhol was the son of Czech immigrants who had come to the United States in the early 20th century. He studied graphic design at the Carnegie Institute of Technology in Pittsburgh, graduated in 1949, and then moved to New York. His success there was as a commercial artist initially: throughout the 1950s he produced many designs for advertisements, as well as illustrations for magazine articles and book covers.

In 1960 Warhol began to paint works on canvas, taking as his subject matter the world of mass media, from advertisements to news headlines to comic strips. At first, Warhol did not use the pristine style with which we associate him, but imitated other artists of the time by dripping paint to mess up the image and distinguish it from its mass-produced source, in works such as *Superman* (1960) and *Popeye* (1961).

From 1962 Warhol started producing paintings of consumer objects such as Coca-Cola bottles, Campbell's soup cans, and Brillo soap-pad boxes, which he reproduced in different formats (sometimes as multiple, repeated images) and combinations of colors. His background in graphic and commercial art was highly relevant to this work, in which he copied the individual style of each brand's packaging methodically. He also began working with the silk-screen printing technique. This process distanced Warhol from any sense of individual expression; even greater distance was achieved by the use of mass-printed photographs from newspapers and magazines.

Warhol also began producing canvases of film and music stars, such as Marilyn Monroe and Elvis Presley. He was not interested in uncovering the real person behind the public persona (as portraiture attempts to); instead his work portrayed them as the products of mass culture and consumer society.

Warhol explored the idea of achieving fame through death and disaster, first with a painting of a newspaper front page, *129 Die in Jet (Plane Crash)* (1962), but also in other works including *Orange Disaster* (1963), depicting an electric chair.

The 1960s was Warhol's creative high point, and during this time he made experimental films. *Sleep* (1963) and *Empire* (1964) were shot from a single camera position. He used the camera to observe the same subject (a man sleeping, and the Empire State Building respectively) over periods of several hours, a technique that seemed designed to induce either boredom or fascination, or both feelings.

In keeping with Warhol's notion that "everybody should be like a machine," in 1962 he set up a large studio space, which he referred to as the "Factory." Here he gathered

Data file

Full name: Andrew Warhola (known as Andy Warhol)

Nationality: American

Style: pop art

Dates: born c1928 in Pittsburgh, PA, died 1987 in New York, NY

Key works:

Campbell's Soup Cans (series of 32 works) 1962

Triple Elvis 1962

Mustard Race Riot 1963

Orange Disaster 1963

Marilyn 1964

Brillo Box (Soap Pads) 1964

Liz 1964

Things to look for:

- consumer objects and images of popular culture
- paring down of images to produce color in dense blocks (using silk-screen printing)

Comparisons: Marcel Duchamp, Roy Lichtenstein, Jeff Koons, Jasper Johns

Glossary terms: pop art, silk-screen printing

People as consumer items

Warhol did not encourage the view of his art as a reflection of his personal beliefs, and was careful to guard his privacy. If people wanted to know about him, he said, they should "look at the surface of my paintings; it's all there, there's nothing more." This very absence of personal involvement in his work became a hallmark of Warhol's style, leaving people to wonder whether his intentions were serious or playful.

His approach to portraying mass-produced products, such as canned food, was no different from his approach to picturing celebrities such as Marilyn Monroe or Elizabeth Taylor. They too were products of mass consumption.

In his portrait of Elizabeth Taylor, *Liz* (1964), Warhol has used strong contrasts of tone in the silk-screen printing process to flatten the contours of Taylor's face, taking away the creases of personality and mood, and leaving only the barest features. Her face is so simplified that it is hard to see what her expression is and even what age she might be. We nevertheless recognize that this is an image of Elizabeth Taylor in the way that we would recognize a familiar brand name or logo on a consumer product. It is a highly artificial picture, and utterly removed from a tangible reality. As in all his work, Warhol is concerned with the reality of image rather than reality itself.

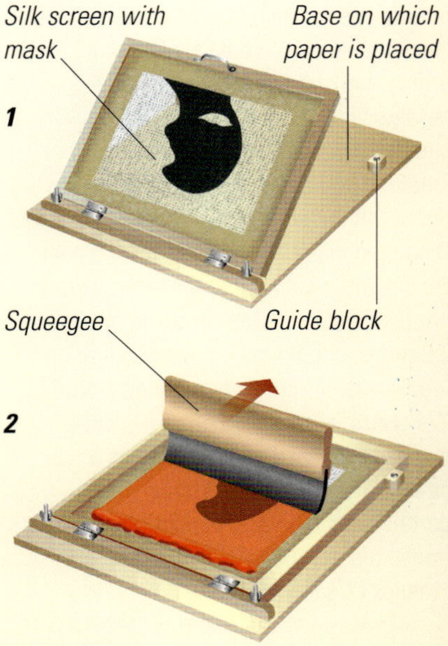

Silk-screen printing *A mask (a negative of the image made from paper, film, or glue, for example) is placed on a silk screen (1). When ink is drawn over the screen with a squeegee (2), it passes through the silk but not through the mask, leaving an image.*

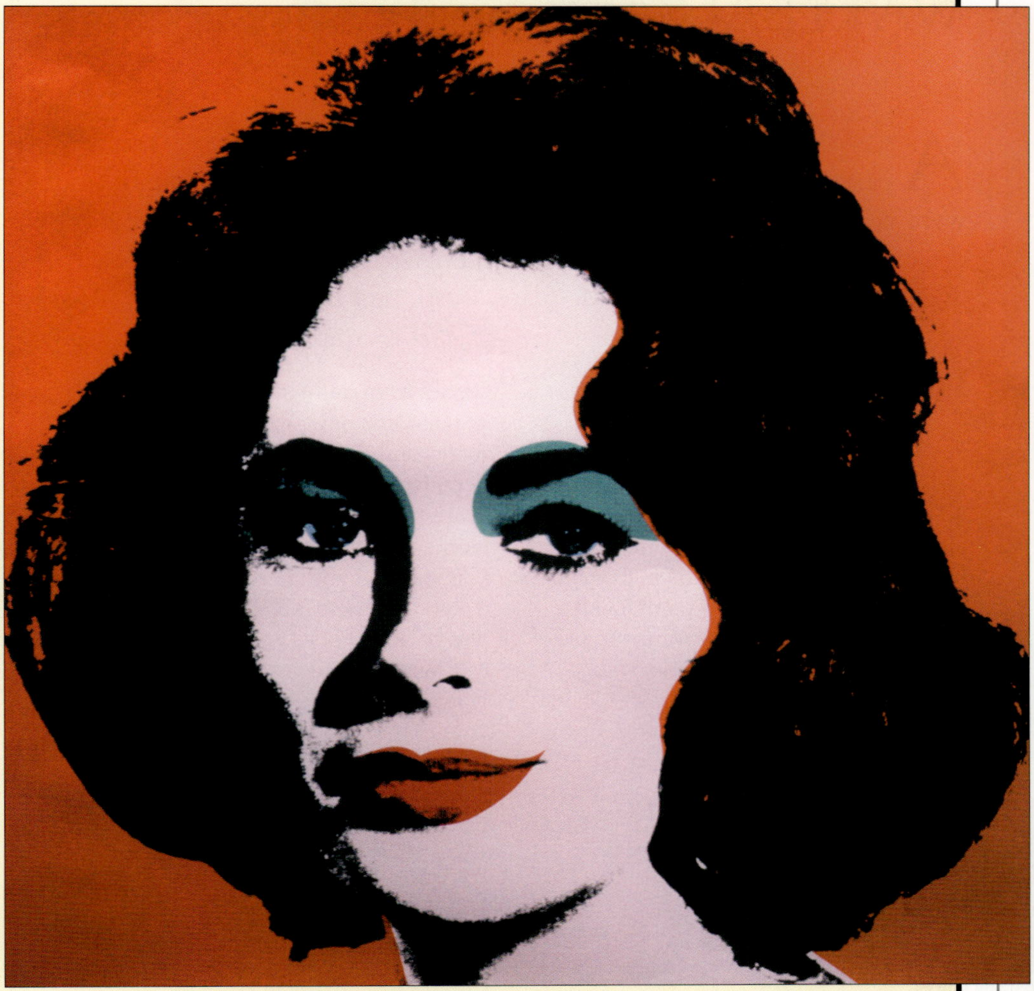

Liz *1964. Screen print on paper. 23 x 23 in (58.5 x 58.5 cm). Private collection.*

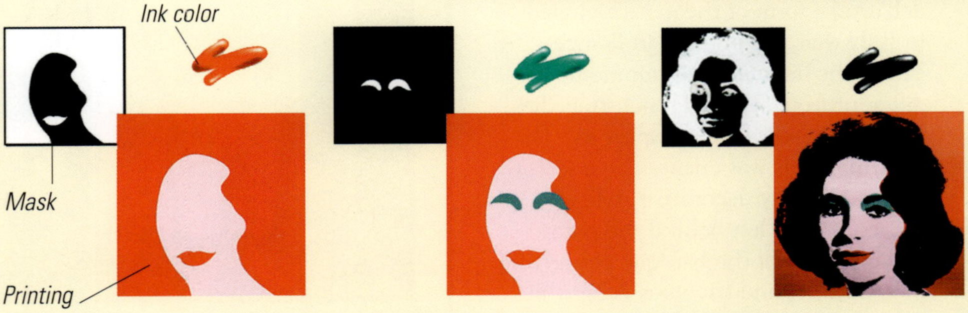

Building up the image *For the Taylor print, Warhol would have used three masks, each corresponding to a different color, making the first print onto colored paper as a fourth color.*

together an entourage, some of whom provided the inspiration and characters for films such as *Chelsea Girls* (1966), but the Factory eventually got out of control. In 1968 Warhol was shot there. He survived, and in the 1970s completed a transformation, as he explained it, from commercial artist to business artist. He produced many portraits for private clients, such as *Mick Jagger* (1975). He also published a magazine and organized multi-media concerts with the pop group Velvet Underground. While all this activity added considerably to his immense wealth, his ability for invention began to run dry. The 1980s saw something of a revival, however, through his collaboration with Francesco Clemente and Jean Michel Basquiat; their styles and subject matter overlapped in work such as *Alba's Breakfast* (1984).

Some of Warhol's final works drew upon great Old Master paintings, such as Botticelli's *Birth of Venus* (1482), and Leonardo's *Last Supper* (c1497), a version of which Warhol produced with a camouflage pattern over the top (*Camouflage Last Supper*, 1986).

Warhol's death did not live up to the glamor of his life: it resulted from complications following a routine gallbladder operation in 1986.

WATTEAU Antoine

ANTOINE WATTEAU CREATED A NEW CATEGORY OF PAINTINGS in the early 18th century: these works were known as *fêtes galantes*, and were characterized by their depiction of refined and elegant people in dreamy, atmospheric pastoral settings, engaged in the pursuits of love and leisure. He painted in a delicate, fresh, and natural style.

Life and work

Born in 1684, Antoine Watteau was to become a key figure of rococo art. He had some early artistic training as an apprentice in his native Valenciennes before going to live in Paris in 1702. His first job there was to paint small devotional works and portraits for a dealer who then sold them in bulk.

From 1705, he worked with Claude Gillot for three years. Gillot was interested in drawing and painting scenes from daily life, the theater, and popular comedy. Watteau copied his works and developed an interest in depicting humorous subjects and grotesque figures. In 1708 Watteau worked with a decorative painter, Claude Audran. He returned to Valenciennes in 1709, but by 1710 he was back in Paris.

Watteau failed to gain a Prix de Rome scholarship that would have enabled him to study in Rome. Many of the judges were so impressed with his paintings, however, that they suggested he submit a work on any subject; they could then judge from that whether he should become a member of the Academy. Watteau did not actually submit a work until 1717. He was busy painting subjects from the commedia dell'arte, a form of theater developed in Italy that was popular in France. This light-hearted entertainment, so different from serious French tragedies, mirrored a new, carefree spirit in painting. This was encapsulated in the detailed, highly decorative style of rococo, which left behind the pomp and grandeur of the baroque period and took a frothy and frivolous delight in depicting the pursuit of happiness.

Watteau's style of painting elegant, refined society in idealized landscapes was given the name *fête galante*, and in 1717 the Academy created a special category for him. His landscapes often included people listening to or playing music, merry young ladies and gentlemen enjoying themselves in parks and gardens, picnicking, courting, and conversing with one another.

Watteau also painted mythological and nude subjects. His works became very popular, partly because many of them were reproduced as engravings and therefore reached a wider public. In 1719 he visited London, but returned to Paris shortly afterward. He lodged with Edmé Gersaint, a picture

Data file

Full name: Jean Antoine Watteau

Nationality: French

Style: rococo

Dates: born 1684 in Valenciennes, died 1721 in Nogent-sur-Marne

Key works:
- *The Music Lesson* 1716
- *Pilgrimage to the Island of Cythera* 1717
- *Gilles and Four Other Characters from the Commedia dell'Arte* 1718–19
- *Venetian Parties* c1719
- *Mezzetin* 1718–20
- *Italian Comedians* c1720
- *Gersaint's Shop Sign* 1720–21

Things to look for:
- elegant and refined figures in atmospheric landscapes, often with classical sculptures
- characters often in theatrical costume or party dress, sometimes playing musical instruments
- delicate and expressive use of brushstrokes
- use of color in a way that recalls the Venetian tradition, and the work of Peter Paul Rubens

Comparisons: François Boucher, Jean-Honoré Fragonard, Titian, Giovanni Bellini, Giorgione, Peter Paul Rubens

Glossary terms: Academy, baroque, engraving, *fête galante*, history painting, Prix de Rome, rococo

Elegance and gallantry

In 1717 Watteau submitted his painting, *Pilgrimage to the Island of Cythera,* to the prestigious Academy as his official "reception piece." To be accepted, an artist's work had to meet various requirements. First, it had to be categorized. The delicate style and idealized content of Watteau's paintings did not fit any of the traditional categories. It had too many figures in it for it to be considered a landscape; the figures were not performing the heroic deeds of history paintings; and it was not a portrait or a still life. However, recognizing the quality of Watteau's work, the judges invented a new category and received him as a painter of *fêtes galantes* (courtship parties). *Fêtes galantes* might also be translated as "elegant party scenes" or "scenes of gallantry."

Pilgrimage to the Island of Cythera shows figures on a mystical, mythological

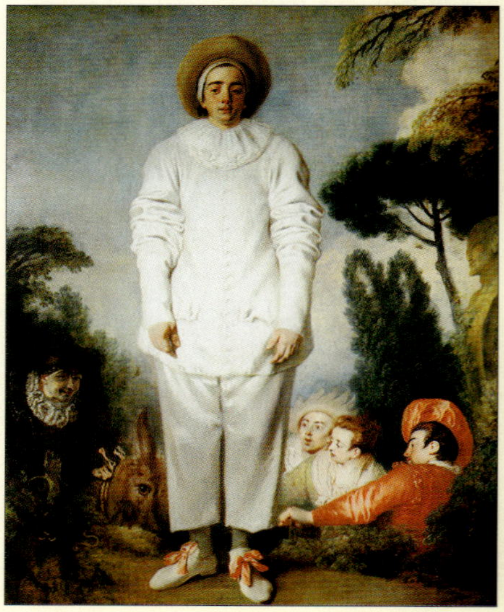

Gilles and Four Other Characters from the Commedia dell'Arte *1718–19. Oil on canvas. 72½ x 58½ in (184 x 149 cm). Musée du Louvre, Paris.*

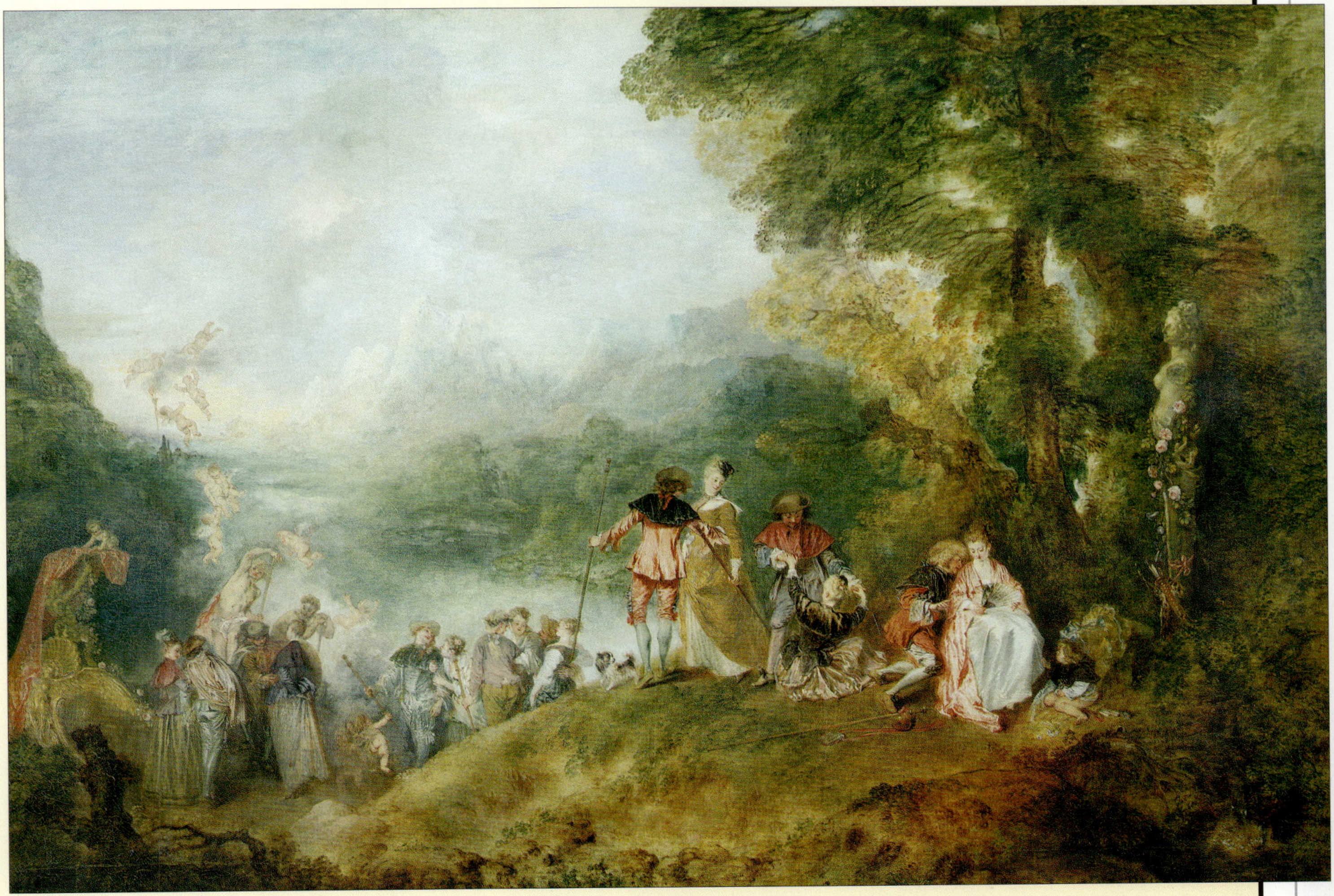

island. Dressed in contemporary party clothes, these figures are not gods and goddesses but fashionable people on a pilgrimage in search of love. Cherubs and baby cupids cavort in the sky, while Venus, the goddess of love, presides over all. The nature of love is depicted in its various stages: from wooing and persuasion on the left to fully fledged love on the right.

The atmosphere and tones are calm, but there are also bright colors and a lively sense of movement. The fresh brushwork and easy use of color reflect Rubens' influence, but are less bold. Watteau's brushstrokes are more delicate and refined. He was also influenced by Venetian painters, such as Titian, whose moody landscapes used light and color brilliantly. In Watteau's fantasy worlds, hazy skies and dark forests add to a sense of mystery and inspire viewers to reflect on the passing of life and its pleasures.

Watteau's painting of *Gilles and Four Other Characters from the Commedia dell'Arte* (1718–19) came out of his interest in the popular Italian theater. Gilles is Pierrot, the naïve fool. The figures stand out against dark foliage and Gilles's clothing is superbly painted. Watteau's virtuoso style always

Pilgrimage to the Island of Cythera *1717. Oil on canvas. 51 x 76 in (130 x 193 cm). Musée du Louvre, Paris.*

conveys the feel of the sumptuous fabrics. Although the characters are from the commedia dell'arte, the painting itself is not intended to be funny. On the contrary, Watteau's works often encourage thoughts about how the characters relate to one another, and what they are feeling or thinking. Gilles's expression is hard to read but he seems awkward and detached. A tinge of melancholy makes us wonder how happy the character really is.

dealer and later his biographer. During this time he made his famous painting, *Gersaint's Shop Sign* (1720–21), to advertise the dealer's shop.

Watteau had always been a moody and slightly melancholic character. On his return to Paris from London his health continued to deteriorate, and in 1721 he died of tuberculosis, aged only 37. Watteau's early death leads many viewers to see his work as melancholic, as if it is prefiguring death by dwelling on the transience of life, but that may not have been his intention. His pictures make us think about the complexities of human relationships, yet they also sparkle with wit, elegance, and refinement.

WEST Benjamin

BENJAMIN WEST WAS THE FIRST AMERICAN-BORN ARTIST to achieve international stature. He became one of the most important neoclassical painters in Britain, and was the most highly paid painter of the period. Patronized by the English king, George III, West was a founding member of the Royal Academy of Arts.

Life and work

Benjamin West received no formal training as a painter. Around 1747, he met a painter named William Williams in Philadelphia, who lent West books on painting and offered him advice. Around 1756, West attracted the attention of Reverend William Smith, the provost of the newly founded College of Pennsylvania, which later became the University of Pennsylvania. Smith was also founder and editor of *American Magazine*, and it was through Smith's support and patronage that West spent a brief period as a successful portrait painter in Philadelphia and New York, before embarking on a trip to Europe under Smith's sponsorship.

West sailed for Italy in 1759. He had been interested in painting mythological and historical subjects before his trip to Italy—he had painted *The Death of Socrates* in 1756—and his four-year stay in Rome provided him with further inspiration. In choosing Italy as his first place for artistic study, West also set a pattern that was to be followed by all the leading American artists in the 18th and 19th centuries. In Rome, West met like-minded painters, such as Nathaniel Dance, Gavin Hamilton, and Anton Raphael Mengs, who were also interested in producing paintings with "noble themes"—that is, scenes taken from Greek and Roman history and classical literature.

In 1763 West moved to London, where he remained for the rest of his life. He continued to practice as a portrait painter, but, five years after his arrival, West received his first commission for a history painting. *Agrippina Landing at Brundisium with the Ashes of Germanicus* (1768) confirmed West as the leading painter in the land, and assured his future as the favorite artist of King George III. *Agrippina Landing* shows the widow bearing back to Rome the ashes of her husband, Germanicus, who, according to the Roman author Tacitus, had been poisoned on the orders of Emperor Tiberius. West portrayed Agrippina disembarking at Brundisium (modern-day Brindisi) with her children, Caligula (the future emperor) and little

Data file

Full name: Benjamin West

Nationality: American

Style: neoclassicism

Dates: born 1738 in Springfield Township, PA, died 1820 in London, England

Key works:
- *Thomas Mifflin* c1758–59
- *Agrippina Landing at Brundisium with the Ashes of Germanicus* 1768
- *The Death of General Wolfe* 1771
- *William Penn's Treaty with the Indians* 1772
- *The Institution of the Order of the Garter* 1787
- *Death on a Pale Horse* 1802
- *Benjamin Franklin Drawing Electricity from the Sky* (oil sketch) c1816

Things to look for:
- linear style
- content of paintings often drawn from classical history or mythology
- contemporary subjects, such as recent history, science, and industry, combined with classical elements or based on classical models
- historically accurate details, such as clothing, topography, and architecture
- themes of heroism, patriotism, and loyalty

Comparisons: Jacques-Louis David, Jean Auguste Dominque Ingres, Joseph Turner, John Singleton Copley, Anton Raphael Mengs, Gavin Hamilton, Nathaniel Dance

Glossary terms: antique, classicism, esthetics, history painting, linear, neoclassicism, painterly, picturesque, putti, rococo, Romanticism

Painting an American hero

West, like his contemporary neoclassicists, rejected the lighthearted subject matter of the rococo, along with its sensual, painterly style. Instead, he favored subjects drawn from Greek and Roman history, which he painted in a harder, more linear style to produce paintings that were esthetically pleasing, intellectually stimulating, and morally uplifting. Of paramount importance was historical accuracy: depictions of clothing, temples, and the landscape had to be as accurate as available knowledge allowed.

Depicting scenes from contemporary history posed a dilemma for the neoclassicist. How to portray a contemporary hero was a question that West successfully tackled in *The Death of General Wolfe* (1771). How to handle a contemporary scientific discovery was another matter. *Benjamin Franklin Drawing Electricity from the Sky* (c1816) is an oil sketch for a never-realized painting.

West first met Benjamin Franklin in Philadelphia, and both lived in London between 1765 and 1775. Despite their close friendship, however, West never painted a portrait of Franklin from life. By the time West painted him conducting his famous electrical experiment, Franklin had been dead for more than 15 years. West is believed to have based Franklin's features on an engraving after a miniature portrait by Jean Baptiste Weyler, painted c1782.

The actual experiment by Franklin, in which he proved the relationship between lightning and electricity, had taken place in June of 1752 in the relative safety of a shed in a field near Philadelphia. Franklin was assisted in his experiment by his son William, who was in his early twenties at the time. In West's interpretation of the event, the main incident illustrated is the

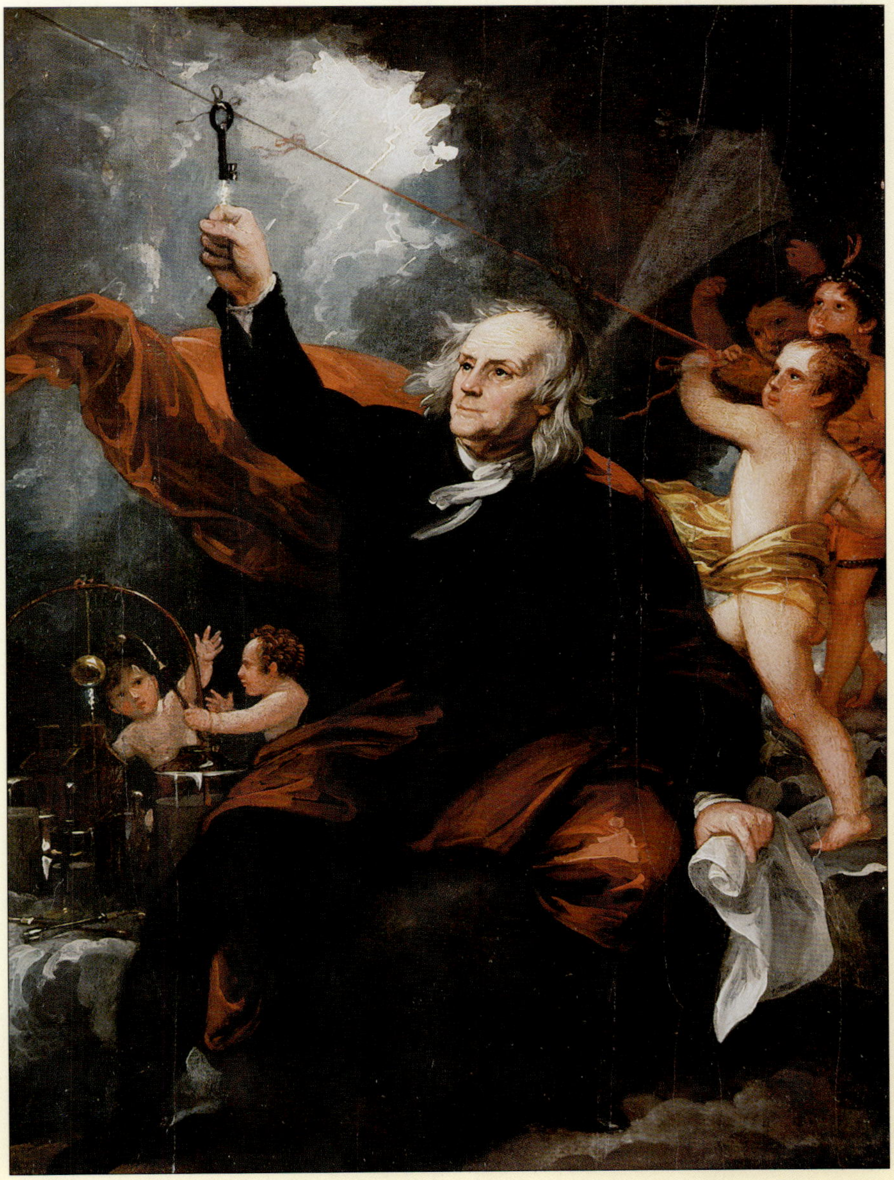

spark of electricity passing from the kite string via the key to Franklin's raised knuckle. Instead of a humble shed and a mere mortal for an assistant, West, in true neoclassical spirit, invented a laboratory set high in the clouds, while celestial putti assist in holding the kite aloft and point to scientific equipment. So strong was the influence of

Benjamin Franklin Drawing Electricity from the Sky *c1816. Oil on paper mounted on canvas. 13 x 10 in (33.5 x 25.5 cm). Philadelphia Museum of Art, PA.*

classicism on West that he chose to fuse one of the latest scientific discoveries with antique, mythological imagery.

Agrippina (the future mother of Nero). West drew on his knowledge of ancient Rome to produce an ambitious historical recreation of the scene that exemplified the neoclassical ideal of decorum, or accuracy.

While his neoclassical subjects brought West to the attention of the critics and the public, it was *The Death of General Wolfe* (1771) that was to be his greatest triumph, leading to his appointment as History Painter to the king. In *The Death of General Wolfe*, West created a new tradition in art: the recent event (the heroic death of Wolfe at the Battle of Quebec) elevated to historical epic. However, instead of the characters appearing in ancient, classical clothing, in this painting they wear contemporary dress. What was important to West was the idea of heroism, not what a hero wore. Furthermore, West demonstrated to the public that heroism was not a virtue confined to the ancient Greeks and Romans, but a contemporary virtue to which all could aspire.

Another relatively recent event in the history of the United States provided the inspiration for *William Penn's Treaty with the Indians* (1772), in which West portrayed the founder of the colony of Pennsylvania making peace with the Lenape Indians in 1682.

From 1773 to 1801, West painted no history pictures, despite the fact that he was still officially the king's History Painter. Instead, he spent his time painting portraits of the royal family, and, from 1778, he also began work on a series of paintings based on biblical themes, for stained-glass windows and altarpieces for churches throughout England. So busy was West's studio that he employed five assistants to work on the large-scale religious commissions that were flowing in. In 1792, West succeeded Sir Joshua Reynolds as President of the Royal Academy, which West had helped to found in 1768. While the Royal Academy only taught drawing, West's studio became the principal school for young American artists abroad, including John Singleton Copley, Gilbert Stuart, Matthew Pratt, and Charles Wilson Peale.

Toward the end of his life, West abandoned his rigorous neoclassical style. *Death on a Pale Horse* (1802), in both style and subject matter, played a seminal role in the birth of the romantic movement, which prevailed in Europe during the 19th century.

WHISTLER James Abbott McNeill

JAMES ABBOTT MCNEILL WHISTLER painted portraits and landscapes, as well as creating sensational interior design schemes. The musical titles he gave his works emphasize the importance to him of the carefully composed color harmonies. Clearly reflected in his work is a cosmopolitan combination of French, British, and American stylistic influences.

Life and work

The son of an army engineer from Massachusetts, Whistler lived in the United States until he was 10. In 1843 his family traveled to Saint Petersburg, Russia, where his father was working, but following his father's death the Whistlers returned to New England. From 1851 Whistler attended West Point Military Academy, but was discharged after four years. Returning to Europe following a brief period working as a topographical engraver, Whistler enrolled at the Ecole Impériale et Spéciale de Dessin in Paris, and also joined the studio of Charles Gleyre.

Whistler always worked in a variety of media, including etching and interior design, as well as painting. Throughout his life he divided his time between London and France, making occasional trips to Italy. His first sets of etchings reflect his love affair with London and France: the *Thames Set* (1858–61) portrays London's river and its inhabitants, while the *French Set* (1858–59) celebrates Bohemian Paris. These etchings were influenced by the realism of Gustave Courbet's work, and its focus on the hardship of working people's lives, along with the stark beauty of nature.

During the 1860s Whistler copied Old Master paintings in order to deepen his education. Having met the painter Henri Fantin-Latour in the Louvre, Whistler was introduced to the leading artists of the realist generation, including Courbet, Alphonse Legros, and Carolus-Duran. Fantin-Latour, who was very interested in music and poetry, encouraged Whistler to pursue these themes, which would dominate his later paintings.

Between 1862 and 1867 Whistler was inspired by Jo Hiffernan, his model and mistress, to paint a group of three paintings of young women in white dresses. He gave these works the title *Symphony in White* (1862–67) and numbered them one to three. This beautiful trio of paintings creates an atmosphere of quiet contemplation which prefigures Whistler's future role as a key figure in the Art for Art's Sake movement of British estheticism and the French symbolist circles of the 1880s and 1890s. The art of Japan was also an important influence upon Whistler throughout his career. In addition to Japanese fans and porcelain in *Symphony in White*, for other paintings of this period he dressed his models in kimonos and surrounded them with decorative Japanese objects.

When the industrialist Frederick Leyland commissioned Whistler to

Data file

Full name: James Abbott McNeill Whistler

Nationality: American

Style: British estheticism, symbolism

Dates: born 1834 in Lowell, MA, died 1903 in London, England

Key works:

- *French Set* 1858–59
- *Symphony in White: No. 1, 2, and 3* 1862–67
- *Arrangement in Gray and Black No. 1: The Artist's Mother* 1871
- *Nocturne: Blue and Gold Old Battersea Bridge* 1872–77
- *Nocturne in Black and Gold: The Falling Rocket* 1875
- Peacock Room 1876
- *Gold and Brown (Self-portrait)* 1896–98

Things to look for:

- subtle tonal color harmonies
- work in many media

Comparisons: Gustave Courbet, Edgar Degas, Henri Fantin-Latour, Albert Moore, John Singer Sargent

Glossary terms: Academy, Art for Art's Sake, Bohemian, estheticism, nocturnes, Old Masters, symbolism

Whistler's visual harmonies

Arrangement in Gray and Black No. 1: The Artist's Mother (1871) synthesizes several aspects of Whistler's career. A portrait of one of his favorite subjects, his mother, the painting draws upon the main colors of his early realist palette: gray and black. Yet the title draws attention to the concept of an "arrangement," anticipating the idea of harmony that dominates his later portraits. Whistler often gave his paintings musical titles, like "symphony" or "nocturne," believing that his work created visual harmonies of color or pattern that were analogous to the harmonies of a musical piece.

Whistler was living with his mother in the London district of Chelsea when this portrait was painted. He had initially planned a standing pose, but this proved too arduous for his mother over the many sittings that her son required of her. He therefore decided to paint her in a seated pose derived from classical tradition.

In this work Whistler painted directly onto a canvas that had not been treated with glue, resulting in a matte surface and very dense color. It was the last painting that Whistler exhibited at the Royal Academy and the first of his works to be purchased by a museum, the Musée de Luxembourg, an institution devoted to the work of contemporary artists.

Arrangement in Gray and Black No. 1: The Artist's Mother *1871. Oil on canvas. 56¾ x 64 in (144 x 162.5 cm). Musée d'Orsay, Paris.*

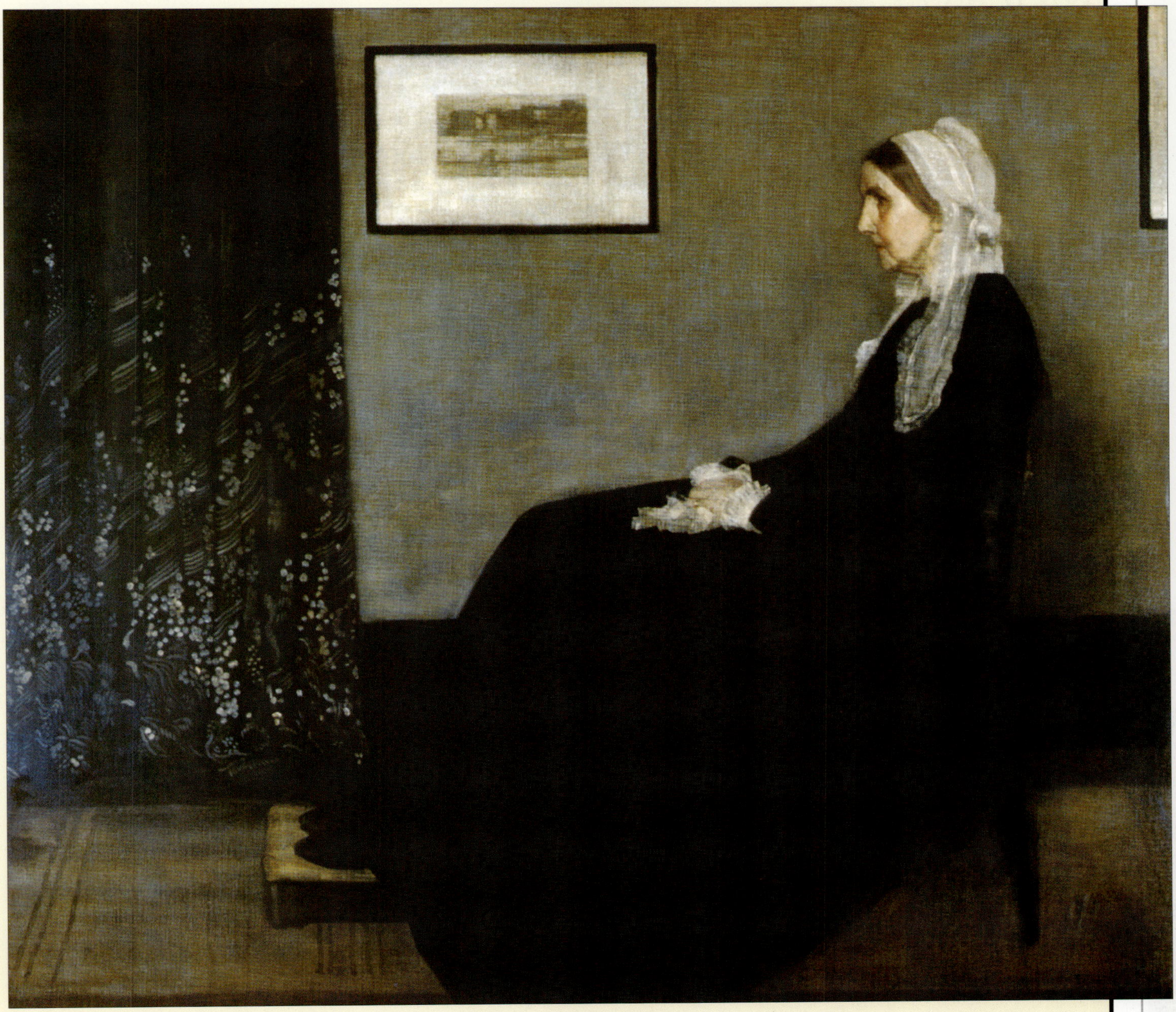

decorate parts of his London home, Whistler created the Peacock Room (1876). The client felt that Whistler had gone beyond the bounds of his commission, and they quarreled. Whistler had a volatile temper, and cultivated controversy throughout his life. In his most famous public debate he charged the art critic John Ruskin with libel for having described his painting *Nocturne in Black and Gold: The Falling Rocket* (1875) as a "paint pot flung in the public's face." Whistler won the case, but was bankrupted by the legal fees he incurred.

Whistler's later painting principally took the form of landscapes and portraits. He gave musical titles to his landscapes of the River Thames, calling them "harmonies" or "nocturnes." In these pastel-colored, hazy vistas, the landmarks of the Thames, as in *Nocturne: Blue and Gold Old Battersea Bridge* (1872–77), appear both poetic and beautiful. He often emphasized one or two colors in his portraits to create a pictorial arrangement, as well as a pyschological study of an individual.

In his "Ten O'Clock Lecture" Whistler described the artist as a dreamer who understands beauty in a deeper way than the rest of humanity. This lecture became a manifesto of the Art for Art's Sake movement, which regarded art and its appreciation as the domain of an artistic elite.

WOOD Grant

INFLUENCED BY NETHERLANDISH PAINTERS, Grant Wood painted scenes of the United States' agricultural heartland, the Midwest. His 1930 work *American Gothic* was criticized as a caricature of farming people, but became one of the nation's favorite images. A committed regionalist, Wood believed that American painters should look to their own country for inspiration and subject matter.

Life and work

Grant Wood was born into a Quaker family on a farm near Anamosa, Iowa. His family moved to nearby Cedar Rapids in 1901 following the death of his father. Wood's first "professional" work was an illustration, *Graduating Seniors* (1908), for the high-school year book. After his own graduation in 1910, Wood studied at the Minneapolis School of Design, Handicraft, and Normal Art. After teaching for a short time, he moved to Chicago in 1913 to work as a designer in a silversmith's shop. In Chicago, Wood established a jewelry design business with fellow craftsman Christopher Haga, but, after the failure of the business, returned to Cedar Rapids in early 1916, where he made his living painting shop signs and decorating interiors.

After serving in the army during World War I, Wood again returned to Cedar Rapids. He held his first exhibition at Killian's department store in 1919, in which he showed 23 small paintings, mostly of buildings and barns along with some landscapes. At this stage, Wood's painting technique consisted of loosely applied brushstrokes in a manner similar to that of the impressionists. Like many young American artists, Wood traveled to Europe to study, in 1920 and 1923. Between trips, Wood exhibited his paintings in Cedar Rapids and completed two commissions, *First Three Degrees of Free Masonry* (1921) for the Masonic Library in Anamosa (later transferred to Cedar Rapids) and the outdoor allegorical mural incorporating portraits of local people, *The Adoration of the Home* (1922), for Henry S. Ely's realty company.

In 1924 Wood lived rent-free in the carriage house of a mansion bought by David Turner that was to serve as a funeral parlor. In exchange for accommodation, Wood provided interior decorations and paintings for the walls. In 1925, he also completed a series of oil paintings based on the theme of quality and craftsmanship for J. G. Cherry Plant, manufacturers of dairy equipment in Cedar Rapids.

In 1927, Wood received a commission for a stained-glass window for the Veterans Memorial Building in Cedar Rapids. While overseeing the window's production in Munich, Germany, in 1928, Wood was inspired by both the old and the new art—the late Gothic and northern Renaissance, as well as the contemporary New Objectivity movement. As a result, he changed his technique and began to use familiar, local subjects for symbolic purposes. He explored this theme in a number of portraits before it became crystalized in the form of *American Gothic* (1930). The painting was an immediate success. It was awarded the Norman Walt Harris Bronze Medal and Purchase Prize at the annual exhibition of American Painting and Sculpture at the Art Institute of Chicago, and established Wood's reputation as an American painter.

In the summer of 1930, Wood was also busy with his first major landscape painting in his new style, *Stone City* (1930). Throughout his career, Wood remained enchanted by the landscape, and his highly organized compositions, with their repeated geometrical forms rendered in a precise, linear style, emphasized and idealized the well-ordered harmony of the rural community in which he lived.

It was an approach to both subject and style that Wood continued to adopt until his death in 1942 from cancer. In his personal statement about his attitude to American regionalism, *Revolt Against the City*, published in 1935, Wood encouraged artists to break free from the cultural domination of the big, eastern cities, and consequently from modernist tendencies in art and literature toward abstractionism. Only by remaining in their native regions did Wood believe that American artists could establish their own, personal style.

Full name: Grant Wood

Nationality: American

Style: American regionalism

Dates: born 1892 in Anamosa, IA, died 1942 in Iowa City, IA

Key works:
- Stained-glass window for Veterans Memorial Building in Cedar Rapids 1928
- *John B. Turner, Iowa Pioneer* 1928–29
- *American Gothic* 1930
- *The Midnight Ride of Paul Revere* 1931
- *Fall Plowing* 1931
- *Daughters of Revolution* 1932
- *Parson Weem's Fable* 1939
- *Spring in Iowa* 1941

Things to look for:
- images of Midwestern rural environments and people, sometimes idealized
- linear precision
- repetition of geometric forms
- smooth surface finish
- elements of satire

Comparisons: Thomas Hart Benton, John Steuart Curry, Andrew Wyeth, Edward Hopper, Otto Dix, Albrecht Dürer, Jan Van Eyck

Glossary terms: abstraction, Gothic, impressionism, modernism, New Objectivity, regionalism, Renaissance

Rediscovering America

Grant Wood, Thomas Hart Benton, and John Steuart Curry made up the triumvirate of American regionalists in the 1930s who rejected European modernism and abstraction in favor of recognizable American subjects, painted in a readable, readily understood style. They were all active in encouraging the search for a native style of art based on a common national experience. For his part, Wood established the Stone City Colony in Iowa. Although shortlived—it lasted just two summers in 1932 and 1933—visiting artists were free to develop a style that was expressive of the geographical area.

Paradoxically, it was outside the United States that Wood found the inspiration for his own style. During the time he spent in Munich overseeing the production of the window for the Veterans Memorial Building in 1928, he visited the museums there and became fascinated by the Netherlandish and German paintings of the 15th and 16th centuries, with their rich patterns and accurately rendered surface details painted using oil glazes. When he returned to the United States, Wood sought a suitable subject on which to try the technique.

During a trip to Eldon, Iowa, Wood came across a house with a porch running across the entire frontage and a Gothic-style window above it. He used a photograph of the house and a quick sketch as compositional aids for *American Gothic* (1930). In the painting, the vertical lines of the house are repeated on the faces of the two figures, as well as on the man's striped shirt and the tines of the pitchfork. Wood's sister Nan and her dentist, Dr B. H. McKeeby, were the models for the figures, who stand motionless and expressionless. Wood supervised all aspects of their clothing and appearance to create the look that he had envisioned.

Over a period of three months, Wood applied thin layers of pigment and oil glaze to Beaverboard—a type of fiberboard used in building to make interior partition walls—to produce a smoothly finished picture in which the background details, such as the plants on the porch, are as clear as the pattern on the woman's apron.

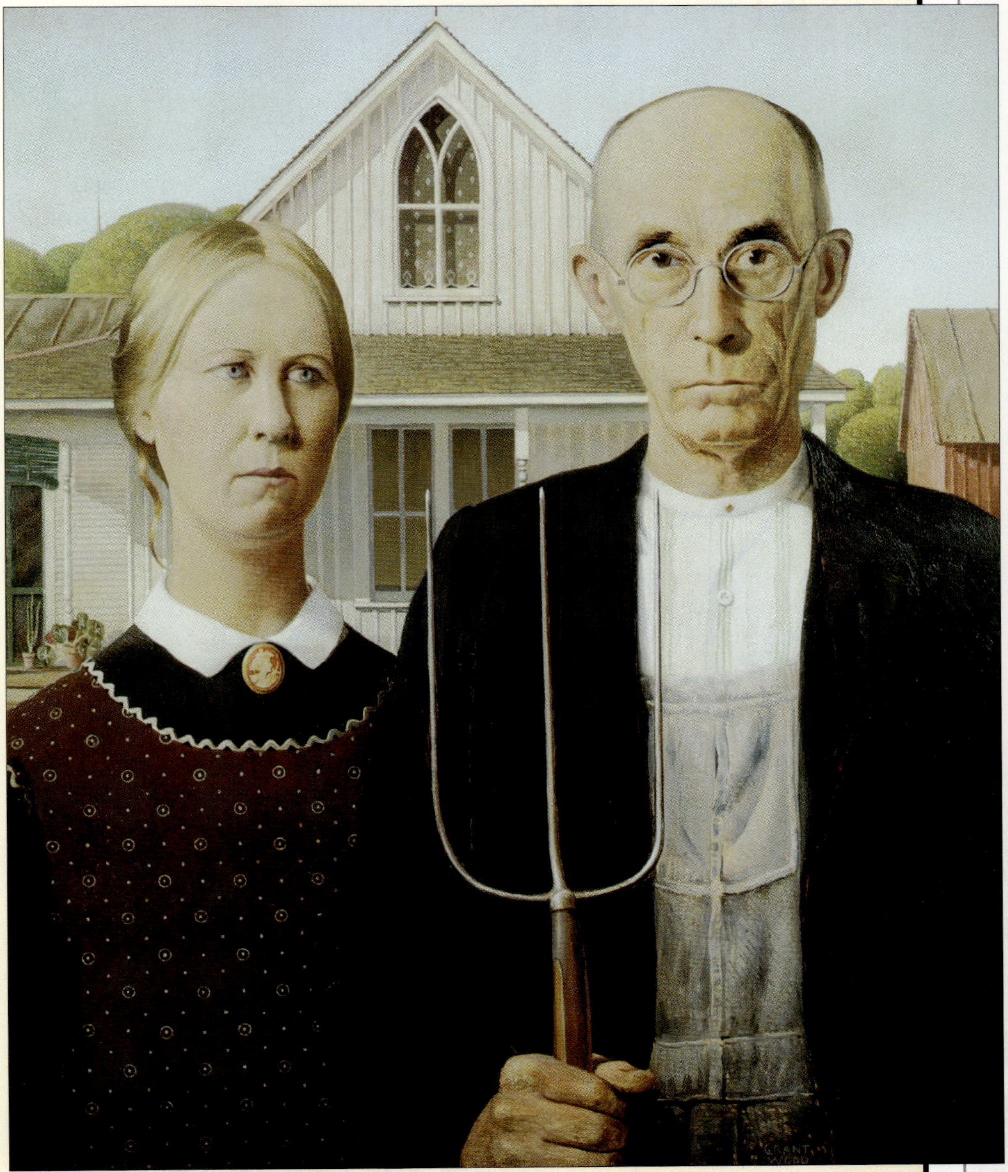

American Gothic *1930. Oil on fiberboard. 29 x 25 in (76 x 63 cm). The Art Institute of Chicago, IL.*

Following the painting's success at the Art Institute of Chicago's annual exhibition, the press erroneously referred to *American Gothic* as an "Iowa Farmer and His Wife." This aroused a storm of protest among many rural Iowans, who felt that Wood had satirized their lifestyle and appearance. Wood defended his painting in an interview in the Des Moines *Sunday Register*, explaining that the people he had attempted to portray were not farmers but small-town folk. Wood claimed that he only ever painted one satirical work, *Daughters of Revolution* (1932), in which three tightlipped women drink tea in front of a reproduction of Emanuel Leutze's painting *Washington Crossing the Delaware* (1850). Wood had had a feud with the Daughters of the American Revolution (DAR) in 1928. When they had realized that the glass for the memorial window was being made in Germany—the United States' enemy only 10 years earlier—they refused to let the window be dedicated. Wood described *Daughters of Revolution* as a "pretty rotten painting, carried by its subject matter."

WYETH Andrew

ANDREW WYETH IS THE MOST CELEBRATED AMERICAN REALIST painter, even though only a small proportion of his work has ever been exhibited or reproduced. Wyeth is a master of traditional painting techniques. His art is a meticulously detailed—and often enigmatic—account of the landscapes and people of two small areas: Chadds Ford in Pennsylvania and Cushing in Maine.

Life and work

Andrew Wyeth is the son of Newell Converse Wyeth, the celebrated illustrator who achieved considerable success with his illustrations for children's classics such as *Treasure Island* and *Robin Hood*. Andrew was tutored at home, where he painted watercolors of the Pennsylvania landscape as well as of the area around Needham, Maine, where the family moved when he was 10 years old. When he was about 15 years old, he began training more formally in his father's studio, drawing from plaster casts and still lifes. At the age of 18, he had his first exhibition of watercolors in a New York gallery.

Unlike many of his contemporaries, Wyeth never studied in Europe. Nevertheless, the influence of European Renaissance art is evident in his work. Wyeth found the opacity of Sandro Botticelli's tempera paintings fascinating, and in the 1930s he began working in this medium. It is a painstakingly slow medium, and Wyeth paints only two or three tempera works a year. Wyeth was also enthralled by the subject matter of Albrecht Dürer's drawings and engravings, as well as the manner in which they had been executed. Wyeth points to two of Dürer's works in particular: *The Young Hare* (1502) and *Large Piece of Turf* (1503), the latter directly inspiring his own drybrush drawing *Grasses* (1941).

While his contemporaries traveled abroad, Wyeth kept to his "own world"—winters in Pennsylvania and summers in Maine. From these two locations came Wyeth's central characters: Karl and Anna Keurner, Christina Olson, and Helga Testorf. The Keurners' farm was over the hill from where Wyeth was born and, over a number of years, he frequently painted pictures of the house and barn, as well as the powerful portraits *Karl Keurner* (1948) and *Anna Keurner* (1971).

When he was 22, Wyeth met his future wife, Betsy Jones, in Maine. He recounts in his autobiography how one day he drove across to Cushing, where he had never been before. Betsy's father was the friend of a man who had bought one of Wyeth's pictures, and the artist wanted to contact him. Betsy's father was away, but the pair got along well enough for Betsy to take Wyeth to see a house she thought would interest

Data file

Full name: Andrew Newell Wyeth

Nationality: American

Style: realism

Dates: born 1917 in Chadds Ford, PA

Key works:
- *Oil Lamp* 1945
- *Winter, 1946* 1946
- *Wind from the Sea* 1947
- *Christina's World* 1948
- *Groundhog Day* 1959
- *The Patriot* 1964
- *Anna Keurner* 1971
- *The Helga Suite* 1971–85

Things to look for:
- carefully rendered surfaces and textures
- sweeping views of the countryside
- solitary figures in landscapes
- when people are absent from works, signs of their presence remain, such as tracks in the snow, or a plate and cup on a table
- the framing edge of the picture used to isolate and give impact to a scene
- understated colors that avoid sharp contrasts and bright hues

Comparisons: Edward Hopper, Grant Wood, Albrecht Dürer, Sandro Botticelli

Glossary terms: abstract expressionism, abstraction, *alla prima*, allegory, drybrush, figurative, impressionism, realism, Renaissance, tempera

A distinctly American voice

Simply because a particular style of art is dominant at any one time, it does not mean that other styles do not continue to thrive. At a time when abstract expressionism was attracting the interest of artists, critics, and the public—not only because it was a brand new mode of art, but also because it was the first one to originate in the United States—some artists rejected abstraction in favor of realism and figurative art.

In Andrew Wyeth, the realists perhaps have their finest painter, yet he himself has denied that he is simply a realist. For Wyeth, what he described as "abstract thought" was important in developing his work from its early stage in drawings and watercolors. If people liked his paintings simply because of the meticulous detail, he felt they were seeing only one side of his art. For Wyeth, realism was not about "optical tricks," and technique was not what truly interested him. What was important for Wyeth was expressing the way he felt at a particular time toward a particular object—whether it was a person, a building, or a piece of land.

While Wyeth may be best known for his paintings of Karl and Anna Keurner, Helga Testorf, and Christina Olson, it is landscape that is the dominant element in his oeuvre. For example, in his most famous work, *Christina's World* (1948), it is the landscape that fills the picture, dwarfing the skinny figure of Christina. It was while Wyeth was painting at the Olsons' in the fall of 1945 that he received the news that his father had been killed after his car stalled on a

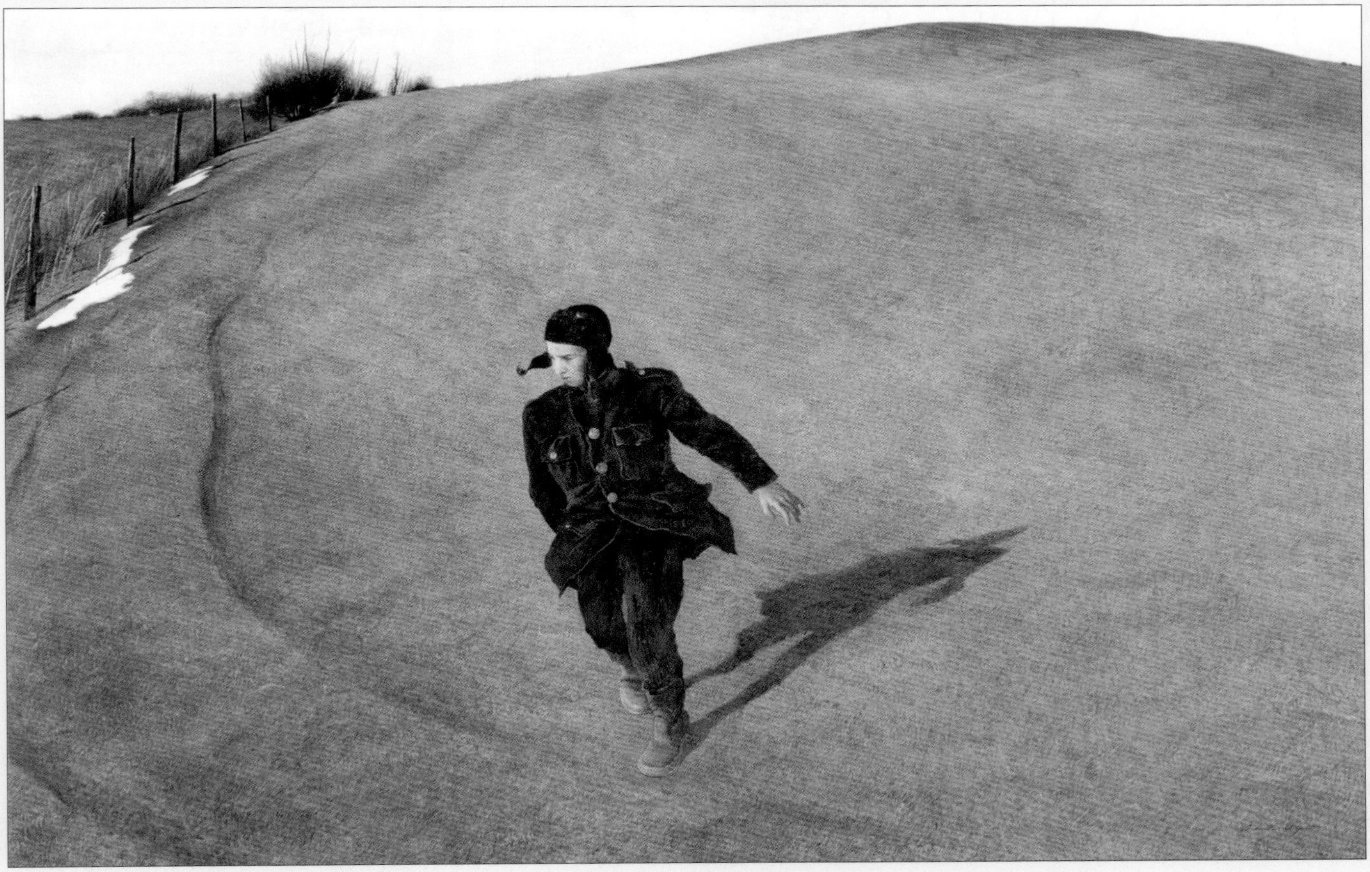

railroad track as a train approached. *Winter, 1946* (1946) is an allegorical work painted shortly after Wyeth returned to Chadds Ford. The subject of the painting is a young boy running down a hill, but because of the hill's sheer size, it dominates the composition and in a sense becomes the true subject. In an interview in *Life* magazine in 1965, Wyeth expressed his regret at never having painted his father and said that the hill in *Winter, 1946* had become his portrait.

Like many of Wyeth's works, *Winter, 1946* captures what the photographer Henri Cartier-Bresson called "the decisive moment." In contrast to photography, Wyeth said that he was interested in the "fleeting moment," not the "frozen moment." Unlike the impressionists' *alla prima* technique of depicting fleeting instances of reality through quick, fractured brushstrokes, Wyeth's method is slow. Each painting begins with pencil sketches, drybrush drawings, and watercolors, from which he distills the "mood" of his first impressions before painting with tempera. The tempera is applied with a dry brush to build up carefully rendered forms and minutely observed details. For Wyeth, tempera provides another link with the land itself: he loves the qualities of the pigments and the earth colors they provide, and has compared them to the dry mud and fields of the Brandywine Valley. Wyeth has likened the painting process itself to building: "...really building in great layers, the way the earth itself was built."

Winter, 1946 *1946. Tempera on board. 31 x 48 in (80 x 121 cm). North Carolina Museum of Art, NC.*

him. This belonged to the Olsons; Christina Olson would become a key subject for his paintings over the next 25 years. At the Olsons', Wyeth's first tempera was *Oil Lamp* (1945), a portrait of Christina's brother, Alvardo. He then turned his attention to Christina. In *Christina Olson* (1947), she is shown seated on the front step of the house, her back against the open door. Wyeth's most famous image of her is the painting *Christina's World* (1948). Also at the Olsons' house, Wyeth painted views from and through the windows, including *Wind from the Sea* (1947) and *Seed Corn* (1948).

From 1971 to 1985, Wyeth produced a third significant body of work, known collectively as *The Helga Suite*, which comprised four tempera paintings, nine drybrush paintings, 63 watercolors, and 164 pencil sketches. These were first exhibited at the National Gallery of Art in Washington, D.C., in 1987. The subject of nearly all the pictures is Helga Testorf, a neighbor of Wyeth's in Chadds Ford. In paintings such as *The Prussian* (1973), *Loden Coat* (1978), *Day Dream* (1980), and *Refuge* (1985), Helga is depicted nude and clothed, indoors and outdoors, at various times of the day, and in different seasons of the year.

ZURBARÁN Francisco de

ZURBARÁN IS BEST REMEMBERED FOR HIS RELIGIOUS WORKS. He was skilled in painting realistic details and creating a mystical, spiritual atmosphere. He was one of the most expressive painters of the Counter-Reformation.

Life and work

Francisco de Zurbarán arrived in Seville at the age of 15. He had intended to train as an apprentice in an artist's workshop, since he was familiar with polychromy (multicolored decoration, usually of sculptural pieces). There were many young artists training in Seville at the same time, and it was here that Zurbarán met and befriended a fellow artist, Diego Velázquez. By 1617 Zurbarán had returned to his birthplace, the southwestern province of Badajos; he lived and worked there for the next 10 years, but none of his work from this period is documented.

In the late 1620s Zurbarán began working on a series of commissions for a Dominican monastery. This led to similar commissions from other religious orders, particularly in Seville. Before the end of the decade, Zurbarán had returned to work there. Through most of the 1630s he continued painting on biblical themes for various religious communities, developing his distinctive style. In 1631 he painted *The Apotheosis of Saint Thomas Aquinas*, his great masterpiece.

In 1634 Zurbarán worked on the decoration of King Philip IV's palace in Madrid. This was probably the result of Velázquez's influence in the royal court. He painted mythological subjects and battle scenes. There he gained access to the king's collection of paintings, which enabled him to study the styles of Venetian painters such as Titian, and the work of contemporary artists such as Peter Paul Rubens and Velázquez. Having made an impression at court, he was appointed Painter to the King.

Returning to Seville in 1635, Zurbarán continued his commissions for monasteries and churches. The influence of Rubens and Titian shows in a few landscape settings, but on the whole his style did not alter greatly. In 1638, Zurbarán worked on an important commission for the Carthusian monastery in Jeréz de la Frontera, creating pieces for the high altar and sacristy. He also completed a commission of a series of eight paintings of scenes from the lives of monks for the Royal Hieronymite Monastery at Guadalupe.

In the 1640s, Zurbarán's life became more difficult. Spain was plunged into economic crisis, and at the end of the decade, there was an outbreak of plague. Commissions were not as plentiful as they had been, and Zurbarán had to look elsewhere for his market. He found trade with the patrons and clients in the newly

A mystical vision

This huge painting is Zurbarán's masterpiece. The composition would have been discussed in detail with members of the dominican college of Saint Thomas Aquinas, who commissioned the work. This is a devotional image: the subject celebrates the contribution to learning made by the college and Saint Thomas, and encourages meditation. The purpose behind the image is to inspire the viewer to lead a devoted and religious life.

This painting is more complex in its structure than many of Zurbarán's other works, and it reveals many of the characteristics of his style. It is clearly divided into two parts. The upper, or "heavenly" part, above the clouds, shows Saint Thomas Aquinas surrounded by the four fathers of the Latin Church (Saints Ambrose, Gregory, Jerome, and Augustine). The Holy Spirit descends from the top of the painting and Saint Thomas gazes up at it as he is taken up into heaven. At the top left of the painting we see Christ and the Virgin Mary, on the right Saints Paul and Dominick (founder of the Dominican Order).

The lower or "earthly" section is distinguished by the architectural features. It shows the founding of the college of Saint Thomas Aquinas by Cardinal Diego de Deza, who kneels opposite Charles I and in front of a piece of paper showing the college charter. They are surrounded by men and monks in attitudes of prayer. Altogether this might appear to be a complicated painting, but it is important to remember its huge size.

The drapery on the figures is modeled rather like monumental sculpture—we can almost feel the weight of the robes covering the four fathers—which is typical of Zurbarán's style. His work also shows a talent for capturing the details of texture and material; also the use of brilliant colors helps a serious painting to come alive.

Full name: Francisco de Zurbarán

Nationality: Spanish

Style: realism, mysticism

Dates: born 1598 in Fuente de Cantos, died 1664 in Madrid

Key works:

Crucifixion 1627

Saint Serapion 1628

The Apotheosis of Saint Thomas Aquinas 1631

Still Life with Oranges, Lemons, and a Cup of Water 1633

Saint Francis in Ecstasy 1639

Annunciation 1650

Things to look for:

- religious subjects, such as scenes of saints, monks, visions, or the Virgin Mary
- monumental and solid figures with very sculpted drapery
- strong contrasts of light and shadow
- realism, especially in still-life details

Comparisons: Michelangelo Merisi da Caravaggio, Georges de La Tour, Diego Velázquez

Glossary terms: chiaroscuro, Counter-Reformation

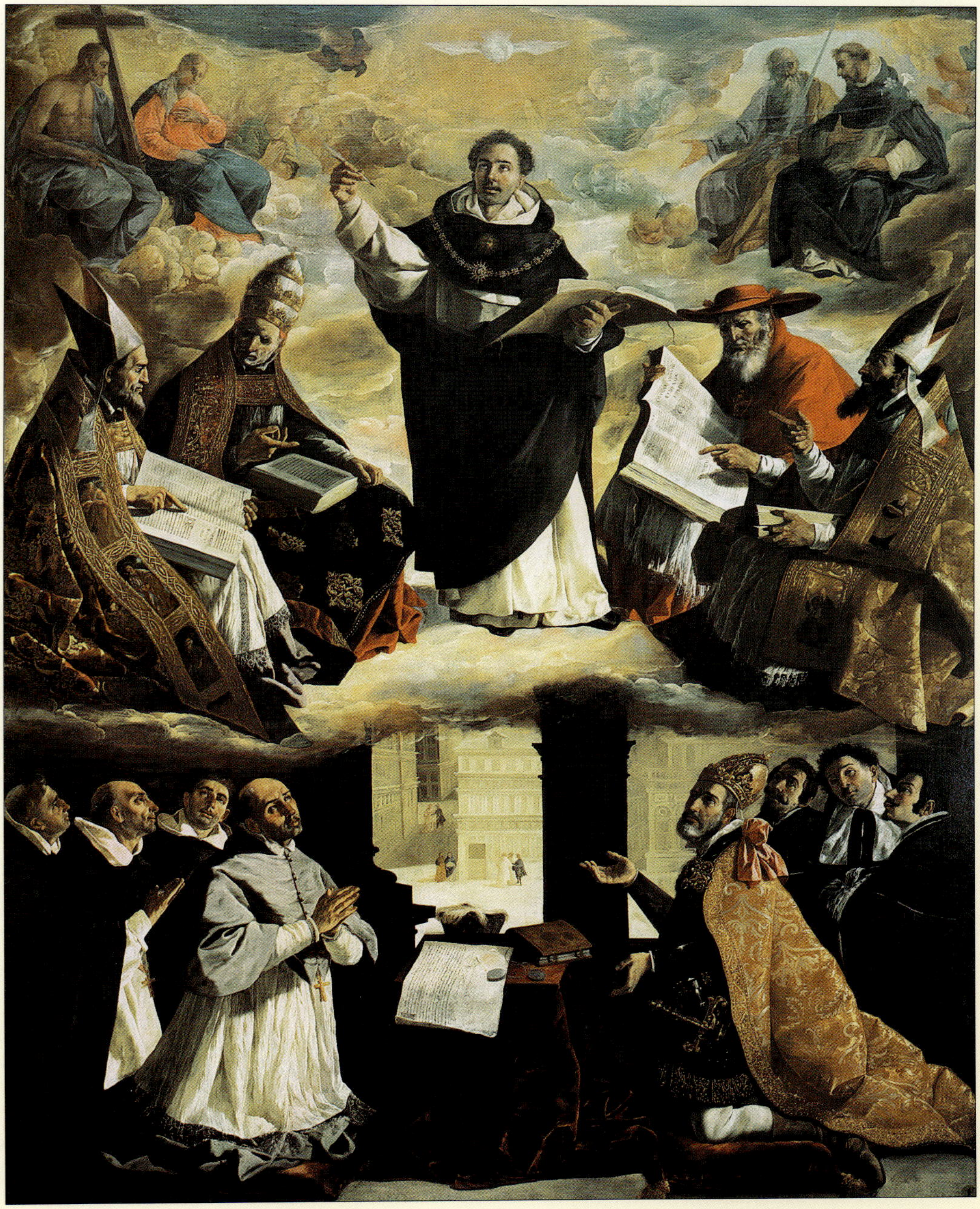

The Apotheosis of Saint Thomas Aquinas *1631.* *Oil on canvas. 187 x 144 1/2 in (475 x 367 cm). Museo del Bellas Artes, Seville.*

Although the figures are symmetrically placed, each figure is individually characterized and interacting with others. By adding realistic touches, Zurbarán helps us to imagine the experience of the saint being taken up to heaven. His evocative art, with attention to chiaroscuro (the contrasts of light and dark), often encourages the viewer to share the mood created, and the pain or ecstasy of the subject.

This was the ideal kind of Counter-Reformation art—a way of drawing people back to the Church by appealing to their minds, to their senses, and to their questions about the mysteries of life and death.

established colonies in the Americas. He and his workshop assistants painted altarpieces and devotional pictures for monasteries in the New World. Mexico, Colombia, and Peru still have works by Zurbarán or his workshop.

Zurbarán returned to Madrid in 1658. He received a commission to decorate a chapel in the monastery of Alcalá de Henares, near Madrid. The influence of Italian painting on his work is clear at this time. In his smaller devotional images, often of the Virgin Mary, his style became softer and more delicate—perhaps in an attempt to imitate his rival, Bartolomé Murillo, who had become the most popular painter in Seville.